ZEUS

A STUDY IN ANCIENT RELIGION

ZEUS

A STUDY IN ANCIENT RELIGION

BY

ARTHUR BERNARD COOK

FELLOW AND LECTURER OF QUEENS' COLLEGE, CAMBRIDGE
READER IN CLASSICAL ARCHAEOLOGY TO THE UNIVERSITY
OF CAMBRIDGE

VOLUME II

ZEUS GOD OF THE DARK SKY
(THUNDER AND LIGHTNING)

χὼ Ζεὺς ἄλλοκα μὲν πέλει αἴθριος, ἄλλοκα δ' ὔει

THEOKRITOS 4. 43

PART II

APPENDIXES AND INDEX

BIBLO and TANNEN
NEW YORK
1965

BIBLO AND TANNEN
BOOKSELLERS and PUBLISHERS, Inc.
63 Fourth Avenue, New York, N.Y., 10003

Reprinted by permission of the
Cambridge University Press
Library of Congress Catalog Card Number: 64-25839

Printed in U.S.A. by
NOBLE OFFSET PRINTERS, INC.
NEW YORK 3, N. Y.

APPENDIX A.

KAIROS.

Kairos as a distinct personification first emerges in the middle of *s.* V B.C., when Ion of Chios composed a hymn in his honour. Pausanias[1] mentions it *à propos* of an altar to him in the north-eastern part of the *Altis* : ' Hard by the entrance into the *Stádion* are two altars. One they call the altar of Hermes *Enagónios*, the other that of Kairos. I am aware that Ion of Chios actually made a hymn to Kairos and in his hymn gives the genealogy of Kairos as the youngest of the sons of Zeus.' It has been conjectured with some probability that this hymn was written for the original dedication of the Kairos-altar at Olympia[2].

Whether Kairos was definitely worshipped elsewhere, we cannot say. Menandros ' spoke of him as a god[3],' and Lysippos ' enrolled him among the gods[4] ' by making his famous effigy. But neither phrase can be pressed to imply a practical cult.

Of the Lysippean Kairos numerous late descriptions and copies are extant[5]. These, however, differ widely among themselves : some must, many may, all might, refer to subsequent modifications of the type. Our earliest and most trustworthy source is Poseidippos (*c.* 270 B.C.), who devotes an epigram to the statue[6]. He informs us that it was fashioned by Lysippos of Sikyon, that it stood on tip-toe as a runner with wings attached to its feet, that it carried a razor in its right hand, that it was long-haired in front but bald behind, and that it was set up ' in the vestibule '—presumably of some Sicyonian building.

But how came Lysippos, the sculptor of athletes, to attempt such a curious piece of allegory? That is a problem which has never been squarely faced. My own conviction is that the statue was not, to speak strictly, allegorical at all. Lysippos, who excelled in the rendering of graceful male forms and is said to have paid special attention to the hair[7], wished simply to portray the Age of Puberty. He therefore modelled a youthful runner, with wings[8] on his feet, holding the razor[9] that had shorn his votive tress for the well known puberty-

---

[1] Paus. 5. 14. 9.

[2] O. Benndorf 'Über eine Statue des Polyklet' in the *Gesammelte Studien zur Kunstgeschichte, eine Festgabe zum 4 Mai 1885 für Anton Springer* Leipzig 1885 p. 11.

[3] Anth. Pal. 10. 52. 1 (Palladas) εὖ γε λέγων τὸν Καιρὸν ἔφης θεόν, εὖ γε, Μένανδρε, | κ.τ.λ.

[4] Himer. *ecl.* 14. 1 ἐγγράφει τοῖς θεοῖς τὸν Καιρόν, κ.τ.λ.

[5] The fullest list is given by Lamer in his admirable article in Pauly—Wissowa *Real-Enc.* x. 1508—1521.

[6] *Anth. Pal.* 16. 275. 1 ff. (Poseidippos).

[7] Plin. *nat. hist.* 34. 65.

[8] These may of course have been a later addition; but similar wings are attached to the feet of the ' Resting Hermes ' at Naples (*Guida del Mus. Napoli* p. 208 f. no. 841, Brunn—Bruckmann *Denkm. der gr. und röm. Sculpt.* pl. 282), which—in the opinion of most critics (*e.g.* M. Collignon *Lysippe* Paris 1904 pp. 112, 115 with fig. 24)—emanated from the school, and reflects the style, of Lysippos.

[9] Lamer *loc. cit.* p. 1516 on grounds which to me seem inadequate denies that Lysippos' Kairos held a razor, and hence infers that even Poseidippos was not describing the original statue.

rite[1]. The resultant figure took the popular fancy, and moralists soon[2] discovered a deep significance in the contrast between the front hair and the back, a significance hardly intended by the sculptor. A further aptitude was perhaps found[3] in the fact that the name *Kairós* is related to the verb *keíro*, 'I shave[4].'

Symbolism, once introduced, grew apace. Gems of the Hellenistic age[5],

Fig. 796.   Fig. 798.   Fig. 797.

when Eros and Psyche were prime favourites[6], added wings on the shoulders (fig. 796 ff.) and a butterfly on the hand (fig. 796 f.). The globe beneath the foot[7] (fig. 798) and the balance suspended in the air (fig. 796 f.) or poised on the razor's edge (fig. 798), are attributes appropriate to divinities of fate such as Nike[8] and

[1] *Supra* i. 23 n. 6.

[2] First in Poseidippos' epigram (*Anth. Pal.* 16. 275. 7 ff.).

[3] Cp. Poll. 2. 33 ἀκαρὴς καιρός and context.

[4] So P. Persson in the *Zeitschrift für vergleichende Sprachforschung* 1895 xxxiii. 288 (καιρός<καρ-ιο-). Dr Giles too told me (Oct. 22, 1911) that, starting from the root of κείρω in the weak grade κρ-, we could assume *kr̥-io-s* > καρ-ιο-s > καιρός, cp. *khr̥-io* > χαρ-ιω > χαίρω.

[5] (*a*) Convex cornelian in the collection of C. Newton-Robinson. Kairos, bearded, with forelock and bald head, wings on shoulders and heels, steps towards the right, holding a butterfly in his right hand and supporting with his left the depressed pan of a balance suspended before him (Furtwängler *Ant. Gemmen* i pl. 43, 49 (=my fig. 796), ii. 207).

(*b*) Gem with the design of (*a*) reversed (Furtwängler *Ant. Gemmen* i pl. 43, 51, ii. 208). This gem appears to be identical with (*b'*).

(*b'*) Gem from the Blacas collection. 'Kairos, bearded, with wings on shoulders and on heels, holding out pair of scales, and a butterfly' (*Brit. Mus. Cat. Gems* p. 143 no. 1199. My fig. 797 is from a cast kindly furnished by Mr A. H. Smith).

(*c*) Convex gem in an unknown collection. Kairos, bearded, with wings on shoulders and heels, runs towards the right. His right foot rests on a ball. His right hand carries a razor, on the edge of which is poised a balance. His left hand is held beneath one of its pans (Furtwängler *Ant. Gemmen* i pl. 43, 50, ii. 207 f.). This gem appears to be identical with (*c'*).

(*c'*) Convex onyx from the Blacas collection. 'Kairos, bald on back of head, bearded, wings on shoulders and heels; runs to r. [with right foot on ball], holding out scales in front [balanced on razor], but without butterfly' (*Brit. Mus. Cat. Gems* p. 143 no. 1200. My fig. 798 is from a cast kindly furnished by Mr A. H. Smith).

[6] *Infra* Append. G *sub fin.* and *supra* p. 645 n. 4.

[7] Kallistrat. ἐκφράσεις 6. 1—4 (' On the statue of Kairos at Sikyon') states that the figure wrought by Lysippos for the Sicyonians was a bronze boy in the bloom of youth, for the most part resembling Dionysos, but with unusual hair—long in front and at the sides, free of tresses at the back—and with winged heels set on a sphere. Nothing is said of razor or scales.

[8] F. Studniczka *Die Siegesgoettin* Leipzig 1898 p. 20 pl. 4, 23, 26 f. See also *supra* i. 48 f. figs. 20, 22.

Nemesis[1]. But the most remarkable innovation of the period remains to be mentioned. The gems in question all represent the nude and agile figure, not merely with well-marked forelock and smooth occiput, but also with a full beard. This can only mean that the verbal misuse of *kairós* for *chrónos*[2] has led to a corresponding typological confusion of Kairos with Chronos.

It is, indeed, likely that confusion became more confounded, since Chronos was constantly interchanged with Kronos[3] and Kronos too appears as a bald-

Fig. 799.

headed god hastening along with a sickle-knife in his hand[4]. Thus we reach the singular result that Kairos 'youngest of the sons of Zeus' has actually been transformed into a figure resembling that of his own grandfather Kronos[5], while by a further surprising coincidence *Krónos*, as we have seen[6], is derivable from the same root as *Kairós*.

Others distinguished the types and continued to portray Kairos as a youthful god. A relief at Turin (fig. 799)[7] shows him, with forelock and tonsure, balancing

---

[1] H. Posnansky *Nemesis und Adrasteia* Breslau 1890 p. 113. See also *supra* pp. 99 n. 1, 734 n. 3.

[2] C. A. Lobeck in his ed. of Soph. *Ai.* Lipsiae 1835 p. 85 n.*.

[3] *Supra* p. 374.

[4] *Supra* p. 550 fig. 426.

[5] We are almost reminded of Zagreus the shape-shifter, who appeared now as a youthful Zeus, now as an aged Kronos (*supra* i. 398 f., 647).

[6] *Supra* p. 549 n. 6.

[7] A. Rivautella—J. P. Ricolvi *Monumenta Taurinensia* Augustæ Taurinorum 1747 ii. 4 ff. no. 22 with pl., E. Curtius 'Die Darstellungen des Kairos' in the *Arch. Zeit.* 1875 xxxiii. 5 f. pl. 1, 1 (photograph of cast = my fig. 799), H. Heydemann *Winckelmannsfest-Progr. Halle* 1879 p. 35 Turin: Museo Lapidario no. 1 (thinks the slab a modern copy of an ancient relief: unconvincing), H. Dütschke *Antike Bildwerke in Oberitalien* Leipzig 1880 iv. 73 f. no. 117, Friederichs—Wolters *Gipsabgüsse* p. 751 no. 1897, A. Baumeister

the scales on the edge of a razor and depressing one pan with his finger[1]. The would-be archaic wings, floating tresses, muscular body, and barocco pose all point to Pergamene influence.

Equipoise on the razor was a trait naturally suggested by the old Greek proverb 'it stands on the razor's edge[2].' An engraved cornelian of imperial date in the Berlin collection figures Kairos himself, scales in hand, treading gingerly along the narrow loom of a steersman's paddle (fig. 800)[3]. And Phaedrus must have seen similar representations in which the light-footed god even trod the razor's edge—*cursu volucri, pendens in novacula*[4],—unless indeed we venture with G. Thiele[5] to translate the last phrase '*weighing* on the razor's edge,' in which case Phaedrus and the Turin relief would be in exact agreement.

Fig. 800.

The recognition of Kairos on Italian soil was attended by a certain grammatical awkwardness. Phaedrus describes the god in words of the masculine gender[6], but names him *Tempus* in the neuter[7], and says that he signifies *occasionem rerum...brevem*[8]. *Occasio*, as the Latin equivalent of *Kairós*, was in fact the name current during the third[9] and fourth[10] centuries of our era; and, being a feminine term, it entailed a change of sex. Ausonius in one of his epigrams[11] professes to expound a group of Kairos and Metanoia carved by

in his *Denkm.* ii. 771 f. fig. 823 ('aus spät-römischer Zeit, aber unzweifelhaft echt'), B. Sauer in Roscher *Lex. Myth.* ii. 900 fig., F. Durrbach in Daremberg—Saglio *Dict. Ant.* iii. 787 fig. 4251 ('la reproduction d'un original grec'), Reinach *Rép. Reliefs* iii. 423 no. 3. Italian marble. Height 0·60ᵐ; breadth 0·65ᵐ.

For an exact *replica* on sale at Florence see Friederichs—Wolters *op. cit.* p. 751 f. no. 1898 n. ; and for a fragmentary relief of the same type at Athens, E. Curtius *loc. cit.* 1875 xxxiii. 6 pl. 2, 4, L. von Sybel *Katalog der Sculpturen zu Athen* Marburg 1881 p. 375 no. 5987, Friederichs—Wolters *op. cit.* p. 751 f. no. 1898.

[1] Cp. Himer. *ecl.* 14. 1 ποιεῖ (*sc.* ὁ Λύσιππος) παῖδα τὸ εἶδος ἁβρόν, τὴν ἀκμὴν ἔφηβον, κομῶντα μὲν τὸ ἐκ κροτάφων εἰς μέτωπον, γυμνὸν δὲ τὸ ὅσον ἐκεῖθεν ἐπὶ τὰ νῶτα μερίζεται· σιδήρῳ τὴν δεξιὰν ὡπλισμένον, ζυγῷ τὴν λαιὰν ἐπέχοντα, πτερωτὸν τὰ σφυρά, οὐχ ὡς μετάρσιον ὑπὲρ γῆς ἄνω κουφίζεσθαι, ἀλλ᾽ ἵνα δοκῶν ἐπιψαύειν τῆς γῆς λανθάνῃ κλέπτων τὸ μὴ κατὰ γῆς ἐπερείδεσθαι.

[2] First in *Il.* 10. 173 ἐπὶ ξυροῦ ἵσταται ἀκμῆς. See further Stephanus *Thes. Gr. Ling.* v. 1692 B—D.

[3] Furtwängler *Geschnitt. Steine Berlin* p. 273 no. 7358 pl. 55, E. Curtius in the *Arch. Zeit.* 1875 xxxiii. 4 pl. 2, 2 (=my fig. 800).

[4] Phaedr. 5. 8. 1.

[5] G. Thiele 'Phaedrus-Studien' in *Hermes* 1906 xli. 577 ff. Dr J. P. Postgate in a letter to me (Aug. 30, 1917) says: 'The absolute use of *pendĕre* is certainly possible though at first strange, and this perhaps has led to the belief that the participle comes from *pendere*. The expression of the thought is compressed in other respects; and Havet reads Curs*or* uolucri pendens in nouacula, Caluus comosa fronte, nudo *occipitio* for curs*u*.' Dr Postgate adds that in *Il.* 10. 173 ἵσταται 'should I suppose be understood of "weighing," a common meaning of ἵστημι, though the commentators do not say so.'

[6] Phaedr. 5. 8. 2 f.   [7] *Id.* 5. 8 *titulus*, 5. 8. 7.   [8] *Id.* 5. 8. 5.

[9] Cato *disticha* 2. 26. 2 fronte capillata, post est Occasio calva.

[10] Paulin. Nolan. *epist.* 16. 4 (lxi. 230 B Migne) unde et Spes et Nemesis et Amor atque etiam Furor in simulacris coluntur, et occipiti calvo sacratur Occasio, et tua ista Fortuna lubrico male nixa globo fingitur (*figuratur* codd. F.P.U.). nec minore mendacio Fata simulantur vitas hominum nere de calathis aut trutinare de lancibus.

[11] Aus. *epigr.* 33 Peiper.

Pheidias (!). *Metánoia* is comfortably Latinised as *Paenitentia*. But the god *Kairós* must needs become the goddess *Occasio*, poised on a little wheel[1], with winged feet and the traditional *coiffure*.

[1] Furtwängler *Ant. Gemmen* i pl. 30, 38, ii. 149 publishes a gem, on which Kairos as a nude youthful runner, with wings on shoulders, winglets on ankles, small round mirror (?) in right hand and whip in left, sets one foot on a four-spoked wheel. Inscription: **L · S · P.**

A limestone relief (height on left 0·40m, breadth at bottom 0·27m) of *s*. iii or iv from Thebes, now at Cairo, shows a youthful figure in military costume, with wreath, shoulder-wings, knife, wheel, and balance, running towards the right. Below are two females, one flying at the same pace, the other left behind in an attitude of dejection. J. Strzygowski *Koptische Kunst* (*Service des Antiquités de l'Égypte: Catalogue général des Antiquités Égyptiennes du Musée du Caire*) Vienne 1904 p. 103 f. no. 8757 fig. 159 calls them Kairos, πρόνοια and μετάνοια. Cp. A. Muñoz in *L'Arte* 1905 viii. 150 fig. 5, O. M.

Fig. 801.

Dalton *Byzantine Art and Archaeology* Oxford 1911 p. 158 with fig. 65 (=my fig. 801). But P. Perdrizet in the *Bull. Corr. Hell.* 1912 xxxvi. 263 ff. fig. 1 takes the subject to be Nemesis trampling on Hybris (*supra* i. 269 fig. 195), with Metanoia behind. Cp. Lamer in Pauly—Wissowa *Real-Enc.* x. 1514. The latter interpretation is probably correct, though the type of Nemesis here is influenced by that of Kairos.

A relief from Thasos, now at Constantinople, has two niches side by side. In the one stands a youthful winged figure in short *chitón* and *himátion*, with balance in right hand and wheel beneath feet. In the other is a pair of draped females, touching bosom of dress with right hand and holding short rod in left. A. Muñoz in *L'Arte* 1906 ix. 212 ff. fig. 1 viewed them as Kairos (or Bios) with Pronoia and Metanoia. But O. Rossbach in

Having rung the changes from youth to eld and from male to female, this Protean personage reappears in Byzantine letters and art, sometimes under the old name of Chronos, sometimes under the new name of Bios.

Georgios Kedrenos (c. 1100 A.D.) states that the masterpieces collected in the House of Lausos[1] at Constantinople included 'the figure by Lysippos representing Chronos, bald behind, long-haired before[2].' Kedrenos' statement is very possibly true[3], though Lamer infers from the name Chronos that we have here to do, not with the original Lysippean figure, but with a bearded copy of it[4] Again, Ioannes Tzetzes (born c. 1110 A.D.) in his historical poem twice over informs us that, when Alexander had let slip an opportunity, Lysippos of Sikyon made him an effigy of Chronos

'Deaf, bald behind, wing-footed on a sphere,
And offering naught but a knife to his follower[5].'

Tzetzes further spends a score of lines on insisting that this was Chronos, not, as sundry wiseacres maintained, Bios[6]. He had already said the same thing in greater detail in one of his letters[7]. And, after him, Nikephoros Blemmydes (1197/8—1272 A.D.) describes the group in almost identical terms[8]. We gather

Roscher Lex. Myth. iii. 157 f. fig. 6 proved that they are Nemesis and the Nemeseis; and P. Perdrizet loc. cit. p. 267 suggested the Nemesis of Alexandreia and the Nemeseis of Smyrna (supra i. 270 fig. 197, 273). Cp. A. Legrand in Daremberg—Saglio Dict. Ant. iv. 54 fig. 5300, Reinach Rép. Reliefs ii. 174 no. 3, Lamer loc. cit.

[1] On this see Kodinos de signis Constantinopolitanis 21 C (p. 37 f. Bekker) = Anonymos πάτρια 2. 36 (p. 170, 4 ff. Preger).

[2] Kedren. hist. comp. 322 C (i. 564 Bekker) καὶ τὸ τὸν χρόνον μιμούμενον ἄγαλμα, ἔργον Λυσίππου, ὄπισθεν μὲν φαλακρόν, ἔμπροσθεν δὲ κομῶν.

[3] See A. Frickenhaus in the Jahrb. d. kais. deutsch. arch. Inst. 1915 xxx. 127.

[4] Lamer in Pauly—Wissowa Real-Enc. x. 1511 f.

[5] Tzetz. chil. 8. 428 ff., 10. 264 ff.

[6] Tzetz. chil. 10. 275 ff.

[7] Tzetz. epist. 70 (p. 61 Pressel) Ἀλεξάνδρῳ ποτὲ τῶν Μακεδόνων τῷ βασιλεῖ παραδραμόντι καιρὸν καὶ μεταμέλου πεῖραν λαβόντι παρὼν ἐκεῖνος ὁ πλάστης ὁ Λύσιππος, Σικυώνιος δ' ἦν ὁ ἀνήρ, θειότατε δέσποτα, ὡς οὔτ' ἀκίνδυνον ἑώρα τὸν βασιλέα ἐλέγχειν, οὔτε μὴν πάντη ἀζήμιον τὸ μὴ τὴν ἑτέρων διαμαρτίαν ἑτέροις ποιεῖσθαι διδάσκαλον, τὴν ἀμφοτέρων κακίαν ἐκπεφευγὼς σοφῶς ἀμφότερα ἔδρασεν. ἐν εἰκόνι καὶ γὰρ τὸν χρόνον ἀγαλματώσας τόν τε βασιλέα τῷ μὴ δοκεῖν ἐλέγχειν κοσμίως ἐξήλεγξε καὶ τῷ κοινῷ τῶν ἀνθρώπων πρακτικὴν τοῦ λοιποῦ τὴν εἰκόνα παραίνεσιν καταλέλοιπεν. ἔχει δὲ οὑτωσὶ τὸ εἰκόνισμα. ἄνθρωπός τις ὁ Χρόνος ἐκείνῳ δεδημιούργηται προκόμιον ἔχων βραχύ, τὰ δ' ἄλλα ὀπισθοφάλακρος καὶ κωφὸς ἱκανῶς, ὥς ἐστιν εἰκάσαι, καὶ γυμνός ἐστιν ὡς διολισθαίνων καὶ ἀναφής· βέβηκε δὲ ἐπὶ σφαίρας εὐδρόμου τινὸς μεταριπτάζων αὐτοῦ τοῖς ποσὶν ἐκείνην ὀξυκινήτως, ὡς ἡ τῶν ποδῶν ὑπαινίττεται πτέρωσις. ἐκείνου δὲ κατόπιν ἕτερος δεδημιούργηται ἄνθρωπος εὐτόνῳ κεχρημένος βαδίσματι, χεῖρά τε ἰδίαν ἐκτείνων, ἐκεῖνον ὡς συλληψόμενος καὶ τοῦτον μετακαλούμενος, ὡς τὸ ἀνεσπασμένον αὐτοῦ τῶν χειλέων δηλοῖ· ὁ δὲ παρέρχεται τε καὶ οἴχεται καὶ κωφεύων οὐκ ἐπαΐει, μάχαιραν δὲ ὀρέγει πρὸς τὸ κατόπιν ἐπανατείνων τὴν χεῖρα, κατακαρδίους πληγὰς αἰνιττόμενος, αἵπερ ἐγγίνονται τοῖς χρόνου καθυστερίζουσιν. οὕτω πως σοφῶς ὁ Λύσιππος ἐνουθέτησε μὴ καθυστερίζειν καιρού, τοιαύτῃ τὸν Χρόνον ἀναστηλώσας γραφῇ, κἂν ἀκαιρηγοροῦντες δοκηταί τινες ἀκρίτως εἶναι βίου ταύτην παραληρῶσιν εἰκόνισμα, μὴ συνιέντες ὡς κ.τ.λ. Cp. epist. 95 (p. 86 Pressel) κωφόν· οἷον τὸν παροιχόμενον χρόνον Λύσιππος μὲν ἐζωγράφησε, κ.τ.λ. with schol. A.B. ἐζωγράφησε· ἀντὶ τοῦ ἠνδριαντούργησεν· ὁ Λύσιππος γὰρ ἀνδριαντοποιός, οὐ ζωγράφος.

[8] Nikeph. Blemmyd. oratio qualem oporteat esse regem 10 (in A. Mai Scriptorum veterum nova collectio Romae 1827 ii. 638) λέγουσί τινες ὅτι καὶ Λύσιππος ὁ ζωγράφος ἐκεῖνος ὁ Σικυώνιος (leg. Σικυώνιος) βουληθεὶς ζωγραφῆσαι καὶ ὡς ἐν παραδείγματι δεῖξαι (leg. δεῖξαι)

that some copy of Lysippos' runner, mounted on a ball, had been amplified by the addition of a second figure portraying the man who has allowed his opportunity to pass by and now pursues it in vain.

Among the wiseacres denounced by Tzetzes must be reckoned his contemporary Theodoros Prodromos (first half of s. xii A.D.), who in an extant epigram[1] describes Bios as a naked man, with wheels beneath his feet and wings about his shins, bearing a balance in his hand, and easily escaping from his pursuer, though holding out hopes of return. The poem is well illustrated by a fragmentary relief (fig. 802)[2] let into the pavement under the steps of the ambo in

ὁποίαν ἔχει τὴν φυγὴν ὁ χρόνος ἐποίησε τοῦτον κωφόν, ὀπιστοφάλακρον (leg. ὀπισθοφάλακρον), πτερόποδα, καὶ ἐπάνω τοῦ τροχοῦ βεβηκότα, μάχαιραν διδόντα κάτωθεν ἱσταμένῳ τινί· κωφὸν μέν, ὡς πρὸς τοὺς αὐτὸν φωνοῦντας, μηδαμῶς αἰσθανόμενον· φαλακρὸν δὲ τὰ ὄπισθεν, ὡς ἀδυνάτου ὄντος ὄπισθεν διώκοντα τινὰ κρατῆσαι αὐτόν· πῶς δέ τις αὐτὸν παραδραμόντα φθάσαι ἰσχύσειε πτερόποδα ὄντα καὶ ἐπὶ σφαίρας ἱστάμενον· διδόντα δὲ ξίφος, διότι οἱ μήτε δυνάμενοι τῆς κόμης κρατῆσαι μήτε φθάσαι φεύγοντα τιτρώσκονται τῷ βέλει τῆς λύπης ὡς τῆς ζημίας ἐπαισθανόμενοι. Id. βασιλικὸς ἀνδριάς 10 (ii. 667 Mai) Λύσιππος ὅθεν ὁ Σικυώνιος, ὅ τι ποτὲ ἐστιν ὁ χρόνος καλῶς συμβολογραφῶν, κωφὸν αὐτὸν ἠγαλμάτωσεν, ὀπισθοφάλακρον, πτερόποδά τε κἀπὶ σφαίρας βεβηκότα, μάχαιράν τινι πρὸς τὸ κατόπιν ὀρέγοντα, δηλῶν ἐντεῦθεν ὡς οὐκ ἂν ἐπιστραφείη καλούμενος, διότι κεκώφευκεν· οὔτε τις αὐτὸν ἐκ τοῦ ὀπίσω παρακατάσχοι δεδραγμένος τῆς κόμης, τὸ γὰρ ὀπισθόκρανον κατεψίλωτο· πῶς δὲ καὶ ὅλως παραδραμόντα τις καταλήψαιτο, τὴν ὀξυκινησίαν τοσαύτην φέροντα κἀκ τῶν ποδῶν κἀκ τῆς βάσεως; ρομφαίαν (ins. ἂν) σπάσαιτο λύπης ὥστε θυμὸν ἀμύσσειν ὁ τῆς ζημίας αἰσθόμενος.

[1] Theod. Prodr. εἰς εἰκονισμένον τὸν βίον (cxxxiii. 1419 A—1420 A Migne)

ἐμὲ τὸν Βίον, ἄνθρωπε, δέξαι σου παραινέτην.
ἔτυχες, εὗρες, ἔλαβες, κατέσχες μου τὰς τρίχας;
μὴ πρὸς ῥᾳστώνην ἐκδοθῇς, μὴ πρὸς τρυφὴν χωρήσῃς,
μηδὲ φρονήσῃς ὑψηλὰ καὶ πέρα τοῦ μετρίου.
γυμνόν με βλέπεις· νόησον γυμνόν μου καὶ τὸ τέλος.
ὑπὸ τοὺς πόδας μου τροχοί· φρίττε μὴ κυλισθῶσι.
περὶ τὰς κνήμας μου πτερά· φεύγω, παρίπταμαί σε.
ζυγὰ κατέχω τῇ χειρί· φοβοῦ τὰς μετακλίσεις.
τί με κρατεῖς; σκιὰν κρατεῖς· πνοὴν κρατεῖς ἀνέμου.
τί με κρατεῖς; καπνὸν κρατεῖς, ὄνειρον, ἴχνος πλοίου.

ἐμὲ τὸν Βίον, ἄνθρωπε, δέξαι σου παραινέτην.
οὐκ ἔτυχες, οὐκ ἔλαβες, οὐκ ἔσχες μου τὰς τρίχας;
μὴ σκυθρωπάσῃς τοῦ λοιποῦ, μηδὲ δυσελπιστήσῃς.
γυμνός εἰμι, καὶ τῶν χειρῶν ἐξολισθήσας τούτων
ἴσως μεταρρυήσομαι πρὸς σὲ καὶ μεταπέσω.
ὑπὸ τοὺς πόδας μου τροχοί· τάχα σοι κυλισθῶσι.
περὶ τὰς κνήμας μου πτερά· τρέχω, προσίπταμαί σοι.
ζυγὰ κατέχω· τάχα σοι τὴν πλάστιγγα χαλάσω.
μὴ τοίνυν ἀποπροσποιοῦ τὰς ἀγαθὰς ἐλπίδας.

There is a line lost from the second of the two stanzas, which were clearly meant to correspond.

[2] O. Jahn in the Ber. sächs. Gesellsch. d. Wiss. Phil.-hist. Classe 1853 pp. 49—59 pl. 4, E. Curtius 'Die Darstellungen des Kairos' in the Arch. Zeit. 1875 xxxiii. 6 f. pl. 1, 2, Friederichs—Wolters Gipsabgüsse p. 752 no. 1899, A. Baumeister in his Denkm. ii. 772 fig. 824, B. Sauer in Roscher Lex. Myth. ii. 900 fig., F. Durrbach in Daremberg—Saglio Dict. Ant. iii. 787 f. fig. 4252, A. Muñoz in L'Arte 1904 vii. 132 ff. fig. 4, O. M. Dalton Byzantine Art and Archaeology Oxford 1911 p. 158 f. fig. 91, Reinach Rép. Reliefs iii. 422 no. 3.

A further fragment of the relief, found by the architect R. Cattaneo in a mason's shop at Venice, was published by him in the drawing here reproduced (R. Cattaneo L'architettura

the Duomo at Torcello near Venice. The relief, which may be dated *c.* 1100 A.D., represents Bios as a half-naked youth hastening on winged wheels from right to left. His left hand, stretched forward, carries the scales; his right, drawn backward, brandishes a knife. In front of him stands a young man, who succeeds in grasping his hair. Behind him stands an old man, who fails in the attempt. To

Fig. 802.

the left of the former is Nike with wreath and palm; to the right of the latter is Metanoia in an attitude of despair. Less elaborate is the symbolism of a later epigram on the same subject by Manuel Philes (*c.* 1275—*c.* 1345), who speaks of life (*bíos*) as a nude youth, with bald head and winged feet, admonishing a frustrated follower[1].

in Italia dal secolo VI al mille circa Venezia 1888 p. 287 fig., trans. Contessa I. Curtis-Cholmeley in Bermani London 1896 p. 334 ff. fig. 165 = my fig. 802) and by A. Muñoz from a photograph (A. Muñoz in *L'Arte* 1906 ix. 214 f. fig. 2). The completed design is discussed by R. von Schneider 'Ueber das Kairosrelief in Torcello und ihm verwandte Bildwerke' in the *Serta Harteliana* Wien 1896 pp. 279—292 with figs., P. Perdrizet in the *Bull. Corr. Hell.* 1912 xxxvi. 264 ff. fig. 2, Lamer in Pauly—Wissowa *Real-Enc.* x. 1513 f.

R. Cattaneo *loc. cit.* was the first to assign this relief to its right place among the decorative sculptures of *s.* x and *s.* xi A.D. A. Muñoz *locc. citt.* first showed that the central figure was that of Bios.

[1] Philes *carm.* 67 (i. 32 Miller) εἰς μειράκιον γυμνόν, εἰκόνα φέρον τοῦ βίου

φεύγω, πτερωτός εἰμι· τί λαβεῖν θέλεις;
τὰς τρίχας; ἀλλ' ἔρρευσαν. ἀλλὰ τοὺς πόδας;
καὶ πῶς πτερωτοὺς εὑρεθέντας ἂν λάβοις;
τὸ σῶμα; γυμνόν ἐστι· τί σπεύδεις μάτην;

Yet another turn of the kaleidoscope, and this shifting personality puts on, if not a fresh form, at least a new colouring. Bios the naked runner on winged wheels, who has hitherto, in accordance with pagan thought, been represented as a good thing eagerly pursued by mankind, is now, within the pale of the medieval Church, viewed as a bad thing itself in hot pursuit of men. A Vatican manuscript of the *Ladder of Paradise* by Saint John Klimax[1], written about the close of *s.* xi A.D., has two relevant miniatures. In the one[2] Bios, a naked youth on wheels, makes after a monk, who bearing a small basket on his shoulder and looking behind him in terror does his best to escape, under the escort of a woman in blue and violet dress called *Aprospátheia*, 'Indifference to the World.' In the

Fig. 803.

other (fig. 803)[3] Bios again appears on his roller-skates, extending a hand to seize the monk, who stands irresolute, hesitating whether or not to abandon for Aprospatheia's sake his wife and children and happy home. A notable picture— one wonders if John Bunyan had somewhere seen the like.

We have traced the career of Kairos *alias* Chronos *alias* Bios for close upon eighteen centuries. It is possible that further investigation might find him with us still, 'offering' as of old 'naught but a knife to his follower.' 'It would be interesting to know,' says Prof. E. A. Gardner[4], 'whether the scythe of Time is the ultimate development of this same symbol, and his hour-glass of the balance.'

$$\text{ἄνθρωπε ταλαίπωρε, λῆξον τοῦ δρόμου,}$$
$$\text{μὴ κατενεχθῆς τῷ δοκεῖν τι λαμβάνειν.}$$
$$\text{σκιὰ γάρ εἰμι, κἂν δοκῶ τέως μένειν.}$$
$$\text{ἀφίπταμαί σου καὶ πρὸς οὐδὲν ἐκτρέχω,}$$
$$\text{καὶ γίνομαι ῥοῦς ἂν συνέξῃς δακτύλοις.}$$

Another MS. of Philes (cod. Paris.) has the *lemma* εἰς τὸν βίον μειράκιον ἐζωγραφημένον, whence A. Muñoz in *L'Arte* 1904 vii. 131 n. 2 justly concludes that the poem alludes to some work of art.

[1] *Supra* p. 134 f. The MS. is cod. Vat. Gr. 394.

[2] A. Muñoz in *L'Arte* 1904 vii. 132 with fig. 2. The three characters are inscribed ὁ βίος, ὁ μοναχός, and ἡ ἀπροσπάθεια, above whose name is written ἡ φυγὴ κόσμου.

[3] A. Muñoz in *L'Arte* 1904 vii. 132 with fig. 3 (part of which = my fig. 803). The inscriptions are ἡ γυνὴ τοῦ μοναχοῦ, οἱ παῖδες τοῦ μοναχοῦ, ὁ βίος, ὁ μοναχός, and in the field ἄπελθε μοναχὲ εἰς καταλύουσαν ἀπροσπάθειαν and ὁ δὲ βίος σκιὰ καὶ ἐνύπνια.

[4] E. A. Gardner *A Handbook of Greek Sculpture* London 1897 ii. 411 n. 1.

The scythe of Time[1] should, I think, rather be derived from the scythe of Death, who was often conceived as a reaper or mower[2] and in folk-celebrations of Mid-Lent was sometimes represented by a straw puppet with a scythe in his hand[3]. The hour-glass of Time likewise copies the hour-glass of Death so frequently figured in the *Danse Macabre*[4] of the Middle Ages. But Time himself is presumably the lineal descendant of the Byzantine Chronos or Bios. And it may well be that the knife, if not the balance, of Bios was modified to suit the popular effigy of Death. After all, the Church's idea of Life has often borne a suspicious resemblance to the world's idea of Death. τίς δ' οἶδεν εἰ τὸ ζῆν μέν ἐστι κατθανεῖν, | τὸ κατθανεῖν δὲ ζῆν κάτω νομίζεται[5] ;

If the main lines of the pedigree are as I have supposed, a further point may be descried. As at the first the razor of Kairos, so at the last the scythe of Time, was a symbol drawn from ritual usage. Such symbols live longest.

APPENDIX B.

THE MOUNTAIN-CULTS OF ZEUS.

Since the mountain-cults of Zeus have not, even in Germany, been made the subject of separate and detailed investigation[6], it seemed worth while to collect the evidence both literary and monumental bearing upon them. The inferences that can be drawn from the evidence have for the most part been already stated[7].

The Greeks worshipped Zeus *Óreios* 'of the Mountain[8],' Zeus *Koryphaîos*

[1] Ancient, medieval, and modern representations of Time are discussed by F. Piper *Mythologie und Symbolik der christlichen Kunst* Weimar 1851 i. 2. 389—409.

[2] J. Grimm *Teutonic Mythology* trans. J. S. Stallybrass London 1883 ii. 848, 1888 iv. 1558, K. Simrock *Handbuch der Deutschen Mythologie*[5] Bonn 1878 p. 479.

[3] J. Grimm *op. cit.* 1883 ii. 772, W. Mannhardt *Wald- und Feldkulte*[2] Berlin 1904 i. 155 f., 412, 418, 421, cp. 420, Frazer *Golden Bough*[3] : The Dying God p. 247.

[4] On the various forms of the *Danse Macabre* see F. Douce *The Dance of Death* London 1833 with 54 pls., E. H. Langlois *Essai historique, philosophique et pittoresque sur les Danses des morts* Rouen 1852 in 2 vols. with 54 pls. and many figs., J. G. Kastner *Les Danses des morts* Paris 1852 with 20 pls. Bibliography in H. F. Massmann *Literatur der Todtentänze* Leipzig 1840 and E. Vinet *Bibliographie méthodique et raisonnée des beaux-arts* Paris 1874 pp. 116—121.

[5] Eur. *Polyeidos frag.* 638 Nauck[2]. See further F. H. M. Blaydes on Aristoph. *ran.* 1477, *infra* Append. N *init.*

[6] R. Beer *Heilige Höhen der alten Griechen und Römer* Wien 1891 pp. x, 86, written as a supplement to F. v. Andrian *Der Höhencultus asiatischer und europäischer Völker* Wien 1891, is a slight and disappointing book. C. Albers *De diis in locis editis cultis pud Graecos* Zutphaniae 1901 pp. 1—92 is likewise quite inadequate (see Gruppe *Myth. Lit.* 1908 pp. 115, 316). The lists given by Welcker *Gr. Götterl.* i. 169 ff., Preller—Robert *Gr. Myth.* i. 116 f., Farnell *Cults of Gk. States* i. 50 ff., 152 ff., Gruppe *Gr. Myth. Rel.* p. 1103 f., though useful, are incomplete.

[7] *Supra* i. 117 ff. *et passim.*

[8] Zeus Ὄρειος. E. Renan *Mission de Phénicie* Paris 1864 p. 396 f. recorded two identical inscriptions on blocks of gritstone formerly used for the lintel of the church-door at *Halalieh*: ἔτους ξνς', μηνὸς Ἀπελλαίου ιε΄, Θρεπτίων (N)εικωνος τοῦ Σωσίππου τοὺς δύο | λέοντας Διὶ Ὀρείῳ, κατ' ὄναρ, ἐκ τῶν ἰδίων, εὐσεβῶν ἀνέθηκεν. The year 257 in the Seleucid era would be 55 B.C., in that of Antioch 209 A.D., in that of Sidon 147 A.D. Renan held

'of the Peak[1],' Zeus *Aktaîos* 'of the Point[2],' Zeus *Akraîos* 'of the Summit[3],'

that the last date agrees best with the lettering. He pointed out that a little lion in white stone, found in 1863 at the foot of the hill on which the church stands, may well have been one of the two lions here mentioned. G. F. Hill in the *Journ. Hell. Stud.* 1911 xxxi. 57 notes that 'the lion, as an inhabitant of the mountain rather than the plain, is naturally sacred to the mountain deity' [cp. 2 Kings 17. 25 f.], in this case to the Mountain Baal, Hellenised as Zeus Ὄρειος, whose consort Astarte (?) rides a lion on coppers of Sidon struck by Severus Alexander (G. F. Hill in the *Brit. Mus. Cat. Coins* Phoenicia pp. cxiii n. 6, 198 pl. 25, 8).

Zeus Ὀρομπάτας. E. Sittig in *Hermes* 1915 l. 158 f. publishes a dedication on a block of dark limestone at Amathous in Kypros: Κυπρ ///////////| Πολυξένου : Αἰνιᾶν[ος θυ]γάτηρ: Εὐβιότα | Παναίτιον Πολυξένου Αἰνιᾶνα, | Διὸς Ὀρομπάτα ἱερέα, τὸν αὐτῆς ἄνδρα, | αὐτὴ καὶ τὰ παιδία. The lettering suggests *s*. iii B.C.; and Sittig regards Ὀρο-μπάτας as = ὀρειβάτης ('Offenbar neigte das Kyprische dazu, β spirantisch zu sprechen; da in dem Dialekte der Ainianen β Verschlusslaut blieb, vollends in einem sakralen Worte, so half man sich bei der Schreibung so, dass man MΠ statt des B setzte, mit dem die Eingeborenen einen anderen Lautwert verbanden'). This is ingenious; but, apart from the fact that μπ for β is unexampled at so early a date, ὀρειβάτης is an epithet which suits Pan (*Anth. Pal.* 16. 226. 1 (Alkaios of Messene)) rather than Zeus. I suspect that Zeus Ὀρομπάτας was a god of streams worshipped by the Ainianes. We hear of Ainianes as settled in Kirrha the harbour of Delphoi (Plout. *quaestt. Gr.* 13 and 26), and of ὀρεμπότης as a Delphic term for 'river' (Plout. *de Pyth. or.* 24 ἀπέπαυσε δὲ τὴν Πυθίαν ὁ θεὸς πυρικάους μὲν ὀνομάζουσαν τοὺς αὐτῆς πολίτας, ὀφιοβόρους δὲ τοὺς Σπαρτιάτας, ὀρεᾶνας δὲ τοὺς ἄνδρας, ὀρεμπότας δὲ τοὺς ποταμούς). On this showing Zeus Ὀρομπάτας resembled his neighbour Zeus Νάιος, a god 'of Streaming Water' (*supra* i. 369). The head of Zeus on coins of the Ainianes (*Brit. Mus. Cat. Coins* Thessaly etc. p. 10 ff. pl. 2, 1, 4, Head *Hist. num.*[2] p. 292), which in the case of coppers struck *c.* 168—146 B.C. often has a thunderbolt in the field (so on two specimens in my collection), may be that of Zeus Ὀρομπάτας.

[1] Zeus Κορυφαῖος. Seleukeia Pieria, at the foot of Mt Koryphaion (Polyb. 5. 59. 4), had a priest of Zeus Ὀλύμπιος and Zeus Κορυφαῖος (*Corp. inscr. Gr.* iii no. 4458, 3 f., 3 ff., = Dittenberger *Orient. Gr. inscr. sel.* no. 245, 3 f. Διὸς Ὀλυμπίου | καὶ Διὸς Κορυφαίου, 27 ff. Διὸς Ὀλυμπίου [καὶ] | τῶν θεῶν τῶν | Σωτήρ[ων] καὶ Διὸς | Κο[ρυφ]αίου, cp. Liban. *legat. ad Iulian.* 79 (ii. 152, 10 f. Foerster) τὸν Δία τόν τε ἐπὶ τῆς κορυφῆς καὶ τὸν ἐν ἄστει, παρ' ὃν εἰσῆλθες ὕπατος, ὅθεν ἐξῆλθες θαρρῶν, ᾧ γέγονας ὀφειλέτης). Philadelpheia in Lydia, at the base of Mt Tmolos, also had a cult of Zeus Κορυφαῖος (*supra* p. 285 n. 0 no. (3) and Addenda *ad loc.*), whose head is seen on an imperial bronze coin of the town (*Brit. Mus. Cat. Coins* Lydia p. 190 pl. 21, 9 = my fig. 804 (from a cast), Head *Hist. num.*[2] p. 655). The title has a variety of meanings in Paus. 2. 4. 5 (Corinth) ὑπὲρ δὲ τὸ θέατρόν ἐστιν ἱερὸν Διὸς Καπετωλίου φωνῇ τῇ Ῥωμαίων· κατὰ Ἑλλάδα δὲ γλῶσσαν Κορυφαῖος ὀνομάζοιτο ἄν, Aristeid. *or.* 1. 8 (i. 11 Dindorf) οὗτος βασιλεύς, πολιεύς, καταιβάτης, ὑέτιος, οὐράνιος, κορυφαῖος, πάνθ' ὅσα αὐτὸς εὗρε μεγάλα καὶ ἑαυτῷ πρέποντα ὀνόματα, Max. Tyr. *diss.* 41. 2 Dübner τὸν Δία...τὸν κορυφαῖον τῆς τῶν ἄστρων περιφορᾶς καὶ δινήσεως καὶ χορείας καὶ δρόμου, cp. Ioul. *or.* 7. 230 D ἀγαγὼν δὲ αὐτὸν ἐπί τι μέγα καὶ ὑψηλὸν ὄρος, Ἐπὶ τούτου, ἔφη, τῆς κορυφῆς ὁ πατὴρ πάντων κάθηται τῶν θεῶν, Cic. *de nat. deor.* 3. 59 (Minerva) quarta Iove nata et Coryphe, Oceani filia, Clem. Al. *protr.* 2. 28. 2 p. 21, 1 f. Stählin (*supra* i. 155 n. 10, to which add Arnob. *adv. nat.* 4. 14 and 16), Orph. *h. Poseid.* 17 b. 3 (Poseidon) ὃς ναίεις κορυφαῖος ἐπ' Οὐλύμποιο καρήνων, Paus. 2. 28. 2 ἐπὶ δὲ τῇ ἄκρᾳ τοῦ ὄρους (sc. of Mt Koryphon near Epidauros) Κορυφαίας ἐστὶν ἱερὸν Ἀρτέμιδος, Steph. Byz. *s.v.* Κορυφαῖον· ὄρος ἐπὶ τῷ Ἐπιδαυρίῳ, ἐν ᾧ τιμᾶται Ἄρτεμις Κορυφαία.

Fig. 804.

[2] Zeus Ἀκταῖος. Dikaiarch. 2. 8 (*Geogr. Gr. min.* i. 107 Müller) ἐπ' ἄκρας δὲ τῆς τοῦ ὄρους (sc. of Mt Pelion) κορυφῆς σπηλαῖόν ἐστι τὸ καλούμενον Χειρώνιον, καὶ Διὸς Ἀκταίου

[3 For note 3 see p. 871.]

(F. Osann, followed by C. Müller, cj. Ἀκραίου) ἱερόν, ἐφ᾽ ὃ κατὰ κυνὸς ἀνατολὴν κατὰ τὸ ἀκμαιότατον καῦμα ἀναβαίνουσι τῶν πολιτῶν οἱ ἐπιφανέστατοι καὶ ταῖς ἡλικίαις ἀκμάζοντες, ἐπιλεχθέντες ἐπὶ τοῦ ἱερέως, ἐνεζωσμένοι κώδια τρίποκα καινά· τοιοῦτον συμβαίνει ἐπὶ τοῦ ὄρους τὸ ψῦχος εἶναι. On this passage see *supra* i. 420 f. The sanctuary of Zeus Ἀκταῖος has been located and partially explored by A. S. Arvanitopoullos in the Πρακτ. ἀρχ. ἑτ. 1911 pp. 305—312 fig. 5 (= my fig. 805). The discoveries there described may be here summarised (brief notice also in *Am. Journ. Arch.* 1913 xvii. 109):

The highest peak of Pelion (1635ᵐ), now called *Plissídi* or *Pliassídi*, has been repeatedly ransacked by treasure-seekers, some of whom coming from *Drákeia* are said to have been devoured by wolves. The rocky eastern side of the summit shows traces of ancient hewn habitations, like those of Demetrias, Pagasai, Phthiotic Thebes, etc., with holes for roof-timbers and coarse tiles perhaps manufactured on the spot. These dwellings are called by the shepherds *Skoleió*, because they resemble the benches in a school.

Close by is a ruined gate of hewn stone (E) with two towers (Π, Π), continued as a wall some 3ᵐ thick, which forms a large elliptical precinct and probably had another gate on the south, though most of the stones have here disappeared. The wall and towers may date from *s*. v B.C. Adjoining this precinct, on the south-east, is another, of whose

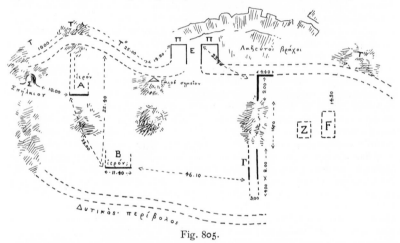

Fig. 805.

wall nothing remains beyond a small portion of the eastern side. The two precincts are separated by a wall of small stones (Γ), again 3ᵐ thick, which was roofed on both sides so as to make a *stoá* for the sale of commodities during festival seasons.

At the north-west end of the large precinct is a steep rock-face, in which is the mouth of a cave (Σ), 2ᵐ across, blocked with stones by the natives in recent times. The walls of the cave appear to have been hewn. Near it are traces of a building (A), which seems to have been of apsidal or horse-shoe shape, like the temple of Athena *Poliás* at Gonnoi (Arvanitopoullos *loc. cit.* p. 316 fig. 6), and was presumably the temple of the divinity worshipped in the cave. Further west was the quadrilateral temple (B) of another related deity: this was on a larger scale, one side partly excavated reaching a length of 11·40ᵐ with a wall 0·55ᵐ thick. Both buildings were carefully constructed of clay, the roofs being supported on trunks of trees. Numerous red tiles and black cover-tiles remain. Miscellaneous finds in this area include small cups of *s*. v—iv B.C., a copper coin of Chalkis of *s*. iv, butts and blades of iron lances, a flat unpainted idol like those of island make, three fragments of votive marble *stêlai*, six *amphorae* buried full of embers and ashes. In the gateway (E) was a fragmentary *stéle* of hard white limestone inscribed in lettering of *s*. iv B.C. [ὁ δεῖνες ἀνέθηκ]αν Μ[ούσ(?)]|αις.

Inside the second precinct are two buildings (F and Z). Of these one (F) is a rectangular structure, built of large hewn blocks, with many roof-tiles. It stands on a slight elevation and, as the finest building on the site, is probably to be identified with the temple of Zeus Ἀκραῖος. Its position outside the large precinct is curious [and may imply that Zeus was a later comer than the deity worshipped in the cave—Cheiron son of Kronos and Philyra (?) A. B. C.]. Arvanitopoullos was unable to complete the excavation of this temple, because at midnight on Aug. 15, 1911, a storm burst on the summit of the mountain, inundated his tent, and forced him to beat a retreat. The small neighbouring structure (Z) was left wholly unexcavated.

³ Zeus Ἀκραῖος. (1) The cult of Zeus Ἀκραῖος on Mt Pelion is attested by an inscription found near *Bupha* on the Gulf of Pagasai and now in the Museum at *Volo* (J. v. Prott and L. Ziehen *Leges Graecorum sacrae* ii no. 82, 1 ff. = O. Kern in the *Inscr. Gr. sept.* iii. 2 no. 1110, 1 ff. [— — — παριστάναι τὰ θύμα]τα λευκὰ ὁλόκληρα [κα]|[θαρὰ ἃ δεῖ θύ]εσθαι τῶι θεῶι καὶ τὰ ἄλλα τὰ ἐθιζόμενα καθὼς [καὶ] | [πρὶν ἐ]γίνετο, τὰς δὲ τούτων δορὰς πωλεῖσθαι ἀπὸ τοῦ [νῦν χρό]|[νου κα]τ' ἐνιαυτὸν ὑπὸ κήρυκα τῆι ἕκτηι ἐπὶ δέκα τοῦ Ἀρτεμισι[ῶνος μη]|νὸς πρὸ τῆς ἐκκλησίας γινομένης ἐννόμου ἀπὸ τοῦ — — — —|ρίου ὑπὸ τῶν προγεγραμ-μένων ἀρχόντων, συμπαρόντων καὶ τοῦ ἱερέ|ως τοῦ Διὸς τοῦ Ἀκραίου καὶ τῶν ἐξεταστῶν, καὶ τὸ ἐκ τούτων | γενόμενον διάφ[ορον ἱερὸν εἶναι] τοῦ Διὸς τοῦ Ἀκραίου . . . . . |νου τὰς ἀγορὰς — — — — — ἄμα τῶι θεῶι συναχθείσῃ | — — κ.τ.λ. (eight lines badly mutilated)) : on this see *supra* i. 421 f. In *s.* ii B.C. the priest of Zeus Ἀκραῖος was a personage of importance, who proposed decrees along with the chief magistrates of the Magnetes (Michel *Recueil d'Inscr. gr.* no. 307, 7 f. = *Inscr. Gr. sept.* iii. 2 no. 1103, 7 f. Ἀδαῖος Ἀδύμο[υ] ὁ ἱερεὺς τοῦ Διὸς τοῦ ['Α]|κραίου, *ib.* iii. 2 no. 1105, 11, 6 f. Θηβαγένης Ἀπολλωνίου ὁ ἱερεὺς τοῦ Διὸς τοῦ | Ἀκραίου, Michel *op. cit.* no. 309, 6 = *Inscr. Gr. sept.* iii. 2 no. 1108, 6 [Λυ]σίας Ἐπιτέλου ὁ ἱερεὺς τοῦ Διὸς τοῦ Ἀκραίου). About 100 B.C. the priest of Zeus Ἀκραῖος was eponymous magistrate of the Magnetes, and those who were charged with the up-keep of the oracle of Apollon Κοροπαῖος took oath by Zeus Ἀκραῖος, Apollon Κοροπαῖος, and Artemis Ἰωλκία (Michel *op. cit.* no. 842 *A*, 1 ff., *B*, 5 ff., 21 f. = Dittenberger *Syll. inscr. Gr.*³ no. 1157, 1 *a*, 1 ff., 1 *bc*, 54 ff., 11, 70 f. = *Inscr. Gr. sept.* iii. 2 no. 1109, 1, 1 ff. ἱερέως Κρίνωνος τοῦ Παρμενίωνος, μηνὸς Ἀρείου δεκάτηι, | Κρίνων Παρμενίωνος Ὁμολιεὺς ὁ ἱερεὺς τοῦ Διὸς τοῦ Ἀκραίου κ.τ.λ., 54 ff. (cited *supra* p. 730 n. 0 *sub fin.*), 11, 70 f. ἱερέως Κρίνωνος τοῦ Παρμενίωνος, μηνὸς Ἀρτεμισιῶνος δεκάτηι, | Κρίνων Παρμενίωνος Ὁμολιεὺς ὁ ἱερεὺς τοῦ Διὸς τοῦ Ἀκραίου κ.τ.λ.). Cp. *Inscr. Gr. sept.* iii. 2 no. 1128, 1 ff. Αὐρ. Τειμασίθεος | Κενταύριος ὁ ἱερ[ε]ὺς τῷ Ἀκραίῳ Δι[ί].

(2) On the Pindos range between Thessaly and Epeiros there was a sanctuary of Zeus Ἀκραῖος (Liv. 38. 2 templum Iovis Acraei), whose figure seated on a rock or throne appears on coins of Gomphoi or Philippopolis (*supra* i. 124 figs. 90—92).

(3) At Trapezous in Arkadia, beneath Mt Lykaion, sacrifices were offered to Zeus Ἀκραῖος (Nikol. Damask. *frag.* 39 (*Frag. hist. Gr.* iii. 377 Müller) ταχὺ δὲ καὶ τοὺς υἱεῖς (*sc.* Κρεσφόντου) ἤθελον (*sc.* οἱ ἐγχώριοι ἀποκτεῖναι), οὓς τότε ὁ μητροπάτωρ (*sc.* Κύψελος) ἄμα τῇ θυγατρὶ κυούσῃ θύειν μέλλων Διὶ Ἀκραίῳ εἰς Τραπεζοῦντα μετεπέμψατο).

(4) At Praisos in eastern Crete, where there was a temple of Zeus Δικταῖος (*supra* i. 660), the god seems to have borne the second appellative Ἀκραῖος. He appears on silver

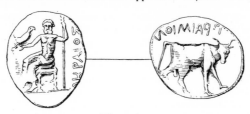

Fig. 806.

coins of the town (*supra* i. 660 n. 3) enthroned with sceptre and eagle and accompanied by the title ΑΚΡΑΙΟΣ (first correctly deciphered by C. T. Seltman) : fig. 806 is from a specimen in my collection. Since the coins in question go back to a date *c.* 400 B.C., this is the earliest known example of ΑΚΡΑΙΟΣ as a numismatic legend.

(5) At Halikarnassos Aphrodite, who shared a temple with Hermes on high ground beside the spring Salmakis (Vitr. 2. 8. 11), probably bore the title Ἀκραία, since the Halicarnassians are known to have, built a temple of Aphrodite Ἀκραία beneath the *akrópolis* of their mother-city Troizen (Paus. 2. 32. 6). Zeus too was worshipped at Hali-karnassos under the same title (Lebas—Waddington *Asie Mineure* no. 501 Διονύσιος | Διὶ Ἀκραίωι εὐχή[ν]). T. Bergk *Exercitationum criticarum specimen VI* Marburgi 1850 p. vi (=*id. Kleine philologische Schriften* ed. R. Peppmüller Halle a. S. 1886 ii. 297), K. Keil in *Philologus* 1854 ix. 454, and G. Wentzel in Pauly—Wissowa *Real-Enc.* i. 1193, would read Ἀκραίῳ for Ἀσκραίῳ in Apollon. *hist. mir.* 13 ἐν τῷ κατὰ τόπους μυθικῷ· ἐν Ἁλικαρ-νασσῷ θυσίας τινὸς τῷ Διὶ τῷ Ἀσκραίῳ συντελουμένης ἀγέλην αἰγῶν ἄγεσθαι πρὸ τοῦ ἱεροῦ καὶ ἵστασθαι· τῶν δὲ κατευχῶν συντελεσθεισῶν προβαίνειν μίαν αἶγα ὑπὸ μηδενὸς ἀγομένην καὶ προσέρχεσθαι τῷ βωμῷ, τὸν δὲ ἱερέα λαβόμενον αὐτῆς καλλιερεῖν. But I have argued in the *Class. Rev.* 1903 xvii. 415 f. that Zeus Ἀσκραῖος, to whom the Lydians brought their first-fruits (Plout. *animine an corporis affectiones sint peiores* 4 οὗτοι συνεληλύθασι...οὐκ

Fig. 807.   Fig. 808.   Fig. 809.

Fig. 810.   Fig. 811.

Ἀσκραίῳ Διὶ Λυδίων καρπῶν ἀπαρχὰς φέροντες), had a cult in Halikarnassos also; that he was an oak-Zeus (Hesych. ἄσκρα· δρῦς ἄκαρπος, cp. O. Schrader *Prehistoric Antiquities of the Aryan Peoples* trans. F. B. Jevons London 1890 p. 226, Prellwitz *Etym. Wörterb. d. Gr. Spr.*[2] p. 59, Boisacq *Dict. étym. de la Langue Gr.* p. 90); and that he is to be seen on imperial coppers of the town as a bearded god crowned with rays and standing between two oak-trees, on each of which is a bird (raven? dove?) (*Brit. Mus. Cat. Coins* Caria, etc. p. 110 no. 83 pl. 19, 2 (=my fig. 807) Trajan, no. 85 (=my fig. 808) Antoninus Pius, p. 111 no. 88 (=my fig. 810) Septimius Severus, W. M. Leake *Numismata Hellenica* London 1854 Asiatic Greece p. 64 (=my fig. 809) Commodus, Overbeck *Gr. Kunstmyth.* Zeus p. 210 f. Münztaf. 3, 12, Head *Hist. num.*[2] p. 619 fig. 305. Fig. 811 Gordianus Pius is from a specimen in my collection). It is of course possible that Ἀκραῖος was a second appellative of Zeus Ἀσκραῖος (cp. *supra* no. (4)).

(6) W. R. Paton in the *Class. Rev.* 1907 xxi. 47 f. publishes an inscription, in lettering of about *s.* i B.C. or *s.* i A.D., found at Myndos: [Πο]σίδεος Κλεωνύμου καθ' ὑοθεσία[ν] | [δὲ] Ποσιδέου καὶ ἡ γυνὴ Ἡδεῖα Ἀπολλωνίδου | [καὶ] οἱ υἱοὶ Κλεώνυμος καὶ Ἀπολλωνίδης | [Ἀλ]ικαρνασσεῖς Διὶ Ἀκραίῳ. Paton proposes Ἀκραίῳ for Ἀσκραίῳ, not only in Apollon.

Zeus *Epákrios* 'on the Summit[1],' Zeus *Karaiós* 'of the Head[2],' Zeus *Lopheítes*

loc. cit., but also in Plout. *loc. cit.* Both passages were emended in the same manner 224 years before by G. Cuper *Apotheosis vel consecratio Homeri* Amstelodami 1683 p. 16.

(7) Imperial coppers of Magnesia ad Maeandrum show Zeus Ἀκραῖος as a nude standing figure, with right hand supported on sceptre, left holding thunderbolt (Imhoof-Blumer *Gr. Münzen* p. 120 no. 312 **AKPAIOC ΜΑΓΝΗΤΩΝ** Geta, *id. Kleinas. Münzen* i. 79 no. 27 **ΜΑΓΝΗΤΩ Ν ZEYC AKPAIOC** Antoninus Pius).

(8) At Smyrna Ulpius Traianus, father of the emperor Trajan, brought an aqueduct to the precinct of Zeus Ἀκραῖος (*Corp. inscr. Gr.* ii no. 3146, 1 ff. ἐκ τοῦ εἰσαχθέντος | ὕδατος ἐπὶ τὸν Δία τὸν | Ἀκραῖον ἐπὶ Οὐλπίου | Τραϊανοῦ τοῦ ἀνθυπάτου, | κ.τ.λ.). *Quasi*-autonomous and imperial coppers show the god's head, usually inscribed **ZEYC AKPAIOC** or **ZEVC AKPAIOC** or **ZEVC AKPAIOC** (*Brit. Mus. Cat. Coins* Ionia p. 253 ff. pl. 27, 1, 2, 5, 6, 8, *Hunter Cat. Coins* ii. 368 ff. pl. 52, 8, Head *Hist. num.*[2] p. 594.

Fig. 812.   Fig. 813.   Fig. 814.

Fig. 812 is from a specimen of mine), or seated figure holding Nike and sceptre, sometimes inscribed **AKPAIOC** or **AKPAIOΣ** (*Brit. Mus. Cat. Coins* Ionia pp. 250 pl. 26, 8, 266, 272 pl. 28, 15, 287 pl. 29, 12 (=my fig. 813), 297, 302 pl. 39, 5, 307 pl. 39, 11 (=*supra* p. 319 fig. 201), *Hunter Cat. Coins* ii. 378 no. 202, 379 no. 203, 389 pl. 52, 18, Head *Hist. num.*[2] p. 594).

(9) At Temnos in Aiolis, on a hill above the Hermos, *quasi*-autonomous coppers of s. iii A.D. bear the bust of Zeus Ἀκραῖος, inscribed **ΣEVC AKPAIO C** (*Brit. Mus. Cat. Coins* Troas, etc. p. 145 no. 22, *Hunter Cat. Coins* ii. 311 no. 7, Head *Hist. num.*[2] p. 557. Fig. 814 is from a specimen of mine).

(10) L. Holstein on Steph. Byz. *s.v.* Μυτιλήνη (ed. Lipsiae 1825 ii. 457) says : 'In Cimeliarchio Mediceo nummus habetur, in cuius uno latere circum Iovem, Neptunum et Plutonem: **ΘΕΟΙ AKPAIOI ΜΥΤΙΛΗΝΑΙΩΝ**. in averso circum caput Iovis: **ZEVC ΒΟΥΛΑΙΟC**. quinam sint θεοὶ ἀκραῖοι...docet Pollux lib. IX. cap. 5. his verbis: Τὰ δὲ δημόσια, ἀκρόπολις· ἦν καὶ ἄκρον ἂν εἴποις καὶ πόλιν· καὶ τοὺς ἐν αὐτῇ θεοὺς, ἀκραίους καὶ πολιεῖς.' This coin, cited by numismatists from Eckhel *Doctr. num. vet.*[2] ii. 504 to Head *Hist. num.*[1] p. 488 inclusive, has disappeared from Head *Hist. num.*[2] p. 562 f.

(11) At Akrai (*Palazzolo*) in Sicily the Museum of Baron Judica had a base inscribed **ΔΙΟΣ | [ ]ΡΑΙΟΥ.** J. Schubring in the *Jahrb. f. Philol. u. Pädag.* Suppl. 1867 iv. 672 fig. 2 supplies ['Aγο]ραίου. But U. von Wilamowitz-Moellendorff in the *Inscr. Gr. Sic. It.* no. 203 with greater probability cj. ['Aκ]ραίου.

See further Schöll—Studemund *anecd.* i. 265 Ἐπίθετα Διός (20) ἀκραίου, Kallim. *h. Zeus* 81 f. ἵζεο δ' αὐτὸς | ἄκρης ἐν πολίεσσιν, Aristeid. *or.* i. 6 (i. 7 Dindorf) τὰς ἀκροπόλεις ἐξεῖλον Διΐ, κ.τ.λ.

---

[1] Zeus Ἐπάκριος. Polyzelos Μουσῶν γοναί *frag.* 1 (*Frag. com. Gr.* ii. 869 f. Meineke) *ap. et. mag.* p. 352, 49 ff. Ἐπάκριος Ζεύς· ἐπ' ἄκρας γὰρ τῶν ὀρῶν ἱδρύοντο βωμοὺς τῷ Διί, οἷον τοῦ Ὑμηττίου, τοῦ Παρνηθίου. Πολύζηλος Μουσῶν γοναῖς· "ἱερὸν γὰρ ὂν (A. Meineke cj. ἱερεὺς γὰρ ὢν, cp. Metagenes Αὖραι *frag.* 4 Meineke *ap.* schol. Aristoph. *av.* 873) τετύχηκας Ἐπακρίου Διός." So Hesych. *s.v.* Ἐπάκριος· Ζεύς. ὁ ἐπὶ τῶν ἄκρων τῶν ὀρῶν

[2 For note 2 see p. 874.]

'of the Crest[1].' These titles, and perhaps certain others[2], proclaim him to be a

ἱδρυμένος. ἐπὶ γὰρ τῶν ὁρῶν τοὺς βωμοὺς αὐτῷ ἵδρυον ὡς ἐπιπολύ, Eustath. *in Od.* p. 1747, 59 ὅθεν καὶ Ζεὺς ἐπάκριος, ᾧ ἐπ' ἄκρων ὀρέων ἱδρύοντο βωμοί. E. Ziebarth in the *Rhein. Mus.* 1900 lv. 502 f. published an inscription from Athens, in which certain ὀργεῶνες let on lease (?) [τὸ ἱερὸν τ]οῦ Διὸς τοῦ 'Επα[κρίου]. But the reading of the appellative is doubtful: ΕΠ/ are the only surviving letters.

[2] Zeus Καραιός. Hesych. *s.v.* Καραιός· Ζεὺς παρὰ Βοιωτοῖς οὕτω προσαγορεύεται· ὡς μέν τινές φασι διὰ τὸ ὑψηλὸς εἶναι, ἀπὸ τοῦ κάρα, *Inscr. Gr. sept.* i no. 3208 on a small unfluted column at Orchomenos in Boiotia [Διὶ] Καραιοῖ | [⋯⋯⋯ ἄρχ]οντος Κλιωνίω (W. Dittenberger *ad loc.* says: 'Vocem ἄρχοντος (aut ἱαραρχίοντος, ἱαρατεύοντος) mediam sumpsi interpositam fuisse inter nomen proprium et adiectivum patronymicum. Sed id quoque fieri potest, ut [Λί]οντος, [Σπένδ]οντος aut aliud simile nomen proprium fuerit'). Maybaum *Der Zeuskult in Boeotien* Doberan 1901 p. 6 draws attention to the proper names derived from this appellative: Καραιόγειτος (Thespiai), Καραΐς (Anthedon), Καράϊχος (Lebadeia, Orchomenos), Καραίων (Orchomenos). E. Sittig *De Graecorum nominibus theophoris* Halis Saxonum 1911 p. 13 extends the list, adding Καραῖος (*Corp. Inscr. Att.* ii. 2 no. 1045, 5 (Athens), *Inscr. Gr. Pelop.* i no. 729, 16 (Hermione), F. Blass in Collitz —Bechtel *Gr. Dial.-Inschr.* iii. 2. 235 f. no. 4942 a, 10 (Aptara in Crete)). The title suits a mountain-god, cp. *Il.* 20. 5 κρατὸς ἀπ' Οὐλύμποιο, 1. 44 κατ' Οὐλύμποιο καρήνων (Eustath. *in Il.* p. 1193, 9 f., Apollon. *lex. Hom.* p. 95, 22 ff. Bekker), *alib.* On Kratinos *Nemesis frag.* 10 see *supra* i. 280 n. 4. Phot. *lex.* Κάριος Ζεύς· ἐν Θεσσαλίᾳ καὶ Βοιωτίᾳ refers more probably to the Carian Zeus (*supra* p. 577), cp. the Boeotian name Καρίων (*Inscr. Gr. sept.* i no. 2787, 5 Kopai, 2974 Koroneia).

Zeus Κλάριος (Aisch. *suppl.* 359 f. ἴδοιτο δῆτ' ἄνατον φυγὰν | ἱκεσία Θέμις Διὸς Κλαρίου, Paus. 8. 53. 9 f. τὸ δὲ χωρίον τὸ ὑψηλόν, ἐφ' οὗ καὶ οἱ βωμοὶ Τεγεάταις εἰσὶν οἱ πολλοί, καλεῖται μὲν Διὸς Κλαρίου (καρίου codd. Vb. M.), δῆλα δὲ ὡς ἐγένετο ἡ ἐπίκλησις τῷ θεῷ τοῦ κλήρου τῶν παίδων ἕνεκα τῶν 'Αρκάδος. ἄγουσι δὲ ἑορτὴν αὐτόθι Τεγεᾶται κατὰ ἔτος· κ.τ.λ.). Farnell *Cults of Gk. States* i. 56, 71 takes Κλάριος to mean 'he who sanctified the original allotment of land,' 'the god of allotments' (κλῆροι) (so already Paus. *loc. cit.* and schol. Aisch. *loc. cit.* παντάπασι (H. Weil corr. πάντα πᾶσι) κληρούντος καὶ κραίνοντος). W. Pape—G. E. Benseler *Wörterbuch der griechischen Eigennamen*[3] Braunschweig 1875 i. 666 cite Hesych. κλάρες· αἱ ἐπὶ ἐδάφου(ς) ἐσχάραι, which might be held to justify Κλάριος = ἐφέστιος (O. Höfer in Roscher *Lex. Myth.* ii. 1212). But F. Solmsen in the *Rhein. Mus.* 1898 liii. 157 f., observing that the Tegeate tribe Κλαρεῶτις (Paus. 8. 53. 6: Schwedler cj. Κλαριῶτις) had tribesmen Κραριῶται (F. Bechtel in Collitz—Bechtel *Gr. Dial.-Inschr.* i. 351 ff. no. 1231, 357 ff. no. 1247), and that the names of the three other tribes 'Ιππο-θοῖτις, 'Απολλωνιᾶτις, 'Αθανεᾶτις are all derived from deities, contends that Zeus Κλάριος is for Zeus *Κράριος, 'ein "höchster Zeus" oder ein "Zeus der Bergeshöhe."' His view is accepted by Adler in Pauly—Wissowa *Real-Enc.* xi. 552 and may well be right.

Zeus Κλάριος of Eustath. *in Dionys. per.* 444 λέγεται δὲ καὶ Διὸς Κλαρίου μαντεῖον εἶναι αὐτόθι (*sc.* at Κλάρος near Kolophon) must not be confounded with Zeus Κλάριος.

[1] Zeus Λοφείτης. A cult of this deity at Perinthos (later known as Herakleia) on the Propontis is evidenced by the following inscriptions: (1) on the back of a rectangular marble altar, between *Rodosto* and *Eregli* (Perinthos), in letters of *s.* ii A.D. Διὶ Λοφείτῃ Ε[ὐ(?)]|δίων Φιλλύδ[ου] | ἱερεὺς νέοις λυ|⋯ρίοις δῶρον (E. Kalinka in the *Arch.-ep. Mitth.* 1896 xix. 67 f., F. Hiller von Gaertringen in the *Ath. Mitth.* 1906 xxxi. 565. Kalinka suggests that the altar was a gift to a corporation of *νέοι αὐράριοι*). (2) From Perinthos: Διὶ Λοφείτῃ | ὑπὲρ Οὐα(τ)ει/νίου Καλλιμά/χου οἱ φίλοι καὶ | οἰκιακοὶ εὐχήν (A. Baumeister in *Philologus* 1854 ix. 392 f. no. 15, F. Hiller von Gaertringen in the *Ath. Mitth.* 1906 xxxi. 565, *id. ib.* 1908 xxxiii. 161 f. Baumeister wrongly supposed that this inscription had come from Herakleia, the small island off the coast of Naxos). (3) From Perinthos: gable with garland, beneath which [Δι]ὶ Λοφείτ(η)ι καὶ | [συ]ναγωγῆι ‾ΝΑ | ⋯ων νέων Πρεῖ[σκ]ος ἐκ τῶν (εἰδ)ίων | καθιέρω[σε]ν (F. Hiller von Gaertringen in the *Ath. Mitth.*

[2 For note 2 see p. 875.]

god of mountain-tops. And, when he is called *Hýpatos* 'the High¹' or

1908 xxxiii. 162 suspects an allusion to the νέοι αὐράριοι (?) of (1) and proposes [συ]ναγωγῇ (τῶ)ν Α[ὑ – –][ρί]ων νέων). The title Λοφείτης was due to the situation of the town: ἡ γὰρ Πέρινθος κεῖται μὲν παρὰ θάλατταν ἐπί τινος αὐχένος ὑψηλοῦ χερρονήσου, σταδιαῖον ἐχούσης τὸν αὐχένα· τὰς δ' οἰκίας ἔχει πεπυκνωμένας καὶ τοῖς ὕψεσι διαφερούσας. αὗται δὲ ταῖς οἰκοδομαῖς ἀεὶ κατὰ τὴν εἰς τὸν λόφον ἀνάβασιν ἀλλήλων ὑπερέχουσι, καὶ τὸ σχῆμα τῆς ὅλης πόλεως θεατροειδὲς ἀποτελοῦσι (Diod. 16. 76). For Zeus Ἐπιλόφιος at Naïssos see *infra* Moesia.

² Gruppe *Gr. Myth. Rel.* p. 1103 n. 2 suggests that Zeus Φαλακρός at Argos (Clem. Al. *protr.* 2. 39. 2 p. 29, 6 f. Stählin οὐχὶ μέντοι Ζεὺς φαλακρὸς ἐν Ἄργει, τιμωρὸς δὲ ἄλλος ἐν Κύπρῳ τετίμησθον;) was a mountain-god. This is probable enough, for the summit of Mt Ida was called Φάλακρον, Φάλακρα, Φαλάκρα, Φαλάκραι, a promontory in Korkyra Φάλακρον, Φαλακρὸν ἄκρον, another in Epeiros Φάλακρον, another in Euboia Φαλάκραι (Stephanus *Thes. Gr. Ling.* viii. 604 B—D). For Zeus Κλάριος see *supra* p. 874 n. 2.

¹ Zeus Ὕπατος was worshipped (1) on Mt Hypatos above Glisas in Boiotia (Paus. 9. 19. 3 ὑπὲρ δὲ Γλισᾶντός ἐστιν ὅρος Ὕπατος καλούμενον, ἐπὶ δὲ αὐτῷ Διὸς Ὑπάτου ναὸς καὶ ἄγαλμα). The mountain, now called *Sagmatás*, rises to a height of 749ᵐ: 'it is bold and rocky, and has a flat summit which is crowned with a monastery of the Transfiguration, founded by Alexis Comnenus. The church of the monastery contains fine mosaics, and stands on the foundations of the temple of Zeus. Both the church and the monastery, as well as two neighbouring chapels, contain many considerable fragments of antiquity built into the walls. The dome of the church is supported by two ancient monolithic columns, with their bases and capitals' (Frazer *Pausanias* v. 61). The view from the monastery embraces the three lakes Kopaïs, Hylike, Paralimne, the Euboean sea, and on the horizon a whole series of mountains—Messapion, Dirphys, Parnes, Kithairon, Helikon, Sphingion, Parnassos, Ptoion (H. N. Ulrichs *Reisen und Forschungen in Griechenland* Berlin 1863 ii. 28 f.). Maybaum *Der Zeuskult in Boeotien* Doberan 1901 p. 6 notes the frequent Boeotian name Ὑπατόδωρος. E. Sittig *De Graecorum nominibus theophoris* Halis Saxonum 1911 p. 13 f. quotes examples of Ὑπατόδωρος from Thebes, Tanagra, Delphoi, Smyrna, of Ὑπατίας from Thebes, of Ὑπατοκλῆς from Rhodes.

(2) He had an altar, founded by Kekrops 'in front of the entry' to the Erechtheion at Athens, where he was served with cakes but no wine- or animal-offerings (Paus. 1. 26. 5 ἔστι δὲ καὶ οἴκημα Ἐρέχθειον καλούμενον· πρὸ δὲ τῆς εἰσόδου Διός ἐστι βωμὸς Ὑπάτου, ἔνθα ἔμψυχον θύουσιν οὐδέν, πέμματα δὲ θέντες οὐδὲν ἔτι οἴνῳ χρήσασθαι νομίζουσιν, 8. 2. 3 ὁ μὲν γὰρ (sc. Κέκροψ) Δία τε ὠνόμασεν Ὕπατον πρῶτος (πρῶτον cod. La.), καὶ ὁπόσα ἔχει ψυχήν, τούτων μὲν ἠξίωσεν οὐδὲν θῦσαι, πέμματα δὲ ἐπιχώρια ἐπὶ τοῦ βωμοῦ καθήγισεν, ἃ πελάνους καλοῦσιν ἔτι καὶ ἐς ἡμᾶς Ἀθηναῖοι). He was on occasion associated with Athena Ὑπάτη and other deities (Dem. *c. Macart.* 66 (a Delphic response) συμφέρει Ἀθηναίοις περὶ τοῦ σημείου τοῦ ἐν τῷ οὐρανῷ γενομένου θύοντας καλλιερεῖν Διὶ Ὑπάτῳ, Ἀθηνᾷ Ὑπάτῃ, Ἡρακλεῖ, Ἀπόλλωνι Σωτῆρι, καὶ ἀποπέμπειν Ἀμφιόνεσσι). Cp. Cougny *Anth. Pal. Append.* 1. 201. 1 ff.= *Corp. inscr. Att.* iii. 1 no. 170, 2 ff. Ὑψιμέδων Ὕπατε, πάτερ εἰρήνης βαθυκά[ρπου,] | σὸν Ἐλαίου (for Ἐλέου) βωμὸν ἱκετεύομεν ἡμεῖς, (scansion!) | Θρήικες οἱ ναίοντες ἀγάκλυτον ἄστυ τὸ [Σά]ρδε[ων(?),] | κ.τ.λ.

(3) The tetrapolis of Marathon sacrificed to him in Gamelion (R. B. Richardson in the *Am. Journ. Arch.* 1895 x. 209 ff. col. 2, 13 Διὶ ὑπ[άτῳ οἷς ΔⱵⱵ(?)]=J. de Prott *Leges Graecorum Sacrae* Lipsiae 1896 Fasti sacri p. 46 ff. no. 26, B 13 Διὶ Ὑπ[άτωι – – – –]).

(4) At Sparta he had a statue of hammered bronze by Klearchos of Rhegion (Paus. 3. 17. 6 (*supra* p. 739 n. 1), 8. 14. 7 τοῦ ἐς Σπαρτιάτας λόγου τὰ ἐπὶ τοῦ ἀγάλματος τοῦ Ὑπάτου Διός).

(5) In Paros on the top of Mt *Kounádos* the little church of the Prophet Elias has built into it boundary-stones belonging to Zeus Ὕπατος, to Aphrodite, to Histie Δημίη (O. Rubensohn in the *Ath. Mitth.* 1901 xxvi. 215). The first of these, a rough block of white marble, is inscribed in lettering of *s.* v B.C. [ὅ]ρος Ὑπάτο· ἀ[τε][λ]έστοι οὐ θέμι[ς]ͅ οὐδὲ γυναι[κ]ὶ (sc. εἰσελθεῖν) (*Inscr. Gr. ins.* v. 1 no. 183 with fig.).

Hýpsistos 'the Most High[1],' there is reason to suspect that the epithet had originally a literal rather than a metaphorical sense.

(6) At Rome the road between the Curia and the Basilica Aemilia yielded a block inscribed Διὶ Ὑπάτωι (*Inscr. Gr. Sic. It.* no. 994).

(7) An honorary inscription of *s.* ii A.D. found at Priene contains the clause ἀναγραψάτω (*sic*) (τό)δε [τ]ὸ ψήφισμα εἰς στήλην λευ|κοῦ λίθου καὶ ἀνατεθή[τ]ω ἐν τῶι ἱερῶ[ι τ]οῦ Διὸς τοῦ Ὑπάτου (*sc.* in Thessaly (?)) (F. Hiller von Gaertringen *Inschriften von Priene* Berlin 1906 no. 71, 28 f.).

(8) M. Schweisthal 'L'image de Niobé et l'autel de Zeus Hypatos au mont Sipyle' in the *Gaz. Arch.* 1887 xii. 224 argues that Zeus on Mt Sipylos was invoked under the name of Ὕπατος, cp. Nonn. *Dion.* 13. 533 ff. ὀψὲ δὲ δύσνιφον οἶδμα καὶ ὑδατόεσσαν ἀνάγκην | Ζεὺς ὕπατος (ὕδατος codd. F. M.) πρήυνε, καὶ ἐκ Σιπύλοιο καρήνων | κλυζομένης Φρυγίης παλιν-άγρετον ἤλασεν ὕδωρ. But ὕπατος is a commonish epithet of Zeus in the poets (Bruchmann *Epith. deor.* p. 141) and is used elsewhere by Nonnos (*Dion.* 33. 162 Ζεὺς ὕπατος καὶ θοῦρος Ἄρης καὶ θέσμιος Ἑρμῆς) without local significance.

Fig. 815.

A leaden anchor, found off the coast of Kyrene and now in the British Museum, bears in relief the ship's name ΣΕΥΣ ΥΠΑΤΟΣ (C. Torr *Ancient Ships* Cambridge 1894 p. 71 f. pl. 8, 45, 46 and 47 (=my fig. 815)). The lettering points to *s.* i A.D.

According to schol. T. *Il.* 13. 837 some persons understood Διὸς αὐγάς as denoting τὰ ὑψηλὰ τῶν ὁρῶν !

[1] Examples of this appellative have been collected, classified, and discussed by E. Schürer in the *Sitzungsber. d. Akad. d. Wiss. Berlin* 1897 pp. 200—225 and F. Cumont *Hypsistos* (Supplément à la *Revue de l'instruction publique en Belgique*, 1897) Bruxelles 1897 pp. 1—15, *id.* in Pauly—Wissowa *Real-Enc.* ix. 444—450 *s.v.* Ὕψιστος. I am under deep obligation to their labours, as the following list will show.

Zeus Ὕψιστος was worshipped (1) at Athens in the Pnyx. For a good survey of the problems that cluster about this much-disputed site see *in primis* J. M. Crow and J. Thacher Clarke 'The Athenian Pnyx' in *Papers of the American School of Classical Studies at Athens* 1885—1886 iv. 205—260. The view adopted from H. N. Ulrichs by

F. G. Welcker *Der Felsaltar des Höchsten Zeus oder das Pelasgikon zu Athen, bisher genannt die Pnyx* Berlin 1852 pp. 1—75 with pl., *id.* 'Pnyx oder Pelasgikon' in the *Rhein. Mus.* 1856 x. 30—76, *id.* 'Ueber C. Bursians "Athenische Pnyx"' *ib.* 1856 x. 591—610, and defended especially by E. Curtius *Attische Studien* i Pnyx und Stadtmauer in the *Abh. d. gött. Gesellsch. d. Wiss.* Phil.-hist. Classe 1862 xi. 53—132 with pls. 1, 2, *viz.* that the so-called Pnyx was an ancient sanctuary of Zeus "Υψιστος with the so-called *bêma* for its altar, is nowadays discredited. But it is generally admitted that in imperial times, when the Pnyx had long ceased to be used for public assemblies, a cult of Zeus "Υψιστος as a healing god was here carried on. In the rock-cut back-wall of the Pnyx, between its eastern angle and the *bêma*, there are more than fifty rectangular niches cut to receive tablets. Many of the tablets that had been in the niches were found by Lord Aberdeen in 1803 buried in the earth at the foot of the wall and are now in the British Museum (*Corp. inscr. Gr.* i nos. 497—506, C. T. Newton in *The Collection of Ancient Greek Inscriptions in the British Museum* Oxford 1874 i nos. 60—70, *Corp. inscr. Att.* iii. 1 nos. 147—156, 237, 238). They are dedications, mostly by women of the lower class, to Zeus "Υψιστος (*Corp. inscr. Att.* iii. 1 no. 148 Σύντροφος | 'Υψίστω Διὶ | χαριστήριον,

Fig. 816.

no. 153 'Ονησίμη εὐχὴν | Διὶ 'Υψίστω with relief representing a female breast) or to θεὸς "Υψιστος (*ib.* no. 237 ......a θεῶ 'Υψί[στω] | [ε]ὐχήν with relief of part of a shoulder) or more often to "Υψιστος alone (*ib.* no. 149 Εὔοδος 'Υψίστω εὐχὴν with relief of a pair of eyes (cp. *ib.* no. 238=C. T. Newton *loc. cit.* no. 69), no. 150 'Ολυμπιὰς 'Υψίστω | εὐχήν with relief of a woman's abdomen, no. 151 Τερτία 'Υψίστω | εὐχήν with relief of a face from the bridge of the nose downwards, no. 152 Κλαυδία Πρέπουσα | εὐχαριστῶ 'Υψίστω with relief of a pair of arms, no. 154 Εὐτυχὶς 'Υψίστω εὐ|χ(ήν) with relief of a female breast (=my fig. 816), no. 155 Εἰσιὰς 'Υψ[ίστω] | εὐ[χήν] with relief of a female breast).

Sporadic inscriptions attest the existence of the same cult elsewhere in Athens. L. Ross *Die Pnyx und das Pelasgikon in Athen* Braunschweig 1853 p. 15 cites three inscriptions discovered in the foundations of a house on the northern slope of the Akropolis (*Ann. d. Inst.* 1843 xv. 330 ff.) and now at Berlin (*Ant. Skulpt. Berlin* p. 270 no. 718 Εὐτυχία | 'Υψίστω | εὐχήν with relief of a female breast, no. 719 Εὔπραξι[s] | εὐχήν with relief of a female breast, no. 720 Εἰσιδότη Διὶ 'Υ|ψίστω with relief of eyebrows, eyes, and bridge of nose. Cp. no. 721 an uninscribed relief from the same spot, representing the middle part of the body of a nude female). A column of Pentelic marble, found to the west of the *Propýlaia*, has Γλαῦκος, | Τρύφαινα, | Λέων | ['Υ]ψίστω | [εὐχὴν] ὑπὲρ | [τῶν γονέων(?)] (*Corp. inscr. Att.* iii. 1 no. 146). A small Ionic capital from the southern slope of the *Akrópolis* is surmounted by a broken eagle, beneath which is inscribed ἀγαθῇ τύχῃ. | 'Ιουλ(ία) 'Ασκληπιανὴ | θεῷ 'Υψίστω ὑπὲ[ρ] | Μαξίμου τοῦ υἱ[οῦ] | εὐχαρισστήριον ἀνέθ[ηκεν].

(2) At Thebes near the Hypsistan Gates (Paus. 9. 8. 5 πρὸς δὲ ταῖς 'Υψίσταις Διὸς ἱερὸν ἐπίκλησίν ἐστιν 'Υψίστου). H. Hitzig—H. Blümner *ad loc.* note that these Gates are assumed to have been on the south-western side of the city, where they are shown, adjoining a hill of Zeus "Υψιστος, in the map given by Frazer *Pausanias* v. 32.

(3) At Corinth three statues of Zeus stood in the open air. One of them had no special title; the second was Χθόνιος; the third, "Υψιστος (Paus. 2. 2. 8 τὰ δὲ τοῦ Διός, καὶ ταῦτα ὄντα ἐν ὑπαίθρῳ, τὸ μὲν ἐπίκλησιν οὐκ εἶχε, τὸν δὲ αὐτῶν Χθόνιον καὶ τὸν τρίτον καλοῦσιν "Υψιστον). We are hardly justified in asserting with Welcker *Alt. Denkm.* ii. 87 that the nameless Zeus was 'ohne Zweifel ein...Zenoposeidon,' or in conjecturing with P. Odelberg *Sacra Corinthia, Sicyonia, Phliasia* Upsala 1896 p. 7 that he was a Zeus ἐνάλιος. Such a god would surely have had a distinctive appellation. See, however, Gruppe *Gr. Myth. Rel.* p. 1094 n. 27, *supra* p. 582 ff.

(4) At Argos Smyrna, the wife of Maenius Apollonius and apparently priestess of Zeus, in an interesting epitaph describes her tomb as a barrow adjoining the sanctuary of Zeus "Υψιστος (*Inscr. Gr. Pelop.* i no. 620, 4=Cougny *Anth. Pal. Append.* 2. 286. 8 ὑψίστου δ' ἠρίον ἄ[γχι Διός]).

(5) At Olympia Zeus "Υψιστος had a couple of altars on the way to the Hippodrome (Paus. 5. 15. 5 πλησίον δὲ καὶ Μοιρῶν βωμός ἐστιν ἐπιμήκης, μετὰ δὲ αὐτὸν 'Ερμοῦ, καὶ δύο ἐφεξῆς Διὸς 'Υψίστου. K. Wernicke's cj. μετὰ δὲ αὐτὸν δύο ἐφεξῆς 'Ερμοῦ καὶ Διὸς 'Υψίστου is unnecessary).

(6) In Skiathos is a marble slab inscribed with a dedication [Διὶ 'Υ]ψίστω καὶ τῇ Πόλει | κ.τ.λ. (*Inscr. Gr. ins.* viii no. 631).

(7) At Hephaistia in Lemnos is a round altar of white marble inscribed in lettering of *s.* ii or iii A.D. 'Επηκόω | θεῷ 'Υψίστω | Βεῖθυς ὁ καὶ | "Αδωνις | εὐχήν (*Inscr. Gr. ins.* viii no. 24).

(8) In Imbros was a slab of white marble, broken at the right side, with the inscription Διὶ 'Υψίσ[τω] | 'Αθηναίω[ν] | 'Αριστων[ος] | εὐχ<ης>ήν (A. Conze *Reise auf den Inseln des Thrakischen Meeres* Hannover 1860 p. 90 pl. 15, 2, *Inscr. Gr. ins.* viii no. 78. In line 4 Conze suggests εὐχῆς (ἔ)ν[εκα]. Wilamowitz says: 'Fortasse Διὶ ὑψίστωι [ὑπὲρ τοῦ δήμου τῶν vel καὶ τῶι δήμωι τῶι] 'Αθηναίω[ν τῶν ἐν 'Ιμβρωι ἀνέθηκεν] 'Αρίστων [patris ἐξ] εὐχῆς ἦν [εὔξατο ὁ δεῖνα]').

(9) Makedonia has furnished dedications from Aigai (L. Duchesne—C. Bayet *Mémoire sur une mission au mont Athos* Paris 1877 no. 136 Διὶ 'Υψίστῳ εὐχὴν Μάκρος Λιβύρνιος Οὐάλης, no. 137 Διὶ 'Υψίστῳ Πο. Αἴλιος Τερεντιανὸς 'Αττικὸς κατ' ὄναρ), Kerdylion (P. Perdrizet in the *Bull. Corr. Hell.* 1895 xix. 110 Μ. Λευκειλιο[s] | Μακλᾶς θεῷ[ι] | 'Υψίστωι χα|ριστήριον), and elsewhere (Delacoulonche *Le berceau de la puissance macédonienne* no. 20 to Zeus "Υψιστος, cited by P. Perdrizet in the *Bull. Corr. Hell.* 1898 xxii. 347 n. 2).

(10) In Thrace we have inscriptions from Anchialos (C. Jireček in the *Arch.-ep. Mitth.* 1886 x. 173 no. 3 **ΔΗΥΨΙΣΙΙΔΕΣ▨** | **ΓΗΠΟΛΥΠΡΟΣ▨** | **▨ΟΝΤΕΙΙΝΩΝ· ΚΑΙΣ** | **ΑΥΤΟΥΕΥΧΑΡΙΣΗ** | **ΡΙΟΝ**, which is read by O. Benndorf *ib.* n. 32ᵃ as Διὶ ὑψίσ[τῳ] ἐ[πόπ]τῃ(?) Πολύ[βι]ος [τ]ῶν τέ[κ]νων καὶ [ἐ]αυτοῦ εὐχαριστήριον) and Selymbria (R. Cagnat *Inscriptiones Graecae ad res Romanas pertinentes* Paris 1911 i. 255 no. 777 Θεῶι ἁγίωι ὑψίστωι | ὑπὲρ τῆς 'Ροιμη|τάλκου καὶ Πυθο|δωρίδος ἐκ τῶν κα|τὰ τὸν Κοιλα[λ]ητι|κὸν | πόλεμον κινδύνου | σωτηρίας εὐξάμενος | καὶ ἐπιτυχὼν Γάιος | 'Ιούλιος Πρόκ(λ)ος χαρι | στ[ήρι]ον).

(11) Moesia. An altar of reddish limestone, found among Roman remains between the villages of *Selenigrad* and *Miloslavci*, and now in the Museum at *Sofia*, is inscribed Ϙ θεῶι 'Υψί[στωι] | ὑπὲρ Αὐφιδίων οἴκων | [......Αὐ]φίδιο[s............] (E. Kalinka *Antike Denkmäler in Bulgarien* Wien 1906 p. 133 f. no. 145). A limestone altar at *Pirot* reads ἀγαθῇ [τύ]χ[η] | Θεῷ ἐπηκόῳ ὑψίστῳ | εὐχὴν ἀνέστησαν | τὸ κοινὸν ἐκ τῶν ἰ|δίων διὰ

ἱερέως | Ἑρμογένους καὶ προ|στάτου Αὐγουστιανοῦ | Ἀχιλλεύς, Αὐρῆλις, Δῖο(ς), Ἀλέ|ξανδρος,
Μόκας, Μο[κι]ανός, | Δομῆτις, Σοφεῖνος, Παυ|λεῖνος, Πύρος, Ἀπολινά|ρις, Μοκιανός, [Σ(?)]ῆ-
λυς | καὶ Ἀλέξανδρος Ἀσκ|ληπιάδου· θία[σος(?)] Σεβαξι|ανὸς θη[···]ρουτας | – – (A. von
Domaszewski in the *Arch.-ep. Mitth.* 1886 x. 238 f. no. 2).

(12) Korkyra (*Corp. inscr. Gr.* ii no. 1869 Φαιακοσίνη Διεὶ Ὑψίστῳ | εὐχήν).

(13) Rome. A round base in the Galleria Lapidaria of the Vatican is inscribed Θεῶι
Ὑψίστωι εὐχὴν ἀνέθηκεν | Κλαυδία Πίστη (*Inscr. Gr. Sic. It.* no. 995).

(14) Crete. T. A. B. Spratt *Travels and Researches in Crete* London 1865 ii. 414 no.
1 pl. 1, 1 Κο[ί]ρανος θε|ῶι ὑψίστωι | εὐχὴν δη|μόσιος (C. Babington's reading *ib.* is wrong)
from Knossos.

(15) Kypros. Dedications to the Θεὸς Ὑψιστος have come to light at *Hagios Tychon*
near Amathous (M. Beaudouin—E. Pottier in the *Bull. Corr. Hell.* 1879 iii. 167 a round
cippus inscribed Θεῷ ὑψίστῳ | Νεικόδημος | κατ[ὰ] χρηματισ|μόν), Golgoi (P. Perdrizet in
the *Bull. Corr. Hell.* 1896 xx. 361 ff. published a series of tablets in yellowish tufa, with
holes for suspension, said to have come from a spot near *Athienau* and then in the hands
of Z. Malis at *Larnaka*: no. 1 Θεῷ Ὑψίστῳ ἀνέθη|κεν Πρόκτυος εὐξαμέ|[ν]η with relief of
two female breasts, no. 2 Θεῷ Ὑψίστῳ εὐξαμέ|[νη – – –] with two eyes painted in black,
cp. no. 3 three square tablets with *phallós* in relief but without inscription, no. 4 several
fragmentary tablets of larger size with remains of painting or drawing, *e.g.* horse), and
Kition (Lebas—Waddington *Asie Mineure* iii no. 2740 read by Perdrizet *loc. cit.* [Θεῷ
Ὑ]ψίστῳ Θέων οἰκοδόμος εὐχήν).

(16) Pisidia. At Oinoanda is a dedication built into the wall near the town-gate
(*Corp. inscr. Gr.* iii Add. no. 4380 n² Χρ(ω)μα|τὶς θεῷ ! Ὑψίστῳ | τὸν λύ|χνον | εὐχ[ήν]=
Lebas—Waddington *Asie Mineure* no. 1231). At Termessos a *cippus*, which once sup-
ported a votive foot (commemorating a visitation or epiphany of the god), is inscribed
Θεῷ ἐπηκόῳ Ὑ|φιστότυχ|ος ὁ καὶ Ἀττα|λιανὸς Ἐρ(μαίου) β´ | Σύρου πατ κα|τὰ τὸ κέλευσιν | αὐτοῦ
ἔστη | ἔ σεν ἔ | σὺν τῷ ἐπόντι | ἴχνει θεοῦ (K. Lanckoroński—G. Niemann—E. Petersen
Städte Pamphyliens und Pisidiens Wien 1892 ii. 76 fig. 27, 220 no. 178. *Eid. ib.* p. 32
rather doubtfully take the name of the dedicator to be 'Hephaistotychos.' F. Cumont
Hypsistos (Supplément à la *Revue de l'instruction publique en Belgique*, 1897) Bruxelles
1897 p. 14 reads Θεῷ ἐπηκόῳ Ὑ(ψ)ίστ(ῳ) Τυχ(ί)ος and Σύρου πά(ππου(?))).

(17) Karia. Ζεὺς Ὑψιστος had cults in Iasos (B. Haussoullier in the *Bull. Corr. Hell.*
1884 viii. 456 a boundary-stone of white marble inscribed Διὸς Ὑψίστου. Zeus had a
temple at Iasos (*Corp. inscr. Gr.* ii no. 2671, 26=Michel *Recueil d'Inscr. gr.* no. 462,
26)), Lagina (C. Diehl—G. Cousin in the *Bull. Corr. Hell.* 1887 xi. 159 no. 67 Διὶ
Ὑψίστῳ| καὶ θειωτ[···]σιλικω Σ[τε]|φανίων ὑπὲρ | αὐτοῦ καὶ | τῶν ἰδίων | πάντων εὐ|χαρισ-
τήρι[ον]. I should conjecture Θείῳ (as at Stratonikeia: see below) τῷ βασιλικῷ, 'the
royal Ζεὺς Ὑψιστος καὶ Θεῖος'), Miletos (O. Kern in the *Ath. Mitth.* 1893 xviii. 267 no. 1
a column of white marble, found at *Palatia* near the big mosque, inscribed Διὸς | Ὑψίστου,
Dittenberger *Orient. Gr. inscr. sel.* no. 755 built into a Byzantine church τὸν ἱερέα τοῦ
ἁγιωτά|του [Θεοῦ Ὑψί]στου Σωτῆρος | Οὐλπιον Κάρπον | βουλευτὴν ὁ στατίων (*sc.* assembly) |
τῶν κατὰ πόλιν κηπου|ρῶν τὸν ἴδιον εὐεργέτη[ν] | ὑπὲρ τῆς ἑαυτῶν σωτηρί[ας], no. 756 built
into the same Byzantine church Οὐλπιον Κάρπον, | τὸν προφήτην τοῦ | ἁγιωτάτου Θεοῦ |
Ὑψίστου, ὁ στόλος τῶν σωληνο|κεντῶν (*sc.* spikers of razor-fish) τὸν ἴδιον εὐ|εργέτην διὰ
πάντων. T. Wiegand in the *Sitzungsber. d. Akad. d. Wiss. Berlin* 1904 p. 87 infers from
these two inscriptions that in early Byzantine days a Christian church was founded on the
site of a temple dedicated to the Θεὸς Ὑψιστος, Mylasa (*Corp. inscr. Gr.* ii no. 2693 e,
1 f. = Lebas—Waddington *Asie Mineure* no. 416, 1 f.=A. Hauvette-Besnault—M. Dubois
in the *Bull. Corr. Hell.* 1881 v. 107 ff. no. 11, B, 1 f. ἐπὶ στεφανηφόρου | Ἀριστέου τοῦ
Μέλανος τοῦ Ἀπολλωνίου ἱερέως Διὸς Ὑψίστου καὶ Τύχης Ἀγαθῆς), Panamara (G. Deschamps
—G. Cousin in the *Bull. Corr. Hell.* 1888 xii. 271 f. no. 57 [Διὶ] Ὑψίστῳ | καὶ Ἑκάτῃ
Σω[τείρᾳ] | [κ]αὶ Διὶ Καπε[τωλίῳ] | [κ]αὶ Τύχῃ τοῦ μ[εγίσσου] | [Αὐτ]οκράτορος Κα[ίσαρος] |
[Τίτου] Αἰλίου Ἀδριανοῦ [Ἀντω][νίνου] Σεβασστοῦ | [···κα]ὶ ταῖς τοῦ Δι[ὸς····] |
[······τολε – – –]), Stratonikeia (Lebas—Waddington *Asie Mineure* no. 515 on a *stéle*
in the form of an altar, with a horse (*supra* i. 20) advancing below, Διὶ Ὑψίστῳ καὶ |

880 Appendix B

Ἀγαθῷ Ἀγγέλῳ, | Κλαύδιος Ἀχιλ|(λ)εὺς καὶ Γαλατ[ί]|α ὑπὲρ σωτηρί[ας] | μετὰ τῶν ἰδίων | πάντων, χαριστ[ή]|ριον, A. Hauvette-Besnault—M. Dubois in the *Bull. Corr. Hell.* 1881 v. 182 f. no. 3 Διὶ Ὑψίστῳ | καὶ Θείῳ Ἀγ|γέλῳ Νέων | καὶ Εὐφροσύ|νη ὑπὲρ τῶν | ἰδίων, no. 4 [Διὶ(?)] Ὑψίστῳ καὶ | Θείῳ Φρό|νιμος καὶ | Πειθὼ κα[ὶ](*sic*) | ὑπὲρ τῶν [ἰ]|δίων χαρι|στήριον, G. Cousin in the *Bull. Corr. Hell.* 1891 xv. 418 f. no. 1 at *Djibi* [Δ]ὶ Ὑψίστ[ῳ] | καὶ Θείῳ Εὐ|τύχης καὶ Σ[υν]|φιλοῦσα, Ἀν|δρέας, Ἀν|τίοχος ὑ|πὲρ ἑαυτῶ[ν] | καὶ τῶν ἰδί|ων χαριστή|ριον), and Tralleis (I. Misthos in the Μουσεῖον καὶ Βιβλιοθήκη τῆς Εὐαγγελικῆς Σχολῆς ἐν Σμύρνῃ 1873—1875 p. 95 no. 89 Θεῷ Ὑψίστῳ | κατ᾽ ὄναρ on a small quadrilateral *stéle*).

(18) Kos. W. R. Paton—E. L. Hicks *The Inscriptions of Cos* Oxford 1891 p. 116 no. 63 record a small *stéle*, with *aedicula* and rosette, inscribed Θεανὸς | Θεῷ Ὑψί|στῳ εὐ|χήν.

(19) Delos. Two votive inscriptions, the one certainly, the other probably, from Rheneia, both dating from the close of *s.* ii B.C. and couched in terms so similar as to be practically identical, record prayers to the Θεὸς Ὕψιστος for speedy vengeance on behalf of

Fig. 817.

two Jewish maidens named Marthine and Heraklea respectively (the names recur in the *Corp. inscr. Gr.* ii Add. no. 2322 *b*[78] and no. 2322 *b*[69] = Lebas—Foucart *Îles* no. 2041 and no. 2039), who had been done to death by violence or witchcraft. The Marthine-inscription, much mutilated, is now in the National Museum at Athens (best published by A. Wilhelm in the *Jahresh. d. oest. arch. Inst.* 1901 iv Beiblatt p. 9 ff. fig. 2). The Heraklea-inscription, better preserved, is in the Museum at Bucharest (*id. ib.* p. 9 ff. fig. 3 = my fig. 817): its text and relief are repeated on the back as well as on the front of the *stéle* (Dittenberger *Syll. inscr. Gr.*[3] no. 1181, 1 ff. ἐπικαλοῦμαι καὶ ἀξιῶ τὸν Θεὸν τὸν | Ὕψιστον, τὸν κύριον τῶν πνευμάτων | καὶ πάσης σαρκός, ἐπὶ τοὺς δόλωι φονεύ|σαντας ἢ φαρμακεύσαντας τὴν τα|λαίπωρον ἄωρον Ἡράκλεαν, ἐχχέαν|τας αὐτῆς τὸ ἀναίτιον αἷμα ἀδίκως, ἵνα οὕτως γένηται τοῖς φονεύ|σασιν αὐτὴν ἢ φαρμακεύσασιν καὶ | τοῖς τέκνοις αὐτῶν, κύριε ὁ πάντα ἐ|φορῶν καὶ οἱ ἄγγελοι Θεοῦ, ᾧ πᾶσα ψυ|χὴ ἐν τῇ σήμερον ἡμέραι ταπεινοῦται | μεθ᾽ ἱκετείας, ἵνα ἐγδικήσῃς τὸ αἷμα τὸ ἀ|ναίτιον ζητήσεις καὶ τὴν ταχίστην (Dittenberger *op. cit.*[2] on no. 816 says: 'Exspectes ἵνα ζητήσῃς τὸ αἷμα τὸ ἀναίτιον καὶ ἐγδικήσῃς τὴν ταχίστην.' The Marthine-text, however, runs: ἵνα ἐγδικήσῃ[ς] | τὸ αἷμα τὸ ἀναίτιον καὶ τὴν ταχίστη[ν],

PLATE XXXIX

Plate XXXIX

Marble *stélé* from Panormos near Kyzikos, now in the British Museum,
with dedication to Zeus *Hýpsistos* and votive reliefs representing Zeus,
Artemis (?), Apollon and a banquet.

See page 881.

omitting the second verb altogether. A. Deissmann, who has a detailed discussion of both *stélai* in his *Licht vom Osten* Tübingen 1908 pp. 305—316 figs. 55—57, thinks that the archetype had ἵνα ἐγδικήσῃς τὸ αἷμα τὸ ἀναίτιον καὶ ζητήσῃς τὴν ταχίστην)). The uplifted hands are those of the suppliant : cp. *infra* no. (33) Aigyptos.

(20) Lydia. Hierokaisareia (A. M. Fontrier in the Μουσεῖον καὶ Βιβλιοθήκη τῆς Εὐαγγελ-ικῆς Σχολῆς ἐν Σμύρνῃ 1886 p. 33 no. φί = P. Foucart in the *Bull. Corr. Hell.* 1887 xi. 95 ιο. 16 at *Sasoba* Λούκιος Θε|ῷ 'Υψίστῳ ε|ὐχήν). Koloe in Maionia (M. Tsakyroglou in the Μουσεῖον καὶ Βιβλιοθήκη τῆς Εὐαγγελικῆς Σχολῆς ἐν Σμύρνῃ 1878—1880 p. 161 no. τκδ' 'Απολλωνίσκος | ὑπὲρ τοῦ υἱοῦ 'Ερ|μογένους Θεῷ | 'Υψίστῳ εὐχήν). Philadelpheia (*Ala-Shehir*) (J. Keil—A. von Premerstein 'Bericht über eine Reise in Lydien und der südlichen Aiolis' in the *Denkschr. d. Akad. Wien* 1910 ii Abh. p. 27 no. 39 on a *stéle* with gabled top ἔτους σξθ' (269 of Actian era = 238/9 A.D., of Sullan era = 184/5 A.D.), μη(νὸς) | Αὐδ(ν)αίου ί. Φλα|βία Θεῷ 'Υψίστῳ | εὐχήν). Sari-*Tsam* (A. M. Fontrier *ib.* 1886 p. 68 no. φνζ' = P. Foucart in the *Bull. Corr. Hell.* 1887 xi. 84 f. no. 4, *a* Τειμόθεος Διαγόρου | Λαβραντίδης (Foucart justly cp. the epithet Λαβρανδεύς) καὶ Μόσχιο[ν] | Τειμοθέου ἡ γυνὴ αὐτοῦ | Θεῶι 'Υψίστωι εὐχὴν τὸν | βωμόν, *b* (by another hand) Διαγόρας, Τειμόθεος, Πύθεος | οἱ Τιμοθέου τοῦ Διαγόρου υἱο[ὶ] | Λαβραντίδαι τὰς λυχναψίας | 'Υψίστῳ ('Υψίστωι Fontrier) ἀνέθηκαν). Silandos (Lebas—Waddington *Asie Mineure* no. 708 Θεῷ 'Υψίστῳ | εὐχὴν ἀνέθη|κε 'Ελένη ὑ|πὲρ Θρασυβού|λου τοῦ υἱοῦ | Θρασυβούλ|ου). *Tchatal Tepe* (K. Buresch *Aus Lydien* Leipzig 1898 p. 119 no. 57 on a small marble altar Θεῷ 'Υψίστῳ 'Α|γαθόπους καὶ | Τελέσειρα εὐ|χήν· ἔτους σν' | μη(νὸς) Δαισίου κ'). *Phata*, three hours east of *Theira* (A. M. Fontrier in the Μουσεῖον καὶ Βιβλιοθήκη τῆς Εὐαγγελικῆς Σχολῆς ἐν Σμύρνῃ 1876—1878 p. 32 on an altar-step Θεῷ 'Υψίστῳ. | Νεικηφόρος 'Ερ|μοκράτου ἱερε[ὺ]ς σὺν καὶ 'Ερμο|[κρ]άτει τῷ ἀδ[ελ]|[φῷ] τὸν βωμὸ[ν]|[ἀνέσ]τησαν· | [ἔτ]ους σκ'). Thyateira (A. Wagener in the *Mémoires de l'académie royale des sciences, des lettres et des beaux-arts de Belgique* Série in 4° Classe de Lettres 1861 xxx. 39 = A. M. Fontrier in the *Revue des études anciennes* 1902 iv. 239 no. 4 a relief of an eagle : on the base is inscribed Μοσχιανὸς Βασιλεὺς | 'Υψίστῳ Θεῷ εὐχήν. J. Keil—A. von Premerstein 'Bericht über eine zweite Reise in Lydien' in the *Denkschr. d. Akad. Wien* 1911 ii Abh. p. 17 f. no. 28 on a small plate of bluish marble in lettering of the end of *s.* ii or *s.* iii A.D. Εὐελ(πί)στ[η] | [Θ]εῷ 'Υψί[σ]|[τ]ῳ εὐχὴ[ν]|[ἀν]έθη[κεν] | [εὐτ]υχῶ[ς], no. 29 on a small altar of similar material and date [Τ]ρυφῶσα | [Θ]εῷ 'Υψίστῳ | εὐχήν). Cp. *Ak Tash* (Temenothyrai?) (*eid. ib.* p. 129 no. 237 on a *stéle* of whitish marble with gabled top, in lettering of *s.* ii A.D., beneath an incised wreath Τύρανις 'Αφ[φι]|άδος 'Υψ[ίστω] | εὐ[χήν]) and *Gjölde* near Koloe (*eid. ib.* p. 97 no. 189 on a *stéle* of whitish marble, in lettering of *s.* i or ii A.D., beneath a sunk panel representing in front view a male (?), with *chitón* and *himátion*, raising the right hand in adoration and holding a staff in the lowered left Θεᾶ 'Υψίστη Γλύκων | εὐχήν). The references to J. Keil—A. von Premerstein were kindly furnished to me by Mr A. D. Nock.

(21) Mysia. At Kyzikos a small cubical base of pink St Simeon marble, found near the theatre, reads [Σ]ωγ[ένης(?)] | Νεικάνδ[ρου] | Διὶ 'Υψίστῳ | εὐχήν (Sir C. Smith—R. de Rustafjaell in the *Journ. Hell. Stud.* 1902 xxii. 207 no. 14, F. W. Hasluck *Cyzicus* Cambridge 1910 p. 271 no. 11). From Panormos (*Panderma*) near Kyzikos came a votive *stéle* of white marble, presented by A. van Branteghem in 1890 to the British Museum (A. H. Smith in the *Brit. Mus. Cat. Sculpture* i. 374 f. no. 817, F. H. Marshall in *The Collection of Ancient Greek Inscriptions in the British Museum* London 1916 iv. 2. 153 no. 1007 with fig. I am indebted to Mr Smith for the photograph by Mr R. B. Fleming from which my pl. xxxix is taken). This relief, which has aroused much interest (see *e.g.* A. S. Murray in the *Rev. Arch.* 1891 i. 10 f. no. 1, H. Lechat—G. Radet in the *Bull. Corr. Hell.* 1893 xvii. 520 f., F. Cumont *Hypsistos* Bruxelles 1897 p. 12 no. 3 pl., P. Perdrizet in the *Bull. Corr. Hell.* 1899 xxiii. 592 f. pl. 4, E. Ziebarth 'ΧΟΥΣ' in the *Ath. Mitth.* 1905 xxx. 145 f., F. Poland *Geschichte des griechischen Vereinswesens* Leipzig 1909 p. 370, F. W. Hasluck *Cyzicus* Cambridge 1910 pp. 207, 271 no. 13, Reinach *Rép. Reliefs* ii. 493 no. 3), represents three deities standing side by side in a sunk panel—Zeus in *chitón* and *himátion*, with a *phiále* in his right hand, a sceptre in his left; Artemis (Persephone, or perhaps

Hekate, according to Murray *loc. cit.*   Dionysos, according to Smith and Reinach *locc. citt.*) in short *chitón*, *chlamýs*, and high boots, with a *phiále* in her right hand, a torch in her left; Apollon in long *chitón* and *himátion*, with a *phiále* in his right hand, a *kithára* in his left, and a snake-twined *omphalós* beside him. Beneath, in low relief, is a banquet of six men, who recline on cushions placed upon a long mattress. On the right a cup-bearer, in a short *chitón*, holds an *oinochóe* in one hand, an *askós* in the other, and draws wine from a large *kratér* partially sunk in the floor. On the left a seated musician plays two flutes, one straight, one curved, while his feet beat time with *kroupézai*. In the centre a girl, stark naked, is dancing, and a man in the costume of a mime-performer, with a pair of long *krótala* in his hands, is running round her at a lively pace. The pediment above is filled with an inscription, whose ligatures point to a date in *s.* ii A.D. Διι·ὶ· ῾Υ·|ψίστῳ·κ(αὶ)·| τῷ χώρῳ Θάλλος | ἐπώνυμος·τὸν·| τελαμῶνα·ἀπέδωκα, 'I Thallos, the name-giver (of the *thíasos*), duly presented the relief to Zeus *Most High* and to the Place (where the *thiasôtai* assemble).' So Marshall *loc. cit.* Perdrizet *loc. cit.* understood: 'Thallos, magistrat éponyme, a voué ce cippe à Zeus céleste et au bourg.' Murray, Smith, and Cumont *locc. citt.* thought χώρῳ a blunder for χορῷ (to which not one of them gives the right accent). Ziebarth *loc. cit.*, following T. Reinach in the *Rev. Et. Gr.* 1894 vii 391, will have it that χῷ was the name of the *thíasos*, cp. T. Wiegand in the *Ath. Mitth.* 1904 xxix. 316 an altar-shaped base of white marble from *Nuserat*, one hour south of *Kebsud* in Mysia, inscribed τὸν Βρομίου μύστην | [ἱ]ερῶν, ἄρξαντα χοῦ, | κ.τ.λ. At Pergamon the Θεὸς ῞Υψιστος, presumably Zeus (M. Fränkel *Die Inschriften von Pergamon* Berlin 1895 ii. 243 f. no. 331 on a small altar of white marble Γλύκινα | Θεῷ ῾Υψίστῳ | εὐχὴν ἀνέθηκα, ἐρωμένη μετὰ τὸν | [ὄνειρον(?) – – –] | [– – – – –] (the last two lines covered with white daub)), was further identified with Helios (*id. ib.* ii. 243 no. 330 on a small altar of white marble from the precinct of Athena ['Ηλ]ίωι, | Θ[ε]ῷὶ | ῾Υψ[ί]στωι, | Τάτιον | ε[ὐ]χήν). At Plakia near Kyzikos was another thank-offering to the Θεὸς ῞Υψιστος (*Corp. inscr. Gr.* ii no. 3669 ἀγαθῆι τύχηι. | Γ. Πεσκέννιος 'Ονήσιμος | Θεῷ ῾Υψίστῳ σωθεὶς ἀν|έθηκα ἐκ μεγάλου κινδ|ύνου μετὰ τῶν ἰδίων. | νείκης εὐχαριστήριον | ἀναθεῖναι (the last two lines are incomplete: *sc.* ἐπέταξεν ὁ θεὸς or the like). On the remarkable dedication to Zeus ῞Υψιστος Βρονταῖος, now in the Tchinili Kiosk at Constantinople, but probably derived from the Cyzicene district, see *supra* p. 833 ff. fig. 793.

(22) Lesbos. Several dedications to the Θεὸς ῞Υψιστος have been found at Mytilene (*Inscr. Gr. ins.* ii no. 115 on a large base or altar of white marble, above and below a relief representing an eagle with spread wings in a great olive-wreath Θεῷ ῾Υψίστω ε[ὐ]χ[α]ριστήριον Μάρκος || Πομπήιος Λυκάων μ[ετ]ὰ τῆς συμβίου Φοίβης | καὶ τῶν ἰδίων, no. 119 on a small base or altar Γ. Κορνήλι(ο)ς | Χρηστίων, Κορ|νηλία Θάλλου|σα, Γ. Κορν<ι>ήλιος | Σεκοῦνδος χει|μασθέντες ἐν | πελάγει Θεῷ ῾Υ|ψίστῳ χρηστήρι|ον (the last word a blunder for χαριστήριον), no. 125 (= A. Conze *Reise auf der Insel Lesbos* Hannover 1865 pp. 5, 12 pl. 5, 3) Θεῷ | ῾Υψίστῳ | Π. Αἴλιος 'Αρ|ριανὸς 'Αλ[έ]|ξανδρος, | βουλευ(τὴς) | Δακίας κο|λωνείας | Ζερμιζεγ[ε]|θούσης, εὐχὴ[ν] | ἀνέθηκεν), and one of these by adding the title Κεραύνιος makes it clear that Zeus is meant (*supra* p. 807 n. 3 no. (3)).

(23) Phrygia. Here too the Θεὸς ῞Υψιστος had a considerable vogue—at Aizanoi (Lebas—Waddington *Asie Mineure* no. 987 = *Corp. inscr. Gr.* iii Add. no. 3842 *d* [ὁ δεῖνα] 'Αλε[ξά]νδρου Ι€Ιόνιος ([Π]ειόνιος Lebas. Cp. Πειονίου = *Pioni* in *Inscr. Gr. Sic. It.* no. 1363, 5 ff., Πιονίου in the *Corp. Inscr. Gr.* iv no. 8866, 9. A. B. C.) | [Θεῷ *vel* Διὶ] ῾Υψίστῳ εὐχήν, at *Hadji-keui* near Aizanoi (A. Körte in the *Ath. Mitth.* 1900 xxv. 405 no. 9 on an altar of half-marble Αὐρ. 'Ασκληπιάδ[ης] | ἐληνθεὶς ἀπ' ὀ|λλων (!) τῶν παθημάτ[ων] | εὐξάμενος Θεῷ ῾Υ[ψ]|ίστῳ μετὰ | τῶν εἰδίων (so Körte. Better ἀπὸ <πο>|λλῶν by lipo-graphy. A. B. C.), at *Yenije* near Akmoneia (W. M. Ramsay *The Cities and Bishoprics of Phrygia* Oxford 1897 ii. 652 f. no. 563 [ἐὰν δέ τις ἕτερον σῶμα εἰσενέγκῃ, ἔσ]ται αὐτῷ πρὸς τὸν θεὸν τὸν ὕψιστον, καὶ τὸ ἀρᾶς δρέπανον εἰς τὸν ὖκον αὐτοῦ [εἰσέλθοιτο καὶ μηδέναν ἐνκατα-λείψαιτο], where the *formula* ἔσται αὐτῷ πρὸς τὸν θεόν and the phrase τὸν θεὸν τὸν ὕψιστον suit the epitaph of a Jew or perhaps a Jewish Christian), at *Hadji-Eyub-li* near Laodikeia (W. M. Ramsay *op. cit.* 1895 i. 78 no. 14 [. . . . .]s Θεῷ ῾Υψέστῳ εὐχήν), at Nakoleia (*Seidi Ghazi*) (W. M. Ramsay in the *Journ. Hell. Stud.* 1884 v. 258 n. 2 no. 9 on a small

slab of marble Θεῷ Ὑψίσ|τῳ εὐ|χὴν Αὐ|ρήλιος | ᾽Ασκλάπω|ν, ἦν ὁμο|λό(γ)ησεν ἐ[ν] | ᾽Ρώμῃ), at *Arslan Apa* in the upper valley of the river Tembrogios or Tembrios (J. G. C. Anderson in W. M. Ramsay *Studies in the History and Art of the Eastern Provinces of the Roman Empire* Aberdeen 1906 p. 211 no. 9 on an altar with a garland in relief [. . . . η] Νικο[μά(?)]χου [. .] | [ἔτου]s τλη′ (=253/4 A.D.)· Αὐρ. ᾽Ιάσων Θεῷ | Ὑψίστῳ εὐχήν). The Θεὸς Ὕψιστος was here, as Anderson saw, Zeus Βέννιος or Βεννεύς the native god of the district (W. M. Ramsay in the *Journ. Hell. Stud.* 1884 v. 259 f. no. 11 on a marble *cippus* from *Karagatch Euren* near *Altyntash*, below a relief representing a bunch of grapes, an eagle, and a radiate head of the sun-god Διὶ Βεννίῳ | Διογένης ὑπὲρ | Διογένους πάππου | καὶ Κλ. Χρυσίου | μάμμης καὶ τῶν | κατοικούντων | ἐν ᾽Ισκόμῃ καθιέρω|σεν. | ᾽Απολλώνιος ᾽Ισγερεανὸς ἐποίει. Ramsay refers the *cippus* 'most probably to the second century after Christ,' adding 'I understand this inscription to be placed by Diogenes on the grave of his grandparents; in preparing the grave Diogenes considers that he is dedicating the spot to Zeus Bennios. The grave is a shrine of Zeus, and the funeral offerings to the dead were considered at the same time as offerings to Zeus.' *Id. ib.* p. 258 f. no. 10 on a *stéle* at Serea (*Kuyujak*), three hours north-west of Nakoleia Μάρκος | Μάρκου | Διὶ Βροντῶν|τι καὶ Βεννεῖ | Σερεανῷ στ|έφανον. Ramsay remarks: 'Here it is evident that Benni-s, or Zeus Benneus, the god of the western side [of the mountains], and Papas, or Zeus Bronton, the god of the eastern side, are expressly identified.' Lebas—Waddington *Asie Mineure* no. 774 = *Corp. inscr. Gr.* iii Add. no. 3857 *l* = G. Perrot—E. Guillaume— J. Delbet *Exploration archéologique de la Galatie et de la Bithynie* etc. Paris 1872 i. 122 f. no. 86 on a cylindrical *cippus* at *Altyntash* ὑπὲρ τῆς αὐτοκράτορος | Νερούα Τραϊανοῦ Καίσαρος | Σεβαστοῦ Γερμανικοῦ | Δακικοῦ νείκης Διὶ Βεννίῳ | Μηνοφάνης Τειμολάου | τὸν βωμὸν ἀνέστησεν | Βεννεισοηνῶν. W. M. Ramsay *The Historical Geography of Asia Minor* (*Royal Geographical Society: Supplementary Papers* iv) London 1890 p. 144 f. (cp. S. Reinach *Chroniques d'orient* Paris 1891 p. 498) was the first to read the concluding line aright as Βεννεῖ Σοηνῶν, Soa being the chief town of the Praipenisseis in the neighbourhood of *Altyntash*), whose priests, the Βεννεῖται, are mentioned in another inscription from the same locality (*Corp. inscr. Gr.* iii no. 3857 between Aizanoi and Kotiaeion Τρύφων Μενίσκου Διὶ | καὶ τοῖς Βεννείταις). W. M. Ramsay in the *Journ. Hell. Stud.* 1887 viii. 512 f. takes Zeus Βέννιος or Βεννεύς to mean 'he who stands on a Car,' cp. the Gallic (Paul. ex Fest. p. 32, 14 Müller, p. 29, 24 f. Lindsay benna lingua Gallica genus vehiculi appellatur, unde vocantur conbennones in eadem benna sedentes), Messapian (W. Deecke in the *Rhein. Mus.* 1882 xxxvii. 385 f. no. 22), and Thraco-Illyrian word *benna* (Steph. Byz. *s.v.* Βέννα, πόλις Θράκης, κ.τ.λ., *Thes. Ling. Lat.* ii. 1907, 48 ff. Bennius, 69 f. Bennus).

(24) Bithynia (?). J. H. Mordtmann in the *Arch.-ep. Mitth.* 1885 viii. 198 no. 18 publishes a miniature base from the coast of Asia Minor inscribed ἀγαθῇ τύχηι· | Θεῷ Ὑψίστῳ | ᾽Ασκληπιόδο|τος Σωσιπά|τρου κατὰ ὄ|ναρ.

(25) Paphlagonia. Inscriptions from the district of Sinope record the cult of the Θεὸς Ὕψιστος (G. Doublet in the *Bull. Corr. Hell.* 1889 xiii. 303 f. no. 7 = D. M. Robinson in the *Am. Journ. Arch.* 1905 ix. 306 no. 29 Θεῷ Ὑψίσ[τ]ῳ | Αἴλιος Θρεπτίων, | Ποντιανός, Σεου|ῆρος, Μάκερ, οἱ | ἀδελφοὶ ('brethren' in a religious sense) εὐξάμενοι) or Θεὸς Μέγας Ὕψιστος (G. Mendel in the *Bull. Corr. Hell.* 1903 xxvii. 333 no. 49 = D. M. Robinson *loc. cit.* p. 304 no. 26 with fig. on a marble altar pierced to serve as base for a post at *Emrilé* near *Chalabdé* Θεῷ Μεγάλ[ῳ] | Ὑψίστῳ εὐχῆ[s] | χά[ριν ἀνέ]θη|κε ....[λ]ος | μετὰ [τῆς γυ]ναι|[κ]ὸς ᾽Ρου[φ]εί[νης]).

(26) Pontos. J. G. C. Anderson—F. Cumont—H. Grégoire *Recueil des Inscriptions grecques et latines du Pont et de l'Arménie* (*Studia Pontica* iii) Bruxelles ii no. 284 Sebastopolis (cited by F. Cumont in Pauly—Wissowa *Real-Enc.* ix. 448).

(27) Bosporos Kimmerios. Gorgippia (*Anapa*) (B. Latyschev *Inscriptiones antiquae Orae Septentrionalis Ponti Euxini Graecae et Latinae* Petropoli 1890 ii. 208 ff. no. 400, 1 ff. (manumission of a slave) Θεῶι Ὑψίστωι παντο|κράτορι εὐλογητῷ, βα|σιλεύοντος βασιλέ|ως [Πολέμωνος] φιλο|γερμα[νι]κοῦ καὶ φιλοπάτ|ριδος, ἔτους ηλτ′ (338 of the Bosporan era = 41 A.D.), μη|νὸς Δείου, Πόθος Στ[]ρά]τωνος ἀνέθηκεν <ἐν> | τῆι [προσ]ευχῆι κατ' εὐχ[ὴ]|ν θρεπτὴν ἑαυτοῦ, ᾗ ὄνο|μα Χρύσα, ἐφ' ᾧ ᾗ ἀνέπα|φος καὶ ἀνεπηρέαστο[s] | ἀπὸ παντὸς κληρο-

ν[όμ]|ου ὑπὸ Δία, Γῆν, Ἥλιο[ν] (cp. *supra* p. 729 n. o), no. 401, 1 ff. = R. Cagnat *Inscriptiones Graecae ad res Romanas pertinentes* Paris 1911 i. 299 no. 911 (manumission of a slave) [Θεῷ 'Τψ]ίσ[τῳ παν]|[τοκράτ]ορι εὐλο[γη]|[τ]ῷ· βασιλεύοντ[ος] | βασιλέως Τιβερίου 'Ι < ω > |ουλίου < λίου > Σαυρομά|του (*sc.* Tib. Iulius Sauromates ii, king of Bosporos in the time of Caracalla) φιλοκαίσαρος καὶ φι|λορωμαίου εὐσεβοῦς | Τειμόθεος Νυμφα|γόρου Μακαρίου σὺν | ἀδελφῆς Ἥλιδος γυ|ναικὸς Νανοβαλα|μύρου κατὰ εὐχὴν | πατρὸς ἡμῶν Νυμ|φαγόρου Μακαρίου | ἀφείομεν τὴν θρεπ|[τὴν ἡμῶν Δ]ωρέαν | [ἐλευθέραν - - -], B. Latyschev *op. cit.* Petropoli 1901 iv. 249 ff. no. 436 *b*, 4 Θεῷ 'Τψίσ[τῳ - -], 15 [- -] Θεῷ 'Τψίστῳ Ποθῆν[ος - -] *i.e.* the name of the god inserted twice in a list of his worshippers).

Tanais (B. Latyschev *op. cit.* Petropoli 1890 ii. 246 ff. nos. 437—467, R. Cagnat *op. cit.* i. 300 ff. nos. 915—921, of which some samples must serve: no. 437, 1 ff. = no. 915, 1 ff. (topped by relief of gable with shield inside and eagle on apex: see L. Stephani in the *Compte-rendu St. Pét.* 1870—1871 p. 230 f. fig.) [Θε]ῷ 'Τψίστωι ὅ ε[ὐχή]. | [β]ασιλεύοντος βα[σιλέως Τιβερίου]|['Ι]ουλίου 'Ροιμητάλκο[υ (*sc.* Tib. Iulius Rhoemetalces, king of Bosporos in the time of Hadrian) φιλοκαίσαρος καὶ] | φιλορωμαίου εὐσε[βοῦς, ἐν τῷ...ἔτει,] | μηνὸς Περειτίου η΄, [ἡ σύνοδος ἡ περὶ] | ἱερέα Πόπλιον Χαρ[ίτωνος (?) καὶ πατέρα συν]|όδου 'Αντ|ίμαχον τοῦ δεῖνος - - -], no. 447, 1 ff. ἀγαθῇ τύχῃ· | Θεῷ 'Τψίστῳ ἐπηκόωι ἡ σύνοδος πε|ρὶ Θεὸν Ὕψιστον καὶ ἱερέα Χόφρασμον | Φοργαβάκου καὶ συναγωγὸν Εὐπρέπην | Συμφόρου καὶ φιλ-αγαθον 'Αντίμαχον Πα|σίωνος καὶ παραφιλάγαθον Σύμφορον Δημη|τρίου καὶ γυμνασιάρχην Β[αλ]ῶδιν Δημητρίου | καὶ νιανισκάρχην Σαυάνων Χοφράσμου καὶ οἱ | λοιποὶ θιασῶται· κ.τ.λ., ño. 449, 1 ff. = no. 918, 1 ff. (with incised decoration of two eagles and a wreath between them: see L. Stephani *loc. cit.* p. 254 ff. fig.) Θεῶι ['Τψίστωι] | βασιλεύοντος β[ασιλέως Τιβερίου] | 'Ιουλίου 'Ρησκουπό[ριδος (*sc.* Tib. Iulius Rhescuporis, king of Bosporos 212—229 A.D.) φιλοκαί]|σαρος καὶ φιλορωμ[αίου εὐσεβοῦς] | ἰσποιητοὶ (= εἰσποιητοί, ' adoptivi ') ἀδελφο[ὶ σεβόμενοι] | [Θεὸ]ν Ὕψιστον ἀν[έστησαν τὸν] | τελαμῶνα ἐνγ[ράψαντες ἑαυτῶν] | τὰ ὀνόματα· | κ.τ.λ., no. 452, 1 ff. = no. 920, 1 ff. [ἀγαθῇ]ι τύχη· | Θε[ῷ 'Τ]ψίστῳ ε[ὐχή.] | βασιλεύοντ[ο]ς βασιλέ[ως Τιβερίου] | ['Ι]ουλίου [Κό]τυος (*sc.* Tib. Iulius Cotys, king of Bosporos *c.* 228—234 A.D.) φιλοκα[ίσαρο]ς καὶ φι|[λορωμαίο]ν εὐσεβοῦς εἰσποιητοὶ | ἀδ[ελφοὶ σ]εβόμενοι Θεὸν Ὕψιστον | ἐνγρά[ψαντ]ες ἑαυτῶν τὰ ὀνόματα | περὶ πρεσβύτερον (*sc.* the senior of the adoptive brethren) Μ.............'Η|ρακλ[είδ]ου καὶ 'Αρίστωνα [Μ]ενε-στράτου καὶ Καλλι|γ[έν]ην Μύ[ρ]ωνος, 'Αλεξίωνα Πατρόκλου, κ.τ.λ. (list of names), 17 τὸν δὲ τελαμῶ[ν]α ἐδωρήσατο τοῖς ἀδελ[φ]οῖς Σαμ[βίω]ν Ἑλπιδίωνος. Φούρτας 'Αγαθοῦ, 'Αγα-θή|μερος Ποπλίου. | ἐν τῷ εκφ΄ ἔτει (525 of the Bosporan era = 228 A.D.), Γορπιαίου α΄, no. 454, 1 ff. ἀγαθῆι τύχηι· | Θε[ῷ 'Τψίστ]ῳ ἐπηκόῳ εὐχῆι· ἡ σύνοδος περὶ | ἱερέα Πάπαν Χρήστου καὶ [σ]υναγωγὸν Νυμ|φέρωτα 'Οχωζιάκου κ[α]ὶ φιλάγαθον Θέωνα | Φαζινάμου κ[α]ὶ παραφι[λ]ά(γ)αθον Φαζίναμ|ον Καλλιστί[ω]νος κα[ὶ γ]υμνασιάρχην Μακάρι|ον Μαστοῦ καὶ νεανισκάρχην Ζήθον Ζήθου | κ[α]ὶ οἱ λοιποὶ θι[α]σῶται· κ.τ.λ.

These inscriptions have been studied by L. Stephani, I. V. Pomjalóvskij, V. V. Látyshev, E. Schürer, E. H. Minns, and others. L. Stephani in the *Compte-rendu St. Pét.* 1870—1871 p. 228 ff. argued that the Θεὸς Ὕψιστος, whose emblem was an eagle, must have been the Greek Zeus, but that the regular omission of the name Zeus implies an incipient Christianisation of his cult. I. V. Pomjalóvskij in the *Transactions of the Sixth* (1884) *Archaeological Congress at Odessa* (published in Russian) Odessa 1888 ii. 24 ff. compared the god with Zeus Σωτήρ, Zeus Στράτιος, Zeus Λαβράϋνδος, Zeus Χρυσαορεύς, etc. and saw no reason to regard his epithets Ὕψιστος, 'Επήκοος as indicative of Christian influence. B. Latyschev *op. cit.* Petropoli 1890 ii. 246 f., in view of the dedication Θεῷ 'Επηκόῳ Ὑψίστῳ by a θίασος Σεβαζιανός (*supra* no. (11)), concluded that here too the god worshipped was *Sabázios*—a possible link between Zeus and the κύριος Σαβαώθ (*supra* i. 234 n. 4, 400 n. 6, 425 n. 2). But E. Schürer 'Die Juden im bosporanischen Reiche und die Genossenschaften der σεβόμενοι θεὸν ὕψιστον ebendaselbst' in the *Sitzungsber. d. Akad. d. Wiss. Berlin* 1897 p. 200 ff. (followed *e g.* by E. H. Minns *Scythians and Greeks* Cambridge 1913 p. 620ff. and F. Cumont in Pauly—Wissowa *Real-Enc.* ix. 448) has made it clear that the worshippers were Bosporan Jews, who however did not scruple to use the gentile *formula* ὑπὸ Δία, Γῆν, Ἥλιον. Their worship was a compromise between the strictly Semitic and the strictly Hellenic ('weder Judenthum noch Heidenthum, son-

The Mountain-cults of Zeus 885

dern eine Neutralisirung beider'). At Tanais, for example, there were several small religious societies (θίασοι, σύνοδοι), each comprising some 15 to 40 members (θιασῶται, θιασῖται, θιεσεῖται, συνοδεῖται). These members were either of recent introduction (εἰσποιητοὶ ἀδελφοί) or of senior standing (πρεσβίτερος). Their officers in descending order were ἱερεύς, πατὴρ συνόδου, συναγωγός, φιλάγαθος, παραφιλάγαθος, γυμνασιάρχης, νεανισκάρχης, γραμματεύς (omissions and transpositions occur). Their aims included the cult of the Θεὸς "Ὕψιστος, the education of the young, and (to judge from similar inscriptions at Pantikapaion) the due burial of the brethren.

(28) **Kappadokia.** An analogous blend of Jewish and Persian beliefs is found in the case of the Ὑψιστάριοι, according to Gregory of Nazianzos, whose own father had belonged originally to this sect (Greg. Naz. *or.* 18. 5 (xxxv. 989 D—992 A Migne) ἐκεῖνος τοίνυν... ῥίζης ἐγένετο βλάστημα οὐκ ἐπαινετῆς...ἐκ δυοῖν τοῖν ἐναντιωτάτοιν συγκεκραμένης, Ἑλληνικῆς τε πλάνης καὶ νομικῆς τερατείας· ὧν ἀμφοτέρων τὰ μέρη φυγὼν ἐκ μερῶν συνετέθη. τῆς μὲν γὰρ τὰ εἴδωλα καὶ τὰς θυσίας ἀποπεμπόμενοι τιμῶσι τὸ πῦρ καὶ τὰ λύχνα· τῆς δὲ τὸ σάββατον αἰδούμενοι καὶ τὴν περὶ τὰ βρώματα ἔστιν ἃ μικρολογίαν τὴν περιτομὴν ἀτιμάζουσιν. Ὑψιστάριοι τοῖς ταπεινοῖς ὄνομα, καὶ ὁ Παντοκράτωρ δὴ μόνος αὐτοῖς σεβάσμιος). Gregory of Nyssa speaks of the same sect as Ὑψιστιανοί (Greg. Nyss. *contra Eunomium* 2 (xlv. 481 D— 484 A Migne) ὁ γὰρ ὁμολογῶν τὸν πατέρα πάντοτε καὶ ὡσαύτως ἔχειν, ἕνα καὶ μόνον ὄντα, τὸν τῆς εὐσεβείας κρατύνει λόγον...εἰ δὲ ἄλλον τινὰ παρὰ τὸν πατέρα θεὸν ἀναπλάσσει, Ἰουδαίοις διαλεγέσθω ἢ τοῖς λεγομένοις Ὑψιστιανοῖς· ὧν αὕτη ἐστὶν ἡ πρὸς τοὺς Χριστιανοὺς διαφορά, τὸ θεὸν μὲν αὐτοὺς ὁμολογεῖν εἶναί τινα, ὃν ὀνομάζουσιν "Ὕψιστον ἢ Παντοκράτορα· πατέρα δὲ αὐτὸν εἶναι μὴ παραδέχεσθαι). See further C. Ullmann *De Hypsistariis, seculi post Christum natum quarti secta, commentatio* Heidelbergae 1823 pp. 1—34, G. Boehmer *De Hypsistariis opinionibusque, quae super eis propositae sunt, commentationem etc.* Berolini 1824 pp. 1—102, W. Boehmer *Einige Bemerkungen zu den von dem Herrn Prof. Dr. Ullmann und mir aufgestellten Ansichten über den Ursprung und den Charakter der Hypsistarier* Hamburg 1826 pp. 1—75, G. T. Stokes in Smith—Wace *Dict. Chr. Biogr.* iii. 188 f.

(29) **Syria.** Palmyra (*Tadmor*) (*Corp. inscr. Gr.* iii no. 4503 = Lebas—Waddington *Asie Mineure* iii no. 2571 *b* on a bilingual altar now at Oxford Διὶ Ὑψίστῳ καὶ ['Ε]|πηκόῳ Ἰού(λιος) Αὐρ(ήλιος) Ἀ|ντίπατρος ὁ καὶ | Ἀλαφώνας Ἀαιλ|αμεῖ τοῦ Ζηνοβί|ου τοῦ Ἀκοπάου | εὐξάμενος ἀνέ|θηκεν, ἔτους δμφ', | Ἀδύναλου κδ' (=Jan. 24, 233 A.D.) = C. J. M. de Vogüé *Inscriptions sémitiques* Paris 1868 p. 74 no. 123*a* iii with translation of the Palmyrene text 'Action de grâces à celui dont le nom est béni dans l'éternité' etc. *Corp. inscr. Gr.* iii no. 4502 = Lebas—Waddington *op. cit.* iii no. 2571 *c* = Dittenberger *Orient. Gr. inscr.* no. 634 on an altar near the great sulphurous spring at the entrance to the town Διὶ Ὑψίστῳ Μεγίστῳ Ἐπηκόῳ Βωλανὸς Ζηνοβίου | τοῦ Αἱράνου τοῦ Μοκίμου τοῦ Μαθθᾶ, ἐπιμελητὴς | αἱρεθεὶς Ἔφκας πηγῆς (I. Benzinger in Pauly—Wissowa *Real-Enc.* v. 2859) ὑπὸ Ἰαριβώλου τοῦ θεοῦ (*supra* p. 814 n. 3) τὸν βω(μ)ὸ(ν) | ἐξ ἰδίων ἀνέθηκεν, ἔτους δου', μηνὸς Ὑπερβερεταίου κ' (=Oct. 20, 162 A.D.). Lebas—Waddington *op. cit.* iii no. 2572 on an altar in the Mohammedan cemetery Διὶ Ὑψίστῳ καὶ Ἐπηκ|όῳ τὸν βωμὸν ἀνέθη|κεν Ἰούλιος Σ.υις ἀπε|λεύθερο(s) Γαίου<s> Ἰου|λίου Βάσσου ὑπὲρ σω|τηρίας Ἰλείβας υἱο(ῦ) | αὐτοῦ, ἔτους ηυ', μη|νὸς Ξανδικοῦ (=April 179 A.D.). Lebas—Waddington *op. cit.* iii no. 2573 on a fragmentary altar from the same site Διὶ Ὑψίστῳ Α[ὐρ.] Διογένης Σωσιβίου ἅμα | Δόμνη εὐξάμενοι καὶ ἐπακουσθέν|τες [- - -] | [- - -]. Lebas—Waddington *op. cit.* iii no. 2574 on a small altar from the same site Διὶ Ὑψίστῳ | καὶ Ἐπηκόῳ | εὐξάμενος | ἀνέθηκεν | Α···ευρος καὶ | Σώπατρος καὶ | Θεῷ Μεγάλῳ | Σαλλούντῳ (?) | Ἐνεουάρει (?) | [-'- -]. Lebas—Waddington *op. cit.* iii no. 2575 on a small bilingual altar from the same site Διὶ Ὑψίστῳ καὶ Ἐπη|κόῳ τὸν βωμὸν ἀν|[έ]θηκεν εὐχαριστ[ῶ]|[ν ὁ δεῖνα] | [- - -] = C. J. M. de Vogüé *op. cit.* p. 68 no. 101, who reads εὐχαριστ[ω]|[s - - -] and renders the Palmyrene text 'Que soit béni son nom à toujours: le bon et le miséricordieux!' etc. M. Sobernheim *Palmyrenische Inschriften* (*Mitteilungen der Vorderasiatischen Gesellschaft* 1905 x, 2) Berlin 1905 p. 38 f. no. 31 on a *stéle* built into the western wall of the steps leading up to the roof of the 'Fahnenheiligtum'; the pilasters of the *stéle* have Corinthian capitals adorned with filleted wreath and winged thunderbolt [Διὶ Ὑψί]στ[ῳ καὶ] Ἐ[πηκόῳ - - -] | [- - -] τῶν κα[ρ]πῶν, οὓς [ἐ]κ [ταύτης] [τῆς χώρας] | [- - -] κατ' ἔτος τ[ε ἀ]γαθῇ ἡμέρᾳ διὰ π[α]ντὸς ε[- - -] |

[– – – ἔτους] δου΄, μηνὶ Ξανδικῷ ϛ (=April 6, 163 A.D.). M. Sobernheim *op. cit.* p. 40 no. 20 on a *cippus* built into the eastern wall of the small court in front of the 'Fahnenheiligtum' Διὶ Ὑψίστῳ καὶ Ἐπηκόῳ ὁ δεῖνα] | ὁ καὶ Ἰαριβω[λέης τοῦ δεῖνα]. M. Sobernheim *op. cit.* p. 40 ff. no. 34 pls. 16, 17 on a bilingual *cippus* in the court before the 'Fahnenheiligtum' Διὶ Ὑψίστῳ καὶ Ἐπηκ[όῳ τὸν βωμὸν] | ἀνέθηκεν Ζαβδίβω[λος τοῦ Ἰαριβωλέους] | τοῦ Λισαμσαίου τοῦ Αἱ[ράνου ὑπὲρ τῆς] | ὑγείας αὐτοῦ καὶ τέκνω[ν καὶ] | ἀδελφῶν, ἔτους ὀμυ΄ Ὑ[περβερεταίου] (=October 132 A.D.) followed by a Palmyrene text, which he translates 'Diesen [Altar] brachte dar dem, dessen Namen in Ewigkeit gesegnet sei,' etc. *Corp. inscr. Gr.* iii no. 4500 = Lebas—Waddington *op. cit.* iii no. 2627. Some 3½ hours from Palmyra on the road to Emesa are three large altars of similar size placed close together; that on the east has a relief representing a large thunderbolt and a bilingual inscription; that on the west has a similar relief and inscription, except for a variant in the Palmyrene text; that in the centre is damaged and appears to have a different emblem but the same inscription Διὶ Ὑψίστῳ καὶ Ἐπηκόῳ ἡ πόλις εὐχήν· | ἔτους εκυ΄, Δύστρου ακ΄ (=March 21, 114 A.D.), ἐπὶ ἀργυροταμιῶν Ζεβείδου Θαιμοαμέδου καὶ | Μοκίμου Ἰαριβωλέους καὶ Ἰαραίου Νουρβήλου καὶ Ἀνάνιδος Μάλχου = C. J. M. de Vogüé *op. cit.* p. 74 f. no. 124, who renders the Palmyrene text 'La ville (de Thadmor) a élevé (cet autel) à celui dont le nom est béni à toujours,' etc. R. Dussaud *Mission dans les régions désertiques de la Syrie* (extr. from the *Nouvelles Archives des missions scientifiques et littéraires* x) Paris 1903 p. 238 no. 2 a dedication, south of Damaskos, Διὶ Μεγίστῳ Ὑψίστῳ (quoted by F. Cumont in Pauly—Wissowa *Real-Enc.* ix. 445). The Syrian Zeus Ὕψιστος is probably *Ba'al-šamin* (M. Sobernheim *op. cit.* pp. 41, 43, 44 f.; *supra* i. 8, 191 f.).

(30) Phoinike. Sanchouniathon of Berytos (*supra* i. 191) in Philon Bybl. *frag.* 2. 12 f. (*Frag. hist. Gr.* iii. 567 Müller) *ap.* Euseb. *praep. ev.* i. 10. 14 f. κατὰ τούτους γίνεταί τις Ἐλιοῦν καλούμενος Ὕψιστος καὶ θήλεια λεγομένη Βηρούθ, οἳ καὶ κατῴκουν περὶ Βύβλον. ἐξ ὧν γεννᾶται Ἐπίγειος ἢ Αὐτόχθων (W. Dindorf reads Ἐπίγειος αὐτόχθων), ὃν ὕστερον ἐκάλεσαν Οὐρανόν· ὡς ἀπ΄ αὐτοῦ καὶ τὸ ὑπὲρ ἡμᾶς στοιχεῖον δι᾽ ὑπερβολὴν τοῦ κάλλους ὀνομάζειν οὐρανόν. γεννᾶται δὲ τούτῳ ἀδελφὴ ἐκ τῶν προειρημένων, ἣ καὶ ἐκλήθη Γῆ, καὶ διὰ τὸ κάλλος ἀπ᾽ αὐτῆς, φησίν, ἐκάλεσαν τὴν ὁμώνυμον γῆν. ὁ δὲ τούτων πατὴρ ὁ Ὕψιστος ἐν συμβολῇ θηρίων τελευτήσας ἀφιερώθη, ᾧ χοὰς καὶ θυσίας οἱ παῖδες ἐτέλεσαν. Here Ἐλιοῦν is but the Phoenician for Ὕψιστος, who naturally weds Βηρούθ because he is the solar Ba'al of Berytos (R. Dussaud *Notes de mythologie syrienne* Paris 1905 p. 140 f.). W. W. Baudissin *Adonis und Esmun* Leipzig 1911 p. 76 supposes a blend of Adonis (killed by the boar) with the 'Kronos' of Byblos. Two votive hands of bronze formerly in the collection of M. Péretié at *Beirut* are dedicated to the Θεὸς Ὕψιστος (M. Beaudouin—E. Pottier in the *Bull. Corr. Hell.* 1879 iii. 265 no. 20 [ἡ δεῖνα] | εὐ\|ξ[α]μέν\|η ὑπὲρ αὐτῆ[ς] | καὶ Θ[ε]οδώ\|ρου ἀνδρὸ[ς] | καὶ τέκνων | Θεῷ Ὑψίστῳ, *ib.* no. 21 Θεῷ Ὑψ|ίστῳ Γηρ|ίων εὐξά|[μ]ενος ἀνέθη|[κ]εν in dotted letters), as is a third described in the *Catalogue de la Collection Hoffmann*, Bronzes, no. 570 (F. Cumont in R. Dussaud *Notes de mythologie syrienne* p. 122). The god in question is presumably Adad or Ramman, the Zeus or Iupiter of Heliopolis (R. Dussaud *ib.* p. 123 f., F. Cumont in Pauly—Wissowa *Real-Enc.* ix. 445). Possibly some confusion of *Ramman* (*supra* i. 576) with *Rama, Ramath, Ramatha,* 'Height' (Beer in Pauly—Wissowa *Real-Enc.* i A. 132), underlies the glosses in Hesych. ῥαμά· ὑψηλή, ῥαμάς· ὁ ὕψιστος θεός, and the aetiological tale in Steph. Byz. *s.v.* Λαοδίκεια· πόλις τῆς Συρίας, ἡ πρότερον Λευκὴ ἀκτὴ λεγομένη καὶ πρὸ τούτου Ῥάμιθα. κεραυνωθεὶς γάρ τις ἐν αὐτῇ ποιμὴν ἔλεγε ῥαμάνθας, τουτέστιν ἀφ᾽ ὕψους ὁ θεός· ῥάμαν γὰρ τὸ ὕψος, ἄθας δὲ ὁ θεός. οὕτω Φίλων. At *Sahin*, five hours from Antarados (*Tortosa, Ṭarṭûs*), is the dedication [Θε]ῷ Ὑψίστῳ Οὐρανίῳ Ὑ[πάτῳ καὶ Ἡλίῳ Ἀνικήτῳ (?)] | [Μί]θρᾳ ὁ βωμὸς ἐκτίσθ[η······] | [ὁ]ρθῶς ἐν τῷ κϙ΄ (=208 A.D.), ἐπ[ικρατείας (?)······] | [ὑπὲ]ρ σωτηρίας Θεο[φ]ρά[στου······] | ἐπὶ ἀρχῆς Σολωμάνο[υ····] (E. Renan *Mission de Phénicie* Paris 1864 p. 103 f., F. Cumont *Textes et monuments figurés relatifs aux mystères de Mithra* Bruxelles 1896 ii. 92 no. 5).

At *Abédat* above the door of the church of Mar-Eusebios in a block inscribed ἀγαθῆι τύχηι· | ἔτους ιζ΄ Καίσαρος Ἀντωνείνου τοῦ κυρίου, | μηνὸς Λώου (=August 154 A.D.), Διὶ Οὐρανίῳ Ὑψίστῳ Σααρναίῳ (a title derived from the ancient name of the village (?)) Ἐπηκόῳ | Γ. Φλάουιος [Γλ]άφυρος ἐκ τῶν ἰδίων τὸν βωμὸν ἀνέθηκα (E. Renan *op. cit.*

p. 234 ff. = R. Cagnat—G. Lafaye *Inscriptiones Graecae ad res Romanas pertinentes* Paris 1906 iii. 406 no. 1060). At Byblos (*Djebeil*), some six hours north of Berytos, is a square statue-base lettered Διὶ Ὑψίστῳ | Πεκουλιάριος | Μάρθας Δ(ημ)η[τρίου(?)]. The upper part of the base shows in relief a bust of the god, facing. He is bearded, and clad in *chitón* and *himátion*, with thunderbolt and sceptre to his right and left (R. Dussaud in the *Rev. Arch.* 1896 i. 299 f. with fig. (inadequate), S. Ronzevalle in the *Revue biblique internationale* 1903 xii. 405 ff. with photographic cut). Ronzevalle *loc. cit.* contends 'que l'*Hypsistos* de Byblos n'est autre que l'antique *Moloch-Kronos* de la même ville': cp. W. W. Baudissin *op. cit.* p. 76 n. 4.

(31) Samaria. On Mt Argarizon (Gerizim) near Neapolis (*Nablûs*) was a sanctuary of Zeus Ὕψιστος, to whom Abraham had devoted himself (Marinos in Damask. *v. Isid. ap.* Phot. *bibl.* p. 345 b 18 ff. Bekker ὅτι ὁ διάδοχος Πρόκλου, φησίν, ὁ Μαρῖνος, γένος ἦν ἀπὸ τῆς ἐν Παλαιστίνῃ Νέας πόλεως, πρὸς ὄρει κατῳκισμένης τῷ Ἀργαρίζῳ καλουμένῳ. εἶτα βλασφημῶν ὁ δυσσεβὴς φησιν ὁ συγγραφεύς, ἐν ᾧ Διὸς Ὑψίστου ἁγιώτατον ἱερόν, ᾧ καθιέρωτο Ἄβραμος ὁ τῶν πάλαι Ἑβραίων πρόγονος, ὡς αὐτὸς ἔλεγεν ὁ Μαρῖνος); cp. Deut. 11. 29, 27. 12 with Gen. 12. 6 f.: Jehovah, from the heathen point of view, was 'a god of the hills' (1 Kings 20. 23). Sanballat built a temple on Mt Gerizim (Ioseph. *ant. Iud.* 11. 8. 4), which during the persecutions of Antiochos iv Epiphanes was dedicated to Zeus Ἑλλήνιος (*id. ib.* 12. 5. 5, Zonar. 4. 19 (i. 317 Dindorf)) or Ξένιος (2 Macc. 6. 2, Euseb. *chron. ann. Abr.* 1850 versio Armenia (ii. 126 Schoene)=Hieron. *chron. ann. Abr.* 1849 (ii. 127

Fig. 818.   Fig. 819.   Fig. 820.

Schoene) in Samaria super verticem montis Garizi Iovis Peregrini delubrum aedificat, ipsis Samaritanis ut id faceret praecantibus). Sanballat's temple was destroyed by Ioannes Hyrkanos i in 129 B.C. (Ioseph. *ant. Iud.* 13. 9. 1). But the mountain remained the centre of Samaritan worship (John 4. 20 f.), and coins of Flavia Neapolis from the reign of Antoninus Pius to that of Volusianus show it topped by a temple (Eckhel *Doctr. num. vet.*[2] iii. 433 ff., T. L. Donaldson *Architectura Numismatica* London 1859 p. 116 ff. no. 33, G. F. Hill in the *Brit. Mus. Cat. Coins* Palestine pp. xxviii ff., 48 f. pl. 5, 14—16 Antoninus Pius, 59 pl. 6, 12 Macrinus, 60 f. nos. 94—100 Elagabalos, 63 nos. 112—115 Severus Alexander, no. 116 f. Philippus Senior, 66 f. pl. 7, 5 Philippus Senior and Philippus Iunior, 68 no. 135 Otacilia Severa, 69 pl. 7, 9 Philippus Iunior, 70 f. pl. 7, 13 Trebonianus Gallus, 73 pl. 7, 19 Volusianus; cp. pl. 39, 7 f., 12, pl. 40, 1, *Hunter Cat. Coins* iii. 278 pl. 77, 25 Antoninus Pius, 281 pl. 77, 27 Volusianus, Head *Hist. num.*[2] p. 803. My figs. 818 and 820 are from F. De Saulcy *Numismatique de la terre sainte* Paris 1874 p. 247 f. pl. 13, 1 Antoninus Pius and pl. 14, 2 Volusianus. Fig. 819 is from a specimen struck by Macrinus, in my collection. Mt Gerizim is often supported by an eagle (*e.g. Brit. Mus. Cat. Coins* Palestine pp. 63 no. 116 f. Philippus Senior, 66 f. pl. 7, 5 Philippus Senior and Philippus Iunior, 69 pl. 7, 9 Philippus Iunior, 73 pl. 7, 19 Volusianus) and sometimes flanked by a star (sun?) on the left and a crescent (moon) on the right (*ib.* p. 71 no. 153 f. Trebonianus Gallus): eagle and heavenly bodies would alike suit the worship of Zeus). Mr G. F. Hill *loc. cit.* p. xxviii f. describes the coin-type as follows: 'It shows two distinct peaks, the steepness of which is certainly exaggerated. On the left-hand peak is the temple which, since it first appears on coins of Pius, is doubtless the temple of Zeus Hypsistos built by Hadrian [E. N. Adler—M. Séligsohn 'Une nouvelle chronique samaritaine' in the *Revue des études juives* 1902 xlv. 82 'le roi Hadrien vint à Sichem et fit du bien aux Samaritains ; il fit construire pour lui un grand temple près du mont Garizim et le nomma Temple de Saphis...Le roi Hadrien prit les battants d'airain qui avaient été mis à la porte du temple de Salomon, fils de David, et les plaça à la porte du temple de Saphis,' *ib.* p. 233 'les battants d'airain que les gens de l'empereur Hadrien avaient enlevés du temple des Juifs à Jérusalem et placés dans le temple construit sur l'ordre d'Hadrien dans l'endroit choisi, le Mont Garizim...les battants d'airain enlevés par Hadrien au temple juif et placés par lui au temple qu'il a construit au pied du Mont Garizim.' Cp. the parallel passages in E. Vilmar *Abulfathi annales Samaritani* Gothæ 1865 and T. G. J. Juynboll *Chronicon Samaritanum, Arabice conscriptum, cui titulus est Liber Josuae* Lugduni Batavorum 1848 cap. 47 p. 188. But the chroniclers' description can hardly refer to a temple on the mountain-*top*. And C. Clermont-Ganneau in the *Journal des Savants* Nouvelle Série 1904 ii. 40 f., in view of the variants *saqaras* lib. Jos., *sapts*, *sîpas* Abu'l Fath, *sapts* chron. Adler, concludes that the god established by Hadrian was Iupiter Sarapis. This is certainly better than Iupiter *Sospes* the conjecture of E. N. Adler—M. Séligsohn *loc. cit.* p. 82 n. 2 or *Caesaris* the suggestion of T. G. J. Juynboll *op. cit.* p. 334 f.]. Behind it is a small erection which may be an external altar. On the other (right-hand) peak is a construction which seems again to be rather an altar than a small temple. Since the mountain is doubtless supposed to be seen from the town, i.e. from the north, this smaller peak must lie to the west of the larger. We may perhaps identify it with the spur west of the main summit on which are the ruins known as *Khûrbet Lôzeh* or *Luzah*, where is still the Samaritans' sacrificing place. The 300 steps by which, in the time of the Bordeaux Pilgrim (A.D. 333), one ascended to the summit [*Palestine Pilgrims' Text Society: Itinerary from Bordeaux to Jerusalem* trans. A. Stewart annot. Sir C. W. Wilson London 1887 p. 18], are indicated on the coins, with chapels at intervals, as on many another *sacro monte* ; but no trace of them has been recorded as surviving to the present day. Along the foot of the mountain was a long colonnade ; an opening gave access to the foot of the stair and to the road, perhaps for wheeled traffic, which wound up the hill between the two peaks, branching about half-way up.' Prokop. *de aed.* 5. 7. 2 states that the Samaritans worshipped the actual mountain-top, but denies that they had ever built a temple on it (τοῦτο δὲ τὸ ὄρος κατ' ἀρχὰς μὲν οἱ Σαμαρεῖται εἶχον· ὡς εὐξόμενοί τε ἀνέβαινον ἐς τὴν τοῦ ὄρους ὑπερβολήν, οὐδένα ἀνιέντες καιρόν· οὐχ ὅτι νεών τινα ἐνταῦθα ᾠκοδομήσαντο πώποτε, ἀλλὰ τὴν ἀκρώρειαν αὐτὴν σεβόμενοι ἐτεθήπεσαν πάντων μάλιστα). He goes on to say (*ib.* 5. 7. 7) that Zenon, emperor of the East, expelled the Samaritans from the mountain, handed it over to the Christians, and built on the summit a church dedicated to the Virgin (τῇ θεοτόκῳ) with a wall, or rather a fence, about it. The *Chronicon Paschale* 327 B (i. 604 Dindorf) for the year 484 A.D. remarks ὁ δὲ βασιλεὺς Ζήνων εὐθέως ἐποίησε τὴν συναγωγὴν αὐτῶν τὴν οὖσαν εἰς τὸ καλούμενον Γαργαρίδην εὐκτήριον οἶκον μέγαν τῆς δεσποίνης ἡμῶν τῆς θεοτόκου καὶ ἀειπαρθένου Μαρίας=Io. Malal. *chron.* 15 p. 382 f. Dindorf. For an account of the ruins still traceable on the mountain see Sir C. W. Wilson 'Ebal and Gerizim, 1866' in *Palestine Exploration Fund: Quarterly Statement for 1873* pp. 66—71 with plan, and for modern celebrations on the site J. A. Montgomery *The Samaritans* Philadelphia 1907 p. 34 ff. with photographic view (*ib.* pp. 322—346 Samaritan bibliography). I. Benzinger in Pauly—Wissowa *Real-Enc.* vii. 767 comments : 'Der Berg verdankt den heiligen Charakter seiner kosmischen Bedeutung : Ebal und G. zusammen sind für Palästina der doppelgipfelige Weltberg, der Gottesberg mit dem Pass dazwischen' —a dogmatic statement of a possible (cp. *supra* p. 422 ff.), but by no means proven, hypothesis.

(32) Ioudaia. The Hebrew Godhead in the later books of the Old Testament, in the Apokrypha, and in the New Testament is often styled (ὁ) Ὕψιστος, sometimes (ὁ) Θεὸς (ὁ) Ὕψιστος or Κύριος (ὁ) Ὕψιστος (details and statistics by E. Schürer in the *Sitzungsber. d. Akad. d. Wiss. Berlin* 1897 p. 214 f.). Cp. Philon *in Flaccum* 7 ὁ τοῦ Ὑψίστου Θεοῦ νεώς, *leg. ad Gaium* 23 ἀπαρχὴν τῷ Ὑψίστῳ Θεῷ, 40 θυσίας ἐντελεῖς ὁλοκαύτους τῷ Ὑψίστῳ

Hýpsistos, however, was obviously susceptible of a less material interpretation. Accordingly, in Hellenistic times, the name of Zeus *Hýpsistos* became attached to the supreme deity of more than one non-Hellenic area. In Syria it meant *Ba'al-šamin*. In Samaria it meant Jehovah. Further denationalised, but still recognisable by his eagle (Athens, Thyateira, Mytilene, Tanais), the *Theòs Hýpsistos*—often called *Hýpsistos* and nothing more—was worshipped throughout the Greek-speaking world in early imperial days. The propagation of his cult was due, partly perhaps to a general trend towards monotheism, but mainly to definite Jewish influence. The Jews of the Dispersion, accustomed to use the term *Hýpsistos* of their own august Godhead, carried it with them into Gentile lands, where they formed small and—truth to tell—somewhat accommodating circles of worshippers (Moesia, Bosporos Kimmerios, Kappadokia). Here and there they continued to light their ceremonial lamps (Pisidia, Lydia) ; but they could hardly be described as whole-hearted devotees of the Mosaic law. Thus

Θεῷ καθ' ἑκάστην ἡμέραν, Ioseph. *ant. Iud.* 16. 6. 2 ἀρχιερέως Θεοῦ 'Υψίστου, Celsus *ap.* Orig. *c. Cels.* 1. 24 μετὰ ταῦτά φησιν ὅτι οἱ αἰπόλοι καὶ ποιμένες ἕνα ἐνόμισαν θεόν, εἴτε "Υψιστον εἴτ' Ἀδωναῖ εἴτ' Οὐράνιον εἴτε Σαβαώθ, εἴτε καὶ ὅπῃ καὶ ὅπως χαίρουσιν ὀνομάζοντες τόνδε τὸν κόσμον, 5. 41 οὐδὲν οὖν οἶμαι διαφέρειν Δία "Υψιστον καλεῖν ἢ Ζῆνα ἢ Ἀδωναῖον ἢ Σαβαὼθ ἢ Ἀμοῦν, ὡς Αἰγύπτιοι, ἢ Παπαῖον, ὡς Σκύθαι, 45 Κέλτος οἴεται μηδὲν διαφέρειν Δία "Υψιστον καλεῖν ἢ Ζῆνα ἢ Ἀδωναῖον ἢ Σαβαὼθ ἤ, ὡς Αἰγύπτιοι, Ἀμοῦν ἤ, ὡς Σκύθαι, Παπαῖον, Lyd. *de mens.* 4. 53 p. 110, 4 ff. Wünsch καὶ 'Ιουλιανὸς δὲ ὁ βασιλεύς, ὅτε πρὸς Πέρσας ἐστρατεύετο, γράφων 'Ιουδαίοις οὕτω φησίν· ' ἀνεγείρω γὰρ μετὰ πάσης προθυμίας τὸν ναὸν τοῦ 'Υψίστου Θεοῦ,' A. Dieterich ' Papyrus magica musei Lugdunensis Batavi ' in the *Jahrb. f. class. Philol.* Suppl. 1888 xvi. 797 verse 23 ff. κατ' ἐπιταγὴν τοῦ 'Υψίστου Θεοῦ 'Ιάω Ἀδωναῖ αβ[λα]ναθαναλβα (cp. A. Audollent *Defixionum tabellae* Luteciae Parisiorum 1904 p. 500 f.), | σὺ εἶ ὁ περιέχων τὰς χάριτας | [ἐ]ν τῇ κορυφῇ λαμπρῇ, C. Wessely *Griechische Zauberpapyrus von Paris und London* Wien 1888 p. 47 pap. Par. 1068 καλὸν καὶ ἱερὸν φῶς τοῦ 'Υψίστου Θεοῦ, *ib.* p. 104 Brit. Mus. pap. 46. 45 ff. = F. G. Kenyon *Greek Papyri in the British Museum* London 1893 i. 66 no. 46, 44 ff. καὶ διατήρησόν με καὶ τὸν παῖδα | τοῦτον ἀπημάντους ἐν ὀνόματι | τοῦ 'Υψίστου Θεοῦ, oracl. *Sib.* 2. 245 Geffcken ἥξει καὶ Μωσῆς ὁ μέγας φίλος 'Υψίστοιο. Aisch. *frag.* 464. 12 Nauck² *ap.* Iust. Mart. *de monarch.* 2 δόξα δ' 'Υψίστου Θεοῦ (δ' om. Clem. Al. *strom.* 5. 14 p. 415, 15 Stählin = Euseb. *praep. ev.* 13. 13. 60) is a Jewish forgery.

(33) Aigyptos. The Jews of Athribis (*Bencha*) in Lower Egypt dedicated a house of prayer to the Θεὸς "Υψιστος (S. Reinach in the *Bull. Corr. Hell.* 1889 xiii. 178 ff. no. 1, cp. *id. Chroniques d'Orient* Paris 1891 p. 579, Dittenberger *Orient. Gr. inscr. sel.* no. 96 ὑπὲρ βασιλέως Πτολεμαίου (*sc.* Ptolemy v Epiphanes (205—181 B.C.) or Ptolemy vi Philometor (181—146 B.C.)) | καὶ βασιλίσσης Κλεοπάτρας | Πτολεμαῖος 'Επικύδου | ὁ ἐπιστάτης τῶν φυλακιτῶν | καὶ οἱ ἐν 'Αθρίβει 'Ιουδαῖοι | τὴν προσευχὴν | Θεῷ 'Υψίστωι). A woman of Alexandreia invokes his aid (*Bulletin de l'Institut Égyptien* 1872—1873 no. 12 p. 116 f. cited by E. Schürer in the *Sitzungsber. d. Akad. d. Wiss. Berlin* 1897 p. 213 and by J. G. C. Anderson—F. Cumont—H. Grégoire *Recueil des Inscriptions grecques et latines du Pont et de l'Arménie* (*Studia Pontica* iii) Bruxelles 1910 i. 17 Θεῷ 'Υψίστῳ καὶ πάντων 'Επόπτῃ καὶ 'Ηλίῳ καὶ Νεμέσεσι αἴρει 'Αρσεινόη ἄωρος τὰς χεῖρας· ἤ (=εἰ) τις αὐτῇ φάρμακα ἐποίησε ἢ καὶ ἐπεχαρέ τις αὐτῆς τῷ θανάτῳ ἢ ἐπιχαρεῖ, μετέλθετε αὐτούς. For the raised hands cp. *supra* no. (19) Rheneia).

(34) Africa. At Hadrumetum in Byzacium several curse-tablets invoke the *Deus Pelagicus Aerius Altissimus* 'Ιάω (A. Audollent *Defixionum tabellae* Luteciae Parisiorum 1904 p. 403 ff. no. 290 ff., *e.g.* no. 293, B adiuro te demon | quicunque es et de|mando tibi ex hanc | die ex hanc ora ex oc | momento ut crucie|tur ; adiuro te per eum | qui te resolvit ex vite | temporibus deum pela|gicum aerium altissimu[m] | Ιαω οι ου ιαιαα ιωιϸε | ο οριυω αηια | Lynceus (*sc.* the name of the horse to be cursed)). *Altissimus*="Υψιστος (F. Cumont in Pauly—Wissowa *Real-Enc.* ix. 449).

their *milieu* on occasion provided a congenial soil for the growth of the Christian church. Indeed, it is sometimes difficult to decide whether a given dedication to the *Theòs Hýpsistos* was the work of a Jew or of a Jewish Christian (Phrygia). After all, *Hýpsistos* was a title that any honest man could use with a clear conscience[1].

Zeus appears as a mountain-god in connexion with the following localities:

Lakonike
Mount Taleton, a peak of Mount Taygeton[2].
The *Akrópolis* at Sparta[3].
Cape Malea[4].
Cape Tainaros (?)[5].

Messene
Mount Ithome[6].

[1] For ὕψιστος as applied to Zeus by the Greek poets see Bruchmann *Epith. deor.* p. 142.

[2] A broken *stéle* of white marble, now at Sparta (M. N. Tod and A. J. B. Wace *A Catalogue of the Sparta Museum* Oxford 1906 p. 43 f. no. 222), mentions Zeus Ταλετίτας along with Auxesia and Damoia (J. de Prott *Leges Graecorum sacrae* Lipsiae 1896 Fasti sacri p. 35 f. no. 14, 1 f. = *Inscr. Gr. Arc. Lac. Mess.* i no. 363, 1 f. cited *supra* i. 730 n. 6). The god derived his title from Mt Taleton (*supra* i. 155 f. pl. xiv), on which horses were sacrificed to Helios (Paus. 3. 20. 4 ἄκρα δὲ τοῦ Ταϋγέτου Ταλετὸν ὑπὲρ Βρυσεῶν ἀνέχει. ταύτην Ἡλίου καλοῦσιν ἱεράν, καὶ ἄλλα τε αὐτόθ' Ἡλίῳ θύουσι καὶ ἵππους· τὸ δὲ αὐτὸ καὶ Πέρσας οἶδα θύειν νομίζοντας. *Supra* i. 180 n. 5). cp. the Cretan sun-god Talos (*supra* i. 719 ff.). The goddesses, Peloponnesian equivalents of Demeter and Kore, were worshipped at the foot of the mountain in Bryseai (*Kalybia Sochiotika*), where traces of an Eleusinion have come to light (H. von Prott in the *Ath. Mitth.* 1904 xxix. 8. *Id. ib.* p. 7 holds that Taleton was not the very summit of Taygeton, but a lower and more accessible crest).

[3] Zeus Ὕπατος (*supra* p. 875 n. 1 no. (4)).

[4] Zeus Μαλειαῖος (Steph. Byz. *s.v.* Μαλέα· ... καὶ ἀπὸ τοῦ Μάλεια Μαλειαῖος Ζεύς).

[5] Tainaros, who founded the Taenarian temple of Poseidon, was the son of Zeus (Steph. Byz. *s.v.* Ταίναρος). *Supra* i. 156.

[6] Zeus Ἰθωμάτας had a cult, but no actual temple (D. Fimmen in Pauly—Wissowa *Real-Enc.* ix. 2306 quoting Oikonomakis Τὰ σωζόμενα Ἰθώμης, Μεσσήνης 1879 p. 14 f.), on the top of Mt Ithome, where he had been brought up by the nymphs Ithome and Neda (Thouk. 1. 103, Paus. 4. 3. 9, 4. 12. 7 ff., 4. 27. 6, 4. 33. 1 f.). Water was carried daily from the spring Klepsydra to his sanctuary (Paus. 4. 33. 1). The statue of him made by Hageladas for the Messenians of Naupaktos was kept in the house of a priest annually chosen (Paus. 4. 33. 2 cited *supra* p. 741 n. 4): its type is reflected on coins of Messene (*supra* p. 741 f. figs. 673, 674). At Messene (M. N. Tod in the *Journ. Hell. Stud.* 1905 xxv. 53 f. no. 11, 1 f. = *Inscr. Gr. Arc. Lac. Mess.* i no. 1399, 1 ff. τειχίοεσ|σα παρ' ἀγλαὸν | ἱρὸν Ἰθώμης Μεσ|σήνη) in *s.* i—ii A.D. the priest of Zeus Ἰθωμάτας was eponymous magistrate (*Inscr. Gr. Arc. Lac. Mess.* i no. 1468, 4 ff. ἐπὶ ἱερέος τοῦ | Διὸς τοῦ Ἰθω|μάτου Ἀπελ|λίωνος τοῦ Φι|λίππου, cp. *ib.* no. 1467, 1 and no. 1469, 1). The yearly festival (*ib.* nos. 1467—1469 record as its officials ἀγωνοθέτης, ἱεροθύται, γραμματεύς, χαλειδοφόρος (= ἀκρατοφόρος, cp. χάλις, 'pure wine')) was called Ἰθωμαῖα (Paus. 4. 33. 2), Ἰθωμαία or Ἰθωμαῖς (Steph. Byz. *s.v.* Ἰθώμη· ... καὶ Ζεὺς Ἰθωμάτας, καὶ ἑορτὴ Ἰθωμαία καὶ Ἰθωμαῖς). It dates back to the time of Eumelos (*s.* viii B.C.), and originally involved a musical competition (Paus. 4. 33. 2 ἄγουσι δὲ καὶ ἑορτὴν ἐπέτειον Ἰθωμαῖα· τὸ δὲ ἀρχαῖον καὶ ἀγῶνα ἐτίθεσαν μουσικῆς. τεκμαίρεσθαι δ' ἔστιν ἄλλοις τε καὶ Εὐμήλου τοῖς ἔπεσιν· ἐποίησε γοῦν καὶ τάδε ἐν τῷ προσοδίῳ τῷ ἐς Δῆλον (Eumel. *frag.* 13 Kinkel, cp. Paus. 4. 4. 1, 5. 19. 10)· 'τῷ γὰρ Ἰθωμάτᾳ καταθύμιος ἔπλετο Μοῖσα | ἁ καθαρὰ < ν κίθαριν (ins. T. Bergk; but see H. W. Smyth *ad loc.*) > καὶ ἐλεύθερα σάμβαλ' ἔχοισα.' οὐκοῦν ποιῆσαί μοι δοκεῖ τὰ ἔπη καὶ μουσικῆς ἀγῶνα ἐπιστάμενος τιθέντας). A tradition of human sacrifice (Nilsson *Gr. Feste* p. 32) attached

Elis
  Mount Olympos[1].
  Olympia[2].
Arkadia
  Mount Lykaion[3].

to Mt Ithome, as to Mt Lykaion (*supra* i. 70 ff.) ; for Aristomenes is said to have slain 300 persons, including Theopompos king of Sparta, as an offering to Zeus Ἰθωμάτας (Clem. Al. *protr.* 3. 42. 2 p. 31, 23 ff. Stählin (=Euseb. *praep. ev.* 4. 16. 12) Ἀριστομένης γοῦν ὁ Μεσσήνιος τῷ Ἰθωμήτῃ Διὶ τριακοσίους ἀπέσφαξεν, τοσαύτας ὁμοῦ καὶ τοιαύτας καλλιερεῖν οἰόμενος ἑκατόμβας· ἐν οἷς καὶ Θεόπομπος ἦν < ὁ (Euseb.) > Λακεδαιμονίων βασιλεύς, ἱερεῖον εὐγενές, Kyrill. Al. *c. Iul.* 4 (lxxvi. 696 D—697 A Migne) Ἀριστομένης μὲν γὰρ ὁ Μεσήνιος τῷ ἐπίκλην Ἰθωμήτῃ Διὶ τριακοσίους ὁμοῦ νεκροὺς ἐχαρίζετο· προσετίθει δὲ τούτοις καὶ τῶν Λακεδαιμονίων βασιλεύσαντα· Θεόπομπος οὗτος ἦν. ἀξιάγαστος ἐντεῦθεν ὁ τῶν θεῶν ὕπατός τε καὶ ὑπέρτατος. ἐπεμειδία γὰρ κατὰ τὸ εἰωθὸς ἀνδράσιν ἀθλίως διολωλόσι, καὶ πλήρη βλέπων τὸν ἐκείνων βωμὸν δαιτὸς εἴσης. ἐντρυφᾶν γὰρ ἔθος αὐτοῖς τῶν ἀνθρώπων συμφοραῖς). Philippos v of Makedonia (in 214 B.C.?) sacrificed to Zeus on Mt Ithome, took the entrails of the ox in both hands, and showed them to Aratos of Sikyon and Demetrios of Pharos, asking each for his interpretation of the omens (Plout. *v. Arat.* 50). The latest notice of Zeus Ἰθωμάτας is in Schöll—Studemund *anecd.* i. 265 Ἐπίθετα Διός (51) ἰθωμήτου, 266 Ἐπίθετα Διός (43) ἰθωμήτου. Nowadays on the highest peak of Ithome the traveller sees a ruined monastery, a branch from that at *Vourkano*: its paved threshing-floor is the scene of the annual festival of the Panagia [Aug. 15], at which the peasants dance crowned with oleander-blossom (Frazer *Pausanias* iii. 437). Among the ruins lives a solitary monk (D. Fimmen *loc. cit.* p. 2307).

   Wide *Lakon. Kulte* p. 22 infers a tree-cult of Zeus Ἰθωμάτας at Leuktron or Leuktra (*Leftro*) in Lakonike from Paus. 3. 26. 6 δ δὲ οἶδα ἐν τῇ πρὸς θαλάσσῃ χώρᾳ τῆς Λευκτρικῆς ἐπ' ἐμοῦ συμβάν, γράψω. ἄνεμος πῦρ ἐς ὕλην ἐνεγκὼν τὰ πολλὰ ἠφάνισε τῶν δένδρων· ὡς δὲ ἀνεφάνη τὸ χωρίον ψιλόν, ἄγαλμα ἐνταῦθα ἱδρυμένον εὑρέθη Διὸς Ἰθωμάτα. τοῦτο οἱ Μεσσήνιοί φασι μαρτύριον εἶναί σφισι τὰ Λεύκτρα τὸ ἀρχαῖον τῆς Μεσσηνίας εἶναι. δύναιτο δ' ἂν καὶ Λακεδαιμονίων τὰ Λεύκτρα ἐξ ἀρχῆς οἰκούντων ὁ Ἰθωμάτας Ζεὺς παρ' αὐτοῖς ἔχειν τιμάς. He justly cp. the figure of Dionysos found in a plane-tree broken by the wind at Magnesia ad Maeandrum (A. E. Kontoleon in the *Ath. Mitth.* 1890 xv. 330 ff. no. 1 = Michel *Recueil d'Inscr. gr.* no. 856). We might also cite in this connexion a modern parallel from Ithome itself. Miss M. Hamilton (Mrs G. Dickins) *Greek Saints and Their Festivals* Edinburgh and London 1910 p. 170 f. writes : 'According to the popular legend, the monks of the monastery of St. Basil on Mount Eva, opposite Ithome, saw one night a flaming tree on the opposite ridge. They crossed the valley and found this ikon of the Panagia on a tree, with a lighted candle beside it. They conveyed it across to their monastery, but it transferred itself miraculously back to the place at which it was found, and the monks believed themselves forced to change to the other ridge. Since then the monastery of St. Basil has been deserted. The trunk of the tree was made into the lintel of the monastery door, and it is said that at the festival it is hacked by the faithful, who take pieces of it as a cure for fever. The ikon is inscribed with reference to the legend— The Guide to the Hill of Ithome—Ὁδηγήτρια τῷ ὄρει Ἰθωμάτει. In celebration of the festival this ikon makes a short tour of the country. On 12th August it goes up from Voulkano to its old home with pomp and ceremony, accompanied by the monks and its worshippers, a goodly company, comprising a large number of babies brought to be baptised on the top of Ithome ... On the 15th a solemn procession reconducts the ikon to the lower monastery, and nine days later it is taken to Nisi, near Kalamata, where a fair ends the celebrations of the district. The rest of the year the ikon remains at Voulkano.'

---

[1] *Supra* i. 100, ii. 758.   [2] Zeus Ὕψιστος (*supra* p. 878 n. o no. (5)).
[3] Zeus Λύκαιος (*supra* i. 63—99, 154 f., 177 f.).

A hill near Tegea[1].
Trapezous[2].

Korinthos
Corinth[3].

Phliasia
Mount Apesas[4].

Argolis
The Larisa at Argos[5].

---

[1] The high place on which stood most of the altars of the Tegeates was called after Zeus Κλάριος (Paus. 8. 53. 9 f. cited *supra* p. 874 n. 2). Sir J. G. Frazer and H. Hitzig— H. Blümner *ad loc.* identify this eminence with the hill of St Sostis. See further *supra* p. 807 n. 2.

[2] Zeus Ἀκραῖος (*supra* p. 871 n. o no. (3)).

[3] Zeus Ὕψιστος (*supra* p. 878 n. o no. (3)).

[4] Apesas (*Phouka*) is a mountain which rises north of Nemea to a height of 873^m. It figured in two distinct myths. On the one hand, Perseus here sacrificed for the first time to Zeus Ἀπεσάντιος (Paus. 2. 15. 3 καὶ ὄρος Ἀπέσας ἐστὶν ὑπὲρ τὴν Νεμέαν, ἔνθα Περσέα πρῶτον Διὶ θῦσαι λέγουσιν Ἀπεσαντίῳ, cp. Stat. *Theb.* 3. 460 ff., 633 ff.), also known as Zeus Ἀπέσας (Steph. Byz. *s.v.* Ἀπέσας· ὄρος τῆς Νεμέας, ὡς Πίνδαρος (*frag.* 295 Bergk[4]) καὶ Καλλίμαχος ἐν τρίτῃ (*frag.* 29 Schneider), ἀπὸ Ἀφέσαντος (*sic*) ἥρωος βασιλεύσαντος τῆς χώρας, ἢ διὰ τὴν ἄφεσιν τῶν ἁρμάτων ἢ τοῦ λέοντος· ἐκεῖ γὰρ ἐκ τῆς σελήνης ἀφείθη. ἀφ' οὗ Ζεὺς Ἀπεσάντιος. Καλλίμαχος δὲ ἐν τοῖς ἰάμβοις (*frag.* 82 Schneider) τὸ ἐθνικὸν Ἀπέσας φησί 'κοὐχ ὧδ' Ἀρείων τῷ Ἀπέσαντι πὰρ Διὶ | ἔθυσεν Ἀρκὰς ἵππος'). On the other hand, Deukalion on escaping from the deluge here built an altar of Zeus Ἀφέσιος (*et. mag.* p. 176, 33 ff. Ἀφέσιος Ζεὺς ἐν Ἄργει τιμᾶται. εἴρηται δὲ ὅτι Δευκαλίων τοῦ κατακλυσμοῦ γενομένου διαφυγὼν καὶ εἰς τὴν ἄκραν τὴν Ἄργου (so H. Usener for Ἀργοῦς) διασωθεὶς ἱδρύσατο βωμὸν Ἀφεσίου Διός, ὅτι ἀφείθη ἐκ τοῦ κατακλυσμοῦ. ἡ δὲ ἄκρα ὕστερον Νεμέα ἐκλήθη ἀπὸ τῶν (τοῦ add. cod. V) Ἄργου βοσκημάτων ἐκεῖ νεμομένων. οὕτως Ἀρρειανὸς ἐτυμολογεῖ ἐν τῷ β' τῶν Βιθυνιακῶν (Arrian. *frag.* 26 (*Frag. hist. Gr.* iii. 591 Müller))). H. Usener *Die Sintfluthsagen* Bonn 1899 pp. 65 ff., 233 (cp. *id.* in the *Rhein. Mus.* 1901 lvi. 482 ff. = *Kleine Schriften* Leipzig—Berlin 1913 iv. 383 ff.) contends that Δευκαλίων presupposes a simpler form *Δεύ-καλος (whence Δευκαλίδαι), 'kleiner Zeus,' 'Zeusknäblein.' Other views are collected by K. Tümpel in Pauly—Wissowa *Real-Enc.* v. 275 f. and Gruppe *Gr. Myth. Rel.* pp. 446 n. 7, 718 e, 1100 n. 1, 1608 n. 3, *id. Myth. Lit.* 1908 p. 456. Imperial coppers of Kleonai represent Mt Apesas as a rock surmounted by an altar with an eagle perched upon it (Rasche *Lex. Num.* Suppl. i. 1836 Septimius Severus, *Brit. Mus. Cat. Coins* Peloponnesus p. 155 pl. 29, 8 = Anson *Num. Gr.* v. 9 no. 57 pl. 2 Iulia Domna, *Hunter Cat. Coins* ii. 154 no. 1 Geta, Imhoof-Blumer and P. Gardner *Num. Comm. Paus.* i. 33 f. Septimius Severus, Iulia Domna, Geta). Traces of the altar of Zeus are still to be seen on the flat rocky summit (É. Puillon Boblaye *Recherches Géographiques sur les ruines de la Morée* Paris 1836 ii. 41 'M. Peytier y a vu quelques ruines qui doivent avoir appartenu à l'autel de Jupiter Apésantius,' E. Curtius *Peloponnesos* Gotha 1852 ii. 505 'der Apesas, auf dem sich bei einer verfallenen Kapelle Palää Ekklesía genannt, noch Ruinen vom Heiligthume des Zeus Apesantios finden ').

[5] Zeus Λαρισαῖος had a roofless *naós* with a wooden statue on the top of the Larisa at Argos (Paus. 2. 24. 3 ἐπ' ἄκρᾳ δέ ἐστι τῇ Λαρίσῃ Διὸς ἐπίκλησιν Λαρισαίου ναός, οὐκ ἔχων ὄροφον· τὸ δὲ ἄγαλμα ξύλου πεποιημένον οὐκέτι ἑστηκὸς ἦν ἐπὶ τῷ βάθρῳ). Near it was a *naós* of Athena containing a three-eyed *xóanon* of Zeus, said to have been the paternal god of Priamos (Paus. 2. 24. 3 f. continues καὶ Ἀθηνᾶς δὲ ναός ἐστι θέας ἄξιος· ἐνταῦθα ἀναθήματα κεῖται καὶ ἄλλα καὶ Ζεὺς ξόανον, δύο μὲν ᾗ πεφύκαμεν ἔχον ὀφθαλμούς, τρίτον δὲ ἐπὶ τοῦ μετώπου. τοῦτον τὸν Δία Πριάμῳ φασὶν εἶναι τῷ Λαομέδοντος πατρῷον, ἐν ὑπαίθρῳ τῆς αὐλῆς ἱδρυμένον, καὶ ὅτε ἡλίσκετο ὑπὸ Ἑλλήνων Ἴλιον, ἐπὶ τούτου κατέφυγεν ὁ Πρίαμος τὸν βωμόν. ἐπεὶ δὲ τὰ λάφυρα ἐνέμοντο λαμβάνει Σθένελος ὁ Καπανέως αὐτόν, καὶ ἀνάκειται

Phalakron (?)[1].
Mount Kokkygion[2].

μὲν διὰ τοῦτο ἐνταῦθα· τρεῖς δὲ ὀφθαλμοὺς ἔχειν ἐπὶ τῷδε ἄν τις τεκμαίροιτο αὐτόν. Δία γὰρ ἐν οὐρανῷ βασιλεύειν, οὗτος μὲν λόγος κοινὸς πάντων ἐστὶν ἀνθρώπων. ὃν δὲ ἄρχειν φασὶν ὑπὸ γῆς, ἔστιν ἔπος τῶν Ὁμήρου (Il. 9. 457) Δία ὀνομάζον καὶ τοῦτον· 'Ζεύς τε καταχθόνιος καὶ ἐπαινὴ Περσεφόνεια.' Αἰσχύλος δὲ ὁ Εὐφορίωνος (frag. 436 b Dindorf, who cp. Prokl. in Plat. Crat. 148 p. 83, 28 f. Pasquali ὁ δὲ δεύτερος δυαδικῶς καλεῖται Ζεὺς ἐνάλιος καὶ Ποσειδῶν) καλεῖ Δία καὶ τὸν ἐν θαλάσσῃ. τρισὶν οὖν ὁρῶντα ἐποίησεν ὀφθαλμοῖς ὅστις δὴ ἦν ὁ ποιήσας, ἅτε ἐν ταῖς τρισὶ ταῖς λεγομέναις λήξεσιν ἄρχοντα τὸν αὐτὸν τοῦτον θεόν. This remarkable figure is mentioned also in schol. Eur. Tro. 16 τὸν δὲ ἕρκειον Δία ἄλλοι ἱστορικοὶ ἀναγράφουσιν ἰδίαν τινὰ σχέσιν περὶ αὐτοῦ ἱστοροῦντες, τρισὶν ὀφθαλμοῖς αὐτὸν κεχρῆσθαί φασιν, ὡς οἱ περὶ Ἀγίαν (frag. 3 (Frag. hist. Gr. iv. 292 f. Müller)) καὶ Δερκύλον (frag. 1 (Frag. hist. Gr. iv. 386 Müller)). I formerly accepted Pausanias' explanation of the three eyes (Class. Rev. 1903 xvii. 174 f., 1904 xviii. 75 f., 325), but later came to the conclusion that it was merely a sophisticated attempt to account for a very primitive feature, plurality of eyes implying superhuman powers of sight and three being a typical plurality (Folk-Lore 1904 xv. 282 ff., 1905 xvi. 275 f.). Excavations in the large court of the Venetian castle on the Larisa have brought to light the tufa foundations (11·70^m broad) of a building orientated towards the east. On the rock were sherds of geometric ware, and 14^m east of the building was a fifth-century inscription mentioning the Τλλεῖς (W. Vollgraff in the Bull. Corr. Hell. 1904 xxviii. 429 no. 11). On the lower terrace of the Larisa, to the east, are the ruined foundations of a second building. These two may well be the temples of Zeus Λαρισαῖος and of Athena respectively (id. ib. 1907 xxxi. 149). Steph. Byz. s.v. Λάρισσα·...καὶ ἡ ἀκρόπολις τοῦ Ἄργους Λάρισσα. καὶ ὁ πολίτης Λαρισσαῖος καὶ Λαρισσεὺς Ζεύς.

[1] Zeus Φαλακρός (supra p. 875 n. 2).

[2] There was a sanctuary of Zeus on the top of Mt Kokkygion (Paus. 2. 30. 2 ἱερὰ δὲ καὶ ἐς τόδε ἐπὶ ἄκρων τῶν ὀρῶν, ἐπὶ μὲν τῷ Κοκκυγίῳ Διός, ἐν δὲ τῷ Πρωνὶ ἐστιν Ἥρας), where Zeus had become a cuckoo in order to woo Hera (schol. vet. Theokr. 15. 64 Ἀριστοτέλης δὲ ἐν τῷ περὶ τῶν Ἑρμιόνης ἱερῶν (frag. 287 (Frag. hist. Gr. ii. 190 f. Müller) = Aristokles frag. (ib. iv. 330 f. Müller): but Grashof's cj. Ἀριστοκλῆς (cp. Ail. de nat. an. 11. 4) for Ἀριστοτέλης codd. is far from certain) ἰδιωτικῶς ἱστορεῖ περὶ τοῦ Διὸς καὶ [τοῦ τῆς (om. Wilamowitz)] Ἥρας γάμου. τὸν γὰρ Δία μυθολογεῖται ἐπιβουλεύειν τῇ Ἥρᾳ μιγῆναι, ὅτε αὐτὴν ἴδοι χωρισθεῖσαν ἀπὸ τῶν ἄλλων θεῶν. βουλόμενος δὲ ἀφανὴς γενέσθαι καὶ μὴ ὀφθῆναι ὑπ' αὐτῆς τὴν ὄψιν μεταβάλλει εἰς κόκκυγα καὶ καθέζεται εἰς ὄρος, ὃ πρῶτον μὲν Θρόναξ (Hemsterhuys cj. Θόρναξ (cp. Paus. 2. 36. 1)) ἐκαλεῖτο, νῦν δὲ Κόκκυξ. τὸν δὲ Δία χειμῶνα δεινὸν ποιῆσαι τῇ ἡμέρᾳ ἐκείνῃ· τὴν δὲ Ἥραν πορευομένην μόνην ἀφικέσθαι πρὸς τὸ ὄρος καὶ καθέζεσθαι εἰς αὐτό, ὅπου νῦν ἐστιν ἱερὸν Ἥρας Τελείας. τὸν δὲ κόκκυγα ἰδόντα καταπετασθῆναι καὶ καθεσθῆναι ἐπὶ τὰ γόνατα αὐτῆς πεφρικότα καὶ ῥιγῶντα ὑπὸ τοῦ χειμῶνος. τὴν δὲ Ἥραν ἰδοῦσαν αὐτὸν οἰκτεῖραι καὶ περιβαλεῖν τῇ ἀμπεχόνῃ. τὸν δὲ Δία εὐθέως μεταβαλεῖν τὴν ὄψιν καὶ ἐπιλαβέσθαι τῆς Ἥρας. τῆς δὲ τὴν μίξιν παραιτουμένης διὰ τὴν μητέρα, αὐτὸν ὑποσχέσθαι γυναῖκα αὐτὴν ποιήσασθαι. καὶ παρ' Ἀργείοις δέ, οἳ μέγιστα (οἱ μέγιστοι codd. Hemsterhuys cj. οἳ μέγιστον vel μάλιστα. Ahrens cj. οἳ μέγιστα) τῶν Ἑλλήνων τιμῶσι τὴν θεόν, τὸ [δὲ (om. Hemsterhuys)] ἄγαλμα τῆς Ἥρας ἐν τῷ ναῷ καθήμενον ἐν [τῷ (om. Wendel)] θρόνῳ τῇ χειρὶ ἔχει σκῆπτρον, καὶ ἐπ' αὐτῷ τῷ σκήπτρῳ κόκκυξ = Eudok. viol. 414^h, cp. Paus. 2. 17. 4, 2. 36. 1). For the chryselephantine statue by Polykleitos see Overbeck Schriftquellen p. 166 f. nos. 932—939, id. Gr. Plastik^4 i. 509—511, Collignon Hist. de la Sculpt. gr. i. 509—512, 516, C. Waldstein (Sir C. Walston) 'The Argive Hera of Polycleitus' in the Journ. Hell. Stud. 1901 xxi. 30—44 with pls. 2, 3, A. B. Cook 'Nephelokokkygía' in Essays and Studies presented to William Ridgeway Cambridge 1913 pp. 213—221 with pl. Cp. supra i. 532. The old name of the mountain, Θρόναξ or Θόρναξ, is said to have meant 'foot-stool' (Hesych. s.v. θόρναξ) and perhaps implies an ancient throne-cult (supra i. 134 f.). On Mt Thornax in Lakonike was a statue of Apollon Θορνάκιος (Hesych. s.v. θόρναξ, cp. Steph. Byz. s.v. Θόρναξ) or Πυθαεύς resembling that at

Mount Arachnaion[1].

Epidauros[2].

Aigina

The mountain of Zeus *Panhellénios*[3].

Amyklai (Hdt. 1. 69, Paus. 3. 10. 8), *i.e.* standing on a throne (Frazer *Pausanias* iii. 351 ff.). The hero Bouphagos shot by Artemis on Mt Pholoe was the son of Iapetos and Thornax (Paus. 8. 27. 17).

[1] Mt Arachnaion above Lessa had altars of Zeus and Hera, on which sacrifices were offered when there was a dearth of rain (Paus. 2. 25. 10 cited *supra* p. 467 n. 2). Frazer *Pausanias* iii. 233 f. says: 'This is the high, naked range on the left or northern side of the road as you go to the Epidaurian sanctuary from Argos. The most remarkable peak is Mt. *Arna*, the pointed rocky summit which rises immediately above the village of *Ligourio*. It is 3540 feet high. The western summit, Mt. *St. Elias*, is a little higher (3930 ft.)... The name Arachnaea is said to have been still used by the peasantry in the early part of this century. The altars of Zeus and Hera...appear to have stood in the hollow between the peaks of *Arna* and *St. Elias*, for there is here a square enclosure of Cyclopean masonry which would appear to have been an ancient place of worship.'

[2] Zeus Κάσιος (P. Kabbadias in the 'Εφ. 'Αρχ. 1883 p. 87 no. 22 = W. Prellwitz in Collitz—Bechtel *Gr. Dial.-Inschr.* iii. 1. 150 no. 3330 = *Inscr. Gr. Pelop.* i no. 1287 a rectangular base of limestone inscribed Διὶ Κασίωι | 'Ελλανοκράτης | 'Ηρακλείδου with

the numeral λα′ and the symbol ,· on which see *infra* Append. L *init*.).

M. Fränkel in the *Inscr. Gr. Pelop.* i. 286 observes: 'Iuppiter Casius notus erat in Graecia, postquam Traianus spolia e victoria contra Getas reportata in eius templum in Cario (*sic*) monte ad Euphratem situm dedicavit [*infra* Append. B Syria]... Hadriani fere aetate collocatus fuerit lapis noster.'

[3] The highest peak in Aigina (531[m]), a landmark for many miles around, is known nowadays as the *Oros*, sometimes also as *Hagios Elias* from the little chapel that crowns its summit. A. Furtwängler *Aegina* München 1906 i. 473 f. reports that excavations carried out in the spring of 1905 discovered an ancient settlement on the mountain-top. The site yielded a quantity of local ware, not unlike that from Troy, and also imported vases of late Mycenaean make. The inhabitants appear to have been Myrmidones, a division of the Thessalian Hellenes (C. Mueller *Aegineticorum liber* Berolini 1817 p. 14 ff.), whose heroes were Aiakos and the Aiakidai. They brought with them the cult of their Zeus 'Ελλάνιος, and Pindar represents the sons of Aiakos, when they prayed for the welfare of Aigina, as standing πὰρ βωμὸν πατέρος 'Ελλανίου (*Nem.* 5. 19). Zeus being a weather-god (*supra* p. 1 ff.), his mountain served as a public barometer (Theophr. *de signis tempest.* 1. 24 καὶ ἐὰν ἐν Αἰγίνῃ [καὶ (om. J. G. Schneider)] ἐπὶ τοῦ Διὸς τοῦ 'Ελλανίου νεφέλη καθίζηται, ὡς τὰ πολλὰ ὕδωρ γίνεται). Tradition said that during a great drought the foremost Hellenes besought Aiakos, as son of Zeus by Aigina daughter of Asopos, to intercede with his father on behalf of all, that Aiakos did so with success, and that on the spot where he had prayed the whole people raised a common sanctuary (Isokr. 9 *Euagoras* 14 f., Diod. 4. 61, Apollod. 3. 12. 6, Clem. Al. *strom.* 6. 3 p. 444, 13 ff. Stählin, schol. Pind. *Nem.* 5. 17, Eudok. *viol.* 13). Accordingly this came to be called the sanctuary of Zeus Πανελλήνιος (Paus. 1. 44. 9 cited *infra* p. 895 n. 1, 2. 29. 7 f., 2. 30. 3 f.). Frazer *Pausanias* iii. 265 describes the site: 'On the northern slope of Mt. *Oros*..., in a wild and lonely valley, there is a terrace supported upon walls of great blocks of trachyte. On this terrace there is a ruined chapel of the Hagios Asomatos (the Archangel Michael), which is entirely built of fine pieces of ancient architecture. About the middle of the terrace there are a number of large flat stones laid at equal intervals, as if they had been the bases of columns.' In the ruins of St Michael's chapel was found a stone block bearing an

Megaris
A height near Megara[1].

archaic Greek inscription (Roehl *Inscr. Gr. ant.* no. 352, Roberts *Gk. Epigr.* i. 146 f. no. 120, F. Bechtel in Collitz—Bechtel *Gr. Dial.-Inschr.* iii. 1. 195 no. 3408, *Inscr. Gr. Pelop.* i no. 6 Κωλιάδαις Ἀβλίων ἐποίησε Ἀλτίλλου), perhaps the base of some offering to Zeus, whose cult was in time superseded by that of the Archangel (cp. G. F. Hill 'Apollo and St. Michael: some analogies' in the *Journ. Hell. Stud.* 1916 xxxvi. 134 ff., especially p. 145). It was however reserved for Furtwängler by the latest excavations of 1905 to produce definite epigraphic evidence that the terrace of Hagios Asomatos was indeed the sanctuary of Zeus Πανελλήνιος (A. Furtwängler *op. cit.* i. 5 f. with the excellent map by H. Thiersch appended to the volume). For Zeus Ἑλλήνιος in the wider sense of the 'Hellenic,' *i.e.* national as opposed to foreign, god see O. Jessen in Pauly—Wissowa *Real-Enc.* viii. 176.

[1] Paus. 1. 44. 9 ἐπὶ δὲ τοῦ ὄρους τῇ ἄκρᾳ (above the Scironian Rocks) Διός ἐστιν Ἀφεσίου καλουμένου ναός· φασὶ δὲ ἐπὶ τοῦ (H. Hitzig cj. ἐπί τον) συμβάντος ποτὲ τοῖς Ἕλλησιν αὐχμοῦ θύσαντος Αἰακοῦ κατά τι δὴ λόγιον τῷ Πανελληνίῳ Διὶ ἐν Αἰγίνῃ †κομίσαντα δὲ ἀφεῖναι καὶ διὰ τοῦτο Ἀφέσιον καλεῖσθαι τὸν Δία. Many attempts have been made to mend this broken passage. T. Panofka *Der Tod des Skiron und des Patroclus* Berlin 1836 pp. 4, 17 would read κομίσαντα δὲ < ἀετον (*sic*) τὴν χελώνην > ἀφεῖναι on the strength of an engraved chalcedony at Berlin (Furtwängler *Geschnitt. Steine Berlin* p. 121 f. no. 2614 pl. 23, T. Panofka *op. cit.* p. 23 pl. 4, 7, E. Braun in the *Ann. d. Inst.* 1836 viii. 317 f., Overbeck *Gr. Kunstmyth.* Zeus p. 267 Gemmentaf. 3, 10 = my fig. 821), which represents Zeus with a sceptre in his left hand, a tortoise in his right, and an eagle at his feet. This is ingenious; for ἤφιει... ἀφεθέντα... used in Paus. 1. 44. 8 of Skiron and his tortoise prepare us for a second tortoise-story in explanation of the title Ἀφέσιος: but, as Frazer *Pausanias* i. 567 f. points out, the sentence remains ungrammatical. C. L. Kayser in the *Zeitschrift für die Alterthumswissenschaft* 1848 vi. 503 cj. ἐν Αἰγίνῃ < καὶ εὐξαμένου ὕδωρ ἀφεῖναι ἐς τὴν Ἑλλάδα γῆν ὑπα > κούσαντά τε ἀφεῖναι. H. G. Lolling in the Ἐφ. Ἀρχ. 1887 p. 214 proposed ἐν Αἰγίνῃ < ἀετὸν ἁρπάσαι τὸ ἱερεῖον εἰς δὲ τὴν ἄκραν > κομίσαντα ἀφεῖναι, cp. schol. Aristoph. *nub.* 52. L. C. Valckenaer (see H. Hitzig in the *Jahrb. f. class. Philol.* 1889 xxxv. 819) had suggested κομίσαντα < ἐνθά > δε, which 'would still leave the verb ἀφεῖναι without either subject or object' (Frazer *loc. cit.*). And J. F. Facius in his edition (Lipsiae 1794 i. 173) had cj. Αἰγίνῃ καὶ ὕσαντά τε ἀφεῖναι. After all this stirabout H. Hitzig and F. Spiro are content to print the passage as it stands.

Fig. 821.

In 1887 H. G. Lolling recognised the site of this sanctuary, about an hour and a half to the south-west of Megara, at a place called *Sta Marmara*, some 850 ft above sea-level, though far below the mountain-crest (H. G. Lolling in the Ἐφ. Ἀρχ. 1887 p. 213 ff. with sketch-plan). D. Philios, who excavated in 1889, discovered a small prostyle temple (6·40ᵐ × 4·75ᵐ) facing south-east. Of this nothing remained except three foundation-ᵒourses and the pavement; but the temple appears to have been of stone and certainly had ‿tone triglyphs. To the north was a Christian tomb (T), long since rifled, showing that sanctity still attached to the spot in Byzantine times: terra-cotta lamps were found, marked with a cross. To the south was a cistern (N), and further east a circular structure (K), three bases (Θ), and a large oblong altar (?)(H). Adjoining this was a line of plinths (M) and a wall (Π—P). West of the precinct, if so it may be termed, lay a complex of chambers built round a court-yard. One chamber (A), which had stone couches set against its walls, contained two pits (α, β) full of ashes. Two other chambers (7 and 8), entered from a *stoá* with bases for pillars (τ, υ, φ (?)), were likewise lined with stone couches. A short staircase led from the *stoá* into another room (9), the centre of which was occupied by a shallow circular depression with a flooring of baked brickwork. From this a channel of baked brick ran into a pit about 0·10ᵐ deep. On the rim of the large sinking, towards the north, was set a square base 0·50ᵐ high. The next room (10) again disclosed a pit o·13ᵐ deep and beside it a base about o·50ᵐ high. The largest chamber of all (11) was probably entered from the court by a door on the south. Round three sides of it were remains of stone seats. The north-east and north-west corners showed traces of a rough mosaic paving. The middle of the floor had five slabs, which had probably served as bases for pillars. Six lesser apartments (1—6) at the south-east angle were built of small stones bonded with clay and were clearly of later construction. The court also contained a hearth of baked bricks (ο), another pit full of ashes (ν), etc. The western portion of the building was protected against water pouring down from a higher level by an extra wall (Γ—Β—Δ), part of which (Β—Δ) was specially strong. And on the southern side the foundations were strengthened by a retaining wall (Ε—Ζ). Miscellaneous finds (at Ω and elsewhere) included the relief of a griffin in limestone, animals in clay (leonine foot, pig's snout), the head of a dove (?) in Pentelic marble, etc. No Mycenaean vases were discovered, but fragments of large *pithoi* with impressed geometric designs, also Corinthian ware in some abundance, and sherds of black-figured and red-figured technique. A few broken vases etc. were inscribed (*Corp. inscr. Gr. sept.* i nos. 3492—3497), of which the most important were a *kylix*-foot incised ΦΕξ or ΦΕϚ =[Διὸς ᾿Α]φεσ[ίου], or [Διὶ ᾿Α]φεσ[ίῳ] (no. 3494) and a stone slab reading ΗΒΡΟ........=῾Ηρω[ος] or ῾Ηρω[ι] (no. 3492). See further D. Philios in the ᾿Εφ. ᾿Αρχ. 1890 pp. 35 ff. (with careful plans and illustrations: pl. 4, 3=my fig. 822), 63 f., H. G. Lolling *ib.* 1890 p. 55 ff., D. Philios in the Πρακτ. ἀρχ.

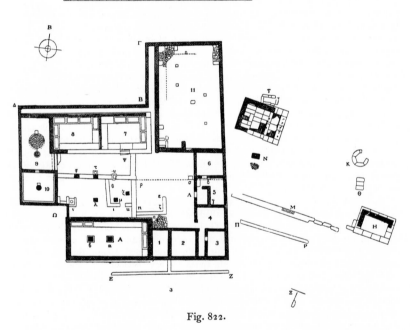

Fig. 822.

ἑτ. 1889 p. 26, W. Doerpfeld in the *Ath. Mitth.* 1889 xiv. 327, and Frazer *Pausanias* ii. 550 f.

The interpretation of the western group of buildings is disputed. H. G. Lolling held that it was originally a private dwelling-house, to which a sanctuary had afterwards been attached; D. Philios, that it was from the first an edifice containing chambers for the priest and the temple-attendants (cp. Paus. 10. 34. 7). I incline to think that the chambers with stone couches (Α, 7, 8) were used for incubation, and that the rooms with circular

Mount Gerania (?)[1].

Attike

The *Akrópolis* at Athens[2].

The Pnyx at Athens[3].

Mount Anchesmos[4].

Mount Hymettos[5].

Mount Parnes[6].

pits and rectangular bases (9, 10) betoken a chthonian cult. On this showing the worship of Zeus Ἀφέσιὸς was associated with that of a local Megarian hero (cp. F. Pfister *Der Reliquienkult im Altertum* Giessen 1909 i. 1 ff. 'Die mythische Königsliste von Megara'), who not impossibly had been regarded as Zeus incarnate. A similar combination occurs *e.g.* at Olympia, and the surviving inscriptions [Διὸς Ἀ]φεσ[ίου] and Ἥρω[ος] are decidedly suggestive.

[1] Paus. 1. 40. 1 τὰς δὲ Σιθνίδας νύμφας λέγουσι Μεγαρεῖς εἶναι μέν σφισιν ἐπιχωρίας, μιᾷ δὲ αὐτῶν [θυγατρὶ (secl. C. G. Siebelis)] συγγενέσθαι Δία, Μέγαρόν τε παῖδα ὄντα Διὸς καὶ ταύτης δὴ τῆς νύμφης ἐκφυγεῖν τὴν ἐπὶ Δευκαλίωνός ποτε ἐπομβρίαν, ἐκφυγεῖν δὲ πρὸς τὰ ἄκρα τῆς Γερανίας (*Makri Plagi* 1370ᵐ above sea-level), οὐκ ἔχοντός πω τοῦ ὄρους τὸ ὄνομα τοῦτο, κ.τ.λ. Cp. Dieuchidas of Megara *frag.* 1 (*Frag. hist. Gr.* iv. 388 Müller) *ap.* Clem. Al. *strom.* 6. 2 p. 443, 9 f. Stählin and *frag.* 11 (*Frag. Hist. Gr.* iv. 290 Müller) *ap.* Harpokr. *s.v.* Γερανία. *Et. mag.* p. 228, 22 ff., telling the same tale, speaks of Μεγαρεὺς ὁ Διὸς καὶ μιᾶς τῶν καλουμένων θηΐδων (L. Dindorf corr. Σιθνίδων) νυμφῶν.

[2] Zeus Ὕπατος (*supra* p. 875 n. 1 no. (2)). Zeus Πολιεύς (*infra* § 9 (h) ii).

[3] Zeus Ὕψιστος (*supra* p. 876 f. n. 1 no. (1)). The Siphnian Zeus Ἐπιβήμιος probably implies a statue of the god on the orator's platform (*infra* Append. N *med.*) ; but it would be unsafe to argue from Siphnos to Athens, and in any case it was not as mountain-god that Zeus supported the speaker (Plout. *praecept. gerend. reip.* 26 κοινόν ἐστιν ἱερὸν τὸ βῆμα Βουλαίου τε Διὸς καὶ Πολιέως καὶ Θέμιδος καὶ Δίκης).

[4] Anchesmos is commonly identified with *Turkovuni*, a range of rocky hills which divides the Attic plain into two unequal parts watered by the Kephisos and the Ilisos respectively (C. Wachsmuth in Pauly—Wissowa *Real-Enc.* i. 2103, H. Hitzig—H. Blümner on Paus. 1. 32. 2). It attains a height of 733ᵐ. Somewhere on this range was a statue of Zeus Ἀγχέσμιος (Paus. 1. 32. 2 καὶ Ἀγχεσμὸς ὄρος ἐστὶν οὐ μέγα καὶ Διὸς ἄγαλμα Ἀγχεσμίου). A. S. Georgiades in the Ἐφ. Ἀρχ. 1920 p. 59 notes foundations on its E. slopes.

[5] On the top of Mt Hymettos (*Monte Matto* or *Trelo-Vuni* 1027·10ᵐ) was an altar (*et. mag.* p. 352, 49 ff. cited *supra* p. 873 n. 1) and statue of Zeus Ὑμήττιος, also altars of Zeus Ὄμβριος and Apollon Προόψιος (Paus. 1. 32. 2 ἐν Ὑμηττῷ δὲ ἄγαλμά ἐστιν Ὑμηττίου Διός· βωμοὶ δὲ καὶ Ὀμβρίου Διὸς καὶ Ἀπόλλωνός εἰσι Προοψίου). Hesych. Ὑμήττιος· Ζεὺς παρὰ Ἀττικοῖς. Clouds on Hymettos portended rain (Theophr. *de signis tempest.* 1. 20 and 24), wind (*id. ib.* 2. 9), and storm (*id. ib.* 3. 6). W. Kolbe in Pauly—Wissowa *Real-Enc.* ix. 138 f. thinks it very probable that the statue of Zeus Ὑμήττιος stood on the small plateau close to the highest point of the mountain, and that the cult of Zeus Ὄμβριος is perpetuated on its ancient site by the chapel of St Elias perched upon a conspicuous crest (508ᵐ) on the eastern slope of the main *massif*, above Sphettos, north of the *Pirnari* Pass, to which chapel in times of drought whole troops of pilgrims still resort (A. Milchhöfer in E. Curtius and J. A. Kaupert *Karten von Attika* Berlin 1883 Text ii. 32).

[6] On Mt Parnes was a bronze statue of Zeus Παρνήθιος and an altar of Zeus Σημαλέος ; also another altar on which sacrifices were made sometimes to Zeus Ὄμβριος, sometimes to Zeus Ἀπήμιος (Paus. 1. 32. 2 καὶ ἐν Πάρνηθι Παρνήθιος Ζεὺς χαλκοῦς ἐστι, καὶ βωμὸς Σημαλέου Διός. ἔστι δὲ ἐν τῇ Πάρνηθι καὶ ἄλλος βωμός, θύουσι δὲ ἐπ' αὐτοῦ ποτὲ μὲν Ὄμβριον τοτὲ δὲ Ἀπήμιον καλοῦντες Δία, *et. mag.* p. 352, 49 ff. cited *supra* p. 873 n. 1). Parnes (*Ozea*) is at once the highest (1413ᵐ) and the most extensive mountain in Attike. C. Bursian *Geographie von Griechenland* Leipzig 1862 i. 252 would locate the statue of Zeus Παρνήθιος and the altar of Zeus Σημαλέος (*supra* p. 4) near Phyle, on the bare rocky ridge

Marathon[1].

Boiotia

Mount Hypatos [2].
Thebes[3].
Orchomenos[4].
Mount Helikon[5].
Mount Kithairon[6].

which the ancients on account of its shape called the Chariot (*supra* p. 815 f.), but the altar of Zeus Ὄμβριος and Ἀπήμιος on some other eminence. Lightning over Parnes, Brilettos, and Hymettos betokened a big storm; over two of the three, a less serious storm; over Parnes alone, fair weather (Theophr. *de signis tempest.* 3. 6). Clouds over the western side of Parnes and Phyle, with a north wind blowing, meant stormy weather (*id. ib.* 3. 10).

[1] Zeus Ὕπατος (*supra* p. 875 n. 1 no. (3)).

[2] Zeus Ὕπατος (*supra* p. 875 n. 1 no. (1)).

[3] Zeus Ὕψιστος (*supra* p. 878 n. 0 no. (2)).

[4] Zeus Καραιός (*supra* p. 874 n. 2).

[5] Zeus Ἑλικώνιος had an altar on Mt Helikon, near the spring Hippokrene, round which the Muses danced (Hes. *theog.* 1 ff. with schol. *ad loc.* 2 ἐν τῷ αὐτῷ γὰρ ὄρει καὶ κρήνη ἦν καὶ βωμός, 4 ἐν Ἑλικῶνι δὲ ἦν ὁ βωμός, ὡς εἴρηται, τοῦ Διὸς τοῦ Ἑλικωνίου). On the north-eastern summit of Helikon (*Zagora* 1527ᵐ) now stands a little roofless chapel of St Elias: it is surrounded by fir-trees, and its walls of small well-jointed polygonal stones probably formed in antiquity the *períbolos* of the altar of Zeus (C. Bursian *Geographie von Griechenland* Leipzig 1862 i. 239, H. N. Ulrichs *Reisen und Forschungen in Griechenland* Berlin 1863 ii. 99, Frazer *Pausanias* v. 158, Maybaum *Der Zeuskult in Boeotien* Doberan 1901 p. 7). See also *supra* i. 132.

[6] Mt Kithairon was sacred to Zeus Κιθαιρώνιος (Paus. 9. 2. 4 ὁ δὲ Κιθαιρὼν τὸ ὄρος Διὸς ἱερὸν Κιθαιρωνίου ἐστίν. This sentence is out of place in its context. H. C. Schubart— E. C. Walz excised it as a gloss. C. L. Kayser in the *Zeitschrift für die Alterthumswissenschaft* 1850 viii. 392 transposed it to stand before καθότι δὲ τοῦ Κιθαιρῶνος κ.τ.λ.). Nominally every sixth year, but really at shorter intervals, the Plataeans held a festival called Δαίδαλα μικρά. Going to an oak-wood near Alalkomenai they set out pieces of boiled flesh, followed the crow that pounced on the flesh, felled the tree on which it perched, and made of it a wooden image called a δαίδαλον. Every fifty-ninth year the Plataeans joined with the Boeotians to celebrate the Δαίδαλα μεγάλα. The various townships drew lots for the fourteen wooden images provided by the Δαίδαλα μικρά. Apparently each township took its image to the river Asopos and placed it on a waggon along with a bridesmaid. Again casting lots for order of precedence, they drove the waggons from the river to the top of Kithairon. Here an altar had been built of blocks of wood with brushwood piled on it. Each township then sacrificed a cow to Hera and a bull to Zeus, and, filling these victims with wine and incense, burnt them along with the images on the altar. The result was a huge column of flame visible at a great distance. The local myth explained that Hera, enraged with Zeus, had once retired to Euboia, and that Zeus, at the advice of Kithairon king of Plataiai, had made a wooden image and put it wrapped up on a bullock-cart, giving out that he was taking to wife Plataia, daughter of Asopos: Hera had flown to the spot, discovered the trickery, and made it up with Zeus (Paus. 9. 3. 1—8). According to Plutarch, Hera had been in hiding on Mt Kithairon (not in Euboia), and the stratagem was suggested to Zeus by Alalkomeneus the autochthon (not by Kithairon): together they cut down a fine oak, shaped it and decked it as a bride and called it Δαιδάλη; the wedding chant was raised, the Tritonid nymphs brought water for the bath, and Boiotia furnished flutes and the band of revellers. Hera with the women of Plataiai in her train came down from Mt Kithairon in jealous anger, but laughed at the ruse and was reconciled to Zeus (Plout. *ap.* Euseb. *praep. ev.* 3. 1. 6). Aristeides before

Mount Laphystion[1].
A mountain near Lebadeia[2].

the battle of Plataiai (479 B.C.) was bidden by the Delphic oracle to pray to Zeus, Hera Κιθαιρωνία, Pan, and the Sphragitid nymphs (Plout. *v. Aristid.* 11): Pausanias, turning towards the Heraion outside Plataiai, prayed to Hera Κιθαιρωνία and the other deities of the Plataean land (*id. ib.* 18). The image of Hera Κιθαιρωνία at Thespiai was a lopped tree-trunk (Clem. Al. *protr.* 3. 46. 3 καὶ τῆς Κιθαιρωνίας "Ηρας ἐν Θεσπείᾳ πρέμνον ἐκκεκομμένον, cp. Arnob. *adv. nat.* 6. 11 ramum pro Cinxia Thespios). She had a sanctuary also at Thebes (schol. Eur. *Phoen.* 24 ἢ ὅτι Κιθαιρωνίας "Ηρας ἐστὶν ἐν Θήβαις ἱερόν). Schöll—Studemund *anecd.* i. 269 Ἐπίθετα "Ηρας (10) κιθαιρωνίας.

In the traditional singing-match between Kithairon and Helikon (for which see Demetrios of Phaleron *ap.* schol. *Od.* 3. 267 and Eustath. *in Od.* p. 1466, 56 ff., Lysimachos (? Lysanias) of Kyrene *frag.* 26 (*Frag. hist. Gr.* iii. 342 Müller) *ap.* schol. Hes. *o.d.* p. 33, 4 ff. Gaisford, cp. Tzetz. *chil.* 6. 917 ff., Hermesianax of Kypros *frag.* 2 (*Frag. hist. Gr.* iv. 428 Müller) *ap.* Plout. *de fluv.* 2. 3) the former sang of the childhood of Zeus (Korinna in the *Berliner Klassikertexte* Berlin 1907 v. 2. 19 ff. no. 284, cp. *ib.* p. 47, =*frag.* 1 Diehl[3]).

[1] On Mt Laphystion near Orchomenos was a precinct and stone statue of Zeus Λαφύστιος. It was here that Athamas was about to sacrifice Phrixos and Helle, when Zeus sent the ram with the golden fleece to aid their escape (Paus. 9. 34. 5, cp. 1. 24. 2). Higher up on the mountain-side was a Herakles Χάροψ; for here, according to the Boeotians, Herakles had brought up the hound of Hades (Paus. 9. 34. 5). Dionysos too was worshipped on the mountain as Λαφύστιος (*et. mag.* p. 557, 51 f. Λαφύστιος· ὁ Διόνυσος, ἀπὸ τοῦ ἐν Βοιωτίᾳ Λαφυστίου ὄρους = Tzetz. *in* Lyk. *Al.* 1237), and his Maenads were Λαφύστιαι (Lyk. *Al.* 1237 with Tzetz. *ad loc.*).

Laphystion has been identified with *Granitsa*, a steep mountain (896ᵐ) of reddish stone with a summit like a crater and warm springs at its north-eastern foot (C. Bursian *Geographie von Griechenland* Leipzig 1862 i. 235 f., Frazer *Pausanias* v. 172, H. Hitzig—H. Blümner on Paus. 9. 34. 5).

That Λαφύστιος must be connected with λαφύσσειν, 'to devour,' is commonly admitted. But beyond this point agreement ceases. Was the god named after the mountain, or the mountain after the god? (1). U. von Wilamowitz-Moellendorff in his ed. 2 of Eur. *H.f.* Berlin 1895 i. 34 n. 67 holds that Mt Laphystion got its name from the crater that engulfed the unwary. And doubtless Zeus Λαφύστιος could have derived his appellation from Mt Laphystion. But we have already (*supra* i. 416 f., 428) seen reason to think that Zeus Λαφύστιος was originally a Thessalian god, and we hear of no Mt Laphystion in Thessaly. (2) Maybaum *Der Zeuskult in Boeotien* Doberan 1901 p. 8 conversely assumes that Mt Laphystion derived its name from Zeus Λαφύστιος. It is then open to us to interpret Λαφύστιος as 'Devouring' with allusion to human sacrifice. For that grim tradition attached to the cult of Zeus Λαφύστιος, not only in Boiotia, but also in Thessaly (*infra* Append. B Thessaliā); and the Dionysos of Orchomenos had an equally sinister reputation (Plout. *quaestt. Gr.* 38, Ant. Lib. 10, Ov. *met.* 4. 1 ff. Frazer *Golden Bough*[3]: The Dying God p. 163 f.). See further P. Buttmann *Mythologus* Berlin 1829 ii. 230, W. Drexler in Roscher *Lex. Myth.* ii. 1850 f., J. W. Hewitt in *Harvard Studies in Classical Philology* 1908 xix. 102 f.

[2] Paus. 9. 39. 4 ἀναβᾶσι δὲ ἐπὶ τὸ μαντεῖον (sc. τοῦ Τροφωνίου) καὶ αὐτόθεν ἰοῦσιν ἐς τὸ πρόσω τοῦ ὄρους, Κόρης ἐστὶ καλουμένη θήρα (καλουμένης θήρας codd. fam. L¹. K. Goldhagen cj. καλουμένης Σωτείρας. H. N. Ulrichs cj. καλουμένης "Ηρας. F. Spiro: 'an θύρα?') καὶ Διὸς Βασιλέως ναός. τοῦτον μὲν δὴ διὰ τὸ μέγεθος ἢ καὶ τῶν πολέμων τὸ ἀλλεπάλληλον ἀφείκασιν ἡμίεργον· ἐν δὲ ἑτέρῳ ναῷ Κρόνου καὶ "Ηρας καὶ Διός ἐστιν ἀγάλματα. ἔστι δὲ καὶ Ἀπόλλωνος ἱερόν. The unfinished temple of Zeus Βασιλεύς is believed to have stood on Mt St Elias, a height which rises west of the castle-hill of *Livadia* at a distance of half an hour from the town. Here the ground is still strewn with big building-blocks, though most of the material was carried off in Turkish times (Sir J. G. Frazer and H. Hitzig—H. Blümner *ad loc.*). The temple seems to have been 46·02ᵐ in length (E. Fabricius *ap.* H. Nissen

Mount Homoloïon (?)[1].

in the *Rhein. Mus.* 1887 xlii. 54). A long inscription, of 175—172 B.C., relating to this temple was found built into the wall of a blacksmith's forge at *Livadia* (*Inscr. Gr. sept.* i no. 3073 = Michel *Recueil d'Inscr. gr.* no. 589 = Dittenberger *Syll. inscr. Gr.*[3] no. 972). It specifies the conditions under which the custodians (ναοποιοί) of the temple of Zeus Βασιλεύς are prepared to place the building-contract with the contractors (ἐργῶναι). The first section (*vv.* 1—89) deals with the slabs (στῆλαι) on which the specification is to be inscribed ; the second (*vv.* 89—164) with the paving-stones to be laid in one of the external colonnades (*v.* 89 ff. εἰς τὸν ναὸν τοῦ | Διὸς τοῦ Βασιλέως εἰς τὴν ἔξω περίστασιν τοῦ σηκοῦ | τῶν εἰς τὴν μακρὰν πλευρὰν καταστρωτήρων ἐργα|σία καὶ σύνθεσις). It appears that the temple was constructed, not by the inhabitants of Lebadeia only, but by the Boeotians in common (*v.* 156 f.), probably—as A. Wilhelm saw—with money supplied by Antiochos iv Epiphanes. Other fragments of the same contract are *Inscr. Gr. sept.* i nos. 3074—3076, A. de Ridder and Choisy 'Devis de Livadie' in the *Bull. Corr. Hell.* 1896 xx. 318—335 (*v.* 58 εἰς τὸ < ν > [ἡμι]κύκλιον is taken to imply an apsidal end to the temple : restoration *ib.* pl. 9. Other Boeotian examples at Arne, Ptoion, Kabeirion, Thespiai are noted by F. Noack in the *Ath. Mitth.* 1894 xix. 424 : cp. *supra* i. 120), A. Wilhelm 'Bauinschrift aus Lebadeia' in the *Ath. Mitth.* 1897 xxii. 179—182.

The Boeotians after vanquishing the Spartans at Leuktra (371 B.C.) established at Lebadeia an ἀγὼν στεφανίτης in honour of Zeus Βασιλεύς (Diod. 15. 53). These games, known as the Βασίλεια, are repeatedly mentioned in inscriptions (*Inscr. Gr. sept.* i Index p. 761, O. Jessen in Pauly—Wissowa *Real-Enc.* iii. 82), one of which has ΒΑΣΙΛΕΙΑ within a bay-wreath (*Inscr. Gr. sept.* i no. 2487). If, as seems probable, Zeus Βασιλεύς was associated with Hera Βασιλίς, the games were quadriennial (*ib.* i no. 3097). Plutarch's story about Aristokleia the κανηφόρος of Zeus Βασιλεύς (Plout. *amat. narr.* 1) implies a ritual procession (Nilsson *Gr. Feste* p. 34).

On the relation of Zeus Βασιλεύς to Trophonios see *infra* Append. K.

[1] Zeus Ὁμολώιος was worshipped in Boiotia (Steph. Byz. *s.v.* Ὁμόλη), particularly at Thebes (Hesych. *s.v.* Ὁμολώιος (Ὁμόλοος cod.) Ζεύς· Θήβησιν οὕτω προσαγορεύεται ὁ Ζεύς) ; and Aristodemos of Alexandreia, who wrote a learned work on Theban antiquities, appears to have derived the name of the Ὁμολωίδες πύλαι at Thebes from their proximity to a Ὁμολώιον ὄρος (Aristodem. Theb. *frag.* 2 (*Frag. hist. Gr.* iii. 309 Müller) *ap.* schol. Eur. *Phoen.* 1119, cp. Steph. Byz. *loc. cit.*). It may be inferred, though not with certainty, that there was a cult of Zeus on this hill (see Maybaum *Der Zeuskult in Boeotien* Doberan 1901 p. 9 f.). A small column, found at Thebes and now in the local Museum, has inscribed in archaic letters on its fluting Διʼ Ὁμολωίοι | Ἀγειμώνδας ἀπὸ δεκά[τας] (P. Foucart in the *Bull. Corr. Hell.* 1879 iii. 130 ff., Roehl *Inscr. Gr. ant.* no. 191, R. Meister in Collitz—Bechtel *Gr. Dial.-Inschr.* i. 227 no. 665, Roberts *Gk. Epigr.* i. 212 no. 198, *Inscr. Gr. sept.* i no. 2456), which is perhaps a clumsy attempt at a hexameter line. Doubtless this column once supported a votive offering in the Theban sanctuary of Zeus Ὁμολώιος. His festival the Ὁμολώια, mentioned in lists of victors from Megara (*ib.* i no. 48, 2) and from Orchomenos in Boiotia (*ib.* i no. 3196, 24 f., no. 3197, 36 f.), was specially discussed by Aristodemos (Aristodem. Theb. *frag.* 2 (*Frag. hist. Gr.* iii. 309 Müller) *ap.* schol. Theokr. 7. 103). The same god was worshipped, not only in Boiotia, but also in Thessaly (Phot. *lex. s.v.* Ὁμολῶος Ζεύς· ἐν Θήβαις καὶ ἐν ἄλλαις πόλεσι Βοιωτίας· καὶ ὁ ἐν Θεσσαλίᾳ ἀπὸ Ὁμολῶας προφήτιδος τῆς Ἐννέως, ἣν προφῆτιν ἐκ Δελφοὺς πεμφθῆναι ὁ Ἀριστοφάνης (*sic cod.* S. A. Naber *corr.* Ἀριστόδημος, *sc.* Aristodem. Theb. *loc. cit.*) ἐν δευτέρῳ Θηβαϊκῶν· Ἴστρος δὲ ἐν τῇ δωδεκάτῃ τῆς συναγωγῆς διὰ τὸ παρʼ Αἰολεῦσιν τὸ ὁμονοητικὸν καὶ εἰρηνικὸν ὅμολον λέγεσθαι (*frag.* 10 (*Frag. hist. Gr.* i. 419 Müller))· ἔστι δὲ Δημήτηρ Ὁμολῴα ἐν Θήβαις = Souid. *s.v.* Ὁμολώιος Ζεύς, cp. Apostol. 12. 67, Arsen. *viol.* p. 381 Walz, Favorin. *lex.* p. 1358, 38 ff., Eudok. *viol.* 414[g] p. 314, 10 ff. Flach). O. Jessen in Pauly—Wissowa *Real-Enc.* viii. 2263 f. remarks that the name of the month Ὁμολώιος, Ὁμολῶος, Ὁμολούιος found in Boiotia, Aitolia, and Thessaly (E. Bischoff *ib.* viii. 2264) implies a wide-spread cult of deities with this appellative, such as Zeus Ὁμολώιος,

Mount Petrachos[1].

Phokis

Delphoi[2].

Demeter Ὁμολωία (*supra*), and Athena Ὁμολωίς (Lyk. *Al.* 520 with schol. and Tzetz. *ad loc.*), and concludes: 'Da der Boiotien und Thessalien gemeinsame Monatsname einen gemeinsamen Kult des Zeus H. wahrscheinlich machen, dürfte Zeus H. ähnlich wie Zeus Olympios von Thessalien nach Mittelgriechenland gekommen sein.' His cult reached Eretria also ; for a fragmentary slab discovered close to the western gate of Eretria is inscribed in lettering of *s.* iii. B.C. Διὸς Ὁμ[ο]||λωῖο[υ] (K. Kourouniotes in the Ἐφ. Ἀρχ. 1897 p. 150 n. 3, who cp. the Theban Ὁμολωίδες πύλαι). See further O. Hoffmann *Die Makedonen, ihre Sprache und ihr Volkstum* Göttingen 1906 p. 105 f. (Λώϊος=Ὁμολώϊος), E. Sittig *De Graecorum nominibus theophoris* Halis Saxonum 1911 p. 14 f. (collects derivatives of Ὁμολώϊος, Λώϊος, and infers from the occurrence of the month Ὁμολόϊος at Eresos in Lesbos (*Inscr. Gr. ins.* ii no. 527, 44) 'Iovem omnes Aeoles, priusquam discesserint, hoc cognomine esse veneratos'), F. Bechtel *Die griechischen Dialekte* Berlin 1921 i. 19, 142, 264. *Supra* p. 857 n. 6, *infra* Append. B Thessalia.

[1] The *Akrópolis* of Chaironeia was a sharp rocky summit named Petrachos (Plout. *v. Sull.* 17). Here Kronos received from Rhea a stone instead of Zeus ; and there was a small statue of Zeus on the top of the mountain (Paus. 9. 41. 6 ἔστι δὲ ὑπὲρ τὴν πόλιν κρημνὸς Πετραχὸς καλούμενος· Κρόνον δὲ ἐθέλουσιν ἐνταῦθα ἀπατηθῆναι δεξάμενον ἀντὶ Διὸς πέτρον παρὰ τῆς Ῥέας, καὶ ἄγαλμα Διὸς οὐ μέγα ἐστὶν ἐπὶ κορυφῇ τοῦ ὄρους). For the extant remains of Chaironeia see C. Bursian *Geographie von Griechenland* Leipzig 1862 i. 205 f., Sir J. G. Frazer on Paus. 9. 40. 5, and H. Hitzig—H. Blümner on Paus. 9. 40. 7 ; for the history of the town, E. Oberhummer in Pauly—Wissowa *Real-Enc.* iii. 2033 ff.

[2] The Delphians originally occupied a town Λυκώρεια higher up on the side of Mt Parnassos (Strab. 418, cp. schol. Ap. Rhod. 4. 1490, Plout. *de Pyth. or.* 1 where W. R. Paton cj. Λυκώρειαν for Λυκουρίαν). H. N. Ulrichs *Reisen und Forschungen in Griechenland* Bremen 1840 i. 120 and C. Bursian *Geographie von Griechenland* Leipzig 1862 i. 179 f. found traces of Λυκώρεια in sundry Hellenic walls still visible on a height to the west of the Corycian Cave. W. M. Leake *Travels in Northern Greece* London 1841 ii. 579 with truer topographical instinct identified the site of the ancient city with the village of *Liakouri*. Here Deukalion had reigned as king (*marm. Par. ep.* 2 p. 3 Jacoby, *ep.* 4 p. 3 f.)—indeed, the town had been founded by survivors of his deluge, who followed the 'howling of wolves,' λύκων ὠρυγαῖς, to the mountain-top (Paus. 10. 6. 2). Another account made its founder Λύκωρος, son of Apollon by the nymph Korykia (Paus. *ib.*, cp. *et. mag.* p. 571, 47 ff.). He is called Λυκωρεύς by schol. Ap. Rhod. 2. 711 (cp. Hyg. *fab.* 161), who adds ἀφ᾽ οὗ Λυκωρεῖς οἱ Δελφοί. Finally Anaxandrides (*supra* p. 238 n. 1) of Delphoi, who wrote a monograph περὶ Λυκωρείας, spoke of Λυκωρεύς as a king (Alexandrides *frag.* 7 (*Frag. hist. Gr.* iii. 107 Müller) *ap.* Steph. Byz. *s.v.* Λυκώρεια).

The town had a cult of Apollon (*et. mag.* p. 571, 47 ff.), who is mentioned as Phoibos Λυκώρειος (Ap. Rhod. 4. 1490), Apollon Λυκωρεύς (Steph. Byz. *s.v.* Ἀνεμώρεια), Phoibos Λυκωρεύς (Euphorion *frag.* 53 in A. Meineke *Analecta Alexandrina* Berolini 1843 p. 95 f., Kallim. *h. Ap.* 19, Orph. *h. Ap.* 34. 1, oracul. *ap.* Euseb. *praep. ev.* 3. 14. 5 = Cougny *Anth. Pal. Append.* 6. 82. 9 f.), or Λυκωρεύς alone (*Anth. Pal.* 6. 54. 1 (Paulus Silentiarius)). There was also a Zeus Λυκώρειος (Steph. Byz. *s.v.* Λυκώρεια·...ἔστι καὶ Λυκώρειος Ζεὺς καὶ Λυκώρειον διὰ διφθόγγου), who was presumably worshipped on the peak known as Λυκώρειον (*id. ib.*) or Λυκωρεύς (Loukian. *Tim.* 3, where for τῷ Λυκωρεῖ I should restore τῷ Λυκωρείῳ), later Λυκορί (schol. rec. Pind. *Ol.* 9. 70). The highest point of Parnassos (2459ᵐ) is still called τὸ Λυκέρι. J. Murray *Handbook for travellers in Greece*[7] London 1900 p. 540 f. says: 'The...summit, locally called Lykeri (8070 ft.), is marked with a wooden cross. At the top of the mountain is a small plain, enclosed in a crater-like basin, and containing a pool generally frozen over... The view on a clear day exceeds in grandeur and interest almost every other prospect of the kind. To the N., beyond the plains of Thessaly, appears Olympus with its snowy tops brilliant in sunlight. Further W.

Euboia
>Mount Oche[1].
>Mount Kenaion[2].

is seen the long chain of Pindus ; on the E. rises Helicon, with other Boeotian mountains. To the S. the summit of Panachaicon is very conspicuous ; Achaia, Argolis, Elis and Arcadia are seen as in a map, while the Gulf of Corinth looks like a large pond. The Aegean and Ionian seas bound the horizon E. and W.' It appears probable that the cult of Zeus Λυκώρειος was displaced or overshadowed by that of Apollon Λυκώρειος. Their common epithet may be connected either with λύκος, 'a wolf' (according to H. N. Ulrichs *op. cit.* i. 118 wolves still haunt the woods of Parnassos : ' In Chrysó sah ich vier Hirten, von denen jeder eine Wolfshaut an einem langen Stocke trug, dessen oberstes Ende aus dem geöffneten Rachen des Thiers hervorsteckte. Sie zogen von Dorf zu Dorf und empfingen an jedem Hause freigebige Geschenke für die Befreiung von diesem gefährlichen Feinde der Herden.' Paus. 10. 14. 7, Ail. *de nat. an.* 10. 26, 12. 40, Plout. *v. Per.* 21 associate wolves with the Delphian Apollon), or with Λύκος, an ancient name for the god of the daylight (?) (*supra* i. 64 n. 3).

When Deukalion, after traversing the flood for nine days and nights in his ark, landed at length on Mt Parnassos, he sacrificed there to Zeus Φύξιος (Apollod. 1. 7. 2, cp. schol. cod. Paris. Ap. Rhod. 2. 1147 Φύξιον δὲ τὸν Δία οἱ Θεσσαλοὶ ἔλεγον, ἤτοι ὅτι ἐπὶ τοῦ Δευκαλίωνος κατακλυσμοῦ κατέφυγον εἰς αὐτόν, ἢ διὰ τὸ τὸν Φρίξον καταφυγεῖν εἰς αὐτόν). This title too is found attached to Apollon (Philostr. *her.* p. 711 Palamedes prays Ἀπόλλωνι Λυκίῳ τε καὶ Φυξίῳ to be delivered from wolves, cp. Souid. *s.v.* Φύξιος).

For Zeus at Delphoi see further *supra* pp. 179 ff., 189 ff., 231 ff., 266 f.

[1] Popular etymology derived the name of Mt Oche ("Οχη) from the union (ὀχή = ὀχεία) of Zeus and Hera, which was said to have taken place there (Steph. Byz. *s.v.* Κάρυστος ·... ἐκλήθη δὲ τὸ ὄρος ἀπὸ τῆς ἐκεῖ ὀχείας, ἤτοι τῶν θεῶν μίξεως Διὸς καὶ "Ηρας, ἢ διὰ τὸ τὰ πρόβατα κυΐσκεσθαι ὀχευόμενα ἐν τῷ τόπῳ· οἱ γὰρ Ἀχαιοὶ τὴν τροφὴν ὀχὴν φασί). The summit of the mountain (1475ᵐ) is nowadays known as *Hagios Elias* (C. Bursian *Geographie von Griechenland* Leipzig 1872 ii. 398).

[2] On the top of Mt Kenaion (677ᵐ), a height untouched by clouds (Sen. *Herc. Oet.* 786 f. hic rupe celsa nulla quam nubes ferit | annosa fulgent templa Cenaei Iovis), an altar and sanctuary of Zeus Κήναιος (Aisch. Γλαῦκος πόντιος *frag.* 30 Nauck² *ap.* Strab. 447, Soph. *Trach.* 237 f., 752 ff., 993 ff., Skyl. *per.* 58 (*Geogr. Gr. min.* i. 47 Müller), Apollod. 2. 7. 7, Steph. Byz. *s.v.* Κάναι·...Καναῖος Ζεὺς οὐ μόνον ἀπὸ τοῦ Καναίου, ἀλλὰ καὶ ἀπὸ τῆς Κάνης, Souid. *s.v.* Κηναῖος· ὁ Ζεύς, Schöll—Studemund *anecd.* i. 265 Ἐπίθετα Διός (57) κηναίου, 266 Ἐπίθετα Διός (49) κηναίου, 274 Ἐπίθετα Διός·....κηναῖος (καναῖος codc. C[1].O[1].), Ov. *met.* 9. 136 f., Sen. *Herc. Oet.* 102, 786 f.). According to Sophokles, Herakles after sacking Oichalia dedicated here altars and a leafy precinct to Zeus Πατρῷος. He offered 100 victims on a pyre of oak, including twelve bulls free from blemish, and put on for the purpose the deadly robe brought to him by Lichas (Soph. *Trach.* 750 ff.). According to Bakchylides, he offered from the spoils of Oichalia nine bulls to Zeus Κήναιος, 'lord of the far-spread clouds,' two to Poseidon, and a cow to Athena (Bakchyl. 15. 17 ff.). Cp. Diod. 4. 37 f., Tzetz. *in* Lyk. *Al.* 50 f., Eudok. *viol.* 436. Fragments of a volute-*kratér* from *Kerch* show Herakles (... ΚΛΗΣ) holding a sacrificial fillet for one of these victims in the presence of ΛΙΧΑΣ and Hyllos (?). All these are wreathed with bay or olive. At their feet is a pile of stones ; in the background, a tripod on a column and a pillar decorated with acanthus-leaves (L. Stephani in the *Compte-rendu St. Pét.* 1869 p. 179 pl. 4, 1, *ib.* 1876 p. 161 pl. 5, 1 = Reinach *Rép. Vases* i. 31, 12, *ib.* i. 50, 3. This vase-painting was attributed by F. Hauser in Furtwängler—Reichhold—Hauser *Gr. Vasenmalerei* iii. 53 f. fig. 24 to the painter Aristophanes *c.* 400 B.C., by J. D. Beazley *Attic red-figured Vases in American Museums* Cambridge Mass. 1918 p. 184 to a contemporary artist, 'the painter of the New York Centauromachy' (Hoppin *Red-fig. Vases* ii. 217 no. 4)). A fragmentary bell-*kratér* in the British Museum has Herakles wreathed with olive and wearing

Cape Geraistos (?)[1].

Thessalia

Mount Oite[2].

a *himátion*. Behind him hangs the poisoned robe (?). In front an altar of unworked stones supports four tiers of blazing logs with the horns of some animal on the top. To left and right of this altar are two youths, Philoktetes (ΦΙΛΟΣΚΕΤ) and Lichas (ΛΙ...), holding meat on spits over the fire. By the altar is an olive-tree, from which hang votive tablets representing a Satyr, a Maenad, and two horsemen ; also, the image of a goddess draped and mounted on a Doric column. To the right is a draped female figure, perhaps Nike, and beyond her Athena (... N .) with *aigís*, spear, and helmet (*Brit. Mus. Cat. Vases* iii. 300 ff. no. E 494 pl. 16). Both vases may depict the sacrifice on Mt Kenaion (A. H. Smith in the *Journ. Hell. Stud.* 1898 xviii. 274 ff.). An inscription from the *Akrópolis* at Athens records an Eretrian coin belonging to Zeus Κήναιος (*Corp. inscr. Att.* i no. 208, 8 f. ['Ερ]ετρικὸν | [Δι]ὸς Κηναίου). *Lithada*, the modern name of Mt Kenaion, is derived from Λιχάδες, the small islands off the point, and appears in Latin documents of *s.* xiii A.D. as *Ponta* (*Punta*) *Litadi* or *Litaldi* (C. Bursian *Geographie von Griechenland* Leipzig 1872 ii. 401 n. 2).

¹ Geraistos, the eponym of Cape Geraistos (*Kavo Mandilo*), was the son of Zeus and brother of Tainaros (Steph. Byz. *s.vv.* Γεραιστός, Ταίναρος).

² Mt Oite (*Katavothra*) rises to a height of 2158ᵐ (Lieut.-Col. Baker in *The Journal of the Royal Geographical Society of London* 1837 vii. 94 says 7071 ft). It was sacred to Zeus (Soph. *Trach.* 1191 τὸν Οἴτης Ζηνὸς ὕψιστον πάγον), whose lightnings played about it (*id. ib.* 436 f., *Phil.* 729 Jebb) ; and the meadows high on the mountain, since they belonged to him, might not be mown (*id. Trach.* 200 ὦ Ζεῦ, τὸν Οἴτης ἄτομον ὃς λειμῶν' ἔχεις).

The traditional pyre of Herakles, son of Zeus, was on the south-eastern shoulder of Oite, known to the ancients as Phrygia (Kallim. *h. Artem.* 159 ὅ γε Φρυγίη περ ὑπὸ δρυὶ γυῖα θεωθείς with schol. *ad loc.* Φρυγία ὄρος Τραχῖνος, ἔνθα ἐκάη ὁ Ἡρακλῆς, Steph. Byz. *s.v.* Φρυγία· ... ἔστι καὶ Φρυγία τόπος τῆς Οἴτης ἀπὸ τοῦ ἐκεῖ πεφρύχθαι τὸν Ἡρακλέα) or Pyra (Theophr. *hist. pl.* 9. 10. 2 white hellebore gathered there for the Amphictionic πυλαία, Liv. 36. 30 M'. Acilius Glabrio offered sacrifice there to Herakles in 191 B.C.) and to the moderns as *Xerovouni* near *Pauliane*. Here, at a spot called *Marmari*, N. Pappadakis in 1920—1921 discovered the remains of a great precinct-wall in *pôros*, within which was a smaller oblong (*c.* 20ᵐ × 30ᵐ) marking the limits of the pyre. A bed of ashes (0·40ᵐ to 0·80ᵐ thick) contained bones of animals, bronze weapons, implements, etc., and pottery ranging from archaic Greek to Roman times. Some of the black-figured sherds bore dedications ΕΡΑΚΛΕΙ or [· · ·]ΚΛΕΙ, and two archaic bronze statuettes (0·09ᵐ and 0·10ᵐ high) represented the hero, with club and bow (?), in violent action. Miscellaneous finds comprised a bronze club, painted architectural tiles, Roman and Thessalian lamps, Megarian bowls, etc. The principal edifice was of Aetolian date, built with large blocks on an older structure of *pôros*: of it there remains the *euthyntería*, part of the west side, and one step of the south side, also part of the paving and of the stereobate for the cult-statue, which seems to have been of the late Roman period. Close by was a Doric *templum in antis* (14ᵐ long) with an altar before it: Pappadakis' suggestion that this building was a treasury is hardly borne out by the presence of the altar. Coins from the site included six or seven coppers belonging to the time of the Aetolian League and silver pieces of the Roman imperial series down to Maximian (286—305 A.D.) [Diocletian, who styled himself *Iovius* (*Class. Rev.* 1904 xviii. 371, *Folk-Lore* 1905 xvi. 315), conferred on Maximian the title *Herculius*]. Of two fragmentary inscriptions one mentions the emperor Commodus (?) [another would-be Herakles (P. v. Rohden in Pauly—Wissowa *Real-Enc.* ii. 2470, 2478 f. See also J. de Witte 'De quelques empereurs romains qui ont pris les attributs d'Hercule' in the *Rev. Num.* 1845 pp. 266—272 pl. 13 f.)]. Lastly, to the north at a higher level was a *stoá*, reconstructed in Aetolian times on the site of an older building. Seven chambers for

Halos[1].
Mount Pelion[2].
Mount Ossa (?)[3].
Mount Homole (?)[4].
Mount Pindos[5].

Makedonia
Mount Olympos[6].

the accommodation of priests and pilgrims opened into a colonnade (40^m long) with octagonal columns. Sundry tiles of this *stoá* are inscribed IHPAH oř IIIPOCH = ἱερά, ἱερὸς Ἡρακλέους (N. Pappadakis in the *Bull. Corr. Hell.* 1920 xliv. 392 f., 1921 xlv. 523).

[1] Halos at the foot of Mt Othrys was founded by Athamas (Strab. 433). There was here a sanctuary and grove of Zeus Λαφύστιος. Tradition said that Athamas, son of Aiolos, had together with Ino plotted the death of Phrixos. The Achaeans were bidden by an oracle to enjoin that the eldest of Athamas' descendants should never enter the Prytaneion. They mounted guard over it, and their rule was that, if any such person entered it, he might leave it only in order to be sacrificed. Many fearing the rule had fled to other lands. If they returned and entered the Prytaneion, they were covered all over with fillets and led out in procession to be slain. The reason given for this strange custom was that once, when the Achaeans in accordance with an oracle were treating Athamas as a scape-goat for the land and were about to sacrifice him, Kytissoros, son of Phrixos, came from Aia in Kolchis and rescued him, thereby drawing down the wrath of the god on his own descendants (Hdt. 7. 197, cp. Plat. *Min.* 315 c). When Phrixos came to Kolchis, he was received by Dipsakos, son of the river-god Phyllis and a local nymph. Phrixos there sacrificed the ram, on which he had escaped, to Zeus Λαφύστιος, and it was a custom for one of his descendants to enter the Prytaneion and sacrifice to the said Zeus (so schol. vulg. Ap. Rhod. 2. 653 καὶ μέχρι τοῦ νῦν νόμος ἕνα τῶν Φρίξου ἀπογόνων εἰσιέναι εἰς τὸ πρυτανεῖον, καὶ θύειν τῷ εἰρημένῳ Διί. But there is an important variant in schol. cod. Paris. καὶ μέχρι νῦν νόμος εἰσελθόντα εἰς τὸ πρυτανεῖον ἕνα τῶν Φρίξου ἀπογόνων θύειν τῷ εἰρημένῳ Διί. The accusative εἰσελθόντα...ἕνα is ambiguous. It might be the subject of θύειν and mean that the man sacrificed to Zeus. It might be the object of θύειν and mean that the man was sacrificed to Zeus. In view of the custom at Halos, the latter alternative is more probable than the former. If so, amend Frazer *Golden Bough*[3]: The Dying God p. 165 n. 1). *Supra* i. 416, ii. p. 899 n. 1.

Coins of Halos show the head of Zeus Λαφύστιος, sometimes filleted, sometimes laureate (*Brit. Mus. Cat. Coins* Thessaly etc. p. 13 pls. 2, 6, 31, 1). On occasion a thunderbolt is added in front of the head on the obverse (W. Wroth in the *Num. Chron.* Third Series 1899 xix. 91 pl. 7, 1) or below Phrixos and the ram on the reverse (*Brit. Mus. Cat. Coins* Thessaly etc. p. 13 no. 3). The coins are coppers of two periods, 400—344 B.C. and 300—200 B.C. (Head *Hist. num.*[2] p. 295 f.).

[2] Zeus Ἀκραῖος (*supra* p. 871 n. 3 no. (1)) and Ἀκταῖος (*supra* p. 869 n. 2). A cloud on Pelion meant rain or wind (Theophr. *de signis tempest.* 1. 22).

[3] Zeus Ὄσσαιος (Schöll—Studemund *anecd.* i. 265 Ἐπίθετα Διός (76) ὀσσαίου, 266 Ἐπίθετα Διός (68) ὀσσαίου) is not necessarily to be taken as the god of Mt Ossa (1950^m). He may be the sender of Rumour (Ὄσσα) the 'messenger of Zeus' (*Il.* 2. 93 f. μετὰ δέ σφισιν Ὄσσα δεδήει | ὀτρύνουσ' ἰέναι, Διὸς ἄγγελος, cp. *Od.* 1. 282 f., 2. 216 f., 24. 413).

[4] Homole or Homolos, one of the northern spurs of Mt Ossa in Magnesia, on which stood the town Homolion (Stählin in Pauly—Wissowa *Real-Enc.* viii. 2259 ff.), was 'the most fertile and best watered of the Thessalian mountains' (Paus. 9. 8. 6, cp. Strab. 443). The Ὁμολωΐδες πύλαι of Thebes were said to have been called after it (Paus. 9. 8. 6 f.; but see *supra* p. 900 n. 1). It is possible that the Theban cult of Zeus Ὁμολώϊος had spread southwards from Mt Homole (Nilsson *Gr. Feste* p. 12 f., *supra* p. 900 n. 1).

[5] Zeus Ἀκραῖος (*supra* p. 871 n. 3 no. (2)).

[6] The cult of Zeus on Mt Olympos has been discussed at some length *supra* i. 100—

Plate XL

The summit of Mount Olympos.

See page 905 *n.* o f.

[By permission of Messrs Boissonnas, Geneva.]

117. My statement that the published illustrations of the mountain are very inadequate (i. 101 n. 3) no longer holds good. A. J. Mann—W. T. Wood *The Salonika Front* London 1920 pl. 7 give a coloured silhouette of Olympos as seen from *Mikra*, the reproduction of a fine original owned by Lieut.-Col. G. Windsor-Clive. And the noble view of the summit here shown (pl. xl) is from a large heliogravure of exceptional merit published by F. Boissonnas of Geneva.

D. Urquhart *The Spirit of the East* London 1838 i. 398 ff. describes with much enthusiasm, but little precision, his ascent of Olympos in 1830 : ' I spent no more than an hour at this giddy height, where the craving of my eyes would not have been satisfied under a week. I seemed to stand perpendicularly over the sea, at the height of 10,000 feet. Salonica was quite distinguishable, lying north-east ; Larissa appeared under my very feet. The whole horizon, from north to south-west was occupied by mountains, hanging on, as it were, to Olympus. This is the range that runs westward along the north of Thessaly, ending in the Pindus. The line of bearing of these heaved-up strata seems to correspond with that of the Pindus, that is, to run north and south, and they presented their escarpment to Olympus. Ossa, which lay like a hillock beneath, stretched away at right angles to the south ; and, in the interval, spread far, far in the red distance, the level lands of Thessaly, under that peculiar dusty mist which makes nature look like a gigantic imitation of an unnatural effect produced on the scene of a theatre. When I first reached the summit, and looked over the warm plains of Thessaly, this haze was of a pale yellow hue. It deepened gradually, and became red, then brown, while similar tints, far more vivid, were reproduced higher in the sky. But, when I turned round to the east, up which the vast shadows of night were travelling, the cold ocean looked like a plain of lead ; the shadow of the mighty mass of Olympus was projected twenty miles along its surface ; and I stood on the very edge, and on my tiptoes' (*ib.* i. 429 f.). On enquiry he found that the shepherds of Olympos ' had no recollection of the "Thunderer" ...but they told me,' he adds, ' that "the stars came down at night on Olympus !" "that heaven and earth had once met upon its summit, but that since men had grown wicked, God had gone higher up"' (*ib.* i. 437, B. Schmidt *Das Volksleben der Neugriechen* Leipzig 1871 i. 35, N. G. Polites Δημώδεις κοσμογονικοὶ μῦθοι Athens 1894 p. 7, cp. p. 41 ff., *id.* Παραδόσεις Athens 1904 i. 122 no. 217, ii. 805).

Later and more scientific ascents were made by L. Heuzey (1856), H. Barth (1862), and H. F. Tozer (1864). Then followed an interval during which brigandage made mountaineering extremely hazardous : for example, in 1911 E. Richter, an engineer of Jena, had to be ransomed by the Porte at a cost of 500,000 francs. But by 1913 political changes had improved the conditions, and the series of ascents was resumed—D. Baud-Bovy and F. Boissonnas (1913), Profs. E. P. Farquhar and A. E. Phoutrides (1914), Major-General Sir W. Rycroft (1918), D. Baud-Bovy, F. Boissonnas, and the son of the latter (1920), M. Kurz and the chamois-hunter Ch. Kakkalos (1921). See further L. Heuzey *Le Mont Olympe et l'Acarnanie* Paris 1860, H. Barth *Reise durch das Innere der Europäischen Türkei* Berlin 1864, H. F. Tozer *Researches in the Highlands of Turkey* London 1869, E. Richter *Meine Erlebnisse in der Gefangenschaft am Olymp* Leipzig 1911, Profs. E. P. Farquhar and A. E. Phoutrides in *Scribner's Magazine* for November 1915 (good photographs), D. W. Freshfield ' The summits of Olympus' in *The Geographical Journal* 1916 xlvii. 293—297, C. F. Meade ' Mount Olympus' in *The Alpine Journal* 1919 xxxii. 326—328 (with photographs taken by Lieutenant-Colonel Wood, R.E., from an aeroplane piloted by Lieutenant-Colonel Todd, R.A.F.), D. Baud-Bovy ' The mountain-group of Olympus : an essay in nomenclature' in *The Geographical Journal* 1921 lvii. 204—213 (with a sketch-map of the *massif* of Olympos and four fine photographs of the summits by F. Boissonnas).

D. Baud-Bovy *loc. cit.* concludes : ' Thus, to sum up, the High Olympus is constituted by two ranges, which, though not parallel, run generally east and west. The northern range is that of Kokkino-Vrako, the southern, that of Bichtes. A high rocky barrier running north and south contains three "stones," three "pipes," or three "brothers," quite separated from each other, the Tarpeian Rock in the south, the Throne of Zeus in

Mount Athos[1].
Aigai, Kerdylion, etc. (?)[2].

Korkyra
Kassiope[3].

the north, and in the centre the Venizelos peak, the highest of the three. The point of junction between this barrier and the northern range is the St. Elias. The joint which unites the central peaks with the southern range is more complicated. It includes the Skolion, which forms the counterpart to the St. Elias on the opposite side of the Megali-Gurna, and the Isto-Cristaci more to the west. The St. Anthony and the domes of Stavoïdia link these two summits to those at the western end of the southern range, of which the Sarai is the most important.' [The peaks seen in pl. xl, from left to right, are —according to Baud-Bovy's nomenclature—(a) the Throne of Zeus (capped by cloud), (b) Peak Venizelos (the true summit), (c) the Cock's Comb, (d) the Virgin, (e) the Tarpeian Rock.]

M. Kurz in *The Alpine Journal* 1921 xxxiv. 173 f. reports that in August 1921 he surveyed the whole mass of Olympos with a photo-theodolite and that he has in preparation a map, covering an area of *c.* 100 square kilometers, on a scale of 1 : 20,000. The heights calculated to date are : Skolion $= \Delta$ 2905.45^m, Pic Venizelos (*Mitka*, 'Needle') $= 2917.85^m$, Throne of Zeus (*Stephan*) $= 2909.94^m$.

[1] Zeus Ἀθῷος (Soph. *Thamyras frag.* 216 Nauck[2], 237 Jebb *ap.* Eustath. *in Il.* p. 358, 40 f. Θρῇσσαν σκοπιὰν Ζηνὸς Ἀθῴου, cp. Aisch. *Ag.* 285 Ἀθῷον αἶπος Ζηνὸς ἐξεδέξατο) was worshipped on Mt Athos (Eustath. *in Il.* pp. 218, 3, 358, 43 f., 953, 45 f., schol. *Il.* 14. 229), where he had a statue (Hesych. *s.v.* Ἀθῶος· ὁ ἐπὶ τοῦ Ἄθω τοῦ ὄρους ἱδρυμένος ἀνδριάς, ὁ Ζεύς) and a sanctuary on the summit (*et. mag.* p. 26, 47 f. Ἀθῴου Διός· Διὸς ἱερὸν ἐν ἄκρῳ Ἄθῳ τῷ ὄρει, Ἀθῴου καλουμένου). For beliefs concerning the mountain-top and its altars see *supra* i. 82 n. 1, 103 n. 4 (Solin. 11. 3 there adduced is dependent on Mela 2. 31). The presence or absence of clouds on Mt Athos betokened rain or fine weather (Theophr. *de signis tempest.* 3. 6, 4. 2). Other allusions are collected by W. Capelle *Berges- und Wolkenhöhen bei griechischen Physikern* (Στοιχεῖα v) Leipzig—Berlin 1916 pp. 1, 27, 32 n. 5, 37, 39. On the various monasteries of this Ἅγιον Ὄρος see the literature cited by E. Oberhummer in Pauly—Wissowa *Real-Enc.* ii. 2068 f. and by C. M. Kaufmann *Handbuch der christlichen Archäologie* Paderborn 1913 p. 120.

[2] Zeus Ὕψιστος (*supra* p. 878 n. 0 no. (9)).

[3] Kassiope, a town and promontory (Ptol. 3. 13. 9 Κασσιόπη πόλις καὶ ἄκρα) in the north-eastern corner of Korkyra, is still called *Kassiopi*. As a convenient haven it figures from time to time in ancient records (L. Bürchner in Pauly—Wissowa *Real-Enc.* x. 2314 f., xi. 1413).—It possessed a temple of Iupiter *Cassius* (Plin. *nat. hist.* 4. 52 et oppido Cassiope temploque Cassi Iovis), at whose altar Nero sang (Suet. *Ner.* 22 ut primum Cassiopen traiecit, statim ad aram Iovis Cassii cantare auspicatus certamina deinceps obiit omnia). Two dedications to Iupiter *Casius* have been found in Korkyra (*Corp. inscr. Lat.* iii no. 576 = Orelli *Inscr. Lat. sel.* no. 1224 P. Hetereius | Rufio | Iovi Casio sac(rum), *Corp. inscr. Lat.* iii no. 577 (cp. p. 989) = Dessau *Inscr. Lat. sel.* no. 4043 M. Valerius Corvi[ni] | [l. L]orico | Iovi Casio v. s.). A ship built of marble and dedicated by a merchant to Zeus Κάσιος was sometimes regarded as the raft of Odysseus, and is compared with the stone ship made by Tynnichos and dedicated by Agamemnon to Artemis Βολοσία at Geraistos (Prokop. *de bell. Goth.* 4. 22 καίτοι οὐ μονοειδὲς τὸ πλοῖον τοῦτό ἐστιν, ἀλλὰ ἐκ λίθων ὅτι μάλιστα πολλῶν ξύγκειται. καὶ γράμματα ἐν αὐτῷ ἐγκεκόλαπται καὶ διαρρήδην βοᾷ τῶν τινα ἐμπόρων ἐν τοῖς ἄνω χρόνοις ἱδρύσασθαι τὸ ἀνάθημα τοῦτο Διὶ τῷ Κασίῳ. Δία γὰρ Κάσιον ἐτίμων ποτὲ οἱ τῇδε ἄνθρωποι, ἐπεὶ καὶ ἡ πόλις, ἐν ᾗ τὸ πλοῖον τοῦτο ἔστηκεν, ἐς τόνδε τὸν χρόνον Κασώπη (sic) ἐπικαλεῖται. κ.τ.λ.).

Autonomous bronze coins of Korkyra from 48 B.C. to 138 A.D. often have for reverse or obverse type the figure of ΖΕΥϹ ΚΑϹΙΟϹ (occasionally ΖΕΥϹ ΚΑϹϹΙΟϹ) seated on a high-backed throne with a sceptre in one hand and sometimes a *phiále* in the other

Korkyra (?)[1].

Kephallenia

Mount Ainos[2].

(*Brit. Mus. Cat. Coins* Thessaly etc. p. 153 ff. pl. 25, 5 (=my fig. 823), 6—11, *Hunter Cat. Coins* ii. 21 pl. 32, 4, Head *Hist. num.*[2] p. 328). Imperial coppers from Antoninus Pius to Geta (138—222 A.D.) repeat the type with legend ZEVC KACIOC Antoninus Pius, KOPKVPAIⲰN KACCIOC M. Aurelius, or KOPKVPAIⲰN M. Aurelius to Geta (*Brit. Mus. Cat. Coins* Thessaly etc. p. 158 ff. pl. 26, 1, *Hunter Cat. Coins* ii. 21

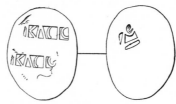

Fig. 823. Fig. 824.

no. 53, 23 nos. 65, 67, 72, Head *Hist. num.*[2] p. 328). Coins of Korkyra, Lakedaimon, Knidos, etc. are found countermarked with various abbreviations of the words Διὸς Κασίου and were probably dedicated in his temple (*Brit. Mus. Cat. Coins* Thessaly etc. p. 158 pl. 25, 14 (=my fig. 824) and 15, Babelon *Monn. gr. rom.* i. 1. 647, 676 f.).

Zeus Κάσιος, an oriental deity (Frau Adler in Pauly—Wissowa *Real-Enc.* x. 2265— 2267 and A. Salač 'ΖΕΥΣ ΚΑΣΙΟΣ' in the *Bull. Corr. Hell.* 1922 xlvi. 160—189) whose cult had been introduced, perhaps *viâ* Delos (A. Salač *ib.* pp. 165, 189), either from Mt Kasion on the Orontes (*infra* Append. B Syria) or from Mt Kasion near Pelousion (*infra* Append. B Aigyptos), was in Korkyra readily identified with the Zeus of Kassiope, a Hellenic god probably connected with Mt Pantokrator (911ᵐ) behind the town. The accidental resemblance of Κάσιος to Κασσιόπη would suffice to ensure his popularity.

[1] Zeus Ὕψιστος (*supra* p. 879 n. 0 no. (12)).

[2] Mt Ainos, the chief mountain of Kephallenia, rises to a height of 1620ᵐ and is known as *Elatovouno* or *Monte Nero* from the dark fir-trees with which it was formerly clad (C. Bursian *Geographie von Griechenland* Leipzig 1872 ii. 372). On it was the sanctuary of Zeus Αἰνήσιος (Strab. 456 μέγιστον δ' ὄρος ἐν αὐτῇ < Αἶνος (*ins.* Xylander)>, ἐν ᾧ τὸ Διὸς Αἰνησίου ἱερόν), to whom the Boreadai prayed when pursuing the Harpyiai (schol. Ap. Rhod. 2. 297 ὅτι δὲ ηὔξαντο οἱ περὶ Ζήτην τῷ Διὶ στραφέντες λέγει καὶ Ἡσίοδος (*frag.* 57 Rzach) 'ἔνθ' οἵ γ' εὐχέσθην Αἰνηίῳ ὑψιμέδοντι.' ἔστι γὰρ καὶ Αἶνος ὄρος τῆς Κεφαληνίας, ὅπου Αἰνησίου Διὸς ἱερόν ἐστιν· οὗ μνημονεύει καὶ Λέων ἐν Περίπλῳ (Leon of Byzantion *frag.* 4 (*Frag. hist. Gr.* ii. 330 f. Müller)) καὶ Δημοσθένης ἐν τοῖς Λιμέσιν (? Demosthenes of Bithynia (*Frag. hist. Gr.* iv. 384 Müller)). But Müller *op. cit.* ii. 331, iv. 365 emends the text to οὗ μνημονεύει Κλέων ἐν τῷ Περὶ λιμένων καὶ Τιμοσθένης ἐν τοῖς Λιμέσιν. The emendation Κλέων is confirmed by *et. gen. s.v.* ἀρετάν·...καὶ Κλέων ἐν τῷ Περίπλῳ (E. Miller *Mélanges de littérature grecque* Paris 1868 p. 41), and Kleon of Syracuse was associated with Timosthenes (*Frag. hist. Gr.* iv. 365 Müller)).

Bronze coins of Pronnoi on the south-eastern coast of Kephallenia, from *c.* 370 B.C. onwards, have *obv.* head of Zeus Αἰνήσιος, laureate, *rev.* a fir-cone, sometimes with twigs (Rasche *Lex. Num.* iv. 1205, *Brit. Mus. Cat. Coins* Peloponnesus p. 89 pl. 18, 7 and 8, Babelon *Monn. gr. rom.* ii. 3. 807 f. pl. 238, 26 and 27, Head *Hist. num.*[2] p. 428).

D. T. Ansted *The Ionian Islands in the year 1863* London 1863 p. 345 f. describes his ascent of Mt Ainos: 'Through a couple of miles of forest of these noble trees, through two or three miles also of hard, granulated snow and some snow recently fallen and very soft, I made my way from the cottage to the top of the mountain. The path is long, but

Sicily
Mount Aitne[1].

nowhere steep. It conducts by a succession of slopes and terraces to the culminating ridge, which is itself of considerable length, and comprises at least half a dozen points of rock, all within twenty feet of the highest point. There is a cairn of stones at the last of these, and the remains of an altar dedicated to Jupiter Enos. Numerous fragments of calcined bones have been taken from the ground at the foot of the altar, where there seems to be a large deposit. This point is not really the highest, being a little to the east of it and ten or fifteen feet lower; the culminating point is about 5,400 feet above the sea. The view from this summit when everything is favourable must be exceedingly grand, as, except the Pindus range which is distant, there is nothing to intercept the view. All around is a rich panorama of islands : Zante at one's feet in all its elegant beauty of form; Ithaca to the east ; beyond it a silver strip of ocean, and then the gulf of Patras, which is seen in all its length to the bay of Lepanto, in the vicinity of Corinth. Athens is not much further in the same direction. A noble chain of snowy mountains shuts in this view towards the south east. Looking down in the direction of Argostoli a minute speck is seen in the water. On the island called Διος (Thios), that looks so small, was once a temple to the father of the gods, and when sacrifice was offered and the smoke was seen by the priests stationed at the altar on this summit, another sacrifice was here made, and the curling incense rising from this lofty point in the thin air was a sign, far and wide, of the completion of the offering. Here above remain the stones of the altar and the burnt bones of the bulls and the goats ; there below, at a distance of several miles, the more solid and beautiful temple is gone—not one stone remains upon another, and there is nothing but the story, probable enough for that matter, to connect the two localities.'

[1] Aitne, the greatest volcano of the ancient world, rises to a height of 10,758 ft (according to the geodetic survey of 1900) and covers not less than 460 square miles, its base being about 90 miles in circumference (K. Baedeker *Southern Italy and Sicily*[16] Leipzig 1912 p. 423. For full details see W. Sartorius Freiherr von Waltershausen *Der Aetna* herausg. von A. von Lasaulx Leipzig 1880 i. ii.).

On the sea-coast at the southern foot of Mt Aitne lay the old town of Katane. And when in 476/5 B.C. Hieron i drove out its inhabitants, settled in their stead 5000 Syracusans with 5000 Peloponnesians, and renamed the place Aitne (Diod. 11. 49), he seems to have erected there a statue of Zeus Αἰτναῖος and instituted a festival called Αἰτναῖα (schol. Pind. *Ol.* 6. 162a ἐν τῇ Αἴτνῃ Διὸς Αἰτναίου ἄγαλμα ἵδρυται, καὶ ἑορτὴ Αἰτναῖα καλεῖται, *ib.* 162 c περιέπει δὲ καὶ θεραπεύει ὁ Ἱέρων καὶ τὸ κράτος τοῦ Διὸς τοῦ κατὰ τὴν Αἴτνην τιμωμένου, schol. Pind. *Nem.* 6 Διὸς ἕνεκεν τοῦ ἐν τῇ Αἴτνῃ· Διὶ γὰρ ἀνάκειται καὶ οὗτος ὁ ἀγών· ἐν γὰρ τῇ Αἴτνῃ Διὸς ἱερόν ἐστι, *ib.* 7 ἐν τῷ ἀγῶνι καὶ ἐν τῇ πανηγύρει τοῦ Αἰτναίου Διὸς ἦγον οἱ περὶ τὸν Ἱέρωνα τοὺς ἐπὶ τοῖς στεφανίταις ἀγῶσι πεποιημένους ἐπινίκους καὶ ᾖδον. κ.τ.λ.). Accordingly Pindar, in odes composed soon after Hieron's new foundation, dwells on the recently established cult (*Nem.* 1. 6 Ζηνὸς Αἰτναίου χάριν, *Ol.* 6. 96 Ζηνὸς Αἰτναίου κράτος, *Pyth.* 1. 29 f. Ζεῦ, ... | ὃς τοῦτ' ἐφέπεις ὄρος, κ.τ.λ., cp. *Ol.* 4. 6 ὦ Κρόνου παῖ, ὃς Αἴτναν ἔχεις κ.τ.λ.). In 461 B.C. the settlers at Katane, driven out in their turn by Douketios and his Sikeloi, captured the Sikel town Inessa (*S. Maria di Licodia*) on the southwestern slope of the mountain and transferred to it the name of Hieron's settlement Aitne (Diod. 11. 76) ; but whether they transferred thither the cult of Zeus Αἰτναῖος also we do not know. Perhaps they did, for in Roman times it seems to have been widely spread. E. Ciaceri *Culti e miti nella storia dell'antica Sicilia* Catania 1911 pp. 34 f., 145 f. cp. Diod. 34. 10 ὅτι ἡ σύγκλητος δεισιδαιμονοῦσα ἐξαπέστειλεν εἰς Σικελίαν περὶ τοὺς Σιβύλλης χρησμοὺς κατὰ Σιβυλλιακὸν λόγιον· οἱ δὲ ἐπελθόντες καθ' ὅλην τὴν Σικελίαν τοὺς τῷ Αἰτναίῳ Διὶ καθιδρυμένους βωμοὺς θυσιάσαντες, καὶ περιφράγματα ποιήσαντες, ἀβάτους ἀπεδείκνυον τοὺς τόπους πλὴν τοῖς ἔχουσι καθ' ἕκαστον πολίτευμα πατρίους θύειν θυσίας.

The cult at Katane-Aitne is attested by coins of the town, issued from shortly before 476 to shortly before 461 B.C. Silver *lítrai* have *obv.* the head of a bald Silenos, *rev.* a thunderbolt with two curled wings and the legend KATA NE often abbreviated (*Brit.*

The Mountain-cults of Zeus 909

Mus. Cat. Coins Sicily p. 42 nos. 8—11, *Hunter Cat. Coins* i. 171 nos. 1—5, G. F. Hill
Historical Greek Coins London 1906 p. 43 pl. 3, 21, Head *Hist. num.*[2] p. 131) or ΑΙΤ
ΝΑΙ likewise abbreviated (*Brit. Mus. Cat. Coins* Sicily p. 43 no. 12 fig., nos. 13—16,
G. F. Hill *op. cit.* p. 44, Head *Hist. num.*[2] p. 132). And a unique silver tetradrachm in
the Hirsch collection at Brussels (*supra* i. 90 f. fig. 62) shows *obv.* ΑΙΤΝΑ ΙΟΝ the
head of a bald Silenos wearing an ivy-wreath (Eur. *Cycl.* 18 ff. Silenos as slave of Polyphemos dwells in a cave on Mt Aitne), with a beetle beneath (Aristoph. *pax* 73 Αἰτναῖον
μέγιστον κάνθαρον and schol. *ad loc.*), *rev.* Zeus Αἰτναῖος sitting on a throne spread with
a lion-skin. He is clad in a *himátion*. His right hand rests on a vine-staff (Strab. 269
ἔχειν τι οἰκείωμα πρὸς τὴν ἄμπελον εἰκὸς τὴν Αἰτναίαν σποδόν); his left holds a thunderbolt
with two curled wings. In the field is an eagle perched on a pine-tree (Diod. 14. 42 εἰς
τὸ κατὰ τὴν Αἴτνην ὄρος ἀπέστειλε γέμον κατ' ἐκείνους τοὺς χρόνους πολυτελοῦς ἐλάτης τε καὶ
πεύκης). On this remarkable coin, which has been taken to represent the cult-statue of
Zeus Αἰτναῖος (Ziegler in Pauly—Wissowa *Real-Enc.* x. 2475 f.), see further Baron L. de
Hirsch in the *Num. Chron.* Third Series 1883 iii. 165 f. pl. 9, 1, B. V. Head *ib.* p. 171 ff.,
G. F. Hill *Coins of Ancient Sicily* London 1903 p. 74 f. pl. 4, 13, *id. Historical Greek
Coins* London 1906 p. 43 ff. pl. 3, 22, G. Macdonald *Coin Types* Glasgow 1905 pp. 94 f.,
97 pl. 3, 6, Head *Hist. num.*[2] p. 131 f. fig. 70. The types of the tetradrachm recall the
famous scene in Aristoph. *pax* 62 ff., where Trygaios tries to reach Zeus, first by clambering
up light ladders towards the sky (*supra* p. 130), and then by mounting an Aetnaean beetle
as a sort of Pegasos. Not improbably there were Dionysiac traits in the cult of Zeus on
Mt Aitne, as there were in his cult on Mt Olympos (*supra* i. 104 ff.).

There is, however, no evidence of a Zeus-cult on Aitne earlier than *s.* v B.C. Hence
the paucity of myths connecting this god with the mountain. Zeus is indeed sometimes
said to have piled Aitne on Typhon (Aisch. *P. v.* 351 ff., Pind. *Pyth.* 1. 13 ff., cp. Strab.
626 f.) or on Enkelados (Lucilius (?) *Aetna* 71 ff., Stat. *Theb.* 11. 8, cp. Verg. *Aen.* 3.
578 ff., Opp. *de venat.* 1. 273 ff.); but Typhon is more properly located in the land of
Arima (*supra* p. 826) or in the Corycian Cave (*supra* p. 448 n. 2), and Enkelados is commonly described as the victim of Athena, not of Zeus. Again, the Palikoi, autochthonous
deities (Polemon *frag.* 83 (*Frag. hist. Gr.* iii. 140 f. Müller) *ap.* Macrob. *Sat.* 5. 19. 26)
of the two volcanic springs in the *Lago dei Palici* (*supra* i. 156. See further L. Bloch in
Roscher *Lex. Myth.* iii. 1281—1295), were fathered upon Zeus. Aisch. Αἰτναῖαι *frag.* 7
Nauck[2] *ap.* Steph. Byz. *s.v.* Παλική made them the children of Zeus by Thaleia daughter
of Hephaistos. *Id. ib. frag.* 6 Nauck[2] *ap.* Macrob. *Sat.* 5. 19. 24 added that Zeus had
named them Παλικοί because they would 'come again' from darkness into light. The
context in Macrob. *Sat.* 5. 19. 17 ff. preserves the Aeschylean version of their myth. The
nymph Thaleia, embraced by Zeus near the Sicilian river Symaithos, became pregnant
and, through fear of Hera, prayed that the earth might swallow her. It did so. But in
due time it opened up and Thaleia's twin sons the Παλικοί 'came again' to light. The
self-transformation of Zeus into a vulture (or eagle?) in order to win the nymph (Rufin.
recognit. 10. 22 and Clem. Rom. *hom.* 5. 13 (ii. 184 Migne)—both cited *supra* i. 106 n. 2 f.)
is a feature of the story, which would have appealed to Aischylos' love of spectacular effect
(cp. the vase-painting *supra* i. 105 f. fig. 76). The so-called interpolator of Servius
(Donatus ?) knows the tale of Zeus and Thaleia, though he is muddle-headed about the
eagle. But Servius himself makes the Palikoi the children of Zeus by the nymph Aitne
(Serv. *in* Verg. *Aen.* 9. 584 Symaethos fluvius est Siciliae [a rege Symaetho dictus], haud
longe ab urbe Carinensi (*leg.* Catinensi), circa quem sunt Palici dei, quorum talis est
fabula: Aetnam nympham [vel, ut quidam volunt, Thaliam] Iuppiter cum vitiasset et
fecisset gravidam, timens Iunonem, secundum alios ipsam puellam, Terrae commendavit,
et illic enixa est. secundum alios partum eius, postea cum de Terra erupissent duo pueri,
Palici dicti sunt, quasi iterum venientes. nam πάλιν ἵκειν est iterum venire. hi primo
humanis hostiis placabantur, postea quibusdam sacris mitigati sunt et eorum immutata
sacrificia. inde ergo 'placabilis ara,' quia mitigata sunt eorum numina. [Palicos nauticos
deos Varro appellat. alii dicunt Iovem hunc Palicum propter Iunonis iracundiam in
aquilam commutasse. alii Vulcani et Aetnae filium tradunt, sed etc.]). Another line of

Akragas[1].

tradition or conjecture speaks of Hephaistos, not Zeus, as father of the Palikoi (Silenos *frag.* 7 (*Frag. hist. Gr.* iii. 101 Müller) *ap.* Steph. Byz. *s.v.* Παλική). Yet another prefers Adranos (Hesych. *s.v.* Παλικοί, cp. Plout. *v. Timol.* 12), the Syrian Hadran (*supra* i. 232 n. 1, ii. 630). It may be surmised that their original connexion was with the Earth rather than with the Sky.

Be that as it may, the cult of Zeus as a mountain-god in the region of Aitne is hardly of great antiquity. The ancient god of the district was the 'Minoan' Kronos (Lyd. *de mens.* 4. 154 p. 170, 6 ff. Wünsch cited *supra* p. 554 n. 3).

[1] Akragas, a joint colony from Rhodes and Gela (C. Hülsen in Pauly—Wissowa *Real-Enc.* i. 1188), had an *akrópolis* named Mt Atabyrion (J. Schubring *Historische Topographie von Akragas in Sicilien während der klassischen Zeit* Leipzig 1870 pp. 21—28 'Die Akropolis'). On the top of it was a sanctuary of Zeus Ἀταβύριος resembling that at Rhodes (Polyb. 9. 27. 7 f. ἐπὶ δὲ τῆς κορυφῆς Ἀθηνᾶς ἱερὸν ἔκτισται καὶ Διὸς Ἀταβυρίου, καθάπερ καὶ παρὰ Ῥοδίοις· τοῦ γὰρ Ἀκράγαντος ὑπὸ Ῥοδίων ἀπῳκισμένου, εἰκότως ὁ θεὸς οὗτος τὴν αὐτὴν ἔχει προσηγορίαν ἣν καὶ παρὰ τοῖς Ῥοδίοις). With Zeus Ἀταβύριος must be identified Zeus Πολιεύς (J. Schubring *op. cit.* p. 24), whose temple on the highest point of the rocky site was built by Phalaris (Polyain. 5. 1. 1 cited *supra* i. 122) in the first half of *s.* vi B.C. Phalaris' famous bull of bronze (Pind. *Pyth.* 1. 95 f., *alib.*) seems to have been the sacred beast of Zeus Ἀταβύριος, the Hellenic successor of a Hittite bull-god (*supra* i. 643 f., cp. 784 f. figs. 567—569. F. Hrozny *Hethitische Keilschrifttexte aus Boghazköi* Leipzig 1919. 1 ff. no. 1 a list of Tešub-cults recording a great bull of silver (i, 34 f.) and several great bulls of iron (ii, 12, 24, 34, 41, iii, 2, 8), one of them with gilded eyes (iv, 3)). The Carthaginians, on capturing Akragas (405 B.C.), carried off the bull, which had a trap-door between its shoulders and pipes in its nostrils (Polyb. 12. 25. 3, Diod. 9. 19 *ap.* Tzetz. *chil.* 1. 646 ff.), to Carthage (Polyb. 12. 25. 3, Diod. 13. 90). Timaios, according to one account, denied that the bull at Carthage had come from Akragas, declaring that the Agrigentines had never possessed the like (Tim. *frags.* 116, 117 (*Frag. hist. Gr.* i. 221 f., 222 Müller) *ap.* Polyb. 12. 25. 1 ff., Diod. 13. 90). But, according to another account, he stated that they had flung the original bull into the sea, and that the bull exhibited at Akragas was only an effigy of the river Gelas (Tim. *frag.* 118 (*Frag. hist. Gr.* i. 222 Müller) *ap.* schol. Pind. *Pyth.* 1. 185). Scipio brought the bull back from Carthage to Akragas (Cic. *Verr.* 4. 73, Diod. 13. 90), where it was still to be seen *c.* 60 B.C. (Diod. 13. 90). See further J. Schubring *op. cit.* p. 24 ff., G. Busolt *Griechische Geschichte* Gotha 1893 i[2]. 422 n. 4.

The temple of Zeus Ἀταβύριος or Πολιεύς is in all probability to be sought beneath the Cathedral of S. Gerlando (bishop of Agrigentum; died Feb. 25, 1101 A.D. Cp. *Acta Sanctorum* edd. Bolland. Februarius iii. 592 C (Pirrus e gestis S. Gerlandi) Cathedrale templum quadrato lapide ac nobili structurâ à fundamentis excitavit, illudóque D. Mariæ (uti à D. Petro fuerat olim dicatum) & D. Iacobo Apostolo consecravit iv die Aprilis) on the highest part of modern *Girgenti* (C. Hülsen *loc. cit.*). J. Schubring *op. cit.* p. 24 says 'dass S. Gerlando auf den Substruktionen eines alten Tempels erbaut ist und unbedenklich erkläre ich die grossen Stufen und Quaderbauten, die aus dem Boden hervorragen, für antike Reste.' But R. Koldewey—O. Puchstein *Die griechischen Tempel in Unteritalien und Sicilien* Berlin 1899 i. 139, while agreeing that S. Gerlando marks the site of the temple, add: 'Leider ist von diesem Bau des Phalaris, dem einzigen sicilischen Tempel des 6. Jahrhunderts v. Chr., über den wir eine historische Nachricht haben, nichts erhalten.' Excavation may yet find traces of it. The substantial remains of a Doric hexastyle peripteral temple of *s.* v B.C. beneath the neighbouring church of S. Maria de' Greci were published by Domenico lo Faso Pietrasanta Duca di Serradifalco *Le Antichità della Sicilia* Palermo 1836 iii. 86 f. pls. 43, 44 as belonging to the temple of Zeus Πολιεύς, but should rather be identified with the temple of Athena (J. Schubring *op. cit.* p. 26, R. Koldewey—O. Puchstein *op. cit.* i. 140 ff., ii pl. 20).

On a hill (75^m high) to the west of the so-called *Porta Aurea*, which led through the southern wall of the lower city towards the sea (Liv. 26. 40), was the vast but unfinished temple of Zeus Ὀλύμπιος (Polyb. 9. 27. 9 καὶ ὁ τοῦ Διὸς τοῦ Ὀλυμπίου νεὼς παντέλειαν (so J. A. Ernesti, followed by F. Hultsch, for πολυτέλειαν codd. F.S. Cluverius cj. συντέλειαν) μὲν οὐκ εἴληφε, κατὰ δὲ τὴν ἐπιβολὴν καὶ τὸ μέγεθος οὐδ' ὁποίου τῶν κατὰ τὴν Ἑλλάδα δοκεῖ λείπεσθαι). When Theron, making common cause with Gelon, had vanquished the huge host of the Carthaginians at Himera (480 B.C.), the Agrigentines used their ·numerous prisoners of war to hew stone for the construction of their largest temples (Diod. 11. 25). The Olympion must have taken many years to build; indeed, it was not yet roofed when in 405 B.C. Akragas was captured by the Carthaginians, and roofless it remained (Diod. 13. 82). In 255 B.C., during the First Punic War, Karthalon besieged and took Akragas; whereupon the remnant of the population fled for refuge to the Olympion (Diod. 23. 14). This great fabric fell gradually into decay. But part of it, supported by three Giants and certain columns, did not collapse till Dec. 9, 1401 A.D. Hence the arms of *Girgenti* (a turreted wall resting on three naked Giants), the mediaeval line *signat Agrigentum mirabilis aula Gigantum*, and the popular name of the ruins *Palazzo de Giganti* (T. Fazellus *de rebus Siculis* Panormi 1558 p. 127 (dec. 1 lib. 6 cap. 1)). In modern times the temple has served as a public quarry, the mole of *Porto Empedocle* being built of its blocks (1749— 1763 A.D.) (R. Koldewey—O. Puchstein *op. cit.* i. 154).

There is a detailed account of the Olympion in Diod. 13. 82 ἥ τε γὰρ τῶν ἱερῶν κατα- σκευὴ καὶ μάλιστα ὁ τοῦ Διὸς νεὼς ἐμφαίνει τὴν μεγαλοπρέπειαν τῶν τότε ἀνθρώπων· τῶν μὲν οὖν (so F. Vogel for γὰρ codd.) ἄλλων ἱερῶν τὰ μὲν κατεκαύθη, τὰ δὲ τελείως κατεσκάφη διὰ τὸ πολλάκις ἡλωκέναι τὴν πόλιν, τὸ δ' (so F. Vogel for δ' οὖν codd.) Ὀλύμπιον μέλλον λαμβάνειν τὴν ὀροφὴν ὁ πόλεμος ἐκώλυσεν· ἐξ οὗ τῆς πόλεως κατασκαφείσης οὐδέποτε ὕστερον ἴσχυσαν Ἀκραγαντῖνοι τέλος ἐπιθεῖναι τοῖς οἰκοδομήμασιν. ἔστι δὲ ὁ νεὼς ἔχων τὸ μὲν μῆκος πόδας τριακοσίους τεσσαράκοντα, τὸ δὲ πλάτος <ἑκατὸν (ins. T. Kidd, J. Schubring)> ἑξή- κοντα, τὸ δὲ ὕψος ἑκατὸν εἴκοσι χωρὶς τοῦ κρηπιδώματος. μέγιστος δ' ὢν τῶν ἐν Σικελίᾳ καὶ τοῖς ἐκτὸς οὐκ ἀλόγως ἂν συγκρίνοιτο κατὰ τὸ μέγεθος τῆς ὑποστάσεως· καὶ γὰρ εἰ μὴ τέλος λαβεῖν συνέβη τὴν ἐπιβολήν, ἥ γε προαίρεσις (so J. J. Reiske for προδιαίρεσις codd.) ὑπάρχει φανερά. τῶν δ' ἄλλων ἢ μέχρι τοίχων (sic codd. J. J. Reiske cj. μετὰ τοίχων. L. Dindorf cj. μέχρι θριγκῶν. F. Vogel cj. μέχρι τεγῶν vel συνεχεῖ τοίχῳ) τοὺς νεὼς οἰκοδομούντων ἢ κύκλῳ κίοσι (so P. Wesseling, followed by F. Vogel, for ἢ κύκλους or κυκλώσει codd. Stephanus cj. ἢ κίοσι) τοὺς σηκοὺς (so J. J. Reiske, followed by F. Vogel, for οἴκους codd. Stephanus cj. τοίχους) περιλαμβανόντων, οὗτος ἑκατέρας τούτων μετέχει τῶν ὑποστάσεων· συνῳκοδομοῦντο γὰρ τοῖς τοίχοις οἱ κίονες (so L. Dindorf for οἱ τοῖχοι τοῖς κίοσιν codd.), ἔξωθεν μὲν στρογγύλοι, τὰ δ' ἐντὸς τοῦ νεὼ ἔχοντες τετράγωνον· καὶ τοῦ μὲν ἐκτὸς μέρους ἐστὶν αὐτῶν ἡ περιφέρεια ποδῶν εἴκοσι, καθ' ἣν εἰς τὰ διαξύσματα δύναται ἀνθρώπινον ἐναρμόζεσθαι σῶμα, τὸ (L. Dindorf cj. τοῦ) δ' ἐντὸς ποδῶν δώδεκα. τῶν δὲ στοῶν τὸ μέγεθος καὶ τὸ ὕψος ἐξαίσιον ἐχουσῶν, ἐν μὲν τῷ πρὸς ἔω μέρει τὴν Γιγαντομαχίαν ἐποιήσαντο γλυφαῖς (so L. Din- dorf for ταῖς γλυφαῖς codd. F.K. ταῖς τε γλυφαῖς cett. codd.) καὶ τῷ μεγέθει καὶ τῷ κάλλει διαφερούσαις (so L. Dindorf for διαφερούσας codd. P.A.K. διαφέρουσαν cett. codd.), ἐν δὲ τῷ πρὸς δυσμὰς τὴν ἅλωσιν τῆς Τροίας, ἐν ᾗ τῶν ἡρώων ἕκαστον ἰδεῖν ἔστιν οἰκείως τῆς περιστάσεως δεδημιουργημένον.

The temple, of which substantial remains still strew the ground, was a Doric pseudo-peripteral building with seven half-columns on the short side and fourteen half-columns on the long side. These columns (lower diameter 4·30^m, upper diameter 3·10^m), engaged externally in the wall of the *naós*, appear internally as rectangular pilasters. If completed, they would have the normal number of twenty flutes, flutes of so vast a size (0·55^m broad) that a man can easily stand in each as in a niche. Beneath the half-column is a moulded base, which is continued along the intercolumniation-wall as a moulded plinth. The stylobate, of four steps surmounted by a projecting cornice, rests on a stereobate measuring 113·45^m × 56·30^m. The architrave (3·20^m high) was formed of three superposed courses of stone. The metopes were single slabs left plain. The pediments were filled with groups representing the Gigantomachy at the eastern end and the capture of Troy at the western end (a few fragments only preserved). The building was throughout of yellowish shell-limestone covered with a fine skin of stucco and decorated with the usual patterns in paint.

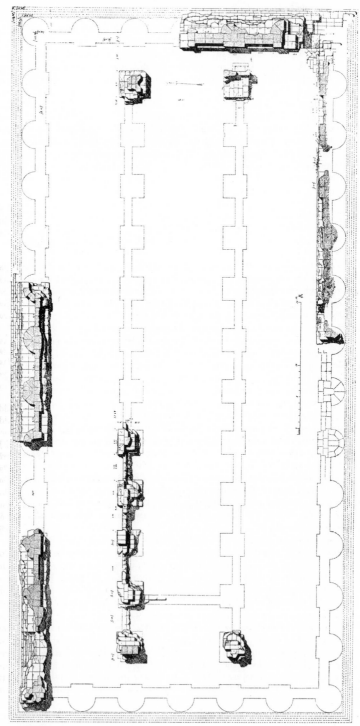

Fig. 825.

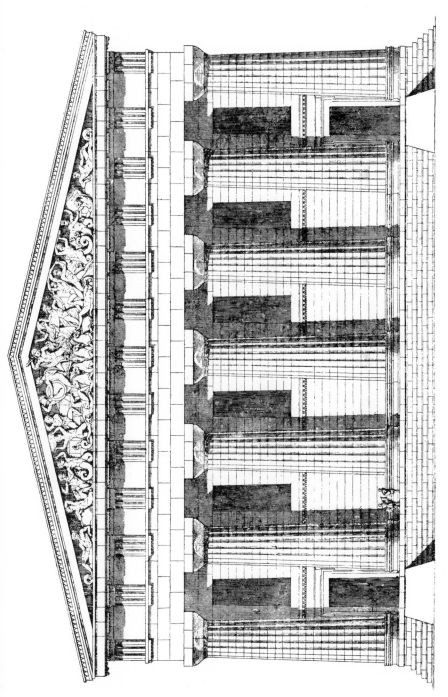

Fig. 826.

Inside, the *naós* ($101 \cdot 16^{m} \times 44 \cdot 01^{m}$) is divided into a nave and two side-aisles by means of two parallel walls, each of which has twelve square pillars engaged in it and forming a series of lateral niches. A cross-wall towards the western end is extant for part of its length. The great altar, as broad as the temple itself, was situated in front of the eastern *façade* at a distance of $50 \cdot 8^{m}$.

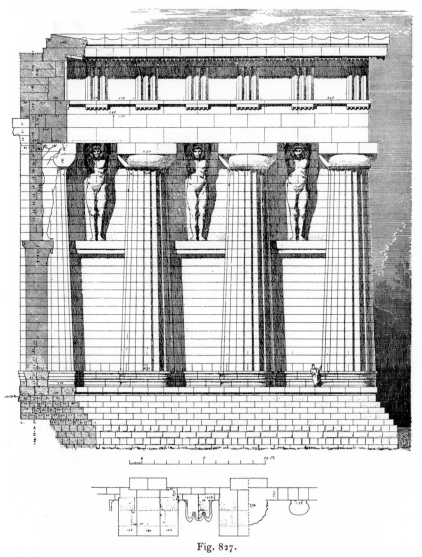

Fig. 827.

    Several points are still unsettled. (1) The temple was in all probability entered at the eastern end through the two outermost intercolumniations (C. R. Cockerell, R. Koldewey—O. Puchstein), not at the western end through a large central doorway (Serradifalco, A. Holm). But it is not clear whether we should assume the existence of two ramps leading up to the side-entries (C. R. Cockerell). (2) The two walls dividing the *naós* into

Plate XLI

The Olympieion at Syracuse.

See page 915 *n.* 2.

Akrai[1].
Syracuse[2].

nave and aisles were either prolonged to meet the western wall of the temple, in which
case the cross-wall marked the beginning of an inner sanctuary or *ádyton* (R. Koldewey—
O. Puchstein), or stopped before reaching the western wall, in which case the cross-wall
marked the beginning of an *opisthódomos* (C. R. Cockerell, Serradifalco, J. Durm, G. Perrot
—C. Chipiez). (3) Many sections of huge Atlantes (7·68m high) have been found in the
temple, and one reconstructed Atlas now lies on his back within the building. But they
are not mentioned by Diodoros, and their original position has been much debated.
C. R. Cockerell (1830) supposed that they stood above the pillars of the nave, supporting
on their upturned arms an entablature intended to carry the transverse beams of the roof.
Serradifalco (1836) was inclined to place them against the pillars of the nave, but at a
lower level. J. Durm (1892), G. Perrot—C. Chipiez (1898), and A. Choisy (1898) reverted
to the position advocated by Cockerell. But R. Koldewey—O. Puchstein (1899), observing
that the southern wall of the temple had fallen outwards and that its ruins included several
blocks belonging to Atlantes, proposed a fresh reconstruction according to which these
gigantic figures were placed high up in the external intercolumniations, each standing on
a cornice and supporting the architrave above his head. J. Durm (1910) finally accepted
Puchstein's restoration in preference to his own. (4) Koldewey and Puchstein speak of
Atlantes and Caryatids. The existence of the latter is inferred, partly from the survival
of a single apparently female head (Serradifalco *op. cit.* iii pl. 25, 2), partly from the fact
that the arms of *Girgenti* figure one female standing between two male Giants—Fama
between Enceladus and Caeus (Serradifalco *op. cit.* iii. 3 fig.).

See further C. R. Cockerell in J. Stuart—N. Revett *Antiquities of Athens and other
places in Greece Sicily etc.* London 1830 iv. 1—10 with frontispiece, vignette, and pls. 1—8
(my fig. 826 is from part of pl. 2), Serradifalco *op. cit.* iii. 52—69 with pls. 20—27, Durm
Baukunst d. Gr.[2] p. 210 f. figs. 138—140 and Index p. 368, *ib.*[3] pp. 104 fig. 72, 141 fig. 112,
401—406 figs. 369—372, 428 with fig. 389, Perrot—Chipiez *Hist. de l'Art* vii. 400 f. pl. 18
and Index p. 673, R. Koldewey—O. Puchstein *op. cit.* i. 153—166 with figs. 134—144
(my fig. 827 is from their fig. 143), ii pls. 22 and 23, B. Pace 'Il tempio di Giove
Olimpico in Agrigento' in the *Mon. d. Linc.* 1922 xxviii ('in corso di stampa').

[1] Zeus Ἀκραῖος (*supra* p. 873 n. o no. (11)).

[2] On a hill (60 ft. high) half-surrounded by the *Fiume Ciani* and overlooking the
Porto Grande of Syracuse stand two weather-worn columns on a broken stylobate—all
that today remains of the once famous temple of Zeus Ὀλύμπιος. This was a Doric peripteral structure of coarse shell-limestone. It had six columns at either end and seventeen
down either side, being about three times as long as it was broad. The columns were
short and thick: one, without a capital, measures *c.* 6·50m in height and *c.* 1·85m in diameter. They were monolithic and had no *éntasis*. The flutes were sixteen in number;
and round the foot ran a small unfluted band, a feature possibly derived from the circular
stone base of a timber prototype. Cornice and gutter were embellished with a revetment
of painted terra cotta. The roofing was of large flat tiles and round cover-tiles. In short,
the building shows every sign of archaism and must be dated *c.* 600 B.C. It is thus one of
the earliest of all Greek temples and quite the oldest surviving temple of Zeus.

It has been supposed that the cult at Syracuse was descended from the cult at Olympia
(R. Koldewey—O. Puchstein *Die griechischen Tempel in Unteritalien und Sicilien*
Berlin 1899 i. 59). But this is far from clear. No doubt the rulers of Syracuse made
repeated dedications in the Olympian *Áltis* (Paus. 6. 12. 1 ff., 6. 19. 7, *Olympia* v. 363 ff.
no. 249, 675 f. no. 661). But is it likely that the filial cult dignified the god with a stone-
built temple more than a century before the parent followed suit? I would rather assume
(with E. Ciaceri *Culti e miti nella storia dell' antica Sicilia* Catania 1911 p. 138) that the
Syracusans brought the cult from their *metrópolis* Corinth. For just outside Corinth, on
the left of the road leading to Sikyon, Pausanias noted a temple which had been burnt
down. Some said that it belonged to Apollon and had been fired by Pyrrhos son of

Achilles; others, that it was the temple of Zeus Ὀλύμπιος and had been accidentally burnt (Paus. 2. 5. 5)—an ominous occurrence which deterred the Corinthians from joining the expedition of Agesilaos against Artaxerxes Mnemon in 396 B.C. (Paus. 3. 9. 2). Of the burnt temple, if I am not mistaken, sundry fragments still subsist. An archaic column-drum and architrave-block of limestone, built into the wall of a late edifice some 500ᵐ to the north of the 'Old Temple,' are attributed by W. Dörpfeld to an ancient Doric fane of even larger size. They resemble in dimensions (cp. W. M. Leake *Travels in the Morea* London 1830 iii. 247 f.) the corresponding members of the temple of Zeus at Olympia. Dörpfeld suggested that they came from the temple of Apollon mentioned by Paus. 2. 3. 6 (W. Dörpfeld in the *Ath. Mitth.* 1886 xi. 307 f.). But, thanks to the excavations of the American School, we now know that this temple of Apollon is none other than the extant 'Old Temple' (R. B. Richardson in the *Am. Journ. Arch.* 1897 i. 464, 1900 iv. 225 f., B. Powell 'The Temple of Apollo at Corinth' *ib.* 1905 ix. 51, 53). Accordingly I should conjecture that the archaic drum and architrave really came from the temple of Zeus Ὀλύμπιος on the left of the Sicyonian road, and that this was in fact the parent of the Syracusan Olympieion. Further excavation will some day test the accuracy of my surmise.

Whatever its precise pedigree, the Syracusan sanctuary was held in high esteem. Here were preserved the tribal lists of Syracuse (Plout. *v. Nic.* 14), and in the *formula* of the civic oath Zeus Ὀλύμπιος took precedence of all other deities except the venerable goddess of hearth and home (*Inscr. Gr. Sic. It.* no. 7 ii, 6 ff. in lettering later than the time of Hieron ii ὅρκιον βουλᾶς κα[ὶ ἀρχόντων (?)] | καὶ τῶν ἄλλων [πολιτᾶν·] | ὀμνύω τὰν Ἱστίαν τῶ[ν Συρακοσίων καὶ τὸν Ζῆνα] | τὸν Ὀλύμπιον καὶ τὰν [.............καὶ τὸν] | Ποσει-δ[ῶνα – – –]). Moreover, for some three hundred years the ἀμφίπολος or priest of Zeus Ὀλύμπιος was eponymous magistrate of the city (Diod. 16. 70 κατέστησε δὲ (*sc.* Timoleon in 343 B.C.) καὶ τὴν κατ᾽ ἐνιαυτὸν ἐντιμοτάτην ἀρχήν, ἣν ἀμφιπολίαν Διὸς Ὀλυμπίου οἱ Συρακούσιοι καλοῦσι. καὶ ἡρέθη πρῶτος ἀμφίπολος Διὸς Ὀλυμπίου Καλλιμένης, καὶ τὸ λοιπὸν διετέλεσαν οἱ Συρακούσιοι τοὺς ἐνιαυτοὺς ἐπιγράφοντες τούτοις τοῖς ἄρχουσι μέχρι τῶνδε τῶν ἱστοριῶν γραφομένων καὶ τῆς κατὰ τὴν πολιτείαν ἀλλαγῆς. τῶν γὰρ Ῥωμαίων μεταδόντων τοῖς Σικελιώταις τῆς πολιτείας (*sc.* in 44 B.C.) ἡ τῶν ἀμφιπόλων ἀρχὴ ἐταπεινώθη, διαμείνασα ἔτη πλείω τῶν τριακοσίων). Every year three candidates, chosen by vote from three clans (*ex tribus generibus*, on which see E. Ciaceri *op. cit.* p. 136 n. 1), cast lots for the office of priest—a rule of succession which was jealously guarded (Cic. *in Verr.* 2. 2. 126 f., cp. 2. 4. 137).

Round the temple grew up a settlement known as Πολίχνα or 'Small Town' (Thouk. 7. 4, Diod. 13. 7, 14. 72), which, never permanently fortified by the Syracusans, was frequently occupied by forces attacking their city.

Hippokrates tyrant of Gela, after vanquishing the Syracusans in the battle on the Heloros (493/2 B.C.), encamped in the sanctuary of Zeus. Having caught the priest and certain Syracusans trying to carry off various votive offerings of gold and in particular the golden *himátion* of Zeus, he taxed them with sacrilege, bade them depart to the city, and would not himself lay hands on the sacred objects (Diod. 10. 28). Others, however, state that the golden *himátion*, which weighed no less than 85 talents (Ail. *var. hist.* 1. 20), was dedicated by Gelon or Hieron after the battle of Himera in 480 B.C. and carried off by Dionysios i (405—367 B.C.), who left a woollen one in its stead with the caustic remark that in summer it would be lighter and in winter warmer wear (Cic. *de nat. deor.* 3. 83 (where *ad Peloponnesum* etc. is due to an obvious confusion), Val. Max. 1. 1. ext. 3, Lact. *div. inst.* 2. 4). The jest is attributed sometimes to Dionysios ii (367—343 B.C.) (Clem. Al. *protr.* 4. 52. 2 p. 40, 18 ff. Stählin, Arnob. *adv. nat.* 6. 21). If these tales are to be trusted, it would seem that Zeus Ὀλύμπιος at Syracuse had a golden *himátion* long before 438 B.C., the year in which Pheidias began his chryselephantine Zeus at Olympia (*supra* p. 757).

The Athenians, when attacking Syracuse in 415 B.C., landed near the Olympieion and encamped there (Thouk. 6. 64 f.). After the fight the Syracusans, though defeated, sent men to guard the Olympieion, lest its treasures should be plundered by the Athenians (Thouk. 6. 70). But the Athenians returned to Katane, and did not go to the sanctuary

Tyndaris[1].

(Thouk. 6. 71), or, if they did, disturbed none of the votive offerings and left the Syracusan priest in charge of them (Paus. 10. 28. 6). That same winter the Syracusans put a garrison in the Olympieion and erected a stockade on the sea-shore to prevent a possible landing (Thouk. 6. 75). In the following year (414 B.C.) a third part of the Syracusan cavalry was posted at Polichna to control the movements of the Athenians at Plemmyrion (Thouk. 7. 4).

Again, in 396 B.C. Himilkon, on his expedition against Dionysios i, took up his quarters in the temple and encamped his forces near by, at a distance of twelve stades from the city (Diod. 14. 62 f.). But Dionysios captured Polichna by storm and in turn pitched his camp at the sanctuary (Diod. 14. 72 and 74).

In 345 B.C. Hiketas tyrant of Leontinoi, in the course of his operations against Dionysios ii, fortified the Olympion with a palisade (Diod. 16. 68).

In 309 B.C. Hamilkar son of Geskon, again with a view to attacking Syracuse, seized τοὺς περὶ τὸ Ὀλύμπιον τόπους (Diod. 20. 29).

In 214 B.C. the Romans, who under M. Claudius Marcellus were then besieging Syracuse, likewise encamped *ad Olympium—Iovis id templum est—mille et quingentos passus ab urbe* (Liv. 24. 33).

The Olympieion was, in fact, a constant centre of military activity. Hence, when we read that Verres at Syracuse carried off *ex aede Iovis religiosissimum simulacrum Iovis Imperatoris, quem Graeci* Οὔριον *nominant, pulcherrime factum* (Cic. *in Verr.* 2. 4. 128, *supra* p. 708), I am inclined to think that the masterpiece in question was a votive figure in the temple of Zeus Ὀλύμπιος, whose position enabled him to control winds and wars alike, rather than a cult-statue erected in some hypothetical temple believed to have stood near the shore adjoining the *empórion* of Achradine (R. Koldewey—O. Puchstein *op. cit.* i. 57).

See further T. Fazellus *de rebus Siculis* Panormi 1558 p. 107 (dec. 1 lib. 4 cap. 1 'Templum hoc prostratum est hodie. Cuius iacentes plures, & erectæ quædam cernuntur columnæ, sed præterea nihil'), V. Mirabella *Dichiarazioni della pianta dell' antiche Siracuse*, etc. Napoli 1613 p. 72 f. ('Di questo Tempio appariscono oggi nõ picciole reliquie, sendovi anco in piede molte colonne scannellate di lavor dorico'), P. Cluverius *Sicilia antiqua*; etc. Lugduni Batavorum 1619 p. 179 ('Exstant hodiéq; eius fani...VII reliquæ columnæ prægrandes, cum aliis quadratorum saxorum fragmentis'), J. Houel *Voyage pittoresque des isles de Sicile, de Malte et de Lipari* Paris 1785 iii. 95 f. pl. 192 (view of remains visible in 1770 : 'Il y avoit alors plusieurs colonnes renversées par terre, avec les chapiteaux : deux seules colonnes étoient encore debout ; mais elles n'avoient plus de chapiteaux'), Serradifalco *op. cit.* iv. 153 f. pls. 28 (view) and 29 (plan, elevation), F. S. Cavallari—A. Holm *Topografia archeologica di Siracusa* Palermo 1883 pp. 24, 53 f., 104, 166 ff., 263 f., 283, 327, 379 f., R. Koldewey—O. Puchstein *op. cit.* i. 58—60, 66—68, ii pl. 8 (careful ground-plan), P. Orsi 'L'Olympieion di Siracusa' in the *Mon. d. Linc.* 1903 xiii. 369—392 with figs. 1—6 and pl. 17 (= my pl. xli), E. Ciaceri *op. cit.* p. 136 ff.

Another handsome temple of Zeus Ὀλύμπιος was founded by Hieron ii in the *Agorá* of Achradine (Diod. 16. 83, Cic. *in Verr.* 2. 4. 119). The Gallic and Illyrian spoils presented to Hieron by the people of Rome (Plout. *v. Marc.* 8) were hung in this temple, but were commandeered by the insurgents under Theodotos and Sosis in 214 B.C. (Liv. 24. 21). The central *kerkís* of the Syracusan theatre bears the name of Zeus Ὀλύμπιος (*Inscr. Gr. Sic. It.* no. 3, 5 Δ Ι Ο Σ Ο Λ Υ Μ Π Ι Ο Υ 'litteris cubitalibus,' cp. M. Bieber *Die Denkmäler zum Theaterwesen im Altertum* Berlin—Leipzig 1920 pp. 49 f., 86, 181) in allusion to the god of Hieron's new temple (F. S. Cavallari—A. Holm *op. cit.* p. 287, R. Koldewey—O. Puchstein *op. cit.* i. 57).

[1] Coppers of Tyndaris struck *c.* 254—210 B.C. or later have sometimes *obv.* a female head (Tyndaris) with *stepháne* or corn-ear (?) and veil, *rev.* ΤΥΝΔΑΡΙΤΑΝ Zeus, half-draped, standing to left, with a thunderbolt in his outstretched right hand and a transverse sceptre in his left (F. von Duhn in the *Zeitschr. f. Num.* 1876 iii. 30 no. 7, cp.

Naxos
Mount Drios[1].

Paros
Mount *Kounádos*[2].

Delos
Mount Kynthos[3].

Rasche *Lex. Num.* x. 527); or *obv.* head of Zeus, laureate, to right, *rev.* ΤΥΝΔΑΡΙΤΑΝ the Dioskouroi standing with, or without, their horses (F. von Duhn *loc. cit.* p. 30 no. 10, p. 30 f. no. 11, *Brit. Mus. Cat. Coins* Sicily p. 236 nos. 9 and 10); or *obv.* head of Zeus, laureate, to right, with star of eight rays behind it, *rev.* ΤΥΝΔΑΡΙΤΑΝ eagle to right, standing with open wings on a thunderbolt (F. von Duhn *loc. cit.* p. 31 no. 12, *Brit. Mus. Cat. Coins* Sicily p. 236 no. 11). See further Imhoof-Blumer *Monn. gr.* p. 33 f., G. F. Hill *Coins of Ancient Sicily* London 1903 p. 201 f., Head *Hist. num.*[2] p. 190. These coins imply the cult, not only of Tyndaris (Helene) and the Tyndaridai (Kastor and Polydeukes), but also of Zeus to whom the children of Tyndareos were early affiliated (*supra* i. 279 f., 780).

Among the ruins of Tyndaris (for which see Serradifalco *op. cit.* v. 48 ff. pls. 29—35) was found a colossal statue of Zeus, finely carved in Greek marble. It is now in the *Cortile Grande* of the Museo Nazionale at Palermo. The head, right arm, left leg, and lower part of right leg were restored by the local sculptor Villareale. But enough of the original remains to show that Zeus stood erect, his right arm raised to hold a long spear or sceptre, his left wholly enveloped in the *himátion* that covered him from the waist downwards. W. Abeken 'Giove Imperatore ossia Urio' in the *Ann. d.' Inst.* 1839 xi. 62—72 pl. A, 1—3 justly compared the figures of Zeus Στρατηγός on a coin of Amastris (*supra* p. 707 fig. 639) and of Zeus Οὔριος on a coin of Syracuse (*supra* p. 708 fig. 643)— a comparison accepted by Overbeck *Gr. Kunstmyth.* Zeus pp. 130—132 no. 25 fig. 12, who ranges the statue from Tyndaris with another colossal statue in the Louvre (Clarac *Mus. de Sculpt.* iii. 42 pl. 311 fig. 683) as forming the first group of his 'Vierte ·Classe.' Probably the inhabitants of Tyndaris had dedicated to Zeus a copy of the Syracusan masterpiece carried off by Verres (*supra* pp. 708, 917 n. o).

The temple of the god is said to have stood on a steep height to the west of the town, which in 1558 A.D. was still known as the Mount of Jove (T. Fazellus *de rebus Siculis* Panormi 1558 p. 205 (dec. 1 lib. 9 cap. 7) 'Extra vrbem occidentem versus, in colle vicino, & vndiq; præciso, qui ab accolis adhuc hodie mons Iouis appellatur, templi Iouis mirabiles cernuntur ruinæ').

[1] Zeus Μηλώσιος (*supra* i. 164 f., 520 n. 2). F. Solmsen in *Glotta* 1909 i. 80 connects Zeus Μηλώσιος_with *μηλώτης, cp. Hesych. *s.vv.* μηλατάν· τὸν ποιμένα. Βοιωτοί and μηλόται· ποιμένες (on which glosses see M. Schmidt *ad locc.*). Different is Zeus Μήλιος on an imperial copper of Nikaia in Bithynia (P. Piovene *I Cesari in metallo mezzano e piccolo raccolti nel Museo Farnese* Parma 1724 ix. 238 pl. 8, 21, Mionnet *Descr. de méd. ant.* Suppl. v. 84 no. 427 (in the Farnese collection) *obv.* ....ΜΙΤΙΑΝΟC head of Domitian, laureate, with countermark of an animal running; *rev.* ΖΕΥΣ ΜΗΛΙΟΣ Zeus seated, holding thunderbolt and sceptrĕ, Waddington—Babelon—Reinach *Monn. gr. d'As. Min.* i. 406 n. 2). O. Jessen in Pauly—Wissowa *Real-Enc.* ii. 1203 cp. Zeus Ἄρνειος (Schöll—Studemund *anecd.* i. 264 Ἐπίθετα Διός no. (1) ἀρνείου, 266 Ἐπίθετα Διός no. (15) ἀρνείου).

[2] *Supra* p. 875 n. 1 no. (5).

[3] Mt Kynthos in the centre of Delos is a granitic cone, which rises to a height of 112·60m (*Délos* i pl. 1. View from the west *ib.* iv. 1 fig. 1). Strab. 485 describes it as ὄρος ὑψηλὸν...καὶ τραχύ, where G. Kramer alters ὑψηλόν, 'high,' into ψιλόν, 'bare.' It is true that the granite and gneiss, of which the mountain is composed (geological detail in *Délos* iv. 1), do not afford the earth required by tree-roots. But, for all that, ὑψηλόν is correct: Kynthos, partly because of its dominating position, partly because of its proximity

to the sea, looks more of a mountain than it really is (*Délos* iv. 1. 196 f.). On the summit is a small plateau, which commands a magnificent view of the Kyklades. When I visited the spot in 1901, it was carpeted with crimson anemones and surrounded by stretches of azure sea.

Here in antiquity was the precinct of Zeus Κύνθιος and Athena Κυνθία (L. Bürchner in Pauly—Wissowa *Real-Enc.* iv. 2473) first excavated by Lebègue in 1873 (J. A. Lebègue *Recherches sur Délos* Paris 1876 pp. 127—172 with plan on p. 127 (=my fig. 828) and list of inscriptions from the sanctuary). Three separate roads (A, B, C), probably processional paths bordered with *stêlai* and statues, led up to the western side of the precinct, where was a gateway (E). Within was a rocky elevation (F) with cuttings for votive slabs etc. (G). The plateau was enclosed by a precinct-wall (I), much of which remains standing on the north, west, and east. At its south-eastern corner was a small temple (S) of late date.

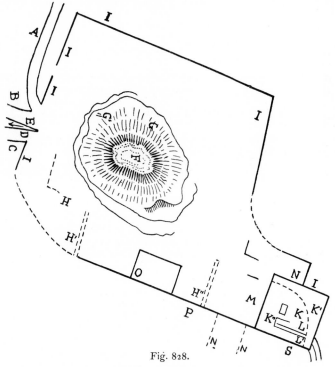

Fig. 828.

The fragments found point to a distyle *templum in antis* of Ionic or composite order with unfluted columns (0·42^m in diameter). At a height of 2^m above the ruins of this temple there was a sacred cistern, into which the water from the roof drained by means of a double conduit (L, L′). The cistern had a mosaic flooring, of which the greater part (K) survives, though a strip to the east (K′) has been destroyed by the collapse of the terrace-wall. The mosaic consists of small white stones and fragments of brick set in cement. An inscription in bluish *tesserae* on a white ground with an oblong framework of bluish stones (K″) records the dedication of the cistern in Roman times (J. A. Lebègue *op. cit.* p. 139 ff. no. 1 Διὶ Κυνθίῳ καὶ Ἀθηνᾷ Κυνθίᾳ | Ἀπολλωνίδης Θεογείτονος | Λαοδικεύς, ὑπὲρ ἑαυτοῦ καὶ | τῶν ἑταίρων, τὸ κατάκλυσ|τον ('cistern'), ἐπὶ ἱερέως Ἀριστομάχου, | ζακορεύοντος Νικηφόρου (after 88/7 B.C.), | ἐπὶ δὲ ἐπιμελητοῦ Κοΐντου Ἀζη(νιέως). My fig. 829 is from photograph no. 1302 in the collection of the Society for the Promotion of Hellenic Studies). Adjoining the cistern was a platform (N), where ashes and fragments of bone, the *débris* of sacrifices,

were buried. South of the rocky summit was an enclosure (O) walled in on the north by
blocks of schist, on the other sides by architectural fragments, *stêlai*, and broken statues.
It contained some thirty urns filled with ashes and animal bones. The urns measured
0·60ᵐ to 0·70ᵐ in height, having rounded handles and a foot, not a pointed base. Miscel-.
laneous finds included a small terra-cotta palmette from the pediment of an *aedicula*, a

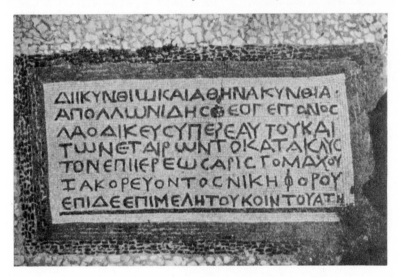

Fig. 829.

colossal hand in Pentelic marble apparently holding a thunderbolt (Zeus Κύνθιος?), a small
head in Parian marble (Apollon?), the lower half of a sun-dial, several altars large and
small (two decorated with *bucrania* and inscriptions were found at some distance from the
temple : J. A. Lebègue *op. cit.* pp. 137, 166 f. nos. 21, 22), etc.

The history of the sanctuary has been well worked out from inscriptions by P. Roussel
Délos Colonie athénienne Paris 1916 pp. 223—228, 290 f., 335, 434 f., whose results are
here summarised (with a few additions in square brackets).

Zeus and Athena, though their association on *akropóleis* etc. is old (Gruppe *Gr. Myth.
Rel.* p. 1217 f.), were not the original occupants of the summit. [In 'Minoan' times it
was probably tenanted by the sky-father (Kronos) and the earth-mother (Rhea), the cave-
temple beneath it (J. A. Lebègue *op. cit.* p. 49 ff. pls. 1, 2) being a Delian parallel to the
sacred caves of Mt Dikte and Mt Ide. The cult of Kronos, however, has left no trace,
unless we can claim as such a broken sherd bearing the letters **KPO**, which was found
buried in charcoal under a limestone slab outside the south-west angle of the cave-temple
(J. A. Lebègue *op. cit.* p. 65 f.). Rhea presumably had lions ; and in this connexion it
should be noted, not only that the late marble statue of a youthful god (Apollon?) erected
on the ancient granite libation-table (?) of the cave-temple had a tree-support covered with
a lion-skin (J. A. Lebègue *op. cit.* pp. 60, 63 ff.), but also that a whole row of lions in
Naxian marble, comparable with the lions of Branchidai (*Brit. Mus. Cat. Sculpture* i. 22 f.
nos. 17 and 18 : no. 17 has on its back a βουστροφηδόν dedication to Apollon in lettering
of early *s.* vi B.C. (Roehl *Inscr. Gr. ant.* no. 483, Roberts *Gr. Epigr.* i. 161 f. no. 133,
Michel *Recueil d'Inscr. gr.* no. 1206, Dittenberger *Syll. inscr. Gr.*³ no. 3 *a*)) and Thera
(F. Hiller von Gaertringen in the *Jahrb. d. kais. deutsch. arch. Inst.* 1899 xiv Arch. Anz.
p. 183 f., *id. Die Insel Thera* Berlin 1904 iii. 28 figs. 16 and 17, 57 regards as a gift to
Apollon the marble lion, bearing a mutilated inscription of *s.* vii B.C. (*Inscr. Gr. ins.* iii
Suppl. no. 1380), which stood on a terrace overlooking the *Agorá* and was later copied

by Artemidoros (*infra*)), adorned a terrace west of the *Límne Trochoeidés* (P. Leroux in the *Comptes rendus de l'Acad. des inscr. et belles-lettres* 1907 pp. 348—353, *ib.* 1908 plan opposite to p. 162). Apparently Rhea had, here as elsewhere (Clem. Al. *protr.* 4. 47. 4 p. 36, 6 ff. Stählin μηδ' (*sc.* ἀμφιβάλλετε) εἰ τὰ ἐν Πατάροις τῆς Λυκίας ἀγάλματα Διὸς καὶ Ἀπόλλωνος Φειδίας πάλιν ἐκεῖνος [τὰ ἀγάλματα] καθάπερ τοὺς λέοντας τοὺς σὺν αὐτοῖς ἀνακειμένους εἴργασται· εἰ δέ, ὥς φασί τινες, Βρυάξιος ἡ τέχνη, οὐ διαφέρομαι· κ.τ.λ., *Inscr. Gr. ins.* iii Suppl. no. 1346 the rock-cut relief of a lion inscribed in *s.* iii B.C. (*supra* i. 117 n. 1) αʹἈπόλλωνι | Στεφανηφόρωι, *b* [τ]εὖξ[ε] λέοντα θεοῖς κεχαρισμένον Ἀρτεμίδωρος | ἐν σεμνῶι τεμένει μνημόσυνον πόλεως. Cp. a statue of Apollon, seated on a tripod over a lion, now in the Villa Albani (S. Raffei *Ricerche sopra un Apolline della Villa Albani* Roma 1821, Clarac *Mus. de Sculpt.* iii. 216 f. pl. 486 B fig. 937 A (wrongly numbered 737 A) = Reinach *Rép. Stat.* i. 249 no. 6, Overbeck *Gr. Kunstmyth.* Apollon p. 231 ff. no. 3 Atlas pl. 23, 30, Müller—Wieseler—Wernicke *Ant. Denkm.* ii. 3. 309 pl. 25, 14, W. Helbig *Führer durch die öffentlichen Sammlungen klassischer Altertümer in Rom*[3] Leipzig 1913 ii. 409 f. no. 1848)), passed on her lions to Apollon.]

Τὸ ἱερὸν τοῦ Διὸς τοῦ Κυνθίου (*e.g. Inscr. Gr. Deli* ii no. 161, *A* 77 f.) or more briefly τὸ Κύνθιον (*e.g. ib.* ii no. 199, *A* 90) does not appear in the extant documents till the very end of *s.* iv B.C. (*ib.* ii no. 145, 1 f., no. 154, *A* 45 f.). Early in *s.* iii (*c.* 281—269 B.C.) the precinct was to a large extent reconstructed and thenceforward contained two small οἶκοι or 'sacred buildings' (F. Dürrbach in the *Bull. Corr. Hell.* 1911 xxxv. 250), on a platform bounded by a strong retaining-wall (*Inscr. Gr. Deli* ii no. 165, 3), together with a ἑστιατόριον or 'banqueting-hall' (*ib.* ii no. 163, *A* 34, cp. T. Homolle in the *Bull. Corr. Hell.* 1890 xiv. 507). The accounts of the ἱεροποιοί for *s.* iii and *s.* ii record various sums spent on repairs to these buildings (*Inscr. Gr. Deli* iii no. 440, *A* 84 f.), but no expenditure on the cult, which seems to have languished (but see *ib.* iii no. 372, *B* 10). According to an inventory of 157/6 B.C., one of the οἶκοι contained a cult-statuette of bronze, eighteen inches high, on a marble base, a bronze incense-burner for processional use, a *kratér* of Corinthian bronze, a marble mortar, twelve wooden couches with small tables beneath them, and sundry portraits and votive paintings (P. Roussel *op. cit.* p. 225 n. 3); the other οἶκος contained a second dozen of wooden couches with small draw-tables beneath them, an old bronze brazier with no bottom to it, two tridents, one of which lacked a tooth, and old iron tongs (*id. ib.* p. 225 n. 4). Despite this poverty, the priest of Zeus Κύνθιος and Athena Κυνθία held the third place in the Delian hierarchy (P. Roussel in the *Bull. Corr. Hell.* 1908 xxxii. 438 f. no. 64, 11 f. and *op. cit.* p. 202).

Better times began in 166 B.C., when Delos became an Athenian colony (P. Roussel *op. cit.* p. 1 ff.). An inventory of 147/6 B.C. records a pair of bronze figures, about a foot in height, representing Zeus and Athena, a table of bronze, another of marble, a tripod, lamps, linen hangings, but no couches; also a gold ring on a ribband, and a silver incense-burner (*id. ib.* pp. 225 nn. 7—9, 401). Other inscriptions, ranging from 158/7 to the middle of *s.* i B.C. or later, show that the *personnel* of the cult consisted in a ἱερεύς, a ζάκορος, and a κλειδοῦχος (lists in P. Roussel *op. cit.* p. 226 [Note the preponderance of well-omened names]). Of these the ἱερεύς held office for a year. So, probably, did the κλειδοῦχος. But the ζάκορος [Boisacq *Dict. étym. de la Langue Gr.* p. 306 suggests that ζάκορος is for *δακορος < *δηι-κορος, cp. νεωκόρος, σηκοκόρος (κορέω, 'I sweep') and δάπεδον : ζάπεδον] could have his tenure prolonged.

So far the cult seems to have had no regular temple. But *c.* 120 B.C. Charmikos, a native of the Attic deme Kikynna, who was priest of Zeus Κύνθιος and Athena Κυνθία, dedicated a *xóanon* (J. A. Lebègue *op. cit.* p. 160 no. 14); and in all probability was the same native of Kikynna who dedicated the *naós* to Zeus Κύνθιος (*id. ib.* p. 161 no. 15), *i.e.* the small Ionic or composite temple noted above. This attracted the attention, not only of Athenians (P. Roussel in the *Bull. Corr. Hell.* 1908 xxxii. 422 f. no. 21, 429 no. 38), but of foreigners—witness a statue of Ptolemy x Soter ii here set up by Areios a notable of Alexandreia (J. A. Lebègue *op. cit.* p. 156 f. no. 11, Michel *Recueil d'Inscr. gr.* no. 1162, Dittenberger *Orient. Gr. inscr. sel.* no. 171) and an altar presented by Philostratos a wealthy banker of Askalon (J. A. Lebègue *op. cit.* p. 166 f. no. 21,

Imbros
  Imbros[1].

Skiathos
  Skiathos[2].

Lesbos
  Mytilene[3].

Chios
  Mount Pelinnaion[4].

Rhodes
  Mount Atabyrion[5].

P. Roussel *op. cit.* p. 227 n. 6). Orientals would naturally regard the mountain-top as one of their own high places. Hence Zeus Κύνθιος came to be associated with the Egyptian divinities (A. Hauvette-Besnault in the *Bull. Corr. Hell.* 1882 vi. 328 f. no. 23 a small column (1ᵐ high) inscribed Διί Κυνθίωι, | Σαράπιδι, Ἴσιδι, | κατὰ πρόσταγμα, | Νεοπτό-λεμος | Φιλωνίδου. | ἐπὶ ἱερέως Δικαίου | τοῦ Δικαίου Ἰωνίδου, | κλειδουχοῦντος | Εὐκράτου Διονυσίου τοῦ Σεύθου, | ζακορεύοντος | Ἀπολλωνίου | τοῦ Δικαίου), and his priest figures among the worshippers of the Syrian Aphrodite Ἀγνή (P. Roussel *op. cit.* pp. 227 n. 8, 266 f., 416 ff. no. 21, *A* col. i, 28). The sanctuary on Mt Kynthos, seemingly untouched by the catastrophe of 88 B.C. (Strab. 486, Plout. *v. Sull.* 11, Appian. *Mithr.* 28, Paus. 3. 23. 3 f.), continued to receive gifts, now a cistern-mosaic (*supra*), now a table etc. (J. A. Lebègue *op. cit.* p. 141 ff. no. 2, P. Roussel *op. cit.* p. 226 n. 14). Finally, about the middle of *s.* i B.C. a priest published on a marble *stéle* the rules of ceremonial purity to be observed by all visitors entering the precinct (J. A. Lebègue *op. cit.* p. 158 f. no. 12, J. v. Prott and L. Ziehen *Leges Graecorum sacrae* Lipsiae 1906 ii. 259 no. 91, P. Roussel in the *Mélanges Holleaux* Paris 1913 p. 276 f. no. 4 and *op. cit.* p. 228 n. 4. Lines 11 ff. run : ἰέναι εἰς τὸ ἱε|[ρὸν τοῦ] Διὸς τοῦ Κυνθίου | [καὶ τῆ]ς Ἀθηνᾶς τῆς Κυνθί|[ας, χερ]σὶν καὶ ψυχῇ καθα|[ρᾷ, ἔ]χοντας ἐσθῆτα λευ|[κήν, ἀνυ]ποδέτους, ἀγνεύοντα[ς] | [ἀπὸ γυν]αικὸς καὶ κρέως· | [μηδὲ . . . . .] εἰσ[φ]έρει[ν] | κ.τ.λ.).

[The Delian cult had spread to Paros as early as *s.* vi B.C. O. Rubensohn in the *Ath. Mitth.* 1901 xxvi. 216 reported that on a hill-top (200ᵐ high) called *Vigla* or *Kastro* in the north-west of that island, the nearest point from which the inhabitants of the town Paros could get a glimpse of Delos, he had discovered a sanctuary with votive inscriptions including an archaic *stéle* lettered ΑΘΗΝΑΙΗΚΥΝΘΙΗ (*Inscr. Gr. ins.* v. 1 no. 210, cp. *ib.* nos. 211, 214). This makes it certain that Athena's connexion with Mt Kynthion was centuries older than the Athenian protectorate. Not impossibly in Delos as at Athens Athena was the legitimate successor of the old ' Minoan' goddess.]

[1] Zeus Ὕψιστος (*supra* p. 878 n. 0 no. (8)).
[2] Zeus Ὕψιστος (*supra* p. 878 n. 0 no. (6)).
[3] Zeus Ἀκραῖος (*supra* p. 873 n. 0 no. (10)).
[4] Mt Pelinnaion (*Hagios Elias*), the highest point (1260ᵐ) of Chios (Strab. 645, Dionys. *per.* 535), derived its name from the leaden grey (πελιτνός, πελιδνός) colour of its rock (L. Bürchner in Pauly—Wissowa *Real-Enc.* iii. 2288, cp. 2290). On it was a cult of Zeus Πελινναῖος (Hesych. *s.v.* Πελινναῖος· ὁ Ζεὺς ἐν Χίῳ), whose Christian supersessor was Saint Elias (*supra* i. 177 ff.).
[5] Mt Atabyrion (*Atayros*), the highest mountain in Rhodes, was crowned with a sanctuary of Zeus Ἀταβύριος (Pind. *Ol.* 7. 87 f. ἀλλ', ὦ Ζεῦ πάτερ, νώτοισιν Ἀταβυρίου | μεδέων, κ.τ.λ. with schol. vet. *ad loc.* ἐπάνω γὰρ τοῦ ὄρους ἵδρυται ὁ Ζεύς (Ἀταβύριον ἄρος ὑψηλότατον ῾Ρόδου οὗ ἄνωθεν ἵδρυται Ζεύς cod. C.), Strab. 655 εἶθ' ὁ Ἀτάβυρις (τάβυρις cod. F.), ὄρος τῶν ἐνταῦθα ὑψηλότατον, ἱερὸν Διὸς Ἀταβυρίου, Lact. *div. inst.* 1. 22 cited *supra* p. 588 n. 1, Steph. Byz. *s.v.* Ἀτάβυρον· ὄρος ῾Ρόδου. ῾Ριανὸς ἕκτῳ Μεσσηνιακῶν (= Herodian. περὶ καθολικῆς προσῳδίας 13 (i. 387, 8 f. Lentz)). τὸ ἐθνικὸν Ἀταβύριος, ἐξ οὗ καὶ Ἀταβύριος Ζεύς, *id. s.v.* Κρητηνία· τόπος ῾Ρόδου, ἐν ᾧ ᾤκουν οἱ περὶ Ἀλθαιμένην, ὃς

χρησθεὶς ὅτι τὸν πατέρα ἀποκτενεῖ ἔφυγε, καὶ νυκτὶ πλοίῳ συναντᾷ ἐν ᾽Ρόδῳ, καὶ ὡς λῃστὰς
νομίσας ἀναιρεῖ τὸν πατέρα. εἰσὶ δὲ ὑπὲρ αὐτοῦ τὰ ᾽Αταβύρια ὄρη, ἀφ᾽ ὧν Ζεὺς ᾽Αταβύριος).

The mountain, as modern travellers report, is a mass of schistose limestone, well
wooded below and dotted with a few large evergreen oaks and pines above. The sanctuary of Zeus is situated on a rounded crest about a hundred paces south-east of the
actual summit. Here at a point 4070 ft above the sea is a walled precinct 120 ft in
length, and within it a pile of ruins lying 3 to 4 ft deep. Bluish blocks quarried on the
mountain, the largest of them 5 ft long, prove the former existence of a Hellenic building on the site. But no columns have survived, and only a single architrave-block with a
simple moulding. The Greek temple was long since reconstructed as a monastery. But
this in turn fell into decay, and nowadays even the little chapel of Hagios Ioannes, which
stands in the middle of the ruins, has lost its roof. North-east of the precinct, somewhat
lower down, in a hollow are the remains of other ancient structures, including a large
vaulted cistern. L. Ross, followed by C. Torr, thought that here may have been a
temple of Athena; but the argument which he drew from Polyb. 9. 27. 7 (cited *supra*
p. 910 n. 1) is insecure. See further W. J. Hamilton *Researches in Asia Minor, Pontus,
and Armenia* London 1842 ii. 61 ff. (ascent from *Embona* Jan. 31, 1837), L. Ross
Reisen auf den griechischen Inseln des ägäischen Meeres Stuttgart—Tübingen 1845 iii.
105 ff. (ascent from *Embona* Sept. 27, 1843), C. Torr *Rhodes in Ancient Times* Cambridge 1885 pp. 1, 75, H. F. Tozer *The Islands of the Aegean* Oxford 1890 p. 220 f.

The local myth is told most fully by Apollod. 3. 2. 1 f. Katreus, son of Minos, was
fated to be killed by one of his own sons. Althaimenes, son of Katreus, to avoid killing
his father, fled from Crete to Rhodes with his sister Apemosyne. He put in at a certain
place which he named Kretenia (κρητινίαν cod. R., followed by R. Hercher and
R. Wagner. κρατινίαν codd. plerique. C. G. Heyne cj. Κρητηνίαν, cp. Steph. Byz. *loc.
cit.*). On climbing Mt Atabyrion he got a view of Crete, and, in memory of his ancestral
deities, built there an altar of Zeus ᾽Αταβύριος. Soon afterwards Hermes fell in love with
Apemosyne and, when he could not catch her (for she was fleet of foot), strewed freshly-
flayed hides in the road. On these she slipped, and thus was violated by her pursuer.
Althaimenes, hearing of her fall, believed the tale about Hermes to be a mere excuse
and killed his sister by leaping upon her. Later, Katreus, anxious to leave his kingdom
to Althaimenes, came to Rhodes and was mistaken for a pirate by the ox-herds, who
chased and pelted him. Katreus told them the truth, but could not gain a hearing
because the dogs were barking. So Althaimenes all unwittingly speared him. On learn-
ing what he had done he uttered a prayer, and in answer thereto was engulfed in a
chasm. Diod. 5. 59, however, probably borrowing his account not from Zenon of
Rhodes (*frag.* 2 (*Frag. hist. Gr.* iii. 177 f. Müller)) but from a later source dependent on
Polyzalos etc. (Gruppe *Myth. Lit.* 1921 p. 380), says that Althaimenes wandered in the
desert till he died of grief and was afterwards, in obedience to an oracle, honoured as a
hero by the Rhodians.

This myth deserves analysis. There is in it, to begin with, a *substratum* of historic, or
at least prehistoric, fact—the intimate relations between 'Minoan' Crete and Rhodes
(H. van Gelder *Geschichte der alten Rhodier* Haag 1900 p. 30 ff., D. Mackenzie in the
Ann. Brit. Sch. Ath. 1905-1906 xii. 222, C. Blinkenberg in *Hermes* 1913 xlviii. 246 f.,
Gruppe *Myth. Lit.* 1921 p. 380) : Minos himself was believed to have dedicated a silver
cup to Athena Πολιάς and Zeus Πολιεύς at Lindos (C. Blinkenberg *Die lindische Tempel-
chronik* Bonn 1915 p. 8 ff. B, 18 ff. Μίνως ἀργύρεον ποτήριον, ἐφ᾽ οὗ ἐπεγέγρα|πτο·
"Μίνως ᾽Αθάναι Πολιάδι καὶ Διὶ Πολιεῖ," ὥς φατι | Ξεναγόρας ἐν τᾶι Α τᾶς χρονικᾶς
συντάξιος, | Γόργων ἐν τᾶι Α τᾶν περὶ ᾽Ρόδου, Γοργοσθένης | ἐν τᾶι ἐπιστολᾶι, ᾽Ιερόβουλος ἐν
τᾶι ἐπιστολᾶι). There is also an element of folk-tale, the story of Katreus fated to be slain
by his own son recalling the *motif* of Odysseus and Telegonos (A. C. Pearson *The Fragments of Sophocles* Cambridge 1917 ii. 105 ff.) or of Laïos and Oidipous (C. Robert
Oidipus Berlin 1915 i. 66 ff.). Lastly there are definite points of aetiology. Apemosyne,
a woman of the royal house, who flees at full speed, falls on the fresh hides, and is then

brutally dispatched by her kinsman, presupposes—I think—a bygone custom or rite (? in the Rhodian month Agrianios) resembling that of the Minyan Oleiai and Psoloeis at the Agrionia of Orchomenos in Boiotia (Plout. *quaestt. Gr.* 38 with Frazer *Golden Bough*[3] : The Dying God p. 163 f.). Her name implies that 'freedom from trouble' was thought to depend on her sacrifice. And the statement that she slipped on freshly-flayed hides suggests that the human victim was wrapped in the skin of the sacred animal (*supra* i. 67 n. 3, cp. *Journ. Hell. Stud.* 1894 xiv. 155 ff.).

Small bronze bulls, which probably served as offerings to Zeus, are sometimes found on Mt Atabyrion (*supra* i. 643 fig. 502). And we have already conjectured that Zeus had here inherited the bronze bulls of the Hittite Tešub (*supra* i. 642 f., ii. 910 n. 1). The common tradition was that certain bronze kine on Mt Atabyrion bellowed when any evil was about to befall Rhodes (schol. vet. Pind. *Ol.* 7. 159 f. εἰσὶ δὲ χαλκαῖ βόες ἐν αὐτῷ, αἵτινες ὅταν μέλλῃ ἄτοπόν τι γενέσθαι, μυκῶνται, 160 c εἰσὶ δὲ καὶ βόες χαλκοῖ ἐπὶ τῷ ὄρει τῆς 'Ρόδου, οἳ ὅταν μέλλῃ τι τῇ πόλει γίνεσθαι κακὸν μυκῶνται, Tzetz. *chil.* 4. 390—393 (=4. 704—706) 'Ρόδιόν ἐστιν ὄρος, | τὴν κλῆσιν 'Αταβύριον, χαλκᾶς πρὶν ἔχον βόας, | αἳ μυκηθμὸν ἐξέπεμπον χωρούσης 'Ρόδῳ βλάβης · | Πίνδαρος (? *Ol.* 7. 87 f.) καὶ Καλλίμαχος (*frag.* 413 Schneider) γράφει τὴν ἱστορίαν). But one authority spoke of a single bull, that of Zeus, as uttering a human voice (Isigonos of Nikaia *frag.* 4 (*Frag. hist. Gr.* iv. 435) *ap.* Kyrill. Al. *c. Iulian.* 3 p. 88 c Aubert (lxxvi. 636 A Migne) καὶ μὴν καὶ 'Ισίγονος ὁ Κιττιεὺς (C. Müller cj. ὁ Νικαιεὺς) ἐν 'Ρόδῳ τῇ νήσῳ τὸν τοῦ Διὸς ταῦρον φησὶν οὐκ ἀμοιρῆσαι λόγου τοῦ καθ' ἡμᾶς. Both versions bear a sinister resemblance to the accounts of the bronze bull made by Perillos for Phalaris at Akragas (*supra* i. 643 f., ii. 910 n. 1) and may likewise be taken to cover a reminiscence of human sacrifice. If the early Cretans tolerated, for ritual purposes, the enclosing of their queen in a wooden cow (*supra* i. 523), the early Rhodians would hardly shrink from burning a *pharmakós* in a bronze bull. Sir J. G. Frazer *Apollodorus* London 1921 i. 307 concludes : 'Atabyrian Zeus would seem to have been worshipped in the form of a bull.' That may have been so, no doubt, in the remote past. But in classical times he was almost certainly anthropomorphic. Rhodian coppers of *c.* 304–189 B.C. or later have *obv.* head of Zeus, wearing bay-wreath, to right ; *rev.* PO rose, often surmounted by radiate solar disk (*Brit. Mus. Cat. Coins* Caria, etc. p. 250 pl. 39, 15 and 16, *Hunter Cat. Coins* ii. 441 no. 38, *Head Hist. num.*[2] p. 640. I have two specimens of the sort in my collection) : the head is presumably that of Zeus 'Αταβύριος. Cp. also *supra* i. 132.

It was not, of course, to be expected that in busy Hellenistic times the good folk of Rhodes would toil up a steep mountain 4000 ft high in order to pay their respects to Zeus. Accordingly we find a chapel of ease built on a more manageable hill adjoining the city-wall (Appian. *Mithr.* 26 αὐτομόλων δ' αὐτῷ (*sc.* Mithridates vi Eupator, in 88 B.C.) λόφον ὑποδεξάντων ἐπιβατόν, ᾗ 'Αταβύριον Διὸς ἱερὸν ἦν, καὶ κολοβὸν τειχίον ἐπ' αὐτοῦ, τὴν στρατιὰν ἐς τὰς ναῦς νυκτὸς ἐπέβησε, καὶ ἑτέροις ἀναδοὺς κλίμακας ἐκέλευσε χωρεῖν ἑκατέρους μετὰ σιωπῆς μέχρι τινὲς αὐτοῖς πυρσεύσειαν ἐκ τοῦ 'Αταβυρίου· κ.τ.λ.). A relic of this urban cult is a block of bluish marble formerly 'built into the wall of a field to the south-west of St. Stephen's Hill, near Rhodes' and now in the British Museum (Sir C. T. Newton in *The Collection of Ancient Greek Inscriptions in the British Museum* Oxford 1883 ii. 121 no. 346 = *Inscr. Gr. ins.* i no. 31 [δόγματι τοῦ κοινοῦ] | [τῶν Διοσαταβυρι]αστᾶν τῶν τᾶς πό|λ[ι]ος δούλων, Εὐλί[μ]ενος γραμματεὺς | [δα]μόσιος ἱερατεύ[σας] Διὸς 'Αταβυρίου | [ὑπὲρ τ]ῶν κυρίων 'Ρο[δίων ἀν]έθηκε Διὶ 'Α[ταβυρίῳ] τού(ς) βοῦς | [χαριστήρ]ιον ⦶. W. Dittenberger *De sacris Rhodiorum* commentatio ii Halis Saxonum 1887 p. viii f. restored the opening lines as above, and proposed for the closing lines [ἀν]έθηκε Διὶ 'Α[ταβυρίῳ] τοῦ βουσ[τάθμου τὸ τειχ]ίον, which is ingenious but less probable. Hence we learn that Eulimenos, a state slave who had been priest of Zeus 'Αταβύριος, dedicated to the god on behalf of the citizens the customary kine, *i.e.* small votive bulls of bronze. He describes himself as commissioned to do so by the public servants, who composed an association of Διοσαταβυριασταί.

Of such associations or religious circles there were at least two in the island. One, in

Crete
Mount Aigaion[1].

the town of Rhodes, founded by a certain Philon, was devoted to Zeus Ἀταβύριος and to the Agathos Daimon (*infra* Append. M) in common (*Inscr. Gr. ins.* i no. 161, 5 f. = H. van Gelder in Collitz—Bechtel *Gr. Dial.-Inschr.* iii. 1. 478 f. no. 3842, 5 f. ('In oppido hodierno, prope hospitium equitum D. Ioannis in basi oblonga marmoris caerulei') καὶ ὑπὸ [Διοσ]αταβυριαστᾶν Ἀγαθοδαιμονιαστᾶν Φιλ(ω)νείων κοινοῦ | θαλλῶι στεφάνωι). The other, at Lindos, established by a man named Euphranor and later headed by one Athenaios of Knidos, worshipped Dionysos, Athena, and Zeus Ἀταβύριος (Sir C. T. Newton *loc. cit.* ii. 135 f. no. 358, 2 ff., 12 ff. = *Inscr. Gr. ins.* i no. 937, 2 ff., 12 ff. = H. van Gelder *loc. cit.* iii. 1. 568 f. no. 4239, 2 ff. ('Found at Mallona near Lindos in 1862... On a circular altar or pedestal of white marble, which has been hollowed out, probably to form a mortar with a hole at the bottom') [– – – – τ]ε[ιμα]θέντα ὑπὸ | τοῦ κοινοῦ τοῦ Διονυσιαστᾶν Ἀθαναϊσστᾶν Διοσ|αταβυριαστᾶν Εὐφρανορ[ίω]ν τῶν σὺν Ἀθηναίῳ Κνιδίῳ | χρυσέῳ στεφάνῳ καὶ ἀνα-γορεύσεσιν ἴσς τὸν ἀεὶ χρόνον. | κ.τ.λ., 12 ff. καὶ τᾶς γυναικὸς αὐτοῦ Ἀρέτης μὲν τειμαθεί|σας ὑπὸ τοῦ κοινοῦ τ[οῦ Διον]υσιαστᾶν Ἀθαν[αϊ]στᾶν Διοσαταβυριαστᾶν | Εὐφρανορίων τῶν σ[ὺν Ἀθηναίῳ Κνιδίῳ καὶ ἀν]αθείσας τῷ κοινῷ (τῷ) | Ἀθανα[ϊστᾶν – – – – τῷ]ν ἀναλωμάτων [– –]). A mutilated inscription on a slab of blackish marble at Netteia (*Apollakia*) near Lindos, where it serves as a threshold in the church of Saint Georgios, contains ritual rules in lettering of *s.* ii B.C. and includes a reference to Zeus Ἀταβύριος (*Inscr. Gr. ins.* i no. 891, 7 [·····]θ[ε]ῖτ[α]ι χο[ρ]εύεται[ι καὶ Διὶ] Ἀτα[β]υρίω[ι – –]). See further F. Poland *Geschichte des griechischen Vereinswesens* Leipzig 1909 pp. 58 f., 181, 237.

The cult of the Rhodian Zeus even found its way to Skythia. At *Kermenchik* (Neapolis?) near *Symph eropol* three inscriptions have come to light recording dedications made *c. s.* i B.C.(?) by one Posideos to Zeus Ἀταβύριος (*Corp. inscr. Gr.* ii no. 2103 b = B. Latyschev *Inscriptiones antiquae Orae Septentrionalis Ponti Euxini Graecae et Latinae* Petropoli 1885 i. 216 no. 242 on a base of grey marble now in the Museum at Odessa Διὶ Ἀταβυρίωι Ποσίδεος Ποσιδέου | χαριστήριον), to Athena Λινδία (*ib.* i. 216 f. no. 243), and to Achilles 'Lord of the Island' (*sc.* Leuke) (*ib.* i. 217 no. 244). E. H. Minns *Scythians and Greeks* Cambridge 1913 pp. 463, 476, 479 treats Posideos, not as a Rhodian, but as an Olbiopolite living at Neapolis and trading with Rhodes. See also M. Rostovtzeff *Iranians & Greeks in South Russia* Oxford 1922 p. 163.

[1] Rhea, when about to bear her youngest son Zeus (Ζῆνα μέγαν, cp. *supra* p. 344 f.), was sent by her parents Ouranos and Gaia to Lyktos, and Gaia received the child to bring him up in Crete. So Rhea came by night first to Lyktos and hid the babe in a steep underground cave on the well-wooded Mt Aigaion (Hes. *theog.* 477 ff. πέμψαν δ' ἐς Λύκτον (γρ. δί (= δίκτον) in marg. cod. E.), Κρήτης ἐς πίονα δῆμον, | ὁππότ' ἄρ' ὁπλότατον παίδων τέξεσθαι ἔμελλε (so G. Kinkel for ἤμελλε τεκέσθαι), | Ζῆνα μέγαν· τὸν μέν οἱ ἐδέξατο Γαῖα πελώρη | Κρήτῃ ἐν εὐρείῃ τραφέμεν ἀτιταλλέμεναί τε. | ἔνθα μιν (so J. G. J. Hermann for μὲν codd., cp. *schol. ad loc.*) ἵκτο φέρουσα θοὴν διὰ νύκτα μέλαιναν | πρώτην ἐς Λύκτον (G. F. Schömann's cj. Δίκτην is mischievous)· κρύψεν δέ ἑ χερσὶ λαβοῦσα | ἄντρῳ ἐν ἠλιβάτῳ, ζαθέης ὑπὸ κεύθεσι γαίης, | Αἰγαίῳ (Salmasius cj. αἰγείῳ, Wilamowitz cj. Αἰγείῳ. But see G. M. Columba *Aigaion* (extr. from the *Memorie della R. Accademia di Archeologia, Lettere e Belle Arti* 1914 iii) Napoli 1914 p. 21 n. 3) ἐν ὄρει πεπυκασμένῳ ὑλήεντι).

Hesiod's connexion of the cave on Mt Aigaion with Lyktos makes it practically certain (*pace* W. Aly in *Philologus* 1912 lxxi. 461) that this was the Psychro Cave on Mt *Lasithi*, some 4½ hours from the ruins of Lyktos, with which it is linked by an ancient road still traceable (so K. J. Beloch in *Klio* 1911 xi. 435 and especially J. Toutain in the *Revue de l'histoire des religions* 1911 lxiv. 290 f., followed by Gruppe *Myth. Lit.* 1921 p. 377). It was partially explored by F. Halbherr and J. Hazzidakis in 1886 (F. Halbherr—P. Orsi 'Scoperte nell' antro di Psychro' in the *Museo Italiano di Antichità Classica* 1888 ii. 905—910 pl. 13, A. Taramelli in the *Mon. d. Linc.* 1899 ix. 411 f.), by Sir A. J. Evans and J. L. Myres in 1894, 1895, 1896 (Sir A. J. Evans in the *Journ. Hell. Stud.* 1897 xvii. 350—361 ('Inscribed Libation Table from the Diktaean Cave')), by

J. Demargne in 1897 (Sir A. J. Evans *The Palace of Minos* London 1921 i. 629), and fully by D. G. Hogarth in 1899—1900 (D. G. Hogarth 'The Dictaean Cave' in the *Ann. Brit. Sch. Ath.* 1899—1900 vi. 94—116 with pls. 8—11 and figs. 27—50, *id.* 'The Birth Cave of Zeus' in *The Monthly Review* 1901 pp. 49—62 with 10 pls.). But these explorers (whom I wrongly followed *supra* i. 150 n. 2, ii. 530) assumed without definite proof that the *Psychro* Cave was the Dictaean Cave—an assumption denounced by W. Aly *Der kretische Apollonkult* Leipzig 1908 p. 47 and simultanequsly refuted by K. J. Beloch in *Klio* 1911 xi. 433—435 ('Dikte') and by J. Toutain 'L'antre de Psychro et le ΔΙΚΤΑΙΟΝ ΑΝΤΡΟΝ' in the *Revue de l'histoire des religions* 1911 lxiv. 277—291 (see *infra* n. on Mt Dikte).

The *Psychro* Cave shows as a dark spot on the mountain-side (*The Monthly Review loc. cit.* pl. 6, 1) some 500 ft above *Psychro*, a village of the inner *Lasithi*-plain (*ib.* pl. 1, 2, pl. 2, 1 f.). It was perhaps originally a swallow-hole, at the time when the *Lasithi*-plain was an upland lake, and an icy pool still remains in its depths. But its religious history was a long one ; for the finds begin with sherds of 'Kamares'-ware in the 'Middle Minoan ii' period (*Ann. Brit. Sch. Ath.* 1899—1900 vi. 101 f. fig. 27) and end with sundry Roman lamps and a silver Byzantine cross. Of the votive bronzes, some are probably 'Middle Minoan' in date, many more 'Late Minoan.' Greek relics of a time subsequent to *c.* 800 B.C. are scarce.

The Cave itself consists of an upper grotto and a steep slope of *c.* 200 ft leading down to a subterranean pool and a series of stalactite halls (plan of grotto *supra* p. 531 fig. 401). The upper grotto contained an altar (3 ft high) of roughly squared stones, close to which lay a libation-table in steatite inscribed with three linear characters (*Ann. Brit. Sch. Ath.* 1899—1900 vi. 114 fig. 50). An adjoining gateway gave access to a paved *témenos* enclosed by a massive 'Cyclopean' wall. At the back of the enclosure were the mouths of natural funnels communicating probably with the lower halls and water-channels in the heart of the hill. In the upper grotto, especially round the altar, the topmost *strata* yielded swords, knives, axes, bracelets, etc. of iron with remains of the earliest Hellenic pottery ; the lower *strata* had scattered objects mainly in bronze—the model of a two-wheeled car drawn by an ox and a ram and intended to carry one or more little figurines (*ib.* p. 108 fig. 39), images of bulls, a knife with a handle ending in a human head (*ib.* p. 111 fig. 44), long hair-pins with ornate ends, lance-points, darts, knives, wire needles, rings, miniature circular shields (?) (*ib.* p. 109 fig. 41), etc.; also hundreds of little plain earthenware cups for food or incense ; a small clay mask with lips, eyelids, and lashes painted in ochre (*ib.* p. 106 fig. 37, 3) ; a great stoup patterned with checker-work etc. and a polyp in lustreless red (*ib.* p. 103 f. figs 31, 32) ; ivory ornaments from sword-hilts, bone articles of the toilet; small altar-like tables in steatite and limestone, three of which bore linear inscriptions (*ib.* p. 114 pl. xi). The *témenos* was less rich in metal, but extraordinarily prolific in sherds of 'Minoan' pottery, *e.g.* fragments of large unpainted *píthoi* with a band of decoration in relief under the rim—embossed double-axe, head of wild goat, rows of *bucrania*, an altar laden with fruit, etc. (p. 104 f. fig. 34). Here too were found the skulls and bones of oxen, wild goats, sheep, large deer, swine, and dogs—clearly the *débris* of animal sacrifices (W. Boyd-Dawkins in *Man* 1902 ii. 162—165 no. 114 identifies *bos domesticus creticus, capra ægagrus, ovis aries, cervus dama, sus scrofa, canis familiaris*).

From the *talus* in the lower halls came other bronzes, including a small statuette crowned with the plumes of Àmen-Râ (*Ann. Brit. Sch. Ath.* 1899—1900 vi. 107 pl. x, 1 f.). This was good early work of the New Empire (*c.* 900 B.C.) and recalls the classical identification of Zeus with Àmen-Râ (*supra* i. 348 ff.).

From the floor of the subterranean pool were dredged many rude bronze statuettes, male and female, nude and draped, with the arms folded on the breast or with one hand raised to the head in a gesture of adoration (*Ann. Brit. Sch. Ath.* 1899—1900 vi. 107 pl. x, 4—14) ; a similar figure in lead (*ib.* p. 107 pl. x, 3) ; sards and other signet stones engraved with wild goats, bulls, and a geometric labyrinth-design (*ib.* p. 112) ; rings, pins, blades, needles. At the head of the pool and in a little lateral chamber opening to

Mount Dikte[1].

the left the crevices and crannies of the stalactite columns, up to the height of a man, were found to be crammed with votive bronzes—blades, pins, tweezers, *fibulae* (*The Monthly Review loc. cit.* pl. 9), with here and there a double axe (*ib.* pl. 8). See *supra* p. 530 ff.

D. G. Hogarth concludes: 'About the pre-eminently sacred character of this Cave there can remain no shadow of doubt, and the *simulacra* of axes, fashioned in bronze and moulded or painted on vases, clearly indicate Zeus of the *labrys* or Labyrinth as the deity there honoured' (*Ann. Brit. Sch. Ath.* 1899—1900 vi. 114).

Among the more important objects obtained from the Cave by Sir A. J. Evans are half the top of a libation-table in black steatite bearing an inscription in two lines (Sir A. J. Evans in the *Journ. Hell. Stud.* 1897 xvii. 350—361 figs. 25 *a*—27 and tab. i), one of which is further extended by a small fragment found by J. Demargne in 1897 (Sir A. J. Evans *The Palace of Minos* London 1921 i. 625—631 figs. 465—467), and a remarkable ·votive tablet of bronze perhaps of the period 'Late Minoan i' (*id. ib.* p. 632 f. fig. 470 re-

Fig. 830.

versed = my fig. 830). The latter, like a lentoid seal of rock crystal found in the Idaean Cave (L. Mariani in the *Mon. d. Linc.* 1895 vi. 178 fig. 12, Furtwängler *Ant. Gemmen* iii. 47 fig. 22, Sir A. J. Evans in the *Journ. Hell. Stud.* 1901 xxi. 141 f. fig. 25), represents the worship of a sacred tree or trees. The ring-dove or wood-pigeon (*columba palumbus*), here perched on one of the three sprays rising from ritual horns, may depict the presence of the deity (? Aphrodite, or her Cretan equivalent Ariadne (cp. *supra* i. 481)). Sun and moon betoken the sky. But the exact significance of the remaining symbols (? cp. *supra* i. 583 n. 4) and linear characters is obscure. The cult of a goddess associated with sacred trees is just what we should expect ἐν ὄρει πεπυκασμένῳ ὑλήεντι. Doves reappear in connexion with the Dictaean Cave (*infra* n. 1).

[1] Zeus Δικταῖος (Kallim. *h. Zeus* 4 πῶς καὶ νῦν (so O. Schneider for καὶ νιν codd. and earlier edd. A. W. Mair cj. καὶ μιν), Δικταῖον ἀείσομεν ἠὲ Λυκαῖον; Schöll—Studemund *anecd.* i. 266 Ἐπίθετα Διός no. (22) δικταίου, Mart. *ep.* 4. 1. 1 f. Caesaris (*sc.* Domitiani) alma dies et luce sacratior illa, | conscia Dictaeum qua tulit Ida Iovem, Min. Fel. *Oct.* 21. 1 ob merita virtutis aut muneris deos habitos Euhemerus exsequitur, et eorum natales, patrias, sepulcra dinumerat et per provincias monstrat, Dictaei Iovis et Apollinis Delphici

et Phariae Isidis et Cereris Eleusiniae, cp. Verg. *georg.* 2. 536 ante etiam sceptrum Dictaei regis, Stat. *Theb.* 3. 481 f. ditior ille animi, cui tu, Dictaee, secundas | impuleris manifestus aves) derived his title from a cave in Mt Dikte, where he was born (Agathokles *frag.* 2 (*Frag. hist. Gr.* iv. 289 Müller) *ap.* Athen. 375 F cited *supra* i. 653 n. 3, Apollod. 1. 1. 6 ὀργισθεῖσα δὲ ἐπὶ τούτοις ʾΡέα παραγίνεται μὲν εἰς Κρήτην, ὁπηνίκα τὸν Δία ἐγκυμονοῦσα ἐτύγχανε, γεννᾷ δὲ ἐν ἄντρῳ τῆς Δίκτης Δία, schol. Arat. *phaen.* 33 ἐγεννήθη μὲν ἐν τῇ Δίκτῃ, μετεκομίσθη δὲ ἐπὶ τὸ ἄντρον τῆς ῎Ιδης, Diod. 5. 70 τὴν δὲ ʾΡέαν ἀγανακτήσασαν, καὶ μὴ δυναμένην μεταθεῖναι τὴν προαίρεσιν τἀνδρός, τὸν Δία τεκοῦσαν ἐν τῇ προσαγορευομένῃ ῎Ιδῃ (Δίκτῃ codd. C. F. G.) κλέψαι καὶ δοῦναι λάθρᾳ τοῖς Κούρησιν ἐκθρέψαι τοῖς κατοικοῦσι πλησίον ὄρους τῆς ῎Ιδης... ἀνδρωθέντα δ᾽ αὐτόν φασι πρῶτον πόλιν κτίσαι περὶ τὴν Δίκταν, ὅπου καὶ τὴν γένεσιν αὐτοῦ γενέσθαι μυθολογοῦσιν· ἧς ἐκλειφθείσης ἐν τοῖς ὕστερον χρόνοις διαμένειν ἔτι καὶ νῦν ἔρματα τῶν θεμελίων, *et. mag.* p. 276, 12 ff. Δίκτη· ὄρος τῆς Κρήτης, καὶ ἄκρα κειμένη κατὰ τὸ Λιβυκὸν πέλαγος... εἴρηται παρὰ τὸ τέκω τίκτω, τίκτα τὶς οὖσα, ἀπὸ τοῦ ἐκεῖ τεχθῆναι τὸν Δία) and reared (Ap. Rhod. 1. 508 f. ὄφρα Ζεὺς ἔτι κοῦρος, ἔτι φρεσὶ νήπια εἰδώς, | Δικταῖον ναίεσκεν ὑπὸ σπέος with schol. *ad loc.*, Arat. *phaen.* 30 ff. εἰ ἐτεὸν δή, | Κρήτηθεν κεῖναί γε (*sc.* the two Bears) Διὸς μεγάλου ἰότητι | οὐρανὸν εἰσανέβησαν, ὅ μιν τότε κουρίζοντα | Δίκτῳ (Zenodotos of Mallos read δίκτῳ = δικτάμνῳ) ἐν εὐώδει, ὄρεος σχεδὸν Ἰδαίοιο, | ἄντρῳ ἐγκατέθεντο καὶ ἔτρεφον εἰς ἐνιαυτόν, | Δικταῖοι Κούρητες ὅτε Κρόνον ἐψεύδοντο with schol. *ad loc.*, Lucr. 2. 633 f. Dictaeos referunt Curetas qui Iovis illum | vagitum in Creta quondam occultasse feruntur (cp. Sil. It. 17. 21 qui Dictaei bacchantur in antro), Dion. Hal. *ant. Rom.* 2. 61 cited *infra*, Arrian. *frag.* 70 (*Frag. hist. Gr.* iii. 599 Müller) *ap.* Eustath. *in Dionys. per.* 498 Ἀρριανὸς δέ φησι· ʿΚρής, οὗ Κρήτη ἐπώνυμος, ὁ τὸν Δία κρύψας ἐν ὄρει Δικταίῳ, ὅτε Κρόνος ἐμάστευεν ἐθέλων ἀφανίσαι αὐτόν,᾽ Serv. *in* Verg. *georg.* 2. 536 ante quam regnaret Iuppiter, qui est in Dictaeo, Cretae monte, nutritus), being fed by bees (Verg. *georg.* 4. 149 ff. nunc age, naturas apibus quas Iuppiter ipse | addidit expediam, pro qua mercede, canoros | Curetum sonitus crepitantiaque aera secutae, | Dictaeo caeli regem pavere sub antro, Colum. *de re rust.* 9. 2 nec sane rustico dignum est sciscitari, fueritne mulier pulcherrima specie Melissa, quam Iuppiter in apem convertit, an (ut Euhemerus poeta dicit) crabronibus et sole genitas apes, quas nymphae Phryxonides educaverunt, mox Dictaeo specu Iovis exstitisse nutrices, easque pabula munere dei sortitas, quibus ipsae parvum educaverant alumnum. ista enim, quamvis non dedeceant poetam, summatim tamen et uno tantummodo versiculo leviter attigit Virgilius, cum sic ait: ʿDictaeo caeli regem pavere sub antro,᾽ Serv. *in* Verg. *Aen.* 3. 104 sanè nati Iovis fabula haec est: Saturnus post quam a Themide oraculo comperit a filio se posse regno depelli natos ex Rhea uxore devorabat, quae natum Iovem pulchritudine delectata nymphis commendavit in monte Cretae Dictaeo; ubi eum aluerunt apes = Lact. Plac. *in* Stat. *Ach.* 387 = Myth. Vat. 1. 104, cp. 2. 16. See further L. Weniger and W. Drexler in Roscher *Lex. Myth.* ii. 2637 ff. *s.vv.* Melissa, Melissaios, Melisseus, Melissos) or a goat (*supra* i. 112 n. 3, 529 n. 4, 653 n. 3, 665 n. 3. See further E. Neustadt *De Jove Cretico* Berolini 1906 pp. 18—43 (ʿDe Amalthea᾽)) or a pig (*supra* i. 653 n. 3) or doves (Moiro of Byzantion *c.* 300 B.C. *frag. ap.* Athen. 491 A—B Ζεὺς δ᾽ ἄρ᾽ ἐνὶ Κρήτῃ τρέφετο μέγας, οὐδ᾽ ἄρα τίς νιν | ἠείδει μακάρων· ὁ δ᾽ ἀέξετο πᾶσι μέλεσσι. | τὸν μὲν ἄρα τρήρωνες ὑπὸ ζαθέῳ τράφον ἄντρῳ, | ἀμβροσίην φορέουσαι ἀπ᾽ Ὠκεανοῖο ῥοάων· | νέκταρ δ᾽ ἐκ πέτρης μέγας αἰετὸς αἰὲν ἀφύσσων | γαμφηλῇς, φορέεσκε ποτὸν Διὶ μητιόεντι. *Supra* i. 182 n. 8), while the Kouretes, or by later confusion the Korybantes, drowned his infant cries with the clashing of their weapons (*supra* i. 150, 530 n. 0, 534, 659, 709. See further O. Immisch in Roscher *Lex. Myth.* ii. 1587 ff., J. Poerner *De Curetibus et Corybantibus* (*Dissertationes philologicae Halenses* xxii. 2) Halis Saxonum 1913 pp. 245—428, Schwenn in Pauly—Wissowa xi. 1441 ff., 2202 ff.).

Ant. Lib. 19 quotes from the *Ornithogonia* of ʿBoios᾽ (*supra* p. 463 n. 1) a queer tale which relates apparently to the Dictaean Cave: ʿIn Crete, they say, there is a cave sacred to bees. Tradition has it that in this cave Rhea gave birth to Zeus, and neither god nor man may enter it. Every year at a definite time there is seen a great glare from the cavern. This happens, so the story goes, when the blood from the birth of Zeus boils out (ἐκζέῃ with allusion to Ζεύς (*supra* i. 31 n. 3)). The cave is occupied by sacred bees,

Plate XLII

Amphora from Vulci, now in the British Museum: Laïos, Keleos, Kerberos, and Aigolios stung by bees in the Dictaean Cave.

See page 929 *n.* 0.

the nurses of Zeus. Laïos, Keleos, Kerberos, and Aigolios dared to enter it that they might draw as much honey as they could. They encased their bodies in bronze, drew the honey of the bees, and saw the swathing-bands of Zeus. Whereupon their bronze armour burst asunder. Zeus thundered aloud and raised his bolt. But the Moirai and Themis intervened; for none might die in that spot. So Zeus made them all into birds, and from them sprang the tribe of birds—blue thrushes (λάιοι), green woodpeckers (κελεοί), birds of an unknown species (κέρβεροι), and owls (αἰγωλιοί). These are good birds to appear and reliable beyond all other birds, because they saw the blood of Zeus.' See further *Folk-Lore* 1904 xv. 388 f. A black-figured *amphora* in the British Museum (*Brit. Mus. Cat. Vases* ii. 122 f. no. B 177 from *Vulci*), hitherto unpublished, has (a) the four marauders stung by the bees in the cave (pl. xlii from a photograph by Mr R. B. Fleming): (b) dancing Maenads and Satyrs.

Other myths attached to the same sacred cavern. Here Anchiale bore the Idaean Daktyloi (Ap. Rhod. 1. 1129 ff. Δάκτυλοι Ἰδαῖοι Κρηταιέες, οὕς ποτε νύμφη | Ἀγχιάλη Δικταῖον ἀνὰ σπέος ἀμφοτέρῃσιν | δραξαμένη γαίης Οἰαξίδος ἐβλάστησεν with schol. *ad loc.*, translated by Varr. *frag.* 3 Baehrens *ap.* Serv. *in Verg. ecl.* 1. 66 quos magno Anchiale partus adducta dolore | et geminis capiens tellurem Oaxida palmis | edidit in Dicta, cp. Vib. Seq. p. 15 Oberlin *s.v.* 'Oaxes'). Here too Zeus, according to one late account, lay with Europe (Loukian. *dial. mar.* 15. 4 ταῦτα ἐκ Φοινίκης ἄχρι τῆς Κρήτης ἐγένετο· ἐπεὶ δὲ ἐπέβη τῇ νήσῳ, ὁ μὲν ταῦρος οὐκέτι ἐφαίνετο, ἐπιλαβόμενος δὲ τῆς χειρὸς ὁ Ζεὺς ἀπῆγε τὴν Εὐρώπην ἐς τὸ Δικταῖον ἄντρον ἐρυθριῶσαν καὶ κάτω ὁρῶσαν· ἠπίστατο γὰρ ἤδη ἐφ' ὅτῳ ἄγοιτο). Minos, their son, used to descend into the Dictaean Cave and thence return with the laws of Zeus (Dion. Hal. *ant. Rom.* 2. 61 ὧν ὁ μὲν (*sc.* Minos) ὁμιλητὴς ἔφη γενέσθαι τοῦ Διός, καὶ φοιτῶν εἰς τὸ Δικταῖον ὄρος, ἐν ᾧ τραφῆναι τὸν Δία μυθολογοῦσιν οἱ Κρῆτες ὑπὸ τῶν Κουρήτων ἔτι νεογνὸν ὄντα, εἰς τὸ ἱερὸν ἄντρον, καὶ τοὺς νόμους ἐκεῖ συνθεὶς ἐκόμιζεν, οὓς ἀπέφαινε παρὰ τοῦ Διὸς λαμβάνειν). Lastly Epimenides claimed to have slept for years in the Cave and to have had visions there (Max. Tyr. 16. 1 ἀφίκετό ποτε Ἀθήναζε Κρὴς ἀνήρ, ὄνομα Ἐπιμενίδης, κομίζων λόγον, οὑτωσὶ ῥηθέντα, πιστεύεσθαι χαλεπόν· ἐν τοῦ Διὸς τοῦ Δικταίου τῷ ἄντρῳ κείμενος ὕπνῳ βαθεῖ ἔτη συχνά, ὄναρ ἔφη ἐντυχεῖν αὐτὸς θεοῖς καὶ θεῶν λόγοις καὶ ἀληθείᾳ καὶ δίκῃ. κ.τ.λ.).

Sir A. J. Evans at first identified Mt Dikte with Mt *Lasithi*, the Dictaean Cave with the *Psychro* Cave, and the city built by Zeus (Diod. 5. 70 cited *supra*) with the ruins at *Goulas* on an outlying spur of the *Lasithi-massif* (Sir A. J. Evans 'Goulas: The City of Zeus' in the *Ann. Brit. Sch. Ath.* 1895—1896 ii. 169 ff.). This made an attractive combination and found many adherents (*supra* p. 925 n. 1). Unfortunately it ignored two essential factors in the situation—the definite statements of ancient topographers (*in primis* Strab. 478 f., Ptol. 3. 15. 3 and 6, cp. Agathokles *frag.* 2 (*Frag. hist. Gr.* iv. 289 Müller) *ap.* Athen. 375 F, schol. Arat. *phaen.* 33 f.; *in secundis* Ap. Rhod. 4. 1635 ff., Loukian. *dial. mar.* 15. 4) and the *provenance* of inscriptions relating to the cult of Zeus Δικταῖος. Discussion of the evidence along these lines led K. J. Beloch in *Klio* 1911 xi. 433 ff. and J. Toutain in the *Revue de l'histoire des religions* 1911 lxiv. 277 ff. to reject the identification of Dikte with *Lasithi* and to insist that Dikte must have been a mountain near Praisos at the eastern end of Crete. Apparently Sir A. J. Evans has himself now given in to this view, for the map prefixed to vol. i of *The Palace of Minos at Knossos* adopts the new equation Aigaion = *Lasithi* and, rightly as I conceive, assigns the name 'Mt Dikta' to the range situated south-west of Praisos. If so, the true Dictaean Cave is still to seek.

The cult of Zeus Δικταῖος in eastern Crete is attested by (1) the civic oath of Itanos in s. iii B.C. (Dittenberger *Syll. inscr. Gr.*² no. 462, 2 ff., *ib.*³ no. 526, 2 ff. = F. Blass in Collitz—Bechtel *Gr. Dial.-Inschr.* iii. 2. 324 f. no. 5058, 2 ff. found at *Eremopoli* [τάδ]ε ὤμοσαν τοὶ Ἰτάνιοι πά[ν][τες] Δία Δικταῖον καὶ Ἥραν καὶ θ[εο]ὺς τοὺς ἐν Δίκται καὶ Ἀθαν[α]ίαν Πολιάδα καὶ θεούς, ὅσσο[ι][ς] ἐν Ἀθαναίαι θύεται, π[ά]ντας | [κ]αὶ Δία Ἀγοραῖον καὶ Ἀπόλλω[ν]α Πύθιον καθ' ἱερῶν νεοκαύ[τ]ων· κ.τ.λ.): (2) the oath of allegiance taken by settlers from Hierapytna, sent probably to occupy conquered territory (Praisos?) (*Corp. inscr. Gr.* ii no. 2555, 11 ff. = F. Blass in Collitz—Bechtel *Gr. Dial.-Inschr.* iii. 2. 311 f. no. 5039, 11 ff. cited *supra* p. 723 n. o): (3) the oath to be taken each year in the month

Dionysios by the *kósmos* or chief magistrate of Praisos in accordance with a treaty of *s.* iii B.C. between that town and Stelai (Michel *Recueil d'Inscr. gr.* no. 440 *A*, 15 ff. = Dittenberger *Syll. inscr. Gr.*² no. 427, *a* 15 ff., *ib.*³ no. 524, *a* 15 ff. cited *supra* p. 731 n. 0. The restoration ὀμνύω Δῆ|[να Δικταῖον] exactly fills the gap and is justified by Strab. 475 τούτων (*sc. Od.* 19. 175—177) φησὶ Στάφυλος (*frag.* 12 (*Frag. hist. Gr.* iv. 507 Müller)) τὸ μὲν πρὸς ἔω Δωριεῖς κατέχειν, τὸ δὲ δυσμικὸν Κύδωνας, τὸ <δὲ> νότιον Ἐτεόκρητας, ὧν εἶναι πολίχνιον Πρᾶσον, ὅπου τὸ τοῦ Δικταίου Διὸς ἱερόν, *id.* 478 εἴρηται δέ, ὅτι τῶν Ἐτεοκρήτων ὑπῆρχεν ἡ Πρᾶσος, καὶ διότι ἐνταῦθα τὸ τοῦ Δικταίου Διὸς ἱερόν· κ.τ.λ.):
(4) a long inscription, dated in 139 B.C., of which one copy was found near Itanos, another at Magnesia ad Maeandrum (Dittenberger *Syll. inscr. Gr.*² no. 929, *ib.*³ no. 685 = R. Cagnat *Inscriptiones Graecae ad res Romanas pertinentes* Paris 1911 i. 345 ff. no. 1021). It deals with a dispute between Itanos and Praisos—later between Itanos and Hierapytna—respecting the territory of Heleia and the island of Leuke. Itanos ultimately appealed to the Roman senate, which entrusted arbitration in the matter to Magnesia. The document in delimiting the territory of Itanos more than once mentions the sanctuary of Zeus Δικταῖος, which must have lain on the border-line of Itanos and Praisos (ii, 37 ff. Ἰτάνιοι πόλιν οἰκοῦν|τες ἐπιθαλάσσιον καὶ χώραν ἔχοντες προγονικὴν γειτονοῦσαν τῶι τοῦ Διὸς τοῦ Δικταίου ἱερῶι, ἔχον|τες δὲ καὶ νήσους καὶ νεμόμενοι, ἐν αἷς καὶ τὴν καλουμένην Λεύκην, 47 ff. οὕτως Ἱεραπύτνιοι τῆς τε νήσου καὶ τῆς χώρας ἀμφισβητεῖν Ἰτανίοις ἐπεβάλαντο, φάμε|νοι τὴν μὲν χώραν εἶναι ἱερὰν τοῦ Ζηνὸς τοῦ Δικταίου, τὴν δὲ νῆσον προγονικὴν ἑαυτῶν ὑπάρ|χειν, iii, 69 ff. τοῦ δὲ ἱεροῦ τοῦ Διὸς ἐκτὸς τῆς διαμφισβητουμένης | χώρας ὄντος καὶ περιοικοδομήμασιν καὶ ἑτέροις πλείοσι[ν ἀ]ποδεικτικοῖς καὶ σημείοις περιλα[μ]βανο|μένου, 81 f. νόμοις γὰρ ἱεροῖς καὶ ἀραῖς καὶ ἐπιτίμοις διεκεκώλυτο ἵνα μηθεὶς ἐν τῷ ἱ|ερῶι τοῦ Διὸς τοῦ Δικταίου μήτε ἐννέμηι μήτε ἐναυλοστατῆι μήτε σπείρηι μήτε ξυλεύηι).

Finally, excavations of the British School at Athens undertaken in 1902 at Heleia (*Palaikastro*) on the eastern coast, south of Itanos (*Eremopoli*) and east of Praisos, located the actual site of the Hellenic temple (R. C. Bosanquet in the *Ann. Brit. Sch. Ath.* 1901—1902 viii. 286 ff.). This was partially explored in 1903 and 1904 (*id. ib.* 1902—1903 ix. 280, *ib.* 1903—1904 x. 246) and fully cleared in 1905 (*id. ib.* 1904—1905 xi. 298 ff.).

The site was an artificially levelled platform half-way down the south-eastern side of a hill. The *témenos* was enclosed by a wall of undressed stones, of which a few courses survive, and can be traced along the north and north-eastern face of the slope for a distance of 36ᵐ. The temple itself has wholly vanished, huge blocks of freestone having been carried off by the villagers of *Palaikastro* about a generation ago. But the position of the altar is fixed by a bed of grey wood-ash, at least 3ᵐ long by 0·25ᵐ thick. Round it were found bronze bowls, miniature shields, and an archaic scarabaeoid seal.

More widely scattered were tiles and architectural terracottas of two distinct periods: (*a*) *Archaic*. Many pieces of a *sima* in low relief decorated with the *motif* of a two-horse chariot, driver, two hoplites, and hound (*Ann. Brit. Sch. Ath.* 1904—1905 xi. 300 ff. pl. 15). Antefixes in the form of a *Gorgóneion* (*ib.* p. 303 fig. 20). *Akrotéria* (?) of large birds (eagles?). The leg of a crouching or running human figure in high relief, probably from the pediment (*ib.* p. 300 fig. 18). Transitional in character is an antefix representing the Gorgon with two snakes rising from her shoulders and two others held in her hands— a pose which recalls that of the 'Minoan' snake-goddess (*ib.* p. 304 fig. 22). (*b*) *Developed style*. Fragments of a deeper *sima* with lion-heads etc. of the conventional sort. Fragments of palmette-shaped antefixes (*ib.* p. 304 fig. 21).

The votive offerings belong mostly to the archaic period (*s.* vii—v B.C.) and comprise: (i) *Bronzes*. At least four large shields decorated with zones of animals. One (0·49ᵐ across) had as central boss the head and forepart of a lion, which pins down a couple of sphinxes and is flanked by two lions rampant on either side of a 'tree-of-life.' A dozen small shields, a miniature cuirass, a miniature helmet. Parts of about fourteen tripods. Eight bowls. Numerous small figures of oxen. (ii) *Terracottas*. About forty lamps and twelve torch-holders (*ib.* p. 307 fig. 23). About thirty large cups or bowls.

A mile to the north-west of the site there was found in 1907 a slab, which records the restoration by Hierapytna (*c.* 145—139 B.C.) of certain statues in the temple of Zeus

Δικταῖος (R. C. Bosanquet *ib.* 1908—1909 xv. 340, S. A. Xanthoudides in the Ἐφ. Ἀρχ.
1908 p. 197 ff. no. 1 fig. 1 ἐπὶ τᾶς Καμιρίδος (*sc.* a tribe at Hierapytna, cp. Steph. Byz.
s.v. Ἱεράπυτνα) κοσμόντων | τῶν σὺμ Βουάω τῷ Ἀμφέροντος, | ἐπεμέληθεν ἐν τῶι ἱερῶι
τῷ | [Ζ (or Τ)]ηνὸς Δικταίω, τὰ ἀρχαῖα | [ἀ]γάλματα θαραπεύσαντες, | [θεὸ]s ἐπισκευῶσαι
καὶ χρυσῶ|[σαι] Ἀθαναίαν, Ἄρτεμιν, Ἄτλαν|[τα, τ]ὰς Σφίγγας ἀστραγαλίσ|[αι] ἐπὶ τῶν
ὑποποδίων, καὶ | [? Ποσ]οιδᾶ, Δία, Ἥρας πρόσωπον, | [? Λατώ]ν καὶ Νίκαν ἀναγράψαι· | [οἶδ'
ἐκ]όσ(μ)ιον, Βούαος Ἀμφέ[[ροντος, Ἀκ]άσσων Βραμισάλ|......s Εὐρυκάρτεος, | ....Εὐρυκάρ-
τεος, | ....νθεος, | ....s Μοιρίλ[ω]|---). A mutilated inscription recording an
agreement between Knossos and Hierapytna, which was found in the church of St Nikolaos
near *Palaikastro* (F. Halbherr in the *Museo Italiano di Antichità Classica* 1890 iii. 612 ff.
no. 36), must likewise have come from the precinct of Zeus Δικταῖος, where it had probably
been set up during the same period of Hierapytna's supremacy.

But by far the most important epigraphic discovery connected with the site was that
of the now famous hymn to Zeus Δικταῖος, first published by R. C. Bosanquet (*Ann. Brit.
Sch. Ath.* 1908—1909 xv. 339—356 pl. 20), restored and translated by G. Murray (*ib.*
pp. 357—365), and expounded at large by Miss J. E. Harrison ('The Kouretes and Zeus
Kouros' *ib.* pp. 308—338, *ead. Themis* Cambridge 1912 pp. 1—29 ('The Hymn of the
Kouretes')). With one exception, already noted (*supra* i. 15 n. 6), I give the text as
printed by G. Murray:

Ἰώ,
Μέγιστε Κοῦρε, χαῖρέ μοι,
Κρόνιε, παγκρατὲς γάνος,
βέβακες
5 δαιμόνων ἁγώμενος·
Δίκταν ἐς ἐνιαυτὸν ἕρ-
πε καὶ γέγαθι μολπᾷ,

Τάν τοι κρέκομεν πακτίσι
μείξαντες ἅμ' αὐλοῖσιν,
10 καὶ στάντες ἀείδομεν τεὸν
ἀμφὶ βωμὸν εὐερκῆ.

Ἰώ, κ.τ.λ.

Ἔνθα γὰρ σέ, παῖδ' ἄμβροτον,
ἀσπιδ[ηφόροι τροφῆες]
15 παρ' Ῥέας λαβόντες πόδα
κ[ρούοντες ἀπέκρυψαν].

Ἰώ, κ.τ.λ.

·   ·   ·   ·   ·
·   ·   ·   ·   ·
20 ·   ·   ·   ·   ·
·   ·   ·   τᾶ]ς καλᾶς Ἀο(ῦ)s.

Ἰώ, κ.τ.λ.

[Ὧραι δὲ βρ]ύον κατῆτος
καὶ βροτο(ὺ)s Δίκα κατῆχε
25 [πάντα τ' ἄγρι' ἄμφεπ]ε ζῷ'
ἁ φίλολβος Εἰρήνα.

Ἰώ, κ.τ.λ.

Ἄ[μιν θόρε, κὲς στα]μνία,
καὶ θόρ' εὔποκ' ἐ[ς ποίμνια,
30 κὲς λήϊ]α καρπῶν θόρε,
κὲς τελεσ[φόρους σίμβλους].

Ἰώ, κ.τ.λ.

[Θόρε κὲς] πόληας ἁμῶν,
κὲς ποντοφόρο(υ)s νᾶας,
35 θόρε κὲς ν[έους πολ]είτας,
θόρε κὲς Θέμιν κ[αλάν].

This hymn, engraved *c.* 200 A.D. but composed *c.* 300 B.C., expresses in cultured
poetical Greek, with a dash of Doric dialect, beliefs that had descended from much earlier
times. It invokes Zeus as the 'greatest Lad of Kronos' line' to come to Dikte for the new
year at the head of the *daímones* (perhaps the gods in general (Plat. *Phaedr.* 246 E στρατιὰ
θεῶν τε καὶ δαιμόνων, cp. *supra* pp. 43, 63 n. 0) rather than the Kouretes in particular
(Strab. 466 δαίμονας ἢ προπόλους θεῶν)) and to take delight in the dance about his altar—
a dance accompanied by harps and pipes. It goes on to tell how the Kouretes once
received him as a babe from Rhea and hid him in safety with the sound of their beating
feet, [how under the reign of Zeus foul Darkness was followed by] fair Dawn, the Seasons
began to be fruitful year by year, Justice spread over the world, and Peace brought wealth
in its train. And now once more comes the invitation to leap in the ritual dance, which
shall ensure full jars, fleecy flocks, crops in the fields, and honey in the hives, prosperity
alike on land and sea, youthful citizens and established Right.

Mount Ide[1].

The god here invoked is clearly thought of as coming from afar to witness, or even to join in, his worshippers' dance—a dance which very possibly originated as a piece of pure magic. But I do not on that account see in him 'a Kouros who is obviously but a reflection or impersonation of the body of Kouretes' (Miss J. E. Harrison *Themis* p. 27) any more than I regard the Bull Dionysos, who is invited to visit his temple at Elis (*carm. pop.* 5 Hiller—Crusius *ap.* Plout. *quaestt. Gr.* 36), as a projection of the Elean women. The *Creator Spiritus* is not lightly to be identified with the *spiritus creatorum*.

[1] Mt Ide bore a name (Ἴδη) which, like many mountain-names (Schrader *Reallex.*[2] p. 88 f.), means 'forest, wood' (F. Solmsen in the *Indogermanische Forschungen* 1908 xxvi. 109 ff., A. Fick *Vorgriechische Ortsnamen* Göttingen 1905 p. 10, *id. Hattiden und Danubier in Griechenland* Göttingen 1909 p. 11 f. ('Ida'), Boisacq *Dict. étym. de la Langue Gr.* p. 365 f.). It had flourishing oak-trees (Dionys. *per.* 503). And it was famous for its cypresses (Theophr. *hist. pl.* 3. 2. 6, 4. 1. 3, Nik. *ther.* 585, Verg. *georg.* 2. 84, Plin. *nat. hist.* 16. 142. Claud. *de rapt. Pros.* 3. 370 ff. confuses Mt Ide in the Troad), which probably stood in some relation to the cult of Rhea (*supra* i. 649 n. 1) or of Zeus (F. Olck in Pauly—Wissowa *Real-Enc.* iv. 1920, 1924, 1926, *supra* i. 558 n. 5); for not only were Cretan cypresses called δρυῖται (Theophr. *caus. pl.* 1. 2. 2), but beams of cypress were used to roof the temple in which were celebrated the rites of Rhea and Zagreus (Eur. *Cretes frag.* 472 Nauck[2] *ap.* Porph. *de abst.* 4. 19 cited *supra* i. 648 n. 1). A fruit-bearing poplar grew in the mouth of the Idaean Cave (Theophr. *hist. pl.* 3. 3. 4 ἐν Κρήτῃ δὲ καὶ αἴγειροι κάρπιμοι πλείους εἰσί· μία μὲν ἐν τῷ στομίῳ τοῦ ἄντρου τοῦ ἐν τῇ Ἴδῃ (so J. G. Schneider for τοῦ ἐν τῷ Ἴδῃ cod. U. τοῦ ἐν τῷ Ἴδης codd. M. V. ἐν τῇ Ἴδῃ edd. Ald. Heins.), ἐν ᾧ τὰ ἀναθήματα ἀνάκειται, ἄλλη δὲ μικρὰ πλησίον· κ.τ.λ., cp. *ib.* 2. 2. 10, Aristot. *mir. ausc.* 69), though Pliny describes it as a willow (Plin. *nat. hist.* 16. 110 salix...una tamen proditur ad maturitatem perferre solita in Creta insula ipso descensu Iovis speluncae durum ligneumque (*sc.* semen), magnitudine ciceris). Iron-coloured stones shaped like the human thumb were found in Crete and known as *Idaei dactyli* (Plin. *nat. hist.* 37. 170, Isid. *orig.* 16. 15. 12, Solin. 11. 14): if these were fossil belemnites (E. Babelon in Daremberg—Saglio *Dict. Ant.* ii. 1465), they were doubtless viewed as thunderbolts (C. Blinkenberg *The Thunderweapon in Religion and Folklore* Cambridge 1911 p. 76 f. ('Thunderstones (Belemnites)')).

Mt Ide, which, as the ancients said, sees the sun before the sunrise (Solin. 11. 6, Prisc. *per.* 527 f. (*Geogr. Gr. min.* ii. 194 Müller)), was not unnaturally associated with the Hellenic sky-god. From *s.* v B.C. onwards we hear of Zeus Ἰδαῖος (Eur. *Cretes frag.* 472 Nauck[2] *ap.* Porph. *de abst.* 4. 19 cited *supra* i. 648 n. 1, Polyb. 28. 14. 3 περὶ τούτων κειμένης ἐνόρκου συνθήκης παρὰ τὸν Δία τὸν Ἰδαῖον, cp. Schöll—Studemund *anecd.* i. 264 f. Ἐπίθετα Διός no. (50) ἰδαίου, 266 Ἐπίθετα Διός no. (42) ἰδαίου, 281 Ἐπίθετα τοῦ Διός... ἰδαῖος. In Nonn. *Dion.* 13. 236 καὶ χθόνα Νωδαίοιο Διὸς κ.τ.λ. G. Falkenburg, G. H. Moser, and Count de Marcellus would read χθονὸς Ἰδαίοιο. J. J. Scaliger cj. χθονὸς ὠδαίοιο. F. Graefe cj. χθόνα Δικταίοιο).

Zeus is never said to have been born on Mt Ide (in Diod. 5. 70 cited *supra* p. 928 n. o the right reading appears to be Δίκτῃ, not Ἴδῃ: at most we have Mart. *ep.* 4. 1. 2 Dictaeum tulit Ida Iovem); the claims of Mt Aigaion (*supra* p. 925 n. 1) and Mt Dikte (*supra* p. 927 n. 1) were too strong. He is, however, said to have been brought by the Kourēes living near Mt Ide to a cave and to have been nurtured there by the nymphs on honey and the milk of the goat Amaltheia (Diod. 5. 70 τὴν δὲ Ῥέαν...τὸν Δία τεκοῦσαν... κλέψαι καὶ δοῦναι λάθρᾳ τοῖς Κούρησιν ἐκθρέψαι τοῖς κατοικοῦσι πλησίον ὄρους τῆς Ἴδης. τούτους δ' ἀπενέγκαντας εἴς τι ἄντρον παραδοῦναι ταῖς Νύμφαις, παρακελευσαμένους τὴν πᾶσαν ἐπιμέλειαν αὐτοῦ ποιεῖσθαι. αὗται δὲ μέλι καὶ γάλα μίσγουσαι τὸ παιδίον ἔθρεψαν καὶ τῆς αἰγὸς τῆς ὀνομαζομένης Ἀμαλθείας τὸν μαστὸν εἰς διατροφὴν παρείχοντο, Ov. *fast.* 5. 115 f. Naïs Amalthea, Cretaea nobilis Ida. | dicitur in silvis occuluisse Iovem, Iuv. 13. 41 et privatus adhuc Idaeis Iuppiter antris) together with Aigokeros or Capricornus (pseudo-Eratosth. *catast.* 27 p. 237 f. Maass <Αἰγοκέρωτος.> οὗτός ἐστι τῷ εἴδει ὅμοιος τῷ Αἰγίπανι. ἐξ ἐκείνου δὲ γέγονεν. ἔχει δὲ θηρίου τὰ κάτω μέρη καὶ κέρατα ἐπὶ τῇ κεφαλῇ. ἐτιμήθη δὲ διὰ τὸ σύν-τροφος εἶναι τῷ Διί, καθάπερ Ἐπιμενίδης ὁ τὰ Κρητικὰ ἱστορῶν φησιν, ὅτι ἐν τῇ Ἴδῃ συνῆν αὐτῷ, ὅτε ἐπὶ τοὺς Τιτᾶνας ἐστράτευσεν (οὗτος δὲ δοκεῖ εὑρεῖν τὸν κόχλον, [ἐν] ᾧ τοὺς συμμά-χους καθώπλισεν), <ἦ> διὰ τὸ τοῦ ἤχου Πανικὸν καλούμενον, ὃ οἱ Τιτᾶνες ἔφευγον. παραλαβὼν δὲ τὴν ἀρχὴν ἐν τοῖς ἄστροις αὐτὸν ἔθηκε καὶ τὴν αἶγα τὴν μητέρα. διὰ δὲ τὸν κόχλον τὸν θαλάσσιον παράσημον ἔχει ἰχθύος, cp. schol. Arat. phaen. 284, Arat. Lat. p. 237 f. Maass, schol. Caes. Germ. Aratea p. 407, 9 ff. Eyssenhardt, Hyg. poet. astr. 2. 28). Adrasteia his nurse made him a golden ball (Ap. Rhod. 3. 132 ff. καί κέν τοι ὀπάσαιμι Διὸς περικαλλὲς ἄθυρμα | κεῖνο, τό οἱ ποίησε φίλη τροφὸς Ἀδρήστεια | ἄντρῳ ἐν Ἰδαίῳ ἔτι νήπια κουρίζοντι, | σφαῖραν εὐτρόχαλον... | ... | χρύσεα μέν οἱ κύκλα τετεύχαται· ἀμφὶ δ' ἑκάστῳ | διπλόαι ἀψῖδες περιηγέες εἱλίσσονται· | κρυπταὶ δὲ ῥαφαί εἰσιν· ἕλιξ δ' ἐπιδέδρομε πάσαις | κυανέη. ἀτὰρ εἴ μιν ἑαῖς ἐνὶ χερσὶ βάλοιο, | ἀστὴρ ὥς, φλεγέθοντα δι' ἠέρος ὁλκὸν ἵησιν. H. Posnansky Nemesis und Adrasteia Breslau 1890 p. 175 f. finds Adrasteia, the infant Zeus, and his ball on a coin of Laodikeia illustrated supra i. 153 fig. 129. More ad rem are the coin-types discussed supra i. 51 f. figs. 27 and 28, 547; for there the cosmic significance of the ball (K. Sittl Der Adler und die Weltkugel als Attribute des Zeus Leipzig 1884 p. 45 ff.) is apparent) and put him to sleep in a golden líknon (Kallim. h. Zeus 46 ff. Ζεῦ, σὲ δὲ Κυρβάντων ἑτάραι προσεπηχύναντο | Δικταῖαι Μέλιαι, σε δ' ἐκοίμισεν Ἀδρήστεια | λίκνῳ ἐνὶ χρυσέῳ, σὺ δ' ἐθήσαο πίονα μαζὸν | αἰγὸς Ἀμαλθείης, ἐπὶ δὲ γλυκὺ κηρίον ἔβρως. | γέντο γὰρ ἐξαπιναῖα Πανακρίδος ἔργα μελίσσης | Ἰδαίοις ἐν ὄρεσσι, τά τε κλείουσι Πάνακρα). Hence in the Rhapsodic theogony Adrasteia, daughter of Melissos and Amaltheia, is associated with her sister Eide (Gruppe Gr. Myth. Rel. p. 1086 n. 0: 'die Göttin Ida?') as protectress of all laws including those of Zeus and Kronos (Orph. frag. 109 Abel ap. Herm. in Plat. Phaedr. p. 148 (p. 161, 15 ff. Couvreur)). Lastly, Zeus was first served in the Idaean Cave by Aetos the beautiful child of Earth (interp. Serv. in Verg. Aen. 1. 394 est et alia fabula. apud Graecos legitur, puerum quendam terra editum admodum pulchrum membris omnibus fuisse, qui 'Αετὸς sit vocatus. hic cum Iuppiter propter patrem Saturnum, qui suos filios devorabat, in Creta insula in Idaeo antro nutriretur, primus in obsequium Iovis se dedit, post vero cum adolevisset Iuppiter et patrem regno pepulisset, Iuno permota forma pueri velut paelicatus dolore eum in avem vertit, quae ab ipso ἀετὸς dicitur Graece, a nobis aquila propter aquilum colorem, qui ater est. quam semper Iuppiter sibi inhaerere praecepit et fulmina gestare: per hanc etiam Ganymedes cum amaretur a Iove dicitur raptus, quos Iuppiter inter sidera collocavit. Cp. supra pp. 751 n. 2, 777). Copper coins of Crete issued by Titus (Rasche Lex. Num. iii. 306, Suppl. ii. 262) and Domitian (J. N. Svoronos Numismatique de la Crète ancienne Mâcon 1890 i. 344 pl. 33, 22 (=my fig. 831), Head Hist. num.² p. 479) have for reverse type an eagle inscribed ΔΙΟΣ ΙΔΑΙΟΥ.

Fig. 831.

Other myths were readily attached to the same locality. It was 'in Idaean caves' that Hermaphroditos was reared by Naiad nymphs (Ov. met. 4. 288 f.) and that the Telchines were wont to work (Stat. silv. 4. 6. 47).

The worship of Zeus on Mt Ide, famous throughout the classical world (Lact. Plac. in Stat. Theb. 4. 105 Ὄlenos Arcadiae civitas, in qua Iovem Amalthea capra dicitur nutrisse, quae in cultum Iovis Idam provocat, montem Cretae, in quo Iuppiter colitur), centred about the Idaean Cave. This was distant from Knossos some twenty miles as the crow flies; but the two were connected by a tolerable road and pilgrims could rest in the shade of trees by the wayside (Plat. legg. 625 A—B). The Cave itself was sacred to Zeus and the meadows near it were regarded as his (Diod. 5. 70 κατὰ δὲ τὴν Ἴδην, ἐν ᾗ συνέβη τρα-φῆναι τὸν θεόν, τό τε ἄντρον ἐν ᾧ τὴν δίαιταν εἶχε καθιέρωται καὶ οἱ περὶ αὐτὸ λειμῶνες ὁμοίως ἀνεῖνται περὶ τὴν ἀκρώρειαν ὄντες). He had repaid his debt to the bees by turning them gold-bronze in colour and making them impervious to wintry weather (id. ib.). Concerning the cavern-ritual we know but little. Votive offerings were to be seen in the entry (Theophr. hist. pl. 3. 3. 4 quoted supra). Pythagoras is said to have gone down into the Cave with Epimenides (Diog. Laert. 8. 3 εἶτ' ἐν Κρήτῃ σὺν Ἐπιμενίδῃ κατῆλθεν εἰς τὸ Ἰδαῖον ἄντρον), who was both a Cretan and a Koures (*supra* p. 191). Fortunately further details are given us by Porph. *v. Pyth.* 17 (cited *supra* i. 646 n. 3). It appears that Pythagoras first repaired to the mystics of Morges, one of the Idaean Daktyloi, by whom he was purified with the thunder-stone (τῇ κεραυνίᾳ λίθῳ—probably a belemnite (*supra*)), at daybreak lying prone beside the sea and at night beside a river, his head wrapped in the fleece of a black ram. He then descended into the Idaean Cave wearing black wool, spent there the customary thrice nine days, made a funeral offering (καθήγισε) to Zeus, saw the throne which was strown for the god once a year, and inscribed on his tomb an epigram entitled 'Pythagoras to Zeus,' which begins ὧδε θανὼν κεῖται Ζάν, ὃν Δία κικλήσκουσιν (*supra* i. 158 n. 2, 646 n. 3, ii. 341 n. 6, 345 n. 1). It is abundantly clear that the cavern-rites were concerned with death as well as birth. Zan or Zeus lay dead. Yet yearly a throne was spread for him, *i.e.* for Zeus come to life again as Zagreus (*supra* i. 646 f.). Pythagoras sought to share his death and resurrection.

Apart from the cave-sanctuary there were in *s.* v B.C.—if we may trust the *Cretans* of Euripides—temples of Zeus Ἰδαῖος roofed with cypress-planks, which were fastened together with glue made of bull's hide. Here the mystics of the god made thunder like Zagreus, feasted on raw flesh, brandished torches for the mountain-mother, and transformed from Kouretes into Bakchoi led thenceforward a life of ceremonial purity (Eur. *Cretes frag.* 472 Nauck[2] *ap.* Porph. *de abst.* 4. 19 cited *supra* i. 648 n. 1). The significance of these rites has already been discussed (*supra* i. 648 ff.).

An archaic *boustrophedón* inscription recording a convention between Gortyna and Rhizenia stipulates that the Rhizeniates shall send the victims to Mt Ide, every other year, to the value of 350 *statêres* (F. Halbherr in the *Am. Journ. Arch.* 1897 i. 204 ff. no. 23, F. Blass in Collitz—Bechtel *Gr. Dial.-Inschr.* iii. 2. 257 f. no. 4985, S. A. Xanthoudides in the Ἐφ. Ἀρχ. 1908 p. 236 θιοί. ἐπὶ τοῖδ(δ)ε Ῥι[ττέν]ι[οι Γ]ορ[τυνίοις αὐτ]όν[ο]μ[ο]ι καύ[τ]όδικοι (space) [τ]ὰ θ[ύ]|ματα παρέκοντες ἐς Βίδαν [τρ]ί[τ]οι [Ϝέ]τει τριακατίος στατέρανς καὶ πεν|τέκοντα). We infer that the celebration on Mt Ide was trieteric (*supra* i. 662, 690 ff., 695 n. 8).

In Hellenistic times the appellative of Zeus was spelled Βιδάτας (= Ϝιδάτας, the god of Mt Ide. So first J. Schmidt in the *Zeitschrift für vergleichende Sprachforschung* 1863 xii. 217 Βιδάτας (Ἰδήτης?), cp. S. A. Xanthoudides *loc. cit.* H. B. Voretzsch in *Hermes* 1870 iv. 273 wrongly assumed connexion with the Phrygian and Macedonian βέδυ (Clem. Al. *strom.* 5. 8 p. 357, 11 ff. Stählin) and concluded that Βιδάτας meant ὑέτιος, ὄμβριος). A treaty of *c.* 150 B.C. between Lyttos and Olous makes the Lyttians swear by Zeus Βιδάτας (*Corp. inscr. Att.* ii. 1 no. 549*b*, 5 ff. = F. Blass in Collitz—Bechtel *Gr. Dial.-Inschr.* iii. 2. 380 f. no. 5147*b*, 5 ff. [ὀμνύω τὰν Ἐστίαν κ]αὶ Τῆνα Βιδάταν καὶ Τῆνα [--] | [--καὶ Ἀπέλλω]να Πύτιον καὶ Λατῶν καὶ [Ἄ]ρ[τεμιν --] | [-- κ]αὶ τὰν Βριτόμαρτιν καὶ τὸς ἄ[λλος θιός --]. Another treaty, of *c.* 100 B.C., between Gortyna and Hierapytna on the one side and Priansos on the other, mentions a temple of Zeus Βιδάτας on the frontier of Priansoŝ (F. Blass in Collitz—Bechtel *Gr. Dial.-Inschr.* iii. 2. 301 ff. no. 5024, 22 f. [-- ἐς τὸ ἱαρὸν τῶ? Ττη]|[νὸς] τῶ Βιδατάω κῆς τὰνς Ἀντρι[--]. Cp. *ib.* 60 and 77 (cited *supra* p. 723 n. 0)).

The oldest cult-cavern of Mt Ide seems to have been the grotto, known locally as *Maurospelaion*, high up on the two-peaked mountain of *Kamares*, the southernmost bastion of the Idaean *massif*. This was first visited in 1894 by A. Taramelli ('A visit to the Grotto of Camares on Mount Ida' in the *Am. Journ. Arch.* 1901 v. 437—451 with map, elevation, plan, and section (map and plan copied by L. Bürchner in Pauly—Wissowa *Real-Enc.* ix. 859 f.)). It was thoroughly explored in 1913 by a party from the British School at Athens (R. M. Dawkins and M. L. W. Laistner 'The Excavation of the Kamares Cave in Crete' in the *Ann. Brit. Sch. Ath.* 1912—1913 xix. 1—34 with figs. 1—8 and pls. 1 (view), 2 (plan), 3 (section), 4—12 (pottery)). The finds included a couple of neolithic sherds, a few pieces of 'Early Minoan' spouted vessels, many handsome vases of 'Middle Minoan i and ii' date, a little 'Middle Minoan iii' ware, and a very little 'Late Minoan,' the series ending with two *Bügelkannen*. The grotto, which is free from snow for only a few months in the year, can hardly have been a dwelling and must rather be regarded as a sanctuary, presumably of the 'Minoan' mountain-goddess Rhea.

A. Taramelli in the *Am. Journ. Arch.* 1901 v. 434 held that it was the cult-centre of Zeus 'Ιδαῖος for the whole commune of Phaistos. But there is no real evidence to connect it with Zeus at all.

The Idaean Cave of classical times has been identified beyond all doubt with the great cavern 500 ft above the plateau of *Nida* (τὰν ϛΙδαν), a fresh grassy level lying to the east of the mountain-top. The actual summit of Ide (*Psiloriti* for Ὑψηλωρείτης), which attains the height of 8060 ft, is occupied by a small Greek monastery of the Holy Cross (*Timios Stauros*). Mr T. Fyfe, who spent a night on the summit, tells me (Jan. 9, 1923) that of the monastery little now remains except the church. This has a western domed compartment (13 ft 6 ins in diameter) with a narrow door leading to an oblong nave (11 ft 6 ins long by 8 ft 3 ins broad) covered by an elliptical dome. Eastwards of this is the sanctuary, entered by a semicircular arch and containing an aumbry opposite to a shallow recess for a seat. At the extreme east end is a built-in altar-table. The whole is very roughly constructed of rubble stone-work and is probably not very ancient, though the circular

Fig. 832.

western portion is said to be older than the remainder. About 3060 ft below the summit, but still at an altitude of some 5000 ft, lies *Nida*. And the Cave in the western side of its mountain-wall is used as a shelter both by shepherds and by travellers making the ascent from *Anogeia* (T. A. B. Spratt *Travels and Researches in Crete* London 1865 i. 9, 19. For *Anogeia* see *supra* i. 163 n. 1). In the summer of 1884 a shepherd named G. Pasparaki, grubbing in the cavern with a stick, chanced to find fragments of terra-cotta lamps, a few pieces of gold foil, and sundry small bronzes. These finds, being talked about, led to a visit the same year from E. Fabricius ('Alterthümer auf Kreta. II Die Idäische Zeusgrotte' in the *Ath. Mitth.* 1885 x. 59—72 with plan and 9 figs., *id.* 'Zur Idäischen Zeusgrotte' *ib.* p. 280 f.) and to a systematic exploration in 1885 by F. Halbherr and G. Aeraki under the auspices of J. Hazzidakis and the Syllogos of Kandia (F. Halbherr ' Scavi e trovamenti nell' antro di Zeus sul monte Ida in Creta' in the *Museo Italiano di Antichità Classica* 1888 ii. 689—768 with numerous figs., pls. 11 (two photographs, of which the second=my fig. 832), 12 (*a* plan, *b—d* sections=my figs. 833—836), and an Atlas of 12 pls., P. Orsi

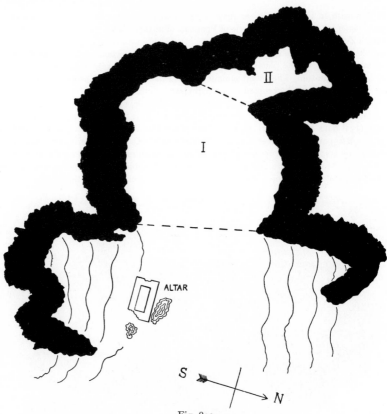

II

I

ALTAR

S

N

Fig. 833.

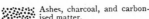 Ashes, charcoal, and carbon-
ised matter.
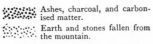 Earth and stones fallen from
the mountain.

Fig. 834.

'Studi illustrativi sui bronzi arcaici trovati nell' antro di Zeus Ideo' *ib.* pp. 769—904 with a few figs., A. L. Frothingham 'Early Bronzes recently discovered on Mount Ida in Krete' in the *Am. Journ. Arch.* 1888 iv. 431—449 with figs. 13—16 and pls. 16—20, H. Thiersch 'Altkretisches Kuretengerät' in the *Jahrb. d. kais. deutsch. arch. Inst.* 1913 xxviii **Arch. Anz.** pp. 47—53 with fig. 1).

The Cave comprises three well-marked divisions: (*a*) the entry; (*b*) chamber I, the *sanctum*; (*c*) chamber II, the *sanctum sanctorum*.

(*a*) On the south side of the entry is a great fallen rock shaped into an altar, the top of which forms an oblong mass (4·80^m long, 1·95^m broad, 0·88^m high) with a wide step all round it (*c.* 1·45^m broad, *c.* 3^m high). Beside it are fragments split off from the parent block and forming deep crannies and cavities, in which many small votive offerings came to light. On the north side are limestone bases of bronze statues etc. formerly erected on

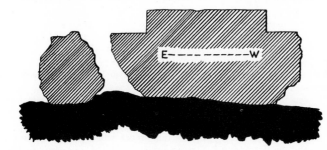

Fig. 835.

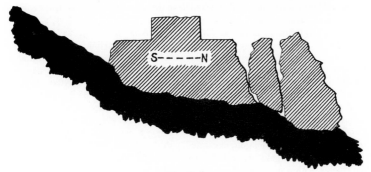

Fig. 836.

the stair-like rocky slope (cp. Theophr. *hist. pl.* 3. 3. 4 cited *supra*). Immediately in front of the Cave numerous objects in bronze, silver, and gold were unearthed.

(*b*) The *sanctum*, entered through a broad yawning aperture (9·50^m high), forms a wide hall (25^m to 31^m across) with rocky walls showing no trace of artificial niches. Snow-drifts have carried down into it a thick bed of earth and stones. This contains patches of black carbonised matter, and has yielded the bulk of the articles in plate-bronze.

(*c*) The *sanctum sanctorum* is a smaller chamber (22^m long, 8^m broad, over 4·50^m high), opening out of the *sanctum* but almost entirely dark. The floor is covered to a depth of several feet with a layer of ashes and charcoal, in which were found fragments of animal-bones half-burnt, several ox-skulls with horns attached, and many terra-cotta lamps.

Below the Cave, on the western edge of the *Nida*-plain, are the foundations of a Roman house once occupied by the custodians of the sanctuary.

The only 'Minoan' object known to have been found in the Cave is a lenticular gem of rock crystal representing a woman, who blows a conch-shell before a group of three sacred trees (Furtwängler *Ant. Gemmen* iii. 47 fig. 22, Sir A. J. Evans *The Palace of Minos at Knossos* London 1921 i. 221 fig. 167, *supra* i. 649 n. 3). This is interesting in view of the tradition that Aigokeros, the *connutricius...Iovis* (Arat. Lat. p. 237 Maass) in the Idaean Cave, was the discoverer of the conch (*supra*). I should conjecture that it was used to make mock-thunder in the rites of Zagreus, the re-born Zeus. It may also be pointed out that Aigokeros or Capricornus was derived from Mesopotamia, where he figures as the constellation *Suḫur-máš*, the 'Fish-goat' (A. Jeremias *Handbuch der altorientalischen Geisteskultur* Leipzig 1913 p. 117 figs. 94—96 and Index p. 362, *id.* in Roscher *Lex. Myth.* iv. 1463 f. figs. 24, 26—29). It is therefore tempting to suppose that Aigokeros came to Crete from the same quarter and along the same route as Zagreus (*supra* i. 651). Further, in Mesopotamian star-lore the constellation *Suḫur-máš* is so intimately related to the constellation *Našru*, Aquila, that the 'Eagle' on occasion takes the place of the 'Fish-goat' (A. Jeremias *locc. citt.*); and the 'Eagle' is personified as the god Zamama (A. Jeremias *Handbuch* p. 129, *id.* in Roscher *Lex. Myth.* iv. 1492). It might be contended, without undue rashness, that we have here the ultimate reason for the Cretan association of Aigokeros with Zeus. But Jeremias goes far beyond this, when he suggests that Zamama and his 'Eagle' are actually the *Urbild* of Zeus and his eagle (*id. ib.*). *Panbabylonismus*!

Votive objects found in the Cave include the following : (1) Convex circular shields of thin bronze, with central boss representing lion's head, eagle or hawk, etc. in high relief and concentric zones of decoration (F. Halbherr *loc. cit.* p. 695 ff. nos. 1—9 Atlas pls. 2—5, 9, 1, 10, 3 f.). (2) A *týmpanon* of thin bronze with a *quasi*-Assyrian representation of Zeus and the Kouretes (*id. ib.* p. 709 f. no. 10 Atlas pl. 1 = *supra* i. 645 pl. xxxv). (3) Cymbals of thin bronze (*id. ib.* p. 712 ff. nos. 1—10 with figs.). (4) Bronze *phiálai*, eight of which are embellished with low reliefs in three distinct styles—Cypriote, Egypto-Phoenician, and Mesopotamian (*id. ib.* p. 718 ff. nos. 1—7 Atlas pls. 6, 7, 8, 9, 2 f., 10, 1 f., 12, 8, 10). (5) Bronze *oinochóai* (*id. ib.* p. 725 Atlas pl. 12, 9, 12 f.). (6) Bronze *lébetes* (*id. ib.* p. 725 ff. nos. 1—5 Atlas pl. 12, 4). (7) Very archaic groups of decorative figures in cast bronze, *e.g.* war-ship with rowers, chariots, warriors, man milking cow, hounds, etc. (*id. ib.* p. 727 ff. nos. 1—14 Atlas pl. 11). (8) Archaic bronze statuettes of nude male and female figures (*id. ib.* p. 732 ff. nos. 1—5 with figs. Atlas pl. 12, 1 f.). (9) Votive animals in bronze (*id. ib.* p. 736 f. nos. 1 sheep (?) with fig., 2 bull, 3 bulls' horns, 4 goats Atlas pl. 12, 3). (10) Ornamental figures in bronze, *e.g.* sphinxes, lion, horse, doves, snakes (*id. ib.* p. 745 ff. with figs. Atlas pl. 12, 18). (11) Handles of vases, rings and feet of tripods, etc. in bronze (*id. ib.* p. 737 ff. with figs. Atlas pl. 12, 11, 14—17, 19 f.). (12) Disks of thin gold decorated with dots or rays (*id. ib.* p. 749 ff. with figs.). A small plaque of thin gold stamped in relief with a procession of four warriors bearing circular shields, within an oblong framework of spirals (*id. ib.* p. 751 with fig.) : this may be of sub-'Minoan' date. Another plaque of gold inscribed ΙΟΥѠΗ | ꓘΑΙΙΗ | . . . . . | ꓤΟϽϽΑ, apparently a 'Gnostic' charm ending with [φυλ]άσσου. A few pieces of jewellery, *e.g.* an oblong plate of gold to which three draped female figures, with *bucrania* between them, are soldered ; from the plate hangs a snake biting its own tail (*id. ib.* p. 752). (13) A small bearded (?) head in amber (*id. ib.* p. 753 f. Atlas pl. 12, 6). (14) Sundry objects in ivory, *e.g.* a bull carved in the round (*id. ib.* p. 754 no. 1 Atlas pl. 12, 7) and a perfume-bottle (?) in the shape of a headless female body (*id. ib.* p. 753 f. no. 2 with figs.). (15) Two pieces of rock-crystal shaped like plano-convex lenses (*id. ib.* p. 756. On the vexed question of classical lenses see H. Blümner *Technologie und Terminologie der Gewerbe und Künste bei Griechen und Römern* Leipzig 1884 iii. 298 ff.). (16) Two small oblong seal-stones of steatite (F. Halbherr *loc. cit.* p. 757 f. with fig.). (17) Phoenician or pseudo-Egyptian majolicas (*id. ib.* p. 758 ff. with figs.). (18) Objects in terra cotta, *e.g.* the archaic figurine of a bull ; the two heads of a god, with a *modius*, and a goddess, with a diadem, embracing ; lamps with acanthus-leaf handles (*id. ib.* p. 759 ff. with fig.). (19) Arrow-heads and lance-heads of iron (*id. ib.* p. 764 with figs.).

Plate XLIII

Mount Juktas, as seen from the west, showing the profile of the 'Pursuer' (Διώκτας).

See page 939 n. 1.

Mount Juktas[1].

(20) A tablet of terra cotta bearing in rubricated characters of Roman date the crucial inscription Δὶ Ἰδαί[ω] | εὐχὴν | Ἀστὴρ ['Α]|λεξάν|δρου (E. Fabricius in the *Ath. Mitth.* 1885 x. 280 f., F. Halbherr *loc. cit.* p. 766).

Thus for more than a millennium—from 'Minoan' to Roman times—men paid their vows to Zeus Ἰδαῖος in the shadow of a great rock and turned again, well content, to the duties that awaited them in the sunlight five thousand feet below.

The cave on Mt Ide called *Arkésion* (*supra* p. 548 f.) has been identified tentatively with the *Kamares* grotto (L. Bürchner in Pauly—Wissowa *Real-Enc.* ix. 861). But its traditional connexion with the Kouretes (*supra* p. 549 n. 1) points rather to identification with the better known Idaean Cave, where in fact the Curetic *týmpanon* was found (*supra*). The name Ἀρκέσιον has been interpreted (L. Bürchner *loc. cit.*) as the 'Bear's Hole' (from ἄρκος, a doublet of ἄρκτος: see Prellwitz *Etym. Wörterb. d. Gr. Spr.²* p. 53, Boisacq *Dict. étym. de la Langue Gr.* p. 78 f.)—a view which might be supported by the existence of a cavern usually described as that of the Bear (*Arkhoudhes*) in the promontory of *Akrotiri*, east of Kydonia (Canea) (Miss D. M. A. Bate in A. Trevor-Battye *Camping in Crete* London 1913 p. 248). After all, bears had some claim to be regarded as the nurses of the infant Zeus (*supra* i. 112 n. 5).

Mr Trevor-Battye *op. cit.* p. 108 ff. describes and illustrates his ascent of the mountain. He says (p. 119 ff.) : ' The actual summit of Ida is a blunted cone with rounded sides. Most of the summit was clear of snow, but on the southern and western sides lay some large melting drifts. The loose stones that pave this cone are laid down flat by the wind. The summit, 8,193 feet high, is now called Stavros... On the tip-top of Ida is a " monastery " : every church in Crete is called a monastery. This particular one is a tiny little building made very strong against the wind ; it is built on the same principle as the mountain-shepherds' huts—of slabs of stone laid one upon the other. At one point only has any mortar been used, just at the springing of the chancel dome. There were tapers inside for the devotees to burn before the ikons... I gathered...that a priest comes once a year to hold a service in this church. The church is surrounded by a walled enclosure that also includes a well of excellent ice-cold water... Beyond the enclosure a circle had been cleared of stones, and here, said Ianni, once a year the people danced. Spratt tells how, as he went up to Ida, he saw forty ibex, and that a group were actually browsing on the summit ; but that was over fifty years ago. I scanned the rocks in' every direction in vain.'

[1] Mt Juktas, an isolated ridge running from south to north towards Knossos and the sea, attains a height of 2720 ft. Its modern Greek name Γιούχτας or Γιούκτας derives from an earlier Διώκτας and means the 'Pursuer' (διώκτης). Such a name of course presupposes a myth, and very fortunately the myth is preserved for us by Kallimachos, who describes the 'pursuit' (διωκτύν) of Britomartis by Minos (Kallim. *h. Artem.* 189 ff., *supra* i. 527 n. 1 : cp. Diod. 5. 76 διωκομένην ὑπὸ Μίνω). The poet tells how Britomartis, to escape the embraces of Minos, plunged from the top of Mt Dikte into the sea, but omits to state what became of her disappointed lover. In all probability he was transformed into the mountain still called the 'Pursuer.' For the outline of Juktas, as seen from the west, is suggestive of a human face. A. Trevor-Battye *Camping in Crete* London 1913 p. 184 with pl. (my pl. xliii is reproduced from a photograph very kindly given me by Mr C. R. Haines) remarks : 'Rocks and mountains often bear a likeness to human lineaments ; every traveller can recall many such resemblances, but none that I have seen have the convincing dignity of the face on Iuktas. The bearded face and the drapery or pillow on which the head reposes occupy the whole of the mountain-top. Seen in the flatness of the mid-day light it is an interesting outline and no more, but at turn of the sun the sculpturing begins. The sun works in masses, as Michelangelo worked ; it carves out the planes of the face as Donatello carved them, letting detail go. So the chiselling continues, a high light here, a deepening shadow there, till with closed eyes the head has sunk down upon its pillow just as the sun is low.' Sir A. J. Evans *The Palace of Minos at Knossos* London 1921 i.

156 with fig. 112 informs us 'that the long ridge of the mountain rising in successive peaks has given rise to a widespread belief in the island that it reproduces the profile of the native Zeus.' It would seem, then, that in the popular interpretation of this natural phenomenon Minos has been dispossessed by Zeus.

The same process of religious expropriation can perhaps be detected in another famous feature of Mt Juktas—the so-called tomb of Zeus. It may be that this celebrated monument really was, as the schol. Kallim. *h. Zeus* 8 (*supra* i. 158 n. 2, cited *infra*) declares it to have been, *ab origine* the tomb of Minos (cp. Sir A. J. Evans in the *Journ. Hell. Stud.* 1901 xxi. 121 n. 3, *id. The Palace of Minos at Knossos* i. 154). The transition from king to god, always possible, becomes peculiarly probable in the case of one who was Διὸς μεγάλου ὀαριστής (*Od.* 19. 179). A lawgiver who claimed to speak with the authority of Zeus might readily be regarded as Zeus incarnate (*supra* i. 662 with n. 1). The tomb has already engaged our attention at some length (*supra* i. 157—163). I shall therefore be content to collect here the ancient allusions to it—a task well, but not quite adequately, performed by J. Meursius *Creta, Cyprus, Rhodus* Amstelodami 1675 pp. 77—81—and to add a brief account of the excavations carried out on the site in 1909 by Sir A. J. Evans and Dr D. Mackenzie (Sir A. J. Evans *The Palace of Minos at Knossos* London 1921 i. 154 ff. figs. 112—114).

Epimenides(?) *ap.* the *Gannat Busamé* (cited *supra* i. 157 n. 3) and *ap.* Isho'dad (cited *supra* i. 663 n. 2). Kallim. *h. Zeus* 8 f. Κρῆτες ἀεὶ ψεῦσται· καὶ γὰρ τάφον, ὦ ἄνα, σεῖο | Κρῆτες ἐτεκτήναντο· σὺ δ' οὐ θάνες, ἐσσὶ γὰρ αἰεί with schol. τάφον· ἐν Κρήτῃ ἐπὶ τῷ τάφῳ τοῦ Μίνωος ἐπεγέγραπτο "Μίνωος τοῦ Διὸς τάφος"· τῷ χρόνῳ δὲ τὸ τοῦ Μίνωος (A. Meineke cj. τὸ "Μίνωος τοῦ") ἀπηλείφθη (Meineke cj. ἀπηλίφη) ὥστε περιλειφθῆναι <"τοῦ (ins. O. Schneider)> Διὸς τάφος." ἐκ τούτου οὖν ἔχειν λέγουσι Κρῆτες τὸν τάφον τοῦ Διός. ἢ ὅτι Κορύβαντες λαβόντες αὐτὸν ἐπὶ τῷ (so Meineke for τοῦ cod. E, τὸ vulg.) κρύψαι διὰ τὸν Κρόνον προσεποιήσαντο τάφον αὐτῷ. Enn. *sacr. hist. frag.* 526 Baehrens *ap.* Lact. *div. inst.* 1. 11 Ennius in Sacra Historia descriptis omnibus quae in vita sua gessit ad ultimum sic ait: 'deinde Iuppiter postquam quinquies terras circuivit omnibusque amicis atque cognatis suis imperia divisit reliquitque hominibus leges mores frumentaque paravit multaque alia bona fecit, inmortali gloria memoriaque adfectus sempiterna monumenta sui reliquit. aetate pessum acta in Creta vitam commutavit et ad deos abiit eumque Curetes filii sui curaverunt decoraveruntque eum (W. von Hartel cj. <ut d>eum); et sepulchrum eius est in Creta in oppido Gnosso et dicitur Vesta hanc urbem creavisse; inque sepulchro eius est inscriptum antiquis litteris Graecis ZAN KPONOY id est Latine Iuppiter Saturni.' hoc certe non poetae tradunt, sed antiquarum rerum scriptores. quae adeo vera sunt, ut ea Sibyllinis versibus confirmentur, qui sunt tales: δαίμονας ἀψύχους, νεκύων εἴδωλα καμόντων, | ὧν Κρήτη καύχημα τάφους ἡ δύσμορος ἕξει (= *oracl. Sibyll.* 8. 47 f. The passage continues, after a comma, θρησκεύουσα θρόνωσιν ἀναισθήτοις νεκύεσσιν). etc. Varr. *ap.* Solin. 11. 7 Varro in opere quod de litoralibus est etiam suis temporibus adfirmat sepulcrum Iovis ibi visitatum (C. Cichorius *Römische Studien* Leipzig—Berlin 1922 p. 212 argues, from a comparison of Varr. *frag.* 364 Bücheler *ap.* Non. Marc. p. 775, 14 ff. Lindsay, that Varro had himself seen the tomb). Cic. *de nat. deor.* 3. 53 tertium (*sc.* Iovem) Cretensem, Saturni filium, cuius in illa insula sepulcrum ostenditur (quoted by Lact. *div. inst.* 1. 11). Diod. 3. 61 γεγονέναι δὲ καὶ ἕτερον Δία, τὸν ἀδελφὸν μὲν Οὐρανοῦ, τῆς δὲ Κρήτης βασιλεύσαντα, τῇ δόξῃ πολὺ λειπόμενον τοῦ μεταγενεστέρου. τοῦτον μὲν οὖν βασιλεῦσαι τοῦ σύμπαντος κόσμου, τὸν δὲ προγενέστερον, δυναστεύοντα τῆς προειρημένης νήσου, δέκα παῖδας γεννῆσαι τοὺς ὀνομασθέντας Κούρητας· προσαγορεῦσαι δὲ καὶ τὴν νῆσον ἀπὸ τῆς γυναικὸς Ἰδαίαν, ἐν ᾗ καὶ τελευτήσαντα ταφῆναι, δεικνυμένου τοῦ τὴν ταφὴν δεξαμένου τόπου μέχρι τῶν καθ' ἡμᾶς χρόνων, *ib.* 6. 5 Vogel (*infra*). *Anth. Pal.* 7. 275. 5 f. (Gaetulicus) τὸν ψεύσταν δέ με τύμβον ἐπὶ χθονὶ θέντο. τί θαῦμα; | Κρῆτες ὅπου ψεῦσται, καὶ Διός ἐστι τάφος (for the cenotaph of Astydamas, a Cydonian drowned between Cape Malea and Crete). Lucan. 8. 871 f. atque erit Aegyptus populis fortasse nepotum | tam mendax Magni tumulo quam Creta Tonantis. Mela 2. 112 Crete...multis famigerata fabulis...maxime tamen eo quod ibi sepulti Iovis paene clarum vestigium, sepulcrum cui nomen eius insculptum est adcolae ostendunt. Stat. *Theb.* 1. 278 f. (Iuno to Iupiter) placet Ida nocens

mentitaque manes | Creta tuos. Tatian. *or. adv. Graec.* 44 τάφος τοῦ 'Ολυμπίου Διὸς καθ'
ὑμᾶς δείκνυται, κἂν ψεύδεσθαί τις τοὺς Κρῆτας λέγῃ. Loukian. *Iup. trag.* 45 εἰ δ' ὁ Ζεὺς ὁ
βροντῶν ἐστι, σὺ ἄμεινον ἂν εἰδείης ἐκεῖθέν ποθεν παρὰ τῶν θεῶν ἀφιγμένος, ἐπεὶ οἵ γε ἐκ
Κρήτης ἥκοντες ἄλλα ἡμῖν διηγοῦνται, τάφον τινὰ ἐκεῖθι δείκνυσθαι καὶ στήλην ἐφεστάναι
δηλοῦσαν ὡς οὐκέτι βροντήσειεν ἂν ὁ Ζεὺς πάλαι τεθνεώς, *de sacrif.* 10 οἱ δ' αὖ Κρῆτες οὐ
γενέσθαι παρ' αὐτοῖς οὐδὲ τραφῆναι μόνον τὸν Δία λέγουσιν, ἀλλὰ καὶ τάφον αὐτοῦ δεικνύουσι·
καὶ ἡμεῖς ἄρα τοσοῦτον ἠπατήμεθα χρόνον οἰόμενοι τὸν Δία βροντᾶν τε καὶ ὕειν καὶ τἆλλα
πάντα ἐπιτελεῖν, ὁ δὲ ἐλελήθει πάλαι τεθνεὼς παρὰ Κρησὶ τεθαμμένος, *philopatr.* 10 ἀλλ' ἔτι
ἀνεμνήσθην τὰ τῶν Κρητῶν, οἳ τάφον ἐπεδείκνυντό μοι τοῦ Διός σου καὶ τὰ τὴν μητέρα θρέψαντα
λόχμια (so M. Solanus and F. Guyet for δόχμια), ὡς ἀειθαλεῖς αἱ λόχμαι αὗται διαμένουσι,
philopseud. 3 τὸ δὲ καὶ πόλεις ἤδη καὶ ἔθνη πολλὰ κοινῇ καὶ δημοσίᾳ ψεύδεσθαι πῶς οὐ γελοῖον;
εἰ Κρῆτες μὲν τοῦ Διὸς τάφον δεικνύοντες οὐκ αἰσχύνονται, κ.τ.λ., *Timon* 6 ἤδη ποτὲ οὖν, ὦ
Κρόνου καὶ 'Ρέας υἱέ, τὸν βαθὺν τοῦτον ὕπνον ἀποσεισάμενος καὶ νήδυμον—ὑπὲρ τὸν 'Επιμενίδην
γὰρ κεκοίμησαι—καὶ ἀναρριπίσας τὸν κεραυνὸν ἢ ἐκ τῆς Οἴτης ἐναυσάμενος μεγάλην ποιήσας
τὴν φλόγα ἐπιδείξαιό τινα χολὴν ἀνδρώδους καὶ νεανικοῦ Διός, εἰ μὴ ἀληθῆ ἐστι τὰ ὑπὸ Κρητῶν
περὶ σοῦ καὶ τῆς ἐκεῖ ταφῆς μυθολογούμενα. Athenag. *supplicatio pro Christianis* 30 p. 40 f.
Schwartz (after quoting Kallim. *h. Zeus* 8 f.) πιστεύων, Καλλίμαχε, ταῖς γοναῖς τοῦ Διὸς
ἀπιστεῖς αὐτοῦ τῷ τάφῳ καὶ νομίζων ἐπισκιάσειν τἀληθὲς καὶ τοῖς ἀγνοοῦσι κηρύσσεις τὸν
τεθνηκότα κἂν μὲν τὸ ἄντρον βλέπῃς, τὸν 'Ρέας ὑπομιμνήσκῃ τόκον, ἂν δὲ τὴν σορὸν ἴδῃς,
ἐπισκοτεῖς τῷ τεθνηκότι, οὐκ εἰδὼς ὅτι μόνος ἀΐδιος ὁ ἀγένητος θεός. Theophil. *ad Autol.* 1. 10
πεύσομαι δέ σου κἀγώ, ὦ ἄνθρωπε, πόσοι Ζῆνές εὑρίσκονται· Ζεὺς μὲν γὰρ ἐν πρώτοις προσ-
αγορεύεται 'Ολύμπιος, καὶ Ζεὺς Λατέριος (*leg.* Λατιάριος), καὶ Ζεὺς Κάσιος, καὶ Ζεὺς
Κεραύνιος, καὶ Ζεὺς Προπάτωρ, καὶ Ζεὺς Παννύχιος, καὶ Ζεὺς Πολιοῦχος, καὶ Ζεὺς Καπετώλιος·
καὶ ὁ μὲν Ζεὺς παῖς Κρόνου, βασιλεὺς Κρητῶν γενόμενος, ἔχει τάφον ἐν Κρήτῃ· οἱ δὲ λοιποὶ
ἴσως οὐδὲ ταφῆς κατηξιώθησαν, *ib.* 2. 3 πρὸς τί δὲ καὶ καταλέλοιπεν ὁ Ζεὺς τὴν "Ιδην; πότερον
τελευτήσας, ἢ οὐκ ἔτι ἤρεσεν αὐτῷ ἐκεῖνο τὸ ὄρος; ποῦ δὲ καὶ ἐπορεύθη; εἰς οὐρανούς; οὐχί.
ἀλλὰ ἐρεῖς εἰς Κρήτην; ναί, ὅπου καὶ τάφος αὐτῷ ἕως τοῦ δεῦρο δείκνυται. Clem. Al.
protr. 2. 37. 4 p. 28, 6 ff. Stählin ζήτει σου τὸν Δία· μὴ τὸν οὐρανόν, ἀλλὰ τὴν γῆν πολυ-
πραγμόνει. ὁ Κρής σοι διηγήσεται, παρ' ᾧ καὶ τέθαπται· Καλλίμαχος ἐν ὕμνοις (*h. Zeus* 8 f.)
"καὶ γὰρ τάφον, ὦ ἄνα, σεῖο | Κρῆτες ἐτεκτήναντο." τέθνηκε γὰρ ὁ Ζεὺς (μὴ δυσφόρει) ὡς
Λήδα (J. Markland cj. ὦ Λήδα), ὡς κύκνος, ὡς ἀετός, ὡς ἄνθρωπος ἐρωτικός, ὡς δράκων.
Philostr. *v. soph.* 2. 4 p. 74 Kayser (Antiochos, a sophist of Aigai in Kilikia, *s.* ii A.D.)
ἄριστα δὲ καὶ ὑπὲρ τῶν Κρητῶν ἀπελογήσατο, τῶν κρινομένων ἐπὶ τῷ τοῦ Διὸς σήματι,
φυσιολογίᾳ τε καὶ θεολογίᾳ πάσῃ ἐναγωνισάμενος λαμπρῶς. Orig. *c. Cels.* 3. 43 μετὰ ταῦτα
λέγει (*sc.* ὁ Κέλσος) περὶ ἡμῶν ὅτι καταγελῶμεν τῶν προσκυνούντων τὸν Δία, ἐπεὶ τάφος αὐτοῦ
ἐν Κρήτῃ δείκνυται, καὶ οὐδὲν ἧττον σέβομεν τὸν ἀπὸ τοῦ τάφου, οὐκ εἰδότες, πῶς καὶ καθὸ
Κρῆτες τὸ τοιοῦτον ποιοῦσιν. ὅρα οὖν ὅτι ἐν τούτοις ἀπολογεῖται μὲν περὶ Κρητῶν καὶ τοῦ Διὸς
καὶ τοῦ τάφου αὐτοῦ, αἰνιττόμενος τροπικὰς ὑπονοίας, καθ' ἃς πεπλάσθαι λέγεται ὁ περὶ τοῦ
Διὸς μῦθος· ἡμῶν δὲ κατηγορεῖ, ὁμολογούντων μὲν τετάφθαι τὸν ἡμέτερον 'Ιησοῦν φασκόντων
δὲ καὶ ἐγηγέρθαι αὐτὸν ἀπὸ τοῦ τάφου, ὅπερ Κρῆτες οὐκέτι περὶ τοῦ Διὸς ἱστοροῦσιν. ἐπεὶ δὲ
δοκεῖ συναγορεύειν τῷ ἐν Κρήτῃ τάφῳ τοῦ Διὸς αὐτῶν· τούτῳ μὲν καὶ καθότι Κρῆτες τοῦτο
ποιοῦσιν, οὐκ εἰδότες, φήσομεν ὅτι καὶ ὁ Κυρηναῖος Καλλίμαχος, πλεῖστα ὅσα ἀναγνοὺς
ποιήματα καὶ ἱστορίαν σχεδὸν πᾶσαν ἀναλεξάμενος 'Ελληνικήν, οὐδεμίαν οἶδε τροπολογίαν ἐν
τοῖς περὶ Διὸς καὶ τοῦ τάφου αὐτοῦ. κ.τ.λ. (a quotation and discussion of Kallim. *h. Zeus* 8 f.,
10, 6 ff.). Min. Fel. *Oct.* 21. 8 eius (*sc.* Saturni) filius Iuppiter Cretae excluso parente
regnavit, illic obiit, illic filios habuit: adhuc (C. A. Heumann cj. illic adhuc) antrum Iovis
visitur et sepulcrum eius ostenditur, et ipsis sacris suis humanitatis arguitur. Cypr. *de*
idol. van. 2 (iv. 567 A Migne) antrum Iovis in Creta visitur (uisitur cod. L. uisitor cod. C¹.
uisitator cod. C². uidetur cod. P. dicitur cod. M. mittitur cod. B.), et sepulcrum eius
ostenditur, et ab eo Saturnum fugatum manifestum est. Porph. *v. Pyth.* 17 (cited *supra* i.
646 n. 3). Arnob. *adv. nat.* 4. 14 aiunt igitur theologi vestri et vetustatis absconditae
conditores, tris (*v.l.* tres) in rerum natura Ioves esse, ex quibus unus Aethere sit patre pro-
genitus, alter Caelo, tertius vero Saturno apud insulam Cretam et sepulturae traditus et
procreatus, *ib.* 4. 25 apud insulam Cretam sepulturae esse mandatum Iovem nobis editum
traditur? Firm. Mat. 7. 6 et a vanis Cretensibus adhuc mortui Iovis tumulus adoratur.

Serv. *in* Verg. *Aen.* 7. 180 antiqui reges nomina sibi plerumque vindicabant deorum...hinc est quod apud Cretam esse dicitur Iovis sepulcrum. Epiphan. *adv. haer.* 1. 3. 42 (ii. 376 Dindorf) καὶ πάλιν φήσαντος (Titus 1. 12) "εἰπέ τις ἴδιος αὐτῶν προφήτης, Κρῆτες ἀεὶ ψεῦσται, κακὰ θηρία, γαστέρες ἀργαί," ἵνα τὸν Ἐπιμενίδην δείξῃ, ἀρχαῖον ὄντα φιλόσοφον, καὶ Μίθρα (*leg.* μάρτυρα) τοῦ παρὰ Κρησὶν εἰδώλου (*v.l.* εἰδωλίου)· ἀφ᾽ οὗπερ καὶ Καλλίμαχος ὁ Λίβυς τὴν μαρτυρίαν εἰς ἑαυτὸν συνανέτεινε, ψευδῶς περὶ Διὸς λέγων, Κρῆτες ἀεὶ ψεῦσται· κ.τ.λ. (Kallim. *h. Zeus* 8 f.). Hieron. *in ep. Paul. ad Tit.* 1 (xxvi. 573 A—C Migne) sunt qui putent hunc versum de Callimacho Cyrenensi poeta sumptum, et aliqua ex parte non errant. siquidem et ipse in laudibus Iovis adversus Cretenses scriptitans, qui sepulcrum eius se ostendere gloriantur, ait : 'Cretenses semper mendaces ; qui et sepulcrum eius sacrilega mente fabricati sunt.' verum, ut supra diximus, integer versus de Epimenide poeta ab apostolo sumptus est ; et eius Callimachus in suo poemate est usus exordio. sive vulgare proverbium, quo Cretenses fallaces appellabantur, sine furto alieni operis in metrum retulit. putant quidam apostolum reprehendendum quod imprudenter lapsus sit et (*alii* ut), dum falsos doctores arguit, illum versiculum comprobarit, quod propterea Cretenses dicuntur (*alii* dicunt) esse fallaces quod Iovis sepulcrum inane construxerint. si enim, inquiunt, Epimenides sive Callimachus propterea Cretenses fallaces et malas bestias arguunt et ventres pigros quod divina non sentiant et Iovem qui regnet in cœlo in sua insula fingant sepultum, et hoc quod illi dixerunt esse verum apostoli sententia comprobatur, sequitur Iovem non mortuum esse sed vivum. Rufin. *recognit.* 10. 23 ipsius denique parricidae, qui et patruos peremit et uxores eorum vitiavit, sororibus stuprum intulit, multiformis magi sepulcrum evidens est apud Cretenses, qui tamen scientes et confitentes infanda eius atque incesta opera et omnibus enarrantes ipsi eum confiteri deum non erubescunt. Caesarius (youngest brother of Gregorios Nazianzenos) *dial.* 2. respons. ad interrogat. 112 (xxxviii. 992 Migne) οἱ δὲ τούτοις πειθόμενοι οὐ θεῷ ἀλλὰ σποδῷ προσκυνοῦσι Διὸς (so Cotelerius for διὰ) τοῦ πατραλοίου καὶ τῶν οἰκείων τέκνων τοὺς γάμους φθείραντος καὶ ἐν τάφῳ παρὰ Κρησὶ (so Cotelerius for κρίσει) φθαρέντος, ὅπερ οὐκ ἔστι θεοῦ. Chrysost. *in ep. Paul. ad Tit.* 3. 1 (lxii. 676 f. Migne) καὶ γὰρ ὅτε τοῖς Ἀθηναίοις διελέγετο, μεταξὺ τῆς δημηγορίας φησίν, "Ἀγνώστῳ Θεῷ"· καὶ πάλιν, "τοῦ γὰρ καὶ γένος ἐσμέν, ὡς καί τινες τῶν καθ᾽ ὑμᾶς ποιητῶν εἰρήκασιν." Ἐπιμενίδης οὖν ἐστιν ὁ εἰρηκώς, Κρὴς καὶ αὐτὸς ὤν· ἀλλὰ πόθεν κινούμενος, ἀναγκαῖον εἰπεῖν τὴν ὑπόθεσιν πρὸς ὑμᾶς· ἔχει δὲ οὕτως· οἱ Κρῆτες τάφον ἔχουσι τοῦ Διὸς ἐπιγραφέντα τοῦτο· "ἐνταῦθα Ζὰν κεῖται, ὃν (*leg.* τὸν) Δία κικλήσκουσι." διὰ ταύτην τὴν ἐπιγραφὴν ὁ ποιητὴς ψεύστας τοὺς Κρῆτας κωμῳδῶν, προϊὼν πάλιν ἐπάγει, αὔξων μᾶλλον τὴν κωμῳδίαν· "καὶ γὰρ τάφον, ὦ ἄνα, σεῖο | Κρῆτες ἐτεκτήναντο· σὺ δ᾽ οὐ θάνες, ἐσσὶ γὰρ αἰεί." κ.τ.λ. Paulin. Nol. 19. 84 ff. (lxi. 515 Migne) Marcus, Alexandrea, tibi datus, ut bove pulso | cum Iove nec pecudes Aegyptus in Apide demens, | in Iove nec civem coleret male Creta sepultum. Kyrill. Al. *c. Iulian.* 10. 342 (lxxvi. 1028 B Migne) γέγραφε δὲ πάλιν περὶ αὐτοῦ (sc. τοῦ Πυθαγόρου) Πορφύριος (*v. Pyth.* 17)· "εἰς δὲ τὸ Ἰδαῖον καλούμενον ἄντρον καταβάς, ἔρια ἔχων μέλανα, τὰς νενομισμένας τριττὰς ἐννέα ἡμέρας ἐκεῖ διέτριψε καὶ καθήγισε τῷ Διί, τόν τε στορνύμενον αὐτῷ κατ᾽ ἔτος θρόνον ἐθεάσατο, ἐπίγραμμά τε (*Anth. Pal.* 7. 746 cited *supra* p. 345 n. 1) ἐνεχάραξεν ἐν τάφῳ, ἐπιγράψας ΠΥΘΑΓΟΡΑΣ ΤΩ, ΔΙΙ, οὗ ἡ ἀρχή,—ὧδε μέγας κεῖται ΖΑΝ, ὃν ΔΙΑ κικλήσκουσιν." κ.τ.λ. Nonn. *Dion.* 8. 114 ff. ἀλλ᾽ ὅτε Δικταίης Κορυβαντίδος ὑψόθι πέτρης | γείτονος Ἀμνισοῖο λεχώιον ἔδρακεν (sc. "Ηρη) ὕδωρ, | ἔνθα οἱ ἀλλοπρόσαλλος ὀρεστιὰς ἤντεεν δαίμων (sc. Ἀπάτη)· | καὶ γὰρ δεῖ παρείμμνε Διὸς ψευδόμενι τύμβῳ | τερπομένη Κρήτεσσιν, ἐπεὶ πέλον ἠπεροπῆες. Theodoret. *interp. ep. Paul. ad Tit.* 1. 12 f. (lxxxii. 861 B Migne) οὐ γὰρ Ἰουδαίων προφήτης Καλλίμαχος ἦν (αὐτοῦ γὰρ ἡ τοῦ ἔπους ἀρχή), ἀλλ᾽ Ἑλλήνων ἦν ποιητής. ἀλλ᾽ ὁ μὲν ποιητὴς διὰ τὸν τοῦ Διὸς τάφον τοὺς Κρῆτας ὠνόμασε ψεύστας. ὁ δὲ θεῖος ἀπόστολος ἀληθῆ τὴν μαρτυρίαν ἐκάλεσεν, οὐ τὴν ποιητικὴν βεβαιῶν μυθολογίαν, ἀλλὰ τῶν Κρητῶν διελέγχων τὸ τῆς γνώμης ἀβέβαιον· ἀντὶ τοῦ, καλῶς ὑμᾶς προσηγόρευσε ψεύστας· τοιοῦτοι γὰρ καθεστήκατε. εἰκὸς δὲ καὶ ἑτέρωθι τὸν καλούμενον Δία τεθνάναι καὶ τούτους μάτην οἰκοδομῆσαι τὸν τάφον. Sedulius Scotus *in ep. Paul. ad Tit.* 1 (ciii. 244 C Migne) *Cretenses semper mendaces.* hoc Epimenides sive Callimachus Cyrenensis de laudibus Iovis contra Cretenses dixit, qui dicebant apud eos sepultum quem raptum putabant in cœlum. Schol. Bern. Lucan. 8. 872 (cited *supra* p. 342). Souid. *s.v.* Πῆκος ὁ καὶ Ζεὺς παραδοὺς τὴν τῆς δύσεως ἀρχὴν τῷ ἰδίῳ υἱῷ Ἑρμῇ τελευτᾷ, ζήσας κ΄ καὶ ἑκατὸν ἔτη· καὶ τελευτῶν ἐκέλευσεν ἀποτεθῆναι τὸ ἑαυτοῦ σῶμα ἐν τῇ Κρήτῃ τῇ νήσῳ <ἐν μνήματι>, ἐν ᾧ ἐπιγέγραπται· ἐνθάδε κεῖται θανὼν Πῆκος ὁ καὶ Ζεύς. μέμνηνται τοῦ τάφου τούτου πλεῖστοι ἐν τοῖς ἰδίοις συγγράμμασι. Kedren. *hist. comp.* 15 D—16 A (i. 28 f. Bekker) ὁ δὲ Κρόνος ἐξωσθεὶς τῆς βασιλείας ὑπὸ τοῦ ἰδίου υἱοῦ Διός, κατελθὼν ἐν τῇ δύσει κρατεῖ τῆς Ἰταλίας. εἶτα ὁ Ζεὺς ὑποχωρήσας τῶν Ἀσσυρίων παραγίνεται πρὸς τὸν πατέρα· ὁ δὲ παραχωρεῖ αὐτῷ βασιλεύειν τῆς Ἰταλίας. καὶ πολλοῖς ἔτεσι βασιλεύσας εἶτα τελευτήσας κατατίθεται ἐν τῇ Κρήτῃ...μετὰ δὲ τὴν τοῦ Διὸς τελευτὴν Φαῦνος ὁ υἱὸς αὐτοῦ ἐβασίλευσεν, ὃς μετωνομάσθη Ἑρμῆς. An attempt to trace the antecedents of the version common to Souidas and Kedrenos will be found *supra* p. 693 n. 4. The sources that mention the burial in Crete are Cramer *anecd. Paris.* ii. 236, 15 ff. (=Diod. 6. 5 Vogel) μέλλων δὲ τελευτᾶν ὁ Ζεὺς ἐκέλευσε τὸ λείψανον αὐτοῦ τεθῆναι ἐν τῇ Κρήτῃ νήσῳ· καὶ κτίσαντες αὐτῷ ναὸν οἱ αὐτοῦ παῖδες ἔθηκαν αὐτὸν ἐκεῖ· ὅπερ μνῆμά ἐστι μέχρι τῆς σήμερον, ᾧ καὶ ἐπιγέγραπται, 'ἐνθάδε κατάκειται Πῖκος ὁ καὶ Ζεύς, ὃν καὶ Δία καλοῦσι,' περὶ οὗ συνεγράψατο Διόδωρος ὁ σοφώτατος χρονογράφος, *ib.* ii. 257, 33 ff. (cited *supra* p. 695), Io. Antioch. *frag.* 5 (*Frag. hist. Gr.* iv. 542 Müller) (cited *supra* p. 695) and *frag.* 6. 4 (*Frag. hist. Gr.* iv. 542 Müller) μέλλων δὲ τελευτᾶν ἐκέλευσε τὸ λείψανον αὐτοῦ ἐν τῇ Κρήτῃ νήσῳ τεθῆναι· καὶ κτίσαντες αὐτῷ ναὸν οἱ αὐτοῦ παῖδες ἔθηκαν αὐτὸν ἐκεῖ ἐν τῇ Κρήτῃ ἐν μνήματι· ὅπερ μνῆμα ἐστιν ἕως τοῦ παρόντος ἐν Κρήτῃ. ἐν τῷ μνήματι ἐπιγέγραπται, 'ἔνθα κεῖται θανὼν Πῖκος ὁ καὶ Ζεύς, ὃν καὶ Δία καλοῦσι,' the *Chronicon Paschale* 44 B—C (i. 80 Dindorf) ἐν ᾧ χρόνῳ Πῖκος ὁ καὶ Ζεὺς ἐτελεύτα, ἐκέλευσεν τὸ λείψανον αὐτοῦ ταφὲν τεθῆναι ἐν τῇ Κρήτῃ νήσῳ· καὶ κτίσαντες αὐτῷ ναὸν οἱ αὐτοῦ παῖδες ἔθηκαν αὐτὸν ἐκεῖ ἐν τῇ Κρήτῃ νήσῳ ἐν μνήματι· ὅπερ μνῆμά ἐστιν ἐν τῇ αὐτῇ Κρήτῃ κείμενον ἕως τοῦ παρόντος, ἐν ᾧ ἐπιγέγραπται, 'ἐνθάδε κεῖται θανὼν Πῖκος ὁ καὶ Ζεύς, ὃν καὶ Δία καλοῦσι'· περὶ οὗ συνεγράψατο Διόδωρος ὁ σοφώτατος χρονογράφος, ὃς καὶ ἐν τῇ ἐκθέσει τοῦ συγγράμματος αὐτοῦ τοῦ περὶ θεῶν εἶπεν ὅτι Ζεὺς ὁ τοῦ Κρόνου υἱὸς ἐν τῇ Κρήτῃ κεῖται (Diod. 3. 61 *supra*). Psell. ἀναγωγὴ εἰς τὸν Τάνταλον (*supra* i. 158 n. 4) p. 348 Boissonade τοιαύτη μὲν καὶ ἡ δευτέρα δόξα περὶ τοῦ Διὸς τοῖς Ἕλλησιν· ἡ δὲ τρίτη ἱστορικωτέρα, καὶ ἴσως ἀληθεστέρα. αὐτόν τε γὰρ καὶ τὸν τούτου πατέρα τὸν Κρόνον οἱ μῦθοι ὁμόθεν ἀπὸ Κρήτης γεννῶσι, καὶ τὸν μὲν οὐκ ἴσασιν ὅπου γῆς κατορώρυκται, τοῦ δὲ τὸν ἐπὶ τῷ τάφῳ δεικνύουσι κολωνόν· εἶτα, τὴν θνητὴν ὑπεραναβάντες φύσιν, ἀγχισπόρους ποιοῦσι τῆς οὐσίας τῆς κρείττονος, καὶ πρὸς τὸ τῆς θειότητος εἶδος μεταβιβάζουσι. τούτῳ δὴ τῷ λόγῳ καὶ Ἑρμῆς προστίθεται ὁ Τρισμέγιστος. τἄλλα γὰρ παραθεωρῶν τοὺς μύθους, τοῦτον δὴ μόνον γυμνὸν ἐξεδέξατο, καὶ πρὸς τὴν ἐκείνου μίμησιν τὸν ἑαυτοῦ παῖδα διερεθίζει τὸν Τάτ (so J. F. Boissonade for τα cod. A. Τάνταλον cod. B).

For references to the tomb of Zeus in writers of the Renaissance and of modern times see *supra* i. 158 ff. A fifteenth-century map of Crete in the British Museum (MS. Add. 15, 760, *f.* 11), published by F. W. Hasluck in the *Ann. Brit. Sch. Ath.* 1905—1906 xii. 214 f. pl. 1, not only marks the *Sepulcru(m) Iouis* but adds a view of it, though—to judge from the representation of the neighbouring *Laberintus* as a circular maze-like structure— this is in the nature of a fancy-sketch.

A. Taramelli in 1899 published a rough plan of Mt. Juktas (*supra* i. 159 fig. 130), and drew special attention to the precinct-wall of 'Cyclopean' masonry, which crowns its northern summit at a height of *c.* 2300 ft above the sea (*supra* i. 160 fig. 132, 161 fig. 133). Within the wall he duly noted the scattered traces of a building, together with much broken pottery including pieces of 'Minoan' *pithoi* (*supra* i. 161 n. 1).

Sir A. J. Evans in 1909 determined the approximate date of the precinct-wall by finding in its inner interstices sherds of 'Middle Minoan i a' ware. 'Middle Minoan i' sherds were also abundant over the rocky surface enclosed by the wall. The cult here carried on passed through two well-marked phases, of 'Middle Minoan' and 'Late Minoan' date respectively.

During the earlier phase offerings were made in the open air at a great altar of ashes. This is represented by two *strata*—a layer of grey ashes yielding ceramic remains of the periods 'Middle Minoan i and ii,' and above it a layer of reddish burnt earth yielding sherds of 'Middle Minoan iii' date. Throughout both *strata* were votive relics in terra cotta—among the ashes, male and female figures, oxen, goats, human limbs (an arm perforated for suspension, two legs joined together), parts of animals (numerous clay ox-horns), 'prayer-pellets' like those of Petsofà (J. L. Myres in the *Ann. Brit. Sch. Ath.* 1902—1903 ix. 382) ; in the burnt earth, larger goats and oxen, the raised arms of a worshipper, clay locks of human hair, flat shell-like coils, and a limestone ladle with traces of an inscription in linear characters (class A). A similar ladle likewise inscribed was found in a deposit of the same date on *Troullos*, a foot-hill of Mt Juktas (S. A. Xanthoudides in the 'Εφ. 'Αρχ. 1909 p. 179 ff. figs. 1—4).

The later phase of the cult ('Late Minoan') witnessed the foundation of a rectangular building with walls of ashlar blocks and outer terrace-walls of rougher construction. The building was approached by an ascent (A—A) and comprised an entrance-chamber (B 1), a magazine (?) (B 2), and an inner room (C). In the floor of B 1 a large hollow has been dug by treasure-hunters. On the walls of B 2 fragments of a plaster-facing are still to be seen. And in C are remains of a paving in white-faced cement. The whole building 'seems to have reproduced the arrangement of a small house of the early Cretan and Aegean "but and ben" type, about 16 × 10 metres in its exterior dimensions' (Sir A. J. Evans *The Palace of Minos at Knossos* London 1921 i. 158 with fig. 114 = my fig. 837).

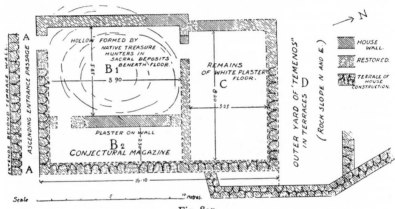

Fig. 837.

Outside the building, to the north, lay a *témenos* of roughly triangular shape supported by terrace-walls.

Here knowledge ends and conjecture begins. Sir Arthur Evans (*op. cit.* p. 158 ff.) surmises that the building described above 'was a little house of shelter and refection for the Goddess on her mountain top, a "Casa Santa,"' etc., and that the *témenos* was 'the hypaethral part of the Sanctuary, well adapted for the exposure of a pillar form of the divinity.' Further, he thinks that a gold signet from Knossos (*supra* p. 48 fig. 19), referable to the period 'Late Minoan ii,' represents 'the Minoan Mother Goddess...bringing down the warrior youth, whether her paramour or actual son, in front of his sacred pillar' —a scene which 'may be even taken to foreshadow the "Tomb of Zeus,"' for 'A later age seems to have regarded these baetylic pillars as actual tombs of divinities.'

Personally I should rather suppose that, just as Kinyras and his descendants were buried in the sanctuary of Aphrodite at Paphos (Ptolemaios of Megalopolis *frag.* 1 (*Frag. hist. Gr.* iii. 66 Müller) *ap.* Clem. Al. *protr.* 3. 45. 4 p. 35, 1 ff. Stählin and *ap.* Arnob. *adv. nat.* 6. 6), just as Erichthonios was buried in the precinct of Athena at Athens (Apollod. 3. 14. 7, *alib.*), just as Hippolytos was buried beside the temple of Aphrodite *Kataskopía* at Troizen (Paus. 2. 32. 3 f., cp. L. R. Farnell *Greek Hero Cults and Ideas of Immortality* Oxford 1921 p. 66)—and the list could be lengthened (see Clem. Al. *protr.* 3. 44. 4 ff. p. 34, 7 ff. Stählin, Arnob. *adv. nat.* 6. 6)—, so Minos the priestly king of Knossos lay buried within the circuit-wall of the mountain-goddess. I should conjecture that during his lifetime he had played the part of Zeus (*supra* i. 662 n. 1, cp. 527 n. 1),

Mount Alysis (?)[1].
Mount Arbios[2].

or rather of Zan the older form of Zeus (*supra* p. 340 ff.), and that after his death he continued to be venerated as Zan or Zeus incarnate. Hence the persistent tradition that the tomb was inscribed ZAN ΚΡΟΝΟΥ (Enn. *loc. cit.*), ΤΑΝ ΚΡΟΝΟΥ (schol. Bern. Lucan. *loc. cit.*), or ὧδε μέγας κεῖται ΖΑΝ ὃν ΔΙΑ κικλήσκουσι (*supra* p. 345). Hence too the ingenious guess of a late grammarian that the inscription originally ran Μίνωος τοῦ Διὸς τάφος (schol. Kallim. *loc. cit.*).

Paganism in due course was superseded by, or at least overlaid with, Christianity. The southern and higher summit of Mt Juktas is topped by a church of Αὐθέντης Χριστός, 'Christ the Lord,' to which there is an annual pilgrimage on August 6, the feast of the Μεταμόρφωσις or 'Transfiguration.' The church contains a chapel of the Panagia (Sir A. J. Evans *op. cit.* i. 154 with n. 7, *supra* i. 162 n. 1).

[1] Schol. Arat. *phaen.* 33 Δίκτῳ· Δίκτον (Δίκτον om. cod. M.) ἀκρωτήριον τῆς Κρήτης πλησίον τῆς Ἴδης τοῦ Κρητικοῦ ὄρους, ἔνθα ἐστὶν Ἀλυσίου Διὸς τέμενος παρὰ τὸ παρακείμενον ἐκεῖ ὄρος Ἄλυσις (so ed. Ald. περὶ τὸ περικείμενον ἄλσος, with ἡ ἄλυσος above ἄλσος cod. A. περὶ τὸ περικείμενον ἄλσος cod. M.). E. Maass cj. ἔνθα ἐστὶν Ἀλσείου Διὸς τέμενος. < ἐκλήθη δὲ οὗτος > παρὰ τὸ περικείμενον ἄλσος. Ἀλύσιος as a hyperdorism for Ἠλύσιος is improbable.

[2] Zeus Ἄρβιος (Steph. Byz. *s.v.* Ἄρβις·...ἔστι καὶ ἐν Κρήτῃ Ἄρβιος ὄρος, ἔνθα τιμᾶται Ἄρβιος Ζεύς). C. Müller in his commentary on Ptol. 3. 15. 3 Ἰνατος πόλις...Ἱερὸν ὄρος... Ἱεράπυτνα and on Anon. *stadiasm. Mar. Magn.* 320 (*Geogr. Gr. min.* i. 506 Müller) identifies Ἱερὸν ὄρος with the mountain of Zeus Ἄρβιος—a view accepted by L. Bürchner in Pauly—Wissowa *Real.-Enc.* viii. 1530 ('Zeus Orbios'!), *ib.* xi. 1814.

R. Pashley *Travels in Crete* Cambridge—London 1837 i. 285 and T. A. B. Spratt *Travels and Researches in Crete* London 1865 i. 295 give illustrations of the cleft at Arvi. Pashley *op. cit.* p. 275 f. would locate the cult of Zeus Ἄρβιος at a point near the shore, where—as he was assured by the villagers of Haghio Vasili—ancient walls, since chiefly used in building the church, were formerly to be seen. Spratt *op. cit.* i. 294 concurred in this opinion. A. Trevor-Battye *Camping in Crete* London 1913 p. 147 f. was even more successful; for he found the memory of Zeus yet living in the locality. He spent an uncomfortable night in a general store at the village of Kalami, where he wanted to skin birds, press plants, and write. The natives, however, dropped in to talk. 'And I am not likely'—he says—'to forget the story of the Hammer of Zeus, for a hammer used to illustrate the story frequently fell very near my head as I skinned a bird on an inverted packing-case. They said that between us and the sea was a gorge in which, in its ultimate and very narrow ravine, one heard the hammer of Zeus. They told me that when the mountain wind was well astir, blow after blow fell upon this chasm with the sound and shock of a titanic hammer. The noise of these repeated blows they said was awe-inspiring. Now the only gorge of this character near there appears to be that which lies below Peuko and runs thence to the sea.... Spratt says of this ravine, that the rock is "singularly rent from summit to base by a yawning fissure, nearly 1000 feet high*." [*Travels and Researches*, I 293.] He connects this rent with volcanic action evidenced in the rocks of the neighbouring valley (Myrtos), and proceeds: "In this remarkable feature, we probably see the reason for the erection of a temple to the God of Thunder at this locality, under the name of Jupiter Arbius. To whom but the God of Thunder could a temple be so appropriately dedicated when associated with such an apparent fracture from some great volcanic movement," etc. I venture to believe that could this distinguished seaman and geologist have listened to the men in the store that night, he would have accepted their story as a much more promising explanation of the temple of Zeus the Thunderer.'

Sir A. J. Evans *The Palace of Minos at Knossos* London 1921 i. 630 f., *à propos* of 'Minoan' libation-tables, says: 'a good specimen of a mottled steatite table of similar shape, though apparently uninscribed, was obtained by me in 1894 from the Knoll of Tartari in the striking cleft of Arvi on the South Coast[2] [[2]Near Viano. The libation table is now in the Ashmolean Museum.], where in later times was a sanctuary of the indigenous

God under the name of Zeus Arbios.' *Id.* in the *Journ. Hell. Stud.* 1894 xiv. 285 f. fig. 16 publishes a green steatite pendant, inscribed with two linear characters, which he got from an early cist-grave at Arvi. There was clearly a ' Minoan' settlement on the site.

The name Ἄρβιος is of doubtful significance. One is tempted to compare it with the Latin *arbor*, since the district abounds in trees. Peuko 'was once a fine pine forest,' and the hollow leading to Kalami 'is filled with ilex, myrtle, pine, oaks and poplars. Lower down near the village grow figs, pomegranates, mulberry, and other more or less cultivated trees' (A. Trevor-Battye *op. cit.* p. 145 f.). Besides, Zeus is known to have been a tree-god in Crete ; for he bore the title Ἐπιρνύτιος (Hesych. *s.v.* Ἐπιρνύτιος· Ζεὺς ἐν Κρήτῃ), which means either metaphorically 'set over the Growing Plants' (H. Voretzsch in *Hermes* 1870 iv. 273, Preller—Robert *Gr. Myth.* i. 130 n. 3, Gruppe *Gr. Myth. Rel.* p. 1109 n. 2, O. Jessen in Pauly—Wissowa *Real-Enc.* vi. 198) or literally 'on the Tree' (as I rendered it in the *Class. Rev.* 1903 xvii. 413 n. 1, cp. Hesych. *s.v.* Ἔνδενδρος· παρὰ Ῥοδίοις Ζεύς· καὶ Διόνυσος ἐν Βοιωτίᾳ), being derived from ἐπί + *ἴρνυς for ἔρνυς = ἔρνος (P. Kretschmer in the *Zeitschrift für vergleichende Sprachforschung* 1890 xxx. 584 'von ἔρνυτες.' Gerhard *Gr. Myth.* i. 161 wrongly prefers the spelling ἐπερνύτιος).

In this connexion we should note that silver *statêres* of Phaistos struck *c.* 360—300 B.C. have *obv.* ƷΟΝΑΧΛƎϽ A youthful, beardless god seated to the left amid the branches of a leafless tree ; his right hand caresses a cock perched on his knee ; his left hand rests on an animal's skin, which passes beneath him and falls over the upper part of his right leg :

rev. ΙΤƷΙΑΦ or ΦΑΙƧΤΙΟΝ (ΦΑΙƧ) A bull standing to the left, or plunging to the right, sometimes with a gad-fly on its back, sometimes surrounded with a bay-wreath (*Brit. Mus. Cat. Coins* Crete etc. p. 63 pl. 15, 10 and 12, Head *Coins of the Ancients* p. 28 pl. 14, 37, *id. Hist. num.*[2] p. 473 fig. 253, *Hunter Cat. Coins* ii. 193 no. 4, J. N. Svoronos *Numismatique de la Crète ancienne* Mâcon 1890 i. 259 f. pl. 23, 24—26

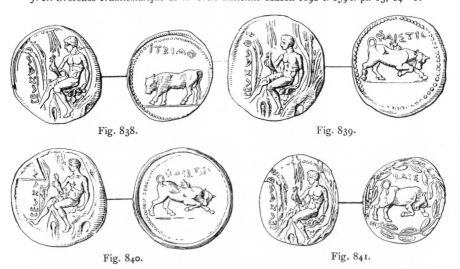

Fig. 838.   Fig. 839.

Fig. 840.   Fig. 841.

(= my figs. 839, 841, 838), Babelon *Monn. gr. rom.* ii. 3. 987 ff. pl. 256, 1—3, Overbeck *Gr. Kunstmyth.* Zeus p. 197 Münztaf. 3, 3, P. Gardner *Types of Gk. Coins* p. 165 f. pl. 9, 17, *Class. Rev.* 1903 xvii. 412 f. fig. 8. My fig. 840 is from a specimen in the McClean collection). Since the tree on these coins of Phaistos is clearly copied from the tree on the Europe-coins of Gortyna (*supra* i. 527 ff. fig. 391 ff.), J. N. Svoronos in the *Rev. Belge de Num.* 1894 pp. 127, 137 infers that it is an oak ; but I adhere to my contention (*supra* i. 527 n. 1) that it is the crown of a pollard willow. Comparison with other Phaestian coins (J. N. Svoronos *Numismatique de la Crète ancienne* i. 260 f. pl. 24, 1 f., 6 f., Babelon

Monn. gr. rom. ii. 3. 989 ff. pl. 256, 4—8) makes it fairly certain that beneath the god is spread a lion (?)-skin, the head of which is touched by his left hand. That we have here to do with a youthful Zeus appears from Hesych. *s.v.* Γελχάνος (for Fελχάνος)· ὁ Ζεὺς παρὰ Κρησίν (so J. V. Perger for κρισίω cod. Musurus cj. 'Ακρισίῳ). We must, I think, conclude that, as at Gortyna Zeus took Europe to wife on a willow-tree (*supra* i. 526 ff.), so in the neighbouring town of Phaistos he had the same or a similar willow-bride.

And here I cannot avoid adding a word on the meaning of the appellative Fελχάνος, which has been often discussed and always misunderstood. Leaving out of account impossible conjectures (for which see O. Jessen in Pauly—Wissowa *Real-Enc.* vii. 969 f.), we have before us two more or less improbable alternatives. (1) Some scholars assume the existence of a Cretan word Fέλκος, a 'cock,' evidenced by the Phaestian coin-type of Fελχάνος holding a cock and by the occurrence of Γέλκος (? Fέλκος misread) as the name of a cock on a late Corinthian vase (Roulez *Vases de Leide* p. 39 n. 4 pl. 10, Reinach *Rép. Vases* ii. 271, *Class. Rev.* 1903 xvii. 413). But the vase-inscription is now read as 'γεκκος?' (A. E. J. Holwerda *Catalogus van het Rijksmuseum van Oudheden te Leiden.* Afdeeling Griekenland en Italie. 1 Deel: Vaatwerk. Leiden 1905 i. 62). And to bring in the Hesychian glosses ἠικανός· ὁ ἀλεκτρυών (A. J. Reinach in *L'Anthropologie* 1910 xxi. 76) and σέρκος· ἀλεκτρυών. καὶ ἀλεκτορίδες σέλκες with Σελχροί· Πέρσαι (T. Panofka in the *Abh. d. berl. Akad. 1840* Phil.-hist. Classe p. 348) is only to darken counsel. (2) Others assume that Fελχάνος is related to *Volcanus*—an assumption made first by G. Secchi 'Giove ϹΕΛΧΑΝΟΣ e l'oracolo suo nell' antro Ideo' in the *Dissertazioni della Pontifica Accademia Romana di Archeologia* Roma 1842 x. 331 ff., later by A. Fick in the *Beiträge zur kunde der indogermanischen sprachen* 1879 iii. 166 f. ('Vielmehr ist Fελχανος von Fελκ glänzen abzuleiten, das in der Form Fλεκ auch in dem Gottesnamen 'Ηʃλέκτωρ 'Τπερίων der Sonnengott wie bei Homer wie in den mythischen Namen 'Ηλέκτρα und 'Ηλεκτρύων erscheint. Gleichen Stammes ist auch ἄβλαξ (=ά-Fλαξ)· λαμπρῶς. Κύπριοι bei Hesych, welches für Digamma beweist.' He defends χ for κ as a Cretan peculiarity, cp. H. Helbig *De dialecto Cretica* Plaviae 1873 p. 13), *id. Vergleichendes Wörterbuch der Indogermanischen Sprachen*[4] Göttingen 1890 i. 133 ('Fελχάνος = Vulcânus'), and last by Walde *Lat. etym. Wörterb.*[2] p. 853 f. ('Doch sind die angeführten Stützen für ein *ʒuelq*- karg und etwas unsicher, dagegen der Anklang von Fελχάνος (mit seinem auffälligen χ) und *Volcanus* so weitgehend, dass beide wohl als identisch und als Lehnworte aus dem Orient zu betrachten sind'). The equation, however, does not satis-factorily explain the χ of Fελχάνος.

Mr B. F. C. Atkinson and I, after a joint consideration of all the *data*, have rejected both these alternatives and reached the conclusion (Feb. 9, 1923) that Fελχάνος means simply 'god of the Willow-tree,' being in fact akin to the English word *willow* (Middle English *wilow*, *wilwe*, Anglo-Saxon *welig*, Dutch *wilg*, Low German *wilge*). My con-tention that Zeus at Phaistos, as at Gortyna, was the consort of a willow-goddess is thus strikingly confirmed. Instead of his usual eagle he has a cock, because that bird as the crest of the Phaestian Idomeneus had a long-standing mythical connexion with the town. Pausanias in describing certain statues by Onatas, which the Achaeans dedicated to Zeus at Olympia, says: 'The one with the scutcheon of the cock on the shield is Idomeneus, the descendant of Minos. They say that Idomeneus was descended from the Sun, who was the sire of Pasiphae, and that the cock is sacred to the Sun and heralds his rising' (Paus. 5. 25. 9 trans. Sir J. G. Frazer). See further G. H. Chase 'The Shield Devices of the Greeks' in *Harvard Studies in Classical Philology* 1902 xiii. 74, 101 f. (nos. lxxvii and lxxviii=eleven vases with cock as shield-sign, one with cock and rosette) and E. Baethgen *De vi ac significatione galli in religionibus et artibus Graecorum et Romano-rum* Gottingae 1887 p. 11 f. ('Sol—Apollo').

The cult of Zeus Fελχάνος has left traces of itself in other places beside Phaistos: (1) *Hagia Triada* (F. Halbherr in the *Rendiconti d. Lincei* 1905 xiv. 381 notes the discovery at *Hagia Triada* of numerous tiles incised with the name of the god Fευχάνος, a dialect form of Fελχάνος). (2) Gortyna (J. de Prott *Leges Graecorum sacrae* Lipsiae 1896 Fasti sacri p. 42 f. no. 20, 1 = F. Blass in Collitz—Bechtel *Gr. Dial.-Inschr.* iii. 2. 248 no. 4963,

The Tallaia range[1].

Bosporos Kimmerios
Gorgippia[2].
Tanais[3].

Moesia
Naissos[4].
Pirot[5].

1 a very archaic inscription in retrograde lettering from the Python (Steph. Byz. *s.v.*
Πύθιον)—[ἱα]ρὰ | τετελημέ[να]...... υι | τῶι [F]ελχανί[ωι] - - αι | ἐν τᾶι πένπτα[ι] - - |
κ.τ.λ.). (3) Knossos (F. Dürrbach—A. Jardé in the *Bull. Corr. Hell.* 1905 xxix. 204 ff.
no. 67, 1 ff. a decree of Lato and Olous ἐπὶ τῶν Αἰθαλέων κοσμιόντων Κνωσοὶ μὲν τῶν | σὺν
Κύδαντι [τ]ῶ(ι) Κύδαντος μηνὸς Ἐλχανίω, Λατοῖ δὲ ἐπὶ τῶν | σὺν Διοκλεῖ τῶ(ι) Ἡρώδα μηνὸς
Βακινθίω, ἐν δὲ Ὀλόντι τῶν σὺν Τη|λεμάχω(ι) τῶ(ι) Γνώμιος μηνὸ[s] Ἀ...νίω, κ.τ.λ., where
the month Ἐλχάνιος probably corresponded with our May—June). (4) Lyttos (G. Doublet
in the *Bull. Corr. Hell.* 1889 xiii. 61 ff. no. 6, 1 ff. - - -|[τ]ῆς δόσεως τοῖς σταρτοῖς
(=στρατοῖς, the classes of the Lyttian population) κατὰ | τὰ πάτρια καὶ Θεοδαισίοις καὶ |
Βελχανίοις· κ.τ.λ. From the sequel it seems likely that the festival Βελχάνια took place
on the kalends of May). (5) Golgoi in Kypros (O. Hoffmann *Die Griechischen Dialekte*
Göttingen 1891 i. 82 f. no. 160, 4 *va la ka ni o*=Fαλκάνιο nom., cp. *ib.* pp. 133, 193.
B. Keil in the *Nachr. d. kön. Gesellsch. d. Wiss. Göttingen* Phil.-hist. Classe 1895 p. 361
n. 1 transcribes Fαλχανίω).

At Magnesia on the Maiandros, a colony from Crete (*supra* i. 483 n. 8), this youthful
god was identified with Apollon (Michel *Recueil d'Inscr. gr.* no. 438, 1 ff., 25 ff.=
O. Kern *Die Inschriften von Magnesia am Maeander* Berlin 1900 p. 16 f. no. 20, 1 ff.
an inscription dating from the end of *s.* iii B.C., which purports to be a decree of the
ancient Cretan confederation in honour of Leukippos the founder of Magnesia πα[ρ]ὰ τοῦ
κοινοῦ τῶν Κρητῶν· | [ἔ]δοξεν Κ[ρ]ηταιέων τῶι κοινῶι συνελ|[θ]ουσᾶν [τ]ᾶμ πολίων πασᾶν ἐς
Βίλκω|να (an unknown place in Crete) ἐς τὸ ἱε[ρ]ὸν τῶ Ἀπέλλωνος τῶ Βιλ|κωνίω, ἀγουμένων
Γορτυνίων ἐπὶ | κόσμω(ι) Κύδαντος τῶ Κυννίω· κ.τ.λ., *ib.* 25 ff. τὸ δὲ ψάφισμα τόδε εἰστάλαν
λιθίναν | ἀναγράψαντας ἀναθέμεν εἰς τὸ ἱερὸν τῶ | Ἀ[πελ]Δωνος τῶ Βιλκωνίω, κ.τ.λ. See
further O. Kern *Die Gründungsgeschichte von Magnesia am Maiandros* Berlin 1894 p. 14 ff.
and in Pauly—Wissowa *Real-Enc.* iii. 472, W. Aly *Der kretische Apollonkult* Leipzig
1908 p. 54 n. 2).

1 The Tallaia range, midway between Oaxos and the sea, reaches a maximum height
of 1092[m]. Here Hermes was worshipped (*supra* i. 730 n. 1) in the wonderful stalactite
cavern of *Melidhoni* described and drawn by R. Pashley *Travels in Crete* Cambridge—
London 1837 i. 126 ff. with pl. Zeus too bore the title Ταλαιός (Hesych. *s.v.* Ταλαιός
cited *supra* i. 729 n. 1) or Ταλλαῖος at Dreros (Dittenberger *Syll. inscr. Gr.*[2] no. 463
(*ib.*[3] no. 527), 14 ff. cited *supra* i. 729 n. 2) and at Olous (Dittenberger *Syll. inscr. Gr.*[2]
no. 514 (*ib.*[3] no. 712), 14 cited *supra* i. 729 n. 3, J. Demargne in the *Bull. Corr. Hell.*
1900 xxiv. 227 no. 1 C 57 ff. cited *supra* i. 729 n. 4. Add F. Dürrbach—A. Jardé in
the *Bull. Corr. Hell.* 1905 xxix. 204 ff. no. 67, 18 f. a decree of Lato and Olous ἔ[ν δὲ]|
[Ὀλόντ]ι ἐν τῶι ἱαρῶ(ι) τῶ Ζηνὸς τῶ [Ταλλ]αίω). He was thus, like the Laconian Zeus
Ταλετίτας (*supra* i. 730, ii. 890 n. 2), related to the Cretan sun-god Talos (*supra* i. 728 ff.).

2 Θεὸς Ὕψιστος (*supra* p. 883 n. 0 no. (27)).

3 Θεὸς Ὕψιστος (*supra* p. 884 n. 0 no. (27)).

4 At Naissos (*Nish*) in Moesia Superior was found a limestone altar inscribed I. O. M.
Pa|terno Ae|pilofio | Sanc(tinius?) Oriens, | Cor(nelia) Mide, P. | Ael(ius) Cocaius | vet-
(eranus) leg(ionis) VII Cl(audiae) Sev(erianae) | ex voto posu(erunt) | Maximo et Aeli|ano
co(n)s(ulibus)=223 A.D. A. v. Premerstein and N. Vulić, who publish the inscription in
the *Jahresh. d. oest. arch. Inst.* 1900 iii Beiblatt p. 130 f. no. 30, take Iupiter *Paternus
Aepilofius* to be the Latin rendering of a local Dardanian or Thracian Zeus Πατρῷος
Ἐπιλόφιος ('on the Crest': cp. *supra* p. 873 f.).

5 Θεὸς Ἐπήκοος Ὕψιστος (*supra* p. 878 n. 0 no. (11)).

Between *Selenigrad* and *Miloslavci*[1].

Thrace
    Anchialos[2].
    Perinthos[3].
    Selymbria[4].

Troas
    Mount Ide[5].

[1] Θεὸς Ὕψιστος (*supra* p. 878 n. 0 no. (11)).
[2] Zeus Ὕψιστος Ἐπόπτης (?) (*supra* p. 878 n. 0 no. (10)).
[3] Zeus Λοφείτης (*supra* p. 874 n. 1).
[4] Θεὸς Ἅγιος Ὕψιστος (*supra* p. 878 n. 0 no. (10)).
[5] Mt Ide, a long range with numerous foot-hills (Strab. 583 σκολοπενδρώδης) and springs (πολυπῖδαξ eight times in the *Il.*, cp. Plat. *legg.* 682 B), derived its name (*supra* p. 932 n. 1) from abundant woods of pine (schol. *Il.* 12. 20), pitch-pine (Plin. *nat. hist.* 14. 128), terebinth (*id. ib.* 13. 54), larch (*id. ib.* 16. 48), ash (Theophr. *hist. pl.* 3. 11. 4, Plin. *nat. hist.* 16. 62), bay (*id. ib.* 15. 131, Dioskor. 4. 145 (147) p. 624 f. Sprengel), fig (Plin. *nat. hist.* 15. 68), and raspberry (*id. ib.* 16. 180). Its inhabitants were familiar with silver fir, oak, plum, filbert, maple, ash, Phoenician cedar, prickly cedar, alder, beech, and sorb (Theophr. *hist. pl.* 3. 6. 5). Here grew the magic herb *aithiopís* (Plin. *nat. hist.* 27. 12, Dioskor. 4. 103 (105) p. 597 Sprengel) and flowers galore (*Il.* 14. 347 ff.). So well-wooded was the mountain that Homer even speaks of a silver fir on its summit reaching through *aér* to *aithér* (*Il.* 14. 286 ff.). A conflagration of the forests on Ide in 1460 B.C. was remembered as an epoch-making event, which led to the discovery of iron by the Idaean Daktyloi (Thrasyllos of Mendes *frag.* 3 (*Frag. hist. Gr.* iii. 503 Müller) *ap.* Clem. Al. *strom.* 1. 21 p. 85, 2 ff. Stählin. Cp. the *Phoronís frag.* 2 Kinkel *ap.* schol. Ap. Rhod. 1. 1129). Here too the herdsman Magnes discovered the loadstone, to which his hobnails and ferule stuck fast (Nikandros *frag.* 101 Schneider *ap.* Plin. *nat. hist.* 36. 127).

Diod. 17. 7 (after Kleitarchos (?): see E. Schwartz in Pauly—Wissowa *Real-Enc.* v. 683 f.) gives an interesting account of Mt Ide: 'There is a tradition that this mountain got its name from Ide daughter of Melisseus. It is the greatest of the ranges near the Hellespont and has in the midst of it a sacred cavern in which, they affirm, the goddesses were judged by Alexandros [Cp. bronze coins of Skepsis, struck by Caracalla, which show the judgment of Eros in place of Paris on Mt ΙΔΗ (F. Imhoof-Blumer in the *Zeitschr. f. Num.* 1883 x. 155 f. fig., *id.* in the *Jahrb. d. kais. deutsch. arch. Inst.* 1888 iii. 291 f. pl. 9, 20, Head *Hist. num.*[2] p. 549)]. It is said that the Idaean Daktyloi too were born here, the first workers of iron, who learnt their craft from the Mother of the Gods. A peculiar phenomenon attaches to this mountain. When the dog-star rises, on the topmost summit so still is the surrounding air that the peak soars higher than the breath of the winds, and the sun is seen coming up before night is over. Its rays are not rounded into a regular disk, but its flame is dispersed in diverse directions so that several fires appear to touch the earth's horizon. A little later and these gather into a single whole, which grows until it becomes 300 ft in diameter. Then, as day increases, the normal size of the sun is completed and produces daylight as usual.' Cp. Lucr. 5. 663 ff., Mela 1. 94 f. The Cretan Ide too (? by confusion with this mountain) was said to see the sun before the sunrise (*supra* p. 932 n. 1).

Coppers of Skamandria struck in *s.* iv B.C. have *obv.* head of Ide wreathed with fir, *rev.* ΣΚΑ (variously arranged) fir-tree or fir-cone (*Brit. Mus. Cat. Coins* Troas, etc. p. 79 pl. 14, 12—14, Head *Hist. num.*[2] p. 548). One specimen names the head [Ι]ΔΗ (Imhoof-Blumer in the *Zeitschr. f. Num.* 1874 i. 139 no. 1 pl. 4, 15 and in his *Kleinas. Münzen* i. 42 no. 2 pl. 2, 2).

One of Mt Ide's summits was known as Γάργαρον or Γάργαρα—probably a Lelegian name, for the Leleges are said to have occupied the district Γαργαρίς (Strab. 610) and the mountain-town Γάργαρος (Steph. Byz. s.v. Γάργαρα, et. mag. p. 221, 26 f. L. Bürchner in Pauly—Wissowa Real-Enc. vii. 757 f. cp. Gargissa some 33 kilometers to the north-east of it). Mt Ide in general was an important centre for the cult of Kybele (A. Rapp in Roscher Lex. Myth. ii. 1653, W. Drexler ib. ii. 2859, O. Jessen in Pauly—Wissowa Real-Enc. ix. 864 f., Schwenn ib. xi. 2287), who as Μήτηρ Ἰδαία (first in Eur. Or. 1453), Mater Idaea, was worshipped far and wide throughout the Roman empire (H. Graillot Le culte de Cybèle Mère des dieux à Rome et dans l'empire romain Paris 1912 Index p. 582 s.v. 'Ida (mont)'). But Gargaron in particular was connected rather with the myth and ritual of Zeus. It was on the height of Gargaron that Here found Zeus the cloud-gatherer (Il. 14. 292 f., cp. 352) and enticed him into the famous dalliance (supra i. 154). It was there that Apollon and Iris saw him sitting in the midst of a fragrant cloud (Il. 15. 152 f.). There in Homeric days Zeus had a precinct and altar (Il. 8. 47 ff. Ἴδην δ' ἵκανεν πολυπί-δακα, μητέρα θηρῶν, | Γάργαρον· ἔνθα δέ οἱ τέμενος βωμός τε θυήεις. | ἔνθ' ἵππους ἔστησε πατὴρ ἀνδρῶν τε θεῶν τε | λύσας ἐξ ὀχέων, κατὰ δ' ἠέρα πουλὺν ἔχευεν. | αὐτὸς δ' ἐν κορυφῇσι καθέζετο κύδεϊ γαίων, | εἰσορόων Τρώων τε πόλιν καὶ νῆας Ἀχαιῶν), on which as on the top of Troy Hektor used to burn for him the thigh-pieces of oxen (Il. 22. 169 ff. ἐμὸν δ' ὀλοφύρεται ἦτορ | Ἕκτορος, ὅς μοι πολλὰ βοῶν ἐπὶ μηρί' ἔκηεν | Ἴδης ἐν κορυφῇσι πολυπτύχου, ἄλλοτε δ' αὖτε | ἐν πόλει ἀκροτάτῃ). For the altar was served by those who claimed to be akin to Zeus and to have his blood running in their veins (Aisch. Niobe frag. 162 Nauck² ap. Plat. remp. 391 E, cp. Strab. 580, Loukian. Dem. enc. 13, οἱ θεῶν ἀγχίσποροι | οἱ Ζηνὸς ἐγγύς, ὧν κατ' Ἰδαῖον πάγον | Διὸς πατρῷου βωμός ἐστ' ἐν αἰθέρι, | κοὔπω σφιν ἐξίτηλον αἷμα δαιμόνων). Gargaros, eponym of the town, was the son of Zeus (Steph. Byz. s.v. Γάργαρα·... ὠνομάσθη δ' ἀπὸ Γαργάρου τοῦ Διός, τοῦ ἐκ τῆς Λαρίσσης ἐν Θεσσαλίᾳ=et. mag. p. 221, 31 f. ὠνόμασται δὲ ἀπὸ Γαργάρου τοῦ Διός, ὡς δηλοῖ Νυμφίος (leg. Νύμφις) ὁ φιλόσοφος (Nymphis frag. 10 (Frag. hist. Gr. iii. 14 Müller)). οὕτως Ἐπαφρόδιτος ἐν ὑπομνήματι θ' Ἰλιάδος, παρατιθέμενος Κλείταρχον Αἰγινήτην λεξικογράφον). And Onetor, priest of Zeus Ἰδαῖος, was 'honoured as a god' by the Trojans (Il. 16. 604 f. Ὀνήτορος, ὃς Διὸς ἱρεὺς | Ἰδαίου ἐτέτυκτο, θεὸς δ' ὡς τίετο δήμῳ). Epicharmos in his Troes made one of his characters pray to the Zeus of Gargara (Epicharm. frag. 130 Kaibel ap. Macrob. Sat. 5. 20. 5 Ζεὺς ἄναξ, ἀν' ἄκρα (ἀνααδαν cod. G. Kaibel cj. ἀν' ἄκρα. F. G. Schneidewin cj. ἀν' Ἴδαν) ναίων Γαργάρων (so A. Meineke for γαργαρα cod.) ἀγάννιφα). Quintus Smyrnaeus did the same in the case of Priam (Quint. Smyrn. 1. 184 f. εὔχετ' ἐς ἱερὸν αἰπὺ τετραμμένος Ἰδαίοιο | Ζηνός, ὃς Ἴλιον αἰ`ν ἑοῖς ἐπιδέρκεται ὄσσοις); for which he had good Homeric authority, since Hekabe bade Priam, when he set out for the hut of Achilles, pour a libation and offer a prayer to Zeus Ἰδαῖος (Il. 24. 287 τῇ, σπεῖσον Διὶ πατρί, καὶ εὔχεο οἴκαδ' ἱκέσθαι κ.τ.λ., 290 f. ἀλλ' εὔχεο σύ γ' ἔπειτα κελαινεφεῖ Κρονίωνι | Ἰδαίῳ, ὅς τε Τροίην κατὰ πᾶσαν ὁρᾶται, κ.τ.λ.), and Priam took her advice (Il. 24. 306 ff. εὔχετ' ἔπειτα στὰς μέσῳ ἕρκεϊ, λεῖβε δὲ οἶνον | οὐρανὸν εἰσανιδών, καὶ φωνήσας ἔπος ηὔδα· | Ζεῦ πάτερ, Ἴδηθεν μεδέων, κύδιστε μέγιστε, | δός μ' ἐς Ἀχιλλῆος φίλον ἐλθεῖν ἠδ' ἐλεεινόν, | πέμψον δ' οἰωνόν, ταχὺν ἄγγελον,' κ.τ.λ.). Virgil and the pseudo-Plutarch associate the cult of Zeus Ἰδαῖος with that of the Phrygian mother-goddess (Verg. Aen. 7. 139 f. Idaeumque Iovem Phrygiamque ex ordine Matrem | invocat (sc. Aeneas), Plout. de fluv. 13. 3 παράκειται δ' αὐτῷ (sc. τῷ Σκαμάνδρῳ) ὄρος Ἴδη, τὸ πρότερον δὲ ἐκαλεῖτο Γάργαρον· ὅπου Διὸς καὶ Μητρὸς Θεῶν βωμοὶ τυγχάνουσιν). Lastly, writers of the Graeco-Roman age treat Gargaron as an appropriate background for the myth of Ganymedes (Loukian. dial. deor. 4. 2, Charid. 7) or that of Paris (Ov. her. 16. 107 f., Loukian. dial. deor. 20. 1).

Imperial bronze coins of Ilion, struck by Faustina Iunior (H. von Fritze in W. Dörpfeld Troja und Ilion Athens 1902 ii. 490 f., 517 pl. 63, 65) and Iulia Domna (fig. 842 from a specimen in my collection), have as reverse type Zeus sitting, with a long sceptre in his right hand and the cult-image of Athena Ἰλιάς in his left, accompanied by the honorific formula ΔΙΑ ΙΔΑΙΟΝ ΙΛΙΕΙC. W. Kubitschek 'Heroenstatuen in Ilion' in the Jahresh. d. oest. arch. Inst. 1898 i. 187 suggests that the coin is one of a series struck by Commodus and his successors to commemorate certain statues of gods and heroes, from which at least three inscribed bases are extant. Accordingly G. F. Hill A Handbook of Greek and Roman Coins London 1899 p. 186 n. 3 would complete the formula by supplying some such word as ἀνέστησαν. See further G. Macdonald *Coin Types* Glasgow 1905 p. 170.

Zeus Ἰδαῖος was worshipped at Skepsis also. Bronze coins of the town, struck by Commodus (*Brit. Mus. Cat. Coins* Troas, etc. p. 84 no. 30) and Caracalla (*ib.* p. 84 pl. 16, 1 = my fig. 843), show ΖΕΥC ΕΙΔΑΙΟ(C) CΚΗΨΙΩΝ clad in a *himátion*, standing with an eagle in his right hand and a long sceptre in his left. An inscription from Skepsis (*Kurshunlu Tepe*) records a priest of Zeus Ἰδαῖος (J. A. R. Munro in the *Journ. Hell. Stud.* 1901 xxi. 236 on a square marble base [ἡ γ]ερουσία | [τὸν] ἱερέα τοῦ Δι[ὸς τ]οῦ Ἰδαίου καὶ | [τῶ]ν Σεβαστῶν Γ[ν][αῖ]ον Φλάβιον Ὀλυ[μ][πι]οδώρου υἱὸν | [Ὀλ]υμ-

Fig. 842.

Fig. 843.

πιόδωρον, | [τὸ]ν ἐκ προγόνω[ν] | [τῆ]s πατρίδος εὐ[εργέ]τ(η)ν καὶ ἑαυ[τῆς σ]υ(μ)ποσιάρχην). Demetrios of Skepsis, who *c.* 150 B.C. compiled an encyclopaedic commentary on *Il.* 2. 814—877, mentions the Trojan claim to possession of the cave where Zeus was born (schol. Ap. Rhod. 3. 134 ἄντρῳ ἐν Ἰδαίῳ· ἢ τῷ τῆς Κρήτης, ἢ τῷ τῆς Τροίας. ἀντιποιοῦνται γὰρ καὶ Τρῶες τῆς τοῦ Διὸς γενέσεως, καθά φησι Δημήτριος ὁ Σκήψιος): cp. *supra* i. 154 n. 2. Other coin-types of Skepsis referable to the same cult are a standing eagle (Imhoof-Blumer *Kleinas. Münzen* i. 45 no. 4), an eagle with open wings in an oak-wreath (*Brit. Mus. Cat. Coins* Troas, etc. p. 83 pl. 15, 13, Imhoof-Blumer *Gr. Münzen* p. 628 no. 230 pl. 8, 6, Head *Hist. num.*[2] p. 549), an eagle standing beside a leafy tree (Imhoof-Blumer *Kleinas. Münzen* i. 46 no. 5 pl. 2, 6).

A noteworthy bust of Zeus in white marble, formerly in the Stroganoff collection, represents the god upborne on the spread wings of an eagle. He is draped in a *himátion* and wears a wreath of pine. Restored: nose, tip of pine-wreath, right foot of eagle. L. Stephani in the *Compte-rendu St. Pét.* 1875 p. 200 ff. Atlas pl. 7, 2 (= my fig. 844) regards this as an effigy of Zeus Ἰδαῖος dating from *s.* i or ii A.D. The association of a Zeus-head with Attis (*supra* p. 297 fig. 189) prepares us to see in the pine-wreath a reminiscence of the tree that figures so largely in the religion of Attis and Kybele (Boetticher *Baumkultus* pp. 142—147, 263 fig. 11, J. Murr *Die Pflanzenwelt in der griechischen Mythologie* Innsbruck 1890 p. 117 f., H. Graillot *op. cit.* p. 121 ff. and Index p. 597 *s.vv.* 'Pin,' 'Pin (pomme de)'). And this connexion certainly seems more probable than any reference to the pine-wreath of the Isthmian victor.

Attempts have been made in modern times to locate the cult-centre of Zeus Ἰδαῖος. J. Thacher Clarke 'Gargara, Lamponia and Pionia: towns of the Troad' in the *Am. Journ. Arch.* 1888 iv. 291—319 notes (*a*) *et. mag.* p. 221, 26 ff. Γάργαρος· πόλις τῆς Ἴδης ἐν ὑψηλῷ τόπῳ κειμένη, ἣν κατῴκουν Λέλεγες· ἐξ ἧς διὰ τὸ κρυῶδες ὑποκατέβησαν οἱ Γαργαρεῖς, καὶ ᾤκισαν αὐτὴν ὑπὸ πεδίον (*an leg.* αὖ τὴν ὑποπόδιον? A.B.C.) Γάργαρον. ἐκείνη δὲ ἐρημωθεῖσα καλεῖται Παλαιὰ Γάργαρος· κ.τ.λ.: (*b*) Strab. 606 μετὰ γὰρ τὸ Λεκτὸν τὸ Πολυμήδιόν ἐστι χωρίον τι ἐν τετταράκοντα σταδίοις, εἶτ' ἐν ὀγδοήκοντα Ἄσσος (so C. Mannert for ἄλσος codd.), μικρὸν ὑπὲρ τῆς θαλάττης, εἶτ' ἐν ἑκατὸν καὶ τετταράκοντα Γάργαρα· κεῖται δὲ τὰ Γάργαρα ἐπ' ἄκρας ποιούσης τὸν ἰδίως Ἀδραμυττηνὸν καλούμενον κόλπον. Assuming Strabon's distances to be cumulative, not consecutive, he infers that Palaia Gargaros is the ruined town with walls of polygonal masonry still to be seen on the top of *Kozlu Dagh* 10 kilometers east-north-east from Assos, that Gargaros on the plain below is the large field of later ruins at the foot of the slope on which lies the Turkish town of *Sazly*, and that the cape mentioned by Strabon is *Katerga Burnu* near Assos.

W. Judeich 'Gargara und der Altar des idäischen Zeus' in the *Jahresh. d. oest. arch. Inst.* 1901 iv. 111—125 figs. 160—163 replies that Strabon's distances are regularly consecutive, not cumulative. Hence Gargaros must be placed further east in the vicinity of *Tschibne*, and Palaia Gargaros should be identified with a ruined stronghold on *Odjak Kaya*, the most westerly summit of the *Dikeli Dagh*, which rises immediately behind *Tschibne* to a height of 780ᵐ. Palaia Gargaros (wrongly equated by Clarke with Lamponeia) was visited by E. Fabricius, who reports that it has terrace-walls of 'Cyclopean'

Fig. 844.

masonry well adapted for the erection of houses and an elliptical *akrópolis* enclosed by a ring-wall (now *c.* 1ᵐ high, *c.* 3ᵐ thick) some 500ᵐ round. On the west side of this wall is a gateway (2·35ᵐ wide) with a square tower. Within, the *akrópolis* is divided by another wall into two unequal parts. In the southern and smaller part, on the highest point of the mountain, are the foundations of a big building, probably a temple. The fragments visible are all of pre-Hellenistic date. When Palaia Gargaros was abandoned, the inhabitants of the new town found it difficult to keep up the cult on the mountain-top and chose a new site for their worship on the southern point of the neighbouring hill *Adatepe* (*c.* 260ᵐ).

Mysia
Kyzikos[1].
Mount Olympos[2].
Pergamon[3].

Here Judeich discovered a rock-cut altar (*loc. cit.* p. 111 ff. figs. 160 view and 161 plan (=my fig. 845)) measuring *c.* 13^m × 15^m and approached by three flights of steps on the

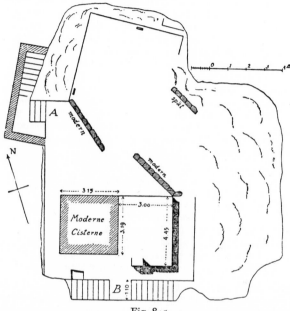

Fig. 845.

west and south sides. A modern cistern constructed on the spot is believed to work cures with its water and probably preserves the sanctity of the ancient altar.

[1] Zeus Ὕψιστος and Θεὸς Ὕψιστος (*supra* p. 881 n. 0 no. (21)).

[2] Zeus Ὀλύμπιος (Mnaseas *frag.* 30 (*Frag. hist. Gr.* iii. 154 Müller) *ap.* schol. T. *Il.* 20. 234 Μνασέας μέν φησιν ὑπὸ Ταντάλου ἡρπάσθαι (sc. Γανυμήδην) καὶ ἐν κυνηγεσίῳ πεσόντα ταφῆναι ἐν τῷ Μυσίῳ Ὀλύμπῳ κατὰ τὸ ἱερὸν τοῦ Ὀλυμπίου Διός). *Supra* i. 116 n. 8, 124.

[3] The district of Pergamon was of old sacred to the Kabeiroi (Paus. 1. 4. 6 ἦν δὲ νέμονται οἱ Περγαμηνοί, Καβείρων ἱεράν φασιν εἶναι τὸ ἀρχαῖον), who as the most ancient deities of the land were worshipped with mystic rites and invoked in stormy weather (Aristeid. *or.* 55 (ii. 709 Dindorf) τοῦτό μοι (Grauert cj. μὲν) πρεσβύτατοι δαιμόνων ἐνταῦθα λέγονται γενέσθαι Κάβειροι, καὶ τελεταὶ τούτοις καὶ μυστήρια, ἃ τοσαύτην ἰσχὺν ἔχειν πεπίστευται ὥστε χειμώνων τε ἐξαισίων (with which word the fragmentary oration ends)). Their cult, attested by the name of a *prýtanis* Κάβειρος (M. Fränkel *Die Inschriften von Pergamon* Berlin 1895 ii. 177 ff. no. 251, 1 and 34, cp. E. Sittig *De Graecorum nominibus theophoris* Halis Saxonum 1911 p. 143 f.), was perhaps at one time carried on in connexion with the apsidal building hidden by the foundations of the great Pergamene altar (*supra* i. 120). They are represented on the large frieze of that altar as two youthful warriors attacking a huge bovine giant with double axe and sword respectively (*supra* i. 110 n. 4). Coppers of Severus Alexander (*Brit. Mus. Cat. Coins* Mysia p. 158 pl. 32, 3) and Gallienus (*ib.* p. 162 pl. 32, 8) show two youthful male figures standing on either side of an altar: one

is handing to the other a ram's head. H. von Fritze in the *Zeitschr. f. Num.* 1901 xxiv. 120 ff. and in the *Abh. d. berl. Akad. 1910* Phil.-hist. Classe Anhang i. 63 f. pl. 6, 1 identifies them with the Kabeiroi, aptly citing a Pergamene decree first published by B. Schroeder in the *Ath. Mitth.* 1904 xxix. 152 ff. no. 1 (Dittenberger *Orient. Gr. inscr. sel.* no. 764, 6 μυστηρίων κατὰ τὰ πάτρια τοῖς μεγάλοις θεοῖς Καβείροις κ.τ.λ., *ib.* 27 καὶ τὰ κριοβόλια τῆς τῶν ἐφήβων μεταπαιδιᾶς πρὸς ἀλλήλους ἕνεκεν). See further E. Thraemer *Pergamos* Leipzig 1888 pp. 263—270 ('Die pergamenischen Kabiren').

The Kabeiroi witnessed the birth of Zeus the lightning-god on the summit of Pergamon, according to an oracle of Apollon (not Apollon Γρύνειος as F. G. Welcker *Sylloge epigrammatum Graecorum*[2] Bonnae 1828 p. 231 and A. Boeckh on *Corp. inscr. Gr.* ii no. 3538 supposed, nor Apollon Χρηστήριος of Aigai as M. Fränkel *op. cit.* ii. 239 thought probable, but Apollon Κλάριος as C. Picard in the *Bull. Corr. Hell.* 1922 xlvi. 190 ff. and in his *Éphèse et Claros* Paris 1922 pp. 461 n. 4, 673 has definitely proved), which bade the Pergamenes, if they would be rid of a plague (that of 166 A.D. (Amm. Marc. 23. 6. 24)), divide their *épheboi* into four groups, chant hymns to Zeus, Dionysos, Athena, and Asklepios, and then for seven days offer thighs on the altars of the same deities, sacrificing a two-year-old heifer to Athena, a three-year-old ox to Zeus, to Zeus Βάκχος (=Zeus Σαβάζιος: *supra* p. 287 n. 2), and to Asklepios, and feasting themselves on bull's flesh (*Corp. inscr. Gr.* ii no. 3538=M. Fränkel *op. cit.* ii. 239 f.=Kaibel *Epigr. Gr.* no. 1035 =Cougny *Anth. Pal. Append.* 6. 172). The oracle begins:

Τηλεφίδαις, οἳ Ζηνὶ πλέον Κρονίδηι βασιλῆϊ
ἐξ ἄλλων τιεσκόμενοι Τευθραντίδα γαῖαν
ναίουσιν καὶ Ζηνὸς ἐρισμαράγοιο γενέθληι
ἠμὲν Ἀθηναίηι πολεμηδόκωι ἀτρυτώνηι
ἠδὲ Δι(ω)νύσωι λαθικηδέϊ φυσιζώιωι
ἠδὲ καὶ εἰητῆρι νόσ(ω)ν Παιήονι λυγρῶν·
οἷσι πάρ' Οὐρανοῦ υἷες ἐθηήσαντο Κάβειροι
πρῶτοι Περγαμίης ὑπὲρ ἄκ(ρι)ος ἀ(σ)τε(ρ)ο(πητ)ὴ(ν)
τικτόμενον Δία, μητρώιην ὅτε (γα)στ(έρα) λῦσ(εν)· κ.τ.λ.

The later passage concerning the sacrifices to the four gods has been quoted *supra* p. 287 n. 2. Of the hymns prescribed one only, that to Zeus, has survived on a fragmentary *stéle* of white marble found on the western terrace of the Akropolis. The text, which is surmounted by a pediment containing reliefs of a *phiále* with two shield-like ornaments, is thus restored by M. Fränkel *op. cit.* ii. 237 ff. no. 324:

    [ἀγ]αθῆι τύχηι.
    [Οὐλύμποιο] μέτωπον, ἄκρην Τειτηνίδα, ναίων,
    [ὦ Ζεῦ δέσποτα,] χαῖρε. λιταζομένωμ πολιητέων
    [κλῦθι, πάτερ μ]ακάρων τε καὶ ἀτρυγέτων ἀνθρώπων,
 5 [λαμπρῶς οὐραν]ίην ἐφέπων ἴτυν αἰγλήεσσαν,
    [δημιοεργὲ βίου] πεφατισμένε σοῖς ὑπὸ φύλοις·
    [τῶν ἀγαθῶν γὰρ] φαῦλα διακρείνας πάρος ὕλης
    [πᾶσιν ἔδωκας χ]ρῆσιν ἐπάρκιον ἡμερίοισιν,
    [νείμας καὶ γαῖάν] τε πολυκλύστον τε θάλασσαν,
10 [αἰθέρα καὶ πά]ντ' ἄλλα, τὰ σὴ ποιήσατο μῆτις.
    [ἐλθέ σε κλητζο]υσι, μάκαρ, μάκαρ, εἴλαος ἡμῖν
    καὶ πτό[λιν ἰθύνο]υσιν ἀμύμοσιν Περγαμίδαισιν,
    ἐλθὲ σὺν ἰητῆρι θεῶμ Παιήονι κλειτῶι
    θεσπεσίην Ὑγίειαν ἐς ἀγλαὰ δώματ' ἄγοντι
15 Εὐνομίηι τε καὶ Εὐστασίηι λιπαρῆι τ' Εἰρήνηι
    Ἥρηι τε ζυγίηι, ἀλόχῳ σέο κυδηέσσηι,
    καὶ Θέμιδι ἀρχ[εγ]όνωι, προυφητίδι καρτεροβούλωι,
    καὶ γάμων [ἄξο]μένηι γλαυκώπιδι Τριτογενείηι
    κ[α]ὶ [παίδων μεδ]έοντι διακτόρωι Ἑρμάωνι
20 [καὶ Μοίραις κλυμέ]νηισιν ἀμύμοσιν Ἀδ[ρηστ]είαις.

[κοίρανος οὐρα]νίαισι κεκασμένος ἦνε[κ]ες ὥραις,
[ἦρι περιστέλλο]ντι κ[ό]μην εὔθρεπτον ἀ[ρ]ούραις
[ἠδὲ θέρει καρπὸν πολι]όσταχυν ἀμώοντ[ι]
[πορφύρεόν τε τρυγῶν]τι βότρυν λιπαρῶι μ[ε]θοπώρω[ι]
25 [καὶ χειμῶνι βροτοῖς] ὥρην εὔκρητον ἄγο[ντ]ι,
[ἐλθὲ πόλιν σώζ]ειμ, μάκαρ, ὄλβιε, καὶ λ[ύε πῆμα,]
[ὅττι κακῶς ὡμῶς τ]ε κατὰ φρένας ἔλλ[αβεν ἡμᾶς.]
[ταρβέομεν γὰρ πάν]τες ἀεὶ κήτεια [πέλωρα]
[λοίμης· ἦ μάλα λ]αὸν ἄρειον ἀμ[ύμονα τρύχει,]
30 [οἴστρωι λυσσηέ]ντι κατ[ασκήπτουσα πολίταις.]
[ἀλλὰ σύ, κάρπιμε] Παι[άν, – – – –].

The older and simpler altar of Zeus, consisting of ashes from the thighs of victims sacrificed to the god (Paus. 5. 13. 8 πεποίηται δὲ (sc. the altar of Zeus at Olympia) ἱερείων τῶν θυομένων τῷ Διὶ ἀπὸ τῆς τέφρας τῶν μηρῶν, καθάπερ γε καὶ ἐν Περγάμῳ κ.τ.λ.), probably occupied the actual summit of the hill (supra i. 120 f. fig. 89). The magnificent altar built by Eumenes ii was situated near the top, on a broad terrace seventy or eighty feet below the temple of Athena (supra i. 118 ff. pl. x and figs. 87, 88). This altar has often been identified with ὁ θρόνος τοῦ Σατανᾶ (Rev. 2. 13); but the phrase refers rather to Pergamon as the centre of the imperial cult (R. H. Charles A critical and exegetical Commentary on the Revelation of St. John Edinburgh 1920 i. 60 f.).

Zeus was associated with Athena (M. Fränkel op. cit. 1890 i. 29 ff. no. 29=Michel Recueil d'Inscr. gr. no. 1215=Dittenberger Orient. Gr. inscr. sel. no. 280 a dedication of c. 223 B.C. βασιλέα Ἄτταλον (sc. Attalos i) | Ἐπιγέν[η]ς καὶ οἱ ἡγεμόνες καὶ στρατ[ιῶ]ται | οἱ συναγωνισάμενοι τὰς πρὸς τοὺς Γ[αλ]άτας | καὶ Ἀντίοχον μάχας χαρισ[τ]ήρια | Διί, Ἀθηνᾶι. | Ἐ(π)ιγόνου ἔργα) or more often with Athena Νικηφόρος (M. Fränkel op. cit. i. 32 ff. nos. 33—37, 43 ff. nos. 51—56, 46 no. 58, 50 f. no. 63, 52 f. no. 65 f., 54 f. no. 69, 124 ff. nos. 214—216, 130 ff. no. 225—the formula in each case being Διὶ καὶ Ἀθηνᾶι Νικηφόρωι). E. Thraemer Pergamos Leipzig 1888 pp. 223—227 infers from their association that the temple of Athena, which is divided by a cross-wall into two approximately equal halves (J. L. Ussing Pergamos Berlin—Stuttgart 1899 pl. 3 after Pergamon ii pl. 3), was in reality a double temple of Zeus and Athena. He notes the Pergamene coin-type of Athena's owl on the thunderbolt of Zeus (Brit. Mus. Cat. Coins Mysia p. 132 pl. 27, 13 ΑΘΗ ΝΑΣ ΝΙΚΗ ΦΟΡΟΥ, Head Hist. num.² p. 536: cp. Brit. Mus. Cat. Coins Pontus, etc. p. 84 pl. 19, 5, Waddington—Babelon—Reinach Monn. gr. d'As. Min. i. 136 pl. 18, 8 similar type on a coin of Amastris) and suspects an allusion to their joint temple in a couplet on the base of a marble herm from the Byzantine wall on the south side of the agorá (M. Fränkel op. cit. ii. 242 no. 325 Ἑρμῆν θυραῖον Ῥοῦφος ἱερεὺς τοῦ Διὸς | εἵδρυσε φύλακα τοῦ νεῶ καὶ ῥύτορα). But his views have not been adopted by the authors of the official Berlin publication.

Zeus figures of course in Pergamene oaths. Eumenes i and the mercenary leaders who rose against him in 263 B.C. swore by Zeus, Ge, Helios, Poseidon, Demeter, Ares, Athena Ἀρεία and ἡ Ταυροπόλος (M. Fränkel op. cit. i. 10 ff. no. 13=Michel op. cit. no. 15= Dittenberger Orient. Gr. inscr. sel. no. 266 quoted supra p. 729 n. o no. (3)). Towards the end of s. ii B.C. public oaths were administered at the altar of Zeus Σωτήρ in the agorá (M. Fränkel op. cit. ii. 177 ff. no. 251, 27 ff.=Michel op. cit. no. 519, 27 ff.=Dittenberger Syll. inscr. Gr.² no. 592, 27 ff. ὅπως δὲ ταῦτα εἰς τὸν ἅπαντα χρόνον διαμένηι | βέβαια Ἀσκληπιάδηι καὶ τοῖς ἀπογόνοις τοῖς | Ἀσκληπιάδου, ἐπιτελεῖν ὁρκωμόσιον τὴν πόλιν | ἐν τῆι ἀγοραι ἐπὶ τοῦ Διὸς τοῦ Σωτῆρος τῶι βωμῶ[ι] | καὶ ὀμόσαι τὰς τιμουχίας, ἦ μὴν ἐμμενεῖν κ.τ.λ.). Among the honours decreed to Attalos iii by Elaia was a golden equestrian statue to be set up on a marble column beside the altar of Zeus Σωτήρ in the agorá (M. Fränkel op. cit. i. 153 ff. no. 246, 9 ff.=Michel op. cit. no. 515, 9 ff. =Dittenberger Orient. Gr. inscr. sel. no. 332, 9 ff. στῆσαι δὲ αὐτοῦ καὶ εἰκόνα χρυσῆν ἔφιππον ἐπὶ στυ|λίδος μαρμαρίνης παρὰ τὸν τοῦ Διὸς [τ]οῦ Σωτῆρος βωμόν, ὅπως ὑπάρχηι ἡ | εἰκὼν ἐν τῶι ἐπιφανε-στάτωι τόπωι τῆς ἀγορᾶς, κ.τ.λ.); but this must refer to the agorá at Elaia, not at Pergamon (M. Fränkel op. cit. i. 156).

Aiolis

Temnos[1].

Lydia

Mount Sipylos[2].

Zeus was worshipped at Pergamon under several other appellatives. The water-supply of the town was a grave matter necessitating repeated changes and improvements to meet the needs of the growing population (F. Gräber *Die Wasserleitungen* (*Pergamon* i. 3) Berlin 1913 Beiblatt 88 bird's-eye view of three conduits and aqueduct). P. Aelius Aristeides (*supra* p. 127) in an epideictic harangue entitled πανηγυρικὸς ἐπὶ τῷ ὕδατι ἐν Περγάμῳ describes how all Asia rejoiced with the Pergamenes when a copious flow of pure water was secured at last, and how he welcomed the good news as a special favour vouchsafed by Zeus Εὐαγγέλιος and Asklepios Σωτήρ (Aristeid. *or.* 55 (ii. 708 Dindorf) εἶναι γὰρ τὸ ὕδωρ πλήθει τε πλεῖστον καὶ κάλλει κάλλιστον ὅσων ἔλαχον πόλεις. ἦγον οὖν οὐχ ὅσον ἡρινὴν ἡμέραν, ἀλλ' οἵαν εἰκὸς ἄγειν Διός τε Εὐαγγελίου καὶ Ἀσκληπιοῦ Σωτῆρος πανταχῇ τιμῶντος. κ.τ.λ.). Zeus Κεραύνιος is represented by two dedications (*supra* p. 808 n. o no. (8)), Zeus Μέγιστος by a small altar of trachyte (M. Fränkel *op. cit.* ii. 243 no. 328, 1 ff. Διὶ Μεγ[ί]‖στῳ Πύρ[ε]‖[σ]ι[s?], cp. *Corp. inscr. Gr.* iii no. 4885, 1), Zeus Μέγιστος Σωτήρ by another of white marble (M. Fränkel *op. cit.* ii. 242 no. 327, 1 ff. Διὶ Μεγίστῳ Σωτῆρι‖ (relief of an eagle in a niche surrounded by tendrils)‖Καπίτων | κατ' ὄνειρον). L. Cuspius Rufinus, the consul of 197 A.D., was priest of Zeus Ὀλύμπιος (M. Fränkel *op. cit.* ii. 297 f. no. 434, 1 ff. a base of white marble inscribed Λ(ούκιον) Κούσπιον Πακτουμήϊ[ον] | Ῥουφῖνον, ὕπατον, ἱερέα Διὸς | Ὀλυμπίου καὶ κτίστην τῆς πατρίδος, | οἱ τὴν ἀκρόπολιν κατοικοῦντες,

Fig. 846.

whose cult was probably introduced in the days of Hadrian the 'Olympian' (*id. ib.* p. 298). H. von Fritze in the *Abh. d. berl. Akad. 1910* Phil.-hist. Classe Anhang i. 55 f. pl. 4, 8 (= my fig. 846) detects the statuary type of the god on a Pergamene coin struck by Hadrian (cp. Overbeck *Gr. Kunstmyth.* Zeus p. 163 Münztaf. 2, 23 with eagle beside the right foot of Zeus). For Zeus Τροπαῖος see *supra* p. 110 n. 9 (add M. Fränkel *op. cit.* i. 137 f. no. 239, 2), for Zeus (?) Ὕψιστος *supra* p. 882 n. o no. (21), for Zeus Φίλιος *infra* Append. N *med.* Coins of Antoninus Pius and Marcus Aurelius, issued at Pergamon, show Zeus enthroned with Nike on his right hand and a long sceptre in his left (H. von Fritze *loc. cit.* p. 55 pl. 4, 12, cp. Mionnet *Descr. de méd. ant.* ii. 602 no. 585).

[1] Zeus Ἀκραῖος (*supra* p. 873 n. o no. (9)).

[2] It has been maintained, though without sufficient reason, that there was a cult of Zeus Ὕπατος on Mt Sipylos (*supra* p. 876 n. o no. (8)), where Zeus was said to have been born (Aristeid. *or.* 22. 270 (i. 440 Dindorf) τὰ μὲν οὖν παλαιὰ μέμνησαι κατὰ τὴν πρώτην ἀκούσας ἀρχήν, ἣν τῷ πατρὶ συνῆρχες, Διός τινα γένεσιν καὶ χορείας Κουρήτων καὶ Ταντάλου καὶ Πέλοπος οἰκισμὸν τῆς πρώτης πόλεως ἐν τῷ Σιπύλῳ γενομένης, cp. *or.* 15. 229 (i. 371 f. Dindorf) ἡ μὲν οὖν πρεσβυτάτη πόλις ἐν τῷ Σιπύλῳ κτίζεται, οὗ δὴ τάς τε θεῶν εὐνὰς εἶναι λέγουσι καὶ τοὺς Κουρήτων χοροὺς περὶ τὴν τοῦ Διὸς μητέρα, *or.* 20. 260 (i. 425 Dindorf) τὰ μὲν ἀρχαῖα Κουρήτων χοροὶ καὶ τροφαὶ καὶ γενέσεις θεῶν καὶ Πέλοπες διαβαίνοντες ἐνθένδε) and to have lain with Semele (schol. B. *Il.* 24. 615 Σίπυλος πόλις ἐστὶ Λυδίας καὶ Ἀχελῷος ποταμὸς ἐκεῖ παρακείμενος. " θεάων " δὲ " εὐνάς," ὅτι ἐκεῖσε Σεμέλη ὁ Ζεὺς συνεκοιμήθη).

A remarkable crag on Mt Sipylos is topped by a rock-cut seat known to the ancients as the 'throne of Pelops' (Paus. 5. 13. 7 Πέλοπος δὲ ἐν Σιπύλῳ μὲν θρόνος ἐν κορυφῇ τοῦ ὄρους ἐστὶν ὑπὲρ τῆς Πλαστήνης μητρὸς τὸ ἱερόν. See further *supra* i. 137 ff. fig. 103), and the sceptre of Pelops was the sceptre of Zeus (*Il.* 2. 100 ff. ἀνὰ δὲ κρείων Ἀγαμέμνων | ἔστη σκῆπτρον ἔχων, τὸ μὲν Ἥφαιστος κάμε τεύχων. | Ἥφαιστος μὲν δῶκε Διὶ Κρονίωνι ἄνακτι, | αὐτὰρ ἄρα Ζεὺς δῶκε διακτόρῳ ἀργεϊφόντῃ· | Ἑρμείας δὲ ἄναξ δῶκεν Πέλοπι πληξίππῳ, | αὐτὰρ ὁ αὖτε Πέλοψ δῶκ' Ἀτρέϊ, ποιμένι λαῶν· | Ἀτρεὺς δὲ θνῄσκων ἔλιπεν πολύαρνι Θυέστῃ, | αὐτὰρ ὁ αὖτε Θυέστ' Ἀγαμέμνονι λεῖπε φορῆναι, | πολλῇσιν νήσοισι καὶ Ἄργεϊ παντὶ ἀνάσσειν, Paus.

Philadelpheia[1].
Mount Tmolos[2].
Tralleis[3].

9. 40. 11 (*supra* i. 406), Quint. *inst. or.* 9. 3. 57 invenitur apud poetas quoque (*sc.* gradatio) ut apud Homerum de sceptro, quod a Iove ad Agamemnonem usque deducit ; et apud nostrum etiam tragicum (*Trag. Rom. frag.* p. 288 f. Ribbeck) ' Iove propagatus (O. Ribbeck cj. *patre prognatus*) est, ut perhibent, Tantalus, | ex Tantalo ortus Pelops, ex Pelope autem satus | Atreus, qui nostrum porro propagat genus '= Diom. *ars gramm.* 2 p. 448, 25 ff. Keil, Quint. *inst. or.* 9. 4. 140 (*Trag. Rom. frag.* p. 289 Ribbeck) ' en impero Argis, sceptra (Sen. *epist.* 80. 7 quotes the line with *regna* for *sceptra*) mihi liquit Pelops').

Coppers of Magnesia ad Sipylum, struck in *s.* ii—i B.C., have *obv.* head of Zeus (or perhaps of Mt Sipylos ?) to right, laureate (*Brit. Mus. Cat. Coins* Lydia p. 137 pl. 15, 1 and 2, p. 139 pl. 15, 7, *Hunter Cat. Coins* ii. 455 no. 3), or *rev.* Zeus standing, in *chitón* and *himátion*, with an eagle on his extended right hand, a transverse sceptre in his left (*Brit. Mus. Cat. Coins* Lydia p. 137 pl. 15, 3), or Zeus and Hermes (?) joining hands with a spear between them (*ib.* p. 138 pl. 15, 4). *Quasi*-autonomous coppers of imperial date (M. Aurelius to Gallienus) repeat the *obv.* head of Zeus (or Mt Sipylos : see *supra* i. 102 n. 5 fig. 75) to right, laureate (*Brit. Mus. Cat. Coins* Lydia p. 139 ff. pl. 16, 2 f., Imhoof-Blumer *Kleinas. Münzen* ii. 521 no. 1). A copper of Philippus Senior has *rev.* a naked Zeus holding a thunderbolt in his left hand and resting with his right on a spear (*Brit. Mus. Cat. Coins* Lydia p. 151 no. 80).

[1] Zeus Κορυφαῖος (*supra* p. 285 n. 0 no. (3), p. 869 n. 1 fig. 804).

[2] According to Eumelos, Zeus was born in Lydia ; and on the top of Mt Tmolos, west of Sardeis, was a place called Γοναὶ Διὸς Ὑετίου and subsequently Δεύσιον (Lyd. *de mens.* 4· 71 p. 123, 14 ff. Wünsch Εὔμηλος δὲ ὁ Κορίνθιος (*frag.* 18 Kinkel) τὸν Δία ἐν τῇ καθ' ἡμᾶς Λυδίᾳ τεχθῆναι βούλεται, καὶ μᾶλλον ἀληθεύει ὅσον ἐν ἱστορίᾳ· ἔτι γὰρ καὶ νῦν πρὸς τῷ δυτικῷ τῆς Σαρδιανῶν πόλεως μέρει ἐπ' ἀκρωρείας τοῦ Τμώλου τόπος ἐστίν, ὃς πάλαι μὲν Γοναὶ Διὸς Ὑετίου νῦν δὲ παρατραπείσης τῷ χρόνῳ τῆς λέξεως Δεύσιον (G. Kinkel prints Δευσίου and is followed by K. Tümpel in Pauly—Wissowa *Real-Enc.* v. 281) προσαγορεύεται). A bronze coin of Sardeis, struck under Iulia Domna, has for its reverse type an infant Zeus seated on the ground with an eagle hovering above him (*Brit. Mus. Cat. Coins* Lydia p. 261 pl. 27, 6=*supra* i. 151 fig. 118). Zeus Σαβάζιος brought the babe Dionysos to Mt Tmolos (Orph. *h. Sabaz.* 48. 1 ff. κλῦθι, πάτερ, Κρόνου υἱέ, Σαβάζιε, κύδιμε δαῖμον, | ὃς Βάκχον Διόνυσον, ἐρίβρομον, εἰραφιώτην | μηρῷ ἐγκατέραψας, ὅπως τετελεσμένος ἔλθῃ | Τμῶλον ἐς ἠγάθεον παρά θ' Ἵππαν (παρ' ἵππαν codd.) καλλιπάρηον. So O. Kern in *Genethliakon* Carl Robert zum 8. März 1910 überreicht von der Graeca Halensis Berlin 1910 p. 90 f. and in his *Orphicorum Fragmenta* Berolini 1922 p. 222 f., W. Quandt *De Baccho ab Alexandri aetate in Asia Minore culto* Halis Saxonum 1913 p. 257 f.). See further K. Buresch *Klaros* Leipzig 1889 p. 16 f., Gruppe *Gr. Myth. Rel.* p. 284 n. 11.

[3] Tralleis (*Aidin*) occupied a high plateau on a southern spur of Mt Messogis. Its *akrópolis* (320ᵐ) overlooks the little river Eudonos, a tributary of the Maiandros (map by C. Humann and W. Dörpfeld in the *Ath. Mitth.* 1893 xviii. 395 ff. pl. 12). The town was said to have been founded by Argives and Thracians (Strab. 649 κτίσμα δὲ φασιν εἶναι τὰς Τράλλεις Ἀργείων καί τινων Θρακῶν Τραλλίων, ἀφ' ὧν τοὔνομα, cp. Steph. Byz. *s.v.* Τραλλία and Diod. 17. 65). A bronze coin struck by M. Aurelius has for reverse type ΤΡΑΛΛΕΥ C ΚΤΙCCΤΗC (*sic*) Tralleus as a soldier, standing to left, with right hand outstretched and left supported on spear (Imhoof-Blumer *Gr. Münzen* p. 203 no. 642 b, Head *Hist. num.*² p. 661).

Larisa, a village higher up on the slopes of Messogis, thirty stades from Tralleis, gave its name to Zeus Λαρίσιος (Strab. 440 (in a list of towns called Λάρισα) καὶ τῶν Τράλλεων διέχουσα κώμη τριάκοντα σταδίους ὑπὲρ τῆς πόλεως ἐπὶ Καΰστρου πεδίον διὰ τῆς Μεσωγίδος ἰόντων κατὰ τὸ τῆς Ἰσοδρόμης Μητρὸς ἱερόν, ὁμοίαν τὴν θέσιν καὶ τὴν ἀρετὴν ἔχουσα τῇ Κρεμαστῇ Λαρίσῃ (so cod. A, with another σ added by the second hand. λαρίσσῃ cett. codd.)· καὶ γὰρ εὔυδρος καὶ ἀμπελόφυτος· ἴσως δὲ καὶ ὁ Λαρίσιος (so cod. A, with another

Appendix B

σ added by the second hand. λαρίσσιος cett. codd.) Ζεὺς ἐκεῖθεν ἐπωνόμασται), as did Larisa on the Caystrian Plain to Apollon Λαρισηνός (Strab. 620 : id. ap. Steph. Byz. s.v. Λάρισσα has Λαρισσηνός). Pythodoros of Tralleis, the friend of Pompey, is mentioned along with Μηνόδωρος, ἀνὴρ λόγιος καὶ ἄλλως σεμνὸς καὶ βαρύς, ἔχων τὴν ἱερωσύνην τοῦ Διὸς τοῦ Λαρισαίου (Strab. 649). The name Λάρισα seems, however, to have been assimilated to the Carian place-names Ἅρπασα, Βάργασα, Μύλασα, Πήδασα, etc. (cp. Ptol. 6. 2. 13 Λάρασα in Media); for Zeus Λαρίσιος or Λαρισαῖος regularly appears on coins and in inscriptions as Zeus Λαράσιος. His cult, the most important of all cults at Tralleis, has been well studied by J. O. Schaefer De Iove apud Cares culto Halis Saxonum 1912 pp. 455—466, to whose collection of evidence I am much indebted.

Tralleis was formerly called Δία (et. mag. p. 389, 55 f. cited supra p. 587 n. 2, cp. L. Bürchner in Pauly—Wissowa Real-Enc. v. 299) and was officially described as sacred to Zeus (Corp. inscr. Gr. ii no. 2926 (of s. iii A.D.) Τι. ΚΛ. Γλύπτον, | Ἀνδρονίκου (υἱ)όν, | τὸν ἀγορα-νόμον, | τὸν ὑπέρτατον | λογιστ(ὴ)ν καὶ | σωτῆρα καὶ | κτίστην τῆς | πατρίδος, | τῆς λαμπρο-τάτης | πόλε(ω)ς τῆς νε|ωκόρου τῶν Σεβαστῶν, | ἱερᾶς τοῦ Διός, κα|τὰ τὰ δόγματα τῆς | συνκλήτου Τραλ|λιανῶν | οἱ μύσται | τῶν ἱερῶν (Lebas—Waddington iii. 203 no. 604 read οἱ μύσται τὸν εὐε[ργέτην])) or to Zeus Λαράσιος (K. Buresch in the Ath. Mitth. 1894 xix. 111 ff. no. 12 (time of Caracalla) Φλάουιον Φ[λ](αουίου) | Διαδούμενον | (ἐπίτροπον?) | τοῦ Σεβαστοῦ ὑπ[α]τικῶν συνγενῆ | ἡ κρατίστη<ι> Κλαυδία | βουλὴ καὶ ὁ δῆ[μο]ς [τῆς] | λαμ-προτάτη[ς μητρο]πόλεως τῆς [Ἀσίας καὶ] | νεωκόρου τῶ[ν Σεβαστῶν] | καὶ ἱερᾶς τοῦ [Διὸς τοῦ Λα]ρασίου κ[ατὰ τὰ δόγματα] | τῆς ἱερωτά[της συνκλή]του Καισα[ρέων Τραλλια]|ν῀ων πόλ[εως] | διὰ τὴν (ὑ)περ(τ)ά[την?] | ἐν ταῖς ἀρχαῖ[ς καὶ λειτουρ]γίαις εὔνοια[ν καὶ] | φιλο-τιμία[ν]). Decrees were set up in the sanctuary of Zeus (A. E. Kontoleon in the Bull. Corr. Hell. 1886 x. 516 no. 4, 2 ff. τὸ δὲ ψήφισμα | [τό]δε ἀναγράψαι εἰς στή|λην λιθίνην καὶ στῆσαι | ἐν τῶι ἱερῶι τοῦ Διός, M. Pappakonstantinou Αἱ Τράλλεις ἤτοι συλλογὴ Τραλλιανῶν ἐπιγραφῶν Athens 1895 no. 42 (of s. iii B.C.) ὁ δῆμος ὁ Σελευκείων (cp. Plin. nat. hist. 5. 108) ... ἀναγράψαι δὲ τὸ ψήφισμα τόδε ἐν στήλη λιθίνῃ καὶ στῆσαι ἐν τῷ [? προ(suppl. J. O. Schäfer)] νάῳ τοῦ Διὸς ἐν τῷ ἐπιφανεστάτῳ τόπῳ) or Zeus Λαράσιος (A. Fontrier in the Bull. Corr. Hell. 1879 iii. 466 ff., v. 11 ff. (of s. iii B.C.) [ἀναγ]ράψαι δὲ τὸ ψήφισμα τόδε ἐ[ίς τ]ὰς περὶ τούτων ἐπι[σκευασθείσας στήλας καὶ στ]ῆσαι μίαν μὲν ἐν τῶι ἱερῶι τοῦ Διὸς τοῦ Λαρ[ασ]ί[ο]υ, τὴν δὲ ἑτέραν | [ἐν τῶι ἱερῶι τῆς Ἀθη]νᾶς, M. Pappakonstantinou in the Ath. Mitth. 1888 xiii. 411 no. 2, 5 ff. ἀνα|[γράψ]αι δ(ὲ) αὐτὸν καὶ εὐεργέτην τῆς πόλε|[ως ὡς καὶ] τὸ ψήφισμα εἰς στήλην λιθίνην | [καὶ στῆ]σαι ἐν τῷ ἱερῷ τοῦ Διὸς τοῦ Λαρα|σίου, κ.τ.λ., A. Rehm in Milet iii. 318 ff. no. 143, 66 ff. (a decree of Seleukeia (Tralleis) cited in a pact of 212/11 B.C. between Miletos and Seleukeia) ἐπὶ δὲ τοῖς ἐψηφισμένοις συν|[τελέσαι θυσία]ν τῶι Διὶ τῶι Λαρασίωι καὶ τῶι Ἀπόλλωνι τοὺς ἱερομνήμονας κα[ὶ] | [τοὺς (8—10 letters missing) καὶ τοὺς θ]ερχ[όλου]ς ἐπευχομένους συνενεγκεῖν ἀμφοτέραις | [ταῖς πόλεσι τὰ ἐψηφισμένα καὶ εἶναι] ἐπὶ σωτηρίαι καὶ εὐτυχίαι· ἀνα|[γράψαι δὲ τὸ ψήφισμα εἰς στήλην λιθίνη]ν καὶ στῆσαι ἐν τῶι ἱερῶι τοῦ | [Διὸς τοῦ Λαρασίου· κ.τ.λ.], T. Macridy in the Jahresh. d. oest. arch. Inst. 1912 xv. 59 f. (a stéle of Hellenistic date from Notion) A, 3 ff. ἀναγράφουσι τὰ ψηφί[σ]|[μ]ατα εἰς στήλας λιθίνας δύο καὶ ἱστᾶσι τὴμ μὲν μίαν παρ' αὑτοῖς ἐν τῶι ἱρῶι τ[οῦ] | [Δ]ιὸς τοῦ Λαρασίου ἐν τῶι ἐπιφανεστάτωι τόπωι, τὴν δὲ ἑτέραν παρ' ἡμῖν κ.τ.λ.). And votive offerings to the god included a couple of eagles (C. Fellows An Account of Discoveries in Lycia London 1841 p. 19=Corp. inscr. Gr. ii Add. no. 2923·b = Lebas—Waddington Asie Mineure iii. 200 no. 597 (beneath a well-carved eagle minus its head) Διογένης Ὀρθί[ων]|ος Θεῷ Διὶ εὐχα[ρ]ιστῶν τούτους | δύ' ἀετοὺς ἀνέ|θηκε. The formula Θεῷ Διὶ is exceptional and sounds like a Latinism, cp. Corp. inscr. Lat. vii no. 80, 1 f. deo | Iovi and the like) and an effigy of Dionysos (M. Pappakonstantinou Αἱ Τράλλεις κ.τ.λ. no. 150 ἀγαθῇ τύχῃ· τῶι Διὶ τὸν Διόνυσον Ἀγαθήμερος ἱερός (on this title see G. Cardinali ' Note di terminologia epigrafica II ' Ἱεροί ' in the Rendiconti d. Lincei 1908 xvii. 165 ff., O. Kern 'Hieroi und Hierai ' in Hermes 1911 xlvi. 300 ff., Link in Pauly—Wissowa Real-Enc. viii. 1471 ff.)).

The priest of the city, presumably the priest of Zeus Λαράσιος, regularly dwelt in the brick palace built there by the kings of Pergamon (Vitr. 2. 8. 9 Trallibus domum regibus Attalicis factam quae ad habitandum semper datur ei qui civitatis gerit sacerdotium). He held office for life (E. Loewy in the *Ath. Mitth.* 1886 xi. 203 f. no. 1 = A. E. Kontoleon in the *Bull. Corr. Hell.* 1886 x. 456 f. no. 8 = J. R. S. Sterrett in the *Papers of the American School of Classical Studies at Athens* 1888 ii. 325 no. 379 = Dittenberger *Orient. Gr. inscr. sel.* no. 499 'On the base or capital of a column' [Γ.] Ἰούλιον, [Γ.] Ἰουλίου Φιλίππου ἀρχιερέως | Ἀσίας υἱόν, Οὐελίνᾳ, Φίλιππον, ἱππέα Ῥω|μαίων (Loewy and Dittenberger give Ῥω|μαῖον), τῶν ἐκλεκτῶν ἐν Ῥώμ[η]ι δικαστῶν, | ἐπίτροπον τῶν Σεβαστῶν, πατέρα Ἰουλί[ου] | Φιλίππου συγκλητικοῦ, στρατηγοῦ Ῥωμαί|ων, ἱερέα διὰ βίου τοῦ Διὸς τοῦ Λαρασίου, J. R. S. Sterrett in the *Ath. Mitth.* 1883 viii. 330 ff. no. 11, 14 ff. = *id.* in the *Papers of the American School* 1885 i. 110 ff. no. 11, 14 ff. (*c.* 200 A.D.) ἐπὶ ἱερέως διὰ βίου τοῦ Δι|ὸς τοῦ Λαρασίου Φλαουίου | Κλειτοσθένους τοῦ κρατί|στου δὶς Ἀσιάρχου, πρῶτο[υ] | Ἀσίας, πατρὸς ὑπατικοῦ κα[ὶ] | πάππου συνκλητικῶν, τῆς | θ' αὐτοῦ πενταετηρίδος, M. Pappakonstantinou Αἱ Τράλλεις κ.τ.λ. no. 12 (a similar inscription) ἐπὶ ἱερέως διὰ βίου τοῦ Διὸς τοῦ Λαρασίου Φλαουίου Κλειτοσθένους κ.τ.λ., *id.* in the *Ath. Mitth.* 1901 xxvi. 239 no. 4 (on a four-sided marble base) [Τ. Φλάουιον] | Στασικλέα Μητροφά|νη τὸν κράτιστον | ἱερέα διὰ βίου τοῦ Διὸς | τοῦ Λαρασίου καὶ ἀγωνοθέτη[ν] | τῶν μεγάλων Ϙ ἱερῶν | εἰσελαστικῶν εἰς ἅπασαν | τὴν οἰκουμένην ~ | ἀγώνων πρώτων Πυθίων | υἱὸν Τ. Φλ. Κλειτοσθένους | ὑπατι-κοῦ ~ ἔγγονον ~ | Τ. Φλ. Κλειτοσθένους, πατρὸς | [ὑπατικοῦ – – – – – –]]). When, in *s.* ii A.D., Tralleis was visited by an earthquake, a Pythian oracle delivered to the priest Kleitosthenes represented the disaster as due to the wrath of Zeus for the city's neglect of Poseidon the earthquake-god and directed that ample atonement should be made to both deities (A. Hauvette-Besnault and Dubois in the *Bull. Corr. Hell.* 1881 v. 340 ff. = Cougny *Anth. Pal. Append.* Add. 6. 104 *b* = O. Kern in *Genethliakon* Carl Robert zum 8. März 1910 überreicht von der Graeca Halensis Berlin 1910 p. 98 ff. with pl. χρησμὸς τοῦ Πυθίου | δοθεὶς Κλειτοσθένει τῷ | ἱερεῖ τοῦ Διὸς ὑπὲρ τῆς | σωτηρίας τῆς πόλεως· |

χειλιετὲς μήνειμα πάτρης Διὸς ἐξαναλύσας
μειλιχίῃ Σεισίχθονι ἐν ἀλσεῖ βωμὸν ἐνείρας
θύεο, μὴ διερεύνω μ' ὦ πόλις, εἰναλίῳ νῦν
ἐννομίην Κρονίδῃ, φοιβῇ χερὶ δὲ ἀρητῆρος,
πυρῶν καὶ καρπῶν τ' ἐπιδράγματα πάντα· καλείσθω
ἀσφάλιος, τεμενοῦχος, ἀπότροπος, ἵππιος, ἀργής·
ὧδε, πόλις, δὲ ὑμνεῖτε δεδραγμένον εἶφι βεβῶτα
οὔ τε βάθρῳ κύκνειον ὅσοι γέρας ἀμφιπένεσθε
ἐν χορῷ εὖ αἰνεῖν Σεισίχθονα καὶ Δ[ί]α μειλαξ

(The last word is a puzzle. O. Kern *loc. cit.* p. 101 n. 1 holds that it is either an unknown adverb or a form comparable with Hesych. μῖλαξ· ἡλικία. ἔνιοι δὲ μέλλαξ· καὶ παρ' Ἑρμίππῳ ἐν Θεοῖς (*frag.* 10 (*Frag. com. Gr.* ii. 392 Meineke)), ἀγνοήσας Ἀρτεμίδωρος· ἐκεῖ γὰρ μῖλάξ ἐστιν. δηλοῖ δὲ τὸν δημοτικόν. J. O. Schaefer *op. cit.* p. 464 f. prefers the first alternative and assumes μεῖλαξ = μειλιχίη. No allusion to the botanical μῖλαξ is probable.) Another priest of *s.* ii A.D., Claudius Meliton, made a dedication to Zeus Λαράσιος Σεβαστὸς Εὐμενής (J. R. S. Sterrett in the *Papers of the American School* 1888 ii. 326 f. no. 381 Διὶ Λαρασί|ῳ Σεβαστῷ | Εὐμενεῖ Κλαύ|δι(ο)ς Μελί▨|των ὁ ἱερεὺς | ἀποκατέ|-στησεν) *ib.* 1885 i. 102) and was there identified with Zeus Λαράσιος (J. B. Lightfoot *The Apostolic Fathers* London 1885 ii. 1. 617 n. 1, J. R. S. Sterrett *loc. cit.* 1888 ii. 327), just as in 128 A.D. he came to Athens and was there identified with Zeus Ὀλύμπιος (P. v. Rohden in Pauly—Wissowa *Real-Enc.* i. 509), or just as in 132 A.D. he came to Dodona and was there identified with Zeus Δωδωναῖος (*id. ib.* i. 512, on the strength of *Corp. inscr. Gr.* ii no. 1822 cited *infra* Append. M. *med.*).

Special interest attaches to the inscription on a small marble base from Aïdin in the Purser collection at Smyrna (W. M. Ramsay in the *Bull. Corr. Hell.* 1883 vii. 276 f. no. 19, *id. The Cities and Bishoprics of Phrygia* Oxford 1895 i. 94 ff., 115 no. 18 [ἀγ]αθῇ τύχῃ· | Λ. Αὐρηλία Αἰ|[μ]ιλία ἐκ προ|γόνων παλλα|κίδων καὶ ἀνί|πτοπόδων θ[υ]|γάτηρ Λ. Αὐρ. Σ[ε]|κούνδου Ση[ί]|ου παλλακεύσα|σα καὶ κατὰ χρη|σμὸν (space) | (space) Διί Ϙ). Sir William Ramsay comments: 'Aurelia Aemilia belonged to a family in which the ancient custom was retained that the women should in their youth be *hetairai* in the service of the temple.'

This custom was common in the native religions of Asia Minor (1) [(1) Strab. p. 559 and 532–3.], but it is somewhat remarkable to find it actually practised by a family bearing Roman names perhaps as late as the third century P.C.' Cp. Ail. *var. hist.* 4. 1 Λυδοῖς ἦν ἔθος πρὸ τοῦ συνοικεῖν τὰς γυναῖκας ἀνδράσιν ἑταιρεῖν, ἅπαξ δὲ καταζευχθεῖσας σωφρονεῖν· τὴν δὲ ἁμαρτάνουσαν ἐς ἕτερον συγγνώμης τυχεῖν ἀδύνατον ἦν (but hardly the references collected by Gruppe *Gr. Myth. Rel.* p. 915 n. 6). The significance of such customs in general is disputed (see *e.g.* M. P. Nilsson *Studia de Dionysiis Atticis* Lundae 1900 pp. 119—121, *id. Gr. Feste* pp. 365—367, Gruppe *Gr. Myth. Rel.* pp. 914—917, F. Cumont *Les Religions Orientales dans le Paganisme Romain*[2] Paris 1909 pp. 143—286, H. Ploss—M. Bartels *Das Weib in der Natur- und Völkerkunde*[10] Leipzig 1913 i. 614—616, 648—654, Frazer *Golden Bough*[3]: Adonis Attis Osiris[3] i. 36 ff., 57 ff.) and investigators have been apt to confuse similar effects produced by dissimilar causes (see E. S. Hartland 'Concerning the Rite at the Temple of Mylitta' in *Anthropological Essays presented to Edward Burnett Tylor* Oxford 1907 pp. 189—202). The Trallian inscription perhaps implies that women, believed to represent a mother-goddess, used to mate with men, believed to represent a father-god, their union being thought to promote the fruitfulness of the land and its occupants. If so, the παλλακίδες may have been comparable with the Egyptian παλλακίδες of Zeus Θηβαιεύς (Hdt. 1. 182 (*supra* i. 348 n. 1), cp. Hekataios of Abdera *frag.* 12 (*Frag. hist. Gr.* ii. 390 Müller) *ap.* Diod. 1. 47 ἀπὸ γὰρ τῶν πρώτων τάφων, ἐν οἷς παραδέδοται τὰς παλλακίδας τοῦ Διὸς τεθάφθαι, κ.τ.λ., Strab. 816 τῷ δὲ Διί, ὃν μάλιστα τιμῶσιν, εὐειδεστάτη καὶ γένους λαμπροτάτου παρθένος ἱερᾶται, ἃς καλοῦσιν οἱ Ἕλληνες παλλάδας (Xylander cj. παλλακάς. W. Dindorf cj. παλλακίδας. But see G. Kramer *ad loc.*)· αὕτη δὲ καὶ παλλακεύει καὶ σύνεστιν οἷς βούλεται, μέχρις ἂν ἡ φυσικὴ γένηται κάθαρσις τοῦ σώματος· μετὰ δὲ τὴν κάθαρσιν δίδοται πρὸς ἄνδρα· πρὶν δὲ δοθῆναι, πένθος αὐτῆς ἄγεται μετὰ τὸν τῆς παλλακείας καιρόν). And the ἀνιπτόποδες recall the priests of Zeus at Dodona (*Il.* 16. 234 ff. Ζεῦ ἄνα, Δωδωναῖε, Πελασγικέ, τηλόθι ναίων, | Δωδώνης μεδέων δυσχειμέρου· ἀμφὶ δὲ Σελλοὶ | σοὶ ναίουσ' ὑποφῆται ἀνιπτόποδες, χαμαιεῦναι), who 'went with unwashen feet and lay on the ground in order that they might be in constant contact with Mother Earth (J. O. Schaefer *op. cit.* p. 462 f. I had hit upon the same explanation years before and published it in the *Class. Rev.* 1903 xvii. 180). The combination of a rite reminiscent of Egyptian Thebes with a rite reminiscent of Dodona is not surprising in view of the analogy already traced between the usages of these two cult-centres (*supra* i. 363 ff.).

Coppers of Seleukeia (Tralleis) first struck late in *s.* iii B.C. (Head *Hist. num.*[2] p. 659) have *obv.* head of Zeus, laureate, to right; *rev.* humped bull, with ΣΕΛΕΥΚΕΩΝ above and magistrate's name below, all within maeander-border (F. Imhoof-Blumer *Lydische Stadtmünzen* Genf—Leipzig 1897 p. 169 pl. 7, 7). Some specimens add ΔΙΟΣ above and ΛΑΡΑΣΙΟΥ below the bull (*id. ib.* p. 169 no. 3). One, in place of the maeander, gives ΔΙΟΣ ΛΑΡΑΣΙΟΥ ΚΑΙ ΔΙΟΣ ΕΥΜΕΝΟΥ (*sic*) (*id. ib.* p. 169 f. no. 4), cp. Dittenberger *Syll. inscr. Gr.*[3] no. 985, 6 ff. (Philadelpheia in Lydia : *s.* i B.C.) Διὸς [γὰρ ἐν τούτωι] | τοῦ Εὐμενοῦς καὶ Ἑστίας τ[ῆς παρέδρου αὐ]|τοῦ καὶ τῶν ἄλλων θεῶν Σωτ[ήρων κ.τ.λ.] and the dedication to Hadrianas Zeus Λαράσιος Σεβαστὸς Εὐμενής cited *supra*. The inference is that Eumenes i was divinised after his death as Zeus Εὐμενής: cp. the divinisation of Eumenes ii in Michel *Recueil d'Inscr. gr.* no. 515, 22 = Dittenberger *Orient. Gr. inscr. sel.* no. 332, 22 θεοῦ βασιλέως Εὐμένου Σωτῆρος (*ib.* 24 f., 45). Coppers of Tralleis struck in early imperial times have sometimes *obv.* head of Zeus, laureate, to right; *rev.* Δ[ΙΟ]Σ ΛΑΡΑΣΙΟΥ ΚΑΙ[ΣΑ]ΡΕΩΝ humped bull standing to left (*Brit. Mus. Cat. Coins* Lydia p. 339 no. 87: my fig. 847 is from a cast of this specimen). Later we find *obv.* ϹΕΥϹΛΑ ΡΑϹΙΟϹ bust of Zeus, laureate, to right, within border of dots; *rev.*

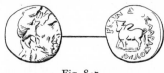

Fig. 847.

ΤΡΑΛ ΛΙΑΝΩΝ Dionysos standing to front, naked, with grape-bunch in raised right hand, *kántharos* in lowered left, within border of dots (*ib.* p. 341 no. 100), or *obv.* ΖΕ ΥϹ bust of Zeus, laureate, to right, within border of dots; *rev.* ΤΡΑΛΛΙΑΝΩΝ humped bull walking to right, within border of dots (*ib.* p. 342 no. 101 f.), or ΤΡΑΛΛ ΙΑΝΩΝ bunch of grapes, within border of dots (*ib.* p. 342 no. 103). Other imperial coppers represent Zeus Λαράσιος as a seated figure, who wears a *himátion* round his legs, holds Nike on his outstretched right hand, and rests upon a sceptre with his left (*ib.* p. 340 no. 93 ΛΑΡΑϹΙΟϹ ΚΑΙϹΑΡΕ ΩΝ time of Nero—Domitian, p. 345 no. 129 ΚΑΙϹΑΡΕΩ ΝΛΑΡΑϹΙ ΟϹ Domitian, cp. p. 354 pl. 37, 7 Gordianus Pius, p. 357 pl. 37, 11 Philippus Senior, p. 362 pl. 41, 11 Gordianus Pius), sometimes with an eagle at his feet (*ib.* p. 350 pl. 37, 2 L. Verus).

Other coins of the town illustrate the myth of Zeus: (1) a copper of Antoninus Pius has *rev.* ΔΙΟϹΓΟΝΑΙ the infant Zeus asleep on a mountain with an eagle hovering above him (Overbeck *Gr. Kunstmyth.* Zeus p. 337 f., Head *Hist. num.*[2] p. 661. *Supra* i. 151 fig. 119, 535 n. 0). Sir W. M. Ramsay *The Historical Geography of Asia Minor* London 1890 p. 13 rightly rejects B. V. Head's former view that the legend is Διὸς Γοναί(ου). Cp. Aristodemos of Thebes *frag.* 6 (*Frag. hist. Gr.* iii. 310 Müller) *ap.* schol. *Il.* 13. 1 μετὰ δὲ τὴν ᾽Ιλίου πόρθησιν ῞Εκτωρ ὁ Πριάμου καὶ μετὰ τὸν θάνατον τὴν ἀπὸ θεῶν εὐτύχησε τιμήν. οἱ γὰρ ἐν Βοιωτίᾳ Θηβαῖοι πιεζόμενοι κακοῖς ἐμαντεύοντο περὶ ἀπαλλαγῆς. χρησμὸς δὲ αὐτοῖς ἐδόθη παύσεσθαι τὰ δεινά, ἐὰν ἐξ ᾽Οφρυνίου τῆς Τρωάδος τὰ ῞Εκτορος ὀστᾶ διακομισθῶσιν εἰς τὸν παρ᾽ αὐτοῖς καλούμενον τόπον Διὸς Γονάς. οἱ δὲ τοῦτο ποιήσαντες καὶ τῶν κακῶν ἀπαλλαγέντες διὰ τιμῆς ἔσχον ῞Εκτορα, κατά τε τοὺς ἐπείγοντας καιροὺς ἐπικαλοῦνται τὴν ἐπιφάνειαν αὐτοῦ. ἡ ἱστορία παρὰ ᾽Αριστοδήμῳ = Cramer *anecd. Paris.* iii. 18, 7 ff. with Bölte in Pauly—Wissowa *Real-Enc.* vii. 1585. (2) A copper of M. Aurelius has *rev.* the infant Zeus suckled by a goat (Mionnet *Descr. de méd. ant.* Suppl. vii. 472 no. 723). (3) A copper of Antoninus Pius has *rev.* the infant Zeus nursed by Rhea, with an eagle on the ground at her feet and three Kouretes clashing their shields about her (F. Imhoof-Blumer *Lydische Stadtmünzen* p. 177 f. pl. 7, 15, *Brit. Mus. Cat. Coins* Lydia p. 347 pl. 36, 5 (*supra* i. 151 fig. 121 from a cast), Head *Hist. num.*[2] p. 661). (4) A copper of Antoninus Pius has *rev.* ΕΙΟΥϹΓΑΜΟ[Ι] Io in long robe and bridal veil led towards the left by Hermes, who wears a *chlamýs* and holds a *caduceus* in his right hand (*Brit. Mus. Cat. Coins* Lydia p. 348 pl. 36, 8, Head *Hist. num.*[2] p. 661). (5) A copper of Antoninus Pius has *rev.* a veiled figure (Io?) sitting in a two-wheeled hooded chariot, which is drawn by a pair of humped bulls and conducted by a naked figure (Hermes?) (*Brit. Mus. Cat. Coins* Lydia p. 348 no. 141). (6) A copper of Tranquillina, now in the British Museum, has *rev.* a male figure (Zeus?) clad in a *himátion* extending his right hand to a fully draped and veiled female figure (Io?), who stands in the entrance of a wattle-shed or hut (perhaps the βούστασις of Aisch. *P. v.*

651 ff. σὺ δ᾽, ὦ παῖ, μὴ ᾽πολακτίσῃς λέχος | τὸ Ζηνός, ἀλλ᾽ ἔξελθε πρὸς Λέρνης βαθὺν | λειμῶνα, ποίμνας βουστάσεις τε πρὸς πατρός, | ὡς ἂν τὸ Δῖον ὄμμα λωφήσῃ πόθου) (so B. V. Head and W. Wroth in the *Num. Chron.* Fourth Series 1903 iii. 337 f. no. 30 pl. 12, 1 (=my fig. 848 from a cast) with the alternative suggestion (*ib.* p. 338 n. 45): 'Or the scene...may possibly refer to a later incident, when Io, at the Egyptian Canobus, is restored to sanity by the gentle touch of Zeus's hand and becomes the mother of Epaphus the ancestor of the Argive Danaoi' [Aisch. *P. v.* 846 ff.], Head *Hist. num.*[2]

Fig. 848.

p. 661). *À propos* of the whole series B. V. Head in the *Brit. Mus. Cat. Coins* Lydia p. cxlvi observes: 'Evidently on these coins we have representations of successive scenes in certain religious mysteries connected with the Io legend, and celebrated by the Trallians in commemoration of their Argive descent, Argos having been the original home of the Io myth.' I doubt the Io-'mysteries.' The coin-types, inscriptions and all, could be equally well explained as copying the subjects of the frescoes or reliefs with which some public edifice at Tralleis was adorned, *e.g.* the octostyle temple (? of Zeus. It has an eagle in its pediment, but a *caduceus* beside

Ionia
    Smyrna[1].
    Ephesos[2].

it or within it) figured on imperial coppers (*Brit. Mus. Cat. Coins* Lydia p. 338 pl. 35, 1, p. 353 no. 161).

The cult of Zeus Λαράσιος spread to Miletos, where a small domestic altar dedicated to him has come to light (T. Wiegand in the *Abh. d. berl. Akad. 1908* Phil.-hist. Classe Anhang i. 27 'am zahlreichsten sind die Zeuskulte, natürlich wiegen die karischen vor, so dass Zeus Labraundios (einmal Λαβρένδιος) durch sechs mit der Doppelaxt geschmückte Altäre vertreten ist, Larasios und Zeus Lepsynos einmal, ebenso der 'Ολύμπιος Πεισαῖος, Κεραύνιος Σωτήρ, Τερμινθεύς, 'Ομοβούλιος und Καταιβάτης; endlich ist ein kleiner Altar Διὸς ἐλπίδων gefunden').

Θεὸς῾Ύψιστος (*supra* p. 880 n. 0 no. (17)).

[1] Zeus 'Ακραῖος (*supra* p. 873 n. 0 no. (8)).

[2] The Zeus-cult of the Ephesians can be traced back to the first half of *s.* vii B.C. (Kallin. *frag.* 4 Bergk[4], 2 Hiller—Crusius *ap.* Strab. 633 ἡνίκα καὶ Σμύρνα ἐκαλεῖτο ἡ ῎Εφεσος· καὶ Καλλῖνός που οὕτως ὠνόμακεν αὐτήν, Σμυρναίους τοὺς 'Εφεσίους καλῶν ἐν τῷ πρὸς τὸν Δία λόγῳ· 'Σμυρναίους δ' ἐλέησον'· καὶ πάλιν· 'μνῆσαι δ' εἴ κοτέ τοι μηρία καλὰ βοῶν | < Σμυρναῖοι κατέκηαν (*ins.* I. Casaubon) >' κ.τ.λ.). But here Zeus was always of less importance than Artemis; and the tradition which located her birth at Ortygia (the glen of *Arvalia*: see O. Benndorf *Forschungen in Ephesos* Wien 1906 i. 76 ff.) boldly appropriated his Kouretes (C. Picard *Éphèse et Claros* Paris 1922 pp. 277 ff., 423 ff.), installing them on Mt Solmissos (Strab. 640 ὑπέρκειται δὲ τοῦ ἄλσους ὄρος ὁ Σολμισσός, ὅπου στάντας φασὶ τοὺς Κουρῆτας τῷ ψόφῳ τῶν ὅπλων ἐκπλῆξαι τὴν ῞Ηραν ζηλοτύπως ἐφεδρεύουσαν, καὶ λαθεῖν συμπράξαντας τὴν λοχείαν τῇ Λητοῖ. κ.τ.λ.).

A bronze coin of Ephesos, struck by Antoninus Pius, has *rev.* Zeus enthroned on a mountain-top (Mt Koressos). He holds in his left hand a thunderbolt and pours from his raised right hand a shower of rain upon a recumbent mountain-god inscribed ΠΕΙΩΝ, who bears a *cornu copiae*. In front of the principal mountain, on the level of the plain, is a distyle temple, above which, in the background, are cypress-trees and two three-storeyed buildings, perched upon rocks. To the left of the same mountain is another three-storeyed building (*Brit. Mus. Cat. Coins* Ionia p. 79 pl. 13, 9 (=*supra* i. 134 fig. 100 from a cast), G. Macdonald *Coin Types* Glasgow 1905 p. 167 f. pl. 6, 9; A. Löbbecke in the *Zeitschr. f. Num.* 1890 xvii. 10 no. 2 pl. 1, 17; O. Benndorf *Forschungen in Ephesos* i. 56 fig. 18 *a* Löbbecke, *b* Cabinet des médailles Paris, *c* British Museum, *d* Gréau collection; Head *Hist. num.*[2] p. 577). High up on the south-eastern side of Mt Koressos is a rock-cut throne, once perhaps regarded as the throne of Zeus (*supra* i. 140 f. fig. 104 f.).

Bronze coins issued at Ephesos by Domitian (*Brit. Mus. Cat. Coins* Ionia p. 75

Fig. 849.

no. 215) and Severus Alexander (*ib.* p. 93 pl. 14, 7 (=my fig. 849 from a cast)) show Zeus 'Ολύμπιος seated to the left, holding the cult-statue of Artemis 'Εφεσία in one hand and a long sceptre in the other. Coppers of Caracalla (*ib.* p. 85 no. 272) and Valerianus Senior (*Hunter Cat. Coins* ii. 337 no. 75) repeat the type, but omit the name of the god. He was worshipped in the Olympieion (Paus. 7. 2. 9 κατὰ τὴν ὁδὸν τὴν ἐκ τοῦ ἱεροῦ παρὰ τὸ 'Ολυμπιεῖον καὶ ἐπὶ πύλας τὰς Μαγνήτιδας). And Hadrian as his vice-gerent shared the honours of his festival (*Corp. inscr. Gr.* ii no. 2810, 17 f. 'Αδριανὰ 'Ο|λύμπια ἐν 'Εφέσωι, iii no. 5913, 30 f.=*Inscr. Gr. Sic. It.* no. 1102, 30 f. ῞Εφεσον τρίς· 'Αδριάνια 'Ολύμ|πια, Βαρβίλληα κ.τ.λ.).

A bronze coin at Ephesos struck by Septimius Severus has *rev.* ΖΕΥϹ ΕΦΕϹΙΟϹ ΠΡΩΤΟϹ ΑϹΙΑϹ Zeus standing with the cult-statue of Artemis 'Εφεσία (Rasche *Lex. Num.* iii. 675, vii. 355, xi. 1256, Eckhel *Doctr. num.*

Magnesia ad Maeandrum¹.
Miletos².

Karia

Halikarnassos³.
Myndos⁴.
Iasos⁵.
Łagina⁶.
Mylasa⁷.
Panamara⁸.
Stratonikeîa⁹.

*vet.*² ii. 514). Others struck by Valerianus (*Brit. Mus. Cat. Coins* Ionia p. 101 no. 357) and Salonina (*supra* p. 743 n. 7 fig. 681) show Zeus naked, striding to right, with thunderbolt in uplifted right hand and eagle on outstretched left.

Finally, the cult-statue of Artemis was called Διοπετές as having fallen from Zeus (Acts 19. 35 τίς γάρ ἐστιν ἀνθρώπων ὃς οὐ γινώσκει τὴν 'Εφεσίων πόλιν νεωκόρον οὖσαν τῆς μεγάλης 'Αρτέμιδος καὶ τοῦ διοπετοῦς; Oikoumenios *comm. in acta apost.* 19. 18—34 (cxviii. 253 Migne) δείκνυσι πολλὴν εἶναι τὴν δεισιδαιμονίαν τῶν 'Εφεσίων ὁ γραμματεὺς ἔκ τε τοῦ κοσμεῖν τὸν ναὸν τῆς 'Αρτέμιδος καὶ τὸ εἴδωλον αὐτῆς τιμᾶν, ὅπερ καὶ Διοπετὲς ἔλεγον ὡς ἐκ τοῦ Διὸς πεπτωκός. ἤτοι γὰρ τὸ ὄστρακον ἔλεγον ἐκεῖνο πάντες (*leg.* πάντως) Διοπετὲς τὸ ἐξ οὐρανοῦ παρὰ τοῦ Διὸς πεμφθέν, ἤτοι καταπτὰν καὶ γενόμενον ἀπ' οὐρανοῦ ἄγαλμα, ἤτοι τὸ Παλλάδιον, καθὼς ἐμύθευον οἱ "Ελληνες πρὸς κατάπληξιν τῶν ἀκεραιοτέρων, ὅπερ ἄνωθεν ἐκ τοῦ Διὸς διαπλασθῆναι ᾤοντο καὶ οὐκ ἐξ ἀνθρώπων. ἢ Διοπετοῦς τοῦ ναοῦ τοῦ Διός, ἤτοι τοῦ στρογγυλοειδοῦς. ἢ καὶ ἱερὸν ἕτερον οὕτως ἐκαλεῖτο παρ' αὐτοῖς=Theophylaktos archbishop of Bulgaria *expos. in acta* text. alt. 29 (cxxv. 1013 Migne) 'καὶ τοῦ Διοπετοῦς.' τὸ εἴδωλον τῆς 'Αρτέμιδος ἐκαλεῖτο Διοπετὲς ὡς ἐκ τοῦ Διὸς πεπτωκός· ἤτοι τὸ ὄστρακον [ἔλεγον] ἐκεῖνο πάντως Διοπετὲς τὸ ἐξ οὐρανοῦ παρὰ τοῦ Διὸς πεμφθὲν ἤτοι καταπτὼν (*leg.* καταπτὰν) καὶ οὐ γενόμενον ὑπὸ ἀνθρώπου ἄγαλμα τῆς 'Αρτέμιδος, καθὼς ἐμύθευον "Ελληνες, Isidoros of Pelousion 4 *epist.* 207 (lxxviii. 1299 Migne) οἱ παρ' "Ελλησι τὰ ξόανα κατασκευάσαντες, φόβον ἐμποιῆσαι τοῖς ὁρῶσι βουλόμενοι, ἔφασκον ὅτι ἐξ οὐρανοῦ παρὰ τοῦ Διὸς ἐπέμφθη ἢ κατέπτη, κρεῖττον ἁπάσης ἀνθρωπίνης χειρός. διὸ καὶ διοπετὲς αὐτὸ καὶ οὐράνιον βρέτας προσηγόρευον = Souid. *s.v.* διοπετές· ἐξ οὐρανοῦ κατερχόμενον. ὅτι οἱ παρ' "Ελλησι τὰ ξόανα κατασκευάζοντες, φόβον ἐμποιῆσαι βουλόμενοι τοῖς ὁρῶσιν, ἔφασκον ὅτι τὸ ἄγαλμα ἐξ οὐρανοῦ παρὰ τοῦ Διὸς ἐπέμφθη καὶ κατέπτη, κρεῖττον ὑπάρχον πάσης ἀνθρωπίνης χειρὸς καὶ ἀνάλωτον. ὅθεν καὶ διοπετὲς αὐτὸ καὶ οὐράνιον βρέτας ἐκάλουν, Sozom. *hist. eccl.* 2. 5 (lxvii. 945 c Migne) γυμνωθέντες δὲ τῆς τοῦ πλήθους ῥοπῆς οἱ νεωκόροι καὶ οἱ ἱερεῖς προύδωκαν τὰ παρ' αὐτοῖς τιμιώτατα καὶ τὰ διοπετῆ καλούμενα). Cp. the passages cited by Stephanus *Thes. Gr. Ling.* ii. 1527 c, to which add Apollod. 3. 12. 3 τὸ διιπετὲς Παλλάδιον, Konon *narr.* 34 τὸ διοπετὲς 'Αθηνᾶς Παλλάδιον, Io. Philop. περὶ ἀγαλμάτων *ap.* Phot. *bibl.* p. 173 b 10 f. διοπετῆ ἐπωνόμασαν. See further Gruppe *Gr. Myth. Rel.* p. 774 n. 2 and P. Saintyves 'Talismans et reliques tombés du ciel' in the *Revue des Études Ethnographiques et Sociologiques* 1909 ii. 175 ff., *Revue d'Ethnographie et de Sociologie* 1910 i. 50 ff., 103 ff.

¹ Zeus 'Ακραῖος (*supra* p. 873 n. 0 no. (7)).
² Zeus "Υψιστος (*supra* p. 879 n. 0 no. (17)).
³ Zeus 'Ακραῖος (*supra* p. 872 n. 0 no. (5)).
⁴ Zeus 'Ακραῖος (*supra* p. 872 n. 0 no. (6)).
⁵ Zeus "Υψιστος (*supra* p. 879 n. 0 no. (17)).
⁶ Zeus "Υψιστος (*supra* p. 879 n. 0 no. (17)).
⁷ Zeus "Υψιστος (*supra* p. 879 n. 0 no. (17)). For Zeus 'Οσογωα or Ζηνοποσειδῶν see *supra* p. 576 ff.; and for Zeus Λαβράϋνδος or Zeus Στράτιος, *supra* pp. 576 ff., 585 ff., 705.
⁸ Zeus "Υψιστος (*supra* p. 879 n. 0 no. (17)). For Zeus Πανάμαρος, Πανήμερος, Πανημέριος see *supra* i. 18 ff.
⁹ Zeus "Υψιστος (*supra* p. 879 n. 0 no. (17)).

Kos
Kos[1].

Bithynia
Prousa ad Olympum[2].

Phrygia
Aizanoi[3].

---

[1] Θεὸς Ὕψιστος (*supra* p. 880 n. o no. (18)).

[2] Zeus Ὀλύμπιος (*supra* i. 116 n. 8, 124). The cult-statue of the god appears on a bronze coin of Prousa, struck by Trajan, with *rev.* ΠΡΟΥCΑΕΙC ΔΙΑ ΟΛΥΜΠΙΟΝ Zeus enthroned to right, resting his right hand on a long sceptre and holding in his left a globe, on which stands a small wreath-bearing Nike (Waddington—Babelon—Reinach *Monn. gr. d'As. Min.* i. 577 pl. 99, 7 (=my fig. 850), Head *Hist. num.*[2] p. 517). A later coin-type gives two agonistic urns, with palms and five balls (? apples, cp. *supra* p. 490 n. o no. (5)) respectively, inscribed ΟΛΥΜΠΙΑ ΠΥΘΙΑ (Waddington—Babelon— Reinach *Monn. gr. d'As. Min.* i. 600 f. pl. 103, 11 Valerianus Senior, 13 Gallienus, 14 Salonina).

A copper of Caracalla shows a youthful figure, in military costume, carrying a sceptre in his left hand and with his right holding a *phiále* above an altar, garlanded and kindled, towards which leaps a boar beneath a fruitful fig (?)-tree with an eagle in its branches (*Brit. Mus. Cat. Coins* Pontus, etc. p. 197 pl. 35, 7, Waddington—Babelon—Reinach *Monn. gr. d'As. Min.* i. 589 pl. 101, 13 (=my fig. 851)). A similar copper of Geta has

Fig. 850.   Fig. 851.   Fig. 852.

rev. ΤΟΝ ΚΤΙCΤΗΝ ΠΡΟΥCΑΕΙC (in exergue) the same figure holding his *phiále* above an altar, garlanded and kindled, at the foot of which are seen the head and forelegs of the sacrificial bull (? boar A.B.C.). Behind is a fruitful fig (?)-tree with an eagle in its branches; to the left, a round temple with an arched entry (*ib.* i. 591 pl. 101, 22 (=my fig. 852)). These coins presumably represent the eponymous hero Prousias (cp. a coin of Commodus *ib.* i. 582 pl. 100, 3 ΠΡΟΥCΑΕΙC ΤΟΝ ΚΤΙCΤΗΝ ΠΡΟΥCΙΑΝ beardless head of hero to right) worshipping Zeus.

[3] Aizanoi (*Tchavdir-Hissar*) (Αἰζανίς only Ptol. 5. 2. 17 *ed. pr.*), the chief town of Aizanitis in Phrygia Epiktetos (Strab. 576), is situated on a high plateau (1085ᵐ above the sea) near the sources of the river Rhyndakos. Herodian. περὶ καθολικῆς προσῳδίας 1 (i. 15, 6 f. Lentz) (cp. περὶ ὀρθογραφίας (ii. 468, 29 Lentz) *ap.* Steph. Byz. *s.v.* Ἀζανοί stated that Aizanoi received its name from Aizen son of Tantalos. Others seem to have held that the town was founded by Azan son of Arkas (Paus. 8. 4. 3). But Hermogenes of Smyrna (?) *frag.* 3 (*Frag. hist. Gr.* iii. 524 Müller) *ap.* Steph. Byz. *s.v.* Ἀζανοί was not content with such commonplace conjectures. He reports the tradition that once in time of dearth the shepherds of the district sacrificed to the gods for fertility, but in vain, till one Euphorbos offered a fox (οὐανοῦν) and a hedgehog (ἔξιν). The gods were satisfied and sent fertility again. Thereupon the people chose Euphorbos as their priest and ruler (ἱερέα καὶ ἄρχοντα), the town being called Ἐξουάνουν after his sacrifice. Cp. the coins of Aizanoi (second half

of *s.* i B.C.) inscribed **EZEANITΩN** (*Brit. Mus. Cat. Coins* Phrygia p. xxiv). Frazer *Pausanias* iv. 192 comments: 'The legend points to the existence of a race of priestly kings or popes, with spiritual and temporal power, such as reigned at Pessinus, Comana, and other cities of Asia Minor (W. M. Ramsay, *Historical Geogr. of Asia Minor*, p. 146 *sq.*).'

The *témenos* of Zeus, which occupies a square terrace ($146\cdot46^m \times 162\cdot96^m$) contrived on a natural hill-top, had a *façade* of twenty-two marble-clad arches with a broad stair-way (30^m across) in their midst. This gave access to a square *stoá* consisting of a double range of Corinthian columns with a handsome *propýlaion* opposite to the stairway. Out-side the *stoá* were gardens, *exédrai*, and statues. Inside the *stoá*, on a stylobate of seven steps, rose the temple, a beautifully finished Ionic structure in blue-grey half-marble, dating apparently from Hadrianic times (A. Körte 'Das Alter des Zeustempels von Aizanoi' in the *Festschrift für Otto Benndorf* Wien 1898 pp. 209—214 with pl. 11 (=my

Fig. 853.

fig. 853)) and in various points inspired by the Athenian Erechtheion. The building was octostyle and pseudo-dipteral with fifteen columns down the long side, two in the *prónaos*, and two in the *opisthódomos*. These last are of interest as having a band of acanthus-leaves beneath their Ionic volutes—a feature which W. J. Anderson—R. P. Spiers *The Architecture of Greece and Rome* London 1902 pp. 98, 154 refer to *s.* i B.C. and claim as the origin of the 'composite' order. The columns are fluted monoliths (height of shaft $8\cdot520^m$: total height $9\cdot504^m$) with a small vase in relief at the top of each flute : sixteen of them are still standing, ten on the northern side and six more at the western end. Oak-leaves and acorns appear among the mouldings of the temple. Round the outside of the *naós*-wall runs a frieze-like band ($0\cdot62^m$ high), with a moulding above and a maeander below, ready to receive inscriptions and already in part inscribed (inside the right *anta* of the *prónaos* and outside the north wall of the *naós*). Under the *naós* is a chamber ($16\cdot157^m \times 9\cdot120^m$) with a semicircular vault, reached by steps from the *opisthódomos* and probably used for the safeguarding of the temple-treasure. It is possible that some dim recollection of this treasure lingered in folk-memory; for the peasants in comparatively modern times, believing that the columns were cast in stone and full of gold, attacked them with pickaxe and hammer, nor did they desist from their futile search till they had filled the temple with faggots and fired the lot! See further C. Texier *Description de l'Asie Mineure* Paris 1839 i. 95—127 pls. 23—34, W. J. Hamilton *Researches in Asia*

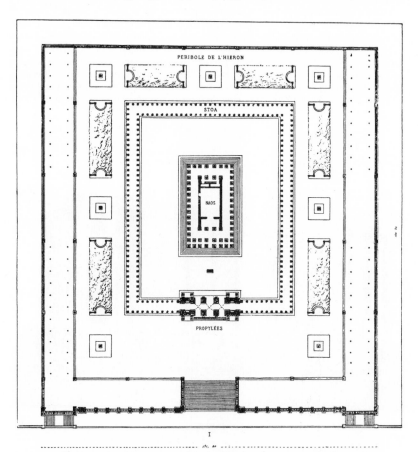

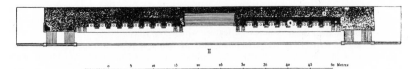

Fig. 854.

Minor, Pontus, and Armenia London 1842 i. 101—104, P. Le Bas *Voyage archéologique en Grèce et en Asie Mineure* Paris 1858 Architecture Asie Mineure i pls. 18—32, Lebas—Reinach *Voyage Arch.* p. 142 ff. Archit. i pls. 18 (=my fig. 854), 19—24, 25 (=my fig. 855), 26—32, F. von Duhn in Durm *Baukunst d. Gr.*[2] Register p. 367 f.

Inscriptions record a priest of Zeus (*Corp. inscr. Gr.* iii Add. no. 3831 *a*¹, 2 ff. Μηνό-
φι|λον Νεικοστράτου | ἱερατεύσαντα τοῦ Δι|ὸς δεκάκις, no. 3831 *a*³, 2 ff. Μενεκλέα | Μενε-
κλέους, υἱὸν τῆς | πόλεως, ἱερατεύσαντα | δὶς τοῦ Διός, no. 3831 *a*⁹, 7 f. ἱερατεύσαντα τοῦ |

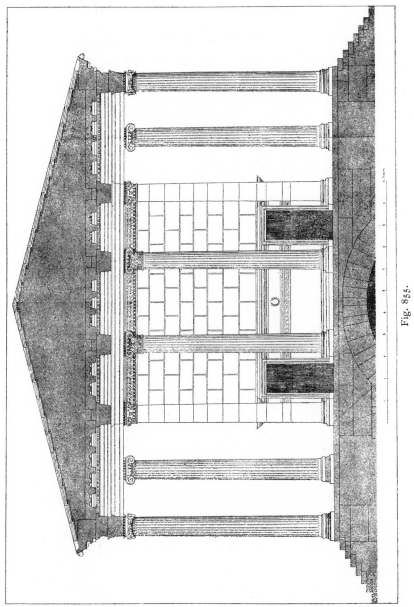

Fig. 855.

[Διός]) and a νεωκόρος of Zeus (*ib.* no. 3831 *a*⁴, 4 ff. Ἰουλι|ανὸν Τρύφω|νος, νεωκό|ρον τοῦ
Διὸς | διὰ βίου, no. 3831 *a*⁷, 2 f. Ὀρδ(εώ)νιον Ἀντιόχου, νε|[ωκ]ό[ρ]ον [τ]ο(ῦ Δ)ιός, cp. no.
3841 *d*, 8 ff. ὁ νεωκόρ[ος] | τ(οῦ Δ)ιός, ἱερὸς | καὶ (ἄσυλ)ος (Α)ἰ(ζα)|[νειτ](ῶν) δῆμος | [ἐκ

Akmoneia[1].
Apameia[2].
Laodikeia ad Lycum[3].

τῶ]ν ἰδίων θεοῦ, no. 3841 g, 1 ff. [τῆς ἱερᾶς καὶ] ἀσύλου καὶ | [νεωκόρο]υ τοῦ Διὸς | [Αἰζανει]τῶν πόλεως | [ἡ φιλοσέβα]στος βουλὴ | [καὶ ὁ νεωκόρ[ος δῆμος | --- | ---). Inside the right *anta* of the *prónaos* is inscribed a letter, in which Avidius Quietus, proconsul of Asia (125—126 A.D.), informs the people of Aizanoi that a long-standing dispute with regard to the temple-estates has been happily settled. He adds three Latin documents dealing with the matter—(*A*) the emperor's rescript, (*B*) his own letter to the imperial procurator, (*C*) the beginning of the procurator's reply (*Corp. inscr. Gr.* iii no. 3835 (cp. *ib.* p. 1064 f.) = *Corp. inscr. Lat.* iii no. 355 = Lebas—Waddington *Asie Mineure* iii nos. 860—863 = Orelli—Henzen *Inscr. Lat. sel.* no. 6955 = Dittenberger *Orient. Gr. inscr. sel.* no. 502, 1 ff. Ἀουίδιος Κουιῆτος Αἰζανειτῶν ἄρχουσι βουλῆι | δήμωι χαίρειν· ἀμφισβήτησις περὶ χώρας ἱερᾶς, ἀνα|τεθείσης πάλαι τῶι Διί, τρειβομένη πολλῶν ἐτῶν, τῆι προνοίᾳ τοῦ | μεγίστου αὐτοκράτορος τέλους ἔτυχε. κ.τ.λ., *A*, 3 f. ager Aezanen|si Iovi dicatus, *B*, 6 f. in ea re|[gione], quae Iovi Aezanitico dicata dicitur).

The neocorate is further evidenced by coins (*Brit. Mus. Cat. Coins* Phrygia p. 28 no. 34 ἐπὶ Ἰου. Οὐλπι. Σευηρείνου ἀρχινεωκόρω (*sic*), no. 35 pl. 5, 6 ἐπὶ Ἰου. Σευηρείνου ἀρχινεωκόρ. with B. V. Head's remarks *ib.* p. xxvi. *Id. ib.*: ‘On a coin of Commodus (*Invent. Wadd.*, Pl. xv. 7) the city claims the title of Neokorate of this divinity (ΝΕΩΚΟΡΩΝ ΤΟΥ ΔΙΟϹ).' Head *Hist. num.*[2] p. 664).

A copper of Phrygia Epiktetos, struck at Aizanoi (F. Imhoof-Blumer in the *Festschrift für Otto Benndorf* Wien 1898 p. 202) probably after 133 B.C., has *obv.* bust of Zeus, laureate, to right, *rev.* ΕΠΙΚΤΗΤΕΩΝ eagle on thunderbolt (*Brit. Mus. Cat. Coins* Phrygia p. 200 pl. 26, 2). *Quasi*-autonomous and imperial coppers of Aizanoi show Zeus standing to left, half-draped in a *himátion*, with an eagle in his right hand, and a long sceptre in his left (*ib.* p. 28 no. 33 f. time of Gallienus; pp. 30 ff., 38 f., 41 f. pl. 5, 8 Augustus, 9 Claudius. Fig. 856 is from a specimen, struck by Caligula, in my collection),

Fig. 856.   Fig. 857.

also the same figure in a tetrastyle temple with arch over central intercolumniation (*ib.* p. 39 no. 113 M. Aurelius). There can be no doubt that we have here the cult-statue of the god. A copper issued by Commodus has *rev.* ΑΙΖΑ ΝΕΙΤ Ω Ν a goat standing to right, with head turned back, suckling the infant Zeus (*ib.* p. 40 pl. 6, 3 (=my fig. 857)). Another copper of Commodus, in the Löbbecke collection, has *rev.* ΑΙΖΑΝΕΙ ΤΩΝ an eagle standing to right on a column, but turning its head backwards, flanked by a flaming altar on the left and a tree on the right (Imhoof-Blumer *Kleinas. Münzen* i. 191 no. 11).

Θεὸς Ὕψιστος (*supra* p. 882 n. o no. (23)).

[1] Infancy of Zeus on a Phrygian mountain (*supra* i. 151 f. figs. 122, 123). Θεὸς Ὕψιστος (*supra* p. 882 n. o no. (23)).

[2] Infancy of Zeus on a Phrygian mountain (*supra* i. 151 f. fig. 124).

[3] Infancy of Zeus on a Phrygian mountain (*supra* i. 151 f. fig. 129). Θεὸς Ὕψιστος (*supra* p. 882 n. o no. (23)).

Nakoleia[1].

Synnada[2].

Upper valley of the Tembrogios or Tembrios[3].

Galatia

Mount Agdos[4].

[1] Θεὸς Ὕψιστος (*supra* p. 882 n. 0 no. (23)).

[2] Infancy of Zeus on a Phrygian mountain (*supra* i. 151 f. fig. 120).

[3] Θεὸς Ὕψιστος = Zeus Βέννιος or Βεννεύς (*supra* p. 883 n. 0 no. (23)).

[4] The myth of Attis has two principal forms—a Lydian version, in which Attis is killed by a boar, and a Phrygian version, in which he mutilates himself under a pine-tree. Since the cult of the Great Mother came to Rome from Pessinous in Phrygia, the Phrygian became the official version and gradually eclipsed its Lydian rival (H. Hepding *Attis seine Mythen und sein Kult* Gieszen 1903 p. 121 f.). The Pessinuntine tradition has been preserved for us by Paus. 7. 17. 10—12 and Arnob. *adv. nat.* 5. 5—7. H. Hepding *op. cit.* p. 37 ff. prints the texts in parallel columns and *ib.* p. 103 ff. discusses their relations and respective sources. Pausanias professes to give the 'local story' (Paus. 7. 17. 10 ἐπιχώριος...λόγος) ; Arnobius, to derive his information from Timotheos the theologian and other equally learned persons, among whom he mentions the priest Valerius (Arnob. *adv. nat.* 5. 5 apud Timotheum, non ignobilem theologorum unum, nec non apud alios aeque doctos super Magna deorum Matre superque sacris eius origo haec sita est, ex reconditis antiquitatum libris et ex intimis eruta, quemadmodum ipse scribit insinuatque, mysteriis, 5. 7 quam Valerius pontifex Iam nomine fuisse conscribit). A. Kalkmann *Pausanias der Perieget* Berlin 1886 p. 247 ff. showed that Pausanias and Arnobius are really dependent on Alexandros Polyhistor, who in turn got his facts from Timotheos, Promathidas, etc. (see Alex. Polyhist. *frag.* 47 (*Frag. hist. Gr.* iii. 233 Müller, cp. *ib.* p. 202) *ap.* Steph. Byz. *s.v.* Γάλλος), and that Arnobius, in addition to Polyhistor, used a Roman source, probably the priest Valerius, thereby contaminating the Pessinuntine tradition of Agdistis with current tales of the Mater Magna and Attis. Hepding summarises the resultant myth, enclosing within square brackets points of divergence between Pausanias and Arnobius :

Zeus let fall seed on the ground [in his sleep (Paus.), when attempting to lie with the Magna Mater who was asleep on the summit of Mt Agdos (Arnob.)]. In due time the earth bore a wild bisexual being named Agdistis. [The gods, fearing him, cut off his male organ of generation (Paus.). He, having irresistible strength and ferocity, did much mischief, till Liber mingled strong wine with the spring at which he used to slake his thirst and thus threw him into a deep sleep. Liber then took an ingenious noose made of bristles and slipped one end round his foot (*plantae.* Hepding translates : 'an einem Baum'), the other round his genitals. The monster, starting up from sleep, drew the noose tight and so castrated himself (Arnob.).] The blood flowed fast, and from the severed member sprang a fruit-tree, [an almond (Paus.), a pomegranate (*malum...cum pomis...punicum*) (Arnob.).] A daughter of the river Sangarios [Nana by name (Arnob.)] picked the fruit and put it in her bosom. [The fruit immediately vanished (Paus.)] and she conceived. [Thereupon her father kept her shut up and tried to starve her ; but the Mother fed her on pomegranates (*pomis*) and other food of the gods (Arnob.).] So she brought forth an infant son, who was exposed [by Sangarios' orders (Arnob.), but tended by a he-goat (Paus.), or found by some one and nurtured on goat's milk (Arnob. : text corrupt). He was called Attis because the Lydian word *attis* means 'scitulus' or because the Phrygian *attagus* means 'hircus' (Arnob.)]. [As the boy grew up, his beauty was more than human, and Agdistis loved him (Paus.). The Mother of the gods loved him for his good looks. So did Agdistis, who ever at his side led him through the woods and presented him with spoils of the chase. Young Attis at first boasted that he had won these himself, but later, under the influence of wine, admitted that they were love-gifts from Agdistis. Hence those that are polluted with wine may not enter his sanctuary (Arnob.).] When Attis was fully grown, he went to Pessinous to wed the king's daughter, [being sent thither by his kinsfolk (Paus.), or summoned by Midas king of Pessinous, who disapproved of the alliance with Agdistis and closed the town to prevent any untoward interruption of the wedding. But the Mother of the gods, aware that the young man's safety depended on his freedom from wedlock, entered the town, uplifting its walls on her head, which has worn a mural crown ever since (Arnob.)]. While the bridal hymn was being sung, Agdistis appeared and drove the whole company mad. [Attis cut off his genitals and so did the father of his bride (Paus.). Gallos mutilated himself and the daughter of his concubine cut off her breasts (Arnob. *adv. nat.* 5. 13 : the text of 5. 7 is confused. A. Kalkmann *op. cit.* p. 248 f. makes it probable that Gallos was king of Pessinous and father of the bride : Midas has been imported from an extraneous source). Attis snatched the pipe borne by Agdistis, and full of frenzy flung himself forth. Falling at length beneath a pine-tree he shore off his genitals and cried : ' Take these, Agdistis,—'twas for their sake thou didst stir up this storm of frenzied mischance.' Attis died from loss of blood. But the Great Mother of the gods collected the severed parts, wrapped them in his garment, and buried them in the ground. Violets sprang from his blood and wreathed the tree. Hence the sacred pines are still covered with garlands. The maiden betrothed to him— Valerius the priest calls her Ia—covered his bosom with soft wool, wept for his hard fate (Arnob.)], as did Agdistis, [and then slew herself. Her blood became purple violets. The Mother of the gods dug beneath Ia (text doubtful), and up came an almond, signifying the bitterness of death. Then she carried the pine, under which Attis had mutilated himself, to her cave, and in company with Agdistis beat her breast about its trunk (texι doubtful) (Arnob.)]. Zeus, when asked by Agdistis to bring Attis to life, refused, but consented that his body should remain incorruptible, [his hair always grow, and his little finger be endowed with perpetual movement. Satisfied with this, Agdistis consecrated Attis' body at Pessinous, and honoured it with yearly rites and a priesthood (Arnob.)].

Throughout this narrative (with which cp. Paus. 1. 4. 5) it is clear that Agdistis is only a Pessinuntine appellation of the Great Mother. So Strab. 469 οἱ δὲ Βερέκυντες, Φρυγῶν τι φῦλον, καὶ ἁπλῶς οἱ Φρύγες καὶ τῶν Τρώων οἱ περὶ τὴν Ἴδην κατοικοῦντες Ῥέαν μὲν καὶ αὐτοὶ τιμῶσι καὶ ὀργιάζουσι ταύτῃ, Μητέρα καλοῦντες θεῶν καὶ Ἄγδιστιν (so I. Casaubon for ἄγεστιν epit. Palat. αἴεστιν codd. plerique) καὶ Φρυγίαν θεὸν μεγάλην, ἀπὸ δὲ τῶν τόπων Ἰδαίαν καὶ Δινδυμήνην καὶ Σιπυλήνην καὶ Πεσσινουντίδα καὶ Κυβέλην, 567 Πεσσινοῦς δ' ἐστὶν ἐμπόριον τῶν ταύτῃ μέγιστον, ἱερὸν ἔχον τῆς Μητρὸς τῶν θεῶν σεβασμοῦ μεγάλου τυγχάνον · καλοῦσι δ' αὐτὴν Ἄγδιστιν (so I. Casaubon for ἀγδίστην codd. *r.o.* ἀγγιδίστην (with ι added over the η) cod. D. ἀγγίδιστιν codd. rell. *Angidistam* Guarino da Verona), Hesych. *s.v.* Ἄγδιστις · ἡ αὐτὴ τῇ Μητρὶ τῶν θεῶν. In Plout. *de fluv.* 13. 3 Αἰγέσθιος ὁ γεννηθεὶς ἐκ τοῦ Διοσφόρου, κόρης Ἴδης ἐρασθείς, συνῆλθεν τῇ προειρημένῃ καὶ ἐγέννησεν ἐξ αὐτῆς τοὺς εἰρημένους Ἰδαίους Δακτύλους. γενομένης δ' αὐτῆς ἄφρονος ἐν τῷ τῆς Ῥέας ἀδύτῳ, Αἰγέσθιος εἰς τιμὴν τῆς προειρημένης τὸ ὄρος Ἴδην μετωνόμασεν R. Unger acutely cj. Ἀγδίστιος (Ἄγδεσις ? A.B.C.) ὁ γεννηθεὶς ἐκ τοῦ Διὸς σπόρου. The same divine name occurs in several inscriptions : (1) *Corp. inscr. Gr.* iii Add. no. 3886, 1 ff.=P. Paris in the *Bull. Corr. Hell.* 1884 viii. 237 f. no. 7, 1 ff. (Eumeneia) ὁ δῆμος ἐτεί[μησεν] | Μόνιμον Ἀρίστων[ος,] | τὸν λαμπαδάρχην, ἱ[ερέα Διὸς] | Σωτῆρος καὶ Ἀπόλλ[ωνος καὶ] | Μηνὸς Ἀσκαηνοῦ [καὶ Μητρὸς] | θεῶν Ἀνγδίστεω[ς καὶ Ἀγαθοῦ] | Δαίμονος καὶ ε(ὐ)σε[βεστάτης Σε]|βαστῆς Εἰρήνης, κ.τ.λ. (2) *Corp. inscr. Gr.* iii no. 3993, 1 ff. (Ikonion) [θ]ε(ο)ὺς σωτῆρας τήν τε Ἀγγ|διστιν καὶ τὴν Μ[ητέ]ρα Βοη|θηνὴν καὶ θεῶν τὴν Μη|τέρα κ.τ.λ. (3) *Ib.* iv no. 6837 (beneath a relief of Kybele, with a pair of lions, seated in an *aedicula* (R. Pococke *A Description of the East, and Some other Countries* London 1745 ii. 2. 212 pl. 98)) Μητρὶ θεῶν Ἀγγιστει Ἀμέριμνος οἰκονόμος τῆς πόλεως | εὐχήν. (4) B. Latyschev *Inscriptiones antiquae Orae Septentrionalis Ponti Euxini Graecae et Latinae* Petropoli 1890 ii. 32 no. 31 (of Roman date ; beneath a relief representing two draped female figures facing, with a girl standing on their right) Πλουσία ὑπὲρ τῶν θυγατέρων κατὰ πρόσταγμα | Ἀγγίσ(τε)ι (the stone has ΑΓΓΙCCCΙ) ἀνέθηκε. On Agdistis see further K. Keil in *Philologus* 1852 vii. 198—201, W. W. Baudissin *Studien zur semitischen Religionsgeschichte* Leipzig 1878 ii. 204 f., 207 f., 216, G. Knaack in Pauly—Wissowa *Real-Enc.* i. 767 f., Gruppe *Gr. Myth. Rel.* pp. 1528 n. 1, 1547.

Another myth connected with Mt Agdos was that of Deukalion (Arnob. *adv. nat.* 5. 5

Ankyra[1].

Lykia

Mount Kragos [2].

in Phrygiae finibus inauditae per omnia vastitatis petra, inquit (*sc.* Timotheus), est quaedam, cui nomen est Agdus, regionis eius ab indigenis sic vocatae. ex ea lapides sumptos, sicut Themis mandaverat praecinens, in orbem mortalibus vacuum Deucalion iactavit et Pyrrha, ex quibus cum ceteris et haec Magna quae dicitur informata est Mater atque animata divinitus). Gruppe *op. cit.* p. 444 n. 4 well cp. Nonn. *Dion.* 13. 522—545.

[1] Coin-type of Zeus seated on a rock (*supra* i. 124).

[2] Mt Kragos is a continuation of Mt Tauros, forming a promontory (*Yedi-Burún*, the 'Seven Capes') on the south-western coast of Lykia. North of it is the range of Anti-kragos. T. A. B. Spratt—E. Forbes *Travels in Lycia, Milyas, and the Cibyratis* London 1847 i. 300 ff. describe their ascent of Kragos (1842): 'In the afternoon we made our way to the opening of a pass leading between the summits of Cragus and Anticragus, now called Mendos and Baba-dagh ;...at daybreak, next morning, (May 27th,) we ascended to a plain which lies between the two chief peaks at a height of four thousand feet... Leaving our attendants and horses...we commenced the ascent of the highest peak of Cragus, which rose precipitously more than two thousand five hundred feet above this alpine plain. The first half of the way was through a thick zone of forest; the remainder was among precipices of bare rock, in the crevices of which lay the accumulated snow of winter... From the sharp and narrow summit of this lofty peak we enjoyed our last look over Lycia ; below us lay the whole expanse of the Xanthian plain, and beyond we could see far into the gorges and yailahs ['summer encampments'] of Massicytus... Such is the steepness of Cragus, that its precipices plunge from the snowy summit to the sea, and from the lofty pinnacle on which we stood we could see the waves breaking white against its base.' Ancient allusions are collected by W. Ruge in Pauly—Wissowa *Real-Enc.* xi. 1567. Strab. 665 is worth quoting : εἶθ' ἑξῆς ὁ 'Αντίκραγος...καὶ μετὰ τοῦτον ὁ Κράγος, ἔχων ἄκρας ὀκτὼ (κράγας ὀκτὼ codd. ἄκρας ὀκτὼ Eustath. *in* Dionys. *per.* 847. ἄκρας δύο Eustath. *in Il.* p. 635, 19. We should probably translate 'eight summits,' not ' eight headlands') καὶ πόλιν ὁμώνυμον. περὶ ταῦτα μυθεύεται τὰ ὄρη τὰ περὶ τῆς Χιμαίρας · ἔστι δ' οὐκ ἄπωθεν καὶ ἡ Χίμαιρα φάραγξ τις, ἀπὸ τοῦ αἰγιαλοῦ ἀνατείνουσα (the glen of *Avlan* : see O. Benndorf— G. Niemann *Reisen in Lykien und Karien* Wien 1884 p. 82 f.).

Kragos had certain caverns known as the θεῶν ἀγρίων ἄντρα. These 'wild gods' appear to have been the eponym Kragos and his family (Steph. Byz. *s.v.* Κράγος, ὄρος Λυκίας. 'Αλέξανδρος δευτέρῳ Λυκιακῶν (Alex. Polyhist. *frag.* 75 (*Frag. hist. Gr.* iii. 235 Müller)). ἀπὸ Κράγου τοῦ Τρεμίλου υἱοῦ, μητρὸς δὲ Πραξιδίκης νύμφης. ἐνταῦθα δ' εἶναι καὶ τὰ ἐπονομαζόμενα θεῶν ἀγρίων ἄντρα. ἀπαθανατισθῆναι γάρ φασι τοὺς περὶ τὸν Κράγον, Eustath. *in* Dionys. *per.* 847 τὸν δὲ ἐνταῦθα Ταῦρον τὸ ὄρος καὶ Κράγον φησὶ φημίζεσθαι, ἀπὸ Κράγου τινὸς ἐπιφανοῦς ἀνδρός, ὃς αὐτόθι θανὼν τιμᾶται. ἐν τούτῳ δέ φασιν οἱ παλαιοὶ τῷ Κράγῳ θεῶν ἀγρίων ἄντρα εἶναι). Kragos and his kin are mentioned also in Panyasis *frag.* 18 Kinkel *ap.* Steph. Byz. *s.v.* Τρεμίλη, in Timagenes *frag.* 2 (*Frag. hist. Gr.* iii. 322 Müller) *ap.* Steph. Byz. *s.v.* Μιλύαι, and in an important inscription from Sidyma (O. Benndorf— G. Niemann *op. cit.* p. 75 ff. no. 53 A, 15 ff. τὴν πρὸς ὑμᾶ[ς καὶ Τλωεῖς καὶ] | Πιναρεῖς γενεαλ[ογίαν Τρεμί][λ]ου καὶ Πραξιδίκης, ἐξ ὧν Τλῶ[ος καὶ] | [Κ]ράγος καὶ Πίναλος ἀνῆκον, δι[αδή][λ]ης γενεαλο[γί]ας καὶ ὑπ' ἐμοῦ πολ|λάκις δεδηλωμένης κατὰ τὰς Πο[λ]υχάρμου καὶ ἑτέρων ἱστορίας, *ib.* C, 9 ff. ἐν δὲ Σιδύμοις, κτίσματι Σιδύμου | υἱοῦ Τλώονι καὶ Χελειδόνος τῆς | Κράγου, 'Απόλλωνα τόπω πρὸς | θαλάσση Λοπτοῖς σπηλαίω | ἀποκρύφω δυσεισόδω ἐκ κορυ|φῆς δὲ φωτούλκον ἄνοιγμα | μεικρὸν ἔχοντι. μέσον εἰς ὃ κα|θοπτεῦσαι θελήσασά τις ἄφνως | ἀψοφητὶ τὸν θεὸν κατη|νέχθη, καὶ λίθος κεῖται πτῶμα | φόβου δεῖγμα κατασκόπων · διὸ καὶ κροτ[οῦ]ν[τε]ς ἐπ' ἄσματι · 'χαῖρε, "Απολλον, ὁ ἐγ Λοπτῶν' | εἰσερχόμενοι φωνοῦμεν τήνδε. The cave-cult of Apollon at Lopta described in this curious record may give us some notion of the θεῶν ἀγρίων ἄντρα : indeed, Apollon himself is on occasion ἄγριος (Orph. *h. Ap.* 34. 5). The Titans too bore the same title (Hesych. ἄγριοι θεοί· οἱ Τιτᾶνες), perhaps as being chieftains or kings (*supra* i. 655 f.). Lobeck *Aglaophamus* ii. 1186 n.[i]

Mount Olympos (?)[1].

Pisidia

Prostanna (?)[2].

justly cp. Plout. *de def. or.* 21 (quoted by Theodoret. *Gr. aff. cur.* p. 129 Gaisford) ἐπεὶ καὶ Σολύμους πυνθάνομαι τοὺς Λυκίων προσοίκους ἐν τοῖς μάλιστα τιμᾶν τὸν Κρόνον· ἐπεὶ δὲ ἀποκτείνας τοὺς ἄρχοντας αὐτῶν, Ἄρσαλον καὶ Δρύον (Ἄρυον Theodoret.) καὶ Τόσοβιν, ἔφυγε καὶ μετεχώρησεν ὁποιδήποτε (τοῦτο γὰρ οὐκ ἔχουσιν εἰπεῖν), ἐκεῖνον μὲν ἀμεληθῆναι, τοὺς δὲ περὶ τὸν Ἄρσαλον σκληροὺς (σκιρροὺς Theodoret.) θεοὺς προσαγορεύεσθαι, καὶ τὰς κατάρας ἐπὶ τούτων ποιεῖσθαι δημοσίᾳ καὶ ἰδίᾳ Λυκίους.

It would seem, then, that Kragos and his relatives were, not only heroified, but actually deified. More than that. Kragos was eventually identified with Zeus himself. For Lyk. *Al.* 541 f. ἔν τε δαιτὶ καὶ θαλυσίοις | λοιβαῖσι μειλίσσωσιν ἀστεργῆ Κράγον is thus expounded by Tzetz. *ad loc.*: ἀστεργῆ δὲ Κράγον τὸν Δία λέγει ἐπεὶ μὴ ἔστερξε τὴν θυσίαν αὐτῶν. λέγονται δὲ θύοντες τοῖς ἄλλοις θεοῖς ἐπιλαθέσθαι τοῦ Διός, ὅθεν φιλονεικίαν αὐτοῖς ἐνέβαλε. Κράγος δὲ ὁ Ζεὺς ἐν Λυκίᾳ τιμᾶται.

[1] *Supra* i. 100 n. 11. Methodios, bishop of the Lycian town Olympos at the beginning of s. iv. A.D., claims to have seen on the summit of this mountain *agnus castus* growing, quite unharmed, round a fire that sprang from the earth (Method. *ap.* Phot. *bibl.* p. 298 b 23 ff. Bekker ἐθεασάμην ἐν Ὀλύμπῳ ἐγώ (ὄρος δέ ἐστιν ὁ Ὄλυμπος τῆς Λυκίας) πῦρ αὐτομάτως κατὰ τὴν ἀκρώρειαν τοῦ ὄρους κάτωθεν ἐκ τῆς γῆς ἀναδιδόμενον, περὶ ὃ πῦρ ἄγνος φυτόν ἐστιν, οὕτω μὲν εὐθαλὲς καὶ χλοερόν, οὕτω δὲ σύσκιον, ὡς ὑπὸ πηγῆς μᾶλλον αὐτὸ δοκεῖν βεβλαστηκέναι. κ.τ.λ.) The good bishop describes the phaenomenon in terms reminiscent of Moses and the burning bush ; and it is noteworthy that Mt Olympos, otherwise called Phoinikous (Strab. 666), iş nowadays named *Musa Dagh*, the 'mountain of Moses.' This mountain rises to a height of *c.* 1000ᵐ due south of the town Olympos on the eastern coast of Lykia. But the perpetual fire is commonly associated with Mt Chimaira (*Yanàr-tash*), a height of some 250ᵐ due north of the same town. Here in fact it is still to be seen—a strong jet of flaming gas that leaps up like a fountain from crevices in the rock. The immediate neighbourhood of the vent is bare of vegetation, but all around, a few paces off, is greenery in abundance. For classical references see W. Ruge in Pauly—Wissowa *Real-Enc.* iii. 2281 ; and for modern description and discussion, E. Petersen—F. von Luschan *Reisen in Lykien Milyas und Kibyratis* Wien 1889 pp. 138—142 ('Die Chimaira') with fig. 65 and pl. 17. In antiquity several such fiery jets were known and the site was called Hephaistion (Sen. *epist.* 79. 3, Plin. *nat. hist.* 5. 100), Hephaistia (Solin. 39. 1), or the mountains of Hephaistos (Plin. *nat. hist.* 2. 236). Skyl. *per.* 100 speaks of a sanctuary of Hephaistos above the harbour Siderous : ὑπὲρ τούτου ἐστὶν ἱερὸν Ἡφαίστου ἐν τῷ ὄρει καὶ πῦρ πολὺ αὐτόματον ἐκ τῆς γῆς καίεται καὶ οὐδέποτε σβέννυται. Hence Hephaistos appears, forging the shield of Achilles, on a copper of Olympos struck by Gordianus iii Pius (Imhoof-Blumer *Monn. gr.* p. 326 f. no. 10 pl. F, 14).

It was, however, only natural that in this town, which lay between Mt Olympos and Hephaistion, there should have been a joint recognition of Zeus and Hephaistos. R. Heberdey—E. Kalinka *Bericht über zwei Reisen in S.W. Kleinasien* Wien 1896 p. 34 no. 42 publish an inscription, in which mention is made of a fine payable θεοῖς Ὀλυμπίοις Διὶ καὶ Ἡφαίστῳ. G. F. Hill in the *Brit. Mus. Cat. Coins* Lycia, etc. p. lxvi compares with it a bronze coin of Olympos at Paris with *obv.* head of Athena to right, *rev.* the ethnic and a thunderbolt.

[2] Prostanna (*Egherdir*) was situated on the shore of Limnai, at the foot of Mt Viarus (Sir W. M. Ramsay *The Historical Geography of Asia Minor* London 1890 p. 407). Imperial coppers of the town have *obv.* Mt Viarus, *rev.* ΠΡ ΟϹ a tree (*Brit. Mus. Cat. Coins* Lycia, etc. pp. cvi, 238 pl. 37, 9, Imhoof-Blumer *Gr. Münzen* p. 175 no. 502 pl. 10, 27), and *rev.* ΠΡΟϹΤΑΝ ΝΕΩΝ Mt Viarus with three trees growing on it and ΟΥΙΑΡΟϹ below (*Brit. Mus. Cat. Coins* Lycia, etc. p. 239 pl. 37, 13 Claudius ii) or Mt Viarus with a pine-tree on its summit and ΒΙΑΡΟϹ below (Imhoof-Blumer *Kleinas.*

Mount Solymos[1].

Münzen ii. 391 no. 10 pl. 14, 5, A. Markl in the *Num. Zeitschr.* 1900 xxxii. 157 no. 4 pl. 7, 4, Head *Hist. num.*[2] p. 709). Since another coin-type of Prostanna shows Zeus seated with Demeter (?) behind him (G. F. Hill in the *Brit. Mus. Cat. Coins* Lycia, etc. p. cvi n. †, Head *Hist. num.*[2] p. 709), it is possible that the cult of the god was connected with the mountain which dominates the town (for views see A. de Laborde, Becker, Hall et L. de Laborde *Voyage de l'Asie Mineure* Paris 1838 p. 111).

[1] Termessos (Termessus Maior) was built, a good 1000ᵐ above sea-level, on Mt Solymos (Strab. 630) or Solyma (*id.* 666), the modern *Güldere Dagh* or *Güllik Dagh.* It was an ideally placed stronghold of the Solymoi, whose eponym Solymos figures on imperial coppers of the town (*Brit. Mus. Cat. Coins* Lycia, etc. pp. xc, 271 no. 27 pl. 41, 12 *rev.* ϹΟΛΥ ΜΟϹ Solymos standing to left, with cuirass, spear, and short sword, 272 no. 36 pl. 41, 14 ϹΟΛΥ ΜΟϹ Solymos enthroned to left, with crested helmet and right hand raised to face, cp. Imhoof-Blumer *Kleinas. Münzen* ii. 410 no. 6 pl. 15, 15 and 411 no. 10 pl. 15, 17, Head *Hist. num.*[2] p. 712). As a warlike hero he was affiliated sometimes to Zeus (Antimachos *frag.* 16 Bergk⁴ *ap.* schol. P.T. *Od.* 5. 283 ὅθεν καὶ οἱ Σόλυμοι ὠνομάσθησαν (δὲ add. T., omissis ὅθεν καὶ οἱ Σόλυμοι) ἀπὸ Σολύμου τοῦ Διὸς καὶ Καλχηδονίας, ὡς 'Αντίμαχος δηλοῖ, Rufin. *recognit.* 10. 21 (Iupiter vitiat) Chalceam nympham, ex qua nascitur Olympus (where O. Höfer cj. *Chalcedonian* and *Solymus*: see his remarks in Roscher *Lex. Myth.* iv. 1154), Steph. Byz. *s.v.* Πισιδία· οἱ Πισῖδαι πρότερον Σόλυμοι, ἀπὸ Σολύμου τοῦ Διὸς καὶ Χαλδήνης), sometimes to Ares (*et. mag.* p. 721, 43 ff. Σόλυμοι (so T. Gaisford for Σόλυμος)· ἔθνος περὶ Κιλικίαν· ἀπὸ Σολύμου τοῦ Καλδήνης τῆς Πισίου καὶ "Αρεως· οἱ νῦν "Ισαυροι).

The principal deity of the town in classical times was Zeus Σολυμεύς. Mionnet *Descr. de méd. ant.* Suppl. vii. 138 no. 228 gives (after Sestini) a coin reading ΖΕΥϹ ϹΟΛΥΜΕΥϹ, and J. Friedlaender in the *Zeitschr. f. Num.* 1885 xii. 6 figures another, at Berlin, with *obv.* ΔΙ[ΟϹ] ϹΟΛΥΜΕΩ[Ϲ] bust of Zeus Σολυμεύς (but see G. F. Hill in the *Brit. Mus. Cat. Coins* Lycia, etc. p. xc n. ‖). The head of Zeus appears as the normal Termessian coin-type *c.* 71—39 B.C., in the time of the Antonines, and from Gordian to Gallienus (*Brit. Mus. Cat. Coins* Lycia, etc. p. 268 ff. pl. 41, 8—11, pl. 42, 1 f., Head *Hist. num.*[2] p. 712). E. Petersen in K. Lanckoroński *Städte Pamphyliens und Pisidiens* Wien 1892 ii. 47 ff. describes the remains of what was probably the temple of Zeus Σολυμεύς. The site is a raised terrace (1054ᵐ) adjoining the southernmost part of the gymnasium and close to a group of other temples (N 3 on the large plan opposite p. 21). Here were found Doric column-drums, Attic bases with portions of shafts and plinths, architrave-blocks, coffering, the right-hand end-block of a pediment, statue-pedestals, and two reliefs from a frieze representing a Gigantomachy (Zeus and Apollon *v.* Giants with serpentine legs). These last were published by G. Hirschfeld in the *Arch. Zeit.* 1881 xxxix. 157—160 figs. *A, B.* Further, a cylindrical base (1·18ᵐ high), which once supported a bronze statue (of Zeus?), is adorned with a relief of a priest presiding at the sacrifice of a humped bull (E. Petersen *op. cit.* ii. 32, 48 f. figs. 7 and 8) and bears the inscription 'Οτάνις ΙΟΓΑΚ | ἱερ(ε)[ύ]s· | Διὶ Σολυμεῖ· | Διονύσιος 'Ηρακλε[ίδου] | 'Αλεξα[ν]-δρε[ύ]s [ἐποίει (?)] (K. Lanckoroński *op. cit.* ii. 206 no. 78). Another base from the same site was set up when a certain Strabon was priest of Zeus Σολυμεύς (*id. ib.* ii. 206 no. 80, 15 ff. ἀνεστάθη | ἐπὶ ἱερέως | Σολυμέως Δι[ὸς] | Στράβωνος [β']). Another carried the statue of a distinguished priest (*id. ib.* ii. 206 no. 79, 1 ff. ἀρχιερέα καὶ ἱερέα Διὸς Σολ[υμέως] | γενόμενον Λαέρτην Να[νναμόου] | Λαέρτου κ.τ.λ., cp. 207 no. 85, 2 ff. [ἀρ]χιερέα αὐτοκράτ-ορος Καίσαρος Σεβαστοῦ | [ἱερ]έα Διὸς Σολυμέως διὰ βίου Λαέ[ρ]την | [Νανναμό]ου φιλόπατριν καὶ πατέρα πόλεως). Other life-priests of Zeus Σολυμεύς are recorded (*id. ib.* ii. 200 no. 39, 4 f. Τι. ΚΛ. Τει|μόδωρον, 200 no. 41, 4 Τι. ΚΛ. Τειμόδωρον, 201 no. 48, 6 ff. Μᾶρ. Αὐρ. Μειδια|νὸν Πλατωνιανὸν | Οὐᾶρον, 208 no. 93, 4 ff. Μᾶρ. | Αὐρ. Μειδιανὸν | Οὐᾶρον).

The same deity was believed to have under his special protection the tombs of the dead, for any violation of their sanctity was punished with a fine usually payable to him. Numerous inscriptions of the sort are given by G. Cousin in the *Bull. Corr. Hell.* 1899

Pontos

Beuyuk Evlia[1].

xxiii. 165—192, 280—286 (*e.g.* p. 169 no. 7, 9 f. ὁ τούτων τι πειράσας ὑπεύθυνος ἔσ|ται Διὶ Σολυμεῖ ✳ ,a, p. 171 no. 13, 7 f. ὁ πειράσας ἐκτεί|σει Διὶ Σολυμεῖ ✳ ,a, p. 173 no. 18, 2 δώσει ὁ πειράσας προστείμου Διὶ Σολυμεῖ ✳ ,β, p. 182 f. no. 41, 5 ff. ὁ τολμήσας | ἢ παραενχειρή|σας ἀποτείσει | Διὶ Σολυμεῖ ἱε|ρὰς καὶ ἀπαραι|τήτους δρα|χμὰς δισχειλίας πεντακοσίας, p. 184 f. no. 44, 5 f. ὁ πειράσας ἐνσχεθήσεται ἐνκλήματι | τυμβωρυχίας καὶ ἐκτείσει Διὶ Σολυμεῖ ✳ ,αφ', p. 188 no. 52, 3 f. ὁ πειράσας ἐκτείσει Διὶ Σολυμεῖ ✳ ,η καὶ τῷ ἱερωτά|τῳ ταμιείῳ ✳ ,η, p. 189 f. no. 54, 7 ff. ὁ τού|των τι πειράσας ἔνοχος ἔσ|ται ἐνκλήματι τυμβωρυχί|ας καὶ ἀραῖς ταῖς εἰς τοὺς κα|τοιχομένους καὶ προσαπο|τείσει Διὶ Σολυμεῖ ✳ ,a. See also pp. 167 f. no. 4, 7 ff., 170 no. 10, 7 f., 171 f. no. 14, 4 ff., 172 no. 15, 8 f., 173 f. no. 20, 10 f., 175 no. 24, 2 ff., 175 f. no. 25, 10 f., 176 no. 26, 7 f., 179 f. no. 34, 7 f., 183 f. no. 43, 9 f., 185 no. 45, 3 ff., 186 f. no. 48, 9 ff., 187 no. 49, 5 ff., 187 no. 50, 3 ff., 187 f. no. 51, 9 f., 188 f. no. 53, 11 f., 191 no. 57, 5 ff., 280 f. no. 62, 6 ff., 283 no. 64, 7 ff., 284 no. 66, 10 f., 285 no. 67, 8 ff., 285 f. no. 68, 9 f.), and a few by K. Lanckoroński *op. cit.* ii. 217 no. 154*, 2 f., 218 no. 167, 6 ff., 218 no. 171ᵃ (= *Corp. inscr. Gr.* iii no. 4366 *k*), 9 f., 219 no. 173, 16 ff., 219 no. 174, 7 f.

G. F. Hill in the *Journ. Hell. Stud.* 1895 xv. 127 f. publishes, among inscriptions copied by E. T. Daniell and Sir C. Fellows, no. 24, 3 ff. ἐκτείσι | τῷ ἱερωτάτω ταμίω | ✳ ,μν κὲ τῷ Διὶ | Σολύμω ✳ ,μν', adding: 'The form Σόλυμος for Σολυμεύς is unusual; it occurs again on an inscription on p. 493 [of a MS. volume transcribed by S. Birch].' The form suggests that the eponymous hero Solymos, by a process already exemplified in the case of Kragos (*supra* p. 971 n. 2), had been raised to the rank of Zeus. Other inscriptions from Termessos attest a cult of Zeus and Dione (*id. ib.* ii. 206 no. 77 on a lintel from the southernmost part of the gymnasium [τοῦ πρώτου ἱερασ]αμένου Διὸς καὶ Διώνης Ἀλφείδου Μολέους | [τὸν ναὸν καὶ τ]ὰ ἐν αὐτῷ ἱερὰ καὶ ἀγάλματα ὁ δῆμος ἐκ τῆς | ὑποστάσεως (*i.e.* ἐκ τῆς ὑποστάσεως τοῦ πρώτου ἱερασαμένου κ.τ.λ.), 219 no. 175ᵃ (= *Corp. inscr. Gr.* iii no. 4366 *m*) completed by G. Cousin in the *Bull. Corr. Hell.* 1899 xxiii. 192 no. 60 on a sarcophagus at the first Gate ἱερεὺς Διὸς καὶ Διώνης | Γάιος Διοτείμου Ἐρ. | Τρ. Γαίου Γεινίου Χυ. τὴν | σωματοθήκην ἑαυτῷ καὶ | Ἀρτέμει Ἐρ. Τρ. Γαίου Γεινί|ου Π. αὐτοῦ· κ.τ.λ.) and a cult of Zeus Ἐλευθέριος (K. Lanckoroński *op. cit.* ii. 203 no. 58, 26 ἱερεὺς Διὸς Ἐλευθερίου Διόδοτος Ἑρμαίου Ἀρ|τείμου ✳ φ', cp. *Brit. Mus. Cat. Coins* Lycia, etc. pp. lxxxix n. ¶, xcii with n.*, 275 no. 55 pl. 42, 2 *obv.* ΤΕΡ ΜΗCCΩΝ head of Zeus, laureate, to right, with Θ below; *rev.* ΕΛΕΥ ΘΕΡΑΤΕ ΡΜΗCCΕ ΗΤΟΚΑΠ ΟΥCΕΧΟ VΓΑ in wreath = ἐλευθέρα Τερμησσὲ | ἡ το(ὺς) κάπους ἔχουσα, which I take to be a tag from some popular chorus (hence the *quasi*-Doric κάπους) performed at a festival of Zeus Ἐλευθέριος).

[1] In 82 B.C. Mithridates vi Eupator, having cleared Kappadokia of the Roman forces, offered a solemn sacrifice to Zeus Στράτιος. Appian. *Mithr.* 66, perhaps following Nikolaos of Damaskos (T. Reinach *Mithridate Eupator roi de Pont* Paris 1890 p. 445 f.), describes the scene in detail (trans. H. White): 'The news of this brilliant and decisive victory spread quickly and caused many to change sides to Mithridates. The latter drove all of Murena's garrisons out of Cappadocia and offered sacrifice to Zeus Stratius on a lofty pile of wood on a high hill, according to the fashion of his country, which is as follows. First, the kings themselves carry wood to the heap. Then they make a smaller pile encircling the other one, on which they pour milk, honey, wine, oil, and various kinds of incense. A banquet is spread on the ground for those present (as at the sacrifices of the Persian kings at Pasargádæ) and then they set fire to the wood. The height of the flame is such that it can be seen at a distance of 1000 stades from the sea, and they say that nobody can come near it for several days on account of the heat. Mithridates performed a sacrifice of this kind according to the custom of his country.' In 74 B.C., when about to enter Paphlagonia, Mithridates repeated the offering. Appian. *Mithr.* 70 (trans. White) says: 'At the beginning of spring Mithridates made trial of his navy and sacrificed to Zeus

Stratius in the customary manner, and also to Poseidon by plunging a chariot with white horses into the sea.'

Imperial coppers of Amaseia, the residence of the Pontic kings (Strab. 561), have been rightly interpreted as referring to this cult (C. Cavedoni in the *Bull. d. Inst.* 1840 p. 70 f.). They exhibit a large altar, sometimes of two stages and flaming. Beside it are two trees with twisted trunks. Above it on some specimens there hovers an eagle, or the sun-god in his *quadriga*, or both. Occasionally a bull is shown lying dead on the upper stage (*supra* i. 602 n. 2. I illustrate four examples. Fig. 858 = Waddington—Babelon—Reinach *Monn. gr. d'As. Min.* i. 38 no. 78 pl. 5, 26 (Paris) Caracalla 206 A.D. ('une victime qui paraît être un chien'!). Fig. 859 = *eid. ib.* i. 38 no. 79 pl. 6, 1 (Paris) Caracalla 206 A.D. Fig. 860 = *eid. ib.* i. 40 no. 96 pl. 6, 7 (A. Löbbecke) Geta 206 A.D. ('un taureau mort'). Fig. 861 is from a specimen, in my collection, struck by Severus Alexander in 232 A.D.).

F. Cumont—E. Cumont *Voyage d'exploration archéologique dans le Pont et la Petite Arménie* (*Studia Pontica* ii) Bruxelles 1906 pp. 136—184 devote a chapter to Amaseia, including a valuable discussion (pp. 145 f., 172 ff.) of Zeus Στράτιος and his cult. Their

Fig. 858.

Fig. 859.

Fig. 860.

Fig. 861.

discoveries may be resumed as follows. Some four miles due east of Amaseia rises a rounded hill (1350ᵐ) known as *Beuyuk Evlia*, 'The Great Saint' (map xiii), and reputed to be the burial-place of a santon or Turkish saint. Every year in May the peasants repair to this otherwise deserted height, slaughter fowls and sheep, and feast merrily in honour of the *Profît Iliyâ*. A clump of large pines crowns the hill-top, venerable trees which are held in such respect that no one will touch them with an axe. (By way of an ancient parallel F. Cumont cites M. Tsakuroglou in the Μουσεῖον καὶ Βιβλιοθήκη τῆς Εὐαγγελικῆς Σχολῆς ἐν Σμύρνῃ 1878—1880 p. 164 no. τλβ′ = S. Reinach *Chroniques d'Orient* Paris 1891 p. 157 an inscription from *Divlit* near Koloë (*Koula*) in Lydia ἔτους τκ′, μη[νὸς] Περειτίουι β′, Αὔρ. | Στρατόνεικος β′, ἐπειδὴ κατὰ | ἄγνοιαν ἐκ τοῦ ἄλσου[ς] ἔκοψα | δένδρα θεῶν Διὸς Σαβαζίου καὶ | Ἀρτέμιδος Ἀναείτις κολασ|θείς, εὐξάμενος εὐχαριστή|ριον ἀνέστησα with Tsakuroglou's note: 'Au-dessus est représenté un homme; à côté de lui, sur la droite, deux arbres, et un seul à gauche. Il est remarquable que la défense de couper du bois dans le bois sacré de Sabazios et d'Artémis Anaïtis subsiste encore aujourd'hui, car les habitants turcs de Santal près de Divlit croient que celui qui coupe du bois est puni par quelque maladie.'

[See further Frazer *Golden Bough*[3] : The Magic Art ii. 40—45].) The summit of the hill forms a flattish space *c*. 250ᵐ across and was enclosed by a *períbolos*-wall, which can still be traced, especially to the south-west. In the middle of the open space a square mound (*c*. 40ᵐ each side) evidently covers some construction, for bits of moulding and the *débris* of cut marble are scattered over the ground. Here in all probability stood a monumental altar. A marble base found on the spot records the name of Cn. Claudius Philon as priest for life (J. G. C. Anderson—F. Cumont—H. Grégoire *Recueil des inscriptions grecques et latines du Pont et de l'Arménie* (*Studia Pontica* iii) Bruxelles 1910 i no. 142 τὸ ἀ[νάθημα] (or ἄ[γαλμα]) | ἐκ τῶν τ[οῦ] | θεοῦ Γναί|ος Κλ(αύδιος) Φίλων | ἱερεὺς διὰ βίου) and two inscriptions from the neighbouring village of *Ebimi* preserve dedications to Zeus Στράτιος (*eid. ib.* i no. 140 on a small limestone altar Διὶ | Στρα|τίῳ | Βασι|λεὺς (a frequent name in Pontos) | εὐχῇ, no. 141 on two portions of a limestone balustrade Διὶ Στρατίῳ [ὁ δῆμος ἐν ἐκκλησίᾳ] κυρίᾳ ἐπὶ τῆς συν◊|αρχίας Πομ[πωνίου........τοῦ?] Κανδίδου, νεωκο|ροῦντος γ´ [..............ο]υ Ἀγριππιανοῦ, ἐκ | τῶν συν(λ)ε[λεγμένων χρημάτω]ν ◊ ἔτους Ϙ ρα´ ◊ (=98/99 A.D.). In line 4 συνα[θροισθέντων κ.τ.λ.] is possible). From these inscriptions we gather that in the year 99 A.D. the cult was administered by συνάρχοντες and νεωκόροι. To the west of the precinct is rising ground formerly covered with buildings. The festivities there celebrated seem to have included dramatic shows—witness the epitaph of the strolling player Gemellos, found at *Ebimi* (F. Cumont in the *Festschrift zu Otto Hirschfelds sechzigstem Geburtstage* Berlin 1903 p. 277 ff. = J. G. C. Anderson—F. Cumont—H. Grégoire *op. cit.* i no. 143 κεῖμε Γεμέλλος ἐγὼ | ὁ πολλοῖς θεάτροις | πολλὰ λαλήσας | καὶ πολλὰς ὁδοὺς | αὐτὸς ὁδεύσας, | καὶ οὐκέτι μου στόμα | φωνὰ[ς] ἀπολύει, | οὐδὲ χειρῶν κρότος | ἔρχετε, ἀλλ᾽ ἀποδοὺς | τὸ δάνιον ('my debt to nature') πεπόρευμε. | ταῦτα πάντα κόνις. The man is as full of quotations as Dikaiopolis).

Other traces of the same cult came to light at *Ghel-Ghiraz*, some sixteen miles west of Amaseia, on the edge of the plain Chiliokomon (*Soulou-Ova*). Here was found a marble altar of *s*. i (?) A.D. dedicated to Zeus Στράτιος (*eid. ib.* i no. 152 Διὶ Στρατίῳ εὐ[χ]ῆς | καὶ εὐσεβίας [χ]ά|ριν Κῦρος καὶ | Φιλέταιρος οἱ | Κλάρου. The letters χ, χ, being crosses, have been effaced by some zealous Mohammedan) and sundry remnants of his temple (Ionic and Corinthian capitals, a column-shaft in red marble, fragments of cornice, blocks of marble) scattered through the village. The temple itself probably stood on a small polygonal plateau cut out on a spur of the mountainous heights above *Ghel-Ghiraz* (map xii).

Lastly, an inscription of Roman date from Athens mentions an offering to Zeus Στράτιος made by four citizens of Amaseia (*Corp. inscr. Att.* iii. i no. 201 ἀγαθῆ τύχῃ · | Διὶ Στρατί[ῳ] | Διότιμος, Ὑψικράτη[ς], | Δρόσερος, Σεύηρος | οἱ Ἀμασεῖς).

F. Cumont justly regards the sacred pines still growing on *Beuyuk Evlia* as comparable with the trees beside the altar on the coins of Amaseia (*supra* figs. 858—861), with the two oaks planted by Herakles at Herakleia Pontike by the altars of Zeus Στράτιος (Plin. *nat. hist.* 16. 239 in Ponto citra Heracleam arae sunt Iovis Στρατίου cognomine, ibi quercus duae ab Hercule satae), and with the sacred plane-trees of Zeus Στράτιος at Labranda (*supra* p. 590). But with equal justice Cumont refuses to see in *Beuyuk Evlia* the scene of Mithridates' pyre, which was visible far out at sea and must therefore have been raised on some such peak as *Ak-Dagh*, the highest summit of the country. As to the nature of Zeus Στράτιος, after renewed consideration of the available *data* (cp. F. Cumont ' Le Zeus Stratios de Mithridate' in the *Revue de l'histoire des religions* 1901 xliii. 47—57), he arrives at the following conclusion: 'Peut-être était-il à l'origine la divinité locale de quelque tribu indigène de la vallée de l'Iris, qui s'assemblait pour l'adorer sur le sommet d'une montagne voisine. A leur arrivée dans le pays, les colons grecs auraient alors, suivant une coutume constante, transformé cette divinité barbare en un Zeus guerrier. Puis, quand une maison d'origine iranienne fonda un royaume dans cette région, elle aurait prétendu reconnaître dans ce Zeus son Ahoura-Mazda, et lui aurait offert des sacrifices nouveaux, imités de ceux qu'accomplissaient les monarques perses. La nature du dieu serait donc composite; elle serait formée d'une réunion des trois éléments,

Kappadokia

Mount Argaios (?)[1].

pontique, grec et iranien, dont la combinaison caractérise la religion comme la civilisation de ces contrées.'

To this I would add but two remarks. Doubtless, as Cumont says, the pyre of Mithridates on the Pontic mountain bears some resemblance to the perpetual fire on the mountain of Zoroastres (Dion Chrys. *or.* 36 p. 92 f. Reiske cited *supra* i. 783 f., ii. 33), and the offering of milk, honey, wine, and oil by Mithridates recalls the offering of oil, milk, and honey by the Magoi (Strab. 733). But these practices can be paralleled from Greek as well as from Persian usage. The big blaze reminds us of the bonfire on the top of Mt Kithairon kindled once in sixty years at the Great Daidala, when the oak-brides of Zeus were burnt (Paus. 9. 3. 1 ff. cited *supra* p. 898 n. 6). And the offering of milk, honey, wine, and oil is suggestive of the usual Hellenic gifts to the dead (see *e.g.* P. Stengel *Die griechischen Kultusaltertümer*[3] München 1920 p. 149 'Man spendet Wein, Wasser, Milch, Honig und Öl, doch selten alles zugleich.' Is the ritual of Aisch. *Pers.* 610 ff. Persian or Greek?). There may after all have been some historica foundation for the folk-belief that a saint lies buried on *Beuyuk Evlia*.

Mt Argaios (*Erjäus*), the culminating point of Antitauros and the highest (3840[m]) peak in Asia Minor, has its summit covered with perpetual snow (Strab. 538, Solin. 45. 4). On the side facing Kaisareia (*Kaiserieh*) this forms a vast slope of glittering white—a fact which perhaps gave its name to the mountain (for ἀργός, ἀργής, ἀργήεις, etc. see Prellwitz *Etym. Wörterb. d. Gr. Spr.*[2] p. 49 f., Boisacq *Dict. étym. de la Langue Gr.* p. 74 f.).

In antiquity few persons reached the summit, and those who did declared that in clear weather they could see both the Euxine and the bay of Issos (Strab. 538)! The ascent readily won its way into the region of the mythical. W. J. Hamilton *Researches in Asia Minor, Pontus, and Armenia* London 1842 ii. 275 reports the following tale: 'A traveller once came from Frangistan, in search of a rare plant which grew only on the summit of Argaeus, having ten leaves round its stalk and a flower in the centre. Here it was said to be guarded by a watchful serpent, which only slept one hour out of the four-and-twenty. The traveller in vain tried to persuade some of the natives to accompany him, and point out the way; none of them would venture, and at length he made the ascent alone. Failing, however, in his attempt to surprise the dragon, he was himself destroyed. The story adds that he was afterwards discovered, transformed into a book, which was taken to Caesareia, and thence found its way back into Frangistan.'

In modern times ascents have been made by Hamilton (1837), Tchihatcheff (1848), and H. F. Tozer with T. M. Crowder (1879). See W. J. Hamilton *op. cit.* ii. 274 ff. (with lithographic pl. view of Mt Argaios as seen from *Kara Hissar*), P. de Tchihatcheff *Asie Mineure* Paris 1853 i. 439 ff. (with fig. 9 view of Mt Argaios, fig. 10 do. as seen from *Erkélet*, fig. 11 do. as seen from *Tomarsé*, fig. 14 plan of Mt Argaios), H. F. Tozer *Turkish Armenia and Eastern Asia Minor* London 1881 pp. 106—131. Tozer says of the summit (*ib.* p. 125 f.): 'The view was quite clear and very extensive, including the long line of the Anti-Taurus to the east, the Allah Dagh and other mountains that run down towards Lycaonia to the south-west, and to the north the vast undulating plains of the interior which we had crossed in coming from Yeuzgatt. One or two small lakes were visible.... We could also trace the depression in which the Halys runs, though the river itself was not in sight. Kaiserieh lay below us...like a dark carpet spread on the bare plain. But far the most remarkable feature was the mountain itself, for the lofty pinnacles of red porphyritic rock, rising from among the snows around and beneath us, veritable *aiguilles*, were as wonderful a sight as can well be conceived [Tozer here gives a striking view of these three needles, which are *c.* 50 feet in height]. The crater or craters, which once occupied the summit, are too much broken away to be easily traceable, the best-marked being that which faces east; but below, all round the base of the mountain, is a belt of volcanic cones. The idea that prevailed among the ancients, that on clear days both the Euxine and the Mediterranean were visible from here, is wholly impossible on account of the distance, and the height of the intervening mountains.' Tozer adds (*ib.* p. 126 f.) : 'As we were climbing about the rocks close by, we found to our great surprise that in places they were perforated with ancient human habitations. One of these wound inwards to a considerable depth with rude niches hollowed in the sides like those which we had seen on the banks of the Halys.... Anyhow there was no question of their being artificial abodes, for besides the niches, the marks of some hard instrument were evident on the roof and sides.'

The capital of Kappadokia, built at the base of Mt Argaios, was named successively Mazaka, Eusebeia, and Kaisareia (Strab. 537 f., Steph. Byz. *s.v.* Καισάρεια). Bronze coins of Eusebeia, struck by Archelaos king of Kappadokia 36 B.C.—17 A.D., have *rev.* Mt Argaios (*Hunter Cat. Coins* ii. 581 no. 1 pl. 62, 15), sometimes with an eagle on its summit (*Brit. Mus. Cat. Coins* Galatia, etc. p. 45 no. 2 pl. 8, 1 (=my fig. 862)). Imperial coins of Kaisareia, in silver and bronze, from Tiberius to Gordianus iii, repeat the type with many interesting variations (*Brit. Mus. Cat. Coins* Galatia, etc. p. 46 ff. pl. 8, 8, 12, pl. 9, 6, 7, 21, pl. 10, 6, 7 (=my fig. 864), 8, 14, 17, 18, 20, pl. 11, 1 (=my fig. 865), 4, 6, 7, 9, 11, 13 (=my fig. 869), 15—19, pl. 12, 1, 2, 3 (=my fig. 873), 4, 7, 9, 12, pl. 13, 1, 2 (=my fig. 875), 3, 4 (=my fig. 877), *Hunter Cat. Coins* ii. 582 ff. pl. 62, 16, 19, 22—24, 25 (=my fig. 868); 26—28, 29 (=my fig. 874), Imhoof-Blumer *Monn. gr.* p. 417 ff. no. 183 ff. pl. H, 1—4, 5 (=my fig. 872), G. Macdonald *Coin Types* Glasgow 1905 p. 167 ff. pl. 6, 10, 11, Head *Hist. num.*[2] p. 752 f. fig. 331. Figs. 863, 866, 867, 870, 871, 876 are from specimens in my collection. See also *supra* i. 603 n. 2). Cp. a red jasper intaglio in the British Museum, which shows Mt Argaios with a wreath above it and a goat's head below (*Brit. Mus. Cat. Gems* p. 135 no. 1107), another from the Blacas collection, which represents the mountain inscribed ΑΡΓΑΙΟC and topped by a radiate figure holding a *patera* in his left hand, a sceptre in his right (*ib.* p. 135 no. 1105), and a third at Berlin, which crowns the summit with an eagle holding a wreath in its beak (Furtwängler *Geschnitt. Steine Berlin* p. 313 no. 8558 pl. 61).

This famous type has been discussed at length by W. Wroth in the *Brit. Mus. Cat. Coins* Galatia, etc. pp. xxxviii—xli and by O. Rossbach in the *Neue Jahrb. f. klass. Altertum* 1901 vii. 406—409. The general shape of the mountain with its crater above and volcanic cones below is adequately rendered. The woods which formerly fringed its sides (Strab. 538 ἀξύλου γὰρ ὑπαρχούσης σχεδόν τι τῆς συμπάσης Καππαδοκίας, ὁ Ἀργαῖος ἔχει περικείμενον δρυμόν, κ.τ.λ.) are represented by trees (figs. 866, 869 ff.). The game inhabiting them is suggested by the lively little picture of the hound chasing the goat or stag (fig. 863). But Argaios was more than a picturesque object or happy hunting-ground. It was to the Cappadocians καὶ θεὸς καὶ ὅρκος καὶ ἄγαλμα (Max. Tyr. *diss.* 8. 8 Dübner cited *supra* i. 102 n. 5). As an ἄγαλμα it is seen on an altar (fig. 869 ff.) or within a temple (fig. 876). It is even worn as a head-dress by Tranquillina (fig. 877), who thus appears as the Tyche of Kaisareia (H. Dressel in the *Zeitschr. f. Num.* 1901 xxiv. 86 f.). Its claim to divinity is stated somewhat differently by Solin. 45. 4 Mazacam sub Argaeo sitam Cappadoces matrem urbium numerant; qui Argaeus nivalibus iugis arduus ne aestivo quidem torrente pruinis caret quemque indidem populi habitari deo (*habitare deum* cod. G) credunt. It remains therefore to ask what deity was believed to inhabit the mountain. W. Wroth rightly rules out Sarapis, though a coin at Paris shows that god holding the mountain in his hand (J. A. Blanchet in the *Rev. Num.* iii Série 1895 xiii. 74 f. pl. 3, 15). This, like the Egyptian symbol (? lotos: cp. *supra* p. 773 fig. 737) which tops the mountain on a coin of Trajan (fig. 863), merely proves that from time to time Sarapis bulked big at Kaisareia. Wroth himself concludes (as does Rossbach *loc. cit.* p. 407 f.) that the naked male figure, who appears on the mountain-top holding globe and sceptre (fig. 867) and sometimes wearing a crown of rays (cp. fig. 868), is the deified emperor. Accordingly he takes the eagle on the mountain (fig. 862) or on the mountain-altar (fig. 869) to be the Roman eagle, interprets the 'two or more figures' sometimes seen on the summit (figs. 870, 872) as ' Imperial personages ?,' and draws attention to a coin of Caracalla at Berlin (J. Friedlaender in the *Zeitschr. f. Num.* 1884 xi. 52 pl. 1, 5, better read by B. Pick in the *Journ. Intern. d'Arch. Num.* 1898 i. 455 ff.) which shows Mt Argaios and a distyle

Fig. 862.

Fig. 863.

Fig. 864.

Fig. 865.

Fig. 866.

Fig. 867.

Fig. 868.

Fig. 869.

Fig. 870.

Fig. 871.

Fig. 872.

Fig. 873.

Fig. 874.

Fig. 875.

Fig. 876.

Fig. 877.

Kilikia
Anazarbos[1].
Mount Olympos (?)[2].

Kypros
Amathous, Golgoi, Kition[3].
Mount Olympos (?)[4].

Assyria
Mount Zagros[5].

Kommagene
Nemroud Dagh[6].

Syria
Chalkis sub Libano (?)[7].

temple below with a star in its pediment and between its columns the inscription ЄІС ЄΩ|ΝΑ ΤΟΥ|С ΚΥΡΙΟΥ (=εἰς αἰῶνα τοὺς κυρίους, an acclamation of the imperial house). Wroth, however, admits 'that before the Imperial age some local divinity— perhaps a mountain-god—was worshipped in connection with Argaeus.'

This is unsatisfactory. The eagle on the mountain-top occurs before the town was renamed Kaisareia (fig. 862 inscribed ΕΥΣ[Ε] ΒΕΙ[Α]), and the eagle on the mountain-altar is much too prominent to be merely a Roman eagle (fig. 869). Gerhard *Gr. Myth.* i. 166, 174 f. did not scruple to speak of a 'Zeus Argäos.' And, though the exact appellation has not yet been found (for Zeus ἀργής see *supra* i. 31 f., 317 f.), he was in all probability on the right track. At least the naked figure with globe and sceptre, the radiate crown, the sun and moon (figs. 869, 873), the star (figs. 871, 876) or stars (fig. 864)—to say nothing of the eagle—are all appropriate to a Hellenistic Zeus. At Kaisareia such an one would readily take on oriental features, *e.g.* the tall headdress with which he appears on a silver coin of Trajan (*Brit. Mus. Cat. Coins* Galatia, etc. p. 52 no. 46 ('Zeus?') pl. 9, 8 (=my fig. 878)). Besides, the two supporters with lances (fig. 870) can then be reasonably explained as the Dioskouroi. It would seem, in fact, that the three rocky pinnacles of the mountain-top were connected with Zeus and the Dioskouroi respectively. I should go further and claim that here, as elsewhere (*supra* pp. 160, 431 f.), the Dioskouroi are

Fig. 878.

anthropomorphic sky-pillars. And I should conjecture that their older aniconic forms were perpetuated by local piety in the curious pillars to right and left of the sacred mountain (figs. 874, 875). The rays that crown these pillars are no accidental adornment. It must often have happened that Dioscuric stars (St Elmo's fires) were to be seen in stormy weather flickering about the *aiguilles* of the summit.

Even so we have hardly exhausted the significance of the coin-types. One of them (fig. 867) apparently attaches a goat's head to the outline of the mountain, low down on its left hand side,—a detail which recalls the goat's head on the gem in the British Museum (*supra*), but is not easy to explain. And what are we to make of the star-like flower or rosette that is found so frequently in the centre of the design? Is this only a stylised rendering of rocks or bushes? Or dare we surmise that popular belief connected the mountain with some magical or mythical flower such as that mentioned by W. J. Hamilton in the tale already told?

[1] Zeus Ὀλύβριος or Ὀλύβρις (*supra* i. 597 n. 4).   [2] *Supra* i. 100 n. 12.

[3] Θεὸς Ὕψιστος (*supra* p. 879 n. o no. (15)).   [4] *Supra* i. 100 n. 14.

[5] Zagreus (*supra* i. 651), whose art-type was borrowed by the Cretan Zeus Ἰδαῖος (*supra* i. 644 ff. pl. xxxv).

[6] Zeus Ὡρομάσδης (*supra* i. 741 ff.).

[7] A bronze coin of *s.* i B.C., probably struck at Chalkis sub Libano (*Anjar*) near

Mount Kasion[1].

Heliopolis (*Ba'albek*), has *obv.* head of Zeus, laureate, to right, *rev.* a temple with two columns, from each of which hangs a fillet, and two steps, on which is the inscription XAΛKI ΔEΩN. Within the temple is a conical stone bound with a fillet (*Brit. Mus. Cat. Coins* Galatia, etc. pp. liv, 279 no. 1 pl. 33, 10 (=my fig. 879), Head *Hist. num.*[1] p. 655 (but not *ib.*[2] p. 783)). W. M. Leake *Numismata Hellenica* London 1854 Asiatic Greece p. 41 had assigned a similar specimen in his collection to Chalkis (*Kinnesrin*) near Beroia (*Aleppo*). De Visser *De Gr. diis non ref. spec. hum.* p. 41 f., 167 treats this conical stone as a primitive ἄγαλμα of

Fig. 879.

Zeus. And he may well be right (*supra* i. 521 n. o), though it should be remembered that Imhoof-Blumer *Monn. gr.* p. 222 f. referred bronze coins with a like *rev.* and *obv.* dolphin round trident (p. 222 no. 60) or head of Hera (p. 223 nos. 63 and 64) to Chalkis in Euboia (so also Head *Hist. num.*[2] p. 360, Anson, *Num. Gr.* v. 19 nos. 133—135).

[1] Mt Kasion (*Djebel-el-Akrá*) rises abruptly from the sea to a height of 5318 ft. The ancients declared that from its summit the sun could be seen in the fourth watch of the night (Plin. *nat. hist.* 5. 80, Solin. 36. 3, Mela 1. 61 (confuses with Mt Kasion in Egypt), Mart. Cap. 680) or at second cock-crow (Amm. Marc. 22. 14. 4). According to Euhemeros the mountain derived its name from a certain king Kasios, who had entertained Zeus (Euhem. *ap.* Euseb. *praep. ev.* 2. 2. 61, Lact. *div. inst.* 1. 22 cited *supra* p. 588 n. 1). Sanchouniathon, as reported by Philon of Byblos, held that Aion and Protogonos had descendants as mortal as themselves named Phos, Pyr, and Phlox, who discovered and taught how to make fire from the friction of wood on wood. They in turn had gigantic sons, who gave their names to the mountains that they occupied—Kassion, Libanos, Antilibanos, and Brathy (cp. Plin. *nat. hist.* 24. 102 herba Sabina, brathy appellata a Graecis, duorum generum est, altera tamarici folio similis, altera cupresso; quare quidam Creticam cupressum dixerunt). Hence sprang Samemroumos (O. Höfer in Roscher *Lex. Myth.* renders 'der hohe Herr des Himmels'), also called Hypsouranios, <and Ousoös (on whom see Gruppe *Cult. Myth. orient. Rel.* i. 392)>, who were named after their mothers, the women of that age being free to mingle with any whom they met (Philon Bybl. *frag.* 2 (*Frag. hist. Gr.* iii. 566 Müller) *ap.* Euseb. *praep. ev.* 1. 10. 9). Synkellos states that Kasos and Belos, sons of Inachos, founded Antiocheia on the Orontes (Synkell. *chron.* 126 A (i. 237 Dindorf), cp. Io. Malal. *chron.* 2 p. 28 Dindorf). Stephanos of Byzantion declares that Mt Kasion in Syria was colonised from Kasos, one of the Kyklades, which was called after Kasos the father of Kleomachos (Steph. Byz. *s.v.* Κάσος, but cp. *id. s.v.* Κάσιον where much the same is said of Mt Kasion in Egypt). The true derivation of the name is still to seek: for modern conjectures see W. W. Baudissin *Studien zur semitischen Religionsgeschichte* Leipzig 1878 ii. 238 f., Frau Adler in Pauly—Wissowa *Real-Enc.* x. 2266 f.

Several myths attached to the mountain. Zeus pursued Typhon to Mt Kasion (Apollod. 1. 6. 3 cited *supra* p. 448 n. 2). The inhabitants of the district, when locusts devastated their crops, besought Zeus to send the *Seleucides aves* (Plin. *nat. hist.* 10. 75 Seleucides aves vocantur quarum adventum ab Iove precibus inpetrant Casii (so Hermolaus Barbarus for *casini* edd. vett. *casmi* cod. F[2]. C. Mayhoff prints *Cadmi*) montis incolae fruges eorum locustis vastantibus. nec unde veniant quove abeant compertum, numquam conspectis nisi cum praesidio earum indigetur). The Antiochenes honoured Triptolemos as a hero with a festival on Mt Kasion (Strab. 750). Some said that Kyparissos, a Cretan boy of great beauty and purity, fled from Apollon or Zephyros to the river Orontes and Mt Kasion, where he was changed into a cypress-tree (interp. Serv. *in* Verg. *Aen.* 3. 680).

In historical times we get repeated allusions to the cult of Zeus on this mountain. When Seleukos i Nikator founded Seleukeia Pieria, he first on the twenty-third day of the month Xanthikos (April) offered sacrifice to Zeus Κάσιος upon Mt Kasion : an eagle carried off a morsel of the sacrificed flesh towards the sea-shore and so showed him the right site (Io. Malal. *chron.* 8 p. 199 Dindorf, cp. *ib.* pp. 199 f., 202 f. *Infra* Append. N *med.*). Trajan, accompanied by Hadrian, visited Seleukeia in the month Apellaios (December) 113 A.D. on his way to fight the Persians (Io. Malal. *chron.* 11 p. 270 Dindorf). Here Trajan dedicated to Zeus Κάσιος silver bowls and a great gilded ox-horn for his victory over the Getai (Souid. *s.v.* Κάσιον ὄρος), while Hadrian commemorated the occasion in a tactful epigram (*Anth. Pal.* 6. 332 (Adrianos) Ζηνὶ τόδ' Αἰνεάδης Κασίῳ Τραϊανὸς ἄγαλμα, | κοίρανος ἀνθρώπων κοιράνῳ ἀθανάτων, | ἄνθετο, δοιὰ δέπα πολυδαίδαλα καὶ βοὸς οὔρου | ἀσκητὸν χρυσῷ παμφανόωντι κέρας, | ἔξαιτα προτέρης ἀπὸ ληΐδος, ἦμος ἀτειρὴς | πέρσεν ὑπερθύμους ᾧ ὑπὸ δουρὶ Γέτας. | ἀλλὰ σύ οἱ καὶ τήνδε, κελαινεφές, ἐγγυάλιξον | κρῆναι εὐκλειῶς δῆριν Ἀχαιμενίην, | ὄφρα τοι εἰσορόωντι διάνδιχα θυμὸν ἰαίνῃ | δοιά, τὰ μὲν Γετέων σκῦλα, τὰ δ' Ἀρσακιδέων). In 129 A.D. Hadrian climbed the mountain by night to witness the sunrise ; but rain came on and, as he was sacrificing, a thunderbolt fell and destroyed both victim and priest (Spart. *v. Hadr.* 14. 3). Perhaps Lucius Verus too paid homage to Zeus Κάσιος, for a medallion, struck in 167 A.D. on account of the victories won in the east by Avidius Cassius, shows the emperor offering Nike to Zeus who is seated on a mountain (Cohen *Monn. emp. rom.*[2] iii. 197 no. 291, *supra* i. 133 f. fig. 99) : this inference, defended by W. Drexler in Roscher *Lex. Myth.* ii. 971 f., is questioned by Frau Adler in Pauly—Wissowa *Real-Enc.* x. 2265. In the spring of 363 A.D. Julian ascended Mt Kasion on a festal day and there sacrificed a hecatomb to Zeus Κάσιος (Amm. Marc. 22. 14. 4, Io. Malal. *chron.* 13. p. 327 Dindorf, cp. Ioul. *misop.* 361 D, Liban. *or.* 14. 69 (ii. 112, 14 Foerster)) : he made the ascent at midday, saw the god (? in a dream), rose up, and received some useful advice (Liban. *or.* 18. 172 (ii. 310, 18 ff. Foerster) εἰς τὸ Κάσσιον ὄρος παρὰ τὸν Κάσσιον ἀναβὰς Δία μεσημβρίας σταθερᾶς εἶδέ τε τὸν θεὸν καὶ ἰδὼν ἀνέστη καὶ συμβουλὴν ἐδέξατο, δι' ἧς πάλιν διαφεύγει λόχον).

But the most interesting evidence with regard to the cult is supplied by the coin-types of Seleukeia. Coppers struck by Trajan and Antoninus Pius have *rev.* a shrine with pyramidal roof resting on four pillars and enclosing a sacred stone, which is filleted. On

Fig. 880.   Fig. 881.   Fig. 882.

Fig. 883.   Fig. 884.

the roof is an eagle with spread wings, and beneath the shrine ΣΕΥϹ ΚΑϹΙΟϹ (*Brit. Mus. Cat. Coins* Galatia, etc. p. 274 pl. 33, 3 (=my fig. 880) Trajan, *Hunter Cat. Coins* iii. 216 f. pl. 74, 32 Trajan) or ΣΕΥϹ ΚΑϹΙΟϹ with star in field (*Brit. Mus. Cat. Coins* Galatia, etc. p. 275 pl. 33, 4 (=my fig. 882), Anson *Num. Gr.* v. 53 no. 354 pl. 8

Kyrrhos[1].
Palmyra[2].
Seleukeia Pieria[3].

Phoinike
Abédat[4].
Berytos[5].
Byblos[6].
Libanos[7].
Sahin[8].

Samaria
Mount Gerizim[9].

Antoninus Pius). Later specimens omit the god's name (*Hunter Cat. Coins* iii. 217 no. 43 Commodus), but show the stone in a tetrastyle temple (*Brit. Mus. Cat. Coins* Galatia, etc. p. 275 no. 50 Septimius Severus, p. 276 no. 52 Caracalla) and add crescent and star in the pediment (*Brit. Mus. Cat. Coins* Galatia, etc. p. 277 no. 57 pl. 33, 7 Elagabalos, no. 58 pl. 33, 8 (= my fig. 884) Severus Alexander (OBO = ὀβολός), Anson *Num. Gr.* v. 53 no. 356 pl. 8 Elagabalos, no. 357 pl. 8 Severus Alexander). Figs. 881, 883 are from examples in my collection.

Zeus Κάσιος must not be confounded with Zeus Κεραύνιος (*supra* p. 809); the stone in the shrine is no thunderbolt. Nor is there any real reason to think with F. Lenormant in Daremberg—Saglio *Dict. Ant.* i. 935 fig. 1206 that the stone was an aerolite worshipped as the Aramaean god Ḳaṣiu (but see Frau Adler in Pauly—Wissowa *Real-Enc.* x. 2266) and Hellenised as Zeus Κάσιος. W. W. Baudissin *op. cit.* ii. 242 observes curtly : ' Der Stein ist Bild des heiligen Berges.' W. Wroth in the *Brit. Mus. Cat. Coins* Galatia, etc. p. lxxii says : ' the conical object has a cavity in the side, which seems further to show that the representation is that of a mountain or the agalma of a mountain.' Accordingly, he takes it to be ' the mountain Kasios—or rather an *agalma* of the mountain ' and compares Mt Argaion on the coins of Kaisareia (*supra* p. 979). A. Salač ' ΖΕΥΣ ΚΑΣΙΟΣ ' in the *Bull. Corr. Hell.* 1922 xlvi. 176 f. rejects the view of Baudissin and Wroth, remarking very justly that on the later coins (figs. 883, 884) the cavity in the sacred stone disappears, the resultant shape being that of an *omphalós* (cp. Overbeck *Gr. Kunstmyth.* Zeus p. 553 n. 4). On the whole it seems safest to conclude that the sacred stone did duty as the god's altar (*supra* i. 521), the hollow in it (Pind. *Pyth.* 4. 206 βωμοῖο θέναρ) being used for libations (*supra* p. 193). A parallel might be found in the sacred stone with a cup-like top represented on some of the earliest *statêres* of Mallos in Kilikia (?) (*Brit. Mus. Cat. Coins* Lycaonia, etc. p. 95 pl. 15, 10—12, Babelon *Monn. gr. rom.* ii. 1. 557 f. pl. 25, 11, Anson *Num. Gr.* v. 17 nos. 117 and 118 pl. 3 : on the doubtful attribution see Imhoof-Blumer *Kleinas. Münzen* ii. 435 f. and Babelon *op. cit.* ii. 1. 561 ff.). The pyramidal or triangular roof topped by an eagle recalls the pyramid of Sandas and would suit a mountain-god (*supra* i. 600 ff.).

A votive inscription from Heddernheim—*Corp. inscr. Lat.* xiii no. 7330 Deo | Casio | Ovinius | v.s.l.m.—has been connected with this Syrian cult (Frau Adler in Pauly—Wissowa *Real-Enc.* x. 2267, A. Salač *loc. cit.* p. 187 f.).

[1] Zeus Καταιβάτης seated on a rock (*supra* i. 124, ii. 15 f. figs. 3 and 4).
[2] Zeus "Υψιστος καὶ 'Επήκοος, less often Zeus "Υψιστος, Zeus Μέγιστος "Υψιστος, Zeus "Υψιστος Μέγιστος 'Επήκοος (*supra* p. 885 n. o n. (29)).
[3] Zeus Κορυφαῖος (*supra* p. 869 n. 1).
[4] Zeus Οὐράνιος "Υψιστος Σααρναῖος 'Επήκοος (*supra* p. 886 n. o no. (30)).
[5] Θεὸς "Υψιστος (*supra* p. 886 n. o no. (30)).
[6] Zeus "Υψιστος (*supra* p. 887 n. o no. (30)).
[7] *Supra* i. 551 with i. 581 f.
[8] Θεὸς "Υψιστος Οὐράνιος "Υπατος (*supra* p. 886 n. o no. (30)).
[9] Zeus 'Ελλήνιος or Ξένιος, Zeus "Υψιστος, Iupiter Sarapis (?) (*supra* p. 887 n. o no. (31)).

Ioudaia
Jerusalem[1].
Aigyptos
Alexandreia[2].
Athribis[3].
Mount Kasion[4].

[1] Hadrian attempted to crush Christianity by erecting a statue of Aphrodite on the site of the Crucifixion and an image of Zeus on the site of the Resurrection (Hieron. *epist.* 58. 3 *ad Paulinum* (xxii. 581 Migne) ab Hadriani temporibus usque ad imperium Constantini, per annos circiter centum octoginta, in loco resurrectionis simulacrum Iovis, in crucis rupe statua ex marmore Veneris a gentibus posita colebatur, existimantibus persecutionis auctoribus quod tollerent nobis fidem resurrectionis et crucis, si loca sancta per idola polluissent. Bethleem nunc nostram et augustissimum orbis locum, de quo Psalmista canit ' Veritas de terra orta est' (Ps. 85. 11), lucus inumbrabat Thamuz, id est Adonidis, et in specu, ubi quondam Christus parvulus vagiit, Veneris amasius plangebatur = Paulin. Nolan. *epist.* 31. 3 (lxi. 326 C—327 A Migne) nam Hadrianus imperator, existimans se fidem Christianam loci iniuria perempturum, in loco passionis < statuam Veneris, in loco resurrectionis (*ins.* A.B.C.) > simulacrum Iovis consecravit, et Bethlehem Adonidis fano profanata est, ut quasi radix et fundamentum ecclesiae tolleretur, si in iis locis idola colerentur, in quibus Christus natus est ut pateretur, passus est ut resurgeret, surrexit ut regnaret iudicatus). So even the pagans realised that the Cross meant Love Divine and the empty Tomb Omnipotence.

[2] Θεὸς ῞Υψιστος καὶ πάντων 'Επόπτης (*supra* p. 889 n. o no. (33)).

[3] Θεὸς ῞Υψιστος (*supra* p. 889 n. o no. (33).

[4] Mt Kasion, a barren sand-dune adjoining Lake Sirbonis, was famous for its sanctuary of Zeus Κάσιος (Strab. 760, Lucan. 8. 858, Plin. *nat. hist.* 5. 68, Solin. 34. 1, Steph. Byz. *s.v.* Κάσιον). According to Sanchouniathon as reported by Philon of Byblos, the descendants of the Dioskouroi, when shipwrecked, were cast up on Mt Kasion and dedicated a temple there (Philon Bybl. *frag.* 2 (*Frag. hist. Gr.* iii. 568 Müller) *ap.* Euseb. *praep. ev.* 1. 10. 20 κατὰ τοῦτον τὸν χρόνον οἱ ἀπὸ τῶν Διοσκούρων σχεδίας καὶ πλοῖα συνθέντες ἔπλευσαν, καὶ ἐκριφέντες περὶ τὸ Κάσσιον ὄρος ναὸν αὐτόθι ἀφιέρωσαν). The story is late, but the sanctuary must indeed have received many a dedication from travellers who had escaped the dangers of the shallow sea and the shifting sand (T. Wiegand in the *Jahrb. d. kais. deutsch. arch. Inst.* 1920 xxxv Arch. Anz. p. 87 f.). Near this spot Cn. Pompeius Magnus the triumvir was murdered as he stepped ashore, on Sept. 29, 48 B.C., and here he was buried (Strab. 760, Vell. Pat. 2. 53, Lucan. 8. 560 ff., Plout. *v. Pomp.* 78—80, Appian. *bell. civ.* 2. 84—86, Dion Cass. 42. 3—5, *alib.*). His partisans erected bronze statues to his memory near Mt Kasion (Appian. *bell. civ.* 2. 86). In the winter of 69—70 A.D. Titus and his army passed from Pelousion to the sanctuary of Zeus Κάσιος, and thence to Ostrakine, Rhinokoroura, etc. *en route* for Jerusalem (Ioseph. *bell. Iud.* 4. 11. 5). In 130 A.D. Hadrian, on his way from Palestine to Egypt, offered a sacrifice (ἐνήγισε) to Pompeius and rebuilt his ruined tomb (Dion Cass. 69. 11, Spart. *v. Hadr.* 14. 4), clearing it of sand and replacing the bronze statues, which had been removed to the *ádyton* of the sanctuary (Appian. *bell. civ.* 2. 86). Hadrian's epigram on the tomb is still extant (*Anth. Pal.* 9. 402 (Adrianos) τῷ ναοῖς βρίθοντι πόση σπάνις ἔπλετο τύμβου). The little town of Kasion made a *spécialité* of intricate woodwork; whence the proverb Κασιωτικὸν ἄμμα (Diogeneian. 5. 44, Apostol. 9. 46, *prov. Bodl.* 527 p. 62 Gaisford, Souid. *s.vv.* ἄμματα, Κάσιον ὄρος, Zonar. *lex. s.v.* ἄμματα). A papyrus of 283 A.D. mentions Casiotic joiners (B. P. Grenfell—A. S. Hunt *The Oxyrhynchus Papyri* London 1898 i. 112 ff. no. 55, 6 Κασιωδῶν). We might have supposed that the local manufacture of Κασιωτικὰ ἱμάτια (Steph. Byz. *s.v.* Κάσιον) or Κασιανὰ ὑφάσματα (Eustath. *in Dionys. per.* 260) rested on a blunder (ἱμάτια or ὑφάσματα for ἄμματα). But Makrisi too speaks of certain fabrics called *qassiah* as made on the spot (Maqrizi *Description topographique et historique de l'Égypte* trad. U. Bouriant Paris 1900 p. 520). Early in *s.* i B.C., if not in

Pelousion[1].

s. ii. B.C., a native of the town made a double dedication in Delos to Zeus Κάσιος along with the Θεὸς Μέγας (*quis*? See *infra* Index i *s.v.* Odessos) and Tachnepsis (a deity new to Egyptologists) (P. Roussel *Les cultes égyptiens à Délos du* IIIᵉ *au* Iᵉʳ *siècle av. J.-C.* Nancy 1916 p. 95 ff. no. 16 Θεῶι Μεγάλωι | καὶ Διὶ Κασίωι καὶ Ταχνήψει | °Ωρος °Ωρου Κασιώτης | ὑπὲρ Λευκίου Γρανίου | τοῦ Ποπλίου 'Ρωμαίου · | γυναῖκα μὴ προσάγειν | μηδὲ ἐν ἐρέοις ἄνδρα · | κατὰ πρόσταγμα, no. 16 *bis* [Θεῶ]ι | [Μεγά]λωι | [καὶ Διὶ Κ]ασίωι καὶ | [Τα]χνήψει | [°Ωρο]ς °Ωρου Κασ(ι)ώτης | [ὑ]πὲρ Λευκίου Γρανίου | τοῦ Ποπλίου 'Ρωμαίου, | κατὰ πρόσταγμα · | γυναῖκα δὲ μὴ προσάγειν | μηδὲ ἐν ἐρέοις ἄνδρα). Similarly a native of Berytos gave a thankoffering in Delos to Zeus Κάσιος (*id. ib.* p. 97 no. 17 Ξενοφῶν | Διονυσίου | Βηρύτιος | Διὶ Κασίωι | χαριστήριον). And, as Roussel remarks, Zeus Κάσιος is again grouped with Egyptian divinities in an inscription from Athens (A. Wilhelm *Beiträge zur griechischen Inschriftenkunde* Wien 1909 p. 136 'sie nennt in den ersten erhaltenen Zeilen Priester verschiedener Gottheiten, so des °Ωρος, Θεὸς 'Αγαθός, Ζεὺς Κάσιος, 'Απόλλων, Διόνυσος, des [Διόνυσος und der] 'Αριάγ[νη?, der Μήτηρ θεῶν, der [Οὐρ]ανία 'Αφροδείτη Νείκη ἐν Κανώπῳ.' A. Salač, who publishes the inscription in the *Bull. Corr. Hell.* 1922 xlvi. 182—187, revises this list as follows : *vv.* 3 f. ['Αρπο]|κράτους, 5 °Ωρου, 6 'Αγαθοῦ δεοῦ, 7 Διὸς Κασίο[υ], 9 'Απόλλωνος, 11 Διονύσο[υ] – – Μητρὸς θεῶν, 13 ἐν Κ[α]νώπῳ (*i.e.* Sarapis at Kanopos (Strab. 801)) – – [Οὐρ]ανίας 'Αφροδείτης, 14 ['Ισιδος Ταποσ]ειριάδος).

J. Clédat in the *Comptes rendus de l'Acad. des inscr. et belles-lettres* 1905 pp. 602—611, *ib.* 1909 pp. 764—774, *ib.* 1911 p. 433 proves that Mt Kasion was not situated, as is commonly held, at *Ras-Bouroun* on the narrow strip of land between the sea and the lake, but at *Mahemdiah* (*Mohamedieh*) some 40 kilometers further to the west, that is, about 15 kilometers east of Pelousion. Here at the western end of the lake and close to the sea rises a rounded sandhill (maximum height 13·30ᵐ: Lucan. 10. 434 f. exaggerates), on which he detected and partially excavated (1) a large (*c.* 20·0ᵐ × 20·0ᵐ) public bath, built of gypsum and baked brick in late Roman times ; (2) a small (9·60ᵐ × 6·0ᵐ) tetrastyle temple facing east, built of gypsum at the eastern extremity of the hill ; (3) numerous tombs, some on the hill, others on the plain, belonging to two Roman and two Byzantine cemeteries. Moreover, in 1909 he noted that a *cippus* of Roman date bore the name of an inhabitant called ΚΑϹΙΟϹ (*loc. cit.* 1909 p. 774). And finally in 1911 he was able to report 'un petit sanctuaire avec niche d'autel en albâtre portant une inscription nabatéenne au nom de Zeus Cassius' (*loc. cit.* 1911 p. 433).

[1] We are further indebted to J. Clédat for the discovery of a temple dedicated to Zeus Κάσιος at Pelousion (J. Clédat 'Le temple de Zeus Cassios à Péluse' in the *Annales du service des antiquités de l'Égypte* Le Caire 1914 xiii. 79—85 with figs. 1—3 and pl. 11). Towards the western end of an elongated mound called by the Arabs *Tell el-Faramah* (Coptic ⲡⲉⲣⲉⲙⲟⲩⲛ) he found the walled camp (*el Kasr*) of the *equites Stablesiani* and to the west of this, at a point but little raised above the level of the surrounding morass, the last remains of a temple built in rosy granite. On the ground lay two columns (7·80ᵐ in length, 1·0ᵐ in diameter) and two architrave-blocks (1·80ᵐ long, 0·96ᵐ high, 0·80ᵐ deep) bearing the central part of a deeply incised inscription, which may be restored *exempli gratia* as follows: [ὑπὲρ αὐτοκράτορος Καίσαρος Τραϊανοῦ 'Αδριανοῦ Σε]βαστοῦ καὶ τοῦ σύ[μπαν]τος αὐτοῦ ο[ἴκο]υ Διὶ Κασίῳ Μ[εγίστῳ θεῷ Πηλουσίου καὶ τοῖς συννάοις θεοῖς] | [ἐπὶ Τίτου Φλαυΐου Τιτιανοῦ ἐπιτροπεύοντος τοῦ ἱε]ροῦ ἀνέθηκεν Και[κίλι]ος Κάσιος Δί[ων 'Απο]λλωνίου τ[οῦ – – –] | [τὸν σηκὸν τοῦ ἱεροῦ καὶ τὸ πρόναον καὶ τὰ ἐν] αὐτοῖς πάντα κοσ[μήσα]ς υνοροσηκ[. . . . .]ιμωματι[– – –] | [– – – αὐ]τοῦ. I cannot make head or tail of the concluding words, unless we may suppose κοσ[μήσα]ς, τὴν ὀροφὴν [τῷ κομ]μώματι [διαποικίλας κ.τ.λ.] or the like. A fragment found to the left of the first block is inscribed ΑΝΟ with ϹΙ beneath it : this might be a portion of [Τραϊ]ανο[ῦ] and [ἐπιτροπεύοντο]ς τ[οῦ]. Another architectural block (2·50ᵐ long, 0·49ᵐ high, 0·90ᵐ deep) bears the central part of a second inscription: [– – – τ]οῦ προγεγραμμένου [– – –]|[– – –] ἐπὶ Τίτου Φλαυΐου Τιτ[ιανοῦ – – –].

A. Salač in the *Bull. Corr. Hell.* 1922 xlvi. 166—176 ('*Zeus Kasios en Égypte*'), not only improves on Clédat's reading of the temple-dedication, but also contrives to throw a good deal of light on its occasion and significance. Hadrian came to Pelousion after his journey in Arabia (Spart. *v. Hadr.* 14. 4), that is, in 130 A.D. (W. Weber *Untersuchungen zur Geschichte des Kaisers Hadrianus* Leipzig 1907 p. 246). By the fall of the thunderbolt on the Syrian Mt Kasion (*supra* p. 982 n. 0) he had already been designated as the favourite of Zeus Κάσιος (*supra* p. 22 ff.)—an honour comparable with the adoption of Alexander the Great by Zeus Ἄμμων. Hence the foundation of a temple of Zeus Κάσιος at Pelousion would glorify the emperor as well as the god (W. Weber *op. cit.* p. 235 f.).

Salač *loc. cit.* further contends that the cult-statue of Zeus Κάσιος at Pelousion, a youthful figure holding a pomegranate (Ach. Tat. 3. 6 ἔστι δ' ἐν τῷ Πηλουσίῳ Διὸς ἱερὸν ἄγαλμα Κασίου· τὸ δ' ἄγαλμα νεανίσκος, Ἀπόλλωνι μᾶλλον ἐοικώς· οὕτω γὰρ ἡλικίας εἶχε· προβέβληται δὲ τὴν χεῖρα καὶ ἔχει ῥοιὰν ἐπ' αὐτῇ· τῆς δὲ ῥοιᾶς ὁ λόγος μυστικός. προσευξάμενοι δὴ τῷ θεῷ καὶ περὶ τοῦ Κλεινίου καὶ τοῦ Σατύρου σύμβολον ἐξαιτήσαντες (καὶ γὰρ ἔλεγον μαντικὸν εἶναι τὸν θεόν) περιῄειμεν τὸν νεών. κατὰ δὲ τὸν ὀπισθόδομον ὁρῶμεν εἰκόνα διπλῆν· καὶ ὁ γραφεὺς ἐνεγέγραπτο· Εὐάνθης μὲν ὁ γραφεύς, ἡ δ' εἰκὼν Ἀνδρομέδα καὶ Προμηθεύς, κ.τ.λ., 8 ἑξῆς δὲ τὸ τοῦ Προμηθέως ἐγεγόνει. κ.τ.λ.), was modelled upon a previously existing cult-statue of Harpokrates, the youthful Horos. This contention is strongly supported by numismatic evidence. In fact, a coin of Pelousion, struck by Trajan, actually shows Harpokrates standing with a sceptre in his left hand and a pomegranate in his right, towards which a little Pan stretches out his hands (G. Dattari *Numi Augg. Alexandrini* Cairo 1901 i. 418 no. 6345 pl. 34). Other coins of the same town, struck by Hadrian in 126/7 A.D., have *obv.* head of the emperor to right, laureate; *rev.* head of Harpokrates to right, wearing the *hem-hem* crown and fillet (V. Langlois *Numismatique des nomes d'Égypte sous l'administration romaine* Paris 1852 p. 39 no. 69 (wrongly described) pl. 3, 1, *Brit. Mus. Cat. Coins* Alexandria etc. p. 351 nos. 44 and 45), or *rev.* a pomegranate (Langlois *op. cit.* p. 39 no. 70, *Brit. Mus. Cat. Coins* Alexandria etc. p. 351 no. 46), while coins of Alexandreia, struck by Hadrian in 137/8 A.D., have *obv.* head of the emperor to right, laureate, with *paludamentum* over shoulder; *rev.* bust of Harpokrates of Pelousion to right, wearing *hem-hem* crown, with *himátion* over left shoulder and pomegranate in front (*ib.* p. 90 nos. 764 pl. 17 and 765, *Hunter Cat. Coins* iii. 457 no. 391). An Egyptian connexion is again presupposed by the statement that Malkandros king of Byblos had a son Palaistinos or Pelousios, who was nurtured by Isis and gave his name to the town that she founded (Plout. *de Is. et Os.* 17. Skyl. *per.* 106 makes Pelousios come ἐπὶ τὸ Κάσιον; Epiphan. *ancor.* 106 (i. 209, 30 Dindorf) makes Kasios worshipped παρὰ Πηλουσιώταις).

But, granting this Egyptian background, we have yet to explain why Zeus in particular was chosen as the successor of the youthful Horos. And here I should conjecture that we must take into account the influence of Crete, where a youthful Zeus had long been recognised. It is noteworthy that, whereas the nursling of Isis is called Horos by Diod. i. 25 and Pelousios by Plout. *de Is. et Os.* 17, he is described as Diktys by Plout. *de Is. et Os.* 8. The name, whatever its origin (Gruppe *Gr. Myth. Rel.* p. 1283 n. 4), recalls the Cretan Diktynna and Mt Dikte and the infant Zeus (*supra* p. 927). It may be objected that Diktys is not expressly associated with Pelousion. But he is expressly associated with the Egyptian taboo on onions (Plout. *de Is. et Os.* 8 τὸ γὰρ ἐμπεσεῖν εἰς τὸν ποταμὸν καὶ ἀπολέσθαι τὸν τῆς Ἴσιδος τρόφιμον Δίκτυν τῶν κρομμύων ἐπιδραττόμενον ἐσχάτως ἀπίθανον· οἱ δὲ ἱερεῖς ἀφοσιοῦνται καὶ δυσχεραίνουσι τὸ κρόμμυον παραφυλάττοντες, ὅτι τῆς σελήνης φθινούσης μόνον εὐτροφεῖν τοῦτο καὶ τεθηλέναι πέφυκεν. ἔστι δὲ πρόσφορον οὔτε ἁγνεύουσιν οὔτε ἑορτάζουσι, τοῖς μὲν ὅτι διψῆν, τοῖς δὲ ὅτι δακρύειν ποιεῖ τοὺς προσφερομένους), and that taboo (as to which see the references collected by J. E. B. Mayor on Iuv. 15. 9) was specially characteristic of Pelousion (Plout. *comm. in Hes. frag.* 11. 52 Dübner *ap.* Gell. 20. 8. 7 'id etiam,' inquit, 'multo mirandum est magis, quod apud Plutarchum in quarto in Hesiodum commentario legi: "cepetum revirescit et congerminat decedente luna, contra autem inarescit adolescente. eam causam esse dicunt sacerdotes Aegyptii, cur Pelusiotae cepe non edint, quia solum olerum omnium contra lunae augmenta atque

Uncertain locality

Mount Hynnarion[1].

damna vices minuendi et augendi habeat contrarias,"' Loukian. *Iup. trag.* 42 ἰδίᾳ δὲ Μεμφίταις μὲν ὁ βοῦς θεός, Πηλουσιώταις δὲ κρόμμυον, καὶ ἄλλοις ἶβις ἢ κροκόδειλος, καὶ ἄλλοις κυνοκέφαλος ἢ αἴλουρος ἢ πίθηκος, Hieron. *comm. in Isa. proph.* 13 (xxiv. 450 C—D Migne) non quo simulacra gentilium in praedam bestiarum et iumentorum exposita sint; sed quo religio nationum simulacra sint bestiarum et brutorum animantium, quae maxime in Aegypto divino cultui consecrata sunt... nam et pleraque oppida eorum ex bestiis et iumentis habent nomina, Κύνων a cane, Λέων a leone, Θμοῦϊς lingua Aegyptia ab hirco, Λύκων a lupo, ut taceam de formidoloso et horribili caepe, et crepitu ventris inflati, quae Pelusiaca religio est, Hieron. *adv. Iovinian.* 2. 7 (xxiii. 296 B Migne) coge Aegyptium ut ovium lacte vescatur; impelle, si vales, Pelusioten ut manducet caepe). Indeed we are told by Sextus Empiricus that no devotee of Zeus Κάσιος in that town would eat an onion (Sext. *Pyrrhon. hyp.* 3. 24. 224 κρόμμυον δὲ οὐκ ἄν τις προσενέγκαιτο τῶν καθιερουμένων τῷ κατὰ Πηλούσιον Κασίῳ Διί, ὥσπερ οὐδὲ ἱερεὺς τῆς κατὰ Λιβύην Ἀφροδίτης σκορόδου γεύσαιτο ἄν. ἀπέχονται δὲ ἐν μὲν ἱεροῖς μίνθης, ἐν οἷς δὲ ἡδυόσμου, ἐν οἷς δὲ σελίνου). Sextus' phrase τῶν καθιερουμένων τῷ...Κασίῳ Διί coupled with that of Achilleus Tatios (*supra*) τῆς δὲ ῥοιᾶς ὁ λόγος μυστικός may fairly be taken to imply that Zeus Κάσιος had mystic rites of initiation—another point of contact with the Cretan Zeus (*supra* i. 648 ff., 663 ff.).

U. Wilcken in the *Archiv für Papyrusforschung und verwandte Gebiete* 1901 i. 555 draws attention to a letter, written from Pelousion by an unskilled hand at some uncertain date (? *s.* ii A.D.), found in the *Fayoum*, and now preserved at Berlin, in which mention is made of Zeus Κάσιος (Zerekli in *Aegyptische Urkunden aus den koeniglichen Museen zu Berlin* herausg. von der Generalverwaltung: Griechische Urkunden no. 827 (P. 7150), 1 ff. Ζοῖς Ἀπ[ολ]λιναρίῳ τῷ ἀδελ|φῷ χαί[ρ]ιν. τὸ προσκύνημά | σου παρὰ τῷ Διὶ τῷ Κασίῳ. γι|νώσκιν σε θέλω ὅτι εὕρη|κα τὴν γυναῖ<κα> τοῦ Ἄχαρις (?) | κα[ὶ] δέδωκα αὐτῇ τὰ γεγρα|μμένα πάντα κ.τ.λ. addressed on the back ἀπό(δος) Ἀπολιναρίῳ ἀ|πὸ Πετρωνίου δρομι|δαρίου ἀπὸ Πη|λουσίου). A circular bronze stamp with long handle in the Leyden Museum shows an Egyptian head-dress, consisting of three bunches of plants with a disk on each, and is inscribed Διὸς Κα|σίου, Ἀθην|ᾶς Ἀππι|ανοῦ ι|[....] (C. Leemans *Description raisonnée des monumens Égyptiens du Musée d'Antiquités des Pays-Bas, à Leide* Leide 1840 p. 111 no. 342, *id. Animadversiones in Musei Antiquarii Lugduno-Batavi inscriptiones Graecas et Latinas* Lugduni Batavorum 1842 p. 28, *Corp. inscr. Gr.* iv no. 7044 *b*, W. Drexler in Roscher *Lex. Myth.* ii. 973 'Bronzespiegel' (!), Gruppe *Gr. Myth. Rel.* p. 1104 n. 1 'Gemme' (!)).

W. W. Baudissin *Studien zur semitischen Religionsgeschichte* Leipzig 1878 ii. 243 infers from Epiphan. *loc. cit.* (Κάσιος δὲ ὁ ναύκληρος παρὰ Πηλουσιώταις (sc. τιμᾶται)) that Zeus Κάσιος was worshipped by sea-faring men. On which Frau Adler in Pauly—Wissowa *Real-Enc.* x. 2266 remarks: 'Daher darf wohl mit dem pelusischen Kulte ein Fund bei Palos in Spanien in Verbindung gesetzt werden; im Meere wurden antike Bleianker aufgefischt mit hebräischen, lateinischen und zwei griechischen Inschriften; die eine galt Aphrodite σώζουσα, die andere Ζεὺς Κάσις σωζ<ων> (die Ergänzung der zwei letzten Buchstaben unsicher), Boletin d. l. Real Ac. d. Historia 1906, XLVIII 157 f.'

Baudissin *op. cit.* ii. 240 was inclined to derive the Pelusiac from the Syrian cult of Zeus Κάσιος, though he added: 'Es ist aber nicht unmöglich, dass der Dienst des Kasios ein *alt*semitischer war, welchen verschiedene semitische Völker aus der gemeinsamen Heimat herübernahmen.' Frau Adler *loc. cit.* adopts the latter view, 'dass beide Kulte auf gemeinsame, ursemitische Wurzel zurückgehen sind.' But Salač in the *Bull. Corr. Hell.* 1922 xlvi. 180, 188 definitely returns to the former view: 'En somme, le culte de Ζεὺς Κάσιος paraît d'origine syrienne; le culte du Mons Casius égyptien semble dérivé de la Syrie.'

[1] Hesych. *s.vv.* Ὑναρεύς· Ζεὺς ἀπὸ τοῦ Ὑναρίου ὄρους, ὑννάς· αἲξ ἀγρία, ὑννή· αἲξ. καὶ τὸ τοῦ ἀρότρου σιδήριον τὸ τέμνον τὴν γῆν <ὕννη>. καὶ ὕννις ὁμοίως, ὕννος· πῶλος ὁ ἐν τῇ γαστρὶ νοσήσας, πρὶν κυνηθῆναι <ἰννός>. Gruppe *Gr. Myth. Rel.* p. 824 n. 7 concludes that Zeus Ὑναριεύς (*sic*) derived his appellative from the goat.

APPENDIX E.

THE KYKLOPS IN FOLK-TALES.

Tales resembling that of Polyphemos have, during the last seventy years, been collected and discussed by a whole series of eminent folklorists. W. Grimm (1857)[1], C. Nyrop (1881)[2], G. Krek (1887)[3], L. Laistner (1889)[4], G. Polívka (1898, 1918)[5], N. G. Polites (1904)[6], P. Sébillot (1904)[7], W. R. Halliday (1916)[8], F. Settegast (1917)[9], and Sir J. G. Frazer (1921)[10] have all said their say, most of them making valuable contributions to the subject. But the palm must be awarded to O. Hackman (1904)[11], who in an exemplary monograph has not merely summarised two hundred and twenty-one variants, but has also added a lucid and logical study of their contents.

Hackman arranges the tales in three groups—A, B, and C. Group A (124 variants) commonly involves two episodes and frequently adds a third:

i The blinding of the giant, which is contrived

either (a) during his sleep by means of a red-hot stake, iron spit, knife, sword, etc. plunged into his one eye,

or (β) as a pretended cure for his defective sight by means of molten tin, lead, oil, pitch, boiling water, etc. poured into his eye.

The former alternative, (a), prevails in southern and western Europe; the latter, (β), in northern and eastern Europe. It is probable that (β) was not a modification of (a), but had a separate and independent origin[12].

---

[1] W. Grimm 'Die Sage von Polyphem' in the *Abh. d. berl. Akad. 1857* Phil.-hist. Classe pp. 1—30 (=*Kleinere Schriften* Gütersloh 1887 iv. 428—462). W. W. Merry in Appendix ii 'On some various forms of the legend of the blinded Cyclops' to his edition of the *Odyssey* Oxford 1886 i.[2] 550—554 summarises nine tales after J. F. Lauer *Homerische Studien* Berlin 1851 p. 319 ff. and W. Grimm *loc. cit.*

[2] C. Nyrop 'Sagnet om Odysseus og Polyphem.' in the *Nordisk Tidskrift for Filologi* 1881 v. 216—255.

[3] G. Krek *Einleitung in die slavische Litteraturgeschichte*[2] Graz 1887 pp. 665—759.

[4] L. Laistner ' Polyphem ' in his *Das Rätsel der Sphinx* Berlin 1889 ii. 1—168.

[5] G. Polívka 'Nachträge zur Polyphemsage' in the *Archiv f. Rel.* 1898 i. 305—336, 378, J. Bolte—G. Polívka *Anmerkungen zu den Kinder- u. Hausmärchen der Brüder Grimm* Leipzig 1918 iii. 374—378.

[6] N. G. Polites Παραδόσεις Athens 1904 ii. 1338—1342 (n. on no. 624).

[7] P. Sébillot *Le Folk-lore de France* Paris 1904 i. 434 f.

[8] W. R. Halliday in R. M. Dawkins *Modern Greek in Asia Minor* Cambridge 1916 p. 217.

[9] F. Settegast *Das Polyphemmärchen in altfranzösischen Gedichten*, eine folkloristisch-literargeschichtliche Untersuchung Leipzig 1917 pp. 1—167. Review by J. Bolte in the *Zeitschrift des Vereins für Volkskunde* 1917 xxvii. 275 f.

[10] Sir J. G. Frazer in Appendix xiii 'Ulysses and Polyphemus' to his edition of Apollodoros London 1921 ii. 404—455 gives an admirable selection of thirty-six variants— quite enough, as he remarks, ' to illustrate the wide diffusion of the tale and the general similarity of the versions.'

[11] O. Hackman *Die Polyphemsage in der Volksüberlieferung* Helsingfors 1904 pp. 1— 241. Review by J. Bolte in the *Zeitschrift des Vereins für Volkskunde* 1905 xv. 460 f. Review by A. van Gennep ' La Légende de Polyphème' reprinted in his *Religions, Mœurs et Légendes* Paris 1908 i. 155—164.

[12] O. Hackman *op. cit.* p. 166 f.

ii The escape of the hero, who gets off
either (a) by clinging under a sheep, goat, ox, etc.,
or more often (β) by putting on a sheep-skin, goat-skin, ox-hide, etc.
Of these alternatives (a), which implies gigantic sheep, was earlier than
(β), which makes less demand on the hearer's credulity.

iii The attempt of the giant to recapture the hero by flinging after him a
magical ring (Dolopathos, Italy, Argyllshire, Basses-Pyrénées, Sieben-
bürgen, Bohemia),
a golden staff (Poland, Servia),
an axe with a golden or silver haft (Russia, Lithuania, Wotyaks),
a sabre (Great Russia),
a copper coin (Little Russia),
a white stone (Altai Mts.).
This episode, which probably formed part of the original tale[1], bulks big
in Russia, Galicia, Italy, and Basses-Pyrénées, but does not occur at all
in Greece.

Group B (50 variants) is marked by another episode :

iv The hero escapes detection by giving his name as 'Self' or 'Myself,'
rarely as 'Nobody' (*Odyssey*, Anjou)[2].
This *motif* belonged originally to a distinct tale, current in northern and
central Europe, which told how a man injured an elfish creature of some
sort—mermaid (Sweden), water-nixie (Germany), wood-nymph (Sweden),
fairy (France), kobold (Rügen), dwarf (Germany), or devil (eastern
Europe)—commonly by means of fire or something hot, and then eluded
the vengeance of his victim's companions by giving his name as 'Myself'
or the like[3].

Group C (47 variants) is a late combination of i (β), the blinding of the
giant by way of cure, with iv, the name-trick. It is found only in Fin-
land, Lettland, and Esthonia[4].

It will be seen from this analysis that the story of Polyphemos, as related by
Homer, includes episode i, the blinding of the giant, in its south-European
form, and episode ii, the escape of the hero, in its earlier and more miraculous
aspect, but omits episode iii, that of the magical ring, altogether[5], substituting
for it episode iv, the originally alien *motif* of the name. Homer, in short, picks
and chooses. He may tolerate a monstrous ram, but he omits mere magic, and
prefers to insert a conspicuous example of human cunning.

As regards the vexed question of ultimate significance Hackman, after
admitting that almost all investigators of the tale (Grimm, Krek, Jubainville,
Cerquand, etc.) have taken the single eye of Polyphemos to be the sun[6], reaches
the cautious conclusion : 'Das Stirnauge des Riesen, das jedenfalls schon der
Grundform angehört hat, war wohl ursprünglich ein die Sonne symbolisirendes
Attribut des Himmels- oder Sonnengottes. Doch hat diese frühzeitig in Verges-
senheit geratene mythologische Bedeutung des Stirnauges nichts mit der Sage
im Übrigen zu tun[7].'

---

[1] *Id. ib.* p. 177 ff. [2] *Id. ib.* p. 204. [3] *Id. ib.* p. 189 ff. [4] *Id. ib.* p. 206 ff.

[5] Unless indeed we may suppose that a trace of the ring-throwing subsists in the stone-
throwing of Polyphemos (A. B. C.). C. Nyrop *loc. cit.* p. 218 suggests *e contra* that the
ring-episode is itself an expansion of the Homeric stone-throwing—a view rejected by
Hackman *op. cit.* p. 177 n. 1.

[6] *Id. ib.* pp. 3 ff., 217 f. [7] *Id. ib.* p. 221 (cp. also p. 218).

With this decision I find myself in substantial agreement. I have already urged, not only that the Kyklops' eye stood for the sun in heaven[1], but also that the Kyklops himself was in the far past a sky-god like Zeus[2]. Moreover I have ventured to compare Odysseus, who plunged a heated bar into the Kyklops' eye, with Prometheus, who thrust a torch into the solar wheel[3]. The comparison might be further strengthened. It now appears that an integral part of the Kyklops-tale was the giant's gift to the hero of a magical ring[4]. This recalls the curious legend that Zeus presented Prometheus with a ring fashioned out of his chains[5]. In Germanic belief, too, the one-eyed Wodan possessed a gold ring from which every ninth night dripped eight other rings of equal weight[6]. It is difficult to avoid the conclusion that the golden rings thrown or dropped by the sky-god were at first but a naïve expression for the daily movement of the solar disk. Nevertheless I concur with Hackman's opinion that the mythological significance of these one-eyed beings had passed into oblivion long before Homer told his immortal tale. *A fortiori* it would be fatuous to seek any such hidden meaning in the modern *Märchen*. I append a few samples from Greece and Italy.

Versions from the Greek area are all more or less defective. At most they preserve episode i (*a*) together with its sequel ii (*a*) or ii (*β*). That is the case with a folk-tale from Athens and with another from Kappadokia :

(1) The Kyklops in a Folk-tale from Athens[7].

Once upon a time there was a king, whose daughter was so lovely that, if—

> ' She bade the sun, he would stand still,
> The morning star, he 'ld twinkle.'

All the princes were eager to marry her. But she refused each one who proffered his love : only the handsomest of them, who had been blessed by his mother, touched her heart at all. In the end she agreed to wed him who should bring her the golden wand of the Famous Drakos[8]. The Famous[9] Drakos was the strongest and fiercest of all the Drakoi ; he had one eye in his forehead, which remained open even when he was asleep, so that none could approach him without being eaten by him. His golden wand, if leant against a door, made it at once fly open. The princes on hearing the terms of betrothal shook with terror. But the handsome prince resolved to obtain the golden wand, or

---

[1] *Supra* i. 313, 323, 462. [2] *Supra* i. 320.
[3] *Supra* i. 325 ff. [4] *Supra* p. 989 n. 1.
[5] *Supra* i. 329 n. 0. [6] *Supra* p. 62 n. 1.

[7] Text in the Δελτίον τῆς Ἱστορικῆς καὶ Ἐθνολογικῆς Ἑταιρίας τῆς Ἑλλάδος Athens 1883 i. 147 ff. Translation (here condensed) in L. M. J. Garnett—J. S. Stuart-Glennie *Greek Folk Poesy* London 1896 ii. 80—87, 444 f. Cp. a very similar tale from Attike in G. Drosinis *Land und Leute in Nord-Euböa* trans. A. Boltz Leipzig 1884 p. 170 ff. ('Die Polyphem-Sage in modern hellenischer Gestalt aus den "Athenischen Märchen" von Frl. Maria Kampúroglu')=Hackman *op. cit.* p. 9 f. no. 1=Sir J. G. Frazer *loc. cit.* p. 439 f. no. 24.

[8] On the Δράκος or Δράκοντας of the modern Greek see B. Schmidt *Das Volksleben der Neugriechen* Leipzig 1871 i. 190—195, N. G. Polites Μελέτη ἐπὶ τοῦ βίου τῶν Νεωτέρων Ἑλλήνων Athens 1871 i. 154—172 ('Δράκοντες'), *id.* Παραδόσεις Athens 1904 i. 219—228 ('Δράκοι'), ii. 990—1002, J. C. Lawson *Modern Greek Folklore and Ancient Greek Religion* Cambridge 1910 pp. 280—283, W. R. Halliday in R. M. Dawkins *Modern Greek in Asia Minor* Cambridge 1916 pp. 219, 225 ff.

[9] With his fixed epithet ' Famous ' cp. the Homeric Πολύφημος.

die in the attempt. So he took the long road, and walked on till he was tired. He sat down under a tree and fell asleep. When he woke, he saw an old woman sifting flour into a great baking-pan. But the flour dropped on to the ground, not into the pan ; for the old woman was blind. The prince sifted the flour for her, put it into her sack, and offered to help her carry it. Pleased with his kindness, she asked what she could do for him in return. He begged her blessing and told her of his quest. 'Listen, my son,' said the old woman : 'thou hast undertaken a hard task, but thy parents' blessing and mine will give thee courage. Go straight along this road to a place where there is much grass, for no man has ever trodden it. Beyond the rising ground to which it leads thou wilt see mountains and ravines ; and thence thou wilt descry afar off a great cavern. Draw near ; and, if thou hear sounds of snoring, thou wilt know that the Drakos is asleep within. Then remain at a distance till the door of the cavern opens ; for he has his flocks inside, and puts in front a great rock, which no man can move. Wait till the Drakos drives out his flock, and then find means to hide thyself in the cavern. When he comes back to sleep and folds his flocks and closes the cavern again, then listen and from the snoring thou wilt know that he is no longer awake. Come down from thy hiding-place and step up to him. Tied to his beard is a golden key. Take these scissors that I give thee, and with them cut the beard and the key together. Then, when he opens the cavern, do thou too go out. Having escaped, take once more the grass-grown road. There thou wilt see a great palace. Lean the key against the door of the palace, and it will open to thee. Upstairs in a great chamber there will be a horse and a dog : before the horse are bones to eat ; before the dog is straw. Change them without a word, giving the bones to the dog ; and the rest thou wilt learn later from the horse.' The prince thanked the old woman, gave her some sequins, and set off. He found the cavern, but heard no snoring. He peeped in, and no one was there. But, seeing within a great caldron full of milk and a bannock as big as a mill-stone, he cut a piece of the bannock, dipped it in the milk, and ate till his hunger was satisfied. Afterwards he espied a hollow high up in the rock, climbed up, and got in. A little later he heard sheep-bells, and concluded that the Drakos was returning with his flocks. So he drew back in his hiding-place, and prayed God to help him. The Drakos entered, pulled-to the rock that closed the cavern, and sat down to eat ; but found that neither the milk nor the bannock satisfied him as usual. Now the old woman had given the prince a powder to throw into the *raki*[1] jar, so that the Drakos might sleep heavily. When, therefore, the Drakos had finished his meal and stirred the fire, he was soon snoring. The prince came softly down, cut the hairs, took the key, and climbed up again into his hiding-place. But, realising that the Drakos, when he found his key gone, would look for it, he got down and took a long pole, sharpened it, put it in the fire and, as soon as it was red-hot, stuck it into the eye of the Drakos. He, being blinded, began to roar. The other Drakoi came running to see what was the matter with their chief. But they could not remove the rock ; and, when they heard his cries, they concluded that he was drunk and went home. Then the Drakos pushed away the stone, sat at the mouth of the cave, and began to fondle and let out his sheep one by one. There was one big, woolly, ram ; and the prince placed himself on his stomach under the wool, and, while the Drakos was fondling it, managed to get out of the cave. Following the old woman's advice, he found the palace, unlocked its door with his key, and saw upstairs a splendid horse fastened with chains and a fine big dog. He

---

[1] A spirit made from grapes (ῥάξ, ῥαγίζω) and flavoured with aniseed.

duly gave the horse's pile of bones to the dog and the dog's heap of straw to the horse. Whereupon they both ate, and then began to talk. The prince related his adventures to them. And they informed him that the old woman was the Good Fate, blinded by the other Fates for her goodness and destined never to recover her sight till she found somebody to love and pity her. They further showed him a chamber containing two beautiful captive princesses, whom he was to set free. The youth did so ; and the princesses gave him the golden wand as his reward. He next loosed the horse and the dog by leaning the wand against them. Then he led the princesses downstairs, placed them on the horse, and took the dog also. But, as he was leaving the palace, the horse and the dog said : 'Look out of the window and see all those different animals. They were once handsome princes, who went out hunting, found this palace door open, and stepped inside. The Drakos saw them and, sprinkling them with a liquid, transformed them into various animals. Now touch them lightly on their backs with the wand, and they will become as they were before.' The prince did as he was bidden ; and the victims of the Drakos, thus restored to human shape, embraced their deliverer and set out for their respective palaces. The prince with the horse and the dog, after locking the Drakos' palace, returned the two princesses to their parents. He also changed the horse and the dog into two princes, who explained that they, in attempting to rescue the princesses of their choice from the Drakos, had been turned into animals by him, but now begged to become the king's sons-in-law. The king bestowed his daughters upon them, and escorted the prince that had saved them all to the door of the princess of whom he was enamoured. She lay dying of grief for his absence, and all the doors of her palace were shut in token of mourning. The prince at once leant the golden wand against each door in turn, reached the princess, and presented her with the wand. The princess embraced him, and they were married with music, drums, and great rejoicings.

(2) The Kyklops in a Folk-tale from Pharasa in Kappadokia[1].

'In a time of old there was a priest. He went to find a goat. He went to a village. There was another priest. He said : "Where are you going?" The priest said : "I am going to find a goat." He said : "Let me come too, that I also may get a goat." They rose up. They went to another village. There was there another priest. And the three of them went to another village. They found another priest. They took that priest also (with them). They went on. They became seven priests. Whilst they were on their way to a village, there was a woman. She was collecting wood. There was also a Tepekozis[2]. The Tepekozis hastened (and) seized the seven priests (and) carried them to his house. In the evening he cooked one priest. He ate him. He was fat. He ate him. He got drunk. The six priests rose up. They heated the spit. They drove it into the Tepekozis' eye. They blinded the Tepekozis. They went into the

[1] I am indebted for this tale to the kindness of my friend Prof. R. M. Dawkins, who took it down at Pharasa in the Antitauros district of Kappadokia (July 23–25, 1911) from the mouth of an urchin named Thomâs Stephánou and dictated the above rendering to me (Nov. 21, 1911). The original is in the local dialect of Greek with some admixture of Turkish words. Text and translation in R. M. Dawkins *Modern Greek in Asia Minor* Cambridge 1916 p. 550 f. no. 25 (cp. W. R. Halliday *ib.* p. 217) = Sir J. G. Frazer *loc. cit.* p. 438 f. no. 23.

[2] *Tepe* means 'hill' and here, presumably, 'head.' *Koz* is for *güz*, 'eye.' The name, therefore, appears to be ' Head-eye' or ' Eye-in-head '—a Turkish Kyklops.

stable. The Tepekozis had seven hundred sheep. They entered the stable. They flayed six sheep. They left the heads and the tails (with the skins). They crawled into the skins. In the morning the Tepekozis rose up. He drove out the sheep. He took them by the head and by the tail. He drove out the seven hundred sheep. He shut the doors[1]. He went inside. He looked for the six priests. He could not find them. He found the six sheep killed. The six priests took the seven hundred sheep. They went to their houses. They gave also a hundred sheep to the wife of the priest whom the Tepekozis had eaten. The woman said : "Where is my priest?" They said : "He has stopped behind to make further gains." And the six priests took a hundred sheep apiece. They went to their houses. They ate. They drank. They attained their destinies.'

More often we meet with single episodes of the Kyklops-tale isolated from their proper context and worked into other narratives. For example, episode i (a), the blinding of the giant with a red-hot spit or the like, was a thrilling incident suitable to a variety of situations and sure to please. It occurs alone on the Greek mainland :

(3) The Blinding of the Kyklops in a Folk-tale from Gortynia[2].

'One of us men in olden days wanted to travel through the whole world. In a certain region he found men who were very tall but had only one eye apiece. The wife of a One-eye, in whose house he lodged, hid him in the evening ; for in the daytime her husband was not there—he was a bad character and ate men. When her husband came home and entered the house, he told her that he smelt something ; but his wife said it was nothing at all. The One-eye didn't believe her. He got up, groped about, found the man, and wanted to eat him. He put him in his apron along with his supper. But when he tasted his bread, without noticing, for his thoughts were elsewhere, he grasped the man too in the hollow of his hand and thrust him into his mouth. But he stuck in a hole of his tooth, without the tooth getting a real grip on him. After he had pulled him out he let him live, to please his wife, since he was hardly worth eating. But next day he changed his mind and again wanted to eat him. His wife then made her husband drunk, got the stranger out secretly and sent him packing. But, before the wife sent him off, he thrust a big burning coal into the eye of the drunken One-eye and blinded him. And so he punished the bad character, who could no longer see to eat men. When he left, the wife asked his name, and he said : "They call me World-traveller[3]" ; for he had seen and learnt much of the world.'

[1] θύρε, plural of θύρι : cp. *Od.* 9. 240, 313, 340 θυρεὸν μέγαν.

[2] Text in N. G. Polites Παραδόσεις Athens 1904 i. 70 f. no. 134 Ὁ μονομμάτης, ii. 752 ff. (recorded at Lasta in the deme Mylaon in Gortynia, a district of the Morea). Translation by K. Dieterich in the *Zeitschrift des Vereins für Volkskunde* 1905 xv. 381 = Sir J. G. Frazer *loc. cit.* p. 441 no. 26. I follow Dieterich.

At Arachova on Mt Parnassos the name Μονόμματοι (or Μονόματοι) is given to a race of wild and impious men believed to inhabit a foreign land of unknown situation and to have but a single eye in their forehead. The same expression is applied to people, who in character and behaviour resemble these mythical savages (B. Schmidt *Das Volksleben der Neugriechen* Leipzig 1871 i. 203). For instance, in Akarnania the natives of Xeromeros detest the uncivilised and unsociable mountaineers of Baltos and speak of them as μονομάται, 'one-eyed' monsters (L. Heuzey *Le Mont Olympe et l'Acarnanie* Paris 1860 p. 259).

[3] " Μὲ λένε Κοσμοτριγυριστή." Cp. *Od.* 1. 1 ff.

The same *motif* is woven into tales of different texture from Zakynthos and Kypros :

(4) The Blinding of the Kyklops in a Folk-tale from Zakynthos[1].

Once upon a time there was a certain king's daughter. Three days after her birth came the Fates, who declared that during the fifteenth year of her life she must hide herself from the sun, on pain of becoming a lizard, falling into the sea, and remaining there for five months. As the destined time drew near, the maid saddened and her father tried to divert his thoughts by travelling. Before he set out on his journey he asked his daughter what he could do for her. She begged him to contract a marriage on her behalf with the Giant of the Mountain[2]. The king then went abroad and reached at last the Giant's town, where he heard say that the Giant meant to marry the fairest maiden in the world. He also made friends with the barber that clipped the Giant's beard and enjoyed the Giant's confidence. The Giant himself proved to be a one-eyed monster, who wore seven veils over his face : he lived with many others of his kind in a hollow mountain, where they dug for treasure and hewed out vast building-stones for their houses. Prompted by the barber, the king claimed to be the Giant's son, and, in proof of his assertion, let the giant strike him with a huge pole: he evaded the blow by receiving it on a big leather bag[3]. He then removed the Giant's veils, and was thanked for his pains. When he broached the subject of his errand, the Giant took him into a chamber apart, showed him many paintings of maidens, and asked whether his daughter resembled any of them. The king replied that these were not worthy even to wash his daughter's feet. The Giant next drew from his breast a miniature, and repeated his question. The king again answered that his daughter's chamber-maid looked like that. So the Giant agreed to wed the king's daughter, if she was as beautiful as her father declared[4]. The king went home and reported his success. His daughter made herself ready, and, in order to avoid the sun-light, came in a litter with her nurse and her nurse's daughter. But, when they were on board ship nearing the coast, the nurse dropped a costly kerchief and begged the princess to have the door of the litter opened that she might recover it. Here-

---

[1] Text unpublished. Translation (here summarised) in B. Schmidt *Griechische Märchen, Sagen und Volkslieder* Leipzig 1877 pp. 98—104 no. 13 ('Der Riese vom Berge'), 230 f.=Hackman *op. cit.* p. 11 f. no. 3. The tale is a variant of a type first described by R. Köhler in L. Gonzenbach *Sicilianische Märchen* Leipzig 1870 ii. 225 ff. as 'das M. von dem Bruder und seiner schönen Schwester' and later studied in detail by P. Arfert *Das Motiv von der unterschobenen Braut in der internationalen Erzählungs-literatur* Rostock 1897 : see J. Bolte—G. Polívka *Anmerkungen zu den Kinder- u. Hausmärchen der Brüder Grimm* Leipzig 1913 i. 79 ff., 1918 iii. 85 ff.

[2] τὸν γίγαντα τοῦ βουνοῦ. In Zakynthos giants, with a long beard on their chin and a single eye that sparkles like fire in their forehead, are said to live underground, where they quarry huge stones for building towers and cause the earthquakes that are so frequent in this island. They are the children of a devil and a *Lámnissa* (Lamia) or a witch ; and their wives spin yarn with spindles of such monstrous size and weight that once, when the giants made war on a certain king, their wives flung these spindles at the enemy and so slew thousands (B. Schmidt *Das Volksleben der Neugriechen* Leipzig 1871 i. 200 f.).

[3] For a similar incident see 'The Scab-pate,' a folk-tale from Astypalaia (J. Pio ΝΕΟΕΛΛΗΝΙΚΑ ΠΑΡΑΜΥΘΙΑ *Contes populaires grecs* Copenhague 1879 p. 162 f., E. M. Geldart *Folk-Lore of Modern Greece* London 1884 p. 157).

[4] A similar situation occurs in a folk-tale from Epeiros (J. Pio *op. cit.* p. 17, E. M. Geldart *op. cit.* p. 37 f. 'The Golden Wand ').

upon the sun shone in, and the princess, transformed at once into a lizard, fell into the sea. The nurse, having thus gained her end, substituted her own daughter for the princess. The Giant of the Mountain came out to meet them, riding on a high horse, with a sceptre in his right hand and a sword in his left. On opening the litter, he and the father of the bride were equally astonished to find an ugly wench instead of a beautiful princess. But, as the nurse explained that in five months' time the bride would regain her good looks, the Giant received her into his mountain along with her mother, though he punished the king by making him an ostler for a term of five years. The Giant's practice was to leave the mountain at dawn and return to it in the evening. He told his young wife that she might enter all the rooms of his castle except one. Curiosity forced her to enter the forbidden apartment, where she found the mother of the giants. This portentous creature was sitting on a stool, holding in one hand a large stone set in plates of gold and in the other an iron staff. Being able to predict the future, she told the would-be queen that she would live to rue her deceit, since the real princess was yet alive and already on her track. The maid fled and told her mother, who, to secure the death of the princess, informed the Giant that his wife was ill and wished all the fish in the harbour to be burnt before her eyes. This was done ; but the princess had already escaped the water and been restored to her former shape. She found her father, who brought her to the Giant. The mother of the giants bade her son treat the nurse's daughter as the nurse's daughter had been minded to treat the princess ; and the false bride was accordingly burnt. The Giant then married the princess and sent her father home a free man. Some months later the giant began to ill-treat his wife, because she was more friendly with his mother than he cared to be. The Giant's wife therefore fled on a ship to her former home. The Giant himself followed her, and bribed a goldsmith to shut him in a large golden coffer and sell him as a saint's relic to the king's daughter. The king's daughter bought the coffer, and proceeded to say her prayers before it. But, while thus engaged, she heard a slight noise, *zicki zicki*, and detected the Giant within. She shrieked aloud. Soldiers came up, ran a red-hot spit through the key-hole of the coffer, and so bored out the eye of the Giant inside it[1]. They then took him and struck him on the ankle-bones till he died.

(5) The Three-eyed Ogre in a Folk-tale from Kypros[2].

A woodcutter's eldest daughter once married a passing merchant, who gave her a hundred and one keys. She might open a hundred chambers in his house, but not the one over. For all that, she opened it. Looking from its window she saw a ghastly sight. First, a corpse was borne out to burial without friends or mourners. Then, her husband appeared among the tombs, made himself a head as big as a sieve, three eyes, enormously long arms and hideous nails. With

---

[1] In a folk-tale from Syra (E. M. Geldart *op. cit.* p. 16 f. ' The two brothers and the forty-nine dragons') the hero kills the Drakoi by thrusting red-hot spits through the chests in which they are concealed.

[2] Text in A. Sakellarios Τὰ Κυπριακά Athens 1868 iii. 136 ff. Translation (here condensed) in É. Legrand *Recueil de contes populaires grecs* Paris 1881 pp. xiv, 115—131 'Le Trimmatos ou l'ogre aux trois yeux.' The tale falls under the thirtieth or ' Bluebeard '-*formula* of J. G. von Hahn *Griechische und albanische Märchen* Leipzig 1864 i. 56, on which see T. F. Crane *Italian Popular Tales* London 1885 p. 77 ff. and J. Bolte—G. Polívka *Anmerkungen zu den Kinder- u. Hausmärchen der Brüder Grimm* Leipzig 1913 i. 13 ff., 370 ff., and especially 398 ff.

these he dug up the dead body and devoured it. At this she fell sick of a fever. Her husband returned, and found reason to suspect her of entering the forbidden room. He transformed himself successively into her mother, her relatives, and her nurse. In this final disguise he induced her to say what she had seen. He then suddenly turned into a Trimmatos or 'Three-eyed' ogre again, and prepared to eat her for not having kept his secret. Kindling a brasier, the flames of which licked the sky, he thrust into it a spit till it became red-hot, and went to fetch his wife. She begged for two hours' respite, slipped out of the window, and besought first a carter and next a camel-driver to hide her from the Trimmatos. The camel-driver took pity on her and concealed her in a bale of cotton. Meantime the ogre had discovered her escape. Starting in pursuit, he soon came up with the carter, who sent him on to the camel-driver. He thrust his glowing spit into each bale belonging to the latter before he was satisfied and took his departure. The spit had wounded his wife's foot. But the camel-driver took her, still in the bale, to the king's palace and told the king her story. The royal physician cured her foot; and she showed such skill in embroidery that the king and queen chose her as their daughter-in-law. She, fearing the vengeance of the ogre, bargained that the wedding should take place at night, that a bridal chamber should be built reached by seven flights of steps, that these steps should be strewn with chick-peas, that two pits should be dug at the bottom of the lowest flight and covered with matting, and that no one should be told a word about it all. Nevertheless the matter came to the ears of the Trimmatos, who, disguised as a merchant, repaired to the palace with negroes in his sacks. His former wife saw through his disguise, and signed to the queen to ask him what wares he had brought. He replied that he had pistachio-nuts, dried apricots, and chestnuts. The bride then said that she was indisposed and would like some of these fruits. The merchant tried to put her off till the morrow; but the king's jester, who was at table, went out to sample the wares and brought back word about the negroes. These were at once put to death. The merchant, however, made his escape. The same night he took the form of a Trimmatos once more, mounted to the bridal chamber, cast the dust of a corpse on the bride-groom to make him sleep soundly, seized the bride and dragged her off to be spitted for his meal. But on the way she gave him a sudden push; he slipped on the chick-peas, and fell into the pit, where he was devoured himself by a lion and a tiger. The bride fainted on the staircase. Next morning the physician brought the happy couple to their senses again; and the subsequent festivities lasted forty days and forty nights.

Again, episode ii (β), the escape of the hero in a sheep-skin, forms part of a wonder-voyage entitled *George and the Storks*, which was related to L. Ross by a native of Psara or Ipsara, an island off the west coast of Chios:

(6) The Blind Kyklops in a Folk-tale from Psara[1].

Long, long ago there lived at Therapia near Constantinople a poor sailor, who bade three of his children—Dimitri, Michael, and George—go out into the world and seek their fortunes. So they took service with a captain and made many trips to Marseilles, Leghorn, Trieste, to Smyrna, to Alexandria, and to other Mediterranean ports. After two years they joined the crew of a fine frigate bound on a voyage of discovery. Passing through the Straits of

---

[1] L. Ross *Erinnerung und Mittheilungen aus Griechenland* Berlin 1863 pp. 279—298 'Georg und die Störche' = O. Hackman *op. cit.* p. 10 f. no. 2 = Sir J. G. Frazer *loc. cit.* p. 440 f. no. 25. I abbreviate from Ross.

Gibraltar into the ocean beyond, they were caught by a terrible storm and driven for months before it. Their provisions were spent and they were starving. When one of their company died, the rest cut up, cooked, and ate his body. Then day by day they drew lots to determine who should be killed and eaten. Some ten days had elapsed when the lot fell on George, who had just had a happy dream of reaching shore. He persuaded his shipmates to spare him till the evening, and at midday land was sighted on the horizon. The crew, overjoyed, thanked God and St Nikolaos, and hastily rowed ashore. Here the three brothers got separated from the others, lost their way, and had to spend the night up a tree. The same thing happened on the morrow, and it was not till the morning of the third day that they got out of the wood.

On the plain beyond they saw a magnificent castle. A narrow door led into a wide courtyard, in which they found a great flock of sheep, but no trace of human beings. The castle too seemed quite unoccupied. They passed from room to room till they entered a banqueting-hall, where a feast was set out. Unable to make anybody hear, they at last sat down to eat, when suddenly through the door came a monstrous, misshapen, blind Drakos. In a voice which froze the blood in their veins he cried : 'I smell the flesh of men, I smell the flesh of men !' Pale with terror, they sprang from their seats. But the Drakos, guided by the sound, stretched out his hideous long claws and seized by the neck first Dimitri and then Michael. He dashed them to pieces on the floor. George alone escaped, being nimble, and slipped out into the courtyard. He found the little door fast-closed and the walls too high to climb. What was he to do? Terror suggested a plan. Whether it was that he had heard of the famous hero Odysseus[1], or thought of it now for himself, he drew his sharp seaman's knife, killed the biggest ram in the flock, stripped off its skin, threw the carcase into a well, wrapped himself in the skin, and attempted to creep out on all fours, as if he were a ram. Meantime the Drakos had finished his horrible meal, and came waddling down the marble steps, shouting : 'You shall not escape me, you shall make me a tasty supper !' He crossed the court to the little door, threw it open, and blocked the way with his ungainly body, leaving just room enough for one sheep to pass. Then he called his ewes one by one, milked them, and let them go through. Last came the rams, with George in their midst. He approached with fear and trembling. But the Drakos only stroked his back, praised his size and strength, and set him too at liberty.

Once safely outside, George fled to the nearest wood, wandered about in it, and on the third day reached a wide plain, where there was a large town built round a king's castle. But again all seemed empty and deserted. This time he did not venture into the castle, but lodged in an ordinary house. He had stayed there for rather more than five months, when one day he caught sight of a great army crossing the plain. He fled in alarm to a bakery and hid in the kneading-trough. Here he was discovered on the third day by the baker and taken before the king, by whom he was kindly treated. For six months he lived with the baker and helped in his work. Then one morning the inhabitants all collected on the plain, and the king despatched his people in troops to England, France, Italy, Smyrna, and the Dardanelles. Before George could ask the reason, they all went off towards a broad river at some distance from the town,

---

[1] It may be thought that this allusion proves the influence of the Homeric narrative. But observe that Odysseus' expedient was *not* that adopted by George. The former clung on beneath a living ram (ii (α)), the latter donned the fleece of a dead ram (ii (β)).

plunged into it, and emerged on the other side as so many bands of storks !
George now woke up to the fact that this was the land of the storks. Six months
later he witnessed their return. A whole cloud of them settled on the further
bank of the river, dived into it, and came out on the near side as men[1]. He
eagerly questioned them about Therapia, and begged the king to send him
thither. The king assured him that this was impossible, unless he would con-
sent to become a stork himself. Anxious to revisit his home, George agreed.
So, when spring came round, he too dived into the river of transformation, and
came out as a fine stork with long red beak, white feathers, and black wings.
He flew to Therapia, married a beautiful she-bird, and built his nest on the roof
of his father's house. He was so tame that he was soon welcomed in, and
picked up crumbs under the low table with his long beak. When his old mother
stroked his head and fed him with tit-bits, he chattered his best and made a
hundred grotesque gestures to show his love and gratitude. But he could not
make his kinsfolk understand that he was their long-lost George. At length he
resolved to play a trick upon his sister Kathinko. She had a pair of silver
armlets, which she had inherited from her grandmother. Waiting his opportunity, he carried off one of these and hid it in his nest. Kathinko and her
mother looked for it in vain ; they never thought of the stork. Meantime summer
slipped away, and the storks departed—George among them. On reaching the
land of the storks he begged the king to contrive his home-coming. So some
weeks later the king had a boat built, laden with food, and launched on a river
which flowed behind the town. He gave George a sack full of his costliest gems,
and let him drift down the strong stream. After some hours the river plunged
into a *katabóthra* and flowed for many hundreds of miles through a rocky
channel. This must have taken weeks, though George lost count of days and
nights in the darkness. At last he saw in the distance a star, which proved to
be the daylight at the end of the channel. His boat was swept out into the open,
and he saw before him the town of Smyrna ; in fact, he found himself on the
river[2] which gushes out of the rocks near that town. He went into the town and
secured a lodging, but returned to his boat the same evening and fetched his
bag of precious stones. Next day he sold a dozen of them to some Jews for two
tons of gold. With this he bought fine clothes, a number of necessaries, and a
big frigate, in which he sailed for Constantinople. He cast anchor off Therapia,
saluted his birthplace by firing a number of guns, and invited on board the elders
of the place. They came in their best clothes, and it so chanced that George's
old father brought their boat alongside. George welcomed them to his table,
but insisted that the old sailor must join their company and gave him a seat next
himself. He sent each man away with a handful of gold pieces, and bade them
come and feast with him on the morrow, only bargaining that the old sailor
should bring his family with him[3]. When the hour arrived, he set wine before
them and told them all of his wonderful experiences. 'Among other things,'
said he, ' I was once a stork, and that here in Therapia.' At this all laughed and
thought it a mere joke. But George proved the truth of his words by bidding a

---

[1] The metamorphosis of storks into men in return for their filial piety is already noticed
by Alexander of Myndos (*c.* 1—50 A.D.) (Ail. *de nat. an.* 3. 23 Ἀλέξανδρος δὲ ὁ Μύνδιός
φησιν, ὅταν ἐς γῆρας ἀφίκωνται (*sc.* οἱ πελαργοί), παρελθόντας αὐτοὺς ἐς τὰς Ὠκεανίτιδας
νήσους ἀμείβειν τὰ εἴδη ἐς ἀνθρώπου μορφήν, καὶ εὐσεβείας γε τῆς ἐς τοὺς γειναμένους
ἆθλον τοῦτο ἴσχειν, κ.τ.λ. See further D'Arcy W. Thompson *A Glossary of Greek
Birds* Oxford 1895 p. 129 and O. Keller *Die antike Tierwelt* Leipzig 1913 ii. 196 f.

[2] The river Meles.   [3] Perhaps a reminiscence of Gen. 42. 14 ff.

servant mount the old sailor's roof and fetch thence the armlet hidden in a stork's nest. He did so, and Kathinko recognised her trinket. Hereupon the old mother would have died of surprise, had she not been kept alive by joy at the recovery of her son. George settled in Therapia, built a fine house there, and maintained his parents in plenty. He endowed his sisters well and married them to honest men. He put up monuments to his luckless brothers and gave a dona-tion to a church for masses to be said on their behalf. His descendants are well-to-do folk still living at Therapia and in the neighbourhood.

Lastly, episode iv, the name-trick, is the main feature of *The Three Thieves*, a very much transmogrified tale from Lesbos :

(7) The Name-trick in a Folk-tale from Lesbos[1].

' Once there was a good man whose fortune was in the sun[2]. He went out on the hill, and saw three thieves who had killed a goat. They told him to cook it. Well, as they say, "a thief among thieves, and a liar among liars[3]"; so he nodded without speaking, and did as he was bid. They asked him his name, and he said Ἀπατός—" Mr Self." When he had cooked the goat, he beat the three thieves soundly with the spit[4], and they ran off howling. People asked them who did it? " Self!" said they, and got laughed at for their pains.'

An Albanian version, recorded at Piana de' Greci near Palermo, recognises two Kyklopes and gives each of them two pairs of eyes :

(8) The Kyklopes in an Albanian Folk-tale[5].

' Once on a time there were two men travelling. Night fell upon them by the way, and it rained and thundered. Poor fellows, just think what a plight they were in ! They saw a light far off and said, "Let's go and see if we can pass the night where that light is." And they went and came to the cave, for a cave it was where the light shone. They went in and saw that there were sheep and rams and two Cyclopes[6], who had two eyes in front and two behind. The Cyclopes saw them come in and said one to the other, " Go to, here we have got something to eat." And they proposed to eat the two men. The poor fellows stayed there two days ; then the Cyclopes felt the back of their necks and said, " Good ! We'll eat one of them to-morrow." Meantime they made them eat to fatten them. For in the evening they would take a sheep and a ram, roast them on spits over the fire, and compel the poor wretches to devour them, entrails and all, just to fatten them. And every now and then they would feel the back of their necks, and one would say to the other, " They're getting on very well ! " But the two men said to each other by words or signs, " Let us see whether we can escape." Now, as I said, two days passed, and on the second day the Cyclopes fell asleep and slumbered with all their eyes open. Nevertheless, when the two men saw the Cyclopes sleeping, they took the spits on which the sheep had been roasted, and they heated them in the fire. Then they took rams' skins

---

[1] Reported by W. H. D. Rouse in *Folk-Lore* 1896 vii. 154 f. =O. Hackman *op. cit.* p. 107 no. 125.

[2] ἡ τύχη του ἦτο 's τὸν ἥλιον, *i.e.* he had no means of subsistence.

[3] κλέφτης μὲ τοὺς κλέφταις, καὶ ψεύτης μὲ τοὺς ψεύταις, *i.e.* do at Rome as the Romans do.

[4] An attentuated form of episode i (*a*).

[5] D. Comparetti *Novelline popolari Italiane* Torino 1875 pp. 308—310 no. 70=O. Hackman *op. cit.* p. 12 f. no. 4=Sir J. G. Frazer *loc. cit.* p. 441 f. no. 27. I transcribe Frazer's rendering.

[6] O. Hackman *op. cit.* p. 13 takes *ciclopi* to be a popular, not a learned, appellation : he cites *ciropiddhu* as a dialect form from Messina (*ib.* p. 16 no. 9 and p. 169).

and clothed themselves in them, and going down on all fours they walked about in the rams' skins. Meanwhile the spits were heated, and each of the men took two, and going softly up to the sleeping Cyclopes, they jabbed the hot spits into their eyes. After that, they went down on all fours like sheep. The Cyclopes awoke blind, and gave themselves up for lost. But they took their stand at the door, each at a doorpost, just as they were, with all the spits sticking in their eyes. They let out all the sheep that were in the cave, saying, "The sheep will go out, and the men will stay in," and they felt the fleeces of the sheep to see whether the men were going out too. But the men had the sheep-skins on their backs, and they went on all fours, and when the Cyclopes felt them, they thought they were sheep. So the men escaped with their life, and when they were some way off, they put off the skins. Either the Cyclopes died or they know themselves what they did. That is the end of the story.'

A Sicilian tale from Erice, which G. Pitrè had from the lips of a girl only eight years old, contains the same two episodes—i (a), the blinding of the giant by means of a hot poker, and ii (β), the escape of the hero by putting on a sheep-skin :

(9) The Kyklops in a Sicilian Folk-tale[1].

' A couple of monks, one big, the other little, were once off on their yearly round, begging for the church, when they lost their way. However, they pushed on and came to a large cave, where a strange creature, a devil if they had but known it, was engaged in making a fire. Hoping to obtain shelter for the night, they entered the cave, and found the monster killing a sheep and roasting it. He had already killed and roasted a score of them, for he kept sheep in his cave. The monster bade the monks eat. At first they refused, saying that they were not hungry. But he forced them to fall to and finish the meal. They then went to bed. The monster took an enormous rock and placed it in front of the cave. Next he seized a huge iron poker with a sharp point, heated it, and thrust it through the neck of the bigger monk. He roasted the body, and asked his companion whether he would help eat it. The little monk said that he would not, because he was already full. The monster thereupon threatened to murder him, unless he would get up and eat. So in sheer terror he sprang up, sat at the table, and took a tiny morsel, but at once cast it on the floor. "Maria!" he cried, "I'm full, I am indeed!" In the course of the night the good man himself got hold of the poker, heated it, and stuck it into the monster's eyes, which gushed out of his head. The monster cried out in pain ; and the monk in alarm slipped on a sheep-skin. Afterwards the monster, feeling his way to the mouth of the cave, raised the stone by which it was shut, and let his sheep out one by one. The monk made his escape among them, and got away to the coast at Trapani, where he told his story to some fishermen. Finally, the monster went fishing, but, being blind, fell over a rock and broke his skull. The sea grew red with his blood. Thus the young man went off, while the monster stayed there.'

Italian versions of the tale, as compared with Greek, are at once more numerous and less defective—a fact which suggests that the original centre of diffusion was Italy rather than Greece. Examples from the Abruzzo and from

---

[1] G. Pitrè *Fiabe novelle e racconti popolari siciliani* Palermo 1875 i (=*Biblioteca delle tradizioni popolari siciliane* iv) p. lxxxviii ff., ii. 1 ff. no. 51 ' Lu munacheddu' (for the dialect see A. Traina *Nuovo vocabolario siciliano-italiano* Palermo 1868)= T. F. Crane *Italian Popular Tales* London 1885 pp. 89 f., 345 n. 31 =O. Hackman *op. cit.* p. 15 no. 8= Sir J. G. Frazer *loc. cit.* p. 437 f. no. 22. I translate from Pitrè.

the neighbourhood of Rome contain, not only episodes i (*a*), the blinding, and ii (β), the escape, but also iii, the *motif* of the magical ring :

(10) The Kyklops in a Folk-tale from Roccascalegna in the Abruzzo[1].

'Four and twenty school-boys once went out for a walk. When they had gone a good distance, night came on. " We had better return," said the youngest of them, " or our master will scold us." " No," cried all the rest, " let us go to yonder inn." They did so, and knocked at the door. A voice from within asked : " Who is it ? " " Friends," they replied. " I'm so glad you've come ! " said Eye-on-forehead. He then made them enter and set about cooking a sheep in a caldron without skinning it first. The boys, disgusted, would not eat. Next day Eye-on-forehead seized a boy, and set about cooking him in the caldron ; but the others would not eat him either. One by one Eye-on-forehead ate them all. Only one was left, the shrewdest of them all, and he said to Eye-on-forehead : " Why do you eat human flesh ? " And Eye-on-forehead answered him : " Out of spite, because I've only one eye." " Then," continued the school-boy, "if I grow you another eye[2], will you let me go free ? " " Yes," replied Eye-on-forehead. Thereupon the boy made the spit red-hot on the hearth, and said to Eye-on-forehead : " Shut your eye." He took that spit and drove it into the eye till it came out the other side. Eye-on-forehead was furious and wanted to eat him ; but how could he see where the rascal was standing? Every day he used to send his sheep out to pasture, and seated himself in the door-way so as to prevent the boy from getting past ; and he felt each sheep as it went by him. One day the boy dropped into the pen, skinned a sheep, put on its fleece and tried walking on all fours. When the time for pasture had come, Eye-on-forehead, thinking he was a sheep, sent him out. Once outside, the boy began to shout : " I'm out ! I'm out ! " Eye-on-forehead, thus informed, took and flung a ring. This ring went straight on to the finger of the boy and he could not stir from where he stood. What could he do ? Eye-on-forehead, groping round, was like to catch him again. But an idea struck him : he would cut off the finger, on which that cursed ring was ; and so he did. Having cut it off, he began to hurry away. Eye-on-forehead found the finger, ate it, and said to the boy as he ran : " So you didn't want me to eat your flesh ? But for all that I've had a taste of it ! " The boy got back home and told his mother all about it.'

(11) The Kyklops in a Folk-tale from the vicinity of Rome[3].

A master was travelling with his servant through a wide wood. They came to a great cavern, where dwelt the Occhiaro ('Bright-eye'), a monster with only

---

[1] G. Finamore *Tradizioni popolari Abruzzesi* Lanciano 1882 i (Novelle) 190 f. no. 38 'Lu fatte dell' uocchie-'n-frónde.' = O. Hackman *op. cit.* p. 17 no. 10. I translate from Finamore. For a very similar version (i (*a*) + ii (β) + iii), likewise from the Abruzzo, see A. de Nino *Usi e costumi Abruzzesi* Firenze 1883 iii (Fiabe) 305—307 = Sir J. G. Frazer *loc. cit.* p. 416 ff. no. 7.

[2] Episode i (*a*) is here crossed by episode i (β), the southern by the northern form (*supra* p. 988). The same contamination is found in a variant from Vasto in the Abruzzo (G. Finamore *Tradizioni popolari Abruzzesi* Lanciano 1886 ii (Novelle) 57 f. no. 68 'La favulette dell' ucchie-'m-brande ' = O. Hackman *op. cit.* p. 17 f. no. 11). Episode (β) takes the place of i (*a*) in a version recorded at Pisa (D. Comparetti (*Novelline popolari Italiane* Torino 1875 pp. 192—195 no. 44 'Il Fiorentino' = O. Hackman *op. cit.* p. 18 f. no. 12 = Sir J. G. Frazer *loc. cit.* p. 418 f. no. 8).

[3] C. Nyrop ' Sagnet om Odysseus og Polyphem ' in the *Nordisk Tidskrift for Filologi* 1881 v. 239—240 = O. Hackman *op. cit.* p. 13 f. no. 5. I translate from Hackman.

one big brilliant eye. The Occhiaro closed the cavern with a great stone, and then slaughtered the servant and ate him up. After that he lay down and went to sleep. The master drew his sword, plunged it into the Occhiaro's eye, and so blinded him. The Occhiaro howled till the cavern rang again. In the night the man slaughtered a sheep and wrapped himself in its skin. Next morning the Occhiaro let the sheep out of the cavern one by one and felt them as he did it. The man in the sheep-skin luckily got out and then mocked at the Occhiaro. He flung him a ring, with which to make himself invisible. The man stuck the ring on his finger. Thereupon the Occhiaro cried : ' Hold fast, ring, till I come.' The man could no longer stir from the spot ; so he chopped the finger off with his sword and made his escape.

To pursue the subject beyond the limits of Greece and Italy would be beside my purpose. But it must of course be borne in mind that the variants noted in classical lands are essentially similar to those collected from the rest of Europe. A single specimen will suffice to make this clear, and may at the same time show how such a tale, drifting along the current of popular mouth-to-mouth transmission, may attach itself to some landmark or salient feature of the countryside and become fixed as a local legend with names of persons and places all complete.

(12) The Kyklops in an English Folk-tale.

In 1879 S. Baring-Gould contributed the following paragraph to W. Henderson's *Folk-Lore of the Northern Counties*[1] : 'At Dalton, near Thirsk, in Yorkshire, is a mill. It has quite recently been rebuilt, but when I was at Dalton, six years ago, the old building stood. In front of the house was a long mound, which went by the name of "the giant's grave[2]," and in the mill was shown a long blade of iron something like a scythe-blade, but not curved, which was said to have been the giant's knife[3]. A curious story was told of this knife. There lived a giant at this mill, and he ground men's bones to make his bread. One day he captured a lad on Pilmoor, and instead of grinding him in the mill he kept him as his servant and never let him get away. Jack served the giant many years and never was allowed a holiday. At last he could bear it no longer. Topcliffe fair was coming on, and the lad entreated that he might be allowed to go there to see the lasses and buy some spice. The giant surlily refused leave ; Jack resolved to take it. The day was hot, and after dinner the giant lay down in the mill with his head on a sack and dozed. He had been eating in the mill and had laid down a great loaf of bone bread by his side, and the knife was in his hand, but his fingers relaxed their hold of it in sleep. Jack seized the moment, drew the knife away, and holding it with both hands drove the blade into the single eye of the giant, who woke with a howl of agony, and starting up

---

[1] W. Henderson *Notes on the Folk-Lore of the Northern Counties of England and the Borders* London 1879 p. 194 f., S. Baring-Gould ' The Giant of New Mills, Sessay ' [Dalton is in the parish of Sessay] in *Folk-Lore* 1890 i. 130 = O. Hackman *op. cit.* p. 33 no. 28 = Sir J. G. Frazer *loc. cit.* p. 430 f. no. 18.

[2] S. Baring-Gould in W. Henderson *op. cit.* p. 196 n. adds : ' I am told by one of our servants from Dalton that at the rebuilding of the farm the mound was opened, and a stone coffin found in it ; but whether this be a kistvaen or a mediæval sarcophagus I cannot tell.'

[3] *Id.* in *Folk-Lore loc. cit.* says further : 'in the mill was shown...the giant's...stone porridge-basin or lather-dish.'

barred the door. Jack was again in difficulties, but he soon found a way out of them. The giant had a favourite dog which had also been sleeping when his master was blinded. Jack killed the dog, skinned it, and throwing the hide over his back ran on all fours barking between the legs of the giant, and so escaped.'

APPENDIX F.

THE DIOSKOUROI AND HELENE IN MODERN FOLK-TALES.

Attention may here be called to a group of modern Greek and Italian folk-tales, which are related to the myth of the Dioskouroi, as I shall presently point out. The group was first recognised as such by that excellent investigator J. G. von Hahn, who included it under his fourth or 'expulsion' *formula*, though he failed fully to perceive its affinity with classical myths[1].

(a) Sun, Moon, and Star in a Folk-tale from Greece.

(1) A good example of the group in question is the modern Greek story of the *Tzitzinaina*, which runs as follows[2]. An old woman once had three daughters, poor and hard-working girls. The eldest said: 'If I had for husband the king's pastry-man, I should eat cake.' The second said: 'If I had his cook, I should taste all the royal dishes.' The third said: 'I would like the king himself. Then I should have all his treasures, and should bear him three children, Sun, Moon, and Star.' It so chanced that the king overheard them talking and granted their several desires. But when the third sister became queen, she was hated by the king's mother. She was about to bring forth Sun, when the king was called off to a war and entrusted her to his mother. This cruel woman bade the midwife put the new-born babe in a box, fling it into the sea, and place a puppy dog instead beside the queen. The same sorry scene was enacted a second and a third time. A cat was substituted for Moon, and a snake for Star, the children being each in turn sent adrift on the sea. The king, disappointed and angry, walled up the queen in the jakes. The children one after the other were washed up at the foot of a mountain, on which dwelt a hermit. He cared for them till they were grown and then sent the two brothers Sun and Moon with their sister Star to the neighbouring town. Meantime the midwife had learnt of the children's escape and, wishing to destroy them, sought out Star and told her that she was beautiful but might be more so, if only she possessed the golden apple kept by forty dragons in a garden. Sun, who had been out to the bazar and bought of a Jew a mysterious box, now opened it, found inside a green winged horse and set out upon him to get the golden apple. The horse caused a flash of lightning and a clap of thunder, under cover of which Sun secured the apple and brought it back to Star. Again the midwife passed by and told Star that she needed, to make her more beautiful still, the golden bough on which all the birds of the world met to sing. Sun remounted his horse, which, as before, promised to lighten and thunder and advised

---

[1] J. G. von Hahn *Griechische und albanesische Märchen* Leipzig 1864 i. 46, T. F. Crane *Italian Popular Tales* London 1885 pp. 17, 325. On the 'expulsion' *formula* see *infra* p. 1012.

[2] Text by G. Ch. B. in the Νεοελληνικὰ ἀνάλεκτα Athens 1871 i. 17 ff., French translation by É. Legrand *Recueil de contes populaires grecs* Paris 1881 pp. 77—93. I have condensed Legrand's version.

his master to take a hatchet to cut a branch from the tree. Sun did so, and returned in safety with the golden bough. Once more the midwife passed by, and this time suggested that Star, to perfect her beauty, needed the Tzitzinaina, who knew the language of the birds and could explain their song. But to obtain the Tzitzinaina proved a harder task. For, when Sun and his horse reached her house and thrice summoned her to come forth, she turned them both into marble, first up to the knees, next up to the thighs, and then up to the waist. At this crisis the young man remembered that he had about him some hairs from the beard of the hermit, which he was to burn if ever he required assistance. He burnt one now. The hermit appeared, and bade the Tzitzinaina restore to life all those whom she had petrified. She sprinkled them with water of immortality and so recovered them. Among the rescued was Moon, whom his brother and sister had lost. The hermit now made the Tzitzinaina act as their mother. She explained to them the language of the birds and everything else that they wanted to know. One day the king met them out and asked them to dine with him on the morrow. The Tzitzinaina told them to take a puppy with them and give it a slice. They did so, and the puppy died. The young folk protested that they had no wish to be poisoned, and invited the king to dine with them on the next day. The Tzitzinaina, when the king sat down to their empty table, clapped her hands thrice and a grand meal appeared. After dinner the king asked Sun, Moon, and Star what they wished for most. They, instructed by the Tzitzinaina, craved the release of the woman hidden in the jakes. She was brought out, washed, clothed, and presented to the king by the Tzitzinaina, who told him all the facts. Thereupon the king in high delight took back his queen to the palace. But the king's mother and the midwife were fastened to four horses, which dragged them along the road and, on being lashed, tore them asunder.

(β) Sun, Moon, and Morning-Star in a Folk-tale from Syra.

(2) A Greek tale from Syra is very similar[1]. A poor old couple once had three hard-working daughters. The eldest of them wished that she had for husband the king's cook: then she would eat of the good things on his table. The next wished for the king's treasurer: then she would have plenty of money. The youngest, for the king himself: then she would bear him three children, Sun, Moon, and Morning-star. The prince[2] overheard them wishing, granted their desires, and married the youngest of them, much against his mother's will. When the young queen was about to bear the children, her mother-in-law bade the midwife substitute a dog, a cat, and a mouse for them, and fling the three children into the river. But the midwife had pity on the little brats and laid them down on a bed of rushes. Here a childless herdsman found them fed by one of his goats. He brought them to his wife, who tended them carefully; and, when they were grown up, he built them a tower to live in. As for the queen, at the time of her confinement the king was absent on a campaign. So his mother put her in the hen-house, and told him on his return that his wife, instead of Sun, Moon, and Morning-star, had given birth to a dog, a cat, and a mouse. The king was so upset that he did not ask what had become of the queen. For long he was inconsolable. At last one day he roused himself, went for a ride, and saw Sun and Morning-star exercising their horses near the tower and Moon watching them from a window. He thought the young folk just like those whom his wife had

---

[1] Text unpublished, German translation by J. G. von Hahn *Griechische und albanesische Märchen* Leipzig 1864 ii. 40 ff. I have condensed the version of von Hahn.

[2] In the sequel he is called king.

promised to bear, and that night he told his mother about them. She taxed the midwife with neglecting her orders. So the midwife went off, obtained by guile an entrance into the tower, and told Moon that she was indeed beautiful, but that she needed one thing to complete her happiness—the branch that makes music. Her brothers Sun and Morning-star consented to get it. They set off, and met a monk, who told them all about it. It was kept by two dragons, who would swallow them if they approached by day, but who snored with open mouth at midnight and might then be shot. The young men followed the monk's directions, shot the dragons, broke off the branch, and brought it back to their sister. The king, who on his rides past the tower had missed them, now told his mother of their return. She again sent the midwife, who paid a second visit to the tower. The girl Moon showed her a tree outside the house, which had grown apace from the planted branch making music continually and producing every morning a dishful of precious stones. The midwife, duly astonished, said that she still needed a mirror showing all towns, villages, lands, and princes. The brothers went off to seek it, and again met the monk. He told them that it was guarded by forty dragons, who by day kept watch, twenty on one side, twenty on the other, and by night slept in a row. About midnight they snored so loud that the mountains re-echoed. The brothers must then tread across their bodies with the greatest care. This they did, and brought the mirror to their sister. The king again noticed their absence and their return. He told his mother. She sent the midwife once more, who said to Moon that the only thing now lacking was the bird Dikjeretto : he understood all languages and by looking in the mirror would be able to tell her what people were saying all the world over. The brothers suspected that this quest would be the death of them. So they gave their sister two shirts, which she was to look at daily : if the shirts turned black, she would know that they had failed. This time, when they met the monk, he refused to help them. However, they pressed on, and the bird by his glance turned first one and then the other into stone. Moon knew of the disaster because the two shirts turned as black as coal. In her grief she set out on horseback to die with her brothers. The monk met her, had compassion on her, and explained that many a prince had failed in this enterprise because they had made the attempt in their clothes. She must strip herself of everything, attack the bird from behind before he was aware of her presence through the rustling of her clothes, and so grasp him by the feet. She did as she was bidden, caught the bird, and asked him where her brothers were. He showed her where they stood, and pointed out a mountain which opened at midday and contained a spring : if she were quick enough, she might slip in and get the water of life from the spring ; if not, the mountain would close upon her, and they would be ruined. The maiden with the bird on her hand performed the feat with the utmost speed ; but even so the mountain as it closed caught a piece of her clothing, and she had to draw her sword and cut it off. She sprinkled her brothers with the water, and they awoke as from a deep sleep. All who had been petrified on the spot were now in turn sprinkled and accompanied the happy party back to the tower, where the herdsman overjoyed at the return of his fosterlings slew forty lambs and poured out wine in abundance : the feasting lasted three days and three nights. The king, hearing of it, went out to see whether the children were there. They showed him the greatest respect, and he invited them to be his guests on the following Sunday. The bird told the young people to take him too along with them, adding that the king was their father. At the royal table both the king's mother and the midwife were present, when the bird from his cage revealed the whole tale. The king sprang up and kissed his children. His wife was fetched from the hen-house, clad in queenly garments, and brought to her children Sun, Moon, and Morning-star. The midwife had her head cut off; and the king's mother was banished from the palace.

(γ) Morning-Star and Evening-Star in a Folk-tale from Epeiros.

(3) A tale from the village of Çagori in Epeiros has some variations of interest[1]. Three sisters once sat on a balcony near the king's castle. The eldest said: 'I wish I sat at the king's table; how I should relish it!' The second said: 'I wish I were in the king's treasury; how I should help myself to money!' The youngest said: 'I wish I were married to the prince; I would bear him a boy and a girl as beautiful as the morning-star and the evening-star[2].' The prince overheard them wishing and granted all their wishes. But, when his young wife was about to be delivered of the children, he had to go off to a war. He entrusted her, therefore, to his mother. She, however, as soon as the little ones were born, put them in a basket and bade the midwife fling it into the river. She also slipped a dog and a cat into the cradle. When the poor wife wanted to see her offspring, she was dismayed indeed at their appearance. The prince now returned victorious from the war, but was so shocked at the news with which he was greeted that for three days he was speechless. Then he gave orders that his wife, who could deny nothing, should be walled up at the entrance of his castle so that only her head showed, and that every one who passed by should spit at her and strike her in the face. Meantime the basket in which the children lay floated to the house of certain dragons, who pulled it out of the water. They kept the children till the age of ten, then put them on a lame horse, and left them in the streets of the town to their fate. People wanted to know where they came from; and the children replied that they themselves did not know. At last the lame nag brought them to the house of a poor old woman, who out of pity took them in. Next morning she was astonished to find a handful of gold coins on the spot where the children had slept. The same thing occurred every morning, and she and they lived happily on the money. One day the king came by and noticed the morning-star on the face of the boy and the evening-star on that of the girl. He sighed and thought of the children that his wife had promised him. Indeed, he became so fond of these two that he brought them into his palace, hunted with them, and would never be without them. But his mother at once perceived who they were, and consulted with the midwife how best to get rid of them. The midwife came to the girl and said: 'You are a beautiful maiden, but you would be more beautiful still, if your brother had the winged horse of the plain.' The brother readily promised to go in quest of it. He rode forth and met an old woman, who told him of a plain near by so large that it took a man six days to cross it, though the winged horse was across it in one. The said horse ate men and beasts. If he would capture it, he must hide behind the thicket by the spring from which it drank, and at the moment when it stooped its head in drinking must leap on to its back and never dismount till it swore by its brother to serve him. The lad carried out her advice to the letter. The horse swore to serve him by its head—by its tail—by its saddle—by its foot—and lastly by its brother. The boy then dismounted, put a bridle on it, and brought it back to his

---

[1] Text unpublished, German translation by J. G. von Hahn *Griechische und albanesische Märchen* Leipzig 1864 ii. 287 ff. As before, I have condensed from von Hahn.

[2] πούλια (*sic*) is the original word, according to von Hahn. But N. Contopoulos *Greek-English Lexicon*[5] Athens 1903 makes πούλια, -ας, mean 'the pleiades, the seven stars in the constellation Taurus.'

sister. The king was so pleased at his success that he gave him a small kingdom. But the grandmother again plotted with the nurse for his destruction. The nurse went a second time to the girl and said : 'You are beautiful, sweetheart, but you would be more beautiful still, if you had the Beauty of the Land.' The brother set out to get her without delay. The Beauty of the Land was a woman beautiful beyond compare, who lived on the far side of a river. Whoever wanted to carry her off had to traverse the dry bed of the river : his horse must there whinny aloud, and, if she heard it whinnying, he would be able to ride through, but, if she heard it not, he and his horse would there and then be turned into stone. When the lad came to the dried up river, he bade the winged horse whinny his loudest. The horse did so, but the Beauty of the Land heard nothing. 'We are lost !' cried the horse. 'Courage !' said the lad, 'whinny once more.' This time the Beauty of the Land heard and answered. The lad rode over and carried her off; and, as they crossed the dry river-bed, a number of people who were petri-fied there came to life again and escorted them home, remaining with them till the marriage between the young man and the Beauty of the Land was celebrated. The king was greatly delighted at all this. But the king's mother plotted once again with the nurse to poison the young people. Soon afterwards the king invited them to a feast. Before they went, the Beauty of the Land revealed everything to her husband, counseling him not to strike in the face the poor walled up woman who was his own mother and at table to eat only of those dishes of which she herself ate. When the bride, the bridegroom, and the bridegroom's sister ate only of the dishes set before the king, the king pressed them to eat of others also. They told him that the rest were poisoned. He hurled the whole meal out of the window with his own hand and ordered another. Afterwards the Beauty of the Land begged him to send for the walled up woman. On her arrival the three young folk stood up and kissed her. The Beauty of the Land told the whole tale to the king, who embraced his children and his wife. But he had his mother and the midwife each bound to four horses and torn into quarters.

(δ) Three Golden Children in a Folk-tale from Euboia.

(4) A variant hails from Hagia Anna, a small town in the north-east of Euboia[1]. The third sister said : 'I would bear the prince three golden children.' She bore a golden child, while her husband was on a campaign ; but the cruel mother-in-law flung it into the hen-house and substituted for it a small dog. When her son returned and asked after the child that his wife had borne, she replied : 'What is to be done ? She is a dog and a dog she has borne.' And the prince made answer : 'Dog though it be, it will watch my house.' The second child she flung into the hen-house and replaced by a cat ; and the prince on his return was told of it and replied : 'Cat though it be, it will clear my house of mice.' For the third child she substituted a snake. Then the prince came back and gave orders that his wife should be flung into the hen-house. There the mother-in-law, who did not want her to die of hunger, brought her food in secret. When the boys had grown up, one day the king bade his heralds summon all his people to assemble before his castle. The boys heard of it, broke their way out of the hen-house and went to the assembly. The king noticed them, and was so pleased with them that he wanted to take them into his castle. But they said that they could not come without their mother ; and, when the king asked 'Who is your mother ?,' they replied 'She is the woman whom you shut up in the hen-house'

---

[1] Text unpublished, German summary by J. G. von Hahn *Griechische und albane-sische Märchen* Leipzig 1864 ii. 291 f. I translate from von Hahn.

and told him all that had happened. Thereupon he brought his wife out of the hen-house, but had his mother bound to two vicious mules and torn asunder by them.

(ε) Two Sons with Apples and a Daughter with a Star in a Folk-tale from Sicily.

(5) A Sicilian parallel to the foregoing tales is entitled *The Herb-gatherer's Daughters*[1]. A herb-gatherer died and left three daughters alone in the world. The eldest said : 'If I were the wife of the royal butler, I would give the whole court to drink out of one glass of water, and there would be some left.' The second said : 'If I were the wife of the keeper of the royal wardrobe, with one piece of cloth I would clothe all the attendants, and have some left.' The youngest said : 'Were I the king's wife, I would bear him three children—two sons with apples in their hands, and a daughter with a star on her brow.' The king happened to overhear them talking and sent for them next morning. The eldest and the second sister made good their promises and received in marriage the royal butler and the keeper of the royal wardrobe. The youngest became queen on condition that, if she failed to bear two sons with apples in their hands and a daughter with a star on her brow, she should be put to death. A few months before the queen's children were born the king went on a campaign. When they were born as she had foretold, the two elder sisters, jealous of her lot, bribed the nurse to substitute little dogs for them and sent word to the king that his wife had given birth to three puppies. He wrote back that she should be taken care of for two weeks and then put into a tread-mill. Meanwhile the nurse carried the babies out of doors and left them for the dogs to eat. Three fairies passed by, admired them, and gave them three gifts—a deer to nurse them, a purse always full of money, and a ring that would change colour when any misfortune befell one of them. The deer nursed the children till they were grown up. Then the fairy that had given the deer came and said : 'Now that you have grown up, how can you stay here any longer?' 'Very well,' said one of the brothers, 'I will go to the city and hire a house.' 'Take care,' said the deer, 'that you hire one opposite the royal palace.' So they all went to the city and hired a palace as directed. The aunts, seeing the apples in the hands of the boys and the star on the brow of the girl, recognised them at once and told the nurse. The nurse visited the girl and said that, to be really happy, she needed the Dancing Water. One of the brothers rode off to get it. On the way he met a hermit, who said : 'You are going to your death, my son; but keep on until you find a hermit older than I.' He met another hermit, who gave him the same direction. He met a third hermit older than the other two, who said : 'You must climb yonder mountain. On the top of it you will find a great plain and a house with a beautiful gate. Before the gate you will see four giants with swords in their hands. When the giants have their eyes closed, do not enter ; when they have their eyes open, enter. Then you will come to a door. If you find it open, do not enter; if you find it shut, push it open and enter. Then you will find four lions. When they have their eyes shut, do not enter ; when their eyes are open, enter, and you will see the Dancing Water.' The lad followed these instructions, filled his bottles with the Dancing Water, and returned in safety to his sister. They had two

---

[1] G. Pitrè *Fiabe novelle e racconti popolari siciliani* Palermo 1875 i (= *Biblioteca delle tradizioni popolari siciliane* iv) 316 ff. no. 36 'Li figghi di lu Cavuliciddaru' (Palermo). There is a slightly condensed translation of this tale in T. F. Crane *Italian popular tales* London 1885 p. 17 ff. I have abbreviated T. F. Crane's version.

golden basons made, and the Dancing Water leaped from one to the other. Again the aunts told the nurse, and again the nurse visited the girl and said that now she wanted the Singing Apple. The same brother rode off to get it. After a time he met the first hermit, who sent him to an older one, <who sent him to an older one still>. He said: 'Climb the mountain; beware of the giants, the door, and the lions; then you will find a little door and a pair of shears in it; if the shears are open, enter; if closed, do not risk it.' The lad did so, and found everything favourable. When he saw the shears open, he went into a room and saw a wonderful tree, on the top of which was an apple. He climbed up and tried to pick the apple, but the top of the tree swayed now this way, now that. He waited until it was still a moment, seized the branch, and picked the apple. He got away in safety and, as he rode home, the apple kept making a sound. Once more the aunts told the nurse, and once more the nurse visited the girl and said that, should she set eyes on the Speaking Bird, there would be nothing left for her to see. The same brother undertook the quest. As before, he met the first hermit, who sent him to the second, who sent him to the third, who said: 'Climb the mountain and enter the palace. You will find many statues. Then you will come to a garden, in the midst of which is a fountain, and on the bason is the Speaking Bird. If it should say anything to you, do not answer. Pick a feather from the bird's wing, dip it into a jar that you will find there, and anoint all the statues. Keep your eyes open, and all will go well.' The lad soon found the garden and the bird. But, when the bird exclaimed 'Your mother has been sent to the tread-mill,' 'My mother in the tread-mill?' he cried, and straightway became a statue like all the rest. In the meantime his sister at home looked at her ring and saw that it had changed its colour to blue. So she sent the second brother after the first. Everything happened to him in the same way. He too met the hermits, found the palace, saw the garden with the statues, and heard the Speaking Bird. And, when the bird said 'What has become of your brother? Your mother has been sent to the tread-mill,' he too cried out 'Alas, my mother in the tread-mill!' and became a statue. The sister now looked at her ring again, and it was black. Thereupon she dressed herself like a page and set out. She met the hermits and received their instructions. The third ended by saying: 'Beware, for, if you answer when the bird speaks, you will lose your life.' When she reached the garden, the bird exclaimed: 'Ah! you here, too? Now you will meet the same fate as your brothers. Do you see them? One, two, and you make three. Your father is at the war. Your mother is in the tread-mill. Your aunts are rejoicing.' She made no answer, but caught it, pulled a feather from its wing, dipped it into the jar, and anointed her brothers' nostrils. The brothers at once came to life again. Then she did the same to all the other statues, the lions, and the giants: all were restored to life. After that she departed with her brothers; and all the noblemen, princes, barons, and kings' sons rejoiced greatly. When they had recovered their life, the palace disappeared; and so did the hermits, for they were the three fairies. On reaching the city they had a gold chain made for the bird; and, the next time that the aunts looked out, they saw in the window of the palace opposite the Dancing Water, the Singing Apple, and the Speaking Bird. 'Well,' said they, 'the real trouble is coming now!' At length the king returned from the war and noticed the palace opposite equipped more magnificently than his own. When he saw the brothers with apples in their hands and the sister with a star on her brow, he cried: 'Gracious! If I did not know that my wife had given birth to three puppies, I should say that those were my children.' Another day, as he stood by the window and enjoyed the Dancing Water and the Singing

Apple, the Speaking Bird spoke to him and bade the sister and brothers invite him to a grand dinner on Sunday. At the dinner the bird got a counter-invitation for them all to dine with the king on the Sunday following. When they were assembled at the king's table, the bird related the whole story, ending with the words: 'These are your children, and your wife was sent to the mill and is dying.' The king at once embraced his children, and went to find his wife, who was at the point of death. He knelt before her and begged her pardon. Then he asked the bird to pronounce sentence on the aunts and the nurse. The bird sentenced the nurse to be thrown out of the window and the aunts to be cast into a caldron of boiling oil. This was done forthwith. Then the bird departed; and the king lived in peace with his children and his wife.

(5) Two Sons with a Gold Star and a Daughter with a Silver Star in a Folk-tale from Brittany.

(6) It must not be supposed that tales of this type are found only in the Greek and Italian area. Here, for example, is a version entitled *The Baker's Three Daughters* from Plouaret in Brittany[1]. An old baker had three daughters, who one evening after supper were talking confidences. The eldest said that she loved the king's gardener. The next, that she loved the king's valet. The youngest, that she loved the king's son, and, what was more, that she would have by him three children—two boys with a gold star on their foreheads and a girl with a silver star. The prince chanced to be taking a walk that evening, accompanied by his gardener and his valet. He overheard the conversation, summoned the girls to his presence next morning, and granted the desires of them all. The young queen was delivered of a fine boy with a gold star in the middle of his forehead. But the jealous sisters, acting on the advice of an old fairy, had secured a midwife, who exposed the babe in a basket on the Seine and substituted a puppy for him. The prince was much distressed, but bowed to the will of God. The babe floated down the river, was picked up by the king's gardener, and reared by the gardener's wife. Again the queen bore a boy with a gold star on his forehead. The midwife exposed him too in a basket on the Seine, and substituted a puppy for him. The prince, who by this time owing to the death of his father was king, was again deeply distressed, but submissive to the will of God. The second boy, like the first, floated down stream, was found by the gardener, and given to the gardener's wife. Once more the queen bore a child—a girl with a silver star in the middle of her forehead. The midwife exposed her in the same manner and substituted a puppy for her. This time the king was very angry: he felt that it was not God's doing, but that there was some mystery behind it all. So he had the queen shut up in a tower, with nothing but bread and water to live upon and a little book to read. The girl, like the boys, was found on the water by the gardener and reared by his wife. In due time their foster-parents died, and the children were taken into the palace by the king, who liked to have them about him. Every Sunday they were to be seen in the royal pew at church, each wearing a head-band to cover up the star: these head-bands puzzled people. One day, when the king was out hunting, an old woman (it was the midwife disguised as a beggar) came to the palace and began to compliment the girl: she was fair indeed, but if only she had the Dancing Water, the Singing Apple, and the Bird of Truth, there would not be her like upon earth! Her eldest brother set out to seek these marvels for her, and, before

---

[1] Text unpublished, French translation by F. M. Luzel in *Mélusine* 1878 i. 206 ff. I have abridged F. M. Luzel's rendering.

he went, gave her a dagger : she was to pull it out of its sheath several times daily for a year and a day ; if ever it would not come out, she might know that he was dead. A day arrived when she failed to draw the dagger : her eldest brother must be dead. The second brother now set out to seek him, and, before he went, gave her a rosary : she was to tell the beads constantly ; if one stuck, she might know that he was dead. A day came when one did stick : he too must be dead. So she bought a horse, dressed as a cavalier, and set out herself in quest of them. She went on and on till she reached a large plain. Here in the hollow of an old tree she saw a little man with a long white beard, who saluted her as the daughter of the king of France. She denied the title, but offered to clip his beard, which must be in his way, she thought. By so doing she delivered him : for five hundred years people had passed that way and no one had helped him. He therefore gave her his blessing, and told her how to find her brothers. Sixty leagues off was a road-side inn, where she was to eat, drink, and leave her horse. Soon afterwards she would find herself close to a very high mountain, terribly hard to climb. A wild wind would burst upon her. There would be hail, snow, ice, and cruel cold to contend with. On either side of the path would be seen many stone pillars—men, who had essayed to climb the mountain, lost heart, and been petrified on the spot. Once at the top, she would see a plain covered with turf and May flowers. Beneath an apple-tree would appear a golden seat. On this she was to sit and feign sleep. A blackbird would then hop down from branch to branch of the apple-tree, and enter a cage beneath it. She was to shut the cage quickly, and would so have secured the Bird of Truth. Next she would cut a branch from the apple-tree with an apple on it ; it would be the Singing Apple. Lastly, she was to fill a phial with water from a fountain beneath the tree ; this was the Dancing Water. On her way down the mountain she was to spill a drop of water on each stone pillar : from every one would come a cavalier, her own two brothers among them. All these directions she faithfully carried out. Passing through the intense cold on the mountain-side she reached the top, where the sky was clear and the air warm, as though it were summer. She sat on the golden seat below the apple-tree, feigned sleep, and duly secured the Bird of Truth, which again addressed her as daughter of the king of France. She next cut a branch of the apple-tree with one apple on it, filled her phial with water from the fountain, sprinkled and set free all the princes, dukes, barons, and cavaliers, who had been turned into stones, and last of all restored to life her own two brothers. They did not recognise their sister : so she hurried on, and got home first. On their arrival they told her how they had failed in the quest, and spoke of a young cavalier of surpassing beauty who had freed them from their fate. Meantime the old king, who loved the children, as he supposed, of his sister-in-law, was glad to see them all back again, and invited them to a banquet. Towards the end of it the young girl placed on the table the Dancing Water, the Singing Apple, and the Bird of Truth, and bade them do their business. So the Water danced, the Apple sang, and the Bird told the whole story to the assembled company. To prove the truth of it he bade the head-bands be removed from the two brothers and their sister : whereupon it was seen that each of the lads had a gold star on his forehead, and the young girl a silver star. The king fainted away. Recovering himself, he went and fetched the queen from her solitary tower. Despite twenty years' imprisonment, she was still beautiful and gracious. She ate and drank a little, and then—died where she sat ! The king, mad with grief and rage, had a furnace heated in the field, into which his sister-in-law and the midwife were cast.

(η) **The Myth of Zethos and Amphion as an 'Expulsion' Tale.**

It would be easy, but needless, to cite other variants. Tales of this type are, in fact, spread throughout the south of Europe, and with sundry modifications and adaptations could be traced yet further afield[1]. J. G. von Hahn, regarding them as essentially tales of 'expulsion' (*Verstossung*), formulated their common characteristics as follows[2]:

(a) Jealous relatives deprive the mother of her new-born children, who are found and brought up at a distance from the father's home by a childless foster-parent.

(b) Beasts are substituted for the new-born children; or the mother is accused of having devoured them.

(c) Expulsion or punishment of the mother.

(d) The children, found again by the father, deliver the mother.

Von Hahn has done good service by thus emphasising the permanent features of the tale. But, when he states that they cannot be illustrated from Greek mythology[3], he has somewhat seriously misconceived the situation and has thereby missed a certain number of interesting parallels. Ancient Greek folk-tales have for the most part come down to us through the discriminating sieve of ancient Greek literature. Sometimes, as in the case of Sophokles, that sieve had a very fine mesh, the result being that the primitive traits still to be seen in Sophoclean dramas are but few. Sometimes, as in the case of Euripides, the mesh was broad, and traits of this kind are comparatively numerous. Nevertheless, Euripides too made his appeal to one of the most aesthetically cultivated audiences of all time; and it is certain that he would not have thought the folk-tale as outlined above immediately suitable for dramatic presentation in the theatre at Athens. How, then, would Euripides, say, have manipulated such a theme to suit his purpose? We may here with some assurance hazard a twofold guess. On the one hand, he would have excised the whole of the second or bestial episode: nowhere in Greek tragedy do we find any precedent for a scene which, to Euripides' gener-

[1] See L. Gonzenbach *Sicilianische Märchen* Leipzig 1870 i. 19 ff. no. 5 'Die verstossene Königin und ihre beiden ausgesetzten Kinder,' *ib.* ii. 206 f., G. Pitrè *Fiabe novelle e racconti popolari siciliani* Palermo 1875 i (= *Biblioteca delle tradizioni popolari siciliane* iv) 328 f. 'La cammisa di lu gran jucaturi e l' auceddu parlanti' (Montevago), *ib.* 330 'Suli e Luna' (Capaci), *ib.* 330 f. 'Stilla d' oru e Stilla Diana' (Casteltermini), *ib.* 331 'Lu Re Turcu' (Noto), *ib.* 331 ff., G. Pitrè *Nuovo saggio de fiabe e novelle popolari siciliane* Imola 1873 (= *Rivista di Filologia Romanza* vol. i fasc. 2 f.) no. 1 'Re Sonnu' (Palermo), G. Finamore *Tradizioni popolari Abruzzesi* Lanciano 1882 i (Novelle) 192 ff. no. 39 'Lu fatte de le tré ssurèlle,' *Il Pentamerone* trans. by Sir R. Burton London 1893 i. 390 ff. 'Fifth Diversion of the Fourth Day,' F. M. Luzel 'Les trois filles du boulanger' (Plouaret) variants in *Mélusine* 1878 i. 209 n. 1, 210 n. 1, R. Koehler *ib.* 213 f., T. F. Crane *Italian Popular Tales* London 1885 p. 325 f., J. F. Campbell *Popular Tales of the West Highlands* Edinburgh 1860 i. p. lxxxiii f., J. Curtin *Fairy Tales of Eastern Europe* London s.a. pp. 91—119 'The Golden Fish, the Wonder-working Tree, and the Golden Bird' (a Hungarian tale of a prince with a golden sun on his breast and a princess with a golden moon on her bosom, who sought a Golden Fish, a branch cut from a Music-tree, and a Golden Bird, all kept in the Glass Mountain beyond the Crimson Sea: the old queen is burned on the public square), L. A Magnus *Russian Folktales* London 1915 pp. 269—273 'The Singing-Tree and the Speaking-Bird' (two princes and a princess seek the Talking-Bird, the Singing-Tree, and the Water of Life on the top of a steep mountain). Most of these authors refer to further sources.

[2] J. G. von Hahn *Griechische und albanische Märchen* Leipzig 1864 i. 46.

[3] *Id. ib.* 'Hellenische und germanische Sage: fehlt.'

ation at least, would have been so outrageous and so unconvincing as that of the supposititious animals or the cannibalistic mother. On the other hand, the poet would have expanded such parts of the story as were susceptible of pathetic treatment, and in particular would have elaborated the final scene of recognition[1]. But I need not follow out this *à priori* enquiry ; for it so happens that there is extant, not indeed a play of Euripides, but at least the summary of a Euripidean play, on a strictly analogous theme.

Apollodoros, who is paraphrasing Euripides' *Antiope*[2], tells the tale of that heroine in these words[3] : ' Antiope was the daughter of Nykteus. Zeus consorted with her, and she, when pregnant, to avoid her father's threats, fled to Epopeus at Sikyon and married him. Nykteus in despair took his own life, after laying his behest upon Lykos to exact vengeance from Epopeus and Antiope. So Lykos made an expedition against Sikyon and captured it : Epopeus he slew, but Antiope he took captive. As she was being led along, at Eleutherai in Boiotia, she gave birth to two sons. They were exposed ; but a herdsman found them and reared them, calling the one Zethos, the other Amphion. Zethos gave his attention to herds of cattle ; but Amphion used to practise harp-playing, for Hermes gave him a lyre. Lykos shut up Antiope and evil intreated her, as did Dirke his wife. At last her bonds dropped off of their own accord, and she escaped by stealth to her sons' homestead, eager to be welcomed by them. They recognised their mother, slew Lykos, bound Dirke to a bull, and, when she had been killed, flung her into a spring that is called Dirke after her.'

The general similarity of Euripides' play to the 'expulsion' *formula* of J. G. von Hahn is sufficiently obvious. The main discrepancy lies in the fact that, according to von Hahn's *formula*, the father of Zethos and Amphion ought to have been Lykos rather than Zeus. But this difficulty vanishes, if with H. Usener we suppose (indeed, we have already supposed it[4]) that *Lýkos* was an ancient god of daylight comparable with Zeus *Lýkaios* : the Theban Lykos will then be a doublet of the Sicyonian Epopeus, two kings bearing the name of the local god. Again, it might be objected that, on von Hahn's showing, Zethos and Amphion should have slain Dirke, but not Lykos. Here the explanation of the difficulty is simpler still. Hyginus, our ultimate authority for the Euripidean character of the narrative[5], has a different ending to it : ' They bound Dirce,' he says, 'by her hair to a bull and slew her. When they were about to slay Lycus, Mercurius forbade them and at the same time ordered Lycus to yield his kingdom to Amphion[6].' Euripides, in short, preserved the main outlines of the old-world tale.

---

[1] On ἀναγνώρισις as a strong point with Euripides see *e.g.* M. Croiset *Histoire de la littérature grecque* Paris 1891 iii. 315 f. Karkinos in his *Thyestes* (*Trag. Gr. frag.* p. 797 Nauck²) *ap.* Aristot. *poet.* 16. 1454 b 21 ff. used certain congenital signs in the shape of stars (ἀστέρας) as the means of effecting such a recognition : this is a parallel to the Breton tale *supra* p. 1011.

[2] This appears from a comparison of Apollod. 3. 5. 5 with Hyg. *fab.* 8, which is headed *eadem Euripidis, quam scribit Ennius.* See also schol. Ap. Rhod. 4. 1090, and the remarks of A. Nauck *Trag. Gr.frag.*² p. 410 ff. An analogous version by Kephalion, a rhetorical historian of Hadrian's age, is preserved by Io. Malal. *chron.* 2 pp. 45—49 Dindorf.

[3] Apollod. 3. 5. 5.

[4] *Supra* i. 64 n. 3, 738.

[5] *Supra* n. 2.

[6] Hyg. *fab.* 8. So the schol. Ap. Rhod. 4. 1090.

(θ) **Stellar names of the children in 'Expulsion' Tales.**

Now Zethos and Amphion were the Theban Dioskouroi[1]. It seems worth while, therefore, to consider whether the features common to the 'expulsion' tales can be paralleled from the numerous classical myths with regard to heroic twins. To begin with, one characteristic of the six 'expulsion' tales cited above is a certain peculiarity of nomenclature. The king's wife bears him children as follows:

1. A boy called *Sun*, a boy called *Moon*, a girl called *Star* (successively).
2. A boy called *Sun*, a girl called *Moon*, a boy called *Morning-star* (simultaneously).
3. A boy with the *Morning-star* on his face, a girl with the *Evening-star* on her face (simultaneously).
4. Three golden children, of whom two at least were boys (successively).
5. Two boys with golden apples in their hands, a girl with a *star* on her brow (simultaneously).
6. Two boys with *golden stars* on their brows, a girl with a *silver star* on her brow (successively).

The children, then, are definitely stellar; and a comparison of the last two tales shows beyond all doubt that the golden apples are tantamount to golden stars. Further, in four, perhaps five, out of the six tales the children consist of two boys and a girl. On both grounds we are forced to compare them with Kastor, Polydeukes, and Helene[2]. Zethos and Amphion too were, as we have before seen[3], intimately related to sun, moon, and stars. Even Romulus and Remus on Roman imperial coins are treated as Dioskouroi and surmounted by a couple of stars[4].

(ι) **Exposure of the children and Punishment of the mother in 'Expulsion' Tales.**

J. Rendel Harris in *The Cult of the Heavenly Twins* argues well in defence of the thesis 'That, in the earliest stages of human evolution, twins are taboo, without distinction between them, and that their mother shares the taboo with them[5].' In conformity with this rule the children of the 'expulsion' tales are regularly exposed as castaways:

1. They are put into boxes and flung into the sea.
2. Orders are given that they should be flung into a river; but they are actually left on a bed of rushes.

[1] *Supra* i. 739, ii. 317, 445.

[2] If this comparison be well founded, the relation of the children to horses may be more than fortuitous:

(1) Sun rides a green winged horse, which can thunder and lighten.

(2) Sun and Morning-star spend their time in exercising their horses: Moon also rides on horseback.

(3) Morning-star and Evening-star are abandoned on a lame horse: Morning-star secures the winged horse of the plain, which eats men and beasts.

(5) The brothers with golden apples and the sister with a star all ride on horseback.

(6) The brothers with golden stars and the sister with a silver star all ride on horseback as cavaliers.

[3] *Supra* i. 739.

[4] Stevenson—Smith—Madden *Dict. Rom. Coins* pp. 761, 914 f., *supra* p. 443 f. figs. 349—351.

[5] J. Rendel Harris *The Cult of the Heavenly Twins* Cambridge 1906 p. 10 ff.

3. They are put into a basket and flung into a river.
4. They are flung into a hen-house.
5. They are thrown out for the dogs to eat.
6. They are put into baskets and floated down the Seine.

Their mother too is (1) walled up in the jakes, or (3) partially walled up at the entrance to the castle, or (6) shut up in a tower, or (5) put into a tread-mill, or (2 and 4) thrown into the hen-house. Here again classical parallels are not far to seek. According to Kephalion, Lykos had the twins Zethos and Amphion exposed near Mount Kithairon, where a childless labourer named Ordion found and reared them; Dirke took their mother Antiope to the same place, fastened a torch to the horns of a wild bull, and gave orders that Antiope should be roped to its neck and so dragged to death, when in the nick of time the twins learned the victim's name from Ordion, set free their mother, and at her request bound Dirke to the bull[1]. As to Kastor, Polydeukes, and Helene, an anonymous narrative, probably drawn from the *Kypria*[2], said that Zeus under the form of a swan had mated with Nemesis under the form of a goose, that Nemesis had laid an egg and left it in the marsh, that a certain shepherd had found it there and brought it to Leda, who kept it carefully in a chest, and that in time Helene was born from this egg and brought up as the child of Leda[3]. A tradition, late in date[4] but early in character[5], added that Kastor and Polydeukes were born of the same egg[6], and used the halves of it as conical caps[7]. Ibykos, a sixth-century lyrical poet, introduced some speaker, presumably Herakles, saying of the twin Moliones:

> The white-horsed youths,
> Sons of Molione, I slew,
> Like-aged and equal-headed and one-bodied,
> Both born in a silver egg[8].

[1] Kephalion *frag.* 6 (*Frag. hist. Gr.* iii. 628 ff. Müller) *ap.* Io. Malal. *chron.* 2 p. 45 ff. Dindorf.

[2] See O. Rossbach in Roscher *Lex. Myth.* iii. 118 ff.

[3] Tzetz. *in* Lyk. *Al.* 88, Apollod. 3. 10. 7. The egg was left ἐν τῷ ἕλει (Tzetz.), ἐν τοῖς ἄλσεσιν (Apollod.: ἄλσεσιν cod. S. ἕλεσιν Preller, δάσεσιν Bekker).

[4] A. Furtwängler in Roscher *Lex. Myth.* i. 1159.

[5] E. Bethe in Pauly—Wissowa *Real-Enc.* v. 1113.

[6] Tzetz. *in* Lyk. *Al.* 88, 506, schol. Kallim. *h. Artem.* 232, schol. *Od.* 11. 298, Hor. *sat.* 2. 1. 26, *ars poet.* 147 with Acron *ad locc.*, Serv. *in* Verg. *Aen.* 3. 328, Fulgent. *myth.* 2. 16, Myth. Vat. 1. 78, 3. 3. 6.

[7] Lyk. *Al.* 506 f., Loukian. *dial. deor.* 26. 1.

Another account said that Iupiter as a swan consorted with Leda, who laid two eggs, one of them containing Castor and Pollux, the other Clytemnestra and Helena (Myth. Vat. 1. 204).

In a sanctuary of Hilaeira and Phoibe at Sparta an egg, hung from the roof by ribbons, was shown as that to which Leda had given birth (Paus. 3. 16. 1). Its position, slung in mid air, suggests that it may have symbolised the moon. Neokles of Kroton stated that the egg from which Helene was born had fallen from the moon, the women there being oviparous and their offspring fifteen times as large as we are, according to Herodoros of Herakleia (*frag.* 28 in *Frag. hist. Gr.* ii. 35, where see C. Müller's note).

[8] Ibyk. *frag.* 16 Bergk[4] *ap.* Athen. 57 F f., cp. Eustath. *in Il.* p. 1321, 33 ff., *in Od.* p. 1686, 45 ff. According to Pherekydes *frag.* 36 (*Frag. hist. Gr.* i. 81 Müller) *ap.* schol. *Il.* 11. 709, Kteatos and Eurytos were the sons of Molione, daughter of Molos, nominally by Aktor, but really by Poseidon: each of them had two heads, four hands, four feet, and one body. They thus closely resembled the composite beings, whom Plato related to the

But whether this egg, like that of Helene, was left in the wilds, we do not know. Far more familiar is the fate of Romulus and Remus. Amulius, king of Alba Longa, gave orders that they together with their mother, the Vestal Ilia, should be thrown into the Tiber. The twins were washed up on the bank, where the shepherd Faustulus found them, suckled by a she-wolf and attended by a woodpecker and a jay. He took them to his wife Acca Laurentia, who reared them. Their mother Ilia became the wife of the river-god Anien or Tiberis[1]. According to another account, Amulius doomed the guilty mother to be flogged to death. Others again said that, owing to the entreaties of his daughter Antho, Amulius commuted her punishment into close imprisonment, but that after his death she was let out[2].

(κ) Quests undertaken by the children in 'Expulsion' Tales.

The quests undertaken by the children in the 'expulsion' tales are not regarded by J. G. von Hahn as essential to this type of story; and in point of fact they are absent altogether from the Eubœan version (4). Still, where they are present, they are likely to repay investigation. Indeed, I suspect that ultimately they will prove to be quite the most interesting portion of the whole. For purposes of comparison, let us enumerate them in order:

1. (*a*) A golden apple kept by forty dragons.
   (*b*) A golden bough, on which all the birds of the world meet to sing.
   (*c*) The Tzitzinaina, who knows the language of all birds and can turn men into stone.
2. (*a*) A branch, which makes music and is kept by two dragons.
   (*b*) A mirror, which shows the whole world and is kept by forty dragons.
   (*c*) The bird Dikjeretto, which can turn men into stone.
3. (*a*) The Winged Horse of the Plain, which swears by its brother.
   (*b*) The Beauty of the Land, who can turn men into stone.
5. (*a*) The Dancing Water, which is guarded by four giants and four lions.
   (*b*) The Singing Apple, which grows on the top of a wonderful tree with shears before it.
   (*c*) The Speaking Bird, which is perched on the bason of a fountain in a garden and can turn men into statues.
6. (*a*)+(*b*)+(*c*) The Dancing Water, the Singing Apple, and the Bird of Truth. The Dancing Water comes from a fountain beneath an apple-tree. On a branch of the tree grows the Singing Apple. A blackbird on the tree is the Bird of Truth. Beside the tree is a golden seat. All these are found in a summery plain on the top of a wintry mountain, the path up which is bordered by cavaliers turned into stone.

It will be seen that the last tale gives the most coherent account of the various objects to be sought. Moreover, it alone makes mention of one detail, the golden seat, which affords a clue to the meaning of all the rest. Whoever can sit on that golden throne thereby establishes his claim to be king, the Dancing Water, the Singing Apple, and the Bird of Truth being in some sort his *regalia*. But this is a matter for further investigation. For the moment I content myself with observing that traces, substantial traces, of similar quests are to be found

---

sun and moon (*supra* i. 311). Cp. Plout. *de frat. am.* 1 τοὺς Μολιονίδας ἐκείνους, συμφυεῖς τοῖς σώμασι γεγονέναι δοκοῦντας.

[1] Serv. *in* Verg. *Aen.* 1. 273.

[2] Dion. Hal. *ant. Rom.* 1. 78 f., Plout. *v. Rom.* 3, Liv. 1. 4. 3.

throughout ancient Greek mythology. The folk-tale hero rides off to get the golden apple kept by forty dragons in a garden[1]. We think of Herakles, the great twin brother of Iphikles, who seeks the golden apples of the Hesperides, apples that grow in the garden of Zeus and are kept by the dragon Ladon[2]. The same folk-tale hero rides a green winged horse, which can thunder and lighten[3]. We are familiar with the winged horse Pegasos, of whom Hesiod wrote:

> In Zeus' home he dwells
> Bearing the thunder-peal and lightning-flash
> For Zeus the wise[4].

[1] *Supra* p. 1003.
[2] K. Seeliger in Roscher *Lex. Myth.* i. 2594 ff.   [3] *Supra* p. 1003.
[4] Hes. *theog.* 285 f., cp. Eur. *Bellerophontes frag.* 312 Nauck² ὑφ' ἅρματ' ἐλθὼν Ζηνὸς ἀστραπηφορεῖ. I do not know any ancient representation of Pegasos as lightning-bearer. But a very remarkable red-figured *hydría* at Paris (De Ridder *Cat. Vases de la Bibl. Nat.* ii. 343 no. 449, J. B. Biot in the *Ann. d. Inst.* 1847 xix. 184 ff., *Mon. d. Inst.* iv pl. 39, 2 (=my fig. 885), Reinach *Rép. Vases* i. 129, 4. R. Eisler *Weltenmantel und Himmelszelt* München

Fig. 885.

1910 i. 84 n. 2 fig. 26 ('Apotropäische Darstellung einer Sonnenfinsternis')) appears to represent him as a constellation in the sky. My friend Prof. E. T. Whittaker, late Astronomer Royal of Ireland, has kindly supplied me with the following note on this unique vase-painting:

'Four stars of approximately equal magnitude will be noticed forming a rectangular figure flanked by two other stars. There are in the northern sky two well-known instances of stars disposed in a rectangle, *viz.* the body of the Plough (Ursa Major) and the great square of Pegasus. Here the addition of Pegasus himself puts the meaning beyond doubt.

The fact that the moon appears as a comparatively thin crescent shows that a time

The hero of another folk-tale captures the Winged Horse of the Plain: he waits till it stoops its head in drinking from a spring, then leaps on to its back, and makes it swear by its brother to serve him[1]. He too can be paralleled by Bellerophontes, who captures Pegasos while drinking at the spring Peirene[2]: and Pegasos, we remember, has Chrysaor for brother[3]. Lastly, the folk-tale hero, who as a new-born babe is put into a box and flung into the sea, while his mother is walled up in the jakes[4], recalls the classical myth of Danae, first shut up in an underground chamber and then sent adrift in a chest on the sea

Fig. 886.

with the infant Perseus. And, when the said folk-tale hero vanquishes the Tzitzinaina that turns men into stone[5], we can but compare Perseus decapitating Medousa and returning in triumph with her petrifying head. The fact is, these modern European folk-tales are—as E. S. Hartland expresses it—'stuff of the kind out of which the classical and other mythologies grew[6].' Such correspondences between the modern illiterate folk-tale and the ancient literary myth are, therefore, to be expected. Parian marble must needs bear a certain resemblance to the Hermes of Praxiteles[7].

either quite early or quite late in the lunation is intended. If the former, the vase must represent the western horizon soon after sunset in spring. If the latter, it represents the eastern sky shortly before sunrise in autumn. No obvious meaning attaches to the short curved lines within or without the moon's disc. The scale on which the moon is represented is much larger than that on which the great square of Pegasus appears.'

[1] *Supra* p. 1006.   [2] Strab. 379.

[3] O. Jessen in Pauly—Wissowa *Real-Enc.* iii. 2484, H. W. Stoll in Roscher *Lex. Myth.* i. 900, F. Hannig *ib.* iii. 1749. *Supra* p. 716 ff.

[4] *Supra* p. 1003 f.

[5] *Supra* p. 1004.

[6] E. S. Hartland *Mythology and Folktales* London 1900 p. 35.

[7] We must, however, bear in mind the warning uttered by that careful student of Greek

(λ) Penalties exacted by the children in 'Expulsion' Tales.

It remains but to notice the extreme savagery with which, in the folk-tales, the guilty parties are punished:

1. The king's mother and the midwife are torn asunder by horses.
2. The king's mother is banished from the palace: the midwife is beheaded.
3. The king's mother and the midwife are torn asunder by horses.
4. The king's mother is torn asunder by mules.
5. The jealous sisters are thrown into a caldron of boiling oil: the nurse is flung from the window.
6. The jealous sister and the midwife are cast into a furnace.

Even here classical mythology, for all its refinement and polish, can offer a gruesome analogy. Zethos and Amphion, as we have already heard[1], bind the ill-starred Dirke to a wild bull, by which she is dragged to death. Nay worse, the scene of her agony was a favourite subject with the sensational art of the Hellenistic age (fig. 886)[2].

APPENDIX G.

ORPHIC THEOGONIES AND THE COSMOGONIC EROS.

The Orphic fragments were collected and discussed with marvellous insight by C. A. Lobeck *Aglaophamus* Regimontii Prussorum 1829 i. 411—ii. 964. A somewhat fuller and handier collection is that of E. Abel *Orphica* Lipsiae-Pragae 1885 pp. 137—273, who, however, does not add a commentary and occasionally refers a fragment to the wrong context. An important supplement is G. Murray 'Critical Appendix on the Orphic Tablets' in Harrison *Proleg. Gk. Rel.*[2] pp. 659 —673 (*supra* p. 118 n. 2). Recently O. Kern in his *Orphicorum fragmenta* Berolini 1922 has produced an admirably careful and complete edition, which includes 'Testimonia' (pp. 1—79), 'Fragmenta' (pp. 80—344), bibliography (pp. 345—350), reference-tables (pp. 351—353), and 'Indices' (pp. 360—407). But the subject is even now far from being exhausted, and a *Corpus* of the monu-

---

folk-tales, Prof. W. R. Halliday, in R. M. Dawkins *Modern Greek in Asia Minor* Cambridge 1916 p. 216 f.: 'It cannot be too strongly insisted that there is no special connexion at all between ancient mythology and modern Greek folk-tales. Wherever it has been traced, there is obvious to the impartial observer either a straining of the evidence or a palpable mistake.'

[1] *Supra* pp. 1013, 1015.

[2] See *e.g.* Collignon *Hist. de la Sculpt. gr.* ii. 532 ff., Herrmann *Denkm. d. Malerei* pl. 43 Text p. 55, E. Bethe in Pauly—Wissowa *Real-Enc.* v. 1170.

I figure *e.g.* the principal design on an Apulian *kratér* from Palazzuolo near Syracuse, now in Berlin (Furtwängler *Vasensamml. Berlin* ii. 926 f. no. 3296 K. Diltheyin the *Arch. Zeit.* 1878 xxxvi. 42 ff. pls. 7 (= my fig. 886) and 8, Reinach *Rép. Vases* i. 421, 2, O. Jessen in Roscher *Lex. Myth.* ii. 2184 ff. fig. 1, J. H. Huddilston *Greek Tragedy in the light of Vase Paintings* London 1898 p. 9 n. 1). On the left Dirke, a pathetic figure with bared breast, is dragged to death by the raging bull. On the right Lykos, caught skulking in a cave by Zethos and Amphion, is about to be dispatched, when Hermes—as in the Euripidean version (*supra* p. 1013)—suddenly intervenes to stay the slaughter. Antiope escapes to the right. The panther-skin hung on the wall of the cave hints at the Dionysiac character of Antiope (*supra* i. 735).

mental evidence is still sorely needed. Of scholars that in modern times have devoted special attention to the Orphic theogonies (P. R. Schuster *De veteris Orphicae theogoniae indole atque origine* Lipsiae 1869, O. Kern *De Orphei Epimenidis Pherecydis theogoniis quaestiones criticae* Berolini 1888, *id.* 'Theogoniae Orphicae fragmenta nova' in *Hermes* 1888 xxiii. 481—488, F. Susemihl 'Die Orphische theogonie' in the *Jahrb. f. class. Philol.* 1874 xx. 666—676, *id. De theogoniae Orphicae forma antiquissima* Gryphiswaldiae 1890, *id.* 'Zu den orphischen Theogonien' in the *Jahrb. f. class. Philol.* 1890 xxxvi. 820—826, *id. Geschichte der griechischen Litteratur in der Alexandrinerzeit* Leipzig 1891 i. 896, F. Lukas *Die Grundbegriffe in den Kosmogonien der alten Völker* Leipzig 1893, pp. 178—195, A. E. J. Holwerda 'De Theogonia Orphica' in *Mnemosyne* N.S. 1894 xxii. 286—329, 361—385, W. Kroll 'De Orphicis addendum' in *Philologus* 1894 liii. 561, P. Tannery 'Sur la première theogonie Orphique' in the *Archiv für Geschichte der Philosophie* 1897 xi. 13—17, Rohde *Psyche*[3] ii. 414—417, and others) none has done better service than O. Gruppe (*Cult. Myth. orient. Rel.* i. 612—675, 'Berichtigung' in the *Jahrb. f. class. Philol.* 1888 xxxiv Anhang 1 f., 'Die rhapsodische Theogonie und ihre Bedeutung innerhalb der orphischen Litteratur' *ib.* 1890 Suppl. xvii. 687—747, *Gr. Myth. Rel.* pp. 419—423, 430—432, 'Älteste orphische Theogonie' in Roscher *Lex. Myth.* iii. 1120—1124, 'Die Lehre von der periodischen Welterneuerung' *ib.* iii. 1139—1149, *Myth. Lit.* 1908 p. 215 f.), whose views—with sundry modifications—are here summarised.

(1) The earliest Orphic Theogony.

Quotations in authors of the classical age (cp. H. Diels *Die Fragmente der Vorsokratiker*[3] Berlin 1912 ii. 167 ff. 'Altbezeugte Fragmente') postulate the existence of an early Orphic theogony, to which even Homer, at least in the Διὸς ἀπάτη, was indebted (*Il.* 14. 201 cp. Plat. *Cratyl.* 402 B—C ; *Il.* 14. 246 cp. Athenag. *supplicatio pro Christianis* 18 p. 20 Schwartz, Krates *ap.* Plout. *de fac. in orbe lun.* 25, Orph. *h. Okean.* 83. 1 f., Hippol. *ref. haeres.* 5. 7 p. 148 Duncker —Schneidewin, 8. 12 p. 424 ; but hardly *Il.* 14. 259 ff. cp. Damaskios *quaest. de primis principiis* 124 (i. 319, 8 ff. Ruelle)). The contents of the poem can be partially reconstructed as follows :—In the beginning was Nyx (Aristot. *met.* 12. 6. 1071 b 26 f., 14. 4. 1091 b 4 ff., Eudemos of Rhodes *ap.* Damaskios *loc. cit.*, Lyd. *de mens.* 2. 8 p. 26, 1 ff. Wünsch). Black-winged Nyx laid a wind-egg, from which in due time sprang gold-winged Eros (Aristoph. *av.* 695 ff.). Apparently heaven and earth were regarded as the upper and lower halves of the vast egg (so in the later theogony of Orph. *frag.* 57 Kern *ap.* Athenag. *supplicatio pro Christianis* 18 p. 20 f. Schwartz, cp. Varro *frag.* 109 Funaioli *ap.* Prob. *in* Verg. *ecl.* 6. 31 p. 354 Lion). Ouranos (Aristot. *met.* 14. 4. 1091 b 5) and Ge (Lyd. *de mens.* 2. 8 p. 26, 2 f. Wünsch) together produced as their offspring Okeanos and Tethys (Plat. *Tim.* 40 E). Fair-flowing Okeanos took to wife Tethys, his sister by the same mother, and so was the first to begin regular wedlock (Orph. *frag.* 15 Kern *ap.* Plat. *Cratyl.* 402 B—C, cp. Aristot. *met.* 1. 3. 983 b 30 f.). Their children were Phorkys, Kronos, Rhea, and others (Plat. *Tim.* 40 E, Cic. *Tim.* 11). The sequel can perhaps be surmised from the Διὸς ἀπάτη. Rhea took Hera to Okeanos and Tethys, who brought up the child in their abode ; and Zeus thrust Kronos down below the earth and the sea (*Il.* 14. 200 ff.). Zeus used to visit Hera clandestinely (*Il.* 14. 294 ff.), repairing to Okeanos for the purpose (Orph. περὶ Διὸς καὶ Ἥρας *frag.* 115 Kern *ap.* Eustath. *in* Dionys. *per.* 1). Not improbably the poem told how, to grace this 'sacred marriage' (Dion Chrys. *or.* 36 p. 99 Reiske, Prokl. *in* Plat. *Tim.* i. 49, 13 f. Diehl cp. *ib.* iii. 248, 5 ff.), Ge sent up golden apples

(Asklepiades of Mende *frag.* 1 (*Frag. hist. Gr.* iii. 306 Müller) *ap.* Athen. 83 C) or apple-trees bearing golden fruit in Okeanos (Pherekydes of Leros *frag.* 33 (*Frag. hist. Gr.* i. 78 f. Müller) *ap.* schol. Ap. Rhod. 4. 1396), or came with branches of golden apples to the wedding and allowed Hera to plant them in her garden by Mt Atlas, where they were protected by the Hesperides and the snake (Pherekydes of Leros *frag.* 33 a (*Frag. hist. Gr.* i. 79 f. Müller) *ap.* Hyg. *poet. astr.* 2. 3, schol. Caes. Germ. *Aratea* p. 383, 1 ff. Eyssenhardt : *id. ap.* pseudo-Eratosth. *catast.* 3 calls it the garden of the gods ; others, the gardens of Zeus (Soph. *Ion frag.* 297 Nauck², 320 Jebb, *ap.* Stob. *flor.* 103. 10 (ed. Gaisford iii. 292) ἐν Διὸς κήποις ἀροῦσθαι (T. Bergk cj. ἀρύεσθαι) μόνον εὐδαίμονος (leg. εὐδαίμονας) ὄλβους) or the plain of Zeus (Aristoph. *av.* 1758 πέδον Διὸς καὶ λέχος γαμήλιον, cp. Eur. *Hipp.* 749 Ζανὸς μελάθρων παρὰ κοίταις (J. G. J. Hermann cj. παρ' εὐναῖς)), or the gardens of Father Okeanos (Aristoph. *nub.* 271), or the meadow of Hera (Kallim. *h. Artem.* 164)). The poem concluded with the sixth generation (Orph. *frag.* 14 Kern *ap.* Plat. *Phileb.* 66 C). O. Gruppe thinks that it was probably composed towards the end of *s.* vii B.C. at Kroton, where Hera *Lakinía* had a garden (Lyk. *Al.* 856 ff. ὄρχατον with Tzetz. *ad loc.* δῆλον τὸν κῆπον λέγειν) and a temple of the Muses (Iambl. *v. Pyth.* 50 after Timaios?) may betoken Orphic influence.

[Here I dissent. It seems to me that clear indications point to an earlier age and a very different locality. If the Διὸς ἀπάτη really presupposes an Orphic theogony, that theogony can hardly be later than *s.* x (see the sober estimates of W. Christ *Geschichte der griechischen Litteratur* ⁵ München 1908 i. 59—62)—a period which accords well with the epic metre and dialect of the extant fragments, not to lay stress on the remote traditional dates of Orpheus himself (O. Gruppe in Roscher *Lex. Myth.* iii. 1064—1073). Moreover, our attention is drawn east-wards rather than westwards : the scene of the Διὸς ἀπάτη is laid on Mt Ide in Phrygia (*supra* i. 154, ii. 950) ; the position assigned by the theogony to Nyx recalls the archaic (*s.* vi) figure of Nyx by Rhoikos at Ephesos (Paus. 10. 38. 6 f.) ; Okeanos and Tethys as forbears are compared by Aristotle with water as the primal substance assumed by Thales of Miletos (Aristot. *met.* 1. 3. 983 b 20 ff.) ; and the cosmic egg, not to mention other points of resemblance, occurs also in the Phoenician theogony (Sanchouniathon as translated by Philon Bybl. *frag.* 2. 2 (*Frag. hist. Gr.* iii. 565 Müller) *ap.* Euseb. *praep. ev.* 1. 10. 2 ἀνεπλάσθη ὁμοίως ᾠοῦ σχήματι κ.τ.λ., cp. *supra* i. 583 n. 4, 785, and Mochos *ap.* Damask. *quaest. de primis principiis* 125 *ter* (i. 323, 6 ff. Ruelle) ᾠόν...τὸ δὲ ᾠὸν ὁ οὐρανός). I infer that the Orphic poem took shape somewhere in Asia Minor as the result of early Ionian speculation brought to bear on primitive Thraco-Phrygian beliefs. A trace of such beliefs may be found in the Lesbian tale of Enorches. A certain Thyestes consorting with his sister Daita or Daito (*v.l.* Daiso, cp. the Lesbian Theodaisia (Nilsson *Gr. Feste* pp. 280 n. 2, 472 n. 2)) produced from an egg a son called Enorches, who founded a temple for Dionysos and called the god after himself Dionysos Ἐνόρχης (Eudok. *viol.* 345, schol. Lyk. *Al.* 212)—a title borne by Dionysos in Samos also (Hesych. *s.v.* Ἐνόρχης) and obviously derived from ὄρχεις, 'testicles' (ἐνόρχης, ἔνορχος, ἔνορχις is elsewhere used *e.g.* of a ram (*Il.* 23. 147, Synes. *epist.* 148) or he-goat (Theokr. 3. 4, Loukian. *dial. deor.* 4. 1) or bull (Aristot. *hist. an.* 9.50. 632 a 20)). Now the names Thyestes and Daito recall at once the banquet of Thyestes, son of Pelops the Phrygian (Bakchyl. 7. 5, Hdt. 7. 8 and 11, Telestes *frag.* 5 Bergk⁴ *ap.* Athen. 625 E—626 A, schol. Pind. *Ol.* 9. 15 a), and imply that in Lesbos as at Mykenai there lingered the memory of ritual cannibalism. H. D. Müller *Mythologie der griechischen Stämme* Göttingen

1861 ii. 154—158 argues that the Mycenaean myth points back to a human sacrifice offered to a Zeus-like deity Θυέστης, the 'Dashing' storm-god (θύω, θύελλα). This etymology is possible (Dionysios i of Syracuse *ap.* Phot. *bibl.* p. 532 b 32 ff. Bekker θυέστην τὸν δοίδυκα ἐκάλει, a pestle being a 'dasher' or 'bruiser': see Boisacq *Dict. étym. de la Langue Gr.* p. 355), though the Lesbian Thyestes appears in a Dionysiac context (Gruppe *Gr. Myth. Rel.* p. 660 n. 1) which relates his name to θυιάδες, θυστάδες, Θυώνη, etc. Be that as it may, the association of human sacrifice with the cult of Dionysos takes us from Lesbos (*supra* i. 656 n. 4 : see also the story told by Ail. *var. hist.* 13. 2 of the Mytilenaean Makareus, priest of Dionysos, and his sons, who μιμούμενοι τὴν τοῦ πατρὸς ἱερουργίαν τῷ βωμῷ τῷ πατρῴῳ προσῆλθον ἔτι καομένων τῶν ἐμπύρων· καὶ ὁ μὲν νεώτερος παρέσχε τὸν τράχηλον, ὁ δὲ πρεσβύτερος ἠμελημένην εὑρὼν σφαγίδα τὸν ἀδελφὸν ἀπέκτεινεν ὡς ἱερεῖον) to Thrace, where the devouring of a dismembered child was not unknown (*supra*, i. 656). Others explained the title Ἐνόρχης by the tale of Polyhymnos (Eudok. *viol.* 345, Tzetz. *in* Lyk. *Al.* 212 : O. Höfer in Roscher *Lex. Myth.* iii. 2657—2661, 3154 f. discusses variants). Dionysos, when his mother was struck by the thunderbolt, groped about for her. A young man named Polyhymnos undertook to show him the way to her, if allowed to consort with him. Dionysos agreed, provided that he found his mother first. Following the advice of Polyhymnos, he went down to Hades and brought her up from the spring at Lerna. Polyhymnos having died, Dionysos by way of keeping his promise attached genitals of fig-wood to himself and leathern *phalloí* of deer-skin. Hence his title Ἐνόρχης. The clue to the understanding of this narrative is the fact that πολύυμνος was an appellative of Dionysos himself (*h. Dion.* 26. 7, Eur. *Ion* 1074 f.), kindred names being found in his *entourage* (Polyhymno his Dodonaean nurse (*supra* i. 111 n. 6), Polymnia mother of Orpheus (schol. Ap. Rhod. 1. 23) and of Triptolemos (schol. *Il.* 10. 435, Eustath. *in Il.* p. 817, 32, Tzetz. *in* Hes. *o. d.* 1 p. 28, 6 f. Gaisford)). The descent of Dionysos and Poly-hymnos is therefore tantamount to a descent of Dionysos Πολύυμνος ; and the obscene pact between the two, which is missing in the version given by Paus. 2. 37. 5, is a piece of aetiology meant to elucidate the Lernaean Φαλλαγώγια. The quest of Dionysos for Semele thus becomes comparable with that of Orpheus for Eurydike (see Harrison *Themis* pp. 420, 523) and again points Thrace-wards.]

(2) The Orphic Theogony of Hieronymos and Hellanikos.

Another Orphic theogony, distinguished as ἡ...κατὰ τὸν Ἱερώνυμον φερομένη καὶ Ἑλλάνικον, εἴπερ μὴ καὶ ὁ αὐτός ἐστιν, is set forth by Damaskios *quaest. de primis principiis* 123 *bis* (i. 317, 15 ff. Ruelle) :—In the beginning was water and slime (Lobeck *Aglaophamus* i. 484, followed by F. Creuzer *Symbolik und Mythologie*[3] Leipzig and Darmstadt 1842 iv. 83, rightly cj. ἰλύς for ὕλη; but cp. Stephanus *Thes. Gr. Ling.* iii. 249 B—C) which thickened into earth. Water, the combining element, and earth, the scattered, together produced a snake with three heads, in the middle that of a god, to one side that of a bull, to the other that of a lion. The snake had wings on its shoulders and was named Chronos the ageless and Herakles (cp. Orph. *h. Herakl.* 12). With it consorted Ananke or Adrasteia, a bodiless being whose arms stretch throughout the world and clasp its extremities : she is described as at once male and female. The snake Chronos begat intelligent (but Lobeck *Aglaophamus* i. 486 n.† cj. νοτερόν for νοερόν, and C. E. Ruelle *ad loc.* approves the change) Aither, boundless Chaos, and misty Erebos. Among these Chronos produced an egg containing male and female elements, a multiplicity of seeds, and a bodiless god (*supra* i. 311 n. 5 : see also

O. Kern *De Orphei Epimenidis Pherecydis theogoniis quaestiones criticae* Berolini 1888 p. 25 f.) with golden wings on his shoulders, the heads of bulls attached to his sides (cp. Orph. *h. Protog.* 6. 3 ταυροβόαν), and on his head a monstrous snake resembling all manner of wild beasts. This god is named Protogonos or Zeus the arranger of all or Pan (Πρωτόγονον ἀνυμνεῖ καὶ Δία καλεῖ πάντων διατάκτορα καὶ ὅλου τοῦ κόσμου, διὸ καὶ Πᾶνα καλεῖσθαι (cp. Orph. *h. Pan.* 11. 12 ἀληθὴς Ζεὺς ὁ κεράστης)). The account given by Damaskios is borne out by Athenag. *supplicatio pro Christianis* 18 p. 20, 22 ff. Schwartz and schol. Greg. Naz. *or.* 31. 16 (E. Norden in *Hermes* 1892 xxvii. 614 f.), who, however, omit the bovine head of the snake, ascribing to it the head of a god between the heads of a snake and a lion, and say nothing of Aither, Chaos, and Erebos. The snake Herakles—they declare—produced a huge egg, which, filled with his force, cracked and broke into halves—the upper heaven, the lower earth. Forth from the egg came a bodiless god (*supra*), Phanes by name. Athenag. *loc. cit.* p. 21, 1 ff. Schwartz adds the sequel. Ouranos and Ge had as their daughters Klotho, Lachesis, Atropos, as their sons the Hekatoncheires Kottos, Gyges, Briareos, and the Kyklopes Brontes, Steropes, Arges. These Ouranos bound and flung into Tartaros, having heard that his sons would dethrone him. Thereupon Ge was angered and bare the Titans, so called 'because they took vengeance (τισάσθην) on great Ouranos the starry' (Orph. *frag.* 57 Kern).

[As to the date and *provenance* of the theogony, we are reduced to guess-work. C. Müller *Frag. hist. Gr.* ii. 450 n.** cj. that Hieronymos was Ἱερώνυμος ὁ Αἰγύπτιος ὁ τὴν ἀρχαιολογίαν τὴν Φοινικικὴν συγγραψάμενος (Ioseph. *ant. Iud.* 1. 3. 6, cp. 1. 3. 9, = Euseb. *praep. ev.* 9. 11. 3, cp. 9. 13. 5, Kedren. *hist. comp.* 11 b c (i. 23 Bekker)), and he is followed *e.g.* by F. Susemihl *Geschichte der griechischen Litteratur in der Alexandrinerzeit* Leipzig 1891 i. 376 n. 6 ; but A. Gudeman in Pauly—Wissowa *Real-Enc.* viii. 1564 enters a *caveat*. Hellanikos is commonly regarded as pseudo-Hellanikos ; but Gudeman *loc. cit.* viii. 121 thinks that the theogony current under his name 'war sicher kein besonderes Buch, sondern der Bericht über die Entstehung der Welt nach einem orphischen Gedicht. H. kann ihn recht gut irgendwo gegeben haben.' If so, the Orphic poem itself cannot have been composed later than *c.* 450 B.C. and may have been a good deal earlier. It exhibits various traces of oriental cosmogony and of Greek philosophy. The complex monsters are more Semitic than Hellenic. The world-creating Herakles is perhaps Phoenician (Gruppe *Gr. Myth. Rel.* p. 499 ; but see *eund.* in Roscher *Lex. Myth.* iii. 1141). So, as was pointed out by E. Zeller (*A History of Greek Philosophy* trans. S. F. Alleyne London 1881 i. 102 n. 4 *fin.*), is primeval slime (Sanchouniathon in Philon Bybl. *frag.* 2. 1 (*Frag. hist. Gr.* iii. 565 Müller) *ap.* Euseb. *praep. ev.* 1. 10. 1 f. καὶ ἐκ τῆς αὐτοῦ συμπλοκῆς τοῦ πνεύματος ἐγένετο Μώτ· τοῦτό τινές φασιν ἰλύν, οἱ δὲ ὑδατώδους μίξεως σῆψιν, with which Gruppe *Cult. Myth. orient. Rel.* i. 386 f. well cp. Diod. 1. 10 φασὶ τοίνυν Αἰγύπτιοι κατὰ τὴν ἐξ ἀρχῆς τῶν ὅλων γένεσιν πρώτους ἀνθρώπους γενέσθαι κατὰ τὴν Αἴγυπτον διά τε τὴν εὐκρασίαν τῆς χώρας καὶ διὰ τὴν φύσιν τοῦ Νείλου. τοῦτον γὰρ πολύγονον ὄντα καὶ τὰς τροφὰς αὐτοφυεῖς παρεχόμενον ῥᾳδίως ἐκτρέφειν τὰ ζωογονηθέντα... ὅταν γὰρ τοῦ ποταμοῦ τὴν ἀναχώρησιν ποιουμένου τὴν πρώτην τῆς ἰλύος ὁ ἥλιος διαξηράνῃ, φασὶ συνίστασθαι ζῷα, τινὰ μὲν εἰς τέλος ἀπηρτισμένα, τινὰ δὲ ἡμιτελῆ καὶ πρὸς αὐτῇ συμφυῆ τῇ γῇ, *ib.* 12 τὸ μὲν οὖν πνεῦμα Δία προσαγορεῦσαι μεθερμηνευομένης τῆς λέξεως, ὃν αἴτιον ὄντα τοῦ ψυχικοῦ τοῖς ζῴοις ἐνόμισαν ὑπάρχειν πάντων οἱονεί τινα πατέρα... τὴν δὲ γῆν ὥσπερ ἀγγεῖόν τι τῶν φυομένων ὑπολαμβάνοντας μητέρα προσαγορεῦσαι, the Egyptian word for 'mother' being μοῦθ (Plout. *de Is. et Os.* 56)=Sanchouniathon's Μώτ : *id. Gr. Myth. Rel.*

p. 431 n. 3 further cites the thickening of water into slime and earth in Mandaite speculation (A. J. H. W. Brandt *Die mandäische Religion* Leipzig 1889 p. 50 ff.)). But a similar view was held by Anaximandros (E. Zeller *op. cit.* i. 255 f.), Diogenes of Apollonia (*id. ib.* i. 294, 296), and Anaxagoras (*id. ib.* ii. 356). Empedokles too had spoken of water as a combining element (*frag.* 34 Diels ἄλφιτον ὕδατι κολλήσας). And the equation of Zeus with Pan is again suggestive of philosophical influence (E. Zeller *op. cit.* i. 101), conceivably that of Herakleitos (*supra* i. 28 ff.). On the whole we may conclude that the Orphic theogony bearing the name of Hieronymos or Hellanikos was the summary of an epic poem drafted somewhere in Ionia *c.* 500 B.C.]

(3) The Theogony of the Orphic Rhapsodies.

But the bulk of the Orphic fragments, quoted by neo-Platonists and others, belongs to a third theogony probably called the ἱερὸς λόγος (Orph. *frag.* 63 Kern *ap. et. mag.* p. 231, 22 ff.) or ἱεροὶ λόγοι (Souid. *s.v.* Ὀρφεύς) and contained in 24 Rhapsodies ascribed by some to Theognetos the Thessalian, by others to Kerkops the Pythagorean (*id. ib.*). Of Theognetos nothing more is known. Epigenes in his work *On poetry attributed to Orpheus* (*ap.* Clem. Al. *strom.* I. 21 p. 81, 11 ff. Stählin) regarded Kerkops the Pythagorean as the author of the Orphic εἰς Ἅιδου κατάβασις and ἱερὸς λόγος (cp. Cic. *de nat. deor.* I. 107). And Pythagorean authorship is not impossible, or even improbable; for Herakleides Lembos *frag.* 8 (*Frag. hist. Gr.* iii. 169 f. Müller) *ap.* Diog. Laert. 8. 7 cites the opening hexameter of a ἱερὸς λόγος ascribed to Pythagoras; Iambl. *v. Pyth.* 146 quotes from another ἱερὸς λόγος or περὶ θεῶν λόγος, believed to be by Pythagoras himself or by his son Telauges, a passage of Doric prose, in which Pythagoras declares that he was initiated at Libethra in Thrace by Aglaophamos and there learnt that Orpheus son of Kalliope, taught by his mother on Mt Pangaion, had enunciated the fundamental significance of number etc.; *id. ib.* 258 f. tells how the rhetorician Ninon professed to divulge Pythagorean secrets contained in a work entitled λόγος ἱερός; Souid. *s.v.* Ἀριγνώτη = Eudok. *viol.* 173 speaks of a ἱερὸς λόγος written by the Pythagorean Arignote; and Plout. *de gen. Socr.* 24 makes Theanor the Pythagorean describe Simmias' story of Timarchos' visit to the Underworld as λόγον...ἱερόν: see further A. Delatte *Études sur la littérature pythagoricienne* Paris 1915 pp. 1—79 ('Un ΙΕΡΟΣ ΛΟΓΟΣ pythagoricien'). The Rhapsodic theogony, according to Damaskios *quaest. de primis principiis* 123 (i. 316, 18 ff. Ruelle), cp. *ib.* 50 (i. 100, 19 f.), 123 *bis* (i. 318, 6 ff.), gave the following sequence of events:—In the beginning was Chronos the ageless, father of Aither and Chaos. Then came the cosmic egg, called also 'the brilliant *chitón*' or 'the cloud' (*ib.* 123 (i. 317, 2 f.) ἤτοι τὸ κυούμενον καὶ τὸ κύον ᾠὸν τὸν θεόν, ἢ τὸν ἀργῆτα χιτῶνα, ἢ τὴν νεφέλην), from which sprang Phanes, otherwise known as Metis or Erikepaios. [As to the meaning of these names valuable information is preserved to us by Io. Malal. *chron.* 4 p. 74 Dindorf ἔφρασε δὲ ὅτι τὸ φῶς ῥῆξαν τὸν αἰθέρα ἐφώτισε τὴν γῆν καὶ πᾶσαν τὴν κτίσιν, εἰπὼν ἐκεῖνο εἶναι τὸ φῶς τὸ ῥῆξαν τὸν αἰθέρα τὸ προειρημένον, τὸ ὑπέρτατον πάντων, οὗ ὄνομα ὁ αὐτὸς Ὀρφεὺς ἀκούσας ἐκ τῆς μαντείας ἐξεῖπε, Μῆτιν, Φάνητα, Ἐρικεπαῖον (*sic*)· ὅπερ ἑρμηνεύεται τῇ κοινῇ γλώσσῃ βουλή, φῶς, ζωοδοτήρ (= Kedren. *hist. comp.* 57 D (i. 102 Bekker) βουλή, φῶς, ζωοδοτήρ, cp. Souid. *s.v.* Ὀρφεύς 7 βουλήν, φῶς, ζωήν = Kedren. *hist. comp.* 84 B (i. 148) βουλή, φῶς, ζωή) and by Nonnos Abbas *collectio et explicatio historiarum quibus Gregorius Nazianzenus in priore invectiva in Julianum usus est* 78 (xxxvi. 1028 C Migne) Περὶ Φάνητος καὶ Ἡρικαπαίου. ἐν τοῖς Ὀρφικοῖς ποιήμασιν εἰσηνέχθη τὰ δύο ταῦτα ὀνόματα μετὰ καὶ ἄλλων πολλῶν· ὧν τὸν Φάνητα εἰσφέρει αἰδοῖον ἔχοντα ὀπίσω περὶ τὴν πυγήν. λέγουσι δὲ αὐτὸν ἔφορον εἶναι τῆς ζωογόνου δυνάμεως· ὁμοίως δὲ καὶ τὸν Ἡρικαπαῖον λέγουσιν ἑτέρας ἔφορον εἶναι δυνάμεως (repeated in a corrupt form by Souid. *s.v.* Φάνης: see G. Bernhardy *ad loc.*). From this it appears that the names Μῆτις and Φάνης had an obvious sense for Greek ears, but that Ἡρικεπαῖος or Ἡρικαπαῖος had not. Presumably Μῆτις (masc.) was a *Kosename* either for πολύμητις, which occurs as an Orphic designation of this deity (Orph. *h. Protog.* 6. 10), or—and this I regard as the more probable view— for μητίετα, the epic appellative of Zeus (*supra* i. 14 n. 1). Φάνης was certainly taken by the Greeks to denote a god of light or daylight or sunlight (*supra* i. 7 n. 6): but of course it remains possible that his name was originally non-Greek; it may *e.g.* have been Thraco-Phrygian, cp. Auson. *epigr.* 48. 3 Mysi Phanacen nominant, 49. 1 Μυσῶν δὲ Φανάκης (F. Creuzer *Symbolik und Mythologie*³ Leipzig and Darmstadt 1840 ii. 226, 1842 iv. 80, Lobeck *Aglaophamus* i. 478 n. ¹, O. Höfer in Roscher *Lex. Myth.* iii. 2248). Ἡρικεπαῖος or Ἡρικαπαῖος is a well-known *crux* (for older views see K. W. Goettling *De Ericapaeo Orphicorum numine* Jenae 1862 (=*id. Opuscula academica* Lipsiae 1869 pp. 206—214); for newer, O. Waser in Pauly—Wissowa *Real-Enc.* vi. 452 f. and K. Beth 'Über die Herkunft der orphischen Erikepaios' (god of *Ericibba*=Eridu) in the *Wiener Studien* 1912 xxxiv. 288—300). If we may rely on Malalas' interpretation ζωοδοτήρ, it is clear that the name was not Greek. I incline to think that it was Thracian or Thraco-Phrygian. Hence its occurrence as a cult-title of Dionysos at Hierokaisareia in Lydia (J. Keil—A. v. Premerstein 'Bericht über eine Reise in Lydien und der südlichen Aiolis' in the *Denkschr. d. Akad. Wien* 1910 ii. Abh. p. 54 f. no. 112 fig. 51=W. Quandt *De Baccho ab Alexandri aetate in Asia Minore culto* Halis Saxonum 1913 p. 181 a round altar of white marble inscribed in lettering of *s.* ii A.D. ἐπὶ ἱεροφάντου | Ἀρτεμιδώρου τοῦ Ἀπολ|λωνίου Μηνόφιλος, Περη|λίας καὶ Σεκοῦνδος Ἀπολ|λωνίου οἱ συγγενεῖς Διο|νύσω Ἡρικεπαίω τὸν βωμόν with wreath below and two garlands supported on ram's-heads). The second element in the compound might be paralleled, as O. Gruppe saw (in Roscher *Lex. Myth.* iii. 2268), from Παντικάπης the river in European Sarmatia and Παντικάπαιον the town in the Tauric Chersonesos. The first element, it seems to me, recurs in the name of the river Ἡριδανός (with which A. Fick *Vorgriechische Ortsnamen* Göttingen 1905 p. 129 and *Hattiden und Danubier in Griechenland* Göttingen 1909 p. 37 compared the river-names Ἀπιδανός in Thessaly, Ἰάρδανος in Lydia, Crete, and Elis). Indeed, if Ἡρι-κεπαῖος meant 'Giver of Life,' I would venture to translate Ἡρι-δανός by 'River of Life'—an appellation suited to that mythical stream (Strab. 215 περὶ τὸν Ἡριδανόν, τὸν μηδαμοῦ γῆς ὄντα, πλησίον δὲ τοῦ Πάδου λεγόμενον, cp. Hdt. 3. 115, Polyb. 2. 16. 6, Plin. *nat. hist.* 37. 31), which was not only a river on earth but also a constellation in heaven (Hes. *frag.* 199 Rzach *ap.* Hyg. *fab.* 152 b, 154, schol. Strozziana *in* Caes. Germ. *Aratea* p. 174, 6 ff. (cp. p. 185, 4 ff.) Breysig, Lact. Plac. *narr. fab.* 2. 2 f., Arat. *phaen.* 359 ff. with schol. *ad loc.* 355, 359, pseudo-Eratosth. *catast.* 37, Caes. Germ. *Aratea* 367 ff., Cic. *Aratea* 143 ff. Baehrens (387 ff.), Mart. Cap. 838, 841, 842, Claudian. *de sext. cons. Hon. Aug.* 175 ff., *Anth. Lat.* i. 2 no. 679. 12 Riese (Priscianus), Nonn. *Dion.* 2. 326 f., 23. 298 ff., 38. 429 ff., Myth. Vat. 3. 6. 21, Eustath. *in* Dionys. *per.* 288) by some called Okeanos (Hyg. *poet. astr.* 2. 32) or the Nile (Hyg. *poet. astr.* 2. 32, pseudo-Eratosth. *catast.* 37, schol. Arat. *phaen.* 359, schol. Caes. Germ. *Aratea* p. 417, 19 Eyssenhardt): see further R. Brown *Eridanus: river and constellation* London 1883, G. Thiele *Antike Himmelsbilder* Berlin 1898 pp. 5, 29 f., 39 f., 49, 124 ff. fig. 50, 147, 164 ff. fig. 72, pls. 2, 4, A. Jeremias *Handbuch der altorientalischen Geisteskultur* Leipzig 1913 pp. 60, 189, *id.* in

Roscher *Lex. Myth.* iv. 1468 fig. 35.] Phanes was also spoken of as Πρωτόγονος (Orph. *frag.* 86 Kern *ap.* Herm. *in* Plat. *Phaedr.* p. 141 (p. 148, 25 ff. Couvreur), Orph. *frag.* 85 Kern *ap.* Prokl. *in* Plat. *Cratyl.* p. 33, 3 ff. Pasquali, *eund. in* Plat. *Tim.* i. 450, 9 ff. Diehl, i. 451, 11 ff., iii. 209, 1 f., Damask. *quaest. de primis principiis* 53 (i. 107, 13 f. Ruelle), 89 (i. 217, 26 f.), 98 (i. 251, 18 ff.), 111 (i. 286, 15 f.), Orph. *h. Protog.* 6. 1, *h. Rhe.* 14. 1, Athenag. *supplicatio pro Christianis* 20 p. 23 Schwartz, Lact. *div. inst.* 1. 5, Nonn. *Dion.* 9. 141 (cp. 157 αὐτογόνου), 12. 34 : see further O. Gruppe in Roscher *Lex. Myth.* iii. 2257 f., O. Höfer *ib.* iii. 3183 f.), Ἀνταύγης (Orph. *frag.* 237, 4 Kern *ap.* Macrob. *Sat.* 1. 18. 12, Orph. *h. Protog.* 6. 9), Φαέθων (Orph. *frag.* 73 Kern *ap.* Lact. *div. inst.* 1. 5), Διόνυσος (Orph. *frag.* 237, 3 Kern *ap.* Macrob. *Sat.* 1. 18. 12 f., Orph. *frag.* 237 p. 250 Kern *ap.* Diod. 1. 11, Prokl. *in* Plat. *Tim.* i. 336, 15 f. Diehl, cp. Orph. *frag.* 239 b, 1 Kern *ap.* Iust. *cohort.* 15 and *frag.* 239 b Kern *ap.* Macrob. *Sat.* 1. 18. 18 cited *supra* i. 187 n. 4, i. 234 n. 4 : see also O. Gruppe in Roscher *Lex. Myth.* iii. 2260), Εὐβουλεύς (Orph. *frag.* 237, 4 Kern *ap.* Macrob. *Sat.* 1. 18. 12 and 17, cp. Orph. *h. Adon.* 56. 3), Πρίηπος ἄναξ (Orph. *h. Protog.* 6. 9), and Ἔρως (*e.g.* Orph. *frag.* 74 Kern *ap.* Prokl. *in* Plat. *Tim.* i. 433, 31 ff. Diehl, Orph. *frag.* 37 Kern *ap.* schol. Ap. Rhod. 3. 26, Orph. *frag.* 82 Kern *ap.* Prokl. *in* Plat. *Tim.* iii. 101, 20 ff. Diehl, Orph. *frag.* 83 Kern *ap.* Prokl. *in* Plat. *Alcib.* i. 66 Creuzer, Orph. *frag.* 170 Kern *ap.* Prokl. *in* Plat. *Tim.* i. 336, 11 ff. Diehl and *ap. eund. in* Plat. *Alcib.* i. 233 Creuzer, cp. Orph. *Arg.* 14 ff.). As μονογενής he was in the time of the emperor Zenon (474—491 A.D.) compared with Christ Himself (*theosoph. Tubing.* 61 in K. Buresch *Klaros* Leipzig 1889 p. 116 f. ὅτι ἐν πολλοῖς Φάνητα φερωνύμως ὁ Ὀρφεὺς προσαγορεύει τὸν μονογενῆ, τὸν υἱὸν τοῦ θεοῦ. κ.τ.λ.). Phanes, when he emerged from the 'white egg' (Orph. *frag.* 70 Kern *ap.* Damask. *quaest. de primis principiis* 55 (i. 111, 17 ff. Ruelle) ἔπειτα δ' ἔτευξε μέγας Χρόνος (so C. A. Lobeck for Κρόνος codd.) αἰθέρι δίῳ | ᾠεὸν ἀργύφεον), contained within him the seed of the gods (Orph. *frag.* 85 Kern *ap.* Prokl. *in* Plat. *Cratyl.* p. 33, 5 f. Pasquali Μῆτιν σπέρμα φέροντα θεῶν κλυτόν, ὅν τε Φάνητα | πρωτόγονον μάκαρες κάλεον κατὰ μακρὸν Ὄλυμπον). Being female as well as male, he begat Nyx, and subsequently consorted with her (Orph. *frag.* 98 Kern *ap.* Prokl. *in* Plat. *Tim.* i. 450, 22 ff. Diehl, Damask. *quaest. de primis principiis* 244 (ii. 116, 4 Ruelle), cp. Prokl. *in* Plat. *Tim.* iii. 170, 4 f. Diehl, Damask. *quaest. de primis principiis* 209 (ii. 92, 22 f. Ruelle)) and by her had three successive pairs of children—Ge or Gaia and Ouranos (Orph. *frag.* 109 Kern *ap.* Herm. *in* Plat. *Phaedr.* pp. 141, 144 (pp. 148, 17 ff., 154, 23 ff. Couvreur)), Rhea and Kronos, Hera and Zeus (Damaskios *quaest. de primis principiis* 244 (ii. 116, 5 ff. Ruelle)). Nyx as queen (Damaskios *quaest. de primis principiis* 209 (ii. 92, 25 ff. Ruelle)) received the sceptre of Phanes or Erikepaios, and in her turn transmitted it to Ouranos, Kronos, Zeus, Dionysos (Orph. *frag.* 107 Kern *ap.* Syrian. *in* Aristot. *met.* N. 4. 1091 b 4 p. 182, 9 ff. Kroll, Alex. Aphr. *in* Aristot. *met.* N. 4. 1091 b 4 p. 821, 5 ff. Hayduck, Prokl. *in* Plat. *Tim.* i. 306, 12 f. and iii. 168, 15 ff. Diehl, Herm. *in* Plat. *Phaedr.* p. 143 (p. 152, 15 ff. Couvreur), Olympiod. *in* Plat. *Phaed.* 61 C p. 2, 21 ff. Norvin, Michael Ephes. *in* Aristot. *met.* N. 4. 1091 b 4 (ed. Berolin. iv. 828 a 8 ff.), Orph. *frag.* 101 Kern *ap.* Prokl. *in* Plat. *Cratyl.* p. 54, 28 ff. Pasquali, Orph. *frag.* 102 Kern *ap.* Alex. Aphr. *in* Aristot. *met.* N. 4. 1091 b 4 p. 821, 19 ff. Hayduck, Syrian. *in* Aristot. *met.* N. 4. 1091 b 4 p. 182, 14 f. Kroll) ; she also had the gift of prophecy (Orph. *frag.* 103 Kern *ap.* Herm. *in* Plat. *Phaedr.* p. 140 (p. 147, 20 ff. Couvreur)). The gods saw with wonderment the light of their creator Phanes shining in the *aithér* (Orph. *frag.* 86 Kern *ap.* Prokl. *in* Plat. *Tim.* i. 435, 3 ff. Diehl (cp. *ib.* iii. 83, 4 ff.), Prokl. *in* Plat. *theol.* 3. 21 p. 161 Portus, Damask

quaest. de primis principiis 113 (i. 291, 18 ff. Ruelle), Herm. *in* Plat. *Phaedr.*
p. 141 (p. 148, 25 ff. Couvreur), cp. Wolf *anecd.* iii. 209). But Zeus with a view to
the ordering of all things consulted both Nyx and Kronos, whom he had already
bound (Orph. *frag.* 164 Kern *ap.* Prokl. *in* Plat. *Tim.* i. 206, 26 ff. Diehl, *id. in*
Plat. *Cratyl.* p. 30 f.) and mutilated after making him drunk on honey (Orph.
frag. 154 Kern *ap.* Porph. *de antr. nymph.* 16 παρὰ δὲ τῷ Ὀρφεῖ ὁ Κρόνος μέλιτι
ὑπὸ Διὸς ἐνεδρεύεται· πλησθεὶς γὰρ μέλιτος μεθύει καὶ σκοτοῦται ὡς ἀπὸ (Lobeck
cj. ὑπὸ) οἴνου καὶ ὑπνοῖ ὡς παρὰ Πλάτωνι (*symp.* 203 B ὁ οὖν Πόρος μεθυσθεὶς τοῦ
νέκταρος, οἶνος γὰρ οὔπω ἦν, εἰς τὸν τοῦ Διὸς κῆπον εἰσελθὼν βεβαρημένος ηὗδεν) ὁ
Πόρος τοῦ νέκταρος πλησθείς· οὔπω γὰρ οἶνος ἦν. φησὶ γὰρ παρ' Ὀρφεῖ ἡ Νὺξ τῷ
Διὶ ὑποτιθεμένη τὸν διὰ μέλιτος δόλον · εὖτ' ἂν δή μιν ἴδηαι ὑπὸ δρυσὶν ὑψικόμοισιν |
ἔργοισιν μεθύοντα μελισσάων ἐριβόμβων, | δῆσον αὐτὸν (Barnes cj. αὐτίκα μιν
δῆσον). ὃ καὶ πάσχει ὁ Κρόνος καὶ δεθεὶς ἐκτέμνεται ὡς ὁ Οὐρανός, cp. Prokl. *in*
Plat. *Cratyl.* pp. 54, 19 and 62, 3 ff. Pasquali). At the advice of Nyx Zeus leapt
upon Phanes and swallowed him (Orph. *frag.* 82 Kern *ap.* Prokl. *in* Plat.
Tim. iii. 102, 2 f. Diehl ὁ δὲ Ὀρφεὺς καὶ ἐπιπηδᾶν αὐτῷ καὶ καταπίνειν δειξάσης
μέντοι τῆς Νυκτός, Orph. *frag.* 167 Kern *ap.* Prokl. *in* Plat. *Tim.* i. 324, 14 ff. Diehl
ταῦτα δὲ καὶ ὁ Ὀρφεὺς ἐνδεικνύμενος καταπίνεσθαι τὸν νοητὸν θεὸν ἔφατο παρὰ τοῦ
δημιουργοῦ τῶν ὅλων· …ὁ δὲ θεολόγος καὶ οἷον ἐπιπηδᾶν αὐτὸν τῷ νοητῷ καὶ καταπίνειν, ὡς ὁ μῦθος ἔφησεν). Having thus with wide open jaws devoured Phanes,
Zeus had within his own belly the body of all things and, since he had digested
the power of that creative god, was himself able to create the universe anew
(Orph. *frag.* 167 a Kern *ap.* Prokl. *in* Plat. *Tim.* i. 324, 29 ff. Diehl ὡς τότε
Πρωτογόνοιο χανὼν μένος Ἡρικεπαίου | τῶν πάντων δέμας εἶχεν ἑῇ ἐνὶ γαστέρι
κοίλῃ, | μῖξε δ' ἑοῖς μελέεσσι θεοῦ δύναμίν τε καὶ ἀλκήν, | τοὔνεκα σὺν τῷ πάντα (παρὰ
codd. E. Abel prints παντὶ E. Diehl cj. πάντα) Διὸς πάλιν ἐντὸς ἐτύχθη.|…πάντα
τάδε κρύψας αὖθις φάος ἐς πολυγηθές | μέλλεν ἀπὸ κραδίης προφέρειν πάλι θέσκελα
ῥέζων, cp. Prokl. *in* Plat. *Cratyl.* p. 62, 3 ff. Pasquali). Inside Zeus were made
afresh the world and all its contents, including gods and goddesses (Orph.
frag. 167 b Kern *ap.* Prokl. *in* Plat. *Tim.* i. 313, 9 ff. Diehl τοὔνεκα σὺν τῷ πάντα
(E. Abel gives παντὶ) Διὸς πάλιν ἐντὸς ἐτύχθη | αἰθέρος εὐρείης ἠδ' οὐρανοῦ ἀγλαὸν
ὕψος, | πόντου τ' ἀτρυγέτου γαίης τ' ἐρικυδέος ἕδρη (E. Abel has εὔρη), | Ὠκεανός
τε μέγας καὶ νείατα τάρταρα γαίης | καὶ ποταμοὶ καὶ πόντος ἀπείριτος ἄλλα τε
πάντα | πάντες τ' ἀθάνατοι μάκαρες θεοὶ ἠδὲ θέαιναι, | ὅσσα τ' ἔην γεγαῶτα καὶ
ὕστερον ὁππόσ' ἔμελλεν, | ἐνγένετο, Ζηνὸς δ' ἐνὶ γαστέρι σύρρα πεφύκει, cp. Prokl.
in Plat. *Parm.* iii (p. 621 Stallbaum), Orph. *frag.* 169 Kern *ap.* Prokl. *in* Plat.
Parm. iv (p. 750 Stallbaum) οὕτως δὲ Ζηνὸς καὶ ἐν ὄμμασι πατρὸς ἄνακτος | ναίουσ'
ἀθάνατοί τε θεοὶ θνητοί τ' ἄνθρωποι | ὅσσα τ' ἔην γεγαῶτα καὶ ὕστερον ὁππόσ'
ἔμελλε, cp. *theosoph. Tubing.* 50 in K. Buresch *Klaros* Leipzig 1889 p. 109 f.).
Accordingly Zeus himself was described by the Orphists in pantheistic terms
(Orph. *frag.* 21 a Kern *ap.* Aristot. *de mundo* 7. 401 a 27 ff. (cp. Clem. Al. *strom.*
5. 14 p. 409, 4 ff. Stählin) διὸ καὶ ἐν τοῖς Ὀρφικοῖς οὐ κακῶς λέγεται:—

Ζεὺς πρῶτος γένετο, Ζεὺς ὕστατος ἀργικέραυνος·
Ζεὺς κεφαλή, Ζεὺς μέσσα, Διὸς δ' ἐκ πάντα τέτυκται·
Ζεὺς πυθμὴν γαίης τε καὶ οὐρανοῦ ἀστερόεντος·
Ζεὺς ἄρσην γένετο, Ζεὺς ἄμβροτος ἔπλετο νύμφη·
Ζεὺς πνοιὴ πάντων, Ζεὺς ἀκαμάτου πυρὸς ὁρμή·
Ζεὺς πόντου ῥίζα, Ζεὺς ἥλιος ἠδὲ σελήνη·
Ζεὺς βασιλεύς, Ζεὺς ἀρχὸς ἀπάντων ἀργικέραυνος·
πάντας γὰρ κρύψας αὖθις φάος ἐς πολυγηθὲς
ἐξ ἱερῆς κραδίης ἀνενέγκατο μέρμερα ῥέζων.

A fuller version of these lines is found in Orph. *frag.* 168 Kern *ap.* Euseb. *praep.*
ev. 3. 9. 1—3=Stob. *ecl.* 1. 1. 23 p. 29, 9 ff. Wachsmuth (cp. Prokl. *in* Plat.
Alcib. i. 233 Creuzer, *id. in* Plat. *Parm.* iii (p. 621 Stallbaum), *id. in* Plat. *Tim.* i.
313, 18 ff. Diehl, *ib.* i. 161, 23 ff., i. 307, 28 ff.) τὸν γὰρ Δία τὸν νοῦν τοῦ κόσμου
ὑπολαμβάνοντες, ὃς τὰ ἐν αὐτῷ ἐδημιούργησεν ἔχων τὸν κόσμον, ἐν μὲν ταῖς θεολογίαις
ταύτῃ περὶ αὐτοῦ παραδεδώκασιν οἱ τὰ Ὀρφέως εἰπόντες·

Ζεὺς πρῶτος γένετο, Ζεὺς ὕστατος ἀργικέραυνος·
Ζεὺς κεφαλή, Ζεὺς μέσσα, Διὸς δ' ἐκ πάντα τέτυκται·
Ζεὺς ἄρσην γένετο, Ζεὺς ἄφθιτος[1] ἔπλετο νύμφη·
Ζεὺς πυθμὴν γαίης τε καὶ οὐρανοῦ ἀστερόεντος·
Ζεὺς βασιλεύς, Ζεὺς αὐτὸς ἁπάντων ἀρχιγένεθλος.
ἓν κράτος, εἷς δαίμων γένετο, μέγας ἀρχὸς ἁπάντων,
ἓν δὲ[2] δέμας βασίλειον, ἐν ᾧ τάδε πάντα κυκλεῖται,
πῦρ καὶ ὕδωρ καὶ γαῖα καὶ αἰθήρ, νύξ τε καὶ ἦμαρ,
καὶ Μῆτις πρῶτος γενέτωρ[3] καὶ Ἔρως πολυτερπής·
πάντα γὰρ ἐν μεγάλῳ Ζηνὸς[4] τάδε σώματι[5] κεῖται.
τοῦ δή τοι κεφαλὴ[6] μὲν ἰδεῖν καὶ καλὰ πρόσωπα
οὐρανὸς αἰγλήεις, ὃν χρύσεαι ἀμφὶς ἔθειραι
ἄστρων μαρμαρέων περικαλλέες ἠερέθονται·
ταύρεα δ' ἀμφοτέρωθε δύο χρύσεια κέρατα,
ἀντολίη τε δύσις τε, θεῶν ὁδοὶ οὐρανιώνων·
ὄμματα δ' ἠέλιός τε καὶ ἀντιόωσα[7] σελήνη·
νοῦς[8] δέ <οἱ[9]> ἀψευδής, βασιλήϊος[10], ἄφθιτος αἰθήρ,
ᾧ δὴ πάντα κλύει[11] καὶ φράζεται, οὐδέ τις ἐστὶν
αὐδὴ οὔτ'[12] ἐνοπὴ οὔτε[13] κτύπος οὐδὲ[14] μὲν ὄσσα
ἣ λήθει Διὸς οὔας ὑπερμενέος Κρονίωνος.
ὧδε μὲν ἀθανάτην κεφαλὴν ἔχει ἠδὲ νόημα·
σῶμα[15] δέ οἱ περιφεγγές[16], ἀπείριτον, ἀστυφέλικτον,
ὄβριμον[17], ὀβριμόγυιον, ὑπερμενὲς ὧδε τέτυκται·
ὦμοι μὲν καὶ στέρνα καὶ εὐρέα νῶτα θεοῖο
ἀὴρ εὐρυβίης· πτέρυγες δέ οἱ ἐξεφύοντο,
τῆς ἐπὶ πάντα ποτᾶθ'· ἱερὴ δέ οἱ ἔπλετο νηδὺς
γαῖά τε παμμήτειρ' ὀρέων τ' αἰπεινὰ κάρηνα·
μέσσῃ δὲ ζώνη βαρυηχέος[18] οἶδμα θαλάσσης
καὶ πόντου· πυμάτη δὲ βάσις χθονὸς ἔνδοθι ῥίζαι
τάρταρά τ' εὐρώεντα καὶ ἔσχατα πείρατα γαίης.
πάντα δ' ἀποκρύψας[19] αὖθις φάος ἐς πολυγηθὲς
μέλλεν[20] ἀπὸ κραδίης προφέρειν πάλι, θέσκελα ῥέζων.

Ζεὺς οὖν ὁ πᾶς κόσμος, ζῷον ἐκ ζῴων καὶ θεὸς ἐκ θεῶν· Ζεὺς δέ, καθὸ νοῦς, ἀφ' οὗ

[1] ἄμβροτος Stob. [2] δὲ om. Stob.
[3] So Prokl. πρωτογενέτωρ codd. *A* Euseb., *F* Stob.
[4] Ζηνὸς μεγάλῳ Stob. Ζηνὸς μεγάλου Prokl. [5] δώματι Prokl.
[6] δ' ἤτοι κεφαλὴ Prokl. δή τοι κεφαλὴν Euseb. [7] Heringa cj. ἀνταυγοῦσα.
[8] Heringa cj. οὖς. [9] So Prokl. Om. Euseb., cod. *F* Stob.
[10] Heringa cj. ἀψευδὲς βασιλήιον.
[11] κλύει cod. *F* Stob. and Prokl. κυκλεῖ Euseb.
[12] οὐδ' Stob. [13] οὐδὲ Stob. οὐδ' αὖ Prokl.
[14] So Prokl. οὔτε Euseb. [15] σῆμα cod. *F* Stob.
[16] πυριφεγγὲς Prokl. [17] ἄτρομον Stob.
[18] βαθυηχέος Prokl. [19] τάδε κρύψας Prokl.
[20] So cod. *F* Stob., cp. Prokl. μέλλει Euseb.

προφέρει πάντα καὶ δημιουργεῖ τοῖς νοήμασι. κ.τ.λ., *ib.* 3. 9. 10 f. δι' ὧν ἀνεπι-
καλύπτως ζῷον μέγα τὸν κόσμον ὑποθέμενος, καὶ τοῦτον Δία προσειπών, νοῦν μὲν
αὐτοῦ τὸν αἰθέρα, σῶμα δὲ τὰ λοιπὰ τοῦ κόσμου μέρη ἀπεφήνατο εἶναι. τοιοῦτος μέν
τις ὁ διὰ τῶν ἐπῶν ὑπογραφόμενος τυγχάνει Ζεύς. ὁ δὲ τῶν ἐπῶν ἐξηγητὴς ἀρξάμενος
μὲν τοῖς ἔπεσιν ἀκολούθως λέγει, Ζεὺς οὖν ὁ πᾶς κόσμος, ζῷον ἐκ ζῴων, θεὸς ἐκ
θεῶν· σαφῶς τὸν θεολογούμενον Δία οὐδὲ ἄλλον ἢ τὸν ὁρώμενον καὶ αἰσθητὸν κόσμον
δηλοῦσθαι διὰ τῶν ἐπῶν ἑρμηνεύσας). Having asked of Nyx how all things might
be both one and divided, he was bidden to wrap *aithér* round the world and tie
up the bundle with the 'golden cord' (Orph. *frag.* 165 f. Kern *ap.* Prokl. *in* Plat.
Tim. i. 313, 31 ff. Diehl, ii. 24, 23 ff., ii. 112, 3 ff. : cp. *Il.* 8. 18 ff. with the sensible
remarks of Dr W. Leaf *ad loc.*). In arranging the universe he was helped by
Dike (Orph. *frag.* 158 Kern *ap.* Prokl. *in* Plat. *remp.* ii. 144, 29 ff. Kroll, *in* Plat.
theol. 6. 8 p. 363 Portus) and Nomos (Orph. *frag.* 160 Kern *ap.* Prokl. *in* Plat.
Tim. i. 315, 11 ff. Diehl, *id. in* Plat. *Alcib.* i. 219 f. Creuzer). Rhea, as the
mother of Zeus, was named Demeter (Orph. *frag.* 145 Kern *ap.* Prokl. *in* Plat.
Cratyl. pp. 80, 10 ff. and 90, 28 ff. Pasquali, *in* Plat. *theol.* 5. 11 p. 267 Portus).
Athena in full armour sprang from the head of Zeus (Orph. *frag.* 174 Kern *ap.*
Prokl. *in* Plat. *Tim.* i. 166, 21 ff. Diehl, cp. Orph. *frag.* 176 Kern *ap.* Prokl. *in*
Plat. *Tim.* i. 169, 1 ff. Diehl) and, as 'leader of the Kouretes,' taught them
rhythmic dancing (Orph. *frag.* 185 Kern *ap.* Prokl. *in* Plat. *Cratyl.* p. 112, 16 ff.
Pasquali) : hence the first Kouretes are said to have been wreathed with olive
(Orph. *frag.* 186 Kern *ap.* Prokl. *in* Plat. *remp.* i. 138, 12 ff. Kroll). Athena was
also the best of the goddesses at weaving and spinning (Orph. *frag.* 178 Kern
ap. Prokl. *in* Plat. *Cratyl.* p. 21, 13 ff. Pasquali). Being herself the wisdom of
the creator and the virtue of the leading gods, she bore the name of Arete
(Orph. *frag.* 175 Kern *ap.* Prokl. *in* Plat. *Tim.* i. 170, 3 ff. Diehl, cp. i. 185, 1 ff.).
Artemis, the lover of virginity (Orph. *frag.* 187 f. Kern *ap.* Prokl. *in* Plat.
Cratyl. p. 105, 18 ff. Pasquali), was also called Hekate (Orph. *frag.* 188 Kern *ap.*
Prokl. *in* Plat. *Cratyl.* p. 106, 25 ff. Pasquali). Zeus and Dione between them
produced Aphrodite, who arose—like her namesake the daughter of Ouranos—
from the seed of the god falling into the sea (cp. Orph. *frag.* 127 Kern *ap.* Prokl.
in Plat. *Cratyl.* p. 110, 15 ff. Pasquali μήδεα δ' ἐς πέλαγος πέσεν ὑψόθεν, ἀμφὶ δὲ
τοῖσι | λευκὸς ἐπιπλώουσιν ἑλίσσετο πάντοθεν ἀφρός· | ἐν δὲ περιπλομέναις ὥραις
ἐνιαυτὸς ἔτικτεν | παρθένον αἰδοίην, ἣν δὴ παλάμαις ὑπέδεκτο | γεινομένην τὸ πρῶτον
ὁμοῦ Ζῆλός τ' Ἀπάτη τε of the first Aphrodite with Orph. *frag.* 183 Kern *ap.*
Prokl. *in* Plat. *Cratyl.* p. 110, 23 ff. Pasquali τὸν δὲ πόθος πλέον εἷλ', ἀπὸ
δ' ἔκθορε πατρὶ μεγίστῳ | αἰδοίων ἀφροῖο γονή, ὑπέδεκτο δὲ πόντος | σπέρμα
Διὸς μεγάλου· περιτελλομένου δ' ἐνιαυτοῦ | ὥραις καλλιφύτοις τέκ' ἐγερσιγέλωτ'
Ἀφροδίτην | ἀφρογενῆ of the second). Zeus also mated with his sister Hera, who
was said to be ἰσοτελής, 'of equal rank,' with him (Orph. *frag.* 163 Kern *ap.*
Prokl. *in* Plat. *Tim.* i. 450, 20 ff. Diehl, cp. *ib.* iii. 249, 2 ff. So also Orph. εὐχὴ
πρὸς Μουσαῖον 16, *id. h. Her.* 16. 2, *id. frag.* 115 Kern *ap.* Eustath. *in* Dionys.
per. 1, Dion Chrys. *or.* 36 p. 99 Reiske). O. Gruppe (*Cult. Myth. orient. Rel.*
i. 637 ff., in the *Jahrb. f. class. Philol.* 1890 Suppl. xvii. 716 ff., *Gr. Myth. Rel.*
p. 432, in Roscher *Lex. Myth.* iii. 1140 f.) contends that the Rhapsodic theogony
further included much that E. Abel (*Orphica* Lipsiae—Pragae 1885 p. 224 ff.)
assigns to the Τελεταί, in particular the whole story of Dionysos. Zeus consorted
with his own mother Rhea or Demeter, both he and she being in the form of
snakes, and had by her a horned, four-eyed, two-faced daughter Phersephone
or Kore, with whom he, again in snake-form, consorted and had for offspring a
horned babe, the chthonian Dionysos or Zagreus (*supra* i. 398 : other notices of

the myth in Ov. *met.* 6. 114, Philostr. *epist.* 30 (58) Hercher, Nonn. *Dion.* 5. 563 ff., Orph. *frag.* 195 Kern *ap.* Prokl. *in* Plat. *Cratyl.* p. 85, 19 ff. Pasquali, Orph. *frag.* 198 Kern *ap.* Prokl. *in* Plat. *theol.* 6. 11 p. 371 Portus, cp. Orph. *frags.* 180, 192 f. Kern with the remarks of Lobeck *Aglaophamus* i. 550 ff. and Orph. *frag.* 43 Kern). Zeus installed Dionysos or Zagreus on his own throne as king of the gods, allowing him to hold the sceptre and wield the lightning, the thunder, and the rain (*supra* i. 398 f., 647 n. 3). The decrees of the Father were confirmed by the Son (Orph. *frag.* 218 Kern *ap.* Prokl. *in* Plat. *Tim.* iii. 316, 3 ff. Diehl κραῖνε μὲν οὖν Ζεὺς πάντα πατήρ, Βάκχος δ' ἐπέκραινε, with which Gruppe *Gr. Myth. Rel.* p. 432 n. 1 aptly cp. Damaskios *quaest. de primis principiis* 245 (ii. 117, 2 ff. Ruelle) καὶ δὴ καὶ ὁ Διόνυσος ἐπικραίνει τὰ τοῦ Διὸς ἔργα, φησὶν Ὀρφεύς, ὁλοποιοῦ τοῦ Διὸς ὄντος). Apollon (Orph. *frag.* 211 Kern *ap.* Prokl. *in* Plat. *Alcib.* i. 83 Creuzer) and the Kouretes (Orph. *frag.* 151 Kern *ap.* Prokl. *in* Plat. *Cratyl.* p. 58, 1 ff. Pasquali, *in* Plat. *Tim.* i. 317, 11 ff. Diehl, *in* Plat. *theol.* 5. 3 p. 253 Portus and 5. 35 p. 322 Portus) were set to keep watch and ward over the infant king, who was nurtured by the Nymphs (cp. Nonn. *Dion.* 24. 43 ff.) like a fruitful olive (Orph. *frag.* 206 Kern *ap.* Clem. Al. *strom.* 6. 2 p. 442, 8 ff. Stählin) till his sixth (?) year (Orph. *frag.* 257 Kern *ap.* Tzetz. *exeg. Il.* p. 26 (ed. G. Hermann Leipzig 1812), cited in this connexion by Lobeck *Aglaophamus* i. 554). But Hera in anger got the Titans to trick the boy by means of certain toys (Orph. *frag.* 34 Kern *ap.* Clem. Al. *protr.* 2. 17. 2 f. p. 14, 7 ff. Stählin (=Euseb. *praep. ev.* 2. 3. 23 f.) τὰ γὰρ Διονύσου μυστήρια τέλεον ἀπάνθρωπα· ὃν εἰσέτι παῖδα ὄντα ἐνόπλῳ κινήσει περιχορευόντων Κουρήτων, δόλῳ δὲ ὑποδύντων Τιτάνων, ἀπατή-σαντες παιδαριώδεσιν ἀθύρμασιν, οὗτοι δὴ οἱ Τιτᾶνες διέσπασαν, ἔτι νηπίαχον ὄντα, ὡς ὁ τῆς Τελετῆς ποιητὴς Ὀρφεύς φησιν ὁ Θράκιος· "κῶνος καὶ ῥόμβος καὶ παίγνια καμπεσίγυια, | μῆλά τε χρύσεα καλὰ παρ' Ἑσπερίδων λιγυφώνων." καὶ τῆσδε ὑμῖν τῆς τελετῆς τὰ ἀχρεῖα σύμβολα οὐκ ἀχρεῖον εἰς κατάγνωσιν παραθέσθαι· ἀστράγαλος, σφαῖρα, στρόβιλος, μῆλα, ῥόμβος, ἔσοπτρον, πόκος, cp. Arnob. *adv. nat.* 5. 19 cuius rei testimonium argumentumque fortunae suis prodidit in carminibus Thracius t'alos, speculum, turbines, volubiles rotulas et teretis pilas et virginibus aurea sumpta ab Hesperidibus mala, *supra* i. 661: on these 'toys' see further Lobeck *Aglaophamus* i. 699 ff. and Harrison *Proleg. Gk. Rel.*[2] p. 490 f.) including a mirror made by Hephaistos (Orph. *frag.* 209 Kern *ap.* Prokl. *in* Plat. *Tim.* ii. 80, 19 ff. Diehl). He was looking at himself in this mirror (Plotin. *enn.* 4. 3. 12, Nonn. *Dion.* 6. 173), when the Titans, having first smeared their faces with gypsum, attacked him with a knife (Nonn. *Dion.* 6. 169 ff., cp. *supra* i. 398, 655 n. 2). To escape them he became a youthful Zeus, an aged Kronos, a babe, a youth, a lion, a horse, a horned snake, a tiger, and a bull (Nonn. *Dion.* 6. 174 ff., cp. *supra* i. 398). A bellowing in mid air from the throat of Hera was the signal for his fate: the Titans with their knife cut up his bovine form (Nonn. *Dion.* 6. 200 ff.) into seven portions (Orph. *frag.* 210 Kern *ap.* Prokl. *in* Plat. *Tim.* ii. 146, 9 ff. Diehl), one for each of themselves (Orph. *frag.* 114, 1 f. Kern *ap.* Prokl. *in* Plat. *Tim.* i. 450, 16 ff. Diehl, Orph. *frag.* 114, 3 ff. Kern *ap.* Prokl. *in* Plat. *Tim.* iii. 184, 3 ff. Diehl, cp. Orph. *frag.* 107 p. 171 f. Kern *ap.* Prokl. *in* Plat. *Tim.* iii. 169, 3 ff. Diehl: similarly Typhon divided the body of Osiris into fourteen (Plout. *de Is. et Os.* 18, 42: see Frazer *Golden Bough*[3]: Adonis Attis Osiris[3] ii. 129 n. 4, Farnell *Cults of Gk. States* v. 17 ff.) or twenty-six pieces, one for each of his assailants (Diod. 1. 21 = Euseb. *praep. ev.* 2. 1. 16: Diod. 4. 6 calls the assailants Titans)); they then set a caldron on a tripod, boiled the portions, pierced them with spits, held them over the fire (Orph. *frag.* 35 Kern *ap.* Clem. Al. *protr.* 2. 18. 1 p. 14, 17 ff. Stählin cited *supra* p. 218, cp. Firm.

Mat. 8. 2), and finally devoured them (Firm. Mat. 6. 3 cited *supra* i. 661 f., Olympiod. *in* Plat. *Phaed.* 61 c pp. 2, 26 and 3, 4 f. Norvin). Thereupon Hekate went to Olympos (Orph. *frag.* 188 Kern *ap.* Prokl. *in* Plat. *Cratyl.* p. 107, 1 ff. Pasquali), Zeus appeared, struck the Titans with a thunderbolt, and gave the limbs of Dionysos to Apollon for burial (Orph. *frag.* 35 Kern *ap.* Clem. Al. *protr.* 2. 18. 2 p. 14, 20 ff. Stählin cited *supra* p. 218). Apollon, at the behest of Zeus, arranged all the limbs in order (Orph. *frag.* 216 b Kern *ap.* Prokl. *in* Plat. *Cratyl.* p. 108, 17 f. Pasquali Οἶνου (=Διονύσου) πάντα μέλη κόσμῳ λαβὲ καί μοι ἔνεικε, Prokl. *in* Plat. *Tim.* ii. 198, 11 ff. Diehl, cp. *ib.* ii. 197, 18 ff.) and took them to Parnassos (Orph. *frag.* 35 Kern *ap.* Clem. Al. *protr.* 2. 18. 2 p. 14, 24 f. Stählin cited *supra* p. 218)—the Titanic caldron being identified with the Delphic tripod (*supra* p. 218 ff.). The Titans had left intact the heart of Dionysos, and this was rescued by Athena (Orph. *frag.* 210 Kern *ap.* Prokl. *in* Plat. *Tim.* ii. 145. 18 ff. Diehl, cp. Prokl. *in* Plat. *Cratyl.* p. 109, 19 ff. Pasquali), who was named Παλλάς because she brandished it (πάλλειν) or because it still beat (πάλλεσθαι) as she brought it to Zeus (Orph. *frag.* 35 Kern *ap.* Clem. Al. *protr.* 2. 18. 1 p. 14, 16 f. Stählin, schol. *Il.* 1. 200, *et. mag.* p. 649, 56 f., *et. Gud.* p. 450, 9 f., Zonar. *lex. s.v.* Παλλάς, Tzetz. *in* Lyk. *Al.* 355, Eudok. *viol.* 746, Favorin. *lex.* p. 1417, 26 ff.: Eustath. *in Il.* p. 84, 43 f. transfers the incident to the Theban Dionysos, and *et. Gud.* p. 450, 11 ff. makes Athena drive off the Titans by 'brandishing' her spear. Lobeck *Aglaophamus* i. 560 n.[e] quotes Souid. *s.v.* κωνοφόροι for the connexion of the heart with Dionysos, and Cornut. *theol.* 6 p. 6, 7 f. Lang for its relation to Rhea). As to what Zeus did with the heart, opinions differed: some said that he placed it in a gypsum image of the boy (Firm. Mat. 6. 4 cited *supra* i. 662), but the common view was that he pounded it into a potion and gave it to Semele to drink, that she conceived thereby, and that Zagreus thus came to life again as Dionysos (Hyg. *fab.* 167 Liber Iovis et Proserpinae filius a Titanis est distractus, cuius cor contritum Iovis Semelae dedit in potionem. ex eo praegnans cum esset facta, Iuno in Beroen nutricem Semeles se commutavit et ait: 'alumna, pete a Iove ut sic ad te veniat, quem ad modum ad Iunonem, ut scias quae voluptas est (J. Scheffer cj. *sit* cp. *fab.* 179) cum deo concumbere.' illa autem instigata petit ab Iove, et fulmine est icta. ex cuius utero Liberum exuit et Nyso dedit nutriendum unde Dionysus est appellatus et Bimater est dictus, Orph. *frag.* 210 p. 231 f. Kern *ap.* Prokl. *h. Ath. Polym.* 7. 11 ff. (E. Abel *Orphica* Lipsiae—Pragae 1885 p. 282) ἣ κραδίην ἐσάωσας ἀμιστύλλευτον ἄνακτος | αἰθέρος ἐν γυάλοισι μεριζομένου ποτὲ Βάκχου | Τιτήνων ὑπὸ χερσί· πόρες δέ ἑ πατρὶ φέρουσα, | ὄφρα νέος βουλῆσιν ὑπ' ἀρρήτοισι τοκῆος | ἐκ Σεμέλης περὶ (Lobeck *Aglaophamus* i. 561 prints κατὰ) κόσμον ἀνηβήσῃ Διόνυσος, Nonn. *Dion.* 24. 47 ff. (Hydaspes to Dionysos) καὶ σὺ φέρεις Ζαγρῆος ὅλον δέμας· ἀλλὰ σὺ κείνῳ | δὸς χάριν ὀψιτέλεστον, ὅθεν πέλες· ἀρχεγόνου γὰρ | ἐκ κραδίης ἀνέτελλες, ἀειδομένου Διονύσου (H. Koechly cj. ἀεξόμενος Διονύσου, but see Nonn. *Dion.* 1. 12), Commod. *instructiones* (an acrostich LIBER PATER etc.) 1. 12. 1 ff. Liberum Patrem certe bis genitum dicitis ipsi. | I n India natus ex Iove Proserpina primum | B elligerans contra Titanas profuso cruore | E xpiravit enim sicut ex mortalibus unus. | R ursus flato (B. Dombart *ad loc.* notes 'spiritui, animae, vitae?' *flato* C (*l* altera (?) manu expunctum). B.A[m].r[1]. *fato* A[t].*r.v.*) suo redditus (F. Oehler cj. *redditur*) in altero ventre. | P ercepit (so B. Dombart for *percipit* codd.) hoc Semele iterum Iovis altera moecha (*Maia r.* Oehler), | A bsciso (so C. *Abscisso* B.A.*r.v.*) cuius utero prope partu (*partum r*[2]. Oehler) defunctae | T ollitur et datur Niso nutriendus alumnus. | E x eo bis natus Dionysus ille vocatur, | Religio cuius in vacuo falsa curatur, | etc.). Thus the upshot of the Titans' murderous onslaught was that their victim was put together again (Cornut. *theol.* 31 p. 62, 10 f. Lang μυθολογεῖται δ' ὅτι διασπασθεὶς ὑπὸ τῶν Τιτάνων συνετέθη πάλιν ὑπὸ τῆς ʽΡέας, κ.τ.λ. = Eudok. *viol.* 272 p. 210, 10 ff. Flach, Ioul. *ap.* Kyrill. Al. *c. Iul.* 2. 44 (lxxvi. 568 B—C Migne) <τῇ> μητρὶ γὰρ ὁ Ζεὺς ἐμίχθη καὶ παιδοποιησάμενος ἐξ αὐτῆς ἔγημεν αὐτὸς τὴν αὐτοῦ θυγατέρα <οὐδὲ κατέσχεν vel simile quiddam ins. Lobeck *Aglaophamus* i. 562 n. ᶠ>, ἀλλὰ μιχθεὶς ἁπλῶς ἄλλῳ παραδέδωκεν αὐτήν. εἶτα οἱ Διονύσου σπαραγμοὶ καὶ μελῶν κολλήσεις) and attained a joyful resurrection (Orph. *frags.* 205, 213, 240 Kern *ap.* Prokl. *in* Plat. *Tim.* iii. 241, 5 ff. Diehl, Iust. Mart. *apol.* 1. 21 (vi. 360 A Migne), 1. 54 (vi. 410 A—B Migne), *cum Tryph. Iud. dial.* 69 (vi. 636 C—638 A Migne), Myth. Vat. 3. 12. 5, Macrob. *comm. in somn. Scip.* 1. 12. 12), whilst the aggressors were visited with condign punishment (Nonn. *Dion.* 6. 206 ff. makes Zeus fling them into Tartaros, as does Prokl. *in* Plat. *Tim.* i. 188, 26 ff., cp. Prokl. *in* Plat. *remp.* i. 93, 22 ff. Kroll; but various offenders, *e.g.* Atlas, were reserved for special fates (Orph. *frag.* 215 Kern *ap.* Prokl. *in* Plat. *Tim.* i. 173, 1 ff. Diehl, Simpl. *in* Aristot. *de cael.* 2. 1. 284 a 1 p. 375, 12 ff. Heiberg, cp. Firm. Mat. ꝑ. 4 cited *supra* i. 662). The bodies of those that had been struck by the thunderbolts were reduced to powder, hence called τίτανος (Eustath. *in Il.* p. 332, 23 ff.: see *supra* i. 655 n. 2), and from their smoking ashes men were made (Olympiod. *in* Plat. *Phaed.* 61 C p. 2, 27 ff. Norvin καὶ τούτους ὀργισθεὶς ὁ Ζεὺς ἐκεραύνωσε, καὶ ἐκ τῆς αἰθάλης τῶν ἀτμῶν τῶν ἀναδοθέντων ἐξ αὐτῶν ὕλης γενομένης γενέσθαι τοὺς ἀνθρώπους, cp. Dion Chrys. *or.* 30 p. 550 Reiske ὅτι τοῦ τῶν Τιτάνων αἵματος ἐσμὲν ἡμεῖς ἅπαντες οἱ ἄνθρωποι). It follows that we are part and parcel of Dionysus (Olympiod. *ib.* p. 3, 2 ff. Norvin οὐ δεῖ ἐξάγειν ἡμᾶς ἑαυτοὺς ὡς τοῦ σώματος ἡμῶν Διονυσιακοῦ ὄντος · μέρος γὰρ αὐτοῦ ἐσμεν, εἴ γε ἐκ τῆς αἰθάλης τῶν Τιτάνων συγκείμεθα γευσαμένων τῶν σαρκῶν τούτου), or he of us (Prokl. *in* Plat. *Cratyl.* p. 77, 24 ff. Pasquali ὅτι ὁ ἐν ἡμῖν νοῦς Διονυσιακός ἐστιν καὶ ἄγαλμα ὄντως τοῦ Διονύσου. κ.τ.λ.). Others taught that men arose from the blood of the Giants (Ov. *met.* 1. 154 ff., interp. Serv. *in* Verg. *ecl.* 6. 41) or from a rain of blood-drops let fall by Zeus (Ioul. *frag. epist.* i. 375, 21 ff. Hertlein ἀποβλέψαντα...εἰς τὴν τῶν θεῶν φήμην, ἣ παραδέδοται διὰ τῶν ἀρχαίων ἡμῖν θεουργῶν, ὡς, ὅτε Ζεὺς ἐκόσμει τὰ πάντα, σταγόνων αἵματος ἱεροῦ πεσουσῶν, ἐξ ὧν που τὸ τῶν ἀνθρώπων βλαστήσειε γένος).

The Rhapsodies, which—as the foregoing summary shows—began with theogony and ended with anthropogony, are supposed by O. Gruppe (*Gr. Myth. Rel.* p. 430, *id.* in Roscher *Lex. Myth.* iii. 1141 ff., cp. *Myth. Lit.* 1908 p. 215) to have been put together at Athens between 550 and 300 B.C., though they did not obtain much recognition till the time of the neo-Pythagoreans. A *provenance* in Pisistratic Athens is suggested, he thinks, by the dedication of this Orphic poem to Mousaios (*theosoph. Tubing.* 61 in K. Buresch *Klaros* Leipzig 1889 p. 117, 3), by the identification of Phanes with Metis which allowed Athena (*infra* § 9 (h) ii (μ)) to be viewed as one aspect of the reborn Erikepaios, by the affiliation of Artemis or Hekate (*supra* p. 1029) to Demeter (Orph. *frag.* 188 Kern *ap.* Prokl. *in* Plat. *Cratyl.* p. 106, 25 ff. Pasquali, Orph. *frag.* 41 Kern *ap.* schol. Ap. Rhod. 3. 467, cp. Kallim. *frag.* 556 Schneider *ap.* schol. Theokr. 2. 12) —a genealogy known to Aischylos (*supra* p. 252), and by the equation of Rhea with Demeter (*supra* i. 398, ii. 1029) which appears also in Euripides (Eur. *Hel.* 1301 ff.) and other fifth-century poets (Pind. *Isthm.* 7 (6). 3 f., Melanippid. *frag.* 10 Bergk⁴ *ap.* Philodem. περὶ εὐσεβείας 51, 11 ff. p. 23 Gomperz : see further Gruppe *Gr. Myth. Rel.* p. 1169 n. 7, O. Kern in Pauly—Wissowa *Real-Enc.* iv. 2755, Farnell *Cults of Gk. States* iii. 32, 312). Bendis (Orph. *frag.* 200 Kern *ap.* Prokl. *in* Plat. *remp.* i. 18, 12 ff. Kroll), the one barbaric deity mentioned in the poem, was worshipped at Athens in 403 B.C. (*supra* p. 115), if not earlier (A. Rapp in Roscher *Lex. Myth.* i. 780, G. Knaack in Pauly—Wissowa *Real-Enc.* iii. 269 f. : Gruppe in Roscher *Lex. Myth.* iii. 1142 suggests that her cult was introduced 'wahrscheinlich durch Peisistratos' thrakische Unternehmungen'). M. Mayer *Die Giganten und Titanen* Berlin 1887 p. 239 f. (cp. *ib.* p. 3 n. 2) notes that Kratinos the younger, a contemporary of Platon the philosopher, in his *Gigantes frag.* 1 (*Frag. com. Gr.* iii. 374 Meineke) *ap.* Athen. 661 E—F ἐνθυμεῖσθε (so A. Meineke for ἐνθύμει δὲ codd. K. W. Dindorf cj. ἐνθυμοῦ (?) δὲ) τῆς γῆς ὡς γλυκύ | ὄζει, καπνός τ᾽ ἐξέρχετ᾽ εὐωδέστερος (T. Bergk cj. εὐωδέστατος); | οἰκεῖ τις ὡς ἔοικεν ἐν τῷ χάσματι | λιβανωτοπώλης ἢ μάγειρος Σικελικός makes fun of the scene in which Zeus was attracted to the Titans' feast by the smell of roast flesh (Orph. *frag.* 34 Kern *ap.* Arnob. *adv. nat.* 5. 19, Orph. *frag.* 35 Kern *ap.* Clem. Al. *protr.* 2. 18. 2 p. 14, 20 ff. Stählin cited *supra* p. 218) and works in a not very appropriate allusion to the χάσμα (Orph. *frag.* 66 a Kern *ap.* Prokl. *in* Plat. *remp.* ii. 138, 8 ff. Kroll, Syrian. *in* Aristot. *met.* 2. 4. 1000 b 14 p. 43, 30 f. Kroll, Simplic. *in* Aristot. *phys.* 4. 1. 208 b 29 p. 528, 14 f. Diels, Orph. *frag.* 66 b Kern *ap.* Prokl. *in* Plat. *Tim.* i. 385, 29 ff. Diehl). Further evidence as to date is at best doubtful. Platon himself has no direct allusion to the Rhapsodies[1]; but it must not be inferred that therefore they are post-Platonic, for they in turn are apparently uninfluenced either by Platon or by later philosophers. Their principal trait, the conception of a world born and re-born, first created by Phanes and then re-created by Zeus, points rather—as Gruppe saw (*Cult. Myth. orient. Rel.* i. 643 ff., *Gr. Myth. Rel.* p. 428 ff., and in Roscher *Lex. Myth.* iii. 1143 ff.)—to ideas that were current in Greece (Anaximandros, Herakleitos, Empedokles) between, say, 550 and 450 B.C. On the whole, then, it may be con- cluded that the Rhapsodic Theogony was composed at Athens (?) *c.* 500 B.C. (?), and consisted in a rehandling of older Orphic materials by a Pythagorising (?) poet. Hence its vogue among neo-Pythagorean writers of the Graeco-Roman age.

(4) Conspectus of the Orphic Theogonies.

For clearness' sake I add a conspectus showing the three chief forms of Orphic theogony. The letters at the side indicate the creation (A) and re-crea- tion (B) of the world: the numerals give the sequence of mythical generations (1—6).

(5) The Cosmic Egg.

The most striking feature of these theogonies is the cosmic egg—a con- ception discussed by R. G. Latham *Descriptive Ethnology* London 1859 i. 439—441, J. Grimm *Teutonic Mythology* trans. J. S. Stallybrass London 1883 ii. 559 n. 4, Costantin in the *Rev. Arch.* 1899 i. 355 ff. fig. 6 f., L. Frobenius *Das Zeitalter des Sonnengottes* Berlin 1904 i. 269—271 ('Die Ureimythe'), M. P. Nilsson 'Das Ei im Totenkult der Alten' in the *Archiv f. Rel.* 1908 xi. 543 and 544 f., and especially F. Lukas 'Das Ei als kosmogonische Vorstellung' in the *Zeitschrift des Vereins für Volkskunde* 1894 iv. 227—243 (this author attempts, not altogether successfully, to distinguish three aspects of the egg in ancient and modern cosmogonies : (1) the world in general is egg-shaped and

---

[1] Mr F. M. Cornford, however, points out to me that Plat. *legg.* 715 E—716 A is apparently paraphrasing not only, as the schol. *ad loc.* saw, Orph. *frag.* 21 Kern Ζεὺς ἀρχή, Ζεὺς μέσσα, Διὸς δ᾽ ἐκ πάντα τέτυκται, but also Orph. *frag.* 158 Kern τῷ δὲ Δίκη πολύποινος ἐφείπετο πᾶσιν ἀρωγός—both lines being probably extant in the Rhapsodic Theogony (cp. E. Abel *Orphica* Lipsiae—Pragae 1885 p. 157 n. 1).

EARLY ORPHIC THEOGONY

composed in Asia Minor(?) *c. s. x* B.C.(?) as the result of Ionic speculation on Thraco-Phrygian beliefs.

A 1

2

Nyx   Ge

Egg

Eros
with golden wings

Ouranos

=   Tethys   etc.

Okeanos

3
4
5
6

Kronos   =   Rhea   etc.

Zeus   =   Hera

sixth generation

ORPHIC THEOGONY OF HELLANIKOS

i.e. Hellanikos' summary of a poem composed in Ionia (?) *c.* 500 B.C. (?) under the influence of oriental cosmogony and of Greek philosophy.

A o

1

Water   Slime becoming Earth

ChronosorHerakles, = Ananke or Adrasteia, a winged snake with a bodiless bisexual heads of bull+god being whose arms en- +lion fold the world

Aither   Chaos   Erebos
among whom Chronos produced

2

Egg

Ge

Ouranos

Protogonos or Zeus or Pan, a bodiless bisexual being with golden wings and heads of bulls and snake; otherwise called Phanes and described as a bodi- less being with heads of snake +god+lion

3

Moirai   Hekatoncheires   Kyklopes   Titanes

RHAPSODIC THEOGONY

composed at Athens (?) *c.* 500 B.C. (?) by a Pythagor- ising (?) poet in touch with the doctrines of other Greek philosophers.

A 1

Chronos   Chaos

Aither

2

Egg

3

Phanes or Metis or Erikepaios, a bisexual being, called also Protogonos, Antauges, Phaethon, Dionysos, Eubouleus, Priapos, Eros, who begat and consorted with Nyx

Ge   Ouranos   Rhea   Kronos   Hera   Zeus

B

4   Zeus, at the advice of Nyx, swallows Phanes and creates the world anew inside himself.

He produces out of his own head Athena who is also Arete.

His union with his sister Hera remains un- fruitful.

4   His union with Dione produces Aphrodite.

4   His union with Semele produces Dionysos.

Zeus as   =   his mother Rhea or
a snake | Demeter as a snake

4   Zeus as   =   Phersephone or Kore, a horned,
a snake | four-eyed, two-faced daughter

5   The chthonian Dionysos or Zagreus, a horned babe, whose murderers the Titanes were slain by Zeus. From their ashes sprang

was originally an egg ('*Weltei*') ; (2) the sun in particular is egg-shaped and was originally an egg ('*Lichtei*', '*Sonnenei*') : (3) the life of all things has been developed like that of a chicken from an egg ('*das Ei als Embryonalzustand*')).

Confining our attention to old-world examples, we note the following : (*a*) EGYPT. Râ as a phoenix (*supra* i. 341) came out of the great egg produced by Seb and Nut (E. A. Wallis Budge *The Gods of the Egyptians* London 1904 ii. 95 f., 107 n. 1, 110, cp. A. Erman *A Handbook of Egyptian Religion* trans. A. S. Griffith London 1907 pp. 26, 81, 157). Ptah the 'Padre dei principii creatore dell' uovo del sole e della Luna' (Lanzone *Dizion. di Mitol. Egiz.* p. 239) was represented as a potter shaping on his wheel the cosmic egg (*id. ib.* p. 250 f. pl. 94, 1). Cp. Sir G. Maspero *The Dawn of Civilization*[4] London 1901 p. 128 with *id. The Struggle of the Nations* London 1896 p. 168 n. 1.

(*b*) INDIA. In Vedic cosmogony Aditi had eight sons, but the eighth, Mārtāṇḍa, the 'Egg-born,' she cast away, having brought him forth to be born and to die (*i.e.* to rise and to set : see the *Rig-Veda* 10. 72. 8 and the remarks of E. W. Hopkins *The Religions of India* Boston etc. 1895 p. 208 n. 2, A. A. Macdonell *Vedic Mythology* Strassburg 1897 p. 13, H. Oldenberg *La religion du Véda* Paris 1903 p. 156 n. 2). Again, according to the *Rig-Veda* 10. 121. 1 (*Vedic Hymns* trans. F. Max Müller (*The Sacred Books of the East* xxxii) Oxford 1891 p. 1), 'In the beginning there arose the Golden Child (Hiraṇyagarbha) ; as soon as born, he alone was the lord of all that is'..., on which Max Müller *ib.* p. 6 observes that the epithet *Hiraṇyagarbha* 'means literally the golden embryo, the golden germ or child, or born of a golden womb, and was no doubt an attempt at naming the sun'—a view endorsed by A. A. Macdonell *Vedic Mythology* Strassburg 1897 pp. 13, 119 : 'In the last verse of this hymn, he is called Prajāpati, "lord of created beings," the name which became that of the chief god of the Brāhmaṇas.' 'This is the only occurrence of the name [*Hiraṇyagarbha*] in the RV., but it is mentioned several times in the AV. and the literature of the Brāhmaṇa period (cp. p. 13). Hiraṇyagarbha is also alluded to in a passage of the AV. (4, 2[8]) where it is stated that the waters produced an embryo, which as it was being born, was enveloped in a golden covering. In the TS. (5, 5, 1[2]) Hiraṇyagarbha is expressly identified with Prajāpati. In the later literature he is chiefly a designation of the personal Brahmā.' A. A. Macdonell *op. cit.* p. 14 : 'The account given in the Chāndogya Brāhmaṇa (5, 19) is that not-being became being ; the latter changed into an egg, which after a year by splitting in two became heaven and earth ; whatever was produced is the sun, which is Brahma'... Similarly in the *Kh*ândogya-upanishad 3. 19. 1 ff. (*The Upanishads* trans. F. Max Müller (*The Sacred Books of the East* i) Oxford 1879 p. 54 f.) : '1. Âditya (the sun) is Brahman... In the beginning this was non-existent. It became existent, it grew. It turned into an egg. The egg lay for the time of a year. The egg broke open. The two halves were one of silver, the other of gold. 2. The silver one became this earth, the golden one the sky, the thick membrane (of the white) the mountains, the thin membrane (of the yoke [*sic!*]) the mist with the clouds, the small veins the rivers, the fluid the sea. 3. And what was born from it that was Âditya, the sun'... Cp. the birth of Prajāpati as described in the Çatapatha Brāhmaṇa 11. 1. 6. 1 f. (*The Ṣatapatha-Brâhmaṇa* trans. J. Eggeling Part V (*The Sacred Books of the East* xliv) Oxford 1900 p. 12) : '1 Verily, in the beginning this (universe) was water, nothing but a sea of water. The waters desired, " How can we be reproduced?" They toiled and performed fervid devotions[1] ([1]Or, they toiled and became heated (with fervid devotion).), when they were becoming heated, a golden egg was produced. The year, indeed, was not then in existence : this golden egg floated about for as long as the space of a year. 2 In a year's time a man, this Pragâpati, was produced therefrom... He broke open this golden egg'... or the birth of Brahma as related in the *Laws of Manu* I. 5 ff. (*The Laws of Manu* trans. G. Bühler (*The Sacred Books of the East* xxv) Oxford 1886 p. 2 ff.) : ' 5 This (universe) existed in the shape of Darkness... 6 Then the divine Self-existent (Svayambhû, himself)... appeared, dispelling the darkness... 8 He, desiring to produce beings of many kinds from his own body, first with a thought created the waters, and placed his seed in them. 9 That (seed) became a golden egg, in brilliancy equal to the sun ; in that (egg) he himself was born as Brahman, the progenitor of the whole world... 12 The divine one resided in that egg during a whole year, then he himself by his thought (alone) divided it into two halves ; 13 And out of those two halves he formed heaven and earth, between them the middle sphere, the eight points of the horizon, and the eternal abode of the waters.' Later Hinduism sometimes represented Brahma as born in a golden egg (*Mahā-Bhārata* 12. 312. 1—7 cited by E. W. Hopkins *The Religions of India* Boston etc. 1895 p. 411), and spoke of a bubble, which contained Viṣṇu as Brahma (*Viṣṇu Purāṇa* I. 2. 45 f.). See further H. Jacobi in J. Hastings *Encyclopædia of Religion and Ethics* Edinburgh 1911 iv. 156—160 and the monograph of K. F. Geldner *Zur Kosmogonie des Rigveda* Marburg 1908.

(c) PERSIA. In Parsi speculation of Sassanian date Ahura the creator made heaven like an egg with the earth for its yolk. *Minokhired* 44. 8—11 (*Dînâ-î Maînôg-î Khirad* trans. E. W. West (*The Sacred Books of the East* xxiv) Oxford 1885 p. 84 f.) : ' The sky and earth and water, and whatever else is within them are egg-like (khâîyak-dîs), just as it were like the egg of a bird. 9. The sky is arranged above the earth (L 19 adds 'and below the earth'), like an egg, by the handiwork of the creator Aûharmazd ; (10) and the semblance of the earth, in the midst of the sky (L 19 has 'and the earth within the sky'), is just like as it were the yolk amid the egg ; [(11) and the water within the earth and sky is such as the water within the egg.]'. Cp. Plout. *de Is. et Os.* 47 εἶθ' ὁ μὲν Ὡρομάζης τρὶς ἑαυτὸν αὐξήσας ἀπέστησε τοῦ ἡλίου τοσοῦτον ὅσον ὁ ἥλιος τῆς γῆς ἀφέστηκε, καὶ τὸν οὐρανὸν ἄστροις ἐκόσμησεν· ἕνα δὲ ἀστέρα πρὸ πάντων οἷον φύλακα καὶ προόπτην ἐγκατέστησε τὸν σείριον, ἄλλους δὲ ποιήσας τέτταρας καὶ εἴκοσι θεοὺς εἰς ᾠὸν ἔθηκεν. οἱ δὲ ὑπὸ τοῦ Ἀρειμανίου γενόμενοι καὶ αὐτοὶ τοσοῦτοι διέτρησαν τὸ ᾠόν· ὅθεν (so D. Wyttenbach, after Xylander, for διατρήσαντος τὸ ᾠὸν γανωθὲν) ἀναμέμικται τὰ κακὰ τοῖς ἀγαθοῖς with the comments of R. Eisler *Weltenmantel und Himmelszelt* München 1910 pp. 410 n. 2 f., 414 n. 2, 537 and J. H. Moulton *Early Zoroastrianism* London 1913 p. 402 n. 4.

(d) PHOINIKE. Of the Phoenician cosmogony we have a threefold account. (i) Eudemos of Rhodes *ap.* Damask. *quaest. de primis principiis* 125 *ter* (i. 323, 1 ff. Ruelle) Σιδώνιοι δὲ κατὰ τὸν αὐτὸν συγγραφέα πρὸ πάντων Χρόνον ὑποτίθενται καὶ Πόθον καὶ Ὀμίχλην, Πόθου δὲ καὶ Ὀμίχλης μιγέντων ὡς δυεῖν ἀρχῶν Ἀέρα γενέσθαι καὶ Αὖραν, Ἀέρα μὲν ἄκρατον τοῦ νοητοῦ παραδηλοῦντες, Αὖραν δὲ τὸ ἐξ αὐτοῦ κινούμενον τοῦ νοητοῦ ζωτικὸν προτύπωμα. πάλιν δὲ ἐκ τούτων ἀμφοῖν Ὠτον γεννηθῆναι κατὰ τὸν νοῦν, οἶμαι τὸν νοητόν. Ὠτος is hardly to be identified with either of the mythical personages so named (O. Höfer in Roscher *Lex. Myth.* iii. 1231 f.) ; nor shall we venture with Gruppe *Cult. Myth. orient. Rel.* i. 349 to take the word as ὦτος, 'the horned owl' (though this bird with crook and flail appears on the coinage of Tyre : see Imhoof-Blumer and O. Keller *Tier- und Pflanzenbilder auf Münzen und Gemmen des klassischen Altertums* Leipzig 1889 p. 32 pl. 5, 22, O. Keller *Die antike Tierwelt* Leipzig 1913 ii. 38 f. pl. 1, 8—other examples in *Brit. Mus. Cat. Coins* Phoenicia pp. cxxvii, 227—233 pls. 28, 9—29, 17, *Hunter Cat. Coins* iii. 263 pl. 76, 31, Head *Coins. of the Ancients* p. 41 pl. 20, 46, p. 61 pl. 29, 36, *id. Hist. num.*[2] p. 799 fig. 352) ; nor yet to treat Ὠτον as a corruption of ᾠόν, the cosmic 'egg' (J. Kopp in his ed. of Damaskios (Frankfurt-am-Main 1826) cj. ᾠόν, and so did F. Creuzer/*Symbolik und Mythologie*[3] Leipzig and Darmstadt 1840 ii. 345 n. 2), though we should thereby reduce all the names in this genealogy to common Greek substantives—χρόνος, πόθος, ὀμίχλη, ἀήρ, αὔρα, ᾠόν. If any change is required, I would rather correct Ὠτον to Μῶτον = the Μώτ of Sanchouniathon's cosmogony (*infra* (iii)).   (ii) Mochos of Sidon (W. Pape—G. E. Benseler *Wörterbuch der griechischen Eigennamen*[3] Braunschweig 1875 p. 969 f.) *ap.* Damask. *quaest. de primis principiis* 125 *ter* (i. 323, 6 ff. Ruelle) ὡς δὲ ἔξωθεν Εὐδήμου τὴν Φοινίκων εὑρίσκομεν κατὰ Μῶχον μυθολογίαν, Αἰθὴρ ἦν τὸ πρῶτον καὶ Ἀὴρ αἱ δύο αὗται ἀρχαί, ἐξ ὧν γεννᾶται Οὐλωμός, ὁ νοητὸς θεός, αὐτό, οἶμαι, τὸ ἄκρον τοῦ νοητοῦ· ἐξ οὗ ἑαυτῷ συνελθόντος γεννηθῆναί φασι Χουσωρόν, ἀνοιγέα πρῶτον, εἶτα ᾠόν, τοῦτον μέν, οἶμαι, τὸν νοητὸν νοῦν λέγοντες, τὸν δὲ ἀνοιγέα Χουσωρόν, τὴν νοητὴν δύναμιν ἅτε πρώτην διακρίνασαν τὴν ἀδιάκριτον φύσιν, εἰ μὴ ἄρα μετὰ τὰς δύο ἀρχὰς τὸ μὲν ἄκρον ἐστὶν Ἄνεμος ὁ εἷς, τὸ δὲ μέσον οἱ δύο ἄνεμοι Λίψ τε καὶ Νότος· ποιοῦσι γάρ πως καὶ τούτους πρὸ τοῦ Οὐλωμοῦ· ὁ δὲ Οὐλωμὸς αὐτὸς ὁ νοητὸς εἴη νοῦς, ὁ δὲ ἀνοιγεὺς Χουσωρὸς ἡ μετὰ τὸ νοητὸν πρώτη τάξις, τὸ δὲ Ὠὸν ὁ οὐρανός· λέγεται γὰρ ἐξ αὐτοῦ ῥαγέντος εἰς δύο γενέσθαι Οὐρανὸς καὶ Γῆ, τῶν διχοτομημάτων ἑκάτερον. The names Οὐλωμός and Χουσωρός are presumably Phoenician, not Greek. Οὐλωμός is commonly regarded as the transliteration of the Hebrew עוֹלָם ('ōlām), 'eternity,' though Gruppe *Cult. Myth. orient. Rel.* i. 514 (cp. i. 349, 642) says : 'Dies Wesen war höchst wahrscheinlich zweigeschlechtig gedacht, da es mit sich selbst den Χουσωρός erzeugt... Demnach scheint es mir (trotz der von Schuster *de vet. Orph. theog. ind. atq. or.* S. 98. Anm. 1 citirten *Kabbala*stelle) zweifellos, dass Οὐλωμός nicht... von עלם "Ewigkeit,' sondern von עלם " Geschlechtstrieb empfinden " abgeleitet ist.' Mr N. McLean, to whom I have referred the point, tells me (Sept. 13, 1916) that Οὐλωμός might perhaps be connected with אוּלָם (ūlām), 'the front, that which is first,' but is more probably the Grecised form of עוֹלָם ('ōlām), 'eternity.' Similarly Count Baudissin sees in 'Οὐλωμός (wohl עוֹלָם)' 'Den Gott der Vorzeit' (W. W. Baudissin *Adonis und Esmun* Leipzig 1911 pp. 503 and 488). Cp. Gen. 21. 33 'And *Abraham* planted a tamarisk tree in Beer-sheba, and called there on the name of the LORD, the Everlasting God' with J. Skinner's note *ad loc.*: ''El 'Ôlâm] presumably the pre-Israelite name of the local *numen*, here identified with Yahwe' etc. Χουσωρός, 'the Opener,' remains obscure. H. Ewald 'Über die phönikischen Ansichten von der Weltschöpfung und den geschichtlichen Werth Sanchuniathon's' in the *Abh. d. gött. Gesellsch. d. Wiss. 1851—1852* Phil.-hist. Classe v. 17 would read Χουσώρ for Χρυσώρ in the anthropogony of Sanchouniathon as given by Philon Bybl. *frag.* 2. 9 (*Frag. hist. Gr.* iii. 566 Müller) *ap.* Euseb. *praep. ev.* I. 10. 11 f. χρόνοις δὲ ὕστερον πολλοῖς ἀπὸ τῆς Ὑψουρανίου γενεᾶς γενέσθαι Ἀγρέα καὶ Ἁλιέα, τοὺς ἄγρας καὶ ἁλείας εὑρετάς, ἐξ ὧν κληθῆναι ἀγρευτὰς καὶ ἁλιεῖς· ἐξ ὧν γενέσθαι δύο ἀδελφοὺς σιδήρου εὑρετὰς καὶ τῆς τούτου ἐργασίας, ὧν θάτερον τὸν Χρυσὼρ λόγους ἀσκῆσαι καὶ ἐπῳδὰς καὶ μαντείας· εἶναι δὲ τοῦτον τὸν Ἥφαιστον, εὑρεῖν δὲ καὶ ἄγκιστρον καὶ δέλεαρ καὶ ὁρμιὰν καὶ σχεδίαν, πρῶτόν τε πάντων ἀνθρώπων πλεῦσαι· διὸ καὶ ὡς θεὸν αὐτὸν μετὰ θάνατον ἐσεβάσθησαν· καλεῖσθαι δὲ αὐτὸν καὶ Δία Μειλίχιον. κ.τ.λ. But Χρυσώρ may well be an attempt to make the Phoenician Χουσωρός intelligible to Greek readers. Be that as it may, Χουσωρός was doubtless 'the Opener' of the cosmic egg (so F. Creuzer *Symbolik und Mythologie*[3] Leipzig

and Darmstadt 1840 ii. 347, 1842 iv. 250, W. Robertson Smith in T. K. Cheyne
—J. S. Black *Encyclopædia Biblica* London 1899 i. 942 n. 9, R. Eisler *Weltenmantel und Himmelszelt* München 1910 ii. 440 n. 6).   (iii) Sanchouniathon in Philon Bybl. *frag.* 2. 1 f. (*Frag. hist. Gr.* iii. 565 Müller) *ap.* Euseb. *praep. ev.* 1. 10. 1 f.

τὴν τῶν ὅλων ἀρχὴν ὑποτίθεται ἀέρα ζοφώδη καὶ πνευματώδη, ἢ πνοὴν ἀέρος ζοφώδους, καὶ χάος θολερόν, ἐρεβῶδες· ταῦτα δὲ εἶναι ἄπειρα, καὶ διὰ πολὺν αἰῶνα μὴ ἔχειν πέρας. 'ὅτε δέ,' φησίν, 'ἠράσθη τὸ πνεῦμα τῶν ἰδίων ἀρχῶν, καὶ ἐγένετο σύγκρασις, ἡ πλοκὴ ἐκείνη ἐκλήθη πόθος. αὕτη δὲ ἀρχὴ κτίσεως ἁπάντων. αὐτὸ δὲ οὐκ ἐγίνωσκε τὴν αὑτοῦ κτίσιν· καὶ ἐκ τῆς αὑτοῦ συμπλοκῆς τοῦ πνεύματος ἐγένετο Μώτ· τοῦτό τινές φασιν ἰλύν, οἱ δὲ ὑδατώδους μίξεως σῆψιν. καὶ ἐκ ταύτης ἐγένετο πᾶσα σπορὰ κτίσεως καὶ γένεσις τῶν ὅλων. ἦν δέ τινα ζῷα οὐκ ἔχοντα αἴσθησιν, ἐξ ὧν ἐγένετο ζῷα νοερά, καὶ ἐκλήθη Ζωφασημίν (Ζωφισημὰν cod. H.), τοῦτ' ἔστιν οὐρανοῦ κατόπται. καὶ ἀνεπλάσθη ὁμοίως ᾠοῦ σχήματι. καὶ ἐξέλαμψε Μὼτ ἥλιός τε καὶ σελήνη ἀστέρες τε καὶ ἄστρα μεγάλα.' Μώτ is another conundrum, of which very various interpretations have been given (W. Drexler in Roscher *Lex. Myth.* ii. 3222 f.). F. C. Movers *Die Phönizier* Berlin 1841 i. 136 equated it with the Egyptian Μούθ, 'Mother' (Plout. *de Is. et Os.* 56 : see further Stephanus *Thes. Gr. Ling.* v. 1219 C—D). H. Ewald *loc. cit.* v. 30 connected it with the Arabic *mâdda*, 'stuff, matter.' W. W. Baudissin *Studien zur semitischen Religionsgeschichte* Leipzig 1876 i. 11 f., 195 supposes מֵי = מֵי 'water'; and Sir G. Maspero *The Struggle of the Nations* London 1896 p. 168 n. 1 likewise says : 'Môt ... is probably a Phœnician form of a word which means *water* in the Semitic languages (ROTH, *Geschichte unserer abendländischen Philosophie*, vol. i. p. 251 ; SCHRÖDER, *Die Phönizische Sprache*, p. 133).' C. C. J. von Bunsen *Aegyptens Stelle in der Weltgeschichte* Gotha 1857 v. 3. 257 n. 25 would correct Μώτ to Μώχ = מֹץ 'mud.' J. Halévy 'Les principes cosmogoniques phéniciens πόθος et μώτ' in the *Mélanges Graux* Paris 1884 p. 59 f. assumes haplography ἐγένετο [ΤΟ]ΜΩΤ and takes Τομώτ to be a Phoenician *Tehômôt* formed with the feminine ending from the Hebrew *Tehôm*, 'deep,' thus obtaining a Phoenician equivalent of the Babylonian Tiāmat. R. Eisler *Weltenmantel und Himmelszelt* München 1910 ii. 440 n. 6 is content with the old (Stephanus *Thes. Gr. Ling.* v. 1219 D) transcription Μώτ = מות *mavet*, 'death.' Mr N. McLean, who has kindly considered the matter for me, inclines (Sept. 13, 1916) to think that מַק (*mak*), 'rottenness,' might have an infinitival form מֹק (*môk*), which would be represented by Μώκ (not Μώχ, as Bunsen proposed). He further notes that Ζωφασημίν is a fairly correct transliteration of צוֹפֵי שָׁמַיִם (*ṣôphē šāmayim*), 'observers of heaven.' The three versions of the Phoenician cosmogony may be set out as follows :

EUDEMOS	MOCHOS	SANCHOUNIATHON
Χρόνος Πόθος = 'Ομίχλη	"Ανεμος Λίψ Νότος or Αἰθήρ = 'Αήρ	'Αὴρ ζοφώδης καὶ = Χάος θολερόν, πνευματώδης ἐρεβῶδες (Πόθος)
'Αήρ = Αὔρα	Οὐλωμός	Μώτ
? Μῶτος	Χουσωρός	Ζωφασημίν
	Οὐρανός ← 'Ωόν → Γῆ	'Ωόν

(6) **The Cosmogonic Eros.**

It will be observed that in several respects the Indian and the Phoenician cosmogonies recall Orphic speculation. In particular, they assign the same primary position to cosmic Desire or Love. According to the *Çatapatha Brāh-maṇa* (*supra* p. 1035) the golden egg was caused by the desire of the waters for reproduction ; according to *The Laws of Manu* (*supra* p. 1036) it was occasioned by similar desire on the part of the divine Self-existent. Eudemos (*supra* p. 1036) spoke of *Póthos* as uniting with Mist to beget Air and Breeze ; Sanchouniathon (*supra* p. 1038) applied the same term *Póthos* to the love of the primeval Wind. These conceptions are akin to that of Eros, who in the early Orphic scheme sprang from the wind-egg laid by Nyx. True, the theogony of Hellanikos dropped the name Eros and substituted for it Protogonos or Zeus or Pan. But the Rhapsodies retained both Eros and Protogonos as alternative appellations of their Phanes or Metis or Erikepaios. It looks as though Eros were in some sense the very soul or self of a deity variously named. Hence his intimate connexion with Wind—a common form of soul (W. H. Roscher *Hermes der Wind-gott* Leipzig 1878 p. 54 ff., Rohde *Psyche*[3] i. 248 n. 1, ii. 264 n. 2, C. H. Toy *Introduction to the History of Religions* Boston etc. 1913 p. 22 f., S. Feist *Kultur Ausbreitung und Herkunft der Indogermanen* Berlin 1913 p. 99, W. Wundt *Völkerpsychologie* Leipzig 1906 ii. 2. 40 ff., *id. Elements of Folk Psychology* trans. E. L. Schaub London 1916 p. 212 f., *infra* § 7 (a)). Miss J. E. Harrison *Proleg. Gk. Rel.*[2] p. 625 n. 3 rightly suspected that a definite doctrine underlay Aristophanes' travesty of the 'wind-egg.' We must, I think, conclude that the Orphic cosmogonies rest in part upon a primitive psychology, which explained desire (ἔρος, ἔρως) as the issuing of the soul from the mouth in the form of a small winged being. That the early Greeks should have entertained such a belief is well within the bounds of possibility : cp. A. E. Crawley *The Idea of the Soul* London 1909 pp. 278 and 280 'In order to see the spiritual world, the savage either anoints his eyes to acquire an extension of sight, or "sends out his soul" to see it. The latter occurs as a theory of imagination[1]. ([1] De Groot, *The Religious System of China*, iv. 105)....' 'The savage holds that when a man desires a thing his soul leaves his body and goes to it. The process is identical with imagination and with magic'... Homeric diction still shows traces of analogous notions. The stock phrase ἔπεα πτερόεντα together with certain less frequent expressions (*Od.* 17. 57, 19. 29, 21. 386, 22. 398 τῇ δ' ἄπτερος ἔπλετο μῦθος, and perhaps *Od.* 7. 36 ὠκεῖαι ὡς εἰ πτερὸν ἠὲ νόημα) presupposes the view that words had actual wings and flew across from speaker to listener, while the *formula* πόσιος καὶ ἐδητύος ἐξ ἔρον ἔντο (*Il.* 1. 469, 2. 432, 7. 323, 9. 92, 23. 57, 24. 628, *Od.* 1. 150, 3. 67, 473, 4. 68, 8. 72, 485, 12. 308, 14. 454, 15. 143, 303, 501, 16. 55, 480, 17. 99, *h. Ap.* 513, cp. *Od.* 24. 489, *h. Ap.* 499) or the like (*Il.* 13. 636 ff., 24. 227, *Theog.* 1064) implies, if pressed, a physical expulsion or dismissal of desire. Not improbably, therefore, the Hesiodic idea that Eros had issued from Chaos (*supra* p. 315), could we trace it to its ultimate origin in the mind of unsophisticated folk, would be found to involve the conviction that the vast void between heaven and earth was a gaping or yawning mouth (χάος for *χάϜος connected with χαῦνος, χάσκω, etc.: cp. οὐρανός, οὐρανίσκος in the sense of 'the mouth's palate' with the remarks of Stephanus *Thes. Gr. Ling.* v. 2405 B—C) from which the divine soul, desirous to create, had flown forth in the guise of Eros. Since winged things in general emerge from eggs, such a belief would naturally, though illogically, be fused with an egg-cosmogony.

Some support for the opinions here advanced is furnished, not indeed by the painted tablet from Tarragona (on which see Addenda to ii. 2 n. 4), but by the occasional numismatic representation of Desire or Love as a winged mannikin proceeding out of the mouth. At Emporion (*Ampurias*) in Hispania Tarraconensis the earliest coins (*s.* iii B.C.), copying the Siculo-Punic *drachmaí*, show a head of Persephone on the obverse and a standing horse crowned by a flying Nike on the reverse side (fig. 887, *a*=A. Heiss *Description générale des monnaies antiques de l'Espagne* Paris 1870 pp. 86, 90 pl. 1 Emporiae 1, Head *Hist. num.*[2] p. 2). Later silver and copper coins of the same town exhibit a most remarkable modification of this originally Carthaginian horse. First, he is transformed into a winged and prancing Pegasos (fig. 887, *b*=Heiss *op. cit.* p. 87 pl. 1 Emporiae 2). Then there emerges from his head a small human head wearing a *pétasos* (Heiss *op. cit.* p. 87 pl. 1 Emporiae 3, cp. 4 f.=fig. 887, *c*, *d*). Finally,

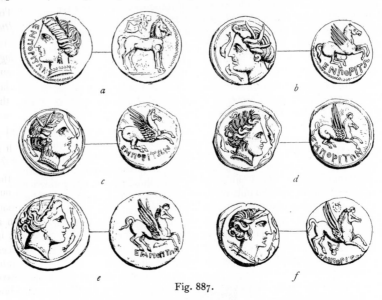

Fig. 887.

this little personage becomes an obvious Eros, his wing formed by the horse's ear, his back by the horse's cheek, his arm and leg by the horse's muzzle (fig. 887, *e*, *f*=Heiss *op. cit.* p. 87 pl. 1 Emporiae 7 f., cp. *ib.* p. 89 f. pl. 2 Emporiae 23—29, 31—35, p. 93 pl. 4 Emporiae 37—43, Head *Hist. num.*[2] p. 2). Gallic imitations of the type sometimes show the winged figure riding the horse (R. Forrer *Keltische Numismatik der Rhein- und Donaulande* Strassburg 1908 p. 39 fig. 68 Pictones, p. 77 f. fig. 144 Pictones).

Once launched from the lips, the small figure representing the desire of the deity might run along his arm and so fare forth into the world to work his will. Silver coins of Kaulonia from *c.* 550 B.C. onwards have as their obverse design a naked male with hair in long ringlets and left foot advanced. In his uplifted right hand is a stalk with pinnate leaves : on or over his outstretched left arm runs a diminutive figure carrying a similar stalk in one (fig. 888) or both hands (figs. 889, 890) and sometimes equipped with a *chlamýs* over his shoulders and wings on his heels (fig. 888). In the field stands a stag, beneath which on many specimens is another stalk of the plant springing from the ground (figs. 889, 890). The design is repeated, incuse, on the reverse side of the coin, though here the small runner is mostly omitted. One specimen (fig. 890) is known bearing the additional legend ΙΚΕΤΕΣΙ(Α), with which festival-name cp. *Od.* 13. 213 Ζεύς σφεας τίσαιτο ἱκετήσιος and the evidence collected by O. Jessen in Pauly—Wissowa *Real-Enc.* viii. 1592 f. (*Brit. Mus. Cat. Coins* Italy p. 334 ff., *Hunter Cat. Coins* i. 126 pl. 9, 8, cp. i. 127 f. pl. 9, 9 f., Babelon *Monn. gr. rom.* ii. 1. 1460 ff. pls. 70, 14 f., 71, 1—6, Garrucci *Mon. It. ant.* p. 155 f. pl. 111, 11—14, p. 186 pl. 125, 17 = my fig. 890, cp. p. 156 f. pl. 111, 15 ff., p. 186 pl. 125, 16, Head *Coins of the Ancients* p. 15 pl. 8, 17 = my fig. 888, cp. p. 15 pl. 8, 18, p. 30 pl. 15, 9, *id. Hist. num.*[2] p. 92 ff. figs. 50 f., G. Macdonald *Coin Types* Glasgow 1905 pp. 36, 97, 132 pl. 3, 7, cp. p. 132 f. pl. 5, 10. Fig. 889 is drawn from a specimen in my collection). Many and wonderful are the explanations of this remarkable

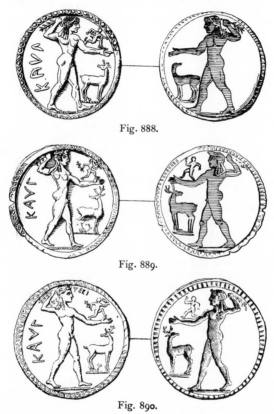

Fig. 888.

Fig. 889.

Fig. 890.

type that have been put forward (for a full list see now Oldfather in Pauly—Wissowa *Real-Enc.* xi. 80—85): *e.g.* Iupiter *Tonans* brandishing a thunderbolt (J. Hardouin *Nummi antiqui populorum et urbium illustrati* Parisiis 1684 p. 244, A. S. Mazzocchi *In Regii Herculanensis Musei Aeneas Tabulas Heracleenses Commentarii* Neapoli 1754 p. 527 f.: see Eckhel *Doctr. num. vet.*[2] i. 168 f.), Dionysos with Οἶστρος (F. M. Avellino in the *Giornale numismatico* 1811—1812 ii. 24 and in his *Opuscoli diversi* Napoli 1833 ii. 108 ff. citing *inter alia* Nonn. *Dion.* 9. 263 f. where Ino lashes the Maenads with sprays of ivy. Note that in *Hunter Cat. Coins* i. 127 pl. 9, 10 = my fig. 891 the small runner is replaced by an ivy-leaf with a long stalk, an attribute which appears again on the reverse of the same coin), Herakles returning from the Hyperboreoi with one of the Kerkopes (F. Streber 'Ueber die Münzen von Caulonia' in

Fig. 891.

the *Abh. d. bayer. Akad. 1837* Philos.-philol. Classe ii. 709 ff.), Apollon with laurel-branch and the purified Orestes (K. O. Müller *Handbuch der Archäologie der Kunst*² Breslau 1835 p. 516, *id. Denkmäler der alten Kunst* Göttingen 1835 i. 8 pl. 16, 72), Apollon as καθαρτής or καθάρσιος with Aristaios (Honoré d'Albert duc de Luynes in the *Nouv. Ann.* i. 426), Apollon with Daphnis or Hyakinthos (J. de Witte in the *Rev. Num.* 1845 p. 400 ff. makes these suggestions, but prefers to follow T. Panofka: see *infra*), Apollon as καθαρτής—or else the Demos of Kaulonia—performing the act of lustration with the genius of ἁγνισμός or καθαρμός on his arm (R. Rochette *Mémoires de Numismatique et d'antiquité* Paris 1840 p. 1 ff. followed by C. Cavedoni in the *Bull. d. Inst.* 1842 p. 90 f.), Apollon as sun-god with a lustral branch and a wind-god dispersing miasmas (W. Watkiss Lloyd 'On the types of the coins of Caulonia' in the *Num. Chron.* 1847 x. 1 ff. followed by P. Gardner *Types of Gk. Coins* p. 85 pl. 1, 1, cp. G. F. Hill *A Handbook of Greek and Roman Coins* London 1899 p. 171 pl. 3, 3), Apollon chasing the thief Hermes (S. Birch 'Notes on types of Caulonia' in the *Num. Chron.* 1845 viii. 163 ff.), the headland Kokinthos with the wind-god Zephyros (Garrucci *Mon. It. ant.* p. 186), 'Some local myth, which has not been handed down to us' (Head *Hist. num.*¹ p. 79 after Eckhel *Doctr. num. vet.*² i. 169). Specially ingenious was the view of T. Panofka 'Über die Münztypen von Kaulonia' in the *Arch. Zeit.* 1843 i. 165 ff.: accepting the identification of the larger figure with Apollon, he regarded the smaller as Kaulon (Steph. Byz. *s.v.* Καυλωνία) or Kaulos, son of the Amazon Kleite and eponymous founder of the town (interp. Serv. *in* Verg. *Aen.* 3. 153), and suggested that both figures bear an olive-branch not without a punning allusion to καυλός, *caulis*. Head *Hist. num.*² p. 93 does not mention Panofka, but adopts and modifies his interpretation: the main figure is the founder Καῦλος, who carries as his emblem a καυλός or 'parsnip' (*pastinaca sativa*); the running genius is Ἀγών (G. F. Hill in the *Journ. Hell. Stud.* 1897 xvii. 80, cp. W. Wroth *ib.* 1907 xxvii. 92), or Hermes Ἀγώνιος (Pind. *Isthm.* 1. 85, cp. *Ol.* 6. 133 ff. with scholl. *ad locc.*) or Δρόμιος (G. Doublet in the *Bull. Corr. Hell.* 1889 xiii. 69 f. publishes an inscription from Polyrrhenion Ἑρμᾶι Δρομίωι, with which S. Eitrem in Pauly—Wissowa *Real-Enc.* viii. 755 cp. Hesych. οὔνιος·...δρομεύς), carrying apparently the same emblem, which is also shown growing beneath the stag. P. Gardner *Types of Gk. Coins* p. 86 came nearer to the truth, when he wrote: 'The most plausible alternative view would be to regard him [the small figure] as an embodiment of the χόλος or wrath of the Apollo, who is about to attack the enemies of the deity....' I hold that he is in fact the soul of the god sent forth to work the divine will. The god himself is Apollon, whose epithets ἑκάεργος, ἑκατηβελέτης, ἑκατηβόλος, ἕκατος, ἑκηβόλος are all connected with ἑκών (A. Fick—F. Bechtel *Die Griechischen Personennamen*² Göttingen 1894 pp. 107, 127, Prellwitz *Etym. Wörterb. d. Gr. Spr.*² p. 133, Boisacq *Dict. étym. de la Langue Gr.* p. 236 f., O. Jessen in Pauly—Wissowa *Real-Enc.* vii. 2664 f., 2799 f., 2800 ff., F. Bechtel *Lexilogus zu Homer* Halle a. d. S. 1914 pp. 114—117) and betoken his magical will-power (cp. *supra* i. 12 n. 1, 14 n. 1). Apollon ἑκηβόλος would thus mean Apollon 'who strikes what he wills' (less probably 'who projects his will'). And I am reminded by Mr F. M. Cornford that Plat. *Cratyl.* 420 C

sought to connect βουλή with βολή—a notion well worth weighing (Boisacq *op.
cit.* pp. 114, 129). However that may be, the καυλός in the hand of the god or
of the god's soul is presumably the magician's rod ; its precise botanical character can hardly be determined.

The nearest analogue to the Cauloniate sprite occurs on a fragmentary votive
pínax of terra cotta found at Rosarno in Calabria and now preserved in the
Antiquarium at Munich (A. Michaelis in the *Ann. d. Inst.* 1867 xxxix. 93—104
pl. D, A. Furtwängler in Roscher *Lex. Myth.* i. 1352 f., Christ—Lauth *Führer
durch d. k. Antiquarium in München* 1891 p. 16 cited by O. Waser in Pauly—
Wissowa *Real-Enc.* vi. 498 f. Fig. 892 is a fresh drawing made from the cast
at Cambridge). This relief, which Furtwängler *loc. cit.* assigned to the period
c. 450—440 B.C., shows Hermes confronting Aphrodite. The type of the goddess
is obviously derived from a cult-statue—witness the rose in her hand and the

Fig. 892.

thymiatérion before her. But the chief interest of the design lies in the little
figure of Eros, who stands on the arm of the goddess and with outstretched hand
expresses her feelings towards the god (Plout. *praec. coniug.* 1 καὶ γὰρ οἱ παλαιοὶ
τῇ Ἀφροδίτῃ τὸν Ἑρμῆν συγκαθίδρυσαν, ὡς τῆς περὶ τὸν γάμον ἡδονῆς μάλιστα λόγου
δεομένης, Harpokr. *s.v.* Ψιθυριστὴς Ἑρμῆς· Δημοσθένης ἐν τῷ κατὰ Νεαίρας (39).
ἦν τις Ἀθήνησιν Ἑρμῆς οὕτω καλούμενος· ἐτιμᾶτο δὲ Ἀθήνησι καὶ Ψίθυρος Ἀφροδίτη
καὶ Ἔρως Ψίθυρος = Souid. *s.v.* Ψιθυριστὴς Ἑρμῆς, *id. s.v.* Ψιθυριστοῦ Ἑρμοῦ καὶ
Ἔρωτος καὶ Ἀφροδίτης· ἅπερ πρῶτος ἐποίησεν, ὥς φησι Ζώπυρος (*Frag. hist. Gr.*
iv. 533 Müller), Θησεύς, ἐπεὶ Φαῖδρα ὥς φασιν ἐψιθύριζε Θησεῖ κατὰ Ἱππολύτου,
διαβάλλουσα αὐτόν. οἱ δὲ ἀνθρωπινώτερόν φασιν Ἑρμῆν Ψιθυριστήν, παρὰ τὸ ἀνθρώπους ἐκεῖ συνερχομένους τὰ ἀπόρρητα συντίθεσθαι, καὶ ψιθυρίζειν ἀλλήλοις περὶ ὧν
βούλονται = Bekker *anecd.* i. 317, 11 ff., Eustath. *in Od.* p. 1881, 1 ff. διὸ καὶ Ψιθύρου
Ἀφροδίτης κατὰ Παυσανίαν (*sc.* the lexicographer Pausanias rather than a slip for
Harpokration) ἱερὸν ἦν Ἀθήνησι καὶ Ἔρωτος δέ· οὗ καὶ Δημοσθένης, φησί, μέμνηται
ἐν τῷ κατὰ Νεαίρας (39). ἐκαλεῖτο δέ, φασι, Ψίθυρος διὰ τὸ τὰς εὐχομένας αὐτῇ πρὸς

τὸ οὖς λέγειν, κ.τ.λ. See further O. Höfer in Roscher *Lex. Myth.* iii. 3198 f. The genesis of the hero Psithyros at Athens (Hesych. *s.v.* ψιθύρα) and of the god Psithyros at Lindos (F. Hiller von Gaertringen in the *Jahrb. d. kais. deutsch. arch. Inst.* 1904 xix Arch. Anz. p. 185 f., H. Usener in the *Rhein. Mus.* 1904 lix. 623 f. (=*id. Kleine Schriften* Leipzig—Berlin 1913 iv. 467 ff.) in an inscription of early imperial date found by R. F. Kinch near the north angle of the temple of Athena : τῷ Ψιθύρῳ νηὸν πολυκείονα τεῦξε Σέλευκος κ.τ.λ.) appears to have resembled that of Eros himself ; the whispered prayer of the worshipper (S. Sudhaus 'Lautes und leises Beten' in the *Archiv f. Rel.* 1906 ix. 185—200), like the heartfelt desire of the deity, was projected in visible form).

Similarly a metope from the north side of the Parthenon (slab no. xxv) shows a diminutive Eros stepping down from behind the shoulder of Aphrodite towards Menelaos, who on the adjoining metope (slab no. xxiv) drops his sword at the sight of Helene clinging to the Palladion (A. Michaelis *Der Parthenon* Leipzig 1870 p. 139 Atlas pl. 4, Friederichs—Wolters *Gipsabgüsse* p. 265 no. 590, Overbeck *Gr. Plastik*[4] i. 424 n.*, A. S. Murray *The Sculptures of the Parthenon* London 1903 p. 79 (misleading) pl. 12, 25 as drawn by Carrey, A. H. Smith *The Sculptures of the Parthenon* London 1910 p. 42 fig. 81 photographic view of metope *in situ*, *ib.* fig. 82 photograph of Eros from the cast at Berlin, C. Prasch-

Fig. 893.

niker 'Die Metopen der Nordostecke des Parthenon' in the *Jahresh. d. oest. arch. Inst.* 1911 xiv. 149 fig. 136 photograph, M. Collignon *Le Parthénon* Paris 1912 p. 29 pl. 39, 25 photograph. In this familiar scene (literary and monumental evidence in Overbeck *Gall. her. Bildw.* i. 626 ff. Atlas pl. 26, 2 ff, Baumeister *Denkm.* i. 745 ff. fig. 798 f., R. Engelmann in Roscher *Lex. Myth.* i. 1970 ff. figs., H. W. Stoll *ib.* ii. 2786 f. figs. 4—6, E. Bethe in Pauly—Wissowa *Real-Enc.* vii. 2832, 2835), especially as represented on the fine red-figured *oinochóe* from Vulci now in the Vatican (fig. 893=*Mus. Etr. Gregor.* ii pl. 5, 2ᵃ, Overbeck *Gall. her. Bildw.* i. 631 f. pl. 26, 12, Baumeister *Denkm.* i. 745 f. fig. 798, P. Weizsäcker in Roscher *Lex. Myth.* iii. 1800 f. fig. 3, J. H. Huddilston *Lessons from Greek Pottery* New York 1902 p. 86 f. fig. 16, Hoppin *Red-fig. Vases* i. 347 no. 7 (by 'The Painter of the Epinetron from Eretria in Athens')), Eros is already so far detached from Aphrodite that he signifies, not the love felt by the goddess, but the love caused by her in the heart of Menelaos. We are well on the way towards later conceptions of the love-god.

In Hellenistic times the favourite types of Eros were those of a boy (*e.g. Ausgewählte griechische Terrakotten im Antiquarium der königlichen Museen zu Berlin* Berlin 1903 p. 17 pl. 20, Winter *Ant. Terrakotten* iii. 2. 325 fig. 6 a flying Eros, said to be from Pagai in Megaris, now at Berlin, holding grapes in his raised right hand and other fruits in a fold of his *chlamýs* : height 0·275ᵐ) or a mere child (*e.g.* O. Rayet *Monuments de l'art antique* Paris 1884 ii pl. (40), 7 with text, L. Heuzey *Les figurines antiques de terre cuite du Musée du Louvre* Paris 1883 p. 21 pl. 35*bis*, 5, M. Collignon in Daremberg—Saglio *Dict. Ant.* i. 1607 fig. 2188, E. Pottier *Les statuettes de terre cuite dans l'antiquité* Paris 1890 p. 129 fig. 44, Winter *Ant. Terrakotten* iii. 2. 320 no. 12 *b* a walking Eros, from Tanagra, formerly in the Barre collection (no. 449), now in the Louvre, with his *chlamýs* drawn over his head : height 0·07ᵐ) or even a babe (*e.g.* L. Stephani in the *Compte-rendu St. Pét.* 1864 p. 202 f. Atlas pl. 6, 2, Winter *Ant. Terrakotten* iii. 2. 313 fig. 4 Eros clinging on to the neck of a swan, found at *Kerch* and now in the Hermitage at Petrograd : height 0·075ᵐ) ; and it is usually assumed that his progressive diminution in size was the natural outcome of fourth-century art with its well-defined *penchant* for youth and beauty (see *e.g.* the clear and sensible statements of O. Waser in Pauly—Wissowa *Real-Enc.* vi. 496 f., 502, 509). It must not, however, be forgotten that this tendency, which was undoubtedly a *vera causa*, gave fresh effect to the very ancient belief in the soul as a tiny winged form sent forth from the lover to compass his desires. That is the ultimate reason—I take it—why Eros with crossed legs and torch reversed became the commonest of all symbols for Death (A. Furtwängler in Roscher *Lex. Myth.* i. 1369, M. Collignon in Daremberg—Saglio *Dict. Ant.* i. 1610 fig. 2192 f., O. Waser in Pauly—Wissowa *Real-Enc.* vi. 508 f., F. Lübker *Reallexikon des klassischen Altertums*⁸ Berlin 1914 p. 1028, C. Robert *Thanatos* (*Winckelmannsfest-Progr. Berlin* xxxix) Berlin 1879 p. 44, Preller—Robert *Gr. Myth.* i. 845, Gruppe *Gr. Myth. Rel.* p. 1050 n. 5, *supra* p. 309) : a resting Eros meant a restful soul. Again, that is why Eros was so constantly associated with Psyche (L. Stephani in the *Compte-rendu St. Pét.* 1877 pp. 53—219, M. Collignon *Essai sur les monuments grecs et romains relatifs au mythe de Psyché* Paris 1877 (inadequate), A. Zinzow *Psyche und Eros* Halle 1881, A. Furtwängler in Roscher *Lex. Myth.* i. 1370—1372, O. Waser in Pauly—Wissowa *Real-Enc.* vi. 531—542 and in Roscher *Lex. Myth.* iii. 3237—3256) : *quasi*-bird and *quasi*-butterfly were kindred conceptions of the soul. Finally, we may discover here one ground at least for the astonishing variety of *genre* occupations attributed to Eros and the Erotes in the Graeco-Roman age. Readers of these lines will probably remember an eloquent passage in which J. W. Mackail *Select Epigrams from the Greek Anthology* London 1890 p. 34 f. describes the wealth of imagination lavished by a single writer, Meleagros, upon the figure of Eros. The poet's words could be illustrated by scores of extant works of art, especially terra-cotta statuettes, engraved gems, and mural paintings. By way of relaxation at the end of a somewhat stiff and stodgy Appendix I subjoin a few specimens.

Eros pervaded the universe and swayed all hearts from the highest to the lowest. Time was when Alkibiades had given offence by carrying a shield of gold and ivory with the device of Eros fulminant (Plout. *v. Alcib.* 16, Athen. 534 E), and an onyx at Berlin dating from the first half of *s.* iv (?) B.C. very possibly shows this deity with his *protégé* (fig. 894 = C. O. Müller *Denkmäler der alten Kunst* Göttingen 1835 ii. 2. 35 pl. 39, 451, Furtwängler *Geschnitt. Steine Berlin* p. 35 no. 355 pl. 7). But in *s.* i B.C. Eros was represented not merely holding a thunderbolt (Furtwängler *Geschnitt. Steine Berlin* p. 160 no. 3708 pl. 29 brown paste : Eros leaning on a pillar with thunderbolt (?) in right hand, sceptre in left and an altar (?) below, *id. ib.* p. 159 no. 3700 pl. 29 dark brown paste : Eros with thunderbolt in right hand, trident in left) but actually breaking it across his knee (fig. 895 = Furtwängler *Ant. Gemmen* i pl. 30, 31, ii. 149 a cornelian in the royal collection at The Hague, *id. Geschnitt. Steine Berlin* p. 90 no. 1628 pl. 17

paste, Reinach *Pierres Gravées* p. 52 no. 16, 1 pl. 51 banded agate, cp. Babelon *Monn. rép. rom.* ii. 8 no. 7 fig. reverse type of a *quinarius* struck by L. Iulius Bursio in 88 B.C.). A sardonyx formerly in the Poniatowski cabinet shows Eros posing as Zeus himself with thunderbolt and sceptre (fig. 896 = T. Cades *Collezione di N° 1400 Impronti delle migliori pietre incise, sì antiche, che moderne, ricavati dalle più distinte Collezioni conosciute dell' Europa* 1ᵐᵃ Classe, A 6, 34 'Genio di Giove': genuine? Lippold *Gemmen* p. 171 pl. 28, 4 says

Fig. 894.   Fig. 895.

'Römisch'). If Eros thus usurped the position of the strongest god, *a fortiori* he superseded the strongest hero. Lysippos is said to have represented Herakles as stripped of his weapons by Eros (*Anth. Pal.* 16. 103. 1 ff. (Tullius Geminus), cp. 16. 104. 1 ff. (Philippos)); and the incident became a commonplace of later art (see *e.g.* M. Collignon in Daremberg—Saglio *Dict. Ant.* i. 1606 fig. 2184, A. Furtwängler in Roscher *Lex. Myth.* i. 1366, 2248 f., O. Waser in Pauly—Wissowa *Real-Enc.* vi. 510, 513 f.). Hence Eros is arrayed in the hero's spoils

Fig. 896.   Fig. 897.

(fig. 897 = Furtwängler *Ant. Gemmen* i pl. 64, 19, ii. 290 a sardonyx cameo of three layers—translucent ground, figure in opaque white, upper surface brown—at Munich; of Roman date. Cp. Furtwängler *ib.* i pl. 62, 2, ii. 280, *id. Geschnitt. Steine Berlin* p. 73 no. 1111 pl. 14 (shown more clearly in C. O. Müller *Denkmäler der alten Kunst* Göttingen 1835 ii. 3. 13 pl. 51, 636) small convex garnet, p. 135 no. 3020 pl. 25 cornelian, p. 135 nos. 3021—3028 pl. 25 pastes, p. 160 nos. 3713—3716 pastes, p. 237 no. 6482 (G. Winckelmann *Monumenti antichi inediti* Roma 1821 i. 39 f. κληδοῦχος! pl. 32) sardonyx), or combines them with those of Zeus in a pantheistic scheme (fig. 898 = Furtwängler *Ant. Gemmen* i pl. 43, 61, ii. 210). In short, Eros plants his foot upon the world (C. O. Müller *Denkmäler der alten Kunst* Göttingen 1835 ii. 3. 13 pl. 51, 633, Furtwängler *Geschnitt. Steine Berlin* p. 276 no. 7440 pl. 55 flat cornelian of imperial date. The *motif* occurs also in sculpture: see A. de Ridder *Les bronzes antiques du Louvre* Paris 1913 i. 87 no. 613 = Reinach *Rép. Stat.* ii. 446 no. 7, Von Sacken *Ant. Bronzen Wien* pl. 14, 1 = Reinach *Rép. Stat.* ii. 447 no. 1, L. Urlichs in the *Bonner Jahrbücher* 1846 ix. 155 pl. 5, 4 = Reinach *Rép. Stat.* ii. 431 no. 4), or takes his seat thereon (fig. 899 = Furtwängler *Ant. Gemmen* i pl. 30, 37, ii. 149), or with a mighty effort carries the globe as if it were a mere ball

Fig. 898.   Fig. 899.   Fig. 900.

(fig. 900 = Furtwängler *Geschnitt. Steine Berlin* p. 160 no. 3722 pl. 29 black paste with bluish band). We are meant to draw the moral: *omnia vincit Amor; et nos cedamus Amori* (Verg. *ecl.* 10. 69). Psyche is no match for the matchless one. Of countless illustrations I give but two: a convex banded agate in my daughter's possession shows Eros with one foot raised on a step in hot pursuit of a butterfly, the animal form of Psyche (fig. 901); and a flat cornelian in my own collection portrays him riding her round a race-course, the goals of which are marked by her butterfly and his weapons respectively (fig. 902). Such allegories, not to say 'sermons in stones,' were keenly relished in the early imperial age. If Eros thus masters the human soul, he enters into all the pleasures and pains of man. Sometimes he is represented as a veritable fay, doing the deeds of mortals with more

Fig. 901.   Fig. 902.

than mortal skill. Thus, like 'the merry Grecian coaster' he sails the blue waters of the Mediterranean, but his boat is nothing more than a wine-jar—no wonder he bears the palm (fig. 903 = T. Cades *op. cit.* I^{ma} Classe, A 6, 57, C. O. Müller *Denkmäler der alten Kunst* Göttingen 1835 ii. 3. 23 f. pl. 55, 702 a cornelian in the Poniatowski collection), or even a *murex*—a cockleshell, as we might say (fig. 904 = T. Cades *op. cit.* I^{ma} Classe, A 6, 59 of unknown *provenance*). Sometimes, again, Erotes and Psychai play the part of ordinary men and women with no trace of divinity beyond the tell-tale wings of bird or butterfly or beetle and a certain exquisite grace that idealizes all—witness a wonderful band of decoration below the main panels on the wall of a dining-room in the house of the Vettii, which pictures Erotes and Psychai as twining garlands, making oil, coining money (?), fulling clothes, and selling wine (Herrmann *Denkm. d. Malerei* pls. 22, 24, 25 Text pp. 34—39, A. Mau *Pompeii its life and art²* trans. F. W. Kelsey New York 1902 pp. 331—337 figs. 163, 165—169, A. Mau *Pompeji in Leben und Kunst* Anhang zur zweiten Auflage Leipzig 1913 p. 48, P. Gusman *Pompéi* Paris 1899 p. 339 with col. pl. 11 opposite p. 388, H. B. Walters *The Art of the Romans* London 1911 p. 102 f. pl. 43). Eros can be the schoolmaster and wield the whip

Fig. 903.   Fig. 904.   Fig. 905.

Fig. 906.

(fig. 905 = Furtwängler *Ant. Gemmen* i pl. 50, 36, ii. 244, E. Gerhard in the *Bull. d. Inst.* 1834 p. 124 no. 31 a cornelian from the Nott collection); Eros can be the schoolboy and suffer the whipping (fig. 906 = T. Cades *op. cit.* 1ᵐᵃ Classe, A 3, 59 'nel Museo Blacas,' *Brit. Mus. Cat. Gems* p. 127 no. 1005 an onyx cameo from the Castellani collection).

It seems a far call from Eros as a great cosmogonic deity to Eros as a diminutive fairy. But ξυνὸν ἀρχὴ καὶ πέρας, and the expression of the one belief may be curiously like the expression of the other. Thus a cornelian formerly in the collection of Sir Henry Russell represents the Orphic Eros seated in the world-egg, already split open to form heaven and earth (fig. 907

Fig. 907.

= C. O. Müller *Denkmäler der alten Kunst* Göttingen 1835 ii. 3. 12 pl. 50, 628, E. Gerhard in the *Bull. d. Inst.* 1839 p. 107 no. 100,

M. Collignon in Daremberg—Saglio *Dict. Ant.* i. 1595 f. fig. 2142, A. Furtwängler in Roscher *Lex. Myth.* i. 1357, *id. Ant. Gemmen* i pl. 50, 37, ii. 244), while one of the most charming of all Pompeian frescoes shows a pair of lovers examining a nestful of tiny Erotes (G. Bechi in the *Real Museo Borbonico* Napoli 1824 i pl. 24, L. Hirt 'Il nido. Idillio' in the *Ann. d. Inst.* 1829 p. 251 ff. pl. E, 1, Herrmann *Denkm. d. Malerei* Text p. 26 fig. 5, Helbig *Wandgem. Camp.* p. 163 no. 821, *Guida del Mus. Napoli* p. 313 no. 1324, from the *Casa del poeta tragico.*

Fig. 908.

Fig. 908, a *replica* from Pompeii *reg.* vii. 12. 26, well published by Herrmann *op. cit.* pl. 17 Text p. 26 = Helbig *op. cit.* p. 164 no. 823, G. Rodenwaldt *Die Komposition der pompejanischen Wandgemälde* Berlin 1909 p. 152 ff. fig. 25, is more completely preserved, but less fine: it has only two Erotes in the nest. A second *replica*, Helbig *op. cit.* p. 164 no 822, omits the girl in the background to the right. See also J. Overbeck—A. Mau *Pompeji*[4] Leipzig 1884 pp. 288, 293, 581).

It was pointed out by F. Piper *Mythologie der christlichen Kunst* Weimar

1847 i. 214—217 that scenes representing Eros and Psyche passed from pagan to Christian *sarcophagi* ((1) R. Garrucci *Storia della Arte cristiana nei primi otto secoli della chiesa* Prato 1879 v. 12 f. pl. 302, 2—5, J. Ficker *Die altchristlichen Bildwerke im christlichen Museum des Laterans* Leipzig 1890 no. 181, W. Lowrie *Christian Art and Archæology* New York 1901 p. 254 fig. 93, L. von Sybel *Christliche Antike* Marburg 1909 ii. 44, 70, 72, 98 n. 1, 103 n. 1, 194, 226 fig. 45, C. M. Kaufmann *Handbuch der christlichen Archäologie* Paderborn 1913 p. 498 fig. 193=a marble *sarcophagus*, found near the catacomb of Praetextatus and now preserved in the Lateran Museum : it dates from the end of *s.* iii or the beginning of *s.* iv A.D. and shows on its main face the Good Shepherd, thrice repeated (bearded in centre, beardless to right and left), amid a vintage of Erotes, which includes a Psyche with butterfly-wings bringing grapes ⁺ɴ an Eros with bird-wings. (2) A. Bosio *Roma Sotterranea* Roma 1632 p. 75 fig., G. Bottari *Sculture e pitture sagre estratte dai cimiterj di Roma* Roma 1737 i. 105 pl. 28 f., E. Z. Platner *Beschreibung der Stadt Rom* Stuttgart 1830—1842 ii. 1. 192 f.=a marble *sarcophagus* from the Vatican catacomb, now under an altar in the chapel of the Madonna della Colonna in St. Peter's : Christ, amid the apostles, adored by a man and his wife ; beneath, a large lamb flanked by twelve smaller lambs ; behind, vines and two palm-trees (phoenix on left palm) ; Christ stands in front of a gateway, the arch of which has a Psyche with butterfly-wings on the left, a wingless Eros with torch on the right. [But R. Garrucci *op. cit.* v. 50 f. pl. 327, 2—4 shows that these figures really represent Sol and Luna respectively.] (3) J. B. L. G. Séroux d'Agincourt *Histoire de l'Art par les monumens* Paris 1823 iii Sculpture p. 4 pl. 4, 3, 5=a *sarcophagus* from the catacomb of S. Pietro e Marcellino (Torrepignatarra) : the column which divides the front bears a relief of Eros embracing Psyche ; the inscription reads *Zacinie cesque* (for *quiesce*) *in pace*. (4) E. Z. Platner *op. cit.* iii. 2. 450= a *sarcophagus* in the Convent of S. Agnese at Rome : both ends show Eros and Psyche with reed and urn to betoken water, and a *cornu copiae* for earth, beneath them ; the centre has inlaid a Christian medallion of S. Agnese. [(5) R. Garrucci *op. cit.* v. 138 pl. 395, 3, L. von Sybel *Christliche Antike* Marburg 1909 ii. 96 fig. 11=a fragmentary *sarcophagus*-lid from the catacomb of S. Callisto at Rome with a medallion supported by two Erotes, adjoining which is the group of Eros and Psyche.] Indeed, early Christian art made constant use of Erotes, winged or wingless, in a variety of *motifs* derived from classical sources (see the examples collected by L. von Sybel *Christliche Antike* Marburg 1906 i col. pl. 1, 2, 169 fig., 175 f. with 176 n. 1, 179, 1909 ii. 96 n. 3). Eros still figured largely in Byzantine carvings and paintings (*e.g.* O. M. Dalton *Byzantine Art and Archaeology* Oxford 1911 p. 216 fig. 130, p. 281 fig. 171). He survived in the *putto* of the early renaissance (F. Wickhoff 'Die Gestalt Amors in der Phantasie des italienischen Mittelalters' in the *Jahrbuch der königlichen preussischen Kunstsammlungen* 1890 xi. 41—53, S. Weber *Die Entwicklung des Putto in der Plastik der Frührenaissance* Heidelberg 1898, O. Waser in Pauly—Wissowa *Real-Enc.* vi. 516), and is still recognizable on our valentines and Christmas-cards.

It would seem, then, that from first to last Eros was simply and essentially a soul-type. If we raise the further question—Whose soul was represented by the Orphic Eros?—, we get an uncertain reply. According to the early Orphic scheme (*supra* pp. 1020, 1034), golden-winged Eros sprang from the egg laid by black-winged Nyx Ἐρέβους...ἐν ἀπείροσι κόλποις (Aristoph. *av.* 695). But who was the consort of Nyx? We are not definitely told. Presumably it was Erebos (so in Hes. *theog.* 123 ff., Akousilaos *frag.* 1 (*Frag. hist. Gr.* i. 100

Müller) *ap.* Damask. *quaest. de primis principiis* 124 (i. 320, 10 ff. Ruelle)—though schol. Theokr. 13. 1 f. says ᾽Ακουσίλλας (Kallierges corr. ᾽Ακουσίλαος) Νυκτὸς καὶ Αἰθέρος (*sc.* υἱὸν εἶπεν τὸν ῎Ερωτα), Antagoras *ap.* Diog. Laert. 4. 26, Cic. *de nat. deor.* 3. 44, Hyg. *fab.* praef. p. 9, 3 ff. Schmidt). But the later Orphic theogonies (*supra* pp. 1022, 1024, 1034) appear to have regarded Chronos as the maker of the cosmic egg. In any case—and this is the main point—it was not Zeus. In the early Orphic theogony Zeus does not figure at all till the fourth generation (*supra* pp. 1020, 1034). In the theogony of Hellanikos he is a name for Protogonos in the second generation (*supra* pp. 1023, 1034). In the Rhapsodies he is one of the children of Phanes in the third generation (*supra* pp. 1026 ff., 1034). We may reasonably infer that the original form of the Orphic cosmogony was independent of, and perhaps anterior to, the recognition of Zeus.

The later Orphists, however, made much of Zeus and viewed him as a pan-theistic power (*supra* p. 1027 ff.). The primitive notion of Chaos as a gaping or yawning mouth (*supra* p. 1039) was transferred to Zeus who, according to the Rhapsodies, opened his jaws wide and swallowed Phanes whole (*supra* p. 1027). Phanes himself was conceived as in some sort a Zeus (*supra* i. 7 n. 6); for Phanes was Protogonos (*supra* p. 1026), and Protogonos was 'Zeus the arranger of all' (*supra* p. 1023). This equation is presupposed by a relief (fig. 909), which seems to have come more than a century since from Rome and is now exhibited in the Royal Museum (no. 2676) at Modena (C. Cavedoni 'Dichiarazione di un bassorilievo Mitriaco della R. Galleria Palatina di Modena' in the *Atti e Memorie delle RR. deputazioni di storia patria per le provincie Modenesi e Parmensi* Modena 1863 i. 1—4 with lithographic pl., A. Venturi *La R. Galleria Estense in Modena* Modena 1883 p. 360 fig. 94, F. Cumont in the *Rev. Arch.* 1902 i. 1—10 with photographic pl. 1, R. Eisler *Weltenmantel und Himmelszelt* München 1910 ii. 399 ff. fig. 47, Reinach *Rép. Reliefs* iii. 61 no. 1). On a thick slab of white marble (0.71ᵐ high, 0.49ᵐ wide) is an oval band enclosing an egg-shaped recess. The band is decorated with the twelve signs of the zodiac, and grouped about it are winged heads representing the four winds of heaven. Within the recess stands a nude youth encumbered with a plethora of attributes. Above his head and beneath his feet are the two halves of an egg, from each of which flames are bursting. A snake coiled round him rears its head on to the upper egg-shell. He has two large wings and a crescent on his back, the head of a lion growing from his front, and the heads of a goat and a ram projecting from his right and left sides. Instead of feet he has cloven hoofs. In his right hand he grasps a thunderbolt, in his left a sceptre. Cavedoni, followed by Cumont, regarded this singular figure as primarily Mithraic, though both ad-mitted the presence of features susceptible of an Orphic interpretation. R. Eisler has done good service by insisting on its Orphic character. The egg-like recess in which the god is placed, the upper and lower shells from which he has emerged, the strange animal-heads on his flanks (*supra* p. 1022 f.), the snake's head appearing above his face (*supra* p. 1023), all mark him as Phanes. He bears thunderbolt and sceptre, because Phanes was one with Zeus. His face is that of the sun-god in Rhodian art, for Phanes was not only called Antauges and Phaethon (*supra* p. 1026) but also identified with Helios (*supra* i. 7 n. 6, 311). Cavedoni took the cloven hoofs to be those of a goat: if so, they hint that Phanes was Pan (*supra* p. 1023). Cumont and Eisler think them bovine: if so, they denote him as Dionysos (*supra* p. 1026). The relief bears two inscriptions. The first, [E]YPHROSY[NE ET] FELIX on the background of the recess, has been intentionally effaced. The second, P   P | FELIX   PATER on

Fig. 909.

either side of the zodiac, must be completed as *p(ecunia) p(osuit) Felix pater* (*sacrorum*). Eisler ingeniously suggests that the relief in question originally adorned the Orphic sanctuary of a certain Felix and Euphrosyne and was subsequently re-dedicated in a Mithraic temple by Felix alone, since women were excluded from the rites of Mithras. That an Orphic monument should thus be re-consecrated in a Mithraic shrine seems likely enough in view of the fact that at Borcovicium (*Housesteads* on Hadrian's Wall) Mithras himself was represented in an oval zodiac with an egg-shell on his head (J. C. Bruce *The Roman Wall*[3] London 1867 p. 399 with fig. on p. 398, *id. Lapidarium Septentrionale* Newcastle-upon-Tyne 1871 ii. 96—98 no. 188 fig., F. Cumont *Textes et monuments figurés relatifs aux mystères de Mithra* Bruxelles 1896 i. 395 fig. 315, R. Eisler *Weltenmantel und Himmelszelt* München 1910 ii. 410 ff. fig. 48 a relief, 1.40^m high, 0.77^m wide, found *in situ* between two Mithraic altars = *Corp. inscr. Lat.* vii nos. 645, 646: Mithras' body emerges from the *Petra genetrix* (Dessau *Inscr. Lat. sel.* nos. 4244, 4248, 4250, cp. 4249); his arms are broken, but his right hand still holds a knife, his left hand a lighted torch), while the lion-headed god, usually described as the Mithraic Kronos or Aion, but more probably explained as Areimanios or Areimanes, the Mithraists' equivalent for Ahriman (F. Legge *Forerunners and Rivals of Christianity* Cambridge 1915 ii. 254 f.), appears with a snake coiled about him, wings attached to his shoulders and haunches, a sceptre held in his left hand, and a thunderbolt on his breast or at his side (*e.g.* Clarac *Mus. de Sculpt.* pl. 559 fig. 1193, Reinach *Rép. Stat.* i. 296 no. 3, F. Lajard *Introduction à l'étude du culte public et des mystères de Mithra en orient et en occident* Paris 1847 pl. 70, C. O. Müller *Denkmäler*

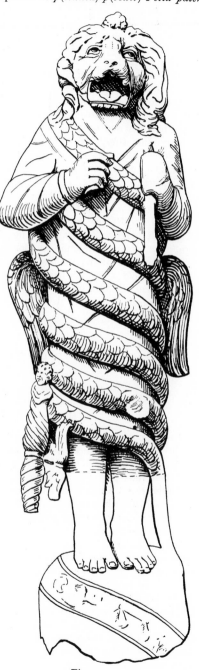

Fig. 910.

der alten Kunst Göttingen 1835 ii. 4. 71 f. pl. 75, 967, F. Cumont *Textes et monuments figurés relatifs aux mystères de Mithra* Bruxelles 1896 ii. 238 f. fig. 68, *id.* in Roscher *Lex. Myth.* ii. 3039 fig. 1, R. Eisler *Weltenmantel und Himmelszelt* München 1910 ii. 412 f. fig. 50 a statue in white marble (1.65ᵐ high, 0.47ᵐ wide at base), found at Ostia in 1797 by the English painter R. Fagan and now erected at the entrance of the Vatican Library: the four wings are adorned with symbols of the seasons, *viz.* the left upper wing with dove and swan, the right upper wing with corn-ears, the right lower wing with grapes, the left lower wing with two palm-trees and reeds; the hands hold keys and a sceptre; the breast is marked with a thunderbolt; the supporting slab shows hammer and tongs to left, *caduceus*, cock, and pine-cone to right, with an inscription (*Corp. inscr. Lat.* xiv no. 65 = Dessau *Inscr. Lat. sel.* no. 4212 C. Valeri|us Heracles pat(er) | et C. Valerii | Vitalis et Nico|mes (*sic*) sacer-do|tes s(ua) p(e)c(unia) p(o)s(ue)r(unt) | D. d. idi. Aug. imp. | Com. | vi et | Septi|miano | cos. = Aug. 13, 190 A.D.). H. Dütschke *Antike Bildwerke in Oberitalien* Leipzig 1878 iii. 180 f. no. 367, F. Cumont *Textes et monuments figurés relatifs aux mystères de Mithra* Bruxelles 1896 ii. 258 f. fig. 96, *id. Die Mysterien des Mithra*² trans. G. Gehrich Leipzig 1911 p. 215 n. 1 pl. 2, 4 (=my fig. 910), Reinach *Rép. Stat.* ii. 477 no. 7 a statue in white Italian marble (1.15ᵐ high, 0.35ᵐ wide) in the Uffizi at Florence: the god wears a sleeved garment; two slot-holes in his back show where the shoulder-wings were attached; his right hand held a key, his left a sceptre; the upper part of the thunderbolt at his side takes the form of a human head; his feet with the sphere on which he stands are restored).

APPENDIX H.

ZEUS *KTÉSIOS.*

(1) The Jars of Zeus *Ktésios.*

Any discussion of Zeus *Ktésios* must start from the *locus classicus* in Athen. 473 B—C ΚΑΔΙΣΚΟΣ. Φιλήμων ἐν τῷ προειρημένῳ συγγράμματι (*sc.* Philemon the Atticist, on whom see W. Christ *Geschichte der griechischen Litteratur*³ München 1898 p. 771 n. 3) ποτηρίου εἶδος. ἀγγεῖον δ' ἐστὶν ἐν (M. P. Nilsson would delete ἐν) ᾧ τοὺς Κτησίους Δίας ἐγκαθιδρύουσιν, ὡς Ἀντικλείδης φησὶν ἐν τῷ Ἐξηγητικῷ (E. Schwartz in Pauly—Wissowa *Real-Enc.* i. 2426, ii. 2597 f. makes it highly probable that the reference is to the Ἐξηγητικόν of Autokleides, not Antikleides,—a valuable source for traditional rites) γράφων οὕτως "Διὸς Κτησίου σημεῖα (G. Kaibel cj. σιπύας) ἱδρύεσθαι χρὴ ὧδε. καδίσκον καινὸν (κενὸν with αι above ε cod. P.) δίωτον ἐπιθηματοῦντα στέψαι τὰ (so Villebrun and C. F. W. Jacobs for στέψαντα. K. W. Dindorf would follow Jacobs, or else read στέψαντα τὰ) ὦτα ἐρίῳ λευκῷ καὶ ἐκ τοῦ ὤμου τοῦ δεξιοῦ καὶ ἐκ τοῦ μετώπου †τοῦ κροκίου† καὶ (K. W. Dindorf would omit καὶ) ἐσθεῖναι (so codd. A.B. ἐσθῆναι cod. P. edd. V. L.) ὅ τι ἂν εὕρῃς καὶ εἰσχέαι (so J. Schweighäuser for εἴσχεαι cod. C. ἴσχεται cod. P. edd. V. L.) ἀμβροσίαν. ἡ δ' ἀμβροσία ὕδωρ ἀκραιφνές, ἔλαιον, παγκαρπία. ἄπερ ἔμβαλε." Cod. C. epitomizes as follows: φησί που Διογένης. εἶτα εἴσχεαι ἀμβροσίαν. ἡ δ' ἀμβροσία, ὕδωρ ἀκραιφνές, ἔλαιον, παγκαρπία· ἄπερ ἔμβαλε. For the word †τοῦ κροκίου†, which I have marked as corrupt, no very satisfactory emenda-

Fig. 911.

tion has been proposed. I. Casaubon cj. ἄωτον κρόκινον κρεμαννύναι, 'lanam suspendito coloris crocei.' Villebrun cj. καὶ ἐκ τοῦ ὤμου τοῦ δεξιοῦ τε καὶ ἐκ τοῦ μετώπου τι κρόκινον ἀρθῆναι (meaning ἀρτηθῆναι!), ὅ τι ἂν εὕρῃς. C. F. W. Jacobs cj. καὶ ἐκ τοῦ ὤμου τοῦ δεξιοῦ τοῦ θεοῦ καὶ ἐκ τοῦ μετώπου κρόκινον κάλυμμα ἐσθῆναι. G. Kaibel cj. < καθέσθαι τὰ ἄκρα > τοῦ κροκίου, 'to let down the ends of the thread.' Tresp *Frag. gr. Kultschr.* p. 47 keeps ἐκ τοῦ μετώπου τοῦ κροκίου, taking κροκίου in the sense of κροκίνου, 'from its forehead smeared with saffron.' But †τοῦ κροκίου† is a *vox nihili*; and there is, to my thinking, much difficulty in ἐσθεῖναι ὅ τι ἂν εὕρῃς. I suspect that we ought to read καὶ ἐκ τοῦ ὤμου τοῦ δεξιοῦ καὶ ἐκ τοῦ μετώπου κρόκινόν τι ἐκτεῖναι, ὅ τι ἂν εὕρῃς, and to translate the whole extract as follows : 'The right way to set up the signs of Zeus *Ktésios* is this. Take a new jar with two ears and a lid to it (ἐπιθηματοῦντα is adj.) and wreath its ears with white wool, and stretch a piece of yellow—anything you can find—from its right shoulder and its forehead, and pour ambrosia into it. Ambrosia is a mixture of pure water, olive oil, and all manner of fruits : empty these ingredients in.'

(2) The Jars of Zeus *Ktésios* funereal in character.

The use of the terms ὦτα, ὦμος, μέτωπον reminded Miss Harrison (*Themis* p. 299) 'of the anthropoid vases of the Troad.' But, though such language may have originated in connexion with *Gesichtsurnen* (*vide* Forrer *Reallex.* pp. 275, 419 and especially J. Schlemm *Wörterbuch zur Vorgeschichte* Berlin 1908 pp. 173—176 figs. a—i), we cannot safely infer that the *kadískos* of Zeus *Ktésios* was of human or partially human shape. The description of it given above recalls rather certain vase-forms developed out of the primitive *píthos* (H. B. Walters *History of Ancient Pottery* London 1905 i. 159) such as the large lidded *amphora* of the 'Dipylon' style, or its lineal descendants (A. Milchhöfer in the *Ath. Mitth.* 1880 v. 177 f., A. Brückner—E. Pernice *ib.* 1893 xviii. 143 ff., P. Wolters in the *Jahrb. d. kais. deutsch. arch. Inst.* 1899 xiv. 128 ff., F. Poulsen *Die Dipylongräber und die Dipylonvasen* Leipzig 1905 pp. 18 ff., 45 ff.) the *próthesis*-vase of the sixth century and the *loutrophóros* of the fifth. Now all these vases were connected with death and the grave. The 'Dipylon' *amphora*, of which I figure a typical specimen (Collignon—Couve *Cat. Vases d'Athènes* p. 40 f. no. 196 Planches p. 5 pl. 11, A. Furtwängler in the *Arch. Zeit.* 1885 xliii. 131, 139 figs., Perrot—Chipiez *Hist. de l'Art* vii. 174 fig. 58, 226 fig. 98, S. Wide in the *Jahrb. d. kais. deutsch. arch. Inst.* 1899 xiv. 196 f. fig. 61. My fig. 911 is from a photograph. Height with lid 0·90ᵐ), stood half-sunk beneath the surface of the ground (cp. A. Brückner—E. Pernice in the *Ath. Mitth.* 1893 xviii. 92 fig. 4 = Perrot—Chipiez *Hist. de l'Art* vii. 56 fig. 4) and—since its bottom is holed—served to convey liquid offerings to the dead beneath it (F. Poulsen *op. cit.* p. 19 'die Vase diente als Hohlaltar, durch welchen man die flüssigen Opfer Milch und Honig, Öl und Wein, vielleicht auch das Blut der Opfertiere hinabströmen lassen konnte'). The lid with its handle in the shape of a vase turned upside down is suggestive of drink-offerings. The procession of chariots above and warriors bèlow would delight the heart of the dead. And snakes moulded in relief round the rim, round the base of the neck, and up either handle sufficiently indicate the funereal character of the whole. The *próthesis*-vase was likewise set up over the grave, as we see from a very remarkable example found at Cape Kolias and now at Athens (Collignon—Couve *Cat. Vases d'Athènes* p. 212 ff. no. 688 Planches p. 14 f. pl. 30; A. Conze in the *Ann. d. Inst.* 1864 xxxvi. 183 ff. with fig., *Mon. d. Inst.* viii pl. 4, 1ᵃ—1ᵉ, pl. 5, 1ᶠ—1ʰ = Reinach *Rép. Vases*

i. 164, 1—5, 165, 1—3, H. von Rohden in Baumeister *Denkm.* iii. 1974 f. fig. 2114, É. Michon in Daremberg—Saglio *Dict. Ant.* ii. 1333 fig. 3280, É. Cuq *ib.* ii. 1377 fig. 3345, 1378 fig. 3346, M. Collignon *ib.* iii. 1319 fig. 4561, O. Crusius in Roscher *Lex. Myth.* ii. 1149 fig. 5, P. Wolters in the *Ath. Mitth.* 1891 xvi. 379 no. 11 fig., Miss J. E. Harrison in the *Journ. Hell. Stud.* 1899 xix. 219 fig. 4, *ead. Proleg. Gk. Rel.*[2] p. 235 fig. 53, *Themis* p. 290 f. fig. 77. I reproduce the drawings given in the *Mon. d. Inst. loc. cit.* Height 0·64ᵐ). The body of the vase shows two successive scenes : (A) the dead man, laid out on a bed, is surrounded by mourners ; beside one of them is the word ΟΙΑΡΟΙ (S. Reinach

Fig. 912.

loc. cit. suggests οἴμοι (?) ; but cp. Souid. *s.v.* οἴαροι· γυναῖκες). (B) The coffin is lowered into the grave by four men, one of whom removes the pall. Mourners stand to right and left ; and there is a tree in the background. Beneath both scenes is a race of four chariots, the goal appearing between two of them. The neck of the vase continues the same sequence of scenes : (A′) In the centre rises an omphaloid tomb painted white. Within it flit four souls represented as small winged *eídola* ; below them is a snake. Round the edge of the tomb runs an inscription, which P. Pervanoglu took to be

ΛΝΔΡΟΣΛ........ΟΙΟΓΛΥ·ΚΛ·ΟΙΕΝΘΛΔΕ ΚΕΙΜΛΙ

S. A. Kumanudis (*Ann. d. Inst.* 1864 xxxvi. 197 n. 2) transcribed the latter part of it as follows :

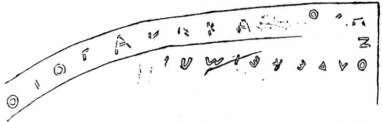

Fig. 913.

A. Conze's illustration is based on a copy by A. Postolakkas. The line was convincingly read by C. Keil: ἀνδρὸς ἀποφθιμένοιο ῥάκος κακὸν ἐνθάδε κεῖμαι—a curiously cynical hexameter. The use of ῥάκος to denote a corpse is defended by *Anth. Pal.* 7. 380. 6 f. (Krinagoras) κεῖται δὲ τῇδε τὠλιγηπελὲς ῥάκος | Εὐνικίδαο, σήπεται δ᾿ ὑπὸ σποδῷ, cp. *ib.* 5. 20. 3 (Rufinus) σῶμα ῥακῶδες and Stephanus *Thes. Gr. Ling.* vi. 2334 D f. On the tomb is placed a vase resembling in shape that which is here described ; and mourners to right and left make lamentation. (B′) A procession of four mourners, two of whom bear offerings (?), approaches the grave. Among the patterns surrounding the neck of the vase will be seen a wavy line clearly derived from the old sepulchral snake. The paintings of this important vase have, unfortunately, suffered much since its discovery: nothing now remains of the inscriptions, the winged souls, or the snake, and little is left of the tomb. Finally, the *loutrophóros* was carved or painted over the tomb of the unmarried (*infra* § 9 (d) ii (β)). ' So war die Grabvase, deren Entwickelung von Hohlaltar zu Monument wir verfolgt haben, aus einem Monument zum Symbol geworden' (F. Poulsen *op. cit.* p. 47).

The 'Dipylon' *amphora*, the *próthesis*-vase, the *loutrophóros*, each in turn served as the σῆμα or σημεῖον of the dead beneath it. In view of these facts how are we to interpret the jars called by Autokleides the σημεῖα of Zeus *Ktésios*? They too may well have been funereal in character. Hence their prophylactic wreathing with white wool and yellow stuff(?). Hence too the necessity for filling them with a mixture of water, oil, and seeds, known as *ambrosía* (cp. Pausanias the Atticist *ap.* Eustath. *in Il.* p. 976, 4 f. κατὰ Παυσανίαν, ὃς λέγει καὶ ὅτι ἀμβροσία γένος τι συνθέσεως ἐξ ὕδατος ἀκραιφνοῦς καὶ μέλιτος καὶ ἐλαίου < καὶ (*inserui*) > παγκαρπίας) : such offerings had come to be conceived as food given by the living to the dead (see *e.g.* P. Stengel *Opferbräuche der Griechen* Leipzig and Berlin 1910 pp. 129 ff., 183 ff.), but were originally a magical means of enabling the dead to make food for the living (see Miss J. E. Harrison *Themis* p. 291 ff.). Similar in character was the offering made to the chthonian Zeus in Eur. *frag.* 912 Nauck[2] (from the *Cretes*, according to L. C. Valckenaer) *ap.* Clem. Al. *strom.* 5. 11 p. 373, 3 ff. Stählin σοὶ τῶν πάντων μεδέοντι χοὴν | πέλανόν τε φέρω (so H. Grotius for φέρων cod. L.), Ζεὺς εἴτ᾿ Ἀίδης | ὀνομαζόμενος στέργεις· σὺ δέ μοι | θυσίαν ἄπυρον (so Abresch for ἄπορον L.) παγκαρπείας (so Grotius for παγκαρπίας L.) | δέξαι πλήρη προχυθεῖσαν (so Valckenaer for προχυτίαν L.). | σὺ γὰρ ἔν τε θεοῖς τοῖς οὐρανίδαις | σκῆπτρον τὸ Διὸς μεταχειρίζεις (so H. van Herwerden for μεταχειρίζων L.) | χθονίων τ᾿ (so F. Sylburg for δ᾿ L.) Ἀίδη (ἄιδηι L.) μετέχεις ἀρχῆς. | πέμψον δ᾿ ἐς (so A. Nauck for μὲν L.) φῶς ψυχὰς ἐνέρων (so Nauck for ἀνέρων L.) | τοῖς βουλομένοις (Grotius cj. πέμψον μὲν φῶς ψυχαῖς ἀνέρων ταῖς βουλομέναις) ἄθλους προμαθεῖν (so Grotius for προσμαθεῖν L.) |

πόθεν ἔβλαστον, τίς ῥίζα κακῶν, | τίνα (F. H. M. Blaydes cj. τίνι) δεῖ (so Grotius for δὴ L.) μακάρων ἐκθυσαμένους (so Valckenaer for ἐκθυσαμένοις L.) | εὑρεῖν μοχθῶν ἀνάπαυλαν.

(3) Zeus *Ktésios* as Forefather buried in the House.

Accordingly I would venture to put forward the following hypothesis with regard to Zeus *Ktésios* and his jars. In Italy the forefather of the family, once buried in the house (Serv. *in* Verg. *Aen.* 5. 64 etiam domi suae sepeliebantur: unde orta est consuetudo ut dii Penates colantur in domibus, *ib.* 6. 152 apud maiores...omnes in suis domibus sepeliebantur. unde [ortum est ut Lares colerentur in domibus, unde] etiam umbras larvas vocamus, nam dii Penates alii sunt. inde est quod etiam Dido cenotaphium domi fecit marito, Isid. *orig.* 15. 11. 1 prius autem quisque in domo sua sepeliebatur. These statements are supported by the custom of burying infants less than forty days old in a *subgrundarium* (Fulgent. *expos. serm. ant.* 7; cp. *Corp. inscr. Lat.* vi no. 27571 = Orelli *Inscr. Lat. sel.* no. 4545 = Dessau *Inscr. Lat. sel.* no. 7938) and by the myths concerning the birth of Romulus (Plout. *v. Rom.* 2), Servius Tullius (Plin. *nat. hist.* 36. 204), and Caeculus (Serv. *in* Verg. *Aen.* 7. 678). They are rightly emphasised by F. Granger *The Worship of the Romans viewed in relation to the Roman Temperament* London 1895 p. 60, *id.* in the *Class. Rev.* 1897 xi. 32 f. W. Warde Fowler *ib.* 1896 x. 394 f., 1897 xi. 33 ff. attempted to minimise their force. But J. E. King *ib.* 1903 xvii. 83 f. suggested that infants were so buried in order to ensure their re-birth, and Frazer *Golden Bough*[3]: The Magic Art i. 105 n. 4 extends his suggestion to cover 'The widespread custom of burying the dead in the house.' A good example of this practice in the Semitic area is the case of Samuel, who was 'buried...in his house at Ramah' (1 Sam. 25. 1). At Bibracte the capital of the Aedui (*Mont Beuvray* in *Saône-et-Loire*) Gallic graves of the third La Tène period (*s.* i B.C.) were found beneath the houses, often under the hearth: see M. Hoernes *Natur- und Urgeschichte des Menschen* Wien und Leipzig 1909 ii. 128, 440, cp. J. Déchelette *Manuel d'archéologie préhistorique* Paris 1914 ii. 3. 948 ff. for an *aperçu* of the town), was known as the Lar or Genius of the home (Plaut. *merc.* 834 familiai Lar pater, Laberius *frag.* 54 *ap.* Non. Marc. p. 172, 26 f. Lindsay Laberius in Imagine: Genius generis nostri parens. For the identification of the Lar with the Genius see further Censorin. *de die nat.* 3. 2 eundem esse Genium et Larem multi veteres memoriae prodiderunt, in quis etiam Granius Flaccus in libro quem ad Caesarem de indigitamentis scriptum reliquit, interp. Serv. (*i.e.* Donatus, according to E. K. Rand in the *Class. Quart.* 1916 x. 158 ff.) *in* Verg. *Aen.* 3. 63 Appuleius de Daemonio Socratis (? a paraphrase of Apul. *de deo Socr.* p. 152 f. Oudendorp): 'Manes,' inquit, 'animae dicuntur melioris meriti, quae in corpore nostro Genii dicuntur, corpori renuntiantes Lemures; cum domos incursionibus infestarent, Larvae appellabantur; contra, si aequi et faventes essent, Lares familiares,' Auson. *technop. de dis* 9 nec Genius domuum, Larunda progenitus Lar, cp. Ov. *fast.* 3. 57 f. Wissowa *Rel. Kult. Röm.*[2] p. 175 denies their identity on grounds that seem to me inadequate) and was conceived as a Iupiter (so at least I have argued in *Folk-Lore* 1905 xvi. 296 ff. noting that the Genius of a man corresponded with the Iuno of a woman (T. Birt in Roscher *Lex. Myth.* i. 1614 f., M. Ihm *ib.* ii. 615 ff.), that according to Caesius (Bassus?), who professed to follow Etruscan authorities, the Penates were Fortuna, Ceres, the Genius Iovialis, and the masculine Pales (Caesius *ap.* Arnob. *adv. nat.* 3. 40, cp. *ib.* 3. 43 Ceres, Pales, Fortuna, Iovialis aut Genius)—this Genius Iovialis being evidently a family god of some kind, not to be confused with the Genius Iovis (Min. Fel. *Oct.* 29. 5, *Corp. inscr. Lat.* i no. 603, 16 with tab. lith. 82=ix no. 3513, 16=Orelli *Inscr. Lat. sel.* no. 2488 *fin.*, cp. no. 1730,=Wilmanns *Ex. inscr. Lat.* no. 105, 25=Dessau *Inscr. Lat. sel.* no. 4906, 16) who was but the Genius of an anthropomorphic Iupiter—, that the Genius was not only affiliated to Iupiter (Fest. p. 359 *a* 14 f. Müller, p. 492, 6 f. Lindsay Tages nomine, Geni filius, nepos Iovis) but actually identified with Iupiter (Aug. *de civ. Dei* 7. 13 quid est Genius? ...hic est igitur quem appellant Iovem. This, however, is a quasi-philosophical conclusion based on the general similarity between the functions of the Genius and those of Iupiter as conceived by Valerius Soranus in his famous couplet (*ib.* 7. 9, cp. Myth. Vat. 3 prooem. p. 152, 28 ff. Bode): Iuppiter omnipotens, regum rerumque deumque (*rerum regumque repertor* Myth. Vat. . G. H. Bode cj. *creator*) | progenitor genetrixque (*genitrixque* Myth. Vat.) deum, deus unus et omnes (*idem* Myth. Vat.)), etc.), who appeared in the form of a snake (Herrmann *Denkm. d. Malerei* pl. 48 Text p. 59, A. Mau in the *Röm. Mitth.* 1896 xi. 29, *id. Pompeii: its Life and Art*[2] trans. F. W. Kelsey New York 1902 p. 271 f. fig. 127, A. Sogliano in the *Mon. d. Linc.* 1898 viii. 268, Talfourd Ely in *Archœologia* 1897 lv. 305 ff. a painting on the back wall of a shrine in the *Casa dei Vettii* at Pompeii, which shows the Genius with *patera* in right hand, *acerra* opened in left, and a face resembling that of Nero (*supra* p. 96); he stands between two dancing Lares, each of whom bears a goat-*rhytón* (cp. *supra* i. 108) and a pail; beneath him a great bearded and crested snake approaches an altar, on which is an egg and fruit. For the snake as a manifestation of the Genius see further T. Birt in Roscher *Lex. Myth.* i. 1623 ff. fig., J. A. Hild in Daremberg—Saglio *Dict. Ant.* ii. 1490 with fig. 3543, W. F. Otto in Pauly—Wissowa *Real-Enc.* vii. 1161 f., E. Küster *Die Schlange in der griechischen Kunst und Religion* Giessen 1913 pp. 146 n. 3, 153 f. ; and for the egg as an offering to the dead, M. P. Nilsson *Das Ei im Totenkultus der Griechen* Lund 1901 pp. 3—12 figs. 1, 2 (Sonderabdruck aus *Från Filologiska Föreningen i Lund, Språkliga uppsatser* ii Lund 1902)).

Similarly we may suppose without any undue temerity that in Greece the forefather of the family, once buried in the house (Plat. *Minos* 315 D οἱ δ' αὖ ἐκείνων ἔτι πρότεροι αὐτοῦ καὶ ἔθαπτον ἐν τῇ οἰκίᾳ τοὺς ἀποθανόντας. No other literary testimony to this custom can be cited; but the assertion here made is fully borne out by actual remains. H. Bulle *Orchomenos* München 1907 i. 67 f. shows that at Orchomenos in Boiotia during early Mycenaean times (*c.* 1700—1500 B.C.) the dead were buried as a rule inside the houses, and quotes parallels from Thorikos, Athens, and Eleusis. In the small settlement of early Mycenaean date on the summit of Mt *Velatouri* at Thorikos round, or in two cases oblong, holes were found hewn in the rock within the houses: the round holes had certainly served as graves, for in them stood large *píthoi* the upper parts of which were safeguarded by circular walls, and in these *píthoi* were remains of human bones (B. Staes in the Πρακτ. ἀρχ. ἐτ. 1893 p. 15 f. pl. B, 3, *id.* in the Ἐφ. Ἀρχ. 1895 p. 228 ff. pl. 11, 3, Frazer *Pausanias* v. 524 f., A. J. B. Wace—M. S. Thompson *Prehistoric Thessaly* Cambridge 1912 p. 222). At Athens a grave of unbaked brick, dating from the şame period and containing four bodies, one of them in a crouching attitude, was discovered between 'Pelasgian' house-walls on the S. slope of the Akropolis (A. N. Skias in the Ἐφ. Ἀρχ. 1902 p. 123 ff. figs. 1—4, A. J. B. Wace—M. S. Thompson *op. cit.* p. 221). In the nekropolis at Eleusis two graves of unbaked brick were found under hearths and mistaken for small altars (A. N. Skias in the Ἐφ. Ἀρχ. 1898 p. 49 ff.

with pl., A. J. B. Wace—M. S. Thompson *op. cit.* p. 222). At Tiryns beneath the walls of the older Mycenaean palace five small stone-built graves with crouched bodies have come to light (W. Dörpfeld in the *Ath. Mitth.* 1907 xxxii p. iii, R. M. Dawkins in *The Year's Work in Class. Stud.* 1907 p. 14). In Thessaly graves have been repeatedly found within houses of the bronze age (Ch. Tsountas Aἱ προϊστορικαὶ ἀκροπόλεις Διμηνίου καὶ Σέσκλου Athens 1908 p. 131 'οἱ νεκροὶ ἐθάπτοντο ἐντὸς τῶν οἰκιῶν ἢ παρ' αὐτάς,' *ib.* p. 383 'τὸ ἔθιμον νὰ θάπτωσι τοὺς νεκροὺς ἐντὸς τῶν οἰκιῶν')}, was viewed as Zeus; for in prehistoric times he had been the representative of the sky-god to his clan. Herein, I take it, lies the ultimate explanation of such cults as that of Zeus Ἀγαμέμνων, who was worshipped at Sparta, if not at Athens (Append. I), Zeus Ἀμφιάραος, who had a popular sanctuary at Oropos (Append. J), Zeus Τρεφώνιος or Τροφώνιος, the great oracular deity of Lebadeia (Append. K), and Zeus Ἀσκληπιός, the healer of Epidauros, Hermione, and Pergamon (Append. L). The same conception will afford us a clue to the cults of Zeus Μειλίχιος and Zeus Φίλιος as well as to the myth of Periphas (Append. M). Most of these buried kings appeared in the guise of snakes. And it is important to observe that Zeus *Ktésios* did so too. A marble *stéle* from Thespiai, now in the Museum at Thebes (inv. no. 330), bears the inscription ΔΙΟΣ | ΚΤΗΣΙΟΥ in lettering of *s.* iii (?) B.C. and below it a relief, partially chipped away to make the block available for building purposes, but still plainly portraying a coiled snake with crest and beard (M. P. Nilsson 'Schlangenstele des Zeus Ktesios' in the *Ath. Mitth.*

Fig. 914.

1908 xxxiii. 279—288 fig.=my fig. 914, Harrison *Themis* p. 297 ff. fig. 79). The discovery of this *stéle* confirmed, as M. P. Nilsson notes, the acute surmise of E. Gerhard *Über Agathodämon und Bona Dea* Berlin 1849 pp. 3, 23 (*Gesammelte akademische Abhandlungen* Berlin 1868 ii. 45 with n. 28) that Zeus *Ktésios* was probably represented as a snake.

(4) The Jars of Zeus *Ktésios* compared with the Jars of the Dioskouroi.

Gerhard further maintained that the jars of Zeus *Ktésios* were comparable with those of the Dioskouroi at Sparta (*e.g. Brit. Mus. Cat. Coins* Peloponnesus p. 122 pl. 24, 6 a silver coin of 250—146 B.C. with rev. Λ Α a lidded *amphora* with a snake twining round it, between the caps of the Dioskouroi surmounted by stars; in the field a monogram and Α. *Ib.* p. 125 pl. 24, 14 a copper of 146—32 B.C. with rev. ΛΑΚΕΔΑΙ Μ·ΝΙΩΝ two *amphorae* with snakes twining round them; in the field two monograms. Fig. 915 = *Einzelaufnahmen* no. 1311, E. Cahen in the *Bull. Corr.*

Fig. 915.

Hell. 1899 xxiii. 599 f. fig. 1 (Perrot—Chipiez *Hist. de l'Art* viii. 442 f. fig. 216) an archaic relief—'sculpture par silhouettage ou découpage'—at Sparta (M. N. Tod and A. J. B. Wace *A Catalogue of the Sparta Museum* Oxford 1906 p. 191 no. 575 fig. 65), which has in the gable an egg (that of Leda??) flanked by two snakes, and in the space below the Dioskouroi facing each other with two lidded *amphorae* between them. Fig. 916—drawn from a photograph kindly given me by Miss J. E. Harrison—shows the relief of Argenidas in the Museo Lapidario at Verona (no. 555, height 0·40ᵐ, breadth 0·72ᵐ. Montfaucon *Antiquity Ex-*

plained trans. D. Humphreys London 1725 Suppl. i. 103 f. pl. 27 no. 1 (inexact),
S. Maffei *Museum Veronense* Veronae 1749 p. 47 fig. 7 (bad) with p. 56,
A. Michaelis in the *Arch. Zeit.* 1871 xxix. 145 n. 37, *Wien. Vorlegebl.* iv pl. 9, 8 *a*,
H. Dütschke *Antike Bildwerke in Oberitalien* Leipzig 1880 iv. 237 no. 538,
A. Furtwängler in Roscher *Lex. Myth.* i. 1170 f. fig., M. N. Tod—A. J. B. Wace
op. cit. p. 113 f. fig. 14, Reinach *Rép. Reliefs* iii. 436 no. 4, Harrison *Themis*
p. 304 f. fig. 84). On a base to the left are statues of the Dioskouroi wearing
pîloi, chitônes (?), and *chlamýdes* (?). Before them is a rectangular altar decorated
with a boar in relief. Behind the altar a large pedestal carries two lidded
amphorae. On a step or low base to the right stands a man, clad in *chitón*
and *himátion* (?), who holds a *phiále* (see H. Heydemann *Mittheilungen aus
den Antikensammlungen in Ober- und Mittelitalien* Halle 1879 p. 5) in his right
hand extended over the altar (?). Away to the right is seen a rocky coast forming
a bay, in which floats a vessel close to the shore. Near the vessel's stern are the
heads of two horned animals (oxen ?). On the further side of the bay two sets

Fig. 916.

of *dókana* (*supra* i. 766 ff.) are set up over a cavern. In the cavern two male
figures are reclining; a third raises his hand with a gesture of surprise or
greeting; a fourth (?) and possibly a fifth (??) follow him into the cave. On the
rocky point to the left of the cave is a cock. And from the *dókana* a snake
makes its way towards the *amphorae*. The scene is accompanied by the inscriptions [ΑΝΔ]ΚΕΙοΝ below the *dókana* and [Δ]ΡΓΕΝΙΔΑΣ ΑΡΙΣΤοΓΕΝ·
ΙΔΔ ΔΙοΣΚοΡοΙΣ | ΕΥΧΔΝ along the lower edge of the slab in lettering
of *s.* ii B.C. (*Corp. inscr. Gr.* ii no. 1949). This relief, found in 1710 A.D. at
Ateste (*Este*) in the country of the Veneti, had perhaps been brought thither
from Venice (A. Boeckh in the *Corp. inscr. Gr. loc. cit.*). It records the gratitude
of one Argenidas, a Spartan (?), who having crossed the sea ·to Venetia (?) in
safety dedicates a thank-offering to the Dioskouroi. It is thus the monumental
counterpart of Catullus' famous poem on his yacht (Cat. 4). The foreground of
the relief shows Argenidas pouring a libation at the altar, which—like many
examples of Italian *àes grave* (*Brit. Mus. Cat. Coins* Italy Index p. 406)—bears
the figure of a boar, and the heads of two sacrificed animals lying on the rocky

shore. The distance gives a very interesting view of the Anakeion (*supra* i. 107 n. 7) or sanctuary at Therapne (?), where the Dioskouroi lived on underground (Alkm. *frag.* 5 Bergk⁴ *ap.* schol. Eur. *Tro.* 210, Pind. *Nem.* 10. 103 f. with schol. *ad loc.*). The reclining figures are the buried heroes themselves. ˙The snake containing their *numen* creeps across from the old sanctuary to the new, intent on tasting the libation of Argenidas), at the Spartan colony Tarentum (see *e.g.* Garrucci *Mon. It. ant.* p. 130 pl. 100, 48, cp. *Brit. Mus. Cat. Coins* Italy p. 160 nos. 1—3, Head *Coins of the Ancients* p. 66 pl. 33, 12, *id. Hist. num.²* p. 58, and especially M. P. Vlasto in the *Journ. Intern. d'Arch. Num.* 1899 ii. 331 f. pl. 17, 1—6 gold *statêres* of Tarentum struck *c.* 281 B.C.: obv. head of Zeus to left with NIK as monogram in the field to right; rev. TAPANTINΩN and NIKAP and on one specimen ΦI, eagle to right on thunderbolt with two *amphorae*, sometimes surmounted by stars, in the field to right, *id. ib.* 1899 ii. 333 f. pl. 17, 16—18 quarter *statêres* of gold with same reverse type, but obverse showing laureate head of Apollon. The presence of the *amphorae* as symbols on these coins is explained by the fact that at Tarentum there was a cult of the Dioskouroi (*supra* i. 35 n. 6 fig. 8). In 1880 A.D. numerous terra-cottas were found at Tarentum, including a series of votive tablets studied by E. Petersen 'Dioskuren in Tarent' in the *Röm. Mitth.* 1900 xv. 3—61 with 2 pls. and many figs. and by G. Gastinel 'Cinq reliefs Tarentins' in the *Rev. Arch.* 1901 i. 46—58 with 4 figs. The tablets are in the form of *naískoi* and were originally painted. As classified by Petersen, they comprise the following types:

A. The Dioskouroi standing without horses (Petersen *loc. cit.* p. 7 fig. 1 and p. 8 fig. 3).

B. The Dioskouroi standing by their horses (Petersen *loc. cit.* p. 15 fig. 1).

C. The Dioskouroi riding (Petersen *loc. cit.* p. 18 fig. 2).

D. The Dioskouroi driving (Petersen *loc. cit.* p. 23 fig. 1).

E. The Dioskouroi on horse-back coming to the *Theoxénia* (Petersen *loc. cit.* p. 24 fig. 6).

F. The Dioskouroi reclining at the feast (Petersen *loc. cit.* p. 27 fig. 2).

It should be observed that the *amphorae* are a constant feature of the Tarentine reliefs (G. Gastinel *loc. cit.* p. 55 cp. the *amphorae* on the cake-moulds from Tarentum: *supra* p. 131), being placed usually on the ground, but sometimes on the *dókana* (cp. *supra* p. 158 ff. fig. 99), or on pillars), in Etruria (Gerhard *Etr. Spiegel* iii. 42 pl. 48, 6 and 8, cp. *supra* i. 770 fig. 564), and at Tauion in Galatia (*Brit. Mus. Cat. Coins* Galatia, etc. p. 24 pl. 5, 1, Head *Hist. num.²* p. 749 coppers of *s.* i. B.C.).

These Dioscuric *amphorae* have been variously explained. E. Petersen in the *Röm. Mitth.* 1900 xv. 41 calls them 'agonistisch' and supposes that jars of wine were given as prizes and contained the drink required for the *Theoxénia* (schol. Pind. *Ol.* 3 argum., 1, cp. 72: see further Nilsson *Gr. Feste* p. 418 ff.). A. Furtwängler in Roscher *Lex. Myth.* i. 1171 hesitates whether to regard them as 'Weinamphoren' implying a ritual use or as merely 'sepulkrale Symbole.' E. Bethe in Pauly—Wissowa *Real-Enc.* v. 1108 takes them to be bottomless vessels, like the great 'Dipylon' vases (cp. *supra* i. 766 n. 9), set up over the grave for the reception of funereal offerings. Gerhard *Gr. Myth.* i. 524 f. long ago described them as 'Aschengefässe.' My friend Dr J. Rendel Harris *Boanerges* Cambridge 1913 p. 377 f. acutely conjectures that in them we have a Greek parallel to the pots used throughout Africa etc. for the burial of a twin or of a twin's *placenta.* Personally I should be content to say that the *amphorae* both of Zeus *Ktésios* and of the Dioskouroi presuppose the custom of *pithos*-burial, and were retained as signs of the divinised dead long after the custom in question had ceased to be. If Zeus *Ktésios* was, as I maintain, an early Greek king buried in his own house, it is certainly permissible to assume that he was buried in a *píthos*. Platon, who states that the primitive Athenians used to bury the dead in their houses (*supra* p. 1060), informs us in the same context that their successors among other old-fashioned burial rites 'sent for women to fill the jars' (Plat. *Minos* 315 C ὥσπερ καὶ ἡμᾶς αὐτοὺς οἶσθά που καὶ αὐτὸς ἀκούων, οἵοις νόμοις ἐχρώμεθα πρὸ τοῦ περὶ τοὺς ἀποθανόντας, ἱερεῖά τε προσφάττοντες πρὸ τῆς ἐκφορᾶς τοῦ νεκροῦ καὶ ἐγχυτριστρίας μεταπεμπόμενοι with schol. *ad loc.* τὰς χοὰς τοῖς τετελευτηκόσιν ἐπιφερούσας, ὡς ἐπὶ τοῦδε. ἔλεγον δὲ καὶ τὸ βλάψαι (βάψαι Zonaras. C. A. Lobeck cj. θάψαι) καταχυτρίσαι (J. G. Baiter cj. ἐγχυτρίσαι), ὡς Ἀριστοφ.ίνης (Aristoph. *vesp.* 289 ὃν ὅπως ἐγχυτριεῖς). λέγονται δὲ καὶ ὅσαι τοὺς ἐναγεῖς καθαίρουσιν, αἷμα ἐπιχέουσαι τοῦ ἱερείου. ἔτι δὲ καὶ αἱ θρηνήτριαι, καὶ δὴ καὶ αἱ μαῖαι αἱ ἐκτιθεῖσαι ἐν χύτραις τὰ βρέφη = Souid. *s.v.* ἐγχυτρίστριαι = *et. mag.* p. 313, 41 ff. (cp. 39 f.) = Zonar. *lex. s.v.* ἐγχυτρίστριαι (cp. *s.v.* ἐγχυτρίζειν), cp. Hesych. *s.vv.* ἐγχυτριεῖς, ἐγχυτρίζειν, schol. Aristoph. *vesp.* 289, Moiris *lex. s.v.* ἐγχυτρισμός, Thom. Mag. p. 264). It seems reasonable to infer that, when *píthos*-burial within the house was abandoned, offerings to the dead were still placed in memorial jars by a special class of mourning-women. My contention is that the σημεῖα of Zeus *Ktésios* were just such memorial jars retained in the house, though their original significance had long been forgotten. The divinity whose presence they betokened would naturally be deemed the guardian of the household stores ; for the master, himself buried in a *píthos*, would know how to protect his own goods bestowed in other *píthoi*.

(5) Zeus *Ktésios* in Literature and Cult.

Hence his title *Ktésios*, 'god of Property,' which occurs in literature from *s.* v B.C. onwards (Aisch. *suppl.* 443 ff. καὶ χρημάτων μὲν ἐκ δόμων πορθουμένων | ... γένοιτ' ἂν ἄλλα Κτησίου Διὸς χάριν, Hippokr. *de insomniis* 4 (xxii. 10 Kühn) καὶ τοῖς θεοῖς εὔχεσθαι, ἐπὶ μὲν τοῖσιν ἀγαθοῖσιν Ἡλίῳ, Διὶ Οὐρανίῳ, Διὶ Κτησίῳ, Ἀθηνᾷ Κτησίῃ, Ἑρμῇ, Ἀπόλλωνι, ἐπὶ δὲ τοῖσιν ἐναντίοισι τοῖσιν ἀποτροπίοισι καὶ Γῇ καὶ ἥρωσιν κ.τ.λ., Hypereid. πρὸς Ἀπελλαῖον *frag.* 13 Blass[2] *ap.* Harpokr. *s.v.* Κτησίου Διός who adds Κτήσιον Δία ἐν τοῖς ταμείοις ἵδρυντο, Menand. *Pseudherakles frag.* 2, 2 f. (*Frag. com. Gr.* iv. 223 f. Meineke) *ap.* Harpokr. *loc. cit.* τὸν δὲ Δία τὸν Κτήσιον | ἔχοντα τὸ ταμεῖον οὐ κεκλεισμένον, Autokleides (?) *ap.* Athen. 473 B—C (*supra* p. 1054 ff.), Plout. *de repugn. Stoic.* 30 ὁ δὲ Ζεὺς γελοῖος, εἰ Κτήσιος χαίρει καὶ Ἐπικάρπιος καὶ Χαριδότης προσαγορευόμενος, ὅτι δηλαδὴ χρυσᾶς ἀμίδας καὶ χρυσᾶ κράσπεδα χαρίζεται τοῖς φαύλοις, τοῖς δ' ἀγαθοῖς ἄξια δραχμῆς ὅταν πλούσιοι γένωνται κατὰ τὴν τοῦ Διὸς πρόνοιαν, Cornut. *theol.* 9 p. 9, 16 f. Lang καὶ Κτήσιον...αὐτὸν (*sc.* Δία) προσαγορεύουσιν, Dion Chrys. *or.* 1 p. 57 Reiske Κτήσιος δὲ καὶ Ἐπικάρπιος ἅτε τῶν καρπῶν αἴτιος καὶ δοτὴρ πλούτου καὶ κτήσεως, οὐ πενίας οὐδὲ ἀπορίας, *or.* 12 p. 413 Reiske Κτήσιος δὲ καὶ Ἐπικάρπιος ἅτε τῶν καρπῶν αἴτιος καὶ δοτὴρ πλούτου καὶ δυνάμεως, Souid. *s.vv.* Διὸς κώδιον (*supra* i. 423 n. 1 = Apostol. 6. 10), Ζεὺς Κτήσιος· ὃν καὶ ἐν τοῖς ταμείοις ἱδρύοντο ὡς πλουτοδότην, Κτήσιος· ὁ Ζεύς, Κτησίου Διός· τὸν Κτήσιον Δία ἐν τοῖς ταμείοις ἱδρύοντο, Schöll—Studemund *anecd.* i. 266 no. 51 (Διός) Κτησίου).

Under this title Zeus was worshipped at Athens (Dem. *in Mid.* 53 Διὶ Κτησίῳ βοῦν λευκόν (*supra* i. 717 n. 2), *Corp. inscr. Att.* iii. 2 no. 3854, 1 f. from the Asklepieion [..κ]αὶ Διὸς | [Κ]τησίου) including the Peiraieus (Antiph. *or.* 1. 16 μετὰ ταῦτα ἔτυχε τῷ Φιλόνεῳ ἐν Πειραιεῖ ὄντα ἱερὰ (C. Wachsmuth *Die Stadt Athen im Alterthum* Leipzig 1890 ii. 1. 146 n. 1 would read ὄντι θύειν ἱερὰ) Διὶ Κτησίῳ, ὁ δὲ πατὴρ ὁ ἐμὸς εἰς Νάξον πλεῖν ἔμελλεν. κάλλιστον οὖν ἐδόκει εἶναι τῷ Φιλόνεῳ τῆς αὐτῆς ὁδοῦ ἅμα μὲν προπέμψαι εἰς τὸν Πειραιᾶ τὸν πατέρα τὸν ἐμὸν φίλον ὄντα ἑαυτῷ, ἅμα δὲ θύσαντα τὰ ἱερὰ ἑστιᾶσαι ἐκεῖνον, ib. 18 ἐπειδὴ γὰρ ἐδεδειπνήκεσαν, οἷον εἰκός, ὁ μὲν θύων Διὶ Κτησίῳ κἀκεῖνον ὑποδεχόμενος, ὁ δ' ἐκπλεῖν τε μέλλων καὶ παρ' ἀνδρὶ ἑταίρῳ αὐτοῦ δειπνῶν, κ.τ.λ., cp. for the domestic celebration Isai. or. 8. 16 καὶ τὰς ἑορτὰς ἤγομεν παρ' ἐκεῖνον πάσας· τῷ Διί τε θύων τῷ Κτησίῳ, περὶ ἣν μάλιστ' ἐκεῖνος θυσίαν ἐσπούδαζε καὶ οὔτε δούλους προσῆγεν οὔτε ἐλευθέρους ὀθνείους, ἀλλ' αὐτὸς δι' ἑαυτοῦ πάντ' ἐποίει, ταύτης ἡμεῖς ἐκοινωνοῦμεν καὶ τὰ ἱερὰ συνεχειρουργοῦμεν καὶ συνεπετίθεμεν καὶ τἆλλα συνεποιοῦμεν, καὶ ηὔχετο ἡμῖν ὑγίειαν διδόναι καὶ κτῆσιν ἀγαθήν, ὥσπερ εἰκὸς ὄντα πάππον) and Phlyeis (Paus. 1. 31. 4 Φλυεῦσι δέ...ναὸς δὲ ἕτερος ἔχει βωμοὺς Δήμητρος Ἀνησιδώρας < καὶ ins. Siebelis > Διὸς Κτησίου καὶ Τιθρωνῆς (Siebelis cj. Τριτώνης) Ἀθηνᾶς καὶ Κόρης Πρωτογόνης καὶ Σεμνῶν ὀνομαζο- μένων θεῶν), at Thespiai (supra p. 1061), at Epidauros (P. Cavvadias Fouilles d'Épidaure Athènes 1893 i. 56 no. 121 = Inscr. Gr. Pelop. i no. 1288 a limestone slab inscribed Διὶ | Κτησίωι | Κράτων. | μη'), at Kárien between Mt Pangaion and the sea (P. Perdrizet in the Bull. Corr. Hell. 1894 xviii. 441 ff. no. 1 = Michel Recueil d'Inscr. gr. no. 774 = Dittenberger Syll. inscr. Gr.² no. 576 a white marble boundary-stone inscribed in lettering of c. 400 B.C. Διὸς Ἑρκείο Πατρώϊο ; καὶ. Διὸ|ς Κτησίο), in the Kyklades Syros (F. Hiller von Gaertringen in Inscr. Gr. ins. v. 1 no. 670 an altar from Psarrianá inscribed in late lettering Διὸς | Κτησίου), Thera (F. Hiller von Gaertringen in Inscr. Gr. ins. iii Suppl. no. 1361 fig. = my

Fig. 917.

fig. 917 a small altar or ἐσχάρα of volcanic stone inscribed Ζεὺς Κτή(σιος)), Anaphe (Corp. inscr. Gr. ii no. 2477, 17 [Διὸς?] τοῦ Κτησίου, which is corrected ib. p. 1091 to [ὁ]πεῖ ὁ [βω]μὸς τοῦ Κτησίου καὶ τὸ ξο[άνι]ον and in Collitz—Bechtel Gr. Dial.-Inschr. iii. 1. 201 ff. no. 3430, 12 to [ὁ]πεῖ ὁ βωμὸς τοῦ Κτησίου καὶ τὸ ξοάνιον = F. Hiller von Gaertringen in the Inscr. Gr. ins. iii no. 248, 13 = Michel Recueil d'Inscr. gr. no. 853, 12 = Dittenberger Syll. inscr. Gr.² no. 555, 13 = J. v. Prott and L. Ziehen Leges Graecorum sacrae ii no. 122, 13. This inscription, which can be dated c. 100 B.C., tells how one Timotheos, anxious to erect a temple of Aphrodite, was bidden by an oracle to do so in the precinct of Apollon Asgelátas: the building-operations necessitated the temporary removal of an altar of Ktésios and an adjacent statuette. It is not certain that the statuette belonged to Ktésios, still less that it represented him. L. Ziehen even denies that Ktésios was originally Zeus Ktésios. In this, however, he is over-sceptical, though no doubt Ktésios was a title applicable to other deities besides Zeus (see O. Höfer in Roscher Lex. Myth. ii. 1578 f.), at Panamara in Karia (G. Deschamps —G. Cousin 'Inscriptions du temple de Zeus Panamaros' in the Bull. Corr. Hell. 1888 xii. 269 f. no. 54, 7 ff. a stéle dedicated by Kleoboulos and Strateia to a series of deities καὶ τοῖς ἐνοικιδίοις θεοῖς Διὶ Κτησίῳ καὶ Τύχῃ καὶ | Ἀσκληπιῷ), at Teos in Ionia (Corp. inscr. Gr. ii no. 3074 on an altar or base of s. ii B.C. Διὸς Κτησίου, | Διὸς Καπετωλίου, | Ῥώμης, | Ἀγαθοῦ δαίμονος = Michel Recueil d'Inscr.

gr. no. 806), in Phrygia (G. Cousin 'Inscription d'Ormellé de Phrygie' in the *Bull. Corr. Hell.* 1884 viii. 503 part of an astragalomantic inscription found at *Tefeny* col. iii, 19 δδδϛα ϙ ιθ′ ϙ Διὸς Κτη|σίου ϙ (*i.e.* the throw 4 +4+4+6+1 = 19 is that of Zeus *Ktésios*) followed by the hexameters θαρσῶν ἐν χειρὶ καὶ ἐ[π′ ἐ]| λπίδος ἐστὶν ὁ χρησμός, ὡς..... | μανύει καὶ τὸν νοσέοντ[α δὲ σώσ|ε]ι· εἰ δέ τι μαντεύῃ χρ[ησμὸς...|. δ]εις ἀπολήιψῃ. I should venture to restore and read the lines as follows : θαρσῶν ἐνχείρει, καὶ ἐπ′ ἐλπίδος ἐστὶν ὁ χρησμός, | ὡς καλὰ μανύει καὶ τὸν νοσέοντα δὲ σώσει· | εἰ δέ τι μαντεύῃ, χρησμοὺς ἡδεῖς ἀπολήιψῃ. See further the clear and helpful observations of W. R. Halliday *Greek Divination* London 1913 p. 213 ff. A. Wagener 'Inscriptions grecques recueillies en Asie Mineure' in the *Mémoires couronnés et mémoires des savants étrangers, publiés par l'Académie Royale des Sciences, des Lettres et des Beaux-Arts de Belgique* 1858 —1861 xxx Classe des Lettres 2. 19 f. no. 2 pl. A inscribed on a white marble *stéle* found at Koloe (*Koula*) with the prefatory remarks of J. de Witte *ib.* p. viii Διὰ Κτήσιον Τατία | Παπίαν τὸν ἑαυτῆ[ς] | ἄνδρα, Τειμοκράτη[ς] | τὸν πατέρα, Καρποφό|ρος τὸν θρέψαντα | κατειέρωσαν. | ἔτους σοα′ μη(νὸς) | Αὐδναίου η′ ; from which it appears that in 175 A.D. (= 261 of the Sullan era) Tatia definitely consecrated her deceased husband Papias as Zeus *Ktésios*—a striking vindication of my view that Zeus *Ktésios* was but the buried ancestor of the clan), at Pergamon in Mysia (H. Hepding in the *Ath. Mitth.* 1910 xxxv. 452 no. 35 a marble altar inscribed [Διὶ Κ]τησίωι | [Μ.] Αὐρήλιος | Μηνογένης | ὁ ἱεροφάντης), and doubtless elsewhere also. At Amastris in Paphlagonia he was recognised as Zeus *Panktésios* (G. Hirschfeld 'Inschriften aus dem Norden Kleinasiens besonders aus Bithynien und Paphlagonien' in the *Sitzungsber. d. Akad. d. Wiss. Berlin* 1888 p. 878 no. 31 on a small marble altar at Amastris inscribed ϙ ΔΙΙ ϙ | ΠΑΝΚΤΗ|ΣΙΩ ϙ). But this was an exceptional flourish. As a rule, Zeus *Ktésios* was a homely power content with worship in a small way—he never has a temple or a statue, but puts up with a jar or a hearth or at most a trumpery altar. I doubt if he ever received a handsomer offering than that of the white ox mentioned by Demosthenes.

(6) The Jars of Zeus in the *Iliad*.

One interesting possibility must not be neglected. We have traced Zeus *Ktésios* back to the days of Aischylos. But the very nature of his cult postulates a hoary antiquity. There is therefore much to be said for an acute suggestion made by Miss Harrison (*Proleg. Gk. Rel.*[2] p. 642), *viz.* that we have a reminiscence of the self-same cult in the Homeric description of the jars of Zeus (*Il.* 24. 527 ff. δοιοὶ γάρ τε πίθοι κατακείαται ἐν Διὸς οὔδει | δώρων, οἷα δίδωσι, κακῶν, ἕτερος δὲ ἑάων· | ᾧ μέν κ′ ἀμμίξας δώῃ Ζεὺς τερπικέραυνος, | ἄλλοτε μέν τε κακῷ ὅ γε κύρεται, ἄλλοτε δ′ ἐσθλῷ· | ᾧ δέ κε τῶν λυγρῶν δώῃ, λωβητὸν ἔθηκε· | καί ἑ κακὴ βούβρωστις ἐπὶ χθόνα δῖαν ἐλαύνει, | φοιτᾷ δ′ οὔτε θεοῖσι τετιμένος οὔτε βροτοῖσιν. For full *apparatus criticus* see A. Ludwich *ad loc.* The most important variants are the omission of line 528 in cod. T. and the substitution of κηρῶν ἔμπλειοι, ὁ μὲν ἐσθλῶν, αὐτὰρ ὁ δειλῶν in the passage as quoted by Plat. *rep.* 379 D, Plout. *quo modo adolescens poetas audire debeat* 6 (but cp. *consolat. ad Apollon.* 7), Euseb. *praep. ev.* 13. 3. 12 (from Plat. *loc. cit.*), Prokl. *in* Plat. *remp.* i. 96, 14 f. Kroll. Dr W. Leaf in 1888 printed δοιοὶ γάρ τε πίθοι κατακείαται ἐν Διὸς οὔδει | δώρων οἷα δίδωσι κακῶν, ἕτερος δὲ ἑάων· | κ.τ.λ. and supposed that 'Zeus has two jars of evil for one of good' (cp. Pind. *Pyth.* 3. 143 ff. ἓν παρ′ ἐσλὸν πήματα σύνδυο δαίονται βροτοῖς | ἀθάνατοι). But in 1898, collaborating with Mr M. A. Bayfield, he was more disposed to admit the possibility that 'there are only two jars spoken of, one of ills and one of blessings.' For κακῶν, ἕτερος δὲ ἐάων = ἕτερος μὲν κακῶν, ἕτερος δὲ ἐάων he cited *Il.* 7. 417 f. But the idiom is by no means rare: to the examples adduced by R. Kühner—B. Gerth *Ausführliche Grammatik der griechischen Sprache* Hannover and Leipzig 1904 ii. 266 add Aristot. *poet.* 1. 1447 b 14 ἐλεγειοποιοὺς τοὺς δὲ ἐποποιοὺς ὀνομάζουσιν, *pol.* 2. 4. 1262 a 26 f. φόνους ἀκουσίους, τοὺς δὲ ἑκουσίους. Moreover, the existence of the variant κηρῶν ἔμπλειοι, ὁ μὲν ἐσθλῶν, αὐτὰρ ὁ δειλῶν, which is not of course 'more careless than the average of Plato's citations' but good evidence of the pre-Aristarchean text, makes it practically certain that the jars were conceived as two in number):

> Two jars lie buried in the floor of Zeus
> Filled with the gifts he gives—evil in this,
> Good in the other. Whensoever Zeus
> The lightning-hurler gives a mingled lot,
> He that receives it falls on evil now
> And now on good. But he to whom Zeus gives
> Of the sorry store is made a very scorn :
> Him evil hunger drives o'er the bright earth,
> Nor gods nor mortals honour him as he goes.

(7) Zeus *Ktésios* compared with the *Di Penates*.

Finally, it should be observed that sundry Greek antiquarians described the Roman *di Penates* as *theoì Ktésioi* (Dion. Hal. *ant. Rom.* 1. 67 τοὺς δὲ θεοὺς τούτους Ῥωμαῖοι μὲν Πενάτας καλοῦσιν· οἱ δὲ ἐξερμηνεύοντες εἰς τὴν Ἑλλάδα γλῶσσαν τοὔνομα οἱ μὲν Πατρῴους ἀποφαίνουσιν, οἱ δὲ Γενεθλίους, εἰσὶ δ' οἳ Κτησίους, ἄλλοι δὲ Μυχίους, οἱ δὲ Ἑρκίους, cp. *ib.* 8. 41 καὶ ὑμεῖς, ὦ θεοὶ Κτήσιοι καὶ ἑστία πατρῴα καὶ δαίμονες οἱ κατέχοντες τοῦτον τὸν τόπον, χαίρετε). The description was apposite ; for the *di Penates*, as divinised ancestors (?? see *Folk-Lore* 1905 xvi. 293 ff.) keeping watch over the *penus*, were in function at least strictly analogous to Zeus *Ktésios*. Perhaps indeed the likeness extended to the signs and symbols of their presence ; for the *Penates* of Lavinium were represented by '*caducei* of iron and bronze together with Trojan pottery' (Timaios *frag.* 20 (*Frag. hist. Gr.* i. 197 Müller) *ap.* Dion. Hal. *ant. Rom.* 1. 67 σχήματος δὲ καὶ μορφῆς αὐτῶν πέρι Τίμαιος μὲν ὁ συγγραφεὺς ὧδε ἀποφαίνεται· κηρύκια σιδηρᾶ καὶ χαλκᾶ καὶ κέραμον Τρωϊκὸν εἶναι τὰ ἐν τοῖς ἀδύτοις τοῖς ἐν Λαουϊνίῳ κείμενα ἱερά. πυθέσθαι δὲ αὐτὸς ταῦτα παρὰ τῶν ἐπιχωρίων), which presumably implies metal snakes coiled about a staff and an earthenware jar (*N.B.* The *tabula Iliaca* in three separate places represents Aineias and Anchises as carrying the *sacra* of Troy in a cylindrical jar (?) with a domed lid : see O. Jahn *Griechische Bilderchroniken* Bonn 1873 p. 35 pl. 1, and cp. Helbig *Wandgem. Camp.* p. 310 no. 1380, *id.* in the *Bull. d. Inst.* 1879 p. 76 f., Preller—Jordan *Röm. Myth.*[3] ii. 322 n. 2). The mention of *caducei* in this connexion sets us thinking. Is it possible that Hermes himself with his chthonian and his phallic traits was of kindred origin? The idea should not be scouted without a careful consideration of the facts brought together by Mr A. L. Frothingham (in the *Am. Journ. Arch.* 1916 xx. 175—211 and a sequel as yet unpublished). See further *supra* p. 383 n. 7.

APPENDIX I.

ZEUS *AGAMÉMNON*.

The evidence for the cult of Zeus Ἀγαμέμνων at Sparta is as follows: Lyk. *Al.* 335 states that Priamos was killed (*supra* i. 39 n. 2 and n. 6) ἀμφὶ τύμβῳ τἀγαμέμνονος, on which Tzetzes remarks Ἀγαμέμνων ὁ Ζεὺς ἐν Λακεδαιμονίᾳ. This is confirmed by Lyk. *Al.* 1124 Ζεὺς Σπαρτιάταις αἱμύλοις κληθήσεται (*sc.* ὁ Ἀγαμέμνων) with Tzetz. *ad loc.* ὅτι Λακεδαιμόνιοι ἱδρύσαντο Ἀγαμέμνονος Διὸς ἱερὸν εἰς τιμὴν τοῦ ἥρωος, Staphylos *frag.* 10 (*Frag. hist. Gr.* iv. 506 Müller) *ap.* Clem. Al. *protr.* 2. 38. 2 p. 28, 17 f. Stählin Ἀγαμέμνονα γοῦν τινα Δία ἐν Σπάρτῃ τιμᾶσθαι Στάφυλος ἱστορεῖ, Athenag. *supplicatio pro Christianis* 1 p. 1 Schwartz ὁ δὲ Λακεδαιμόνιος Ἀγαμέμνονα Δία...σέβει.

For his cult at Athens the evidence is slighter: Lyk. *Al.* 1369 ff. πρῶτος μὲν ἥξει Ζηνὶ τῷ Λαπερσίῳ | ὁμώνυμος Ζεύς, ὃς καταιβάτης μολὼν | σκηπτῷ πυρώσει πάντα δυσμενῶν σταθμά with Tzetz. *ad loc.* Λαπέρσαι δῆμος τῆς Ἀττικῆς (U. von Wilamowitz-Moellendorff cj. Λακωνικῆς), ἔνθα Ἀγαμέμνονος Διὸς ἱερόν ἐστιν. ὁ ὁμώνυμος οὖν τῷ Λαπερσίῳ Διὶ ὁ Ἀγαμέμνων, κ.τ.λ. The cj. Λακωνικῆς is supported by Soph. *frag.* 871 Nauck², 957 Jebb, *ap.* Strab. 364 νὴ τὼ Λαπέρσα (*sc.* the Dioskouroi), νὴ τὸν Εὐρώταν τρίτον, | νὴ τοὺς ἐν Ἄργει καὶ κατὰ Σπάρτην θεούς, Rhian. *ap.* Steph. Byz. *s.v.* Λαπέρσα θηλυκῶς, ὄρος Λακωνικῆς, οὗ μέμνηται Ῥιανὸς ἐν Ἠλιακῶν πρώτῳ· ἀπὸ τῶν Λαπερσῶν Διοσκούρων. τὸ ἐθνικὸν Λαπερσαῖος. See further W. Pape—G. E. Benseler *Wörterbuch der griechischen Eigennamen*³ Braunschweig 1875 ii. 773.

With regard to the interpretation of this evidence ancient and modern views have differed widely: Metrodoros of Lampsakos, who allegorized Homer (Tatian. *or. adv. Graec.* 37), took Agamemnon to be the *aithér* (Hesych. Ἀγαμέμνονα· τὸν αἰθέρα Μητρόδωρος ἀλληγορικῶς). Eustath. *in Il.* p. 168, 11 ff. is hardly more satisfactory: δοκεῖ εὐλόγως παρὰ Λάκωσι Ζεὺς Ἀγαμέμνων ἐπιθετικὸς εἶναι, ὡς ὁ Λυκόφρων λαλεῖ· Ἀγαμέμνων τε γὰρ εὐρυκρείων καὶ Ζεὺς εὐρυμέδων. εἰ δὴ ταὐτὸν εὐρυκρείων καὶ εὐρυμέδων, λέγοιτ' ἂν διὰ τοῦτο διθυραμβικώτερον καὶ Ἀγαμέμνων Ζεύς, καθότι καὶ εὐρυκρείων. Welcker *Gr. Götterl.* ii. 183 regards Ἀγαμέμνων as a title of Zeus, 'Erzwalter.' Gruppe *Gr. Myth. Rel.* p. 157 renders 'Zeus...der "grosse Sinner"' and *ib.* n. 22 cites the vase inscriptions ΑΛΑΜΕϟΜΟΝ and ΑΛ·ΜΕϟΜΟ·(P. Kretschmer *Die Griechischen Vaseninschriften* Gütersloh 1894 p. 168 ff.) as implying an original *Ἀγαμέδμων (W. Prellwitz in the *Beiträge zur kunde der indogermanischen sprachen* 1891 xvii. 171 f., 1894 xx. 306 f., *id. Etym. Wörterb. d. Gr. Spr.*² p. 3) with which he compares such names as Ἀγαμήδης, Ἀγαμήστωρ. Wide *Lakon. Kulte* pp. 12 f., 333 f., following F. Deneken in Roscher *Lex. Myth.* i. 2449 f., holds that a god Ἀγαμέμνων (ἀγα-+μεμ-), 'der viel sinnende, viel Sorge tragende, mächtig schirmende und schützende,' whose partner was originally Ἀλεξάνδρα, came to be identified with Zeus. On the etymology see, however, K. Brugmann—A. Thumb *Griechische Grammatik*⁴ München 1913 p. 89: 'Dass uridg. -*nm*- auch zu -*μν*- geworden sei, glauben wir nicht. Man nimmt an, Ἀγα-μέμνων sei aus *-μενμων (zu ai. *mánman-*) entstanden (DE SAUSSURE, Mém. 4, 432). Wäre das richtig, so könnte die besondere Behandlung der Gruppe -*nm*- aus der Mitwirkung der anderen Nasale des Wortes oder aus Volksetymologie (vgl. θρασυ-μέμνων 'mutig standhaltend') erklärt werden. Aber die attische Nebenform Ἀγαμέσμων (KRETSCHMER, Vas. 168 f.) weist auf *Ἀγα-μέδμων als Grundform (vgl. PRELLWITZ, BB. 17, 171 f.

20, 306 f.). Hieraus ging einerseits durch Anlehnung an Πολυ-φράσμων u. a. (§ 88 Anm. 2) die Form Ἀγαμέσμων hervor; Ἀγαμέμνων anderseits zeigt die gleiche Behandlung des δμ wie att. μεσό-μνη neben ion. μεσό-δμη (§ 58), ὕμνος aus *ὕδμος (falls zu ὕδω, ὑδέω, s. W. SCHMID, Rhein. Mus. 61, 480; anders, aber unwahrscheinlich EHRLICH, Rhein. Mus. 62, 321 ff., vgl. ferner P. MAAS, Philol. 66, 590 ff.), kret. μνῴᾱ neben ion. δμώς: in einzelnen griechischen Dialekten wurde also δμ zu νμ (vgl. *ŋm* aus *gm* § 87, 6) und dieses weiter zu μν (vgl. neuir. *meamna*=altir. *menme* 'mens') zu einer Zeit, wo der Wandel von uridg. *-nm-* zu -μμ- schon längst vollzogen war[1]. ([1] Dass *dm-* schon uridg. zu *nm-* geworden sei und hierauf unser μν beruhe (so zuletzt JOHANSSON, IF. 3, 227), ist unwahrscheinlich.) Aus diesem Dialektgebiet stammt die Form Ἀγα-μέμνων. Anders KRETSCHMER a. a. O., FICK, Gött. gel. Anz. 1894 S. 234. 241 (der in μεσό-μνη ursprüngliches -δμν- vermutet) und SCHULZE, Gött. gel. Anz. 1896 S. 236 (der in μεσόμνη, Ἀγαμέμνων "durch eine Art von Metathesis δμ zu βν und weiter zu μν" geworden sein lässt unter Mitwirkung des in den beiden Wörtern vorausgehenden μ); vgl. aber auch STOLZ, Innsbrucker Festschr. zur 50. Philol.-Vers. (1909) 13 ff.' Farnell *Cults of Gk. States* iv. 50 without venturing upon philological ground assumes that 'the two names [Ζεύς and Ἀγαμέμνων] were originally quite distinct and became conjoined owing to some later fusion of cults.' But A. Furtwängler in Roscher *Lex. Myth.* i. 96 'ein chthonischer Zeus' and K. Wernicke in Pauly—Wissowa *Real. Enc.* i. 721 'vielleicht ein chthonischer Gott' had already pointed the way to a better solution of the problem. In the *Class. Rev.* 1903 xvii. 277, cp. *Folk-Lore* 1904 xv. 299, 301, I contended that the hero was a Zeus all along, the local champion or king being as such the embodiment of the god. Even in Homer there are traces of this belief. Agamemnon's stock epithet ἄναξ ἀνδρῶν is suggestive of a divine appellation (cp. Verg. *Aen.* 1. 65 divom pater atque hominum rex, Hes. *theog.* 923 θεῶν βασιλῆι καὶ ἀνδρῶν), and in *Il.* 2 478 he is described as ὄμματα καὶ κεφαλὴν (S. A. Naber cj. φθογγὴν) ἴκελος Διὶ τερπικεραύνῳ. See further *supra* p. 1060 f.

APPENDIX J.

ZEUS *AMPHIÁRAOS*.

The worship of Zeus Ἀμφιάραος at Oropos is attested by Dikaiarch. 1. 6 (*Geogr. Gr. min.* i. 100 Müller) ἐντεῦθεν εἰς Ὠρωπὸν δι' Ἀφιδνῶν καὶ τοῦ Ἀμφιαράου Διὸς ἱεροῦ ὁδὸν ἐλευθέρῳ βαδίζοντι σχεδὸν ἡμέρας προσάντη πάντα. The text is not free from corruption. For the manuscript's διαδαφνιδὸν L. Holstein and others read διὰ Δελφίνιον (cp. Strab. 403), C. Müller in *Frag. hist. Gr.* ii. 256 διὰ Ψαφιδῶν (cp. Strab. 399); *id.* in *Geogr. Gr. min.* i. 100 accepts C. Wordsworth's cj. δι' Ἀφιδνῶν or else δι' Ἀφίδνων. For the manuscript's ὁδὸν...πρόσαντα C. Müller, after I. Casaubon, proposes ὁδὸς...προσάντης πᾶσα, but prints ὁδὸν... προσάντη [πάντα]. Casaubon wanted to expunge Διός. But he was certainly wrong. The hero Amphiaraos had come to be reckoned as a god: cp. Soph. *El.* 836 ff. οἶδα γὰρ ἄνακτ' Ἀμφιάρεων χρυσοδέτοις | ἕρκεσι κρυφθέντα γυναικῶν· καὶ νῦν ὑπὸ γαίας | ... | πάμψυχος ἀνάσσει with Cic. *de div.* 1. 88 Amphiaraum autem sic honoravit fama Graeciae, deus ut haberetur, atque ut ab eius solo, in quo est humatus, oracula peterentur, Paus. 1. 34. 2 θεὸν δὲ Ἀμφιάραον πρώτοις Ὠρωπίοις κατέστη νομίζειν, ὕστερον δὲ καὶ οἱ πάντες Ἕλληνες ἥγηνται. That he was under the protection of Zeus appears from Pind. *Nem.* 9. 58 ff. ὁ δ᾽ Ἀμφιάρῃ σχίσσεν κεραυνῷ παμβίᾳ | Ζεὺς τὰν βαθύστερνον χθόνα, κρύψεν δ᾽ ἄμ᾽ ἵπποις, | δουρὶ Περικλυμένου πρὶν νῶτα τυπέντα μαχατὰν | θυμὸν αἰσχυνθῆμεν, 10. 13 ff. γαῖα δ᾽ ἐν Θήβαις ὑπέδεκτο κεραυνωθεῖσα Διὸς βέλεσιν | μάντιν Οἰκλείδαν, πολέμοιο νέφος, Apollod. 3. 6. 8 Ἀμφιαράῳ δὲ φεύγοντι παρὰ ποταμὸν Ἰσμηνόν, πρὶν ὑπὸ Περικλυμένου τὰ νῶτα τρωθῇ, Ζεὺς κεραυνὸν βαλὼν τὴν γῆν διέστησεν. ὁ δὲ σὺν τῷ ἅρματι καὶ τῷ ἡνιόχῳ Βάτωνι, ὡς δὲ ἔνιοι Ἐλάτωνι (so R. Wagner after Sommer, who suggested Ἐλάτωνι or Ἐλατίῳ. L. Dindorf cj. Ἐλάτῳ. ἐλάτῶ R. ἐλάττωνι *Rᵃ. ἐλάττωνον P. Rᵇ. Rᶜ. ἐλάττω V. L. N. T.), ἐκρύφθη, καὶ Ζεὺς ἀθάνατον αὐτὸν ἐποίησεν.

As a parallel to this famous scene H. Usener in the *Sitzungsber. d. kais. Akad. d. Wiss. in Wien* Phil.-hist. Classe 1897 cxxxvii. 3. 2, 4, 37 (=*id. Kleine Schriften* Leipzig—Berlin 1913 iv. 200 ff., 234) cites the belief that Theodoric the Great, king of the Ostrogoths, did not die in 526 A.D., but entered the earth as a living man seated on his black charger. I am, however, inclined to lay more stress on analogies drawn from the classical area, *e.g.* that of Erechtheus (*supra* p. 793 f.) or those of Latinus and Aeneas (*Class. Rev.* 1904 xviii. 363, *Folk-Lore* 1905 xvi. 286). Such cases may be taken to imply that the early king, who during his life had been credited with magical powers of making a thunderstorm, was after his death frankly identified with the weather-god. Moreover dead kings, being chthonian powers, can give oracles, send dreams, and bestow health on those that consult them in the right way. Hence at the popular Amphiareion near

Fig. 918. Fig. 919.

Oropos (on which see F. Dürrbach *De Oropo et Amphiarai sacro* Paris 1890, E. Bethe in Pauly—Wissowa *Real-Enc.* i. 1893 ff. fig., Frazer *Pausanias* ii. 466 ff. pl. 9, figs., and for recent finds etc. F. Versace in the *Ath. Mitth.* 1908 xxxiii. 247—272, H. Lattermann *ib.* 1910 xxxv. 81—102, B. Leonardos in the Ἐφ. Ἀρχ. 1913 p. 237, *ib.* 1916 pp. 118—121, besides reports in the Πρακτ. ἀρχ. ἑτ. 1903 p. 33 f., 1904 p. 27 f., 1906 p. 83 f., 1913 p. 114) the marble cult-statue of Amphiaraos (Paus. 1. 34. 2) appears to have borne a close resemblance to Asklepios. An autonomous copper of the town, dating from *s.* ii B.C. or later, has for obverse type the head of Amphiaraos bearded and laureate, and for reverse a snake coiled round a staff with the legend Ω ΡΩ ΠΙΩ N (É. de Cadalvène *Recueil de médailles grecques inédites* Paris 1828 p. 168 no. 1 = Overbeck *Gall. her. Bildw.* i. 151 Atlas pl. 6, 10=my fig. 918. Other specimens show *obv.* a beardless head described as Apollon (A. v. Sallet in the *Zeitschr. f. Num.* 1898 xxi. 208 f. pl. 4, 10) or Amphiaraos (Head *Hist. num.*² p. 392—a bad guess, unless the head is really bearded, as stated by Cadalvène *op. cit.* p. 168 no. 2, cp. *Brit. Mus. Cat. Coins* Attica etc. p. 115 pl. 20, 5) or even a female (U. Köhler in the *Ath. Mitth.* 1879 iv. 250 f. fig., 259 ff.), *rev.* a dolphin coiled round a trident with the legend ΩΡΩ ΠΙΩΝ). Another copper of Oropos, struck by Gallienus, has *rev.* ΩΡΩ[Π Ι Ω]N Amphiaraos enthroned to left, his left hand grasping a sceptre and his right extended over a snake (*Brit. Mus. Cat. Coins* Attica etc. p. 115 pl. 20, 6, Imhoof-Blumer and P. Gardner *Num. Comm. Paus.* iii. 153 pl. EE, 18

=my fig. 919). Imhoof-Blumer and P. Gardner justly remark that 'On these coins Amphiaraus is represented exactly in the guise of Asclepius, as a god rather than as a hero.' B. I. Leonardos in the Πρακτ. ἀρχ. ἑτ. 1887 p. 62 f. reports the discovery in the Amphiareion at Oropos of a small statue, *minus* head and extremities, 'παριστὰν δὲ βεβαίως τὸν 'Αμφιάραον ὡς τὸν 'Ασκληπιόν, στηριζόμενον ἐπὶ ῥάβδου περὶ ἣν ἑλίσσεται ὄφις,' and of a small relief representing a similar Amphiaraos and Hygieia seated on a rock beside him (cp. 'Εφ. 'Αρχ. 1885 p. 102 no. 4, 3 = *Corp. inscr. Gr. sept.* i no. 311, 3, 'Εφ. 'Αρχ. 1885 p. 106 no. 6, 3 = *Corp. inscr. Gr. sept.* i no. 372, 3, *ib.* i no. 412, 11), while above them appears the head of Pan another partner in their cult (Paus. 1. 34. 3).

The hero's name offers a variety of problems. 'Αμφιάραος had a clipped form "Αμφις (Herodian. περὶ παθῶν *frag.* 104 (ii. 205, 16 ff. Lentz) *ap. et. mag.* p. 93, 50 ff. = Zonar. *lex. s.v.* 'Αμφίς, cp. *et. mag.* p. 159, 31, cites Aisch. *frag.* 412 Nauck[2]). A possible doublet is "Αμφιος, brother of Adrastos and son of Merops the seer of Perkote who foresaw the doom of his sons at Troy (*Il.* 2. 830 ff., 11. 328 ff.); and he in turn has been regarded (E. Bethe in Pauly—Wissowa *Real-Enc.* i. 1949) as originally identical with "Αμφιος, son of Selagos, who lived at Paisos and was slain at Troy (*Il.* 5. 612 ff., Tzetz. *Hom.* 89 f. *N.B.*: *Il.* 2. 828 'Απαισοῦ = *Il.* 5. 612 Παισῷ). See further H. Usener in E. Bethe *Thebanische Heldenlieder* Leipzig 1891 p. 65, *id. Götternamen* Bonn 1896 p. 355, *id.* in the *Sitzungsber. d. kais. Akad. d. Wiss. in Wien* Phil.-hist. Classe 1897 cxxxvii. 3. 40 ff. (= *id. Kleine Schriften* Leipzig—Berlin 1913 iv. 237 ff.), who holds that "Αμφιος gave rise, on the one hand to 'Αμφίων (cp. *et. mag.* p. 92, 41 ff.), on the other to 'Αμφιάραος, 'Αμφιάρεως, 'Αμφιάρης. It may, however, be doubted whether Usener has said the last word on the subject; for the etymology of the name 'Αμφιάραος is still far from clear. F. G. Welcker *Der epische Cyclus*[2] Bonn 1882 p. 322 takes 'Αμφιάραος to mean 'der Beter' (ἀράομαι). P. Kretschmer *Die Griechischen Vaseninschriften* Gütersloh 1894 pp. 32, 123 argues that 'Αμφιάρηος, for *'Αμφ-ιάρηϝος, was derived from ἱαρεύς (stem ἱαρηϝ-) and meant ἀρχιέρεως, but that 'Αμφιάραος was formed by popular etymologizing from ἀράομαι. A. Fick *Die Griechischen Personennamen*[2] Göttingen 1894 p. 438 f. connects with "Αρης: 'Dasselbe Element ist in ἀμφι-άρηος Zeus.' Similarly J. Rendel Harris *Boanerges* Cambridge 1913 p. 225 suggests that at Argos Areïos (Ap. Rhod. 1. 118, Orph. *Arg.* 148, cp. Pherekyd. *frag.* 75 (*Frag. hist. Gr.* i. 90 Müller) *ap.* schol. *Od.* 11. 289) and Amphiaraos were twin-brothers. But all these views are *risquées*. At most we can assert that there is a tendency (satirised in the person of 'Αμφίθεος by Aristoph. *Ach.* 46 ff.) for divine and heroic names to begin with 'Αμφι-. Such names need not point to the existence of twins (*pace* J. Rendel Harris *op. cit.* p. 224 f.), but might on occasion refer to some twofold aspect of Zeus (*supra* p. 445), who is *e.g.* ἀμφιθαλής, 'god of both parents,' in Aisch. *cho.* 394 f. καὶ πότ᾽ ἂν ἀμφιθαλὴς | Ζεὺς ἐπὶ χεῖρα βάλοι; (see a good note by T. G. Tucker *ad loc.*). Thus H. Usener in the *Rhein. Mus.* 1898 liii. 336 f. (= *id Kleine Schriften* iv. 266 f.) regards 'Αμφιτρύων (τρύω, τρυπᾶν, κ.τ.λ.) as 'der nach Osten und Westen den Donnerkeil entsendende und damit durchbohrende Gewitter-gott,' an ancient *Sondergott* (*supra* p. 13 n. 1) absorbed into the all-prevailing personality of Zeus. I should myself put the matter somewhat differently. To my thinking Amphitryon, like Amphiaraos, was a king who played the part of a human Zeus and was named accordingly.

APPENDIX K.

ZEUS *TREPHÓNIOS* OR *TROPHÓNIOS*.

For the cult of Zeus Τρεφώνιος or Τροφώνιος at Lebadeia Rohde *Psyche*³ i. 125 n. 1 cites the following evidence: Strab. 414 Λεβάδεια δ' ἐστίν, ὅπου Διὸς Τροφωνίου μαντεῖον ἵδρυται, χάσματος ὑπονόμου κατάβασιν ἔχον, καταβαίνει δ' αὐτὸς ὁ χρηστηριαζόμενος, Liv. 45. 27 Lebadiae quoque templum Iovis Trophonii adit (*sc.* L. Aimilius Paullus in 167 B.C.): ibi cum vidisset os specus, per quod oraculo utentes sciscitatum deos descendunt, sacrificio Iovi Hercynnaeque facto, quorum ibi templum est, etc., Iul. Obseq. *prod.* 110 (96 B.C.) Lebadiae Eutychides in templum Iovis Trophonii digressus tabulam aeneam extulit, in qua scripta erant quae ad res Romanas pertinerent, [add Ampel. 8. 3 ibi (*sc.* Ar͟g͟is in Epiro!*—* unless we may assume that a mention of Lebadeia has dropped out of the text, or that *pictum est* is to be supplied from the preceding clause) Iovis templum Trophonii (so D. *hyphonis* C.), unde est ad·inferos descensus ad tollendas sortes: in quo loco dicuntur ii qui descenderunt Iovem ipsum videre], Hesych. *s.v.* Λεβάδεια· πόλις Βοιωτ[ε]ίας, ἔνθα καὶ μαντεῖον Διὸς τὸ ἱερὸν κατεσκεύαστο [? *leg.* μαντεῖον Διός, <Τροφωνίου> τὸ ἱερὸν κατασκευάσαντος], Phot. *lex.* (p. 154 Hermann) *s.v.* Λεβάδια· πόλις Βοιωτίας, ἐν ᾗ Διὸς μαντεῖον, Τροφωνίου κατασκευάσαντος, *Corp. inscr. Gr. sept.* i no. 3090=R. Meister in Collitz—Bechtel *Gr. Dial.-Inschr.* i. 162 f. no. 423 Ἵππων Ἐπινίκαν Νικίαο | Διὶ Τρεφωνίοι on a square base formerly supporting a statue of Epinike (on the back of the same base was recorded the manumission of Athanon (*Corp. inscr. Gr. sept.* i no. 3080 *infra*); on its right side, that of Hermaïa (*ib.* no. 3081 *infra*): later the base was used for a statue of Drusus Caesar (*ib.* no. 3103)), *ib.* no. 3098=L. Stephani *Reise durch einige Gegenden des nördlichen Griechenlandes* Leipzig 1843 p. 70 f. no. 47 pl. 5 Διονύσῳ Εὐσταφύλῳ | κατὰ χρησμὸν Διὸς | Τροφωνιου, *Corp. inscr. Gr. sept.* i no. 3077, 3 ὁ ἱερεὺς τοῦ Διὸς τοῦ Τροφωνίου Τροφωνιανός (the priest being named after his god, as Maybaum *Der Zeuskult in Boeotien* Doberan 1901 p. 11 f. remarks).

Further, at Lebadeia—as I urged in *Folk-Lore* 1904 xv. 301—Zeus bore the significant title Βασιλεύς (*Corp. inscr. Gr. sept.* i no. 3073, 89 f. and 93=Michel *Recueil d'Inscr. gr.* no. 589, 89 f. and 93=Dittenberger *Syll. inscr. Gr.*³ no. 972, 89 f. and 93 εἰς τὸν ναὸν τοῦ Διὸς τοῦ Βασιλέως in an important inscription of *s.* ii B.C. dealing with the half-built temple on Mt St. Elias to the W. of *Livadia* (Paus. 9. 39. 4, *supra* p. 900 n. 0), *Corp. inscr. Gr. sept.* i no. 3080, 1 ff. =R. Meister in Collitz—Bechtel *Gr. Dial.-Inschr.* i. 165 no. 430, 1 ff. [τὸ Fί]διο[ν] δουλι[κὸν | π]αιδάριον Ἀθάνωνα τῦ Δὶ τεῖ Βασιλεῖ κὴ τεῖ Τρεφωνίει ἱαρὸν εἶμεν τὸν πάν[τα | χ]ρόνον ἀπὸ τᾶσδε τᾶς ἀμέρας, *Corp. inscr. Gr. sept.* i no. 3081, 2 f. =R. Meister in Collitz—Bechtel *Gr. Dial.-Inschr.* i. 164 f. no. 429, 2 f. τὰν Fιδίαν δούλαν Ἑρμαῖαν τεῖ Δὶ τεῖ Βασιλεῖ κὴ τῦ Τρε[φ]ωνίυ ἱαρὰν εἰμ[εν] | τὸν πάντα χρόνον, *Corp. inscr. Gr. sept.* i no. 3083, 6 ff.=R. Meister in Collitz—Bechtel *Gr. Dial.-Inschr.* i. 163 no. 425, 6 ff.=Michel *Recueil d'Inscr. gr.* no. 1392, 6 ff. τὸν | Fίδιον θεράποντα Ἀν|δρικὸν τῦ Δὶ τῦ Βασιλεῦ | κὴ τῦ Τρεφωνίυ ἱαρὸν εἴ|μεν παρμείναντα πὰρ | τὰν ματέρα Ἀθανοδώ|ραν Fέτια δέκα, *Corp. inscr. Gr. sept.* i no. 3085, 2 ff. τὸ ἴδιον δουλικὸν παι[δάριον | Σωκράτην, παραμείναντα Κι......] καὶ Ἀριστοκίδι, τὸ[ν πάντα | χρόνον ἱερὸν κατὰ τὴν] ἀνάθ[ε]σιν τῷ Διὶ τῷ Βα[σιλεῖ], *ib.* no. 3091, 1 ff. =R. Meister in Collitz—Bechtel *Gr. Dial.-Inschr.* i. 162 no. 422, 1 ff.=Michel *Recueil d'Inscr. gr.* no. 1115, 1 ff. Νέων Φασκώ[νδαο] | ἀγωνοθετεί[σας] | τὰ Βασίλεια | τὸ ἐληοχρίσ[τιον] | ἀνέθεικε τοῖ [Δὶ] | τοῖ Βασιλε[ῖ] κ[ὴ τῆ] | πόλι in an inscription which can be dated shortly after 250 B.C., cp. Polyb. 20. 5. 5, 8, 14, *Corp. inscr. Gr. sept.* i no. 3096, 1 f. Διὶ Βασιλεῖ | καὶ τῇ πόλει Λεβαδέων | κ.τ.λ., *ib.* no. 4136, 1 ff. = M. Holleaux in the *Bull. Corr. Hell.* 1890 xiv. 19 ff. no. 10, 27 ff. = Dittenberger *Syll. inscr. Gr.*³ no. 635 *B*, 27 ff. Καλλικλίδας Λοκρὸς ἐς ᾿Οπόεντος καταβὰς ἐν Τρεφώ|νιον ἀνάνγειλε Λεπάδειαν τοῖ Δὶ τοῖ Βασιλεῦ ἀνθέμεν | κὴ τοῖ Τρεφωνίοι, κ.τ.λ., 32 f. ὅστις δέ κα τῶ | Διὸς τῶ Βασιλεῖος ἐπιμελειθείει τῶ ναῶ, τὸν στέφανον | ὕσετη in the record of an oracle delivered soon after 178 B.C.).

In view of the foregoing passages and inscriptions I would venture to reconstruct the story of the Lebadean cult as follows. Once upon a time there lived in the locality a king of the old magical sort (*supra* i. 12 ff.), who controlled the weather for his people (*supra* i. 79) and passed as a human Zeus (*supra* i. 247 (?), 545 n. 5, 547 (?), 662, 737 (?), ii. 24, 192, 794, 833, 897 n. 0, 940 n. 0, 944 f. n. 0, Append. H (3) and (4), Append. I, Append. J, *infra* Append. L *sub fin.*, Append. M *med.*)—one of those who in epic days came to be called Διοτρεφέες βασιλῆες (*Il.* 1. 176, 2. 98, 196, 445, 14. 27, *Od.* 3. 480, 4. 44, 63, 7. 49, *h. Dion.* 11, Hes. *theog.* 82, 992: see H. Ebeling *Lexicon Homericum* Lipsiae 1885 i. 311 f.) because it was remembered that they were at least intimately related to the sky-god (either by descent (schol. *Il.* 1. 176 citing Hes. *theog.* 96 ἐκ δὲ Διὸς βασιλῆες, Hesych. *s.v.* Διοτρεφέων), or by special favour (*Il.* 2. 196 f. with Eustath. *in Il.* p. 199, 20 ff. ἐνταῦθα δὲ καὶ ἐφερμηνεύει, διὰ τί Διογενεῖς καὶ Διοτρεφεῖς τοὺς βασιλεῖς λέγει, οὐχ ὅτι ἐκ Διὸς τὸ γένος ἕλκουσιν, ἀλλ᾿ ὅτι ἐξ ἐκείνου αὐτοῖς ἡ τιμή. φησὶ γάρ· "τιμὴ δ᾿ ἐκ Διός ἐστιν," ἡ τῆς βασιλείας δηλαδή. ἀφιδρύματα γὰρ ὡσανεὶ Διὸς ἐδόκουν εἶναι οἱ βασιλεῖς, cp. *ib.* p. 316, 33 f.) : the relation is moralised by Themist. *or.* 6 p. 79 A—B ἡ δὲ εἰς ἀνθρώπους ἀρετή καὶ πραότης καὶ εὐμένεια...μὴ καὶ μᾶλλόν ἐστιν ἐγγυτέρα τῷ κοινωνοῦντι τῆς φύσεως ; αὕτη ποιεῖ θεοείκελον, αὕτη θεοειδῆ, οὕτω Διοτρεφὴς γίνεται βασιλεύς, οὕτω Διογενής, οὕτως αὐτῷ τὴν θειότητα ἐπιφημίζοντες οὐ ψευσόμεθα). Now Διοτρέφης, Διειτρέφης, and similar names have a shortened form Τρέφων (A. Fick *Die Griechischen Personennamen*² Göttingen 1894 p. 269), and Τρέφων by the addition of a common suffix would become Τρεφώνιος. Hence our local king, when dead and buried, was still consulted as Zeus Τρεφώνιος or—since he was responsible for the crops (*supra* i. 79)—as Zeus Τροφώνιος (Max. Tyr. 41. 2 τὸν Δία...τὸν καρπῶν τροφέα, cp. Zeus ᾿Οπωρεύς in *Corp. inscr. Gr. sept.* i no. 2733 = Roehl *Inscr. Gr. ant.* no. 151 = R. Meister in Collitz—Bechtel *Gr. Dial.-Inschr.* i. 213, 396 no. 567 an early inscription from Akraiphia Κρίτων καὶ Θειόσδοτος τοῖ | Δὶ τῶπωρεῦ. Other appellatives of Zeus with the same general significance are collected and discussed by H. Usener *Götternamen* Bonn 1896 p. 243 n. 67, Gruppe *Gr. Myth. Rel.* p. 1109 n. 1). In support of this explanation it should be noted that, when Q. Titius and Salvenius obtained from Trophonios at Lebadeia prophecies concerning Sulla, ἀμφότεροι...ταὐτὰ περὶ τῆς ὀμφῆς ἔφραζον· τῷ γὰρ ᾿Ολυμπίῳ Διὶ καὶ τὸ κάλλος καὶ τὸ μέγεθος παραπλήσιον ἰδεῖν ἔφασαν (L. Cornelius Sulla *rer. gestar. frag.* 16 Peter *ap.* Plout. *v. Sull.* 17). Further, Paus. 9. 39. 10 compares the oracular building to a κρίβανος or 'baking jar,' *i.e.* one of the domical earthen ovens still used in the east for baking bread (J. H. Middleton in the *Journ. Hell. Stud.* 1888 ix. 313 f.). It was in fact the *thólos*-tomb of an old Boeotian king (cp. schol. Loukian. p. 255, 21 ff. Rabe). Those who descended into it to consult the divinised dead took honey-cakes in their hands (Aristoph. *nub.* 506 ff., Paus. 9. 39. 11, Poll. 6. 76, Loukian. *dial. mort.* 3. 2, Max. Tyr. 14. 2, Hesych. *s.v.* μαγίδες) for the reptiles that they might encounter (Philostr. *v. Apoll.* 8. 19 p. 335 Kayser, schol. Aristoph. *nub.* 508 = Souid. *s.v.* Τροφωνίου κατὰ γῆς παίγνια, Eudok. *viol.* 930) because the man who first penetrated its recesses found there two snakes and appeased them with honey-cakes (schol. Aristoph. *nub.* 508). It was even said that the oracle was delivered by a snake (schol. Aristoph. *nub.* 508 = Souid. *s.v.* Τροφωνίου κατὰ γῆς παίγνια) or snakes (Souid. *s.v.* μελιτοῦττα), to which the inhabitants threw honey-cakes. Snakes, it would seem, were as sacred to Trophonios as they were to Asklepios (Paus. 9. 39. 3): indeed, in the cave from which flowed the stream Herkyna there stood images of Trophonios and Herkyna with snakes coiled about their staves so that they resembled Asklepios and Hygieia (Paus. *ib.*). According to the story current in the district, Herkyna (a sort of Demeter, cp. Lyk. *Al.* 152 f. Ἐνναία... | Ἔρκυνν' Ἐρινὺς κ.τ.λ. with Tzetz. *ad loc.* Ἔρκυνν' Ἐρινὺς ἐπώνυμα Δήμητρος. κ.τ.λ., Hesych. Ἑρκύνια (so S. Potter for Ἑρκήνια)· ἑορτὴ Δήμητρος. Nilsson *Gr. Feste* p. 353 says: 'wohl eine Fruchtbarkeit spendende Quellgöttin, der arkadischen Demeter ähnlich'), playing with Kore, had lost a goose, which flew into a cave and hid beneath a stone till Kore came in and found it: the stream springing from the spot, whence Kore had lifted the stone, was called Herkyna. And in the temple of Herkyna near the bank of the stream a maiden was still to be seen with a goose in her hands (Paus. 9. 39. 2 f.). The story reminds us that Zeus, to win Nemesis or Leda, transformed himself into a goose (*supra* i. 279 n. 4, 760 n. 2). It may, I think, be divined that the goose in the hands of the maiden was Zeus himself in animal form. For that Zeus was associated with Herkyna appears from Paullus' sacrifice 'Iovi Hercynnaeue' (*supra* p. 1073). L. Stephani in the *Compte-rendu St. Pét.* 1863 p. 94 finds an illustration of the Lebadean tale on a *rhytón*, shaped like a bull's head, found at Ruvo and now in the Jatta collection, which shows (*a*) Zeus seated with thunderbolt and sceptre, and (*b*) a maiden pursuing a goose (published by T. Avellino in the *Bull. Arch. Nap.* 1856 Nuova Serie iv. 114 f. pl. 11, 2, 1, 3 = Reinach *Rép. Vases* i. 483, 4, 3, 6): but this is perhaps a mere juxtaposition of the sublime with the ridiculous (Maybaum *Der Zeuskult in Boeotien* Doberan 1901 p. 19 detects 'eine Genrescene'). Be that as it may, Trophonios was not only a dead man, but also a living god (Loukian. *dial. mort.* 3. 1 f.), and as such received the rites due to a god (Charax *frag.* 6 (*Frag. hist. Gr.* iii. 637 f. Müller) *ap.* schol. Aristoph. *nub.* 508 καὶ θύουσιν αὐτῷ ὡς θεῷ), being, as we have seen, frequently identified with Zeus (in Cic. *de nat. deor.* 3. 55, Arnob. *adv. nat.* 4. 14, with a chthonian Hermes: cp. Paus. 9. 39. 7). This, however, does not preclude a certain likeness to Amphiaraos; for Trophonios too was swallowed by the earth at a place in Lebadeia, where there was a hole (βόθρος) of Agamedes and a *stéle* beside it (Paus. 9. 37. 7, cp. 9. 39. 6?). The name Καταβάσιον sometimes given to the oracular building (schol. Aristoph. *nub.* 508 = Souid. *s.v.* Τροφωνίου κατὰ γῆς παίγνια) bears a superficial resemblance to that of Zeus Καταιβάτης, but means presumably the sacred spot 'to which men descend' (cp. Dikaiarchos περὶ τῆς εἰς Τροφωνίου καταβάσεως (*Frag. hist. Gr.* ii. 266 ff. Müller), and a work by Plutarch with the same title— no. 181 in the catalogue of Lamprias (W. Christ *Geschichte der griechischen Litteratur*[5] München 1911 ii. 1. 371 n. 4)). J. Vürtheim 'De Eugammonis Cyrenaei Telegonia' in *Mnemosyne* 1901 xxix. 27—30 regards both Agamedes and Trophonios as hypostases of Zeus: 'Sed indigetando ex uno hoc Iove (vel Mercurio) dii tres sunt facti, e quibus unus Clymenus (i.e. Ζεὺς Κλύμενος vel Περικλύμενος) avum repraesentabat, secundus Trophonius antiquo nomine servato vates fiebat, tertius Agamedes (i.e. sagacissimus) indolem prudentem τοῦ χθονίου θεοῦ indicabat; deinde e dis mutati in reges mythicos (ut Amphiaraus ille)' etc....'Vidimus igitur Iovem τροφώνιον χθόνιον e spelunca sua in lucem quasi protractum in duos heroas abiisse, quemadmodum Amphiaraus est natus e Iove Amphiarao et subterraneus Iuppiter plurimis locis *cognominibus variis* invocabatur, qualia sunt Ζεὺς Εὔβουλος vel Εὐβουλεύς, Βουλαῖος, Κλύμενος᾽ etc. But this explanation leaves unexplained the peculiar character of the Καταβάσιον. I much prefer to suppose that it was the *thólos* of an ancient Lebadean king, who in his day played the part of Zeus. The worship of Zeus Βασιλεύς, which— as we have seen—flourished at Lebadeia, implies a similar, though not identical, tradition. We may, in fact, conceive of the local cult as having developed along the following divergent lines:

Διοτρεφὴς βασιλεύς

[Τρέφων ?]   Zeus Βασιλεύς

(Zeus) Τρεφώνιος

(Zeus) Τροφώνιος

Trophonios is said to have been succeeded at Lebadeia by St Christopher the martyr (schol. Loukian. p. 255, 15 ff. Rabe); but see Frazer *Pausanias* v. 198 f. and H. Hitzig—H. Blümner on Paus. 9. 39. 4.

APPENDIX L.

ZEUS *ASKLEPIÓS*.

The cult of Zeus ᾿Ασκληπιός at Epidauros, Hermione, and Pergamon is attested by a considerable body of evidence, inscriptional, literary, and monumental.

(1) Zeus *Asklepiós* in Inscriptions.

M. Fränkel in the *Inscr. Gr. Pelop.* i no. 1000 Epidauros [Γᾶ(?)]ος ᾿Ιο[ύ]λιος ᾿Α[σια]|τικός, ἱεραπολή|σας ἔτους πα᾽, | κελεύσα[ν]τι | Διὶ ᾿Ασκληπιῷ | Σωτῆρι. |

with the numeral ιθ᾽ and the symbol 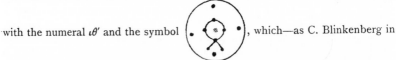, which—as C. Blinkenberg in

the *Nordisk Tidsskrift for Filologi* Tredie Række 1894—1895 iii. 175 ff. and in the *Ath. Mitth.* 1899 xxiv. 384, 391 showed—represents the wreath of Asklepios. P. Kabbadias in the ᾿Εφ. ᾿Αρχ. 1884 p. 24 no. 65 = *id. Fouilles d'Épidaure* Athènes 1893 i. 58 no. 136 inserted a comma between Διὶ and ᾿Ασκληπιῷ, but E. Thraemer in Pauly—Wissowa *Real-Enc.* ii. 1661 and M. Fränkel *loc. cit.* rightly reject it. M. Fränkel in the *Inscr. Gr. Pelop.* i no. 1022 Epidauros − − − − − − ν − − − −|− − − − ος Διογνήτου ἱερεὺς | ᾿Ασκληπιῷ Διὶ κατὰ ὄναρ. | with the numeral ϛϛ᾽. *Id. ib.* i no. 1086 Epidauros Παταῖος − − − | πυρο[φορή]σας | ᾿Ασ-

κληπιῶι | Διὶ Τελείωι. | with the numeral ϙζ᾽ and the symbol , which

C. Blinkenberg in the *Nordisk Tidsskrift for Filologi* Tredie Række 1894—1895 iii. 175 f. took to be 'le rameau...comme un signe de la soumission et du respect le plus profond' and in the *Ath. Mitth.* 1899 xxiv. 385, 392 described as 'Zweig (oder Baum?),' 'wahrscheinlich...ein Palmenzweig,' while M. Fränkel in the *Inscr. Gr. Pelop.* i. 188 calls it 'Ramus olivae s. quercus.' C. Blinkenberg in the *Ath. Mitth.* 1899 xxiv. 385 n. 2 read the name of the dedicator as Π̊ΑΙΛΙΟ⊂ *i.e.* Πόπλιος Αἴλιος and put a comma between Ἀσκληπιῶι and Διί. M. Fränkel in his note on the *Inscr. Gr. Pelop.* i no. 1086 thinks Blinkenberg's reading possible, but demurs to his punctuation. The inventory-symbols, which appear to have been added to the inscriptions *c.* 306 A.D. (*Inscr. Gr. Pelop.* i. 186), suffice to prove that at Epidauros Asklepios was then known as Zeus Ἀσκληπιὸς Σωτήρ and Zeus as Asklepios Ζεὺς Τέλειος. A. Boeckh in the *Corp. inscr. Gr.* i no. 1198 = M. Fränkel in the *Inscr. Gr. Pelop.* i no. 692 = W. Prellwitz in Collitz— Bechtel *Gr. Dial.-Inschr.* iii. 1. 185 no. 3396 Hermione Ξενότιμος Πολυκλέος | Δάματρι Χθονίαι, Διὶ Ἀ(σκ)λαπιῶι, where K. O. Müller *Die Dorier*[2] Breslau 1844 i. 403 n. 3 corrected M. Fourmont's reading ΔΙΙΑΡΓΙΛΑΠΙΩΙ to ΔΙΙΑΣΚΛΑ-ΠΙΩΙ. P. Kabbadias *Fouilles d'Épidaure* i. 58 and W. Prellwitz *loc. cit.* assume a series of three deities; but A. Boeckh *loc. cit.* and M. Fränkel *loc. cit.* treat Διὶ Ἀσκλαπιῶι as one god.

(2) Zeus *Asklepiós* in Literature.

Their view is supported by E. Thraemer *loc. cit.*, who adds : 'Besonders häufig findet sich Zeus A. bei Aristeides, nicht etwa ein blos rhetorischer Ausdruck für die Hoheit des Gottes, sondern Anlehnung an einen ganz bestimmten Kult der Stadt Pergamos. Dieser hat mit dem schon in hellenistischer Zeit blühenden vorstädtischen Asklepieion freilich nichts zu thun, ist vielmehr eine Neuschöpfung des 2. Jhdts. v. Chr., seine Stätte die grösste Ruine der Unterstadt, die früher Basilika genannte, jetzt in Berlin für Thermen gehaltene Anlage über dem Selinos. Dass wir es hier mit dem Tempel und ἄλσος des Zeus A. zu thun haben, werde ich demnächst an anderem Orte nachweisen.' See further K. Pilling *Pergamenische Kulte* Naumburg a. S. 1903 p. 23 ff. (cited by Gruppe *Myth. Lit.* 1908 p. 271) and Gruppe *Gr. Myth. Rel.* pp. 295, 1094 n. 19, 1456 n. 4. Cp. Aristeid. *or.* 6. 37 (i. 64 f. Dindorf) καὶ Διὸς Ἀσκληπιοῦ νεὼν οὐκ ἄλλως οἱ τῇδε ἱδρύσαντο. ἀλλ' εἴπερ ἐμοὶ σαφὴς ὁ διδάσκαλος, εἰκὸς δὲ παντὸς μᾶλλον, ἐν ᾧ δὲ ταῦτ' ἐδίδαξε τρόπῳ καὶ τοῖς ἱεροῖς λόγοις εἴρηται, οὗτός ἐσθ' ὁ τὸ πᾶν ἄγων καὶ νέμων σωτὴρ τῶν ὅλων καὶ φύλαξ τῶν ἀθανάτων, εἰ δὲ θέλεις τραγικώτερον εἰπεῖν, ἔφορος οἰάκων, σώζων τά τε ὄντα ἀεὶ καὶ τὰ γιγνόμενα. εἰ δ' Ἀπόλλωνος παῖδα καὶ τρίτον ἀπὸ Διὸς νομίζομεν αὐτόν, αὖθις αὖ καὶ συνάπτομεν τοῖς ὀνόμασιν, ἐπεί τοι καὶ αὐτὸν τὸν Δία γενέσθαι λέγουσί ποτε, πάλιν δὲ αὐτὸν ἀποφαίνουσιν ὄντα τῶν ὄντων πατέρα καὶ ποιητήν, *or.* 23. 283 (i. 456 Dindorf) ὁ δὲ στέφανος ἦν ἐκ τοῦ ἱεροῦ τοῦ Διὸς Ἀσκληπιοῦ (for the wreath of Asklepios C. Blinkenberg in the *Nordisk Tidsskrift for Filologi* Tredie Række 1894—1895 iii. 176 f. and in the *Ath. Mitth.* 1899 xxiv. 391 cites, not only the Epidaurian symbol, but also a red-figured *kratér* from Boiotia, now at Athens (Collignon—Couve *Cat. Vases d'Athènes* p. 626 f. no. 1926), published by O. Kern in the Ἐφ. Ἀρχ. 1890 p. 131 ff. pl. 7 = Reinach *Rép. Vases* i. 515, 1 f., which shows (*a*) Asklepios on a couch feeding a huge snake from a Boeotian cup in his right hand and holding an egg in his left hand, the wall hung with four garlands, (*b*) Hygieia seated, grasping a sceptre with her left hand and extending her right towards a girl, who carries a basket of fruits and cakes and an *oinochóe*, the wall hung with three garlands and votive limbs, and a Messenian copper of Roman date (*Brit. Mus. Cat. Coins* Peloponnesus p. 112 pl. 22, 16, Imhoof-Blumer and P. Gardner *Num. Comm. Paus.* ii. 66 pl. P, 1 f.), on which

Asklepios appears with a large wreath by his side), *or.* 23. 290 (i. 464 Dindorf) καὶ ἅμα λαμβάνω τινὰ ἐπιστολὴν πρὸ ποδῶν κειμένην τοῦ Διὸς Ἀσκληπιοῦ, *or.* 26. 332 (i. 516 Dindorf) μετὰ δὲ ταῦτα βουλομένοις ἡμῖν κοινῇ περὶ τοῦ ἀναθήματος συνεδόκει καὶ τῷ ἱερεῖ καὶ τοῖς νεωκόροις ἀναθεῖναι ἐν Διὸς Ἀσκληπιοῦ, ταύτης γὰρ οὐκ εἶναι χώραν καλλίω· καὶ οὕτω δὴ τοῦ ὀνείρατος ἡ φήμη ἐξέβη. καὶ ἔστιν ὁ τρίπους ὑπὸ τῇ δεξιᾷ τοῦ θεοῦ, εἰκόνας χρυσᾶς ἔχων τρεῖς, μίαν καθ' ἕκαστον τὸν πόδα, Ἀσκληπιοῦ, τὴν δὲ Ὑγιείας, τὴν δὲ Τελεσφόρου. κ.τ.λ.

(3) Zeus Asklepiós in Art.

In art the type of Asklepios was not uninfluenced by that of Zeus. Furtwängler *Masterpieces of Gk. Sculpt.* p. 186 ff. regards a whole series of standing Asklepios-statues as copies of a Myronian original representing Zeus (Strab. 637 notes a Zeus by Myron formerly grouped with an Athena and a Herakles by the same sculptor at Samos, but later erected by Augustus in an *aedicula* on the Capitol at Rome): 'The restful conception that marks the older type of Zeus exactly suited the mild character of Asklepios.' Overbeck *Gr. Plastik*[4] i. 379 holds that 'das Ideal des Asklepios wesentlich als eine geistreiche Umbildung des von Phidias ausgeprägten Zeusideales erscheint, eine Umbildung, die unter Beibehaltung der meisten charakteristischen Formen doch vermöge ihrer Herabsetzung auf ein reiner Menschliches die Hoheit des Weltregierers durch die herzliche Milde und Klugheit des hilfreichen Heilgottes zu ersetzen weiss': accordingly he traces the canonical bearded type of Asklepios to the cult-statue of the god by Pheidias' pupil Alkamenes at Mantineia (Paus. 8. 9. 1). E. Reisch in the *Eranos Vindobonensis* Wien 1893 p. 21 f. assumes that this statue showed the god standing as on imperial coppers of Mantineia (*Brit. Mus. Cat. Coins* Peloponnesus p. 187 pl. 35, 9, Imhoot-Blumer and P. Gardner *Num. Comm. Paus.* ii. 93 pl. S, 15, Rasche *Lex. Num.* v. 183 f.), and that the same figure appearing with inverted sides on Athenian silver ((i) ΜΕΝΕΔ ΕΠΙΓΕΝΟ *Brit. Mus. Cat. Coins* Attica etc. pp. xliv, 63 pl. 11, 6, Imhoof-Blumer and P. Gardner *Num. Comm. Paus.* iii. 150 pl. ΕΕ, 2, E. Beulé *Les monnaies d'Athènes* Paris 1858 p. 331 ff., Head *Hist. num.*[2] p. 383 accepting J. Sundwall's date, 177 B.C.; (ii) ΔΙΟΚΛΗΣ ΛΕΩΝΙΔΗΣ E. Beulé *op. cit.* p. 401, Head *op. cit.*[2] p. 386 dating *c.* 86 B.C. to time of Augustus) and copper coins (*Brit. Mus. Cat. Coins* Attica etc. p. 109 pl. 19, 4, Imhoof-Blumer and P. Gardner *Num. Comm. Paus.* iii. 150 pl. ΕΕ, 3 f., E. Beulé *Les monnaies d'Athènes* Paris 1858 p. 331) attests the existence in the Asklepieion at Athens of a similar statue by Alkamenes or one of his pupils. But, after all, the coins adduced by Reisch exhibit common poses of Asklepios (the coppers of Mantineia show *schema* iii of E. Thraemer's classification in Roscher *Lex. Myth.* i. 636; the silver and copper coins of Athens, *schema* i *ib.* i. 634 f.), and it is far from certain that they were intended to portray cult-statues, let alone works by Alkamenes. We are on firmer ground in observing that Kolotes, who helped Pheidias with his Zeus at Olympia (Plin. *nat. hist.* 34. 87, 35. 54), made a wonderful ivory statue of Asklepios for Kyllene (Strab. 337). If this, like Zeus at Olympia, was a seated figure, Kolotes paved the way for Thrasymedes of Paros, whose chryselephantine Asklepios at Epidauros (bibliography in Svoronos *Ath. Nationalmus.* p. 148 n. 1) was half the size of the Zeus Ὀλύμπιος at Athens (Paus. 2. 27. 2) and was, by a natural blunder, attributed to Pheidias himself (Athenag. *supplicatio pro Christianis* 17 p. 19, 15 f. Schwartz). Thrasymedes' cult-statue was decidedly Zeus-like in appearance—witness the silver (*Brit. Mus. Cat. Coins* Peloponnesus p. 156 pl. 29, 14, Imhoof-Blumer and P. Gardner

Num. Comm. Paus. i. 43 pl. L, 3, W. Wroth in the *Num. Chron.* Third Series 1892 xii. 14 f. pl. 1, 17, J. N. Svoronos in the *Journ. Intern. d'Arch. Num.* 1901 iv. 11 fig. 6 enlarged=*id. Ath. Nationalmus.* p. 150 fig. 104, Head *Hist. num.*[2] p. 441) and copper coins of Epidauros (*Brit. Mus. Cat. Coins* Peloponnesus p. 159 pl. 29, 22 f., cp. *ib.* p. 158 pl. 29, 19, Imhoof-Blumer and P. Gardner *Num. Comm. Paus.* i. 43 pl. L, 4 f., J. N. Svoronos in the *Journ. Intern. d'Arch. Num.* 1901 iv. 10 f. figs. 3—5 enlarged=*id. Ath. Nationalmus.* p. 150 f. figs. 105—107, Head *Hist. num.*[2] p. 442), and an imperial copper of Kleonai (Imhoof-Blumer *Monn. gr.* p. 133, *id.* and P. Gardner *Num. Comm. Paus.* i. 32, Head *Hist. num.*[2] p. 441). The god is seated to the left with his left foot advanced, holding a long sceptre high up in his left hand and extending his right hand over the head of a coiled snake. Beneath his seat (silver coins) or behind it (coppers) lies a dog (see H. Gaidoz 'À propos des chiens d'Épidaure' in the *Rev. Arch.* 1884 ii. 218—222, O. Keller *Die antike Tierwelt* Leipzig 1909 i. 141, F. Orth in Pauly—Wissowa *Real-Enc.* viii. 2576 f.). The seat itself is sometimes a high-backed throne (silver and copper coins), sometimes a mere stool (silver coins). Other Zeus-like types of Asklepios seated occur on coppers of Argos—perhaps after the group by Xenophilos and Straton (Paus. 2. 23. 4), which followed the main lines of Thrasymedes' work (Imhoof-Blumer and P. Gardner *Num. Comm. Paus.* i. 40 f. pl. K, 47, *Brit. Mus. Cat. Coins* Peloponnesus p. 151 no. 166),

| Fig. 920. | Fig. 921. | Fig. 922. | Fig. 923. |

Rhegion (*Brit. Mus. Cat. Coins* Italy p. 381 f., Garrucci *Mon. It. ant.* p. 165 pl. 115, 12 f., Head *Hist. num.*[2] p. 111. The shape of the seat varies from throne to high-backed chair), the Magnetes in Thessaly—an adaptation of Thrasymedes' statue (Imhoof-Blumer *Choix de monn. gr.*[1] pl. 1, 26, *id. Monn. gr.* p. 133 no. 2[a], Head *Hist. num.*[2] p. 300), Trikke (T. Panofka 'Asklepios und die Asklepiaden' in the *Abh. d. berl. Akad. 1845* Phil.-hist. Classe p. 353 pl. 1, 13, *Brit. Mus. Cat. Coins* Thessaly etc. p. 52 pl. 11, 13, Head *Hist. num.*[2] p. 311 'Asklepios seated, feeding serpent with bird, or resting on crooked staff'! Fig. 922, from a well-preserved specimen of mine, shows the god to have a sceptre and the bird to be a goose (cp. Loukian. *Alex.* 13 f. cited *infra*)), Ainos (*Ant. Münz. Nord-Griechenlands* ii. 1. 1. 199 pl. 5, 28), Anchialos (*ib.* ii. 1. 1. 272 pl. 8, 2), Bizye (Rasche *Lex. Num.* i. 154, 1548, Suppl. i. 295), Serdike (*ib.* viii. 673, Suppl. i. 295), Mytilene (*Brit. Mus. Cat. Coins* Troas, etc. p. 201 pl. 40, 3=*supra* p. 260 fig. 172, p. 206 pl. 41, 4), Pergamon—perhaps after the statue of Phyromachos (Polyb. 32. 27. 4, Diod. 31 *frag.* 46 Bekker (ii. 2. 128 Dindorf), Souid. *s.v.* Προυσίας *bis*: diverse possibilities are mooted by P. Smith *Dict. Biogr. Myth.* iii. 608, W. Wroth in the *Num. Chron.* Third Series 1882 ii. 14 ff., W. Amelung 'Der Asklepios des Phyromachos zu Pergamon' in the *Röm. Mitth.* 1903 xviii. 1 ff., H. von Fritze in *Nomisma* 1908 ii. 19 f. Rasche *Lex. Num.* i. 154, Mionnet *Descr. de méd. ant.* ii. 604 no. 595, Suppl. v. 443 no. 1018, T. Panofka 'Asklepios und die Asklepiaden' in the *Abh. d. berl. Akad. 1845* Phil.-hist. Classe p. 352 f.

pl. 1, 8, p. 353 pl. 1, 17, W. M. Leake *Numismata Hellenica* London 1856 Asiatic Greece p. 98, *Brit. Mus. Cat. Cöins* Mysia p. 121 pl. 25, 9, cp. *ib.* p. 156 pl. 32, 1, Head *Hist. num.*[2] p. 534), Herakleia Salbake (*Brit. Mus. Cat. Coins* Caria, etc. pp. 116, 120 pl. 20, 9), Neapolis in Samaria (*Brit. Mus. Cat. Coins* Palestine p. 65 f. pl. 7, 3): cp. coins of Antoninus Pius (Rasche *Lex. Num.* i. 154, Suppl. i. 295 f., Cohen *Monn. emp. rom.*[2] ii. 381 no. 1138). The same Zeus-like figure appears on gems (Furtwängler *Geschnitt. Steine Berlin* p. 111 no. 2356, *supra*

Fig. 924.

i. 357 n. 4, a small convex 'plasma,' which I reproduce in fig. 923 from T. Panofka 'Asklepios und die Asklepiaden' in the *Abh. d. berl. Akad. 1845* Phil.-hist. Classe p. 289 pl. 1, 10. Asklepios (? Zeus Ἀσκληπιός) is enthroned to the left with serpent-sceptre: on the back of the throne, behind his head, stands a Nike; beneath his left foot lies a ram's-head; in his right hand is a pine-cone, possibly resting on a *phiále* (?); before his feet is a second pine-cone (cp. Asklepios at Sikyon as described by Paus. 2. 10. 3 ἐσελθοῦσι δὲ ὁ θεός ἐστιν οὐκ ἔχων γένεια, χρυσοῦ καὶ ἐλέφαντος, Καλάμιδος δὲ ἔργον· ἔχει δὲ καὶ σκῆπτρον καὶ ἐπὶ τῆς ἑτέρας χειρὸς πίτυος καρπὸν τῆς ἡμέρου with Sir J. G. Frazer's note *ad loc.*). Furtwängler *op. cit.* p. 124 no. 2677 pl. 24 a cornelian = Asklepios (?) seated on a stool gazing at a beardless head held in his right hand, a serpent-staff before him, *ib.* p. 248 no. 6753 pl. 48 a cornelian = Asklepios (?) with portrait features, seated on a stool, plucking fruit and placing it in a basket on an altar (?), a serpent-staff before him). Indeed, Asklepios was commonly conceived as a kindly, human Zeus,

Fig. 925.

conversant with the ways of men and able to cure their ailments. The difference between Zeus and Asklepios may be readily grasped, if we set side by side two reliefs of Pentelic marble found in the precinct at Epidauros (Staïs *Marbres et Bronzes: Athènes*[2] p. 42 f. no. 173 f., P. Kabbadias in the 'Εφ. 'Αρχ. 1885 p. 48 ff. pl. 2, 6 and 1894 p. 11 ff. pl. 1, *id. Fouilles d'Épidaure* Athènes 1893 i. 22 pl. 9, 21, A. Defrasse—H. Lechat *Épidaure* Paris 1895 p. 83 ff. with figs., Brunn—Bruckmann *Denkm. der gr. und röm. Sculpt.* pl. 3, Collignon *Hist. de la Sculpt.*

gr. ii. 186 f. fig. 88). Svoronos *Ath. Nationalmus.* pp. 148—154 no. 173 f. pl. 31 (cp. my figs. 924, 925) has made out a strong case for supposing that they were metopes from the temple of Asklepios, carved in *s.* iv B.C. On his showing the one (fig. 924) represents Zeus seated on a throne, the arms of which are supported by winged sphinxes and end in rams'-heads. His right hand held a sceptre; his left was extended. An ample *himátion*, draped over the back of the throne and round the legs of the god, left bare his broad chest. His head wore a metal wreath (holes for attachment remain), and his feet were shod with sandals of strap-work. Altogether he was an august and imposing figure. The other relief (fig. 925) shows Asklepios, very similar in attitude and costume, but curiously diverse in effect. A comfortable man with soft, podgy body, he sits on a cushioned chair with easy back, crosses his feet, and talks with a gesture of his right hand. He might be a Harley Street consultant prescribing for a patient. The same humanity and affability are characteristic of Asklepios, even when an attempt is made to emphasise his Zeus-hood by means of external attributes. For instance, an alliance-copper of Pergamon and Ephesos, struck by Commodus, has Asklepios standing, in his right hand the serpent-staff, in his left a Nike, who offers a wreath to Artemis (Rasche *Lex. Num.* vi. 888,

Fig. 926.

Suppl. i. 295: but cp. *Brit. Mus. Cat. Coins* Mysia p. 164 pl. 33, 4), while coppers of Caracalla show Asklepios with little Telesphoros to the left and the cosmic globe to the right (Rasche *Lex. Num.* i. 158, Stevenson—Smith—Madden *Dict. Rom. Coins* p. 775 f., Cohen *Monn. emp. rom.*[2] iv. 178 no. 329 f. P·M·TR·P·XVIII·IMP·III·COS· IIII·P·P·S·C· first brass, cp. *ib.* iv. 179 no. 331 do. do. without Telesphoros. Fig. 926 is from a second brass in my collection. For other examples of Asklepios with the globe see Rasche *Lex. Num.* Suppl. i. 298 f.: E. Loewe *De Aesculapi figura* Strassburg 1887 p. 75 n. 7).

(4) *Asklepiós* and the Snake.

Next we must note the constant association of this human Zeus with a snake. Asklepios himself on occasion took that form. He travelled from Epidauros to Sikyon as a snake drawn by mules; and from the roof of his temple in the latter town hung a small figure of Aristodama, the mother of his son Aratos, riding on a snake (Paus. 2. 10. 3): the creature so ridden was presumably none other than the god, who was believed to have consorted with Aristodama in snake-form (Paus. 4. 14. 7 f., cp. Gruppe *Gr. Myth. Rel.* p. 866 n. 1). Again, it was as a snake that Asklepios came from Epidauros to Epidauros Limera on the east coast of Lakonike: he slipped out of the ship and dived into the earth not far from the sea at a place where altars, planted about with olive trees, were erected to him (Paus. 3. 23. 7: see F. W. Hasluck in the *Ann. Brit. Sch. Ath.* 1907—1908 xiv. 179). At Lebena in Crete there was a famous temple of Asklepios (Paus. 2. 26. 9, Philostr. *v. Apoll.* 4. 34 p. 152 f. Kayser), where incubation was practised (Kaibel *Epigr. Gr.* no. 839, 1 f.=Cougny *Anth. Pal. Append.* i. 303. 1 f.): the divine snake sent by Asklepios to guide his priest the son of Aristonymos to the temple-spring and forty-seven years later sent on a similar errand to show Soarchos, priest in his father's room, how to replenish the failing spring (see the interesting inscription from Lebena (*Leda*) published by T. Baunack in *Philologus* 1890 xlix. 578 ff. and R. Meister *ib.* 1891 l. 570 ff.) should probably be viewed 'als Inkarnation des Gottes selbst' (Gruppe *Gr. Myth. Rel.*

p. 1448 n. 7). Whether the snake followed by Antinoe, daughter of Kepheus and granddaughter of Aleos, when she refounded Mantineia on its historical site (Paus. 8. 8. 4 f.), was Asklepios (as Miss Harrison apparently assumes in *Themis* p. 381 n. 5) is very doubtful. In 293—291 B.C. Asklepios was fetched from Epidauros to Rome and duly domiciled on the island in the Tiber; he arrived in the guise of a golden snake (Liv. 10. 47. 7, *per.* 11 Aesculapi signum... anguem...in quo ipsum numen esse constabat, Ov. *met.* 15. 622 ff. especially 669 f. cristis aureus altis | in serpente deus etc., 737 erigitur serpens, etc., cp. *fast.* 1. 291 f., Val. Max. 1. 8. 2 anguis, Plout. *quaestt. Rom.* 94 τοῦ δράκοντος, Plin. *nat. hist.* 29. 72 anguis, Aur. Vict. *de vir. ill.* 22. 1—3 anguis, Sidon. *epist.* 1. 7. 12 serpentis Epidaurii : see further O. Richter *Topographie der Stadt Rom*[2] München 1901 p. 282 f., H. Jordan—C. Hülsen *Topographie der Stadt Rom im Alterthum* Berlin 1907 i. 3. 633—635)—a belief commemorated on coppers of the *gens Rubria* (Babelon *Monn. rép. rom.* ii. 406 ff. nos. 5 f. and 9 figs., *Brit. Mus. Cat. Rom. Coins* Rep. i. 312 pl. 38, 5, i. 313 n. 1 fig. under date *c.* 86 B.C.) and on bronze medallions of Antoninus Pius (Gnecchi *Medagl. Rom.* ii. 9 pl. 43, 1 = my fig. 927 and

ii. 9 pl. 43, 2, *Brit. Mus. Cat. Medallions* p. 7 no. 4 pl. 8, 3, cp. p. 7 no. 5, Fröhner *Méd. emp. rom.* p. 51 ff. figs., Baumeister *Denkm.* i. 140 fig. 150, Stevenson—Smith—Madden *Dict. Rom. Coins* p. 20 fig. Father Tiber, reclining amid his waters, rests his left elbow on an urn, holds a reed in his left hand, and extends his right to greet the snake on its arrival. The galley, whose steersman and rowers(?) are visible, passes under the Pons Fabricius towards the island, where buildings and a tree mark the new home of the god). Lastly, Lucian in his *Alexandros or the*

Fig. 927.

Sham Seer tells how an impostor from Abonou Teichos, a coast-town in Paphlagonia, purchased a large tame snake at Pella in Makedonia (Loukian. *Alex.* 7), and with the aid of a confederate spread the news that Asklepios and his father Apollon were about to visit the Abonotichians (*ib.* 10). The rascals had made a snake's head of linen, painted it with a human expression, given it a mouth that could open and shut by means of horse-hairs, and added a black forked tongue that worked in the same way (*ib.* 12). Thus equipped Alexandros went to Abonou Teichos, where the worthy inhabitants were already digging the foundations of a new temple to greet the advent of the gods, buried a goose's egg containing a young reptile in the mud after dark (*ib.* 13) and duly discovered 'the new-born Asklepios' next morning to the astonishment of the bystanders (*ib.* 14). Alexandros now became the exhibitor of the god. He took into his bosom 'the Asklepios from Pella,' twined its body round his neck and let its tail hang down, but kept its head hidden under his armpit and showed the linen mask instead (*ib.* 15). The people were astounded at the miraculously rapid growth of the snake (*ib.* 16). Bithynians, Galatians, Thracians came flocking in; pictures, portraits, and images, some of bronze, some of silver, were made; and the god was named Glykon in obedience to an oracle of his own (*ib.* 18 εἰμὶ Γλύκων, τρίτον αἷμα Διός, φάος ἀνθρώποισι). From this time onwards Alexandros drove a roaring trade in oracles (*ib.* 19 ff.). A tube consisting of the windpipes of cranes introduced into the artificial head enabled an assistant outside to make 'the linen Asklepios' answer questions and deliver 'autophone oracles' (*ib.* 26). The fame of Glykon spread to Italy and made a sensation at Rome (*ib.* 30 ff.). Mysteries were instituted with hierophants, *daidoûchoi*, and a full ceremonial lasting three days (*ib.* 38 ff.). Alexandros even petitioned the emperor that new coins might be struck with an obverse design of Glykon and a reverse of himself bearing the *stémmata* of Asklepios and the *hárpe* of Perseús (*ib.* 58). The whole narrative is sufficiently amazing. But perhaps more amazing still is the fact that much collateral evidence can be quoted in its support. Copper coins of Abonou Teichos from the reigns of Antoninus Pius, Lucius Verus, Geta, Severus Alexander, Gordianus Pius, and Trebonianus Gallus represent the new-fangled god as a snake with a more or less human face (*Brit. Mus. Cat. Coins* Pontus, etc. p. 83 pl. 19, 1=my fig. 928, Waddington—Babelon—Reinach *Monn. gr. d'As. Min.* i. 129 ff. pl. 17, 12, 13, 16 (=my fig. 929), 19 with legend ΓΛΥΚΩΝ, cp. pl. 17, 20, 21, 22, Head *Hist. num.*[2] p. 505). Coppers of Nikomedeia in Bithynia struck by Caracalla and Maximus give the snake a definitely human head (M. Dumersan *Description des médailles antiques du cabinet de feu M. Allier de Hauteroche* Paris 1829 p. 70 pl. 11, 10, *Brit. Mus. Cat. Coins* Pontus, etc. p. 187 no. 48, Waddington—Babelon—Reinach *Monn. gr. d'As. Min.* i. 513, 545 pl. 94, 12=my fig. 930, pl. 94, 13 f.,

Fig. 928.   Fig. 929.   Fig. 930.

562 pl. 97, 14). Amulets appear to confuse him with the Khnemu-snake (*supra* i. 357 n. 4, W. Drexler in Roscher *Lex. Myth.* ii. 1258 ff., cp. for Egyptian snake-worship in general T. Hopfner *Der Tierkult der alten Ägypter nach den griechisch-römischen Berichten und den wichtigeren Denkmälern* (*Denkschr. d. Akad. Wien* 1913 ii Abh.) Wien 1913 p. 136 ff.). Thus an agate in the Behr collection showed Khnemu as a lion-headed snake, with a radiate crown, accompanied by several inscriptions—XNOVBIC in the field, ΓΛΥΚѠΝΑ in front, ΙΑѠ beneath, and a magical *formula* on the other side of the stone (F. Lenormant *Description des médailles et antiquités composantes le cabinet de M. le baron Behr* Paris 1857 p. 228 no. 76, *id.* in the *Gaz. Arch.* 1878 iv. 183, E. Babelon in the *Rev. Num.* iv Série 1900 iv. 28 fig. 6). Again, a red jasper in the Sorlin-Dorigny collection at Constantinople has Asklepios standing with a raven(?) behind his shoulder and a human-headed or lion-headed snake before him (F. Lenormant 'Un monument du culte de Glycon' in the *Gaz. Arch.* 1878 iv. 179 ff. with fig., E. Babelon in the *Rev. Num.* iv Série 1900 iv. 27 f. fig. 5). Two inscriptions from Apulum (*Carlsburg*) prove that the cult of Glykon reached Dacia (*Corp. inscr. Lat.* iii no. 1021=Dessau *Inscr. Lat. sel.* no. 4079 Glyconi | M. Ant. | Onesas | iusso dei | l. p., *Corp. inscr. Lat.* iii no. 1022 Gl(y)co | M. Aur. | Theodo|tus ius|so dei p.). A third inscription found at *Blatsche* between Skoupoi (*Uskub*) and Stoboi associates the beast with the false prophet (*Corp. inscr. Lat.* iii Suppl. no. 8238=Dessau *Inscr. Lat. sel.* no 4080 Iovi et Iuno|n. [et] Dracco|n. et Dracce|nae et Ale|xandro Epi|tynchanus [C. | F]uri Octavi[ani] | c. v.

posuit). See further F. Cumont 'Alexandre d'Abonotichos' in the *Mémoires de l'Académie Royale des Sciences de Belgique* 1887 xl. 13 ff., 37 ff. and in Pauly—Wissowa *Real-Enc.* v. 1634 f., vii. 1468 f., E. Babelon 'Le faux prophète Alexandre d'Abonotichos' in the *Rev. Num.* iv Série 1900 iv. 1—30 with 6 figs., W. Drexler in Roscher *Lex. Myth.* i. 1692 f., Gruppe *Gr. Myth. Rel.* p. 1487, O. Weinreich 'Alexandros der Lügenprophet und seine Stellung in der Religiosität des II. Jahrhunderts n. Chr.' in the *Neue Jahrb. f. klass. Altertum* 1921 xlvii. 129—151. The main point to bear in mind—a point commonly missed—is that the populace regarded Asklepios as essentially serpentiform.

(5) The Name *Asklepiós*.

This leads us to consider the question whether Ἀσκληπιός originally meant 'Snake' and nothing more. The name occurs in a puzzling variety of forms:

Ἀγλαόπης (Hesych. Ἀγλαόπης· ὁ Ἀσκληπιός. Λάκωνες. So Musurus for . γλαόπης cod., cp. Bekker *anecd.* i. 329, 23, Souid. *s.v.* ἄγμασι, Zonar. *lex. s.v.* ἄγμασι).

Ἀγλαπιός (G. Dickins in the *Ann. Brit. Sch. Ath.* 1904—1905 xi. 131 f. no. 1 fig. 1 publishes a *stéle* at Thalamai (*Koutiphari*) inscribed ΛΑΝΙΚΙΑ | ΑΝΕ⊗ΘΚΕ | ΤΩΙΑΓΛΑΠΙΩΙ in lettering which M. N. Tod *ib.* assigns to *c.* 350 B.C. ,and W. Kolbe in *Inscr. Gr. Arc. Lac. Mess.* i no. 1313 to *s.* v B.C.).

Ἀσκληπιός in epic, Ionic, Attic. Ἀσσκληπιός thrice in Attic inscriptions (K. Meisterhans *Grammatik der attischen Inschriften*[3] Berlin 1900 p. 89 n. 770), cp. Ἀσσκληπιάδης (*id. ib.* p. 89 n. 771), Ἀσσκληπιόδωρος (*id. ib.* p. 89 n. 772).

Ἀσκλαπιός in non-Ionic dialects. Ἀσκαλπιός in a Gortynian inscription (F. Halbherr in the *Mon. d. Linc.* 1889 i. 38 ff. C, 7 ΑΣΚΑΛΠΙΟΝ). Ἀσκλειπιός in a Spartan inscription (*Corp. inscr. Gr.* i no. 1444, 10 ΑΣΚΛΕΙΠΙΟΥ) turns out to be a mistaken reading (H. J. W. Tillyard and A. M. Woodward in the *Ann. Brit. Sch. Ath.* 1906—1907 xiii. 212 ΑΣΚΛΗΠΙΟΥ, *Inscr. Gr. Arc. Lac. Mess.* i no. 602, 10). Ἀσχλαπιός in a Boeotian inscription (*Inscr. Gr. sept.* i no. 3191 f., 3 ΑΣΧΛΑΠΙΩ, 37 f. [ΑΣΧ]ΛΑΠΙΩ Orchomenos), cp. Ἀσχλάπων (Collitz—Bechtel *Gr. Dial.-Inschr.* i. 397 no. 571ᵃ, 10 Akraiphia), but Ἀσκλαπίχιος (*ib.* i. 174 no. 476, 40 Orchomenos).

Αἰσχλαβιός in the alphabet of Megara or Corinth on the leg of an archaic bronze statuette from Bologna (*Corp. inscr. Gr.* iii no. 6737, 2, Roehl *Inscr. Gr. ant.* no. 549, 2, *Inscr. Gr. Pelop.* i no. 356, 2, Roberts *Gk. Epigr.* i. 146 no. 118 (*c*), 2 ΑΙΣΧΛΑϞΙΟΙ).

Αἰσκλαπιός in the oldest Epidaurian inscription (P. Cavvadias *Fouilles d'Épidaure* Athènes 1893 i. 37 no. 8 on a bronze *phiále*, to be dated at the beginning of *s.* v B.C., if not earlier still, *Inscr. Gr. Pelop.* i no. 1202 ΤΟΙΑΙΜΚΛΑΠΙΟΙ) and in an inscription from Troizen (E. Legrand in the *Bull. Corr. Hell.* 1893 xvii. 90 ff. no. 4, 3, *Inscr. Gr. Pelop.* i no. 771, 3 ΤΩΙΑΙΣΚΛΑΠ[ΙΩΙ]).

Αἰσκλαπιεύς in another early Epidaurian inscription (P. Cavvadias *Fouilles d'Épidaure* Athènes 1893 i. 37 no. 10 from the rim of a bronze vessel ΙΙΙΙΜΙ϶ΠΑΛϞΣΙΑ⊣=τ' Αἰσκλαπιεῖ μ' [ἀνέθηκε—]).

Aisclapius in an inscription painted on an Etruscan cup (H. Jordan in the

Ann. d. Inst. 1884 lvi. 357 f. pl. R, Wilmanns *Ex. inscr. Lat.* no. 2827 *b*, Dessau *Inscr. Lat. sel.* no. 2958 ΛISCLΛPΙ).

Aesclapius in an inscription at Narona (*Corp. inscr. Lat.* iii no. 1766 AESCLAPIO, cp. *ib.* iii no. 1767, 1 [AE]SCLAPIO).

Aiscolapius in an inscription found in the Tiber (*Corp. inscr. Lat.* vi no. 30846, Dessau *Inscr. Lat. sel.* no. 3833).

Aescolapius in a trilingual (Latin, Greek, Phoenician) inscription on the base of a bronze column at *Santuacci* in Sardinia (*Corp. inscr. Lat.* x no. 7856, 1, Dessau *Inscr. Lat. sel.* no. 1874, 1, *Inscr. Gr. Sic. It.* no. 608, 1 AES-COLAPIO) and in two inscriptions from Rome (*Corp. inscr. Lat.* vi no. 30849, Dessau *Inscr. Lat. sel.* no. 3834 ; *Corp. inscr. Lat.* vi no. 30847, Dessau *Inscr. Lat. sel.* no. 3835).

Aisculapius in an inscription from the Tiber-island (*Corp. inscr. Lat.* vi no. 12, Dessau *Inscr. Lat. sel.* no. 3837).

Aesculapius, the normal form in Latin.

Esculapius on a bronze plate from the *ager Praenestinus* (*Corp. inscr. Lat.* xiv no. 2846, Dessau *Inscr. Lat. sel.* no. 3838).

In view of Asklepios' early connexion with Thessaly, special importance must be attached to the names Ἀσκαλαπιάδας at Iolkos (H. G. Lolling in the *Ath. Mitth.* 1883 viii. 115 no. 9, 1, Collitz—Bechtel *Gr. Dial.-Inschr.* i. 378 no. 1284, 1 [Ἀσ]καλαπιάδ[ας]) and Ἀσκαλαπιόδωρος at Phalanna (H. G. Lolling in the *Ath. Mitth.* 1883 viii. 109 f. line 3, Collitz—Bechtel *Gr. Dial.-Inschr.* i. 384 no. 1330, 5 ΑΣΚΑΛΑΓΙΟΔΟΥΡΟΙ), since these point to an original Thessalian *Ἀσκαλαπιος (E. Thraemer in Pauly—Wissowa *Real-Enc.* ii. 1642): cp. Collitz—Bechtel *Gr. Dial.-Inschr.* iii. 1. 186 no. 3398 *b*, 21 Hermione ΛΣΚΑΛΑ gen. of Ἀσκαλᾶς, J. H. Mordtmann in the *Ath. Mitth.* 1885 x. 13 no. 1 near Kotiaeion Ἀσκλᾶς καὶ Ἀσκληπᾶ[ς] | οἱ Ἀσκληπᾶ (A. Fick in the *Beiträge zur kunde der indo-germanischen sprachen* 1901 xxvi. 319). The ultimate meaning of Ἀσκληπιός has been much debated, and is still questionable. The ancients—children in philo-logy—jumped to the conclusion that the second element in the name was ἤπιος, 'mild,' and used this word (Lyk. *Al.* 1054 with Tzetz. *ad loc., et. mag.* pp. 154, 45 ff., 434, 15 ff., Tzetz. *chil.* 6. 991, 10. 712, Eustath. *in Il.* pp. 463, 34 f., 860, 9 ff., *in Od.* p. 1447, 48 f., Cornut. *theol.* 33 p. 70, 5 ff. Lang (?), cp. *Corp. inscr. Att.* iii. 1 Add. no. 171 *b*, 8 and 13=*carm. pop.* 47, 6 and 11 Bergk[4]=Cougny *Anth. Pal. Append.* 4. 53. 4 and 9) or its compounds ἠπιοδώτης, ἠπιόδωρος, ἠπιόφρων (Bruchmann *Epith. deor.* p. 51, Gruppe *Gr. Myth. Rel.* p. 1441) of the god himself—Demosthenes is even said to have sworn by Ἀσκλήπιος, not Ἀσ-κληπιός (Plout. *de vit. decem orat.* 8, Herodian. περὶ καθολικῆς προσῳδίας 5 (i. 123, 1 ff. Lentz), Eustath. *in Il.* p. 463, 37 ff., *in Od.* p. 1447, 64 ff., Favorin. *lex.* p. 296, 40 f.),—and Ἠπιόνη, Ἠπιώ of his partner (Cornut. *theol.* 33 p. 71, 2 ff. Lang : see further Gruppe *Gr. Myth. Rel.* p. 1441 n. 9, E. Thraemer in Pauly—Wissowa *Real-Enc.* vi. 186 ff.). But the first element puzzled them. They tried ἀσκεῖν (schol. *Il.* 4. 195, Eustath. *in Il.* p. 463, 35 f., Favorin. *lex.* p. 296, 43 f.), ἀσκελές (*et. mag.* p. 154, 43 ff., 47 ι., *et. Gud.* p. 83, 39 ff., Orion p. 9, 14 ff., Tzetz. *in Lyk. Al.* 1054, Favorin. *lex.* p. 296, 38 ff.), Ἄσκλης a supposed king of Epidauros (Tzetz. *in* Lyk. *Al.* 1054, Favorin. *lex.* p. 296, 41 ff., cp. *et. mag.* p. 154, 45 ff., Eustath. *in Il.* p. 463, 34 f.), Αἴγλη the mother of Asklepios (P. Cavvadias *Fouilles d'Épidaure* Athènes 1893 i. 35 f. no. 7, 50 ff. = Isyll. 19 f. Weir Smyth). Modern scholars have gone from bad to worse, starting with ἄλκω, 'I help,' whence an assumed *Ἀλξηπιος (A. F. Pott in the *Zeitschrift für vergleichende Sprach-forschung* 1857 vi. 401), and, after numerous blind alleys (see E. Thraemer in

Roscher *Lex. Myth.* i. 616 and in Pauly—Wissowa *Real-Enc.* ii. 1643), ending in the *quartier juif* with *ish-kalbi*, 'l'homme-chien' (C. Clermont-Ganneau in the *Revue critique* 1884 p. 502). Much more attractive is the view first put forward in 1860 by Welcker *Gr. Götterl.* ii. 736, *viz.* that 'Ασκληπιός is akin to ἀσκάλαβος, 'lizard,'—a word which may well have had at one time a wider meaning and denoted 'snake.' This idea has commended itself, not only to mythologists (J. Maehly *Die Schlange im Mythus und Cultus der classischen Völker* Basel 1867 pp. 6, 8 f., M. Mayer *Die Giganten und Titanen* Berlin 1887 p. 93 n. 105, L. Deubner *De incubatione* Lipsiae 1900 p. 37, Gruppe *Gr. Myth. Rel.* p. 1443 ff.), but also to philologists. C. Angermann in *Studien zur griechischen und lateinischen Grammatik* herausgegeben von G. Curtius und K. Brugmann 1876 ix. 247 f. would trace both 'Ασκληπιός and ἀσκάλαβος, ἀσκαλαβώτης (perhaps also the bird-names ἀσκαλώπας, σκολόπαξ, and the insect-name σκολόπενδρα) to a root *skalp* or *skarp*, a lengthened form of *skar*, 'springen, sich hin und her bewegen.' A. Vaniček *Griechisch-lateinisches etymologisches Wörterbuch* Leipzig 1877 ii. 1079 says: '(σκαλ-π, σκλα-π, σκλη-π) 'Α-σκληπ-ιό-s m. (urspr. Schlange).' A. Fick in the *Beiträge zur kunde der indogermanischen sprachen* 1901 xxvi. 313—323 'Asklepios und die heilschlange,' followed by Prellwitz *Etym. Wörterb. d. Gr. Spr.*[2] p. 58, holds that Asklepios was originally a snake and explains the Thessalian *'Ασκαλαπιος and the Cretan 'Ασκαλπιός by the help of the Hesychian glosses σκαλαπάζει· ῥέμβεται and σκαλπάζειν· ῥεμβωδῶς βαδίζειν. Thus 'Ασκληπιός would mean 'Creepy-crawly'—a likely enough name for a snake. 'Ασκάλαβος, 'lizard,' and ἀσκάλαφος, a species of 'owl' (Apollod. 2. 5. 12, Ov. *met.* 5. 538 ff., interp. Serv. *in* Verg. *Aen.* 4. 462 f.) that haunts holes in the rock (cp. Apollod. 1. 5. 3, 2. 5. 12 : see further D'Arcy W. Thompson *A Glossary of Greek Birds* Oxford 1895 p. 36), are very possibly related forms, if not also σκολόπαξ, ἀσκολόπας, ἀσκαλώπας, 'woodcock' (*id. ib.* pp. 36, 155).

(6) Thessalian Kings as impersonations of Zeus.

The explanation of 'Ασκληπιός as formerly denoting a snake is perfectly compatible with the belief that the original bearer of the name was a Thessalian king. Drakon of Thebes, Ophis of Salamis, Python of Delphoi, etc. were all recognised as kings by Euhemeristic writers (see W. H. Roscher *Lex. Myth.* i. 1201, O. Höfer *ib.* iii. 925 f., R. Wagner in Pauly—Wissowa *Real-Enc.* v. 1646 f.). But here, as elsewhere (*supra* i. 662), Euhemerism had a foundation in fact. Greeks and Romans alike regarded the soul of the dead as able to manifest itself in the form of a snake (the evidence is conveniently summarised by E. Küster *Die Schlange in der griechischen Kunst und Religion* Giessen 1913 p. 62 ff., cp. W. Wundt *Völkerpsychologie* Leipzig 1906 ii. 2. 72 ff., *id. Elements of Folk Psychology* trans. E. L. Schaub London—New York 1916 pp. 190 ff., 214, 368, O. Waser 'Über die äussere Erscheinung der Seele' etc. in the *Archiv f. Rel.* 1913 xvi. 354 ff.). A deceased king might well appear as a great beneficent snake, or at least be accompanied by such. And, when his soul-animal had come to be viewed as a mere attendant or attribute, explanatory myths would arise. Thus Asklepios was said to have reared his snake in an oak growing in a glen of Mt Pelion called Pelethronion (Nik. *ther.* 438 ff. with schol. and Eutekn. *ad loc.*: *Class. Rev.* 1904 xviii. 83. Cp. the story told of Melampous by Apollod. 1. 9. 11), or again to have been placed by Zeus in the sky as the constellation Ophiuchus (*supra* i. 755 n. 9) because he had raised from the dead Hippolytos son of Theseus (pseudo-Eratosth. *catast.* 6, Hyg. *poet. astr.* 2. 14) or Glaukos son of Minos (Hyg. *poet. astr.* 2. 14). Such tales are late and of little value. It is more important to note that the earliest home of Asklepios was in central Thessaly (E. Thraemer in Roscher *Lex. Myth.* i. 623 and more fully in Pauly—Wissowa *Real-Enc.* ii. 1643 ff., 1662 f.), and that at Trikke he had an underground *ádyton* (P. Cavvadias *Fouilles d'Épidaure* Athènes 1893 i. 34 ff. no. 7, 27 ff. πρῶτος Μᾶλος ἔτευξεν Ἀπόλλωνος Μαλεάτα | βωμὸν καὶ θυσίαις ἠγλάϊσεν τέμενος. | οὐδέ κε Θεσσαλίας ἐν Τρίκκηι πειραθείης | εἰς ἄδυτον καταβὰς Ἀσκληπιοῦ, εἰ μὴ ἐφ' ἁγνοῦ | πρῶτον Ἀπόλλωνος βωμοῦ θύσαις Μαλεάτα. Cp. J. Ziehen 'Über die Lager des Asklepiosheiligtums von Trikka' in the *Ath. Mitth.* 1892 xvii. 195—197 and especially P. Kastriotes Τὸ ἐν Τρίκκῃ τῆς Θεσσαλίας Ἀσκληπιεῖον Athens 1903, *id.* 'Τρίκκης Ἀσκληπιεῖον' in the Ἐφ. Ἀρχ. 1918 pp. 65—73) comparable with the Καταβάσιον of Trophonios at Lebadeia, which we have already (*supra* p. 1076) taken to be the *thólos* of an ancient king (A. J. B. Wace—M. S. Thompson *Prehistoric Thessaly* Cambridge 1912 p. 272 Index record *thólos*-tombs at Dhimini, Ghura, Kapakli, Marmariani, Rakhmani (?), Sesklo, Zerelia (?)). Moreover, there is reason to think that in early days Thessalian kings were wont to pose as Zeus. Salmoneus, the very type of a would-be Zeus (*supra* i. 12, 318), was a king hailing from Thessaly (Apollod. 1. 9. 7, schol. Aristoph. *ran.* argum. 4, Souid. *s.v.* Σαλμωνεύς. See further J. Ilberg in Roscher *Lex. Myth.* iv. 290). Keyx, who declared that his wife was Hera, and Alkyone, who dubbed her husband Zeus (Apollod. 1. 7. 4, schol. *Il.* 9. 562, Eustath. *in Il.* p. 776, 19 ff., schol. Aristoph. *av.* 250. K. Wernicke in Pauly—Wissowa *Real-Enc.* i. 1580 f. suggests that the story in this form goes back to the Hesiodic Κήυκος γάμος), were commonly described as king and queen of Trachis in south Thessaly (schol. Aristoph. *av.* 250, Loukian. *Alcyon* 1, Ov. *met.* 11. 268 ff., 382 ff., Lact. Plac. *narr. fab.* 11. 10. See further K. Wernicke *loc. cit.* and H. W. Stoll in Roscher *Lex. Myth.* i. 249 ff., ii. 1181 f.). Ixion, king of the Thessalian Lapithai, aspired to the hand of Hera, while conversely Zeus was enamoured of Ixion's wife Dia (*Class. Rev.* 1903 xvii. 420, 1906 xx. 378)—a case paralleled by that of Hera in love with the Thessalian Iason and Zeus in love with Medeia (*supra* i. 248). Now it is a very noteworthy fact that all these names, indeed the great bulk of the personages considered in the present discussion,—Amphiaraos, Trophonios, Asklepios, Askalaphos, Salmoneus, Alkyone, Ixion, Iason—belonged to the family of Aiolos (see the pedigree conveniently set forth by Gerhard *Gr. Myth.* ii. 223 ff.). The inference is that this custom of regarding the king as Zeus was characteristic of the Aeolians settled in Thessaly and central Greece. Asklepios, like the rest, was *ab origine* a king (he is ἄναξ in *h. Asklep.* 5, Aristoph. *Plout.* 748, Herond. 4. 1 and 18, P. Cavvadias *Fouilles d'Épidaure* Athènes 1893 i. 36 no. 7, 79, *Corp. inscr. Gr.* i no. 2292, 1 (Delos)= Kaibel *Epigr. Gr.* no. 803. 1 = Cougny *Anth. Pal. Append.* 1. 225. 1 (see R. Wünsch in the *Archiv f. Rel.* 1904 vii. 95 ff.); βασιλεύς in *Corp. inscr. Gr.* iii no. 5974 B, 1 (Rome)= *Inscr. Gr. Sic. It.* no. 967 *b*, 1 = Kaibel *Epigr. Gr.* Add. no. 805 a, b *tit.*= Cougny *Anth. Pal. Append.* 1. 247 β n., Ail. *de nat. an.* 9. 33, Orph. εὐχὴ πρὸς Μουσαῖον 37, Cougny *op. cit.* 6. 180. 2 f. Ἀσκλαπιὸς Καῖσαρ in W. R. Paton—E. L. Hicks *The Inscriptions of Cos* Oxford 1891 p. 130 no. 92, 5 f., *ib.* p. 153 no. 130, 4 f.= Collitz—Bechtel *Gr. Dial.-Inschr.* iii. 1. 375 f. no. 3672, 5 f. is the deified Claudius), who played the part of Zeus during his life and was worshipped as Zeus after his death (E. Thraemer in Roscher *Lex. Myth.* i. 620 and in Pauly—Wissowa *Real-Enc.* ii. 1654 f. draws attention to the fact that several Greek localities could point to an alleged grave of Asklepios: Cic. *de nat. deor.* 3. 57 Aesculapiorum...secundus, secundi Mercurii frater. is, fulmine percussus, dicitur humatus esse Cynosuris, Clem. Al. *protr.* 2. 30. 3 p. 22, 14 Stählin οὗτος μὲν οὖν κεῖται κεραυνωθεὶς ἐν τοῖς Κυνοσουρίδος ὁρίοις

Zeus *Asklepiós*   1089

with schol. *ad loc.* p. 305, 31 Stählin κώμη Λακεδαίμονος, Lyd. *de mens.* 4. 142 p. 164, 8 ff. Wünsch δεύτερος Ἰσχύος τοῦ Ἐλάτου καὶ Κορωνίδος,<ὃς ἐν τοῖς Κυνοσ­ουρίδος suppl. C. B. Hase> ὁρίοις ἐτάφη, cp. *Acta Sanctorum* edd. Bolland. Octobris ix. 546 ('Passio S. Philippi episc., Severi presb. et Hermæ diac.' I. 8) ignis ille divinus...et Scolapium medicum in monte Cynozuridos fulminatum consecrationem mereri ʼin gentibus fecit, where cod. Bodecense rightly reads *Æsculapium* and the Bollandist editors wrongly (?) comment : 'apud Cynozurim Thessaliæ urbem sepultus' (*ib.* ix. 549). Cic. *de nat. deor.* 3. 57 tertius, Arsippi et Arsinoae,...cuius in Arcadia non longe a Lusio flumine sepulcrum et lucus ostenditur, Lyd. *de mens.* 4. 142 p. 164, 10 ff. Wünsch τρίτος Ἀρσίππου καὶ Ἀρσινόης τῆς Λευκίππου·...καὶ τάφος αὐτῷ ἐν Ἀρκαδίᾳ. Clem. Rom. *hom.* 6. 21 (ii. 213 Migne) Ἀσκληπιὸς ἐν Ἐπιδαύρῳ (*sc.* κεῖται), Rufin. *recognit.* 10. 24 in Epidauro Aesculapii (*sc.* sepulcrum demonstratur). Cp. Tert. *ad nat.* 2. 14 Athenienses...Aesculapio et matri inter mortuos parentant with Mommsen *Feste d. Stadt Athen* pp. 217 n. 4, 218, 222 and F. Kutsch *Attische Heilgötter und Heilheroen* Giessen 1913 p. 16 ff.).

(7) Telesphoros.

Such an one might even be called Zeus Τέλειος (cp. the dedication Ἀσκληπιῶι Διὶ Τελείωι *supra* p. 1076). Further, the citle τελεσφόρος, 'bringing the end, bringing to maturity' (see Stephanus *Thes. Gr. Ling.* vii. 1971 C ff.), appropriate to the divine monarch (*h. Zeus* I. f. Ζῆνα θεῶν τὸν ἄριστον ἀείσομαι ἠδὲ μέγιστον,|εὐρύοπα, κρείοντα, τελεσφόρον, κ.τ.λ.) and actually found on a Phrygian altar as his appellative (*supra* p. 838 n. 1), was a likely epithet of his human counterpart. And here it will be remembered that antiquity often associates with Asklepios a subordinate deity Telesphoros, who has been the subject of much speculation (L. Schenck *De Telesphoro deo* Göttingen 1888, W. Wroth 'Telesphorus' in the *Journ. Hell. Stud.* 1882 iii. 283—300, *ib.* 1883 iv. 161 f., *ib.* 1884 v. 82 n. 2, Frazer *Pausanias* iii. 70 f., S. Reinach 'Télesphore' in the *Rev. Ét. Gr.* 1901 xiv. 343—349=*id. Cultes, mythes et religions* Paris 1906 ii. 255—261, Gruppe *Gr. Myth. Rel.* p. 1455 n. 1, *alib., id. Myth. Lit.* 1908 p. 622, Harrison *Themis* p. 382 f.). We shall not be far wrong, if we regard him as the procreative power of Asklepios, split off from the god, to whom he at first belonged by way of appellative, and endowed with a separate and secondary personality. The existence of *Grabphalli* (*supra* i. 53 n. 1) and the birth-myths of Romulus and Servius Tullius (*supra* p. 1059) lead us to suppose that the buried ancestor in his procreative capacity might take the form of a simple *phallós* (with this interchange of human and phallic shapes cp. the statue of Nabu at Calah figured in two aspects by C. F. Lehmann-Haupt in Roscher *Lex. Myth.* iv. 685 f.). Accordingly we sometimes meet with representations of Telesphoros as a *phallós* draped to look like a man or a boy. C. M. Grivaud de la Vincelle *Recueil de monumens antiques, la plupart inédits, et découverts dans l'ancienne Gaule* Paris 1817 i. 86 f., ii. pl. 10, 1—5 (of which 1, 3=my fig. 931) and pl. 11, 5 (Reinach *Rép. Stat.* ii. 75 no. 1, J. A. Dulaure *Histoire abrégée de différens cultes²* Paris 1825 ii. 242 f.) published a bronze statuette, found some forty years earlier in a tomb near Amiens, which shows a bearded male figure clad in a short tunic, a cape with a peaked hood (*bardocucullus*), and boots (*caligae*): the upper part—head, hood, and cape—can be lifted off, revealing a body that consists in an erect *phallós*. Similarly T. Panofka 'Asklepios und die Asklepiaden' in the *Abh. d. berl. Akad. 1845* Phil.-hist. Classe pp. 324, 357 pl. 6, 5 and 5 a (=my fig. 932, C. O. Müller—F. Wieseler *Denkm. d. alt. Kunst* Göttingen 1856 ii. 4. 4 pl. 61, 789, Reinach *Rép. Stat.* ii.

469 no. 8 f.) published a bronze statuette at Copenhagen (L. Müller *Description des antiquités du Musée-Thorvaldsen* Section i et ii Copenhague 1847 p. 162 f. no. 50 height without the peak 3 Danish inches, with it 4, S. B. Smith *Kort Veiledning i Antikkabinettet i Kjøbenhavn* Kjöbenhavn 1864 p. 38 no. 123 a), which repeats the type, except that the figure is a beardless youth and wears no sandals. One whose function is to bring to maturity might well be portrayed as either man or boy. Asklepios himself was beardless on occasion (Paus. 2. 10. 3 Sikyon (*supra* p. 1080), 2. 13. 5 Phlious, 8. 28. 1 Gortys. Furtwängler *Masterpieces of Gk. Sculpture* pp. 277 n. 5, 300, E. Thraemer in Pauly—Wissowa *Real-Enc.* ii. 1690 f., 1693 ff.) or even infantile (Paus. 8. 25. 11 Thelpousa, 8. 32. 5 Megalopolis. *Corp. inscr. Gr.* iii no. 5974 A, B (Rome)=*Inscr. Gr. Sic. It.* no. 967

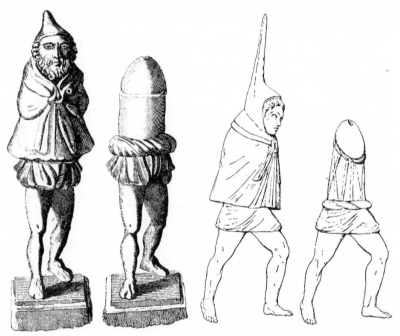

Fig. 931.   Fig. 932.

a, b = Kaibel *Epigr. Gr.* Add. no. 805 a, b = Cougny *Anth. Pal. Append.* 1. 247 a, β: Overbeck *Gr. Plastik*[4] ii, 181). The Copenhagen bronze is inscribed OMORION (Panofka *loc. cit.*), which could be connected with Zeus Ὁμόριος (Steph. *Thes. Gr. Ling.* v. 1984 A quotes the title from Polyb. 2. 39. 6; but see *supra* i. 17 n. 4) or Ὅριος (Dion. Hal. *ant. Rom.* 2. 74)=Iupiter *Terminus* or *Terminalis* (*supra* i. 53. 520 n. 2. Cp. Aug. *de civ. Dei* 4. 11 ipse in aethere sit Iuppiter,... in Iano initiator, in Termino terminator. E. Samter 'Die Entwickelung des Terminuskultes' in the *Archiv f. Rel.* 1913 xvi. 137—144 argues that the boundary-stone could not have been originally sacred to Iupiter, because at its erection offerings were placed in the hole prepared for it (Siculus Flaccus in the *Grom. vet.* i. 141 Lachmann)—a procedure suggestive of a chthonian rather than of a celestial power. But the lord of the property, who had been a celestial Iupiter during his life would be a chthonian Iupiter after his death). B. Borghesi in the *Bull. d. Inst.*

1831 p. 182 ff. and E. Gerhard in the *Ann. d. Inst.* 1846 xviii. pl. S, *ib* .1847 xix. 327 ff. drew attention to a white marble Hermaphrodite-term, found near Ravenna, which is inscribed (Orelli—Henzen *Inscr. Lat. sel.* no. 5648 = *Corp. inscr. Lat.* xi no. 351) IOV · TER · M | VAL · ANT · | AN · TI · CO · | V · L · S · | *ᚭ ramus*, *i.e.*, according to Borghesi, Iov(i) Ter(minali) M(arcus) Val(erius) Ant(onius) Antico v(otum) l(ibens) s(olvit), or, as Mommsen suggested, M. Val(erius) Ant(iochus) An(nii) Ti(beriani) co(mes). It should be noted also that a *denarius* of Augustus, struck

Fig. 933.   Fig. 934.

c. 29—27 B.C., has *obv.* head of Octavian, *rev.* IMP | CAESAR an ithyphallic term of Octavian with a bay-wreath on his head and a winged thunderbolt at his feet (Babelon *Monn. rép. rom.* ii. 64 no. 153 fig., cp. *ib.* ii. 65 no. 155 fig., *Brit. Mus. Cat. Rom. Coins* Rep. ii. 16 no. 4360 f. pl. 60, 5 f., cp. *ib.* ii. 16 no. 4362 pl. 60, 7 = my fig. 933, Emp. i. pp. cxxiii f., 102 nos. 628—630 pl. 15, 10 f., cp. *ib.* i. 104 no. 637 pl. 15, 16, A. Boutkowski *Dictionnaire numismatique* Leipzig 1881 i. 333 f. no. 732, cp. *ib.* i. 334 no. 733. Fig. 934 is from a specimen in my collection),—an excellent illustration of a mortal monarch aping the sky-god and credited with superhuman propagatory powers. See also Addenda *ad loc.*

APPENDIX M.

ZEUS *MEILÍCHIOS.*

(1) Zeus *Meilíchios* on the Kephisos.

Zeus was worshipped under the title *Meilíchios* far and wide through the Hellenic world. *In primis* Athens had long been a centre of his cult. Pausanias, noting the objects of interest along the Sacred Way from Athens to Eleusis, remarks :

'When you have crossed the Kephisos there is an ancient altar of Zeus *Meilíchios.* At this altar Theseus was purified by the descendants of Phytalos after he had slain various brigands including Sinis, who was related to him through Pittheus[1].'

Plutarch's account is rather fuller :

'So Theseus went on and came to the Kephisos. Here he was met by men of the clan Phytalidai, who were the first to salute him. He begged them to purify him. Thereupon they cleansed him with the customary rites, offered Milichian sacrifices, and feasted him in their home, whereas up to that time no man had shown him hospitality by the way. His return is said to have fallen on the eighth day of the month Kronios, Hekatombaion as it is called nowadays[2].'

Dates of this sort are not invented at random, and we may fairly suppose that the local festival of Zeus *Meilíchios* was celebrated by the Phytalidai in their

---

[1] Paus. 1. 37. 4.   [2] Plout. *v. Thes.* 12.

ancestral house[1] on Hekatombaion 8[2]. Plutarch adds that, in return for their entertainment, Theseus gave them charge over a sacrifice at the Oschophoria[3]. In the old Attic myth two points deserve to be stressed. On the one hand, Zeus *Meilíchios* was a god able to purify a man from the stain of kindred bloodshed: we have already noted that the skins of animals sacrificed to him were used in purificatory rites[4]. On the other hand, the festival of this god was observed 'at home[5]' by a clan traditionally associated with the fig-tree and its fruit[6]: in fact, the descendants of Phytalos appear to have had special duties in regard to Zeus *Meilíchios*, much as the descendants of Anthos had in regard to Zeus *Lýkaios*[7].

(2) The Title *Meilíchios*.

We are, therefore, at once confronted with the difficult question: What is the meaning of *Meilíchios*? Does it denote 'the Kindly One' (*meílichos*, *meilíchios*)[8], a deity whose wrath could be readily appeased by the quaking man-slayer? Or does it rather signify 'the god of Figs' (*meílicha*)[9] with special

---

[1] Cp. Paus. 1. 37. 2 quoted *infra* n. 6.

[2] In the calendar of Mykonos (J. de Prott *Leges Graecorum sacrae* Lipsiae 1896 Fasti sacri p. 13 ff. no. 4, 29 ff., Michel *Recueil d'Inscr. gr.* no. 714, 29 ff., Dittenberger *Syll. inscr. Gr.*[2] no. 615, 29 ff.) Hekatombaion 7 is marked by the sacrifice of a bull and ten lambs to Apollon Ἐκατόμβαιος and by the sacrifice of a full-grown victim and ten lambs to Acheloios—a god who at Athens was closely connected with Zeus Μειλίχιος (*infra* p. 1117 f.). It seems possible that this Myconian festival on Hekatombaion 7 was the equivalent of an Athenian festival on Hekatombaion 8. But further evidence is lacking.

[3] Plout. *v. Thes.* 23: see J. Töpffer *Attische Genealogie* Berlin 1889 p. 251 f., Mommsen *Feste d. Stadt Athen* p. 286 n. 2.

[4] *Supra* i. 422 ff.

[5] Plout. *v. Thes.* 12 καὶ δεομένου καθαρθῆναι τοῖς νενομισμένοις ἁγνίσαντες καὶ Μειλίχια θύσαντες εἱστίασαν οἴκοι.

[6] Paus. 1. 37. 2 ἐν τούτῳ τῷ χωρίῳ Φύταλόν φασιν οἴκῳ Δήμητρα δέξασθαι, καὶ τὴν θεὸν ἀντὶ τούτων δοῦναί οἱ τὸ φυτὸν τῆς συκῆς· μαρτυρεῖ δέ μοι τῷ λόγῳ τὸ ἐπίγραμμα (Cougny *Anth. Pal. Append.* 3. 24) τὸ ἐπὶ τῷ Φυτάλου τάφῳ· ἐνθάδ' ἄναξ ἥρως Φύταλός ποτε δέξατο σεμνὴν | Δήμητραν, ὅτε (A. Meineke cj. Δήμητρ' ᾧ τότε L. Dindorf and C. G. Cobet cjj. Δήμητρ' ὅπποτε) πρῶτον ὀπώρας καρπὸν ἔφηνεν, | ἣν ἱερὰν συκῆν θνητῶν γένος ἐξονομάζει· | ἐξ οὗ δὴ τιμὰς Φυτάλου γένος ἔσχεν ἀγήρως. *Infra* p. 1103 n. 3.

[7] *Supra* i. 71 ff.

[8] Cornut. *theol.* 11 p. 12, 2 ff. Lang προσαγορεύουσι δὲ καὶ μείλιχον (F. Osann cj. μειλίχιον; but Aristeid. *or.* 1. 3 (i. 4 Dindorf) has εἰ δέ πη σφαλλόμεθα, ὁ μείλιχος (*sc.* Zeus) ἡμῖν κεκλήσθω) τὸν Δία, εὐμείλικτον ὄντα τοῖς ἐξ ἀδικίας μετατιθεμένοις, οὐ δέοντος ἀδιαλλάκτως ἔχειν πρὸς αὐτούς: cp. Liban. *or.* 57. 12 (iv. 154 Foerster) Σευῆρος δὲ χρηστός τε ἦν ἐν τοῖς ῥήμασι καὶ τιμήσειν ἔλεγε τῇ πραότητι τὸν Μειλίχιον Δία, κ.τ.λ., *Anth. Pal.* 9. 581. 4 f. (Leon Philosophos?) μηδὲ νοήσω, | Ζηνὸς Μειλιχίοιο λαχὼν θρόνον, ἀνέρος οἶτον. A highly moral explanation: but high morals are out of place in an early cult-title. Phrynichos the 'Atticist' (on whom see Sir J. E. Sandys *A History of Classical Scholarship*[2] Cambridge 1906 i. 323 ff.) in Bekker *anecd.* i. 34, 12 ff. Δικαιόσυνος Ζεύς· ὁ ἐπὶ τοῖς δίκαιά τε καὶ ἄδικα δρῶσι τεταγμένος. ὥσπερ καὶ ὁ ἐπὶ τοῖς μείλιχα μειλίχιος καὶ ὁ ἐπὶ τοῖς φίλα φίλιος adduces would-be parallels. But Zeus Δικαιόσυνος is a late divinity (D. M. Robinson in the *Am. Journ. Arch.* 1905 ix. 302 no. 24 near *Gherzeh* (Karousa) Διὶ Δικαιοσύνωι | Μεγάλωι | Πύθης Διονυσίου | στρατηγῶν | χαριστήριον, cp. schol. *Il.* 13. 29, Eustath. *in Il.* p. 918, 47), and Zeus Φίλιος is probably euphemistic (Append. N). On Zeus Ἅγιος see *supra* i. 192, 400 n. 6, 565 n. 2.

[9] Figs were called μείλιχα, 'sweets,' in Naxos—witness Athen. 78 c Νάξιοι δέ, ὡς Ἀνδρίσκος (*frag.* 3 in *Frag. hist. Gr.* iv. 304 Müller) ἔτι δ' Ἀγλαοσθένης (*frag.* 5 in *Frag. hist. Gr.* iv. 294 Müller) ἱστοροῦσι, Μειλίχιον καλεῖσθαι τὸν Διόνυσον διὰ τὴν τοῦ συκίνου

reference to the Phytalidai and their fig-culture? Arguments in support of either interpretation lie near to hand.

In may be urged that Zeus was notoriously sympathetic with the outcast and the vagabond. He was worshipped as *Hikésios*, 'the Suppliant's god[1],'

καρποῦ παράδοσιν. διὸ καὶ πρόσωπον τοῦ θεοῦ παρὰ τοῖς Ναξίοις τὸ μὲν τοῦ Βακχέως Διονύσου καλουμένου εἶναι ἀμπέλινον, τὸ δὲ τοῦ Μειλιχίου σύκινον. τὰ γὰρ σῦκα μείλιχα καλεῖσθαι, where T. Reinesius' proposed alteration of Μειλίχιον...Μειλιχίου...μείλιχα into Μόρυχον...Μορύχου...μόρυχα (cp. Souid. *s.vv.* Μόρυχος, μωρότερος Μορύχου) is a good example of misplaced ingenuity.

[1] At Athens in *s.* vi B.C. (Poll. 8. 142 τρεῖς θεοὺς ὀμνύναι κελεύει Σόλων, Ἱκέσιον, Καθάρσιον, Ἐξακεστῆρα, *i.e.* Zeus under three diverse aspects (cp. Poll. 1. 24), as observed by W. Dindorf *ad loc.*, G. F. Schoemann *Griechische Alterthümer*[4] Berlin 1902 ii. 145, 276 = *id. Antiquités recques* trans. C. Galuski Paris 1887 ii. 185, 331, O. Jessen in Pauly—Wissowa *Real-Enc.* viii. 1592. The recognition of Zeus Ἐξακεστήρ (Hesych. Ἐξακεστήριος· ὁ Ζεύς. καὶ ἡ "Ηρα) is perhaps not unconnected with the fact that Solon's own father was Ἐξηκεστίδης. The oath by this triad of Zeuses was inscribed on the ἄξονες (Hesych. τρεῖς θεοί· παρὰ Σόλωνι ἐν τοῖς ἄξοσιν

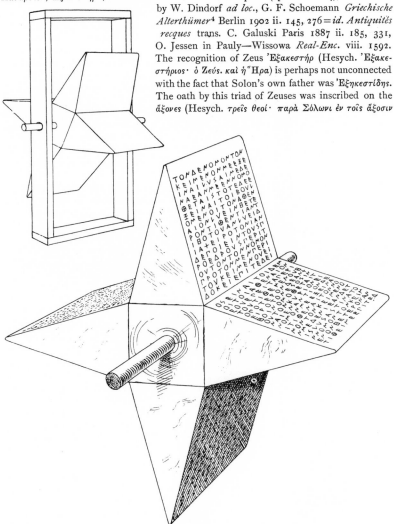

Fig. 935.

ὅρκῳ τέτακται <τρεῖς θεοὺς ἐπιμαρτύρεσθαι?>. ἔνιοι κατὰ τὸ Ὁμηρικόν (sc. *Il.* 2. 371, 4. 288, 7. 132, 16. 97, *Od.* 4. 341, 7. 311, 17. 132, 18. 235, 24. 376 αἳ γάρ, Ζεῦ τε πάτερ καὶ Ἀθηναίη καὶ Ἄπολλον)), which are said to have been wooden axles revolving in oblong frames kept in the Prytaneion (Plout. *v. Sol.* 25 καὶ κατεγράφησαν εἰς ξυλίνους ἄξονας ἐν πλαισίοις περιέχουσι στρεφομένους, ὧν ἔτι καθ' ἡμᾶς ἐν Πρυτανείῳ λείψανα μικρὰ διεσώζετο). Another account says rather enigmatically that they were square in shape, but that when laid in the direction of their acute angle they produced a triangular appearance (Polemon *frag.* 48 (*Frag. hist. Gr.* iii. 130 Müller) *ap.* Harpokr. *s.v.* ἄξονι· οἱ Σόλωνος νόμοι ἐν ξυλίνοις ἦσαν ἄξοσι γεγραμμένοι...ἦσαν δέ, ὥς φησι Πολέμων ἐν τοῖς πρὸς Ἐρατοσθένην, τετράγωνοι τὸ σχῆμα. διασώζονται δὲ ἐν τῷ Πρυτανείῳ, γεγραμμένοι κατὰ πάντα τὰ μέρη. ποιοῦσι δ' ἐνίοτε φαντασίαν τρίγωνον, ὅταν ἐπὶ τὸ στενὸν κλιθῶσι τῆς γωνίας). The Solonian laws were also inscribed on κύρβεις set up in the Stoa Basileios (Aristot. *resp. Ath.* 7. 1 = Aristot. *frag.* 352 Rose *ap.* Harpokr. *s.v.* κύρβεις, Souid. *s.v.* κύρβεις, Plout. *v. Sol.* 25, schol. Aristoph. *av.* 1354, cp. Aristot. *de mundo* 6. 400 b 30 f.), and these κύρβεις are described as stones standing upright like pillars, surmounted by an apex or cap (Apollod. *frag.* 26 (*Frag. hist. Gr.* i. 432 f. Müller) *ap.* Harpokr. *s.v.* κύρβεις·...κύρβεις φησὶν Ἀπολλόδωρος ἐν τοῖς περὶ θεῶν ἔχειν ἐγγεγραμμένους τοὺς νόμους. εἶναι δ' αὐτοὺς λίθους ὀρθοὺς ἑστῶτας, ὡς ἀπὸ μὲν τῆς στάσεως στήλας, ἀπὸ δὲ τῆς εἰς ὕψος ἀναστάσεως (*leg.* ἀνατάσεως) διὰ τὸ κεκορυφῶσθαι κύρβεις ἐκάλουν, ὥσπερ καὶ κυρβασίαν τὴν ἐπὶ τῆς κεφαλῆς τιθεμένην, cp. Souid. *s.v.* κύρβεις, Phot. *lex. s.v.* κύρβεις, schol. Aristoph. *av.* 1354). One ancient grammarian attempts to identify the κύρβεις with the ἄξονες, stating that in both cases a large brick-shaped body as long as a man had fitted

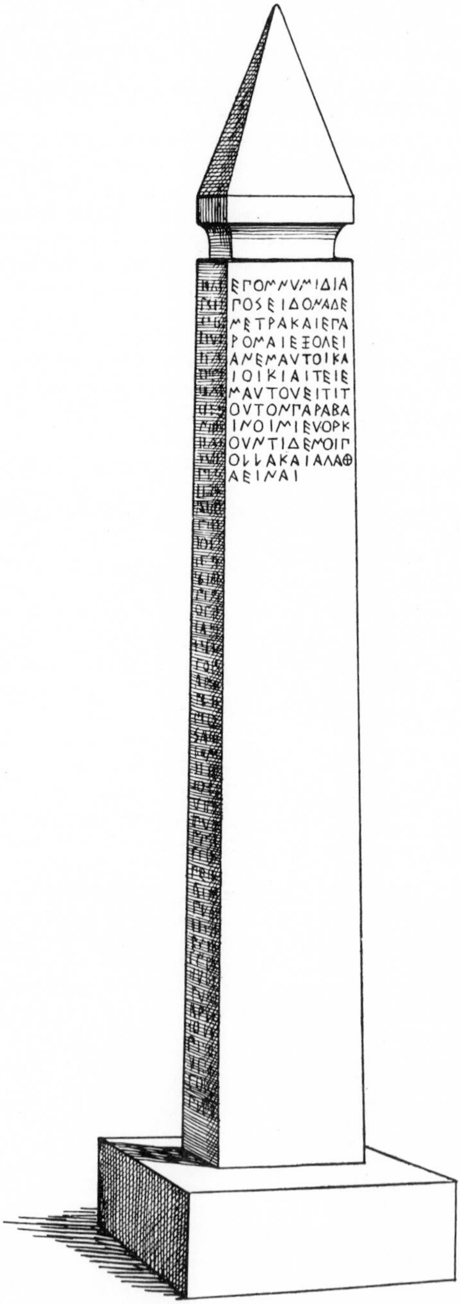

ΕΓΟΜΝΥΜΙΔΙΑ
ΓΟΣΕΙΔΟΝΑΔΕ
ΜΕΤΡΑΚΑΙΕΓΑ
ΡΟΜΑΙΕΞΟΛΕΙ
ΑΝΕΜΑΥΤΟΙΚΑ
ΙΟΙΚΙΑΙΤΕΙΣ
ΜΑΥΤΟΥΕΙΤΙΤ
ΟΥΤΟΝΓΑΡΑΒΑ
ΙΝΟΙΜΙΕΝΟΡΚ
ΟΥΝΤΙΑΣΜΟΙΓ
ΟΛΛΑΚΑΙΑΛΛΑΘ
ΑΕΙΝΑΙ

Fig. 936.

to it quadrangular pieces of wood, whose sides were flat and covered with lettering, and that pivots at either end enabled readers to move and turn about the text (Aristophanes (of Byzantion) *ap*. Souid. *s.v.* κύρβεις·...'Αριστοφάνης δὲ ὁμοίας εἶναί φησι τοῖς ἄξοσι·...ἀμφοτέρων δὲ τὸ κατασκεύασμα τοιοῦτον· πλινθίον τι μέγα, ἀνδρόμηκες, ἡρμοσμένα ἔχον τετράγωνα ξύλα, τὰς πλευρὰς πλατείας ἔχοντα καὶ γραμμάτων πλήρεις· ἑκατέρωθεν δὲ κνώδακας, ὥστε κινεῖσθαι καὶ μεταστρέφεσθαι ὑπὸ τῶν ἀναγινωσκόντων). On the whole it seems clear that the wooden ἄξονες of the Prytaneion are to be distinguished from the stone κύρβεις of the Stoa Basileios. The ἄξονες were apparently shaped as in fig. 935, the κύρβεις as in fig. 936 (on the former is inscribed *frag.* 149 (I. B. Télfy Συναγωγὴ τῶν 'Αττικῶν νόμων *Corpus iuris Attici* Pestini et Lipsiae 1868 p. 39 f.) *ap*. Dem. *c. Timocr.* 33; on the latter, *frag.* 562 (Télfy *op. cit.* p. 137) *ap*. Dem. *c. Timocr.* 151). Neither shape was chosen at random. The wheel of Nemesis (*supra* i. 269 ff.) had a long history behind it and was related (*supra* i. 267) to that wheel, which in India symbolised *ṛta*, the course of nature, the right path, in short, law and order (W. Simpson *The Buddhist Praying-wheel* London 1896 p. 89 ff., H. Oldenberg *La religion du Véda* Paris 1903 p. 163 ff., Harrison *Themis* p. 526 f., F. M. Cornford *From Religion to Philosophy* London 1912 p. 172 ff.). It seems highly probable that Solon inscribed his laws on wooden ἄξονες because he wished to represent them as the σεμνὰ θέμεθλα Δίκης (Solon *frag.* 2. 14 Hiller—Crusius). At the same time the shape chosen would be convenient for purposes of reference or consultation : my friend Dr P. Giles tells me that in the parish church of Great Yarmouth documents are, or were, arranged *à la* Solon. Individual enactments appear to have been copied on stones of the characteristic wedge-like form, as may be seen from an extant fragment (*Corp. inscr. Att.* iv. 1. 2 no. 559 with figs.) first published by S. A. Koumanoudes, to whose brilliant article in the 'Εφ. 'Αρχ. 1885 pp. 215—218 figs. 1—3 I am indebted for the main idea of my restoration in fig. 935 (Koumanoudes fits his wedges on to an axle that is circular, not square, in section). Again, it seems likely that the κύρβεις—as indeed I conjectured in the *Class. Rev.* 1904 xviii. 86—copied the primitive idols of Zeus. Their shape, to judge from Apollodoros' words (*supra* p. 1094 n. o), was identical with that of Zeus Στορπᾶος, Zeus Πάσιος, Zeus Πατρῷος, etc. (*supra* i. 520 n. 2, ii. 815 fig. 781). If so, the implication is that the laws were the very voice of Zeus (cp. Gruppe *Gr. Myth. Rel.* pp. 426 n. 1, 1001 n. 5). There was a tradition that Solon had tried to express his laws in hexameter verse and had begun with a couplet invoking Zeus: πρῶτα μὲν εὐχώμεσθα Διῒ Κρονίδῃ βασιλῆϊ | θεσμοῖς τοῖσδε τύχην ἀγαθὴν καὶ κῦδος ὀπάσσαι (Plout. *v. Sol.* 3). The original form of his famous oath may have been πρὸς Διὸς ἱκεσίοιο καθαρσίου ἐξακέσαντος (cp. for the last word Pyth. *carm. aur.* 66) or the like. Analogous to the κύρβεις as inscribed obelisks were the Egyptian κύρβεις of the Colchians (Ap. Rhod. 4. 279 ff. with schol. *ad loc.*), not to mention the pillar of Zeus Τριφύλιος (*supra* i. 662). Cp. also the marble obelisk from Kition, the base of which bears a votive inscription for Esmun (*Corp. inscr. Sem.* i no. 44 pl. 8 fig. 44, Perrot—Chipiez *Hist. de l'Art* iv. 385 fig. 203, Ohnefalsch—Richter *Kypros* pp. 173 ff., 416 pl. 80, 5. Seleukos, a grammarian of Alexandreia, wrote a whole treatise τῶν Σόλωνος ἀξόνων (*Frag. hist. Gr.* iii. 500 Müller), and modern writers have devoted much attention to them, *e.g.* E. Caillemer in Daremberg—Saglio *Dict. Ant.* i. 589, G. Busolt *Griechische Geschichte* Gotha 1895 ii.[2] 290 ff., E. Szanto in Pauly—Wissowa *Real-Enc.* ii. 2636, Lübker *Reallex.*[8] pp. 153, 963 f., and the literature there cited. E. Beulé *Les monnaies d'Athènes* Paris 1858 p. 399 f. fig. would recognize Solon with one of his ἄξονες on a copper coin of Athens: but see K. Lange in the *Ath. Mitth.* 1881 vi. 68 f. fig., Imhoof-Blumer and P. Gardner *Num. Comm. Paus.* iii. 152 pl. ΕΕ, 16 f.).

Similarly at Thera in *s.* vi B.C. the same appellative occurs without the name of Zeus (*supra* i. 143 in three rock-cut inscriptions). Elsewhere name and title appear together : so at Kos in *s.* iv B.C. (A. Hauvette-Besnault and M. Dubois in the *Bull. Corr. Hell.* 1881 v. 224 no. 12 on a slab fixed in the pavement of an ancient chapel of S. John Διὸς 'Ικεσίου | Σιμωνιδᾶν=W. R. Paton—E. L. Hicks *The Inscriptions of Cos* Oxford 1891 p. 161 no. 149=Collitz—Bechtel *Gr. Dial.-Inschr.* iii. 1. 376 no. 3674=Michel *Recueil d'Inscr. gr.* no. 796=Dittenberger *Syll. inscr. Gr.*[3] no. 929) and at Delos in *s.* iii B.C.

and even as *Hikétas*, himself 'the Suppliant[1],'—a remarkable title dependent, 1 think[2], upon the very primitive notion[3] that a stranger suddenly
appearing in the midst of the community may well be a god on his travels[4].

(T. Homolle in the *Bull. Corr. Hell.* 1879 iii. 471 f. no. 4 on a square base of white
marble Διονύσιος Νίκωνος | Παλληνεὺς ἐπιμελητὴς | γενόμενος Δήλου | ὑπὲρ τοῦ δήμου τοῦ |
'Αθηναίων Διὶ 'Ικεσίωι). More doubtful is an inscription of *s.* ii B.C. from Netteia in
Rhodes (*Inscr. Gr. ins.* i no. 891, 2 on a slab of blackish marble [οἱ ἐπιμή]νιοι ἀεὶ τοὶ
αἱ[ρ]εθέ[ντες 'Ικε]σίωι φθόϊ[s] ἐγ λ- , where F. Hiller von Gaertringen *ad loc.* supplies Διὶ
and notes that φθόϊs = φθόϊας, 'cakes').

¹ Roehl *Inscr. Gr. ant.* Add. nov. no. 49a with fig. = my fig. 937 a rough calcareous

Fig. 937.

boundary-stone (0·35ᵐ long, 0·30ᵐ high,
0·10ᵐ—0·11ᵐ thick), found at Sparta and
preserved in the Museum at Teuthis (*Di-
mitzana*), bearing the retrograde inscrip-
tion Διοικέτα, | Διώλευθερ[ω] = Roberts
Gk. Epigr. i. 249 no. 244 = R. Meister
in Collitz—Bechtel *Gr. Dial.-Inschr.* iii.
2. 6 no. 4407. E. S. Roberts *ad loc.*
remarks: 'The change of the final σ of
Διὸs in l. 1 to the *spiritus asper* is remarkable; still more so the contraction
in Διώλ. of l. 2 after disappearance of
the *h* = σ. Stolz (*Wiener Stud.* VIII.
1886, p. 160), who summarily rejects
this explanation, suggests a genitive Δίω

on the analogy of o-stems, and compares Lat. *Iovos*, *Eph. ep.* I. 14 no. 21, *Iovo*, *Herm.*
XIX. 453. Elsewhere certainly final σ does not disappear in Laconian, even where the
next word begins with a vowel.' But R. Meister *ad loc.* is content to assume the change
of σ into *h*; and so is A. Thumb in K. Brugmann *Griechische Grammatik*⁴ München 1913
p. 171, citing Cypriote parallels.

² H. Roehl *loc. cit.* refers to Eustath. *in Od.* p. 1807, 9 f. καὶ ὁ ἱκετεύσας καὶ ὁ τὴν
ἱκετείαν δεξάμενος ἤτοι κατὰ τοὺς παλαιοὺς εἰπεῖν ἱκετοδόχος ἱκέται εἰσὶν ἀλλήλοις. For the
supposed reciprocal sense Eustathios cp. ξένος, προστρόπαιος, χρήστης.

G. Murray *The Rise of the Greek Epic*² Oxford 1911 p. 291 ('this Zeus of Aeschylus is
himself the suppliant; the prayer which you reject is his very prayer, and in turning from
your door the helpless or the outcast you have turned away the most high God. The
belief was immemorially old') comes much nearer the mark, though I cannot accept the
explanation which he adds in a footnote *ib.* p. 291 n. 1 ('Ζεὺς 'Αφίκτωρ...is a "projection"
of the rite of Supplication').

³ Frazer *Golden Bough*³: Spirits of Corn and Wild i. 216 ff., 252 f. (the story of
Lityerses compared with the harvest customs of Europe, after W. Mannhardt *Mythologische Forschungen* Strassburg 1884 p. 18 ff.).

⁴ This is definitely stated in *Od.* 17. 483 ff. 'Αντίνο', οὐ μὲν κάλ' ἔβαλες δύστηνον
ἀλήτην· | οὐλόμεν', εἰ δή πού τις ἐπουράνιος θεός ἐστι,— | καί τε θεοὶ ξείνοισιν ἐοικότες
ἀλλοδαποῖσι, | παντοῖοι τελέθοντες, ἐπιστρωφῶσι πόληας, | ἀνθρώπων ὕβριν τε καὶ εὐνομίην
ἐφορῶντες (cp. Hes. *o.d.* 121 ff.), and is implied in the history of Barnabas and Paul
(*supra* i. 193 n. 3. See too Acts 28. 1—6), the myths of Philemon and Baucis (Ov. *met.* 8.
616 ff., Lact. Plac. *narr. fab.* 8. 7—9), Pelargus or Pelasgus (*Class. Rev.* 1904 xviii. 81 f.),
Lykaon (*supra* i. 79 n. 6. There is a reminiscence of the Homeric passage in Nikolaos
Damask. *frag.* 43 (*Frag. hist. Gr.* iii. 378 Müller) ὅτι Λυκάων ὁ Πελασγοῦ υἱός, βασιλεὺς
'Αρκάδων, ἐφύλαττε τὰ τοῦ πατρὸς εἰσηγήματα ἐν δικαιοσύνῃ. ἀποστῆσαι <δὲ> βουλόμενος
καὶ αὐτὸς τῆς ἀδικίας τοὺς ἀρχομένους, ἔφη τὸν Δία ἑκάστοτε φοιτᾶν παρ' αὐτὸν ἀνδρὶ ξένῳ
μοιούμενον εἰς ἔποψιν τῶν δικαίων τε καὶ ἀδίκων = Souid. *s.v.* Λυκάων), and many others.

Zeus *Meilichios* 1097

Similarly the poets spoke of Zeus, not only as *hiketésios*[1], *hikésios*[2], and
It is reasonable to surmise that the possible divinity of the stranger even helped to establish the law of hospitality (other contributory causes in Schrader *Reallex*. p. 269 ff., Frazer *Golden Bough*[3]: Taboo p. 130, W. Wundt *Elements of Folk Psychology* trans. E. L. Schaub London 1916 p. 340 ff.). Ἱκέτης or ξένος—who could tell?—might turn out to be Zeus himself. 'Some have entertained angels unawares' (Heb. 13. 2).

At a later stage of religious development Zeus is conceived, not as the actual ἱκέτης or ξένος, but as his unseen attendant. Thus *e.g.* the Phaeacian Echeneos says to Alkinoos: ἀλλ᾽ ἄγε δὴ ξεῖνον μὲν ἐπὶ θρόνου ἀργυροήλου | εἴσον ἀναστήσας, σὺ δὲ κηρύκεσσι κέλευσον | οἶνον ἐπικρῆσαι, ἵνα καὶ Διὶ τερπικεραύνῳ | σπείσομεν, ὅς θ᾽ ἱκέτῃσιν ἅμ᾽ αἰδοίοισιν ὀπηδεῖ· | κ.τ.λ. (*Od.* 7. 162 ff. with the sequel in line 178 ff.), and Odysseus to Polyphemos: ἀλλ᾽ αἰδεῖο, φέριστε, θεούς· ἱκέται δέ τοί εἰμεν. | Ζεὺς δ᾽ ἐπιτιμήτωρ ἱκετάων τε ξείνων τε, | ξείνιος, ὃς ξείνοισιν ἅμ᾽ αἰδοίοισιν ὀπηδεῖ (*Od.* 9. 269 ff.). Cp. *Od.* 14. 158 f., a variant of *Od.* 19. 303 f.

Ultimately Zeus becomes Ἱκέσιος and Ξένιος (cp. Ap. Rhod. 2. 378 Ζηνὸς Εὐξείνοιο Γενηταίην ὑπὲρ ἄκρην with schol. *ad loc.* cited *supra* p. 617 n. 1), the god who protects suppliants and strangers in general.

[1] *Od.* 13. 213 f. Ζεύς σφεας τίσαιτο (C. G. Cobet cj. Ζεὺς δέ σφεας τίσαιθ᾽) ἱκετήσιος, ὅς τε καὶ ἄλλους | ἀνθρώπους ἐφορᾷ καὶ τίνυται ὅς τις ἁμάρτῃ with schol. *ad loc.* ἱκέσιος· ἱκετῶν ἐπόπτης and Eustath. *in Od.* p. 1739, 18 f. ἱκετήσιος δὲ Ζεὺς δοκεῖ πρωτότυπον εἶναι τοῦ ἱκέσιος (*id. ib.* p. 1576, 14), Tzetz. *alleg. Od.* 13. 46 ὁ Ζεὺς ὁ ἱκετήσιος, Hesych. *s.v.* ἱκετήσιος· ὁ ἐπὶ τῶν ἱκετῶν Ζεύς· ἢ ὁ τοὺς ἱκέτας ἐλεῶν.

[2] Aisch. *suppl.* 343 βαρύς γε μέντοι Ζηνὸς ἱκεσίου κότος, 616 f. ἱκεσίου Ζηνὸς κότον | μέγαν προφωνῶν κ.τ.λ., Soph. *Phil.* 484 πρὸς αὐτοῦ Ζηνὸς ἱκεσίου, Eur. *Hec.* 345 πέφευγας τὸν ἐμὸν ἱκέσιον Δία, Aristot. *de mundo* 7. 401 a 23 f. καθάρσιός τε καὶ παλαμναῖος καὶ ἱκέσιος καὶ μειλίχιος, ὥσπερ οἱ ποιηταὶ λέγουσι=Stob. *ecl.* 1. 1. 36 p. 45, 21 f. Wachsmuth, Ap. Rhod. 2. 215 ff. ἱκεσίου πρὸς Ζηνός, ὅτις ῥίγιστος ἀλιτροῖς | ἀνδράσι,... | λίσσομαι with schol. *ad loc.*, 2. 1131 ff. ἀλλ᾽ ἱκέτας ξείνους Διὸς εἵνεκεν αἰδέσσασθε | ξεινίου ἱκεσίου τε· Διὸς δ᾽ ἄμφω ἱκέται τε | καὶ ξεῖνοι· ὁ δέ που καὶ ἐπόψιος ἄμμι τέτυκται, 4. 358 f. πού τοι Διὸς ἱκεσίοιο | ὅρκια; 4. 700 ff. τῷ καὶ ὀπιζομένη Ζηνὸς θέμιν ἱκεσίοιο, | ὃς μέγα μὲν κοτέει, μέγα δ᾽ ἀνδροφόνοισιν ἀρήγει, | ῥέξε θυηπολίην with the whole context (Iason and Medeia, on reaching the hall of Kirke, sit in silence at her hearth as is the wont of suppliants. Medeia hides her face in both hands; and Iason fixes in the ground the sword with which he has slain Apsyrtos. Kirke understands, and performs the appropriate rites of atonement. She holds above their heads a young pig, slits its throat, and sprinkles their hands with its blood. Then she makes propitiation with drink-offerings, καθάρσιον ἀγκαλέουσα | Ζῆνα, παλαμναίων τιμήορον ἱκεσιάων (708 f.). Her attendants carry forth all defilement (cp. *Il.* 1. 314), while she, standing by the hearth, burns *pélanoi* and expiatory offerings without wine as she prays to the Erinyes and Zeus. Finally, she raises Iason and Medeia, and bids them sit on seats to question them), Cornut. *theol.* 11 f. p. 12, 4 ff. Lang (sequel to passage cited *supra* p. 1092 n. 8) διὰ τοῦτο γὰρ καὶ ἱκεσίου Διός εἰσι βωμοὶ καὶ τὰς Λιτὰς ὁ ποιητὴς ἔφη τοῦ Διὸς εἶναι θυγατέρας, κ.τ.λ., Dion Chrys. *or.* 1 p. 56 f. Reiske (of Zeus) πρὸς δὲ τούτοις Ἱκέσιός τε καὶ Φύξιος καὶ Ξένιος...Ἱκέσιος δὲ ὡς ἂν (Reiske suggests ὢν for ἂν) ἐπήκοός τε καὶ ἵλεως τοῖς δεομένοις, Φύξιος δὲ διὰ τὴν τῶν κακῶν ἀπόφευξιν (L. Dindorf restores ἀπόφυξιν), Ξένιος δὲ ὅτι καὶ τοῦτο ἀρχὴ φιλίας μηδὲ τῶν ξένων ἀμελεῖν μηδὲ ἀλλότριον ἡγεῖσθαι μηδένα ἄνθρωπον=*or.* 12 p. 413 Reiske (of Zeus) πρὸς δὲ αὐτοῖς Ἱκέσιός τε καὶ <Φύξιος καὶ> Ξένιος...Ἱκέσιος δὲ ὡς ἂν ἐπήκοός τε καὶ ἵλεως τοῖς δεομένοις, Φύξιος δὲ διὰ τὴν τῶν κακῶν ἀπόφυξιν, Ξένιος δὲ ὅτι δεῖ μηδὲ τῶν ξένων ἀμελεῖν μηδὲ ἀλλότριον ἡγεῖσθαι ἀνθρώπων μηδένα, Clem. Al. *protr.* 2. 37. 1 p. 27, 23 f. Stählin καλός γε ὁ Ζεὺς ὁ μαντικός, ὁ ξένιος, ὁ ἱκέσιος, ὁ μειλίχιος, ὁ πανομφαῖος, ὁ προστροπαῖος, Heliod. 2. 22 ὁ δὲ Κνήμων θαυμάσας, Ἀλλ᾽ ἢ Ξενίου Διός, ὡς ἔοικεν, εἰς αὐλὰς ἥκομεν, ὦ πάτερ, οὕτως ἀπροφάσιστος ἡ θεραπεία καὶ πολὺ τὸ εὐνοῦν τῆς γνώμης ἐμφαίνουσα. Οὐκ εἰς Διός, ἔφη, ἀλλ᾽ εἰς ἀνδρὸς Δία τὸν Ξένιον καὶ Ἱκέσιον ἀκριβοῦντος, Anth. Pal. 11. 351. 7 f. (Palladas) ἀλλά σε πρὸς πύκτου Πολυδεύκεος ἠδὲ καὶ αὐτοῦ | Κάστορος ἱκνοῦμαι καὶ Διὸς ἱκεσίου, Orph. *Arg.* 107 f. οὐ γὰρ

hiktaîos (?)[1], 'the god of suppliants,' but also as *hiktér*[2], and *aphíktor*[3], 'the suppliant.' Again, Zeus was known as *alástoros*[4] or *alástor*[5], 'he that brings a curse[6],' *Palamnaîos*, 'he of the Violent Hand[7],' *prostrópaios*, 'he of the

ἄτιμοι | ἱκεσίου Ζηνὸς κοῦραι Λιταί, Nonn. *Dion.* 18. 18 πρὸς Διὸς ἱκεσίοιο, τεοῦ, Διόνυσε, τοκῆος, Tryphiod. *exc. Il.* 278 πεφύλαξο Διὸς σέβας ἱκεσίοιο, Schöll—Studemund *anecd.* i. 265 (Διός) 49 ἱκεσίου, *ib.* i. 266 (Διός) 44 ἱκεσίου.

[1] Aisch. *suppl.* 385 μένει τοι Ζηνὸς ἱκταίου κότος. So U. von Wilamowitz-Moellendorff (1914) with cod. M. E. Fraenkel in the *Zeitschrift für vergleichende Sprachforschung* 1913 xlv. 168 n. 2 accepts Dindorf's cj. ἱκτίου 'das wohl eine Kompromissbildung zwischen ἱκέσιος und ἱκτήριος ist genau wie Lykophrons ἵκτης, ἵκτιδες eine solche zwischen ἱκέτης, -τις und ἱκτήρ; vgl. auch die umgekehrte Beeinflussung, die ἱκετηρία (im Gegensatz zu ἱκτήριος) durch ἱκεσία, ἱκετεία erfahren hat ([E. Fraenkel *Griechische Nomina agentis* Strassburg 1910] I, S. 52 ff. mit Anm. 2).'

[2] Aisch. *suppl.* 478 f. ὅμως δ' ἀνάγκη Ζηνὸς αἰδεῖσθαι κότον | ἱκτῆρος· ὕψιστος γὰρ ἐν βροτοῖς φόβος. W. Headlam renders 'Zeus Petitionary.'

[3] Aisch. *suppl.* 1 f. Ζεὺς μὲν ἀφίκτωρ ἐπίδοι προφρόνως | στόλον ἡμέτερον. 'Zeus Petitionary' (W. Headlam).

[4] Cramer *anecd. Oxon.* i. 62, 10 ff. παρὰ δὲ τὸ ἀλαστῶ ῥῆμα, ἀλάστωρ ὁ Ζεύς, ἐπὶ τῶν χαλεπῶν τι πρασσόντων· παρηκτικὴ δὲ ἡ εὐθεῖα παρὰ τὴν ἀλάστορος γενικήν· Αἰσχύλος Ἰξίονι (*frag.* 92 Nauck²) "πρευμενὴς ἀλάστορος," καὶ Φερεκύδης (*frag.* 114ª (*Frag. hist. Gr.* i. 99 Müller)) "ὁ Ζεὺς δὲ Ἱκέσιος καὶ ἀλάστορος καλεῖται." With πρευμενὴς ἀλάστορος A. Nauck *ad loc.* cp. Aisch. *Eum.* 236 (Orestes to Athena) δέχου δὲ πρευμενῶς ἀλάστορα | κ.τ.λ. and Bekker *anecd.* i. 382, 29 f. ἀλάστορος· ἀντὶ τοῦ ἀλάστορα, ἀπὸ εὐθείας τῆς ὁ ἀλάστορος, Αἰσχύλος (*frag.* 294 Nauck²) "μέγαν ἀλάστορον" εἶπεν. Farnell *Cults of Gk. States* i. 67 reasonably supposes that Pherekydes spoke of Zeus ἱκέσιος καὶ ἀλάστωρ (*sic*) in relation to Ixion (*supra* i. 198 n. 3).

[5] Orph. *h. daem.* 73. 2 ff. cited *infra* Append. M *fin.*, cp. *supra* i. 504 n. 2. The title provoked much learned discussion: Cornut. *theol.* 9 p. 10, 20 ff. Lang λέγεται δ' (*sc.* ὁ Ζεύς) ὑπό τινων καὶ ἀλάστωρ καὶ παλαμναῖος τῷ τοὺς ἀλάστορας καὶ παλαμναίους κολάζειν, τῶν μὲν ὠνομασμένων ἀπὸ τοῦ τοιαῦτα ἁμαρτάνειν ἐφ' οἷς ἔστιν ἀλαστῆσαι καὶ στενάξαι, τῶν δὲ ἀπὸ τοῦ ταῖς παλάμαις μιάσματα ἀνέκθυτα (ἀνέκπλυτα codd. N. B. G.) ἀποτελεῖν = Eudok. *viol.* 414⁸, Hesych. *s.v.* ἀλάστωρ· πικρὸς δαίμων. Ζεύς, *et. Gud.* p. 32, 35 ff. ἀλάστωρ· ὁ Ζεὺς ὁ ἐποπτεύων τοὺς ἀλαστὰ καὶ χαλεπὰ ποιοῦντας. ἢ ὁ ἀσεβής, ἢ ὁ κακοποιός. οὕτως Ἡρωδιανός (περὶ καθολικῆς προσῳδίας 2 = i. 49, 13 f. Lentz reading ὑποπτεύων for ἐποπτεύων· cp. ii. 937, 27 n. Lentz), *et. mag.* p. 57, 25 ff. ἀλάστωρ· ὁ ἁμαρτωλός, ἢ ὁ φονεύς, ἢ ὁ ἔφορος τοὺς φόνους Ζεύς...ἐπὶ δὲ τοῦ Διός, ὅτι ἀλάστωρ Ζεύς, ἀπὸ τοῦ τοῖς τὰ ἀλαστὰ πάσχουσιν ἐπαμύνειν· ἢ ὁ τὰ ἀλαστὰ (τουτέστι τὰ χαλεπὰ) τηρῶν, Eustath. *in Il.* p. 474, 22 f. παρὰ δὲ τοῖς ὕστερον καὶ Ζεὺς ἀλάστωρ, ὃν ἐλάνθανεν οὐδέν, ἢ ὁ τοῖς ἀλαστὰ πάσχουσιν ἐπαμύνων κατὰ τοὺς παλαιούς, *ib.* p. 763, 36 f. ὅθεν καὶ Ζεὺς ἀλάστωρ καὶ φθόνος καὶ δαίμων ἀλάστωρ ἐπενοήθη λέγεσθαι = Favorin. *lex.* p. 1692, 43 f. ὅθεν καὶ Ζεὺς ἀλάστωρ καὶ ὁ φθονερὸς δαίμων ἐπενοήθη λέγεσθαι.

[6] The derivation of the word is doubtful (cjj. in A. Vaniček *Griechisch-lateinisches etymologisches Wörterbuch* Leipzig 1877 i. 788 f., L. Meyer *Handb. d. gr. Etym.* i. 293 f., Prellwitz *Etym. Wörterb. d. Gr. Spr.*² p. 23, Boisacq *Dict. étym. de la Langue Gr.* p. 41), but its meaning is sufficiently clear (see K. Wernicke in Pauly—Wissowa *Real-Enc.* i. 1292 f.).

[7] Aristot. *de mundo* 7. 401a 23 (cited *supra* p. 1097 n. 2) = Stob. *ecl.* 1. 1. 36 p. 45, 21 Wachsmuth, Cornut. *theol.* 9 p. 10, 20 ff. Lang (cited *supra* p. 1098 n. 5), Orion in F. W. Sturz's ed. of *et. Gud.* p. 628, 17 ff. παλαμναῖος ὁ τοὺς αὐτοχειρὶ φονεύσαντας τιμωρούμενος καὶ Ζεὺς Παλαμναῖος ἐν Χαλκίδι, *et. Gud.* p. 448, 28 ff. παλαμναῖος· σημαίνει δὲ δύο, ὁ τοὺς αὐτοχειριφονεύσαντας τιμωρούμενος καὶ ὁ ἐπί τινι βιάσματι κατεχόμενος, *ib.* p. 449, 21 f. καὶ Ζεὺς δὲ Παλαμναῖος λέγεται ἐν Χαλκίδι, *et. mag.* p. 647, 43 f. παλαμναῖος· ὁ τοὺς αὐτοχειρὶ φονεύσαντας τιμωρούμενος, Ζεὺς Παλαμναῖος. λέγεται καὶ ἐν Χαλκίδι Παλαμναῖος (cod. D. omits the last word), Souid. *s.v.* παλαμναῖος = Phot. *lex. s.v.* παλαμ-

appeal[1],'—titles which applied primarily to the sinner, secondarily to the god concerned with his sin. Less ambiguous and further removed from primitive conceptions are the cult-names *Litaîos*, 'god of Prayers[2],' and *Kathársios*, 'god

ναῖος· φονεὺς ἢ μιαρός· παλαμναῖοι γὰρ λέγονται οἱ διὰ χειρὸς ἀνδροφονοῦντες· παρὰ τὴν παλάμην· καὶ Ζεὺς Παλαμναῖος, ὁ τοὺς τοιούτους τιμωρούμενος· καὶ προστροπαῖος ὁ προστρέπων τὸ ἄγος αὐτοῖς, Favorin. *lex.* p. 221, 54 καὶ Ζεὺς δέ φασι Παλαμναῖος, ὁ τοὺς φονεῖς καταρρίπτων, Schöll—Studemund *anecd.* i. 265 (Διός) 87 παλαμναῖον, *ib.* i. 266 (Διός) 69 παλαμναίου. Cp. Ap. Rhod. 4. 708 f. (cited *supra* p. 1097 n. 2) and Clem. Al. *protr.* 2. 39. 2 p. 29, 6 f. Stählin οὐχὶ μέντοι Ζεὺς Φαλακρὸς ἐν "Αργει, Τιμωρὸς (J. Bernays cj. σινάμωρος) δὲ ἄλλος ἐν Κύπρῳ τετίμησθον;

In a church near Gomphoi (*Musáki*) Leake found a plain quadrangular altar inscribed in large deeply-cut letters ΖΗΝΙ | ΠΑΛΑΜΝΙѠ (W. M. Leake *Travels in Northern Greece* London 1835 iv. 523 f. pl. 44 no. 220, Lebas—Foucart *Peloponnèse* ii no. 1194, *Inscr. Gr. sept.* ii no. 291).

[1] Clem. Al. *protr.* 2. 37. 1 p. 27, 23 f. Stählin (cited *supra* p. 1097 n. 2), Souid. *s.v.* παλαμναῖος = Phot. *lex. s.v.* παλαμναῖος (cited *supra* p. 1098 n. 7), Eustath. *in Od.* p. 1807, 11 f. προστρόπαιός τε γὰρ Ζεὺς ἐν ῥητορικῷ λεξικῷ (E. Schwabe *Aelii Dionysii et Pausaniae Atticistarum fragmenta* Lipsiae 1890 p. 254, 7 ff.: see further Sir J. E. Sandys *A History of Classical Scholarship*[2] Cambridge 1906 i. 323 and L. Cohn in Pauly—Wissowa *Real-Enc.* vi. 1478 ff.), ᾧ ἄν τις, φασί, προστρέποιτο δεόμενος. καὶ προστρόπαιος ὁ ἱκέτης, ὁ πρός τινα δηλαδὴ δεητικῶς τρεπόμενος (*supra* p. 1096 n. 2). It follows that Zeus, who in one respect was προστρόπαιος, in another was ἀποτρόπαιος: cp. Bekker *anecd.* i. 427, 5 f. ἀποδιοπομπεῖσθαι· ἀποπέμπεσθαι πρὸς τὸν προστρόπαιον Δία καὶ οἰονεὶ καθαίρεσθαι ἢ ἱλάσκεσθαι, schol. Plat. *Crat.* 396 E ἀποδιοπομπεῖσθαί φασι τὸ ἀποτρέπεσθαι τὸν προστρόπαιον Δία καὶ οἰονεὶ καθαίρεσθαι τὰ δεινά, schol. Plat. *legg.* 854 B ἀποδιοπομπήσεις· τὰς ἀποστροφὰς τὰς γιγνομένας ὑπὸ τοῦ ἀποτροπαίου Διός, διὰ τὸ καθαίρεσθαι τὰ δεινά· ἢ τὰς ἀπομπομπὰς τὰς πρὸς τὸν προστρόπαιον Δία καὶ οἰονεὶ καθάρσεις καὶ Διαλμούς, schol. Aischin. *de fals. leg.* 323 προστρόπαιός ἐστιν ὁ εἰς ἑαυτὸν ἐπισπώμενος τὰ κακά, ὅπερ ἐστὶν ἐναντίον τοῦ (so H. Sauppe for τῷ cod. f.) ἀποτρόπαιος, τοῦ ἀποτρέποντος τὰ κακά. διὸ καὶ Διὶ ἀποτροπαίῳ θύομεν, οὐκέτι μέντοι καὶ προστροπαίῳ (on which see O. Höfer in Roscher *Lex. Myth.* iii. 3154).

The essence of a προστροπή was that the supplicator and the supplicated should both be turned towards each other and thus brought into such immediate connexion that the thing asked must needs be granted. If possible, direct contact was established by the clasping of knees, chin, etc. (C. Sittl *Die Gebärden der Griechen und Römer* Leipzig 1890 pp. 163 ff., 282 f.). Failing that, *quasi*-contact was made by means of outstretched arms, etc. (*id. ib.* pp. 186 ff., 283, 296). But in any case the two parties were face to face.

[2] Coppers of Nikaia in Bithynia, struck by Nero (M. P. Lambros in the *Bull. Corr. Hell.* 1878 ii. 508 f. pl. 24, 1 = my fig. 938 ΔΙΟΣ | ΛΙΤΑΙΟΥ) and Antoninus Pius (*supra* i. 37 n. 1 ΔΙ|ΟC ‖ ΛΙΤΑΙΟΥ), show the altar of Zeus Λιταῖος (Head *Hist. num.*[2] p. 517). O. Höfer in Roscher *Lex. Myth.* ii. 2064 explains the title as 'Father of the Litai' with reference to the remarkable passage in *Il.* 9. 502 ff. καὶ γάρ τε Λιταί εἰσι, Διὸς κοῦραι μεγάλοιο, | χωλαί τε ῥυσαί τε παραβλῶπές τ' ὀφθαλμώ, | αἵ ῥά τε καὶ μετόπισθ' Ἄτης ἀλέγουσι κιοῦσαι. | ἡ δ' Ἄτη σθεναρή τε καὶ ἀρτίπος, οὕνεκα πάσας | πολλὸν ὑπεκπροθέει, φθάνει δέ τε πᾶσαν ἐπ' αἶαν | βλάπτουσ' ἀν-

Fig. 938.

θρώπους· αἱ δ' ἐξακέονται ὀπίσσω. | ὃς μέν τ' αἰδέσεται κούρας Διὸς ἆσσον ἰούσας, | τὸν δὲ μέγ' ὤνησαν καί τ' ἔκλυον εὐχομένοιο· | ὃς δέ κ' ἀνήνηται καί τε στερεῶς ἀποείπῃ, | λίσσονται δ' ἄρα ταί γε Δία Κρονίωνα κιοῦσαι | τῷ Ἄτην ἅμ' ἕπεσθαι, ἵνα βλαφθεὶς ἀποτίσῃ (see for variants A. Ludwich *ad loc.*, for imitations Quint. Smyrn. 10. 300 ff. Λιταῖς δ' ἀποθύμια ῥέξεις, | αἵ ῥα καὶ αὐταὶ Ζηνὸς ἐριγδούποιο θύγατρες | εἰσί, κ.τ.λ., Orph.

of Purification[1].' The exact relationship of all these appellatives and the growth of the religious beliefs implied by them are still far from clear. Perhaps we shall come within measurable distance of the truth by assuming that development proceeded on some such lines as follow:

Arg. 107 f. cited *supra* p. 1097 n. 2, and for a parody *Anth. Pal.* 11. 361. 1 ff. (Automedon)). How Zeus could have begotten such creatures, 'halt wrinkled squinting,' was a puzzle (Bion Borysthenites *frag.* 44 Mullach *ap.* Clem. Al. *protr.* 4. 56. 1 p. 43, 29 ff. Stählin, Herakleitos *quaestt. Hom.* 37, Porph. *quaest. Il.* 97, 21, Eustath. *in Il.* p. 768, 28 ff.). But symbolism proved a ready solvent (*vide* the comments of Herakleitos *quaestt. Hom.* 37, schol. *Il.* 9. 502 f., Porph. *quaestt. Il.* 97, 21, Eustath. *in Il.* p. 767, 60 ff., Cornut. *theol.* 12 p. 12, 5 ff. Lang, Eudok. *viol.* 606, Cramer *anecd. Paris.* iii. 239, 32 ff., cp. Hesych. *s.v.* Αἶται (H. Stephanus restored Λιταί)). Dr W. Leaf *A Companion to the Iliad* London 1892 p. 185 can still write: 'The epithets applied to them indicate the attitude of the penitent: halting, because he comes with hesitating steps; wrinkled, because his face betrays the inward struggle; and of eyes askance, because he dares not look in the face the man he has wronged' (cp. the same scholar's note on *Il.* 9. 503, repeated in his joint ed. with the Rev. M. A. Bayfield). I am sorry to dissent from Dr Leaf, to whom all lovers of Homer are so deeply indebted. But to me it seems far more probable that the Litai were physically deformed and loathsome like the Erinyes, to whom they were akin. I suppose them to have been essentially the prayers of the injured man taking shape as vengeful sprites. In the last analysis they were simply the soul of the victim issuing from his mouth in visible form, maimed because he was maimed, and clamouring for vengeance. The personification is not unlike that implied in Gen. 4. 10 'the voice of thy brother's blood crieth unto me from the ground' (with Dr J. Skinner's note *ad loc.*). For the soul as Erinys see Harrison *Proleg. Gk. Rel.*[2] p. 213 ff. No doubt all this belongs to the dim background of Greek religion and has already been half-forgotten by the Homeric writer, who conceives the Litai, not as the wrathful prayers of the injured man, but as the penitential prayers of his injurer. The apologue thus acquires a new moral value. It is, however, largely couched in language appropriate to the earlier conception (Ate, swift of foot, drives many a man to do mad deeds. Then come the Litai and effect the cure. If a man respects them, they help him and hear his prayer. If a man flouts them, they go and pray to Zeus that Ate may fall upon such an one, drive him mad, and make him pay the price), and in particular its description of the Litai as misshapen and hideous is an abiding relic of its former significance. The passage is, in fact, an αἶνος (like *Il.* 19. 91 ff. or the oracle in Hdt. 6. 86) misinterpreted and misapplied by a later moralist. But, however understood, it contributes little or nothing to an explanation of Zeus Λιταῖος. The altar at Nikaia was surely voted to him as 'Hearer of Prayers' for the restored health of the emperor or for some other benefit vouchsafed to a grateful public.

[1] Zeus was worshipped as Καθάρσιος at Athens (Poll. 8. 142 (cp. 1. 24) cited *supra* p. 1093 n. 1) and at Olympia (Paus. 5. 14. 8 πρὸς αὐτῷ δέ ἐστιν Ἀγνώστων θεῶν βωμός, καὶ μετὰ τοῦτον Καθαρσίου Διὸς καὶ Νίκης, καὶ αὖθις Διὸς ἐπωνυμίαν Χθονίου. E. Curtius *Die Altäre von Olympia* (*Abh. d. berl. Akad. 1881* Phil.-hist. Classe) Berlin 1882 p. 39 no. 21 rightly assumes that Zeus Καθάρσιος and Nike had here a common altar. So, with some hesitation, does W. Dörpfeld in *Olympia* i. 83 no. 18. C. Maurer *De aris Graecorum pluribus deis in commune positis* Darmstadii 1885 p. 17 adopts the same view. But K. Wernicke 'Olympische Beiträge i' in the *Jahrb. d. kais. deutsch. arch. Inst.* 1894 ix. 96 no. 18 f. thinks otherwise). For literary allusions see Aristot. *de mundo* 7. 401 a 23 (cited *supra* p. 1097 n. 2) = Stob. *ecl.* 1. 1. 36 p. 45, 21 Wachsmuth, Ap. Rhod. 4. 708 f. (cited *supra* p. 1097 n. 2), Plout. *de carn. esu* 2. 1 ὦ Ζεῦ καθάρσιε, Orph. *h. Zeus* 15. 8 f. σεισίχθων, αὐξητά, καθάρσιε, παντοτινάκτα, | ἀστράπιε (so G. Hermann for ἀστραπαῖε), βρονταῖε, κεραύνιε, φυτάλιε Ζεῦ.

MAN-SLAYER.

(1) The bloodguilty man, appearing suddenly as a suppliant stranger, is deemed a god (Zeus Ἱκέτας, ἱκτήρ, ἀφίκτωρ, ἀλάστωρ, κ.τ.λ.)[1].

(2) The suppliant or stranger is not himself mistaken for a god, but is thought to have a divine escort (Zeus ὅς θ᾽ ἱκέτῃσιν ἅμ᾽ αἰδοίοισιν ὀπηδεῖ, Zeus ὃς ξείνοισιν ἅμ᾽ αἰδοίοισιν ὀπηδεῖ)[2].

(3) Suppliants and strangers in general are supposed to be *protégés* of the god (Zeus Ἱκέσιος, ἱκετήσιος, ἱκταῖος (?), Zeus Ξένιος)[3].

VICTIM.

(1) The soul (κήρ) of the murdered man becomes a wrathful spirit (ἐρινύς). His curses (ἀραί), prayers (λιταί), and penalties (ποιναί) all pursue the guilty.

(2) Hence arises the whole tribe of avenging deities (Κῆρες, Ἐρινύες, Ἀραί, Ἀράντιδες[4], Λιταί[5], Ποιναί, κ.τ.λ.).

(3) With the progress of religion deities of this low type are subordinated to a high god[6], especially to Zeus[7] (cp. Zeus Τιμωρός[8]).

The protective and the punitive powers of Zeus are fused
(Zeus Ἱκέσιος, Παλαμναῖος, προστρόπαιος).

---

[1] *Supra* pp. 1096, 1098.   [2] *Supra* p. 1097 n. 0.

[3] *Supra* pp. 1093, 1097, 1097 n. 0, 1097 n. 2.

A marble statue of Zeus Ξένιος by Papylos, a pupil of Praxiteles, was owned by C. Asinius Pollio (Plin. *nat. hist.* 36. 34 Iuppiter hospitalis Papyli (*pamphili* Gelenius),

Fig. 939.

Praxitelis (K. L. von Urlichs cj. *Pasitelis*) discipuli). At Sparta—the former home of ξενηλασία—Zeus Ξένιος was grouped with Athena Ξενία (Paus. 3. 11. 11 with H. Hitzig

[4-8 For notes 4, 5, 6, 7, and 8, see page 1102.]

Zeus *Meilíchios* as an angry god readily appeased by the man-slayer might conveniently be ranged under this joint-category, his title being interpreted as 'the Kindly One.'

and H. Blümner *ad loc.* Wide *Lakon. Kulte* p. 9 aptly cites Philostr. *v. Apoll.* 4. 31 p. 149 Kayser περιστάντες δὲ αὐτὸν οἱ Λακεδαιμόνιοι ξένον τε παρὰ τῷ Διὶ ἐποιοῦντο κ.τ.λ.). A broken relief in the Terme Museum (fig. 939) shows Zeus Ξένιος as a traveller sitting with a rumpled *himátion* over his knees and a knotted stick in his left hand, while he extends his right in welcome to a draped figure before him and offers a seat on his own eagle-decked couch (Matz—Duhn *Ant. Bildw. in Rom* iii. 146 f. no. 3772, P. Arndt *La Glyptothèque Ny-Carlsberg* Munich 1896 p. 64 fig. 34, Reinach *Rép. Reliefs* iii. 330 no. 2, R. Paribeni *Le Terme di Diocleziano e Il Museo Nazionale Romano*[4] Roma 1922 p. 217 no. 546). The lower border of the relief bears an archaising inscription, which G. Kaibel in *Inscr. Gr. Sic. It.* no. 990 transcribes [ὁ δεῖνα ...]ѵους καθ᾽ ὕπνον ἀνέθηκα Διεὶ Ξενίωι ... (facsimile in W. Helbig *Führer durch die öffentlichen Sammlungen klassischer Altertümer in Rom*[3] Leipzig 1913 ii. 173 ff. no 1405 fig. 38).

[4] Hesych. Ἀράντισιν (Musurus cj. ἀραντίσιν)· Ἐρινύσι. Μακεδόνες. See O. Crusius in Roscher *Lex. Myth.* i. 470, ii. 1165, K. Tümpel in Pauly—Wissowa *Real-Enc.* ii. 379, O. Hoffmann *Die Makedonen, ihre Sprache und ihr Volkstum* Göttingen 1906 p. 95 f.

[5] *Supra* p. 1099 n. 2.

[6] A. Rapp in Roscher *Lex. Myth.* i. 1328.

[7] This can be best made out in the case of the Erinyes. The following sequence of extracts attests their increasing subordination to Zeus: *Il.* 19. 86 ff. ἐγὼ δ᾽ οὐκ αἴτιός εἰμι, | ἀλλὰ Ζεὺς καὶ Μοῖρα καὶ ἠεροφοῖτις Ἐρινύς, | οἵ τέ μοι εἰν ἀγορῇ φρεσὶν ἔμβαλον ἄγριον ἄτην | κ.τ.λ. (see further E. Hedén *Homerische Götterstudien* Uppsala 1912 p. 134 f.), Aisch. *Ag.* 55 ff. ὕπατος δ᾽ ἀΐων ἤ τις Ἀπόλλων | ἢ Πὰν ἢ Ζεὺς... | ὑστερόποινον | πέμπει παραβᾶσιν Ἐρινύν, 744 ff. παρακλίνασ᾽ ἐπέκρανεν | δὲ γάμου πικρὰς τελευτάς, | δύσεδρος καὶ δυσόμιλος | συμένα Πριαμίδαισιν, | πομπᾷ Διὸς ξενίου | νυμφόκλαυτος Ἐρινύς (see W. Kausche 'Mythologumena Aeschylea' in the *Dissertationes philologicae Halenses* Halis Saxonum 1888 ix. 182 f.), Verg. *Aen.* 12. 849 ff. hae (*sc.* the three Furies) Iovis ad solium saevique in limine regis | apparent, acuuntque metum mortalibus aegris, | si quando letum horrificum morbosque deum rex | molitur, meritas aut bello territat urbes. | harum unam celerem demisit ab aethere summo | Iupiter, etc., Val. Flacc. 4. 74 f. gravis orantem procul arcet Erinys, | respiciens celsi legem Iovis.

[8] *Supra* p. 1099 n. o. Gruppe *Gr. Myth. Rel.* p. 1116 n. 9 cites as a doubtful analogue Hesych. Ζητήρ· Ζεὺ(ς) ἐν Κύπρῳ=Favorin. *lex.* p. 828, 36 f. F. Guyet in J. Alberti's note on Hesych. *loc. cit.* says: 'An Ζητήρ a ζάω, unde Ζὰν, Ζῆν, & Ζεὺς, a ζέω.' This derivation would have satisfied the Greeks themselves (*supra* i. 11 n. 5, 31 n. 3), and in Kypros a Zeus Ζητήρ might have been regarded as a Grecised equivalent of the Semitic θεὸς ζῶν (W. W. Baudissin *Adonis und Esmun* Leipzig 1911 pp. 450—510 'Jahwe der lebendige Gott'). But it is far more probable that Ζητήρ means 'Avenger' and is related to ζη-μία, ζη-τρός, κ.τ.λ. (on which see A. Vaniček *Griechisch-lateinisches etymologisches Wörterbuch* Leipzig 1877 i. 756, Prellwitz *Etym. Wörterb. d. Gr. Spr.*[2] p. 168, Boisacq *Dict. étym. de la Langue Gr.* p. 309). *Supra* p. 444 n. 7.

His Roman equivalent was Iupiter *Ultor*. Dessau *Inscr. Lat. sel.* no. 9239 (a dedication found at Clunia in Spain) Iovi Aug. | Ultori sacrum | L. Valerius Paternus | mil. leg. x Gem. | optio 7 Censoris exs | voto perhaps has reference to the death of Nero. Pertinax at the last besought Iupiter *Ultor* to avenge his assassination (Iul. Capit. *v. Pert.* 11. 10). Domitian, Septimius Severus, Alexander Severus, Pupienus, and Gallienus issued coins with the legend IOVI VLTORI (Rasche *Lex. Num.* iv. 902 ff., Suppl. iii. 158 f., Stevenson—Smith—Madden *Dict. Rom. Coins* p. 486 fig.). I figure a 'first brass' of Alexander Severus in my collection (fig. 940) and a medallion struck in two bronzes by the same emperor, 224 A.D. (F. Gnecchi in the *Rivista italiana di numismatica* 1888 i. 286 no. 12 pl. 8, 7 (=my fig. 941) *rev.*: JOVI VLTORI P·M·TR·P·III· and COSPP· Hexastyle temple with triumphal chariot and statues as *akrotéria*; statuary

Very different is the explanation propounded by Monsieur S. Reinach in an able and persuasive paper already noticed[1]. The altar of Zeus *Meilíchios*, at which the Phytalidai purified Theseus[2], was not far from the spot called *Hierà Syké*, the 'Sacred Fig-tree,' where Demeter first revealed to Phytalos the fruit of the fig[3]. It is, therefore, tempting to surmise that Theseus was purified 'avec du suc des figuiers sacrés (?)[4]' and that *Meilíchios* meant originally the 'god of Figs' (*meilicha*)[5]. Whether we accept Monsieur Reinach's further contention that the word *sykophántes* meant the hierophant of this fig-cult[6], or not, we must admit that the contiguity of a place named the 'Sacred Fig-tree' affords strong support to his derivation of *Meilíchios*. Moreover, Zeus *Meilíchios* was, according to the myth, a purificatory power, and another purifying Zeus bore the title *Sykásios*, which presumably denotes the 'god of Fig-gathering' (*sykázein*)[7]. The case for a local fig-cult might indeed be made even stronger. When Plouton carried off Kore, he was said to have descended into the earth beside the Eleusinian Kephisos at a point known as *Erineós*, the 'Wild Fig-tree[8].' Again, Sir James Frazer thinks that the site of the ancient altar dedicated

also in pediment. Within the temple sits Iupiter *Ultor* with thunderbolt and sceptre.

Fig. 940.

Fig. 941.

Round the temple is a large *porticus* with eight arches a side, and three arched entrances surmounted by statues).

[1] *Supra* p. 291 n. 2.   [2] *Supra* p. 1091 f.

[3] *Supra* p. 1092 n. 6. Cp. Plout. *symp.* 7. 4. 4, Athen. 74 D, Philostr. *v. soph.* 2. 20, Hesych. *s.v.* ἱερά, Phot. *lex. s.v.* ἱερὰ συκῆ, et. *mag.* p. 469, 17, Eustath. *in Od.* p. 1964, 12 f.

[4] On figs as a means of purification see Boetticher *Baumkultus* p. 437 f., J. Töpffer *Attische Genealogie* Berlin 1889 pp. 249 f., 252, Gruppe *Gr. Myth. Rel.* p. 910, F. Olck in Pauly—Wissowa *Real-Enc.* vi. 2148 f.

[5] *Supra* p. 1092.   [6] *Supra* p. 291 n. 2.

[7] Eustath. *in Od.* p. 1572, 58 f. λέγεται δὲ καὶ Συκάσιος Ζεὺς παρὰ τοῖς παλαιοῖς, ὁ Καθάρσιος. τῇ γὰρ συκῇ ἐχρῶντο φασὶν ἐν καθαρμοῖς, Hesych. Διὶ Συκασίῳ (so Musurus for διὸκασίῳ cod.)· παραπεποίηται παρὰ τὸ συκοφαντεῖν. From these two passages it may be inferred that there was a cult of Zeus Συκάσιος with cathartic rites, and that some comedian had used the phrase Διὶ Συκασίῳ with a sly reference to συκάζειν in the sense of συκοφαντεῖν or worse (Stephanus *Thes. Gr. Ling.* vii. 1014 A).

[8] Paus. 1. 38. 5, cp. Plat. *Theaet.* 143 B.

When Zeus was pursuing a Titan named Sykeas or Sykeus, Ge rescued her son by sending up a fig-tree to shelter him: the scene was laid at Sykea in Kilikia (Athen. 78 A—B περὶ δὲ τῆς προσηγορίας τῶν σύκων λέγων Τρύφων ἐν δευτέρῳ φυτῶν ἱστορίας Δωριωνά φησιν ἐν Γεωργικῷ ἱστορεῖν Συκέαν, ἕνα τινὰ τῶν Τιτάνων, διωκόμενον ὑπὸ Διὸς τὴν μητέρα Γῆν ὑποδέξασθαι καὶ ἀνεῖναι τὸ φυτὸν εἰς διατριβὴν τῷ παιδί, ἀφ' οὗ καὶ Συκέαν πόλιν εἶναι ἐν Κιλικίᾳ, Steph. Byz. *s.v.* Συκαῖ, Eustath. *in Od.* p. 1764, 13 ff.). Kreuzer in

to Zeus *Meilíchios* may now be covered by the church of Saint Sabas[1]. If so[2], is it a mere coincidence that this Greek martyr, whose festival falls on the first of May, was said to have been hung by his hands upon a fig-tree[3]?

There is, it would seem, much to be said in favour of both these views—that which regards Zeus *Meilíchios* as a god 'Kindly' towards the fugitive man-slayer and that which takes him to have been originally a 'god of Figs.' Nevertheless I find myself unable to adopt either opinion; for both alike are based on the circumstances of one particular cult-centre without regard to the other localities in which Zeus *Meilíchios* is known to have been worshipped. Our survey must be wider before we can safely venture on an interpretation of the disputed appellative.

(3) Zeus *Meilíchios* on the Attic coast.

Between the harbours of Zea and Mounichia the Attic coastline shows various groups of rock-cut niches[4]. At one point[5], four hundred metres in a north-westerly direction from the island of *Stalida*, the foothill displays a grotto and beside it a recess, originally lined with red stucco and still framed by pilasters and an architrave with palmettes above it. The decoration appears to date from the fourth century B.C. Some ninety metres further towards the west other niches of different shapes and sizes are to be seen carved in an old quarry-face[6]. To judge from votive reliefs found in the vicinity, the whole site was once sacred to Zeus *Meilíchios* and to a kindred deity Zeus *Phílios*[7]. Agathe Tyche, regarded

Roscher *Lex. Myth.* iv. 1617 connects this myth with the belief that the fig-tree was lightning-proof (Plout. *symp.* 4. 2. 1, 5. 9, Lyd. *de mens.* 3. 52 p. 49, 22 Bekker = *ib.* 4. 96 p. 111, 3 f. Bekker = p. 181, 18 f. Wünsch, 4. 4 p. 69, 1 Wünsch, *de ostent.* 45 p. 98, 15 ff. Wachsmuth, Theophanes Nonnos *epitome de curatione morborum* 259, Geopon. 11. 2. 7, cp. Plin. *nat. hist.* 15. 77: see Rohde *Psyche*[3] ii. 406 f., Gruppe *Gr. Myth. Rel.* p. 785 n. 6, F. Olck in Pauly—Wissowa *Real-Enc.* vi. 2145, and especially T. H. Martin *La foudre l'électricité et le magnétisme chez les anciens* Paris 1866 p. 194 f.).

[1] Frazer *Pausanias* ii. 493.

[2] F. Lenormant *Monographie de la Voie Sacrée Éleusinienne* Paris 1864 p. 312 accepts the view of F. C. H. Kruse *Hellas* Leipzig 1826 ii. 1. 173 that the site of the altar is marked by the little church of St Blasios (Sir W. Gell *The Itinerary of Greece* London 1819 p. 31).

[3] *Acta Sanctorum* edd. Bolland. Maii i. 46 (De Sancto Saba, martyre apud Græcos.) *Antiqua MSS. Menæa, quæ Divione apud Petrum Franciscum Societatis Iesu asservari reperimus anno MDCLXII, referunt hisce Kalendis Maji* S. Sabam, in fico digitis suis appensum, & sic gloriosa vita functum, *&* addunt hoc distichon.
"Ηνεγκε καρπὸν πρωϊμένης συκῆς   [*lege* "Ηνεγκε καρπὸν πρωίμης συκῆς κλάδος
Κλάδος τὸν χειροδεσμοῖς ἐκκρεμαμένον   Τὸν χειροδέσμοις ἐκκρεμαμένον (*sic*) Σάβαν.]
Σάβαν.
Attulit fructum præmaturæ ficus
Ramus, suspensum è digitis vinctis Saban.
     M. and W. Drake *Saints and their Emblems* London 1916 p. 113 confuse this St Sabas with St Sabas the Gothic martyr (April 12), who suffered under Athanaricus in 372 A.D. (G. T. Stokes in Smith—Wace *Dict. Chr. Biogr.* iv. 566).

[4] A. Milchhöfer in E. Curtius—J. A. Kaupert *Karten von Attika* Berlin 1881 Erläuternder Text Heft i p. 60 f., C. Wachsmuth *Die Stadt Athen im Alterthum* Leipzig 1890 ii. 1. 146 ff., A. Furtwängler in the *Sitzungsber. d. kais. bayr. Akad. d. Wiss.* Phil.-hist. Classe 1897 p. 406 ff., W. Judeich *Topographie von Athen* München 1905 p. 383.

[5] E. Curtius and J. A. Kaupert *Atlas von Athen* Berlin 1878 p. 35 pl. 12, 1.

[6] E. Curtius and J. A. Kaupert *op. cit.* p. 35 pl. 12, 2.

[7] *Infra* Append. N *med.*

as consort of the latter[1], had a separate precinct near by[2], as had also on a larger scale Asklepios[3].

Zeus *Meilíchios* was sometimes represented as a kingly figure enthroned. A fourth-century relief of white stone, found near the Tsocha theatre in the Peiraieus and now in the National Museum at Athens, shows him approached by three devotees (fig. 942)[4]. Within an architectural framework the god is seated towards the right on a throne, the arm of which is adorned with the usual sphinx and ram's-head (?)[5]. Clad in a *himátion* only, he holds a sceptre in one hand, a *phiále* in the other. Before him is a rectangular altar. From the right draws near a simple family-group of man[6], woman, and child, with gestures of greeting. Above, on the architrave, is the dedication:

'Aristarche, to Zeus *Meilíchios*[7].'

A second relief from the same find-spot adds more to our knowledge of the god (fig. 943)[8]. As before, he is seen within a framework of architecture, which bears the inscription:

'——toboule, to Zeus *Milíchios*[9].'

As before, he is enthroned on the left with a *phiále* in his right hand[10], while a group of worshippers advances towards him from the right. But this time he grasps a *cornu copiae* in his left hand, and they bring a pig to sacrifice at his altar. Behind the altar stands a boy with something in a shallow basket: between the man and woman is seen a grown girl supporting a deep basket on her head. The *cornu copiae*, one of the rarer attributes of Zeus[11], marks him as a sort of Plouton, able to dispense abundance. The pig, again, though its bones strewed the altar of Zeus *Lýkaios*[12], was an animal commonly sacrificed to Zeus in his chthonian capacity—Zeus *Bouleús* at Mykonos[13], Zeus *Eubouleús* at Delos[14].

---

[1] *Infra* Append. N *init.*

[2] Ch. D. Tsountas in the 'Εφ. 'Αρχ. 1884 p. 169 line 44, W. Judeich *op. cit.* p. 383 n. 9.

[3] W. Judeich *op. cit.* p. 388 n. 16.

[4] Staïs *Marbres et Bronzes: Athènes*[2] p. 245 f. no. 1431, Svoronos *Ath. Nationalmus.* p. 436 f. pl. 70, 4, P. Foucart in the *Bull. Corr. Hell.* 1883 vii. 507 ff. pl. 18 (=my fig. 942), Farnell *Cults of Gk. States* i. 117 pl. 2, *a*, *Einzelaufnahmen* no. 1246, 2 with Text v. 21 by E. Löwy, Harrison *Proleg. Gk. Rel.*[2] p. 19 f. fig. 3, Reinach *Rép. Reliefs* ii. 363 no. 1. Height 0·30^m, breadth 0·40^m.

[5] *Supra* i. 407 n. 1.

[6] Not the priest (Foucart *loc. cit.*), but the husband (Svoronos *loc. cit.*) or son (Löwy *loc. cit.*) of the dedicant Aristarche.

[7] *Corp. inscr. Att.* ii. 3 no. 1579 'Αριστάρχη Διὶ Μειλιχίωι. Rather: 'Αρι(σ)τάρχη κ.τ.λ.

[8] I. Ch. Dragatses in the 'Εφ. 'Αρχ. 1886 p. 49 f. no. 1, Farnell *Cults of Gk. States* i. 117, A. Furtwängler in the *Sitzungsber. d. kais. bayr. Akad. d. Wiss.* Phil.-hist. Classe 1897 p. 408, Harrison *Proleg. Gk. Rel.*[2] p. 21 f. fig. 6. My illustration is from a photograph kindly placed at my disposal by Miss Harrison. Height 0·36^m, breadth 0·24^m. Traces of colouring subsist on Zeus and his horn (red, yellow), etc.

[9] *Corp. inscr. Att.* ii. 3 no. 1579 *b* —τοβούλη Διὶ Μιλιχίω[ι]. Miss Harrison *loc. cit.* after Dragatses prints [Κριτο]βόλη Διὶ Μειλιχίῳ. But this is inexact. The name of the dedicator should be longer, perhaps ['Αρι]τοβούλη (F. Bechtel *Die Attischen Frauennamen* Göttingen 1902 pp. 6, 9); and the name of the god has no ε.

[10] I. Ch. Dragatses *loc. cit.* says τὴν μὲν δεξιὰν ἐπὶ τῶν μηρῶν ἀναπαύοντα—another inexactitude.

[11] *Supra* i. 361, 501 f., 598 n. 1.   [12] *Supra* i. 82.

[13] *Supra* i. 668, 717 n. 3.   [14] *Supra* i. 669 n. 2, 717 n. 3.

The abundance vouchsafed by Zeus *Meilíchios* and the pig provided by his worshippers are alike illustrated by a passage in Xenophon's *Anabasis*[1]:

'Next they sailed across to Lampsakos, where Xenophon was met by a seer

Fig. 942.

Fig. 943.

from Phlious, Eukleides son of Kleagoras. Kleagoras was the man who painted the frescoes in the Lvkeion. This Eukleides congratulated Xenophon on his

[1] Xen. *an*. 7. 8. 1—6.

escape and asked him how much money he had. Xenophon told him on oath that he would not even have enough to take him home, unless he sold his horse and personal belongings. Eukleides did not believe him. But when the men of Lampsakos sent gifts by way of welcome to Xenophon and he offered sacrifice to Apollon, he bade Eukleides stand beside him. And he on seeing the victims said that he believed in Xenophon's lack of funds. "But I know," he added, "that even if funds are ever forthcoming there is some hindrance in your way—yourself, if nothing else." To this Xenophon agreed. "The fact is," said Eukleides, "Zeus *Meilíchios* is hindering you." And he went on to ask if Xenophon had already sacrificed to that deity "as I," said he, "used at home to have sacrifice made and to present whole burnt-offerings on your behalf." Xenophon replied that since leaving home he had not sacrificed to this god. So Eukleides counselled him to have sacrifice made to the god in his usual manner and declared that things would improve. Next day Xenophon advanced to Ophrynion : there he had sacrifice made and presented whole burnt-offerings of pigs in accordance with his ancestral custom, and the omens were favourable[1]. That very day Bion and Nausikleides arrived with money for the troops. They were entertained by Xenophon and, as to the horse which he had sold at Lampsakos for fifty darics, hearing that it was a favourite mount and suspecting that he had parted with it through poverty, they bought the animal back again and handed it over to its master, refusing to take the purchase-money from him.'

That the god who thus sent wealth in return for whole burnt-offerings of pigs was in fact an Underworld power appears further from other votive reliefs, nine or more in number, found in 1878 near the north-east angle of the Munichian Gate[2]. These show the same deity in the guise of a monstrous snake[3], usually bearded (figs. 944[4], 945[5]) and towering above his human worshippers (fig. 946)[6]. P. Foucart, to whom we are indebted for the first collection and discussion of these reliefs, pointed out that in no case is the name of the dedicator accompanied by that of his deme. It follows that the worshippers were strangers, resident

---

[1] ἐθύετο καὶ ὡλοκαύτει χοίρους τῷ πατρίῳ (πατρῴῳ cod. Eton. etc. followed by Bornemann) νόμῳ, καὶ ἐκαλλιέρει (Xen. *an*. 7. 8. 5).

[2] P. Foucart in the *Bull. Corr. Hell.* 1883 vii. 507 ff. draws up the list.

[3] On the chthonian character of the snake see *supra* pp. 1060, 1061.

[4] *Ant. Skulpt. Berlin* p. 270 no. 722 with fig., R. Kekulé von Stradonitz *Die griech-ische Skulptur²* Berlin 1907 p. 202, P. Foucart in the *Bull. Corr. Hell.* 1883 vii. 509 no. 6, Harrison *Proleg. Gk. Rel.²* p. 17 f. fig. 1 a *stéle* of Hymettian marble inscribed in lettering of *s*. iv. B.C. - - - Διὶ Μειλιχίωι (*Corp. inscr. Att.* ii. 3 no. 1581). Height 0·58ᵐ, breadth 0·31ᵐ. I am again indebted to Miss Harrison for the photograph from which my fig. 944 is drawn.

P. Foucart in the *Bull. Corr. Hell.* 1883 vii. 509 no. 7 describes a relief in the Louvre representing a snake reared upright, with the inscription Ἀσκληπιάδης | Ἀσκληπιοδώρου | Διὶ Μιλιχίωι (*Corp. inscr. Att.* ii. 3 no. 1580).

[5] Svoronos *Ath. Nationalmus.* p. 438 pl. 70, 3 (=my fig. 945), P. Foucart in the *Bull. Corr. Hell.* 1883 vii. 510 no. 8 with fig., *id.* in Daremberg—Saglio *Dict. Ant.* iii. 1700 f. fig. 4892, Harrison *Proleg. Gk. Rel.²* p. 20 fig. 4 a relief inscribed in lettering of *s*. iv. B.C. Ἡρακλείδης τῶι θεῶι (*Corp. inscr. Att.* ii. 3 no. 1583). Height 0·33ᵐ, breadth 0·19ᵐ. J. N. Svoronos *loc. cit.* notes that τῶι θεῶι might mean either Διὶ Μειλιχίωι or Ἀσκληπιῶι (*id.* in the *Journ. Intern. d'Arch. Num.* 1901 iv. 503—507).

[6] *Ant. Skulpt. Berlin* p. 271 no. 723 with fig., R. Kekulé von Stradonitz *Die griech-ische Skulptur²* Berlin 1907 p. 202, P. Foucart in the *Bull. Corr. Hell.* 1883 vii. 509 no. 5, Harrison *Proleg. Gk. Rel.²* pp. 17, 19 fig. 2, Reinach *Rép. Reliefs* ii. 31 no. 4 a *stéle* of Hymettian marble without inscription. My fig. 946 is from a transparency in the collection of Newnham College, Cambridge. Height 0·42ᵐ, breadth 0·23ᵐ to 0·25ᵐ. The gigantic snake approached by a woman and two men might, again, be either Zeus Μειλίχιος or Asklepios.

aliens, freedmen, or slaves. And Foucart suggests[1] that they formed a *thíasos* of Phoenician settlers, who had brought with them to the crowded port of Athens *Ba'al Milik* or *Melek* or *Molok*, their own 'Lord King'[2] : *Ba'al* they translated as *Zeús* and *Milik* they transliterated as *Milíchios*[3]. This view has commended

Fig. 944.

[1] P. Foucart in the *Bull. Corr. Hell.* 1883 vii. 511 ff., *id.* in Daremberg—Saglio *Dict. Ant.* iii. 1700 f.

[2] On the problematic Malakba'al- or Melekba'al-*stêlai* see E. Meyer in Roscher *Lex. Myth.* i. 2871, ii. 3107, and on Moloch in general E. Meyer and A. Jeremias *ib.* ii. 3106 ff., F. X. Kortleitner *De polytheismo universo* Oeniponte 1908 pp. 216—227. My friend and colleague the Rev. Prof. R. H. Kennett has suggested 'that Moloch, to whom first-born children were burnt by their parents in the valley of Hinnom,...may have been originally the human king regarded as an incarnate deity': for this important hypothesis see Frazer *Golden Bough*[3] : Adonis Attis Osiris[3] ii. 219 ff. ('Moloch the King').

[3] Cp. P. Foucart in the *Bull. Corr. Hell.* 1883 vii. 513 n. 4: 'M. Renan avait fait remarquer que la forme la plus vraisemblable est Milik, que la leçon Δία Μιλίχιον se rencontre

dans plusieurs des manuscrits d'Eusèbe où est traduit un passage de Sanchoniaton sur le dieu phénicien [Euseb. *praep. ev.* 1. 10. 12 Δία Μειλίχιον. G. H. A. Ewald in W. W. Bau-dissin *Studien zur semitischen Religionsgeschichte* Leipzig 1876 i. 15 took Μειλίχιος here to be a Grecised form of the Semitic word for 'sailor,' and Baudissin himself *ib.* p. 36 n. 2 says : 'Insofern der oben S. 15 erwähnte Μειλίχιος '' der Schiffer'' die Bezeichnung Ζεύς

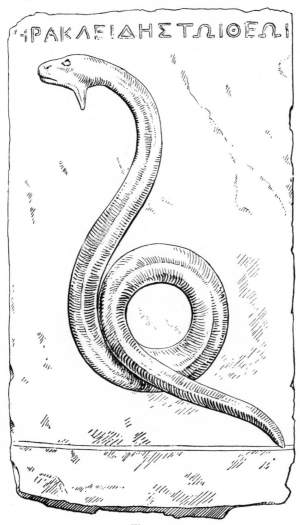

ΗΡΑΚΛΕΙΔΗΣ ΤΩΙΟΘΕΩΙ

Fig. 945.

erhält, haben wir eine Gottheit in diesem Namen zu suchen, die kaum eine andere als Mel-kart sein kann (s.m. *Jahve et Moloch* S. 28 f.). Μελικέρτης, dessen Name sicher das phönicische *Melkart* ist, gilt bei den Griechen als Meergottheit...' Cp. Gruppe *Cult. Myth. orient. Rel.* i. 398, *Gr. Myth. Rel.* p. 908 n. 3. *À propos* of the Semitic word for 'sailor' my friend Mr N. McLean writes to me (April 10, 1917): 'The word occurs in the form *mallāḥ* in Hebrew, Aramaic, & Arabic. Arabic borrowed it from Aramaic; & it is said to

itself to sundry scholars including M. Clerc[1], H. Lewy[2], M. Mayer[3], O. Höfer[4], W. Prellwitz[5], and in a modified form to S. Reinach[6]. But Miss Harrison in-

Fig. 946.

have come to Hebrew & Aramaic as a loanword from Assyrian, where the form is *Malaḫu*.' The last statement is further guaranteed by the Rev. C. H. W. Johns (April 11, 1917)], qu'enfin Silius Italicus (III, 104 [103 ff. lascivo genitus Satyro nymphaque Myrice | Milichus indigenis late regnarat in oris | cornigeram attollens genitoris imagine frontem]) cite Milichus comme un dieu punique (*Mémoires de l'Académie des Inscriptions*, t. 23, p. 267). L'orthographe constante [?] des bas-reliefs du Pirée vient confirmer cette opinion.' F. C. Movers *Die Phönizier* Berlin 1841 i. 326 f. had already connected the words Μειλίχιος, *Milichus*, and *Melech*.

[1] M. Clerc *Les métèques athéniens* (*Bibliothèque des écoles françaises d'Athènes et de Rome* lxiv) Paris 1893 p. 127 ff.

[2] H. Lewy *Die semitischen Fremdwörter im Griechischen* Berlin 1895 p. 242 f.

[3] M. Mayer in Roscher *Lex. Myth.* ii. 1521.

[4] O. Höfer in Roscher *Lex. Myth.* ii. 2561 : but cp. *ib.* p. 2562.

[5] Prellwitz *Etym. Wörterb. d. Gr. Spr.*[2] p. 286.

[6] S. Reinach *Chroniques d'Orient* Paris 1891 p. 683 holds that in Zeus Μειλίχιος we may see the fusion of an original Greek with an incoming oriental god : 'une forme grecque et une forme orientale, distinctes à l'origine, ont été confondues par le même syncrétisme qui a assimilé Héraklès à l'Hercule latin.' Similarly in the *Rev. Ét. Gr.* 1906 xix. 348

dicates an obvious difficulty: 'Unfortunately for this interesting theory we have no evidence that "Moloch" was ever worshipped in snake form[1].' And R. Dussaud further contends that in point of fact the Phoenicians recognised no such deity as *Milk*[2]. We must turn a deaf ear to all Semitic Sirens and seek an explanation nearer home.

Miss Harrison herself maintains that the cult of Zeus *Meilíchios* was a case of 'superposition.' The worship of the sky-god Zeus had ousted that of an older earth-demon *Meilíchios* : hence the snake inappropriate to the former, but natural to the latter; hence too the euphemistic title common to many a buried hero. 'Zeus,' we are told, 'is one of the few Greek gods who never appear attended by a snake. Asklepios, Hermes, Apollo, even Demeter and Athene have their snakes, Zeus never[3].' 'And the truth is nothing more or less than this. The human-shaped Zeus has slipped himself quietly into the place of the old snake-god.... It is not that Zeus the Olympian has "an underworld aspect"; it is the cruder fact that he of the upper air, of the thunder and lightning, extrudes an ancient serpent-demon of the lower world, Meilichios. Meilichios is no foreign Moloch, he is home-grown, autochthonous before the formulation of Zeus[4].' 'When we come to the discussion of hero-worship, it will be seen that all over Greece the dead hero was worshipped in snake form and addressed by euphemistic titles akin to that of Meilichios[5].' That Miss Harrison's shaft has hit the target and indeed gone near to piercing the bull's-eye, I shall not deny. The snake-form and euphemistic title of Zeus *Meilíchios* are rightly explained as the appanage of a chthonian power resembling the divinised dead. But why need we make the rather unlikely assumption that a sky-cult has been superposed on an earth-cult? Because—says Miss Harrison—Zeus never has a snake as his attribute. That, surely, is a misleading statement. I have already adduced much evidence connecting both the Thraco-Phrygian Zeus[6] and the Graeco-Libyan Zeus[7] with the snake. To recall but a single case: the coinage of Dion in Makedonia shows Zeus standing with a snake at his side[8]. Should we not rather conclude that the

(*id. Cultes, Mythes et Religions* Paris 1908 iii. 104): 'C'est plus tard seulement...qu'on l'identifia, par exemple au Pirée, à quelque *baal-melek* phénicien.' Cp. Harrison *Proleg. Gk. Rel.*[2] p. 18 n. 1: 'The possibility of a *contaminatio* between the Phenician Baal and Zeus Meilichios cannot be lightly dismissed. For a discussion of the subject see especially Clermont-Ganneau, *Le dieu Satrape*, p. 65, on the river Meilichos at Patrae, and La-grange, *Études sur les Religions Sémitiques*, p. 105.'

[1] Harrison *Proleg. Gk. Rel.*[2] p. 18. Not but what there is ample evidence of serpent-worship among the Semites: see *e.g.* S. Bochart *Hierozoicon* rec. E. F. C. Rosenmüller Lipsiae 1796 iii. 125—250, F. X. Kortleitner *De polytheismo universo* Oeniponte 1908 pp. 191 ff., 323 f., J. Skinner on Gen. 3. 1 ff., R. H. Kennett 'Ark' in J. Hastings *Encyclopædia of Religion and Ethics* Edinburgh 1908 i. 791—793. The sanctity of the serpent in Phoinike (Philon Bybl. *frag.* 9 (*Frag. hist. Gr.* iii. 572 f. Müller) *ap.* Euseb. *praep. ev.* 1. 10. 46 ff.) may in part account for its frequency as a *motif* in Phoenician art (*e.g.* Perrot—Chipiez *Hist. de l'Art* iii. 658, with fig. on p. 628, 759 fig. 543, 833 fig. 597, F. Poulsen *Der Orient und die frühgriechische Kunst* Leipzig—Berlin 1912 p. 193 Index *s.vv.* 'Schlangen, Schlangenkopf,' E. Küster *Die Schlange in der griechischen Kunst und Religion* Giessen 1913 p. 48).

[2] R. Dussaud 'Milk, Moloch, Melqart' in the *Revue de l'histoire des religions* 1904 xlix. 163—168, Gruppe *Myth. Lit.* 1908 p. 643.

[3] Harrison *Proleg. Gk. Rel.*[2] p. 18 f.

[4] *Ead. op. cit.* p. 19.   [5] *Ead. op. cit.* p. 20 f.
[6] *Supra* i. 392 ff., 428.   [7] *Supra* i. 358 ff., 428.
[8] *Supra* i. 102 n. 4, 113 fig. 84.

local king, reverenced during his life-time as Zeus incarnate, was after his death worshipped as an anguiform soul under the euphemistic appellation of Zeus 'the Kindly One'? On this showing Zeus *Meilíchios* falls into line with a whole string of deities already discussed—Zeus *Ktésios*[1], Zeus *Agamémnon*[2], Zeus *Amphiáraos*[3], Zeus *Trophónios*[4], Zeus *Asklepiós*[5]. Moreover, from the new standpoint the circumstances of the cult on the Kephisos are readily intelligible. The head of a clan, dead and buried, would be just the personage required on the one hand to purify a man from the stain of kindred bloodshed, on the other to promote the fertility of the fig-trees. His title *Meilíchios*, 'the Kindly One[6],'— originally a euphemistic name[7]—would lend itself equally well to two false inter-

---

[1] Append. H.   [2] Append. I.   [3] Append. J.
[4] Append. K.   [5] Append. L.

[6] E. Maass *De Aeschyli Supplicibus commentatio* Gryphiswaldiae 1890 p. xxxvii n. 4 says: 'Juppiter Μελισσαῖος (Hesych. s.v. [Μελισσαῖος· ὁ Ζεύς]) a μέλισσα abstracto (= ἠπιότης) videtur derivatus, ut sit idem ac μειλίχιος.' But Zeus Μελισσαῖος presumably means Zeus 'of the Bees' (cp. Nik. *ther*. 611). Whether the allusion is to the infant Zeus of Crete nurtured by bees (*supra* i. 150, ii. 928 f. n. 0, 932 f. n. 1) or to Aristaios the bee-keeper worshipped as Zeus in Arkadia (*supra* i. 372 n. 7) or to some unidentified cult, we cannot say. Gruppe *Gr. Myth. Rel.* p. 908 f.: 'Das gewöhnlichste Mittel, die Geister zu versöhnen, ist die Bewirtung mit Honig; wahrscheinlich nach ihm heisst das Entsühnen μειλίσσειν. Nach der besänftigenden Honigspende sind wahrscheinlich Zeus und Dionysos Meilichios genannt worden.' But, as Gruppe himself is aware (*op. cit.* p. 908 n. 2 f.), the connexion of μειλίσσειν with μέλι is very doubtful: see now Boisacq *Dict. étym. de la Langue Gr.* pp. 620, 624.

[7] Euphemism is and always has been a *vera causa* in popular life. I once stayed at Lavancher, a village near the Mer de Glace: the little inn, which had languished under the name *L'hôtel du Mauvais Pas*, was doing well as *L'hôtel Beau-Séjour*! Similarly with Greek and Latin place-names: the Ἄξενος became the Εὔξεινος (Strab. 298 f., Ov. *trist.* 4. 4. 55 ff., Mela 1. 102, Plin. *nat. hist.* 4. 76, 6. 1, Solin. 23. 16, Isid. *orig.* 13. 16. 7), *Maleventum* was improved into *Beneventum* (Liv. 9. 27, Plin. *nat. hist.* 3. 105, Fest. p. 340 *b* 7 f. Müller, p. 458, 35 f. Lindsay, Paul. ex Fest. p. 34 Müller, p. 31, 17 ff. Lindsay, Steph. Byz. *s.v.* Βενεβεντός, Prokop. *de bell. Goth.* 1. 15); it was even supposed that *Epidamnus* had been changed into *Dyrrhachium* (Mela 2. 56, Plin. *nat. hist.* 3. 145, Fest. p. 340 *b* 9 Müller, p. 458, 37 Lindsay) and *Egesta* into *Segesta* (Fest. p. 340 *b* 3 ff. Müller, p. 458, 31 ff. Lindsay) for the sake of avoiding an evil omen. Frazer *Golden Bough*[3]: Taboo p. 392 ff. collects many examples of euphemistic substitutes for common words, which for one reason or another were taboo. He might have added to his store from Greek usage. When the ancient Greek spoke of his 'left hand' as ἀριστερά or εὐώνυμος, of 'night' as εὐφρόνη, of 'death' as εἴ τι πάθοις, of 'the dead' as οἱ πλείονες (see O. Höfer in Roscher *Lex. Myth.* iii. 2560 f.), when the modern Greek calls the small-pox Συγχωρεμένη, the 'Gracious One,' or Εὐλογία, the 'Blessing' (G. F. Abbott *Macedonian Folklore* Cambridge 1903 p. 236), and the Devil himself ὁ καλὸς ἄνθρωπος, 'the Good man,' or ὁ κατάκαλος, 'the Beloved' (B. Schmidt *Das Volksleben der Neugriechen* Leipzig 1871 i. 176), these complimentary phrases are best explained as due to downright euphemism. Cp. Eustath. *in Od.* p. 1398, 50 ff., *et. mag.* p. 144, 20 ff. Further instances are adduced by writers on rhetoric to illustrate the trope *antíphrasis*: see Anonymos περὶ τρόπων 14 (C. Walz *Rhetores Graeci* Stuttgartiae et Tubingae 1835 viii. 722, 10 f.), Tryphon περὶ τρόπων 15 (Walz *op. cit.* viii. 755, 11 ff.), Gregorios of Corinth περὶ τρόπων 18 (Walz *op. cit.* viii. 773, 20 ff.), Kokondrios περὶ τρόπων 6 (Walz *op. cit.* viii. 785, 27 ff.), Choiroboskos περὶ τρόπων 13 (Walz *op. cit.* viii. 812, 11 ff.). An example will serve: Helladios *ap.* Phot. *bibl.* p. 535 a 4 ff. Bekker ὅτι τὸ μὴ λέγειν δύσφημα πᾶσι τοῖς παλαιοῖς μὲν φροντὶς ἦν, μάλιστα δὲ τοῖς Ἀθηναίοις. διὸ καὶ τὸ δεσμωτήριον οἴκημα ἐκάλουν, καὶ τὸν δήμιον κοινόν [a euphemism for a euphemism!], τὰς δὲ Ἐρινύας Εὐμενίδας ἢ σεμνὰς θεάς, τὸ δὲ μύσος ἄγος, τὸ δὲ ὄξος μέλι καὶ τὴν χολὴν

γλυκεῖαν, τὸν δὲ βόρβορον ὀχετόν. οἱ δὲ γραμματικοὶ τὰ τοιαῦτα κατὰ ἀντίφρασιν ὀνομάζουσιν. οἶδα δέ τινας, φησί, τῶν φιλολόγων καὶ τὸν πίθηκον ὀνομάζοντες καλλίαν.

Confining our attention to the titles of Greek divinities, we note the following cases:—
(1) The Erinyes were known as Ἀβλαβίαι (Dittenberger *Syll. inscr. Gr.*[2] no. 600, *b* 67, Michel *Recueil d'Inscr. gr.* no. 839, *B* 18 Erythrai in the first half of *s.* iii B.C.), Εὐμενίδες, Σεμναί.

(2) Hades was Ἀγήσανδρος (Hesych. *s.v.*, Favorin. *lex.* p. 18, 22), Ἀγησίλαος (Aisch. *frag.* 406 Nauck[2] *ap.* Athen. 99 B, cp. Hesych. *s.v.* Ἀγεσίλαος (so Musurus for ἄγες, λαὸς cod.) = Favorin. *lex.* p. 17, 7 f., Kallim. *lavacr. Pall.* 130 Ἀγεσίλᾳ cited by *et. mag.* p. 8, 32 f. as Ἀγεσιλάῳ, Kaibel *Epigr. Gr.* no. 195. 2 = Cougny *Anth. Pal. Append.* 2. 551. 2 ἔπ' Ἀγεσίλας for the meaningless inscr. ΕΠΑΓΕΣΙΜΗ, Lact. *div. inst.* 1. 11 Plutoni, cui cognomen Agesilao (*v.l.* Agelasto) fuit. So Nik. *frag.* 74, 72 *ap.* Athen. 684 D Ἡγεσιλάου, *Anth. Pal.* 7. 545. 4 (Hegesippos) ἡγησίλεω... Ἀιδος), Εὐβουλεύς (*supra* p. 118 n. 4), Εὐειδής (Hesych. *s.v.* Εὐκλής cited *supra* p. 118 n. 3), Εὐκλῆς (*supra* p. 118 n. 3), Εὐχαίτης (J. Franz in the *Ann. d. Inst.* 1842 xiv. 136 ff. no. 1, 24 an oracle of Klaros, *s.* ii A.D., found at Kallipolis on the Thracian Chersonese: see Kaibel *Epigr. Gr.* no. 1034. 23, W. H. Roscher in his *Lex. Myth.* i. 1397, K. Buresch *Klaros* Leipzig 1889 p. 81 ff., H. von Prott in the *Ath. Mitth.* 1899 xxiv. 257 f., O. Jessen in Pauly—Wissowa *Real-Enc.* vi. 880, and C. Picard *Éphèse et Claros* Paris 1922 pp. 212, 389, 673, 694, 696 (following Buresch), Ἰσοδαίτης (Hesych. *s.v.*: see further O. Höfer in Roscher *Lex. Myth.* ii. 551 f., Preller—Robert *Gr. Myth.* i. 804 n. 7, Gruppe *Gr. Myth. Rel.* pp. 1430 n. 1, 1432 n. 2, 1557 n. 3, Harrison *Proleg. Gk. Rel.*[2] pp. 440, 481 n. 1, *Themis* p. 157), Κλύμενος (C. Scherer in Roscher *Lex. Myth.* i. 1783, R. Engelmann, W. H. Roscher, and W. Drexler *ib.* ii. 1228 f.), Πασιάναξ (on Megarian (?) imprecatory tablets of lead published by E. Ziebarth 'Neue attische Fluchtafeln' in the *Nachr. d. kön. Gesellsch. d. Wiss. Göttingen* Phil.-hist. Classe 1899 p. 120 no. 21, 1, 3, 7 and p. 121 no. 22, 1. O. Höfer in Roscher *Lex. Myth.* iii. 1664 cp. the Pythian oracle quoted by Phlegon of Tralleis *Olympiades seu chronica frag.* 1 (*Frag. hist. Gr.* iii. 603 Müller) = Cougny *Anth. Pal. Append.* 6. 20. 5 f. ἀτιμάζοντες Ὀλύμπια πασιάνακτος | Ζηνός), Περικλύμενος (Hesych. *s.v.*: so Salmasius and Soping for περίκλυμος cod.), Πλούτων (*supra* i. 503 f.), Πολύαρχος (Cornut. *theol.* 35 p. 74, 15 Lang), Πολυδαίμων (Orph. *h. Plout.* 18. 11: see Gruppe *Gr. Myth. Rel.* p. 400 n. 2, O. Höfer in Roscher *Lex. Myth.* iii 2637), Πολυδέγμων (*h. Dem.* 17, 31, 430, Cornut. *theol.* 35 p. 74, 15 Lang: see further Gruppe *Gr. Myth. Rel.* p. 400 n. 2, 809 n. 1, O. Höfer in Roscher *Lex. Myth.* iii. 2639 f.), Πολυδέκτης (*h. Dem.* 9 with the note of E. E. Sikes *ad loc.*, Cornut. *theol.* 35 p. 74, 14 Lang: see further Gruppe *Gr. Myth. Rel.* pp. 400 n. 2, 867 n. 5, H. W. Stoll and O. Höfer in Roscher *Lex. Myth.* iii. 2640), Πολύξενος? (Kallim. *frag.* 478 Schneider *ap. et. Flor.* p. 189 Κλυμένου...πολυξείνοιο. In Soph. *O.C.* 1569 f. ἐν πύλαισι | ...πολυξέστοις S. Musgrave restored πολυξένοις. Cp. Aisch. *suppl.* 157 f. τὸν πολυξενώτατον | Ζῆνα τῶν κεκμηκότων, where T. Birt would read Δία for Ζῆνα with the citation in *et. Gud.* p. 227, 43 διὰ (*sic*) and in Cramer *anecd. Oxon.* ii. 443, 13 Διὰ (*sic*). Again, in Aisch. *frag.* 228 Nauck[2] Ζαγρεῖ τε νῦν με καὶ πολυξένῳ < > | χαίρειν cited by *et. Gud.* p. 227, 40 f. and by Cramer *anecd. Oxon.* ii. 443, 10 f. Hermann supplied πατρί, Schneidewin Διί. See further O. Höfer in Roscher *Lex. Myth.* iii. 2561 and 2742), Πυλάοχος (Plout. *de Is. et Os.* 35), πυλάρτης (*Il.* 8. 367 with schol. *ad loc.*, 13. 415, *Od.* 11. 277, Mosch. 4. 86, Apollon. *lex. Hom.* p. 137, 25 ff., Hesych. *s.v.* πυλάρταο κρατεροῖο, *et. mag.* p. 696, 48 ff., Eustath. *in Il.* pp. 718, 20 f., 914, 18 f., 940, 5 f., *in Od.* p. 1684, 43 f., Favorin. *lex.* p. 1601, 28 ff.: see further Gruppe *Gr. Myth. Rel.* p. 400 n. 1, O. Höfer in Roscher *Lex. Myth.* iii. 3326). *Infra* Append. N *med.*

(3) Persephone was Μελίβοια? (Lasos *frag.* 1 Bergk[4] *ap.* Athen. 624 E Δάματρα μέλπω κόραν τε Κλυμένοι' ἄλοχον Μελίβοιαν, | ὕμνων ἀναγνῶν Αἰολῇδα | βαρύβρομον ἁρμονίαν: but E. Hiller—O. Crusius read ἄλοχον | μελιβόαν ὕμνων ἀναγνεων | Αἰολίδ' ἀνὰ κ.τ.λ.), Μελιτώδης (Theokr. 15. 94 with schol. *ad loc.*, Porph. *de antr. nymph.* 18. In Kokondrios περὶ τρόπων 6 (Walz *op. cit.* viii. 786, 8) καὶ Μελιτώνην τὴν Περσεφόνην Boissonade *anecd.* iii. 292 cj. μελιτώδη), Μελινδία? (Io. Malal. *chron.* 3 p. 62 Dindorf: Rohde *Psyche*[3] i. 206 n. 2 cj. Μελίνοια).

pretations. Some, narrowing its range overmuch, would see in it the description of a god specially gracious to the repentant man-slayer. Others, wrongly associating it with *meilicha*, 'figs,' would point in triumph to the Sacred Fig-tree of the Phytalidai.

(4) Zeus *Meilichios* on the Hills near Athens.

There must have been another sanctuary of Zeus *Meilichios* on the northern slope of the Nymphs' Hill, now crowned by the Observatory. For here two dedications to the god have come to light, one inscribed on a round pillar[1], the other on a quadrangular base[2]. The latter associates him with Helios, possibly as being a god of fertility[3].

The eastward prolongation of the Nymphs' Hill, on which stands the church of Saint Marina, had in antiquity its own cult of Zeus : a couple of rock-cut inscriptions on the southern slope mark the limits of his precinct[4]. Whether the god here also had fertilising powers, we cannot tell ; but at the present day women who come to supplicate Saint Marina for children 'go through the performance of sliding down the great sloping rock in front of the church[5].'

(4) Hekate was Ἀρίστη (C. Wessely *Griechische Zauberpapyrus von Paris und London* Wien 1888 p. 57 pap. Par. 1450 καὶ Ἀρίστη Χθονία), Εὐκολίνη (Kallim. *frag.* 82ᵈ Schneider χαῖρ', Εὐκολίνη, *ap. et. Sorbon.* (cited by T. Gaisford in his note on *et. mag.* p. 392, 27), *et. Ultraiect.* (cited by D. Ruhnken *epist. crit.* ii. 181), *et. Flor.* p. 133, cp. *et. mag.* p. 392, 27 f., Cramer *anecd. Paris.* iv. 182, 23 ff., Souid. *s.v.* Εὐκολίνη), Καλλίστη (Hesych. *s.v.*), Κράταιις (Ap. Rhod. 4. 829 with schol. *ad loc.* : see further H. W. Stoll and O. Höfer in Roscher *Lex. Myth.* ii. 1408 f.).

(5) A daughter of Zeus by Persephone was Μειλινόη ? (so C. A. Lobeck for Μηλινόη in Orph. *h. Melin.* 71. 1).

(6) An Arcadian bear-goddess (?) was Καλλιστώ (Harrison *Myth. Mon. Anc. Ath.* p. 402 ff. fig. 26, R. Franz ' De Callistus fabula' in the *Leipziger Studien zur classischen Philologie* 1890 xii. 233—365, *id.* in Roscher *Lex. Myth.* ii. 931—935, Farnell *Cults of Gk. States* ii. 438, Frazer *Pausanias* iv. 191, Gruppe *Gr. Myth. Rel.* pp. 194 f., 942 n. 8, *alib.*, O. Keller *Die antike Tierwelt* Leipzig 1909 i. 176 f.).

(7) The bogus snake-god of Abonou Teichos was Γλύκων (*supra* Append. L p. 1083 ff.).

Such titles have a twofold aspect. Their value is at once negative and positive. On the one hand, they are substitutes for names that were taboo. 'It is especially,' says Dr Farnell (*Cults of Gk. States* iii. 137), 'in the cults of the powers of the lower world, in the worship of Hades and Persephone, and more especially still in the mysteries, that we discern in many Greek communities a religious dislike to pronounce the proper personal name, either because of its extreme holiness or because of its ominous associations, and to conceal it under allusive, euphemistic, or complimentary titles.' On the other hand, these titles often aim at securing by magical means the blessing that they describe : you call your god what you wish him to be, in order to make him so. See some shrewd remarks by W. R. Halliday *Greek Divination* London 1913 p. 33 f. : ' Here, in part (there are other elements also) lies the efficacy of Euphemism. You call the Fairies " Kindly Ones "; behind the conscious motive of putting them into a good temper, and the fear of effecting a connection with them by uttering their name, is further the comfort that you derive by persuading yourself to believe that 'they are kindly : the fact that you call them kindly makes them kindly.' Μειλίχιος is a case in point.

[1] *Corp. inscr. Att.* ii. 3 no. 1584 Διὶ Μειλιχίωι | Ξωπυρίων.

[2] *Corp. inscr. Att.* ii. 3 no. 1585 Ἡλίωι καὶ Διὶ Μειλ[ιχίωι] | Μαμμία.

[3] Mommsen *Feste d. Stadt Athen* pp. 421 n. 4, 424.

[4] *Corp. inscr. Att.* i no. 504 ϹΟΙΔ:ϷΟϞΟΗ and a little lower down no. 505 ΗΟΡΟϹ.

[5] Miss M. Hamilton *Greek Saints and their Festivals* Edinburgh and London 1910 p. 58 f. Cp. *supra* i. 563 n. 4.

At Alopeke (*Angelokepoi, Ampelokepoi*) near Mount Lykabettos[1] Zeus again appears to have borne a chthonian character. A roughly squared block of Pentelic marble, found in an ancient well of this locality, has the upper part of its front face engraved as follows[2] in lettering of the late fifth century B.C. :

HI E P O N :	Sanctuary
ΔI O Ϩ :M I	of Zeus *Mi-*
Ⱶ I X I O :A	*líchios*, (G)-
HϨ :AΘH N	e, Athen-
AI A Ϩ	aia.

The grouping of the god with Ge, if not also the discovery of his boundary-stone in a well, is significant of his underground nature.

(5) Zeus *Meilíchios* on the Ilissos.

Yet another Athenian cult seems to have connected Zeus *Meilíchios* as a god of fertility with underground waters. In 1893 A. N. Skias, when exploring

Fig. 947

[1] S. Reinach 'Le sanctuaire d'Athéna et de Zeus Meilichios à Athènes' in the *Bull. Corr. Hell.* 1892 xvi. 411—417.

[2] S. A. Koumanoudes in the 'Εφ. 'Αρχ. 1889 pp. 51—54 no. 1 = *Corp. inscr. Att.* iv. 1. 3 no. 528[1] ἱερὸν | Διὸς Μι|λιχίου, (Γ)|ῆς, 'Αθην|αίας. The reading (Γ)ῆς, here adopted by A. Kirchhoff, was suggested independently by Semitelos and Diels (O. Kern in the *Ath. Mitth.* 1891 xvi. 10 n. 2), and is accepted by O. Höfer in Roscher *Lex. Myth.* ii. 2558 f., Mommsen *Feste d. Stadt Athen* pp. 421 n. 3, 424, W. Larfeld *Handbuch der griechischen Epigraphik* Leipzig 1898 ii. 1. 69.

the bed of the Ilissos, discovered in the two reservoirs beneath the rocky barrier of the later Kallirrhoe four slabs carved in relief. Of these slabs two were found close together in the basin[1] adjoining the chapel of Saint Photeine, and with

Fig. 948.

them a colossal head of Herakles wearing the lion-skin. One of the two reliefs in question (fig. 947)[2] shows Zeus, with a sceptre in his left hand and a *phiále* (?) in

---

[1] Marked B in W. Wilberg's plan of the excavations (Πρακτ. ἀρχ. ἑτ. 1893 pl. A).

[2] A. N. Skias in the 'Εφ. 'Αρχ. 1894 p. 133 ff. fig., Svoronos *Ath. Nationalmus.*

his right, seated on a rock (?)[1]. Before him is an altar of rude stones. Beyond it stand two female worshippers, presumably mother and daughter, conceived on a smaller scale than the god himself. The moulding above bears traces of fifth-century letters, which were read by Skias as a dedication to Zeus *Náios*[2]: they may equally well, indeed better, be completed as a dedication to Zeus *Meilíchios*[3]. The second relief (fig. 948)[4] represents Zeus holding a jug in both hands as he sits on a horned and bearded head, which is inscribed in lettering of the Alexandrine age *Achelôios*[5]. Behind Zeus stands a female (?)—perhaps Kallirrhoe, daughter of Acheloios,—fronting us with a *cornu copiae* in her left hand and a *phiále* in her right. Before Zeus stand Hermes and Herakles. Hermes has a trefoil *oinochóe* in his right hand, the *caduceus* in his left. Herakles, equipped with lion-skin and club, extends his right hand with something in it (another *oinochóe* ?) towards Zeus. To either side of the heads of Zeus and Herakles are two holes of doubtful significance.

It is not quite certain that either of these reliefs figures Zeus *Meilíchios*. But it is probable that both do so. The former bears a general resemblance to the *Meilíchios*-reliefs of the Peiraieus (figs. 942, 943)[6], though it shows a more primitive type of altar and dispenses with architectural framework. The latter represents a chthonian Zeus of some sort; for it associates him closely with Acheloios[7] and Kallirrhoe (?). Now somewhere in the immediate neighbourhood

pl. 130, 2 (=my fig. 947). The dimensions of the slab, which is now preserved in the National Museum (no. 1779), are as follows: breadth 0·31^m, height 0·22^m.

[1] Cp. Svoronos *op. cit.* pl. 130, 3 (no. 1781), *infra* p. 1119 n. 0.

[2] ΕΟΙ ΝΕΝΝΑΙ = [ὁ δεῖνα ἀν]έθηκεν Ναΐ[ῳ Διΐ]. The lettering is hardly later than *c.* 450 B.C.

[3] Skias himself supposes that the god portrayed is Zeus Μειλίχιος, who *qua* watery chthonian Zeus might—he thinks—bear the title Νάιος. But it is surely simpler to restore [Διὶ Μειλιχίωι κατ' εὐχὴν ἀν]έθηκεν Ναΐ[άς] or Νάν[ιον] or the like.

[4] P. Kabbadias in the 'Εφ. 'Αρχ. 1893 p. 137 n. 1, A. N. Skias *ib.* 1894 p. 137 ff. pl. 7 (=my fig. 948), Svoronos *Ath. Nationalmus.* pl. 131 (larger, but not so clear), Reinach *Rép. Reliefs* ii. 351 no. 3 (summary sketch). The slab, now in the National Museum (no. 1778), measures: greatest height 0·85^m, breadth below 0·53^m, breadth above 0·60^m, thickness of base 0·16^m, thickness of background *c.* 0·10^m.

[5] ΑΧΕΛΩΙΟΣ.   [6] *Supra* p. 1105 f.

[7] A votive relief of Pentelic marble (height 0·42^m, breadth 0·49^m, thickness 0·08^m: it had originally a tenon for insertion in a mortise), found at Megara (F. Wieseler ' Ueber ein Votivrelief aus Megara' in the *Abh. d. gött. Gesellsch. d. Wiss.* Phil.-hist. Classe 1875 xx. 6. 1—39) and now in the Berlin Museum (*Ant. Skulpt. Berlin* p. 251 f. no. 679 with fig.), is referable to the early part of *s.* iv. B.C. (Furtwängler *Samml. Sabouroff* Sculptures pl. 27 = my fig. 949). On the back wall of a cavern is carved the head of Acheloios, and immediately beneath it is set a table for offerings. Ranged round the cavern we see a semicircle of divinities. Zeus in the centre is flanked by Pan (horns) and Kore (torches). Next to Pan is Demeter (?); next to Kore, Plouton (?—possibly Agathos Daimon) (*phiále, cornu copiae*). The reclining youth on the extreme left and the seated female figure on the extreme right are insufficiently characterised as deities (Apollon ?? Aphrodite ?? cp. Paus. 1. 44. 9) and more probably represent the eponymous hero Megaros and his mother, one of the nymphs called Sithnides, who was beloved by Zeus (Paus. i. 40. 1, cp. *et. mag.* p. 228, 21 ff. where the hero is called Megareus): the fact that they alone occupy the ground-level would not justify the inference that they are merely the dedicators of the *ex voto*.

The nearest parallel to this relief as a whole is furnished by the rock-carvings at the entrance to the marble-quarries of Paros: see J. Stuart—N. Revett *The Antiquities of Athens* London 1816 iv pp. ix, 34 f., ch. 6 pl. 5, Müller—Wieseler *Denkm. d. alt. Kunst*

of the reservoirs above-mentioned must be located[1] that sanctuary of the Nymphs and Acheloios, which with its votive statuettes and images still makes a pretty picture in the pages of Platon. It will be remembered how Sokrates and Phaidros one thirsty day stretched themselves on the turf beneath a great plane-tree, cool water bubbling up at their feet, the air ringing with a chorus of cicalas, and blossoms of *agnus castus* perfuming the whole place[2]. It is reasonable to suppose that the Zeus of our reliefs had a precinct adjoining this sacred spot. And the supposition squares well with sundry further considerations. To the north, and close at hand, lay the vast temple of Zeus *Olýmpios*, begun by Peisistratos, continued by Antiochos iv Epiphanes, and ended by Hadrian. Zeus indeed had been established here from time immemorial. 'They say,' writes Pausanias, 'that Deukalion built the old sanctuary of Zeus *Olýmpios*, and in proof that Deukalion dwelt at Athens they point to a grave not far from the present temple[3].' If early graves were to be seen in the vicinity, we might look to find the cult of a chthonian Zeus[4], who would be readily brought into connexion with the powers of sub-

ii. 4. 11 pl. 63, 81 , A. Michaelis in the *Ann. d. Inst.* 1863 xxxv. 314 f., 328, Lebas—

Fig. 949.

Reinach *Voyage Arch.* p. 110 f. pl. 122, Reinach *Rép. Reliefs* ii. 360 no. 1, *Inscr. Gr. ins.* v. 1 no. 245.

   [1] A. N. Skias Συμβολαὶ εἰς τὴν Ἀθηναικὴν τοπογραφίαν pp. 13—16 (=Ἑστία 1894 p. 292), *id.* in the Πρακτ. ἀρχ. ἐτ. 1893 p. 123.

   [2] Plat. *Phaedr.* 230 B–C.   [3] Paus. 1. 18. 8.

   [4] A. N. Skias in the Πρακτ. ἀρχ. ἐτ. 1897 p. 81 ff. suggests that the small Ionic temple

terranean springs. Pliny, or his authority, was probably[1] thinking of the site, when he remarked : 'At Athens during a rainy summer Enneakrounos is colder than the well in the garden of Zeus, but in dry seasons the latter is freezing-cold[2].' More than that. Midway between the Kallirrhoe-bar and the Olympieion are the foundations of a small temple built in Roman times and subsequently transformed into a Christian church[3]. This little edifice perhaps marks the very ground where Zeus *Meilíchios* was worshipped[4].

on the Ilissos (J. Stuart—N. Revett *The Antiquities of Athens* London 1762 i. 7 ff., ch. 2 pls. 1—8, A. N. Skias *loc. cit.* p. 73 ff. with pl. A′ by A. N. Lykakes, W. Dörpfeld in the *Ath. Mitth.* 1897 xxii. 227 f., J. N. Svoronos in the *Journ. Intern. d'Arch. Num.* 1901 iv. 243 ff., C. Wachsmuth in Pauly—Wissowa *Real-Enc.* Suppl. i. 190 f.), which was standing as the church of the Παναγία εἰς τὴν Πέτραν till towards the close of the eighteenth century, had originally some connexion with Zeus Φίλιος, a doublet of Zeus Χθόνιος. He relies on a fragmentary votive relief (Πρακτ. ἀρχ. ἐτ. 1897 p. 83 f. pl. A′ fig. A′, Svoronos *Ath. Nationalmus.* pl. 130, 3 (no. 1781)) of *s.* iv or iii B.C. found in one of the numerous tombs adjoining the temple: it represents a sceptred god sitting on a rock with an altar before him. But W. Judeich *Topographie von Athen* München 1905 p. 371 f. makes out a strong case for regarding the sanctuary as that of the Μήτηρ ἐν Ἄγρας.

[1] But see W. Judeich *op. cit.* p. 182 n. 6.

[2] Plin. *nat. hist.* 31. 50 Athenis Enneacrunos nimbosa aestate frigidior est quam puteus in Iovis horto, at ille siccitatibus riget.

[3] A. N. Skias in the Πρακτ. ἀρχ. ἐτ. 1893 p. 130 ff. pl. A with inset (=my fig. 950). The temple was a peripteral building with 6 columns on each short side and 9 on each long side : the *naós* was amphiprostyle with 4 columns at either end (Skias *loc. cit.* p. 131 fig.). The order appears to have been Doric (?). When the temple became a church, the *prónaos* was transformed into a ἅγιον βῆμα. Beneath the sacred table was a pit (Γ in fig. 950) for relics, which were bestowed in an old Greek sepulchral urn of black stone with four handles. Several tombs of Christian date were found on the site.

[4] That is my conjecture. A. N. Skias, who has a better right to speak, contends (Πρακτ. ἀρχ. ἐτ. 1893 p. 132 f.) that here was the spot known in *s.* xv A.D. as the 'precinct of Hera' (Anon. Vindob. 7 in C. Wachsmuth *Die Stadt Athen im Alterthum* Leipzig 1874 i. 735 f. πρὸς δὲ νότον τούτων ἔστιν οἶκος βασιλικὸς πλὴν ὡραῖος, εἰς ὃν κατερχόμενος ὁ δοὺξ κατὰ καιρὸν εἰς εὐωχίαν ἐκινεῖτο· ἐκεῖ ἐστι καὶ ἡ Ἐννεάκρουνος (νεάκρουνος cod.) πηγὴ ἡ Καλλιρρόη, εἰς ἣν λουόμενος ἀνήρχετο εἰς τέμενος τὸ τῆς Ἥρας λεγόμενον καὶ προσηύχετο· νῦν δὲ μετεποιήθη εἰς ναὸν τῆς ὑπεραγίας Θεοτόκου ὑπὸ τῶν εὐσεβῶν). But W. Judeich *Topographie von Athen* München 1905 p. 371 n. 12 decides with greater probability that this and other early allusions to a 'temple de Junon' (Wachsmuth *op. cit.* i. 736 n. 1) referred to the Christian church on the Ilissos-'island' (see R. Rangabé in the *Bull. d. Inst.* 1850 p. 134 ff.), which had been wrongly identified with Hadrian's temple of Hera and Zeus Πανελλήνιος (Paus. 1. 18. 9 Ἀδριανὸς δὲ κατεσκευάσατο μὲν καὶ ἄλλα Ἀθηναίοις, ναὸν Ἥρας καὶ Διὸς Πανελληνίου κ.τ.λ., Dion Cass. 69. 16 τόν τε σηκὸν τὸν ἑαυτοῦ, τὸ Πανελλήνιον ὠνομασμένον, οἰκοδομήσασθαι τοῖς Ἕλλησιν ἐπέτρεψε, καὶ ἀγῶνα ἐπ' αὐτῷ κατεστήσατο (*sc.* Ἀδριανός), Philostr. *v. soph.* 2. 1. 7 καὶ μὴν καὶ ἐλειτούργησεν (*sc.* Ἡρώδης) Ἀθηναίοις τὴν τ' ἐπώνυμον καὶ τὴν τῶν Πανελληνίων, 2. 17. 1. μηδ' εἰ τὴν τῶν Πανελληνίων Ἀθήνησιν εὐκλεῶς ἦρξεν (*sc.* Ῥοῦφος, cp. *Corp. inscr. Att.* iii. 1 no. 17), Hieron. *chron. ann. Abr.* 2148 (Euseb. *chron.* ii. 167 Schoene) Hadrianus cum insignes et plurimas aedes Athenis fecisset agonem edidit bibliothecamque miri operis instruxit). The real site of the temple of Zeus Πανελλήνιος at Athens is unknown : future excavators will doubtless discover it.

Meantime extant inscriptions confirm the literary sources and add somewhat to our knowledge of the god and of his festival. The name appears to have had a distinctly political origin. In late republican or early imperial times the Achaean League was revived as τὸ τῶν Ἀχαιῶν καὶ Βοιωτῶν καὶ Λοκρῶν καὶ Φωκέων καὶ Εὐβοέων κοινόν, or more briefly τὸ κοινὸν τῶν Ἀχαιῶν, ἡ σύνοδος τῶν Πανελλήνων : their council met at Argos under the presidency of a στρατηγὸς τῶν Ἀχαιῶν. But in 131 A.D. Hadrian instituted a new Πανελλήνιον on grander lines: it met at Athens and included all the Greek states, not merely those of the Peloponnese. Thenceforward the revived Achaean League naturally dropped its pretension to be Panhellenic (see W. Dittenberger's notes on the *Corp. inscr. Att.* iii. 1 no. 18, on *Syll. inscr. Gr.*³ no. 842, 2 f., and on *Orient. Gr. inscr. sel.* no. 504, 1 f., 11). Hadrian not only founded a temple of Zeus Πανελλήνιος (*Corp. inscr. Att.* iii. 1 no. 13, 10 [ναὸν Πανελλ]ηνίου Διὸς ἐφ[ιδρύσατο (*sc.* Ἀδριανός)]), but also himself assumed the title Πανελλήνιος (*ib.* iii. 1 no. 12, 26 ff. [τ]ὰς δωρεὰς ὡ[ς ἕκασται ἐδόθησαν ὑπὸ τοῦ] | μεγίσ[του Αὐτοκράτορ]ος Καίσαρος Τραϊα[νοῦ Ἀδριανοῦ Σεβαστοῦ] | Ὀλυμπί[ου Πανελληνίου], *Inscr. Gr. sept.* i no. 70, 1 f. τὸν δὶς αὐτοκράτορα Κ[αίσαρα Τρ]αϊανὸν Ἀδρια[νὸν] | Σεβαστὸν Ὀλύμπιον Π[ύθι]ον Πανελλήνιον, *ib.* i no. 71, 1 f. [τὸν δὶς αὐτοκράτορα Καίσαρα Τραϊανὸν Ἀδριανὸν

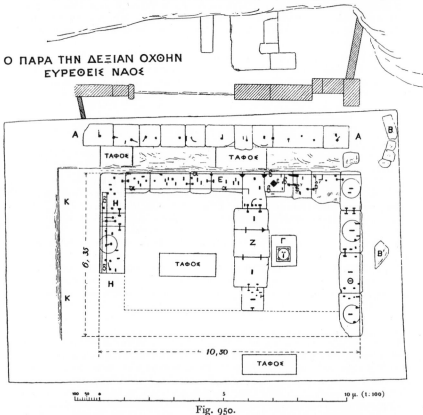

Ο ΠΑΡΑ ΤΗΝ ΔΕΞΙΑΝ ΟΧΘΗΝ
ΕΥΡΕΘΕΙΣ ΝΑΟΣ

Fig. 950.

Σεβαστὸν Ὀλύμπιον Πύθιον Πανελλήνιον], *ib.* i no. 72, 1 ff. τὸν δὶς αὐτοκράτορα Καίσαρα Τραϊανὸν | Ἀδριανὸν Σεβαστὸν Ὀλύμπιον Πύθιον | Πανελλήνιον, *ib.* i no. 3491, 1 ff. τὸν δὶς αὐτοκράτορα Καίσαρα [θεοῦ Τραϊανοῦ Παρθικοῦ υἱόν], | θεοῦ Νέρβα υἱωνόν, Τραϊανὸν Ἀδριανὸν Σεβαστὸν Ὀλύμ]πιον Πανελλήνιον νέον Πύθιον, G. Radet in the *Bull. Corr. Hell.* 1887 xi. 480 no. 60, 1 f. *Kirk-Agatsch* from Thyateira [αὐτ]οκράτορα Τραϊανὸν Ἀδριανὸν Καίσαρα Σ[εβαστόν, | ...κ]αὶ Πανελλήνιον) presumably as being the earthly representative and vice-gerent of Zeus (*Folk-Lore* 1905 xvi. 314). After his death the divinised Hadrian had as priest the president of the great Panhellenic council (*Corp. inscr. Att.* iii. 1 no. 681, 2 ff. τὸν ἄρχο[ντα τῶν] | σεμνο[τάτων Παν]ελλήνω[ν καὶ ἱερέα] | θεοῦ Ἀδ[ριανοῦ Παν|ελ]ληνί[ου καὶ ἀγω]ν[ο]θ[έ]τ[ην τῶν Παν|ελλη]ν[ίων.....],? cp. *ib.* iii. 2 no. 3872, 1 ff. θεὸν |[Ἀδριανόν?] – – – Πανε[λλην...], Dittenberger *Orient. Gr. inscr. sel.* no. 504, 1 f. Aizanoi ὁ ἄρχων τῶν

With his cult on the Ilissos I would connect both a local myth and a local custom.

(6) The Myth of Periphas.

Antoninus Liberalis in his *Metamorphoses*, a valuable work preserved to us by a single manuscript at Heidelberg, gives the following account of Periphas:

'Periphas was sprung from the soil in Attike before Kekrops the son of Ge appeared. He became king of the ancient population, and was just and rich and holy, a man who offered many sacrifices to Apollon and judged many disputes and was blamed by no one. All men willingly submitted to his rule and, in view of his surpassing deeds, transferred to him the honours due to Zeus and decided that they belonged to Periphas. They offered sacrifices and built temples to him, and called him Zeus *Sotér* and *Epópsios* and *Meilíchios.*

Πανελλήνων καὶ ἱερεὺς θεοῦ 'Αδριανοῦ Π[ανελληνίου] | καὶ ἀγωνοθέτης τῶν μεγάλων Πανελ-ληνίων, *ib.* no. 507, 1 f. ὁ ἄρχων τῶν Πανελλήνων καὶ ἱερεὺς θεοῦ 'Αδριανοῦ Πανελληνίου | καὶ ἀγωνοθέτης τῶν μεγάλων Πανελληνίων). It would even seem that at Athens the god Hadrian took over the temple of Zeus 'Ολύμπιος (so W. Dittenberger *Orient. Gr. inscr. sel.* no. 504 n. 6 understands Dion Cass. 69. 16 cited *supra*). Cp. *Corp. inscr. Gr.* ii no. 1822(Epeiros) an altar inscribed αὐτοκ[ράτορι Τραϊα]|νῶι 'Αδρια[νῶι Σε]βασ[τῶι,] | 'Ολυμπίωι, Διὶ Δωδωναί[ωι]. The foundation of the Πανελλήνιον in 131 A.D. (P. Cavvadias *Fouilles d'Épidaure* Athènes 1893 i. 43 no. 35, 1 ff. = Dittenberger *Syll. inscr. Gr.*³ no. 842, 1 ff. ἔτους γ' τῆς καθιερώσεως τοῦ Διὸ[ς] | τοῦ 'Ολυμπίου καὶ τῆς κτίσεος | τοῦ Πανελληνίου) was commemorated (Dion Cass. and Hieron. *chron. locc. citt.*) by means of an ἀγών (*Corp. inscr. Att.* iii. 1 no. 10, 13 f. (ἀ)[ντ]άρχοντος τοῦ ἱερωτάτου ἀ(γ)[ῶ]νος τοῦ] (Π)αν(ελ)ληνίου, cp. *ib.* iii. 1 no. 681, 6 ff. [ἀγω]|ν[ο]θ[έ]τ[ην τῶν Παν|ελλη]ν[ίων .....], *ib.* iii. 1 no. 682, 1 ff. [ἀγωνοθετήσ]αντα - - - [? Πανελλη]νίων, *ib.* iii. 1 no. 1199, 5 f. ἐπὶ ἀγωνοθέ[του τῶν μεγά]|λων Πανελληνίων, Dittenberger *Orient. Gr. inscr. sel.* no. 504, 2 ἀγωνοθέτης τῶν μεγάλων Πανελληνίων, *ib.* no. 507, 2 ἀγωνοθέτης τῶν μεγάλων Πανελληνίων) known as the Πανελλήνια (*Corp. inscr. Att.* iii. 1 no. 32, 5 τὸ εἰς τὰ Πανελλ[ήνια], *ib.* iii. 1 no. 127, 3 f. Πανελλήνια | ἐν 'Αθήναις, *ib.* iii. 1 no. 128, 5 νεικήσας κατὰ τὸ ἑξῆς Πανελλήνια | κ.τ.λ., 10 f. Πανελ|λήνια | δὶς | 'Αθή(νας), *Olympia* v. 347 ff. no. 237, 8 f. α' 'Αδρειάνεια ἐν Ζμύρνῃ καὶ ἐν 'Εφέσωο καὶ τὰ πρώτως Πα|νελλήνια ἀχθέντα ἐν 'Αθήναις πρῶτος κηρύκων, *Corp. inscr. Gr.* i no. 1068 i, 1 f. = *Inscr. Gr. sept.* i no. 49, 7 Megara Πανελλήνια | ἐν 'Αθήναις, E. L. Hicks *The Collection of Ancient Greek Inscriptions in the British Museum* iii. 2. 237 f. Oxford 1890 no. 611, 7 Ephesos Πανελλήνια ἐν 'Αθήναις, στάδιον, *ib.* iii. 2. 238 f. no. 613, 8 f. Ephesos ['Α]θήναις παῖ[δων Παν|ελ]λήνια γ̄, *ib.* iii. 2. 239 f. no. 615, 5 Ephesos 'Αθήνας παίδων Πανελλήνια, J. R. S. Sterrett in *Papers of the American School of Classical Studies at Athens* Boston 1888 iii. 291 f. no. 413, 15 f. Kara Baulo Πανελλήνε(ι)α | ἐν 'Αθήναις). The name μεγάλα Πανελλήνια (*Corp. inscr. Att.* iii. 1 no. 17, 3 [τῶν μεγ]άλων Πανελ[ηνίων] or [τῶν ἄ]λλων Πανελλ[ήνων], *ib.* no. 1199, 5 f. ἐπὶ ἀγωνοθέ[του τῶν μεγά]|λων Πανελληνίων, Dittenberger *Orient. Gr. inscr. sel.* no. 504, 2 ἀγωνοθέτης τῶν μεγάλων Πανελληνίων, *ib.* no. 507, 2 ἀγωνοθέτης τῶν μεγάλων Πανελληνίων) implies that the contest was organised also as a *pentaeterís* on the analogy of the Panathenaia (Mommsen *Feste d. Stadt Athen* p 168 ff. tries to make out that the Panhellenia at Athens was modelled on the Eleutheria at Plataiai). Few further details of the festival are on record (with *Corp. inscr. Att.* iii. 1 no. 1141, 20 f. καὶ ἐκ Παν[ελ]|ληνίου οὐθέν cp. *ib.* iii. 1 no. 1184, 20 ff. [με]τ[ὰ τὰ]ς Σεβαστο-φορικὰς νομὰς πάσας τὰς διὰ Πανελληνίων ἐπ' ἴσης οἵ τε ἔφηβοι καὶ οἱ πε|[ρὶ τὸ Δι]ογενείον θύσαντες καὶ σπείσαντες ἐν τῶ Διογενείω τὰ ἐξιτήρια εὐωχήθησαν, ο[ὐδε]νὶ δὲ ἄλλω συνετέλε-σαν οἱ ἔφηβοι ἢ κατὰ τὸ ἀναγκαῖον τῶ καψαρίω μόνω. Mommsen *op. cit.* p. 168 f. argues that the *épheboi*, who began their course in Boedromion, must have ended it in Metageitnion: accordingly, if their concluding feast took place after the Panhellenia, we may refer the Panhellenia also to Metageitnion, *i.e.* to August or September. The relevance of *Corp. inscr. Att.* iii. 1 no. 85, 1 ff. οἱ Πανέλληνες | ΑΡΙΣΤΑ[Ν] | ...... | καρποῦ ἀπαρχῆς is doubtful : see W. Dittenberger *ad loc.*)).

Indignant at this, Zeus wished to consume his whole house with a thunderbolt. But when Apollon, whom Periphas used to honour exceedingly, begged Zeus not to destroy him utterly, Zeus granted the request. He came into the home of Periphas and found him embracing his wife. Grasping them both in his hands, he turned Periphas into an eagle; his wife, who begged him to make her too a bird to bear Periphas company, into a vulture. So upon Periphas he bestowed honours in return for his holy life among men, making him king over all the birds, and granting him to guard the sacred sceptre and to draw near to his own throne; while Periphas' wife he turned into a vulture, and suffered to appear as a good omen to men in all their doings[1].'

From what source Antoninus Liberalis, a compiler of the second century A.D. or later[2], drew this singular narrative is unknown[3]; nor are its incidents—apart from a casual reference in Ovid[4]—cited elsewhere. Nevertheless the story as it stands is instructive. Certain traits are late and must be suppressed. Thus the writer, or his authority, is inclined to etymologise[5] and, worse still, to moralise. His tale belongs to a well-defined group, in which an early king (Salmoneus is typical) poses as Zeus and is consequently punished by the real Zeus. This implies, as I have elsewhere pointed out[6], that, when the essential divinity of the old-world king had little by little faded into oblivion, posterity treated his claim to be Zeus as sheer impiety calling for the vengeance of the genuine god. Yet the author of our tale, with illuminating inconsistency, makes Zeus himself bestow upon the blasphemer altogether exceptional 'honours in return for his holy life.' I take it, then, that Periphas was an Attic king, who in the dim past had played the *rôle* of Zeus and made his petty thunder for some unsophisticated folk. It may even be that his name *Períphas*, 'the Brilliant[7],' was a recognised epithet of Zeus[8]; for an Orphic hymn salutes Zeus *Astrápios*, the lightning-god, as *períphantos*[9]. Now we have repeatedly found a human Zeus of this sort figuring among the kings of Thessaly descended from Aiolos[10]. It is therefore of interest to observe that Lapithes, the eponymous king of the Thessalian Lapithai, was either father[11] or son of a Periphas, who wedded Astyagyia

[1] Ant. Lib. 6.

[2] G. Wentzel in Pauly—Wissowa *Real-Enc.* i. 2573 ('schwerlich vor dem 2. Jhdt. n. Chr.'), W. Christ *Geschichte der griechischen Litteratur*[3] München 1898 p. 778 ('aus der Zeit der Antonine'). See further E. Oder *De Antonino Liberali* Bonn 1886 pp. 1—61.

[3] H. Usener in the *Rhein. Mus.* 1868 xxiii. 357 (=*id. Kleine Schriften* Leipzig—Berlin 1913 iv. 66) says: 'wahrscheinlich von Boios,' and O. Schneider *Nicandrea* Lipsiae 1856 p. 43 had reached the same conclusion before him. M. Wellmann in *Hermes* 1891 xxvi. 507 n. 2 thinks otherwise: 'Vermuthlich ist Nikander Quelle.'

[4] Ov. *met.* 7. 399 f. Palladias arces: quae te, iustissima Phene, | teque, senex Peripha, pariter videre volantes. Lact. Plac. *narr. fab.* 7. 20 merely echoes Ovid (M. Schanz *Geschichte der römischen Litteratur*[2] München 1899 ii. 1. 237 f.): venisse etiam Athenas, ubi Phineum (*sic*) et Peripham in aves conversos.

[5] He harps on derivatives of φαίνω, real or supposed: Περίφας...φανῆναι...φήνην... ἐπιφαίνεσθαι.

[6] *Class. Rev.* 1903 xvii. 277, *Folk-Lore* 1904 xv. 300.

[7] Περίφας = περιφανής (Gerhard *Auserl. Vasenb.* iii. 86), περίφαντος, περιφαής. Cp. Πολύφας, Ὑπέρφας. For other explanations see O. Höfer in Roscher *Lex. Myth.* iii. 1971 f.

[8] H. Usener in the *Rhein. Mus.* 1868 xxiii. 357 (=*id. Kleine Schriften* Leipzig—Berlin 1913 iv. 66 f.).

[9] Orph. *h. Zeus* Astrápios 20. 1 ff. κικλήσκω μέγαν, ἀγνόν, ἐρισμάραγον, περίφαντον, | ...ἀστράπιον Δία, παγγενέτην, βασιλῆα μέγιστον, | κ.τ.λ. adduced by O. Höfer *loc. cit.*

[10] *Supra* p. 1088.

[11] Epaphroditos *Homerica frag.* 16 Luenzner *ap.* Steph. Byz. *s.v.* Λαπίθη.

daughter of Hypseus and became by her the father of Antion and the grand-father of Ixion[1]. J. Töpffer in an important article[2] insisted on the point that Periphas was at once an Attic autochthon and a Thessalian king : he compared other cases of the same bilocation[3] and, following up the clue thus afforded, reached the conclusion that in prehistoric times some Thessalian tribe (Lapithai? Dryopes?) migrated southwards through Euboia to north-eastern Attike, and so on by sea to the southern parts of the Argolid. Töpffer's hypothesis has been accepted by P. Weizsäcker[4] and is, I think, helpful in any attempt to unravel the tangled skein of Attic religion. For, in view of their traditional descent from Aiolos, we shall probably be right in supposing that these immigrants were Aeolians (not Achaeans[5]), who, swarming off from Thessaly in days before the great Athenian *synoikismós*, settled in Attike and planted the worship of their[6] Zeus *Olýmpios* on the northern bank of the Ilissos. The leader of the settlement, regarded by his subjects as the human representative of the sky-god, would later on be reverenced in the same neighbourhood as Zeus *Sotér* and *Epópsios* and *Meilíchios*. All these titles, whose connotation was subsequently enlarged in a variety of directions, were from the first applicable to the buried king. To begin with, he was *Sotér*, because on him depended the preservation and perpetuation of the family line. Custom prescribed that at a banquet libation should be made from the first mixing-bowl to Zeus *Olýmpios* and the Olympians, from the second to the Heroës, from the third to Zeus *Sotér*, otherwise styled *Téleios*[7]. The sequence suggests that this final offering was in its essence simply

---

[1] Diod. 4. 69, who—according to E. Schwartz (Pauly—Wissowa *Real-Enc.* v. 674)—is here excerpting from an earlier mythographical handbook.

[2] J. Töpffer 'Theseus und Peirithoos' in *Aus der Anomia* Berlin 1890 pp. 30—46.

[3] Theseus, Peirithoos, Boutes, Ixion, Phorbas, Phaleros, Mopsos, etc. Töpffer remarks *inter alia* that Perithoidai, a deme of the tribe Oineis (A. Milchhöfer in Pauly—Wissowa *Real-Enc.* ii. 2195, with map to face p. 2204, places it to the N.W. of Athens on the near side of Mt Aigaleos), was said to have been founded by Peirithoos son of Ixion, and that the Athenian custom of extending a special welcome to Thessalians was motived by the friendship of Theseus and Peirithoos (Ephoros *frag.* 37 (*Frag. hist. Gr.* i. 243 Müller) *ap.* Phot. *lex. s.v.* Περιθοῖδαι, Souid. *s.v.* Περιθοῖδαι, Apostol. 14. 19).

[4] P. Weizsäcker in Roscher *Lex. Myth.* iii. 1762.

[5] The commonly received opinion that the Achaeans were an Aeolian people is subjected to shrewd criticism by J. A. K. Thomson *Studies in the Odyssey* Oxford 1914 p. 117 ff. See further A. Fick 'Äoler und Achäer' in the *Zeitschrift für vergleichende Sprachforschung auf dem Gebiete der indogermanischen Sprachen* 1911 xliv. 1 ff., *eund.* 'Älteste griechische Stammverbände' *ib.* 1914 xlvi. 67 ff., G. Dottin *Les anciens peuples de l'Europe* Paris 1916 p. 143 ff.

[6] A. Fick *loc. cit.* 1914 xlvi. 97.

[7] Poll. 6. 15 κρατῆρες δὲ ὁ μὲν πρῶτος Διὸς Ὀλυμπίου καὶ Ὀλυμπίων θεῶν, ὁ δὲ δεύτερος ἡρώων, ὁ δὲ τρίτος Διὸς Σωτῆρος Τελείου, ὅτι καὶ τὰ τρία πρῶτα τέλειος ἀριθμός, 6. 100 ὥσπερ καὶ Διὸς Σωτῆρος ὁ τρίτος κρατὴρ ἱερὸς ἦν, Schol. Pind. *Isthm.* 6 (5). 10 τὸν δὲ τρίτον κρατῆρα Διὸς Σωτῆρος ἔλεγον, καθὰ καὶ Σοφοκλῆς ἐν Ναυπλίῳ (*frag.* 392 Nauck[2], 425 Jebb)·
'Ζεῦ παυσίλυπε καὶ Διὸς σωτηρίου | σπονδὴ τρίτου κρατῆρος.' τὸν μὲν γὰρ πρῶτον Διὸς Ὀλυμπίου ἐκίρνασαν, τὸν δὲ δεύτερον ἡρώων, τὸν δὲ τρίτον Διὸς Σωτῆρος, καθὰ καὶ Αἰσχύλος ἐν Ἐπιγόνοις (*frag.* 55 Nauck[2])· 'λοιβὰς Διὸς μὲν πρῶτον ὡραίου γάμου | "Ηρας τε.' εἶτα· 'τὴν δευτέραν γε (C. G. Schütz cj. δὲ) κρᾶσιν "Ηρωσιν νέμω.' εἶτα· 'τρίτον (A. Nauck cj. τρίτην) Διὸς Σωτῆρος εὐκταίαν λίβα.' Διὸς δὲ Σωτῆρος ἔλεγον τὸν τρίτον διὰ τὸ τοὺς τούτου πίνοντας σταθεροὺς γίνεσθαι, τοὺς δὲ μετὰ τοῦτον εἰς ἄτην καὶ ἀνομίαν καὶ ἀσέλγειαν τρέπεσθαι. ἔλεγον δὲ αὐτὸν καὶ Τέλειον διὰ τὸ τέλειον εἶναι τὸν τρίτον ἀριθμὸν ἀρχὴν ἔχοντα καὶ μέσον καὶ τέλος, schol. Plat. *Phileb.* 66 D τὸ τρίτον τῷ Σωτῆρι : ἐκ μεταφορᾶς εἴρηται τοῦ ἐν ταῖς

συνουσίαις ἔθους· Σοφοκλῆς ἐν Ναυπλίῳ καταπλέοντι. ἐκιρνῶντο γὰρ ἐν αὐταῖς κρατῆρες τρεῖς. καὶ τὸν μὲν πρῶτον Διὸς Ὀλυμπίου καὶ θεῶν Ὀλυμπίων ἔλεγον, τὸν δὲ δεύτερον ἡρώων, τὸν δὲ τρίτον Σωτῆρος, ὡς ἐνταῦθά τε καὶ δὴ καὶ ἐν Πολιτείᾳ (Plat. rep. 583 B). ἔλεγον δὲ αὐτὸν καὶ Τέλειον, ὡς Εὐριπίδης Ἀνδρομέδᾳ (frag. 148 Nauck²) καὶ Ἀριστοφάνης Ταγηνισταῖς (frag. 33 Meineke), schol. Plat. Charm. 167 A—B τὸ τρίτον τῷ Σωτῆρι: ἐπὶ τῶν τελείως τι πραττόντων. τὰς γὰρ τρίτας σπονδὰς καὶ τὸν τρίτον κρατῆρα ἐκίρνων τῷ Διὶ τῷ Σωτῆρι. τέλειος γὰρ ὁ τρία ἀριθμός, ἐπειδὴ καὶ ἀρχὴν καὶ μέσον καὶ τέλος ἔχει, καὶ πρῶτος οὗτος τῶν ἀριθμῶν ἀρτιοπέριττος. Τέλειος δὲ καὶ ὁ Ζεύς, ὥστε κατὰ λόγον τρίτον τῷ Διὶ σπένδεταί τε καὶ ὁ κρατὴρ τρίτος τίθεται. Σοφοκλῆς Ναυπλίῳ· 'καὶ Διὸς σωτηρίου | σπονδὴ τρίτου κρατῆρος,' καὶ Πλάτων Πολιτείαις καὶ ἐνταῦθα, Hesych. s.v. τρίτος κρατήρ· Σοφοκλῆς Ναυπλίῳ καταπλέοντι. ἐν ταῖς συνουσίαις ἐκιρνῶντο κρατῆρες τρεῖς. καὶ τὸν μὲν πρῶτον Διὸς Ὀλυμπίου καὶ θεῶν Ὀλυμπίων ἔλεγον· τὸν δὲ δεύτερον ἡρώων· τὸν δὲ τρίτον Σωτῆρος, schol. Arat. phaen. 14 τὴν μὲν πρώτην σπονδὴν εἶναι θεῶν τῶν Ὀλυμπίων, δευτέραν δὲ ἡρώων, καὶ τρίτην Διὸς Σωτῆρος, Souid. s.v. τρίτου κρατῆρος· τοῦ Σωτῆρος, ὃν καὶ Τέλειον ἔλεγον. τὸν μέν γε (G. Bernhardy cj. μὲν γὰρ) πρῶτον Ὀλυμπίων φασί· τὸν δὲ β' Ἡρώων, <τὸν δὲ γ' Σωτῆρος ins. T. Gaisford>. Πλάτων Πολιτείᾳ· τὸν (G. Bernhardy cj. τὸ) δὲ γ' Ὀλυμπικῶς τῷ Σωτῆρί τε καὶ Ὀλυμπίῳ (cp. Plat. rep. 583 B) = Phot. lex. s.v. τρίτου κρατῆρος· τοῦ Σωτῆρος, ὃν καὶ Τέλειον ἔλεγον. τὸν μὲν πρῶτον Ὀλυμπίων φασί, τὸν δὲ δεύτερον ἡρώων, τὸν δὲ τρίτον Ὀλυμπικῶς τῷ Σωτῆρί τε καὶ Ὀλυμπίῳ, ib. s.v. τρίτος κρατήρ· Διὸς Τελείου Σωτῆρος· πρῶτος γὰρ τέλειος ἀριθμὸς ὁ τρία, ὅτι ἔχει ἀρχὴν καὶ τέλος καὶ μέσα, ὡς Φιλόχορος ἐν τῷ περὶ Ἡμερῶν (frag. 179 (Frag. hist. Gr. i. 414 Müller)), Apostol. 10. 5 a κρατὴρ τρίτος Διὸς Σωτῆρος· εἰώθασι γὰρ ἐν συμποσίοις οἱ παλαιοὶ κιρνᾶν κρατῆρα πρῶτον Ὀλυμπίῳ Διί, δεύτερον τοῖς ἥρωσι, τὸν δὲ τρίτον Διὸς Σωτῆρος. Σοφοκλῆς τοῦτο μαρτυρεῖ ἐν Ναυπλόῳ (A. Boeckh corr. Ναυπλίῳ)· 'Ζεῦ παυσίλυπε (P. Wolters in the Ath. Mitth. 1903 xxxviii. 197 notes a skýphos at Athens (no. 12351) with incised inscription ΠΑΓϹΙΑΓΠΟϹ) καὶ Διὸς σωτηρίου | σπονδαὶ τρίτου κρατῆρος,' 10. 77 a 'λοιβὰς <Διὸς> μὲν πρῶτον ὡραίου γάμου | Ἥρας τε.· εἶτα· 'τὴν δευτέραν <γε> κρᾶσιν Ἥρωσιν νέμω,' 17. 28 τρίτου κρατῆρος ἐγεύσω (a proverb in ancient dactylic metre: supra i. 444)· ἐπὶ τῶν μεμυημένων τὰ τελεώτατα καὶ σωτηριωδέστερα. τρεῖς δὲ ἦσαν κρατῆρες· καὶ τὸν μὲν πρῶτον ἔλεγον Ὀλυμπίων, τὸν δὲ δεύτερον ἡρώων, <τὸν δὲ τρίτον Σωτῆρος ins. T. Gaisford>. Πλάτων ἐν Πολιτείᾳ· τὸν (leg. τὸ) δὲ τρίτον Ὀλυμπικῶς τῷ Σωτῆρί τε <καὶ> Ὀλυμπίῳ. S. A. Naber on Phot. lex. s.v. τρίτου κρατῆρος says: 'Boethi observatio est.' A. C. Pearson on Soph. frag. 425 Jebb remarks: 'It is clear that our passage was a stock instance with the grammarians, and that all the quotations given above are derived from a common source: this was in all probability Didymus, from whom they may have passed to Diogenian, and thence to the Platonic scholia.' Another tradition is evidenced by Souid. s.v. κρατήρ· τρεῖς κρατῆρας ἵστασαν ἐν τῷ δείπνῳ· α' Ἑρμῇ, β' Χαρισίῳ (T. Hemsterhuys cj. Χάρισιν), γ' Διὶ Σωτῆρι.

A kratér or stámnos of Apulian ware from Fasano, now in the British Museum (Brit. Mus. Cat. Vases iv. 226 no. F 548, P. Wolters in the Ath. Mitth. 1903 xxxviii. 198 n. 2), has its body decorated with (a) a vine-wreath, from which hang two branches with a comic mask between them and a rosette on either side; (b) an ivy-wreath. On its neck is painted in white ΔΙΟΣ ΣΩΤΗΡΟΣ (Corp. inscr. Gr. iv no. 8470 c).

Literary allusions to the third bowl of Zeus Σωτήρ will be found e.g. in Pind. Isthm. 6 (5). 10 ff., Aisch. suppl. 27 f., Ag. 244 ff., 1385 ff., cho. 577 f. with 1073 f., Eum. 759 f., frag. 55 Nauck², Soph. frag. 392 Nauck², 425 Jebb, Eur. frag. 148 Nauck² (?), Aristoph. tagenistaí frag. 33 Meineke (?), Plat. Charm. 167 A—B, rep. 583 B, Phileb. 66 D, legg. 692 A, epist. 7. 334 D, 340 A, Antiphanes ágroikoi frag. 5 Meineke ap. Athen. 692 F, Euboulos kybeutaí frag. 1 Meineke ap. Athen. 471 D—E, Alexis tokistés or katapseudómenos frag. 3 Meineke ap. Athen. 692 F f., frag. fab. inc. 12 Meineke ap. Athen. 466 D—E (a goblet inscribed in golden letters ΔΙΟΣ ΣΩΤΗΡΟΣ), Diphilos Sappho frag. 1 Meineke ap. Athen. 487 A, Philochoros frag. 18 (Frag. hist. Gr. i. 387 Müller) ap. Athen. 38 C—D, Diod. 4. 3, Philonides de unguentis et coronis ap. Athen. 675 B—C, Eumath. 1. 14 (τέταρτον (sic) ἐπίνομεν Σωτῆρι Διί).

The chthonian character of the god is well brought out by Aischylos. In suppl. 24 ff. the chorus of Danaïdes prays: ὧν πόλις, ὧν γῆ καὶ λευκὸν ὕδωρ | ὕπατοί τε θεοὶ καὶ βαρύ-

drink for the soul of a dead man. As such it was duplicated by the cup of unmixed wine drunk after dinner in the name of the Agathos Daimon[1]. Both

τιμοι | χθόνιοι θήκας κατέχοντες, | καὶ Ζεὺς Σωτὴρ τρίτος, οἰκοφύλαξ | ὁσίων ἀνδρῶν, κ.τ.λ. In *Ag.* 1385 ff. Klytaimestra describes the third and fatal blow dealt by her hand: καὶ πεπτωκότι | τρίτην ἐπενδίδωμι, τοῦ κατὰ χθονός | Διὸς (so R. Enger for ἄιδου codd.) νεκρῶν Σωτῆρος εὐκταίαν χάριν, where W. Kausche 'Mythologumena Aeschylea' in the *Dissertationes philologicae Halenses* Halis Saxonum 1888 ix. 179 and A. W. Verrall (ed. 1889) adhere to the manuscript reading, but W. Headlam (trans. 1904) and U. von Wilamowitz-Moellendorff (ed. 1914) rightly accept Διός.

[1] With regard to the Agathos Daimon various opinions have been held: see E. Gerhard *Über Wesen, Verwandtschaft und Ursprung der Dämonen und Genien* Berlin 1852 pp. 12 f., 30 (=*Abh. d. berl. Akad. 1852* Phil.-hist. Classe pp. 248 f., 266), K. Lehrs *Populäre Aufsätze aus dem Alterthum*[2] Leipzig 1875 i. 173 ff. ('Dämon und Tyche'), E. Saglio in Daremberg—Saglio *Dict. Ant.* i. 131, K. Wernicke in Pauly—Wissowa *Real-Enc.* i. 746 f., Preller—Robert *Gr. Myth.* i. 541 ff., Rohde *Psyche*[3] i. 254 n. 2, Gruppe *Gr. Myth. Rel.* p. 1087 n. 2, Nilsson *Gr. Feste* p. 401 f., Harrison *Themis* p. 277 ff.

On the whole it seems probable that the *Agathòs Daímon* or 'Good Spirit' was originally the male ancestor of the family addressed by a euphemistic title (*supra* p. 1112 n. 7). As such, he was a giver of fertility and wealth, a sort of Plouton or chthonian Zeus, equipped with a *cornu copiae* (Cornut. *theol.* 27 p. 51, 11 ff. Ἀγαθὸς δὲ Δαίμων... προστάτης...καὶ σωτὴρ τῶν οἰκείων ἐστὶ τῷ σώζειν καλῶς τὸν ἴδιον οἶκον... τὸ δὲ τῆς Ἀμαλθείας κέρας οἰκεῖον αὐτῷ φόρημά ἐστιν, ἐν ᾧ ἅμα πάντα ἀλόῆσκει τὰ κατὰ τοὺς οἰκείους καιροὺς φυόμενα, κ.τ.λ.). An Athenian relief shows him as a bearded man carrying his horn and associated with his usual partner, Agathe Tyche (L. Stephani in the *Compte-rendu St. Pét.* 1859 p. 111, R. Schöne *Griechische Reliefs aus athenischen Sammlungen* Leipzig 1872 p. 55 pl. 26, 109. The inscriptions run: ...ι... | ἀνέθηκ... | Ἀγαθὸς Δα[ίμω]ν ['Αγ]α[θὴ] Τύχη): cp. *Brit. Mus. Marbles* xi. 90 ff. pl. 47, *Brit. Mus. Cat. Sculpture* iii. 232 no. 2163, Reinach *Rép. Reliefs* ii. 481 no. 5. A relief from Thespiai represents a similar figure seated before an altar (?) with a *phiále* in his right hand, a horn in his left (G. Körte in the *Ath. Mitth.* 1878 iii. 408 no. 189, O. Kern *ib.* 1891 xvi. 24 f. fig.). And another relief from Thespiai completes the likeness to Zeus by the addition of throne, sceptre, and eagle (O. Kern in the *Ath. Mitth.* 1891 xvi. 24 f. fig. = my fig. 951, Harrison *Proleg. Gk. Rel.*[2] p. 356 f. fig. 107, *infra* Append. N *init.* Inscribed: Ἀγέστροτο[s], | Τιμοκρά-τεια, | Πιωτάλλεια, | Ἐμπεδονίκα | Ἀγαθοῖ Δήμον[ι] (*Inscr. Gr. sept.* i no. 1815)). Hence, although the contention of J. Neuhaeuser *De Graecorum daemonibus particula prior* Berolini 1857 p. 10 ff. that the word δαίμων was in the beginning 'ipsius summi numinis appellatio' is justly dismissed by Gruppe *Gr. Myth. Rel.* p. 1087 n. 2, we can understand the reasoning of Paus. 8. 36. 5 Μεγαλοπολίταις δὲ διὰ τῶν ἐπὶ τὸ ἕλος ὀνομαζο-μένων πυλῶν, διὰ τούτων ὁδεύουσιν ἐς Μαίναλον

Fig. 951.

παρὰ τὸν ποταμὸν τὸν Ἑλισσόντα ἔστι τῆς ὁδοῦ ἐν ἀριστερᾷ Ἀγαθοῦ Θεοῦ ναός· εἰ δὲ ἀγαθῶν οἱ θεοὶ δοτῆρές εἰσιν ἀνθρώποις, Ζεὺς δὲ ὕπατος θεῶν ἐστιν, ἐπόμενος ἄν τις τῷ λόγῳ τὴν ἐπίκλησιν ταύτην·Διὸς τεκμαίροιτο εἶναι. Others besides Pausanias took the Agathos Theos to be a sort of Zeus. Tiberius Claudius Xenokles, after serving as fire-bearer, set up an altar at Epidauros in 224 A.D. to the local Agathos Theos, whom he represented as a chthonian Zeus with a sceptre in his right hand, a *cornu copiae* in his left, and a snake wriggling below](P. Cavvadias *Fouilles d'Épidaure* Athènes 1893 i. 45 no. 44, Harrison *Themis* p. 285 f. fig. 75, M. Fränkel in the *Inscr. Gr. Pelop.* i no. 1059 with numeral πθ′ and circle no. 2 *ib.* p. 186 possibly meant for a snake emerging from its hole (?)); cp. another block erected at Epidauros in 187 A.D. by Tiberius Claudius Pollio, after service as *hierapólos*, to the Agathos Theos and to Agathe (P. Cavvadias *op. cit.* i. 44 f. nos. 41—41ᵃ, M. Fränkel *loc. cit.* i no. 997: Agathos Theos has numeral ξγ′ and circle no. 1 *ib.* p. 186 possibly meant for a snake emerging from its hole (?); Agathe has numeral ξϛ′). The same explanation might well be given of the Zeus-like Theos Megas at Odessos in Thrace,

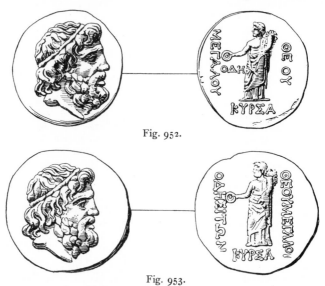

Fig. 952.

Fig. 953.

where silver tetradrachms were struck in *s.* ii B.C. with *obv.* a bearded male head wearing a fillet, *rev.* the bearded god standing with *phiále* and *cornu copiae* (B. Pick in the *Jahrb. d. kais. deutsch. arch. Inst.* 1898 xiii. 155 f. pl. 10, 20 = my fig. 952, Head *Hist. num.*² p. 276 fig. 167, inscribed ΘΕΟΥ ΜΕΓΑΛΟΥ ΟΔΗ and ΚΥΡΣΑ below. *Hunter Cat. Coins* i. 418 pl. 28, 4 = my fig. 953 inscribed ΘΕΟΥΜΕΓΑΛΟΥ ΟΔΗΣΙΤΩΝ and ΚΥΡΣΑ below. For later variants see *Brit. Mus. Cat. Coins* Thrace etc. p. 137 ff. fig., *Hunter Cat. Coins* i. 418 f. pl. 28, 5, Head *Hist. num.*² p. 276 f., and especially B. Pick in the *Jahrb. d. kais. deutsch. arch. Inst.* 1898 xiii. 157 ff. pl. 10, 15 ff. and *Ant. Münz. Nord-Griechenlands* i. 2. 524 ff. pl. 4 f.).

Fig. 954.

Fourth-century sculptors *more suo* represented the Agathos Daimon in younger form. Plin. *nat. hist.* 34. 77 mentions among the bronzes of Euphranor to be seen at Rome 'a statue of Bonus Eventus holding a *patera* in its right hand, a corn-ear and poppies in its left.' Fröhner *Méd. emp. rom.* p. 35 f. fig. detected the type on a bronze medallion struck by Hadrian (Gnecchi *Medagl. Rom.* ii. 3 no. 3) and Furtwängler *Masterpieces of Gk. Sculpt.* p. 349 f. fig. 149 with pl. 6, 37, id.

Ant. Gemmen i pl. 44, 9 ff., ii. 211 f. illustrated it from gems and coins of Galba etc. (in fig. 954 I add the reverse of an unpublished copper of Antoninus Pius in my collection):

cp. also a cameo plaque of blue glass now in the British Museum (*Brit. Mus. Marbles* iii Frontisp., F. Robiou in Daremberg—Saglio *Dict. Ant.* i. 737 fig. 870, Reinach *Rép. Reliefs* ii. 462 no. 5, C. Davenport *Cameos* London 1900 p. 24 f. pl. 3, Harrison *Themis* p. 302 f. fig. 82), which Taylor Combe *Brit. Mus. Marbles loc. cit.* already recognised as a copy of Euphranor's statue. Plin. *nat. hist.* 36. 23 in his list of marble works by Praxiteles at Rome includes 'the statues of Bonus Eventus and Bona Fortuna on the Capitol.' W. Klein *Praxiteles* Leipzig 1898 p. 156, greatly daring, would identify the Praxitelean Bonus Eventus with the bronze original of the Madrid Hypnos and its numerous congeners, *e.g.* the bronze statuette of a horn-bearing Hypnos at Vienna (*id. ib.* p. 140 fig. 21). Be that as it may, the common assumption that Pliny's *Bonus Eventus* and *Bona Fortuna* are the Latinised forms of *Agathòs Daímon* and *Agathè Týche* is probably correct.

Not till Hellenistic times do we get evidence of the Agathos Daimon conceived as a snake. This belief was especially prevalent in Egypt; but it seems to have spread from thence to Delos, and even to Rome. According to the foundation-legend of Alexandreia, when the city-walls began to rise, a snake of huge size and majestic bearing attacked the workmen and hindered their work. Alexander the Great bade his men assemble on the following day to slay the monster. This was done on the site of the later Stoa. An elaborate tomb was built for the snake, and Alexander had garland-shops erected near by 'in order that the beast, commonly thought to do service in temples—it is called Agathos Daimon—, might itself be worshipped as a deity' (Iul. Valer. 1. 28 p. 37, 15 ff. Kuebler. The concluding words are: 26 ff. ut quod haec bestia famulitium quoddam templis praestare videbatur—daemon <enim> melior appellatur—, ipse quoque divina quadam religione coleretur). When the snake's tomb was finished, certain blocks of the architrave over the columns of the entrance gave way, and from them were seen to issue numerous snakes (cp. *supra* i. 205 f.). These crept about and entered the *penetralia* of the newly built houses. Soothsayers declared that they too were presiding Daimones to be worshipped in every house as *di Penates*. Hence the custom at Alexandreia that on definite days wheaten meal is thrown for the snakes to eat and the upper classes, with garlands, go up to the temple of the Heros, who is served by snakes of this sort (Iul. Valer. 1. 29 p. 38, 18 ff. Kuebler. Cp. pseudo-Kallisth. 1. 32 ἱδρυμένου δὲ τοῦ πυλῶνος τοῦ ἱεροῦ ἐξαίφνης πλὰξ μεγίστη ἐξέπεσεν ἀρχαιοτάτη πλήρης γραμμάτων, ἐξ ἧς ἐξῆλθον ὄφεις πολλοί, καὶ ἑρπύζοντες εἰσῆλθον εἰς τὰς ὁδοὺς τῶν ἤδη τεθεμελιωμένων οἰκιῶν. [τὴν πόλιν γὰρ ἔτι παρὼν Ἀλέξανδρος καθίδρυσεν τῇ αὑτοῦ δυνάμει ἰαννουαρίου πρώτῃ καὶ αὐτὸ τὸ ἱερόν.] ὅθεν τούτους τοὺς ὄφεις σέβονται οἱ θυρωροὶ ὡς Ἀγαθοὺς Δαίμονας εἰσιόντας εἰς τὰς οἰκίας· οὐ γάρ εἰσιν ἰοβόλα ζῷα with the addition in cod. A ἐκέλευσε δὲ ὁ Ἀλέξανδρος τοῖς φύλαξι τῶν οἴκων σῖτον δοθῆναι. οἱ δὲ λαβόντες, ἀλήσαντες καὶ ἀθηροποιησάμενοι τὴν ἡμέραν (C. Müller cj. ταύτῃ τῇ ἡμέρᾳ) τοῖς ἐνοικοῦσι θάλλους διδόασιν· ὅθεν καὶ μέχρι τοῦ δεῦρο τοῦτον τὸν νόμον φυλάττουσι παρ᾽ Ἀλεξανδρεῦσι, Τύβι (so C. Müller for Τύβη) κε΄ τὰ μὲν κτήνη στεφανοῦσθαι, θυσιάζεσθαι <δὲ> τοῖς Ἀγαθοῖς Δαίμοσι τοῖς προνοουμένοις τῶν οἰκιῶν, καὶ διασώσεις (διαδόσεις? C. Müller) τῶν ἀθηρῶν ποιεῖσθαι). See further Plout. *amat.* 12 ἐν Αἰγύπτῳ ποτὲ γείτονας ἑώρων δύο διαμφισβητοῦντας ὄφεως προσερπύσαντος εἰς τὴν ὁδόν, ἀμφοτέρων μὲν Ἀγαθὸν Δαίμονα καλούντων, ἑκάτερου δ᾽ ἔχειν ἀξιοῦντος ὡς ἴδιον, Lamprid. *v. Heliogab.* 28. 3 Aegyptios dracunculos Romae habuit, quos illi Agathodaemonas vocant, C. Wessely *Griechische Zauberpapyrus von Paris und London* Wien 1888 p. 81 pap. Par. 2427 ff. (part of a charm to secure wealth, in which a waxen man begs with his right hand, holds in his left a wallet and a staff with a snake coiled about it, and has a coiled snake on his belt and upon the crown of his head) εἰς δὲ τὸν δράκοντα τὸ | ὄνομα τοῦ Ἀγαθοῦ Δαίμονος, ὅ ἐστιν, | ὡς λέγει Ἐπαφρόδιτος, [ὅ ἐστιν] τὸ ὑποκείμ(ενον)· | φρη αν ωϊ φωρχω φνννν ρορψις | οροχωωϊ, ὡς δὲ ἐν τῷ χάρτῃ δ (sic) εὑρό(ν), | μετεβλήθη τὸ πραγματικὸν οὕτως· | αρπονκνουφι ὁ, Philon Bybl. *frag.* 9 (*Frag. hist. Gr.* iii. 572 Müller) ap. Euseb. *praep. ev.* 1. 10. 48 ff. Φοίνικες δὲ αὐτὸ (sc. the snake) Ἀγαθὸν Δαίμονα καλοῦσιν. ὁμοίως καὶ Αἰγύπτιοι Κνήφ ἐπονομάζουσι· προσθέασι δὲ αὐτῷ ἱέρακος κεφαλὴν διὰ τὸ πρακτικὸν τοῦ ἱέρακος…ἔτι μὴν οἱ Αἰγύπτιοι ἀπὸ τῆς αὐτῆς ἐννοίας τὸν κόσμον γράφοντες περιφερῆ κύκλον ἀεροειδῆ καὶ πυρωπὸν χαράσσουσι, καὶ μέσα τεταμένον ὄφιν ἱερακόμορφον, καὶ ἔστι τὸ πᾶν σχῆμα ὡς τὸ παρ᾽ ἡμῖν θῆτα, τὸν μὲν κύκλον κόσμον μηνύοντες τὸν δὲ μέσον ὄφιν συνεκτικὸν τούτου Ἀγαθὸν Δαίμονα σημαίνοντες. Nero, who in Egypt called himself ὁ Ἀγαθὸς Δαίμων τῆς | οἰκουμένης (Corp. inscr. Gr. iii no. 4699, 3 f. = Dittenberger Orient. Gr. inscr. sel. no. 666, 3 f.), struck billon coins there with the reverse type of a serpent enfolding corn-ears and poppy-heads, inscribed NEO·ΑΓΑΘ·ΔΑΙΜ = νέος Ἀγαθὸς Δαίμων (Brit. Mus. Cat. Coins Alexandria p. 20 f. pl. 26, 171 = my fig. 955, Hunter Cat. Coins iii. 413, Head Hist. num.² p. 863, E. Saglio in Daremberg—Saglio Dict. Ant. i. 131 fig. 174, Harrison Themis p. 277 fig. 66). And a remarkable contorniate medal shows him as the νέος Ἀπόλλων, νέος Διόνυσος (supra pp. 96 n. 3, 254), and νέος Ἀγαθὸς Δαίμων rolled into one (fig. 956 from a specimen in my collection. Obv.: Head of Nero to right, with bow and arrow in front of him, and ivy-leaf behind him. The usual compendium ⱷ here appears on Nero's face, the P encircling his eye and the E marking his nostril and mouth. Also the muscles of his neck are peculiarly rendered in the form of an ivy-leaf. Rev.: Bearded and crested snake approaching a portable altar with dependent fillets). The antechamber of a Graeco-Egyptian catacomb at Kom el Chougafa has its doorway flanked by two such snakes equipped with thýrsos and winged caduceus (F. W. von Bissing Les bas-reliefs de Kom el Chougafa Munich 1901 pl. 1). Another rock-cut tomb, known locally as 'the grave of

Fig. 955.

Fig. 956.

Adam and Eve,' in the garden of the late Sir John Antoniadis at Alexandreia has its innermost niche occupied by the relief of a large snake coiled on a couch with gay-coloured cushions (H. Thiersch Zwei antike Grabanlagen bei Alexandria Berlin 1904 p. 6 ff. figs. 6 f., p. 16 f. pl. 5 f.). This challenges comparison with a relief from Delos, which shows a large bearded snake similarly installed on a couch between a bearded male figure bearing phiále and cornu copiae to the right and a female figure bearing oinochóe and cornu copiae to the left: these personages, who both have a modius on their heads and are draped alike in chitón and himátion, should be interpreted as Agathos Daimon (hardly Sarapis or Plouton) and Agathe Tyche (M. Bulard in the Bull. Corr. Hell. 1907 xxxi. 525 ff. fig. 24, Reinach Rép. Reliefs ii. 326 no. 2). Agathos Daimon is, in fact, here represented both in his animal and in his human form. Similarly a marble statue at Berlin, which portrays Antinoos as Agathos Daimon, makes him a youthful Dionysiac figure resting his hand on a cornu copiae with a snake twined about it (Ant. Skulpt. Berlin p. 146 f. no. 361 fig., Clarac Mus. de Sculpt. pl. 947 fig. 2427, E. Saglio in Daremberg—Saglio Dict. Ant. i. 131 fig. 173). A small relief of s. iii A.D. in the Palazzo Massimo alle Terme again groups Agathos Daimon with Agathe Tyche (F. von Duhn in Matz—Duhn Ant. Bildw. in Rom iii. 144 no. 3764 says Sarapis (?) with Alexandreia (?). F. Grossi Gondi 'Di una singolare rappresentazione mitologica sincretistica del culto romano' in the Bull. Comm. Arch. Comun. di Roma 1910 xxxviii. 150—160 fig. 1 decides for Serapis with Isis (Isityche)). It represents the former as a coiled snake with

had their counterpart in another Greek custom. 'Food that fell from the tables,' says Athenaios, 'they used to assign to their dead friends.' And by way of proof he quotes from Euripides the couplet descriptive of the love-sick Sthenoboia, who believes that Bellerophontes is dead:

> Never a crumb falls from her finger-tips
> But she must cry: 'For the Corinthian guest[1]!'

Athenaios might have added the Pythagorean precept not to pick up food from the floor, a precept utilised by Aristophanes in his *Heroes* and duly recorded by Aristotle *On the Pythagoreans*[2].

a bearded human head wearing a *modius*, the latter as a draped goddess likewise wearing a *modius* and holding a leafy spray (hardly corn-ears) in her right hand, a *cornu copiae* in her left, while a large jar projects from the ground beside her.

Agathos Daimon was, on this showing, a chthonian power essentially akin to Zeus *Sotér*. As a fertilising agent he was naturally brought into connexion with Dionysos (see bibliography at the beginning of this note), with whom he is even identified (Philonides *de unguentis et coronis ap.* Athen. 675 B). The postprandial draught of unmixed wine is referred to Agathos Daimon by Aristoph. *eq.* 105 ff., *vesp.* 525, *pax* 300 with scholl. *ad locc.*, Antiphanes *lampás frag.* 1 Meineke *ap.* Athen. 486 F and 487 B, Theophr. *ap.* Athen. 693 C—D, Aelius Dionysios *ap.* Eustath. *in Od.* p. 1471, 32 ff., Ail. *var. hist.* 1. 20, Hesych. *s.v.* Ἀγαθοῦ Δαίμονος πόμα = Bekker *anecd.* i. 209, 14 ff., i. 334, 4 ff. = Apostol. 1. 10. Cp. also the Ἀγαθοδαιμονισταί (Hesych. *s.v.*) or Ἀγαθοδαιμονιασταί (Aristot. *eth. Eud.* 3. 6. 1233 b 3 f., *Inscr. Gr. ins.* i no. 161, 5 = Collitz—Bechtel *Gr. Dial.-Inschr.* iii. 1. 478 f. no. 3842, 5 καὶ ὑπὸ [Διοσ]αταβυριαστᾶν Ἀγαθοδαιμονιαστᾶν Φιλ(ω)νείων κοινοῦ κ.τ.λ., with Plout. *symp.* 3. 7. 1). The toast Ἀγαθοῦ Δαίμονος is distinguished from the toast Διὸς Σωτῆρος by Eriphos *frag.* 3 Meineke *ap.* Athen. 693 C, Xenarchos *dídymoi frag.* 1 Meineke *ap.* Athen. 693 B—C, Diod. 4. 3, Poll. 6. 100, Athen. 692 F, Souid. *s.v.* Ἀγαθοῦ Δαίμονος, schol. Aristoph. *pax* 300, cp. Philochoros *frag.* 18 (*Frag. hist. Gr.* i. 387 Müller) *ap.* Athen. 38 C—D and *frag.* 19 (*Frag. hist. Gr.* i. 387 Müller) *ap.* Athen. 693 D—E, and never really confused with it (Diphilos *Sappho frag.* 1 Meineke *ap.* Athen. 487 A Ἀρχίλοχε, δέξαι τήνδε τὴν μετανιπτρίδα | μεστὴν Διὸς Σωτῆρος, Ἀγαθοῦ Δαίμονος is a case of asyndeton, not of apposition. Cp. *e.g.* Herond. 2. 67 f.).

A *kántharos* with knotted handles from Athens (Nicole *Cat. Vases d'Athènes Suppl.* p. 272 f. no. 1173, C. Watzinger in the *Ath. Mitth.* 1901 xxvi. 74 no. 17 fig., P. Wolters *ib.* 1913 xxxviii. 198 n. 2) has round its neck a yellow ivy-wreath, above which is painted in white ΑΓΑΘΟΥ ΘΕΟΥ. A small vase at Kentoripa (*Centorbi*) is inscribed ΑΓΑΘΟΥΔΑΜΟϵ, which is perhaps to be read as Ἀγαθοῦ Δαίμονος rather than as Ἀγαθοδάμου (*Inscr. Gr. Sic. It.* no. 2406, 109, P. Wolters *loc. cit.*). Cp. a fragment of black ware with relief-decoration and the inscription ΗΣΤΥ+ΗΣ = [Ἀγαθ]ῆς Τύχης round its neck, found on the W. slope of the Akropolis at Athens (A. Koerte in the *Ath. Mitth.* 1896 xxi. 294, P. Wolters *loc. cit.*).

[1] Athen. 427 E τοῖς δὲ τετελευτηκόσι τῶν φίλων ἀπένεμον τὰ πίπτοντα τῆς τροφῆς ἀπὸ τῶν τραπεζῶν· διὸ καὶ Εὐριπίδης περὶ τῆς Σθενεβοίας φησίν, ἐπειδὴ νομίζει τὸν Βελλεροφόντην τεθνάναι, 'πεσὸν δέ νιν λέληθεν οὐδὲν ἐκ χερός, | ἀλλ' εὐθὺς αὐδᾷ "τῷ Κορινθίῳ ξένῳ"' (Eur. *frag.* 664 Nauck[2]). The Euripidean passage is parodied by Kratin. *fab. inc. frag.* 16. 4 (*Frag. com. Gr.* ii. 179 ff. Meineke) *ap.* Athen. 782 D—E, Aristoph. *thesm.* 404 f. with schol. *ad loc.*, cp. Hesych. *s.v.* Κορίνθιος ξένος.

[2] Aristot. *frag.* 190 Rose *ap.* Diog. Laert. 8. 34 φησὶ δ' Ἀριστοτέλης...παραγγέλλειν αὐτὸν (sc. Πυθαγόραν)...τὰ...πεσόντ' ἀπὸ τραπέζης μὴ ἀναιρεῖσθαι, ὑπὲρ τοῦ ἐθίζεσθαι μὴ ἀκολάστως ἐσθίειν ἢ ὅτι ἐπὶ τελευτῇ τινος ('sive quod essent mortuo destinata' Ambrosius revised by C. G. Cobet)· καὶ Ἀριστοφάνης δὲ τῶν ἡρώων φησὶν εἶναι τὰ πίπτοντα, λέγων ἐν τοῖς Ἥρωσι (*frag.* 2 (*Frag. com. Gr.* ii. 1070 f. Meineke)) 'μηδὲ γεύεσθ' ἅττ' ἂν ἐντὸς (I. Casaubon and W. Canter, followed by C. Jacobitz, cjj. ἐκτὸς) τῆς τραπέζης καταπέσῃ' = Souid. *s.v.* Πυθαγόρα τὰ σύμβολα.

Secondly, the buried chieftain was *Epópsios* because he kept an eye on his descendants and watched over their interests[1]. The title was, however, susceptible of a wider meaning. So Zeus *Epópsios*[2] came to be revered as the guardian of suppliants[3], the observer of right and wrong[4], the avenger of impious deeds[5]. Like Zeus *Panóptes*[6], he readily took on a solar complexion[7]. And it may be that the story of Zeus transforming himself into a hoopoe (*épops*)

[1] Cp. the important passage Hes. *o. d.* 121 ff. αὐτὰρ ἐπεὶ δὴ τοῦτο γένος κατὰ γαῖ' ἐκάλυψε, | τοὶ μὲν δαίμονές εἰσι Διὸς μεγάλου διὰ βουλὰς | ἐσθλοί, ἐπιχθόνιοι, φύλακες θνητῶν ἀνθρώπων, | [οἵ ῥα φυλάσσουσίν τε δίκας καὶ σχέτλια ἔργα | ἠέρα ἑσσάμενοι πάντη φοιτῶντες ἐπ' αἶαν,] | πλουτοδόται· καὶ τοῦτο γέρας βασιλήιον ἔσχον. For *apparatus criticus* see A. Rzach *ad loc. Infra* Append. M *fin.*

The adjective ἐπόψιος is used in this sense by Soph. *Phil.* 1040 f. ἀλλ', ὦ πατρῷα γῆ θεοί τ' ἐπόψιοι, | τείσασθε κ.τ.λ., the substantive ἔποψις by Strab. 676 εἶτ' 'Αμφίλοχον... συμβαλεῖν εἰς μονομαχίαν πρὸς τὸν Μόψον, πεσόντας δ' ἀμφοτέρους ταφῆναι μὴ ἐν ἐπόψει ἀλλήλοις, the verb ἐποπτεύω by Aisch. *cho.* 489 of the buried Agamemnon ὦ γαῖ', ἄνες μοι πατέρ' ἐποπτεῦσαι μάχην, *cho.* 1 of Hermes *Chthónios* 'Ερμῆ Χθόνιε πατρῷ' ἐποπτεύων κράτη cited by Aristoph. *ran.* 1126, 1138 ff., *Eum.* 220 of the Eumenides τὸ μὴ τίνεσθαι μηδ' ἐποπτεύειν κότῳ, *cho.* 984 ff. of Helios ὡς ἴδῃ πατήρ, | οὐχ οὑμός, ἀλλ' ὁ πάντ' ἐποπτεύων τάδε | "Ηλιος, ἄναγνα μητρὸς ἔργα τῆς ἐμῆς, *Ag.* 1270 of Apollon ἐποπτεύσας δέ με, *Eum.* 224 of Athena δίκας δὲ Παλλὰς τῶνδ' ἐποπτεύσει θεά, *cho.* 1064 f. of God καί σ' ἐποπτεύων πρόφρων | θεὸς φυλάσσοι κ.τ.λ., *Ag.* 1578 f. of the gods in general φαίην ἂν ἤδη νῦν βροτῶν τιμαόρους | θεοὺς ἄνωθεν γῆς ἐποπτεύειν ἄχη (see further F. H. M. Blaydes on Aristoph. *ran.* 1126). Similarly ἐφορᾶν is used of Zeus in Od. 13. 213 f. (cited *supra* p. 1097 n. 1), Archil. *frag.* 84 Hiller—Crusius *ap.* Stob. *ecl.* 1. 3. 34 p. 58, 11 ff. Wachsmuth (Clem. Al. *strom.* 5. 14 p. 412, 3 ff. Stählin, Euseb. *praep. ev.* 13. 13. 54) ὦ Ζεῦ, πάτερ Ζεῦ, σὸν μὲν οὐρανοῦ κράτος, | σὺ δ' ἔργ' ἐπ' ἀνθρώπων ὁρᾷς | λεωργὰ καὶ θεμιστά (so Liebel for κάθεμιστα or the like), σοὶ δὲ θηρίων | ὕβρις τε καὶ δίκη μέλει, Soph. *El.* 174 f. ἔτι μέγας οὐρανῷ | Ζεύς, ὃς ἐφορᾷ πάντα καὶ κρατύνει. For Zeus "Εφορος see *supra* i. 737 n. 8.

[2] *Supra* i. 737 n. 9.

[3] Ap. Rhod. 2. 1123 ἀντόμεθα πρὸς Ζηνὸς 'Εποψίου with schol. Paris. *ad loc.* 'Εποψιος δὲ ὁ ἔποπτος (J. Alberti corr. ἐπόπτης), 1131 ff. (cited *supra* p. 1097 n. 2).

[4] Kallim. *h. Zeus* 81 ff. ἵζεο δ' αὐτὸς | ἄκρῃς ἐν πολίεσσιν, ἐπόψιος οἵ τε δίκῃσι | λαὸν ὑπὸ σκολιῆς, οἵ τ' ἔμπαλιν ἰθύνουσιν.

[5] Orph. *Arg.* 1035 ἀλλά οἱ οὔτι λάθον Δί' ἐπόψιον οὐδὲ θέμιστας.

[6] *Supra* i. 459 ff.

[7] A stone pillar (height 1·0m, breadth 0·23m), found on the site of Itanos (*Erimopoli*) in E. Crete and now serving as a lintel in a cottage near the lighthouse on *Capo Sidero*, bears the following inscription in letters of *s.* iv B.C. or earlier: Πάτρων Διὶ | 'Επ[ο]ψί[ω]ι | ἀνέ[θ]ηκε. | τροπα[ὶ] χειμεριναί. | εἴ τινι τού|των : ἐπιμε|λές : κατὰ | τὴν : χοι|ράδα : τὴν | μικρὰν | καὶ τὴν στή|λην: ὁ ἥλιος | τρέπεται (F. Halbherr in the *Museo Italiano di antichità classica* 1890 iii. 585 f. no. 4 = Michel *Recueil d'Inscr. gr.* no. 1181 = Dittenberger *Syll. inscr. Gr.*[3] no. 1264). The original position of the pillar was such that a line drawn from it to a certain small rock visible at sea, and prolonged thence to the horizon, would mark the precise spot where the sun rose at the winter solstice. Halbherr *ad loc.* cp. schol. Aristoph. *av.* 997 φησὶ δὲ Καλλίστρατος ἐν Κολωνῷ ἀνάθημά τι εἶναι αὐτοῦ (*sc.* Μέτωνος) ἀστρολογικόν and Ail. *var. hist.* 10. 7 ὅτι Μέτων ὁ Λευκονοιεὺς ἀστρολόγος ἀνέστησε στήλας καὶ τὰς τοῦ ἡλίου τροπὰς κατεγράψατο. The rosette or star, which figures so frequently on coins of Itanos (J. N. Svoronos *Numismatique de la Crète ancienne* Mâcon 1890 i. 201 ff. pl. 18, 21 ff., pl. 19, 5, 16, 19, 22 f., 25 ff., *id.* in the *Bull. Corr. Hell.* 1894 xviii. 115, 117 f., *Brit. Mus. Cat. Coins* Crete etc. p. 51 f. pl. 12, 6 ff., pl. 13, 4, 7 f., Babelon *Monn. gr. rom.* ii. 3. 895 ff. pl. 244, 1 ff., 20, pl. 245, 3, 7 ff., Anson *Num. Gr.* vi. 11 no. 114 pl. 1, Head *Hist. num.*[2] p. 469 f.), was in all probability a solar symbol. And Zeus on Cretan soil tended to become a sun-god (*supra* i. 545 ff.).

For 'Επόψιος as a title of Apollon see *supra* i. 737 n. 9.

to win Lamia[1] owes something to popular confusion with the title *Epópsios*[2]. Thirdly, the king was *Meilíchios*—a coaxing or cajoling appellation[3], which he shared with various chthonian powers[4].

Two other points in the narrative of Antoninus Liberalis call for remark. Periphas, transformed into an eagle, was set to guard the sacred sceptre and had leave to approach the very throne of Zeus[5]. Much the same is said of

[1] W. Crönert in the *Archiv für Papyrusforschung und verwandte Gebiete* 1901 i. 109 n. 1 drew attention to an unnoticed fragment of Philodem. περὶ εὐσεβείας (in the series of photographs issued by the Oxford Philological Society vi. 206) on the amours of Zeus: [ὧν ἦν καὶ Νέμ]ϵϛις, [ἣν | φη]σιν (T) ὁ τὰ Κύ[πρια | γ]ράψας ὁμοιωθῆ|[ν]α<ι> χηνί, Διὰ <δὲ> αὐτ[ὴν | δ]ιώκειν καὶ μιγῆν[αι, | τὴν δ]ὲ ὠιὸν τεκεῖν, | [ἐξ] οὗ γενέσθαι τὴ[ν | 'Ελ]ένην. ὥσ[π]ϵ[ρ αὖ | Λή]δας ἐρασθεὶς [ἐ|γ]ένετο κύκνο[ς, | Εὐ]ρώπης δὲ ταῦ|[ρος], Λαμίας δὲ ἔ|[πο]ψ (so F. Blass), Δανάης δὲ χ[ρυ|σός]. καὶ παρ' Ἀπολ[λω|νίδη] καὶ παρ' Εὐ[ρι|πίδ]η λέγεται... With this allusion to the hoopoe O. Höfer in Roscher *Lex. Myth.* iii. 2566 well cp. Clem. Rom. *hom.* 5. 13 (ii. 184 Migne) Λαμίᾳ ἐπεμορφώθη ἔποψ, Rufin. *recognit.* 10. 22 Lamiam (*sc.* stuprat) mutatus in upupam.

[2] Aisch. *frag.* 304, 1 Nauck[2] *ap.* Aristot. *hist. an.* 9. 49 B. 633 a 19 τοῦτον δ' ἐπόπτην ἔποπα τῶν αὑτοῦ κακῶν | κ.τ.λ. (F. G. Welcker *Die Griechischen Tragödien* Bonn 1839 i. 384, followed by many scholars, attributed the fragment to Sophokles' *Tereus*: see A. C. Pearson on Soph. *frag.* 581 Jebb). Cp. Hesych. ἔποψ· ἐπόπτης. δυνάστης. καὶ εἶδος ὀρνέου.

There were, no doubt, other reasons, which made the hoopoe a suitable vehicle for Zeus, especially his fine feathered crest or crown and his widely-recognized magical powers (to the evidence cited by S. Bochart *Hierozoicon* rec. E. F. C. Rosenmüller Lipsiae 1796 iii. 111 f. add the *Kyranídes* 1. 7. 11 ff. in F. de Mély—C. É. Ruelle *Les Lapidaires de l'antiquité et du moyen âge* Paris 1898 ii (Les Lapidaires grecs). 20 ff. with 235 f. [ἔποψ] ζῷόν ἐστιν ἐν ἀέρι πτώμενον ὃ καλεῖται ἔποψ, ἐπτάχρωμον βασίλειον ἔχον μήκει δακτύλων β', ἁπλούμενον καὶ συστελλόμενον· αὐτὸ δὲ τετράχρωμον, ὡς εἰπεῖν, πρὸς τὰς δ' τροπὰς τοῦ ἐνιαυτοῦ· οὗτος καλεῖται κουκούφας καὶ ποῦπος, ὡς ἐγράφη τὰ περὶ τούτου ἐν τῇ πρώτῃ τῇ βίβλῳ 'ἀρχαϊκῇ' καλουμένῃ. ἔστι δὲ τὸ ζῷον ἱερόν. λαβὼν οὖν τὴν τούτου καρδίαν ἔτι παλπροῦσαν κάταπιε ἀντίκρυ τοῦ ἡλίου ὥρας πρώτης ἀρχομένης ἢ ὀγδόης ἀρχομένης· ἔστω δὲ ἡμέρα Κρόνου, σελήνης ἀνατολικῆς οὔσης· καὶ ἐπίπιε γάλα βοὸς μελαίνης μετ' ὀλίγου μέλιτος ἐκ τοῦ συνθέματος αὐθωρόν, ἵνα ἡ καρδία ὑγιὴς καταποθῇ, καὶ ἔσῃ προγινώσκων τὰ ἐν οὐρανῷ καὶ γῇ, καὶ εἴ τις κατὰ ψυχὴν ἔχει τι καὶ ὅσα κατὰ τὰ κλίματα καὶ κατὰ πόλεις γίνεται καὶ τὰ μέλλοντα ἅπασιν ἀνθρώποις· ...ἐὰν δὲ καὶ ἑτέραν καρδίαν καὶ ἧπαρ ἔποπος βάλῃς ἐν τῷ συνθέματι, κρεῖττον ἔσται καὶ ἔτι μνημονικώτερον ποιεῖ... The sequel deals with a yet more potent charm, in which, among other ingredients, is καὶ τὸ βασίλειον τὸ ἐπὶ τῆς κεφαλῆς τοῦ ἔποπος). On his relations to the cuckoo, hawk, woodpecker, and bee-eater see E. Oder 'Der Wiedehopf in der griechischen Sage' in the *Rhein. Mus.* 1888 xliii. 541—556, D'Arcy W. Thompson *A Glossary of Greek Birds* Oxford 1895 pp. 54—57, S. Bochart *op. cit.* iii. 107—115, J. Grimm *Teutonic Mythology* trans. J. S. Stallybrass London 1883 ii. 681 f., C. Swainson *The Folk Lore and Provincial Names of British Birds* London 1886 pp. 106—109, O. Keller *Die antike Tierwelt* Leipzig 1913 ii. 60—63.

Horapoll. *hierogl.* 1. 55 εὐχαριστίαν γράφοντες, κουκούφαν ('hoopoe') ζωγραφοῦσι· διότι τοῦτο μόνον τῶν ἀλόγων ζώων, ἐπειδὰν ὑπὸ τῶν γονέων ἐκτραφῇ, γηράσασιν αὐτοῖς τὴν αὐτὴν ἀποδίδωσι χάριν·...ὅθεν καὶ ἐπὶ τῶν θείων σκήπτρων κουκούφα προτίμησίς ἐστι (cp. Ail. *de nat. an.* 10. 16, 16. 5) looks like a parallel to the tale of Periphas, but perhaps based on a misconception; for the erectile crest of the hoopoe, when laterally compressed (H. Lydekker *The Royal Natural History* London 1895 iv. 57 ff., col. pl., A. H. Evans *The Birds of Britain* Cambridge 1916 p. 108 f. fig.), bears a superficial resemblance to the regular sceptre of the gods (see *e.g.* C. Leemans on Horapoll. *loc. cit.* with fig. 54).

[3] *Supra* p. 1112 n. 7.

[4] See O. Höfer in Roscher *Lex. Myth.* ii. 2558, 2563.

[5] Ant. Lib. 6 (*supra* p. 1121 f.) διδοῖ φυλάσσειν τὸ ἱερὸν σκῆπτρον καὶ προσιέναι πρὸς τὸν ἑαυτοῦ θρόνον.

Merops an early king of Kos[1]. Behind such traditions lie definite beliefs. It was supposed, as I have elsewhere contended[2], that, when the divine king died, his soul escaped as a bird and in that shape continued to watch over the fortunes of his realm. Further, his divinity was transmitted to his successor in outward and visible form as an eagle-tipped sceptre to be handed down from king to king. Thus the soul of Agamemnon, for instance, became an eagle[3]; and the sceptre which had descended to him from Zeus[4], with an eagle perched upon it[5], was worshipped at Chaironeia as the chief of the gods[6]. The sceptre originally belonged

[1] Schol. *Il.* 24. 293 οἱ δέ, ὅτι Μέροψ ὁ Κῷος ἀπαύστως ἐπένθει τὴν γυναῖκα, ξενίσας δὲ τὴν 'Ρέαν (C. Robert cj. "Ηραν) μετεβλήθη καὶ συμπάρεστιν ἀεὶ τῷ Διί, Eustath. *in Il.* p. 1351, 29 f. φέρεται δὲ μῦθος καὶ ὅτι Μέροψ Κῷος, ἀπαύστως τὴν γυναῖκα πενθῶν θανοῦσαν, ξενίσας 'Ρέαν, μετεβλήθη εἰς ἀετόν, καὶ σύνεστιν ἀεὶ τῷ Διί. It may be suspected that originally Merops was metamorphosed, not into an eagle, but into a bee-eater (μέροψ), cp. Ant. Lib. 18 and D'Arcy W. Thompson *A Glossary of Greek Birds* Oxford 1895 p. 116 f.

[2] *Folk-Lore* 1904 xv. 386 ff., cp. *ib.* 1905 xvi. 312, 1906 xvii. 165 ff., 313 ff.

[3] Plat. *rep.* 620 B τὴν δ' ἐπὶ τούτῳ 'Αγαμέμνονος (*sc.* ψυχήν)· ἔχθρᾳ δὲ καὶ ταύτην τοῦ ἀνθρωπίνου γένους διὰ τὰ πάθη ἀετοῦ διαλλάξαι βίον. It would not be safe to conclude that Agamemnon's choice was due to Platonic fancy: Platon constantly founds on folk-belief (*supra* i. 310 f., 357 n. 4, ii. 43 ff., 63 n. o).

[4] *Il.* 2. 100 ff. (Hephaistos made the sceptre for Zeus, from whom it passed successively to Hermes, Pelops, Atreus,. Thyestes, and Agamemnon) with schol. *ad loc.* and Eustath. *in Il.* p. 181, 13 ff.

[5] Aristoph. *av.* 509 ff. ΠΕ. ἦρχον δ' οὕτω σφόδρα τὴν ἀρχὴν ὥστ' εἴ τις καὶ βασιλεύοι | ἐν ταῖς πόλεσιν τῶν Ἑλλήνων, 'Αγαμέμνων ἢ Μενέλαος, | ἐπὶ τῶν σκήπτρων ἐκάθητ' ὄρνις, μετέχων ὅ τι δωροδοκοίη with schol. *ad loc.* ἐν γὰρ τοῖς σκήπτροις τῶν βασιλέων ἦν ἀετός. But see *supra* i. 406 f.

[6] Paus. 9. 40. 11 f. θεῶν δὲ μάλιστα Χαιρωνεῖς τιμῶσι τὸ σκῆπτρον ὃ ποιῆσαι Διί φησιν "Ομηρος "Ηφαιστον, παρὰ δὲ Διὸς λαβόντα Ἑρμῆν δοῦναι Πέλοπι, Πέλοπα δὲ 'Ατρεῖ καταλιπεῖν, τὸν δὲ 'Ατρέα Θυέστῃ, παρὰ Θυέστου δὲ ἔχειν 'Αγαμέμνονα· τοῦτο οὖν τὸ σκῆπτρον σέβουσι, δόρυ ὀνομάζοντες. καὶ εἶναι μέν τι θειότερον οὐχ ἥκιστα δηλοῖ τὸ ἐς τοὺς ἀνθρώπους ἐπιφανὲς ἐξ αὐτοῦ· φασὶ δ' ἐπὶ τοῖς ὅροις αὐτῶν καὶ Πανοπέων τῶν ἐν τῇ Φωκίδι εὑρεθῆναι, σὺν δὲ αὐτῷ καὶ χρυσὸν εὕρασθαι τοὺς Φωκεῖς, σφίσι δὲ ἀσμένοις ἀντὶ χρυσοῦ γενέσθαι τὸ σκῆπτρον. κομισθῆναι δὲ αὐτὸ ἐς τὴν Φωκίδα ὑπὸ 'Ηλέκτρας τῆς 'Αγαμέμνονος πείθομαι. ναὸς δὲ οὐκ ἔστιν αὐτῷ δημοσίᾳ πεποιημένος, ἀλλὰ κατὰ ἔτος ἕκαστον ὁ (H. C. Schubart, followed by H. Hitzig—H. Blümner, cj. ὁ κατὰ ἔτος ἕκαστον) ἱερώμενος ἐν οἰκήματι ἔχει τὸ σκῆπτρον· καὶ οἱ θυσίαι ἀνὰ πᾶσαν ἡμέραν θύονται, καὶ τράπεζα παράκειται παντοδαπῶν κρεῶν καὶ πεμμάτων πλήρης. The worship of sceptre or spear was characteristic of a primitive age: .Iust. 43. 3. 3 per ea tempora adhuc reges hastas pro diademate habebant, quas Graeci sceptra dixere. nam et ab origine rerum pro signis inmortalibus veteres hastas coluere, ob cuius religionis memoriam adhuc deorum simulacris hastae adduntur, Philon Bybl. *frag.* 1. 7 (*Frag. hist. Gr.* iii. 564 Müller) *ap.* Euseb. *praep. ev.* 1. 9. 29 οἱ παλαίτατοι τῶν βαρβάρων, ἐξαιρέτως δὲ Φοίνικές τε καὶ Αἰγύπτιοι, παρ' ὧν καὶ οἱ λοιποὶ παρέλαβον ἄνθρωποι, θεοὺς ἐνόμιζον μεγίστους τοὺς τὰ πρὸς τὴν βιωτικὴν χρείαν εὑρόντας, ἢ καὶ κατά τι εὐποιήσαντας τὰ ἔθνη· εὐεργέτας τε τούτους καὶ πολλῶν αἰτίους ἀγαθῶν ἡγούμενοι ὡς θεοὺς προσεκύνουν, καὶ εἰς τὸ χρεὼν μεταστάντας ναοὺς κατασκευασάμενοι στήλας τε καὶ ῥάβδους ἀφιέρουν ἐξ ὀνόματος αὐτῶν, καὶ ταῦτα μεγάλως σεβόμενοι, καὶ ἑορτὰς ἔνεμον αὐτοῖς τὰς μεγίστας Φοίνικες. Examples of the cult are collected by De Visser *De Gr. diis non ref. spec. hum.* p. 90 f. § 94 ff. and Frazer *Pausanias* v. 210 ff., *Golden Bough*[3]: The Magic Art i. 365. It is possible that the object reverenced by the Chaeroneans was a sceptre found in the grave of some 'Minoan' chief (cf. C. Schuchhardt *Schliemann's Excavations* trans. E. Sellers London 1891 p. 250 f., Perrot—Chipiez *Hist. de l'Art* vi. 978 f., W. Dörpfeld *Troja und Ilion* Athen 1902 i. 385, 398, R. M. Dawkins in the *Ann. Brit. Sch. Ath.* 1904—1905 xi. 284, H. R. Hall *Ægean Archæology* London 1915 pp. 57, 242). H. C. Schubart in

to the king as weather-maker, and the eagle on it was no mere decoration[1]

Philologus 1860 xv. 400 thought that it was housed in a portable wooden shrine (οἴκημα !). But F. Thiersch in the *Abh. d. bayer. Akad.* 1858 Philos.-philol. Classe viii. 445 with far greater probability explained that the priest for the time being used a room (οἴκημα) in his own house as chapel for the *chose sacrée*. The annual tenure of his office seems to have been a method of ensuring his bodily competence (*Folk-Lore* 1904 xv. 394 ff.).

[1] K. Sittl *Der Adler und die Weltkugel als Attribute des Zeus* (Besonderer Abdruck aus dem vierzehnten Supplementbande der Jahrbücher für classische Philologie) Leipzig 1884 pp. 3—42 contains a rich collection of material. Here we are concerned only with the eagle in relation to the sceptre (cp. *supra* i. 127 fig. 96, 128 f. pl. xii, 200 f. fig. 146, 251 pl. xxii, 501 f. pl. xxxi, 590 fig. 450, 596 fig. 454, ii. 104 fig. 65, 512 fig. 390)—a combination which should be compared with the cuckoo-on-sceptre (*supra* i. 134 f., 532 fig. 399), the cock-on-column (G. von Brauchitsch *Die panathenäischen Preisamphoren* Leipzig and Berlin 1910 p. 106 ff. fig. 33 ff., R. Garrucci *Storia della Arte Cristiana* Prato 1881 iv. 59 pl. 251, 1), the woodpecker-on-post (Dion. Hal. *ant. Rom.* 1. 14: see *Class. Rev.* 1904 xviii. 375, Furtwängler *Ant. Gemmen* i. pl. 24, 10, ii. 119, Harrison *Themis* p. 101 f. fig. 17, W. R. Halliday *Greek Divination* London 1913 p. 265. I figure (scale ⅔) an engraved cornelian at Corpus Christi College, Cambridge (J. H. Middleton *The Lewis Collection of Gems and Rings* London 1892 p. 50 no. 26), which shows a warrior consulting the woodpecker of Mars at Tiora Matiene (Dion. Hal. *loc. cit.*)), the hawk-on-pillar (D. G. Hogarth *Excavations at Ephesus* London 1908 pp. 157 pl. 22, 1 a, 161 f. pl. 25, 1 ff., 198, W. M. Flinders Petrie *Tanis* London 1888 ii. 2. 9, J. T. Bent *The Ruined Cities of Mashonaland*[3] London 1895 p. 180 ff.), the dove-on-sceptre (*Encyclopædia Britannica*[9] London 1886 xx.

Fig. 957.

340 *s.v.* ' Regalia,' *ib.* xxi. 385 *s.v.* ' Sceptre,' *Folk-Lore* 1906 xvii. 315, *The Daily Graphic* for Dec. 14, 1907 p. 8 fig.), and the like.

The earliest literary allusions (Pind. *Pyth.* 9 ff. εὕδει δ' ἀνὰ σκάπτῳ Διὸς αἰετός, κ.τ.λ. with schol. *ad loc.* and Soph. *frag.* 799 Nauck[2], 884 Jebb, *ap.* schol. Aristoph. *av.* 515 ὁ σκηπτροβάμων αἰετός, κύων Διός) are at least suggestive of vitality. Cp. Append. N *med.* And classical numismatic art conceived of the bird as alive and active. On an archaic silver obol (?) of Galaria or Galarina in Sicily he is unusually large and prominent (*Brit. Mus. Cat. Coins* Sicily p. 64 fig., P. Gardner *Types of Gk Coins* p. 89 pl. 2, 1 f., G. F. Hill *Coins of Ancient Sicily* London 1903 p. 90 f. fig. 12, Head *Hist. num.*[2] p. 139 *obv.* ϹΑΛΑ, Dionysos standing with *kántharos* and vine-branch; *rev.* ΣΟΤΕΡ retrograde, Zeus enthroned with eagle-sceptre). On coppers of Ptolemy vi Philometor (*Brit. Mus. Cat. Coins* The Ptolemies, Kings of Egypt p. 80 pl. 19, 2, *Hunter Cat. Coins* iii. 388 ΠΤΟΛΕΜΑΙΟΥ ΒΑΣΙΛΕΩΣ and ΕΥΛ (the regent Eulaios)) and of Antiochos viii Grypos (*Brit. Mus. Cat. Coins* Seleucid Kings of Syria p. 90 pl. 24, 4, *Hunter Cat. Coins* iii. 102 f. pl. 70, 1 ΒΑΣΙΛΕΩΣ ΑΝΤΙΟΧΟΥ ΕΠΙΦΑΝΟΥΣ with ΙΕ to left, ΒꟼΡ (= 120 B.C.) and ear of corn below, *ib.* iii. 103 pl. 70, 2) the Macedonian eagle appears shouldering a sceptre. On a gold coin struck by Koson, king of Thrace (??) under the Romans, *c.* 42 B.C. the eagle carries a sceptre and a wreath (*Brit. Mus. Cat. Coins* Thrace p. 208 fig., *Hunter Cat. Coins* i. 436, *Ant. Münz. Berlin* Paeonia etc. iii. 2. 23 fig., Head *Hist. num.*[2] pp. 272, 289). *Denarii* struck *c.* 49 B.C. by one Terentius Varro *pro quaestore* have *obv.* VARRO · PRO Q, a filleted bust of Iupiter (*Terminalis* ?) to right ; *rev.* MAGN · PRO COS (*Magnus pro consule*) in exergue, a sceptre upright between an eagle and a dolphin (emblems of earth, air, and sea ?) (Babelon *Monn. rép. rom.* ii. 343, 485 f. fig., *Brit. Mus. Cat. Rom. Coins* Rep. ii. 362 nos. 64, 65 pl. 100, 16, 66, 363 nos. 67, 68 pl. 100, 18, 69). An *aureus* of Q. Caecilius Metellus Pius Scipio, 48—46 B.C., has *obv.* METEL · PIVS SCIP · IMP, a bust of Iupiter (*Terminalis*?)

but an actual embodiment of Zeus[1], which conferred upon its holder the powers of the sky-god. This belief has left traces of itself throughout the historical period of Greece and Rome[2]; indeed, it appears to have lingered on[3] well into the middle ages[4]. In a sense it is still with us[5]. But if the mythopoeic mind fitly transformed any ancient king into an eagle[6], it did so in the case of Periphas with a clear conscience. For Periphas, as son or father of Lapithes[7], was near akin to the Phlegyai[8], whose very name marks them as an 'Eagle'-tribe[9].

In conclusion, the devotion of Periphas to Apollon is adequately explained, either by the fact that in the Lapith genealogy Lapithes and Kentauros were

Fig. 958.

to right, with an eagle's head and sceptre below (Babelon *Monn. rép. rom.* i. 278 f. fig., *Brit. Mus. Cat. Rom. Coins* Rep. ii. 571 fig.: there are *denarii* with the same type—Babelon *op. cit.* i. 279, *Brit. Mus. Cat. Rom. Coins* Rep. ii. 571 no. 4 pl. 121, 2, no. 5). A first brass of Hadrian has *rev.* PROVID ENTIADEORVM and S·C·, an eagle flying with a sceptre towards the emperor, who stands with a roll in his left hand (Cohen *Monn. emp. rom.*[2] ii. 208 no. 1207. Fig. 958 is from a specimen in my collection. Cohen *ib.* no. 1208 fig. shows a second brass with the same design).

[1] *Supra* i. 105 f. fig. 76, 164 n. 4, 532 figs. 395—400, 543 n. 6, and especially ii. 187 n. 8, 751 f.

[2] *Supra* p. 1133 n. 1.

[3] Cp. R. Garrucci *Storia della Arte Cristiana* Prato 1881 iv. 76 pl. 226, 5.

[4] Mrs H. Jenner *Christian Symbolism* London 1910 p. 41 f.: 'The Eagle is chiefly used to suggest the inspiration of the Holy Spirit to saints of the Old Law, such as David and Elisha, but it is not common.' This is illustrated by a plate from an English MS. of *s.* xi now in the British Museum (Cotton. Tib. C. vi), which shows David inspired by the eagle on his sceptre (Mrs Jenner by an odd slip says 'dove'): above is the hand of God, holding a horn full of rays. My friend Mr G. F. Hill kindly directs me to a discussion of the inspiration-type by C. R. Morey 'East Christian Paintings in the Freer Collection' in the *University of Michigan Studies*, Humanistic Series 1914 xii. 35 ff.

[5] *Supra* p. 1133 n. 1 the dove-on-sceptre.

[6] In addition to Periphas (*supra* p. 1121 f.), and Merops (*supra* p. 1131 f.), the shape-shifter Periklymenos underwent the same transformation (Hes. *frag.* 14, 3 f. Rzach *ap.* schol. Ap. Rhod. 1. 156, Ov. *met.* 12. 556 ff., Hyg. *fab.* 10). ? Cp. Furtwängler *Ant. Gemmen* i pl. 26, 71 and 72, ii. 132, if not also i pl. 25, 42, ii. 128.

[7] *Supra* p. 1122.

[8] See the pedigrees in Gerhard *Gr. Myth.* p. 227 f. ('Lapithen und Phlegyer').

[9] Hes. *sc. Her.* 133 f. (arrows) ὄπισθε | μόρφνοιο φλεγύαο καλυπτόμενοι πτερύγεσσιν, Hesych. *s.v.* φλεγύας· ἀετὸς ξανθός, ὀξύς, Souid. *s.v.* φλεγύας· ὁ ἀετός, *et. mag.* p. 795, 57 ff. φλεγύας, ἔστιν ἀετός, ἀπὸ τοῦ φλέγειν καὶ λαμπρὸς εἶναι. οἱ δέ, ὄρνεον παραπλήσιον γυπί. Ἡσίοδος Ἀσπίδι, 'μορφνοῖο φλεγύαο,' τουτέστι μέλανος ἀετοῦ, Eustath. *in Il.* p. 933, 27 f. ῥήτωρ δέ τις, κατὰ στοιχεῖον συντάξας ἅπερ ἐπόνησε, λέγει καὶ ὅτι φλεγύας ξανθὸς ἀετός, κατὰ γλῶσσάν τινα, ὡς ἔοικεν. A. Fick in the *Zeitschrift für vergleichende Sprachforschung auf dem Gebiete der indogermanischen Sprachen* 1914 xlvi. 77 f. renders φλεγύας 'der Schwarzadler' and adds: 'Das Wort wird soviel als "braun, dunkel" bedeutet haben: wie αἴθων braun, αἴθαλος Russ von αἴθειν brennen, so φλεγύας von φλέγω brennen, engl. *black* zu germ. *blek* (φλέγειν).' See further my paper on 'Descriptive animal names in Greece' in the *Class. Rev.* 1894 viii. 381 ff. and, for the bird-tribes of Greece and Italy, an appendix by W. R. Halliday *Greek Divination* London 1913 p. 277 ff.

The central slab from the Eastern Frieze of the Parthenon

1. The relief as extant in the British Museum.

Plate XLIV

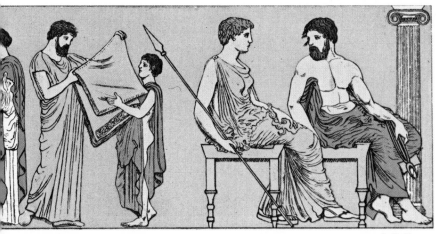

E. T. T.

...g the ritual Apotheosis of the King and Queen at Athens:
...elief with flat coloration and metal accessories restored.

See page 1135 ff.

the sons of Stilbe by Apollon[1], or by the contiguity of the Olympieion to the Pythion[2]. In any case it is noteworthy that at Ardettos, just across the Ilissos, Athenian jurors used to swear by Apollon *Patrôios*, Demeter, and Zeus *Basileús*[3].

The myth of Periphas comes to us from an age that had largely forgotten its own antecedents. Few, if any, citizens even of Periclean Athens would have dared to assert that on the banks of the Ilissos there once lived a line of kings claiming to be Zeus incarnate. Nevertheless that is the real gist of the tale, and I do not see how we are to avoid accepting it as a genuine echo of bygone beliefs. After all, Periclean Athens, democratic to the core, still had its 'king' and still remembered that divinity clung about him[4]. If any doubted, he had but to lift his eyes to the scene carved by Pheidias' direction above the main doorway of the Parthenon. The central slab of the eastern frieze (pl. xliv)[5] represents a ritual apotheosis[6]. The 'king' and 'queen' of Athens receive from

[1] Diod. 4. 69.

[2] Frazer *Pausanias* ii. 189 ff., v. 519 ff., W. Judeich *Topographie von Athen* München 1905 p. 344 f.

[3] Poll. 8. 122 ὤμνυσαν δὲ ἐν Ἀρδήττῳ δικαστηρίῳ Ἀπόλλω Πατρῷον καὶ Δήμητρα καὶ Δία Βασιλέα.

[4] We must be careful here to rule out invalid evidence. Some statements, which *prima facie* connect the Athenian king with Zeus, or Zeus with the Athenian king, will not bear closer scrutiny.

The βασιλεύς of republican Athens, during his year of office, sat in the Στοὰ Βασίλειος (Paus. 1. 3. 1 with the notes of Sir J. G. Frazer and H. Hitzig—H. Blümner *ad loc.*, E. A. Gardner *Ancient Athens* London 1902 pp. 386 f., 518 f., W. Judeich *op. cit.* p. 295 ff.), which is sometimes said to have been named after Zeus Βασιλεύς (Hesych. *s.v.* Βασίλειος Στοά δύο εἰσὶν Ἀθήνῃσιν Βασίλειοι Στοαί, ἥ τε τοῦ λεγομένου Βασιλέως Διὸς καὶ ἡ τοῦ Ἐλευθερίου = Favorin. *lex.* p. 355, 13 f., Bekker *anecd.* i. 222, 29 f. Βασίλειος Στοά· Ἀθήνῃσι δύο εἰσὶ Βασίλειοι Στοαί, ἡ τοῦ λεγομένου Βασιλέως Διὸς καὶ ἡ τοῦ Ἐλευθερίου); but this seems to be a misconception due to a transcriber's error (cp. Harpokr. *s.v.* Βασίλειος Στοά ...δύο εἰσὶ στοαὶ παρ' ἀλλήλας, ἥ τε τοῦ Ἐλευθερίου Διὸς καὶ ἡ Βασίλειος. ἔστι δὲ καὶ τρίτη τις, ἡ πάλαι μὲν Ἀνάκτιος καλουμένη, Ποικίλη δὲ μετονομασθεῖσα, Souid. *s.v.* Βασίλειος Στοά· δύο εἰσὶ στοαὶ παρ' ἀλλήλας, ἥ τε τοῦ Ἐλευθερίου Διὸς καὶ ἡ Βασίλειος. ἔστι δὲ καὶ τρίτη, ἡ πάλαι μὲν Πανάκτιος (P. J. de Maussac cj. Πεισιανάκτειος cp. Diog. Laert. 7. 5 and Souid. *s.vv.* Ζήνων and Πεισιανάκτιος Στοά, G. Bernhardy cj. Πεισιανάκτιος) ἐκαλεῖτο, νῦν δὲ μετωνομάσθη Ποικίλη, whence Meursius in Hesych. *loc. cit.* restored δύο εἰσὶν Ἀθήνῃσι στοαὶ ἥ τε Βασίλειος λεγομένη τοῦ βασιλέως καὶ ἡ Διὸς τοῦ Ἐλευθερίου).

Cic. *de nat. deor.* 3. 53 Διόσκουροι etiam apud Graecos multis modis nominantur. primi tres, qui appellantur Anactes Athenis, ex rege Iove antiquissimo et Proserpina nati, Tritopatreus, Eubuleus, Dionysus. This passage forms part of the Catalogue of the gods, the origin of which has been much disputed. J. B. Mayor *ad loc.* would trace it back to Kleitomachos, who became head of the New Academy in 129 B.C. W. Michaelis *De origine indicis deorum cognominum* Berlin 1898 finds its ultimate source in the pseudo-Aristotelian *péplos*, which he attributes to an unknown Rhodian author of *s.* ii. B.C. W. Bobeth *De indicibus deorum* Leipzig 1904 thinks that the Catalogue was first drafted in 100—50 B.C. Gruppe *Myth. Lit.* 1908 p. 199 refers it to Aristokles of Rhodes, whose *floruit* falls in *s.* i. B.C. In any case the allusion to 'Zeus a very ancient king' betrays the influence of Euhemeros (*supra* i. 662, 758).

[5] Pl. xliv, 1 is drawn from the best available photographs of the actual slab, *viz.* A. H. Smith *The Sculptures of the Parthenon* London 1910 pls. 34—36, supplemented by the casts of it in the Cambridge collection. Pl. xliv, 2 gives a restoration of the same.

[6] So at least I ventured to suggest in the *Class. Rev.* 1904 xviii. 371, cp. Frazer *Golden Bough*[3]: The Dying God p. 89 n. 5. Other interpretations (which to me,

their attendants the sacred *péplos* and two cushioned *díphroi*. Of these *díphroi* one is being handed to the 'queen,' the other with a footstool[1] is reserved for the 'king.' He is a very noteworthy personage. Alone of all the figures on the frieze, he is clad simply in a long *chitón* with short sleeves and in shoes—doubt-less the Cretan garment[2] and royal footgear[3], which we know to have been his distinctive attire. Court etiquette is conservative and these articles of apparel were reminiscent of 'Minoan' predecessors. But, to complete his costume, he needs a *himátion*; and it seems not unreasonable to conjecture that he is about to put on immortality in the shape of Athena's *péplos*[4]. This done, the 'king'

I confess, seem inadequate) regard the scene as (1) the priest receiving the new *péplos* (most archaeologists); (2) the priest folding up and putting away the old *péplos* (G. F. Hill 'The east frieze of the Parthenon' in the *Class. Rev.* 1894 viii. 225 f., E. A. Gardner *A Handbook of Greek Sculpture* London 1897 ii. 291 f., *id. Ancient Athens* London 1902 p. 332 ff.); (3) the priest, about to sacrifice, handing his own *himátion* to the boy, cp. the vase shown in the *Arch. Zeit.* 1879 xxxvii pl. 4 (A. Flasch *Zum Parthenon-Fries* Würzburg 1877 p. 99 ff., Friederichs—Wolters *Gipsabgüsse* p. 277 f., Sir C. Waldstein 'The Panathenaic festival and the central slab of the Parthenon frieze' in the *Am. Journ. Arch.* 1885 i. 10 ff., *id. Essays on the Art of Pheidias* Cambridge 1885 p. 229 ff. ('The central slab of the Parthenon frieze and the Copenhagen plaque') pls. 11 f.); (4) the βασιλεύς, before sacrifice, about to put on his *protónion* (W. Watkiss Lloyd 'On the Central Groups of the Eastern Frieze of the Parthenon' in *Transactions of the Royal Society of Literature* Second Series (1892) xvi. 73 ff.); (5) the priest receiving a carpet (στρωμνή, cp. Dittenberger *Syll. inscr. Gr.*[3] no. 589, 9 and 44 f.) to be spread before the seats of the gods for a theoxeny (E. Curtius in the *Jahrb. d. deutsch. arch. Inst.* 1894 ix *Arch. Anz.* p. 181, Miss J. E. Harrison in the *Class. Rev.* 1895 ix. 91, 427 f. ('The central group of the east frieze of the Parthenon: peplos or στρωμνή?')). See also E. Petersen 'Peplosübergabe' in the *Arch. Zeit.* 1877 xxxv. 136 f., A. Michaelis 'Peplos und Priestermantel' in the *Festschrift für Johannes Overbeck* Leipzig 1893 p. 178 ff., A. H. Smith in the *Brit. Mus. Cat. Sculpture* i. 156 ff., *id. A Guide to the Sculptures of the Parthenon* London 1908 p. 75 ff., *id. The Sculptures of the Parthenon* London 1910 p. 53, Furtwängler *Masterpieces of Gk. Sculpt.* p. 427, *id.* in the *Class. Rev.* 1895 ix. 274 ff.

[1] E. Petersen *Die Kunst des Pheidias am Parthenon und zu Olympia* Berlin 1873 p. 247 n. 1.

[2] Poll. 7. 77 ἐκαλεῖτο δέ τι καὶ Κρητικόν, ᾧ Ἀθήνῃσιν ὁ βασιλεὺς ἐχρῆτο.

[3] Poll. 7. 85 ὑποδημάτων δὲ εἴδη βασιλίδες· ἐφόρει δὲ αὐτὰς ὁ βασιλεὺς Ἀθήνῃσιν.

[4] If it be objected that the βασιλεύς had no right to masquerade in the costume of Athena, various considerations may be urged in his defence. At the Greater Mystery of Pheneos in Arkadia the priest put on the mask of Demeter *Kidaría* before smiting the Underground Folk with rods (Paus. 8. 15. 3). The obverse of a gold *statér* with the name and types of Alexander the Great is believed by C. T. Seltman to exhibit the head of Demetrios Poliorketes wearing the helmet of Athena (*Num. Chron.* Fourth Series 1909 ix. 267 ff. pl. 20, 3). A Melian copper of imperial date shows a bearded male figure inscribed T | V | [X] | H, with left arm carrying a child and right arm resting on a pillar (Imhoof-Blumer *Gr. Münzen* p. 23 no. 66 pl. 2, 8), presumably a benefactor of Melos represented as her Tyche holding the infant Ploutos (so Furtwängler *Masterpieces of Gk. Sculpt.* p. 382 n. 3). The colossal statues of the Nemroud Dagh include Antiochos i of Kommagene, who in the accompanying inscription speaks of himself as Τύχης νέας (*supra* i. 744 n. 3). Conversely, the gold octadrachms and silver decadrachms etc. of the deified Arsinoe ii give her a horn like that of Zeus *Ámmon* (J. N. Svoronos in the *Journ. Intern. d'Arch. Num.* cited *supra* p. 773 fig. 739, C. T. Seltman *Num. Chron.* Fourth Series 1909 ix. 269, Head *Hist. num.*[2] p. 850). Again, it might be pointed out that a woman's *péplos* is really the same garment as a man's *himátion*, both being essentially an oblong piece of woollen cloth folded for wear. But the true defence of the βασιλεύς is more

and 'queen' will take their places on the *díphroi* set for them between the deities enthroned on either hand[1]. With Zeus and Hera on the one side, Athena and Hephaistos on the other[2], they will appear with all the credentials of divinity.

But it is time to pass from the local myth of Periphas to the local custom of the Diasia[3].

probably to be sought in the fact that on certain ritual occasions men were expected to don women's raiment—a custom on which I have said my say elsewhere (*Class. Rev.* 1906 xx. 376 f.). Miss Harrison has suggested to me (July 30, 1917) an explanation, which—if sound—would not only meet the objection here noted but also add much to the significance of the whole procedure. The 'king,' on my showing, is about to assume the *péplos* of Athena. Yes, but the *péplos* may be simply the 'Weltenmantel,' which Athena had taken over from the early Attic kings. Such a garment could be appropriately worn by the 'king,' who thus came by his own again. R. Eisler *Weltenmantel und Himmelszelt* München 1910 i. 58 ff., 77 ff., ii. 326 seems (though he is not very clear about it) to regard Athena's *péplos* as a cosmic robe. I fail to see that he has proved the point. When he states that the 'Praxiergidenpriesterinnen' ἀμφιέννουσιν ἐν ἑορταῖς τὸν πέπλον Διὶ Μοιραγέτει 'Απόλλωνι (*op. cit.* i. 59), he is indulging in an ungrammatical (Πραξιεργίδαι should be masculine, and ἀμφιέννουσιν is not Greek at all) and highly improbable ('Διὶ...appellativisch (wie divus)') restoration of the mutilated text *Corp. inscr. Att.* i no. 93, 11 f.=J. V. Prott and L. Ziehen *Leges Graecorum sacrae* ii no. 14, 11 f. cited *supra* p. 231 n. 8.

[1] Similarly Philip of Macedon, immediately before his assassination at Aigai in 336 B.C., εἴδωλα τῶν δώδεκα θεῶν ἐπόμπευε...σὺν δὲ τούτοις αὐτοῦ τοῦ Φιλίππου τρισκαιδέκατον ἐπόμπευε θεοπρεπὲς εἴδωλον, σύνθρονον ἑαυτὸν ἀποδεικνύντος τοῦ βασιλέως τοῖς δώδεκα θεοῖς (Diod. 16. 92).

[2] It seems likely that Pheidias had already employed the same principles of composition for the trophy erected at Delphoi as a tithe from the spoils of 'Marathon.' The account given by Paus. 10. 10. 1—2 has led to much discussion, which is conveniently summarised by H. Hitzig—H. Blümner *ad loc.* Personally, I hold that the grouping of this remarkable monument was as follows:

[Three national worthies]	Five ἐπώνυμοι	ATHENA as goddess of Athens	MILTIADES	APOLLON as god of Delphoi	Five ἐπώνυμοι	[Three later ἐπώνυμοι]

Three out of the ten ἐπώνυμοι, viz. Oineus, Hippothoon, and Aias, are not mentioned in the text of Pausanias (probably a clerical error, cp. E. Curtius in the *Nachr. d. kön. Gesellsch. d. Wiss. Göttingen* Phil.-hist. Classe 1861 p. 369 ff.=*id. Gesammelte Abhandlungen* Berlin 1894 ii. 365 f.). Later, when the ten tribes were increased to thirteen, the Athenians added at one end of the row three figures of the new ἐπώνυμοι, Antigonos, Demetrios Poliorketes, Ptolemy ii Philadelphos, and balanced them at the other end by three more figures of national worthies, Kodros, Theseus, Phyleus. It will be observed that, on this showing, the arrangement of the Delphic trophy definitely anticipated that of the eastern frieze of the Parthenon (I accept the view of A. S. Arvanitopullos 'Phylen-Heroen am Parthenonfries' in the *Ath. Mitth.* 1906 xxxi. 38 ff. pl. 4 f. that the ten standing men of the eastern frieze are the eponymous heroes of the Attic tribes):

Head of Panathenaic procession	Five ἐπώνυμοι	Six seated DEITIES	KING and QUEEN of Athens with their attendants	Six seated DEITIES	Five ἐπώνυμοι	Head of Panathenaic procession

In both cases alike Pheidias' design portrays a virtual apotheosis—humanity raised to the rank of surrounding deities.

[3] The best collection of sources will be found in O. Band *Die Attischen Diasien* Berlin 1883 pp. 3—10. The remainder of this excellent monograph suffers from undue compression and is admittedly incomplete.

(7) The Diasia.

Towards the close of the seventh century (636? 632? 628? B.C.) Kylon, an Athenian noble who had married the daughter of Theagenes tyrant of Megara, resolved with Theagenes' help to make himself tyrant of Athens. In answer to an enquiry the Delphic god bade him seize the Akropolis 'at the greatest festival of Zeus.' Kylon, who had been an Olympic victor, naturally took this to be the festival at Olympia. So he waited till it came round and then made his *coup*, which proved a disastrous failure[1]. Thoukydides' comment concerns us :

'Whether the greatest festival spoken of was in Attike or elsewhere, was a point which he did not perceive and the oracle did not reveal. For the Athenians too have what is called the Diasia, a festival of Zeus *Meilichios*, greatest of any, held outside the city, at which all the people offer sacrifice—many not victims but sacrifices peculiar to the country[2].'

The difficulties of the Thucydidean style[3] and the doubts attaching to the text · have, I think, hindered scholars from asking the obvious question : Why did the oracle regard the Diasia as a suitable day for setting up a tyranny at Athens? The explanation is twofold : partly, no doubt, because the gathering of the populace outside the city would leave the coast clear for Kylon's attempt ; but partly also because the Diasia was the festival of Zeus *Meilichios*, who represented the line of ancient kings. Kylon might in fact have acted under their auspices and been accepted as their successor. His presumptuous error spoiled what was, in reality or pretence, quite a pretty piece of politico-religious plotting[5].

[1] Thouk. 1. 126, Hdt. 5. 71, Aristot. *de Athen. rep. frag.* 8 p. 110, 14 ff. Blass— Thalheim, Herakleides Pontikos *frag.* 1. 4 (*Frag. hist. Gr.* ii. 208 Müller), Cic. *de leg.* 2. 28, Plout. *v. Sol.* 12 f., Paus. 1. 28. 1, 1. 40. 1, 7. 25. 3, Hesych. *s.v.* Κωλών(ε)ιον ἄγος, Souid. *s.v.* Κυλώνειον ἄγος, schol. Aristoph. *eq.* 445.

[2] Thouk. 1. 126 εἰ δὲ ἐν τῇ Ἀττικῇ ἢ ἄλλοθί που ἡ μεγίστη ἑορτὴ εἴρητο, οὔτε ἐκεῖνος ἔτι κατενόησε τό τε μαντεῖον οὐκ ἐδήλου. ἔστι γὰρ καὶ Ἀθηναίοις Διάσια ἃ καλεῖται, Διὸς ἑορτὴ Μειλιχίου μεγίστη, ἔξω τῆς πόλεως, ἐν ᾗ πανδημεὶ θύουσι, πολλοὶ οὐχ ἱερεῖα ἀλλὰ θύματα ἐπιχώρια with schol. *ad loc.* ἱερεῖα· πρόβατα and θύματα· τινὰ πέμματα εἰς ζώων μορφὰς τετυπωμένα ἔθυον.

[3] B. Jowett *ad loc.* would punctuate differently, reading either (1) ἔστι γὰρ καὶ Ἀθηναίοις, Διάσια ἃ καλεῖται, Διὸς ἑορτὴ Μειλιχίου μεγίστη, κ.τ.λ. 'For the Athenians also have a greatest festival of Zeus, namely, of Zeus Meilichius, the Diasia as it is called' ; or (2) ἔστι γὰρ καὶ Ἀθηναίοις Διάσια, ἃ καλεῖται Διὸς ἑορτὴ Μειλιχίου μεγίστη, κ.τ.λ. 'For the Athenians also have a festival of Zeus, namely, the Diasia, which is called the greatest festival of Zeus Meilichius.' E. C. Marchant *ad loc.* translates as in (2).

[4] E. F. Poppo—J. M. Stahl *ad loc.* cj. Διάσια ἣ καλεῖται. C. F. Hermann in *Philologus* 1867 ii. 1 ff. cj. ἐν ᾗ πανδημεὶ θύουσι πολλὰ οὐχ ἱερεῖα, κ.τ.λ. T. Hemsterhuys on Loukian. *Tim.* 7 cj. ἀλλ' ἀγνὰ θύματα ἐπιχώρια. O. Band *op. cit.* p. 4 regards the words ἔστι—μεγίστη as a probable and ἔξω—ἐπιχώρια as a certain interpolation.

[5] In view of Kylon's connexion with Theagenes, note that the cult of Zeus at Megara bore some resemblance to the cult of Zeus on the Ilissos. A relief from Megara, like that from the Kallirrhoe-basin, associates Zeus with Acheloios (*supra* p. 1117 n. 7). Megara, like the Ilissos-bank, had its myth of the deluge (Paus. 1. 40. 1). And at Megara too there was an Olympieion with a famous statue of Zeus (Paus. 1. 40. 4 μετὰ ταῦτα ἐς τὸ τοῦ Διὸς (τοῦ Διὸς τὸ cod. Monac.) τέμενος ἐσελθοῦσι καλούμενον Ὀλυμπιεῖον ναός ἐστι θέας ἄξιος· τὸ δὲ ἄγαλμα οὐκ ἐξειργάσθη τοῦ Διὸς ἐπιλαβόντος τοῦ Πελοποννησίων πολέμου πρὸς Ἀθηναίους,... τῷ δ' ἀγάλματι τοῦ Διὸς πρόσωπον ἐλέφαντος καὶ χρυσοῦ, τὰ δὲ λοιπὰ πηλοῦ τέ ἐστι καὶ γύψου· ποιῆσαι δὲ αὐτὸ Θεόκοσμον λέγουσιν ἐπιχώριον, συνεργάσασθαι δέ οἱ Φειδίαν. ὑπὲρ δὲ τῆς κεφαλῆς τοῦ Διός εἰσιν Ὧραι καὶ Μοῖραι· δῆλα δὲ πᾶσι τὴν Πεπρωμένην μόνῳ οἱ πείθεσθαι, καὶ τὰς ὥρας τὸν θεὸν τοῦτον νέμειν ἐς (so H. C. Schubart—E. C. Walz for εἰς) τὸ δέον. ὄπισθε δὲ τοῦ ναοῦ κεῖται ξύλα ἡμίεργα· ταῦτα ἔμελλεν ὁ Θεόκοσμος ἐλέφαντι

It remains to determine the place, time, and character of the Diasia. O. Band[1] and A. Mommsen[2] conclude in favour of the Ilissos-site. Not without reason ; for here Zeus had been worshipped since the days of Deukalion[3], and here, on the north bank of the river, just outside the Themistoclean wall[4], there was convenient space for the people to assemble[5]. They did so on Anthesterion 22 or 23[6], which in the time of Plutarch would have corresponded with March 22 or 23[7]. The inference to be drawn from this dating is that the Diasia, like the Lesser Mysteries of Agra (*c.* Anthesterion 20[8]) or the *Pithoigía, Chóes,* and *Chýtroi* (Anthesterion 11—13[9]), had a character at once chthonian and agrarian[10]. Zeus *Meilíchios,* the buried king, was the giver of animal and vegetable life.

καὶ χρυσῷ κοσμήσας τὸ ἄγαλμα ἐκτελέσειν τοῦ Διός, *supra* i. 2 n. 2). Imperial coppers of Megara show a seated Zeus holding a Nike (*Brit. Mus. Cat. Coins* Attica etc. p. 122 pl. 22, 1 = my fig. 959, Imhoof-Blumer and P. Gardner *Num. Comm. Paus.* i. 4 f. pl. A, 3, Head *Hist. num.*[2] p. 394) or an eagle (Imhoof-Blumer and P. Gardner *op. cit.* i. 5), which may be meant for Theokosmos' masterpiece, and a Zeus striding to the right with

Fig. 959.　　　　　　　　　　Fig. 960.

thunderbolt and eagle (Imhoof-Blumer and P. Gardner *op. cit.* i. 5 pl. A, 4 = my fig. 960, Head *Hist. num.*[2] p. 394), in which—since the god sometimes has a base—we must recognise another statue (cp. Paus. 1. 40. 6 Διὸς Κονίου in a context cited *supra* p. 257 n. 4, Paus. 1. 43. 6 καὶ ἐν τῷ ναῷ τῷ πλησίον Μούσας καὶ χαλκοῦν Δία ἐποίησε Λύσιππος).

[1] O. Band *Die Attischen Diasien* Berlin 1883 p. 11.

[2] Mommsen *Feste d. Stadt Athen* p. 421 f.

[3] Paus. 1. 18. 8, *supra* p. 420.

[4] Schol. Aristoph. *nub.* 408 ἑορτὴ Διὸς 'Αθήνησι τὰ Διάσια, ἐν ᾗ πανδημεὶ ἔξω τείχους συνόντες ἑορτάζουσιν (a paraphrase of Thouk. 1. 126 cited *supra* p. 1138 n. 2) = Favorin. *lex.* p. 492, 36 f.

[5] See A. N. Skias in the Πρακτ. ἀρχ. ἐτ. 1893 pl. A.

The Ilissos-site is highly probable, but not absolutely certain ; for the Kephisos-site (W. Judeich *Topographie von Athen* München 1905 p. 362 n. 5) likewise had claims to high antiquity and convenient proximity. It is not, however, so aptly described by the phrases ἔξω τῆς πόλεως, ἔξω τείχους, and its festal day appears to have been Hekatombaion 8 (*supra* p. 1091 f.).

[6] Schol. Aristoph. *nub.* 408 Διασίοισιν· ἑορτὴ 'Αθήνησι Μειλιχίου Διός. ἄγεται δὲ μηνὸς 'Ανθεστηριῶνος η' φθίνοντος. This would be Anthesterion 22 or 23, according as that month was 'full' (30 days) or 'hollow' (29 days): see the discussion and tables in A. Schmidt *Handbuch der griechischen Chronologie* Jena 1888 p. 200 ff.

[7] Plout. *v. Sull.* 14 ἐλεῖν δὲ τὰς 'Αθήνας αὐτός φησιν ἐν τοῖς ὑπομνήμασι (*frag.* 13 (*Hist. Rom. frag.* p. 131 Peter)) Μαρτίαις καλάνδαις, ἥτις ἡμέρα μάλιστα συμπίπτει τῇ νουμηνίᾳ τοῦ 'Ανθεστηριῶνος μηνός, ἐν ᾧ κατὰ τύχην ὑπομνήματα πολλὰ τοῦ διὰ τὴν ἐπομβρίαν ὀλέθρου καὶ τῆς φθορᾶς ἐκείνης δρῶσιν, ὡς τότε καὶ περὶ τὸν χρόνον ἐκεῖνον μάλιστα τοῦ κατακλυσμοῦ συμπεσόντος, *infra* § 9 (h) ii (e).

[8] Mommsen *Feste d. Stadt Athen* p. 406, *supra* i. 692 f.

[9] Mommsen *op. cit.* p. 384 ff., *supra* i. 684.

[10] *Supra* i. 687.

The ritual of the Diasia is imperfectly known. Thoukydides' statement that many, in lieu of 'victims,' offered 'sacrifices peculiar to the country' is annotated by the scholiast, who remarks (1) that 'victims' means sheep (*próbata*), and (2) that the 'sacrifices peculiar to the country' were cakes moulded into the forms of animals[1]. Both observations are credible. On the one hand, we have seen that the 'fleece of Zeus' was stripped from a victim sacrificed to Zeus *Meilíchios* or to Zeus *Ktésios*[2]. On the other hand, we hear[3] of a cult of Artemis at Syracuse, in which rustic singers were decked with a loaf that had wild beasts moulded upon it[4], a wallet full of mingled grain, and wine in a goat-skin for distribution to all and sundry. They wore garlands, had stag-horns on their foreheads, and carried a crook in their hands. Thus equipped they vied with each other in song : the victor received the loaf of the vanquished and stopped in Syracuse ; the vanquished went about the neighbouring villages collecting food for themselves. Their songs were full of mirth and merriment, and ended with the stanza:

Here's wealth for you !
Here's health for you !
We bring you what the goddess sends,
A boon and blessing to her friends !

It would seem that at Athens the god, and at Syracuse the votary, accepted the cake or loaf moulded with animal forms as a surrogate for the animals themselves in accordance with a well-known principle of ancient ritual[5].

[1] *Supra* p. 1138 n. 2.
[2] *Supra* i. 422 ff. O. Band *Die Attischen Diasien* Berlin 1883 p. 4 (following E. F. Poppo on Thouk. 1. 126) *à propos* of the scholion ἱερεῖα· πρόβατα says curtly 'Immo χοίρους.'
[3] Schol. Theokr. *proleg.* B εὕρεσις τῶν βουκολικῶν b p. 3, 2 ff. Wendel (cp. *anecd. Estense* 3. 1 p. 7, 11 ff. Wendel, Prob. *in* Verg. *ecl.* p. 347 f. Lion, Diomed. *ars gramm.* 3 p. 486, 27 ff. Keil: Probus and Diomedes connect the custom with the cult of Diana *Lyaea* ᾄδειν δέ φασιν αὐτοὺς ἄρτον ἐξηρτημένους θηρίων ἐν ἑαυτῷ πλέονας τύπους ἔχοντα καὶ πήραν πανσπερμίας ἀνάπλεων καὶ οἶνον ἐν αἰγείῳ ἀσκῷ, σπονδὴν νέμοντας τοῖς ὑπαντῶσι, στέφανόν τε περικεῖσθαι καὶ κέρατα ἐλάφων προκεῖσθαι καὶ μετὰ χεῖρας ἔχειν λαγωβόλον. τὸν δὲ νικήσαντα λαμβάνειν τὸν τοῦ νενικημένου ἄρτον· κἀκεῖνον μὲν ἐπὶ τῆς τῶν Συρακουσίων μένειν πόλεως, τοὺς δὲ νενικημένους εἰς τὰς περιοικίδας χωρεῖν ἀγείροντας ἑαυτοῖς τὰς τροφάς· ᾄδειν (so H. Schaefer for διδόναι codd.) δὲ ἄλλα τινὰ παιδιᾶς καὶ γέλωτος ἐχόμενα καὶ εὐφημοῦντας ἐπιλέγειν· 'δέξαι τὰν ἀγαθὰν τύχαν, | δέξαι τὰν ὑγίειαν, | ἃν φέρομες παρὰ τᾶς (so F. G. Schneidewin for τῆς E[b]. A.T. τοῦ K.) θεοῦ, | ἃν ἐκαλέσσατο (ἐκλελάσκετο K. A. H. Ahrens cj. ᾇ 'κελήσατο C. Wendel cj. ἐκλάσκετο or ἐλακήσατο) τήνα (*carm. pop.* 42 Bergk[4], 45 Hiller—Crusius).
[4] ? cp. Athen. 646 E ἔλαφος πλακοῦς ὁ τοῖς Ἐλαφηβολίοις ἀναπλασσόμενος διὰ σταιτὸς καὶ μέλιτος καὶ σησάμου.
[5] Serv. *in* Verg. Aen. 2. 116 et sciendum in sacris simulata pro veris accipi. unde, cum de animalibus quae difficile inveniuntur est sacrificandum, de pane vel cera fiunt et pro veris accipiuntur. Lobeck *Aglaophamus* ii. 1079 ff. and Frazer *Golden Bough*[3]: Spirits of Corn and Wild ii. 95 n. 2 have made full collections of the literary evidence. Countless archaeological finds illustrate the same principle: see W. H. D. Rouse *Greek Votive Offerings* Cambridge 1902 p. 295 ff. To take a single case, the pig for sacrifice might be replaced by a dog dressed in a pig-skin (so on a red-figured *kylix* at Vienna (Masner *Samml. ant. Vasen u. Terracotten Wien* p. 40 f. no. 321 fig. 24, F. Studniczka 'Ein Opferbetrug des Hermes' in the *Jahrb. d. kais. deutsch. arch. Inst.* 1891 vi. 258 ff. fig., J. E. Harrison—D. S. MacColl *Greek Vase Paintings* London 1894 p. 25 pl. 33, 1)), or by a terra-cotta pig (so with those from the precinct of Demeter and Kore at Tegea (*Brit. Mus. Cat. Terracottas* pp. xxxviii f., 78 no. B 46, A. Milchhöfer in the *Ath.*

Kylon's mistake suggests that already in the seventh century the Diasia was past its zenith. But popular rites die hard. Two hundred years later old-fashioned folk still thought of the family feast and the public fair. Aristophanes makes Strepsiades tell with gusto how once at the Diasia he roasted a haggis for his kinsmen[1], and how on a like occasion he spent an obol on a toy-cart for his little son[2]. This is the last that we hear of the festival for more than half a millennium. Then came Lucian with his marvellous talent for galvanizing the past into a semblance of life. In the *Ikaromenippos* Zeus asks 'why the Athenians had dropped the Diasia all those years[3].' In the *Timon* Hermes jogs the memory of Zeus himself:

'What, Father! Don't you know Timon—son of Echekratides, of Kollytos? Many's the time he's entertained us on perfect sacrifices, the wealthy *parvenu* of the whole hecatombs, with whom we used to feast like lords at the Diasia[4].'

In the *Charidemos* there is a reference to literary competitions at the same festival[5].

A stage more remote from the original facts was Eumathios Makrembolites, the Byzantine novelist (second half of *s.* xii A.D.) who penned the *Romance of Hysmine and Hysminias*. He laid its scene in the imaginary towns of Eurykomis and Aulikomis and dealt largely with the circumstances of the Diasia. The hero, Hysminias, wearing a bay-wreath, a long *chitón*, and sacred shoes[6], went as herald of Zeus from the former to the latter town, where he was received as a god[7] and entertained in the name of Zeus[8], but proved himself to be very human by falling in love with Hysmine the daughter of his host. She, however, was betrothed to another; and her parents, who had escorted the herald back to Eurykomis, offered there at the altar of Zeus a sacrifice for the future happiness of their daughter. Thereupon an eagle swooped down and carried off the sacrifice. The parents were much upset at this evil omen[9]. But some of the bystanders took it to be a most auspicious sign[10]. And a friend of Hysminias pointed out to him that he might be the eagle, and carry off the bride[11]—which he proceeded to do. We need not trace at greater length his rather banal escapades and adventures. But we should note that the god, whom he served so unworthily, is throughout spoken of as Zeus or Zeus *Pátrios*[12] or Zeus *Phílios*[13] or Zeus *Sotér*[14]

Mitth. 1879 iv. 171, 174, C. A. Hutton *Greek Terracotta Statuettes* London 1899 p. 3 f.) or from that of Persephone at Tarentum (Sir A. J. Evans in the *Journ. Hell. Stud.* 1886 vii. 24, W. H. D. Rouse *op. cit.* p. 301)), or even by a ham-shaped coin (so with the curious coppers from the fountain at Nîmes (L. de la Saussaye *Numismatique de la Gaule Narbonnaise* Blois 1842 p. 159 pl. 20, 36, G. Long in Smith *Dict. Geogr.* ii. 414 f. fig., A. Boutkowski *Dictionnaire Numismatique* Leipzig 1884 ii. 1. 1738 f. no. 2833 fig., E. Muret—M. A. Chabouillet *Catalogue des monnaies gauloises de la Bibliothèque Nationale* Paris 1889 p. 61 no. 2839, H. de la Tour *Atlas de monnaies gauloises* Paris 1892 no. 2839 pl. 7, G. F. Hill *A Handbook of Greek and Roman Coins* London 1899 p. 3 f. fig. 2, Babelon *Monn. gr. rom.* i. 1. 675 f.)).

[1] Aristoph. *nub.* 408 ff.   [2] *Id. ib.* 861 ff.

[3] Loukian. *Icaromen.* 24.

[4] Loukian. *Tim.* 7.   [5] Loukian. *Charid.* 1, cp. 3.

[6] Eumath. 1. 1 f., 1. 7, 4. 3, 4. 24, 5. 3, 8. 10, 8. 13, cp. 8. 19, 8. 21.

[7] *Id.* 1. 3 δέχομαι παρ' αὐτοῖς οὐχ ὡς κῆρυξ, ἀλλ' ὡς θεός.

[8] *Id.* 1. 10 Διασίωι καιρός, καταιτρυφήσωμεν τὰ Διάσια· ὅλοι γευώμεθα τῆς ἑορτῆς, ὅλοι τῆς πανηγύρεως. Ζεὺς παρὰ τῇ τραπέζῃ, καὶ Διὸς τράπεζα, ὅτι καὶ ὁ κῆρυξ οὗτος Διός: cp. 6. 2.

[9] *Id.* 6. 10.   [10] *Id.* 6. 11.

[11] *Id.* 6. 13.   [12] *Id.* 6. 10.   [13] *Id.* 3. 9, 5. 18.

[14] *Id.* 4. 2, 5. 15, 6. 2, 6. 15, cp. 1. 14.

or Zeus *Xénios*[1], but never as Zeus *Meilíchios*—a sufficient proof that the author, though he works up his material with some care, has not preserved to us a trustworthy record of Athenian cult.

The scholiast on Lucian, who here and there makes valuable remarks, tells us more than once that the Diasia was kept at Athens 'with gloomy looks,' such as befitted the worship of the dead[2]. This agrees well with other indications concerning the ritual of Zeus *Meilíchios*. An old Attic calendar, the lettering of which has been referred to the early part of *s.* v B.C., mentions 'sober' offerings to *Milíchios* side by side with offerings to Meter at some date before the end of Gamelion[3]. Now 'sober' offerings consisted in the main of honey[4], and were specially, though not exclusively, given to chthonian powers (Gaia[5], the *Bona Dea*[6], Dis[7], Hekate[8], the Eumenides[9], Kerberos[10]) and the souls of the dead[11]. The same might be said of the pigs sacrificed to Zeus *Meilíchios* at the Peiraieus[12] and by Xenophon 'in accordance with his ancestral custom[13].' In short, we have every reason to conclude that at Athens the cult of Zeus *Meilíchios* was essentially chthonian—the worship of a buried king, who during his life-time had been hailed as the sky-god incarnate and still was present to bless his people with increase of field and flock and family.

[1] Eumath. 5. 8 f., 5. 14 f., 6. 1 f., 6. 9, 11. 3.
At the altar of this deity, who is called indifferently Zeus Σωτήρ or Zeus Ξένιος, the parents sacrifice about the third watch of the night (*id.* 5. 15, 6. 5, 6. 14, 6. 16, cp. 10. 9).

[2] Schol. Loukian. *Icaromen.* 24 p. 107, 15 f. Rabe Διάσια· ἑορτὴ Ἀθήνησιν, ἣν ἐπετέλουν μετά τινος στυγνότητος θύοντες ἐν αὐτῇ Διὶ Μειλιχίῳ, *Tim.* 7 p. 110, 27 f. Rabe Διάσια· ἑορτὴ Ἀθήνησιν οὕτω καλουμένη, ἣν εἰώθεσαν μετὰ στυγνότητος τινος ἐπιτελεῖν θύοντες Διὶ τῷ Μειλιχίῳ, *Tim.* 43 p. 117, 14 ff. Rabe ἀποφράς·...ἐτελεῖτο δὲ ταῦτα κατὰ τὸν Φεβρουάριον μῆνα, ὅτε καὶ τοῖς καταχθονίοις ἐνήγιζον. καὶ πᾶς οὗτος ὁ μὴν ἀνεῖτο τοῖς κατοιχομένοις μετὰ στυγνότητος πάντων προϊόντων † ἕτερον † τρόπον, ὃν καὶ τὰ Διάσια στυγνάζοντες ἦγον Ἀθηναῖοι. M. du Soul marked ἕτερον as corrupt. T. Hemsterhusius cj. ἐνέρων. Graeven cj. οὐχ ἕτερον. O. Band *Die Attischen Diasien* Berlin 1883 p. 6 regards ἕτερον as euphemistic. If alteration is needed, perhaps we should read σκυθρωπότερον. Cp. Hesych. Διάσια· ἑορτὴ Ἀθήνησι. καὶ σκυθρωποὺς ἀπὸ τῆς ἑορτῆς ἣν ἐπετέλουν μετά τινος στυγνότητος θύοντες, on which M. Schmidt acutely observes: 'Fortasse comicus dixerat βλέποντας Διάσια.'

[3] *Corp. inscr. Att.* i no. 4 *A*, 3 ff., J. de Prott *Leges Graecorum sacrae* Lipsiae 1896 Fasti sacri p. 1 ff. no. 1 A, 3 ff. θάρ[γελοι? - - - Διὶ Μ]|[ι]λιχίοι : ε[- - - - - νεφ]|[ά](λι)α : Μετρὶ : [ἐν Ἄγρας - - -]|[.]σπυριχεια - - - - - - -. Mommsen *Feste d. Stadt Athen* p. 421 infers that Zeus *Milíchios* and Meter (=Demeter) were worshipped in or near Agra on the Ilissos : cp. *supra* p. 1118 n. 4.

[4] W. H. Roscher *Nektar und Ambrosia* Leipzig 1883 p. 64 n. 167, *id. Über Selene und Verwandtes* Leipzig 1890 p. 49 n. 199, W. Robert-Tornow *De apium mellisque apud veteres significatione et symbolica et mythologica* Berolini 1893 p. 144, *Journ. Hell. Stud.* 1895 xv. 20 f.   [5] Ap. Rhod. 2. 1271 ff.   [6] Macrob. *Sat.* 1. 12. 25.

[7] Sil. It. 13. 415 f. For bees and honey in relation to Demeter and Persephone see *supra* i. 443 n. 6 f., ii. 1113 n. 0 no. (3).

[8] Ap. Rhod. 3. 1035 f.

[9] Aisch. *Eum.* 106 f., Soph. *O.C.* 98 ff., 480 ff. with schol. *ad loc.*, Paus. 2. 11. 4.

[10] Verg. *Aen.* 6. 417 ff., Souid. *s.v.* μελιτοῦττα=schol. Aristoph. *Lys.* 601.

[11] *Il.* 23. 170 f., *Od.* 10. 518 ff., 11. 26 ff., 24. 67 f., Aisch. *Pers.* 607 ff., Eur. *Or.* 114 f. with schol. *ad loc.*, *I.T.* 159 ff., 633 ff., Ap. Rhod. 2. 1271 ff., Souid. *s.v.* μελιτοῦττα= schol. Aristoph. *Lys.* 601. See further H. Usener 'Milch und Honig' in the *Rhein. Mus.* 1902 lvii. 177—195 (=*id. Kleine Schriften* Leipzig—Berlin 1913 iv. 398—417) and S. Eitrem *Opferritus und Voropfer der Griechen und Römer* (*Videnskapsselskapets Skrifter.* II. Hist.-Filos. Klasse. 1914. No. i) Kristiania 1915 pp. 102—105.

[12] *Supra* p. 1105.   [13] *Supra* p. 1107.

(8) *Zeus* *Meilíchios* at Argos.

Outside Athens the cult of Zeus *Meilíchios* seems to have borne a similar character. Thus at Argos there was a seated statue of Zeus *Meilíchios*, made of white marble by Polykleitos (so it was said) to purify the people from the stain of kindred bloodshed[1]. Argive coppers of imperial date show several types of Zeus. Coins of Hadrian (fig. 961) and Lucius Verus give his head alone[2]. Others, struck by Antoninus Pius, Marcus Aurelius, and Lucius Verus (fig. 962), represent

Fig. 961.   Fig. 962.   Fig. 963.   Fig. 964.

him enthroned with a *phiále* in his right hand and a sceptre in his left[3]. Others of Septimius Severus and Plautilla (fig. 963) make him hold an eagle or a Nike in place of the *phiále*[4]. On others, again, struck by Hadrian, Marcus Aurelius (fig. 964), Septimius Severus, Iulia Domna, Plautilla, and Valerianus Senior, he stands, naked, with a sceptre in his right hand and an eagle at his feet[5]; while yet another, by Plautilla, figures him striding, naked, with eagle and thunderbolt in his hands[6]. F. Imhoof-Blumer and P. Gardner suggest that the Zeus enthroned with *phiále* and sceptre (fig. 962) may be Zeus *Meilíchios*, and add that the head

---

[1] Paus. 2. 20. 1 f. with Sir J. G. Frazer and H. Hitzig—H. Blümner *ad loc.* The statue has been attributed to the elder Polykleitos by Overbeck *Schriftquellen* p. 168 no. 941 and *Gr. Kunstmyth.* Zeus p. 50 f. (but see *infra*), G. Löschcke in the *Arch. Zeit.* 1878 xxxvi. 11 n. 12, Collignon *Hist. de la Sculpt. gr.* i. 486, to the younger Polykleitos by H. Brunn *Geschichte der griechischen Künstler* Stuttgart 1857 i. 280 f. and in the *Sitzungsber. d. kais. bayr. Akad. d. Wiss.* Phil.-hist. Classe 1880 p. 469, Overbeck *Gr. Plastik*[4] i. 508 f. (but see *supra*). Both attributions are called in question by C. Robert *Archaeologische Maerchen aus alter und neuer Zeit* Berlin 1886 p. 102, Furtwängler *Masterpieces of Gk Sculpt.* p. 224, E. A. Gardner *A Handbook of Greek Sculpture* London 1897 ii. 332 n. 1. To me it seems clear (1) that Pausanias meant the elder and more famous Polykleitos, but (2) that marble was an improbable material for such a statue by him, and (3) that an obvious ground for the false ascription of the seated Zeus to him lay in the fact that he was the sculptor of the seated Hera (*supra* i. 134 f.).

[2] Imhoof-Blumer and P. Gardner *Num. Comm. Paus.* i. 36 pl. K, 27 = my fig. 961, Rasche *Lex. Num.* i. 1082.

[3] Imhoof-Blumer and P. Gardner *op. cit.* i. 36 pl. K, 25 = my fig. 962.

[4] Imhoof-Blumer and P. Gardner *op. cit.* i. 36 pl. K, 26 = my fig. 963.

[5] Imhoof-Blumer and P. Gardner *op. cit.* i. 36 pl. K, 28 = my fig. 964, *Brit. Mus. Cat. Coins* Peloponnesus p. 148 pl. 28, 10 Hadrian, p. 150 Septimius Severus (with wrong reference to pl. 28, 21), *Hunter Cat. Coins* ii. 154 pl. 39, 13 Valerianus Senior, Rasche *Lex. Num.* i. 1083 Iulia Domna, Suppl. i. 1034 Plautilla. Imhoof-Blumer and P. Gardner *loc. cit., id.* in the *Brit. Mus. Cat. Coins* Peloponnesus p. 148 n.* cp. Paus. 2. 20. 3 τούτων δὲ ἀπαντικρὺ Νεμείου Διός ἐστιν ἱερόν, ἄγαλμα ὀρθὸν χαλκοῦν, τέχνη Λυσίππου (where H. C. Schubart cj. < τὸ > ἄγαλμα, but H. C. Schubart— E. C. Walz and Kayser omit ἱερόν with cod. Leid. a).

[6] Imhoof-Blumer and P. Gardner *op. cit.* i. 36, Rasche *Lex. Num.* Suppl. i. 1034.

of Zeus (fig. 961) being 'decidedly fine and early' is perhaps 'a reminiscence of the head of Polycleitus' statue[1].' But, in view of the large number of Argive Zeuses[2], these conjectures are admittedly uncertain.

(9) Zeus *Meilichios* at Sikyon.

From Argos to Sikyon[3], as the crow flies, is less than five-and-twenty miles. But in their representation of Zeus *Meilichios* Argives and Sicyonians differed *toto caelo*. The former could boast a masterpiece shown to visitors as the work of Polykleitos himself ; the latter were content with an artless pyramid, not even anthropomorphic[4]. Why Zeus was given this peculiar shape, we are not told.

[1] Imhoof-Blumer and P. Gardner *op. cit.* i. 36.

[2] In addition to references already given (*supra* i. 117 Zeus 'Αφέσιος, 122 f. Zeus Λαρισαῖος, 134 f. Zeus as a cuckoo, 320 and 462 Zeus with three eyes, 448 and 456 Zeus Νέμειος, 461 Zeus Πανόπτης, ii. 704 ff. Zeus as a cuckoo, 712 ff. Zeus as partner of Hera, 875 n. 2 Zeus Φαλακρός, 892 n. 5 Zeus Λαρισαῖος, Λαρισσεύς) see Paus. 2. 19. 7 Δαναὸς δὲ ταῦτά τε ἀνέθηκε καὶ πλησίον κίονας ἐκ < > Διὸς καὶ Ἀρτέμιδος ξόανον (so most MSS. and H. C. Schubart, who indicated the *lacuna* : he is followed by Sir J. G. Frazer and H. Hitzig—H. Blümner. Some of the older editors read ἐς Διὸς with cod. Paris c. H. C. Schubart—E. C. Walz, L. Dindorf, and F. Spiro print καὶ Διὸς after cod. Vindob. a. Clavier cj. ὡς Διὸς. A. Kuhn cj. ξόανα) where we should perhaps correct ἐκ Διὸς <κελεύσματος> (cp. *supra* i. 371 n. 1) and suppose a pillar-cult of some sort, 2. 19. 8 βωμὸς 'Γετίου Διὸς (*infra* § 9 (h)), 2. 20. 6 καὶ Διός ἐστιν ἐνταῦθα ἱερὸν Σωτῆρος, 2. 21. 2 πρὸ δὲ αὐτοῦ πεποίηται Διὸς Φυξίου βωμός, 2. 22. 2 πέραν δὲ τοῦ τάφου (*sc.* of Pelasgos) χαλκεῖόν ἐστιν οὐ μέγα, ἀνέχει δὲ αὐτὸ ἀγάλματα ἀρχαῖα Ἀρτέμιδος καὶ Διὸς καὶ Ἀθηνᾶς. Λυκέας μὲν οὖν ἐν τοῖς ἔπεσιν ἐποίησε Μηχανέως τὸ ἄγαλμα εἶναι Διός, καὶ Ἀργείων ἔφη τοὺς ἐπὶ Ἴλιον στρατεύσαντας ἐνταῦθα ὀμόσαι παραμενεῖν (so H. C. Schubart—E. C. Walz for παραμένειν codd.) πολεμοῦντας, ἔστ' ἂν ἢ τὸ Ἴλιον ἕλωσιν ἢ μαχομένους τελευτὴ σφᾶς ἐπιλάβῃ· ἑτέροις δέ ἐστιν εἰρημένον ὀστᾶ ἐν τῷ χαλκείῳ κεῖσθαι Ταντάλου. The word χαλκεῖον, which has been much misunderstood (see H. Hitzig—H. Blümner *ad loc.*), presumably means a bronze *cista*. On the lid of it stood three archaic figures—an arrangement familiar to us from extant specimens (*e.g.* the 'Ficoroni'-*cista*, on which see Gerhard *Etr. Spiegel* ii. 14 ff. pl. 2, P. O. Bröndsted *den Ficoronische Cista* Kjöbenhavn 1847, E. Braun *Die Ficoronische Cista des collegio Romano* Leipzig 1849, O. Jahn *Die Ficoronische Cista* Leipzig 1852, Baumeister *Denkm.* i. 453 f. fig. 500, Forrer *Reallex.* p. 148 f. fig. 146; the handle of another *cista* from Palestrina in *Brit. Mus. Cat. Bronzes* p. 106 no. 643). Lykeas, as an Argive poet (Paus. 1. 13. 8 f., 2. 19. 5, 2. 23. 8), followed local tradition. And it is possible that the bones in the *cista* really were those of some early chieftain worshipped after his death as Zeus Μηχανεύς (for whom see *infra* § 9 (h) i). Argive inscriptions further allude to the cult of Zeus Νέμειος (*Inscr. Gr. Pelop.* i no. 602, 14 ff. καὶ θύσαν|τα τῶ Δὶ τῶ Νεμείω ἑκατόμ|βην, *ib.* no. 606, 11 f. = *Corp. inscr. Gr.* i no. 1123, 12 f. =W. Prellwitz in Collitz—Bechtel *Gr. Dial.- Inschr.* ii. 1. 131 f. no. 3293, 12 f. θύσαντά τε καὶ τῶ Δὶ τῶ Νεμείω ἑκα|τόνβαν πρῶτον καὶ μόνον) and Zeus Ὕψιστος (*Inscr. Gr. Pelop.* i no. 620, 4 =Kaibel *Epigr. Gr.* no. 465. 8 = Cougny *Anth. Pal. Append.* 2. 286. 8 cited *supra* p. 878 n. o no. (4)).

[3] I pass by Epidauros, because the evidence for a cult of Zeus *Meilichios* in that town is small—in fact depends on the suggested interpretation of a single letter. See J. Baunack 'Zu den Inschriften aus Epidauros' in *Philologus* 1895 liv. 37 : 'Nr. 125 h. bei K. [= P. Kabbadias *Fouilles d'Épidaure* Athènes 1893 p. 57] nur Ἀφροδίτας μιλιχίας. Bl. (Askl. S. 123) [=C. Blinkenberg *Asklepios og hans fraender i Hieron ved Epidauros* Kobenhavn 1893 p. 123 no. 7] merkt darauf einen Zwischenraum von etwa 2 Zeichen an und hierauf ein Δ, was er ansprechend als den Anfang einer zweiten Inschrift Δ[ιὸς μιλιχίου] erklärt,' *Inscr. Gr. Pelop.* i no. 1272 in letters of *s.* iii B.C. ΑΦΡΟΔΙΤΑΣΜΙΛΙΧΙΑΣ| |ᴅᴎ= Ἀφροδίτας Μιλιχίας. Δι[ὸς Μιλιχίου].

[4] Paus. 2. 9. 6 cited *supra* i. 520 n. 2.

I do not, of course, mean to imply that the Sicyonians were averse from the Zeus-types

It is tempting to conjecture that his pyramid betokened a buried king. For tombs of pyramidal form occur sporadically from Egypt to Italy[1]; and, if Eumelos

of later art. A 'third brass' of Geta shows Zeus seated with a *phiále* in his right hand, a sceptre in his left (Rasche *Lex. Num.* viii. 912, Imhoof-Blumer and P. Gardner *Num. Comm. Paus.* i. 29). A copper of Caracalla (?) has CI KVW N Zeus standing to the left, naked, with thunderbolt in right hand, sceptre in left (*Brit. Mus. Cat. Coins* Peloponnesus p. 55, Imhoof-Blumer and P. Gardner *op. cit.* i. 29 pl. H, 10 = my fig. 965): cp. the obverse type of a *quasi*-autonomous coin in *Numismata antiqua* in tres partes divisa, collegit Thomas Pembrochiæ et Montis Gomerici comes Londinii 1746 ii pl. 28, 11, Rasche *Lex. Num.* viii. 910 Zeus standing, naked, with Nike in his right hand and a sceptre in his left. Imhoof-Blumer and P. Gardner *loc. cit.* rightly see in the British Museum coin an illustration of Paus. 2. 9. 6

Fig. 965.

τῆς δὲ ἀγορᾶς ἐστιν ἐν τῷ ὑπαίθρῳ Ζεὺς χαλκοῦς, τέχνη Λυσίππου (cp. Overbeck *Gr. Kunstmyth.* Zeus p. 151 f.).

[1] A good collection of evidence is got together by R. Rochette 'Sur la pyra, comme type de monument funéraire' in the *Mémoires de l'Institut National de France* Académie des Inscriptions et Belles-Lettres 1848 xvii. 388—401, who derives pyramidal tombs from pyramidal pyres. Without necessarily subscribing to this view, we may admit that pyres and similar structures of funerary import must be taken into account along with actual tombs. A rough classification of the relevant monuments according to form would include (*a*) stepped pyramids, (*b*) smooth-sided pyramids, (*c*) stepped pyramids on plinths, (*d*) smooth-sided pyramids on plinths. Examples are :—

(*a*) The stepped pyramid at Saqqâra built by Zosiri of the third dynasty (G. Maspero *The Dawn of Civilization*[4] London 1901 p. 359, E. A. Wallis Budge *A History of Egypt* London 1902 i. 193, 218 f. fig., J. H. Breasted *A History of Egypt* New York 1911 p. 113 f. fig. 63, E. Bell *The Architecture of Ancient Egypt* London 1915 p. 23 ff. fig.), or that at Riqqeh, whose occupant is unknown (G. Maspero *op. cit.*[4] p. 359 n. 3), or again that at Mêdûm built by Snofrûi the last king of the third dynasty, though this at least was probably meant to be cased with polished stone (G. Maspero *op. cit.*[4] p. 359 f. fig., E. A. Wallis Budge *op. cit.* ii. 24 f. fig., J. H. Breasted *op. cit.* p. 115 fig. 64, E. Bell *op. cit.* p. 25 f. fig.). The form has traceable antecedents, *viz.* the four-sided *tumulus* → the brick-built *mastaba* → the stone-built *mastaba* → a series of stone-built *mastaba* superposed = a stepped pyramid.

(*b*) The fully developed pyramids of Egypt, those of Kenchreai (A. Blouet etc. *Expédition scientifique de Morée* Paris 1833 ii. 92 pl. 55, 1—3, Frazer *Pausanias* iii. 212—214, v. 565 f.) and *Ligourio* near Epidauros (A. Blouet etc. *op. cit.* ii. 164 pl. 76, 2 f., Frazer *Pausanias* iii. 233, v. 570), that at *Astros* in Kynouria (W. Vischer *Erinnerungen und Eindrücke aus Griechenland* Basel 1857 p. 327), that of Cestius on the *via Ostiensis* (A. Schneider *Das alte Rom* Leipzig 1896 pl. 4, 15, O. Richter *Topographie der Stadt Rom*[2] München 1901 p. 355, H. Jordan—C. Huelsen *Topographie der Stadt Rom im Alterthum* Berlin 1907 i. 3. 179 f.), if not also the one formerly existing near the Mausoleum of Hadrian and known to the middle ages, or earlier (Acron *in* Hor. *epod.* 9. 25), as the *sepulcrum Scipionis* or *Romuli* (O. Richter *op. cit.*[2] p. 280, H. Jordan—C. Huelsen *op. cit.* i. 3. 659 f., H. Jordan *ib.* Berlin 1871 ii. 405 f.). A pyramid of the sort is grouped with a warrior or gladiator (*bustuarius?*) in two different gem-types (E. Saglio in Daremberg—Saglio *Dict. Ant.* i. 755 fig. 898, Reinach *Pierres Gravées* p. 65 no. 73, 5 pl. 65 ; Reinach *op. cit.* p. 83 no. 90 pl. 80).

(*c*) The stepped tomb of 'Kyros' on the site of Pasargadai (C. F. M. Texier *Description de l'Arménie, la Perse et la Mésopotamie* Paris 1852 ii. 152 ff. pls. 81—83, Perrot—Chipiez *Hist. de l'Art* v. 597 ff. figs. 375—377, J. Fergusson *A History of Architecture in all Countries*[3] London 1893 i. 196 ff. figs. 84—86) can hardly be said to have a plinth, but forms the starting-point for such edifices as the lion-tomb at Knidos (Sir C. T. Newton *A*

is to be trusted, the eponymous king Sikyon, son of Marathon son of Epopeus, came of a family in which we have already seen reason to suspect successive incarnations of Zeus[1]. To be sure, there were rival traditions with regard to Sikyon. Hesiod made him the son of Erechtheus[2]. Asios the Samian genealogist[3] took him to be the son of Metion son of Erechtheus, and this view was preferred by the Sicyonians themselves[4]. Finally, Ibykos deemed him the son of Pelops[5]. But the variants each and all suggest close connexion with Zeus. *Erechtheús*, the 'Cleaver,' was a cult-title of Zeus the lightning-god[6]. *Metion* is

History of Discoveries at Halicarnassus, Cnidus, and Branchidæ London 1862—1863 i pls. 61—66, ii. 480—511, *id. Travels & Discoveries in the Levant* London 1865 ii. 214 ff., *Brit. Mus. Cat. Sculpture* ii. 214 ff. no. 1350, J. Fergusson *op. cit.*[3] i. 284 f. fig. 164 P. Gardner *Sculptured Tombs of Hellas* London 1896 p. 224 ff. fig. 77), the Mausoleion of Halikarnassos, the stepped tomb at Mylasa (M. G. F. A. Comte de Choiseul-Gouffier *Voyage pittoresque de la Grèce* Paris 1782 i. 144 ff. pls. 85—89, *Antiquities of Ionia* published by the Society of Dilettanti London 1797 ii. 26 pls. 24—26, C. Fellows *An Account of Discoveries in Lycia* London 1841 p. 75 f. with pl.), and that near Delphoi (E. Dodwell *Views and Descriptions of Cyclopian, or, Pelasgic Remains, in Greece and Italy* London 1834 p. 20 pl. 36 f.).

(*d*) A good specimen of the smooth-sided pyramid on plinth is the tomb of 'Zechariah' in the Valley of Jehoshaphat near Jerusalem (T. H. Horne *Landscape Illustrations of the Bible* London 1836 i pl. 93 with text). See also *supra* i. 515 n. 5 fig. 388, ii. 814 f. fig. 781, cp. i. 600 ff. figs. 465—468.

Further cp. the pyramids built above the rock-cut tombs of the Maccabees at Modin (Macc. 1. 13. 25—30, Ioseph. *ant. Iud.* 13. 6. 5, Euseb. *onomasticon de locis Hebraicis s.v.* Μοδεΐμ p. 290, 4 ff. F. Larsow—G. Parthey = Hieron. *de situ et nominibus locorum Hebraicorum s.v.* 'Modeim' p. 291, 6 ff. F. Larsow—G. Parthey: see V. Guérin *Description géographique, historique et archéologique de la Palestine* Paris 1868—1880 Seconde partie—Samarie ii. 55 ff. with two pls., Troisième partie—Galilée i. 47 ff., Perrot—Chipiez *Hist. de l'Art* iv. 361), the three pyramids built near Jerusalem by Helene, sister and wife of Monobazos Bazaios king of Adiabene (Ioseph. *ant. Iud.* 20. 4. 3, *bell. Iud.* 5. 2. 2, 5. 3. 3, 5. 4. 2, Paus. 8. 16. 5, Euseb. *hist. eccl.* 2. 12. 3, Hieron. *epist.* 108. 9 (xxii. 883 Migne): see W. Otto in Pauly—Wissowa *Real-Enc.* vii. 2836 f.), the pyramid, decorated with Argive shields, beneath which the followers of Proitos and Akrisios were buried (Paus. 2. 25. 7), the pyramidal tombs built by Hieron ii at Agyrion in Sicily (Diod. 16. 83), those made for horses at Agrigentum (Plin. *nat. hist.* 8. 155), the rock-cut 'Sepolcro Consolare' at Palazzola (Palazzuolo) above the Alban Lake (A. Nibby *Viaggio antiquario ne' contorni di Roma* Roma 1819 ii. 125 f.), the 'Sepolcro di Pompeo' or, as the folk of the district call it, 'di Ascanio' on the *via Appia* near Albano (A. Nibby *op. cit.* ii. 110—112), and another tomb near Capua (J. C. Richard de Saint-Non *Voyage pittoresque ou description des royaumes de Naples et de Sicile* Paris 1781—1786 ii. 249).

All these and other related types (cones etc.) ought to be made the subject of a thoroughgoing investigation. It would, no doubt, be found that the structures in question were produced by a combination of factors, some of practical exigency, some of symbolic significance. I shall content myself with suggesting that one root-idea was that of a mountain reaching up to heaven—an idea comparable with those of the sky-pillar (*supra* p. 44 ff.), the soul-ladder (*supra* p. 121 ff.), the stepped or spiral tower (*supra* p. 128 f.).

[1] *Supra* i. 245 ff.

[2] Hes. *frag.* 229 Flach, 102 Rzach *ap.* Paus. 2. 6. 5.

[3] E. Bethe in Pauly—Wissowa *Real-Enc.* ii. 1606, W. Christ *Geschichte der griechischen Litteratur*[5] München 1908 i. 125.

[4] Asios *frag.* 11 Kinkel *ap.* Paus. 2. 6. 5.

[5] Ibyk. *frag.* 48 Bergk[4] *ap.* Paus. 2. 6. 5.   [6] *Supra* p. 793.

but another form of *metíeta, metióeis*, Zeus the 'Magician[1].' And Pelops too we have regarded as in some sense a human Zeus[2]. Nevertheless I should not insist on the Sicyonian pyramid as sepulchral in character; for it must not be forgotten that at Tegea the pyramid-on-pillar was a favourite type for the representation of deities in general[3].

(10) Zeus *Melíchios* at Tegea.

From Tegea comes a dedication, of *s.* ii B.C. or earlier, to Zeus *Melíchios*[4]. W. Immerwahr holds that the cult was of recent introduction[5]. But Tegea was an ancient Arcadian town[6], and there is some ground for thinking that the Tegeates, like the Athenians, recognised the divinity of their early kings. At Athens—it will be remembered—the dead king seems to have been known as Zeus *Sotér* or *Téleios*[7]; and at Tegea Zeus *Téleios* had an altar and a square image (presumably a pyramid-on-pillar) of the usual Arcadian type[8]. Moreover, there are scattered indications that something rather like the Erechtheion and its royal worship existed at one time in Tegea. Aleos, the founder of the town[9], was, like Erechtheus[10], a *quasi-*
divine king, whose head as
shown on autonomous coppers
closely resembles that of Zeus
(fig. 966)[11]. His house, like the
house of Erechtheus, was still
to be seen in Pausanias' time[12].
Again, Aleos instituted the cult
of Athena *Aléa*[13] and estab-

Fig. 966.

lished his kingdom in connexion with her sanctuary[14]. This suggests that he stood to her in the same sort of relation as Erechtheus to Athena *Poliás*. Further hints help to fill in the picture: Athena *Aléa* had a sacred couch in her temple[15], was served by a boy-priest[16], and on occasion received the

[1] *Supra* i. 14 n. 1.   [2] *Supra* i. 139.   [3] *Supra* i. 520 n. 1, ii. 814 f.

[4] O. Hoffmann *Die Griechischen Dialekte* Göttingen 1891 i. 33 no. 49, Michel *Recueil d'Inscr. gr.* no. 1092, *Inscr. Gr. Arc. Lac. Mess.* ii no. 90 Διὶ Μελιχί|ωι Μικύλο|ς ἀνέθηκε where F. Hiller von Gaertringen notes: 'Forma Λ et dativus in -ωι alterius, sed Μελ-pro Μειλ_quarti potius saeculi a. Chr. esse videtur.'

[5] Immerwahr *Kult. Myth. Arkad.* p. 30.

[6] There was another Τεγέα in Crete, founded by Talthybios (Steph. Byz. *s.v.* Τέγεα) or Agamemnon (Vell. Pat. 1. 1. 2). Conversely, Tegea in Arkadia had its ὅρος...Κρήσιον (Paus. 8. 44. 7).

[7] *Supra* p. 1123.

[8] Paus. 8. 48. 6 πεποίηται δὲ καὶ Διὸς Τελείου βωμὸς καὶ ἄγαλμα τετράγωνον· περισσῶς γὰρ δή τι τῷ σχήματι τούτῳ φαίνονταί μοι χαίρειν οἱ Ἀρκάδες.

[9] Paus. 8. 45. 1.   [10] *Supra* p. 793 f.

[11] *Brit. Mus. Cat. Coins* Peloponnesus p. 202 pl. 37, 19 (=my fig. 966), *Hunter Cat. Coins* ii. 163, W. M. Leake *Numismata Hellenica* London 1856 European Greece p. 98, F. Imhoof-Blumer and P. Gardner *Num. Com. Paus.* ii. 108 f. pl. V, 23, Head *Hist. num.*[2] p. 455: autonomous copper struck after *c.* 146 B.C. *obv.* ΑΛΕΟΣ Bearded head of Aleos to right, wearing fillet; *rev.* ΤΕΓΕΑΤΑΝ Athena handing to Kepheus the hair of the Gorgon, while Sterope holds up a vase to receive it. In the field are two monograms.

[12] Paus. 8. 53. 10.   [13] Paus. 8. 4. 8, 8. 45. 4.

[14] Paus. 8. 4. 8.   [15] Paus. 8. 47. 2.

[16] Paus. 8. 47. 3 ἱερᾶται δὲ τῇ Ἀθηνᾷ παῖς χρόνον οὐκ οἶδα ὅσον τινά, πρὶν δὲ ἡβάσκειν καὶ οὐ πρόσω, τὴν ἱερωσύνην with Sir J. G. Frazer and H. Hitzig—H. Blümner *ad loc.*

gift of a *péplos*[1]. Notice too that, just as the safety of Athens depended on the snake kept in the Erechtheion[2], so the safety of Tegea depended on a lock of Medousa's hair which Athena had given to Kepheus son of Aleos[3]. The coins represent Kepheus' daughter Sterope receiving it in a jar (fig. 966)[4]. And it is permissible to conjecture that both at Athens and at Tegea the original talisman[5] was the soul of the ancestral king living on as a snake[6] in his burial jar[7]. The comparison will even take us a step further. The perpetual lamp of the Erechtheion[8] was but a civilised form of the perpetual fire burning on the common hearth of a primitive folk[9]. Now Pausanias says: 'The Tegeates have also what they call the common hearth of the Arcadians.... The high place on which stand most of the altars of the Tegeates is called after Zeus *Klários*[10] : plainly the god got his surname from the lot (*kléros*) cast on behalf of the sons of Arkas. The Tegeates celebrate a festival here every year[11].' Zeus *Klários* gave his name to the first of the four Tegeate tribes *Klareôtis*, *Hippothoîtis*, *Apolloniâtis*, *Athaneâtis*[12]. But the legend of the lot is probably due to a mis-

---

[1] Paus. 8. 5. 3.

[2] Frazer *Pausanias* ii. 168—170 collects the evidence. The precise position of the snake's hole is doubtful (W. Judeich *Topographie von Athen* München 1905 p. 250 f., M. L. D'Ooge *The Acropolis of Athens* New York 1908 p. 209). H. N. Fowler in the *Papers of the American School of Classical Studies at Athens 1882—1883* Boston 1885 would seek it somewhere under the N. porch of the Erechtheion, a view approved by M. P. Nilsson in the *Journ. Hell. Stud.* 1901 xxi. 329. Not improbably it is covered by the small round cistern of Turkish (?) origin still to be seen in the N.W. corner of the crypt beneath the N. porch (Πρακτικὰ τῆς ἐπὶ τοῦ Ἐρεχθείου ἐπιτροπῆς Athens 1853 pl. 3 = F. Thiersch in the *Abh. d. bayer. Akad. 1857* Philos.-philol. Classe viii pl. 3 will provide a coloured plan and section. See also P. Cavvadias—G. Kawerau *Die Ausgrabung der Akropolis* Athens 1907 pl. Γ′, and the remarks of E. M. Beulé *L'Acropole d'Athènes* Paris 1854 ii. 251 f., D'Ooge *op. cit.* p. 207).

[3] Paus. 8. 47. 5, cp. Apollod. 2. 7. 3, Phot. *lex. s.v.* πλόκιον Γοργάδος, Souid. *s.v.* πλόκιον Γοργάδος, Apostol. 14. 38.

[4] Cp. *Brit. Mus. Cat. Coins* Peloponnesus p. 203 pl. 37, 20, *Hunter Cat. Coins* ii. 163, W. M. Leake *Numismata Hellenica* London 1856 European Greece p. 98, F. Imhoof-Blumer and P. Gardner *Num. Comm. Paus.* ii. 108 pl. V, 22, Head *Hist. num.*[2] p. 455 : *obv.* Head of Eileithyia (?) with torch at her shoulder; *rev.* [T]ΕΓΕΑΤΑΝ and type as above described. In the field are two monograms.

[5] For other classical examples see Frazer *Pausanias* iv. 433 f. and *Golden Bough*[3] : Taboo p. 317, *ib.*[3] : Balder the Beautiful i. 83 n. 1.

[6] K. Tümpel in Roscher *Lex. Myth.* ii. 1108 says 'βόστρυχος; ob vielmehr Schlange?'— an acute suggestion.

[7] *Supra* Append. H.

[8] Strab. 396, Plout. *v. Num.* 9, *v. Sull.* 13, Paus. 1. 26. 6 f., schol. *Od.* 19. 34.

[9] Sir J. G. Frazer 'The Prytaneum, the Temple of Vesta, the Vestals, Perpetual Fires' in the *Journal of Philology* 1885 xiv. 145 ff., *id. Pausanias* iv. 441 f., *id. Golden Bough*[3] : The Magic Art ii. 253 ff., *ib.*[3] : Adonis Attis Osiris[3] ii. 174, *id. Totemism and Exogamy* London 1910 ii. 491, iii. 239.

[10] The high place in question (684[m] above sea-level) lies to the N. of the town and is now occupied by the modern village of Mertzaouzi. Another height (706[m]) to the N.W. of the town, the ancient citadel, is crowned by the village of Hagios Sostis (V. Bérard in the *Bull. Corr. Hell.* 1892 xvi. 541 with pl. 13).

[11] Paus. 8. 53. 9 f. cited *supra* p. 874 n. 2.

[12] Paus. 8. 53. 6, *supra* p. 164 n. 6. G. Gilbert *Handbuch der griechischen Staats-alterthümer* Leipzig 1885 ii. 127 notes that, according to inscriptional evidence (*Corp.*

taken attempt to explain the title *Klários*, which has been better interpreted by F. Solmsen as 'god of the High Place' (*Klários* for **Krários*)[1]. Be that as it may[2], Zeus *Klários* was not improbably the old divine king buried under the common hearth of his people. If such were really the beliefs of the Tegeates, the cult of Zeus *Melíchios*, whether imported or not, would flourish in their midst.

(ii) Zeus *Meílichos* or *Mílichos* in Boiotia.

At Orchomenos in Boiotia, the great stronghold of the Aeolian Minyai[3], Zeus was worshipped under the title *Meílichos*. Towards the close of the third century B.C. a certain Anticharidas, priest of the god, brought forward a decree for the construction of a fountain in or near his sanctuary, the *Meilíchion*, in order that persons sacrificing there might have a convenient supply of drinkable water[4]. The connexion with water recalls the *Meilíchios*-cults of Athens[5] and prepares us to find that here too Zeus was a chthonian god with fertilising powers. Now Orchomenos the eponym of the town is said to have been the son

inscr. Gr. i nos. 1513, 1514 = F. Bechtel in Collitz—Bechtel *Gr. Dial.-Inschr.* 1. 351 ff. no. 1231 = Michel *Recueil d'Inscr. gr.* no. 888 = *Inscr. Gr. Arc. Lac. Mess.* ii. no. 36 and F. Bechtel *loc. cit.* i. 357 ff. no. 1246 = *Inscr. Gr. Arc. Lac. Mess.* ii no. 38. Add *Inscr. Gr. Arc. Lac. Mess.* ii no. 6, 83 and 89, ii nos. 39, 40, 41, 173, 174), the names of the tribes were ἐπ᾽Ἀθαναίαν, Κραριῶται, Ἱπποθοῖται, Ἀπολλωνιᾶται. On their topographical distribution see V. Bérard in the *Bull. Corr. Hell.* 1892 xvi. 549 with pl. 13.

[1] *Supra* p. 874 n. 2.

[2] *Alii aliter.* (1) M. Schmidt on Hesych. κλάρες· αἱ ἐπὶ ἐδάφους (so M. Musurus for ἐδάφου) ἐσχάραι suggests that Zeus Κλάριος of Tegea drew his title hence.

If Zeus Κλάριος was a god 'of Hearths,' his annual festival was presumably for the purpose of furnishing the people with new fire (Frazer *Golden Bough*[3]: Index p. 271 f.). This adds significance to a curious incident in the history of the town. According to Paus. 8. 53. 10, the Lacedaemonians once marched against the Tegeates at the time of the festival: 'It was snowing, and the Lacedaemonians were cold and weary with the weight of their weapons. But the Tegeates unbeknown to them kindled a fire and, not being incommoded by the chill, got under arms, marched out against the Lacedaemonians, and beat them in the action.' According to Polyain. 1. 8, when the Lacedaemonians were attacking Tegea, Elnes(?) king of the Arcadians bade the men of military age to charge downhill against the enemy at midnight, but the old men and children to kindle a huge fire outside the town at the same hour. The Lacedaemonians turned in astonishment towards the glare, and so fell a prey to the onslaught from the height. Both accounts presuppose the fire-festival of Zeus Κλάριος.

(2) Immerwahr *Kult. Myth. Arkad.* p. 29 takes Zeus Κλάριος to be 'god of Branches,' *i.e.* of suppliant-boughs, cp. Hesych. †κλάριοι (Immerwahr rightly adopts M. Schmidt's cj. κλάροι)· κλάδοι and Aisch. *suppl.* 354 ff. ΠΕΛ. ὁρῶ κλάδοισι νεοδρόποις κατάσκιον | νεύονθ᾽ ὅμιλον τόνδ᾽ (so J. G. J. Hermann for τῶνδ᾽) ἀγωνίων θεῶν followed by 359 f. cited *supra* p. 874 n. 2.

[3] On the Minyai as Aeolians see A. Fick in the *Zeitschrift für vergleichende Sprachforschung auf dem Gebiete der indogermanischen Sprachen* 1911 xliv. 2 f., 5, *ib.* 1914 xlvi. 70, 76 f., 85 ff., 93, 102 ff.

[4] *Corp. inscr. Gr.* i no. 1568, R. Meister in Collitz—Bechtel *Gr. Dial.-Inschr.* i. 191 no. 495 with i. 394, *Inscr. Gr. sept.* i no. 3169, Michel *Recueil d'Inscr. gr.* no. 701, Dittenberger *Syll. inscr. Gr.*[3] no. 994 Δαμοτθίδαο ἄρχοντος, | ἱαρειάδδοντος | Ἀντιχαρίδαο Ἀ[θ]ανοδώρω, (ἀ π)όλις Διὶ Μειλί(χ)[υ.] | Ἀντιχαρίδας Ἀθανοδώρω ἔλ[ε]ιξε· δεδόχθη τῦ δάμυ, ὅπω[ς] ἔχω(ν)|θι τῶν πολιτάων τὺ (θ)ύ(ο)ν(τ)ες ἔ[ν] | (τ)ῦ Μειλιχίν ο(ὕδ)ατι χρειεῖσθη [πο]|τίμυ, κατασκευάττη κ(ρ)[άναν] | ἐν τῦ ἱαρῦ εἶ πὰρ τὸ (ἱ)αρ[όν, εἴ κα] | δοκί ἔ[ν] καλλίστο[ι εἶμεν].

[5] *Supra* p. 1115 ff.

of Zeus[1] by the Danaid Hesione[2] or by Hermippe daughter of Boiotos[3]. Alleged descent from Zeus presupposes a line of kings believed to incarnate Zeus. Was one of them that Minyas, of Aeolian ancestry[4], whose name was attached by the Orchomenians to their famous prehistoric *thólos*[5]? It would seem so; for among the relics of funerary cult discovered by Schliemann within the *thólos*, relics ranging from 'Minoan' to Roman times[6], was a slab of white marble inscribed with a late dedication to Zeus *Téleios* and Hera *Teleía*[7]. The old pre-Greek king, whose underground cupola with its rosettes of glittering bronze mimicked the midnight sky[8], was indeed aptly succeeded by an Aeolian dynast reverenced as a nether Zeus[9]. With all the prestige of immemorial tradition behind him such an one would watch over the fortunes of his people. For instance, in or about the year 329 B.C., as we know from an inscription formerly (1868) to be seen in the court of the neighbouring monastery[10], Orchomenian troopers, who

---

[1] Eustath. *in Il.* p. 272, 31 ὁ Βοιώτιος δὲ τῷ τοῦ Διὸς Ὀρχομενῷ ἐπωνόμασται.

[2] Schol. Ap. Rhod. 1. 230 Ἡσιόνης (Ἰσιόνης cod. Paris.) δὲ τῆς Δαναοῦ καὶ Διὸς γίνεται Ὀρχομενός, ἀφ' οὗ καὶ ἡ πόλις Ὀρχομενὸς καλεῖται (ἐκλήθη cod. Paris). Rufin. *recognit.* 10. 21 Hippodamiam et Isionen Danai filias (*sc.* vitiat Iupiter), quarum unam Hippodamiam < matrem (*inserui*) > Olenus, Isionen vero Orchomenus sive Chryses habuit. O. Höfer in Roscher *Lex. Myth.* iii. 939 f. conjectures that the mother's name was Ἰσονόη: but see G. Weicker in Pauly—Wissowa *Real-Enc.* viii. 1240.

[3] Schol. D. *Il.* 2. 511 τὸν ἐν τῇ Βοιωτίᾳ λέγει Ὀρχομενόν, τὸν ὑπὸ Μινύου βασιλευθέντα, τὸν ὀνομασθέντα ἀπὸ Ὀρχομενοῦ τοῦ Διὸς υἱοῦ καὶ Ἑρμίππης τῆς Βοιωτοῦ.

[4] Ap. Rhod. 3. 1094 Αἰολίδην Μινύην with schol. *ad loc.* (cod. Paris.) Αἰολίδην δὲ τὸν Μινύαν λέγει, οὐχ ὡς ὄντα υἱὸν τοῦ Αἰόλου, ἀλλ' ὡς μητρόθεν ἀπ' ἐκείνου καταγόμενον. Σισύφου γὰρ τοῦ Αἰόλου παῖδες Ἄλμος καὶ Πορφυρίων, Χρυσογόνης δὲ τῆς Ἄλμου καὶ Ποσειδῶνος Μινύας. ὥστε ἐκ μητρὸς μὲν Αἰολίδης ὁ Μινύας, πατρὸς δὲ Ποσειδῶνος.

[5] The genealogy of Minyas is very variously given: see *in primis* schol. Pind. *Isthm.* 1. 80 τοῦτον δὲ τὸν Μινύαν οἱ μὲν Ὀρχομενοῦ γενεαλογοῦσιν, ὡς Φερεκύδης (*frag.* 84 (*Frag. hist. Gr.* i. 92 Müller)), ἔνιοι δὲ ἔμπαλιν τὸν Ὀρχομενὸν Μινύου, ἔνιοι δὲ ἀμφοτέρους Ἐτεοκλέος γενεαλογοῦσι, Διονύσιος (*quis*? Perhaps the Rhodian, cp. schol. Pind. *Pyth.* 1. 109, *Nem.* 3. 104) δὲ τὸν Μινύαν Ἄρεος ἀναγράφει, Ἀριστόδημος (*sc.* ὁ Ἀλεξανδρεύς, cp. schol. Pind. *Isthm.* 1. 11) δὲ Ἀλεοῦ τὸν Μινύαν, καὶ τοὺς Ἀργοναύτας δὲ Μινύας ἐντεῦθεν γράφει προσηγορεῦσθαι with K. Tümpel's article in Roscher *Lex. Myth.* ii. 3016 ff.

[6] H. Schliemann *Orchomenos* Leipzig 1881 p. 56 ff. = *id.* 'Exploration of the Boeotian Orchomenus' in the *Journ. Hell. Stud.* 1881 ii. 137 ff., Perrot—Chipiez *Hist. de l'Art* vi. 439 f., Frazer *Pausanias* v. 189, 191.

[7] H. Schliemann *Orchomenos* p. 58 = *id.* in the *Journ. Hell. Stud.* 1881 ii. 139 ('a slab of marble broken on the left side, with the inscription:— ... ΕΙΩΗΡΑΤΕΛΕΙΑ which Professor Sayce [May he be forgiven! A.B.C.] holds to be the end of an hexameter'), *Inscr. Gr. sept.* i no. 3217 [........Δι Τελ]είῳ, Ἥρᾳ Τελείᾳ.

[8] *Supra* i. 751 f.

[9] Notice *Inscr. Gr. sept.* i no. 3218 Orchomenos [...............τὸ]ν ἑαυτῶν γυμνασί-αρχον | ....ίου Ἑρμῇ καὶ Μινύᾳ, which proves a definite cult of Minyas. In 1889 a herm of white marble was found near the church of Haghios Charalambos on a small hill to the W. of Thespiai: beneath the *phallós* was inscribed τοὶ ἱεράρχαι ἀνέθεαν | τοὶ ἐφ' Ἵππωνος ἄρχοντος | τοῖς Δαιμόνεσσι· | κ.τ.λ. (P. Jamot in the *Bull. Corr. Hell.* 1895 xix. 375 ff. no. 28, Dittenberger *Syll. inscr. Gr.*[2] no. 752, Michel *Recueil d'Inscr. gr.* no. 1102). This inscription (*c.* 300 B.C.) associates Hermes with certain Δαίμονες. May we venture to conclude that they were the souls of bygone Thespian kings?

[10] The monastery named after the Κοίμησις τῆς Θεοτόκου, the 'Falling Asleep of the Mother of God,' is believed to occupy the site of the ancient temple of the Charites (Frazer *Pausanias* v. 186, H. Hitzig—H. Blümner on Paus. 9. 38. 1, K. Baedeker *Greece* Leipsic 1889 p. 188, J. Murray *Handbook for Travellers in Greece*[7] London 1900 p. 562).

had served with Alexander the Great in Asia, returned home and testified their gratitude by a votive offering to Zeus *Sotér*[1].

At Thespiai, another ancient city of Boiotia, Zeus *Milichos* had a consort *Milíche*[2]. Since Thespios, the eponymous hero of the place, was said to have been an Athenian and the son of Erechtheus[3], or of Teuthras son of Pandion[4], we may legitimately compare the cult with that of Zeus *Meilíchios* at Athens. Accordingly, we are not surprised to learn that Thespiai made much of Zeus *Saótes*, the local equivalent of Zeus *Sotér*. Pausanias heard all about him:

'The Thespians have in their town a bronze image of Zeus *Saótes*. The story they tell of it is this. Once upon a time, when a snake (*drákon*) was ravaging the town, the god commanded that every year a youth, chosen by lot, should be given to the monster. They do not, they say, remember the names of the victims who thus perished. But they add that, when the lot fell on Kleostratos, his lover Menestratos resorted to the following expedient. He had a bronze breastplate made with a fish-hook on each of its plates, pointing upwards. This breastplate he put on, and offered himself willingly to the snake; for he meant by his offering to kill the monster, though he died for it. Hence Zeus got the name of *Saótes* (the "Saviour.")[5].'

So the Greeks had their own version of Slingsby and the Snapping Turtle! Indeed, the episode is but one variety of a world-wide myth, that of the dragon-slayer[6]. We must not, therefore, too hastily assume that the snake in question was the animal form of a divinised ancestor. Not improbably, however, the Boeotian Zeus *Saótes*, like the Elean *Sosípolis*[7], appeared on occasion as a snake, so that the old snake-myth, which originated elsewhere in a different connexion, would in Boiotia readily attach itself to the ancestral theriomorphic Zeus.

A relic of his cult has survived in a votive relief of white marble found at *Sialesi* and now in the Berlin collection (fig. 967)[8]. This monument, which might be good Attic work of the fourth century B.C., shows a bearded man and a boy approaching a cave in a rocky hill-side. The man holds an egg-shaped object, perhaps a honey-cake[9], in his raised right hand. And a large snake writhes out of the cave to get it. If *Sialesi* is rightly identified with the site of the ancient Eteonos[10] (later Skarphe), the cave may well represent the burying-

---

[1] P. Foucart in the *Bull. Corr. Hell.* 1879 iii. 452 ff., R. Meister in Collitz—Bechtel *Gr. Dial.-Inschr.* i. 170 f. no. 470, *Inscr. Gr. sept.* i no. 3206, Michel *Recueil d'Inscr. gr.* no. 1112 [τοὶ ἱππότη το]ὶ̀ ἐν τὰν Ἀσία[ν] στ[ρατευσάμενοι βα]σιλεῖο]s' Ἀλεξάνδρω στραταγίοντος, ...|. ὀδωρίω ϝιλαρχίοντος, Διὶ Σωτεῖρι ἀν[έθιαν · κ.τ.λ.].

[2] P. Foucart in the *Bull. Corr. Hell.* 1885 ix. 404 no. 15, *Inscr. Gr. sept.* i no. 1814 Θυνοκλῖδας Διονου|σίω Διὶ Μιλίχυ κὴ Μι|λίχη (an inscription of s. ii or iii B.C.).

[3] Diod. 4. 29, Paus. 9. 26. 6 (with Thespia daughter of Asopos as alternative eponym).

[4] Steph. Byz. *s.v.* Θέσπεια, Eustath. *in Il.* p. 266, 6 f.

[5] Paus. 9. 26. 7 f.

[6] See Sir J. G. Frazer on Paus. 9. 26. 7·and the authorities cited *supra* i. 178 n., 782.

[7] Paus. 6. 20. 5. See further C. Robert 'Sosipolis in Olympia' in the *Att. Mitth.* 1893 xviii. 37—45 and the excellent article of L. Weniger in Roscher *Lex. Myth.* iv. 1222 ff.

[8] *Ant. Skulpt. Berlin* p. 271 no. 724 fig., C. O. Müller—A. Schöll *Archaeologische Mittheilungen aus Griechenland* Frankfurt a/M. 1843 p. 97 no. 103 ('Opfer an die (Asklepios-) Schlange für einen (kranken) Knaben'), R. Kekulé von Stradonitz *Die griechische Skulptur*[2] Berlin 1907 p. 202 fig. ('Weihrelief an Zeus Meilichios'), Reinach *Rép. Reliefs* ii. 14 no. 1 ('Hommage au serpent d'Asklépios'), Harrison *Proleg. Gr. Rel.*[2] p. 20 f. fig. 5 and *Themis* p. 282 f. fig. 73. I am indebted to Miss Harrison for the photograph, from which my fig. 967 was drawn. Height 0·265ᵐ, breadth 0·495ᵐ to 0·505ᵐ.

[9] So Harrison *Themis* p. 282.

[10] C. O. Müller—A. Schöll *loc. cit.*, *Ant. Skulpt. Berlin loc. cit.*

place of Oidipous in the sanctuary of Demeter. Lysimachos of Alexandreia[1] in his work on *Theban Marvels* wrote as follows[2]:

'When Oidipous died, his friends thought to bury him in Thebes. But the Thebans, holding that he was an impious person on account of the misfortunes which had befallen him in earlier times, prevented them from so doing. They carried him therefore to a certain place in Boiotia called Keos and buried him there. But the inhabitants of the village, being visited with sundry misfortunes, attributed them to the burying of Oidipous and bade his friends remove him

Fig. 967.

from their land. The friends, perplexed by these occurrences, took him up and brought him to Eteonos. Wishing to bury him secretly, they interred him by night in the sanctuary of Demeter—for they did not know the locality. When the facts transpired, the inhabitants of Eteonos asked the god what they should do. The god bade them not to move the suppliant of the goddess. So Oidipous is buried there, and'—adds Lysimachos—'the sanctuary is called the *Oidipódeion.*'

Demeter at Eteonos bore the surname *Euryódeia*[3] and was certainly an earth-goddess[4]. Oidipous, buried in her precinct with the honours due to a suppliant[5], would naturally be viewed as a beneficent chthonian power. In this capacity he would almost certainly be anguiform. Indeed, P. Kretschmer has argued that the name *Oidípous*, 'Swell-foot,' actually denoted a snake, being a euphemistic

---

[1] W. Christ *Geschichte der griechischen Litteratur*[5] München 1911 ii. 1. 184.

[2] Lysimachos *frag.* 6 (*Frag. hist. Gr.* iii. 336 f. Müller) *ap.* schol. Soph. *O.C.* 91, citing Arizelos, of whom nothing further is known (*Frag. hist. Gr.* iv. 340 Müller).

[3] Hesych. Εὐρυοδεία· μεγαλάμφοδος (so Musurus for μεγαλάμφεδα cod.). καὶ ἡ Δημήτηρ οὕτως ἐν Σκαρφείᾳ (so M. Schmidt for Σκαρφίᾳ cod.). καὶ ἡ γῆ.

[4] *Et. mag.* p. 396, 24 ff. εὐρυοδεία·...'ἀπὸ χθονὸς εὐρυοδείης' (*Il.* 16. 635, *Od.* 3. 453, 10. 149, cp. 11. 52), μέγα τὸ ἕδος ἐχούσης, ὅ ἐστιν ἕδρασμα. ἐστι δὲ ἐπίθετον τῆς γῆς.
Cp. schol. *Od.* 16. 118'Ἀρκείσιος Εὐρυοδίας (W. Dindorf cj. Εὐρυοδείας) καὶ Διός Eustath. in *Od.* p. 1796, 34 ἰστέον δὲ ὅτι γενεαλογοῦσι Διὸς μὲν καὶ Εὐρυοδίας Ἀρκείσιον, which presupposes a union of Zeus with the earth-goddess.

[5] Similarly in the Attic version Oidipous at Kolonos ἱκέτευεν ἐν τῷ ἱερῷ τῶν θεῶν Δήμητρος καὶ Πολιούχου Ἀθηνᾶς (Androtion *frag.* 31 (*Frag. hist. Gr.* i. 374 Müller) *ap.* schol. *Od.* 16. 271. The passage continues καὶ Διός. ἀγόμενος < δὲ > ὑπὸ Κρέοντος κ.τ.λ. But W. Dindorf, following J. T. Struve, *corr.* καὶ βίᾳ ἀγόμενος ὑπὸ Κρέοντος κ.τ.λ.).

appellation for the swollen coils of the creature appropriate to a chthonian hero[1].

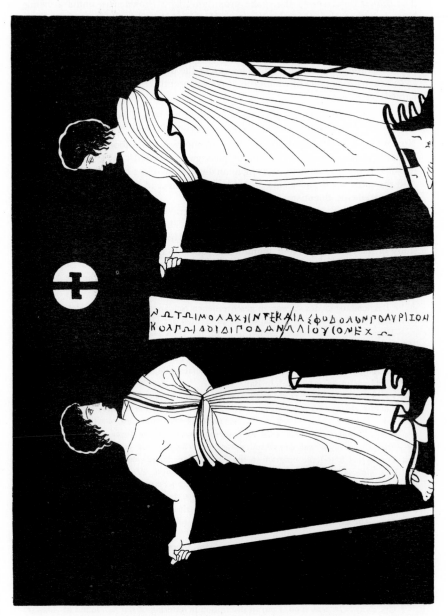

[1] P. Kretschmer *Die Griechischen Vaseninschriften* Gütersloh 1894 p. 191 n. 3 'Οἰδίπους erinnert an einen anderen rätselhaften mythischen Namen, den des frommen Sehers Μελάμπους: beides sind chthonische Heroen... Chthonische Wesen haben einen Schlangenleib statt der Füsse:... Sollten nicht "Schwellfuss" und "Schwarzfuss" euphemis-

Again, the buried hero would be responsible for the growth of all living things. The *Sialesi* relief shows the snake propitiated by a grown man and a growing boy—a sufficiently suggestive picture. Moreover, a red-figured *amphora* from Basilicata, now in the Naples collection (fig. 968)[1], represents two youths, with *himátia* and sticks, standing to right and left of a *stéle*, which marks the grave of Oidipous. In the background hangs a pair of *haltêres*[2], the sign of their devotion. But the most interesting feature of the design is the inscription on the *stéle*, a metrical couplet in which the grave apparently (though the speaker is not named) announces:

> Mallows and rooty asphodel upon my back I bear,
> And in my bosom Oidipodas, Laïos' son and heir[3].

Now mallows and asphodel were the common vegetable food of the Boeotian peasant, as we learn from a famous passage of Hesiod[4]. We may therefore reasonably regard this vase-painting as an illustration of the Boeotian *Oidipódeion*. And the more so, if—as seems probable—the dialect of the inscription contains sundry would-be Boeotisms[5].

It appears, then, that Oidipous in his grave played a part not easily distinguishable from that of Zeus *Meilíchios*[6]. There is, I think, that much of truth in a venturesome view advanced by O. Höfer, who after an exhaustive study of the hero's myth and monuments comes to the tentative conclusion that Oidipous after all may be but a hypostasis of the chthonian Zeus[7]. Sophokles knew what he was about in making the old king summoned hence by the

---

tische Bezeichnungen des schwarzen geschwollenen Schlangenleibes sein, welcher diesen Heroen natürlich genommen wurde, als sie zu Helden der Dichtung wurden?'

[1] Heydemann *Vasensamml. Neapel* p. 415 f. no. 2868 pl. 7, B. Quaranta in the *Real Museo Borbonico* Napoli 1833 ix pl. 28, J. Millingen *Ancient Unedited Monuments* Series ii London 1826 p. 86 ff. pl. 36, Inghirami *Vas. fitt.* iv. 18 ff. pl. 315. Fig. 968 is copied from Millingen's coloured plate and Heydemann's facsimile of the inscription.

[2] Heydemann *loc. cit.* says 'ein Ball.'

[3] νώτωι < μὲν > μολάχην τε καὶ ἀσφόδολον πολύριζον | κόλπωι δ' Οἰδιπόδαν Λαΐου < υ >ἱὸν ἔχω (Cougny *Anth. Pal. Append.* 2. 120). A. Boeckh in the *Corp. inscr. Gr.* iv no. 8429 quotes Eustath. *in Od.* p. 1698, 25 ff. ἐφυτεύετο ἐν τοῖς τάφοις τὸ τοιοῦτον φυτόν (*sc.* ὁ ἀσφόδελος), ὡς δηλοῖ καί τι τῶν παρὰ τῷ Πορφυρίῳ ἐπιγραμμάτων λέγον ὡς ἀπό τινος τάφου ὅτι νώτῳ μὲν μαλάχην καὶ ἀσφόδελον πολύριζον, κόλπῳ δὲ τὸν δεῖνα ἔχω and surmises that Porphyrios found the epigram in the Aristotelian *péplos* (see Eustath. *in Il.* p. 285, 24 f.)—a view already put forward by Jahn *Vasensamml. München* p. cxxiv n. 914. Boeckh *loc. cit.* further cp. Auson. *epitaph.* 21. 1 f. (p. 79 Peiper) Hippothoum Pyleumque tenet gremio infima tellus: | caulibus et malvis terga superna virent, whence E. Curtius would read Ἱππόθοόν τ' ἠδὲ Πύλαιον for τὸν δεῖνα in Eustath. *loc. cit.*

[4] Hes. *o.d.* 41 with K. W. Goettling—J. Flach *ad loc.*, and H. G. Evelyn White in the *Class. Quart.* 1920 xiv. 128 f.

[5] μολάχην for μαλάχην, ἀσφόδολον for ἀσφόδελον, Οἰδιπόδαν for Οἰδιπόδην, if not also (as Dr P. Giles suggests to me), Λαΐο=Λαΐω for Λαΐου. J. Millingen *loc. cit.* p. 87 n. 5 says 'according to the Æolic dialect'; P. Kretschmer *op. cit.* p. 224 f., 'in attischem Dialekt,' regarding μολάχην as a blend of μαλάχην and μολόχην (Athen. 58 D), ἀσφόδολον as a case of vulgar assimilation. *Decernant peritiores.*

[6] Cp. *Inscr. Gr. sept.* ii no. 1329 an inscription in lettering of *s.* ii B.C. found at *Akketsí* near Thebes Λυσίμαχο[s] | Μειλιχίοις.

[7] O. Höfer in Roscher *Lex. Myth.* iii. 743 'Ist Oidipus vielleicht eine Hypostase des Ζεὺς χθόνιος?' This suggestion should not be tossed on one side till the evidence adduced *ib.* p. 741 ff. has been carefully weighed.

thunders of Zeus *Chthónios*[1]. When the moment of departure comes and Theseus remains 'holding his hand before his face to screen his eyes, as if some dread sight had been seen, and such as none might endure to behold[2],' the poet with consummate tact leaves the secret untold. But the mythologist may be forgiven, if he hazards the conjecture that Oidipous was then and there transformed into a snake.

(12) Zeus *Meilíchios* in Thessaly.

The demolition of a mosque at Larissa in Thessaly brought to light two fragments of an Ionic architrave inscribed as follows[3]:

> Makon, son of Omphalion, (dedicated) the temple
> to Zeus *Meilíchios* and to *Enhodía*[4] and to the City[5].

The cult of the chthonian Zeus here had civic importance, and may fairly be connected with the founder of the state, Akrisios[6], who—struck on the foot and slain by the *dískos* of Perseus—was buried in a *herôion* outside the town[7] or else in the temple of Athena on the akropolis[8]. Akrisios was represented by Attic vase-painters of *s.* v B.C. as a bearded king, twice with a long sceptre[9], once with a long staff and a wreath of olive[10]. He had a divine doublet in Akrisias, the

---

[1] Soph. *O. C.* 1606 κτύπησε μὲν Ζεὺς Χθόνιος κ.τ.λ. *Supra* p. 805 n. 6.

[2] Soph. *O. C.* 1650 ff.

[3] *Ath. Mitth.* 1886 xi. 336, S. Reinach in the *Rev. Arch.* 1887 ii. 79, *id. Chroniques d'Orient* Paris 1891 p. 346, G. Fougères in the *Bull. Corr. Hell.* 1889 xiii. 392 no. 9, *Inscr. Gr. sept.* ii no. 578 Μάκων Ὀμφαλίωνος τὸν να[ὸν] | Διὶ Μειλιχίωι καὶ Ἐνοδίᾳ καὶ Πό[λει].

[4] For this appellation of Hekate at Larissa cp. *Inscr. Gr. sept.* ii no. 575, 2 f. εὔξατο: δ' Ἀγέ[τ]ορ | ϝαστικᾶι :'Ενοδίαι.

[5] Cp. *Inscr. Gr. sept.* ii no. 31, 2 (Hypata) Ἑρμᾶι καὶ τᾶι πόλε[ι], no. 94, 5 (Larissa Kremaste) Ἑρμᾶι καὶ τᾶι πόλει.

[6] Hellanikos *frag.* 29 (*Frag. hist. Gr.* i. 49 Müller) ap. schol. Ap. Rhod. 1. 40 = Favorin. *lex.* p. 1156, 25 f., Steph. Byz. *s.v.* Λάρισσα.

[7] Pherekyd. *frag.* 26 (*Frag. hist. Gr.* i. 77 Müller) *ap.* schol. Ap. Rhod. 4. 1091 = Eudok. *viol.* 40 = Favorin. *lex.* p. 99, 16 ff., Apollod. 2. 4. 4, cp. Paus. 2. 16. 2. Hyg. *fab.* 63 lays the scene in Seriphos and makes Akrisios struck on the head, cp. *fab.* 273. Further confusion in Lact. Plac. *in* Stat. *Theb.* 1. 255 = Myth. Vat. 2. 111 (Perseus hurls the Gorgon's head at Akrisios and turns him into stone!).

[8] Antiochos *frag.* 15 (*Frag. hist. Gr.* i. 184 Müller) *ap.* Clem. Al. *protr.* 3. 45. 1 p. 34, 9 f. Stählin.

[9] (1) On a red-figured *kratér* from Caere, now at Petrograd (Stephani *Vasensamml. St. Petersburg* ii. 281 ff. no. 1723, E. Gerhard *Danae, ein griechisches Vasenbild*(*Winckelmannsfest-Progr.* Berlin xiv) Berlin 1854 with col. pl., Welcker *Alt. Denkm.* v. 275 ff. pl. 17, 1, Overbeck *Gr. Kunstmyth.* Zeus pp. 406 f., 411 f. Atlas pl. 6, 2 f., Baumeister *Denkm.* i. 405 f. fig. 447 f., P. Hartwig *Die griechischen Meisterschalen der Blüthezeit des strengen rothfigurigen Stiles* Stuttgart—Berlin 1893 p. 396 f., J. D. Beazley *Attic red-figured Vases in American Museums* Cambridge Mass. 1918 p. 94 ('The Foundry Painter'), Hoppin *Red-fig. Vases* i 458 f. no. 17).

(2) On another red-figured *kratér* from Caere, now at Petrograd (Stephani *op. cit.* ii. 139 ff. no. 1357, F. T. Welcker in the *Mon. ed. Ann. d: Inst.* 1856 p. 37 f. pl. 8, Welcker *Alt. Denkm.* v. 283 ff. pl. 17, 2, Overbeck *op. cit.* Zeus p. 412 f. Atlas pl. 6, 4, Reinach *Rép. Vases* i. 244, 1, J. D. Beazley in the *Ann. Brit. Sch. Ath.* 1911–1912 xviii. 226 no. 16 and *op. cit.* p. 46 f. fig. 28 ('The Eucharides Painter'), Hoppin *Red-fig. Vases* i. 359 no. 20).

[10] On a red-figured *hydría* at Boston (P. Hartwig 'Danaé dans le coffre' in the *Mon.*

Phrygian Kronos[1]. It seems probable, therefore, that Akrisios was the royal embodiment of a sky-god[2]. And the story of his death from the *diskos* of Perseus, like that of Hyakinthos' death from the *diskos* of Apollon[3], is best explained as a genuine solar myth[4]. Whether Akrisios or Akrisias, as O. Gruppe supposes[5], was originally a mountain-god, is doubtful[6]. Still more so is Gruppe's attempt[7] to equate him with *Arkésios* or *Arkeísios*, a clipped form of *Arkesílaos*[8], god of the underworld[9]. Ruling out such questionable possibilities, we must yet concede that Akrisios was likely enough to live on in the popular memory as a buried beneficent Zeus.

(13) Zeus *Meilíchios* in the Archipelago, Asia Minor, etc.

The cult of Zeus *Meilíchios* was wide-spread in the islands of the Archipelago. Rock-cut inscriptions at Thera show that Zeus *Melíchios* was adored by the intimates of a certain Polyxenos[10] and that *Melíchios* received the offering of a 'singed' victim[11]. Boundary-stones inscribed 'Of Zeus *Meilíchios*' have been found at *Palaiopolis* in Andros[12], at Arkesine in Amorgos[13], and in the district of

Piot 1903 x. 55—59 pl. 8, J. D. Beazley *op. cit.* p. 51 f. fig. 32 ('The Painter of the Diogenes Amphora'), Hoppin *Red-fig. Vases* i. 206 no. 1).

[1] Hesych. Ἀκρισίας· Κρόνος, παρὰ Φρυξίν.

[2] On Kronos as a sky-god see *supra* p. 548 ff.

[3] Greve in Roscher *Lex. Myth.* i. 2760, G. Fougères in Daremberg—Saglio *Dict. Ant.* iii. 305, S. Eitrem in Pauly—Wissowa *Real-Enc.* ix. 9 f.

[4] *Pace* S. Eitrem *loc. cit.* p. 16.

[5] Gruppe *Gr. Myth. Rel.* pp. 182 n. 2, 1105 n. 1 starting from ἄκρις = *ocris* derives Ἀκρίσιος from the former, *Ocrisia* from the latter and cp. Hesych. Ἄκρια· ἡ Ἀθηνᾶ ἐν Ἄργει, ἐπί τινος ἄκρας ἱδρυμένη, ἀφ' ἧς καὶ Ἀκρίσιος (so Musurus for ὀκρίσιος). M. Schmidt suggests ὁ Ἀκρίσιος) ὠνομάσθη. ἔστι δὲ καὶ ἡ Ἥρα καὶ Ἄρτεμις καὶ Ἀφροδίτη προσαγορευομένη ἐν Ἄργει, κατὰ τὸ ὅμοιον ἐπ' ἄκρῳ ἱδρυμέναι, cp. Methodios *ap. et. mag.* p. 52, 40 f. Ἀκρίσιος· ὁ ἥρως, ἀπὸ τῆς ἐν τῷ Ἄργει ἄκρας. οὕτως Μεθόδιος.

[6] A. Fick *Die ehemalige Spracheinheit der Indogermanen Europas* Göttingen 1873 p. 411 proposed to connect the Phrygian Ἀκρισίας with Hesych. ἄκριστιν· κλέπτριαν (C. A. Lobeck cj. πέπτριαν). ἀλετρίδα. Φρύγες. This, though groping in the dark, is better than *et. mag.* p. 52, 41 f. ὁ δὲ Ὧρος ἀπὸ τοῦ ἀκρίζω Ἀκρίσιος, ὡς παρὰ τὸ θαυμάζω θαυμάσιος. ἢ παρὰ τὸ κρίσις κρίσιος, καὶ ἀκρίσιος, ὁ ἄκριτος καὶ ὠμός. [ἀκρίζω δὲ σημαίνει τὸ ἄκροις ποσὶ πορεύεσθαι· κ.τ.λ.].

[7] Gruppe *Gr. Myth. Rel.* pp. 253, 778, 1105 n. 1.

[8] A. Fick in the *Beiträge zur kunde der indogermanischen sprachen* 1906 xxx. 279 : 'Ἀρκείσιος [*Od.* 14. 182, 16. 118, *alib.*] würde richtig Ἀρκέσσιος = Ἀρκεσίλαος heissen ; den anlass zu der entstehung gab die schreibung mit *einem σ*.'

[9] Cp. *et. mag.* p. 144, 33 ff. cited *supra* p. 549 n. 1.

[10] With *Inscr. Gr. ins.* iii Suppl. no. 1316 Ζεὺς Μηλί|χιος τῶν | περὶ Πολύ|ξενο|ν (fig.) cp. the other rock-cut inscriptions from the same locality *ib.* no. 1317 Ζε(ὺ)s | τ[ῶ]ν περ[ὶ Λ]άκιον and *ib.* no. 1318 Ζεὺs | τῶν περὶ Ὀλ[υμ]|πιόδωρον. *Supra* i. 144 n. 2 with i. 143 n. 13.

[11] *Inscr. Gr. ins.* iii no. 406 (*supra* i. 144 n. 1).

[12] E. Pernice in the *Ath. Mitth.* 1893 xviii. 9 f. no. 4 = *Inscr. Gr. ins.* v. 1 no. 727 on a large unworked stone ΔΙΟΣ | ΜΕΛΙΧΙ∩ (fig.) = Διὸs | Με(ι)λιχίο(υ). E. Pernice and F. Hiller von Gaertringen *locc. citt.* regard the line after Ο as a mere crack.

[13] *Inscr. Gr. ins.* vii no. 89 on a rough stone in letters of s. iii or iv B.C. [Δι]ὸs Μειλιχίου, *ib.* no. 90 on a fragmentary slab of marble with lower moulding [Διὸs Μει]λιχίου. Note also *ib.* no. 92 on a small white marble base of Roman date Διὸs Σωτῆρος, *ib.* no. 93 on a broken block of bluish marble in letters of s. iii B.C. Διὸs | Σωτῆρο[s], *ib.* no. 94 on a fragment of rough bluish marble Διὰ Τελ[είωι], *ib.* no. 91 on a large marble slab

Saint Anna beyond *Bounáki* at Chios¹. A dedication to the same god has been recorded at Chalkis in Euboia². Nisyros had its sect of Diosmilichiastai³, and Crete a joint-cult of Zeus *Melíchios* and Hera *Melichía*⁴.

Our search might be extended eastwards into Asia Minor and Egypt, westwards into Sicily and Italy. An altar 'Of Zeus *Meil[íchios]*,' discovered at Knidos by Sir Charles Newton, is now in the British Museum⁵. Xenophon sacrificed pigs to Zeus *Meilíchios* at Ophryníon⁶: but we have no reason to think that there was a local cult of this deity. Achilleus Tatios (?*s.* vi. A.D.⁷) brings Kleitophon and Leukippe, the hero and heroine of his novel, to Alexandreia, his own native town.

ΔΙΟΣΑΝΑΛΩΙΟΥ = Διὸς 'Ανα(δ)ώ(τ)ου, 'of Zeus who sendeth up his Gifts from Below'—an obviously chthonian god (cp. *supra* p. 321 n. 1).

Other Zeus-cults of the same town: *ib.* no. 88 on a rough altar of bluish marble in letters of *s.* iv B.C. [Δ]ιὸς'Αποτροπαίο (cp. P. Kabbadias *Fouilles d'Épidaure* Athènes 1893 i. 56 no. 119=*Inscr. Gr. Pelop.* i no. 1285 Epidauros, not later than *s.* iii B.C. Διὸς 'Αποτροπαίου, O. Rayet in the *Rev. Arch.* 1887 i. 107 ff. = Michel *Recueil d'Inscr. gr.* no. 839 B, 19 f., C, 2 ff. = Dittenberger *Syll. inscr. Gr.³* no. 1014 *b*, 69 f., *c*, 114 ff. Erythrai, a sale of priesthoods dating from the first half of *s.* iii B.C. Διὸς | 'Αποτροπαίου καὶ 'Αθηνᾶς 'Αποτροπαίας ⌐Α⌐ ⊦ ⊦, ἐπώνιον· ⊦ [⊦] and Διὸ[s] | ['Αποτ]ροπαίου καὶ 'Αθηνᾶς 'Αποτ[ρο]]-[παί]ας ⊢⌐Α⌐, ἐπωνίου ⌐), *ib.* no. 95 a metrical inscription on a marble slab Μνημοσύνης καὶ Ζηνὸς 'Ολυμ[πίου ἀγλαὰ τέκνα cp. Cougny *Anth. Pal. Append.* 4. 33. 1], | κ.τ.λ., *supra* i. 194 f.

¹ A. G. Paspates Τὸ Χιακὸν γλωσσάριον Athens 1888 p. 421 f. no. 58 on Chian marble ΔΙΟΣ | ΜΙΛΙΧΙ [..]=Διὸς | Μιλιχί[ου].

At *Mestá*, six kilometers S.E. of the capital, is a place still called *Olýmpi*, where was a cult of Zeus *Olýmpios* and Herakles (Paspates *op. cit.* p. 410 no. 24 Διὸς'Ολυ[μπίου] | καὶ 'Ηρακλεῦς).

² *Corp. inscr. Gr.* ii no. 2150 ΕΡΜΙΩΝΜΕΙΛΙΧΙΟΥΔΙΛΙΟΝΙ which A. Boeckh *ad loc.* would read as'Ερμίων Μειλιχί(ωι) Δι(ὶ ἀ)ν(έ)[θηκεν].

³ A. E. Kontoleon in the *Ath. Mitth.* 1890 xv. 134, S. Reinach *Chroniques d'Orient* Paris 1891 p. 702, *Inscr. Gr. ins.* iii no. 104 a cylindrical base of white marble now serving as pedestal for an *eikón* in the church at *Mandráki* i ff. Γνωμαγόραν Δωροθέου | Νεισύριον | κ.τ.λ., *ib.* 13 ff. καὶ στεφανωθέντα ὑπὸ'Ερμαϊζόντων χ|ρυσέοις στεφάνοις πλεονάκις, καὶ ὑπὸ 'Αφρο|δισιαστᾶν Σύρων καὶ ὑπὸ Διὸς Μιλιχιαστᾶν, | [καὶ] τειμαθέντα ὑπὸ αὐτῶν καὶ στεφανω-θέν|[τα ὑπὸ Διον]υσιαστᾶν Εὐ[ρυθεμιδ]ίων τῶν σὺν | [τῷ δεῖνι – – –]. I should prefer to read (with Kontoleon and Reinach) Διοσμιλιχιαστᾶν, cp. Διοσαταβυριαστᾶν (*supra* p. 924 f. n. 0).

⁴ F. Halbherr in the *Museo Italiano di antichità classica* 1890 iii. 621 f. no. 39 Hierapytna=J. Baunack in *Philologus* 1889 xlviii. 399 f. no. 3 Herakleion, a small altar inscribed ΖΗΝΙΜΗΛΙ|ΧΙΩΚΔΗΡΑ|ΜΗΛΙΧΙΑ|ΣΩΤΑΣΥΠΕ|ΡΠΑΡΔΑΛΑ| ΕΥΧΗΝ=Ζηνὶ Μηλι|χίῳ κα(ὶ)"Ηρᾳ | Μηλιχίᾳ. | Σώτας ὑπὲ|ρ Παρδάλα | εὐχήν.

⁵ Sir C. T. Newton *A History of Discoveries at Halicarnassus, Cnidus, and Branchidæ* London 1862—1863 i pl. 92 no. 40, ii. 755 (cp. 470) no. 40, R. Schoell in the *Rhein. Mus.* 1887 xlii. 478 ff., E. L. Hicks *The Collection of Ancient Greek Inscriptions in the British Museum* iv. i. 24 f. Oxford 1893 no. 817. Newton, followed by Schoell, read ΔΙΟΣ ΜΕΙ as Διὸς Μεγ[ίστου]. But Hicks gives ΔΙΟΣ ΜΕΙ/ with Φ below ΔΙΟΣ and interprets as Διὸς Μειλ[ιχίου] with inventory number. In addition to this mark of ownership the altar bears a second inscription, which Schoell took to be a modified hexameter [ἀθα]νάτοις | [θυ]όεντα | [δα]μιουργὸς 'Αρ[πο]κρᾶ(s) ἱδρύσατο | βωμόν. Hicks reads [ἀθα]νάτοις | [θυ]όεντα | [δα]μιουργὸς 'Αρ| ⬛ κρᾶσ ϛ ἱδρύσατο | βωμόν, and suggests with hesitation that ϛ may be a numeral. He thinks that the name, Harpokras or the like, was substituted for that of an earlier dedicator. *Non liquet.*

⁶ *Supra* p. 1107.   ⁷ W. Schmid in Pauly—Wissowa *Real-Enc.* i. 245.

'By a stroke of luck,' says Kleitophon[1], 'we happed upon a sacred month of the great god, whom the Greeks call Zeus and the Egyptians Serapis[2]. The festivities included a torch-lighting; and I saw that remarkable sight. It was evening and the sun sank. Yet night was nowhere to be seen. Another sun made its appearance, or rather the small change of that gold piece. There before my eyes was the city rivalling the sky in beauty. On the one hand I saw Zeus *Meilíchios*, on the other the temple of Zeus *Ouránios*[3]. So, after breathing a prayer to the great god and beseeching him that our troubles might at last come to a standstill, we reached the lodging hired for us by Menelaos.'

It may be inferred from this passage, not only that the Alexandrines had a statue of Zeus *Meilíchios* and a temple of Zeus *Ouránios*[4], but also that the former was a god of the underworld, the latter a god of the upperworld. Both are appropriately mentioned at a moment when the twinkling lamps below seemed to reflect the twinkling stars above. At Alaisa or Halaesa (*Castel Tusa*), founded or re-founded in 403 B.C. by the Sikel king Archonides ii[5] on the north coast of Sicily, an inscription records among other topographical features 'the road past the *Meilichieîon*[6].' And, finally, an Oscan road-makers' tablet of *c.* 200 B.C. from Pompeii states that the aediles M. Suttius and N. Pontius laid out the Via Pompeiana, now known as the *Strada Stabiana*, with a breadth of three perches as far as the temple or precinct of Iupiter *Milichius*[7].

Further indications of the cult might be sought in theophoric names[8] such as Meilichios, a magistrate of Hierapolis in Phrygia[9], or Meilichion, a woman of Elateia in Phokis[10].

[1] Ach. Tat. 5. 2.   [2] *Supra* i. 188 ff.

[3] ἐθεασάμην δὲ καὶ τὸν Μειλίχιον Δία, καὶ τὸν Διὸς Οὐρανίου (so C. B. Hase, W. A. Hirschig, and S. Gaselee for οὐράνιον codd.) νεών.

[4] *Supra* i. 8, 565 n. 2, 647 n. 7.

[5] B. Niese in Pauly—Wissowa *Real-Enc.* ii. 565.

[6] *Corp. inscr. Gr.* iii no. 5594 col. dextra, 15 f. = *Inscr. Gr. Sic. It.* no. 352 i, 15 f. κατὰ τᾶς ὁδοῦ τᾶς παρὰ τὸ | Μειλιχιεῖον ἐς τὸν ῥοῖσκον κ.τ.λ.

Coppers of Alaisa, struck during Timoleon's war with the Carthaginians (340 B.C.), have *obv.* ΞΕΥΣ ΕΛΕΥΘΕΡΙΟΣ head of Zeus; *rev.* ΑΛΑΙΣΙΝΩΝ ΣΥΜΜΑΧΙΚΟΝ torch between two ears of corn (G. F. Hill *Coins of Ancient Sicily* London 1903 p. 175, Head *Hist. num.*[2] p. 126). Coppers of the same town, struck after *c.* 241 B.C., have *obv.* a head of Zeus, usually to left, wearing a bay-wreath; *rev.* an eagle to left, standing with open wings (*Brit. Mus. Cat. Coins* Sicily p. 27, *Hunter Cat. Coins* i. 166 pl. 12, 6, Rasche *Lex. Num.* i. 269 f., Suppl. i. 425, Head *Hist. num.*[2] p. 126).

[7] H. Grassmann in the *Zeitschrift für vergleichende Sprachforschung* 1867 xvi. 103, J. Zvetaieff *Sylloge inscriptionum Oscarum* Petropoli 1878 i. 41 ff. no. 62, 5 ff., ii pls. 10, no. 5, and 10[a], R. S. Conway *The Italic Dialects* Cambridge 1897 i. 58 f. no. 39, 5 ff., C. D. Buck *A Grammar of Oscan and Umbrian* Boston 1904 p. 239 f. no. 3, 5 ff. *iussu* via Púmpaiiana ter|emnattens perek. III ant kai|la Iúveís Meeílíkiieís (= iidem viam Pompeianam terminaverunt perticis III usque ad aedem (cp. *caeli templa* in De Vit *Lat. Lex.* *s.v.* 'templum' § 2) Iovis Milichii).

[8] E. Sittig *De Graecorum nominibus theophoris* Halis Saxonum 1911 p. 15.

[9] Imhoof-Blumer *Kleinas. Münzen* i. 238 f. no. 21, *Brit. Mus. Cat. Coins* Phrygia p. lxvii ...ΙΑΛΟ[Σ] | ΜΕΙΛΙΧΙΟΣ on the reverse of a copper struck by Augustus.

[10] *Inscr. Gr. sept.* iii. 1 no. 174 a cone of grey limestone found near the E. foundation-wall of the temple of Athena *Kranaía* at Elateia and now preserved in the local museum at *Drachmani*: the cone has a hole in its truncated top and is inscribed on the side ΜΕΙΛΙΧΙΟΛ | ΔΑΜΟΣΤΡΑΤΑ | ΜΙΚΑ | ΧΟΙΡΙΝΑ = Μειλίχιο[ν], | Δαμοστράτα, | Μίκα, | Χοιρίνα. P. Paris in the *Bull. Corr. Hell.* 1887 xi. 345 f. no. 15 at first read Μειλίχιο[ς], but concluded in favour of Μειλίχιο[ν].

(14) Conclusions with regard to Zeus *Meilíchios*.

It remains to gather up the results of our enquiry. Early Greek kings, especially such as could claim descent from Aiolos, were held to be embodiments of the sky-god Zeus, and as weather-makers for the community bore a sceptre tipped with the lightning-bird. Even when dead and buried the king continued to help his people. He preserved and perpetuated the tribe (Zeus *Sotér*). He brought its young folk to his own state of maturity (Zeus *Téleios*). He watched over its interests (Zeus *Epópsios*). Hence, like other chthonian powers, he was fitly addressed by a coaxing appellation—'the Kindly One' (Zeus *Meilíchios*). Regents of this sort, at once human and divine, were, strictly speaking, *daímones* rather than *theoí*; and there is much to be said for O. Schrader's brilliant suggestion that in name, as in nature, they were the equivalent of the Latin *Lares*[1]. They are best described in two passages of poetry which, though separated by a thousand years, yet derive mutual support and illustration from each other, and serve to assure us that the belief common to both was latent, if not patent, throughout the whole course of Greek history. Hesiod, looking

---

[1] Schrader *Reallex.* p. 29 : 'Es steht daher nichts im Wege, für δαίμων ein Grundform *δασι-μων anzusetzen, und den ersten Bestandteil dieses Wortes *δασι- unter Annahme eines bekannten Lautwandels (δάκρυμα : lacrima) dem lat. *lasi- (*lăres, lărium) "Geist eines Verstorbenen". zu vergleichen.' The context rightly maintains that previous derivations (from δαήμων, 'knowing,' or from δαίομαι, 'I divide,' or from the Sanskrit root *div*, 'to shine') are all unsatisfactory. I regret to see that Prellwitz *Etym. Wörterb. d. Gr. Spr.*[2] p. 103 and Boisacq *Dict. étym. de la Langue Gr.* p. 162 still cling to δαίομαι.

The word *δασι-μων is perhaps related to the name Δάσιμος or Δάξιμος. Δάσιμος Πύρρου is engraved on a bronze helmet from Anxia (*Anzi*) now in the British Museum (*Brit. Mus. Cat. Bronzes* p. 48 no. 317, Roehl *Inscr. Gr. ant.* no. 547, Roberts *Gk. Epigr.* i. 272 no. 269, *Inscr. Gr. Sic. It.* no. 655); and Δάξιμος Πύρρω, presumably a descendant of the same family, is mentioned in the bronze *tabulae Heracleenses* (*Inscr. Gr. Sic. It.* no. 645 i, 5, 9, ii, 1, 5, 8, R. Meister in Collitz—Bechtel *Gr. Dial.-Inschr.* iii. 2. 88 no. 4629 i, 5, 9, ii, 1, 5, 8, F. Solmsen *Inscriptiones Graecae ad inlustrandas dialectos selectae* Lipsiae 1905 no. 18 i, 5, 9, ii, 1, 5, 8). The *l*-form of this name occurs in ΛΑΣΙΜΟΣ ΕΓΡΑΨΕ, an inscription on an Apulian *amphora* from Canusium (*Canosa*) now in the Louvre (*Corp. inscr. Gr.* iv no. 8486, *Wien. Vorlegebl.* 1889 pl. 11, 3, Reinach *Vases Ant.* p. 64 ff. Millin ii pl. 37 ff. with bibliography, P. Kretschmer *Die Griechischen Vaseninschriften* Gütersloh 1894 p. 217 f.). The foregoing can hardly be separated from the definitely Messapian name ΔΑΞΙΜΑϚ (J. P. Droop in *Ann. Brit. Sch. Ath.* 1905—1906 xii. 139 f. fig. 1, 2 *Ceglie Messapica*) and the Grecised or Latinised Δάσιος (Appian. *Hannib.* 31 and 45), Δάξιος (*Brit. Mus. Cat. Coins* Thessaly etc. p. 68 no. 52 ΔΑΖΙΟΣ on a coin of Dyrrhachion, cp. *Brit. Mus. Cat. Coins* Italy p. 130 no. 1 f. ΔΑΞΟΥ on coins of Arpi, *ib.* p. 144 no. 4 ΔΑΞΕΝΙ and no. 6 ΔΑΞΥ on coins of Salapia, *Hunter Cat. Coins* i. 53 no. 1 pl. 4, 10 ΔΑΞΟΥ on a coin of Arpi), *Dasius, Dasumius,* etc. (De Vit *Onomasticon* ii. 568 f., R. S. Conway *The Italic Dialects* Cambridge 1897 ii. Index iii p. 566, F. Münzer, Stein and Groag in Pauly—Wissowa *Real-Enc.* iv. 2218 f., 2222 ff.).

A. Zimmermann in the *Zeitschrift für vergleichende Sprachforschung* 1915 xlvii. 192 holds that the *-da* of *Larunda* is identical with the Δα- of Δαμάτηρ and regards *Larunda* δαιμόνων μήτηρ (G. Goetz—G. Gundermann in the *Corpus glossariorum Latinorum* Lipsiae 1888 ii. 121, 17) as a literal translation (cp. *eid. ib.* ii. 265, 62 δαίμονες ἤτοι θεοὶ κατοικίδιοι· lares dicitur et lar).

For a useful vindication of the view that the *Lares* were originally the souls of deified ancestors see Miss M. C. Waites 'The nature of the Lares and their representation in Roman art' in the *Am. Journ. Arch.* 1920 xxiv. 241—261.

backward to the Golden Age when men lived 'as gods' and the soil was fruitful to the uttermost, says:

> But since the earth hath covered o'er this race
> They are *daímones* by the will of mighty Zeus,
> Good spirits that tread the ground and guard mankind,
> Givers of wealth—a guerdon meet for kings[1].

The late writer of an Orphic hymn strikes the self-same note:

> I bid the *daímon* to draw near, dread chief,
> The Kindly Zeus, begetter and life-giver,
> Great Zen, much-roaming[2], curse-bringer[3], king of all,
> Wealth-giving where he enters house full-force,
> Or now again chilling the poor man's blood.
> The keys of grief and gladness both are thine[4].

The *daímon*, in short, was the *theós* incarnate[5]. And the Agathos Daimon *par excellence* was Zeus *Meilíchios*.

APPENDIX N.

ZEUS *PHILIOS*.

It was pointed out by H. Usener[6] that every important conception of a god tends to express itself verbally in more ways than one. The result is a succession of divine appellatives, practical synonyms which vary from time to time and from place to place. In accordance with this principle we find the Greeks worshipping, not only Zeus *Meílichos* or *Meilíchios*, 'the Kindly One,' but also Zeus *Phílios*, 'the Friendly One.' The former title gradually became old-fashioned and wore out. The latter, with its appeal to the language of daily life, seemed more up-to-date, promised a business-like return, and consequently acquired a vogue of its own. Of course old centres remained more or less faithful to the old name, the connotation of which was enlarged in various directions. But new centres accepted, fixed, and popularised the novel epithet, which in its turn was filled with fresh meaning and expanded into an ever widening circle of applicability. Nevertheless Zeus *Phílios* was from the outset essentially akin to Zeus *Meilíchios*, as may be seen from a brief survey of the relevant monuments and literary allusions[7].

---

[1] Hes. *o.d.* 121 ff. cited *supra* p. 1130 n. 1.　　　[2] *Supra* p. 1096 n. 4.

[3] *Supra* p. 1098 n. 5.

[4] Orph. *h. daem.* 73. 1 ff. (ΔΑΙΜΟΝΟΣ, θυμίαμα λίβανον) δαίμονα κικλήσκω πελάσαι ἡγήτορα φρικτόν, | μειλίχιον Δία, παγγενέτην, βιοδώτορα θνητῶν, | Ζῆνα μέγαν, πολύπλαγκτον, ἀλάστορα, παμβασιλῆα, | πλουτοδότην, ὁπότ' ἄν γε βρυάζων οἶκον ἐσέλθῃ, | ἔμπαλι δὲ ψύχοντα βίον θνητῶν πολυμόχθων · | ἐν σοὶ γὰρ κλῇδες λύπης τε χαρᾶς τ'.ὀχέονται. *Supra* i. 504 n. 2, ii. 1098 n. 5.

[5] The relation of δαίμων to θεός is a thorny topic, which cannot be dismissed in a sentence, but must not here be pursued. See further J. A. Hild in Daremberg—Saglio *Dict. Ant.* ii. 9 ff., O. Waser in Pauly—Wissowa *Real-Enc.* iv. 2010 f., Harrison *Proleg. Gk. Rel.*[2] pp. 587, 624, 657, *ead. Themis* pp. 307, 386.

[6] H. Usener *Götternamen* Bonn 1896 p. 56 ff. ('Erneuerung des Begriffs').

[7] The evidence is well presented in Roscher *Lex. Myth.* iii. 2305—2308 by that excellent enquirer O. Höfer, to whose article I am much indebted.

(1) Zeus *Philios* at Athens.

We begin with Athens. The priest of Zeus *Philios* was a personage of importance, who in the time of Augustus had a reserved seat at the theatre[1]. On the northern slope of the Nymphs' Hill, where—as we have already seen[2]—Zeus *Meilichios* was worshipped, Zeus *Philios* too had obtained a footing as far back as *s.* iv B.C. For here in the archonship of Hegesias (324—323 B.C.) certain *e-ranistai* or club-feasters dedicated to him a *stéle* of Pentelic marble bearing a relief (fig. 969)[3], which closely resembles the offering of [? Aris]toboule to Zeus *Meilichios* (fig. 943)[4]. The club-feasters too represent Zeus enthroned on the left with a *phiále* in his right hand, while a pig is brought to the altar before him. The pig is proof enough that Zeus *Philios*, despite the eagle at his side, was a chthonian god[5]—a god much like the Agathos Daimon, as Miss Harrison adroitly shows by figuring together this relief and another from Thespiai (fig. 951)[6]. But what—it will be asked—had feasters to do with a chthonian god

Fig. 969.

---

[1] *Corp. inscr. Att.* iii. i no. 285 = Michel *Recueil d'Inscr. gr.* no. 860. 46 = Roberts—Gardner *Gk. Epigr.* ii. 467 ff., no. 260 ΙΕΡΕΩΣΔΙΟΣΦΙΛΙΟΥ in letters referable to the Augustan age.

[2] *Supra* p. 1114.

[3] Svoronos *Ath. Nationalmus.* pl. 219, 1, Harrison *Proleg. Gk. Rel.*[2] p. 357 fig. 107. My fig. 969 is from a photograph kindly supplied to me by Miss Harrison. The *stéle* is inscribed: ἐραν(ι)σταὶ Διὶ | Φιλίωι ἀνέ|θεσαν ἐφ' Ἡ|γησίου ἄρχον|τος (*Corp. inscr. Att.* ii. 3 no. 1330).

[4] *Supra* p. 1105 f.

[5] *Supra* p. 1105.

[6] *Supra* p. 1125 n. 1.

akin to a divinised ancestor? In view of our discovery[1] that at an ordinary banquet food was assigned 'to dead friends' and drink offered to the father of the clan under the titles of Zeus *Sotér* and Zeus *Téleios*, we may well suppose that a dinner-club would reverence its deceased founder as Zeus *Phílios* and think of him as still a sharer in the common festivity. His presence would transform the meal into a communion[2] and safeguard the participants against the intrusion of evil[3] without in any way diminishing their social merriment.

In the other world too Zeus *Phílios* was a feaster, as appears from an Attic relief of fourth-century style, now in the Jacobsen collection at Ny Carlsberg (fig. 970)[4]. Within an architectural framework we see the man-turned-god

Fig. 970.

recumbent on a couch, with a *cornu copiae* in his left hand, a *phiále* in his right, and a table bearing flat and pointed cakes (*pyramídes* made of wheat and honey[5]) at his side. On the foot of the couch sits a goddess holding in both hands a fillet or perhaps rather a garland for the neck (*hypothymís*[6]), the carving

---

[1] *Supra* p. 1129.

[2] On communion with the dead by means of food see *e.g.* Frazer *Golden Bough*[3]: Spirits of Corn and Wild ii. 154. *Infra* p. 1170 ff.

[3] An important consideration during a repast, when the mouth must be opened and bad spirits as well as good food might gain a ready entrance. In the *Journ. Hell. Stud.* 1902 xxii. 22 ff. I have argued that the common *kóttabos*-stand was originally a feasters' gong intended to keep evil at a distance.

[4] *Ny Carlsberg Glyptotek: Billedtavler til Kataloget over Antike Kunstvaerker* Kiøbenhavn 1908 no. 95, A. Furtwängler 'Sogenanntes "Todtenmahl"-Relief mit Inschrift' in the *Sitzungsber. d. kais. bayr. Akad. d. Wiss.* Phil.-hist. Classe 1897 i. 401—414 with fig. (=my fig. 970), Harrison *Proleg. Gk. Rel.*[2] p. 354 ff. fig. 106, *ead. Themis* p. 312 f. fig. 90.

[5] Stephanus *Thes. Gr. Ling.* vi. 2250 D.   [6] *Id. ib.* viii. 338 D ff.

of which would be eked out by means of colour. Behind the goddess stands a naked cup-bearer, dipping his right hand into the *kratér* so as to fill the *phiále* in his left. Then, on a smaller scale, we have two women and a man approaching from the left with hands raised in adoration. The architrave above carries an inscription, which throws a good deal of light (together with some darkness) on the scene represented :

> 'Aristomache, Olympiodoros, Theoris dedicated (this) to Zeus *Epitéleios Phílios* and to *Philía* the mother of the god and to Tyche *Agathé* the god's wife[1].'

We gather that the dedicators are worshipping their kinsman transformed into a chthonian Zeus—*Epitéleios* because he has himself come 'to maturity[2],' *Phílios* because he will be 'friendly' to his friends. The goddess associated with him is in all probability his wife, Tyche *Agathé* as the inscription calls her. An Agathe Tyche makes an appropriate partner for one who is essentially an Agathos Daimon. This being so, we should have expected *Philía*, the feminine form of *Phílios*, to be a second title attached to Tyche. Instead of that, it is treated as the name of a third deity, who is described as the mother of the god. Possibly the curious distribution of divine names was motived by the fact that the dedicators too were three in number—a man, his wife, and his mother[3]. Possibly also an effigy of *Philía* was added in paint on the smooth background between Zeus *Epitéleios Phílios* and Tyche *Agathé*.

But this does not exhaust the interest of our relief. The artist has, somewhat unexpectedly but quite justifiably, used for his Zeus *Phílios* the familiar type of a *Totenmahl* or hero-feast[4]. Now Mr J. C. Lawson[5] in a chapter marked by equal insight and eloquence has gone far towards proving, partly from ancient literature[6],

---

[1] Ἀριστομάχη, | Ὀλυμπιόδωρος, | Θεωρὶς | ἀνέθεσαν Διὶ Ἐπιτελείωι Φιλίωι καὶ τῆι μητρὶ τοῦ θεοῦ Φιλίαι | καὶ Τύχηι Ἀγαθῆι τοῦ θεοῦ γυναικί. Since the names of the three dedicators are inscribed above their respective figures, and Theoris heads the procession, it seems that the order of precedence should be Θεωρίς, Ὀλυμπιόδωρος, Ἀριστομάχη.

[2] Cp. Plat. *legg.* 784 D μήτε γὰρ εἰς γάμους ἴτω μήτε εἰς τὰς τῶν παίδων ἐπιτελειώσεις with Hesych. *s.v.* ἐπιτελείωσις· αὔξησις. Zeus Ἐπιτέλειος would thus be only another form of Zeus Τέλειος, whose priest at Athens was drawn from the ancient clan of the Bouzygai and occupied a special seat in the theatre (*Corp. Inscr. Att.* iii. 1 no. 294 = Michel *Recueil d'Inscr. gr.* no. 860. 55 = Roberts—Gardner *Gk. Epigr.* ii. 467 ff. no. 251 ἱερέως | Διὸς Τελεί|ου βουζύγου in lettering (fig. 971) not earlier than *s.* ii A.D.).

ΙΕΡΕΩΣ
ΔΙΟΣΤΕΛΕΙ
ΟΥΒΟΥΣΥΓΘ
Fig. 971.

[3] So Harrison *Proleg. Gk. Rel.*[2] p. 356.

[4] Lübker *Reallex.*[8] p. 1052 gives a brief bibliography, to which should be added Gruppe *Gr. Myth. Rel.* p. 1049 n. 1, Harrison *Proleg. Gk. Rel.*[2] pp. 349—362, 614, *ead. Themis* pp. 307—316.

[5] J. C. Lawson *Modern Greek Folklore and Ancient Greek Religion* Cambridge 1910 pp. 543—606 ('The union of gods and men'). The statement 'that Easter falls in the same period of the year as did the great Eleusinian festival' (*ib.* p. 572) is a slip, which has hindered the critics from appreciating the real merits of this important chapter.

[6] Soph. *Ant.* 574 f., [653 f.,] 804 f., 810 ff., 891 ff., 1203 ff., 1240 f., [Eur. *Tro.* 445, *Or.* 1109, *I. A.* 460 f.,] Artemid. *oneirocr.* i. 80 θεῷ δὲ ἢ θεᾷ μιγῆναι ἢ ὑπὸ θεοῦ περανθῆναι νοσοῦντι μὲν θάνατον σημαίνει (θανάτου σημεῖον cod. B.)· τότε γὰρ ἡ ψυχὴ τὰς τῶν θεῶν συνόδους τε καὶ μίξεις μαντεύεται, ὅταν ἐγγὺς ᾖ τοῦ καταλιπεῖν τὸ σῶμα ᾧ ἐνοικεῖ κ.τ.λ., 2. 49 ἀποθανεῖν δοκεῖν καὶ ἐκκομισθῆναι καὶ κατορυγῆναι...ἀνδρὶ...ἀγάμῳ γάμον προαγορεύει· τέλη μὲν γὰρ ἀμφότερα τοῖς ἀνθρώποις εἶναι νενόμισται καὶ ὁ γάμος καὶ ὁ θάνατος. ἀεὶ δὲ

partly from modern folk-song[1], that the Greeks of old aspired to an actual marriage-union with the deities of the underworld, a union to be fore-shadowed here in mystic rites and consummated hereafter in very truth. Every man would one day enter the bridal chamber of Persephone, every woman that of Hades[2]. If this daring belief is rightly credited to them—and the evidence for it is strong—, then we may, I think, venture to interpret the popular scheme of the hero-feast as a naïve representation of the dead man's marriage-banquet. Wedded at last to the queen of the nether world, he is actually feasting in her company. His garland and cakes recall

'the white sesame-grains
And myrtle-berries and poppy-head and water-mint[3]'

appropriate to any bridegroom. Were they not the magic means by which he

δείκνυνται ὑπ' ἀλλήλων. ὅθεν καὶ τοῖς νοσοῦσι τὸ γαμεῖν θάνατον προαγορεύει· καὶ γὰρ τὰ αὐτὰ ἀμφοτέροις συμβαίνει τῷ τε γαμοῦντι καὶ τῷ ἀποθανόντι, οἷον παραπομπὴ φίλων ἀνδρῶν τε καὶ γυναικῶν καὶ στέφανοι καὶ ἀρώματα καὶ μύρα καὶ συγγραφὴ κτημάτων, 2. 65 ἐπειδὴ καὶ ὁ γάμος ἔοικε θανάτῳ καὶ (ἐπειδὴ καὶ cod. B.) ὑπὸ θανάτου σημαίνεται, ἐνταῦθα καλῶς ἔχειν ἡγησάμην ἐπιμνησθῆναι (ὑπομνησθῆναι cod. B.) αὐτοῦ. γαμεῖν παρθένον τῷ νοσοῦντι θάνατον σημαίνει· ὅσα γὰρ τῷ γαμοῦντι συμβαίνει, τὰ αὐτὰ καὶ τῷ ἀποθανόντι.

Mr Lawson might have found further support for his theory in the rich storehouse of ancient Greek epitaphs. Turning over the leaves of the *Anthology* I lit upon the following: *Anth. Pal.* 7. 13. 2 f. (Leonidas or Meleagros) Ἤρινναν... | Ἀίδας εἰς ὑμέναιον ἀνάρπασεν, 7. 183. 2 (Parmenion) Ἀίδης τὴν Κροκάλης ἔφθασε παρθενίην, 7. 401. 9 (Krinagoras) χθὼν ὦ δυσνύμφευτε, 7. 492. 6 (? Anyte of Mitylene) νυμφίον ἀλλ' Ἀίδην κηδεμόνι εὑρόμεθα, 7. 507[b] (? Simonides =*frag.* 124 B Bergk[4], 105 Hiller—Crusius) οὐκ ἐπιδὼν νύμφεια λέχη κατέβην τὸν ἄφυκτον | Γόργιππος ξανθῆς Φερσεφόνης θάλαμον, 7. 547. 3 f. (Leonidas of Alexandreia) κατέστενε δ' οὐχ Ὑμεναίῳ, | ἀλλ' Ἀίδα νύμφαν δωδεκέτιν κατάγων, cp. 7. 221. 5 f. Ἀίδη δυσκίνητε, τί τὴν ἐπέραστον ἑταίρην | ἥρπασας; ἢ καὶ σὴν Κύπρις ἔμηνε φρένα; Cougny *Anth. Pal. Append.* 2. 43 = Kaibel *Epigr. Gr.* no. 50 ἐνθάδε τὴν πάσης ἀρετῆς ἐπὶ τέρμα μολοῦσαν | Φαναγόραν κατέχει Φερσεφόνης θάλαμος, Cougny 2. 122 a. 3 f. = Kaibel no. 35 a. 3 f. ἔθανες, Διονύσιε, καὶ τὸν ἀνάγκης | κοινὸν Φερσεφόνης πᾶσιν ἔχεις θάλαμον, Cougny 2. 127. 3 f. Γλαυκιάδης... | ἦλθ' ἐπὶ πάνδεκτον Φερσεφόνης θάλαμον, 2. 214. 3 f. = Kaibel no. 201. 3 f. συγκέχυται γενέτας δὲ Ποσείδιππος κλυτὸν ἔρνος | ζαλωτὸν πέμψας Περσεφόνας θαλάμοις, Cougny 2. 268. 1 f. = Kaibel no. 570. 1 f. οὐχ ὁσίως ἥρπαξας ὑπὸ [χθόνα], κοίρανε Πλουτεῦ, | πενταέτη νύμφην κ.τ.λ.

See also R. Foerster *Der Raub und die Rückkehr der Persephone* Stuttgart 1874 p. 73 n. 3, E. Maass *Orpheus* München 1895 p. 219, Gruppe *Gr. Myth. Rel.* p. 865 n. 1.

[1] *E.g.* A. Passow *Popularia carmina Graeciae recentioris* Lipsiae 1860 no. 364. 6 ff. Κ' ἐγὼ πάγω νὰ παντρεφτῶ νὰ πάρω μιὰ γυναῖκα, | Πῆρα τὴν πλάκα πεθερὰ, τὴ μαύρη γῆ γυναῖκα | Κι' αὐτὰ τὰ λιανολίθαρα ὅλα γυναικαδέρφια ('For I must go to marry me, to take a wife unto me; | The black earth for my wife I take, the tombstone as her mother | And yonder little pebbles all her brethren and her sisters'—from the dirge of an old man: Bostitsa), *ib.* no. 374. 8 f. Ἐψὲς ἐγὼ παντρεύθηκα, ἐψὲς ἀργὰ τὸ βράδυ. | Ὁ ᾄδης εἶν' ὁ ἄντρας μου, ἡ πλάκ' ἡ πεθερά μου ('Yesterday was my marriage-day, late yestere'en my wedding, | Hades I for my husband have, the tomb for my new mother'—from the dirge of a young girl). Cp. *ib.* nos. 38, 65, 152, 180, 370, 380, 381, G. F. Abbott *Macedonian Folklore* Cambridge 1903 p. 256 n. 1.

[2] This had been remarked by E. Maass *Orpheus* München 1895 p. 219: 'Jedes Weib, das stirbt, vermählt sich nach alter Anschauung dem Hades; die Männer und Jünglinge betreten ihrerseits den Thalamos der Persephone.' B. Schmidt *Das Volksleben der Neugriechen* Leipzig 1871 i. 232 f. had already drawn attention to this group of ideas, citing ancient and modern illustrations. See further O. Schrader *Totenhochzeit* Jena 1904 pp. 1—38 and S. Reinach in the *Rev. Arch.* 1921 ii. 141—143.

[3] Aristoph. *av.* 159 f. τὰ λευκὰ σήσαμα | καὶ μύρτα καὶ μήκωνα καὶ σισύμβρια.

was empowered to impregnate his bride[1]?   Raised from mortal to immortal

[1] Schol. Aristoph. *pax* 869 πλακοῦς γαμικὸς ἀπὸ σησάμων πεποιημένος, διὰ τὸ πολύγονον, ὥς φησι Μένανδρος (*frag.* 435 (*Frag. com. Gr.* iv. 318 Meineke)).   A. de Gubernatis
La mythologie des plantes Paris 1882 ii. 347 refers to L. G. Gyraldus *Operum quæ extant
omnium* Tomus Secundus Basileae 1580 p. 485, 24 ff. Quale est illud, quod de nubentibus
dici vulgo solebat, Sesamum aut hordeum sere, aut proijce: cum fœcunditatem, &
multiplicem generationem ac fœtum significare volebant.   Sunt enim huiusmodi semina
multæ fœcunditatis, & vt Græci dicunt, πολύγονα. Sed quod de sesamo dicimus, aliqui ex
eo placentam fieri solitam in nuptijs, eadem ratione tradunt.'

Boetticher *Baumkultus* pp. 445—455 begins his article on the myrtle by distinguishing
a lucky aspect of the plant as sacred to Aphrodite from a sepulchral aspect of it as sacred
to chthonian deities.   He finds a connecting link in the cult of Venus *Libitina*, Aphrodite
Epitymbía, etc.   I should rather suppose that both aspects are referable to the quickening
qualities of the evergreen.   When a long journey was to be taken afoot, the mere carrying
of myrtle-twigs prevented fatigue.   Twisted into rings without the use of iron, they cured
swelling of the groin (Plin. *nat. hist.* 15.. 124).   To dream of a myrtle-wreath meant
marriage with a free-born woman and a prospect of long-lived children (Artemid. *oneirocr.*
1. 77).   Etc., etc.   A shrub of such vivifying or revivifying potency was well fitted to be
a life-token.   Accordingly we hear of two sacred myrtles, which grew before the temple
of Quirinus and by their fertility or barrenness portended the fortunes of the patricians
and plebeians respectively (Plin. *nat. hist.* 15. 120 f.).   See further A. de Gubernatis *op.
cit.* ii. 233— 236, H. Friend *Flowers and Flower Lore* London 1883 ii. 688 Index *s.v.*
'Myrtle,' R. Folkard *Plant Lore, Legends, and Lyrics* London 1884 pp. 454—457.
These authors by no means exhaust the topic, which deserves fuller investigation.   It
might, for example, be discovered that the myrtle-wreath worn by the initiate at Eleusis
(Aristoph. *ran.* 156, 328 ff. with schol. *ad loc.*, Istros *frag.* 25 (*Frag. hist. Gr.* i. 421
Müller) *ap.* schol. Soph. *O. C.* 681: illustrated *supra* i. 220 f. fig. 163, E. Lübbert in the
Ann. d. Inst. 1865 xxxvii. 82 ff. pl. F = L. Stephani in the *Compte-rendu St. Pét.* 1868
p. 160 = F. Lenormant in Daremberg—Saglio *Dict. Ant.* ii. 570 fig. 2637 = Reinach *Rép.
Vases* i. 313, 1 f.) or by the Orphic devotee (*supra* p. 555) marked him as the prospective
consort of a chthonian deity.   The botanical fact underlying these beliefs is the poly-
spermous nature of the myrtle: ' The fruit is a purplish berry, consisting of the receptacle
and the ovary blended into one succulent investment enclosing very numerous minute
seeds ' (*The Encyclopædia Britannica*[11] Cambridge 1911 xix. 115).

The poppy has an even greater wealth of tiny seeds.   Hence its made for fertility, and became the attribute of various mother-goddesses. A. de Gubernatis *op. cit.* ii. 284 quotes from
L. G. Gyraldus *op. cit.* ii. 468, 39 f. the *dictum* 'papauer fertilitatis & vrbis symbolum fuit'
[where, however, we should restore *orbis*, cp. Cornut. *theol.* 28 p. 56, 8 ff. Lang ἀνατιθέασι
δ' αὐτῇ (*sc.* τῇ Δήμητρι) καὶ τὰς μήκωνας κατὰ λόγον· τό τε γὰρ στρογγύλον καὶ περιφερὲς
αὐτῶν παρίστησι τὸ σχῆμα τῆς γῆς σφαιροειδοῦς οὔσης, ἥ τε ἀνωμαλία τὰς κοιλότητας καὶ τὰς
ἐξοχὰς τῶν ὀρῶν, τὰ δ' ἐντὸς τοῖς ἀντρώδεσι καὶ ὑπονόμοις ἔοικε, σπέρματά τε ἀναρίθμητα
γεννῶσιν ὥσπερ ἡ γῆ].   The poppy of Demeter (Gruppe *Gr. Myth. Rel.* p. 1179 n. 2) was
passed on to Rhea (*id. ib.* p. 1542 n. 1) and to Isis (W. Drexler in Roscher *Lex. Myth.* ii.
450 ff. fig.).   Kanachos made for the Sicyonians a chryselephantine Aphrodite with a
poppy in one hand, an apple in the other (Paus. 2. 10. 5): and here again the influence
of Demeter may be suspected; for certain persons derived the old name of Sikyon,
Μηκώνη, from the ' poppy,' μήκων, which Demeter there first discovered (*et. mag.* p. 583,
56 f. : but cp. Ov. *fast.* 4. 531 ff., Serv. and interp. Serv. *in* Verg. *georg.* i. 212).   Poppy-
heads, as well as myrtle-wreaths, played their part in the Eleusinian initiation (*supra* i.
425 f. fig. 307 f.).

Lastly, σισύμβριον or ' bergamot-mint' (*mentha aquatica*) was used for the bridegroom's garland (schol. Aristoph. *av.* 160), not merely because its branches, leaves, etc.
were sweet-scented (Theophr. *hist. pl.* 6. 6. 2 and *frag.* 4, 27 *ap.* Athen. 689 D, Nik.
georg. frag. 2. 57 *ap.* Athen. 684 B), but on account of its aphrodisiac properties.   If the

rank, henceforward he can read a deeper meaning in the old-world wedding-chant:

'I have fled the bad, I have found the better[1].'

It looks as though the primitive mind conceived of death itself as simply due to the fact that the chthonian deity (whether goddess or god) had claimed another consort[2]. The summons has been sent. The call must be obeyed. But—

'Who knows if life be death and death be life[3]?'

In the embrace of Persephone the dead man becomes the chthonian king. Borne off by Hades the dead woman becomes the chthonian queen. We can understand now the familiar saying

'Whom the gods love dies young[4],'

and find a further significance in the representation of Death as Love[5].

wearing of a wreath made from it betokened disease (Artemid. *oneirocr.* 1. 77), that was due to the fact that the plant in question was recognised as a cure for diseases (Nik. *ther.* 896). Greeks called it the garland of Aphrodite, Romans the herb of Venus (Dioskor. 2. 154 (155) p. 271 Sprengel); and the medical writers enable us to guess the reason, cp. Dioskor. 2. 154 (155) p. 272 Sprengel δύναμιν δὲ ἔχει θερμαντικήν· ἁρμόζει δὲ πρὸς στραγγουρίας καὶ λιθιάσεις τὸ σπέρμα σὺν οἴνῳ πινόμενον, *id.* 2. 155 (156) p. 272 Sprengel of another variety ἔστι δὲ θερμαντικόν, οὐρητικόν, Galen. *de simplicium medicamentorum temperamentis ac facultatibus* 8. 18. 20 (xii. 124 Kühn) θερμαινούσης καὶ ξηραινούσης κατὰ τὴν τρίτην τάξιν ἐστὶ δυνάμεώς τε καὶ κράσεως. καὶ τὸ σπέρμα δ' αὐτοῦ λεπτομερές τε καὶ θερμόν ἐστιν, ὅθεν σὺν οἴνῳ τινὲς αὐτὴν διδόασι κ.τ.λ., *id. ib.* 8. 18. 21 (xii. 124 Kühn) of the other variety ὅταν μὲν ξηρὸν ᾖ, τῆς τρίτης ἐστὶ τάξεως τῶν ξηραινόντων τε ἅμα καὶ θερμαινόντων, κ.τ.λ. On mint in general see A. de Gubernatis *op. cit.* ii. 226–228, H. Friend *op. cit.* ii. 687 Index *s.v.* 'Mint,' R. Folkard *op. cit.* p. 439 f. *Supra* i. 257 n. 5.

1 ἔφυγον κακόν, εὗρον ἄμεινον (*carm. pop.* 20 a Hiller—Crusius)—an early dactylic line (cp. *supra* i. 444) first found in Dem. *de cor.* 259 (cited *supra* i. 392 n. 4) as a *formula* used by initiates in the rites of *Sabázios*, and from him apparently quoted by Hesych. *s.v.* It is given as a marriage-rubric by Pausanias the Atticist *ap.* Eustath. *in Od.* p. 1726, 19 ff. καὶ παροιμία δηλοῖ παρὰ Παυσανίᾳ λέγουσα 'ἔφυγον κακόν, εὗρον ἄμεινον,' ἣν ἔλεγέ, φησιν, ἀμφιθαλὴς παῖς Ἀθήνησιν, ἐστεμμένος ἀκάνθαις μετὰ δρυΐνων καρπῶν, λίκνον βαστάζων πλῆρες ἄρτων, αἰνισσόμενος τὴν ἐκ τοῦ παλαιοῦ βίου ἐπὶ τὸ κρεῖττον μεταβολήν=Zenob. 3. 98, Diogeneian. 4. 74, Plout. 1. 16, Apostol. 8. 16, Phot. *lex.* and Souid. *s.v.*, cp. Porph. *de abst.* 1. 1. Probably the so-called proverb was a very ancient charm employed in the mysteries to facilitate the transition from the lower to the higher life, a transition culminating in the divine marriage (see Lobeck *Aglaophamus* i. 646 ff.). Subsequently it was transferred, with some loss of meaning, to ordinary human marriages.

2 Cp. the Celtic tales of the Otherworld-visit, which I have summarised in *Folk-Lore* 1906 xvii. 143 ff. (*supra* i. 239).

3 Eur. *Polyeidos frag.* 638 Nauck[2] (*supra* p. 868), cp. Eur. *Phrixus frag.* 833 Nauck[2]. In Aristoph. *ran.* 1477 f. τίς οἶδεν εἰ τὸ ζῆν μέν ἐστι κατθανεῖν, | τὸ πνεῖν δὲ δειπνεῖν, τὸ δὲ καθεύδειν κώδιον; the attempts of the editors to extract sense from the latter line are far from convincing. I fancy Aristophanes is poking fun at the prospect held out to every pious believer, the hero-feast (δειπνεῖν) and the poppy-head (for κώδιον read κώδυον, cp. Theophr. *hist. pl.* 6. 8. 1 and *ap.* Athen. 680 E, or κωδία, cp. Aristoph. *frag.* 166 Dindorf *ap.* Harpokr. *s.v.* κωδία). Life hereafter was to be one perpetual banquet in the bridal chamber of Persephone: if the new immortal tired of it, he had at least the poppy-capsule to lull him to sleep and to renew his generative powers. Those who retain κώδιον in the text should still interpret the word of the initiate's equipment, the 'fleece of Zeus' (*supra* i. 422 ff.).

4 Menand. *disexapaton frag.* 4 (*Frag. com. Gr.* iv. 105 Meineke). Cp. Kaibel *Epigr. Gr.* no. 340. 8=Cougny *Anth. Pal. Append.* 2. 585. 8.   5 *Supra* pp. 309, 1045.

Nor was this union one of merely physical fruition. The Greek was capable of rising to greater heights, and the title *Philios* had from the first a moral connotation. True, Aristotle denied the possibility of love (*philía*) between man and God :

'For love, we maintain, exists only where there can be a return of love. But love towards God does not admit of love being returned, nor at all of loving. For it would be strange if one were to say that he loved Zeus[1].'

But popular usage was against him[2]. Whether parched with drought[3], or drenched with rain[4], the man in the street cried out upon 'loved Zeus.' And the like intimacy is attested by half-a-dozen poets from Theognis to Antipatros of Thessalonike[5]. On a red-figured *kýlix* by the potter Sosias Herakles, when admitted to Olympos, makes the same naïve ejaculation[6]. Moreover, the name *Díphilos*, 'loved by Zeus,' was of common occurrence[7]. No doubt this mutual love did not amount to much. But the root of the matter was there, and its growth was fostered by mystic teaching. On the grandest page of extant Greek literature[8] the Platonic Sokrates tells how Diotima of Mantineia (supposed to be a priestess of Zeus *Lýkaios*[9] and in any case, as her name shows, 'honoured of Zeus') once made plain to him the mysteries of Eros. The initiate, she said, must mount by successive grades from desire of a single beautiful body to desire of all beautiful bodies, and from beauty of body to beauty of soul involving the beauty of customs and laws. Thence he will launch out boldly into the beauty of knowledge until, crossing its wide sea and nearing his journey's end, on a sudden he catches sight

---

[1] Aristot. *mag. mor.* 2. 11. 1208 b 28 ff. τὴν γὰρ φιλίαν ἐνταῦθά φαμεν εἶναι οὗ ἐστὶ τὸ ἀντιφιλεῖσθαι, ἡ δὲ πρὸς τὸν θεὸν φιλία οὔτε ἀντιφιλεῖσθαι δέχεται οὔθ' ὅλως τὸ φιλεῖν· ἄτοπον γὰρ ἂν εἴη εἴ τις φαίη φιλεῖν τὸν Δία.

[2] Indeed, he was against himself—witness his brief but pregnant utterance with regard to the Final Cause in *met.* 12. 7. 1072 b 3 f. κινεῖ δὴ ὡς ἐρώμενον, κινούμενον δὲ τἄλλα κινεῖ. He is groping his way towards the stupendous discovery that ' God is love.'

[3] Marc. Ant. *comment.* 5. 7 ὦ φίλε Ζεῦ (*infra* § 9 (b)).

[4] *Anth. Pal.* 5. 166. 6 (Asklepiades) Ζεῦ φίλε (*infra* § 9 (b)).

[5] Theogn. 373 Hiller—Crusius Ζεῦ φίλε, θαυμάζω σε· κ.τ.λ., Eupol. χρυσοῦν γένος *frag.* 13 (*Frag. com. Gr.* ii. 541 f. Meineke) *ap.* Poll. 10. 63 ἀλλ', ὦ φίλε Ζεῦ, κατάχυτλον τὴν ῥῖν' ἔχεις, Aristoph. *eccl.* 378 f. καὶ δῆτα πολὺν ἡ μίλτος, ὦ Ζεῦ φίλτατε, | γέλων παρέσχεν, κ.τ.λ., Philem. *Pyrrhos frag.* 1. 7 f. (*Frag. com. Gr.* iv. 22 Meineke) *ap.* Stob. *flor.* 55. 5 εἰρήνη 'στίν· ὦ Ζεῦ φίλτατε, | τῆς ἐπαφροδίτου καὶ φιλανθρώπου θεοῦ, Kallim. *ep.* 7. 4 Schneider, 6. 4 Wilamowitz Κρεωφύλῳ, Ζεῦ φίλε, τοῦτο μέγα, *Anth. Pal.* 5. 108. 4 (Antipatros) ἦ ῥα μάτην, Ζεῦ φίλε, βοῦς ἐγένου. It is obvious that the phrases Ζεῦ φίλε, ὦ φίλε Ζεῦ, ὦ Ζεῦ φίλτατε expressed a variety of moods—indignation, astonishment, delight, etc. But the point is that all alike are colloquial, herein differing somewhat from such usages as *Il.* 1. 578 πατρὶ φίλῳ ἐπίηρα φέρειν Διί, Pind. *Nem.* 10. 104 ff. ἀμέραν τὰν μὲν παρὰ πατρὶ φίλῳ | Δὶ νέμονται, τὰν δ' ὑπὸ κεύθεσι γαίας κ.τ.λ.

[6] Furtwängler *Vasensamml. Berlin* ii. 549 ff. no. 2278, C. Lenormant in the *Ann. d. Inst.* 1830 ii. 232 ff., *Mon. d. Inst.* i pl. 24 = Reinach *Rép. Vases* i. 70, 2, Furtwängler—Reichhold—Hauser *Gr. Vasenmalerei* iii. 13 ff. pl. 123, Perrot—Chipiez *Hist. de l'Art* x. 503 ff. fig. 285, Pfuhl *Malerei u. Zeichnung d. Gr.* i. 457 ff., iii. 137 fig. 418. Further bibliography in Hoppin *Red-fig. Vases* ii. 421 ff. no. 1. *Corp. inscr. Gr.* iv no. 8291, a Ǝ⋈ΙꙨVƎꓘ.

[7] Pauly—Wissowa *Real-Enc.* v. 1152—1156 record twenty-two bearers of the name. See also K. Meisterhans *Grammatik der attischen Inschriften*[3] Berlin 1900 p. 74 n. 644 a.

[8] I am weighing my words: that is my deliberate opinion.

[9] Schol. Aristeid. p. 468, 15 f. Dindorf.

of Absolute Beauty, timeless, changeless, formless,—the beatific vision which shall

make amends
For all our toil while on the road.

Embracing this, he will at last beget no phantom forms of virtue, for it is no phantom that he clasps, but virtues true to type, for he has the very truth. And here he will live for ever as one that is indeed 'loved of God' and a sharer in immortality. That is the hope of which Sokrates, persuaded himself, is fain to persuade others also[1]. To summarise or paraphrase such a passage is, of course, to ruin its effect, and is little short of blasphemy to boot. I can but call attention to the one word *theophilés*, 'loved of God[2].' Platon had it from the mystics. And Theon of Smyrna (*s.* ii. A.D.) informs us that the initiate passed upwards through five stages, *viz.* purification, the tradition of the rite, the eyewitnessing of it, the binding and putting on of the garlands in order to communicate it to others, and finally the resultant felicity of dwelling in the 'love of God' (*theophilés*) and sharing in the life divine[3].

These beliefs formed a point of contact between paganism and Christianity. The hero-feast is an antecedent of the celestial banquet, a favourite theme in the art of the catacombs[4]. And if the Greeks looked forward to 'the good fare of the blest[5]' in the bridal chamber of Hades or Persephone, John can say 'Blessed are they which are bidden to the marriage supper of the Lamb[6].' The conception, cherished by the Church[7], has inspired not a few modern mystics :

---

[1] Plat. *symp.* 209 E—212 B. Faith, Hope, and Charity unite in this triumphant climax.

[2] The relevant words are: τεκόντι δὲ ἀρετὴν ἀληθῆ καὶ θρεψαμένῳ ὑπάρχει θεοφιλεῖ γενέσθαι καὶ εἴπερ τῳ ἄλλῳ ἀνθρώπων, ἀθανάτῳ καὶ ἐκείνῳ. On the later Platonic conception of ἀθανασία I have said my say in *The Metaphysical Basis of Plato's Ethics* Cambridge 1895 p. 96 ff. See also R. K. Gaye *The Platonic Conception of Immortality and its Connexion with the Theory of Ideas* (Hare Prize Essay 1903) London 1904.

[3] Theon Smyrn. *mathem.* p. 14, 18 ff. Hiller καὶ γὰρ αὖ τὴν φιλοσοφίαν μύησιν φαίη τις ἂν ἀληθοῦς τελετῆς καὶ τῶν ὄντων ὡς ἀληθῶς μυστηρίων παράδοσιν. μυήσεως δὲ μέρη πέντε. τὸ μὲν προηγούμενον καθαρμός· οὔτε γὰρ ἅπασι τοῖς βουλομένοις μετουσία μυστηρίων ἐστιν, ἀλλ' εἰσὶν οὓς αὐτῶν εἴργεσθαι προαγορεύεται, οἷον τοὺς χεῖρας μὴ καθαρὰς καὶ φωνὴν ἀξύνετον ἔχοντας, καὶ αὐτούς δὲ τοὺς μὴ εἰργομένους ἀνάγκη καθαρμοῦ τινος πρότερον τυχεῖν. μετὰ δὲ τὴν κάθαρσιν δευτέρα ἐστὶν ἡ τῆς τελετῆς παράδοσις· τρίτη δὲ ‹ ἡ ins. C. A. Lobeck › ἐπονομαζομένη ἐποπτεία· τετάρτη δέ, ὃ δὴ καὶ τέλος τῆς ἐποπτείας, ἀνάδεσις καὶ στεμμάτων ἐπίθεσις, ὥστε καὶ ἑτέροις, ἅς τις παρέλαβε τελετάς, παραδοῦναι δύνασθαι, δᾳδουχίας τυχόντα ἢ ἱεροφαντίας ἤ τινος ἄλλης ἱερωσύνης· πέμπτη δὲ ἡ ἐξ αὐτῶν περιγενομένη κατὰ τὸ θεοφιλὲς καὶ θεοῖς συνδίαιτον εὐδαιμονία (so I. Bouillaud for εὐδαιμονίαν cod. A.). See Lobeck *Aglaophamus* i. 38 ff.

[4] W. Lowrie *Christian Art and Archæology* New York 1901 pp. 221—223, L. von Sybel *Christliche Antike* Marburg 1906 i. 181—209 (the best account), C. M. Kaufmann *Handbuch der christlichen Archäologie* Paderborn 1913 pp. 269—274, 358.

[5] Aristoph. *ran.* 85 ἐς μακάρων εὐωχίαν, cp. Plat. *Phaid.* 115 D. Notice the schol. Aristoph. *loc. cit.* ἢ ὡς περὶ τετελευτηκότος λέγει, ὡσανεὶ εἶπε τὰς μακάρων νήσους· ἢ ὅτι ᾿Αρχελάῳ τῷ βασιλεῖ μέχρι τῆς τελευτῆς μετὰ ἄλλων πολλῶν συνῆν ἐν Μακεδονίᾳ, καὶ μακάρων εὐωχίαν ἔφη τὴν ἐν τοῖς βασιλείοις διατριβήν. If Hades was known as ᾿Αγησίλαος, Πολύαρχος, and the like (*supra* p. 1113 n. 0 no. (2)), it is at least possible that he bore the title ᾿Αρχέλαος. Aristophanes' *sous-entendu* would thus gain in point.

[6] Rev. 19. 9 with the context.

[7] A. Dieterich *Eine Mithrasliturgie²* Leipzig and Berlin 1910 pp. 129—134.

He lifts me to the golden doors ;
   The flashes come and go ;
All heaven bursts her starry floors,
   And strows her lights below,
And deepens on and up ! the gates
   Roll back, and far within
For me the Heavenly Bridegroom waits,
   To make me pure of sin.
The sabbaths of Eternity,
   One sabbath deep and wide—
A light upon the shining sea—
   The Bridegroom with his bride !¹

How much, or how little, of all this is to be found in our relief, it is not easy to say. The title *Epitéleios* suggests the mystic marriage, and the stress laid on *Phílios* and *Philía* tends to confirm the suggestion. We must leave it at that.

The matter-of-fact spectator, who cared little for mysteries or mystical symbolism, saw in Zeus *Phílios* a god of good company, given to feasting in both this world and the next. Accordingly, Diodoros of Sinope, a poet of the new comedy, who flourished early in *s.* iii B.C.², makes him the discoverer of the parasite and his ways:

'Twas Zeus the Friendly, greatest of the gods
Beyond all doubt, that first invented parasites.
For he it is who comes into our houses,
Nor cares a rap whether we're rich or poor.
Wherever he espies a well-strown couch
With a well-appointed table set beside it,
Joining us straightway like a gentleman
He asks himself to breakfast, eats and drinks,
And then goes home again, nor pays his share.
Just what I do myself ! When I see couches
Strown and the tables ready, door ajar,
In I come quietly, all in order due—
I don't disturb, not I, my fellow-drinker.
Everything set before me I enjoy,
Drink, and go home again, like Zeus the Friendly³.

The inference to be drawn from the fourth-century reliefs and the third-century comedy is that at Athens Zeus *Phílios*, like Zeus *Sotér*⁴, Zeus *Xénios*⁵, and other

¹ Tennyson *St. Agnes' Eve* 25 ff.
² J. Kirchner in Pauly—Wissowa *Real-Enc.* v. 660, Lübker *Reallex.*⁸ p. 293.
³ Diod. Sinop. ἐπίκληρος *frag.* 1. 5 ff. (*Frag. com. Gr.* iii. 543 ff. Meineke) *ap.* Athen. 239 A ff.
⁴ *Corp. inscr. Att.* ii. 1 no. 305, 10 ff. = *Inscr. Gr.* ed. min. ii—iii. 1 no. 676, 10 ff. ἐπειδὴ ο[ἱ ἐπιμεληταὶ πάσας] ἔθ[υόν τε τὰς θ|υ]σίας τῶ[ι Διὶ τῶι Σωτῆρι καὶ τ]εῖ Ἀθη[ναῖ τεῖ | Σω]τείρ[αι καὶ τῶν ἄλλων ἐπεμε]λήθησα[ν μετὰ | το]ῦ ἱερ[έως καλῶς καὶ φιλοτίμω]ς, ἐπεμελήθη|[σα]ν δὲ [καὶ τῆς στρώσεως τῆς κλί]νης καὶ τῆς κ|[οσ]μή[σεως τῆς τραπέζης· κ.τ.λ.] in a decree of 277/6 B.C.
⁵ Pyrgion Κρητικὰ νόμιμα *frag.* 1 (*Frag. hist. Gr.* iv. 486 f. Müller) *ap.* Athen. 143 E—F ἦσαν δὲ καὶ ξενικοὶ θᾶκοι καὶ τράπεζα τρίτη δεξιᾶς (I. Casaubon cj. ἐκ δεξιᾶς or ἐν δεξιᾷ) εἰσιόντων εἰς τὰ ἀνδρεῖα· ἣν Ξενίου τε Διὸς ξενίαν τε προσηγόρευον.

chthonian powers[1], had a couch set for him and a table spread. The rite was private rather than public, belonging essentially to family worship[2] and being in effect a communion between the dead and the living[3]. A. Furtwängler[4] justly compares the *lectisternia*, which are commonly held to have been a Roman adaptation of the Greek *Theoxénia*[5]. Be that as it may, the comparison is of interest. For it is possible, perhaps even probable, that at the Greek feast, as at its Roman equivalent, the god was represented in visible shape. But in what shape? Our only clue is the Roman custom. Livy mentions 'heads of gods' placed on the couches[6]. Pompeius Festus (*s.* ii A.D.)—an excellent authority, since he abridged the important dictionary of Verrius Flaccus (*c.* 10 B.C.)[7]— states that these 'heads of gods' were properly termed *struppi* and consisted in bundles of *verbenae* or 'sacred plants[8].' Elsewhere Festus, *à propos* of *stroppus* in the sense of a priestly head-dress or wreath, informs us that at Tusculum an

[1] Furtwängler *Samml. Sabouroff* Sculptures p. 28 f., A. Milchhöfer in the *Jahrb. d. kais. deutsch. arch. Inst.* 1887 ii. 31 (with list of deities).

[2] The ἐρανισταί (*supra* p. 1161 f.) formed a *quasi*-family, worshipping—we have conjectured—its deceased founder as its ancestor.

[3] *Supra* p. 1162 n. 2. See also Nilsson *Gr. Feste* p. 419.

[4] A. Furtwängler in the *Sitzungsber. d. kais. bayr. Akad. d. Wiss.* Phil.-hist. Classe 1897 i. 405.

[5] F. Robiou 'Recherches sur l'origine des lectisternes' in the *Rev. Arch.* 1867 i. 403—415, F. Deneken *De Theoxeniis* Berolini 1881, (G.) Wackermann *Ueber das Lectisternium* Hanau 1888 pp. 1—28, G. E. Marindin in Smith—Wayte—Marindin *Dict. Ant.* ii. 15—17, C. Pascal 'De lectisterniis apud Romanos' in the *Rivista di filologia* 1894 xxii. 272—280, *id. Studî di antichità e mitologia* Milano 1896 p. 19 ff., W. Warde Fowler *The Roman Festivals* London 1899 pp. 200, 218, 273, *id. The Religious Experience of the Roman People* London 1911 pp. 263 ff., 268, 318 f., A. Bouché-Leclercq in Daremberg—Saglio *Dict. Ant.* iii. 1006—1012, Nilsson *Gr. Feste* p. 161 f., Wissowa *Rel. Kult. Röm.*[2] pp. 61, 269 f., 311, 315, 421 ff.

[6] Liv. 40. 59 terra movit : in foris (K. A. Duker cj. *fanis*) publicis, ubi lectisternium erat, deorum capita, quae (K. A. Duker and J. N. Madvig cjj. *qui*) in lectis erant,'averterunt se, lanaque (J. Scheffer cj. *laenaque*, G. Cuypers and J. Marquardt cjj. *lanxque*) cum integumentis (F. van Oudendorp cj. *intrimentis*), quae Iovi opposita (C. Sigone and J. Scheffer cjj. *apposita*) fuit, decidit = Iul. Obseq. 61 in lectisternio Iovis terrae motu deorum capita se converterunt. lana cum integumentis, quae Iovi erant apposita, decidit.

[7] M. Schanz *Geschichte der römischen Litteratur*[2] München 1899 ii. 1. 319 ff., Sir J. E. Sandys *A History of Classical Scholarship*[2] Cambridge 1906 i. 200.

[8] Fest. p. 347, 34 f. Müller, p. 472, 15 f. Lindsay struppi vocantur in pulvinaribus <fasciculi de verbenis facti, qui pro de>orum capitibus ponuntur = Paul. ex Fest. p. 346, 3 Müller, p. 473, 4 f. Lindsay struppi vocabantur in pulvinaribus fasciculi de verbenis facti, qui pro deorum capitibus ponebantur. Cp. Paul. ex Fest. p. 64, 5 Müller, p. 56, 12 Lindsay capita deorum appellabantur fasciculi facti ex verbenis.

Serv. *in* Verg. *Aen.* 12. 120 verbena proprie est herba sacra sumpta de loco sacro Capitolii, qua coronabantur fetiales et paterpatratus foedera facturi vel bella indicturi. abusive tamen verbenas iam vocamus omnes frondes sacratas, ut est laurus, oliva vel myrtus. etc. Cp. Plin. *nat. hist.* 22. 5, 25. 105 ff., interp. Serv. *in* Verg. *ecl.* 8. 65, Donat. *in* Ter. *Andr.* 4. 3. 11.

S. Eitrem in the *Class. Rev.* 1921 xxxv. 20 finds an illustration of these *struppi* in a painting of *s.* v B.C. in the *Tomba del Letto funebre* at Corneto (F. Poulsen *Fra Ny Carlsberg Glyptoteks Samlinger* Copenhagen 1920 i fig. 34, F. Weege *Etruskische Malerei* Halle (Saale) 1921 pls. 23, 24) : 'on a mighty lectus you see on the torus not two recumbent defuncts, but *two green crowns*, surmounted by the Etruscan (and Roman) pointed head-dress, the *tutulus*.'

object known as *struppus* was placed on the couch of Castor[1]. We gather, then, that at the *lectisternia* Iupiter and the gods in general were originally represented by twisted bundles of herbs. These bundles seem to have been padded and clothed as puppets ; for in 179 B.C., shaken by an earthquake, the wool and wrappings attached to Iupiter slipped off revealing his true inwards to the confusion of all present[2]. Later, if we may trust the evidence of a Roman lamp (fig. 972)[3] and certain Roman coins (figs. 973, 974, 975)[4], the puppets of the

Fig. 973.

Fig. 974.

Fig. 972.

Fig. 975.

---

[1] Fest. p. 313 *a* 12 ff. Müller, p. 410, 6 ff. Lindsay stroppus est, ut Ateius Philologus (L. Ateius Praetextatus *frag.* 7 Funaioli) existimat, quod Graece στρόφιον vocatur, et quod sacerdotes pro insigni habent in capite. quidam coronam esse dicunt, aut quod pro corona insigne in caput inponatur, quale sit strophium. itaque apud Faliscos diem (so Antonius Augustinus for *idem* codd.) festum esse, qui vocetur Struppearia, quia coronati ambulent; et a Tusculanis, quod in pulvinari inponatur Castoris, struppum vocari=Paul. ex Fest. p. 312, 1 Müller, p. 411, 1 ff. Lindsay stroppus, quod Graece στρόφιον dicitur, pro insigni habebatur in capitibus sacerdotum ; alii id coronam esse dixerunt. Cp. Plin. *nat. hist.* 21. 3.

[2] Liv. 40. 59 and Iul. Obseq. 61 cited *supra* p. 1170 n. 6.

Cp. the woollen effigies of the Lares hung up at the cross-roads during the Compitalia (Paul. ex Fest. p. 121, 17 f. Müller, p. 108, 27 ff. Lindsay ; Fest. p. 237 *b* 34 ff. Müller, p. 272, 15 ff. Lindsay = Paul. ex Fest. p. 239, 1 ff. Müller, p. 273, 7 ff. Lindsay. See further Frazer *Golden Bough*[3]: Spirits of Corn and Wild ii. 94 ff., 107 f.), if not also the saying that the gods had woollen feet (Apollod. *frag.* 41 (*Frag. hist. Gr.* i. 435 Müller) *ap*. Macrob. *Sat.* 1. 8. 5, Petron. *sat.* 44. 18, Porph. *in* Hor. *od.* 3. 2. 31 f.).

[3] Fig. 972 shows the relief on the handle of a terra-cotta lamp first published by P. S. Bartoli—G. P. Bellori *Le antiche lucerne sepolcrali* Roma 1691 ii pl. 34 (A. Bouché-Leclercq in Daremberg—Saglio *Dict. Ant.* iii. 1011 fig. 4381, H. B. Walters *History of Ancient Pottery* London 1905 ii. 412). Sarapis and Isis, Selene and Helios, are here represented by half-length busts set on the couch. A similar bust of white marble, obtained in the Levant by Mr W. Simpson and now in my possession (height 3¾ inches : *kálathos* broken off: traces of paint (?) on face, chest, etc.: eye-holes and breast-jewel once filled in with glass or other glittering substance), was very possibly used at some *lectisternium* of Sarapis (cp. *e.g. Brit. Mus. Cat. Coins* Pontus, etc. p. 101 no. 57 a copper of Sinope struck by Caracalla : *rev.* Zeus Sarapis on couch to left, with eagle on right hand, sceptre in left, Stevenson—Smith—Madden *Dict. Rom. Coins* p. 507).

Another lamp-handle with a similar design, found at Pesaro, is suspect as being derived from the *Lucernae fictiles Musei Passerii* Pisauri 1739—1751 iii pl. 51 (A. Bouché-Leclercq *loc. cit.* iii. 1011 fig. 4382) : see the exposure by H. Dressel in the *Röm. Mitth.* 1892 vii. 144 ff. (150 'una solenne impostura'), H. B. Walters *History of Ancient Pottery* ii. 408.

[4] *Denarii* of the *gens Coelia*, struck *c.* 61 B.C., have for reverse type a *lectisternium*

lectisternia appear to have developed into half-length busts. Indeed, on one occasion, when Seleukos was sending back to Athens the statues of Harmodios and Aristogeiton carried off by Xerxes, the Rhodians invited the venerable bronzes to a public banquet and installed them bodily on the sacred couches[1]. So much for progressive anthropomorphism. The vegetable bundles, which formed the primitive effigies[2], may be taken to imply that the souls of the dead were conceived as animating the yearly vegetation[3]. And the same belief may underlie the rites of Iupiter *Dapalis*[4] and Iupiter *Farreus*[5], in which Mr Warde

surmounted by a half-figure and flanked by two trophies. The front is inscribed L·CALDVS | VII·Ꞷ·EΓꞶ. (= *Lucius Caldus septemvir epulo*). To left and right is the legend, read downwards, C·CALDVS | IMP·A (or AꞨ)·X (= *Gaius Caldus imperator augur decemvir sacris faciundis*). Below is CⲘVS·III·VIR (= *Caldus triumvir monetalis*). See Morell. *Thes. Num. Fam. Rom.* i. 100 ff., ii pl. Coelia I, IA, IB, Babelon *Monn. rép. rom.* i. 373 ff. with six figs., G. F. Hill *Historical Roman Coins* London 1909 p. 76 ff. pl. 10, 44, *Brit. Mus. Cat. Rom. Coins* Rep. i. 475 pl. 47, 23 f., pl. 48, 1. Figs. 973—975 are from specimens in my collection. The identification of the personage seen above the couch has long been disputed. He is either the moneyer's father, L. Coelius Caldus, as *septemvir epulo* preparing the feast for Iupiter (Rasche *Lex. Num.* ii. 659 f., T. Mommsen *Histoire de la monnaie romaine* Paris 1870 ii. 506, Babelon *loc. cit.*, G. F. Hill *op. cit.* p. 78), or— more probably—the effigy of Iupiter himself eating the sacrificial meal (see the remarks of S. Havercamp in Morell. *op. cit.* i. 102, Stevenson—Smith—Madden *Dict. Rom. Coins* p. 507, H. A. Grueber in *Brit. Mus. Cat. Rom. Coins* Rep. i. 474 n. 2).

The two *epula Iovis*, which took place on Sept. 13, the foundation-day of the Capitoline temple, and on Nov. 13, were in relation to the *ludi Romani* and *ludi plebei* respectively (Wissowa *Rel. Kult. Röm.*[2] pp. 127, 423, 453 ff.). Iupiter had a *lectulus*, Iuno and Minerva each a *sella* (Val. Max. 2. 1. 2), while the magistrates and senate took the meal before them *in Capitolio* (Liv. 38. 57, 45. 39, Gell. 12. 8. 2 f., Dion Cass. 39. 30, 48. 52). See further E. Aust in Roscher *Lex. Myth.* ii. 732, 734 f., W. Warde Fowler *The Roman Festivals* London 1899 p. 215 ff., *id.* *The Religious Experience of the Roman People* London 1911 pp. 172 f., 336, 338, 353. Hence the title of Iupiter *Epulo* (*Corp. inscr. Lat.* vi no. 3696 found in the Forum at Rome=Dessau *Inscr. Lat. sel.* no. 4964, with the criticisms of G. Wissowa in Pauly—Wissowa *Real-Enc.* vi. 265, who prefers T. Mommsen's reading (*Bull. d. Inst.* 1873 p. 51 f.) [*magistri*] *quinq*(*uennales*) | [*collegi*] *teib*(*icinum*) *Rom*(*anorum*), *qui* | [*s*(*acris*) *p*(*ublicis*) *p*(*raesto*) *s*(*unt*)], *Iov*(*i*) *Epul*(*oni*) *sac*(*rum*) | etc. to that of E. Bormann and H. Dessau *qui* | .... *Iov*(*is*) *epul*(*o*), *sac*(*ris*) | [*p*(*ublicis*) *p*(*raesto*) *s*(*unt*)] : | etc.).

[1] Val. Max. 2. 10. 1 *ext*.

[2] Masurius Sabinus *ap.* Serv. *in* Verg. *Aen.* 2. 225 Masurius Sabinus delubrum, effigies, a delibratione corticis ; nam antiqui felicium arborum ramos cortice detracto in effigies deorum formabant, unde Graeci ξόανον dicunt. Cp. Serv. *in* Verg. *Aen.* 4. 56, Paul. ex Fest. p. 73, 1 Müller, p. 64, 6 f. Lindsay, pseudo-Ascon. *in* Cic. *div. in Caec.* p. 101, 16 f. Baiter (in J. C. Orelli's ed. of Cicero Turici 1833 v. 2. 101). But a closer parallel may be found in the Corn-maiden (*supra* i. 397 n. 4 pl. xxviii).

[3] *Supra* i. 687.

[4] Cato *de agr.* 132 dapem hoc modo fieri oportet : Iovi Dapali culignam vini quantam vis polluceto. eo die feriae bubus et bubulcis et qui dapem facient. cum pollucere oportebit, sic facies : 'Iuppiter Dapalis, quod tibi fieri oportet in domo familia mea culignam vini dapi, ei<us> rei ergo macte hac illace dape pollucenda esto.' manus interluito, postea vinum sumito : 'Iuppiter Dapalis, macte istace dape pollucenda esto, macte vino inferio esto.' Vestae, si voles, dato. daps Iovi assaria pecuina (pecuina v.) urna vini. Iovi caste profanato sua contagione. postea dape facta serito milium, panicum, alium, lentim. The adjective *dapalis*, 'sumptuous,' is most frequently found as an epithet of *cena* (*Thes. Ling. Lat.* v. 35, 29 ff.).

[5] Gaius *inst.* 1. 112 farreo in manus (Göschen, followed by P. Krüger—W. Studemund,

Fowler conjectures that Iupiter himself was originally identified with the flesh, the wine, and the bread consumed by his worshippers[1].

It is possible, then, that the communion-feast of Zeus *Philios* approximated to, and paved the way for, the *agápe* or 'love-supper' of the early Christian Church[2]. Nevertheless the evidence is indirect and by no means conclusive. We shall be on surer, if lower, ground in returning to the cult-monuments of Attike.

(2) Zeus *Philios* on the Attic coast, etc.

To the west of the *Asklepieîon* near the strand of Zea there appears to have been a common sanctuary of Zeus *Meilíchios* and Zeus *Philios*[3]. Votive reliefs from the site show the latter god in the same types (anthropomorphic and theriomorphic) as the former.

On the one hand, a slab of Pentelic marble, found on the eastern slope of Mounichia at a point two hundred paces from the sea, represents him (fig. 976)[4] as a kingly personage enthroned towards the right with a sceptre (painted) in his hand. He is approached by a woman and a girl—Mynnion and her daughter, as we infer from the inscription added above in lettering of *s.* iv B.C. :

'[M]ynnion dedicated (this) to Zeus *Philios*[5].'

A fragmentary relief of white marble, found later in the same locality, was clearly of similar type[6]. On the left are seen the head of Zeus, his left shoulder, and his left hand holding a sceptre. On the right a bearded man and a youthful figure draw near with right hand raised in the attitude of adoration : behind them there

---

cj. *manum*) conveniunt per quoddam genus sacrificii, quod Iovi Farreo fit, in quo farreus panis adhibetur ; unde etiam confarreatio dicitur ; etc.

[1] W. Warde Fowler *The Religious Experience of the Roman People* London 1911 p. 141 'The cult-title [*Farreus*] should indicate that the god was believed to be immanent in the cake of *far*, rather than that it was offered to him (so I should also take I. Dapalis, though in later times the idea had passed into that of sacrifice, Cato, *R. R.* 132), and if so, the use of the cake was sacramental.' A shrewd and scholarly verdict. Wissowa *Rel. Kult. Röm.*[2] p. 119 'die heilige Handlung gilt dem Juppiter, welcher von dem zur Anwendung kommenden *farreum libum* den Beinamen Farreus erhält' is inadequate. B. J. Polenaar on Gaius *inst.* 1. 112 cp. *Adorea* as goddess of martial glory (Hor. *od.* 4. 4. 41) *a farris honore* (Plin. *nat. hist.* 18. 14) : but the derivation of the word from *ador*, though assumed by the ancients, is doubtful or worse (see F. Stolz in the *Indogermanische Forschungen* 1899 x. 74 f., Walde *Lat. etym. Wörterb.*[2] p. 13 *s.v.* 'adōria').

[2] On the Christian ἀγάπαι consult A. Kestner *Die Agape oder der geheime Weltbund der Christen* Jena 1819, E. H. Plumptre in Smith—Cheetham *Dict. Chr. Ant.* i. 39 ff., R. St. J. Tyrwhitt *ib.* i. 625 ff., H. Leclercq in F. Cabrol *Dictionnaire d'archéologie chrétienne et de liturgie* Paris 1907 i. 775—848, A. J. Maclean in J. Hastings *Encyclopædia of Religion and Ethics* Edinburgh 1908 i. 166—175.

[3] *Supra* p. 1104.

[4] R. Schöne *Griechische Reliefs* Leipzig 1872 p. 53 f. no. 105 pl. 25, Friederichs—Wolters *Gipsabgüsse* p. 370 no. 1128, *Einzelaufnahmen* no. 1247, 2 with Text v. 22 by E. Löwy, Svoronos *Ath. Nationalmus.* p. 354 f. no. 1405 pl. 59 (=my fig. 976), Reinach *Rép. Reliefs* ii. 362, 7 (wrongly described *ib.* p. 363 as 'Hommage à Zeus Meilichios'). Height 0·22[m], breadth 0·21[m].

[5] *Corp. inscr. Att.* ii. 3 no. 1572 [M]ΥΝΝΙΟΝΔΙΙΦΙΛΙΩΙΑΝΕΘ[ΗΚΕΝ]= [Μ]ύννιον Διὶ Φιλίωι ἀνέθ[ηκεν].

[6] I. C. Dragatses in the 'Εφ. 'Αρχ. 1885 p. 89 f. no. β', Svoronos *Ath. Nationalmus.* p. 355. Height 0·16[m], breadth 0·30[m].

are traces of a third head. The whole is enclosed by an architectural framework, which bears the inscription:

'Hermaios (dedicated this) to Zeus *Phílios*[1].'

On the other hand, the same site yielded two reliefs representing a snake accompanied by the words:

'—— dedicated (this) to Zeus *Phílios*[2].'

Fig. 976.

As before[3], we must suppose that the snake figures the soul of the divinised dead, here conciliated by the euphemistic title Zeus 'the Friendly One.' *Phílios* is virtually a synonym of *Meilíchios*[4].

Other reliefs, which probably derive from the same cult-centre in the Peiraieus,

---

[1] *Corp. inscr. Att.* ii. 3 Add. no. 1572*b* ΕΡΜΑΙΟΣΔΙΙΦΙΛΙΩΙ =ʹΕρμαῖος Διὶ Φιλίωι.

[2] (1) I. C. Dragatses in the Δελτ. ʼΑρχ. 1888 p. 135, *Corp. inscr. Att.* iv. 2 no. 1572*c* a fragmentary marble slab inscribed ϽΙΛΙ and ΞΝ=[– – – Διὶ Φ]ιλί[ωι] | [ἀνέθηκ]εν above the relief of a snake. (2) I. C. Dragatses in the Δελτ. ʼΑρχ. 1888 p. 135 no. 3, Svoronos *Ath. Nationalmus.* p. 355 the relief of a snake with the inscription Διὶ Φ[ιλί]ωι [ἀνέθηκ]εν.

[3] *Supra* p. 1111.

[4] This explains the otherwise inexplicable gloss of Hesych. φιλιός (Soping *corr.* φίλιος, M. Schmidt *cj.* ἀφάδιος?)· ὁ ἀποτρόπαιος, κατʼ εὐφημισμ[έν]όν.

repeat the types in question but, having no inscribed dedication, cannot be assigned with assurance to either god. Two examples will suffice. A fourth-century relief in Pentelic marble (fig. 977)[1] shows, within an architectural border, Zeus enthroned towards the right, holding a *phiále* in his right hand and a sceptre (painted) in his left. Before him kneels a woman, who with a well-known gesture of supplication stretches out both hands to clasp his knees[2]. Behind her stands a second woman, with right hand uplifted. They are accompanied by a couple of children. The scene is closed by two *hieródouloi*—a boy carrying a flat basket on his right hand while he grasps a ram with his left, and a girl sup-

Fig. 977.

porting a large round basket on her head. The fact that in reliefs of this sort the father is so often escorted by his son, the mother by her daughter, suggests that the god, whether *Meilíchios* or *Phílios*, was in any case worshipped as *Téleios*.

More difficult to interpret is another fourth-century relief (fig. 978)[3] representing a cylindrical altar with a snake coiled about it and a pair of snakes, both bearded, in heraldic pose to right and left. Have we here a votive tablet honouring the same god under all three aspects?

The chthonian character of Zeus *Phílios* is borne out by his ability to witness oaths and to send dreams. Greek dialogues, letters, and speeches abound in such phrases as 'by Zeus the Friendly[4],' 'by the Friendly Zeus[5],' 'by the Friendly

[1] Friederichs—Wolters *Gipsabgüsse* p. 375 no. 1139, *Einzelaufnahmen* no. 1245, 3 with Text v. 20 by E. Löwy, Staïs *Marbres et Bronzes: Athènes*[2] p. 242 no. 1408, Svoronos *Ath. Nationalmus.* p. 357 f. no 1408 pl. 65 (=my fig. 977), Reinach *Rép. Reliefs* ii. 363 no. 2. Height 0·25ᵐ, breadth 0·40ᵐ.

[2] C. Sittl *Die Gebärden der Griechen und Römer* Leipzig 1890 pp. 163 ff., 282 f., Svoronos *op. cit.* p. 358.

[3] Svoronos *op. cit.* p. 441 no. 1441 pl. 71 (=my fig. 978). Height 0·15ᵐ, breadth 0·24ᵐ.

[4] πρὸς Διὸς Φιλίου Plat. *Phaedr.* 234 E, *Minos* 321 C, Ioul. *epist.* 3. 2. Cp. πρὸς Διὸς Φιλίου τε καὶ Ἐταιρείου Sokrat. *epist.* 27. 1 p. 627 Hercher.

[5] πρὸς Φιλίου Διός Ioul. *or.* 2 p. 123, 9 Hertlein, *or.* 3 p. 165, 23 Hertlein, Aineias of Gaza *epist.* 1.

One[1],' 'yes, by the Friendly One[2],' 'no, by your Friendly One and mine[3].'

Fig. 978.

Friends in general swore by Zeus *Phílios*[4], who came to be looked upon as the overseer and guardian of friendship[5], or ultimately as a god of love who would

[1] πρὸς Φιλίου Plat. *Euthyphr.* 6 B, *Gorg.* 500 B, 519 E, Loukian. *Herod.* 7, *rhet. praecept.* 4, *de dipsad.* 9, Themist. *or.* 1. 17 A p. 19, 6 Dindorf, Prokop. *epist.* 75, 103, 116, 132.

[2] ναὶ τὸν Φίλιον Aristoph. *Ach.* 730 with schol. *ad loc.* νὴ τὸν Φίλιον Pherekrat. κραπάταλοι *frag.* 16. 4 (*Frag. com. Gr.* ii. 293 Meineke) *ap.* Phot. *lex. s.v.* Φίλιος Ζεύς = Souid. *s.v.* Φίλιος.

[3] μὰ τὸν Φίλιον τὸν ἐμόν τε καὶ σόν Plat. *Alcib.* 1 109 D, imitated by Aristain. *epist.* 2. 14 μὰ τὸν Φίλιον "Ἐρωτα (D. Wyttenbach *om.* "Ἐρωτα as a gloss) τὸν ἐμόν τε καὶ σόν and Synes. *epist.* 49 p. 660 Hercher and 59 p. 672 ναὶ μὰ τὸν Φίλιον τὸν ἐμόν τε καὶ σόν, 103 p. 700 οὐ μὰ τὸν Φίλιον τὸν ἐμόν τε καὶ σόν, 129 p. 716 νὴ τὸν Φίλιον τὸν ἐμόν τε καὶ σόν, 95 p. 694 οὐ μὰ τὸν Ὁμόγνιον τὸν ἐμόν τε καὶ σόν. We have a similar usage of the possessive pronoun (one of those little touches, which show that on occasion Greek religion could be personal as well as civic) in Eur. *Andr.* 602 f. ἥτις ἐκ δόμων | τὸν σὸν λιποῦσα Φίλιον (*sc.* Δία) ἐξεκώμασε | κ.τ.λ., *Hec.* 345 (cited *supra* p. 1097 n. 2).

[4] Menand. ἀνδρόγυνος *frag.* 6 (*Frag. com. Gr.* iv. 85 Meineke) *ap.* Phot. *lex. s.v.* Φίλιος Ζεύς = Souid. *s.v.* Φίλιος '…μαρτύρομαι τὸν Φίλιον, ὦ Κράτων, Δία, Loukian. *Toxar.* 11 f. ΜΝΗΣ. ὁμούμεθα, εἴ τι καὶ ὅρκου δεῖν νομίζεις. τίς δέ σοι τῶν ἡμετέρων θεῶν—ἆρ' ἱκανὸς ὁ Φίλιος; ΤΟΞ. καὶ μάλα·… ΜΝΗΣ. ἴστω τοίνυν ὁ Ζεὺς ὁ Φίλιος, ἦ μὴν κ.τ.λ., schol. rec. Soph. *Ai.* 492 p. 211, 6 ff. ἐφεστίου Διός· τοῦ τιμωμένου ἐν τῇ οἰκίᾳ καὶ ἐφορῶντος τὴν συνοίκησιν ἡμῶν. Ἐφέστιον Δία προτείνουσιν οἱ συνοικοῦντες· οἱ δὲ φίλοι Φίλιον· οἱ δὲ ἐν μιᾷ τάξει καταλεγόμενοι καὶ μιᾷ συμμορίᾳ, Ἑταιρεῖον· οἱ δὲ ξένοι, Ξένιον· οἱ δὲ ἐν ὅρκοις συμφωνίας ποιοῦντες, "Ὁρκιον· οἱ δὲ δεόμενοι, Ἱκέσιον· οἱ δὲ ἀδελφοί, Ὁμόγνιον = schol. Eur. *Hec.* 345.

[5] Phrynichos the 'Atticist' (*c.* 180 A.D.) in Bekker *anecd.* i. 34, 14 (cited *supra* p. 1092 n. 8), *ib.* i. 71, 7 Φίλιος· ὁ φιλίας ἔφορος θεός, Phot. *lex. s.v.* Φίλιος Ζεύς = Souid. *s.v.* Φίλιος· ὁ τὰ περὶ τὰς φιλίας ἐπισκοπῶν, *et. mag.* p. 793, 43 Φίλιος Ζεύς· ὁ τὰ περὶ τῆς φιλίας (F. Sylburg cj. τὴν φιλίαν) ἐπισκοπῶν, Olympiod. *in* Plat. *Gorg.* 500 B (published by

have all men dwell together in amity[1]. A title with such claims to popularity was naturally included among the stock epithets of Zeus[2].

An oblong slab of limestone found in the precinct of Asklepios at Epidauros bears a dedication to Zeus *Phílios* 'in accordance with a dream' and adds, as symbol of the god, a branch of olive or oak enclosed in a circle[3]. It must not be

A. Jahn in the *Neue Jahrbücher für Philologie und Pädagogik* Suppl. 1848 xiv. 364 f.) ἐπὶ τὸν ἔφορον τῆς φιλίας φέρει αὐτόν, ἵνα εἰδὼς ὅτι θεός ἐστιν ὁ τῆς φιλίας προστάτης μὴ πάλιν παίξῃ· ὁ γὰρ παίζων εἰς φίλον τὸν προστάτην ταύτης θεὸν παίζει, schol. Plat. *Gorg.* 500 Β Διὸς ἦν ἐπώνυμον παρ' Ἀθηναίοις ὁ Φίλιος, ἐκ τοῦ εἶναι τῶν φιλικῶν καθηκόντων αὐτὸν ἔφορον, Thom. Mag. *ecl. voc. Att.* p. 382 Ritschl Φίλιος ὁ τῆς φιλίας ἔφορος θεός, Favorin. *lex.* p. 1188, 57 Φίλιος, ὁ φιλίας ἔφορος, p. 1832, 62 f. Φίλιος Ζεύς, ὁ τὰ περὶ τῆς φιλίας ἐπισκοπῶν. With these scholastic definitions cp. such passages as Liban. *epist.* 19 καὶ ταύτην τίνομεν τῷ Φιλίῳ τὴν δίκην ὅτι δὴ φίλων ἡμῖν ἐφάνη τι τιμιώτερον, 1204 ὑπέμνησα Φιλίου Διός and context.

[1] Dion Chrys. *or.* 1 p. 56 f. Reiske Ζεὺς γάρ...ἐπονομάζεται...καὶ Φίλιός τε καὶ Ἑταιρεῖος ...Φίλιος δὲ καὶ Ἑταιρεῖος ὅτι πάντας ἀνθρώπους ξυνάγει καὶ βούλεται εἶναι ἀλλήλοις φίλους, ἐχθρὸν δὲ ἢ πολέμιον μηδένα = *or.* 12 p. 412 f. Reiske Ζεὺς γάρ...ὀνομάζεται...καὶ Φίλιος καὶ Ἑταιρεῖος...Φίλιος δὲ καὶ Ἑταιρεῖος ὅτι πάντας ἀνθρώπους ξυνάγει καὶ βούλεται φίλους εἶναι ἀλλήλοις, ἐχθρὸν δὲ ἢ πολέμιον οὐδένα οὐδενός, Eustath. *in magnam quadragesimam oratio praeparatoria* 44 (= Eustath. *opusc.* p. 86 Tafel) πονηροὶ οἱ μὴ ἀγαπῶντες· πονηροὺς δὲ ὁ Φίλιος οὐ προσίεται.

[2] Aristot. *de mund.* 7. 401 a 22 ἑταιρεῖός τε καὶ φίλιος καὶ ξένιος = Stob. *ecl.* i. 1. 36 p. 45, 19 f. Wachsmuth (translated by Apul. *de mund.* 37 alii Hospitalem Amicalemque), Loukian. *Tim.* 1 TIM. ὦ Ζεῦ φίλιε καὶ ξένιε καὶ ἑταιρεῖε καὶ ἐφέστιε καὶ ἀστεροπητὰ καὶ ὅρκιε καὶ νεφεληγερέτα καὶ ἐρίγδουπε καὶ εἴ τί σε ἄλλο οἱ ἐμβρόντητοι ποιηταὶ καλοῦσι, καὶ μάλιστα ὅταν ἀπορῶσι πρὸς τὰ μέτρα, Tzetz. *in Lyk. Al.* 288 Φύξιος δὲ ὁ Ζεὺς καὶ Φίλιος καὶ Ἑταιρεῖος καὶ Ἐφέστιος καὶ Ὁμόγνιος καὶ ἄλλα μυρία καλεῖται πρὸς τὰ συμβαίνοντα καὶ γινόμενα καὶ μετονομαζόμενος· κ.τ.λ., Achilleus (Tatios) *comment. frag. in* Arat. *phaen.* 2 f. p. 84, 16 ff. Maass λέγεται γὰρ καὶ βουλαῖος Ζεὺς καὶ ξένιος καὶ ἑταιρειος (*leg.* ἑταιρεῖος) φίλιος φυτάλμιος ἐπικάρπιος, schol. Arat. p. 332, 10 f. Maass ὥς εἰσι (φασί) γενέτωρ φράτριος ὁμόγνιος ἑταιρεῖος φίλιος ἱκέσιος ξένιος ἀγοραῖος βουλαῖος βρονταῖος καὶ τὰ ὅμοια (*sc.* ἐπίθετα Διός), Schöll—Studemund *anecd.* i. 267 no. 100 φιλίου (*sc.* Διός), 274 φίλιος (*sc.* Ζεύς), 282 φίλιος (*sc.* Ζεύς).

In particular the epithets Ξένιος and Φίλιος are often combined: Plout. *v. Arat.* 54 δίκας γε μὴν ὁ Φίλιππος οὐ μεμπτὰς Διὶ Ξενίῳ καὶ Φιλίῳ τῆς ἀνοσιουργίας ταύτης τίνων διετέλεσε, Himer. *or.* 6. 3 φέρε οὖν κἀνταῦθα Φιλίῳ Διὶ κρατῆρα στήσωμεν καὶ τὸν Ξενίου βωμὸν λόγων ξενίαις ἀμείψωμεν, Ioul. *or.* 8 p. 327, 8 ff. Hertlein ἄγοι μὲν θεὸς εὐμενής, ὅποι ποτ' ἂν δέῃ πορεύεσθαι, Ξένιος δὲ ὑποδέχοιτο καὶ Φίλιος εὔνους, Heliod. *Aeth.* 6. 2 πρὸς Ξενίων καὶ Φιλίων θεῶν, schol. Eur. *Hec.* 791 χθονίους μὲν (*sc.* οὐ δείσας) διὰ τὸ ἄταφον ἐᾶσαι φονεύσαντα, οὐρανίους δὲ διὰ τὸν Ξένιον καὶ Φίλιον Δία (here actually contrasted with the chthonian powers!), schol. Eur. *Andr.* 603 Φίλιον'...ἢ λείπει τὸ Δία, ἵν' ᾖ Φίλιον Δία, ὡς Ξένιον Δία, schol. Aristoph. *eq.* 500 Ζεὺς Ἀγοραῖος· ὡς Ζεὺς Ξένιος ἢ Μειλίχιος ἢ Φίλιος, οὕτω καὶ Ἀγοραῖος.

See also Aineias of Gaza *epist.* 8, Prokop. *epist.* 15, Eumath. 3. 9, 5. 18 (*supra* p. 1141 n. 13). And cp. Loukian. *Prom. s. Caucas.* 6 πάνυ φιλανθρώπου τοῦ Διὸς πεπειραμένος.

[3] P. Kabbadias in the Ἐφ. Ἀρχ. 1883 p. 31 no. 12, *id. Fouilles d'Épidaure* Athènes 1893 i. 60 no. 161, M. Fränkel in the *Inscr. Gr. Pelop.* i no. 1296 [Δ]ιὶ Φιλίω | Πύροιος | κατ' ὄναρ with the numeral νθ′ and the symbol 🌿 in circle, on which see *supra* p. 1076 f.

The garland of Zeus *Phílios* is mentioned in an inscription from Kyrene (*Corp. inscr. Gr.* iii no. 5173, 3 ff. = Kaibel *Epigr. Gr.* no. 873, 1 ff. = Cougny *Anth. Pal. Append.* 1. 280. 1 ff. ἀ(γ)ρεῖ δ' Ἄρτεμις ἀ(γ)[ροτέ]ρη, καλοῖς ἐνὶ [πέπλ]οις, | Μαρκιανὴν ἱερῷ δερκομένη (θ)[αλάμῳ]| ᾿| ο[ὗ Δ]ιὸς ἀρητὴρ [ἤρᾶ]το, πατὴρ ἱερήων, | [ἄρ]τ[ι πυ]κ[νὸ]ν Φιλίο(υ) [σ]τέμμ' ἀν[α]δησάμενος· | κ.τ.λ. The restoration is doubtful : see G. Kaibel and E. Cougny *ad loc.*).

hastily assumed that Zeus *Phílios* was only another name for Asklepios[1], though the two deities were certainly of similar origin and somewhat similar character.

But we have yet to notice three remarkable cults of Zeus *Phílios* at Megalopolis in Arkadia, at Pergamon in Mysia, and at Antiocheia on the Orontes, respectively.

(3) Zeus *Phílios* at Megalopolis.

Pausanias in describing the enclosure sacred to the Greek Goddesses at Megalopolis says:

'Within the precinct is a temple of Zeus *Phílios*. The image is by Polykleitos the Argive and resembles Dionysos ; for its feet are shod with buskins and it has a cup in one hand, a *thýrsos* in the other. On the *thýrsos* is perched an eagle, though this does not agree with what is told of Dionysos. Behind the said temple ⁚ a small grove of trees surrounded by a wall. People are not allowed to enter it, but before it are images of Demeter and Kore some three feet in height. Within the precinct of the Great Goddesses there is also a sanctuary of Aphrodite[2].'

So the temp'e of Zeus *Phílios* had a grove of awful sanctity behind it, over which Demeter and Kore mounted guard. I take this to mean that Zeus *Phílios*, himself a chthonian god, was reckoned as the consort of these chthonian goddesses, and was held to be jointly responsible with them for the yearly yield of corn and wine. Hence his approximation to the type of Dionysos. The singular Dionysiac Zeus is attributed by J. Overbeck[3] to Polykleitos the younger on the ground that his more famous namesake was dead and buried years before the foundation of Megalopolis (371—368 B.C.). But H. Brunn[4] suggested that the statue was a work of Polykleitos the elder, brought from some other Arcadian town to grace the new federal centre. Two arguments incline me towards Brunn's view. In the first place, Pausanias is elsewhere careful to distinguish the younger sculptor from his more illustrious predecessor[5], so that, rightly or wrongly, our author must have meant the elder Polykleitos. In the second place, Polykleitos the elder, bowing to the authority of local tradition, represented Hera with a highly peculiar sceptre[6] : he may well have done the same for this cult-statue of Zeus. It is not, however, necessary to suppose with Brunn that the statue was brought from another town : cult-statues are not easily transplanted. I should rather conceive of the situation as follows. Megalopolis had a quarter or, as Stephanos the geographer says, a 'half' called *Orestía* after Orestes[7], who had spent a year of exile in the *Orésteion*[8]. Now in the only other *Orésteion* known

---

[1] Cp. *supra* p. 1076 ff.

[2] Paus. 8. 31. 4 f. (*supra* i. 112 n. 2) τοῦ περιβόλου δέ ἐστιν ἐντὸς Φιλίου Διὸς ναός, Πολυκλείτου μὲν τοῦ Ἀργείου τὸ ἄγαλμα, Διονύσῳ δὲ ἐμφερές· κόθορνοί τε γὰρ τὰ ὑποδήματά ἐστιν αὐτῷ, καὶ ἔχει τῇ χειρὶ ἔκπωμα, τῇ δὲ ἑτέρᾳ θύρσον, κάθηται δὲ ἀετὸς ἐπὶ τῷ θύρσῳ· καίτοι γε τοῖς (R. Porson cj. τοῖς γε) ἐς Διόνυσον λεγομένοις τοῦτο οὐχ ὁμολογοῦν ἐστι. τούτου δὲ ὄπισθεν τοῦ ναοῦ δένδρων ἐστὶν ἄλσος οὐ μέγα, θριγκῷ περιεχόμενον. ἐς μὲν δὴ τὸ ἐντὸς ἔσοδος οὐκ ἔστιν ἀνθρώποις· πρὸ δὲ αὐτοῦ Δήμητρος καὶ Κόρης ὅσον τε ποδῶν τριῶν εἰσιν (Siebelis cj. ἐστιν) ἀγάλματα. ἔστι δὲ ἐντὸς τοῦ περιβόλου τῶν Μεγάλων Θεῶν καὶ Ἀφροδίτης ἱερόν.

[3] Overbeck *Gr. Kunstmyth.* Zeus pp. 51 f., 228 ff., 563, *Gr. Plastik*[4] i. 533, 537.

[4] H. Brunn in the *Sitzungsber. d. kais. bayr. Akad. d. Wiss.* Phil.-hist. Classe 1880 p. 468 f.

[5] Paus. 6. 6. 2.　　　　　　　　　[6] *Supra* i. 134 f., ii. 893 n. 2.

[7] Steph. Byz. *s.v.* Μεγάλη πόλις.

[8] Eur. *Or.* 1643 ff. with schol. See N. Wedd *ad loc.* and Frazer *Pausanias* iv. 413.

to us Orestes and Pylades were revered by the Scythians as *Phílioi Daímones*[1]. Not impossibly, therefore, the Arcadian Orestes likewise was a *Phílios Daímon* worshipped after his death as Zeus *Phílios*. Orestes was the son of Agamemnon; and it is probable enough that he, like his father[2], was remembered as a human Zeus. His name *Oréstes*, whatever its origin[3], would pass muster as a title of Zeus the mountain-god[4]. In any case there was good reason for the retention of this pre-Megalopolitan cult : the appellative *Phílios* was a most desirable omen for a town which combined the inhabitants of some forty Arcadian villages[5].

(4) Zeus *Phílios* at Pergamon.

From Arkadia we pass to Pergamon. 'The Pergamenes themselves,' says Pausanias, 'claim to be Arcadians of the band which crossed into Asia with Telephos[6].' It is not, therefore, surprising to find that Pergamon too had its cult of Zeus *Phílios*. An inscribed block from the wall of the *Traianeum* speaks of that splendid structure (fig. 979)[7] as the temple of Iupiter *Amicalis* and the emperor Trajan. The inscription is probably of 113—114 A.D. and intimates that, thanks to the liberality of one Iulius Quadratus, the joint cult is to be honoured with a penteteric festival, which shall take rank with the existing Pergamene festival of Roma and Augustus[8]. The competitions thus established

---

[1] In Loukian. *Toxar.* 7 the Scythian states that his compatriots honour Orestes and Pylades on account of their mutual loyalty and devotion, adding καὶ τοὔνομα ἐπὶ τούτοις αὐτῶν ἐθέμεθα Κοράκους καλεῖσθαι· τοῦτο δέ ἐστιν ἐν τῇ ἡμετέρᾳ φωνῇ ὥσπερ ἂν εἴ τις λέγοι 'Φίλιοι Δαίμονες.' He also mentions a bronze tablet in the *Orésteion* inscribed with the tale of their sufferings, which Scythian children had to get by heart, and ancient paintings on the temple-wall illustrating the record. Possibly Κόρακοι = (Διός)κοροι.

[2] *Supra* Append. I.

[3] Recent discussion of Orestes and his myth is conveniently summarised by Gruppe *Myth. Lit.* 1908 pp. 576 ff., 620 ff.

[4] *Supra* i. 100 ff., 117 ff., ii. Append. B.

[5] Diod. 15. 72, Paus. 8. 27. 3 ff. Prof. J. B. Bury in the *Journ. Hell. Stud.* 1898 xviii. 19 says of the temples enumerated by Pausanias at Megalopolis : ' Those which he saw on the north side [of the river Helisson] suggest no federal association.' Is not this to ignore the obvious connotation of the title *Phílios* ?

[6] Paus. 1. 4. 6. See further W. Ridgeway *The Early Age of Greece* Cambridge 1901 i. 180 f. and A. C. Pearson on Soph. Μυσοί *frag.* 409 ff. Jebb.

Orestes enters into the myth of Telephos (O. Höfer in Roscher *Lex. Myth.* iii. 958— 961) and is figured on the small inner frieze of the grand altar of Zeus (H. Winnefeld in *Pergamon* iii. 2. 191 f., 219, 223, 228, Beilage 6, D, 7, 42, pl. 33, 4, Overbeck *Gr. Plastik*[4] ii. 285 fig. 201 c, C. Robert in the *Jahrb. d. kais. deutsch. arch. Inst.* 1887 ii. 245 ff. fig. D, *id. ib.* 1888 iii. 104, A. Trendelenburg in Baumeister *Denkm.* ii. 1271 f. fig. 1429, O. Höfer *loc. cit.* p. 960).

[7] *Pergamon* v. 2. 1—54 with numerous illustrations and an Atlas of plates (my fig. 979 is after pl. 34 the restored view) forms a monograph on the *Traianeum* by H. Stiller. See also E. Pontremoli and M. Collignon *Pergame, restauration et description des monuments de l'acropole* Paris 1900 pp. 153—160 with figs. and pls. 11 f.

[8] T. Mommsen in the *Corp. Inscr. Lat.* iii Suppl. no. 7086, 18 ff. = M. Fränkel *Die Inschriften von Pergamon* (= *Pergamon* viii. 2) Berlin 1895 ii. 203 ff. no. 269, 9 ff. with facsimile [placere ut certamen illud,] quod in honorem templi Iovis Amicalis et | [Imp. Caes. divi Nervae f. Ner]vae Traiani Augusti Germanici Dacici | [pontif. max. est const]itutum εἰσελαστικὸν in civitate | [Pergamenorum, eiusdem con]dicionis sit, cuius est, quod in honorem Romae | [et divi Aug. ibi agitur, it]a ut ea impendia, quae propter id certamen | [fieri oportebit, cedant in] onus Iuli Quadrati clarissimi viri | [eorumque a]d quos ea res pertinebit. The official description *ib.* 13 = 5 [ἀγὼν δεύτ]ερος παρ' ὑμεῖν ἱερὸς

are called in another inscription the Traianeia Deiphileia[1]. From the double nomenclature and from the absence of earlier foundations beneath the temple M. Fränkel justly infers that the cult of Trajan was superposed on a previously existing cult of Zeus *Phílios* (Latinised as Iupiter *Amicalis*), who formerly had

Fig. 979.

no temple but only an open-air altar[2]—presumably that detected by J. Schrammen on the highest point of the hill[3]. When it was decided to institute the cult of Trajan, who himself had some pretensions to the name of Zeus[4], the best

is borne out by Dion Cass. 51. 20 καὶ ἔλαβον καὶ οἱ Περγαμηνοὶ τὸν ἀγῶνα τὸν ἱερὸν ὠνομασμένον ἐπὶ τῇ τοῦ ναοῦ αὐτοῦ (*sc.* Αὐγούστου) τιμῇ ποιεῖν.

[1] E. L. Hicks *The Collection of Ancient Greek Inscriptions in the British Museum* iii. 2. 233 f. Oxford 1890 no. 605, 9 Τραϊάνεια Δειφίλεια ἐν Περγάμῳ ἀνδρῶν πυγμ(ήν·), where Hicks wrongly supposes that the games 'may have been endowed by one Δίφιλος (*sic*).' Δειφίλεια, as M. Fränkel *loc. cit.* saw, are the games of Ζεὺς Φίλιος.

[2] M. Fränkel *Die Inschriften von Pergamon* (=*Pergamon* viii. 2) Berlin 1895 ii. 206.

[3] *Supra* i. 120 f. fig. 89.

[4] A fragmentary inscription from Hermione speaks of Trajan as Zeus *Embatérios* (*Corp. inscr. Gr.* i no. 1213=*Inscr. Gr. Pelop.* i no. 701 ------- | [Κ]αίσαρα θεὸν θεο[ῦ] | Σεβαστὸν Γερμανικὸν | Δακικόν, Δία Ἐμβατήριον, | ἡ πόλις). L. Dindorf in Stephanus *Thes. Gr. Ling.* iii. 810 A cp. Apollon Ἐμβάσιος (O. Jessen in Pauly—Wissowa *Real-Enc.* v. 2485) and Ἐπιβατήριος (*id. ib.* vi. 28). We can contrast Apollon Ἐκβάσιος (*id. ib.* v. 2155), Artemis Ἐκβατηρία (*id. ib.* v. 2158). Such epithets denote a deity invoked by the voyager before he embarks or after he disembarks, as the case may be. The deity in question might chance to be of mortal stock: on the quay at Alexandreia was τὸ λεγόμενον Σεβάστιον, Ἐπιβατηρίον Καίσαρος νεώς (Philon *leg. ad Gai.* 22: see further O. Puchstein in Pauly—Wissowa *Real-Enc.* i. 1385, O. Jessen *ib.* vi. 28). Hesych. Ἐπιβήμιος· Ζεὺς ἐν Σίφνῳ has been wrongly added to this group of travel-titles (O. Jessen *ib.* vi. 28), or altered to Ἐπιδήμιος (R. Förster in the *Ath. Mitth.* 1894 xix. 372 f., citing a marble block at *Karadjadagh-Köi* on the *Ulutshar* in Bithynia, which is inscribed Διὶ Ἐπιδημίῳ | Κλαύδιο(ς) Σεῆρο|ς Ὀφελίων οἰκο|νόμος κ(αὶ) Ἡλιὰς | ὑπὲρ τέκνων | κ(αὶ) τῶν βοῶν | εὐχῆς χάριν | ἀνεστήσα|μεν): Zeus 'on the Step' is better explained as a god standing beside the

course seemed to be to maintain the old altar of ashes on the hill-top and to erect a new temple, which should be shared on equal terms by Zeus *Phílios* and the divinised emperor. Copper coins of Pergamon, struck by Trajan, illustrate the inscription from the *Traianeum* in two ways. On the one hand, they put

Fig. 980.　　　　　　Fig. 981.　　　　　　Fig. 982.

Trajan himself more or less on a par with Zeus *Phílios*. Thus the emperor's head occupies the obverse, the god's head the reverse, of a coin (fig. 980)[1]. Or, the emperor's head on the obverse is balanced by a seated figure of the god on the reverse (fig. 982)[2]. Or, the emperor in military costume stands beside the

orator on his platform and inspiring his utterance (cp. Welcker *Gr. Götterl.* ii. 207, Farnell *Cults of Gk. States* i. 162). *Supra* p. 897 n. 3.

The southern or townward face of Trajan's Arch at Beneventum, which like the Pergamene temple dates from the year 113—114, represents in the two panels of its attic (*a*) the Capitoline triad awaiting the arrival of Trajan : Iuno is escorted by Mercurius and Ceres, Minerva by Liber and Hercules; (*b*) Trajan approaching the *area Capitolina* : accompanied by Hadrian as emperor designate and followed by two lictors, he has reached the temple of Iupiter *Custos*, on the left of which, before the entrance-arch, are seen Roma, the Penates Publici Populi Romani, and the consuls. These two panels, separated only by the dedicatory inscription (*Corp. inscr. Lat.* ix no. 1558 = Dessau *Inscr. Lat. sel.* no. 296 imp. Caesari divi Nervae filio | Nervae Traiano Optimo Aug. | Germanico Dacico, pontif. max., trib. | potest. XVIII, imp. VII, cos. VI, p. p., | fortissimo principi, senatus p. q. R.), form a single composition—Iupiter handing his own thunderbolt to Trajan, who is thereby recognised as his vice-gerent (figs. 983, 984 are from photographs by R. Moscioni (nos. 15308, 15309)). See further E. Petersen 'L'arco di Traiano a Benevento' in the *Röm. Mitth.* 1892 vii. 239—264 with cut, especially p. 251 f., A. L. Frothingham in the *Comptes rendus de l'Acad. des inscr. et belles-lettres* 1897 p. 379 f., A. von Domaszewski 'Die politische Bedeutung des Traiansbogens in Benevent' in the *Jahresh. d. oest. arch. Inst.* 1899 ii. 173—192 with figs., especially p. 175 ff., F. Wickhoff *Roman Art* trans. Mrs. S. A. Strong London 1900 pp. 105—110 with figs., *ead. Roman Sculpture* London 1907 pp. 214—227 with pls. 63—66, especially p. 215 f., *ead. Apotheosis and the After Life* London 1915 pp. 85—87 pl. 10, Reinach *Rép. Reliefs* i. 58—66, especially p. 64 no. 1 f. For the title *Optimus* see *supra* p. 100 n. 6.

The significance of the imperial figure on the summit of Trajan's Column at Rome has been already considered (*supra* p. 100 ff.).

[1] Overbeck *Gr. Kunstmyth.* Zeus p. 228 Münztaf. 3, 23, *Brit. Mus. Cat. Coins* Mysia p. 141 pl. 28, 12, H. Stiller in *Pergamon* v. 2. 53 fig. 2, H. von Fritze in the *Abh. d. berl. Akad. 1910* Phil.-hist. Classe Anhang i. 55 pl. 4, 5. I figure a specimen from my collection : obv. ΛΥΤΤΡΛΙΛ ΝΟϹϹϹΒΛ, rev. ϹΕΥϹ ΦΙΛΙΟϹ (=obv. Αὐτοκράτωρ Τραϊανὸς Σεβαστός, rev. Ζεὺς Φίλιος).

[2] Rasche *Lex. Num.* vi. 872, *Brit. Mus. Cat. Coins* Mysia p. 141 no. 259, H. Stiller in *Pergamon* v. 2. 53 fig. 1 = my fig. 982, H. von Fritze *loc. cit.* p. 55 pl. 4, 4 : obv. ΛΥΤΤΡΛΙ ΛΝΟϹϹΕΒΛϹΤ, rev. ΦΙΛΙΟϹϹΕΥϹ ΠΕΡΓΛ (=obv. Αὐτοκράτωρ

seated god within the same temple (fig. 981)[1]. On the other hand, the coins
equate the cult of Zeus *Phílios* and Trajan with the cult of Roma and Augustus.
The obverse shows Zeus *Phílios* and Trajan in their temple, the reverse Roma

Fig. 983.

and Augustus in theirs[2]. Or, the obverse has Trajan, the reverse Augustus, as
sole occupants of their respective fanes[3].

Τραϊανὸς Σεβαστός, rev. Φίλιος Ζεὺς Περγαμηνῶν). A copper of Lucius Verus gives
the reverse type on a larger scale (*Brit. Mus. Cat. Coins* Mysia· p. 148 no. 293,
H. Fritze *loc. cit.* p. 55 pl. 4, 6) with the legend: ΕΠΙϹΤΡΑΑΤVΛ.... ΚΡΑ
ΤΙΠΠΟVΠΕΡΓΑΜΗΝΩΝΒ ΝΕΟΚΟΡ (=ἐπὶ στρατηγοῦ Ἀτυλλίου Κρατίππου,
Περγαμηνῶν βʹ νεωκόρων).

   [1] Rasche *Lex. Num.* vi. 872, *Brit. Mus. Cat. Coins* Mysia p. 142 no. 262, H. Stiller
in *Pergamon* v. 2. 53 fig. 3 = my fig. 981: rev. ΦΙΛΙΟϹ ΖΕVϹ ΤΡΑΙΑ ΝΟϹΠΕΡΓ
ΑΜΗΝΩΝ. Cp. a copper of Traianus Decius (H. von Fritze *loc. cit.* p. 55 pl. 8, 18).

   [2] Rasche *Lex. Num.* vi. 872 ff., *Brit. Mus. Cat. Coins* Mysia p. 142 pl. 28, 10,
H. Stiller in *Pergamon* v. 2. 53 fig. 5, H. von Fritze *loc. cit.* pp. 55, 83 ff. pl. 8, 12:
obv. ΦΙΛΙΟϹ ΣΕVϹ ΑVΤ ΤΡΑΙΑΝΟ ϹΕΒΠΕ[Ρ] or ΠΕΡΓΑΜΗ, rev. ΘΕΛ
ΡΩΜΗ [Κ]Λ[ΙΘ]Ε[Ω] ϹΕΒΛϹ ΤΩ.

   [3] Rasche *Lex. Num.* vi. 873, *Brit. Mus. Cat. Coins* Mysia p. 142 pl. 28, 11, *Hunter*

The cult of Zeus *Phílios* on the mountain at Pergamon was, if I am right in my conjecture[1], derived from the cult of Zeus *Phílios* the 'Mountaineer[2]' of Megalopolis. But the original connexion with *Oréstes* had long since been for-

Fig. 984.

gotten, or at best left a mere trace ot itself in the traditional link between Orestes and Telephos[3]. It was, however, remembered that Zeus *Phílios* somehow stood for the founder of the state. This may be inferred from the fact that, when

Cat. Coins ii. 282 no. 57, H. Stiller in *Pergamon* v. 2. 53 fig. 4, H. von Fritze *loc. cit.* p. 84 pl. 8, 17: obv. CT ΡΠΩΛ ΛΙΩΝΟϹ ΤΡΑΙΑ ΝΟ Ϲ or CΤΡΠΩΛΛΙ ΩΝΟϹΤΡΑΙΑ ΝΟϹΕΠΙ, rev. ΑVΓ Ο V ϹΤΟϹ ΠΕΡΓΑ (=obv. ἐπὶ στρατηγοῦ Πωλλίωνος· Τραϊανός, rev. Αὔγουστος· Περγαμηνῶν).

[1] *Supra* p. 1179.
[2] *Supra* p. 1178 f.
[3] *Supra* p. 1179 n. 6. Note that Τήλεφος, a clipped form of Τηλεφάνης (F. Bechtel— A. Fick *Die Griechischen Personennamen*[2] Göttingen 1894 p. 374) was, like 'Ορέστης (*supra* p. 1179), a name which would fitly describe a mountain-god (cp. *Od.* 24. 83, Aristoph. *nub.* 281, Menand. Λευκαδία *frag.* 1, 4 (*Frag. com. Gr.* iv. 158 f. Meineke) *ap.* Strab. 452, and the like).

the Pergamenes invented an eponymous hero Pergamos[1], they portrayed him (fig. 985)[2] with the features of Zeus *Phílios*.

Whether Zeus *Phílios* at Pergamon was in any sense Dionysiac, we can hardly determine. A *phiále* in his hand (figs. 981, 982) is no proof. Nor can we lay stress on the curious association of Telephos with the vine[3]. The most we

Fig. 985.　　　　　　　　　　　　Fig. 986.

can say is that a buskined Zeus of the Arcadian type[4] would not be out of place in a town which recognised Zeus *Sabázios*[5] and Zeus *Bákchos*[6].

Popular enthusiasm, or policy, having thus raised the emperor to the level of Zeus *Phílios*, went a step further and identified the two. An alliance-coin of Thyateira and Pergamon (fig. 986)[7] surrounds the laureate bust of Trajan with

---

[1] H. von Fritze *loc. cit.* p. 69 n. 1 points out that Pergamos is first mentioned as founder of the state in two mutually complementary inscriptions of *c.* 50 B.C. published together by H. Hepding in the *Ath. Mitth.* 1909 xxxiv. 329 ff.: ὁ δῆμος ἐτίμησεν | Μιθρα-δάτην Μηνοδότου τὸν διὰ γένους ἀρχιερέ[α] | καὶ ἱερέα τοῦ Καθηγεμόνος Διονύσου διὰ γένο[υς,] | ἀπο[κα]ραστήσαντα τοῖς πατρώιοις θεοῖς τ[ήν τε πόλιν] | καὶ [τὴν] χώραν καὶ γενόμενον τῆς πατρίδος μ[ετὰ Πέργαμον] | καὶ Φιλέταιρον νέον κτίστην and ὁ δῆμος ἐτίμησεν | [Μιθραδάτη]ν Μηνοδότου τὸν διὰ γέν[ους ἀρχιερέα | καὶ ἱερέα τοῦ Κα]θηγεμόνος Διονύσου, ἀποκα[ταστήσαντα | τοῖς πατ]ρῴοις θεοῖς τήν τε πόλιν καὶ τὴν χώρα[ν καὶ γενόμενον | τῆς πατ]ρίδος μ[ε]τ[ὰ Π]έργαμο[ν καὶ Φ]ιλέταιρον νέον κτ[ίστην]. On the hero Pergamos and his cult see further O. Höfer in Roscher *Lex. Myth.* iii. 1958 f.

[2] *Brit. Mus. Cat. Coins* Mysia p. 136 pl. 28, 1, H. von Fritze *loc. cit.* p. 67 pl. 3, 14 and 19=my fig. 985, Head *Hist. num.*[2] p. 536: *quasi*-autonomous coppers inscribed ΠΕΡΓΑΜΟΣ and ΠΕΡΓΑΜΟΣ ΚΤΙΣ ΤΗΣ.

[3] When the Greeks sailed against Troy, they lost their way and attacked Mysia by mistake. Telephos, king of the Mysians, went out against the invaders and slew many of them, but fled before Achilles and, tripping over a vine, was wounded in the thigh by that hero's spear (Apollod. *epit.* 3. 17). This occurred because Dionysos was angry with Telephos for depriving him of his due honours (schol. *Il.* 1. 59 f., cp. Eustath. *in Il.* p. 46, 35 ff. (Telephos' horse stumbles over a vine by the design of Dionysos), Tzetz. *in Lyk. Al.* 211 (Dionysos repays Achilles' sacrifices by causing to spring up a vine-shoot, which entangles Telephos), Dictys Cretensis 2. 3 (Telephus, pursued by Ulysses among the vine-yards, trips over a vine-stem and is speared by Achilles in the left thigh)). The story is given without detail by Pind. *Isthm.* 8. 109 f. ὃ καὶ Μύσιον ἀμπελόεν | αἵμαξε Τηλέφου μέλανι ῥαίνων φόνῳ πεδίον. On the golden vine presented to Telephos' wife Astyoche by Priamos see *supra* p. 281 n. 4.

[4] *Supra* p. 1178.　　　　　　[5] *Supra* p. 287 n. 2.

[6] *Supra* pp. 287 n. 2, 954 n. o.

[7] *Brit. Mus. Cat. Coins* Lydia p. 320 pl. 41, 5 (my fig. 986 is from a cast of the coin), H. von Fritze *loc. cit.* p. 100: ΑΥΝΕΡΤΡΑΙΑΝΟ Ν[CΕ]ΓΕΡ ΔΑΚΙ-ΦΙΛΙΟΝ ΔΙΑ (=αὐτοκράτορα Νέρουαν Τραϊανὸν Σεβαστὸν Γερμανικὸν Δακικὸν Φίλιον Δία).

the cunningly-worded legend : 'The emperor Nerva Traianus [Augustus] Germanicus Dacicus Zeus *Philios*.' The mind of the reader passes upward from names of human import through titles recording hard blows struck and magnificent triumphs won to the final claim of supreme beneficent godhead. Moreover, the whole is thrown into the accusative case with a subtle suggestion of some verb denoting honour, if not worship[1]. Adulation of the man has reached its limit. And, after all, a god who starts as a buried king ends not unfittingly as a divinised emperor.

Pergamon, in common with other cities of Asia Minor, frankly regarded the reigning sovereign as lord of heaven and earth, and did not hesitate to portray him in this capacity as a cosmic Zeus. A wonderful copper piece from the Pergamene mint (fig. 987)[2] exhibits Commodus in the form of a youthful Zeus with short hair and slight beard, naked and erect, a thunderbolt in his right hand, a sceptre in his left. He has an eagle with spread wings at his feet, and is flanked by two recumbent figures— Gaia on the right with a turreted crown and a *cornu copiae*, Thalassa on the left with a head-dress of crab's-claws and a steering paddle. In the field are busts of Helios and Selene. A unique coin, struck at Pergamon and now in the cabinet of T. Prowe at Moscow (fig. 988)[3], repeats the theme with variations.

Fig. 987.

Thalassa and Gaia stand side by side, the former with bare breast, crab's-claws on her head, and a steering paddle in her uplifted hand, the latter with covered

Fig. 988.

Fig. 989.

[1] G. F. Hill *A Handbook of Greek and Roman Coins* London 1899 p. 186, G. Macdonald *Coin Types* Glasgow 1905 pp. 161, 170, H. von Fritze *loc. cit.* p. 78 ff.

[2] *Brit. Mus. Cat. Coins* Mysia p. 151 pl. 30, 4 = my fig. 987: rev. [ΕΠΙ]CΤΡΜΑΙΓ Λ. ΥΚΩΝΙΑΝ[ΟΥ] ΠΕΡΓΑΜΗΝΩ ΝΝΕΟΚΟΡΩ Ν·Β (= ἐπὶ στρατηγοῦ Μ. Αἰλίου Γλυκωνιανοῦ, Περγαμηνῶν νεωκόρων β'). H. von Fritze *loc. cit.* p. 56 f. pl. 4, 7 publishes another specimen from the Gotha collection.

[3] H. von Fritze *loc. cit.* p. 56 f. pl. 4, 11: rev. ΕΠΙCΤΡ ΜΗΝΟ Γ ΕΝΟΥC Β ΝΕΩ[ΚΟ] ΡΩΝ ΠΕΡΓΑΜΗΝ ΩΝ (= ἐπὶ στρατηγοῦ Μηνογένους, β' νεωκόρων Περγαμηνῶν).

breast, wheat-ears on her head, and a *cornu copiae* on her arm. Both join hands to support a nude, youthful Zeus with the features of Geta, who holds a sceptre in his left hand and brandishes a thunderbolt in his right. Below him is his eagle with spread wings, grasping a wreath in his talons. Further variations are found on another unique copper, struck by Caracalla at Laodikeia in Phrygia and now in our national collection (fig. 989)[1]. Gaia and Thalassa have changed places: behind the one corn-ears spring from the ground; behind the other a dolphin plunges into the sea. On their joined hands, instead of Zeus, stands Caracalla with a radiate crown on his head holding *phiále* and sceptre, while beneath him hovers his eagle bearing a wreath.

(5) Zeus *Phílios* at Antiocheia.

Lastly, we turn to Antiocheia on the Orontes, where the worship of Zeus *Phílios* was established by Theoteknos, governor of the city under Maximinus ii and an apostate from the Christian faith[2]. Eusebios in his *Ecclesiastical History*[3] pens an ugly portrait of this persecutor[4]:

'The root of all the mischief grew in Antiocheia itself[5]—Theoteknos, a horror, a humbug, and a villain, whose character belied his name; he was supposed to keep the town in order. He set all his forces against us. He threw himself with zest into the task of hunting our people out of their holes and corners in every possible way, as though they had been a gang of thieves and malefactors. He went all lengths in slandering and accusing us. And, after causing tens of thousands to be put to death, he finally set up an idol of Zeus *Phílios* with a deal of quackery and imposture. He invented foul rites for it, initiations of an irreligious sort, and abominable modes of purification. He even exhibited before the emperor the portentous signs by means of which it was supposed to produce oracles[6].'

Theoteknos may well have augured a great success for his new cult, partly on general and partly on special grounds.

On the one hand, the Antiochenes had always been devoted to the worship of Zeus. Long before their city was built, Triptolemos—so they said—had founded Ione on the slope of Mount Silpion and had constructed there a sanctuary of Zeus *Némeios*, later renamed Zeus *Epikárpios*[7]. Subsequently Perseus

---

[1] *Brit. Mus. Cat. Coins* Phrygia p. 316 pl. 37, 12 (= my fig. 989), H. von Fritze *loc. cit.* p. 57: rev. ·ΕΠΙ·Π·ΑΙΛ ΠΙΓΡΗ ΤΟϹ ΑϹΙΑΡΓ ΛΑΟΔΙΚΕΩΝΝ ΕΩΚΟΡΩΝ· (=ἐπὶ Π. Αἰλίου Πίγρητος Ἀσιάρχου γʹ, Λαοδικέων νεωⁿ ʹρων).

[2] G. T. Stokes in Smith—Wace *Dict. Chr. Biogr.* iv. 1011.

[3] Euseb. *hist. eccl.* 9. 2 f.

[4] In 304 A.D. he did to death S. Theodotos and the Seven Virgins of Ankyra (*Acta Sanctorum* edd. Bolland. Maii iv. 147—165, T. Ruinart *Acta primorum martyrum sincera & selecta*[2] Amstelaedami 1713 pp. 336—352, A. Gallandius. *Bibliotheca veterum patrum antiquorumque scriptorum ecclesiasticorum* Venetiis 1768 iv. 114—130).

[5] We have here a buried hexameter: ὧν πάντων ἀρχηγὸς ἐπʹ αὐτῆς Ἀντιοχείας.

[6] Euseb. *hist. eccl.* 9. 3 τελευτῶν εἴδωλόν τι Διὸς Φιλίου μαγγανείαις τισὶ καὶ γοητείαις ἱδρύεται, τελετάς τε ἀνάγνους αὐτῷ καὶ μνήσεις ἀκαλλιερήτους ἐξαγίστους τε καθαρμοὺς ἐπινοήσας, μέχρι καὶ βασιλέως τὴν τερατείαν διʹ ὧν ἐδόκει χρησμῶν (*leg.* χρησμοὺς) ἐκτελεῖν ἐπεδείκνυτο. Cp. the loose translation of Rufin. *hist. eccl.* 9. 3 apud Antiochiam simulacrum quoddam Iovis Amicalis nuper consecratum artibus quibusdam magicis et impuris consecrationibus ita compositum erat, ut falleret oculos intuentium et portenta quaedam ostentare videretur ac responsa proferre. C. F. Crusé renders τελετάς τε ἀνάγνους κ.τ.λ. 'after reciting forms of initiation' etc., clearly taking ἀνάγνους to be ἀναγνούς—an ingenious error.

[7] Liban. *or.* 11. 51 (i. 2. 453, 1 ff. Foerster), *supra* i. 236 n. 10. Cp. *Chron. Paschale*

visited Ione and, when a storm burst so that the river Orontes, then called Drakon, overflowed its banks, bade the inhabitants pray for deliverance. Thereupon a ball of lightning fell from the sky and stopped at once the downpour and the flood. Perseus kindled a fire from the blaze, took it to his own palace in Persia, and taught the Persians to reverence it as divine. He also established for the men of Ione a sanctuary of Immortal Fire[1]. In the Hellenistic age this sanctuary on Mount Silpion was known as that of Zeus *Keraúnios*[2]. Again, the foundation of Antiocheia itself was directly associated with the cult of Zeus. Libanios in his panegyric of the town says[3]:

'The settlement began with Zeus *Bottiaîos*[4], erected by Alexander, and the hill called Emathia after Alexander's home.'

i. 76 Dindorf ἔκτισαν οὖν ἐκεῖ οἱ αὐτοὶ ᾿Ιωνῖται ἱερὸν Κρονίωνος (but see *supra* i. 237 n. 1) εἰς τὸ Σίλπιον ὄρος and perhaps Liban. *legat. ad Iulian.* 79 (ii. 152, 10 ff. Foerster) cited *supra* p. 869 n. 1.

Zeus *Νέμειος* appears on a billon coin of Alexandreia with *sélinon* (?)-wreath, *aigís*, and star (*Brit. Mus. Cat. Coins* Alexandria p. 17 no. 130 pl. 1 (=my fig. 990), Head *Hist. num.*[2] p. 862, Overbeck *Gr. Kunstmyth.* Zeus pp. 218, 248, O. Höfer in Roscher *Lex. Myth.* iii. 116). These coins were struck by Nero in 67—68 A.D. to commemorate his triumphant tour through Greece in 67 A.D. (Eckhel *Doctr. num. vet.*[2] iv. 53).

Fig. 990.

As to the title ᾿Επικάρπιος, my friend Mr G. F. Hill in the *Journ. Hell. Stud.* 1915 xxxv. 150 kindly draws my attention to Methodios *ap. et. mag.* p. 58, 20 ff. ᾿Αλδήμιος ἤ ῎Αλδος, ὁ Ζεύς, ὃς (codd. D. Vb. omit ὃς) ἐν Γάξῃ τῆς Συρίας τιμᾶται· παρὰ τὸ ἀλδαίνω, τὸ αὐξάνω· ὁ ἐπὶ τῆς αὐξήσεως τῶν καρπῶν. Μεθόδιος (οὕτως Μεθόδιος cod. Vb.). Cp. S. Bochart *Geographia sacra, seu Phaleg et Canaan*[4] Lugduni Batavorum 1707 lib. ii cap. 14 p. 748 'Ego Jovem illum Phœnices linguâ suâ vocasse puto בעל חלדא *baal-halda* dominum sæculi, vel בעלחלדים *baal-aldim* dominum sæculorum'—a most ingenious explanation of the alternatives ῎Αλδος and ᾿Αλδήμιος.

[1] Pausanias the chronographer (cp. Io. Tzetz. *schol. in exeges. Iliad.* in L. Bachmann *Scholia in Homeri Iliadem* Lipsiae 1835 p. 833, 28 f. Παυσανίας δὲ ὁ ἱστορικὸς ἐν τῷ περὶ ᾿Αντιοχείας κτίσεως γράφει πλατύτερον. κ.τ.λ.) *ap.* Io. Malal. *chron.* 2 p. 37 f. Dindorf= *Chron. Paschale* i. 72 f. Dindorf ὁ δὲ αὐτὸς Περσεὺς ἔκτισε τοῖς ᾿Ιωνίταις ἱερόν, ὃ ἐπωνόμασε πυρὸς ἀθανάτου.

[2] Io. Malal. *chron.* 8 p. 199 Dindorf says of Seleukos i Nikator after the foundation of Seleukeia καὶ εὐχαριστῶν ἀνῆλθεν εἰς ᾿Ιώπολιν καὶ μετὰ τρεῖς ἡμέρας ἐπετέλεσεν ἑορτὴν ἐκεῖ τῷ Κεραυνίῳ Διὶ ἐν τῷ ἱερῷ τῷ κτισθέντι ὑπὸ Περσέως τοῦ υἱοῦ Πίκου καὶ Δανάης, τῷ ὄντι εἰς τὸ Σίλπιον ὄρος, ἔνθα κεῖται ἡ ᾿Ιώπολις, ποιήσας τὴν θυσίαν τῇ πρώτῃ τοῦ ᾿Αρτεμισίου μηνός.

[3] Liban. *or.* 11. 76 (i. 2. 461, 18 ff. Foerster).

[4] With Zeus *Βοττιαῖος* cp. Zeus *Βώττιος* of Βωττία, a village on the Orontes (Io. Malal. *chron.* 8 p. 200 Dindorf cited *infra* p. 1188), which doubtless claimed connexion with Βοττία, Βοττιαία, Βοττιαιίς, the district round Pella in Makedonia (E. Oberhummer in Pauly—Wissowa *Real-Enc.* iii. 794 f.). Since the Bottiaeans of Makedonia were said to have been brought by one Botton from Crete (Aristot. *frag.* 443 Rose *ap.* Plout. *v. Thes.* 16 and *quaestt. Gr.* 35, Strab. 279, 282, 329 *frag.* 11, Konon *narr.* 25, *et. mag.* p. 206, 1 ff.), it is possible that Zeus *Βοττιαῖος* was ultimately of Cretan origin. The story of the clay loaves etc. told by Konon *loc. cit.* probably has some basis in Bottiaean ritual. Coppers struck at Pella, under Philippos v and later (Head *Hist. num.*[2] p. 243), with the monogram ₿ (for Βοττεατῶν) have obv. head of Zeus wreathed with bay (*Brit. Mus. Cat. Coins* Macedonia, etc. p. 13, *Hunter Cat. Coins* i. 352) or oak (*Brit. Mus. Cat. Coins* Macedonia, etc. p. 13 fig., *Hunter Cat. Coins* i. 352 (?)), rev. winged thunderbolt.

Further on he adds[1]:

'The whole thing was ordained of God. Forty furlongs from this city of ours there was a city bearing the name of Antigonos and built by Antigonos. Here Seleukos was sacrificing after his victory[2]. The bull had been slaughtered, the altars had received their customary portion, the fire was already licking up the sacrifice and burning fiercely, when, lo, Zeus moved from his sceptre[3] his own companion and favourite bird and despatched him to the altar. He flew down into the midst of the flame, caught up the thigh-pieces all ablaze, and bore them off[4]. As the event attracted the looks and thoughts of all and was manifestly due to divine interposition, Seleukos bade his son[5] mount a horse, pursue the flight from the ground, and guide his horse by the bridle according to the route taken by the bird; for he wished to know what it would do with its booty. Seleukos' son riding his horse, with upturned eyes, was led by the flight to Emathia. There the eagle stooped and deposited his burden on the altar of Zeus *Bottiaîos*, erected by Alexander when he was cheered by the sight of the spring[6]. So all men, even without special powers of interpretation, could see that Zeus meant them to build a city on the spot. And thus it came about that the settlement intended and commenced by Alexander was carried to completion, while the chief of the gods[7] by means of his own omen became our founder.'

Similar tales were current with regard to Alexander's foundation of Alexandreia[8] and Seleukos' foundation of Seleukeia Pieria[9]. Ioannes Malalas, of whose sixth-century chronicle a Greek abridgment (not to mention the fuller Slavonic version[10]) is extant, gives the Antiochene story[11], adding a touch or two of his own to heighten the interest. Thus, instead of connecting Zeus *Bottiaîos* with the hill Emathia, he harrows our feelings by the assertion that at Bottia, a village over against Iopolis, Seleukos, when founding Antiocheia, sacrificed a maiden named Aimathe (*sic*) by the hand of the chief priest and initiator Amphion, between the city and the river, on Artemisios, *i.e.* May, 22, at daybreak, as the sun rose—a most circumstantial narrative. He goes on to say that Seleukos founded also the sanctuary of Zeus *Bóttios*[12]. Again, Antiochos iv Epiphanes built for the Antiochenes, presumably on Mount Silpion, a magnificent temple of Iupiter *Capitolinus*, of which we are told, not only that its roof had gilded coffers, but that its walls were overlaid with beaten gold[13]. Tiberius either completed or restored the structure[14]. Antiochos Epiphanes also erected in the temple, which he had built, or more probably beautified, for Apollon at Daphne, a copy of the Olympian Zeus, said to have been as large as the original[15]. This statue was perhaps in-

[1] Liban. *or*. 11. 85—88 (i. 2. 464, 10 ff. Foerster).
[2] Seleukos i Nikator, after vanquishing Antigonos in Phrygia (301 B.C.).
[3] *Supra* p. 1132 ff.   [4] *Infra* fig. 1001.   [5] Antiochos i Soter.
[6] See Io. Malal. *chron*. 10 p. 234 Dindorf.
[7] (ὁ Ζεὺς) ὁ τῶν θεῶν κορυφαῖος.
[8] Iul. Valer. 1. 30 p. 39, 9 ff. Kuebler, pseudo-Kallisth. 1. 32 (context *supra* p. 1127 n. o).
[9] *Supra* p. 981 n. 1.
[10] Prof. J. B. Bury informs me that such a version exists, but is not yet published in accessible shape. On Malalas see further K. Krumbacher *Geschichte der byzantinischen Litteratur von Justinian bis zum Ende des Oströmischen Reiches*[2] München 1897 p. 325 ff., Sir J. E. Sandys *A History of Classical Scholarship*[2] Cambridge 1906 i. 390 f.
[11] Io. Malal. *chron*. 8 p. 199 ff. Dindorf.
[12] *Id. ib*. 8 p. 200 Dindorf.
[13] Liv. 41. 20. Cp. Gran. Licin. 28 p. 6, 5 f. Flemisch duos colossos duodenum cubitorum ex *aere* unum Olympio, alterum Capitolino Iovi de*dicaverat*.
[14] Io. Malal. *chron*. 10 p. 234 Dindorf ὁ δὲ Τιβέριος Καῖσαρ ἔκτισεν ἐν τῇ αὐτῇ ᾿Αντιοχείᾳ πόλει ἱερὸν μέγα Διὸς Καπετωλίου. The word ἔκτισεν must not be pressed.
[15] Amm. Marc. 22. 13. 1 eodem tempore die xi Kalend. Novembrium amplissimum

tended to represent Antiochos himself[1]; for it seems to have been part of that ruler's policy always to foster the cult, and on occasion to assume the *rôle*, of Zeus[2]. Thus he struck handsome silver pieces showing on the obverse side an

Fig. 991.

idealised portrait-head of himself, sometimes with twin stars at the ends of his diadem[3], and on the reverse Zeus enthroned with a Nike in his hand. The Nike extends a wreath towards the god. And the accompanying legend reads 'Of King Antiochos, the God Made Manifest' (fig. 991)[4], or 'Of King Antiochos, the God Made Manifest, Bearer of Victory' (fig. 992)[5]. Another imposing type has on the obverse the head of the monarch, wreathed with wild-olive and bearded as if he were indeed Zeus *Olýmpios*, on the reverse Zeus enthroned with Nike in the act of crowning him (fig. 993)[6] or his pompous inscription (fig. 994)[7]. It is very possible that this coin commemorates the erection of the Olympian Zeus at Daphne. Be that as it may, the

Fig. 992.

statue was probably made of gold and ivory, like its original at Olympia.

Daphnaei Apollinis fanum, quod Epiphanes Antiochus rex ille condidit iracundus et saevus, et simulacrum in eo Olympiaci Iovis imitamenti aequiparans magnitudinem, subita vi flammarum exustum est. But Liban. *or.* 11. 94 ff. (i. 2. 467, 1 ff. Foerster) and Sozom. *hist. eccl.* 5. 19 agree that the sanctuary of Apollon Δαφναῖος was the work of Seleukos i Nikator. Presumably Antiochos Epiphanes added to its attractions. Overbeck *Gr. Kunstmyth.* Zeus p. 58 by an odd blunder takes Ammianus to mean that Antiochos dedicated at Daphne a statue of Apollon in the guise of Olympian Zeus!

[1] We may fairly suspect that the same intention prompted Antiochos' sacrilegious treatment of the temples at Jerusalem and on Mt Gerizim (*supra* i. 233, ii. 887 n. 0 no. (31)).

[2] See E. R. Bevan 'A note on Antiochos Epiphanes' in the *Journ. Hell. Stud.* 1900 xx. 26—30, *id. The House of Seleucus* London 1902 ii. 154 ff., G. F. Hill *Historical Greek Coins* London 1906 p. 144.

[3] Tetradrachms with rev. ΒΑΣΙΛΕΩΣ ΑΝΤΙΟΧΟΥ or ΑΝ ΤΙΟΧΟΥ Apollon seated on the *omphalós* have obv. head of Antiochos with diadem surmounted by a star (*Brit. Mus. Cat. Coins* Seleucid Kings of Syria p. 34 pl. 11, 1) or with diadem ending in two eight-rayed stars (*Hunter Cat. Coins* iii. 41 pl. 66, 9). They bear witness to the early deification of the king.

[4] *Brit. Mus. Cat. Coins* Seleucid Kings of Syria p. 35 pl. 11, 8, *Hunter Cat. Coins* iii. 44 pl. 66, 13, Head *Hist. num.*[2] p. 762. I figure a specimen from my collection.

[5] *Brit. Mus. Cat. Coins* Seleucid Kings of Syria p. 35 pl. 11, 7 = my fig. 992, *Hunter Cat. Coins* iii. 47 f. pl. 66, 17 (cp. 18), Head *Hist. num.*[2] p. 762, *Bunbury Sale Catalogue* 1896 ii. 65 no. 494.

[6] E. Babelon *Les rois de Syrie* Paris 1890 pp. xciv f., 71 pl. 12, 11 (= my fig. 993).

[7] *Brit. Mus. Cat. Coins* Seleucid Kings of Syria p. 36 pl. 11, 9 = my fig. 994, *Hunter*

Alexander ii Zabinas, when beaten by Antiochos viii Grypos in 123—122 B.C., retired to Antiocheia and, in order to pay his troops, bade men enter the temple of Zeus and remove from the god's hand the Nike of solid gold, remarking that

Fig. 993.

Fig. 994.

Zeus had lent him victory![1] A unique *statér* of gold, formerly in the Montagu collection (fig. 995)[2], was doubtless struck by Zabinas from this stolen Nike[3]. A few days later he attempted to carry off the whole statue of Zeus with its vast weight of gold, but was caught in the act and forced by popular outcry to flee from the city[4].

Fig. 995.

The statue, however, did not escape for long the cupidity of the Syrian kings Antiochus ix Kyzikenos, son of Antiochos vii Sidetes, being in need of money, gave orders that the golden Zeus, fifteen cubits high, should be melted down and replaced by a copy in inferior material with gilded sheathing[5]. It was presumably in connexion with the cult of Zeus *Olýmpios* that Antiochos Epiphanes held games

Cat. Coins iii. 48 no. 50, E. Babelon *Les rois de Syrie* Paris 1890 p. xciv f., Head *Hist. num.*[2] p. 762 f. The head is usually described as laureate.

[1] Iust. 39. 2. 5.

[2] *Montagu Sale Catalogue* 1896 i. 92 no. 716 pl. 9=my fig. 995.

[3] E. Babelon *Les rois de Syrie* Paris 1890 p. cxlix f.

[4] Iust. 39. 2. 6, Diod. *excerpta de virt. et vit.* 35 p. 145, 42 ff. Dindorf.

[5] Clem. Al. *protr.* 4. 52. 3 p. 40, 22 ff. Stählin ʾΑντίοχος δὲ ὁ Κυζικηνὸς ἀπορούμενος χρημάτων τοῦ Διὸς τὸ ἄγαλμα τὸ χρυσοῦν, πεντεκαίδεκα πηχῶν τὸ μέγεθος ὄν, προσέταξε χωνεῦσαι καὶ (J. Markland cj. κἀκ) τῆς ἄλλης τῆς ἀτιμοτέρας ὕλης ἄγαλμα παραπλήσιον ἐκείνῳ πετάλοις κεχρυσωμένον ἀναθεῖναι πάλιν. Cp. Arnob. *adv. nat.* 6. 21 Antiochum Cyzicenum ferunt decem (F. Orsini cj. *quindecim*) cubitorum Iovem ex delubro aureum sustulisse et ex aere bracteolis substituisse fucatum.

of unusual significance at Daphne[1], not to mention the high jinks[2] which earned him the *sobriquet* of *Epimanés*. Antiochos Grypos followed suit[3]. And in later times the Olympic contests of Daphne obtained a wide celebrity[4]. Diocletian is said to have built a sanctuary of Zeus *Olýmpios* in the *Stádion* at Daphne—a statement of uncertain value[5]. Meantime in Antiocheia itself Commodus had built a temple of Zeus *Olýmpios* with an adjoining portico known as the *Xystón*[6]. Didius Iulianus had added a *Pléthron*[7], which was later doubled in size by Argyrios and Phasganios[8], and still further enlarged by Proklos[9]. The whole complex of buildings was evidently modelled on its counterpart at Elis and was meant to accommodate athletes preparing for the Olympia, which were actually held at Daphne. At Daphne too there was a temple of Zeus *Sotér*, built to commemorate a crisis in the history of the city. For at dawn on Apellaios, *i.e.* December, 13 in the year 115 Antiocheia was shaken by a great earthquake with most disastrous results. The survivors founded this temple and inscribed upon it the words:

'The saved set up (this edifice) for Zeus the Saviour[10].'

The earthquake was preceded by many thunderbolts and unusual winds[11]; and so severe was it that the tops of Mount Kasion were broken off and threatened destruction to the town below[12]. Finally, there was the ancient cult of Zeus

---

[1] Polyb. 31 *ap.* Athen. 194 C—195 F and 439 B—D.

[2] *E.g.* Polyb. 31 *ap.* Athen. 195 F (=439 D) ὑπὸ τῶν μίμων ὁ βασιλεὺς εἰσεφέρετο ὅλος κεκαλυμμένος καὶ εἰς τὴν γῆν ἐτίθετο, ὡς εἷς ὢν δῆτα τῶν μίμων· καὶ τῆς συμφωνίας προκαλουμένης ἀναπηδήσας ὠρχεῖτο καὶ ὑπεκρίνετο μετὰ τῶν γελωτοποιῶν. Was this sheer foolery, or the take-off of some resurrection-rite?

[3] Poseidonios of Apameia 28 *frag.* 31 (*Frag. hist. Gr.* iii. 263 Müller) *ap.* Athen. 210 D—E and 540 A—B.

[4] Liban. *or.* 60. 6 f. (iv. 315, 5 ff. Foerster)=Io. Chrys. *de Babyla c. Iul.* 19 (ii. 568 A Montfaucon), Liban. *epist.* 763 Wolf, Io. Malal. *chron.* 9 p. 224 f. Dindorf (see P. Perdrizet in the *Bull. Corr. Hell.* 1900 xxiv. 290 f.), 12 pp. 289 f., 307 Dindorf, 16 p. 396 Dindorf. Cp. Liban. *or.* 10. 30 (i. 2. 409, 15 ff. Foerster).

[5] Io. Malal. *chron.* 12 p. 307 Dindorf ἔκτισε δὲ ἐν αὐτῷ τῷ σταδίῳ Δάφνης ἱερὸν Ὀλυμπίου Διός, καὶ ἐν τῇ σφενδόνῃ τοῦ αὐτοῦ σταδίου ἔκτισεν ἱερὸν τῇ Νεμέσει. C. O. Müller *Antiquitates Antiochenae* Gottingae 1839 p. 62 f. thinks it far more likely that the temple of Zeus Ὀλύμπιος at Daphne was founded by Antiochos Epiphanes. Overbeck *Gr. Kunstmyth.* Zeus p. 59 dismisses the claims of Diocletian ('wohl ohne allen Zweifel verkehrt') and attributes to Antiochos Epiphanes merely a redecoration of the temple ('nur eine neue Ausschmückung des Zeusheiligthums von Daphne, nicht dessen Gründung'). But is it certain that Malalas is referring to the big temple of Zeus? A small shrine in the *Stádion* would be appropriate enough.

[6] Io. Malal. *chron.* 12 p. 283 Dindorf καὶ εἰς τὴν ἀρχὴν δὲ τὴν κάτω τοῦ Ξυστοῦ ἔκτισεν ἱερὸν τῷ Ὀλυμπίῳ Διί.

[7] Io. Malal. *chron.* 12 p. 290 Dindorf Πλεθρίν.

[8] Liban. *or.* 10. 9 ff. (i. 2. 403, 22 ff. Foerster).

[9] Liban. *or.* 10. 1 ff. (i. 2. 401, 2 ff. Foerster).

[10] Io. Malal. *chron.* 11 p. 275 Dindorf οἱ σωθέντες ἀνέστησαν Διὶ Σωτῆρι. Eustath. *in* Dionys. *per.* 916 quotes the dedication as οἱ ζήσαντες (ζητήσαντες cod. *y*.) ἀνέστησαν θεῷ (ἐν θεῷ cod. *y*. H. S. Reiner cj. ἀνεστήσαμεν) Σωτῆρι, which amounts to much the same thing.

[11] Dion. Cass. 68. 24.

[12] Dion. Cass. 68. 25. See further Iuv. 6. 411, Aur. Vict. *de Caes.* 13. 10, cp. *epit.* 13. 12, Oros. *hist. adv. pag.* 7. 12. 5, Euagrios *hist. eccl.* 2. 12, Synkell. *chron.* 348 A (i. 657 Dindorf), Euseb. *vers. Armen. in ann. Abr.* 2130 (= 116 A.D.), Hieron. *in* Euseb. *ann. Abr.* 2130 (= 116 A.D.), Zonar. 11. 22 (iii. 68 f. Dindorf).

Kásios on Mount Kasion, where Julian offered a belated hecatomb[1]. The devotion of the Antiochenes to Zeus—a devotion grafted perhaps upon the *Baʻal*-worship of their predecessors—might further be inferred from their coin-types. Antiochos iv Epiphanes (175—164 B.C.) inaugurated a system of municipal coinage and struck coppers at 'Antiocheia near Daphne,' which had as reverse design Zeus wrapped in a *himátion* with a wreath in his outstretched hand (fig. 996)[2]—sign and symbol of the Olympic sports that he held at Daphne[3]. Alexandros i Bala (150—145 B.C.), who claimed to be the son of Antiochos iv, repeated his father's type of a wreath-bearing Zeus[4]. Other Seleucid kings in all probability issued coins with Zeus-types at Antiocheia, *e.g.* Demetrios ii

Fig. 996.   Fig. 997.

Nikator in his first reign (146—140 B.C.)[5] and Antiochos viii Grypos (121—96 B.C.)[6] Passing from the regal to the autonomous coinage of the town, we have coins struck for the *tetrápolis*[7] of Antiocheia by Daphne, Seleukeia in Pieria, Apameia, and Laodikeia (149—147 B.C.) with a head of Zeus as obverse and a thunderbolt as reverse type[8], or with two Zeus-like heads—probably meant for the Demoi of Antiocheia and Seleukeia—as obverse and Zeus enthroned, Nike in one hand, a sceptre in the other, as reverse type (fig. 997)[9]. The autonomous issues of 'the metropolis of the Antiochenes' (s. i B.C.) show the head of Zeus wearing bays and Zeus enthroned as before but enclosed in a

[1] *Supra* p. 981 n. 1.

[2] *Brit. Mus. Cat. Coins* Seleucid Kings of Syria p. 40 pl. 13, 1, *Hunter Cat. Coins* iii. 50 f. pl. 66, 20, E. Babelon *Les rois de Syrie* Paris 1890 p. 79 pl. 14, 6 (=my fig. 996), Head *Hist. num.*[2] p. 763.

[3] *Supra* p. 1188 ff.

[4] *Brit. Mus. Cat. Coins* Seleucid Kings of Syria p. 56 pl. 17, 1, *Hunter Cat. Coins* iii. 66 no. 65 f., Head *Hist. num.*[2] p. 765 f.

[5] *Brit. Mus. Cat. Coins* Seleucid Kings of Syria p. 61 no. 29 obv. head of Zeus to right, laureate; rev. ΒΑΣΙΛΕΩΣ ΔΗΜΗΤΡΙΟΥ ΘΕΟΥ ΦΙΛΑΔΕΛΦΟΥ ΝΙΚΑΤΟΡΟΣ, with Μ Ν in exergue, Apollon seated on the *omphalós*, holding arrow and bow.

[6] *Hunter Cat. Coins* iii. 100 pl. 69, 20 obv. Head of Antiochos viii to right, diademed; rev. ΒΑΣΙΛΕΩΣ ΑΝΤΙΟΧΟΥ ΕΠΙΦΑΝΟΥΣ, with ⊕ and $\underset{A}{Ε}$, Zeus enthroned to left, holding Nike with a wreath on his right hand and a long sceptre in his left.

[7] Strab. 749.

[8] *Brit. Mus. Cat. Coins* Galatia, etc. p. 151 no. 1, p. 152 pl. 18, 7, *Hunter Cat. Coins* iii. 142 nos. 2—4, Head *Hist. num.*[2] p. 778.

[9] *Brit. Mus. Cat. Coins* Galatia, etc. p. 152 pl. 18, 6 (= my fig. 997), cp. pl. 18, 8, *Hunter Cat. Coins* iii. 141 no. 1, cp. p. 142 no. 8, Head *Hist. num.*[2] p. 778. G. Macdonald in the *Hunter Cat. Coins* iii. 141, followed by B. V. Head *loc. cit.*, supposes that the mint was Seleukeia, not Antiocheia. The usual interpretation of the two bearded heads is borne out by the reverse legend ΑΔΕΛΦΩΝ ΔΗΜΩΝ.

large bay-wreath (fig. 998)[1]. In imperial times the head of Zeus sometimes occupies the obverse (fig. 999)[2], while his eagle in one guise or another very commonly fills the reverse[3]. We see the great bird grasping a thunderbolt[4], or holding a wreath in his beak and a bay-branch in his talons[5], or gripping a *caduceus* with his jaws and a palm-branch with his right claw as he rests

Fig. 998.   Fig. 999.

Fig. 1000.   Fig. 1001.   Fig. 1002.   Fig. 1003.

on a garlanded altar (fig. 1000)[6], or again perched with wreath in beak on the thigh of an animal-victim (fig. 1001)[7]—altar and thigh alike recall the city's foundation-myth—[8], or bestriding a bay-wreath with the three Charites in it (fig. 1002)[9], or soaring beneath the imperial head (fig. 1003)[10]. Here and there

[1] *Brit. Mus. Cat. Coins* Galatia, etc. p. 153 ff. pl. 18, 9, 11, 12, pl. 19, 1 (cp. my fig. 998 from a specimen of mine, which likewise shows Nike wreathing the city's title), *Hunter Cat. Coins* iii. 143 ff. pl. 71, 28, 30, 34, Head *Hist. num.*[2] p. 778.

[2] From a specimen in my collection. Cp. *Brit. Mus. Cat. Coins* Galatia, etc. p. 162 f. pl. 19, 11 and pl. 20, 3. The reverse shows Boule (?), in *chitón* and *himátion*, dropping a pebble into the voting-urn.

[3] *Brit. Mus. Cat. Coins* Galatia, etc. p. 158 ff., *Hunter Cat. Coins* iii. 148 ff., Head *Hist. num.*[2] p. 779 f.

[4] *Brit. Mus. Cat. Coins* Galatia, etc. p. 175 pl. 21, 9 Nero: ΕΤΟΥΣ ΒΙΡ · Ι (year 112 of the Caesarean era, reckoned from 49 B.C.: see B. Pick in the *Zeitschr. f. Num.* 1887 xiv. 312 n. 3).

[5] *Brit. Mus. Cat. Coins* Galatia, etc. p. 177 pl. 22, 2 Otho: ΕΤΟΥϹΑ (year 1 of the emperor's reign!).

[6] *Ib.* p. 179 pl. 22, 5 Vespasian: ΕΤΟΥϹΝΕΟΥ ΙΕΡΟΥ Ε (new sacred year 5 = 73–74 A.D., reckoned from Sept. 2 to Sept. 1, the Syrian year of Augustus: see B. Pick *loc. cit.* p. 331 ff.).

[7] *Brit. Mus. Cat. Coins* Galatia, etc. p. 192 pl. 23, 5 Marcus Aurelius: ΓΕΡϹΑΡΔΗ ΜΕΞΑΙ ΥΠΑ ΤΓ (=Γερμανικὸς Σαρματικός, δημαρχικῆς ἐξουσίας αι΄, ὕπατος γ΄).

[8] *Supra* p. 1188.

[9] *Ib.* p. 196 pl. 23, 11 Caracalla: ΔΗΜΑΡ Χ · ΕΞ · ΥΠΑ · Τ · Δ (=δημαρχικῆς ἐξουσίας, ὕπατος τὸ δ΄).

[10] *Ib.* p. 196 pl. 23, 12 Caracalla: ΔΗΜΑΡΧΕ ΞΥΠΑΤΟϹΤΟ Δ (=δημαρχικῆς ἐξουσίας, ὕπατος τὸ δ΄). See F. Imhoof-Blumer 'Zur griechischen Münzkunde' in the *Revue Suisse de Numismatique* 1898 p. 45 f.

a little touch implies that the emperor, whose bust appears on the obverse, is posing as the very Zeus. Thus Nero[1], Domitian[2], and Nerva[3] are all invested with the *aigís*. It is clear, then, that for centuries the inhabitants of Antiocheia had been familiar with the Hellenic Zeus and had known emperors who claimed to be his visible vicegerents.

On the other hand Maximinus ii, like Diocletian[4] and Galerius[5] before him,

---

[1] *Brit. Mus. Cat. Coins* Galatia, etc. p. 175 pl. 21, 9: ΝΕΡѠΝΚΑΙϹΑΡ ϹΕ-ΒΑϹΤΟϹ.

[2] *Ib.* p. 182 pl. 22, 8: ΑΥΤΚΛΙϹΑΡΔΟΜΙΤΙΑΝΟϹϹΕΒΓΕΡΜ.

[3] *Ib.* p. 183 pl. 22, 9: ΑΥΤΝΕΡΟΥΑϹ ΚΑΙϹϹΕΒ. On these coins of Domitian and Nerva the *aigís* is reduced to a mere fringe of snakes passing over the further shoulder. It is, however, certain that there ought to have been noticed in the British Museum catalogue.

[4] Eumenius *panegyr. Constantio Caesari* 4, *pro restaur. schol.* 10, 16, Lact. *de mortibus persecut.* 52, Aur. Vict. *de Caes.* 39. 18, 39. 33, 40. 1, 40. 8, Dessau *Inscr. Lat. sel.* no. 621 Rome (= *Corp. inscr. Lat.* vi no. 254 = Orelli *Inscr. Lat. sel.* no. 1047) Genio Iovii Aug., | Iovia porticu eius a fundamentis absoluta | excultaque, | etc., no. 623 Sirmium (= *Corp. inscr. Lat.* iii no. 3231 = Orelli—Henzen *Inscr. Lat. sel.* no. 5560a = Wilmanns *Ex. inscr. Lat.* no. 1059) I. O. M. et | G.h.l. (= Genio huius loci) pro | salute dd. | nn. Iovio | et Herculio Augg. nn. (= dominorum nostrorum, Iovio et Herculio Augustis nostris), no. 634 Thessalonike Herculi Augusto | Iovius . . . . (the words *et Herculius* have been erased) Augg. (e)t | Herculius et Iovius nobb. Caess., no. 8930 Alexandreia (S. de Ricci in the *Comptes rendus de l'Acad. des inscr. et belles-lettres* 1908 p. 793) Iovi Auguste, vincas, cp. no. 659 Carnuntum (*Corp. Inscr. Lat.* iii no. 4413 = Orelli *Inscr. Lat. sel.* no. 1051) D.S.I.M. (= Deo Soli Invicto Mithrae), | fautori imperii sui, | Iovii et Herculii | religiosissimi Augusti et Caesares | sacrarium restituerunt.

A gold medallion of Diocletian and Maximianus, formerly in the Cabinet de France, had rev. IOVIO ET HERCVLIO The two emperors pouring a libation over a tripod: in the field above, nude statues of Iupiter, with thunderbolt, and Hercules, with club, set on a garlanded altar. In exergue S M V R or S M T (Rasche *Lex. Num.* iv. 917 f., 932, Suppl. iii. 162, Cohen *Monn. emp. rom.*² vi. 480 no. 7, Stevenson—Smith—Madden *Dict. Rom. Coins* p. 487, Gnecchi *Medagl. Rom.* i. 12 no. 3). A bronze medallion of Diocletian, at Paris, has obv. IOVIO DIOCLETIANO AVG Half-length bust of Diocletian, with bay-wreath, sceptre, and *himátion* only—in imitation of Iupiter (Rasche *Lex. Num.* iv. 917, Suppl. iii. 162, Fröhner *Méd. emp. rom.* p. 256 f. fig., Cohen *Monn. emp. rom.*² vi. 429 f. no. 142 fig., Gnecchi *Medagl. Rom.* ii. 124 no. 3 pl. 124, 1, cp. ii. 124 no. 4). A smaller bronze medallion, in the Vatican, has obv. IOVI DIOCLETIANO AVG A similar bust of Diocletian, with radiate crown (*id. ib.* iii. 78 no. 40 pl. 158, 11): this medallion, if IOVI is not a mere blunder for IOVIO, baldly identifies the god with the emperor. Another at Paris has rev. IOVI CONSERVATORI AVG A hexastyle temple, with wreath in pediment and architrave inscribed IOVIVS AVG, containing emperor as Iupiter enthroned with thunderbolt and sceptre (Fröhner *Méd. emp. rom.* p. 255, Cohen *Monn. emp. rom.*² vi. 443 no. 275 fig., Gnecchi *Medagl. Rom.* ii. 124 no. 7 pl. 124, 3 corroded and retouched, cp. *id. ib.* ii. 124 no. 8 at Florence): similar medallions at Paris, struck by Maximianus, repeat the reverse type, but show the emperor as Iupiter standing with thunderbolt, sceptre, and eagle (Rasche *Lex. Num.* iv. 931 f., Fröhner *Méd. emp. rom.* p. 255 fig., Gnecchi *Medagl. Rom.* ii. 128 nos. 6 f. pl. 126, 6 and 7). A gold piece, formerly in the Cabinet de France, had rev. PRIMI XX IOVI AVGVSTI Iupiter seated, with thunderbolt and sceptre. In exergue TR (Cohen *Monn. emp. rom.*² vi. 458 no. 393 with n. 1 'IOVI est sans doute mis pour IOVII, et encore dans ce cas la légende n'est-elle pas trop compréhensible').

The title *Iovius* was, no doubt, suggested by the name *Dio*cletianus, the origin of which is uncertain. W. Ramsay in Smith *Dict. Biogr. Myth.* i. 1011 says of Diocletian:

or Licinius[1] and Licinius Iunior[2] after him, had assumed the title *Iovius*[3]—

'From his mother, Doclea, or Dioclea, who received her designation from the village where she dwelt, he inherited the appellation of *Docles* or *Diocles*, which, after his assumption of the purple, was Latinized and expanded into the more majestic and sonorous Diocletianus' [Aur. Vict. *epit.* 39. 1]. But T. Mommsen in the *Corp. inscr. Lat.* iii. 283 argues that the home of Diocletian was Salona, not Doclea. And Patsch in Pauly—Wissowa *Real-Enc.* v. 1251 notes that Doclea came to be called Dioclea (Aur. Vict. *epit.* 39. 1), Διόκλεια (Constantinus Porphyrogenitus *de administrando imperio* 29 (iii. 126 Bekker)), Διόκληα (*id. ib.* 35 (iii. 162 Bekker)) in consequence of the conjecture that Diocletian was born there.

[5] *Chronicon Paschale* (i. 512 Dindorf) 275 B Μαξιμιανὸς 'Ιόβιος ἐπιφανέστατος Καῖσαρ, 275 C Μαξιμιανοῦ 'Ιοβίου Καίσαρος, 275 D Μαξιμιανοῦ 'Ιοβίου *bis*, Dessau *Inscr. Lat. sel.* no. 634 cited *supra* p. 1194 n. 4, no. 658 Aquincum (= *Corp. inscr. Lat.* iii no. 3522) pro salute dd. | nn. | [M]aximiano | Iovo invic. | Aug. et Maximino | Caes. (=dominorum nostrorum Maximiani Iovii invicti Augusti et Maximini Caesaris) | Iulius Valeria[n]u|s et Aurel. Maxim[us] ddvv. col. | Aq. (=duoviri coloniae Aquinci), cp. no. 659 cited *supra* p. 1194 n. 4, no. 661 Solva near Leibnitz in Stiria (= *Corp. inscr. Lat.* iii no. 5325) divo| Iovio | Maximiano | ordo Sol., no. 8931 Alexandreia (S. de Ricci in the *Comptes rendus de l'Acad. des inscr. et belles-lettres* 1909 p. 146) Iovi Cae[s]ar, vincas.

[1] Dessau *Inscr. Lat. sel.* no. 676 Canusium (= *Corp. inscr. Lat.* ix no. 6026) d. n. Iovio Licinio invicto semper Aug.

Rasche *Lex. Num.* iv. 932, Suppl. iii. 163, cites from A. Banduri *Numismata imperatorum a Trajano Decio ad Palæologos Augustos* Lutetiæ Parisiorum 1718 ii. 195 and other sources a coin showing the head of Licinius with the legend IOVIVS LICINIVS AVG. On this Eckhel *Doctr. num. vet.*[2] viii. 67 remarks : ' *Iovius.* Hujus appellationis auctor Diocletianus, quam is transmisit in Gal. Maximianum, hic in Maximinum, mox Licinium, scilicet lege adoptionis, Licinius denique in filium. Haec confirmata numis vidimus, tum iis, quae supra de hereditariis his nominibus in numis Constantii Chlori exposui. Atque hujus cum Iove cognationis causa tot Licinius numos cum ejus dei effigie feriri jussit, quot ante eum nemo, neque ingratus is adversus nepotem fuit. Nam ut Hercules olim filio Maximiano leoninum capitis integumentum, ita Iuppiter Licinio fulmen impertivit, quod ille, ut in antica nonnullorum ejus numorum videre est [*ib.* p. 64], manu terrifica vibrat, sed cujus aciem Constantinus Enceladus apud Hadrianopolin obtundet.' Cohen *Monn. emp. rom.*[2] vii. 198 f. nos. 98—100 with fig. gives examples, in small bronze and in bad billon or potin, of the type described by Eckhel.

I add a few specimens from my collection which illustrate the relation of Licinius (figs. 1004—1006) and Licinius Iunior (fig. 1007) to Iupiter *Conservator*. It is amusing to see the thunderbolt in the hand of the emperor (figs. 1004, 1005) replaced by a mere *mappa* (figs. 1006, 1007).

[2] Copper coins struck by Licinius and his son have obv. DD. NN. IOVII LICINII INVICT. AVG. ET CAES. Laureate busts of the two Licinii supporting between them a figure of Fortuna (or Victoria, or a trophy); rev. I. O. M. ET FORT. CONSER. (or VICT. CONSER., or VIRTVTI) DD. NN. AVG. ET CAES. Iupiter and Fortuna (or Victoria, or a trophy). In exergue SMKA or SMKB or SMNA (or SMKA· SMKΓ or SMKΔ̄, or SMNTA or SMATE) (Rasche *Lex. Num.* iv. 932, 1740, 1746, Cohen *Monn. emp. rom.*[2] vii. 210 f. nos. 1—3 with fig. of no. 2).

[3] Euseb. *hist. eccl.* 9. 9. 1 *bis* 'Ιόβιος Μαξιμῖνος Σεβαστὸς Σαβίνῳ, Dittenberger *Syll. inscr. Gr.*[2] no. 420, 22 ff. (=G. Deschamps and G. Cousin in the *Bull. Corr. Hell.* 1888 xii. 101 ff. no. 22, 22 ff.) an inscription from the precinct of Zeus *Panámaros* (*supra* i. 18 ff.) honouring a certain priest and priestess ἐφ' ὧν ἱερωμένων καὶ | ἡ θειότης τοῦ δεσπότου | ἡμῶν, τοῦ ἀηττήτου Σεβαστοῦ | 'Ιοβίου Μαξιμίνου ἐν τῇ πα[τρ]ίδι | ἐπέλαμψεν καὶ τὰ ληστήρια | ἐξέκοψεν.

A bronze medallion of Maximinus, now at Paris, has obv. IOVIVS MAXIMINVS NOB CAES A bust of the emperor, laureate and armed, holding sceptre and *mappa* (Cohen

struck perhaps by the fact that, so far as names were concerned, *Iovius* Maximinus was a tolerable imitation of Iupiter *Optimus Maximus*. Theoteknos in importing the novel cult very probably designed to win the favour of his imperial master. *Quasi*-Dionysiac rites practised in the name of Zeus would be quite in the line of the profligate *Iovius*.

Alas for his calculations. A few pages further on Eusebios[1] tells us what happened:

'Theoteknos too was summoned by Justice, who had no intention of forgetting the harm he did to Christians. On the strength of the *xóanon*[2] that he had set up at Antiocheia he expected to take life easily, and was in fact already promoted by Maximinus to the post of governor. But Licinius had no sooner set foot in the city of the Antiochenes than he ordered all impostors to be brought in, and put the prophets and priests of the new-fangled *xóanon* to the torture, asking them how they came to play such a lying part. Hard pressed by the tortures, they could conceal the facts no longer, but explained that the whole mystery was a fraud contrived by the wily Theoteknos. Thereupon Licinius punished them all according to their deserts. He first condemned Theoteknos, and then the partners of his imposture, to death, after inflicting upon them the greatest possible torments.'

For all that, the cult of Zeus *Phílios* once started was not easily suppressed. Fifty years later Julian wintered at Antiocheia (362—363 A.D.) and, as we gather from his own *Misopógon*, was diligent in visiting the temple of Zeus *Phílios*[3].

Fig. 1004.   Fig. 1005.

Fig. 1006.   Fig. 1007.

Monn. emp. rom.[2] vii. 155 no. 134 fig., Gnecchi *Medagl. Rom.* ii. 132 no. 1 pl. 129, 5 roughly retouched). Another, with the same legend, had for obverse type the bare head of Maximinus (Rasche *Lex. Num.* iv. 932, Suppl. iii. 163, Cohen *Monn. emp. rom.*[2] vii. 155 no. 135, Gnecchi *Medagl. Rom.* ii. 132 no. 2). One of his coppers, struck at Antiocheia, ventures on a new title: rev. IOVIO PROPAGAT. ORBIS TERRARVM Maximinus, with bay-wreath and *toga*, stands holding Victoria on a globe: to the right is a burning altar; on either side of him, the letter A and a star; in the exergue, ANT (Cohen *Monn. emp. rom.*[2] vii. 153 no. 130 fig.).

[1] Euseb. *hist. eccl.* 9. 11. 5 f.

[2] For the implications of this term see now an excellent paper by Miss F. M. Bennett 'A study of the word ΞΟΑΝΟΝ' in the *Am. Journ. Arch.* 1917 xxi. 8—21.

[3] Ioul. *misopog.* p. 446, 10 ff. Hertlein ἡ Σύρων ἧκει νουμηνία, καὶ ὁ καῖσαρ αὖθις εἰς Φιλίου Διός· εἶτα ἡ πάγκοινος ἑορτή, καὶ ὁ καῖσαρ εἰς τὸ τῆς Τύχης ἔρχεται τέμενος. ἐπισχὼν δὲ τὴν ἀποφράδα πάλιν ἐς Φιλίου Διὸς τὰς εὐχὰς ἀναλαμβάνει κατὰ τὰ πάτρια. καὶ τίς ἀνέξεται τοσαυτάκις εἰς ἱερὰ φοιτῶντος καίσαρος, ἐξὸν ἅπαξ ἢ δὶς ἐνοχλεῖν τοῖς θεοῖς, κ.τ.λ. Cp. Liban. *or.* 1. 122 (i. 1. 141, 19 ff. Foerster) ἧκε δέ ποτε εἰς Διὸς Φιλίου θύσων κ.τ.λ.

Again, Libanios the Antiochene, when petitioning Theodosios to protect the pagan temples against the depredations of the Christian monks (384[1] A.D.), expressly notes that certain temples—those of Tyche, Zeus, Athena, and Dionysos—are still untouched[2].

Antiocheia was a city where Christians and pagans jostled each other in the street[3]; and it is possible that, as the former found their centre in the great Constantinian church, so the latter had a nucleus and rallying-point in the temple of Zeus *Philios*. Indeed, between the two rival cults there was a certain superficial resemblance. On the one hand, Zeus *Philios* was a god of love, who brought even enemies together[4], encouraged love-feasts among the faithful here, and held out hopes of a celestial banquet hereafter[5]. If his initiations and purifications[6] savoured somewhat of *Sabázios*, it must be remembered that the Hebrew Godhead was by successive pagan blunderers confused with Iupiter *Sabazius*, Bacchus, Liber *Pater*, and Dionysos[7]. On the other hand, the Christians themselves—as I shall hope to prove in a third volume—had not scrupled to employ the art-types of Zeus and Dionysos for the representation of Christ, and that on objects of the most solemn and sacred character.

The strongest support for this assertion, so far as Antiocheia was concerned, is to be derived from the famous chalice recently published by Dr G. A. Eisen. It appears that early in the year 1910 certain Arabs, who were digging a cellar or a well at *Antakieh* (Antiocheia), lit upon underground chambers partially choked with *débris*. In the *débris* were embedded various objects of value. In addition to the chalice of carved silver that is here in question, there was a second chalice of plain silver with inscriptions of the sixth or seventh century A.D.; there were also three silver book-covers decorated with saints and referable to the fourth or fifth century; and there was a large ceremonial cross inscribed on front and back, not to mention a sackful of crumbled silver fragments. A 'smaller cross, likewise of silver, supposed to be from the same find, passed into the possession of Monsieur W. Froehner. Since the spot where these objects were discovered was, according to local tradition, the site of an ancient cathedral[8], it is clear that we have to do with a church-treasure

---

[1] Libanios ed. R. Foerster iii. 80 n. 3.

[2] Liban. *or.* 30. 51 (iii. 116, 1 ff. Foerster) εἰπέ μοι, διὰ τί τὸ τῆς Τύχης τοῦτο σῶν ἐστιν ἱερὸν καὶ τὸ τοῦ Διὸς καὶ τὸ τῆς Ἀθηνᾶς καὶ τὸ τοῦ Διονύσου; ἆρ᾽ ὅτι βούλοισθ᾽ ἂν αὐτὰ μένειν; οὔ, ἀλλ᾽ ὅτι μηδεὶς τὴν ἐπ᾽ αὐτὰ δέδωκεν ὑμῖν ἐξουσίαν.

[3] The most careful and thorough-going monograph on Antiocheia in general is still C. O. Müller *Antiquitates Antiochenae* Gottingae 1839 pp. viii, 134 with map and pl. of coins etc. Other works of importance in particular directions are J. M. Neale *A History of the Holy Eastern Church. The Patriarchate of Antioch* London 1873 pp. lx, 229, R. Förster 'Antiochia am Orontes' in the *Jahrb. d. kais. deutsch. arch. Inst.* 1897 xii. 103— 149 with twelve figs. and pl. 6, *id.* 'Skulpturen von Antiocheia' *ib.* 1898 xiii. 177—191 with figs. and pl. 11, S. Krauss 'Antioche' in the *Revue des Études Juives* 1902 xlv. 27— 49 (classical records largely supplemented from Rabbinic sources), K. Bauer *Antiochia in der ältesten Kirchengeschichte* Tübingen 1919 pp. 1—47, H. Dieckmann *Antiochien, ein Mittelpunkt urchristlicher Missionstätigkeit* Aachen 1920 pp. 1—56.

[4] *Supra* p. 1176 f.

[5] *Supra* p. 1161 ff.

[6] *Supra* p. 1186.

[7] *Supra* i. 234 n. 4.

[8] Mr C. L. Woolley in *The Times Literary Supplement* for July 10, 1924 p. 436 tells a very different tale. He says of the chalice: ' I believe myself to be fully justified

buried either accidentally by earthquake or intentionally to escape some threatened danger. The treasure trove, at first divided among the finders and widely
dispersed (two pieces were carried off to Mesopotamia), was recovered piecemeal
by Messieurs S. and C. Kouchakji and forwarded to Monsieur G. Kouchakji in
Paris. Here the principal chalice, coated with oxide to a thickness of several
millimetres, was skilfully deoxidised by Monsieur A. André. He found the silver
matrix already crystalline in texture and so brittle that he dared not rectify a
compression of the cup caused by a blow received in ancient times[1]. In 1914
the chalice, for safety's sake, was sent over to Messieurs H. and F. Kouchakji
in New York, where since 1915 it has been exhaustively studied by Dr Eisen[2],
formerly Curator of the California University Academy of Sciences.

    The chalice stands 0·19^m in height and measured originally about 0·15^m in
diameter. It consists of three parts—an inner bowl rudely hammered out of a

in stating that it was found in a small mound close to Ma'arit il Na'aman, a village
situated' south of Aleppo, on the Aleppo-Homs railway, about a hundred miles from
Antioch. It was discovered, together with a silver cup or bowl and a silver crucifix, by
a peasant, who sold it for £3 to a man in Ma'arit il Na'aman, who sold it for £70 to
a group of three antiquity dealers at Aleppo.... I derive my information from the dealers
concerned, who had no motive for telling me an untruth and were able to give me a very
fair description of the object before any photographs of it had been published.'
    This account is detailed and circumstantial. But, in reply to enquiries, Messrs Kouchakji
have informed me by cable (Nov. 9, 1924) that they confirm Dr Eisen's statement. They
say: ' Arabs found chalice in Antioch.... Woolley's information absolutely incorrect.'
    [1] In 341 A.D., when the 'Golden' Basilica of Antioch, begun by Constantine the
Great and finished by his son Constantius ii, was consecrated, the chalice must have
been one of its most cherished possessions. Some twenty years later, in 362, Julian,
uncle of Julian the Apostate, came to Antioch, closed the churches, and plundered their
valuables (Io. Monach. Rhod. vit. S. Artemii 23 (xcvi. 1272 c—D Migne)). It is said
that after a futile attempt to intimidate Theodoros, the 'guardian of the treasures' in the
great church, he condemned him to torture and death, and that flinging the sacred
vessels on the ground he treated them to the grossest indignities (Sozom. hist. eccl. 5. 8,
Theodoret. eccl. hist. 3. 12, cp. Ruinart acta prim. mart.[2] p. 588 ff.)—a story of very
doubtful historicity (Seeck in Pauly—Wissowa Real-Enc. x. 94). Dr Eisen, however,
accepts the tale, and even suggests that the compression of the chalice may be the result
of its sacrilegious mishandling by Julian. In that case the chalice must have been
concealed again either during the invasion of Chosroes i, who in 538 burned Antioch
but spared the Cathedral, or more probably during the conquests of Chosroes ii, who
captured Syria in 611. The later date would account for the association of the chalice
with the objects of early Byzantine art enumerated above.
    [2] G. A. Eisen 'Preliminary Report on the Great Chalice of Antioch containing the
Earliest Portraits of Christ and the Apostles' in the Am. Journ. Arch. 1916 xx. 426—437
with pl. 19 and four figs., id. 'The Plate with seven Loaves and two Fishes on the Great
Chalice of Antioch' ib. 1917 xxi. 77—79 with fig., id. 'The Date of the Great Chalice of
Antioch' ib. 1917 xxi. 169—186 with five figs., id. 'Chalice of Antioch and Its Portraits
of Christ, Apostles and Evangelists' in the New Era Magazine for January 1920
pp. 12—15 with four figs., id. 'Identification of Seated Figures on Great Chalice of
Antioch' ib. for June and July 1920 pp. 414—417, 526—528 with six figs., id. The Great
Chalice of Antioch New York 1923 pp. 1—194 with two diagrams and an atlas of sixty
photogravures and etchings. The last-mentioned publication is a monograph de luxe,
the plates of which include three whole-page photographs—life-size, enlarged, and larger
still—of every figure on the chalice together with an attempted drawing of each head.
The accompanying text is less satisfactory, being verbose, over-credulous, and disfigured
by unnecessary slips. The book as a whole is obviously meant for wealthy art-lovers

a

The Chalice of Ant

Plate XLVII

b

See page 1197 ff. *with fig.* 1008.

thick sheet of silver, the rim of which has been bent outwards over itself and left with uneven edge; an outer shell or container of carved open-work, for which the inner bowl now serves as a background ; and a support, comprising knop and foot, turned on the lathe out of a solid block of silver. The inner bowl is wholly unadorned and was, when found, quite distinct and separable from the outer shell : the two have since been cemented together for fear of breakage. The base exhibits simple but good decorative work ; the knop, surrounded by a wreath of lozenge-shaped leaves, parts lotus-petals above from lotus-petals below. The shell or container is carved *à jour* with an intricate design. Six vines with double stems rise from the ground-line and cover the whole available surface with a complicated growth of branches. Amid the profusion of tendrils, leaves, and grape-bunches many living creatures can be made out—doves and other birds, a couple of snails, a rabbit, a butterfly, a grasshopper, etc. Moreover, twelve spaces are reserved in the foliage for as many seated persons, arranged in two horizontal alternating rows. These twelve persons fall into two distinct groups, of which one occupies the front, the other the back of the chalice. On the obverse side (pl. xlvii, *a*) Christ appears as a beardless man, enthroned, with a lamb standing at his right hand. Above his head flies one of the birds, perhaps a dove[1]. His right arm is extended[2]; his left, which is missing, may have held a roll[3]. Beneath his footstool an eagle with spread wings rests upon a basket of fruit[4]. And round him are ranged five of his followers, who turn towards him raising the right arm with a gesture of salutation. On the reverse side (pl. xlvii, *b*) Christ is represented as a boy, sitting on a round-backed throne, with his right hand held out and a roll in his left. He is again surrounded by five of his followers, who raise their arms as before. Most of the ten, if not all[5], hold

rather than scholars, and it is to be hoped that it will be followed at no distant date by a better documented students' edition.

I am indebted to Dr Eisen for sending me his three articles in the *New Era Magazine* (now out of print) and to Messrs Kouchakji Frères for presenting me, not only with a copy of the big monograph, but also with the special silver-prints from which pl. xlvii and fig. 1008 were made.

[1] G. A. Eisen *The Great Chalice of Antioch* p. 7 : 'over his head soars the Holy Ghost in the form of a dove.'

[2] *Id. ib.* p. 7 : 'at his right hand is a plate with loaves and fishes.' *Id. ib.* p. 27 : 'The objects on the plate are: seven loaves of bread, two fishes, an oval object with minute spheres and a bunch of pointed leaves.' Dr Eisen gives an enlarged drawing ($\frac{6}{7}$) of the plate in the *Am. Journ. Arch.* 1917 xxi. 78 fig. 1. I confess that, on the photographs, it looks to me like an ordinary bunch of grapes, partly hidden by over-lying tendrils (the supposed fish) and partly resting on a round piece of background (the supposed plate) left to connect it with the sheep below. But I suspect that the artist originally intended to represent a bird's nest with eggs and later modified his design.

[3] As on the reverse side of the chalice.

[4] G. A. Eisen *The Great Chalice of Antioch* p. 7: 'a basket with bread.' *Id. ib.* p. 180: 'The Eagle, perched on one of the Baskets, can only symbolize the Roman Empire, now partaking of the Christian religion as administered by St. Peter and St. Paul.' I see nothing but a basket of fruit, such as might be expected in any vintage scene, and an eagle which is in relation to the figure above, not to the basket below.

[5] Dr Eisen in the *Am. Journ. Arch.* 1917 xxi. 180 f. fig. 4 and in *The Great Chalice of Antioch* pp. 31 ff., 41 describes the object in the left hand of no. 2 as possibly the handle of a sword and that in the left hand of no. 5 as resembling a bag or purse. Neither description is free from doubt, and it is more probable that in every case a roll was intended.

rolls in their hands. Two (nos. 12 and 9 on fig. 1008) show the right arm wound
with phylactery-bands (?)[1]. Finally, the upper part of the shell is encircled by a
narrow strip of thin silver, to which are attached fifty-eight rosettes[2].

It should be noticed that the chalice, long after it was made, came to be
gilded, and that at two different dates—at first with pale whitish gold, and later
with deep reddish gold. The first gilding affected the whole outer surface of the
shell ; the second did not extend to its lower part, and was carried out in much
thicker gold leaf. Both layers of gold are largely worn away by the fingering of
reverent hands, especially in the case of persons and objects that would be
deemed most sacred. There are no inscriptions on the chalice. But, between
the first and second gildings, upon many of the chairs (perhaps upon all) were
added poorly scratched *graffiti* representing a variety of emblems[3], which—if
they can be deciphered—may help to show how the seated figures were interpreted[4] at some doubtful date before the final gilding.

[1] See Dr Eisen in the *Am. Journ. Arch.* 1917 xxi. 182 ff. fig. 5 and *e contra*
Prof. F. C. Burkitt in *The Cambridge Review* 1923—1924 xlv. 254 (long tight sleeves,
not phylacteries).

[2] G. A. Eisen *The Great Chalice of Antioch* pp. 7, 19 f., 125 claims that the rosette
above the hand of Christ on the obverse side of the chalice is in reality a six-pointed star,
the Star of the Nativity.

[3] Dr Eisen in the *New Era Magazine* for June 1920 p. 415 figures four of the *graffiti*
from the chairs of nos. 2 (two crossed bars or keys), 6 (tree? or *ankh*? [amulet A. B. C.]),
7 (water jug), 9 (arch with circle [coin C. Renz] above it). The rest are less distinct and
as yet undeciphered. See further *The Great Chalice of Antioch* p. 29 f.

[4] In his initial publication of the chalice Dr Eisen held that its twelve figures portray
Christ in older and younger form together with ten of his Apostles. He noted also the
suggestion that they are the Baptist with the Lamb at his side, and Christ with ten
Apostles. But the number ten was hard to justify; and careful study of the features of
each portrait led to the conviction that figures 1 and 8 are related, that figures 2 and 5
possess much in common, and that the heads of figures 10 and 11 are quite different in
formation from the rest. Satisfied that the two central figures 1 and 8 are indeed Christ
as a man and Christ as a youth, Dr Eisen next observed that 2 closely resembles St Peter
as portrayed in the Catacombs (J. Wilpert *Die Malereien der Katakomben Roms* Freiburg
1903 pl. 94) and in the Viale Manzoni Hypogeum at Rome (*Not. Scavi* 1920 p. 123 ff.)—an
identification seemingly confirmed by the discovery on seat 2 of the *graffito* representing
two crossed bars or keys. The identity of the other figures remained doubtful till it
was remarked that no. 6, unlike the rest, has a band round his head but no side-lock of
hair. This suggested a Greek as distinct from a Jew, and in that case he must necessarily
be St Luke. But, if so, the figures are not all Apostles. Those grouped with St Luke may
then be St Matthew (9), St Mark (7), and St John (10). At this point again *graffiti* were
helpful. Tradition said that St Mark had been a water-carrier (Alexandros Monachos
(*s.* vi A.D.) *laudatio S. Barnabae Apost.* 1. 13 in the *Acta Sanctorum* edd. Bolland.
Antverpiæ 1698 Junius ii. 440 D λόγος γὰρ ἦλθεν εἰς ἡμᾶς ἀπὸ γερόντων ὅτι ὁ τὸ κεράμιον
βαστάζων τοῦ ὕδατος, ᾧ κατακολουθῆσαι προσέταξεν ὁ Κύριος τοῖς μαθηταῖς, Μάρκος ἦν ὁ υἱὸς
τῆς μακαρίας Μαρίας, Severus Bishop of El-Eschmounein in Upper Egypt *History of the
Patriarchs of the Coptic Church of Alexandria* trans. B. T. A. Evetts Paris 1907 1. 1 p. 17
in the *Patrologia Orientalis* i. 139 'And he (*sc.* Mark) was among the servants who poured
out the water which our Lord turned into wine, at the marriage of Cana in Galilee. And it
was he who carried the jar of water into the house of Simon the Cyrenian, at the time of
the sacramental Supper') ; and on his chair is scratched a water-jar. St Matthew sat at the
receipt of custom; his *graffito* is an archway with a circle above it, presumably the city-
gate with a coin in evidence. St Luke, as a physician, has for his emblem an obvious

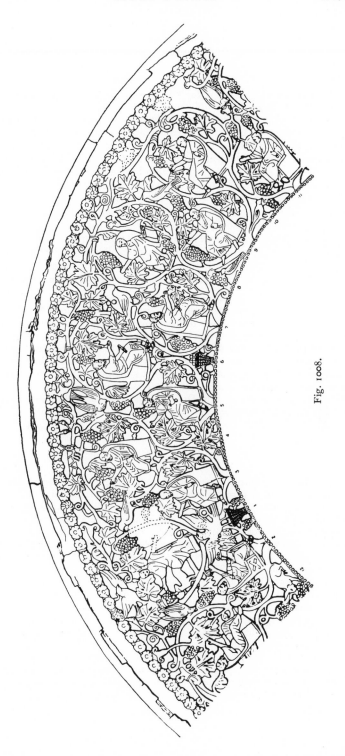

Fig. 1008.

To determine the date of the chalice is a task of primary importance. Sound criticism will rely, not on any *à priori* notions as to what the early Church could or could not have done, but on definite considerations of shape, *technique*, style, and subject.

Now the outer shell or container is essentially an ovoid bowl, without handles, supported on a round knop with a low and narrow foot-stand. A cup so constructed suffers from one obvious defect. It is top-heavy and would be easily upset. Such a shape could hardly have been popular for long together. Nor was it. Bronze coins of uncertain denomination struck by Simon Maccabaeus in 136/5 B.C. have for reverse type a closely similar chalice with knop, short stem, and small foot[1]. But silver shekels and half-shekels dating from the First Revolt of the Jews in 66/7—70 A.D. have for obverse type a chalice with smaller knop, longer stem, and broader foot[2]. Coins of the Second Revolt in 132—135 A.D. substitute either a one-handled jug[3] or a two-handled *amphora*[4], and do not enable us to trace further the evolution of the chalice. But this at least is clear, that on Palestinian soil the old top-heavy chalice was passing out of use as early as 66 A.D. Elsewhere too the same holds good. Two silver cups of similar shape belonging to the Pierpont Morgan collection, exhibited in the Metropolitan Museum of Fine Arts, are justly regarded as excellent samples of Hellenistic work[5]. And silver cups of a like pattern depicted in frescoes from Herculaneum[6]

amulet. Again, if 10 is St John, the other beardless figure (11) must be his brother, St James the son of Zebedee. Moreover, St Peter (2) would naturally be balanced by St Paul (3). And the resemblance of the older man 5 to figure 2 suggested St Peter's brother, St Andrew. Lastly, it was surmised that figures 12 and 4, seated respectively on the right and left hand of Christ are St James the Lord's brother and St Jude, his nearest relatives on earth. It is claimed that figure 12 alone is clad in linen, which would suit the tradition that St James despised woollen clothes even in winter and habitually wore thin linen garments (Euseb. *hist. eccl.* 2. 23. 6 οὐδὲ γὰρ ἐρεοῦν ἐφόρει ἀλλὰ σινδόνας). These are the main arguments advanced by Dr Eisen, whose proposed identifications may be conveniently shown in tabular form :

Front (12) James the Brother of the Lord	(1) CHRIST as Man	(4) Jude		(6) Luke	(8) CHRIST as Boy	(10) John		**Back**
	(2) Peter	(3) Paul	(5) Andrew		(7) Mark	(9) Matthew	(11) James the Son of Zebedee	

Dr G. H. Rendall in a letter to me (Feb. 16, 1924) very pertinently suggests that 5 may be, not St Andrew, but St Barnabas, whose association with Antioch was most intimate. Accepting the attribution of the *Epistle to the Hebrews* to St Barnabas, Dr Rendall points out that we should thus have represented on the chalice the whole canon of the New Testament [*plus* James, son of Zebedee]. His shrewd conjecture of course postulates a date at which the canon was complete. But I see no difficulty in supposing that, at the time when the *graffiti* were added, those who added them believed the ten seated figures to include portraits of all the New-Testament writers.

[1] *Brit. Mus. Cat. Coins* Palestine p. 185 ff. pl. 20, 11—14.

[2] *Ib.* p. 269 ff. pl. 30, 1—9.

[3] *Ib.* p. 288 ff. pl. 33, 5 f., 9 f., 14 f., pl. 34, 4—10, 20.

[4] *Ib.* p. 303 f. pl. 35, 14, pl. 36, 1—3, p. 306 pl. 36, 10.

[5] Miss G. M. A. Richter in *Art in America* 1918 vi. 171 ff. with pl., *Am. Journ. Arch.* 1918 xxii. 349 f. fig. 1.

[6] *Antichità di Ercolano* Napoli 1760 ii (Pitture ii) p. 287 (= Roux—Barré *Herc. et Pomp.* iv Peintures 3ᵉ Série p. 219 pl. 115) preparations for a festival, including a silver jug, a silver cup, three wreaths, a palm-branch, etc., cp. *ib.* ii pp. 118, 157 a similar but deeper vessel, standing on a square plinth, with a couple of wreaths in it.

must be dated before the fatal year 79 A.D. Plate was naturally imitated in less costly materials ; and here again the evidence is in favour of an early date. Very similar to the chalice of Antioch, though without its knop, is a glass vessel in another painting from Herculaneum [1]. Precisely parallel to the chalice in contour and proportions is a small glass cup from Syria, now in a private collection in New York : this, on account of its shallow spiral fluting, has been assigned to the first century A.D. [2] The main point is that after the first century the chalice-shape is entirely superseded. Dr Eisen is, so far as I know, justified in concluding : ' Not one single specimen of this form and with such proportions has been found of a date later than the first century A.D.' [3]

The *technique* of the chalice is compatible with the same early date. Knop, stem, and foot are chased in solid silver—a procedure somewhat uncommon, but known to occur in Graeco-Roman times [4]. The rest of the container is of carved open-work, the so-called *opus interrasile*, which is more than once mentioned by the elder Pliny and seems to have been fashionable at Rome in the seventies [5]. Dr Eisen supposes that this shell of open silver was from the first meant to cover the bowl of plain silver within it. But here I demur. Open-work was regularly used with an eye to colour-contrast, and no toreutic artist worthy of the name would have cased a silver bowl in a silver holder [6]. Dr Eisen further maintains that the inner bowl, which is of crude and unfinished appearance, was more ancient than the outer shell and, when that shell was made, must have been already regarded as a venerable relic, too sacred to alter or amend [7]. But many months ago Dr Minns suggested to me that very likely the inner bowl

[1] *Ib.* ii p. 111 a glass goblet full of eggs.

[2] G. A. Eisen in the *Am. Journ. Arch.* 1917 xxi. 170 fig. 1, 1, 172, *id. The Great Chalice of Antioch* p. 143.

[3] G. A. Eisen in the *Am. Journ. Arch.* 1917 xxi. 171. Note, however, that Dr Eisen himself in the *New Era Magazine* 1920 p. 12 and in *The Great Chalice of Antioch* pp. 136, 180 has figured a pottery lamp from a fourth-century grave at Gezer, on which a very similar cup is seen flanked by a pair of doves. Dr Eisen holds that this is a pious representation of the Antiochene chalice with two dove-like souls gazing upon it ! I see in it merely a traditional *motif*, which could, if necessary, be traced back to the days of Nestor. It might, I think, reasonably be urged that the old-fashioned cup has become stereotyped as a decorative detail and should not be taken to imply that cups of this pattern were still in common use. After all, heraldic shields do not portray the equipment of the modern soldier.

The force of the argument from shape is—I concede—to some extent lessened by the possibility that, for ritual purposes, an archaic form might be deliberately preferred. But are we really prepared to maintain that the chalice is the product of an archaising art ?

[4] E. Saglio in Daremberg—Saglio *Dict. Ant.* i. 801. A good example is the vase from Herculaneum, now at Naples, representing the apotheosis of Homer (J. Millingen *Ancient Unedited Monuments* Series ii London 1826 p. 25 f. pl. 13, J. Overbeck *Pompeji*[4] Leipzig 1884 p. 624 f. figs. *b, c, Guida del Mus. Napoli* p. 411 no. 25301 fig. 93).

[5] Plin. *nat. hist.* 12. 94 interrasili auro, 33. 140 interradimus alia.

[6] We can hardly escape from this improbability by urging that the silver holder was richly gilt and so provided the requisite contrast in colour. For even the first of its gildings appears to have been added when the chalice had been in use for years (*The Great Chalice of Antioch* pp. 17 f., 139).

[7] He points out that in form it resembles the mysterious cup taken from Jerusalem by the Romans and figured, along with the holy vessels of Herod's temple, on the Arch of Titus at Rome (*Am. Journ. Arch.* 1917 xxi. 170 fig. 1, 4). Since Vespasian is said to have erected before the city-gate of Antioch the bronze Cherubim, which Titus his son had

was later, not earlier, than the shell. He argued that the inner bowl appropriate
to the shell would be of glass; and this, when broken, might well have been replaced by a silver substitute of later and clumsier make[1]. If so, the shell cannot
be earlier than the introduction of open-work over glass. And when did that
take place? We think first, no doubt, of the finest extant example, the silver-gilt
kántharos found in 1871 in a tomb to the north of Tiflis and now preserved in the
Hermitage at Petrograd[2]. Here a vessel of dark violet glass was actually blown
into shape within the holder and still bears in places the impress of the silver
upon it. Stephani, who published this splendid cup—it is six inches high,—
assigns it on account of its hunting-scene to a date *c.* 200 A.D.; and we note in
passing that the rosettes round its rim recall those of the Antioch chalice. But
other examples of the art are of much earlier date. To the period of Augustus
or Tiberius belongs a *skýphos* of open-work lead formerly in the Slade collection
and now in the British Museum[3]. This curious work, perhaps a goldsmith's
model, has blown within it a cup of azure glass, which shows through oval
openings in a band about its waist. Above are Bacchic scenes in relief with
incised inscriptions[4]. Below is another relief of vine-tendrils and grape-bunches.
The two handles also are decorated with masks. Earlier still may be placed the
skýphos found in 1876 at Varpelev in Zealand and now in the Museum at Copenhagen[5]. It is a bowl of deep blue glass, the upper part of which is covered with
a decorative design of vine-leaves, ivy-leaves, etc. in open-work silver. It was
found with coins of Probus (276—282 A.D.), but is itself Greek work[6] of the early

---

found in the temple of Solomon (Io. Malal. *chron.* 10 p. 260 f. Dindorf), it is just think-
able that this silver cup of special sanctity was presented on the same occasion to the
Antiochenes. Dr Eisen, however, does not press the point (*Am. Journ. Arch.* 1917 xxi.
171 f.) and obviously inclines to a different and a more heroic hypothesis. With the fall of
Jerusalem Antioch became the main centre of Christianity in the east. May not the inner
bowl of the chalice have been brought thither from Jerusalem? May it not even have been
the very vessel used in Apostolic times by the infant Church? Nay more, might it not
conceivably have been the actual Cup of the Last Supper? No wonder that in the great
Syrian capital, where the disciples were first called Christians, those who obtained possession of a relic so precious lavished all the resources of early imperial art upon its external
embellishment.

[1] E. H. Minns in *The Cambridge Review* of Feb. 15, 1924 (xlv. 216). Sir Martin
Conway in *The Burlington Magazine* for Sept. 1924 (xlv. 109) independently makes the
same conjecture: 'I suggest,' he says, 'that this original was of coloured glass.' Mr F.
Kouchakji in a letter to me (March 4, 1924) replies by anticipation: 'So far all the open-
work over glass cups that have come down to us from antiquity are very small. None of
them possessed a glass cup of the size of the inner cup. Then, if a fine glass cup had been
broken, it would have been replaced by a finished cup and not by a crudely made one,
never finished.'

[2] L. Stephani in the *Compte-rendu St. Pét.* 1872 p. 143 ff. Atlas pl. 2, 1 and 2 (in
colours), E. Saglio in Daremberg—Saglio *Dict. Ant.* i. 808 fig. 981, H. Blümner *Technologie
und Terminologie der Gewerbe und Künste bei Griechen und Römern* Leipzig 1887 iv.
405 n. 1, A. Kisa *Das Glas im Altertume* Leipzig 1908 ii. 602 ff. with figs. 208, 208a.

[3] Gerhard *Ant. Bildw.* p. 327 pl. 87, 1—4, A. Kisa *op. cit.* ii. 602 with figs. 335,
335 a, 335 b.

[4] (a) DOMITILLAE | STATILIO CONIVGI, (b) SALVS | GEN · HVM. Below the foot is an
inscription in relief: (c) · FM · AVG 𝆮. Clearly (a) and (b) are later than (c).

[5] C. Engelhardt in the *Aarbøger for nordisk Oldkyndighed og Historie* 1877 p. 354
with col. pl. 1, A. Kisa *op. cit.* ii. 604 f. with fig. 209.

[6] Witness the wave-pattern round its rim, broken by the single word ΕΥΤΥΧѠC.

first century, or earlier[1]. Kisa goes further and claims that already in Ptolemaic times craftsmen had begun to cover glass cups with gold and silver[2]. How else are we to understand Athenaios' statement that 'two glass vessels of open-work gold' were carried in the pageant of Ptolemy ii Philadelphos[3]? After this it may be conceded that the *technique* of the Antioch chalice is no bar to accepting the first-century date suggested by its shape.

A third criterion may be sought in the style of the chalice-decoration. Mr T. Davies Pryce in a recent letter to me (Nov. 12, 1924) says : 'Apart from the Christian figures, the decorative elements are undoubtedly similar to those used by the first and second century *sigillata* potters.'[4] The vines, though not so purely naturalistic as those of the Augustan age[5], are as yet untouched by the incipient stylisation of the third century[6] and show little, if any, trace of that formality which as time went on became more and more marked[7] till it culminated in the Coptic art of the sixth century[8]. Mr W. A. Watkins draws my attention (Nov. 15, 1924) to the fact that the vines on the chalice resemble, on the one hand, the vine in the Catacomb of Domitilla, which likewise springs from the ground with a double stem and has birds and Cupids among its

---

[1] A. Kisa *op. cit.* ii. 604 notes that its handles, inlaid with gold, resemble those of Alexandrine silver cups found *e.g.* at Bosco Reale.

[2] *Id. ib.* ii. 600.

[3] Kallixenos of Rhodes περὶ 'Αλεξανδρείας 4 (*Frag. hist. Gr.* iii. 62 Müller) *ap.* Athen. 199 F ὑάλινα διάχρυσα δύο.

[4] Mr Pryce's arguments include the following: (*a*) The vine-scroll is comparable with that on a sherd from Wroxeter dated 90—110 or 120 A.D. (J. P. Bushe-Fox *Excavations on the Site of the Roman Town at Wroxeter Shropshire, in 1912* (*Reports of the Research Committee of the Society of Antiquaries of London* No. 1) Oxford 1913 p. 38 f. no. 23 fig. 12). (*b*) The eagle with outspread wings and head turned to right or left was a common stock-type with the potters of *s.* i and ii A.D. (F. Oswald—T. Davies Pryce *An Introduction to the study of Terra Sigillata* London 1920 pls. 6, 4 ; 7, 2 ; 9, 4). (*c*) The rabbit eating grapes appears in the period Domitian—Trajan (*eid. ib.* pl. 19, 5). (*d*) The basket with outspread rim and externally concave sides occurs often on pottery of 100—150 A.D. (*eid. ib.* pl. 17, 4 in a vintage scene with birds, J. Déchelette *Les vases céramiques ornés de la Gaule Romaine* Paris 1904 ii. 154 f. types 1082 and 1087). (*e*) The repeated rosette frequently forms an upper bordering in Italian *sigillata* designs and is sometimes copied by the later or first-century Gaulish *sigillata* potters.

[5] A silver bowl of this period, formerly in the Blacas collection and now in the British Museum, is covered with exquisitely natural vine-leaves and tendrils in gilded *repoussé*-work (*Brit. Mus. Cat. Silver Plate* p. 22 no. 82 pl. 11).

[6] A circular mirror of about *s.* iii A.D., found in a woman's grave near Sofia and now in the British Museum, has a frame of silver-gilt bronze with a somewhat schematised vine-scroll and peacocks worked *à jour* on a backing of wood (*ib.* p. 28 no. 106 pl. 15).

[7] *E.g.* L. von Sybel *Christliche Antike* Marburg 1909 ii figs. 45 (*sarcophagus* in the Lateran Museum at Rome), 46 (*sarcophagus* in San Lorenzo at Rome), 74 (ivory throne at Ravenna) = R. Garrucci *Storia della arte cristiana nei primi otto secoli della chiesa* Prato 1881 v pl. 302, 2 f., v pl. 306, 1—4, vi pl. 414 f.

[8] Sir Martin Conway in *The Burlington Magazine* for Sept. 1924 (xlv. 106 ff.) compares the chalice with the sculptured semidome of a Coptic niche now in the Cairo Museum (*s.* vi), with the back and front of a carved ivory fragment in the same collection (*s.* v–vi), with a panel of the ivory throne at Ravenna (*c.* 550 A.D.), etc. Accordingly he would date the chalice *c.* 550 A.D. (*ib.* p. 110). But on all the monuments cited by him the vines are far advanced in stylisation.

branches[1], on the other hand, the vine-scroll in the Catacomb of Praetextatus, where again birds are seen among the vine-leaves[2]. The cemetery of Domitilla on the Via Ardeatina is believed to go back to Apostolic times[3], while that of Praetextatus on the Via Appia is referred to the second century[4]. The two representations of Christ as a young man and as a boy are imperfectly preserved, but appear to be idealistic rather than realistic figures. The head of the latter at any rate is, as Dr Eisen duly notes[5], reminiscent of a well-known Scopaic type. The other seated persons are at least to some extent individualised[6] and were almost certainly interpreted as portraits at the time when the *graffiti* were added. We know so little at present about the history of Greek portrait-sculpture in the east during the first few centuries of the Christian era that it is peculiarly difficult to date a given work, especially when executed on a small scale[6]. But if we might assume (a somewhat doubtful assumption) that the development of later Greek portraiture followed the same lines as that of Roman portraiture, we should have little hesitation in referring these life-like but not over-realistic heads to the Flavian period (69—96 A.D.). The preceding Augustan and Julio-Claudian art (31 B.C.—68 A.D.) had been more idealistic and aristocratic. Trajanic portraits (98—117 A.D.), though still life-like, are harder and less sympathetic. In the Hadrianic age (117—138 A.D.) we get a marked loss of individualism owing to the revival of old Hellenic ideals. Antonine and Aurelian carving (138—180 A.D.) is pictorial in effect : loose locks contrast with polished faces and there is a glint of light on plastic eyes. Realism returns with the third century, but is accompanied by various tell-tale innovations, *e.g.* very short hair shown by pick-marks on a roughened surface. Had the work been later than this, we should have looked to find standing figures frontally arranged with formal hair and eyes monotonously drilled. On the whole it may be contended that the style of the seated persons suits best the end of the first or, possibly, the beginning of the second century A.D. But, I repeat, the scarceness of strictly comparable work and above all the smallness of the scale—each head is only three-eighths of an inch in height—make certainty unattainable.

It remains to speak of the subject represented on the chalice. The nearest parallels were pointed out by Prof. F. C. Burkitt[7] and Sir Martin Conway[8], who both aptly cite a gilded glass or *fondo d'oro* published by Garrucci (fig. 1009)[9].

---

[1] G. B. de Rossi *Roma sotterranea* edd.[1] J. S. Northcote—W. R. Brownlow London 1869 p. 73 with fig. 10 (ed.[2] 1879 ii. 120 ff. fig. 26), R. Garrucci *op. cit.* Prato 1881 ii. 23 pl. 19, 1. The vine spreads over the vaulted roof in the oldest portion of the catacomb.

[2] G. B. de Rossi *op. cit.* ed.[1] p. 78 with fig. 12 (ed.[2] ii. 148 ff. fig. 37), R. Garrucci *op. cit.* ii. 43 f. pl. 37, 1. The vine occupies the third (autumnal) zone of decoration on the Crypt of St Januarius, who was martyred in 162 A.D.

[3] W. Lowrie *Christian Art and Archæology* New York 1901 p. 65 f., C. M. Kaufmann *Handbuch der christlichen Archäologie* Paderborn 1913 p. 127.

[4] C. M. Kaufmann *op. cit.* p. 127 f.

[5] G. A. Eisen in the *New Era Magazine* for June 1920 p. 416, *id.* *The Great Chalice of Antioch* pp. 63 ff., 74.

[6] Whether this individualisation was in any degree due to tooling or retouching of the original figures before the first gilding of the shell is a point that calls for careful investigation.

[7] In *The Cambridge Review* 1923—1924 xlv. 253 f.

[8] In *The Burlington Magazine* for Sept. 1924 (xlv. 109).

[9] R. Garrucci *Vetri ornati di figure in oro trovati nei cimiteri dei cristiani primitivi di Roma* Roma 1858 p. 40 f. pl. 18, 4 (not 3, as both Prof. Burkitt and Sir M. Conway cite

This shows a youthful Christ (CRISTVS) seated with a group of eight or more[1] Saints to right and left of him. As on the chalice, they occupy high chairs with a rounded back, most of them holding rolls, two extending their right hands. The highest pair is inscribed PETRVS and [PA]V[LVS]. The lowest four are TIMOTEVS, SVSTVS, SIMON, FLORVS—Roman Christians of the third or fourth century[2]. The glass itself is assigned to the age of Pope Damasus (366—384 A.D.)[3].

Fig. 1009.

But the makers of these gilded glasses often gave new names to old designs, and Prof. Burkitt[4] rightly traces the type back to a ceiling in the Catacomb of Petrus and Marcellinus. J. Wilpert holds that the ceiling in question dates from the middle of *s.* iii and depicts the Judgment with the Saints as assessors[5].

It is clear that we have here one element in the design of the Antioch chalice. But that is not all. Prof. Burkitt[6] very justly observes that the left arm of the

it), *id. Storia della arte cristiana nei primi otto secoli della chiesa* Prato 1881 iii. 159 f. pl. 187, 4 (more complete)=my fig. 1009, C. M. Kaufmann *Handbuch der christlichen Archäologie* Paderborn 1913 p. 623 fig. 253, 7. On the vestments lettered Ɪ and Ɉ see Garrucci *Storia* iii. 160.

[1] Originally, perhaps, ten: the glass is broken away to right and left.

[2] Timotheus was martyred in 301 (?), Sustus *i.e.* Xystus (Sixtus ii) in 258 A.D.

[3] H. Vopel *Die altchristlichen Goldgläser* Freiburg i. B. 1899 p. 58.

[4] Cp. Vopel *op. cit.* p. 58 n. 1.

[5] J. Wilpert *Ein Cyclus christologischer Gemälde aus der Katakombe der heiligen Petrus und Marcellinus* Freiburg im Breisgau 1891 p. 17 pl. 1—2, 1, pl. 3—4, 1

[6] In *The Cambridge Review* 1923—1924 xlv. 254.

Christ above the eagle (no. 1) and much of the adjoining space are due (*vide* the key-plan) to a restoration by Monsieur André. He suggests that the disturbing blank was originally filled with a second lamb, the figure being conceived as that of the Good Shepherd. And, if it be objected that the Good Shepherd should be standing not seated, the unusual position is defended by a fifth-century mosaic in the mausoleum of Galla Placidia at Ravenna[1]. It might have been defended by a second-century painting in the cemetery of Callistus at Rome, which shows Christ seated, lyre in hand, between two sheep—the type of the Good Shepherd being definitely influenced by that of Orpheus[2]. I incline therefore to think that Prof. Burkitt's acute divination of the original design is right and that Christ was represented on the chalice in the Orphic or seated type of the Good Shepherd with a sheep on either hand[3]. In this connexion it is interesting to recall that Tertullian, writing between 217 and 222 A.D., mentions chalices of the anti-Montanist party as decorated with representations of the Good Shepherd[4]. It is possible that he had in view cheap imitations of such a masterpiece as the chalice of Antioch.

The combination of the Judge and the Shepherd accounts for much, but not quite for everything. We have yet to explain the eagle beneath his feet. An eagle commonly suggests Zeus, and not least at Antioch where his cult was so familiar[5]. But what exactly is the link between the Shepherd-Judge and Zeus? It is, I think, to be found in the conception of the Divine Ruler, which would easily attach itself either to the figure of the Judge on his judgment-seat or to the seated type of the Shepherd[6]. Dr Eisen[7] remarks that the central figure

---

[1] R. Garrucci *Storia della arte cristiana nei primi otto secoli della chiesa* Prato 1881 iv. 41 pl. 233, 2, W. Lowrie *Christian Art and Archæology* New York 1901 p. 330 f. fig. 141, C. M. Kaufmann *Handbuch der christlichen Archäologie* Paderborn 1913 p. 456.

[2] G. B. de Rossi *Roma sotterranea* edd.[1] J. S. Northcote—W. R. Brownlow London 1869 p. 373 col. pl. 11, 2 (ed.[2] 1879 i. 455, ii col. pl. 18, 2), R. Garrucci *op. cit.* ii. 10 pl. 4, 1, L. von Sybel *Christliche Antike* Marburg 1906 i. 245 f. fig., 1909 ii. 106, C. M. Kaufmann *op. cit.* p. 275 f. fig. 102.

It is a curious coincidence, if nothing more, that the Phoenician Ba'al-ḥammân is represented by a Cypriote terra cotta as sitting on a throne with a ram standing on either side of him (*supra* i. 354 pl. xxvi, 1).

[3] Dr Eisen in a letter to Dr F. J. Foakes Jackson, of which a copy was sent to me by Messrs Kouchakji (March 15, 1924), says: 'An original photograph taken before the cleaning shows that there was no lamb on the other side, and that the design was probably one: branches, leaves, tendrils and bunches of grapes. There is a total absence of symmetry in any part of the Chalice design.' [!]

[4] Tertull. *de pud.* 7 a parabolis licebit incipias, ubi est ovis perdita a domino requisita et humeris eius revecta. procedant ipsae picturae calicum vestrorum, si vel in illis perlucebit interpretatio pecudis illius, utrumne Christiano an ethnico peccatori de restitutione conlineet, *ib.* 10 sed cederem tibi, si scriptura Pastoris, quae sola moechos amat, divino instrumento meruisset incidi, si non ab omni concilio ecclesiarum etiam vestrarum inter apocrypha et falsa iudicaretur, adultera et ipsa et inde patrona sociorum, a qua et alias initiaris, cui ille, si forte, patrocinabitur pastor quem in calice depingis, prostitutorem et ipsum Christiani sacramenti, merito et ebrietatis idolum et moechiae asylum post calicem subsecuturae, de quo nihil libentius libas quam ovem paenitentiae secundae (cp. *ib.* 13).

[5] *Supra* p. 1186 ff.

[6] The seated Shepherd in the mausoleum of Galla Placidia 'is clothed in imperial purple' (W. Lowrie *op. cit.* p. 331).

[7] G. A. Eisen in the *Am. Journ. Arch.* 1916 xx. 432, 434, *id. ib.* 1917 xxi. 172, 174 fig. 2, 10 ff., 179, *id. The Great Chalice of Antioch* pp. 31, 34, 143, 147, 179.

enthroned with a footstool bears a strong resemblance in costume, pose, and general effect to the figure of Augustus on a silver *skýphos* from Bosco Reale[1]. He notes also that on this toreutic triumph, as on the chalice of Antioch, the central figure appears twice—once seated to receive the submission of the barbaric Germans, once enthroned amid the gods as master of the universe. I submit that the artist of the chalice has given to Christ the aspect and position of a divinised emperor[2]. Now Roman emperors were often acclaimed by Greek adulation as Zeus incarnate[3]; and a bust of Zeus, referred to the first or second century A.D., is supported on an eagle with spread wings[4]. We are not, therefore, surprised to find that the head of Caracalla on a coin of Antioch struck between 213 and 217 A.D. has a similar eagle beneath it[5]. In view of these facts it becomes a legitimate conjecture that the eagle beneath the seated Christ marks him as at once human and divine, the true claimant to the throne of Zeus[6].

So, then, the Shepherd-Judge is also the Divine Ruler. And, if it be argued that this multiple *rôle* is not likely to go back to the first century, I should answer that it is already implied by a great passage in the Gospel[7]: ' But when the Son of man shall come in his glory, and all the angels with him, then shall he sit on the throne of his glory: and before him shall be gathered all the nations : and he shall separate them one from another, as the shepherd separateth the sheep from the goats.'

It amounts to this. For the Christian artist—trained, it may be, in a pagan school—Christ has dispossessed all rivals and has taken his seat on the very throne of Zeus. But the chalice has a reverse as well as an obverse design, and we have still to ask Why this duplication of Christ in younger form? and Wherein lies the special appropriateness of the vine-symbolism? The problem, so put, suggests its own solution. The boyish figure seated on the divine throne

---

[1] A. Héron de Villefosse in the *Mon. Piot* 1899 v. 133 ff. pls. 31—33 = Reinach *Rép. Reliefs* i. 92 no. 2 f., 93 no. 1 f., 94 no. 1 f.

[2] For a later variation on the same theme see the well-known ivory *pyxís* at Berlin (R. Garrucci *op. cit.* vi. 60 pl. 440, 1, L. von Sybel *op. cit.* ii. 253 fig. 77, C. M. Kaufmann *op. cit.* pp. 366, 552 fig. 142), which likewise has Christ seated *en face* on a round-backed throne, with a roll in his hand and a footstool at his feet. He is flanked by two seated Apostles (St Peter and St Paul), who raise their hands in salutation. The other ten stand to right and left of him.

The position assigned to the two foremost Apostles suits their ' Dioscuric' character (*supra* p. 606). Zeus is supported by the Dioskouroi (*supra* i. 35 fig. 8, ii. 1230 tailpiece) ; Christ, by St Peter and St Paul (*supra* i. 51 fig. 24, ii. 1207 fig. 1009).

[3] See *e.g.* the examples that I collected in *Folk-Lore* 1905 xvi. 308 ff.

[4] *Supra* p. 951 n. 0 with fig. 844.

[5] *Supra* p. 1193 fig. 1003. The head of Trajan on silver coins struck at Tyre is often supported by an eagle with closed wings (*Brit. Mus. Cat. Coins* Phoenicia p. 300 f. pl. 36, 1, 3—6, *Hunter Cat. Coins* iii. 268 f. pl. 77, 5). Some specimens, which have the same obverse type, but for reverse Tyche seated with the Orontes at her feet, are assigned doubtfully by G. F. Hill to Tyre (*Brit. Mus. Cat. Coins* pp. cxxxvii f., 302 pl. 36, 9), by G. Macdonald to Antioch (*Hunter Cat. Coins* iii. 163 f. pl. 72, 19).

[6] I do not deny that the eagle here may have had a further significance. C. M. Kaufmann *op. cit.* p. 286 discusses its appearance in Christian art ' als...Symbol der Auferstehung...und zwar der in Christo gebotenen felix reparatio temporum (vgl. Ps. 103, 5) im Jenseits.'

[7] Matthew 25. 31 f. Aischylos long since had made Agamemnon, his divine ruler, an ἀγαθὸς προβατογνώμων (*Ag.* 795).

in the midst of his trusty followers is, to those at least who have in mind the coinage of Lydia and Kilikia[1], reminiscent of the child Zeus or Dionysos seated on his throne with the Kouretes grouped about him ; and the framework of grape-vines adds point to the analogy.

On the whole, piecing together the evidence of shape, *technique*, style, and subject, I conclude that the chalice of Antioch was made at some date not far removed from the year 100 A.D.[2] ; that it was then adorned with figures of Christ sitting in Judgment with the Saints[3], ten in number merely because ten was a typical plurality[4] ; and that these assessors were later, by means of *graffiti*, identified with individual Apostles and canonical authors, including perhaps all the recognised writers of the New Testament[5]. Further, I hold that the decoration of the chalice, though essentially Christian, owes certain of its features to pagan antecedents, in particular to Anatolian representations of Zeus and Dionysos[6]. Here, as elsewhere, the art-types of the Greek Father and Son were both taken into the service of the conquering creed and alike used to portray the form of Him who said : 'I and the Father are one[7].'

[1] *Supra* i. 152 f. figs. 125—128, i. 646 f.

[2] Prof. Strzygowski, after personal inspection of the chalice and prolonged study of its detail, refers it to the first century A.D. (J. Strzygowski 'Der "Silberkelch von Antiochia"' in the *Jahrbuch der asiatischen Kunst* 1924 pp. 53—61 pl. 28 f., especially p. 61). But when he attributes the Berlin *pyxis* also to the first century (*ib.* p. 59), we part company.

[3] *Supra* p. 1207.

[4] M. H. Farbridge *Studies in Biblical and Semitic Symbolism* London 1923 p. 140 ff. (citing E. W. Bullinger *Number in Scripture* Bromley 1894 p. 243).

[5] *Supra* p. 1200 n. 4.　　　　　[6] *Supra* p. 1209 f.　　　　　[7] John 10. 30.

ADDENDA

ii. 2 n. 4. The painted marble tablet from Tarragona, though accepted as genuine by more than one archaeologist of repute (F. Ladelci in the *Atti dell' Accademia pontificia de' nuovi Lincei* 1885 xxxviii. 4. 122 ff. pl. 1, Milani *Stud. e mat. di arch. e num.* 1899—1901 i. 36 ff. fig. 4, A. L. Frothingham in the *Am. Journ. Arch.* 1916 xx. 209—211 fig. 41), has recently been denounced as a forgery by the eminent connoisseur of Iberian antiquities P. Paris 'Le faux sarcophage égyptien de Tarragone' in the *Rev. Arch.* 1921 ii. 146—157 with figs. 1—6. I have not myself seen the tablet; but Mr T. W. I. Bullock of Queens' College, Cambridge, who has kindly interviewed on my behalf J. R. Mélida y Alinari, director of the Museo Arqueologico Nacional at Madrid, and F. A. Ossorio, keeper of the Greek and Roman antiquities, reports (Sept. 21, 1923) that both these authorities regard, and always have regarded, the fragment as a mere fabrication.

ii. 7 n. 1. Add Eunap. *v. Aedesii* 37 (p. 20 Boissonade) τὸ τῶν ὁμιλητῶν ἄριστον πρὸς μυστηριώδη τινὰ σιωπὴν καὶ ἱεροφαντικὴν ἐχεμυθίαν ἐπιρρεπὲς ἦν καὶ συνεκέκλιτο.

ii. 31 n. 7. So also Loukian. *somn.* 2 ὦ Ζεῦ τεράστιε, cp. Aristoph. *pax* 41 f. οὐκ ἔσθ' ὅπως | τοῦτ' ἐστὶ τὸ τέρας οὐ Διὸς σκαταιβότου (*supra* p. 15 n. 1) and Eustath. *in Od.* p. 1885, 8 f. Διὸς δὲ τέρας ἀλληγορικῶς μὲν τὸ ἐξ ἀέρος· τοιοῦτον γὰρ ἦ, ὡς ἐρρέθη, δίχα νέφους βροντή. ἄλλως δὲ διὰ τὸ πᾶν τέρας ἀνάγεσθαι εἰς ἐκεῖνον, καθὰ καὶ πᾶσαν ὀμφήν· διὸ καὶ πανομφαῖος ἐλέγετο Ζεύς. See further O. Höfer in Roscher *Lex. Myth.* v. 369.

ii. 32. The relief of Zeus Κραταιβάτης is now figured by Svoronos *Ath. Nationalmus.* pl. 219, 8 (=my fig. 1010).

Fig. 1010.

ii. 38 n. 5. Mr A. D. Nock points out to me (Oct. 4, 1921) that Paulin. Nolan. *carm.* 5. 37 ff. is transplanted from Auson. *ephem.* 3. 37 ff. See M. Schanz *Geschichte der römischen Litteratur* München 1904 iv. 1. 33, 238 f.

ii. 44. Platon's comparison of the Galaxy with 'the undergirders of triremes' perhaps rests on another folk-belief. W. Gundel *Sterne und Sternbilder im Glauben des Altertums und der Neuzeit* Bonn—Leipzig 1922 p. 46 says that the Milky Way is sometimes conceived as 'ein gewaltiges Seil.' This would explain, not only the Platonic cable, but also the yet more famous σειρὴν χρυσείην of *Il.* 8. 19 ff. A golden rope hung from heaven to earth may well have been a popular conception of the Galaxy. And, if Zeus bound it περὶ ῥίον Οὐλύμποιο (*ib.* 25), we recall that 'the stars came down at night on Olympus' (*supra* p. 905 n. 0).

ii. 44 n. 4. The late Mr H. G. Evelyn White kindly supplied me (Sept. 23, 1921) with a Coptic parallel to the Manichaean 'pillar of light.' It occurs in an apocalyptic Gospel from Dêr Abû Makâr in the Wady'n Natrûn (*New Texts from Dêr Abû Makâr* no. 3, folio 117^{recto}): 'There shall be a pillar (cⲧϩ\oc=στῦλος) of light, like unto silver, in Amenti (Hades): all mankind that is shall come to the place of judgment. But ye upon your thrones within the wall shall order the judgment. But the rest of the just—they who shall not be able to attain to the measure of the judgment—shall sit (or rest, remain) upon a pillar (στῦλος) of light, that they may behold them who do judgment and them who have judgment done upon them.' Mr Evelyn White further noted (Oct. 24, 1921), after Dr M. R. James, a 'great pillar' in the judgment-scene of oracl. Sib. 2. 238 ff. Geffcken

ἡνίκα δ' ἀναστήσῃ νέκυας μοῖραν καταλύσας | καὶ καθίσῃ Σαβαὼθ Ἀδωναῖος ὑψικέραυνος | ἐς θρόνον οὐράνιον [τε] μέγαν δέ τε κίονα πήξῃ, | ἥξει δ' ἐν νεφέλῃ πρὸς ἄφθιτον ἄφθιτος αὐτός | ἐν δόξῃ Χριστὸς κ.τ.λ.

ii. 45 n. 1. After repeated inspection of the marble (in the spring of 1922) and examination of a good photograph I incline to think that the arch is intentional, that the pillar is topped by an *abacus*, and that the inscription should be read as ⊥ΕΥΣ.

ii. 50 ff. F. Haug 'Die Irminsul' in *Germania* 1918 ii. 68—72 contends that there was but one *Irminsûl*, that of Eresburg, probably a huge oak-tree lopped of its boughs but still rooted in the ground, till it was destroyed by Charles the Great in 772 A.D. Haug makes light of Widukind's evidence for a second *Irminsûl* at Scheidungen, and gives short shrift to the view of Müllenhoff and Mogk that there were several or even many such pillars. He regards the first element in the name as either adjectival ('mächtige, starke, erhabene Säule') or substantival ('für *Irmin(e)ssul*, d. h. Säule des Gottes oder Halbgottes Irmin').

ii. 50 n. 2. C. Petersen 'Zioter (Zeter) oder Tiodute (Jodute), der Gott des Kriegs und des Rechts bei den Deutschen' in *Forschungen zur Deutschen Geschichte* 1866 vi. 223—342 must be read with caution.

ii. 51 n. 5. Mr B. Dickins has sent me the following notes in criticism (Oct. 8, 1920) of the view advocated by J. Grimm, K. Simrock, and others:—

'The evidence on which this view is based appears to be as follows:

(*a*) *Stephens, No.* 5, taken from Hickes' edition of the A.S. Runic Poem, which glosses ⤃ as both *ear* and *tir*: this poem was however derived from the burnt Cott. Otho B. 10, which seems to have had the characters but no names, the latter being added by Hickes from

(*b*) *Stephens, No.* 9, taken from Cott. Dom. A. 9, the writer or copyist of which was an ignorant person who confused ⤃ and ↑ as he had previously failed to distinguish between the names of ᛗ and ᛘ.

(*c*) *Stephens, No.* 10, taken from St Gall, 4to, No. 270, p. 52, which gives the value and name of ⤃ as *z* and *aer* respectively. This is a pretty faithful copy of the A.S. 28 letter futhorc only partially assimilated to the phonology of O.H.G.; e.g. þ is still preserved, though its name has become *dorn*, and ↑ retains the name *ti* and the value *t*, though the name and value of ᛗ have become *tag* and *t*.

Later a more drastic attempt is made to harmonize the Latin alphabet, the English futhorc and the sounds of O.H.G. þ disappears, though its name *þorn* in the form *dorn* is attached to ᛗ; the A.S. name of ᛗ (*dæg*) is changed to *tac* and attached to ↑, while ⤃, for which O.H.G. had no use in its proper value *ea*, is baptised *ziu*, which corresponds with A.S. *tiw* (found also in the alphabets as *ti* and *tir*).

However the equation of Bavarian *Er* and A.S. *ear* is etymologically unsound, and the association of ⤃ with the god *Ziu* is quite fortuitous, for the following reasons:—

(1) The use of ⤃ to represent the sound of *z* [ts] is by no means universal; cf. e.g. Stephens Nos. 13 and 18 where varieties of the Latin *z* are used and No. 20, where the last letter of the Northumbrian futhorc ⤳ (*gaar*) is similarly thrust into the gap.

(2) ⤃ is a specifically English letter invented to represent the *ēa* which arose from Gmc. *au*: it is not found in inscriptions outside the English area, and where it occurs in O.H.G. futhorcs and alphabets it is legitimate to assume that it has been borrowed from England.

(3) The sound *z* [z], which existed in the parent Gmc. and was represented by ↓ in the old futhark, disappeared both in English and German, though the letter kept its place in the series and was sometimes used in the later Runic alphabets to fill the vacant place of the Latin *x*. When, therefore, by the Fourth Sound-Shifting a new *z* [ts] developed

in O.H.G. it was necessary to find a fresh symbol. Now ᛏ was the last letter of the 28 letter English futhorc found, for instance, on the Thames scramasax [the characters for guttural *c* and *g* seem to have been confined to Northumbria] ; moreover O.H.G. had no use for an *ea* character.

Put shortly, the association of the character ᛏ with the name of the god Ziu appears to be due to the following causes :

By a sound-change peculiar to O.H.G. (the Fourth Sound-Shifting) the dentals experienced a general shift round, $þ > d > t > z$, the effect of which was the loss of *þ* and the appearance of a new sound *z* [ts]. The disappearance of *þ* was welcomed rather than otherwise, since it was an alien which could not be found a place in the Latin alphabet, but it was necessary to find a symbol for *z*. ᛏ happened not to be needed in its proper A.S. value of *ea*, and moreover to be the last letter of the non-Northumbrian futhorc. It was therefore taken over, but its original name *ear* discarded in order to avoid the confusion which would arise if the initial of the name of a letter were other than the letter itself. Naturally it inherited the name *ziu* which in its shifted form was no longer appropriate to its original possessor ᛏ.'

ii. 57 n. 4. Recent articles on 'Jupiter-columns' are listed by W. Deonna in the *Rev. Ét. Gr.* 1917 xxx. 348, *ib.* 1918 xxxi. 434. Add F. Hertlein 'Zu älteren Funden des Juppitergigantenkreises' in *Germania* 1917 i. 101—105 with 2 figs., *id.* 'Der Zusammenhang der Juppitergigantengruppen' *ib.* 1917 i. 136—143 with 9 figs. R. Forrer 'Zur Frage der Juppitergigantensäulen' in the *Römisch-germanisches Korrespondenzblatt* 1912 v. 60 f. questions Hertlein's Germanic interpretation of the columns on two grounds ((1) 'dass an vielen Orten, so z. B. in Zabern, die neben Juppitergigantenresten auf Inschriften gefundenen Personennamen nicht germanische sondern keltische sind'; (2) 'dass schon auf vorrömisch gallischen Münzen eine verwandte Darstellung Platz gegriffen hat').

ii. 86. On the group from *Luxeuil* see now É. Espérandieu in the *Rev. Arch.* 1917 i. 72—86 with two figs. (summarised in the *Am. Journ. Arch.* 1918 xxii. 220). Espérandieu argues that the rider was Iupiter with an astral wheel, that the horse should be restored in a rearing or galloping posture, and that the human head supporting its foot was part of a giant with snaky legs.

ii. 90. Mr C. D. Bicknell notes a second example—*British Museum : A Guide to the Antiquities of Roman Britain* London 1922 p. 20 f. fig. 10 'Half of a stone octagon, with reliefs in niches of the deities presiding over the days of the week, was found by Horsley in the mill at Chesterford, Essex, where it had been used by the local blacksmith as a water-trough for cooling his iron.'

ii. 90. The 'Jupiter-column' had a long history in front of it as well as behind it— witness the sacred pillars reverenced by thousands today in France and Spain. Miss J. E. Harrison 'The Pillar and the Maiden' in the *Proceedings of the Classical Association* 1907 v. 65—77 has drawn attention to the cult of La Vierge du Pilier at Chartres and to the multiplied pillar-shrines of her Cathedral (bibliography by U. Chevalier *Répertoire des sources historiques du moyen âge* Montbéliard 1895 p. 661 ff.). Similarly at Zaragoza the Apostle James (Santiago) built a chapel on the spot where he had seen a vision of the Virgin poised on a pillar of jasper and attended by angels (A. F. Calvert *Valladolid, Oviedo, Segovia, Zamora, Avila, & Zaragoza* London 1908 p. 158 ff. with pls. 348 and 349 Our Lady del Pilar).

ii. 93 ff. The Column of Mayence continues to provoke discussion. To the bibliography (ii. 93 n. 3) add F. Quilling 'Zur grossen Juppitersäule von Mainz' in the *Römisch-germanisches Korrespondenzblatt* 1913 vi. 49—53, K. Körber *Die grosse Juppitersäule im Altertumsmuseum der Stadt Mainz* Mainz 1915 pp. 1—28 with 10 pls. and 9 figs. (reviewed by K. Wigand in the *Römisch-germanisches Korrespondenzblatt* 1915 viii. 47 f.), F. Drexel 'Zur Mainzer Jupitersäule' in the *Römisch-germanisches Korrespondenzblatt* 1915 viii. 67—69, F. Quilling 'Zur grossen Juppitersäule in Mainz' in *Germania* 1917 i. 43—45, *id. Die Jupiter-Säule des Samus und Severus* Leipzig 1918 pp. 1—236 with many figs. (reviewed by F. Drexel in *Germania* 1919 iii. 28—32, J. P. Waltzing in *Le Musée Belge* 1921 xxv. 221—226, cp. *Class. Rev.* 1922 xxxvi. 141), F. Quilling *Die Nerosäule des Samus und Severus* Leipzig 1919 pp. 1—32 with 2 figs. ('Nachtrag' to the 1918 volume by the same author), *id. Die Juppiter-Votivsäule der Mainzer Canabarii. Eine neue Erklärung ihres Bildschmuckes* Frankfurt 1919 pp. 1—16 with figs. and 2 pls. (reviewed by F. Drexel in *Germania* 1919 iii. 127 f.).

Of points made since my section on the subject (*supra* p. 93 ff.) was written the most important is the discovery by P. T. Kessler, assistant of the Mayence Museum, that two drums of the column have hitherto been incorrectly placed. Kessler observed that in its first, fourth, and fifth drums the run-holes for lead ('Gussrinnen') were contrived at the back of the shaft. If the same rule was followed for the second and third drums, we must suppose that their front figures were Volcanus and the goddess with the scales. This supposition is confirmed by the fact that a lance-tip carved beneath Ceres' altar on the lower edge of the second drum is now seen to be the point of Neptunus' staff on the first drum —an adjustment further certified by an incised mark ('Versatzmarke') on the two adjacent edges. Another mark above the helmet of Virtus on the second drum is likewise found to fit on to its prolongation below the figure of Pax on the third drum. The whole rearrangement may be set out as follows:

	IVNO *Regina*	Luna		Sol
	Genius Neronis	Lar	Bacchus	Lar
	VENVS	Pax	Iuno *Sancta*	VESTA
	VOLCANVS	Virtus	CERES	Honos
	Victoria	MARS	DIANA	NEPTVNVS
UPPER PLINTH	Inscription	Castor	APOLLO	Pollux
LOWER PLINTH	IVPITER	MERCVRIVS and Maia (?)	Hercules	MINERVA and Fortuna
	FRONT	LEFT SIDE	BACK	RIGHT SIDE

(left vertical label: SHAFT OF THE COLUMN)

Quilling now maintains that the entire monument refers to its dedicators, the Canabarii. Virtus and Honos are (as Maass suggested) personifications of Mayence and Castel. Victoria between Mars and Neptunus denotes the success of the fourteenth legion, formerly stationed at Mayence, over the British Boudicca in 61 A.D. Volcanus is there to avert the risk of fire from the corn-ears of Ceres, who represents the harbour-quarter. The goddess with the scales is the patron of Mayence market. She that sets foot on the cow's head and she that has the horse (?) stand for cattle-breeding. Pax is for petty trade. The Genius Neronis becomes the Genius Canabensium. Apollo hails from the Vicus Apollinensis. Etc., etc. But Quilling's views succeed one another at such a pace that the foregoing identifications are, for aught I know, already superannuated.

ii. 97 n. o. H. Mattingly in the *Journ. Rom. Stud.* 1920 x. 38 described an *aureus* of Nero, which has *rev.* IVPPITER LIBERATOR Iupiter enthroned to left with a thunderbolt in his right hand and a sceptre in his left—a thin disguise for the emperor himself. Mr Mattingly supposed that this coin was struck at Corinth (?) in 67 A.D. (*Brit. Mus. Cat. Rom. Coins* Emp. i pp. clxxxiii f., 214 no. 110 pl. 40, 15), but he is careful to state that its authenticity has been very seriously questioned (*ib.* p. clxxxiv n. 1). Coppers of l'atrai, issued under Nero, show *rev.* IVPPITER LIBERATOR Iupiter, nude, standing to left with an eagle on his right hand and a sceptre in his left (Eckhel *Doctr. num. vet.*² ii. 243, 256, B. Pick in the *Zeitschr. f. Num.* 1890 xvii. 180 ff.).

ii. 98 n. 3. On the statuette from Woodchester see also Farnell *Cults of Gk. States* ii. 529 pl. 31, *a* ('must be a fragment of a statue of Artemis Tauropolos, standing on the bull and carrying a torch'), and S. Reinach in the *Rev. Arch.* 1913 i. 29 fig. 3 ('Cérès'), i. 422 ('Déméter-Cérès').

ii. 106 n. 2. Add R. Traquair and A. J. B. Wace 'The Base of the Obelisk of Theodosius' in the *Journ. Hell. Stud.* 1909 xxix. 60—69 with 7 figs.

ii. 121 ff. on Thracian tattooing. P. Wolters in *Hermes* 1903 xxxviii. 265—273 explains the name Ἐλαφόστικτος (Lys. *or.* 13. 19 Θεόκριτον τὸν τοῦ Ἐλαφοστίκτου καλούμενον) as appropriate to a Thracian painted or tattooed. See further O. Crusius in *Philologus* 1903 lxii. 125—132 (reported in the *Am. Journ. Arch.* 1903 vii. 477 f.).

At *Dikili-Tasch* near Philippoi have been found terra-cotta figures of prehistoric (neolithic?) date, which show male heads tattooed, with pointed beards (*Bull. Corr. Hell.* 1921 xlv. 543 fig. 15).

ii. 131 n. 1. W. B. McDaniel 'The Holiness of the Dischi Sacri' in the *Am. Journ. Arch.* 1924 xxviii. 24—46 figures and discusses eleven such disks ; he sees in them (p. 44) 'a sort of compound seal, a composite of signets, peculiar in its design to Tarentum, used for commercial purposes'... 'Pressed in the wax of Tarentum or upon a seal of clay or gypsum.'

ii. 136 ff. Anent the 'Ladder of Salvation' Mr G. G. Coulton kindly refers me to a passage in the *vita fratris Leonis* (*Analecta Franciscana* Ad Claras Aquas (Quaracchi) 1897 iii. 71, 19 ff.) semel etiam frater Leo vidit in somnis, quod divinum iudicium parabatur, et in prato quodam Angelis tubicinantibus congregabatur gentium innumerabilis multitudo. et ecce duae scalae, quarum una erat alba, altera rubea, fuerunt positae, una ab una parte illius prati, altera ab alia, quarum proceritas usque ad coelos a terra tendebatur. apparuit autem Christus in summitate scalae rubeae quasi offensus graviter et iratus ; et beatus Franciscus erat aliquantulum inferius prope ipsum. qui amplius descendens, fratres suos fortissime clamando vocabat dicens : 'venite, fratres, venite, accedite ad Dominum, qui vos vocat. confidite, ne timeatis.' fratres autem multi currebant ex admonitione Patris et incipiebant ascendere scalam rubeam confidenter. cum autem sic ascenderent, unus cadebat de tertio gradu, alius de quarto, alius de decimo, alii de medio, alii de summo. beatus autem Franciscus ad tantam fratrum ruinam motus compassione, pro filiis iudicem precabatur. Christus vero ostendebat manus et latus, in quibus plagae eius renovari videbantur ; et inde sanguis recentissime distillabat, et dicebat : 'ista fecerunt mihi fratres tui.' et dum beatus Franciscus perseveraret misericordiam pro filiis postulando, post brevem morulam aliquantulum per scalam rubeam descendebat et clamabat dicens : 'confidite, fratres, ne desperetis, currite ad scalam albam et ascendite, quia ibi suscipiemini et per eam intrabitis coelum.' currentibus autem fratribus ad scalam albam ex admonitione paterna, ecce beata Virgo apparuit in summitate scalae et recipiebat eos ; et ingrediebantur regnum sine labore. Cp. Bartholomaeus de Pisis *de conformitate vitae beati Francisci ad vitam Domini Iesu Redemptoris nostri* 8. 2 *de fratre Leone* (*Analecta Franciscana* Ad Claras Aquas (Quaracchi) 1906 iv. 191, 18 ff.), S. Alfonso de' Liguori *Glories of Mary* (extr. from *The Christian Remembrancer* Oct. 1855) London 1856 p. 25 f., *The Church Quarterly Review* 1902—1903 lv. 55.

ii. 146. A similar sacred trunk adorned with the spoils of the chase was to be seen at Autessiodurum (*Auxerre*), a town of the Senones in Gallia Lugudunensis, as late as the beginning of *s.* v A.D. (*Acta Sanctorum* edd. Bolland. Maius i. 57 C—E (Stephanus Africanus Presbyter *vita S. Amatoris Episcopi Autissiodorensis* 4. 24) Eo autem tempore quo hæc gesta sunt, Germanus quidam nomine, nobili germine procreatus, territorium Autissiodorense visitatione propria gubernabat : cui mos erat tirunculorum potius industriis indulgere, quam Christianæ religioni operam dare. Is ergo assiduo venatui invigilans, ferarum copiam insidiis atque artis strenuitate frequentissime capiebat. Erat autem arbor pyrus in urbe media, amoenitate gratissima, ad cujus ramusculos ferarum ab eo deprehensarum capita pro admiratione venationis nimiæ dependebant. Quem celebris vir ejusdem civitatis Amator Episcopus, his frequens compellabat eloquiis : Desine, quæso, vir bonorum splendidissime, hæc jocularia, quæ Christianis offensa, Paganis vero imitanda sunt, exercere. Hoc opus idololatricæ culturæ est, non Christianæ elegantissimæ disciplinæ. Et licet hoc vir Deo dignus indesinenter perageret, ille tamen nullo modo admonenti se acquiescere voluit aut obedire. Vir autem Domini iterum atque iterum eum hortabatur, ut non solum à consuetudine male arrepta discederet, verum & ipsam arborem, ne Christianis offendiculum esset, radicitus extirparet. Sed ille nullatenus aurem placidam applicare voluit admoneti. In hujus ergo persuasionis tempore, quadam die præfatus Germanus ex urbe in prædia sui juris secessit. Tunc B. Amator, opportunitatem operiens, sacrilegam arborem cum radicibus abscidit ; & ne aliqua ejus incredulis esset memoria, igni concremandam illico deputavit : oscilla vero, quæ tamquam trophei cujusdam certaminis umbrâ dependentia ostentabant, longius à civitatis terminis projici præcepit. Protinus autem [aliquis], gressus suos ad aures sæpedicti Germani retorquens, dictis animum incendit ; atque iram suis suasionibus exaggerans, ferocem effecit : ita ut oblitus sanctæ religionis, cujus fuerat ritu atque munere consecratus, mortem viro beatissimo minitaret : & ne ei aliquo modo quorumdam Christianorum conventus furenti resisteret, turbam secum agrestem coadunans civitati improvisus advenit. The upshot was unexpected. Amator, to escape the wrath of Germanus, fled the town, made his way to Augustodunum (*Autun*), and besought Julius, governor of the province, to sanction the nomination and consecration of Germanus to the episcopal throne of *Auxerre* in the room of himself. 'For,' said the saint, 'God has revealed to me that my life draweth to a close.' A few days later Amator died, while Germanus became bishop in his stead and ruled the see well (S. Baring-Gould *The Lives of the Saints*[2] Edinburgh 1914 v. 13 f.). Amator's festival falls on May 1).

There are points about this curious narrative which suggest that we have here in an attenuated, Christianised, form a Gallic parallel to the cult of Diana *Nemorensis*.

ii. 157 n. o. F. Courby *Les vases grecs à reliefs* Paris 1922 pp. 509—513 ('Oenochoés à portraits de reines') enumerates four examples and sundry fragments, which commemorate Arsinoe ii, Berenike ii, and Ptolemy iv Philopator. With unimportant variations, all repeat the same type, derived—according to Courby—from a statue of Arsinoe ii with the attributes of Tyche set up by Ptolemy ii Philadelphos (Athen. 497 B—c) in her temple at Alexandreia (Plin. *nat. hist.* 37. 108) together with an obelisk eighty cubits high (*id. ib.* 36. 67 f.).

ii. 174. In the *Rev. Arch.* 1920 i. 172 C. Picard attempts to discredit the *omphalós* found by F. Courby within the temple of Apollon. He suggests that it is perhaps a mere weight and that its inscription may not after all be archaic. But Mr C. T. Seltman, who at my request has made a careful examination of the original stone, sends me (Jan. 11, 1923) the following report: 'After our trip to Delphi, from which we returned four days ago, I must write and tell you what I think about *the* Omphalos, which is now placed in the Museum there. It seems to me that the suggestion of its being a forgery can only be born of madness or malice! The thing is smaller than one expected it to be, but it is to my thinking impossible that it should be a fake. The ⊓ upon it is clear as are ΛΑ; but the *sigma* of ΛΑΖ is so mutilated by a large fracture in the stone that it might be almost any letter.'

ii. 176 n. 1. On Themis at Delphoi see also F. Courby in the *Fouilles de Delphes* ii. 1. 81, who notes the inscription restored by G. Colin in the *Bull. Corr. Hell.* 1903 xxvii. 107 no. 684 B, 14 f. ἐφιορκοῦντι δὲ [Θέμις] καὶ Ἀπόλλων Πύθιος καὶ Λατὼ καὶ Ἄρτεμ[ις καὶ] Ἑστία καὶ πῦρ ἀθάνατον καὶ θεοὶ πά[ντες καὶ πᾶσαι κακίστωι ὀλέθρωι τὴν] | σωτηρίαν μοι [ἀφέλωσι]ν, κ.τ.λ.

In the hymn composed by Aristonoös of Corinth and inscribed on the Athenian Treasury at Delphoi we read how Apollon first occupied the oracular seat πείσας Γαῖαν ἀνθοτρόφον | Θέμιν τ' εὐπλόκαμον θεάν (G. Colin in the *Fouilles de Delphes* iii. 2. 213 ff. no. 191, 18 f.).

ii. 176 n. 2. W. H. Roscher 'Die Bedeutung des E zu Delphi und die übrigen γράμματα Δελφικά' in *Philologus* 1900 lix. 21—41 labours to prove that the mystic εἶ is for πρόσει, εἴσει, '"komm her" oder "Willkommen."' This, to my mind, is quite impossible Greek.

ii. 190 n. o. Further references for the history of *rhytá* are given by F. W. von Bissing in the *Jahrb. d. Deutsch. Arch. Inst.* 1923/24 xxxviii/ix Arch. Anz. pp. 106—109.

ii. 193. On the evolution of the tripod see now K. Schwendemann 'Der Dreifuss' in the *Jahrb. d. Deutsch. Arch. Inst.* 1921 xxxvi. 98—185 with figs. 1—30. *Id. ib.* p. 183 f. discusses the relation of the tripod to Zeus on vases and coins.

ii. 193 n. 2. Cp. the twelfth-century fonts at Winchester etc. (C. H. Eden *Black Tournai Fonts in England* London 1909 pp. 1—32 with good plates), which in appearance at least perpetuate this ancient form of libation-table.

ii. 195 n. 1. A. Furtwängler 'Zum platäischen Weihgeschenk in Delphi' in the *Sitzungsber. d. kais. bayr. Akad. d. Wiss.* Phil.-hist. Classe 1904 pp. 413—417 (*Am. Journ. Arch.* 1905 ix. 477) figures the upper surface of the highest extant step of the Plataean tripod, and explains three symmetrically arranged slots in it as due to tenons which passed through the top step of the base and thus tethered the tripod-feet to the second step. If so, we must suppose that the legs of the tripod were drawn somewhat closer together than I have placed them (*supra* p. 194 fig. 134). Furtwängler's inference, however, is not quite secure, since the serpent-coil, which he too takes to have been the central support of the caldron, has left no trace whatever on the second step. It may be that the three slots in question served merely for dowels fastening this step to the one above it, in which serpent-coil and legs were alike embedded.

Re the Plataean tripod see now R. M. Dawkins in *Folk-Lore* 1924 xxxv. 234 f., 380.

ii. 208 f. In this connexion Miss H. Richardson of Newnham College drew my attention (Oct. 24, 1924) to Plout. *de sera num. vind.* 22 566 D ἅμα δ' ἐπειρᾶτο προσάγων ἐπιδεικνύειν αὐτῷ τὸ φῶς ἐκ τοῦ τρίποδος, ὡς ἔλεγε, διὰ τῶν κόλπων τῆς Θέμιδος ἀπερειδόμενον εἰς τὸν Παρνασόν· καὶ προθυμούμενος ἰδεῖν οὐκ εἶδεν ὑπὸ λαμπρότητος, ἀλλ' ἤκουε παριὼν φωνὴν ὀξεῖαν γυναικὸς ἐν μέτρῳ φράζουσαν ἄλλα τέ τινα καὶ χρόνον, ὡς ἔοικε, τῆς ἐκείνου τελευτῆς. We have here, apparently, Themis on the Delphic tripod impregnated by the central pillar of light (=Apollon: cp. *supra* p. 178).

ii. 222 n. 2. On Iason swallowed by the snake see further P. Ducati 'Giasone e il serpente' in the *Rendiconti d. Lincei* 1920 xxix. 52—64 (p. 53 fig. 1 *kýlix* from *Cervetri*, p. 61 fig. 3 bronze *kýathos* from Felsina).

ii. 229 n. 7. Zeus as Artemis wooing Kallisto is the subject of a painting by F. Boucher (1703—1770 A.D.) (W. Hausenstein *Der nackte Mensch in der Kunst aller Zeiten* München 1918 p. 122 fig. 84).

ii. 281 n. 4. For the golden vine overhanging the entrance to Herod's temple Mr G. C. Armstrong quotes also Ioseph. *de bell. Iud.* 5. 5. 4.

ii. 282. Mr B. F. C. Atkinson has kindly supplied me (Apr. 28, 1922) with a *Note on the Name Sabazios* :—

'I suggest the following etymology for *Sabazios*. The second part I believe to be *Zios*, *Dios*, the Phrygian Zeus. The change of *d* to a sound represented by *zeta* in Thracian is frequent and seems regular, whether it be, as Kretschmer suggests (*Einleitung* p. 196), due to "Assibilation des *d* vor *i*," or whether, as is perhaps more probable, a change of *d* to the voiced dental spirant *đ* took place over the whole Illyrian—Thracian—Phrygian language area. The disappearance of intervocalic digamma may be due to conscious assimilation by Greek transcribers to Gk. Δία, Διός, etc., although it is well to remember in this connection that there is a form of the stem that contains no *μ* (Skt. *dyām*, Gk. Ζῆν, Lat. *diem*).

The first part of the compound adapts itself with surprising regularity to the root given by Brugmann as *ƙeμā, which appears with varying ablaut in Skt. *çávişṭhas*, *çvātrás*, *çváyati*, *çúras*, Gk. κύος, κῦρος and Boeotian τὰ ππάματα. The root has the general meaning of "swell," "be important," "be master," "possess." *Sabazios* would thus mean originally "Lord Zeus."

There seems to be another possible etymology for the first part of the compound. The root occurring in Skt. *kávis*, Gk. κοέω, Lat. *caueo*, Goth. *us-skáus* may be in evidence here. If this is the case, the initial *s* can be explained in two ways. It may represent an *s*- sound and illustrate the Thracian treatment of the I.-E. combination *sq*-. More probably we have in Thracian that form of the stem that shows no initial sibilant (as in the examples cited from Skt., Gk., and Lat.), in which case concealed beneath *sigma* is the sound *tş* (final in Eng. *thatch*). The Messapian and Lycian inscriptions, if correctly interpreted by Deecke, throw light on this view. There we find *sigma* or *zeta* used for a sound that represents the I.-E. velar (Messap. *zis* for *quis*, a proper name *Plazet* with genitive *Plaχtas*; Lyc. *sättäre*, "four," etc.: vd. Deecke in *Bezz. Beit.* Vols. xii, xiii, xiv), though it is true that it is the labialised velar that in these cases undergoes palatalisation. In this case *Sabazios* would mean "Zeus the wise one" with a hint at prophetical power (cf. *caueo*), somewhat resembling "*augur Apollo.*" Then we could regard the *Sauadai* or *Saboi*, whose connection with the god seems obvious, as his "wise ones" or "seers."

The former of these two etymologies is perhaps the more straightforward; but there is no real barrier to the second (though it would scarcely have been possible apart from the evidence of the Messapian and Lycian inscriptions). In either case the *beta* represents a *v*-sound, as the alternative forms (*Saouazios*, *Sauazios*, *Saoazios*, *Savazios*, *Sabadius*) make clear, and this derives almost certainly from an earlier *u*. The *a* of the first syllable, whether it represent older *e* or *o*, is assimilated to the following *a*, a practice which seems regular in Illyrian and Thracian (cf., for example, *Delminium* but *Dalmatae*, *-poris* but *-para*). Thus the former etymology would give us *Savađios*, the latter *Tşavađios*.'

ii. 282 n. 2. P. Roussel—J. Hatzfeld in the *Bull. Corr. Hell.* 1909 xxxiii. 511 no. 29 publish a marble slab, from a house N.W. of the *agorá* of Theophrastos in Delos, inscribed in late lettering Δειεὶ Σαβαζίω(ι) --- | κατ' εὐχὴν Μο--- | του γεγονότος --- | ἐν Δήλωι Αἰλ[ίου?] ---. See also P. Roussel *Délos Colonie athénienne* Paris 1916 p. 276 n. 7.

ii. 285 n. o no. (3). The relief from Philadelpheia (*Ala-Shehir*) in Lydia, hitherto incorrectly described, is figured from a photograph (=my fig. 1011) by J. Keil—A. von Premerstein 'Bericht über eine zweite Reise in Lydien' in the *Denkschr. d. Akad. Wien* 1911 ii Abh. p. 84 no. 2. A bearded man standing erect, in *chitón* and *himátion*, holds his garment with his left hand. With his right hand he pours a libation from a *phiále* into a *kratér*, set on the ground, about which two snakes are twined, apparently drinking out

Fig. 1011.

of it. Behind the *kratér* is seen a tree (oak ??), from which a snake lowers itself towards the *phiále*.

ii. 290 n. o. Sir W. M. Flinders Petrie 'Funereal Figures in Egypt' in *Ancient Egypt* 1916 pp. 151—162 draws attention to the existing African custom of treasuring in the family the head of the deceased father and uses it to elucidate certain sepulchral practices of the ancient Egyptians. He shows that in many burials of prehistoric times the head was removed and later replaced in the grave, if not lost or buried elsewhere ; that in tomb-shafts of the fourth dynasty a stone image of the head was provided in case the actual head should be lost or injured ; that at the break-up of the Old Kingdom a stone image of the mummy came into vogue ; and that the addition of hands, arms, etc. led on to the fully developed *ushabti* figures of the seventeenth and following dynasties.

P. D. Chantepie de la Saussaye *The Religion of the Teutons* Boston and London 1902 p. 303 notes relevant facts in the Scandinavian area.

ii. 295 n. 1. On Ἄδαμνα=Ἄττις see now W. Vollgraff 'De voce thracia ἀδαπταῖς' in *Mnemosyne* 1921 xlix. 286—294 (summarised by S. Reinach in the *Rev. Arch.* 1921 ii. 406 f.).

ii. 322 n. 6. In the Hesychian gloss on the word κυνακίας J. Alberti rightly conjectured διδόμενοι for διδομένου. He is followed by Wide *Lakon. Kulte* p. 68.

ii. 326. See now Miss M. A. Murray *The Witch-Cult in Western Europe* Oxford 1921.

ii. 345. The *formula* of the Cretan mystics (βοῦς μέγας) may help to clear up an obscure epigram of Kallimachos—'οὗτος ἐμὸς λόγος ὔμμιν ἀληθινός· εἰ δὲ τὸν ἡδὺν | βούλει, Πελλαίου βοῦς μέγας εἰν Ἀίδῃ' (Kallim. *ep.* 15. 5 f. with A. W. Mair's note *ad loc.*).

ii. 345 n. 6. On the survival of this *formula* into the middle ages see some interesting remarks by W. Deonna in the *Rev. Arch.* 1921 ii. 412.

ii. 386. The *pétasos* as a sky-symbol possibly meets us again on the tomb of Porsenna at Clusium as described by Varro *ap.* Plin. *nat. hist.* 36. 91—93 (92 pyramides stant quinque...ita fastigatae ut in summo orbis aeneus et petasus unus omnibus sit inpositus, ex quo pendeant exapta catenis tintinabula, etc.). For discussion and attempted restorations see Quatremère de Quincy and the Duc de Luynes in the *Ann. d. Inst.* 1829 i. 304—309, *Mon. d. Inst.* i pl. 13, G. Dennis *The Cities and Cemeteries of Etruria*[3] London 1883 ii. 345—358, J. Martha *L'Art Étrusque* Paris 1889 p. 206 ff., Durm *Baukunst d. Etrusk.*[2] p. 140 ff. fig. 165.

ii. 388 n. 4. Janifórm busts of Zeus and Hermes are implied by the word Διέρμαι (Prokl. *in* Plat. *Alcib.* i. 68 f. Creuzer καὶ περὶ ἕκαστον τῶν θεῶν πλῆθός ἐστι δαιμόνων ἀμύθητον καὶ ταῖς αὐταῖς ἐπωνυμίαις ἀποσεμνυνόμενον τῶν ἡγουμένων θεῶν· Ἀπόλλωνες γὰρ καὶ Δίες καὶ Διέρμαι καλούμενοι χαίρουσιν, ἅτε δὴ καὶ τὴν ἰδιότητα τῶν οἰκείων θεῶν ἀποτυπούμενοι).

ii. 397 n. 0. R. B. Onians in the *Class. Rev.* 1924 xxxviii. 5 takes Zeus Ἠλακατεύς to mean Zeus 'of the Spindle,' who spins the thread of fate (cp. *Od.* 4. 207 f. ῥεῖα δ' ἀρίγνωτος γόνος ἀνέρος ᾧ τε Κρονίων | ὄλβον ἐπικλώσῃ γαμέοντί τε γεινομένῳ τε).

ii. 465. For horned female deer see L. P. Hatch 'A Doe with Horns' in *The American Naturalist* 1870 iii. 279, W. J. Hays 'Does with Horns' *ib.* 1870 iii. 548—550 and in *The Academy* 1870 i. 103.

ii. 479 n. 8. J. Kohler 'Bräuche und Mythen der Arandas' [=the Arunta] in the *Zeitschrift des Vereins für Volkskunde* 1916 xxvi. 283 'hier bildet die Milchstrasse einen grossen Fluss: sie ist mit hohen Bäumen besetzt und von Wasserquellen umgeben, wo Beerenfrüchte in Hülle und Fülle wachsen.'

ii. 479 n. 10. See also D. A. Mackenzie in *Folk-Lore* 1922 xxxiii. 159.

ii. 482. For the Milky Way conceived as a tree cp. W. Gundel *Sterne und Sternbilder im Glauben des Altertums und der Neuzeit* Bonn—Leipzig 1922 p. 46 : 'Für sich steht die Auffassung der Bakaïri die einen gewaltigen Trommelbaum darin erblicken' (citing K. von den Steinen *Unter den Naturvölkern Zentral-Brasiliens* Berlin 1894 pp. 360, 436).

ii. 483. Mr R. Campbell Thompson, in a letter passed on to me by Mr Sidney Smith, says : 'The *kiškanû* is not a common plant, and is rarely, if ever, used in the medical texts. Yet there are three kinds of it—*ṣalmu*, *piṣu*, and *samu*—black, white, and red? (or yellow). I doubt it being the *astragalus* now. I looked about always in Mespot for anything which would coincide and I confess I am baffled. There is nothing at Eridu now—which is as flat and bare, save for low scrub growth in parts, as one's hand. It can hardly be a very special tree, since it is to be found at the mouth of the rivers.'

ii. 484. A. Nehring in the *Mitteilungen der Schlesischen Gesellschaft für Volkskunde* 1916 xviii. 23 argues that the original form of the name was the vocative Ἄπελλον, because only in the vocative is the ε unaccented, and only unaccented ε becomes o under the influence of a following ω (o). This argument was cited by A. H. Krappe in a letter to J. Rendel Harris, who comments: 'He should have added that, with the second syllable unstressed, it was easy to explain the Thessalian Ἄπλουν' (F. Bechtel *Die griechischen Dialekte* Berlin 1921 i. 172).

ii. 486. The ultimate acceptance of the bay as the tree *par excellence* of Apollon can be well illustrated from a unique *statér* of *s.* iv B.C., struck by some uncertain town in Crete and now preserved in the Hunterian collection at Glasgow (P. Gardner *Types of Gk. Coins* p. 165 pl. 9, 15 and 16, J. N. Svoronos *Numismatique de la Crète ancienne* Mâcon 1890 i. 331 pl. 31, 8, *Hunter Cat. Coins* ii. 200 pl. 43, 7, Head *Hist. num.*[2] p. 479). *Obv.* Apollon, seated to right on the trunk of a bay-tree, holding a wreath in his left hand. *Rev.* Apollon, seated to right on the trunk of a bay-

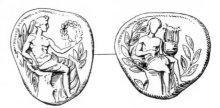

Fig. 1012.

tree, holding a lyre in his left hand. Fig. 1012 is drawn from a cast kindly supplied to me by Mr G. Macdonald.

ii. 493. I am indebted to Mr B. F. C. Atkinson for the following important communication (Feb. 25, 1922) :—'*Note on Apollo and the Apple.* It seems to me that the philological obstacles to this connection are not insurmountable. Professor E. H. Sturtevant (*Pronunciation of Greek and Latin*, Chicago 1920 pp. 91 ff.) has shown that, while in Greek the unvoiced stops were *lenes*, that is, pronounced without force, and the voiced stops were *fortes*, the reverse was true in Latin. This is the reason why in certain cases of transliteration from one language into the other $g(\gamma)$ and $k(\kappa)$, $d(\delta)$ and $t(\tau)$, $b(\beta)$ and $p(\pi)$ are interchangeable: for references and examples see my article on "Apollo and the Apple" in the *Bulletin of the John Rylands Library, Manchester*, 1922 vii. 138—140. I have in this article tried to show that in respect of the sets of stops which are *fortes* or *lenes* there is a probability of the Illyrian dialects agreeing with Latin rather than Greek. If then, as I have ventured to surmise, the god's name were borrowed by thė Greeks from an Illyrian dialect, in which the form had a voiced stop and was connected with the stem meaning "apple," which runs through the northern languages and appears probably in the name of *Abella* in Campania, the unvoicing of the stop in transmission, that is to say, the change from *b* to *p*, need cause us no surprise. The suggestion is somewhat strengthened by the occurrence of the proper names *Abellio* (dat. *Abellioni*) in an inscription from Salona on the Dalmatian coast (*Corp. inscr. Lat.* iii no. 2169, 3) and *Abello* (gen. *Abellonis*) in another from Mursa in Pannonia Inferior (*ib.* iii no. 10271, 3).'

ii. 496 n. 0. On Zeus Περφερέτας or Φερφερέτας as worshipped by the Phrouroi (originally conservators of a particular stretch of the Sacred Way?) see now F. Stählin *Das hellenische Thessalien* Stuttgart 1924 p. 90 n. 7.

ii. 498 n. 2: 'Has it been noticed etc.?' The answer is, Yes. See Campbell Bonner in the *Am. Journ. Philol.* 1900 xxi. 433—437.

ii. 500 f. I have doubted, and still doubt, Artemis' northern *provenance*. But see, on the other side, an interesting paper by Mr J. Whatmough 'Inscribed fragments of stags-horn from North Italy' in the *Journ. Rom. Stud.* 1921 xi. 245—253. He would equate Ἄρτεμις, not only with Βριτόμαρτις (= Ϝριτόμαρτις), but also with *Rehtia* at Este and *Rit-* in Magrè.

ii. 542. W. Gaerte 'Die Bedeutung der kretisch-minoischen Horns of Consecration' in the *Archiv f. Rel.* 1922 xxi. 91 n. 2 interprets the problematic object between the horns of my fig. 415 f. as the sun between the peaks of an 'Erdsymbol' (mountains).

ii. 575 n. 4. The coin of Euromos that shows the local Zeus with a stag (cp. ii. 575 n. 1) suggests that Zeus has here replaced Artemis Ἐφεσία. Note that the similar Zeus on coins of Mylasa was, like Artemis at Ephesos (ii. 408 n. 0), linked to the ground with fillets (ii. 574), and that the Zeus of Euromos is covered with dots, which may represent breasts (ii. 592 ff.).

ii. 578 n. 4. Add A. Rehm in *Milet* iii. 330 ff. no. 146, A 17 ff. ἵνα δὲ καὶ διαμνημονεύη-ται τὸν ἀεὶ χρόνον καὶ τηρῆται τὰ δεδογμένα, συνέταξαν τὰ περὶ τούτων ἐψηφισμένα ἀ|ναγράψαι ἐν τοῖς ἑαυτῶ ἱεροῖς τῶι τε τοῦ Διὸς τοῦ Ὀσογῶ καὶ τοῦ Διὸς | τοῦ Λαβραύνδου· συνετέλεσαν δὲ καὶ εὐχὰς καὶ θυσίας | τοῖς τε προειρημένοις θεοῖς καὶ τῆι Ἑστίαι καὶ Ἀπόλλωνι Δι|δυμεῖ, B 71 ff. ὅπως δὲ τὰ ἐψηφισμένα ὑπὸ τοῦ δήμου | τίμια μνημονεύηται εἰς τὸν ἀεὶ χρόνον, ἀναγράψαι τόδε τὸ ψήφισμα ἐ[ν] | τοῖς ἱεροῖς τῶι τε τοῦ Διὸς τοῦ Ὀσογῶ καὶ τοῦ Διὸς τοῦ Λαβραύνδου. ἵνα δ[ὲ] | ἕκαστα γίνηται μετὰ τῆς τῶν θεῶν εὐμενείας, τὸμ μὲν στεφανηφόρον | μετὰ τοῦ ἱερέω τῆι Ἑστίαι θῦσαι καὶ τὸν ἱερέα τοῦ Ἀπόλλωνος τοῦ Διδυμέ|ως καὶ τοὺς ἱερεῖς τόν τε τοῦ Διὸς τοῦ Ὀσογῶ καὶ τὸν τοῦ Διὸς τοῦ Λαβραύ|δου προσαγαγεῖν θυσίαν τοῖς θεοῖς καὶ εὐχὰς ποιήσασθαι συνενεγκεῖν | ταῖς πόλεσιν ἀμφοτέραις τὰ ἐψηφισμένα (in a treaty between Miletos and Mylasa, 209/8 B.C.).

ii. 583. E. W. Fay in the *Class. Quart.* 1917 xi. 215 derives Ποτ-ειδάϝων from *ποτι-, 'lord,' and EID, 'to swell.'

ii. 587. Unexpected confirmation of O. Höfer's conjectural Zeus Σπάλαξος has recently come to hand. The British Museum has acquired an imperial bronze coin of Aphrodisias in Karia, on which he actually appears. Mr G. F. Hill kindly allows me to illustrate it here for the first time (fig. 1013). *Obv.* ΚΡΙϹΠΕΙΝΑ ΑΥΓΟΥϹΤΑ Bust of Crispina to right. *.Rev.* ϹΕΥϹϹΠ Α Λ[Α]ΞΟϹ ΑΦΡΟΔΕΙϹΙ [Ε]ΩΝ Zeus Σπάλαξος (less probably Σπάλωξος) enthroned to left with Nike in right hand and long sceptre in left.

Fig. 1013.

ii. 596 fig. 499. In J. G. C. Anderson—F. Cumont—H. Grégoire *Recueil des inscriptions grecques et latines du Pont et de l'Arménie* (*Studia Pontica* iii) Bruxelles 1910 i. 161 f. no. 146 H. Grégoire gives a photographic cut of the whole relief, a facsimile of its inscription (which he transcribes as Ζώβη (or Ζιώβη) | θεᾷ (or θεαῖς) | .... σι though various other letters are visible in lines 4, 5, 6), and a commentary.

ii. 619 n. 4. On the Mithraeum of Allmendingen, excavated 1824—1825, see further Lohner in *Der Schweizerische Geschichtsforscher* 1834 viii (wrongly numbered ix). 430 ff. pl. 5, F. Cumont *Textes et monuments figurés relatifs aux mystères de Mithra* Bruxelles

1896 ii. 505 figs. 450—455. Seven little hatchets of bronze were found, inscribed IOVI, MIИERVAE, etc.

ii. 625 n. 3. Mr A. J. B. Wace, lecturing to the Classical Society at Cambridge on Nov. 27, 1922, described how in the last season's 'dig' at Mykenai the British School had excavated various tombs outside the town. In the entrance to tomb no. 515 were found two sealstones, dating from s. xv B.C., with an almost identical device. Above a stepped base stands a 'Minoan' goddess, flanked by a pair of lions erect upon their hind legs. On her head she supports a double axe, which rises from the centre of a couple of two-headed snakes connected by crossbars—apparently a serpentine substitute for the more usual 'horns of consecration' (cp. *Brit. Mus. Cat. Jewellery* p. 54 f. no. 762 pls. 6 and 7). Fig. 1014 is enlarged ¾ from a cast supplied to me by the British Museum. The main difference between the two stones is that on this one the lions' tails curl upwards, on the other downwards. Mr Wace aptly drew attention to Hesych. *s. vv.* κύβηλις· μάχαιρα. ἄμεινον δὲ πέλεκυν, ᾧ τὰς βοῦς καταβάλλουσι, κυβηλῖσαι· πελεκῖσαι· κύβηλις γὰρ ὁ πέλεκυς, and accordingly proposed to call the goddess Kybele (*id.* in the *Journ. Hell. Stud.* 1921 xli. 264 'Kybele or Rhea').

Fig. 1014.

ii. 632 n. 6. Add an axe of dark brown schist, decorated with zigzags and spirals and ending in the forepart of a lioness, found in a 'Middle Minoan iii' vase at Mallia (*Comptes rendus de l'Acad. des inscr. et belles-lettres* 1925 p. 23 f. fig.).

ii. 633 ff. The axes borne by Roman lictors may be illustrated from a fragmentary marble relief now affixed to a wall of the Cryptoporticus on the Palatine. Fig. 1015 is from a photograph taken by my friend and colleague Mr A. Munro, Fellow of Queens' College, Cambridge. It will be observed that the haft of every axe is surmounted by a head (lion, man, ram).

The 'Tomb of the Lictor' at Vetulonia takes its name from an iron double axe (0.27ᵐ long) hafted on to an iron rod surrounded by eight hollow rods of iron (last published by D. Randall-MacIver *Villanovans and Early Etruscans* Oxford 1924 p. 145 fig. 56 after O. Montelius *La civilisation primitive en Italie depuis l'introduction des métaux* Stockholm 1904 Série B pl. 194, 5). Cp. *Sil. It.* 8. 483 ff.

ii. 637. Four fine examples of carving in amber (Eros *v.* Anteros, Bacchant, female bust, 'Tiergruppe') are figured by H. Maionica in the *Führer durch das K. K. Staatsmuseum in Aquileia* Wien 1910 p. 71 ff. Finer still (*c.* 0·40ᵐ high) is the archaic *koûros* of Fiumicino (S. Reinach in the *Rev. Arch.* 1924 ii. 237).

ii. 645 n. 4. See now Sir A. J. Evans in the *Journ. Hell. Stud.* 1925 xlv. 53 ff.

ii. 660. A small double axe of ivory (fig. 1016: scale ⅓), now in my possession, is said to have come from Pharsalos, but was more probably found at Pherai. With it were an ivory *fibula* of 'spectacle'-type and two bronze pendants of the Hallstatt period.

Fig. 1015.

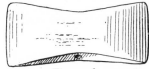

Fig. 1016.

ii. 667. Cp. Furtwängler *Geschnitt. Steine Berlin* p. 312 no. 8514 pl. 71 a red jasper of imperial date showing a crab with a comic mask as its carapace.

ii. 693 n. 4. See now an interesting study by W. R. Halliday 'Picus-who-is-also-Zeus' in the *Class. Rev.* 1922 xxxvi. 110—112.

ii. 716. F. J. M. De Waele 'ΧΡΥΣΑΩΡ' in *Le Musée Belge* 1924 xxviii No. 1 (January) holds that ἄορ in this compound retains its original sense, 'arrow.' See *Class. Rev.* 1924 xxxviii. 92.

ii. 725 figs. 660, 661. A. della Seta *Italia antica* Bergamo 1922 p. 252 fig. 281 shows this statue as it stands in the Galleria dei Candelabri of the Vatican, with a bow restored in its right hand and an eagle in its left !

ii. 739. On statuettes of Zeus the thunderer see now S. Casson in the *Journ. Hell. Stud.* 1922 xlii. 211 f. figs. 4—6. He claims that a crude example of the type from Dodona (C. Carapanos *Dodone et ses ruines* Paris 1878 p. 32 no. 16 pl. 13, 4, S. Casson *loc. cit.* p. 211 f. fig. 4 (*b*)=my fig. 1017) is 'of the Geometric period.' If so, this would be the earliest known representation of Zeus in the round. Unfortunately it is not quite certain that Zeus was intended. The subject *may* be a fighting man, not a thundering god. The holes in his hands would suit spear and shield at least as well as they would suit thunderbolt and eagle. The absence of a helmet, however, tells in favour of Zeus.

Fig. 1017.   Fig. 1020.

ii. 741 f. K. A. Rhomaios in the 'Αρχ. Δελτ. 1920—21 vi. 169—171 figs. 3—6 (of which figs. 5 and 6=my figs. 1018 and 1019) publishes an archaic bronze statuette of Zeus, found in a wonderful state of preservation at Ambrakia in Aitolia and now installed in the National Museum at Athens (no. 14984. Height 0·165^m; with base, 0·188^m. Patina, blackish green). The god advances brandishing a bolt in his raised right hand and supporting an eagle on his outstretched left. Yet the action of his legs and arms is by no means strenuous. It agrees rather with the pose of Hageladas' Zeus on the coins of Messene (ii. 742 fig. 673 f.). Accordingly Rhomaios regards the new statuette as made under the influence of Hageladas' work, which he dates *c.* 480 B.C. (cp. C. Robert *Archaeologische Maerchen aus alter und neuer Zeit* Berlin 1886 p. 92 ff. and Collignon *Hist. de la Sculpt. gr.* i. 318). But that is definitely to reject the testimony of Paus. 4. 33. 2 (see Sir J. G. Frazer and H. Hitzig—H. Blümner *ad loc.*). It is safer to conclude that the new statuette was an early faithful copy (*c.* 480 B.C.), Hageladas' masterpiece a later improved copy (*c.* 455 B.C.), of the same cult-statue on Mt Ithome, which itself was a modification of the ancient strenuous type (*c.* 490 B.C.). We thus obtain the *stemma*:

Strenuous type (*c.* 490)
fig. 669

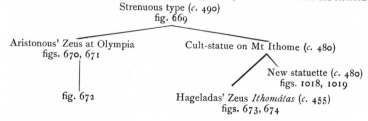

Aristonous' Zeus at Olympia
figs. 670, 671

Cult-statue on Mt Ithome (*c.* 480)

New statuette (*c.* 480)
figs. 1018, 1019

fig. 672

Hageladas' Zeus *Ithomátas* (*c.* 455)
figs. 673, 674

ii. 741 f. fig. 674. A rare variety of this Messenian tetradrachm shows Zeus holding, not only an eagle, but also a long sceptre in his left hand. Fig. 1020 is from a well-preserved specimen formerly in the Mavrocordato collection (J. N. Svoronos in the *Journ. Intern. d'Arch. Num.* 1912 xiv. 29 no. 2052 pl. Z', 8) and now in mine. A second

Fig. 1018.　　　　　　　　　　Fig. 1019.

example from the same dies, as I am informed by Mr C. T. Seltman, was in the collection of E. F. Weber (*Sammlung Consul Eduard Friedrich Weber† Hamburg* München 1908 i. 136 no. 1983 pl. 25). The variation of type is presumably due to the die-sinker and does not reproduce the original aspect of Hageladas' work.

ii. 743 n. 5. More complete is a later example now in my collection (fig. 1021). Zeus, with abundant hair and wreath of large bay-leaves, advances brandishing a three-spiked thunderbolt (one end broken) in his right hand and supporting an eagle erect on his left wrist. Height 3⅜ inches. Careful work of the Hellenistic age.

ii. 744 n. 3. The Pourtalès *amphora* is now in the Louvre (G 204): see E. Pottier *Vases antiques du Louvre* 3ᵐᵉ Série Paris 1922 p. 204 f. pl. 129, J. D. Beazley *Attic red-figured Vases in American Museums* Cambridge Mass. 1918 p. 38 ('in the style of the Berlin painter'), Hoppin *Red-fig. Vases* i. 65 no. 45.

ii. 757 fig. 700. A second and better preserved specimen of this important coin has lately come to light. I am indebted to Mr C. T. Seltman for the casts from which my

Fig. 1021.

illustration of it (fig. 1022) is drawn. The obverse is from the same die as that of fig. 701 ; the reverse, from the same die as that of fig. 700.

Fig. 1022.

ii. 771 fig. 735. For Zeus enthroned with a lotos in his hand cp. an Arabian imitation of a tetradrachm of Alexander, showing a beardless god enthroned to left with a flower instead of an eagle in his right hand (B. V. Head in the *Num. Chron.* New Series 1880 xx. 303 ff. pl. 15, 3, G. F. Hill in the *Brit. Mus. Cat. Coins* Arabia etc. p. lxxxii pl. 50, 5).

ii. 774 n. 4. Miss M. E. H. Lloyd tells me (Oct. 7, 1922) that at Pitigliano in Grosseto during May and June the leaves of the *giglio* (*iris fiorentina*) are hung up outside the windows as a charm against lightning. The plant in leaf, before being hung up, is taken to the church to be blessed by the priest.

ii. 798. Mrs A. Strong 'Treasure from Vatican Rubbish' in *The Illustrated London News* 1922 clxi. 380 fig. 1 (=my fig. 1023) publishes, among other fragments of sculpture

Fig. 1023.

found by W. Amelung in *magazzini* of the Vatican, a neo-Attic relief of *s*. i A.D., which shows 'a composite divinity, carrying the thunderbolt of Zeus, the trident of Poseidon, and the sword of Ares, while behind him an eagle perches upon a large cornucopia.' See also S. Reinach in the *Rev. Arch.* 1923 i. 176.

ii. 799 n. 2. A fine bronze trident, which can be converted at will into a bident, was found in the Tomba del Tridente at Vetulonia and is figured by Milani *Stud. e mat. di arch. e num.* 1905 iii. 85 fig. 415 *a*, *b*.

ii. 800 n. 1. A photograph of this vase with the restorations removed is now published by H. Schaal *Griechische Vasen aus frankfurter Sammlungen* Frankfurt am Main 1923 pl. 30, a.

ii. 802. Mr E. J. Seltman kindly informs me (Aug. 24, 1923) that he has recently seen a terra cotta of the same questionable sort on sale at Naples. He describes it as being 'About 6 inches high, and 4 broad. Hollow. On the back, in the centre, a round boss with **T . A͞T**. On the front appear at the top, from left to right, the heads of Poseidon, Zeus, and Hades. Below [Zeus] is the thunderbolt, the trident below Poseidon, and below Hades his bidens. Underneath, an inscription of three short lines beginning **DIS——**.'

ii. 805 n. 6. For recent discussion of the three-bodied monster see A. Brückner in the *Jahrb. d. Deutsch. Arch. Inst.* 1923/24 xxxviii/ix Arch. Anz. pp. 113—115.

ii. 807 n. 5 no. (3). V. Chapot in the *Bull. Corr. Hell.* 1902 xxvi. 168 no. 8 publishes the following inscription from a marble block, hollowed out to serve as a trough, in the village of *el-qābūsīje* (Seleukeia Pieria): ὁ δῆμος καὶ ἡ προβουλὴ (perhaps a misreading of [ἱε]ρ[ὰ] βουλὴ) Ϙ | [Γ]νάϊον Πομπήϊον Ζήνωνα, τὸν διὰ βί|ου νεωκόρον τοῦ Νεικηφόρου Κεραυν|ν[ίο]υ καὶ πατέρα τῆς πόλεως, κ.τ.λ. with date ἔτους δϚ' = 95 or 155 A.D.

ii. 818. G. Kazarow 'Nouvelles inscriptions relatives au Dieu Thrace Zbelsourdos' in the *Rev. Arch.* 1913 i. 340 ff. adds two from the village *Golémo-Sélo* in the district *Dupnitza*: (1) Κυρίῳ | θεῷ προ|γονικῷ Ζβελ|σούρδῳ Φλ. ᾿Α|μάτοκος Φλ. ᾿Α|[μ]ατόκου υἱὸς | εὐξά[μ]ενος ἀ|νέθηκεν. (2) Τῷ κυρίῳ | Διὶ Ζβελ|σούρδῳ | ἀνέθηκεν | Τ. Φλα. ᾿Αμά|το[κ]ος Τ. | Φ[λ. ᾿Αματόκου υἱός].

C. F. Lehmann-Haupt 'Der thrakische Gott Zbelsurdos' in *Klio* 1921 xvii. 283—285 notes also V. Dobrusky *Archäol. Bericht des bulgar. Nationalmuseums* 1907 i. 152 no. 203 an inscription from the village *Chatrovo* in the district *Dupnitza* Διὶ Ζβε[λ]|σούρδῳ | τῷ κυρίῳ Βελβαβρι|ηνοὶ κωμῆται | ἀνέθη|καν.

ii. 822 n. 13. C. F. Lehmann-Haupt *loc. cit.* proposes Cic. *in Pis.* 85 a te Iovis *Zbelsurdi* fanum etc.

ii. 823. J. Whatmough 'The *Iovilae*-dedications from S. Maria di Capua' in the *Class. Quart.* 1922 xvi. 181—189 would connect them with the cult of Iuno *Lucina* as goddess of motherhood and procreation.

ii. 826 n. 3. With the gong at Dodona cp. those discussed by J. Jüthner 'Die Schelle im Thiasos' in the *Jahresh. d. oest. arch. Inst.* 1904 vii. 146—150.

ii. 837 n. 1. The Phrygian Zeus ἐξ αὐλῆς is hardly to be connected with Plat. *Axioch.* 371 A—Β εἰ δὲ καὶ ἕτερον βούλει λόγον, ὃν ἐμοὶ ἤγγειλε Γωβρύης, ἀνὴρ μάγος· ἔφη κατὰ τὴν Ξέρξου διάβασιν τὸν πάππον αὐτοῦ καὶ ὁμώνυμον, πεμφθέντα εἰς Δῆλον,...ἐκ τινῶν χαλκέων δέλτων, ἃς ἐξ Ὑπερβορέων ἐκόμισαν Ὦπίς τε καὶ Ἑκαέργη, ἐκμεμαθηκέναι μετὰ τὴν τοῦ σώματος λύσιν τὴν ψυχὴν εἰς τὸν ἄδηλον χωρεῖν τόπον, κατὰ τὴν ὑπόγειον οἴκησιν, ἐν ᾗ βασίλεια Πλούτωνος οὐχ ἥττω τῆς τοῦ Διὸς αὐλῆς, ἅτε τῆς μὲν γῆς ἐχούσης τὰ μέσα τοῦ κόσμου, τοῦ δὲ πόλου ὄντος σφαιροειδοῦς, οὗ τὸ μὲν ἕτερον ἡμισφαίριον θεοὶ ἔλαχον οἱ οὐράνιοι, τὸ δὲ ἕτερον οἱ ὑπένερθεν, οἱ μὲν ἀδελφοὶ ὄντες, οἱ δὲ ἀδελφῶν παῖδες.

ii. 869 n. 2. For Mt Pelion and its cults see now F. Stählin *Das hellenische Thessalien* Stuttgart 1924 pp. 41—43.

ii. 873 n. 2. Cp. Zeus Καραός of Akarnania (K. A. Rhomaios in the Ἀρχ. Δελτ. 1918 iv. 117 ff.=*Suppl. Epigr. Gr.* i. no. 213 (near Astakos) ἱεραπόλοι Διὸς Καραοῦ· | κ.τ.λ. of s. ii B.C.).

ii. 874 n. 2 (on p. 875). Φάλακρον in Epeiros is not to be distinguished from Φάλακρον in Korkyra.

Schrader *Reallex.*[2] ii. 245 compares Zeus Φαλακρός with the ancient Roman Divus Pater Falacer (Varr. *de ling. Lat.* 5. 84, cp. 7. 45), on whom see G. Wissowa in Pauly—Wissowa *Real-Enc.* vi. 1967 f. or in his *Rel. Kult. Röm.*[2] p. 240 n. 4.

ii. 892 n. 4 line 9. The word ἔθυσεν is well corrected by A. Meineke to ἴθυσεν, *i.e.* ran in the Nemean games (K. Tümpel in Pauly—Wissowa *Real-Enc.* ii. 622).

ii. 897 n. 5. Mr C. W. Blegen has kindly furnished me (Aug. 16, 1924) with the following note :—'Trial excavations conducted by the American School in 1923 and 1924 brought to light near the summit of Mt. Hymettus a large deposit of ancient pottery. It seems to have been deliberately placed in a great heap and carefully covered with earth and ashes, and is probably, therefore, formed of votive offerings discarded from a small shrine or altar. These vases, of many different shapes and sizes, date almost exclusively from the Geometric Period ; and some of them bear incised inscriptions. The material is sadly fragmentary, only one inscription being sufficiently preserved to give an idea of its content. It is of a coarsely vituperative nature, recalling the archaic inscriptions of Thera, and unfortunately gives no clue to the character of the shrine. A slight scattering of sherds of classical pottery and a few fragments of Roman lamps were also found.

The small mountain sanctuary which once occupied this lofty position accordingly appears to have flourished chiefly during the Geometric Age, though it continued to be visited in a small way till Roman times.

Since no trace of a building has yet been discovered, it is possible that the cult possessed merely an open altar.

Until further evidence is forthcoming there can be no certainty in identifying definitely this cult; but it is tempting to conjecture that we have here the site of the worship of Zeus Ombrios, which, according to Pausanias, was somewhere on Mt. Hymettus.'

See now *Am. Journ. Arch.* 1924 xxviii. 337 (citing *Art and Archaeology* 1924 xvii. 285 f. and *Archaeological Institute of America: 42d Annual Report of the Managing Committee of the American School at Athens, 1922—1923* p. 16 f.) and *Journ. Hell. Stud.* 1924 xliv. 255 f.

ii. 903 n. 2. For Mt Oite see now F. Stählin *Das hellenische Thessalien* Stuttgart 1924 p. 192 ff.

ii. 904 n. 1. W. Vollgraff in the *Ann. Brit. Sch. Ath.* 1907—1908 xiv. 225 : 'Two hours south-east of Almyró, near Paralia, are the insignificant ruins of a large building of the classical period, within a rectangular temenos. It seems to me that these can only be the remains of a temple belonging to the neighbouring city of Halos. Mr. [N. I.] Giannopoulos' view that this is the sanctuary of Zeus Laphystios may perhaps be correct, though no proof can at present be adduced. In the small trial excavation which I made here, a few fragments of black-glazed pottery were found, but nothing of the prehistoric age.'

ii. 904 n. 3.   For Mt Ossa and its cults (no sign of Zeus) see F. Stählin *Das hellenische Thessalien* Stuttgart 1924 p. 40 f.

ii. 904 n. 4.   F. Stählin *Das hellenische Thessalien* Stuttgart 1924 p. 46 f. describes Homolion and states that on its *akrópolis* (233^m above sea-level), beneath the unroofed chapel of St Elias, remains of a temple have come to light together with glazed sherds of the fifth and fourth centuries B.C.   Close by was found the foot of a colossal statue (*c.* 5^m high) with a thunderbolt represented on its sandal.   This is now preserved in the Museum at Volo, and may fairly be taken as implying the local cult of Zeus ['Ομολώιος?].

ii. 904 n. 6.   H. Scheffel 'Eine antike Opferstätte auf dem Olymp' in the *Ath. Mitth.* 1922 (published 1924) xlvii. 129 f. reports that in the summer of 1923 he climbed the highest peak of Mt Olympos and found there no trace of ancient cult, but that on one of the neighbouring summits (*c.* 2900^m high, *i.e. c.* 100^m below the true top) he recognised remains of an altar and, strewn among the stones of the peak, some hundreds of sherds, badly weathered and broken.   Perhaps one half of their number showed traces of ancient black glaze, and the fragments collected must have come from several dozen vessels— small cups, jugs, bowls, etc., mostly of late classical times.   Scheffel justly identifies this with the altar of Zeus mentioned by Solin. 8. 6 (*supra* i. 103 n. 1).

F. Stählin *Das hellenische Thessalien* Stuttgart 1924 pp. 5—11 gives a good description of the mountain with concise geological, topographical, and historical notes.

But by far the most important source for exact knowledge of Olympos is now M. Kurz *Le Mont Olympe* (*Thessalie*) Paris—Neuchâtel 1923.   This well-written and brilliantly illustrated monograph contains a historical introduction (pp. 7—35), a full record of successive explorations (pp. 37—157), chapters on cartography (pp. 159—186) and toponomy (pp. 187—207), with sundry appendixes (pp. 209—232). Its illustrations include 3 photographic panoramas, 14 plates, and 2 coloured maps, one of which (scale 1 : 20,000) is a special survey made by the author (*supra* p. 906 n. o).

ii. 910 n. 1.   B. Pace 'Il tempio di Giove Olimpico in Agrigento' in the *Mon. d. Linc.* 1922 xxviii. 173—252 with pls. 1—3 and figs. 1—31 gives a historical account of the temple and of the attempts hitherto made to recover its arrangements (pp. 175—198), a fresh discussion of its plan, elevation, roof, doors, Atlantes, and sculpture (pp. 199—236), and an Appendix on ancient buildings with *façades* involving an uneven number of columns (pp. 237—252). The main conclusions reached by the author are as follows. The temple had a central nave and two side aisles (κρυπτοὶ περίπατοι, cp. Athen. 206 A). The cross-wall at the western end of the nave marked the beginning of an *ádyton*, which could be entered also from the aisles. The building was hypaethral, the central nave being left open like an *atrium*, though the *ádyton* and the side aisles were roofed over. Whether it had pediments is doubtful (R. Pierce on p. 208 ff. is clear that it had not, and on pl. 3 restores it without them). The metopes at either end were carved ; those of the long sides were plain. The Atlantes and Caryatids were not placed in the external intercolumniations (*supra* p. 914 fig. 827), but engaged in the internal pilasters of the hypaethral nave (N. Maggiore 'Nota sulla collocazione dei così detti giganti nell' Olimpico agrigentino' in *Due opuscoli archeologici* Palermo 1834 p. 21). No ramps are assumed.

ii. 920 n. o.   C. Picard in 1923 reconstructed from remains of sculpture in the Artemision at Delos two lionesses with heads raised in attendance on the goddess. He supposes that this group was set up near the Keraton or altar of horns (G. Glotz *La civilisation égéenne* Paris 1923 p. 476).

ii. 922 n. o.   See now Rubensohn 'Das Delion von Paros' in the *Jahrb. d. Deutsch. Arch. Inst.* 1923/24 xxxviii/ix Arch. Anz. pp. 118—121.

ii. 929 n. o.   W. Aly *Der kretische Apollonkult* Leipzig 1908 p. 47 n. 4 regards the hound of Praisos (Theophr. περὶ ἔρωτος *frag.* 113 Wimmer *ap.* Strab. 478, cp. Ant. Lib. 36 (*supra* i. 720 n. 4), schol. *Od.* 19. 518, schol. Pind. *Ol.* 1. 91 a) as a sort of Kerberos, guardian of the Dictaean Zeus.

ii. 933 n. o.   See now M. M. Gillies 'The Ball of Eros (Ap. Rhod. iii. 135 ff.)' in the *Class. Rev.* 1924 xxxviii. 50 f.

ii. 957 n. 2 on Zeus at Sardeis. E. Littmann in *Sardis* vi. 1. 13 (cp. *ib.* pp. 42, 70) quotes from two Lydian inscriptions the four following phrases :

no. 4 (inv. 1), b 4 f. *fakmũt Hũdãnś | Artəmuk vqbahẽnt*, 'then him may Hũdãnś and Artemis destroy.'

no. 23 (inv. 7), 1   *Hũdãn. Artimuũ daquve.śt*, 'is sacred to Hũdãnś and Artemis' (?).

no. 23 (inv. 7), 3 f. *Hūdāns̄ Tavśaś | Artimuk Ibśimsis katsarlokid*, 'Hūdāns̄ Tavśaś and Artemis of Ephesos will punish.'

no. 23 (inv. 7), 10 *Hūdānk Artimuk katsarlokid*, 'Hūdāns̄ as well as Artemis will punish.'

W. H. Buckler *ib.* p. 13 very acutely suggests that *Hūdāns̄ Tavśaś* is Ζεὺς Ὑδηνός. He observes : '*Hyde* was the ancient, or one of the ancient names, of Sardis (STRAB. XIII, 4. 6), and as in the third century B.C. one could speak of the Carian god Komyros without also calling him Zeus (LYKOPH. *Al.* 459 : καταίθων θύσθλα Κωμύρῳ, and TZETZES *ad loc.*), so one could probably have mentioned Hūdāns̄ without the additional name *Tavśaś*. The Old-Indian god Dyaus (*Dyāúṣ̄*) is the same as Zeus, and since *t* in Lydian often takes the place of *d*, *Tavśaś* might represent *D(y)avś-aś*, and this would be very similar to Dyaus. In the big stele (No. [23]) sacred to *Hūdāns̄* and *Artemis*, the god mentioned **before** Artemis must be an important one. We know.that Zeus' temple shared the precinct of Artemis at Sardis, that Tmolos disputed with Crete the honor of Zeus' birthplace, that Zeus was very important in Lydia, being mentioned and depicted on coins of Sardis and many other towns, in short that next to Artemis he was by far the most important local deity.... The termination of *Hūdāns̄* does not seem to be found in any other Lydian adjective denoting origin, but we cannot be sure that it is not a possible form, and it certainly suggests the Greek termination Σαρδι-ανός, or -ηνός. Or perhaps *Hūdāns̄* is no adjective, but the original name of the Lydian Zeus.'

Id. ib. vi. 2. 11 and 44 retains *Tavśaś*=Ζεῦσις (Hesych. *s.v.* Μηδινεύς cited *supra* p. 312 n. 5), but now transliterates *Pλdāns̄* (not *Hūdans̄*) and refers to O. A. Danielsson 'Zu den lydischen Inschriften' in the *Skrifter utgifna af Kungl. Humanistiska Veten-skaps-Samfundet i Uppsala* 1917 xx. 2. 24 f., who compares *Tavśaś* with the man's name *Tavσâs, gen. Tavσâδος (Dittenberger *Syll. inscr. Gr.*[3] no. 46 *a* 64=F. Bechtel in Collitz—Bechtel *Gr. Dial.-Inschr.* iii. 2. 743 ff. no. 5727 *a* 64 from Halikarnassos), and equates *Pλdāns̄* with Ἀπόλλων (-λd-=-λλ-, cp. Carian Ὑσσωλδος= Ὑσσωλλος in the last-mentioned inscription).

Mr Buckler informs me (May 19, 1924) that his identification of *Tavśaś* with Ζεύς has been accepted by Professors A. H. Sayce and J. Fraser. Dr P. Giles, whom I consulted on the point (Dec. 27, 1924), sees no objection.

The Zeus-cults of Lydia in general are listed by J. Keil ' Die Kulte Lydiens ' in *Anatolian Studies presented to Sir William Mitchell Ramsay* edd. W. H. Buckler— W. M. Calder Manchester 1923 pp. 259—261. The list includes no fewer than twenty-five appellatives, eight of which are epithets in -ηνός.

ii. 962 n. o on the Zeus-cults of Miletos. Add A. Rehm in *Milet* i. 7. 290 ff. no. 203 b 12 f. (cult-regulation of *c.* 130 B.C.) the priest τοῦ Δήμου τοῦ Ῥωμαίων καὶ τῆς Ῥώμης must have been τελεσθεὶς Διὶ | Τελεσιουργῷ, *ib.* i. 7. 299 ff. no. 204 a 13 f. (cult-regulation of *s.* i A.D.) the priest of Asklepios must have been τελεσθὶς Διὶ Τελεσ[ι]ουργῶι with remarks on p. 297 f., *ib.* i. 7. 347 nos. 275 (' in der zweischiffigen Halle ') small altar of white marble decorated with a double axe, to left and right of which is inscribed in late Hellenistic lettering Δι||ὸς Λα||βρα|υν||δέ|ω||s, 276 (' in der zweischiffigen Halle ') small altar decorated with a double axe, beneath which in late Hellenistic letters is Διὸς Λαβρα|ύνδου, 277 (' in der zweischiffigen Halle ') small altar of grey-blue marble decorated with a double axe, to left of which is Λέων | Ἱεροκλείους | Διὶ | Λαβραύνδωι, 278 (' in der Füllung der Justiniansmauer ') small altar of white-grey marble decorated with a double axe, round which is inscribed Δι||ὸς | Κε||ρα|υνίου.

ii. 970 n. o. Other inscriptions relating to Agdistis are as follows : (1) P. Jouguet in the *Bull. Corr. Hell.* 1896 xx. 398 f.=Dittenberger *Orient. Gr. inscr. sel.* no. 28 small slab of white marble, on sale at Gizeh in 1896 but possibly brought from the Fayum, in lettering of reign of Ptolemy ii Philadelphos ὑπὲρ βασιλέως Πτολεμαίου | τοῦ Πτολεμαίου καὶ βασιλίσσης | Ἀρσινόης Μόσχος ὁ ἱερεὺς | τὸν ναὸν καὶ τὸ τέμενος | Ἀγδίστει ἐπηκόωι | ἱδρύσατο.

(2) J. Keil—A. v. Premerstein ' Bericht über eine dritte Reise in Lydien ' in the *Denkschr. d. Akad. Wien* 1914 i. Abh. p. 18 ff. no. 18=O. Weinreich 'Stiftung und Kultsatzungen eines Privatheiligtums in Philadelpheia in Lydien' in the *Sitzungsber. d. Heidelb. Akad. d. Wiss.* Phil.-hist. Classe 1919 Abh. xvi. 1—68=Dittenberger *Syll. inscr. Gr.*[3] no. 985 a *stéle* of whitish marble, found at Philadelpheia in Lydia and con-taining in late Hellenistic script (*s.* i or ii (?) B.C.) the regulations of an οἶκος, or private sanctuary, of Agdistis established by one Dionysios in accordance with a dream vouchsafed to him by Zeus. The inscription enumerates the deities who have altars in the 'house' (vv. 1—11), gives a long list of ritual and moral prescriptions (vv. 12—50), mentions Agdistis as the guardian and mistress of the 'house' (vv. 50—60), and ends with a

solemn prayer to Zeus Σωτήρ (vv. 60—64). The first and last portions are as follows:
1 ff. ἀγαθῆι τ[ύχηι]. | ἀνεγράφησαν ἐφ᾽ ὑγιείαι κα[ὶ κοινῆι σωτηρίαι] | καὶ δόξηι τῆι ἀρίστηι
τὰ δοθέ[ντα παραγγέλμα]|τα Διονυσίωι καθ᾽ ὕπνον π[ρόσοδον διδόν]|τ᾽ εἰς τὸν ἑαυτοῦ οἶκον
ἀνδρά[σι καὶ γυναιξὶν] | ἐλευθέροις καὶ οἰκέταις· Διὸς [γὰρ ἐν τούτωι] | τοῦ Εὐμενοῦς (*supra*
p. 960 n. 0) καὶ Ἑστίας τ[ῆς παρέδρου αὐ]|τοῦ καὶ τῶν ἄλλων θεῶν Σωτ[ήρων καὶ Εὐδαι]|-
μονίας καὶ Πλούτου καὶ Ἀρετῆς [καὶ Ὑγιείας] | καὶ Τύχης Ἀγαθῆς καὶ Ἀγαθοῦ [Δαίμονος καὶ
Μνή]|μης καὶ Χαρίτων καὶ Νίκης εἰσιν ἱδ[ρυμένοι βωμοί]. | τούτ[ωι] δέδωκεν ὁ Ζεὺς παραγγέλ[-
ματα τούς τε ἁ]|γνισμοὺς καὶ τοὺς καθαρμοὺς κα[ὶ τὰς θυσίας ἐπι]|τελεῖν κατά τε τὰ πάτρια καὶ
ὡς νῦν [εἴθισται]· κ.τ.λ. 50 ff. [τὰ παραγγέλμα]|τα ταῦτα ἐτέθησαν παρὰ Ἀγγδιστιν [τὴν
ἁγιωτάτην] | φύλακα καὶ οἰκοδέσποιναν τοῦδε τοῦ ο[ἴκου, ἥτις ἀγαθὰς] | διανοίας ποιείτω
ἀνδράσι καὶ γυναιξὶν [ἐλευθέροις καὶ] | δούλοις, ἵνα κατακολουθῶσι τοῖς ὧδε γ[εγραμμένοις, καὶ
ἐν] | ταῖς θυσίαις ταῖς τε ἐμμήνοις καὶ ταῖ[ς κατὰ ἐνιαυτὸν ἁ]|πτέσθωσαν, ὅσοι πιστεύουσιν
ἑα[υτοῖς ἄνδρες τε καὶ] | [γυ]ναῖκες, τῆς γραφῆς ταύτης, ἐν [ἧι τὰ τοῦ θεοῦ παραγγέλ]|[μα]τά
εἰσιν γεγραμμένα, ἵνα φαν[εροὶ γίνωνται οἱ κατα]|[κολου]θοῦ[ντ]ες τοῖς παραγγέλ[μασιν καὶ οἱ
μὴ κατακολου]|[θοῦν]τες. [Ζεῦ] Σωτή[ρ], τὴν ἀφή[γησιν ταύτην ἵλεως καὶ] | [εὐμεν]ῶς προσ-
δέχου καὶ προ[space for *c.* 18 letters] | [πάρεχ]ε ἀγαθὰς ἀμοιβάς, [ὑγίειαν, σωτηρίαν,
εἰρήνην, ἀσφάλεια]ν ἐπὶ γῆς καὶ ἐπὶ θα[λάσσης ἐμοί τε καὶ τοῖς] | [εἰσπορευο]μένοις ὁμοίω[ς].

(3) J. Keil 'Denkmäler des Meter-Kultes' in the *Jahresh. d. oest. arch. Inst.* 1915
xviii. 73 f. fig. 45 republishes (cp. A. Conze in the *Arch. Zeit.* 1880 xxxviii. 4 pl. 3, 3) a
fragmentary votive relief of grey-blue marble, now in the Estense collection at Vienna,
which represents a goddess (Agdistis) standing, with a *kálathos* on her head, a *phiále* in
her right hand, and a large *týmpanon* in her left, between two lions. To her right stands
a youthful god (Attis) in short *chitón* and *chlamýs*. To her left (now missing) stood an
elderly god (Zeus), whose hand held a sceptre. On the left margin of the relief is a small
torch-bearing maiden. Below, in lettering of *s.* iii B.C., is inscribed Ἀναξιπόλη [— —]
[Ἀ]γδίστε[ι ἀνέθηκεν]. I am indebted to Mr B. F. C. Atkinson for a notice of this
inscription.

ii. 1059 on burial in the house. See further H. J. Rose *The Roman Questions of
Plutarch* Oxford 1924 p. 202 (note on *quaestt. Rom.* 79).

ii. 1065 n. 0. H. Bolkestein 'The Exposure of Children at Athens and the ἐγχυτρίστριαι' in *Classical Philology* 1922 xvii. 222—239 (summarised in the *Class. Quart.*
1923 xvii. 206), arguing 'that the current idea as to the normality of *expositio* is totally
unfounded,' interprets ἐγχυτρίζειν 'to throw into a pit (χύτρος = βόθρος), to sacrifice in a
pit to the dead' and so 'to burn up, to destroy,' ἐγχυτρίστριαι 'women who sacrificed to
the dead.'

ii. 1089. G. Seure 'ΤΕΛΕΣΦΟΡΟΣ-ΤΙΛΕΣΠΟΡΟΣ' in the *Rev. Ét. Gr.* 1918
xxxi. 389—398, following up a suggestion of S. Reinach 'Télesphore' *ib.* 1901 xiv.
343—349=*id. Cultes, Mythes et Religions* Paris 1906 ii. 255—261, contends that Telesphoros, though Greek in appearance, was Thracian in origin. He points out that a
Thracian name *Τιλε-σπόρις, *Τιλε-σπόρος, of legitimate formation but of unknown significance, might well have been Hellenised into Τελεσφόρος.

ii. 1101 n. 3. F. Hiller von Gaertringen in the *Sitzungsber. d. Akad. d. Wiss. Berlin*
1921 p. 442 publishes an inscription from the western slope of the *Akrópolis* at Athens,
where it was built into the wall of a later *Lésche*: ἱιερὸν | Διὸς Ξενί|ο Θυμαιτί|δος φρα|τρίας.
He infers that the phratry Thymaitis had a sanctuary of Zeus Ξένιος near the *Lésche*.

ii. 1102 n. 0. On the relief in the Terme Museum (fig. 939) see further P. Perdrizet
'D'une certaine espèce de reliefs archaïsants' in the *Rev. Arch.* 1903 ii. 211—218 with
pl. 13.

ii. 1118. G. Welter 'Das Olympieion in Athen' in the *Ath. Mitth.* 1922 (published
1924) xlvii. 61—71 with pls. 7—10 marks an important advance in our knowledge of the
Olympieion.

(1) Within the eastern portion of its foundations there has come to light the lowest
course of a pre-Peisistratic *perístasis*, of which the N. wall was uncovered by F. C.
Penrose, the W. by Welter. The wall was 2·50^m thick, and the *perístasis* measured
30·50^m broad by *c.* 60^m long. This was τὸ ἀρχαῖον ἱερόν built by Deukalion (Paus. 1.
18. 8).

(2) The temple of the Peisistratidai, begun *c.* 515 B.C., was a more ambitious structure,
having the same proportions, size, and plan as its Hellenistic—Hadrianic successor. It
was designed as an Ionic dipteral building with eight columns on the short side and
twenty on the long side. Its length and breadth (107·70^m × 42·90^m) make it comparable

with the great Ionic temples of eastern Greece—the Artemision at Ephesos ($109 \cdot 20^m \times 55 \cdot 10^m$) and the second Heraion at Samos ($108 \cdot 73^m \times 52 \cdot 41^m$). The foundations, continuous for the outermost columns, separate for the inner rows, are laid in neat polygonal courses of Akropolis-limestone and Kara-stone with a *euthyntería* of hard *pôros*. The stylobate had three steps of *pôros*. No column-bases have been found. But unfluted drums of *pôros* show a lower diameter of $2 \cdot 42^m$ and enable us to conclude that the height of the shafts was *c.* 16^m.

Welter suggests that the Peisistratidai, as a counterbast to the Delphic activities of the Alkmaionidai, not only rebuilt the Telesterion at Eleusis (520—515 B.C.), but also tried to establish a panHellenic Zeus-cult at Athens. He thinks that these two enterprises were not unconnected. Hippias dealt in oracles (Hdt. 5. 93, cp. 90), Hipparchos in dreams (Hdt. 5. 36); and Hipparchos was at one time under the influence of Onomakritos (Hdt. 7. 6). Such men might well honour Zeus as the supreme god of the Orphic cosmogony. But, with the fall of the mystically-minded Peisistratidai, the vast temple was left unfinished, and the democracy reverted to the worship of Athena.

Fig. 1024.

ii. 1133 n. 1. With fig. 957 cp. the Roman mural relief of Mars and Apollo with an oracular bird on a pillar in a cage (G. P. Campana *Antiche opere in plastica* Roma 1842—1851 pl. 19, *Brit. Mus. Cat. Terracottas* p. 381 no. D 507, Von Rohden—Winnefeld *Ant. Terrakotten* iv. 1. 20 f. figs. 29—32).

ii. 1143 fig. 964. A specimen in the British Museum (fig. 1024 from a cast) shows the type somewhat more clearly.

CORRIGENDA

ii. 19 line 2. For 'Kynados' read 'Kounados.'

ii. 67 n. 3. For 'p. 377^t' read 'p. 57.'

ii. 115 n. 2 line 4. For 'οπερ' read 'ὅπερ.'

ii. 120 n. 1 last quotation. For 'Ομηρος' read '"Ομηρος.'

ii. 133 n. 0. For 'Gaulminus' read 'Gualminus' *bis.*

ii. 182 n. 1 line 5. For '*Nalionalmus.*' read '*Nationalmus.*'

ii. 209 n. 2 line 10. For 'Ολμον' read '"Ολμον.'

ii. 241 n. 4 line 6 from bottom of page. For 'Pherekyde' read 'Pherekydes.'

ii. 298 n. 2. For 'Modius' read 'Modius|.'

ii. 423 n. 3 *sub fin.* For 'Riøbenhavn' read 'Kiøbenhavn.'

ii. 436 n. 7. For '376 f.' read '22 ff.'

ii. 547 n. '2' should be numbered n. '4,' and n. '3' should be numbered n. '5.'

ii. 565 n. 2 line 5. For 'η' read 'ῆ.'

ii. 664 n. 1 line 10. For '*syrinx*' read '*sẏrinx.*'

ii. 714 n. 2 line 2. For 'Εκάτης' read ''Εκάτης.'

ii. 729 n. 0 line 15 from bottom of page. For 'ii 208 f.' read 'ii. 208 f.'

ii. 774 n. 1 line 7. For 'Vishna' read 'Vishnu.'

ii. 784 n. 7. For 'Kentoripai' read 'Kentouripai.'

ii. 806 n. 8. For 'ἀστεροπήτης' read 'ἀστεροπητής.'

ii. 808 n. 0 line 11. For 'δ' read 'δ'.'

ii. 829 line 23. For 'they delay' read 'thy delay.'

ii. 868 n. 6 line 4. For '*pud*' read '*apud.*'

ii. 874 n. 2 last line. For '874' read '873.'

ii. 916 n. 0 line 15. For 'Ολύμπιος' read ''Ολύμπιος.'

ii. 960 n. 0 line 13 from bottom of page. For 'Hadrianas' read 'Hadrian as.'

ii. 968 n. 0 line 2. For 'νεωκόρ[ος' read 'νεωκόρ]ος.'

ii. 975 n. 0 line 7 from bottom of page. For 'Περειτίου β′' read 'Περειτίου ιβ′.'

ii. 977 n. 0 line 14. For 'historica' read 'historical.'

ii. 1088 line 14 from bottom of page. For '*inscr. Gr.* i' read '*inscr. Gr.* ii.'

ii. 1093 n. 1 line 5. For '*recques*' read '*grecques.*'

ii. 1128 n. 0 line 1. For 'Αγαθὸν' read ''Αγαθὸν.'

ii. 1140 n. 3 line 4. For '*Lyaea*' read '*Lyaea*).'

ii. 1178 line 7. For 'Greek' read 'Great.'

Bronze medallion of Commodus,
struck 185 A.D. (Gnecchi *Medagl.
Rom.* ii. 59 f. no. 74 pl. 83, 2).
Supra p. 1209 n. 2.

INDEX I

PERSONS PLACES FESTIVALS

The contents of each item are arranged, as far as possible, under the following heads: *Cults Epithets Festivals Oracles Rites Priests Personations Myths Metamorphoses Genealogy Functions Etymology Attributes Types Identifications Assimilations Associations Comparisons Relations Supersedure.*

In the Genealogies f. = father, m. = mother, s. = son, d. = daughter, b. = brother, st. = sister, gf. = grandfather, gm. = grandmother, gs. = grandson, h. = husband, w. = wife.

The larger numerals refer to pages, the smaller numerals to foot-notes.

Agathe Tyche (*cont.*)
  Associated with Agathos Daimon 1125_1
    1128_0 cp. 1228
  See also Tyche Ἀγαθή
Agathodaemones 1127_0
Agathodaimoniastai 925_0 1129_0
Agathodaimonistai 1129_0
Agathoi Daimones
  Cult: Alexandreia 1127_0
  Type: snakes 1127_0
Agathos Angelos
  Cult: Stratonikeia $880_{0(0)}$
  See also Theios Angelos
Agathos Daimon
  Cults: Alexandreia 1127_0 1128_0 Athens
    1125_1 Delos 1128_0 Eumeneia in
    Phrygia 970_0 Kentoripa (?) 1129_0
    Philadelpheia in Lydia 1229 Phoi-
    nike 1127_0 Rhodes the town 925_0
    Teos 1066 Thespiai 1125_1 1161
  Epithet: Νέος 98_0
  Rite: cup of unmixed wine drunk
    after dinner 1125 1129_0
  Personated by Antinoos 1128_0 Nero 98_0
    1128_0 Philippus i of Rome 970_0
  Functions: chthonian 1129_0 fertility
    1125_1 1129_0 male ancestor 1125_1
    wealth 1125_1
  Attributes: corn-ears 98_0 *cornu copiae*
    1117_7 (?) 1125_1 1128_0 eagle 1125_1
    phiále 1125_1 1128_0 poppy-heads 98_0
    sceptre 1125_1 *skhent* 98_0
  Types: animal and human 1128_0
    bearded 1125_1 beardless 1126_0 Eu-
    phranor 1126_0 1127_0 Praxiteles 1127_0
    snake 98_0 1127_0 1128_0
  Identified with Dionysos 1129_0 Kneph
    1127_0 1128_0
  Assimilated to Zeus 1125_1
  Associated with Agathe Tyche 1125_1
    1128_0 cp. 1228 Zeus Ἀταβύριος 925_0
  Compared with Zeus Ἐπιτέλειος Φίλιος
    1163 Zeus Φίλιος 1161
  In relation to Dionysos 1129_0
  —— toast of 1129_0
Agathos Deos (*sic*)
  Cult: Athens 985_0
Agathos Theos
  Cults: Athens 1129_0 Epidauros 1126_0
    Megalopolis 1125_1
  Function: a sort of Zeus 1126_0
  Attributes: cornu copiae 1126_0 sceptre
    1126_0 snake 1126_0
  Associated with Agathe 1126_0
Agathyrsi tattooed 123_0
Agaue 347_0 (?)
Agdestis (?) 970_0
Agdistios (?) 970_0
Agdistis
  Cults: Egypt 1228 Ikonion 970_0 Panti-
    kapaion 970_0 Pessinous 970_0 Phila-
    delpheia in Lydia 1229 Phrygia 970_0
  Epithets: Ἐπήκοος 1228 [τὴν ἀγιωτάτην]
    φύλακα καὶ οἰκοδέσποιναν τοῦδε τοῦ
    ο[ἴκου] 1228

Agdistis (*cont.*)
  Myths: 969_4 970_0 castrated by himself
    969_4 castrated by the gods 969_4
    Liber 969_4
  Attributes: kálathos 1229 *phiále* 1229
    týmpanon 1229
  Type: standing between two lions
    with *kálathos* on head, *phiále* in
    right hand and *týmpanon* in left,
    flanked by Attis and Zeus 1229
  Identified with Kybele 970_0 Mother of
    the gods 970_0 Rhea 970_0
  Associated with Attis and Zeus 1229
Agdos, Mt
  Myths: Agdistis 969_4 970_0 Deukalion
    970_0 971_0 Zeus and the Magna
    Mater 969_4
Agedincum
  Cults: Mars 99_3 Vesta 99_3 Volcanus
    99_3
Agesandros (= Hades) $1113_{0(2)}$
Agesilaos (= Hades) $1113_{0(2)}$ 1168_5
Agesipolis 7
Agis 7
Agis, f. of Amphikles 421
Aglaopes (*sc.* Asklepios) 1085
Aglaophamos 1024
Aglapios (*sc.* Asklepios) 1085
Aglibolos
  Cult: Emesa 814_3
Agnes, St 1050
Agnostoi Theoi
  Cult: Olympia 1100_1
Agnostos Theos
  Cult: Athens 942_0
Agon
  Cult: Kaulonia (?) 1042
Agonium 19_0
Agra
  Cults: Meter 554_2 Meter ἐν Ἄγρας
    1142_3 (?) Zeus Μιλίχιος 1142_3 (?)
  Rites: Lesser Mysteries (*c.* Anthe-
    sterion 20) 1139
Agreus 715_4 1037
Agrigentum
  Cults: Athena 910_1 Zeus Ἀταβύριος
    910_1 Zeus Ὀλύμπιος 911_0 ff. 1227
    Zeus Πολιεύς 910_1
  —— coins of 667 667_3 Olympion at
    911_0 ff. *Porta Aurea* at 910_1 tombs
    for horses at 1146_0
Agrionia 164_6 924_0
Agyieus See Apollon *Epithets* Ἀγυιεύς
    and Zeus *Epithets* Ἀγυιεύς
Agyieus, the Hyperborean 169
Agyrion 1146_0
Ahriman
  Attributes: key 1054 sceptre 1053
    thunderbolt 1053
  Types: lion-headed 664_1 1053 with
    wings on shoulders and haunches,
    snake coiled about him, key in
    right hand, sceptre in left, and
    thunderbolt on breast or at side
    1053 f.

Apollo

Epithet: Delphicus 927_1
Associated with Hercules and Diana
59_0
In relation to Castor and Pollux 95 f.
Diana 99 f.

Apollon

Cults: Achaeans (?) 458 Acharnai 163
Aigai in Aiolis 954_0 Aigina 184
Akraiphia 238_0 Alabanda 97_0 247_0
248_0 714_2 Amyklai 458 894_0 Anaphe 816_4 1066 Antiocheia in Chrysaoris (= Alabanda) 714_2 Antiocheia
on the Orontes (?) 1192_5 Ardettos
1135 Argos 163 173_4 Athens 163
163_4 184 255 730_0 $875_{1(2)}$ 985_0 1121
Aulai 249_2 Axos 816_4 Babylonia (?)
456 Badinlar, in Phrygia 567 f. Bas-
sai 405_3 Bilkon 948_0 Branchidai
920_0 Byzantion 167 f. Corinth 210_0
915_2 (?) 916_0 Crete 457 948_0 Daldeia
250 f. Daphne near Antiocheia on
the Orontes 1188 Delos 223_3 249_2
452 ff. 854 Delphoi 457 839 1216
Didyma near Miletos 317 f. 317_2
Dorylaeion 281 Eleuthernai (Eleu-
therna) 456_7 $491_{0(6)}$ $492_{0(0)}$ Epidau-
ros $487_{3(1)}$ Erythrai in Ionia 730_0
Eumeneia in Phrygia 571 970_0
Gortyna 723_0 731_0 Gryneia $489_{0(4)}$
Halikarnassos 163 Hiera in Lesbos
$488_{0(2)}$ Hierapolis in Phrygia 567
Hierapytna 723_0 Mt Hymettos 897_5
Hyperboreoi 501 844 Illyria 458
Itanos 929_0 Kalymna $808_{0(11)}$ Karia
573_{10} 574_1 574_2 574_3 Katane 486_5
Kaulonia 1042 f. Keratia in Attike
237_0 Klaros $489_{0(4)}$ Knidos 729_0
Koloe 568 f. Korkyra 730_0 Kroton
237_0 Kypros 246_1 Lakonike 322 322_6
Larisa on the Caystrian Plain 958_0
Lebadeia 899_2 Mt Lepetymnos 832
Leukas 782 Lopta 971_2 Lykia 453
458 f. Lykoreia 901_2 902_0 Lyttos
723_0 934_0 Magnesia ad Maeandrum
249_2 948_0 Magnesia ad Sipylum 729_0
Magnesia in Thessaly 730_0 Make-
donia 458 Cape Malea (Maleai)
$488_{0(0)}$ Megalopolis 160_5 163 Megara
165_3 185 Messene 458 Miletos 237_0
250 255 457 486_5 1220 Mykonos
1092_2 Myrrhinous 730_0 Mytilene
$488_{0(2)}$ Neapolis in Campania 486_5
Olbia $493_{0(7)}$ Olymos 586_2 Orchia (?)
in Lakonike 439 Oropos (?) 1071
Panormos near Kyzikos $882_{0(0)}$
Patara 210 921_0 Peiraieus $487_{3(1)}$
Pergamon 729_0 Phlyeis 251 Praisos
731_0 Prasiai in Lakonike $487_{3(1)}$
Priansos 723_0 Mt Ptoïon 455
Rhegion 680 Rhithymna $492_{0(0)}$
Samos 223_3 Selinous $489_{0(0)}$ Skias
in Arkadia (?) 439 Skythia 292_4
Sparta 255 246_1 $487_{3(1)}$ Stelai in
Crete 731_0 Sybrita 731_0 Tarentum

Apollon *(cont.)*
1064 Tarsos 570 Tegea 163 Thera
920_0 921_0 Mt Thornax in Lakonike
893_2 Thrace 458 Thyateira 562
Tilphossa 439 Tralleis 958_0 Trikke
$487_{3(1)}$ 1088 Troy 453 Tyana (?)
570

Epithets: ἄγριος 971_2 Ἀγυιεύς 163 f. 456_7
Ἀγυιεύς Ἀλεξίκακος 163_4 Ἀγυιεύς
Προστατήριος Πατρῷος Πύθιος Κλάριος
Πανιώνιος 163_4 Αἰγλήτης 816_4 Ἄκτιος
255 782 Ἀμάδοκος (?) 452 Ἀμυκλαῖος
255 ἄναξ 252_1 Ἀρχηγέτης 237_0 567
Ἀσγελάτας 1066 Ἀσκραῖος 255 486_5
ἄστρων ἡγεμών 255_3 Αὐλαείτης (Αὐ-
λαΐτης, Αὐλίτης, Αὐλητής) 249_2 ἀφή-
τωρ 180 841 βακχεύς (?) 253_2 Βάκχος
253_3 Βιλκώνιος 948_0 βιοδώτης 252_0
Βοηνός 568 ff. Βραγχιάτης 255 Γενέ-
τωρ 223_3 Γοιτόσυρος 293_0 Γρύνειος
954_0 Δαφναῖος 265_0 1189_0 Δαφνη-
φόρος 265_0 Δαφνίτας 265_0 Δειραδιώτης
173_4 210_0 Δελφίνιος 189_8 205_1 230
237_0 456_7 Δήλιος 255 Διδυμαῖος 317 f.
Διδυμεύς 317_2 1220 Διδύμων γενάρ-
χης 317_2 Διονυσοδότης (less probably
Διονυσόδοτος) 251_2 Δονάκτας (?) 249_3
Δοναστάς (?) 249_3 Δονητής (?) 249_3
Δρομαῖος 456_7 Δρύμαιος 486_5 Δρύμας
486_5 Ἑβδομαγενής 237_0 ἑβδομαγέτης
237_0 Ἑβδομεῖος 237_0 238_0 Εἰκάδιος
456 Ἑκάεργος 1042 ἑκατηβελέτης
1042 ἑκατηβόλος 1042 Ἑκατόμβαιος
1092_2 Ἕκατος 1042 Ἐκβάσιος 1180_4
ἐκηβόλος 1042 Ἐλευθέριος 97_0 ἐλπι-
δοδώτης 252_0 Ἐμβάσιος 1180_4 ἐνόλ-
μιος, ἐνολμίς, ἔνολμος 209_2 ἐν Πάνδοις
729_0 Ἐπιβατήριος 1180_4 Ἐπικούριος
405_3 Ἐπόψιος 1130_7 Ἐρεθίμιος 630
εὔλυρος 253_3 ξάθεος 204_1 ξηλοδοτήρ (?)
204_1 252_0 ξηνοδοτήρ 204_1 252_0 ξηνό-
φρων 204_1 ξωογόνος 204_1 Θορνάκιος
893_2 Θύϊος 250 ἰήϊος 246_1 Ἰσότιμος
714_2 Καρινός 167 f. Κάρνειος 456_7
458 κισσεοχαίτης 246_1 κισσεύς 253_2
Κίσσιος (less probably Κισσέος) 247_0
248_0 Κλάριος $489_{0(4)}$ 954_0 Κοροπαῖος
730_0 $871_{3(1)}$ Κόρυδος 458 Κουρίδιος
322_6 Κτίστης 98_0 κυνηγέτης 237_0
Λαιρμηνός (Λαρμηνός, Λαρβηνός, Λει-
μηνός, Λυρμηνός) 567 f. Λαόδοκος (?)
452 Λαρισηνός 958_0 Λάφριος 599
Λητοΐδης (Λητοΐδας) 455 $490_{0(5)}$ Λο-
ξίας 204_1 Λύκειος 255 453 458 λυκηγενής 455_0 Λυκηγενής (?) 453 Λύκιος
453 729_0 902_0 Λυκωρεύς 901_2 Μαλεάτας (Μαλεάτης) $487_{3(1)}$ 1088 Μαλεάτας Σωτήρ $487_{3(1)}$ Μαλόεις $488_{0(2)}$
μάντις (?) 253_2 Μοιραγέτης 237_0 231
1137_0 (?) Μουσηγέτης 237_0 Μύλας
or Μυλάντιος 260_0 Μύστης 250 f.
Νόμιος 252 Νουμήνιος 456 Νυμφη-
γέτης 237_0 ξυνοδοτήρ 252_0 ὁ ἐκ Λοπ-
τῶν 971_2 ὁ προπάτωρ θεὸς Ἥλιος
Πύθιος...Τυριμναῖος 562 Ὀρχιεύς 439

Asklepios (cont.)
  πυροφορεῖν 413$_7$ 1076 sacrifice of
    three-year-old ox 287$_2$ 954$_0$
  Priest: Alexandros of Abonou Teichos
    1083 ff.
  Personated by Claudius 1088
  Myths: buried in Arkadia 1089 buried
    in Epidauros 1089 buried at Kyno-
    soura in Lakonike 1088 f. Ophiu-
    chus 1087 raises dead at Delphoi
    241$_4$ raises Glaukos from dead 1087
    raises Hippolytos from dead 394$_2$
    1087 rears his snake on Mt Pelion
    1087 slain by Zeus at Delphoi 241$_4$
    struck by thunderbolt 23 f.
  Metamorphosed into snake 1082 ff.
  Genealogy: descended from Aiolos
    1088 f. of Aratos by Aristodama
    (w. of Kleinias) 1082 h. of Epione
    (Epio) 1086 s. of Aigle 1086 s. of
    Apollon 1077 1083 s. of Apollon by
    Aigla (Koronis) 488$_{0(0)}$ s. of Ar-
    sippos by Arsinoe d. of Leukippos
    1089 s. of Ischys by Koronis 1089
    s. of Koronis 833$_0$
  Function: healing 127 954$_0$
  Etymology: 1085 ff.
  Attributes: dog 1079 globe 1082 goose
    1079 human-headed or lion-headed
    snake (Glykon or Khnemu) 1084
    Nike 1080 pine-cone 1080 f. ram's-
    head 1080 raven (?) 1084 sceptre
    1079 snake 1077 1079 1111 snake
    coiled round sceptre 1080 snake
    coiled round staff 1075 1082 wreath
    1076 ff.
  Types: Alkamenes 1078 bearded 1078
    beardless 1080 1090 infant 1090
    on couch, feeding snake 1077
    Kalamis 1080 f. Phyromachos 1079
    seated 1078 ff. seated with goose in
    right hand and sceptre in left 1079
    seated with pine-cone in right hand
    and snake round sceptre in left
    1080 standing 1078 1084 standing
    with serpent-staff in right hand
    and Nike in left 1082 Thrasymedes
    of Paros 1078 f. with sceptre and
    pine-cone 1081 Xenophilos and
    Straton 1079
  Identified with Apollon 241$_4$ Ophiou-
    chos 241$_4$ Zeus 1076 ff.
  Assimilated to Zeus 1078 ff.
  Associated with Apollon Μαλεάτας
    487$_{3(1)}$ Artemis 1082 Herakles 241$_4$
    Hygieia and Telesphoros 1078
    Telesphoros 1082
  Compared with Herakles 241$_4$ Tropho-
    nios 1075
  Contrasted with Zeus 1081 f.
  In relation to Zeus Φίλιος 1178
  —— grave of 1088 f. underground
    ἄδυτον of 1088 variant forms of
    the name 1085 f.
Askles 1086

Asopos, the river 898$_6$
Asopos, the river-god 898$_6$ 1151$_3$
Assklepios (sc. Asklepios) 1085
Assos
  Cults: (Athena) Παρθένος 728$_0$ Octa-
    vianus 728$_0$ Zeus Ὁμονῶος 857$_6$
    Zeus Σωτήρ 728$_0$
Assyria
  Cult: Baal or Bel 694$_0$
Assyrioi (= Syrioi)
  Cult: Adonis 296$_4$
  —— tattooed 123$_0$
Astakos, s. of Poseidon 665$_3$
Astakos in Akarnania 666$_0$
Astakos in Bithynia, coins of 665$_3$
Astarte
  Cult: Chytroi 157$_1$
  Type: riding lion (?) 869$_0$
Asterioi 663
Asterion 663
Astrabakos 421
Astraios 230
Astrapai
  Cult: Bathos 827
Astrape, personification of lightning 828
  851
Astros 1145$_{1(b)}$
Astyagyia 1122
Astynome, m. of Aphrodite 693$_4$ 694$_0$
Astyoche, w. of Telephos 281$_4$ 1184$_3$
Ataburus 588$_1$
Atabyrion, Mt, in Rhodes
  Cults: Athena (?) 923$_0$ Zeus Ἀταβύριος
    922$_5$ 923$_0$ 924$_0$ 925$_0$
  Myths: Althaimenes 923$_0$ Apemosyne
    923$_0$ Katreus 923$_0$
Atabyrion, Mt, in Sicily See Agrigentum
Atabyris (Tabyris) See Atabyrion, Mt, in
  Rhodes
Atalante
  Myth: dedicates oak to Artemis in
    Arkadia 412
Ate 1099$_2$ 1100$_0$
Atella, coins of 831$_{1(2)}$
Athamas
  Myths: founds Halos 904$_1$ golden
    ram 899$_1$ plots death of Phrixos
    904$_1$
  Genealogy: h. of Ino 904$_1$ s. of Aiolos
    and f. of Phrixos 904$_1$
  —— eldest descendant of, must never
    enter Prytaneion 904$_1$
Athanaïstai 925$_0$
Athaneatis, a Tegeate tribe 1148 cp. 1149$_0$
Athena
  Cults: Achaeans (?) 458 Agrigentum
    910$_1$ Aliphera (?) 782 Alopeke 1115
    Antiocheia on the Orontes 1197
    Argos 502$_2$ 892$_5$ 893$_0$ 1144$_2$ 1156$_5$
    Assos 728$_0$ Mt Atabyrion in
    Rhodes (?) 923$_0$ Athens 259$_0$ 729$_0$
    730$_0$ 757 875$_{1(2)}$ 922$_0$ 944$_0$ 1147
    1169$_4$ 1230 Boiotia 731$_0$ Chersonesos
    Taurike 729$_0$ Delos 919$_0$ 920$_0$ 921$_0$
    922$_0$ Delphoi 231 Eilenia 625

Athens (cont.)
793 f. Eros Ψίθυρος 1043 Ge 729_0
Hadrian 1120_0 1121_0 Harpokrates
985_0 Helios 729_0 1114 Hera 1119_4
Herakles 163_4 $875_{1(2)}$ 1116 f. Hermes
1117 Hermes Καταιβάτης 14 Hermes
Χθόνιος 14 Hermes Ψιθυριστής 1043
Heroës 1123 Hestia Βουλαία 259_0
Horos 985_0 Isis Ταποσειριάς 985_0
Kallirrhoe, d. of Acheloios 1117 (?)
Kronos 554_2 Leto 163_4 St Marina
1114 Meter ἐν Ἄγρας 1119_0 1142_3 (?)
Moirai 231_8 Mother of the gods
985_0 Nymphs 1118 Παναγία εἰς τὴν
Πέτραν 1119_0 Philia 1163 St Pho-
teine 1116 Poseidon 729_0 730_0 Psi-
thyros the hero 1044 (Sarapis) ἐν
Κανώπῳ 985_0 ἡ ὑπεραγία Θεοτόκος
1119_4 Tyche Ἀγαθή 1163 Zeus 729_0
730_0 817 1229 Zeus Ἀγαμέμνων (?)
1061 Zeus Ἀστραπαῖος 815 Zeus
Βασιλεύς 730_0 Zeus Βουλαῖος 259_0
Zeus Ἐλευθέριος 1135_4 Zeus Ἐλευ-
θέριος (=Domitian) 97_0 Zeus Ἐλευ-
θέριος (=Hadrian) 98_0 Zeus Ἐλευ-
θέριος Ἀντωνῖνος Σωτήρ Ὀλύμπιος (?)
(=Antoninus Pius) 101_1 Zeus
Ἐξακεστήρ 1093_1 Zeus Ἐπιτέλειος
Φίλιος 1163 Zeus Ἐπόψιος 1121
1123 Zeus Ἐρεχθεύς 793 Zeus
Ἑρκεῖος 730_0 Zeus Ἱκέσιος 1093_1
Zeus Καθάρσιος 1093_1 1100_1 Zeus
Κάσιος 985_0 Zeus Καταιβάτης 20 f.
Zeus Κήναιος (Κηναῖος) 903_0 Zeus
Κτήσιος 1065 Zeus Μειλίχιος 1091 f.
1103 1114 ff. 1121 1123 1149 1151
1161 Zeus Μοιραγέτης 231_8 Zeus
Μόριος 20 Zeus Νάιος 1117 (?) Zeus
Ξένιος 1229 Zeus Ὀλύμπιος 20 1078
1118 1123 Zeus Ὀλύμπιος (=
Hadrian) (?) 959_0 Zeus Πανελλήνιος
1119_4 1120_0 Zeus Πατρῷος 111_0
Zeus Πολιεύς 897_2 Zeus Στράτιος
976_0 Zeus Σωτήρ 1121 1123 1147
1169 Zeus Τέλειος 1123 1147 1163_2
Zeus Τροπαῖος 111_0 Zeus Ὕπατος
163_4 $875_{1(2)}$ 897_2 Zeus Ὕψιστος
$876_{1(1)}$ 897_3 Zeus Φίλιος 1161 ff.
Zeus Φράτριος 730_0
Festivals: Anthesteria (Anthesterion
11—13) 1139 City Dionysia 244_2
Diasia (Anthesterion 22 or 23)
1137 ff. Lenaia 244_2 Megala Panhellenia 1121_0 Panathenaia 1121_0
Panhellenia 1119_4 1121_0 Pyanopsia
or Pyanepsia 237_0 Thargelia 237_0
Rites: Bacchants cover their breasts
with iron bowls 346_0 burial within
the house 1060 1065 ἐγχυτρίστριαι
1065 ἔφυγον κακόν, εὗρον ἄμεινον
1166_1 first-fruits taken to Delphoi
816 f. need-fire brought from Delphoi 816 f. πιθοιγία (Anthesterion
11) 1139 procession to Delphoi
headed by axe-bearers 628 817 847

Athens (cont.)
sacred tripod fetched from Delphoi
816 f. sacrifice of pig to Zeus Φίλιος
1161 sacrifice of white ox to Zeus
Κτήσιος 1065 1067 χόες (Anthesterion
12—13) 1139 χύτροι (Anthesterion
13) 1139 wearing of white-poplar
470 women slide down rock to
obtain children 1114
Priestess: πυρφόρος 817_0
Myths: Akropolis struck with trident
by Poseidon 793 Deukalion 1118
1139 1229 Erichthonios 944_0
Kekrops $875_{1(2)}$ Periphas 1121 ff.
sea-water on Akropolis 581
—— Asklepieion at 1078 coins of 232_0
674_1 675_1 1078 Erechtheion at 24
789_7 792 965_0 1148 Kyklops in folk-
tale from 990 ff. old Hekatompedon
at 757_1 Olympieion at 1118 ff. 1135
1229 f. Parthenon at (See Parthenon)
Prytaneion at 1094_0 1095_0 Pythion
at 201_1 202_1 1135 Stoa Basileios at
1094_0 1095_0 1135_4 Stoa Poikile at
1135_4 Stoa of Zeus Ἐλευθέριος at
1135_4 talisman of 1148
Athos, Mt
Cult: Zeus Ἀθῷος 906_1
—— altars on 906_1 Macrobii on 500
monasteries on 906_1
Athribis
Cult: Theos Ὕψιστος $889_{0(33)}$ 984_3
Athtar 430_4
Atlas
Cult: Heleia 931_0
Genealogy: f. of Alkyone 414_2
See also Index II Atlantes
Atlas, Mt
Myths: garden of Hera 1021 Hes-
perides 1021
Atreus
Myth: sceptre of Zeus 547_2 956_2 1132_4
1132_6
Genealogy: s. of Pelops and f. of
Agamemnon 957_0
Etymology: 569_2
Atropos 1023
Attabokaoi 310_2
Attaleia in Pamphylia
Cult: Zeus Τροπαιοῦχος 111_0
Attalos
Etymology: 569_2
Attes 292_3 296_4 297_0
See also Attis
Attes, s. of Kalaos 444
Attike
Cults: Zeus Ἀγαμέμνων (?) 1069 Zeus
Μειλίχιος 291_2
Myth: Theseus purified by Phytalidai
at altar of Zeus Μειλίχιος 291_2
Attis
Cults: Hierapolis in Phrygia 306_1
Ostia 297 ff. 303_2 Pessinous 970_0
Phrygia 313 Rome 303_3 306_5
Epithets: Aeternus (?) 306_4 αἰπόλος

Boreadai
Myth: pursue Harpyiai 907$_2$
Boreas
Cult: Thrace 380
Myth: pursues Oreithyia 380
Genealogy: f. of Zetes and Kalaïs by Oreithyia, d. of Erechtheus 444
Etymology: 494 ff.
Types: bifrontal 341$_0$ 380 444 horse 830$_7$ Janiform (dark + light) 387 winged man 380
Compared with Zeus 444
—— land beyond blast of 465
See also Hyperborean Maidens, Hyperboreoi
Bormos 295$_2$
Bosco Reale, *skýphos* from 1209
Bosporos
Cult: Zeus Οὔριος 707
Bosporos Kimmerios
Cults: Ge 729$_0$ Helios 729$_0$ Theos Ὕψιστος 883$_{0(27)}$ 884$_{0(0)}$ 885$_{0(0)}$ Zeus 729$_0$
Bŏttia (Bŏttiaia, Bŏttiaiis), district in Makedonia
Rite: clay loaves etc. (?) 1187$_4$
Myth: Botton 1187$_4$
Bŏttia, village on the Orontes
Cult: Zeus Βώττιος 1187$_4$
—— maiden sacrificed at 1188
Botton 1187$_4$
Boubastis
Identified with Artemis 252
Boubastos 671
Boucheta (Bouchetos, Boucheton, Bouchetion)
Myth: Themis riding on ox comes thither during Deukalion's flood 267$_5$ 348$_5$
Boukatia 233
Boule
Cult: Antiocheia on the Orontes (?) 1193$_2$
Bousbatos
Cult: Thrace 501$_3$
Identified with Artemis 501$_3$
Boutes
Genealogy: s. of Poseidon 793$_{12}$
Bouthrotou (Bouthrotos) 348
Cult: Zeus 348
Myth: founded by Helenos on spot where escaped sacrificial ox fell 348$_6$
Bouzygai 1163$_2$
Bouzyge 217$_2$
Bovianum Undecimanorum
Cult: Venus *Caelestis* 68$_2$
Brachmanes 7$_2$
Brahma 1035
Myth: birth 1036
Brahmā
Cult: India 367 774$_1$
Myth: Vishnu 774$_1$
Genealogy: h. of Sarasvatī 774$_1$
Function: solar (?) 774$_1$

Brahmā (*cont.*)
Attribute: lotos 774$_1$
Types: four-faced 367 seated on lotos 774$_1$
Identified with Hiraṇyagarbha 1035
Brahman 1035
Branchidai
Cult: Apollon 920$_0$
—— as centre of earth 167 *omphalós* (?) at 180 oracular centre at 170$_1$ votive lions at 920$_0$
Brasiai
Myth: Semele and Dionysos 671
Brathy, Mt 981$_1$
Brauronia 228$_4$
Bria
Cult: Dioskouroi 313
—— coins of 313
Briareos 1023
—— pillars of 422
Bricia See Brixia
Bridget, St 116
Brilettos, Mt 898$_0$
Brioc, St 116
Briseis 726
Britanni tattooed 123$_0$
Britomartis
Cult: Lyttos 934$_0$
Myth: pursued by Minos 939$_1$
Etymology: 1220
Brittany, two sons with gold star and daughter with silver star in folktale from 1010 f. 1013$_1$
Brixia, a goddess at Luxovium 86 86$_3$
Brixia in Cisalpine Gaul
Cult: Iupiter *Iurarius* 726$_0$
Brontai
Cults: Bathos 827 Orphists 141$_1$ 827
Brontaios 833$_7$
Bronte, horse of Helios 828 851
Bronte, personification of thunder 28 828 851
Bronteas 833$_7$
Brontes 784 828 851 1023
Brundisium
Etymology: 30$_3$
Bruttii
Cult: Zeus 709
—— coins of 709 831$_{1(2)}$
Bryaxis 921$_0$
Brygos 245$_5$ 777$_2$ 800
Bryseai
Cult: Auxesia and Damoia 890$_2$
Buddha, ladder of 129$_3$
Bunarbashi in Phrygia
Cult: Zeus Βροντῶν 835$_4$
Burdigala
Rite: *natalici viribus* 306$_4$
Byblis 413$_1$
Byblos in Phoinike
Cults: Adonis (?) 886$_{0(30)}$ Kronos (?) 886$_{0(30)}$ 887$_{0(0)}$ Moloch 887$_{0(0)}$ Zeus Ὕψιστος 887$_{0(0)}$ 983$_6$
Myths: Berouth 886$_{0(30)}$ Elioun Ὕψιστος 886$_{0(30)}$ Epigeios (Autochthon)

Clunia in Spain
  Cult: Iupiter *Augustus Ultor* 1102₈
Clusium, tomb of Porsenna at 1219
Collorgues, carved slabs from 690
Commodus
  Cult: Pergamon 1185
  Personates Zeus 1185
Compitalia 1171₂
Coralli 108 111₀
Cordeilla   See Cordelia (Cordalia)
Cordelia (Cordalia) 325 f.
Corinium in Dalmatia
  Cult: Ianus *Pater* 325
Corinth
  Cults: Apollon 915₂ (?) 916₀ Apollon
    Δειραδιώτης 210₀ Iupiter *Liberator*
    (Nero) (?) 1214 Zenoposeidon (?)
    878₀(3) Zeus 878₀(3) Zeus Καπετώλιος
    (=Κορυφαῖος) 869₁ Zeus 'Ολύμπιος
    916₀ Zeus"Υψιστος 878₀(3) 892₃ Zeus
    Χθόνιος 878₀(3)
Corne, Mt
  Cult: Diana 403
Corneto, *Tomba del Letto funebre* at 1170₈
Corvus 664₁
Corycian Cave 449₀
Crater 664₁
Crete
  Cults: Apollon Βιλκώνιος 948₀ Apollon
    Πύθιος 457 Diktynna 986₀ Kronos
    548 f. Pikos who is also Zeus (?)
    697₀ Talos 890₂ 948₁ Tan 342₀
    Zagreus 352 667 Zan 344 f. Zeus
    344 f. 352 354 727 743₇ Zeus 'Ασ-
    τέριος 230₉ Zeus Βοττιαῖος (?) 1187₄
    Zeus 'Ελαφρός 599 Zeus 'Επιρνύτιος
    946₀ Zeus 'Ιδαῖος 932₁ ff. Zeus Ξένιος
    1169₅
  Rites: bovine omophagy 539 Kouretes
    sacrifice children to Kronos 548
  Myths: Adiounios Tauros 349 birth of
    Zeus 1228 925₁ 927₁ 932₁ Botton
    1187₄ nurses of Zeus 228 reign of
    Kronos and Rhea 548 Talos 645₀
    Zeus a prince slain by wild boar
    and buried in Crete 522 727
  In relation to Delphoi 189₈ Rhodes
    923₀
  —— coins of 743₇ 933₀ tomb of Zeus
    in 219 940₀ ff.
Culśanś 378   See also Ianus
Cuprius, Vicus 401
Curiatii 363 f.
Cuthbert, St 116
Cygnus 477₇   See also Olor
Cynthianum 419₃   See also Genzano

Daai (Daoi, Dahae), a Scythian tribe
  312₅
Daci 114₀
—— tattooed 123₀
Daeira 312₅
Daes (?), consort of Daeira 312₅
Dahae   See Daai
Daidala Megala 898₆ 977₀

Daidala Mikra 898₆
Daidale 898₆
Daidalos
  Myth: makes dancing-ground for Ari-
    adne 600 f.
  Genealogy: f. of Iapyx 30
  Function: sculptor 322₇ 739₁
Daimon
  Epithets: ἡγήτορα φρικτόν, | μειλίχιον
    Δία, παγγενέτην, βιοδώτορα θνητῶν, |
    Ζῆνα μέγαν, πολύπλαγκτον, ἀλά-
    στορα, παμβασιλῆα, | πλουτοδότην,
    κ.τ.λ. 1160₄
  Identified with Zeus 1160₄ Zeus Μει-
    λίχιος 1160₄
  —— Orphic hymn to 1160
Daimones
  Cult: Thespiai 1150₉
  Epithets: ἐσθλοί, ἐπιχθόνιοι, φύλακες
    θνητῶν ἀνθρώπων, |...| πλουτοδόται
    1130₁ 1160
  Function: buried kings (?) 1150₉
  Etymology: 1159₁
  Associated with Hermes 1150₉
Daiso   See Daita or Daito
Daita or Daito (Daiso), m. of Enorches
  1021
Daktyloi
  Cult: Mt Ide in Crete 232₀ 929₀
  Epithets: πολέων μοιρηγέται ἠδὲ πάρ-
    εδροι | μητέρος 'Ιδαίης 232₀
  Rites: head wrapped in fleece of black
    ram 934₀ lying prone beside sea and
    river 934₀ purification with thunder-
    stone (belemnite ?) 934₀
  Myths: born in Dictaean Cave 929₀
    born on Mt Ide in Phrygia 949₅
    discover iron 949₅ learn iron-work-
    ing from Mother of the gods 949₅
  Genealogy: sons of Aigesthios (Ag-
    destis ?) by Ide 970₀ sons of Anchiale
    929₀
  See also Index II Stones, thumb-shaped
Daldeia
  Cult: Apollon Μύστης 250 f.
  —— coin of 251₁
Dalmatia 440₂
Damaskos
  Cults: Zeus Κεραύνιος 807₅(2) Zeus
    Μέγιστος"Υψιστος 886₀(0)
Damastes 626 f.
Damoia
  Cults: Bryseai 890₂ Sparta 890₂
Damokles 703
Dan
  Cult: Boiotia 342₀ 344₀ cp. 583₀
  See also Zeus
Danaë
  Myths: consorts with Zeus 1131₁ sent
    to sea in coffer 671 1018
  Genealogy: m. of Perseus 464 m. of
    Perseus by Pikos 1187₂
Danaïdes: Hesione 1150 Hippodameia
  1150₂ Isonoe (?) 1150₂ Polydora 486
Danaoi 961₀

Eros (*cont.*)
    as Zeus with thunderbolt and sceptre (?) 1045
    Identified with Erikepaios 1039 Metis (masc.) 1039 Phanes 1026 1039 Protogonos 1039 Zeus 1028
    Assimilated to Herakles 1046 Zeus 1045 ff.
    Associated with Psyche 1045
    In relation to Ker 315_3 Psyche 315_3 Wind 1039 Zeus 316_2 316_5
    Survives as early Renaissance *putto* 1050
Erotes
    Types: coining money (?) 1047 f. fulling clothes 1048 *genre* 1047 f. making oil 1047 in nest 1049 selling wine 1048 twining garlands 1047 winged 1050 wingless 1050
    Associated with Psychai 1047 f.
Erymne, old name of Tralleis 587_2
Erysichthon
    Myths: Dotion 497_5 683 f. 848 Prasiai 497
    —— hunger of 683 f.
Erysichthon the Giant 684_4
Erythrai in Ionia
    Cults: Ablabiai $1113_{0(1)}$ Apollon 730_0 Athena Ἀποτροπαία 1157_0 Demeter 730_0 Zeus 730_0 Zeus Ἀποτρόπαιος 1157_0
Esculapius (*sc.* Aesculapius) 1086
Ešmun
    Cults: Kition 1095_0 Phoinike 314_0
    Type: obelisk 1095_0
    Identified with Dionysos Σαβάζιος 314_0 Kadmilos 314_0
Esquilinus, Mons 401
Essir-keui in Bithynia
    Cult: Zeus Βροντῶν 835_5
Este
    Cult: Rehtia 1220
Esus
    Cults: Gallia Belgica 547_0 Gallia Lugudunensis 547_0 619
    Attribute: axe 619
    Associated with Iovis and Volcanus 547_0 619 Mercurius and Rosmerta (?) 547_0
Eteo-Cretans at Praisos 930_0
Eteokles
    Genealogy: f. of Orchomenos and Minyas 1150_5 s. and b. of Oidipous 825_2
Eteonos
    Cults: Demeter Εὐρυόδεια 1152 Oidipous 1151 ff.
    Myth: Oidipous 1152
Etruria
    Cults: Aesculapius 1085 f. Ani (=Ianus) 338_3 Charon 627_3 803 Culśanś 378 Dioskouroi 431 f. 1064 god of the Underworld 805 f. 850 Tina (=Iupiter) 338_3 Tiv 339_0 Uni (=Iuno) 338_3 Usil 339_0
    —— gold necklace from 528

Etrusci, lightning-lore of 5_5 805 mirrors of 160
Euboia, three golden children in folk-tale from 1007 f.
Eubouleus (=Hades) 118_4 $1113_{0(2)}$
    Functions: one of the first three Dioskouroi 1135_4 s. of the nether Zeus (?) 119_0
    Identified with Phanes 1026
Euboulos 190_0
Euchaites (=Hades) $1113_{0(2)}$
Eudaimonia
    Cult: Philadelpheia in Lydia 1229
Eudoxos 222
Eueides (=Hades) $1113_{0(2)}$
Euhemeros 342_0 554_3 588 927_1 928_0 981_1 1087 1135_4 cp. 940_0
Eukleia, the goddess 118_3
Eukleia, the festival 118_3
Eukleides, s. of Kleagoras 1106 f.
Eukles (=Hades) 118_3 $1113_{0(2)}$
    See also Euklos
Euklos (=Hades) 118_3
    See also Eukles
Eukoline (=Hekate) $1114_{0(4)}$
Eumeneia in Phrygia
    Cults: Agathos Daimon (=the emperor Philippus i) 970_0 Apollon 571 970_0 εὐσεβεστάτη Σεβαστὴ Εἰρήνη (=Marcia Otacilia Severa, w. of Philippus i) 970_0 Men Ἀσκαηνός 970_0 Meter Theon Ἄνγδιστις (=Ἄνγδιστις) 970_0 Zeus Σωτήρ 970_0
    —— coins of 565 f. 571
Eumenes i divinised as Zeus Εὐμένης 960_0 1228 f.
Eumenes ii divinised as Theos Βασιλεὺς Εὐμένης Σωτήρ 960_0
Eumenides
    Rites: libation of μελίκρατον (water and honey) 1142_9 νηφάλια 1142
    Genealogy: daughters of Nyx 825_1
    Function: avenge bloodshed 1130_1
    —— euphemistic names of $1113_{0(1)}$
Eumolpos, a flute-player 670
Euneidai 245_5
Euneos 245_5
Eunomia 954_0
Euphorbos, priestly ruler of Aizanoi 964_3
Euphranor 1126_0 1127_0
Euphronios 121_3
Euripides, portrait-herm of (with Sophokles) 389 tomb of, struck by lightning 9
Euromos
    Cults: Dionysos 575_1 Dioskouroi 574 f. Zeus 572_7 573_4 574 f. 1220 Zeus Εὐρωμεύς (?) 589_0
    Priests: dedicate temple-columns 580
    —— coins of 572 ff. 1220 site of 588_7
Europe
    Myth: Zeus 348 929_0 1131_1
    Compared with Themis 267_5
Euros
    Type: horse 830_7

Galerius
  Personates Iupiter 1194
Galla Placidia, Mausoleum of 1208 1208_6
Galli
  Rite : use vervain for casting lots and
    chanting oracles 395_2
Gallia Aquitanica, coins of 1040
Gallia Belgica
  Cults: Esus 547_0 Mercurius 547_0
    Rosmerta (?) 547_0
Gallia Lugudunensis
  Cults: Esus 547_0 619 Iovis 547_0 619
    pear-tree 1215 f. Volcanus 547_0
    619
  —— burial within the house in 1059
    tombstones dedicated *sub ascia* in
    547_0
Gallos, king of Pessinous (?) 970_0
Ganymedes
  Myths : buried on Mt Olympos in
    Mysia 953_2 Mt Gargaron (Gargara)
    950_0 golden vine 281_4 Tantalos
    212_5 953_2 Zeus 188_0 281_4 933_0
  Genealogy : f. of Ballenaios by Mede-
    sigiste 270_5
  Types: with eagle 188_0 189_0 with eagle
    and golden vine (?) 281_4
Gargaris, the district 949_5
Gargaron (Gargara), Mt 949_5 ff.
  Cult: Zeus 950_0 ff.
  Myths: Ganymedes 950_0 Paris 950_0
    Zeus consorts with Hera 950_0
Gargaros, the town 950_0 951_0 f.
Gargaros, s. of Zeus at (by ?) Larissa in
    Thessaly 950_0
Gaza
  Cults: Bes 674 Janiform god and
    goddess 673 f. Kronos (?) 675 Mar-
    nas 675 Rhea (?) 675 Satyric god
    674 Zeus Ἀλδήμιος or Ἄλδος 675
    1187_0 Zeus Κρηταγενής 675
  —— coins of 673 ff. cosmic picture at
    828
Gazaka
  Cult: fire 34_1
Ge
  Cults: Alopeke 1115 Athens 729_0
    Bosporos Kimmerios 729_0 Cher-
    sonesos Taurike 729_0 Delphoi 176_1
    841 Dodona 350_1 Karia 729_0 Knidos
    729_0 Magnesia ad Sipylum 729_0
    Paphlagonia 729_0 Pergamon 729_0
    955_0 Phaselis 729_0 Smyrna 729_0
    Sparta $487_{3(1)}$ 729_0 Thermos in
    Aitolia 729_0
  Epithets: Εὐρυστέρνα 176_1 Εὐρύστερνος
    176_1 Θεμέλη ($= Σεμέλη$) 279_3 Θέμις
    176_1 266 f. (?) 268_0 841 (?) Θυώνη
    279_3 Καρποφόρος 214_4 μᾶ 294_0 μέλαινα
    176_1 μήτηρ 1023
  Rite: οὐλαί, οὐλόχυται 18_6
  Myths: golden apples 1020 f. Palikoi
    909_0 sends up fig-tree to shelter
    Sykeas or Sykeus 1103_8
  Genealogy: d. of Elioun Ὕψιστος by

Ge (*cont.*)
    Berouth $886_{0(30)}$ d. of Phanes by
    Nyx 1026 m. by Ouranos of Klotho,
    Lachesis, Atropos, the Hekaton-
    cheires Kottos, Gyges, Briareos,
    and the Kyklopes Brontes, Steropes,
    Arges 1023 m. of Aetos 933_0 m. of
    Eros by Ouranos 315_4 m. of Kekrops
    1121 m. of Manes by Zeus 312 m.
    of Okeanos and Tethys by Ouranos
    1020 m. of Titanes by Ouranos 1023
    m. of Typhon by Tartaros 448_2 m.
    of Zeus 294_0 w. of Zeus 294_4
  Functions: fertility 267 crops 350_0
  Attributes: kteís 268_0 lamp 268_0 mar-
    joram 268_0 *omphalós* 231 239 841
    sword 268_0
  Type: praying Zeus to rain 21_4
  Identified with Apia (Api) 293_0 Chthonie
    351_1 Semele 279_3 Themis 176_1
  Associated with Poseidon 176_1 Zeus
    266 f. 294_4 Zeus and Helios 729_0
    $884_{0(0)}$ Zeus, Helios, and Erinyes
    728_0 f. Zeus Μιλίχιος and Athenaia
    1115
  —— *omphalós* of 231 239 1216
  See also Gaia
Gebeleïzis
  Cult: Getai 227 805 822
  Etymology : 227_4 805 822 f.
  Identified with Salmoxis (Zalmoxis)
    227 822
  See also Zibeleïzis
Gela
  Myth : Entimos and Antiphemos are
    bidden to beware of τὸν Τετράωτον
    322_6 322_7
Gelas, the river in Sicily
  Type: bull 910_1
Geloni tattooed 123_0
Gemini 430 477_8
  —— Didyma named after (?) 318
Genes, river in Pontos 617
Genetaean headland
  Cults: Zeus Γενηταῖος 616 Zeus Εὔ-
    ξεινος 617 1097_0 Zeus Ξένιος 617
Genii
  In relation to Manes, Lemures, Larvae,
    Lares *familiares* 1059
Genius
  Cult: Mogontiacum 96_2
  Epithet: generis nostri parens 1059
  Genealogy: f. of Tages 1060 s. of
    Iupiter 1060
  Attributes: acerra 1060 *patera* 1060
  Types: anthropomorphic 1060 snake
    1060
  Identified with Iupiter 1060 Lar
    1059
  Assimilated to Nero 1060
  —— of a man corresponds with Iuno
    of a woman 1059 on Iupiter-
    columns (?) 71
Genius Caeli Montis
  Cult: Rome 400_{11}

Haeva
  Cult: Batavi 64_0
Hageladas 741 ff. 749 890_6 1222 1223
Hageladas, the younger (?) 742_3 742_4
Hagia Triada
  Cults: Dionysos (?) 522 524 double axe
    522 Velchanos $947_{0(1)}$ Zagreus (?)
    522 (Zeus) $Fευχάνος$ $947_{0(1)}$
  Rite: sacrifice of bull 517 522
  —— *sarcophagus* of painted limestone
    from 516 ff. 652 657 677 692 845
Hagios Onuphrios, spear-head from 799
Haimonioi
  Cult: Korybas 295
Haimos, Mt 108
  Myth: Zeus fights Typhon 449_0
Halaesa See Alaisa
Halieus 715_4 1037
Halikarnassos
  Cults: Aphrodite ('Ακραία?) $872_{0(5)}$
    Apollon 'Αγυιεύς 163 Artemis 164_8
    Hermes $872_{0(5)}$ Zeus 'Ακραῖος $872_{0(5)}$
    cp. $872_{0(6)}$ 963_3 Zeus 'Ασκραῖος
    $872_{0(5)}$ Zeus Κώμυρος 1228 Zeus
    Λαβράϋνδος 585_3
  Myth: Pegasos 721_2
  —— coins of 721_2 $872_{0(5)}$ the Mauso-
    leion at $1146_{0(0)}$
Hallowmas 326_4
Hallstatt, axe-heads from 618 632_6 635
Halmos, s. of Sisyphos and f. of Chryso-
  gone 1150_4
Halos
  Cult: Zeus Λαφύστιος 904_1 1226
  —— coins of 904_1
Ham 35
Hamar (Hamer) 660_1
Hapi Kema 772_1
Hapi Mehit 772_1
Hariasa 57_3
Harii tattooed 123_0
Harma near Mykalessos 815_7 816_0
Harma near Phyle 815 831_0 898_0
Harmodios 1172
Harpasa 958_0
Harpasos, s. of Kleinis 463_1
Harpe = Phaiakia or Korkyra 448_0
Harpe, w. of Kleinis 463_1
Harpokrates
  Cults: Athens 985_0 Pelousion 986_0
  Function: youthful Horos 986_0
  Attributes: hem-hem crown 986_0 pome-
    granate 986_0 sceptre 986_0
  Associated with Pan 986_0
Harpolykos 713 (?)
Harpy
  In relation to Eros 315_3
Harpyiai
  Myth: pursued by Boreadai 907_2
Hathor 409_0
Hati 305_0
Hebe
  Epithet: πότνια 584_0
  Type: introduction of Herakles to
    Olympos 737

Hebrews 115_2
Hecate
  Cult: Rome 835_6
  Genealogy: m. of Ianus by Caelus
    368_3
  See also Hekate
Heddernheim
  Cult: Deus *Casius* 983_0
Hegesilaos (=Hades) $1113_{0(2)}$
Heimdallr 305_0
Hekaerge (Arge) 452 452_{11} 501 1226
Hekaergos 452 f.
Hekate
  Cults: Lagina 714_2 Panamara $879_{0(17)}$
    Panormos near Kyzikos (?) $882_{0(0)}$
    Rome 307_0 Stratonikeia 714_2 714_3
  Epithets: 'Αρίστη Χθονία $1114_{0(4)}$
    Δαδοφόρος 714_3 Εὐκολίνη $1114_{0(4)}$
    θεῶν μήτηρ 328_7 καλλιγένεθλος 328_7
    Καλλίστη $1114_{0(4)}$ Κράταιις $1114_{0(4)}$
    μεγασθενής 328_7 πολυώνυμος 328_7
    προθυραία (προθύραιε?) 328_7 Σώτειρα
    $879_{0(17)}$ Χθονία $1114_{0(4)}$ Χθονική (*sic*)
    695_0
  Festival: πανηγύρεις 714_2
  Rite: libation of honey 1142_8
  Priest: hierofanta 307_0
  Genealogy: d. of Demeter 1032
  Attributes: kálathos with crescent 714_2
    torch 714_2
  Types: *Hecatae* 307_0 holding torches
    187_4 (?)
  Identified with Artemis 1029 1032
    Bendis 314_0 Kabeiro 314_0 Semira-
    mis 695_0
  Associated with Zeus 714_2 714_3 (Zeus)
    Βροντῶν 835_6 838
  See also Hecate
Hekatoncheires
  Genealogy: sons of Ouranos by Ge
    1023
Hektor
  Cult: Thebes in Boiotia 961_0
  Myths: Apollon 459 buried at Ophry-
    nion 961_0 sacrifices to Zeus 950_0
    cp. 8
  In relation to Paris 447_5 Zeus 8
Heleia 930_0
  Cults: Artemis 931_0 Athena 931_0 Atlas
    931_0 Hera 931_0 Leto (?) 931_0 Nike
    931_0 Poseidon (?) 931_0 Zeus 931_0
    Zeus Δικταῖος 930_0 931_0 932_0
  See also Palaikastro
Helene
  Cult: Tyndaris 918_0
  Myths: brought up as d. of Leda 1015
    dedicates electrum cup, modelled
    on her own breast, in temple of
    Athena at Lindos 346_0 Menelaos
    1044
  Genealogy: d. of Tyndareos 918_0 d.
    of Zeus by Leda and st. of Klytai-
    mestra 1015_7 d. of Zeus by Nemesis
    1131_1
  Type: radiate 432_2 (?)

Helene (*cont.*)
   Associated with Dioskouroi 432_2 (?)
    1003 ff.
   —— in folk-tales 1003 ff.
Helenos
   Myth : founds Bouthroton (Bouthrotos)
    in Epeiros 348_6
Heliadai 479
Heliades
   Myths : escort Parmenides up Milky
    Way 42 f. 476 shed tears of amber
    484 499_4
   Metamorphosed into alders 472 black-
    poplars 472 484 f. larches (?) 402_0
    472_9 oaks 472_{10} poplars 472 483 495
   Types : mourning 479 transformation
    into trees 473 ff.
Helikon, Mt
   Cults : St Elias 898_5 Zeus Ἑλικώνιος
    898_5
   Myths : Muses dance round Hippo-
    krene and altar of Zeus 898_5 singing-
    match with Mt Kithairon 899_0
Heliopolis in Syria
   Cults : Iupiter $886_{0(30)}$ Iupiter *Heliopo-*
    litanus 745_1 Zeus $886_{0(30)}$
Helios
   Cults : Alexandreia $889_{0(33)}$ Apollonia
    in Illyria 485 Athens 729_0 1114
    Badinlar, in Phrygia 568 Bosporos
    Kimmerios 729_0 Chersonesos Tau-
    rike 729_0 Edessa 428 Eresos 729_0
    Gythion 259_0 Karia 729_0 Magnesia
    ad Sipylum 729_0 Paphlagonia 729_0
    Pergamon 729_0 955_2 1185 Phaselis
    729_0 Rhodes 469 Sahin in Phoi-
    nike (?) $886_{0(30)}$ Smyrna 729_0 Sparta
    729_0 Mt Taleton 890_2 Thermos in
    Aitolia 729_0
   Epithets : Ἀνίκητος (?) $886_{0(30)}$ ἠλέκτωρ
    499_2 499_3 499_4 Νέος 98_0 ὁ προπάτωρ
    θεὸς...Πύθιος Ἀπόλλων Τυριμναῖος
    562 ὃς πάντ' ἐφορᾷς καὶ πάντ' ἐπα-
    κούεις 728_0 πατήρ 1130_1
   See also Elektor, Hyperion
   Festival : Tlapolemeia 469
   Rite : sacrifice of horses on Mt Taleton
    890_2
   Priest : ἱερεύς 562_2
   Personated by Nero 98_0 254 254_5
   Myths : Auriga 477_7 Cygnus 477_7
    Eridanus 477_7 Hyades 477_7 Phae-
    thon 473 ff.
   Genealogy : f. of Elektryone (Alek-
    trona) 499 f. of Pasiphae 947_0 f. of
    Phaethon by Klymene 473_3 f. of
    Triopas by Rhodos 684_2 forefather
    of Idomeneus 947_0
   Attributes : cock 947_0 torch 478 wreath
    of white-poplar 469
   Types : bust 1185 bust on couch 1171_3
    colossal 254_5 in four-horse chariot
    975_0 on horseback 473 475 475_6 478
    radiate bust with crescent (!) 664_1
    radiate head, facing 469_7 seated 479

Helios (*cont.*)
   Identified with Antoninus Pius 321 f.
    Apollon 164_1 562 568 Apollon and
    Dionysos 253 f. Lairmenos 568
    Mithras $886_{0(30)}$ (?) Phanes 1051
    Theos Hypsistos $882_{0(0)}$ Tyrimnos
    562
   Associated with Monimos and Azizos
    428 Selene 1171_3 Zeus and Ge 729_0
    $884_{0(0)}$ Zeus, Ge, and Erinyes 728_0 f.
    Zeus, rivers, earth, and chthonian
    powers 728_0 Zeus Μειλίχιος 1114
   Supersedes Apollon 730_0
   Superseded by Phoibos Ἀπόλλων 500
   —— connected with Aurelii 321 gates
    of 41 horses of 828 851
Hell
   Types : gaping monster 138_0 harrowing
    of Hell 138_0
Hellanikos 1023
Hellas personified 853
Helle
   Myth : golden ram 899_1
Hellenes, the Thessalian tribe 894_3
Helloi 677
Hellos 677 f. 848
Hemithea
   Cults : Kastabos 670 f. Tenedos 670 f.
    847
   Myths : sent to sea in a coffer 669 ff.
    swallowed by earth 670
   Functions : childbirth 671 cures 671
    earth 670 f. 673
Henny-penny 54_3
Heos (Eos)
   Myths : *psychostasia* 734 supplicates
    Zeus 753_3
   Genealogy : m. of Memnon by Tithonos
    281_4 cp. 734
Hephaistia in Lemnos
   Cult : Ἐπήκοος Theos Ὕψιστος $878_{0(7)}$
Hephaistion (Hephaistia) in Lykia 972_1
Hephaistos
   Cults : Mt Aitne 630 Olympia 706_5
    Olympos in Lykia 972_1 Siderous
    972_1
   Epithet : Ὀλύμπιος in Lykia 972_1
   Myths : presents Polytechnos with
    double axe 693 sceptre of Zeus
    547_2 956_2 1132_4 1132_6 shield of
    Achilles 972_1
   Genealogy : f. of crabs 665 667 f. of
    Palikoi 910_0 f. of Thaleia and gf.
    of Palikoi 909_0
   Attributes : blue *pilos* 386_5 dogs 630
    double axe 709 f. perpetual fire 630
   Identified with Chrysor 715 Hadran
    630 Ptah 34_1 Zeus Μειλίχιος 715
   Associated with Athena 1137 Zeus 972_1
   —— road-making sons of (= Atheni-
    ans) 817 cp. 628_4
Hephaistos, Mts of, in Lykia 972_1
Hera
   Cults : Aigion 210_0 Amastris 707 Mt
    Arachnaion 894_1 Argos 290_0 515

Hippothoïtis, a Tegeate tribe 1148 1149_0
Hippothoon 1137_2
Hippothoos, s. of Lethos 1154_3
Hipta 347_0 (?) 957_2 (?)
Hiram 425
Hiranyagarbha 1035
  Identified with Brahmā 1035 Prajāpati 1035
Histie See Hestia
Hittites
  Cults: Artemis (?) 410_1 bull of bronze or iron or silver 910_1 dagger-god (akin to Kronos?) 550 ff. 845 god with grape-bunches and corn-ears 564 f. lion-god (akin to Kronos?) 550 ff. Sutekh 621 f. 623 Tešub 766_1 767_0 910_1 winged deities 457 youthful god bearing double axe 599_2 youthful god on lioness (?) 552
  In relation to Amazons 560 Artemis Χιτώνη (?) 410_1 Iupiter *Dolichenus* 615 Tenedos 662 Zeus 'Αταβύριος in Rhodes 615
  —— axes of 560 double eagle of 779_2 reliefs of, from Babylon 766_1 767_0 reliefs of, at Eyuk 620 f. reliefs of, from Sinjerli 767_0 rock-carvings of, at Boghaz-Keui 550 ff. 845 thunder-weapon of 790
Hlóðyn 66_0
Hludana 65_1 See also Hluθena
Hluθena 65_1 See also Hludana
Hǫdhr
  Myth: stabs Baldr with lance of mistletoe 305_0
Holda 66_0
  Functions: snow 66_0 spinning 65 66_0 winter 65 66_0
  Identified with Minerva 65 66_0 94_1
  In relation to Milky Way 66_0
Holden 66_0
Holl 66_0
Holle 66_0
Holmos (?) 209_2
Holy Cross Day 326_4
Homer, apotheosis of 1203_4 indebted to early Orphic theogony 1020 omits mere magic 989 portrait-herm of (with Hesiod) 389
Homole (Homolos), Mt
  Cult: Zeus 'Ομολώιος (?) 904_4
Homolion
  Cults: St Elias 1227 Zeus 'Ομολώιος (?) 1227
  —— bronze rings from 166_2
Homoloïa, d. of Enyeus 900_1
Homoloïa, festival of Zeus 'Ομολώιος 900_1
Homoloïon, Mt, near Thebes in Boiotia
  Cult: Zeus 'Ομολώιος (?) 900_1
Homonoia
  Cult: Dorylaeion 280_1
  Epithet: Σεβαστή 280_1
Homoroka 558_0

Honos
  Type: with sheathed sword and captured armour 99
  —— on column of Mayence 96 100
Hopladamos (Hoplodamos?) 291_0
Horae
  Associated with Ianus 336_9
Horai
  Genealogy: daughters of Zeus by Themis 37_1 94_2
  Functions: attendants of Zeus 94_2 seasons 479 year 94_2
  Etymology: 94_2
  Types: four Seasons pass over starry globe beside Tellus reclining under vine 373 four Seasons sent forth from the *orbis annuus* held by Iupiter 372 f.
  Associated with Apollon and Pan (?) 165_0 Zeus 94_2
  —— as attribute of Zeus 1138_5 symbols of 1054
Horatii 363 f.
Horatius Cocles, statue of, struck by lightning 9
Horkos
  Genealogy: s. of Eris 723_0 s. of Zeus 723_0
Horomazes See Ahura Mazdâh
Horos
  Cults: Athens 985_0 Denderah 773_0 Egypt 255 Koptos 450_0
  Myths: eye swallowed by Typhon 450_0 nursed by Isis 986_0
  Genealogy: s. of Isis 126
  Etymology: 255
  Types: child seated on lotos 773_0 hawk on lotos 774_0 holding genitals of Typhon 450_0
  Identified with Apollon 252 255
  —— ladder of 126 soul of, identified with Orion 450_0
Hortensii 147
Hrimnir 682
Hūdãnś (= 'Υδηνός?)
  Cult: Sardeis 1227 f.
  But see Pλdãnś
Hulda 66_0
Hulle 66_0
Hungary, prince with golden sun and princess with golden moon in folktale from 1012_1
Hunni
  Myth: sword of Mars 548_0
Hyades 274 f.
Hyades, the constellation 477
Hyakinthia 246_1
Hyakinthos
  Myth: slain by *diskos* of Apollon 1156
  In relation to Apollon $491_{0(6)}$ (?) 1042 (?) Dioskouroi 435 (?)
Hyde, old name of Sardeis 1228
Hydisos
  Cult: Zeus "Αρειος 705 f. 848
  —— coins of 705 f.

Hydra
  Myth: Herakles 665₃
Hygieia
  Cults: Oropos 1072 Philadelpheia in
    Lydia (?) 1229
  Epithet: θεσπεσίη 954₀
  Attributes: sceptre 1077 snake 1075
  Type: seated 1072 1077
  Identified with Salus 94₃
  Associated with Amphiaraos and Pan
    1072 Asklepios and Telesphoros
    1078
  Compared with Herkyna 1075
Hyllos 902₂ (?)
Hymenaios 1164₀
Hymettos, Mt
  Cults: Apollon Προόψιος 897₅ Zeus 873₁
    Zeus Ὄμβριος 897₅ 1226 Zeus Ὑμήτ-
    τιος 897₅
Hynnarion, Mt
  Cult: Zeus Ὑνναρεύς 987₁
  Etymology: 987₁
Hypaipa
  Cult: youthful hero with double axe
    and bay-branch in guise of Apollon
    Τύριμνος 564
Hypata
  Cults: Hermes 1155₅ Polis 1155₅
Hypatios, St 32 f.
Hypatos, Mt
  Cult: Zeus Ὕπατος 875₁(₁) 898₂
Hyperbios 712
Hyperborean Land 465
Hyperborean Maidens, arrival of, in Delos
    453₃ bring bronze tablets to Delos
    1226 grave of, in Delos 466 names
    of 452 f.
Hyperboreoi 493 ff.
  Cults: Apollon 501 844 Artemis Ὀρ-
    θία (?) 501
  Epithets: δᾶμον...Ἀπόλλωνος θεράποντα
    465 χιλιετεῖς 465 500₄
  Rites: offerings sent to Apollon at
    Delos 497 ff. with pl. xxvi περφερέες
    495₆ sacred things wrapped in
    wheaten straw 497 498₂ 500 f. sacri-
    fice of asses to Apollon 463 f. 843
  Myths: Apollon 459 ff. 484 493 843
    Delos 452 f. Delphoi 169 452 499
    844 Herakles 466 1041 (?) Kroisos
    465
  Etymology: 494 ff. 495₆
  In relation to Agyieús-pillars 169 499 f.
    amber-routes 493 f. 497 ff. China (?)
    495
Hyperes, king of Troizen 414₂
Hyperion
  Epithet: ἠλέκτωρ 499₂ 947₀
  Function: sun 947₀
Hyperoche 452 f. 466 501
Hyperochos 452
Hyperphas 1122₇
Hypnos
  Cult: Sikyon 321₁
  Epithet: Ἐπιδώτης 321₁

Hypnos (*cont.*)
  Genealogy: b. of Thanatos 317
  Attribute: horn 1127₀
  Types: 1127₀
Hypseus 1123 *
Hypsistarioi 885₀(₂₈)
Hypsistianoi 885₀(₂₈)
Hypsistos
  Cults: Ak Tash (Temenothyrai?) in
    Lydia 881₀(₂₀) Ioudaia 888₀(₃₂)
    889₀(₀) Kappadokia 885₀(₂₈) Sari-
    Tsam in Lydia 881₀(₂₀)
  Epithet: Παντοκράτωρ 885₀(₂₈)
  Rite: lamp-lighting 881₀(₂₀)
  Worshippers: Ὑψιστάριοι or Ὑψιστιανοί
    885₀(₂₈)
  See also Elioun, Theos Hypsistos
Hypsouranios 715₄ 981₁ 1037
Hyria 30
Hysmine 1141
Hysminias 1141

Ia, betrothed to Attis 970₀
Iakchos
  Epithet: Νέος 97₀
  Personated by Antinoos 97₀
Ialysos
  Cult: Elektryone (Alektrona) 499
Iambe
  Myth: Demeter 821 851
Ian
  Identified with Zan 341 344 353 842
  —— in the Salian hymn 330₀ 331₀ 341
  See also Ianus
Iana
  Epithet: Arquis 339₆
  Functions: arches 339₆ moon 339₆
  Etymology: 338₆ 340₂
  See also Diana
Ianiculum 368₃
Ianos See Ianus
Ianus
  Cults: Aenona 325 Corinium in Dal-
    matia 325 Etruria 378 Falerii 373
    Iulia Apta 325 Lambaesis 369₀
    Noricum 324 Ouxenton (?) 386₁
    Philadelpheia in Lydia 374 Rome
    364 ff. Salonae (?) 325 Tusculum (?)
    368₂ Volaterrae (?) 383
  Epithets: anni origo 336₁₀ annorum
    nitidique sator pulcherrimc mundi
    336₁₀ antiquissimus divom 335₁
    Augustus 325 biceps 336₁₀ Cameses
    or Camises (?) 330₀ 331₀ Conser-
    vator (?) 327 327₁₁ Culšanš 378
    Curiatius 364 deorum deus 337₄
    divom deus 337 duonus (duenos?)
    330₀ 331₀ duonus Cerus (duenos
    Ceros?) 330₀ 331₀ 724₀ ἔφορος πάσης
    πράξεως 338₃ ἔφορος τοῦ παντὸς
    χρόνου 336₈ Geminus 324 337₄ 338₃
    358 360 365 lucifer annorum 336₁₀
    Iunonius 336₈ Matutinus 338 Pater
    325 335₁ 336₅ 337₄ 338 369₀ 377₁
    Pater Augustus 325 Ποπάνων 338₃

Iphikles (*cont.*)
   In relation to Herakles 445 447₅
   See also Iphiklos (=Iphikles)
Iphiklos (=Iphikles) 451 f.
   See also Iphikles
Iphiklos, s. of Phylakos
   Myth: cured by Melampous 452 684 f.
Iphithea (?) 353₃
Iphitos, king of Elis 466 f.
Ipsara See Psara
Irbos (=Virbius?) 421
Iring
   Identified with Ziu (?) 51 f.
   —— road of 52
Iris
   Type: with spread wings and out-
      stretched arms 473
Irmin
   Etymology: 52₆ 1212
   Identified with Ziu 52 114
   In relation to Armenios (?) 54 114
Irminsûl 50 ff.
   —— as effigy of sky-god 57 as link
      between earth and heaven 82 as
      prototype of column at Mayence
      109 as support of sky 56 as vehicle
      of sky-god 56 f. as wooden trunk 74
      1212 compared with *Agyieús*-pillar
      166 178 compared with Diana-pillar
      157 166
Isauroi 973₁
Ischys, s. of Elatos 1089
Isinoe (?), d. of Danaos 1150₂
Isis
   Cults: Athens 985₀ Delos 922₀
   Epithets: Pharia 928₀ Ταποσειριάs 985₀
   Rites: effigy of Osiris buried in pine-
      tree 303₂ libation of milk from
      golden bowl shaped like female
      breast 347₀
   Myths: founds Pelousion 986₀ nurses
      Diktys 986₀ nurses Horos 986₀
      nurses Pelousios 986₀
   Function: earth 557₁
   Attributes: leafy spray (?) 1129₀ *mo-
      dius* (?) 1129₀ poppy 1165₁
   Types: bust on couch 1171₃ double
      bust (with Apis) 392 enthroned
      under arch 362
   Identified with Demeter 252 Tethys
      481₉
   Associated with Sarapis (Serapis)
      1128₀ (?) 1171₃ Zeus Κύνθιοs and
      Sarapis 922₀
   —— soul of, identified with Kyon by
      Greeks, with Sothis by Egyptians
      450₀
Isityche 1128₀ (?)
Islands of the Blest 36 117 465
Isodaites (=Plouton) 1113₀ (2)
Isopata, gold ring from 49₁
Ištar
   Attribute: axe (*i.e.* woodpecker?) 696₀
   Associated with Sin and Sibitti 545₀
Isthmia, the festival 490₀ (5) 951₀

Istia See Hestia
Istros, springs of 465 494
Italy
   Cults: Lares 1059 Penates 1059 Picus
      696₀
   Rite: burial within the house 1059
   —— coins of 1063
Itanos
   Cults: Apollon Πύθιοs 929₀ Athena
      Πολιάs 929₀ Hera 929₀ Zeus Ἀγορ-
      αῖοs 929₀ Zeus Δικταῖοs 929₀ cp.
      930₀ Zeus Ἐπόψιοs 1130₇
   —— coins of 1130₇ oath of 929₀
Ithake, coins of 706₅ the cave in 42
Ithomaiă (Ithomaiă, Ithomaïs) 741₄ 890₆
Ithome, Mt
   Cult: Zeus Ἰθωμάταs 741 ff. 890₆ 1222
   Festival: Ithomaiă (Ithomaiă, Itho-
      maïs) 741₄ 890₆
   Rites: human sacrifice 890₆ water
      from Klepsydra brought daily to
      sanctuary of Zeus 890₆
   Myth: Zeus brought up by nymphs
      Ithome and Neda 890₆
Ithome, the nymph 890₆
Iulia Apta
   Cult: Ianus *Vaeosus* 325
Iuno
   Cults: Aquincum 68₂ Blatsche 1084
      Mogontiacum 96₁ 96₂ Rome 364
      Thibursicum Bure 68₂ Urbs Sal-
      via (?) 803
   Epithets: Augusta 61₀ *Caelestis* 68₂
      Cinxia 899₀ *Lucetia* 61₀ *Lucina*
      59₃ 60₀ 61₀ 1226 *Pronuba* 61₀ *Regina*
      59₃ 87₃ 95₁ 96 96₁ 96₂ 98 *Sancta*
      96 98 *Sororia* 364
   Festivals: Kalendae Martiae 61₀ *Kalen-
      dae Octobres* 364
   Rite: brandishing torches 61₀
   Metamorphosed into Beroe 1031
   Functions: Kalendae 336₈ light 61₀
      marriage 61₀ motherhood 1226
      procreation 1226 spring 59 61₀
      94₁
   Attributes: flower 61₀ girdle (?) 61₀
      iris (?) 61₀ lily 61₀ peacock 60₀ 67
      sceptre 98 f. torch or torches 59 61₀
      two snakes (?) 61₀
   Types: bearing babe and flower 61₀
      bearing babe and lily or iris (?) 61₀
      bearing babe and torch 60₀ bearing
      patera and sceptre 60₀ bearing
      torch or torches 59 clad in goat-
      skin (?) 60₀ grouped with children
      60₀ 61₀ standing on cow 99₀ veiled
      60₀ with foot on head of cow 98 f.
      with foot on head of ox 98₃
   Identified with Frija 59 94₁ Luna,
      Diana, Ceres, Proserpina 256
   Associated with Hercules and Minerva
      89 Iupiter *Optimus Maximus* 96₁
      96₂ Mercurius and Ceres 1181₀
      Mercurius, Hercules, Minerva 57 ff.
      Mercurius and Minerva 89

Iupiter (cont.)

Functions: aether 1090 celestial 1090
(See also sky) chthonian 1090 container and sustainer of the world
110_5 earth·803 father and mother
of the gods 1060 flesh, wine, and
bread 1173 (?) good weather 94_2
holder of scales 734_3 lightning by
night 725_0 nocturnal sky 725_0 nur-
ture 365_4 oak-tree 570_0 sea 803 sky
337 340 f. 373 803 (See also celestial)
thunder 830_6 Thursday 70 treaties
725_0 universe 335_5 a younger Ianus
335 ff.

Attributes: bay-wreath 751_2 dog (?)
367_1 dolphin 803 f. double axe
609 eagle 400_{11} 751_2 81_2 eagle on
globe 95_2 feretrum 601 f. 613 fork
850 mallet 620 sceptre 400_{11} 81_2
spear 711 f. 848 thunderbolt 803 f.
810 ff. 850 trident 803 f. 850 trophy
1195_2 two-pronged fork 803 ff.
violet mantle 803 wheel 57_6 1213

Types: advancing with thunderbolt,
trident, and fork 803 f. bearded
head 331 334 bundle of herbs
clothed as puppet 1171 bust 1133_1
bust with thunderbolt in right
hand and spear in left 712 on
column 46 eating sacrificial meal (?)
1172_0 enthroned on a pillar 47 flint
(unhafted neolithic celt?) 546_0
grasping or hurling thunderbolt in
chariot 82 831_1 cp. 76_0 handing
thunderbolt to Trajan 1181_0 on
horseback with uplifted bolt 82
Janiform 326 ff. protecting emperor
104_1 seated with thunderbolt in
right hand and sceptre in left 1103_0
1194_4 1214 seated with Victory in
right hand and sceptre in left
1103_0 (fig. 940) sending forth the
four Seasons from the orbis annuus
372 f. standing with eagle on right
hand and sceptre in left 1214
standing with sceptre in raised
right hand and thunderbolt in
lowered left—751 standing with
spear (sceptre?) in raised right
hand and thunderbolt in lowered
left 708_5 standing with thunderbolt
in lowered right hand and sceptre
in raised left 70_1 standing with
thunderbolt (?) in outstretched
right hand and spear in raised left
711 f. standing with thunderbolt,
sceptre, and eagle 285_0 1194_4
standing with thunderbolt and
sceptre under arch 367 standing
with thunderbolt and sceptre in
four-horse chariot driven by Victory
331 334 $831_{1(2)}$ tree-trunk 109

Identified with Donar 64_0 95_2 Genius
1060 Ianus 328 365 Jehovah 1197
Sucaelus 620 Theos Hypsistos

Iupiter (cont.)

$886_{0(30)}$ Thor 620 Vediovis (?) 726_0

Assimilated to Hercules 95_2

Associated with Fontes 369_0 Fontes
and Minerva 401_0 Fortuna 1195_2
Genius Fontis 369_0 Genius huius
loci 1194_4 Hercules 1194_4 Iuno
Regina 96_1 96_2 Lares 751 Mater
Phrygia 950_0 Victoria 1195_2

In relation to emperor 708 Erinys
1102_7 Furiae 1102_7 Hercules 95_2
Ianus 328_6 331 335 ff. 353 842

—— acorn of (walnut) 775_0 beard of
(silver-bush) 775_0 chariot of 76_0 82
331 334 830_6 831_1 flame of (a flower)
775_0 footprints of 37_2 pullus Iovis
35_0 regalia of 811 f. statue of, made
of armour 46_3 throne of 1102_7 and
Ianus on coins 331 ff. and Ianus in
the Salian hymn 328 ff.

See also Diespiter, Iupater

Iupiter, the planet 480_5

Iustitia 99_1

Iuturna

Genealogy: w. of Ianus 368_3 394_3

Iůvilas 823 1226

Ivrîz 564 f.

Ixion

Myths: Hera 1088 Zeus 1098_4

Genealogy: descended from Aiolos
1088 s. of Antion s. of Periphas
s. (or f.) of Lapithes 1122 f.

Jachin 426 f.

Jacob and Esau 451_1 ladder of 127 f. 129_1
136

Jains, sacred column of 150_2

James, St, b. of the Lord

Type: on chalice of Antioch 1202_0

James, St, s. of Zebedee

Type: on chalice of Antioch 1200_4
1202_0

Janina

Etymology: 350

—— folk-tale from 678 f.

Jehovah

Cults: Mt Gerizim $887_{0(31)}$ Ioudaia
$888_{0(32)}$ $889_{0(0)}$

Epithets: Κύριος "Υψιστος $888_{0(32)}$ Theos
Ζῶν 1102_8 Theos "Υψιστος $888_{0(32)}$
$889_{0(0)}$ "Υψιστος $888_{0(32)}$ $889_{0(0)}$

Rite: θυσίαι ἐντελεῖς ὁλόκαυτοι...καθ'
ἑκάστην ἡμέραν $888_{0(32)}$

Priest: ἀρχιερεύς $889_{0(0)}$

Function: hills $887_{0(31)}$

Identified with Bacchus 1197 Dionysos
1197 'El 'Ôlâm 1037 Iupiter Sabazius 1197 Liber Pater 1197 Zeus
"Υψιστος 889

Jerusalem

Cults: Aphrodite (Venus) 984_1 Liber
Pater (supposed) 282_0 Zeus (Iupiter)
984_1

—— Antiochos iv Epiphanes and 1189_1
'cup-marks' at 793_4 golden vine

Kallirrhoe (Kalliroe), d. of Acheloios (*cont.*)
   Associated with Acheloios and Zeus
      Μειλίχιος (?) 1117 Hestia, Kephisos,
      Apollon Πύθιος, Leto, Artemis
      Λοχία, Eileithyia, Acheloios, the
      Geraistian birth-nymphs, Rhapso
      183
Kallirrhoe, d. of Okeanos 716
Kalliste (= Hekate) $1114_{0(4)}$
Kallisto
   Cult: Arkadia $1114_{0(6)}$
   Myth: Zeus 228_4 228_7 1217
   Metamorphosed into bear 228 f.
   Function: bear-goddess (?) $1114_{0(6)}$
Kalydon
   Myth: Calydonian boar 799
Kalymna
   Cults: Apollon $808_{0(11)}$ Zeus Κεραύνιος
      $808_{0(11)}$
Kāma
   Cult: India 774_1
   Function: love 774_1
Kamares, Mt
   Cults: Rhea (?) 934_0 Zeus Ἰδαῖος (?)
      935_0
   —— Maurospelaion on 934_0 935_0
Kameiros, relief-ware from 614 f.
Kamikos 30
Kamise, st. and w. of Ianos 330_0
Kanachos 1165_1
Kanai (Kane)
   Cult: Zeus Καναῖος 902_2
Kanake 684_2
Kandaules 559
Kane See Kanai
Kanobos (Kanopos)
   Cult: Sarapis 985_0
   Myth: Io, touched by Zeus, becomes
      m. of Epaphos 961_0
Kapaneus
   Myth: struck by lightning 23 824 f.
   Genealogy: f. of Sthenelos 824_5 892_5
Kappadokia
   Cults: Mt Argaios 977_1 ff. Hypsistos
      $885_{0(28)}$ Zeus Δακιηνός 616 Zeus
      Στράτιος 594_8 595_0
   —— coins of 296_0 Kyklops in folk-tale
      from 992 f.
Kar, s. of Phoroneus 168_1 257_4
Karbina 29
Karia
   Cults: Apollon 573_{10} 574_1 574_2 574_3
      Dionysos Μάσαρις 565_2 Ge 729_0
      Helios 729_0 Zeus 573 f. 705 729_0
      745_1 Zeus Ἐλευθέριος 763_1 Zeus
      Κάριος 577 Zeus Λαβραδεύς 559 f.
      572
   —— coins of 573 f.
Karia, *akrópolis* of Megara 168_1 257_4
Karia, personification of the district 320_0
Karien, near Mt Pangaion
   Cults: Zeus Ἑρκεῖος Πατρῷος 1066 Zeus
      Κτήσιος 1066
Karkinar 666_2
Karko 666_2

Karmania
   Cult: Ares 464
Karmanor 190_0
Karme 190_0
Karneades 237_0
Karneia 237_0
Karousa
   Cult: Zeus Δικαιόσυνος Μέγας 1092_8
Karyanda
   Festival: bull-sports 582_5
Karystos
   Rite: Hyperborean offerings 497
Kasion, Mt, in Egypt 984_4 f.
   Cult: Zeus Κάσιος 907_0 984_4 f.
   Myth: temple founded by descendants
      of Dioskouroi 984_4
   Etymology: 981_1
Kasion, Mt, in Syria 981_1
   Cults: Triptolemos 981_1 Zeus Κάσιος
      907_0 981_1 ff. 1191 f.
   Rites: hecatomb 982_0 incubation 982_0 (?)
   Myths: Kyparissos 981_1 *Seleucides aves*
      981_1 Zeus fights Typhon 449_0 981_1
   Etymology: 981_1
   —— injured by earthquake 1191
Kasion, town in Egypt 984_4 f.
Kasios, eponym of Mt Kasion in Egypt
   Cult: Pelousion 986_0 987_0
   Epithet: ὁ ναύκληρος 987_0
Kasios, eponym of Mt Kasion in Syria 981_1
Ḳaṣiu, an Aramaean god 983_0
Kasmilos
   Identified with Hermes 314_2
   See also Kadmilos
Kasos, f. of Kleomachos 981_1
Kasos, one of the Kyklades 981_1
Kasos, s. of Inachos 981_1
Kassiope
   Cults: Iupiter *Casius* (*Cassius*) 906_3
      Zeus (?) 907_0 Zeus Κάσιος (Κάσσιος)
      906_3 907_0
Kastabos
   Cult: Hemithea 670
   Myth: Staphylos and his daughters
      Molpadia, Rhoio, Parthenos 670 f.
Kastalia 460
Kastalios 190_0
Kastor
   Epithet: ἱππόδαμος 436
   Genealogy: b. of Polydeukes 317 1015_7
      cp. 1097_2 s. of Zeus by Leda 1015_7
   Type: fights Calydonian boar 799
   See also Dioskouroi
Katabasion of Trophonios at Lebadeia
      1075 f. 1088
Kàtane 908_1
   Cult: Apollon 486_5
   —— coins of 486_5
   See also Aitne
Kato Zakro, clay seal-impression from
      623 652
Katreus
   Myth: 923_0 924_0
   Genealogy: s. of Minos and f. of Al-
      thaimenes and Apemosyne 923_0

Kithairon, Mt (*cont.*)
δαλα) on altar of wood piled with brushwood 898₆ 977₀ sacrifice of bulls to Zeus and cows to Hera, these victims being filled with wine and incense 898₆
Myths : singing-match with Mt Helikon 899₀ Zeus pretends marriage with Plataia, d. of Asopos 898₆
Kithairon, king of Plataiai 898₆
Kition in Kypros
Cults: Aphrodite 807₅(₄) Esmun 1095₀ Keraunios and Keraunia 807₃(₁) Theos Ὕψιστος 879₀(₁₅) 980₃ Zeus Κεραύνιος 807₅(₄) (Zeus?) Κεραύνιος and (?) Κεραυνία 807₃(₁)
Klareotis, a Tegeate tribe 1148 cp. 1149₀
Klaros
Cults : Apollon Κλάριος 489₀(₄) Zeus Κλάριος 873₂
Myth: contest of Kalchas with Mopsos 489₀(₄)
Klazomenai, *sarcophagi* of 521₅
Kleagoras 1106
Kleanthes' *Hymn to Zeus* 854 ff.
Klearchos of Rhegion 739 875₁(₄)
Kleinis 463₁ 501
Kleite, m. of Kaulon or Kaulos 1042
Kleomachos, s. of Kasos 981₁
Kleonai, coins of 892₄ 1079
Kleophema, w. of Phlegyas 488₀(₀)
Kleophrades 733
Kleostratos 1151
Klepsydra, spring on Mt Ithome 890₆
Klodones 133₀
Klotho 212₅ 1023
Klymene, m. of Phaethon 473₃ 479 (?)
Klymenos (= Hades) 1113₀(₂)
Klymenos, f. of Erginos
Function: hypostasis of Zeus (?) 1075
Klytaimestra
Genealogy: d. of Zeus by Leda and st. of Helene 1015₇
——— ghost of, seen in mirror 206₂
Kneph
Cult: Egypt 1127₀
Type : hawk-headed snake 1127₀
Identified with Agathos Daimon 1127₀ 1128₀
Knidos
Cults: Apollon Λύκιος 729₀ Ge 729₀ Zeus 729₀ Zeus Μέγιστος (?) 1157₅ Zeus Μειλίχιος 1157
——— Triopion at 684₂
Knossos
Cults: Elchanos (?) = Velchanos 948₀(₃) Rhea 520₅ 548 Theos Ὕψιστος 879₀(₁₄) two double axes 537 Zeus Ἐλχάνος (?) = Fελχάνος 948₀(₃)
Myths: founded by Hestia 940₀ founds Brundisium 30₃
——— ancient grove of cypresses at 520₅ clay seal-impressions from 552₁ 652 coins of 491₀(₆) gold ring from 49 f. incised gem from 623 oath of 731₀

Knossos (*cont.*)
road from, to Idaean Cave 933₀ tomb of Zeus at 695₀ wall-painting from 528 f.
Kodros
Myth: dressed as woodman with double axe or bill-hook 627₆
——— on trophy at Delphoi 1137₂
Koios 915₀ (?)
Kokkygion, Mt
Cults: Hera Τελεία 893₂ Zeus 893₂
Myth: Zeus married to Hera 893₂
——— formerly called Thronax (Thornax?), later Kokkyx 893₂
Kokynthos, headland of Bruttii 1042 (?)
Kolchis
Cult: Phasis 471
Myth: Phrixos 904₁
Kolchoi
Cult: Diana 411
Myth: Orestes 421₃
——— Egyptian *kýrbeis* of 1095₀
Kolikantzaroi See Kallikantzaroi
Koloe
Cults : Apollon Βοζηνός 568 Apollon Ταρσεύς 568 f. Theos Ὕψιστος 881₀(₂₀) Zeus Κτήσιος 1067 Zeus Σαβάζιος 285₀
Kolonai
Myth: Kyknos, s. of Poseidon 669
Kolonos
Cults: Athena Πολιοῦχος 1152₅ Demeter 1152₅ Zeus (?) 1152₅ Zeus Χθόνιος 1154 f.
Myth: Oidipous 1152₅
Kolophon
Myth: Polytechnos 693
Kolotes 1078
Komana in Kappadokia
Cult: Ma 616
——— priestly kings at 965₀
Komana in Pontos, priestly kings at 965₀
Koptos
Cult: Horos 450₀
Korakoi (= Philioi Daimones)
Cult: Skythia 1179₁
Etymology: 1179₁ (?)
Kore
Cults: Eleusis 314₀ 314₂ Megalopolis 1178 Megara 1117₇ Nysa in Lydia(?) 564 Paros 131 Phlyeis 1066 Samothrace 314₀ 314₂ Selinous 489₀(₀) Tegea 1140₅
Epithets: Μελίβοια (?) 1113₀(₃) Πασικράτεια 489₀(₀) Πρωτογόνη 1066
Rite: bridal hymn 132₂
Myths: carried off by Plouton 345₆(₂) consorts with Zeus 1029 Herkyna 1075 Plouton 1103
Genealogy: d. of Zeus by Rhea or Demeter 1029 m. by Zeus of the chthonian Dionysos or Zagreus 1029 w. of Klymenos (= Hades) 1113₀(₃)
Function: Corn-maiden 295₂

Larisa, old name of Tralleis 587$_2$
Larisa on the Caystrian Plain
  Cult: Apollon Λαρισηνός 958$_0$
Larisa on Mt Messogis
  Cult: Zeus Λαράσιος 958$_0$ ff. Zeus Λα-
    ρισαῖος 958$_0$ Zeus Λαρίσιος 957$_3$ f.
Larissa in Thessaly
  Cults: Akrisios 1155 Athena 1155 En-
    hodia 1155 Enhodia Φαστικά 1155$_4$
    Polis 1155 Zeus Μειλίχιος 1155 f.
  Myths: Akrisios slain by Perseus 1155
    Gargaros, s. of Zeus 950$_0$
Larissa Kremaste
  Cults: Hermes 1155$_5$ Polis 1155$_5$
  —— compared with Larisa on Mt
    Messogis 957$_3$
Larunda
  Genealogy: m. of Lar 1059
  Etymology: 1159$_1$
Larvae
  In relation to Manes, Genii, Lemures,
    Lares *familiares* 1059
Lasimos 1159$_1$
Latinus 1071
Latinus Silvius 404$_0$
Latmos, Mt 589
Lato See Leto
Latos, oath of 730$_0$
Lavinium
  Cult: Penates 1068
  —— *caducei* of iron and bronze to-
    gether with Trojan pottery pre-
    served at 1068
Lear 325 f. See also Llyr
Lebadeia
  Cults: Apollon 899$_2$ St Christopher
    1076 chthonian Zeus (or Hermes)
    233$_0$ St Elias 899$_2$ Hera 899$_2$ Her-
    kyna 1073 1075 Kronos 899$_2$ Tro-
    phonios (Trephonios) 899$_2$ 1073 ff.
    Zeus 899$_2$ Zeus Βασιλεύς 899$_2$ 900$_0$
    1073 f. 1076 Zeus Τρεφώνιος or Τρο-
    φώνιος 1061 1073 ff.
  Festival: Basileia 900$_0$
  Rite: honey-cakes offered to snakes
    1074 f.
  Myth: Trophonios (Trephonios) swal-
    lowed by earth 1075
  —— *bóthros* of Agamedes at 1075 con-
    tract for building temple of Zeus
    Βασιλεύς at 900$_0$ *Katabásion* at 14
    1075 f. 1088 Κόρης θήρα (?) near 899$_2$
Lebedos 662
Lebena
  Cult: Asklepios 1082
  Rite: incubation 1082
  —— temple-spring at 1082
Lebuinus, St 117
Lectisternia See Index II
Leda
  Myths: consorts with Zeus 1015$_7$ 1131$_1$
    cp. 941$_0$ keeps egg of Nemesis in
    chest 1015 lays two eggs contain-
    ing Castor and Pollux, Clytemnestra
    and Helena 1015$_7$

Leda (*cont.*)
  Attribute: Phrygian cap 432$_2$ (?)
  —— egg of (?) 1062
Leibethra (Libethra)
  Rite: mysteries 1024
Leicester
  Cult: Janiform god 325 f.
  Rite: workmen begin the year's work
    in underground chamber sacred to
    Janiform god 325 f.
  Myth: Cordelia buries King Lear in
    underground chamber beneath the
    Soar 325 f.
Leimon 164$_6$
Leïs 414$_2$
Leleges 354$_9$ 458$_1$ 666$_0$ 949$_5$ 951$_0$
Lemnos
  Cults: Bendis 314$_0$ crabs 664 f. Dio-
    nysos 314$_0$ Kabeiroi 663 ff.
Lemures
  In relation to Manes, Genii, Larvae,
    Lares *familiares* 1059
Lenaia 236 244$_2$
Leo 43$_4$ 734$_3$
Leochares 281$_4$
Leon (*leg.* Λεόντων, *sc.* πόλις)
  Cult: lion 987$_0$
Leonard, St 134
Leonidas 6
Lepetymnos
  Cult: Mt Lepetymnos 832
Lepetymnos, Mt
  Cults: Apollon 832 Lepetymnos 832
  Myth: two ravens 832
Lerne (Lerna)
  Cult: Dionysos Σαώτης 599$_2$
  —— spring at 1022
Lesbos
  Cult: Dionysos Ἐνόρχης 1021
  Festival: Theodaisia 1021
  Rite: cannibalism 1021
  Myths: Enorches 1021 head of Orpheus
    290$_0$
  —— name-trick in folk-tale from
    999
Leto (Lato)
  Cults: Argos 455 Athens 163$_4$ Badinlar,
    in Phrygia 567 568$_6$ Delphoi 1216
    Gortyna 723$_0$ Heleia (?) 931$_0$ Hiera-
    pytna 723$_0$ Lyttos 723$_0$ 934$_0$ Pha-
    leron 183 Priansos 723$_0$
  Epithets: Ἀσιᾶτις 455 Μήτηρ 567
    568$_6$
  Myths: aided by Kouretes on Mt Sol-
    missos 962$_2$ bears Apollon and
    Artemis to Zeus in Lykia 455$_2$
    Kleinis 463$_1$
  Genealogy: m. of Apollon 237$_0$ 484
    m. of Apollon and Artemis by Zeus
    453 m. of Apollon and Artemis 456
    m. of Artemis 465 501
  Etymology: 455
  Associated with Apollon 567 Apollon
    and Artemis 183 202$_1$ 203$_0$ 317$_2$
  In relation to Artemis 501

Leukas
   Cult: Apollon $A\kappa\tau\iota os$ 782
   Rite: ox sacrificed to flies 782
Leuke, d. of Okeanos 468
Leuke, island in Euxine sea 925_0
Leuke Akte $886_{0(30)}$
Leukippides 438_2
Leukippos, b. of Aphareus 438_2 1089
Leukophrys, old name of Tenedos 669
Leukothea 211
Leukothea, st. of Tenes 670
Leuktron or Leuktra in Lakonike
   Cult: Zeus '$I\theta\omega\mu\acute{a}\tau as$ 891_0
Libanos, Mt
   Cult: Zeus (Abad) 983_7
   Myth: Libanos 981_1
Liber
   Cults: Jerusalem (supposed) 282_0
     Rome 307_0
   Epithets: *Bimater* 1031 *bis genitus*
     1031 *Pater* 220_0 244_4 256 282_0 1031
     1197
   Festival: Magna Corona 244_4
   Priest: archibucolus 307_0
   Myths: Agdistis 969_4 born in India
     1031 descent to the dead 256 reared
     by Nysus 1031 slain by Titans 1031
   Genealogy: s. of Iupiter by Proserpina
     1031
   Function: triumphs 244_4
   Attributes: bay 244_4 ivy 244_4
   Identified with Apollo and Sol 256 f.
     Apollon 244_4 Dionysos 220_0 1031
     Jehovah 1197 Osiris 244_4
   Associated with Minerva and Hercules
     1181_0
Libera (?) 98_1
Libethra See Leibethra
Libye, the country
   Cult: Aphrodite 987_0
   Rite: taboo on garlic among priests of
     Aphrodite 987_0
Libye
   Type: double bust (with Triton) 392
Lichades 903_0
Lichas 902_2 903_0
Licinius
   Personates Iupiter 1195
Licinius Iunior
   Personates Iupiter 1195
Ligourio $1145_{1(b)}$
Liguria
   Myth: Kyknos 477
Ligurians
   In relation to Illyrians and Iberians
     340_3
   —— rock-engravings of 688_0
Lindos
   Cults: Athena 346_6 925_0 Athena $\Pi o\lambda\iota\acute{a}s$
     923_0 Dionysos 925_0 Psithyros the
     god 1044 Zeus '$A\tau a\beta\acute{v}\rho\iota os$ 925_0 Zeus
     $\Pi o\lambda\iota\epsilon\acute{v}s$ 923_0
   Festival: Sminthia 250_2
   Myth: Helene dedicates electrum cup
     to Athena 346_0

Linos 164_5 164_6
Lips in Phoenician cosmogony 1037 f.
Litai 1097_2 1098_0 1099_2 1100_0 1101
   Functions: avenging deities 1101
     prayers of injured man 1100_0 1101
     prayers of injurer 1100_0
   Type: halt, wrinkled, squinting 1099_2
     1100_0
Liternum
   Cult: Mater deum 306_4
   Rite: (vires) condidit 306_4
Lithuanians
   Cults: Sondergötter 13_1 wind-god (*Wejo-*
     patis) 445_1
   Myth: Road of the Birds 38 462
   —— star-lore of 158_1
Lityerses 295_2 1096_3
Livia, fresco from house of 145 ff.
Livinus, St 117
Ljod 682
Llyr
   Cult: Celts 326
   Identified with Ianus 326
Loki 305_0
Longinus, the blind soldier 305_0
Lopta, near Sidyma
   Cult: Apollon 971_2
Lotis
   Metamorphosed into lotus-tree 486_2
Lousoi
   Cult: Artemis 646
Loxo 452_{11}
Lucania
   Cult: Zeus 709
   —— coins of 709
Ludi Plebei 1172_0
Ludi Romani 1172_0
Lugdunum
   Cults: Mars 99_3 Vesta 99_3 Volcanus 99_3
   Rite: vires excepit et a Vaticano trans-
     tulit 306_4
Lugdunum Convenarum
   Cult: Fagus 402_1
Luke, St
   Attribute: amulet 1200_3 1200_4
   Type: on chalice of Antioch 1200_4
     1202_0
Luna
   Function: Monday 70
   Attribute: torch 1050
   Types: bust with crescent on head
     555_0 colossal 254_5 driving chariot 96
   Identified with Diana, Ceres, Iuno,
     Proserpina 256
   Associated with Sol 59_0 96 98 555_0 1050
Lupercalia 20_0
Lussoius See Luxovius
Luxovium in Germania Superior
   Cults: Brixia (Bricia) 86_3 Iupiter (?)
     1213 Luxovius (Lussoius) 86_3
Luxovius (Lussoius) 86 86_3
Lydia
   Cults: Zeus 1228 Zeus '$A\sigma\kappa\rho a\hat{\imath} os$ $872_{0(5)}$
     Zeus $K\acute{a}\rho\iota os$ 577 Zeus $K\epsilon\rho a\acute{v}\nu\iota os$
     $807_{5(6)}$ Zeus $M\eta\delta\epsilon\acute{v}s$ ($M\eta\delta\iota\nu\epsilon\acute{v}s$) 312_5

Oaxos 929_0 See also Axos
Occasio 862 f.
Oceanus, the constellation 481
Oche, Mt
  Cult: Zeus superseded by St Elias 902_1
  Myth: union of Zeus with Hera 902_1
Ocrisia
  Etymology: 1156_5
Octavianus See Augustus
Odessos in Thrace
  Cult: Theos Megas 1126_0
  —— coins of 1126_0
Odhin
  Myths: fights the fire-demon Surtr 305_0 hangs on the tree as a sacrifice to Odhin 305_0 overcome by Fenrir 305_0 rides down to Mimir's well 305_0 rides through the hall of serpents on Nastrand 305_0
  Genealogy: f. of Vidharr 305_0
  Attribute: broad hat 386
  Type: one-eyed 682
Odrysai
  Cult: Dionysos 269_1 661 f. (?)
  —— coin of 661 f.
Odysseus
  Myths: axes as marriage-test 690 Kyklops 990 997 offers meal to dead 18_6 prays Zeus for omen 8 Telegonos 676 923_0 Telephos 1184_3 tree-bed 690
  Functions: fire-god (?) 697 hero 698 sun-god (?) 697
  —— raft of 906_3
Oea in Tripolitana 360_2
Ogur (Ogut) in Galatia
  Cult: Zeus Βροντῶν 835_5
Ogygos 824_6
Oichalia 902_2
Oidipodeion at Eteonos 1152 1154
Oidipodes (= Oidipous) 1154_3 1154_5
Oidipous
  Cult: Eteonos 1151 ff.
  Myths: as explained by S. Freud 451_0 Eteonos 1152 Keos 1152 Kolonos 1152_5 Laïos 923_0 summoned by Zeus Χθόνιος 829 Thebes 1152
  Metamorphosed into snake (?) 1155
  Genealogy: f. and b. of Eteokles and Polyneikes 825_2 s. of Laïos 1154_3
  Function: hypostasis of Zeus Χθόνιος (?) 1154
  Etymology: 1152 f.
  Type: anguiform 1152 ff.
  Compared with Melampous 1153_1 Zeus Μειλίχιος 1154
  —— grave of 1154
Oineus 1137_2
Oinoanda
  Cult: Theos Ὕψιστος $879_{0(16)}$
Oinomaos, house of, at Olympia 706 $808_{0(15)}$ sacrifice of 706
Oistros (?) 1041

Oite, Mt 903_2 1226
  Cults: Herakles 903_2 Zeus 903_2
  Myths: Dryope 486 pyre of Herakles 941_0 (?) (T. Faber cj. Αἴτνης)
  —— meadows that might not be mown on 903_2 pyre of Herakles on 903_2
Oitosyros (Goitosyros, Gongosyros), the Scythian Apollon 293_0
Okeanos
  Epithets: ἀθανάτων τε θεῶν γένεσιν θνητῶν τ' ἀνθρώπων 481_9 ἀψόρροος 481_8 θεῶν γένεσις 481_9 καλλίρροος 1020 μέγας 1027 ὅς περ γένεσις πάντεσσι τέτυκται 481_9 πατήρ 1021
  Myths: Hera 343_0 Themis 37_1
  Genealogy: f. of Leuke 468 f. of Phorkys, Kronos, Rhea, etc. by Tethys 1020 h. of Tethys 473 cp. 343_0 s. of Ouranos by Ge 1020
  Functions: celestial river 516 seed of sky-god (?) 481_9
  Types: recumbent with head-dress of crab's-claws 665_3
  Identified with Eridanus the constellation 1025 Neilos 1025 Osiris 481_9
  —— at first none other than Milky Way 481 garden of 1021 woods of Persephone beyond 472
Olaf, St 135
Olbia
  Cult: Apollon $493_{0(7)}$
  —— coins of $493_{0(7)}$ leaden *bucrania* and double axes from 540
Olbia, m. of Astakos 665_3
Oleiai 924_0
Olen 455
Olenos in Aitolia
  Cult: Zeus 933_0
  Myth: Zeus nurtured by goat Amaltheia 933_0
Olenos, s. of Zeus by Hippodameia d. of Danaos 1150_2
Olor, the constellation 477 477_8
Olous
  Cult: Zeus Ταλλαῖος 948_1
  —— oath of 730_0 treaty of 934_0
Olymos
  Cults: Apollon 586_2 Artemis 586_2
Olympe, coins of 161 ff. 499
Olympia
  Cults: Agnostoi Theoi 1100_1 Ares (?) 706_5 Hephaistos 706_5 Hera 706_5 Hermes 231_8 $878_{0(5)}$ Hermes Ἐναγώνιος 859 Heros- 897_0 Kairos 859 Kronos 554_2 Moirai 231_8 $878_{0(5)}$ Myiodes 783 Nike 1100_1 Pelops 471 Zan 349 Zeus 349 757 ff. 849 916_0 947_0 955_0 1078 1222 1224 Zeus Ἀπόμυιος 783 Zeus Ἄρειος 706 Zeus Ἑρκεῖος $808_{0(15)}$ Zeus Καθάρσιος 1100_1 Zeus Καταιβάτης 21 Zeus Κεραύνιος $808_{0(15)}$ (Zeus) Μοιραγέτας 231_8 Zeus Ὀλύμπιος 758_0 761 Zeus Ὅρκιος 722 726 f. Zeus Ὕψιστος 231_8 $878_{0(5)}$ 891_2 Zeus Χθόνιος 1100_1

Philadelpheia in Lydia (*cont.*)
monia 1229 Hestia 960$_0$ 1229
Hygieia (?) 1229 Ianus 374 Mneme
1229 Nike 1229 Ploutos 1229 Theoi
Σωτῆρες 960$_0$ 1229 Theos Ὕψιστος
881$_{0(20)}$ Tyche Ἀγαθή 1229 Zeus
Εὐμένης (=Eumenes i) 960$_0$ 1229
Zeus Κορυφαῖος 285$_0$ 869$_1$ 957$_1$
1217 f. Zeus Σωτήρ 1228 f.
Rite: procession of Ianus on *Kalendae
Ianuariae* 374
—— coins of 363 869$_1$
Philai
Cults: Osiris 773$_0$ Zeus Ἐλευθέριος
(=Augustus) 97$_0$
Philandros, s. of Apollon 218$_0$
Philemon
Myth: 1096$_4$
Philia
Cult: Athens 1163
Genealogy: m. of Zeus Ἐπιτέλειος
Φίλιος 1163 1169
Associated with Zeus Ἐπιτέλειος Φίλιος
and Tyche Ἀγαθή 1163
Philioi Daimones (Orestes and Pylades)
Cult: Skythia 1179
Philioi Theoi 1177$_2$
Philip of Macedon
Associated with the twelve gods 1137$_1$
Philippopolis in Thessaly See Gomphoi
Philippopolis in Thrace, coins of 490$_{0(5)}$
Philoktetes 903$_0$
Philomela
Metamorphosed into swallow 693
Philonome 669
Philyra
Genealogy: m. of Aphros and Cheiron
by Kronos 695$_0$ m. of Cheiron by
Kronos 871$_0$
Phlegyai
Etymology: 1134
Phlegyas 463$_1$ 488$_{0(0)}$
Phlious
Cults: Asklepios 1090 Zeus Μειλίχιος
1106 f.
Phlox 981$_1$
Phlyeis
Cults: Apollon Διονυσοδότης (less pro-
bably Διονυσόδοτος) 251$_2$ Athena
Τιθρωνή 1066 Demeter Ἀνησιδώρα
1066 Kore Πρωτογόνη 1066 Semnai
1066 Zeus Κτήσιος 1066
Phobos
Cult: Selinous 489$_{0(0)}$
Phoenicians
In relation to 'Minoan' culture 662
—— sacred pillars of 423 425
See also Phoinike
Phoibe
Cults: Delphoi 500 Sparta 1015$_7$
Function: earth 500
Type: Gigantomachia 399$_1$
Associated with Hilaeira 1015$_7$
In relation to Gaia and Themis 500
Phoibe, one of the Heliades 500$_{11}$

Phoibos
Cults: Delphoi 839 Kurshumlu in
Phrygia 839 Lykoreia 901$_2$
Epithets: Ἀπόλλων 500 844 Λυκώρειος
or Λυκωρεύς 901$_2$ 902$_0$
Functions: interpreter of Zeus 500 sky
500
Etymology: 500 500$_{12}$
In relation to Zeus 500 844 Zeus Βρον-
τῶν 839
Supersedes Helios 500
Phoinike
Cults: Agathos Daimon 1127$_0$ Baʻal
Milik (Melek, Molok) 1108 bene-
factors of society 1132$_6$ Ešmun
314$_0$ Kabeiroi 314$_0$ Kadmilos 314$_0$
Rešef (Rešup) 630 Theos Ὕψιστος
886$_{0(30)}$ Zeus Ὄρειος 868$_8$
Myth: cosmic egg 1036 ff.
—— snake sacred in 1111$_1$
Phoinike, old name of Tenedos 662
Phoinikous, a name of Mt Olympos in
Lykia 972$_1$
Phokis
Cults: Athena 731$_0$ Hera Βασίλεια 731$_0$
Poseidon 731$_0$ Zeus Βασιλεύς 731$_0$
Phol 844$_6$
Etymology: 110$_5$
Identified with Apollo (?) 110$_5$ 844
Balder (?) 110$_5$ 844 St Paul (??) 110$_5$
Pholoe, Mt 894$_0$
Phorkys
Genealogy: s. of Okeanos by Tethys
1020
Phoroneus 168$_1$ 257$_4$
Phos 981$_1$
Phosphoros 430$_4$ 430$_5$ 478$_2$ (?) 609$_1$
Photeine, St 1116
Phrixos
Myths: golden ram 899$_1$ 904$_1$ received
by Dipsakos 904$_1$ Zeus Λαφύστιος
904$_1$ Zeus Φύξιος 902$_0$
Genealogy: s. of Athamas and f. of
Kytissoros 904$_1$
—— tomb 471
Phrygia
Cults: Agdistis 970$_0$ Akrisias 1155 f.
Attis 313 Deos (Dios) 278 ff. Kronos
1156 Mother of the gods 970$_0$
Mother of the gods Τηρείη 697
Papas 292 ff. 313 836 Rhea 970$_0$
Semele 279 Zeus Βαγαῖος 294$_0$(?)
295$_2$ 569 Zeus Βέννιος or Βεννεύς
883$_{0(0)}$ 969$_3$ Zeus Βροντῶν 835 f.
838 f. 852 Zeus Δίος 836 Zeus
Κεραύνιος 807$_{5(5)}$ Zeus Πάπας or
Παπᾶς 292$_4$ Zeus Σαβάζιος 282
Zeus Τετράωτος 322 842
Festivals: arbor intrat 303$_2$ Ballenaion
270$_5$
Rite: man bound in sheaf 498$_2$
Priests: Βεννεῖται 883$_{0(0)}$
Myth: Lityerses 295$_2$
—— coins of 296$_0$
Phrygia, Mt, pyre of Herakles on 903$_2$

Syracuse
Cults: Artemis Λυαία 1140₃ Hestia
916₀ Poseidon 916₀ Zeus Ἐλευθέριος
763₁ Zeus Ὀλύμπιος 915₂ 916₀ 917₀
Zeus Οὔριος 708 917₀ 918₀
Rite : contest of rustic singers wearing
stag-horns 1140
Priest : ἀμφίπολος of Zeus Ὀλύμπιος as
eponymous magistrate 916₀
—— celt from 509 coins of 110₆ 708 918₀
Syria
Cults: Hadran 910₀ Keraunios 807₃₍₂₎
Zeus 745₁ Zeus Καταιβάτης 15 f.
(Zeus ?) Κεραύνιος 807₃₍₂₎ Zeus
Ὕψιστος 886₀₍₀₎
—— coins of 761 816₄ 1189 f. Sun,
Moon, and Morning-Star in folk-
tale from 1004 ff.
Syrna 451₁
Syros
Cult : Zeus Κτήσιος 1066

Taautos   See Thoth
Tabai
Cult : Zeus 743₇
—— coins of 743₇
Tabala
Cult : youthful hero, radiate, on horse-
back bearing double axe 564
Tabiti, the Scythian Hestia 293₀
Tabyris   See Atabyris
Tachnepsis
Cult : Delos 985₀
Tacitus, M. Claudius, statue of, struck
by lightning 10
Tages
Genealogy : s. of Genius and gs. of
Iupiter 1060
Tainaros, Cape
Cults : Poseidon 890₅ Zeus (?) 890₅
Tainaros, s. of Zeus 890₅
Taleton, Mt 890
Cult : Helios 890₂
Rite : sacrifice of horses to Helios 890₂
Tallaia range
Cults : Hermes 948₁ Zeus Ταλλαῖος (?)
948₁
Talos
Cult : Crete 890₂ 948₁
Myth : nail and vein 645₀
Function : sun 890₂ 948₁
Type : stone-throwing 491₀₍₆₎
Compared with Zeus 948₁
Talthybios
Myths : Agamemnon and Briseis 726
Tegea in Crete 1147₆
Tammuz
Cults : Bethlehem 984₁ Eridu 483
Associated with Aphrodite (Venus) 984₁
Šamaš 483
Compared with Adonis and Zeus 345
Zeus 347
Tan
Cults : Crete 662 Hierapytna 342₀
Polyrrhenion 342₀

Tan (*cont.*)
—— tomb of 342₀
See also Zeus
Tanagra, vases from 123₀
Tanais
Cults : Theos Ὕψιστος 884₀₍₀₎ 948₃
Theos Ὕψιστος Ἐπήκοος 884₀₍₀₎
Tanit
Cult : Carthage 69₀
Identified with Iuno *Caelestis* 68₂ Venus
Caelestis 68₂
Tantalos
Myths : Ganymedes 953₂ golden hound
212₅ Pelops 212₅ perpetual thirst
134₁ Mt Sipylos 956₂
Genealogy : f. of Aizen 964₃ f. of Pelops
438 957₀ s. of Zeus 957₀
Taouion   See Tauion
Taranis 32
Tarantos in Bithynia
Cult : Zeus Ταρανταῖος 32₃
Taranucnus·32
Taras
Etymology : 31 f.
Tarentum 31
Cults : Apollon 1064 Dioskouroi 1064
Persephone 1141₀ pillar 29 45 131
161 166 Venti 464 Zeus 762 ff. 1064
Zeus Ἐλευθέριος 763₁ Zeus Καται-
βάτης 29 ff. 45 131 161 559 845
Festival : Theoxenia 1064
Rite : sacrifice of asses to the Winds
464
—— cake-moulds(?) from 131 802 1064
1215 coins of 763₁ 1064 compound
seals (?) from 1215 Dioscuric reliefs
from 1064 disk from 462₀ gold
sceptre from 763₁ persistence of
'Minoan' cult at 543
Tarentum in the Campus Martius 32
Tarraco (Tarragona), coins struck at 604
painted tablet from 2₄ 481₉ 1039 1211
Tarragona   See Tarraco
Tarsos
Cults : Apollon Ταρσεύς 570 Ba'al-tars
761 f. Herakles (Sandas) 560 845
Sandas (Herakles) 560
Rite : sword of Apollon washed in
water from the Kydnos 570 f.
Myths : Herakles 570₄ Perseus 570₄
Titanes 570₄
—— coins of 101₁ 550₃ 571 761 f.
Tartaros (Tartara) 827₇ 1023 1032
Epithet : εὐρώεντα 1028
Tartaros
Genealogy : f. of Typhon by Ge 448₂
Tat (= Thoth)
Genealogy : s. of Hermes Τρισμέγιστος
943₀
Tauion
Cults : Dioskouroi 1064 Zeus 754₁
—— coins of 754₁ 789₉ 1064
Taurini
Cult : Aeternus 306₄
Rite : viribus Aeterni taurobolio 306₄

Termessos (Termessus Maior) (*cont.*)
$\theta\acute{\epsilon}\rho\iota o s$ 974_0 Zeus $\Sigma o\lambda\upsilon\mu\epsilon\acute{\upsilon}s$ 973_1 f.
Zeus $\Sigma\acute{o}\lambda\upsilon\mu o s$ 974_0
Festival : Eleutheria (?) 974_0
—— coins of 973_1 974_0
Terminus
Rite : offerings placed in hole 1090
Function : terminator 1090
Terra
Myth : Palici 909_0
Tešub
Cults : Hittites 766_1 767_0 910_1 list of 910_1
Attributes : axe 767_0 lightning-fork 767_0
Type : standing with axe and lightning-fork 766_1 767_0
Tethys
Myth : nurses Hera 343_0
Genealogy : d. of Ouranos by Ge 1020 m. of Phorkys, Kronos, Rhea, etc. by Okeanos 1020 w. of Okeanos 473
Identified with Isis 481_9
Tetraotos, a god
Cult : Sikanoi (?) 322
See also Apollon $T\epsilon\tau\rho\acute{a}\omega\tau o s$, Zeus $T\epsilon\tau\rho\acute{a}\omega\tau o s$
Tetraotos, a Phoenician freebooter 322_6 323_0
Teukros 472
Teuthras
Genealogy : f. of Thespios 1151 s. of Pandion 1151
Thagimasada See Thamimasadas
Thalamai
Cults : Asklepios 1085 Pasiphaa 31 Zeus $Ka\beta\acute{a}\tau as$ 17 f. 31
Thalassa
Cults : Laodikeia on the Lykos 1186 Pergamon 1185
Attributes : crab's-claws 665_3 1185 dolphin 1186 steering-paddle 1185
Types : androgynous 558_0 recumbent 1185 standing 1185 f. with head-dress of crab's-claws 665_3 1185
Thalatth 558_0
Thaleia, d. of Hephaistos
Genealogy : m. of Palikoi by Zeus 909_0
Thales 1021
Thalna 709 f.
Thamimasadas (Thagimasada), the Scythian Poseidon 293_0
Thanatos
Genealogy : b. of Hypnos 317
Type : Eros with crossed legs and torch reversed 309 1045 1166
Thanr 709 f.
Thargelia 237_0
Thasos
Cults : Bendis 314_0 Dionysos 314_0 Zeus $K\epsilon\rho a\acute{\upsilon}\nu\iota o s$ $808_{0(10)}$
—— antefix from 123_0 coins of 388_0 relief from 863_1
Thea Hypsiste
Cult : Gjölde in Lydia $881_{0(20)}$

Theai Megalai See Megalai Theai
Theanor 1024
Thebarma
Cult : fire 34_1
Thebes in Boiotia
Cults : Artemis 412 Demeter $\dot{o}\mu o\lambda\acute{\omega}a$ 900_1 cp. 901_0 Hektor 961_0 Hera $K\iota\theta a\iota\rho\omega\nu\acute{\iota}a$ 899_0 Meilichioi 1154_6 Zeus $\dot{o}\mu o\lambda\acute{\omega}\iota o s$ 900_1 Zeus $\ddot{\Upsilon}\psi\iota\sigma\tau o s$ $878_{0(2)}$ 898_3
Festivals : Daphnephoria 455_8 Homoloïa 900_1
Myths : Drakon 1087 Ogygos 824_6 Oidipous 1152
—— coins of 110_7 $\dot{o}\mu o\lambda\omega\acute{\iota}\delta\epsilon s$ $\pi\acute{\upsilon}\lambda a\iota$ at 900_1 901_0 904_4 $\ddot{\Upsilon}\psi\iota\sigma\tau a\iota$ $\pi\acute{\upsilon}\lambda a\iota$ at $878_{0(2)}$
Thebes in Egypt
Cults : Amen 774_0 Zeus $\Theta\eta\beta a\iota\epsilon\acute{\upsilon}s$ 960_0
Rite : $\pi a\lambda\lambda a\kappa\acute{\iota}\delta\epsilon s$ of Zeus $\Theta\eta\beta a\iota\epsilon\acute{\upsilon}s$ 960_0
—— relief from 863_1
Theios Angelos
Cult : Stratonikeia $880_{0(0)}$
See also Agathos Angelos
Thelpousa
Cult : Asklepios 1090
Themele (= Semele) 279_3
Themis
Cult : Delphoi 176_1 500 1216
Epithets : $\dot{a}\rho\chi\acute{\epsilon}\gamma o\nu o s$ 954_0 $Bo\upsilon\lambda a\acute{\iota}a$ 258_3 $\epsilon\ddot{\upsilon}\beta o\upsilon\lambda o s$ 37_1 258_3 $\epsilon\ddot{\upsilon}\kappa\tau a\acute{\iota}a$ 723_0 $\epsilon\dot{\upsilon}\pi\lambda\acute{o}\kappa a\mu o s$ $\theta\epsilon\acute{a}$ 1216 $\dot{\iota}\kappa\epsilon\sigma\acute{\iota}a$ 873_2 $\kappa a\lambda\acute{\eta}$ (?) 931_0 $\dot{o}\rho\theta\acute{o}\beta o\upsilon\lambda o s$ 258_3 $\dot{o}\rho\kappa\acute{\iota}a$ 723_0 $o\dot{\upsilon}\rho a\nu\acute{\iota}a$ 37_1 $\pi\iota\nu\upsilon\tau\acute{\eta}$ 258_3 $\pi\rho o\phi\hat{\eta}\tau\iota s$ $\kappa a\rho\tau\epsilon\rho\acute{o}\beta o\upsilon\lambda o s$ 954_0
Rite : leap 931_0
Myths : Boucheta 267_5 348_5 consorts with Zeus 37_1 Delphoi 239_0 Deukalion 267_5 348_5 971_0 gives oracle to Kronos 928_0 impregnated by pillar of light (= Apollon) 1217
Genealogy : m. of Horai by Zeus 37_1 94_2
Function : supports orator 893_3
Etymology : 268_1
Types : riding on ox 348_5 seated on tripod 206_1 1217
Identified with Ge 176_1
Associated with Moirai 929_0 Zeus 258 723_0 Zeus and Apollon 730_0 Zeus and Dike 897_3 Zeus and Dionysos 261 f.
Compared with Europe 267_5
In relation to Zeus 873_2
—— a possible doublet of Thetis 268
Themisonion
Cults : Dioskouroi (?) 313 Lyk(abas ?) $\Sigma\acute{\omega}\zeta\omega\nu$ 312_5 313_8
—— coins of 312_5 313
Theodaisia $948_{0(4)}$ 1021
Theodoric the Great 1071
Theodoros, sculptor of *tabula Iliaca* 45_1
Theodotos, St 1186_4
Theognetos, the Thessalian 1024
Theoi Agnostoi See Agnostoi Theoi

Theseus (*cont.*)
  Myths: clears road to Delphoi 628
    Damastes 626 f. Phaidra and Hip-
    polytos 1043 Phytalidai 291₂ 1091
    1103 Prokoptes 626 f. Prokroustes
    626 f. Sinis 627₆ 1091 Skiron 627₆
  Genealogy: f. of Hippolytos 1087 gs.
    of Pittheus 1091
  Attributes: double axe 626 ff. 847
    sword 627₆
  Type: attacking Centaur 628
  Associated with Kodros and Phyleus
    1137₂ Peirithoos and Herakles 211₂
Thespia, d. of Asopos 1151₃
Thespiai
  Cults: Agathos Daimon (Demon)
    1125₁ 1161 St Charalambos 1150₉
    Daimones 1150₉ Dionysos Σαώτης (?)
    599₂ Hera Κιθαιρωνία 899₀ Hermes
    1150₉ Miliche 1151 Mousa (Mosa)
    238₀ Zeus Κτήσιος 1061 1066 Zeus
    Μίλιχος 1151 Zeus Σαώτης 599₂
    1151
  Myth: snake slain by Menestratos 1151
  —— apsidal temple of 900₀
Thespios, eponym of Thespiai
  Genealogy: s. of Erechtheus 1151 s.
    of Teuthras s. of Pandion 1151
Thesprotia, caldron of 133₀
Thessalonike
  Cults: Hercules *Augustus* 1194₄ Prino-
    phoros 411₆
  —— coins of 411₆
Thessaly
  Cults: pillar 166₂ (?) Zeus Κάριος 873₂
    Zeus Λαφύστιος 899₁ Zeus Ὁμολώιος
    900₁ Zeus Ὕπατος (?) 876₀(7) Zeus
    Φύξιος 902₀
  Rites: burial within the house 1061
    φοιβονομεῖσθαι 500₁₂
  Myth: Salmoneus 825 833 1088
  —— kings of, personate Zeus 1087 ff.
Thetis
  Myths: Mnemon 670 supplicates Zeus
    45₁ 753₃
  Etymology: 268₂
  Type: with head-dress of crab's-claws
    665₃
  Compared with Metis 12
Thibursicum Bure
  Cult: Iuno *Caelestis* 68₂
Thmouis
  Cult: he-goat 987₀
Thoas 421₃
Tholathes (?) 558₀
Thor
  Cults: Gothia 620 Lapps (?) 423₃ 533₂
  Rite: erection of beam pierced by iron
    nail (?) 533₂
  Myths: brings to life his goats when
    cooked in caldron 63₁ 213₀ leads
    Thorolfr Mostrarskegg to Iceland
    533₂
  Genealogy: f. of Magni 64₀ s. of
    Hlóðyn 66₀

Thor (*cont.*)
  Functions: fertility 63₁ thunder 547₀
  Etymology: 32
  Attributes: club 64₀ hammer 547₀
    mallet 620 sword 305₀ thistle 775₀
  Type: bearded 64₀
  Identified with Iupiter 620
  —— carved on high-seat pillar 533₂
    temple of 533₂
Thorikos
  Rite: burial within the house 1060
Thornax, Mt, in Lakonike
  Cult: Apollon Θορνάκιος or Πυθαεύς
    893₂
Thornax, w. of Iapetos 894₀
Thoth
  Epithet: Astennu 700₀
  Myth: gives wings etc. to the gods
    553
  Identified with Hermes Τρισμέγιστος
    611
  See also Tat
Thoukydides, portrait-herm of (with
  Herodotos) 389 f.
Thourioi 118₂ 119
Thouros
  Identified with the planet Ares and
    Baal or Bel 694₀
Thrace
  Cults: Apollon 458 Artemis 411
    Artemis Βασίλεια 500 f. Axieros
    314 f. Axiokersa 314 f. Axiokersos
    314 f. Bendis 303₂ 314₀ 411 501
    Boreas 380 Bousbatos 501₃ Dionysos
    269 ff. Dionysos Βάλιν 270 (Diony-
    sos) Ἰαμβαδούλης 820₃ 821 851
    Dionysos Σαβάζιος 314₀ Dios 277 ff.
    288 313 824 842 Dios Νῦσος 313
    Erikepaios (Erikapaios) (?) 1025
    Kabeiroi 313 ff. Κύριος Θεὸς Προγον-
    ικὸς Ζβελσοῦρδος 1225 Κύριος Zeus
    Ζβελσοῦρδος 1225 rider-god 821 823
    Zeus Διόνυσος 282 (Zeus) Ζάλμο-
    ξις (?) 230 822 Zeus Ζβελσοῦρδος
    817 ff. 833 851 Zeus Ζβελσοῦρδος ὁ
    Κύριος 1225 (Zeus) Ζιβελεῖζις (?) 822
    (Zeus) *Ζιβελεσσοῦρδος (?) 822
  Rite: human omophagy 1022
  Myths: Kosingas 130 Salmoxis 226
    Tereus 692 f.
  —— as link between Germany and
    Greece 114 coins of 1133₁ (?) kings
    of 271₀
  See also Thracians, Thraco-Phrygians
Thracians tattooed 121 123₀
Thraco-Phrygians
  Cults: Dionysos 268 ff. 663 673 Dios
    277 ff. 663 842 Dios Νῦσος 842
    Erikepaios (Erikapaios) (?) 1025
    Father and Son 313 Phanes (?)
    1025 Semele 673 842 Zeus 1111
  Myth: death and burial of Dionysos
    at Delphoi 218 ff.
  —— prepared to accept Christianity
    288

Vesta (*cont.*)
Associated with Mars and Volcanus
99$_3$ Volcanus 99
—— on column of Mayence 96 99 100
Vestalia 20$_0$
Vettersfelde, celt ·from 509 f.
Vettii, frescoes from house of 1047 f.
Vetulonia, 'Tomb of the Lictor' at 1221
'Tomb of the Trident' at 1225
Via Egnatia 495
Viarus, Mt
Cult: Zeus (?) 973$_0$
—— on coins of Prostanna 972$_2$ f.
Vichy
Cult: Iupiter *Sabasius* (=*Sabazius*)
285$_0$
—— silver *bratteae* from 285$_0$
Victoria
Cults: Divitia 64$_0$ Rome 1195$_2$ Urbs
Salvia 803
Attributes: palm-branch 99 811$_5$ wreath
811$_5$
Types: on globe 1196$_0$ writing on
shield 57$_6$ (fig. 22, 3 *b*)
Associated with Iupiter 1195$_2$
—— on column of Mayence 96 98 on
Iupiter-columns 57$_6$ 59$_0$ 71
Vidharr 305$_0$
Virae
Epithet: Querquetulanae 402$_0$
Virbius
Cults: Neapolis in Campania 421 Nemi
392 ff.
Priest: flamen Virbialis 421$_1$
Myth: Diana 393
Functions: consort of Diana 392 ff.
842 growth 421 f. mythical proto-
type of *rex Nemorensis* 399
Etymology: 397$_0$ 398$_0$ 399 399$_5$ 421 f.
Type: Janiform (with Hippolytos)
392 ff. 420 f. 842
In relation to Diana 414 417 842
Irbos (?) 421
Virbius, Clivus, at Rome 400 f. 421
Virbius, river in Lakonike (?) 394$_2$ 421
Vires
Function: testicles personified 306$_4$
Associated with Deus Magnus Pantheus
306$_4$ Fons and (Aqua) Ventina 306$_4$
Lymphae 306$_4$ Neptunus 306$_4$ Nym-
phae 306$_4$
Virgin, the
Cults: Athens 1119$_0$ 1119$_4$ Chartres
1213 Mt Gerizim 888$_{0(0)}$ Mt Juktas
945$_0$ Zaragoza 1213
Epithets: ἀειπάρθενος 888$_{0(0)}$ *del Pilar*
1213 *du Pilier* 1213 ἡ ὑπεραγία
Θεοτόκος 1119$_4$ Θεοτόκος 888$_{0(0)}$
1150$_{10}$ Παναγία 891$_0$ 945$_0$ Παναγία
εἰς τὴν Πέτραν 1119$_0$
Festival: Aug. 15 891$_0$
Supersedes Charites 1150$_{10}$
Virgins, the Seven, of Ankyra 1186$_4$
Virgo
Epithets: spicifera, iusti inventrix,

Virgo (*cont.*)
urbium conditrix, ...lance vitam et
iura pensitans 734$_3$
Identified with Mater divum, Pax,
Virtus, Ceres, dea Syria 734$_3$
Virtus
Type: with banner 99
Identified with Virgo 734$_3$
—— on column of Mayence 96 100
Virvinus, spring in Lakonike (?) 394$_2$
Vishnu
Cults: India 367 774$_1$
Myths: Brahmā 774$_1$ in bubble as
Brahma 1036 Paraśu-rāma 660$_1$
Rāma-ćandra 660$_1$
Genealogy: h. of Lakshmī 774$_1$ h. of
Sarasvatī 774$_1$
Function: solar (?) 774$_1$
Attribute: lotos 367 774$_1$
Types: four-handed 774$_1$ seated be-
neath starry arch 367
—— sixth incarnation of 660$_1$ seventh
incarnation of 660$_1$
Vitellia, goddess 404$_0$
Vitellia, town in Latium 404$_0$
Vitellii 404$_0$
Volaterrae
Cults: Hermes (?) 383 Ianus (?) 383
—— coins of 382 f.
Volcanus
Cults: Agedincum 99$_3$ Gallia Lugudun-
ensis 547$_0$ 619 Lugdunum 99$_3$
Genealogy: f. of Palicus by Aetna 909$_0$
Function: elemental fire 100
Etymology: 947$_0$
Identified with Donar 63$_1$ Velchanos (?)
947$_0$
Associated with Esus and Iovis 619
Mars and Vesta 99$_3$ Vesta 99
—— on column of Mayence 96 100
on Jupiter-columns 57$_6$ 59$_0$ smithy
of 784
Volsung 682
Vulci, tomb-painting at 641
Vulturnus 368$_3$

Weaving Damsel 66$_0$
Wind-gods   See Venti
Winds   See Anemoi
Wodan
Rite: sacrifice at beginning of summer
62$_1$
Myth: contest with Fenris-wolf 62$_1$
Functions: leader of Wild Hunt or
Furious Host 62$_1$ sky-god 62$_1$
Attributes: chariot or coach 62$_1$ gold
helmet 62$_1$ gold ring 62$_1$ 990 throne
62$_1$
Type: one-eyed 62$_1$
Identified with Mercurius 59 63$_0$ 69 94$_1$
386$_6$
In relation to Ziu 62$_1$
Woodchester, statuette from 98$_3$ 1214

Xenioi Theoi 1177$_2$

Zethos (*cont.*)

Myths : Dirke 1013 1015 1019 Lykos 1019$_2$

Genealogy : b. of Amphion 317 s. of Zeus by Antiope 1013 s. of Zeus or Epopeus 445

Functions : herdsman 1013 one of the Theban Dioskouroi 1014

Etymology : 445$_2$

Type : on column 428

In relation to Zetes 445

Zeus

Cults : Abédat in Phoinike 886$_{0(30)}$ 983$_4$ Achaeans ·458 Adrianoi in Mysia 127 Aeolians 901$_0$ Agra 1142$_3$ (?) Agrigentum 911$_0$ ff. 1227 Aigai in Aiolis 259$_0$ Aigai in Makedonia 878$_{0(9)}$ 906$_2$ Aigina 894$_3$ 895$_0$ 895$_1$ Aigion 742 f. 749 826$_6$ Ainianes 869$_0$ Mt Ainos 907$_2$ Mt Aitne 908$_1$ 909$_0$ 910$_0$ Aitne (formerly Katane) 908$_1$ 909$_9$ Aixone 730$_0$ Aizanoi 882$_{0(23)}$ (?) 965$_0$ ff. Akarnania 743$_7$ 1226 Akmoneia 312$_5$ Akrai in Sicily 915$_1$ Akraiphia 97$_0$ 1074 Alaisa (Halaesa) 1158$_6$ Alban Mt 808$_{0(16)}$ Alexandreia 1158 1187$_0$ Alopeke 1115 Altyntash in Phrygia 883$_{0(0)}$ Mt Alysis (?) 945$_1$ Amaseia 975$_0$ f. Amastris 707 848 918$_0$ 1067 Amathous 598 f. 869$_0$ Ambrakia 1222 Amorgos 258$_3$ Anaphe 1066 Anazarbos 980$_1$ Mt Anchesmos 897$_4$ Anchialos in Thrace 878$_{0(10)}$ 949$_2$ Andros 1156 Ankyra in Galatia 754$_1$ 835$_5$ 971$_1$ Antandros 815 Antigoneia on the Orontes 1188 Antiocheia in Chrysaoris (= Alabanda) 714$_2$ Antiocheia on the Maiandros 259$_0$ Antiocheia on the Orontes 428 1178 1186 ff. 1188$_{14}$ 1196 f. Apameia on the Orontes 1192 Mt Apesas 892$_4$ Aphrodisias in Karia 585$_3$ 1220 Arabia (?) 1224 Mt Arachnaion 894$_1$ Mt Arbios 945$_2$ 946$_0$ Ardettos 1135 Mt Argaios 980$_0$ Mt Argarizon (See Mt Gerizim) Argos 164$_5$ 164$_6$ 179 808$_{0(14)}$ 874$_2$ 878$_{0(4)}$ 892$_5$ 893$_0$ 893$_1$ 1099$_6$ 1143 f. 1143$_5$ 1144$_2$ 1230 Arkadia 760 f. 793 849 Arkesine 1156 1156$_{13}$ 1157$_0$ Arslan Apa in Phrygia (?) 883$_{0(0)}$ Assos 728$_0$ 857$_6$ Mt Atabyrion in Rhodes 922$_5$ 923$_0$ 924$_0$ 925$_0$ Mt Atabyrion in Sicily 910$_1$ Athens 20 f. 97$_0$ 98$_0$ 111$_0$ 231$_8$ 259$_0$ 729$_0$ 730$_0$ 793 815 875$_{1(2)}$ 876$_{1(1)}$ 897$_2$ 897$_3$ 903$_0$ 976$_0$ 985$_0$ 1061(?) 1065 1078 1091 f. 1100$_1$ 1103 f. 1114 ff. 1121 ff. 1135$_4$ 1147 1149 1151 1161 ff. 1169 1229 Mt Athos 906$_1$ Attaleia in Pamphylia 111$_0$ Attike 291$_2$ 1069 (?) Attouda 743$_7$ Axos 816$_4$ Babylon 128$_4$ 675 714$_1$ Bejad in Phrygia 292$_4$ Beuyuk Evlia near Amaseia 974$_1$ ff. Bithy

Zeus (*cont.*)

nia 271$_0$ 292$_4$ 815 835$_5$ 1180$_4$ Blaudos in Mysia 284$_0$ Boiotia 238$_0$ 731$_0$ 873$_2$ 875$_{1(1)}$ 900$_1$ Bosporos 707 Bosporos Kimmerios 729$_0$ Bōttia on the Orontes 1187$_4$ Bouthroton (Bouthrotos) 348 Bruttii 709 Bunarbashi in Phrygia 835$_4$ Byblos 887$_{0(0)}$ 983$_6$ Celts (See Keltoi) Chaironeia (sceptre of Zeus) 547$_2$ Chalkis 1098$_7$ Chalkis in Euboia 1157 Chalkis sub Libano 981$_0$ Chersonesos Taurike 729$_0$ Chios 922$_4$ 1157$_1$ Corinth 869$_1$ 878$_{0(3)}$ 892$_3$ 916$_0$ Crete 230 344 f. 352 354 599 697$_0$ 727 743$_7$ 925 ff. 1169$_5$ 1187$_4$ (?) Damaskos 807$_{5(2)}$ 886$_{0(0)}$ Daphne, near Antiocheia on the Orontes 1191 Delos 259$_0$ 907$_0$ (?) 919$_0$ 920$_0$ 921$_0$ 922$_0$ 985$_0$ 1095$_0$ 1096$_0$ 1105 1217 Delphoi 179 f. 231 ff. 244 816 841 901$_2$ 902$_0$ Demotionidai 728$_0$ Denderah 97$_0$ Didyma near Miletos 317 317$_2$ 318$_0$ Mt Dikte 927$_1$ 928$_0$ 929$_0$ Diokaisareia in Kilikia (?) 810 Dion in Makedonia 1111 Dionysopolis in Phrygia 285 Divlit near Koloë 975$_0$ Dodona 214 350 350$_6$ 353 693$_3$ 763$_1$ 826 855$_2$ 960$_0$ Doliche 745$_1$ Dorylaeion 280 f. 280$_1$ 292$_4$ 835$_4$ 836 Dreros 948$_1$ Mt Drios 918$_1$ Ebimi near Amaseia 976$_0$ Egypt 1023 Elaia in Aiolis 955$_0$ Mt Elakataion in Thessaly 397$_0$ Elasson in Thessaly 808$_{0(13)}$ Elis 728$_0$ 783 Emathia, hill at Antiocheia on the Orontes 1187 f. Ephesos 728$_0$ 743$_7$ 962$_2$ Epidauros 894$_2$ 1061 1066 1076 f. 1144$_3$ (?) 1157$_0$ 1177 f. Eresos 729$_0$ Eretria 901$_0$ Erythrai in Ionia 730$_0$ 1157$_0$ Essir-keui in Bithynia 835$_5$ Eumeneia in Phrygia 970$_0$ Euromos 572$_7$ 573$_4$ 574 f. 589$_0$ (?) 1220 Galaria or Galarina 1131$_1$ Galatia 835$_5$ Mt Gargaron (Gargara) 950$_0$ ff. Gaza 675 1187$_0$ Genetaean headland 616 f. 1097$_0$ Cape Geraistos (?) 903 Mt Gerizim 887$_{0(30)}$ 888$_{0(0)}$ 983$_9$ Ghel-Ghiraz near Amaseia 976$_0$ Golgoi (?) 948$_{0(5)}$ Gomphoi 871$_{3(2)}$ 1099$_0$ Gortyna 723$_0$ 731$_0$ 947$_{0(2)}$ (?) Graeco-Libyans 1111 Gümbet in Phrygia 835$_4$ Günjarik in Phrygia 835$_4$ Gythion 31 259$_0$ Hagia Triada 947$_{0(1)}$ Halikarnassos 585$_3$ 872$_{0(5)}$ 963$_3$ 1228 Halos 904$_1$ 1226 Heleia 930$_0$ 931$_0$ 932$_0$ Mt Helikon 898$_5$ Hephaistia in Lemnos 878$_{0(7)}$ (?) Herakleia ad Latmum 585$_3$ Herakleia Pontike 976$_0$ Hermione 100$_6$ 1061 1077 Hierapolis in Phrygia 570 571$_6$ Hierapytna 342$_0$ 723$_0$ 929$_0$ cp. 930$_0$ 1157$_4$ Mt Homole (Homolos) (?) 904$_4$ Homo-

Zeus (*cont.*)

973$_0$ Prousa ad Olympum 292$_4$ 964$_2$
Prymnessos 835$_4$ Rhodes 615 922$_5$
923$_0$ 924$_0$ 925$_0$ 946$_0$ Rhodes the
town 924$_0$ 925$_0$ Rome 724$_0$ 808$_{0(17)}$
835$_6$ 876$_{0(6)}$ Salamis 110$_9$ Sardeis
1227 f. Seleukeia Pieria 807$_{5(3)}$ 809
869$_1$ 981$_1$ f. 983$_3$ 1192 1225 Selge
492$_{0(0)}$ Selinous 489$_{0(0)}$ Selymbria
878$_{0(10)}$ (?) Serdike 744$_0$ Serea in
Phrygia 883$_{0(0)}$ Sicily 808$_{0(18)}$ 812 ff.
Sikyon 97$_0$ 1144 ff. Sillyon 572$_{11}$ (?)
Mt Silpion 1186 f. 1188$_{14}$ (?) Sinope
1171$_3$ Siphnos 897$_3$ 1180$_4$ Mt Sipylos 876$_{0(8)}$ 956$_2$ (?) Skepsis 951$_0$
Skiathos 878$_{0(6)}$ 922$_2$ Skythia 292$_4$
925$_0$ Smyrna 280$_1$ 319 729$_0$ 873$_{0(8)}$
962$_1$ Mt Solymos 973$_1$ f. Sparta 98$_0$
110$_9$ 259$_0$ 261$_0$ 321$_1$ 436 728$_0$ 729$_0$
739$_1$ 875$_{1(4)}$ 890$_2$ 890$_3$ 948$_1$ 1061
1069 1096$_1$ 1101$_3$ Stelai in Crete
731$_0$ Stratonikeia 585$_3$ (cp. 586$_3$)
714 ff. 714$_3$ 963$_9$ Suwasa in Kappadokia 594 f. Sybrita 731$_0$ Syracuse
708 763$_1$ 915$_2$ 916$_0$ 917$_0$ 918$_0$ Syria
745$_1$ 807$_{3(2)}$ (?) 886$_{0(0)}$ Syros 1066
Tabai 743$_7$ Cape Tainaros (?) 890$_5$
Tallaia range (?) 948$_1$ Tarantos in
Bithynia 32$_3$ Tarentum 29 ff. 45 131
161 559 762 ff. 763$_1$ 1064 Tavium
754$_1$ Tegea 807 815 850 873$_2$ 892$_1$
1147 ff. Temnos 873$_{0(9)}$ 956$_1$ Tenedos (?) 662 Teos 1066 Termessos
(Termessus Maior) 321$_1$ 973 f. the
tetrapolis of Marathon (See Marathon) Thalamai 17 f. 31 Thasos
808$_{0(10)}$ Thebes in Boiotia 878$_{0(2)}$
898$_3$ 900$_1$ Thebes in Egypt 960$_0$
Thera 17 817 1066 1095$_0$ 1156 Ther-
mos in Aitolia 729$_0$ Thespiai 599$_2$
1061 1066 1151 Thessaly 873$_2$
876$_{0(7)}$ (?) 899$_1$ 900$_1$ 902$_0$ Thrace
230 (?) 282 817 ff. 833 851 1225
Thraco-Phrygians 1111 Thyateira
808$_{0(0)}$ 1184 f. Mt Tmolos 957$_2$
Tralleis 958$_0$ ff. Trapezous in Arkadia 871$_{3(3)}$ 892$_2$ Troy 8 950$_0$
Tyana 569 722$_5$ Tyndaris 917$_1$ 918$_0$
Tyre 424$_0$ Venasa 616 Mt Viarus (?)
973$_0$

Epithets: Ἀβοζηνός 570 Ἀγαμέμνων
1061 1069 f. 1112 Ἀγαμήδης (?) 233$_0$
1075 ʺΑγιος 1092$_8$ ἀγκυλομήτης 549$_7$
ἀγνός 1122$_9$ Ἀγοραῖος 51$_1$ 260$_0$ 929$_0$
1177$_2$ Ἀγυιεύς 165 Ἀγχέσμιος 897$_4$
Ἀέριος 808$_{0(0)}$ Ἀθῷος 906$_1$ αἰγίοχος
830$_7$ Αἰθέριος 727$_{3(3)}$ Αἰνήσιος 907$_2$
Αἰτναῖος 908$_1$ 909$_0$ ἀκαμάτου πυρὸς
ὁρμή 1027 ἀκοντιστὴρ κεραυνοῦ 705$_3$
Ἀκραῖος 319 730$_5$ 869 871$_3$ 872$_0$ 873$_0$
892$_2$ 904$_2$ 904$_5$ 915$_1$ 922$_3$ 956$_1$ 962$_1$
963$_1$ 963$_3$ 963$_4$ ἀκρολοφίτας (See also
Λοφείτης, Ἐπιλόφιος) 343$_0$ Ἀκταῖος
869 904$_2$ ἀλάστορος 1098 ἀλάστωρ
1098 1101 Ἀλδήμιος or ʺΑλδος 675

Zeus (*cont.*)

1187$_0$ ἀληθὴς Ζεὺς ὁ κεράστης (= Pan)
1023 ʺΑλσειος (?) 945$_1$ Ἀλύσιος (?)
945$_1$ Ἀμβούλιος 261$_0$ ἄμβροτος (ἄφθιτος) νύμφη 1027 f. ʺΑμμων 388 986$_0$
1136$_4$ Ἀμφιάραος 232 794 1061
1070 ff. 1076 1112 ἀμφιθαλής 1072
ἀναδωδωναῖος (sic) 855$_2$ Ἀναδώτης
321$_1$ 1157$_0$ ἄναξ 855$_2$ 950$_0$ 956$_2$ 960$_0$
ἄναξ ἀνάκτων 337$_4$ Ἀπεσάντιος 892$_4$
Ἀπέσας 892$_4$ Ἀπήμιος 897$_6$ 898$_0$
Ἀπόμυιος 781 ff. 850 Ἀποτρόπαιος
1157$_0$ ἀποτρόπαιος 1099$_1$ ʺΑρβιος 945$_2$
946$_0$ Ἀργαῖος (?) 980$_0$ ἀργής 980$_0$
ἀργικέραυνος 806$_8$ 858 1027 f. ʺΑρειος
705 ff. 848 ἀριστοτέχνης 693$_3$ ʺΑρνειος
918$_1$ ʺΑρσηλις (?) 559$_6$ ἄρσην 1027 f.
ἀρχή 1033$_1$ ἀρχὸς ἁπάντων ἀργικέραυνος 1027 Ἀσβαμαῖος 569 Ἀσείς
321$_0$ ἀσελγής 348$_2$ Ἀσκλαπιός 1077
Ἀσκληπιός 794 1061 1076 ff. 1112
Ἀσκληπιὸς Σωτήρ 1076 f. Ἀσκραῖος
872$_{0(5)}$ Ἀστέριος 230 ἀστεροπητής
723$_0$ 727$_{3(1)}$ 806$_8$ 954$_0$ 1177$_2$ Ἀστραπαῖος 815 850 Ἀστράπιος 1122
ἀστράπιος 806$_8$ 815$_4$ 1100$_1$ Ἀστράπτων 817$_2$ 817$_3$ 850 ἀστράπτων 817$_3$
Ἀταβύριος in Rhodes 922$_5$ 923$_0$
924$_0$ 925$_0$ Ataburius 588$_1$ αὐξητής
1100$_1$ αὐτὸς ἁπάντων ἀρχιγένεθλος
1028 Ἀφέσιος 179 266 f. (?) 841 892$_4$
895$_1$ 896$_0$ 897$_0$ 1144$_2$ ἀφίκτωρ 1096$_2$
1098 1101 Βαγαῖος 294$_0$ (?) 295$_2$ 569
Βάκχος 287 954$_0$ 1184 Βάλλος 271$_0$
βαρύγδουπος 204$_1$ Βασιλεύς 727$_{3(1)}$
730$_0$ 731$_0$ 869$_1$ 899$_2$ 900$_0$ 1073 f.
1076 1135 1135$_4$ (?) βασιλεύς 954$_0$
1027 f. 1095$_0$ βασιλεὺς μέγιστος 1122$_9$
βασιλικὸς 879$_{0(17)}$ Βελχάνος (?) = Ϝελ-
χάνος 948$_{0(4)}$ Βεννεύς 883$_{0(0)}$ 969$_3$
Βέννιος 883$_{0(0)}$ 969$_3$ Βῆλος 128$_4$ 210$_2$
675 Βιδάτας 723$_0$ 934$_0$ Βοζιος (?)
570 Βόλλαιος 259$_0$ Βόρειος 380 Βοτ-
ταῖος 1187 f. Βουλαῖος 259$_0$ 260$_0$
317$_2$ 824$_4$ 824$_8$ 873$_{0(10)}$ 897$_3$ 1076
1177$_2$ Βουλεύς 258$_3$ 1105 Βρονταῖος
833 ff. 852 882$_{0(0)}$ 1100$_1$ 1177$_2$ Βρον-
τήσιος (= Iupiter Tonans) 111$_0$ 835$_6$
βροντοποιός 807$_2$ Βροντῶν 280$_1$ 805$_6$
835 f. 838 f. 852 883$_{0(0)}$ Βροντῶν
(= Iupiter Tonans) 835$_6$ Βροντῶν καὶ
Ἀστράπτων 817 Βροντῶν καὶ Πατὴρ
Θεός 836$_2$ Βροντῶν Νεικήτωρ Πατὴρ
836$_3$ Βωζιος (Βοζιος) 570 Βώττιος
1187$_4$ 1188 Γαιβόλος (?) 18$_3$ Casius
588$_1$ γενέτης (sc. Διονύσου) 616$_4$
γενέτωρ 1177$_2$ Γενηταῖος 616 Γιγαν-
τοφόνος 449$_0$ Γογγυλάτης 260$_0$ 824$_4$
824$_7$ Γοναῖος (?) 961$_0$ Δάης (?) 312$_5$
δαίμων 856 Δακινός 616 Δακίης (?)
616$_1$ Δάκιος (?) 616$_1$ Δάος 312$_5$ Δει-
πάτυρος (See Deipatyros) Διδυμαῖος
317 Διδύμων γενάρχης 317$_2$ Δικαιόσυνος 1092$_8$ Δικαιόσυνος Μέγας 1092$_8$
δικηφόρος 806$_1$ Δικταῖος 342$_0$ 723$_0$

Zeus (cont.)

γενής 238₀ 587 675 731₀ Κρονίδης 204₁ 321₁ 954₀ 1095₀ Κρόνιος (See Μέγιστε Κοῦρε...Κρόνιε) Κρονίων 734₃ 831₀ 950₀ 956₂ 1028 1099₂ 1219 Κρόνου παῖς 908₁ Κρόνου υἱός 957₂ Κτεβάτης (=Καταιβάτης) 16₁ Κτήσιος 3₀ 321 384₀ 1054 ff. 1112 1140 κύδιμε δαῖμον 957₂ κύδιστ' ἀθανάτων 855 κύδιστος 728₀ 950₀ Κύνθιος 919₀ 920₀ 921₀ 922₀ Κύριος Ζβελσοῦρδος 1225 Κύριος Θεὸς Προγονικὸς Ζβελσοῦρδος 1225 Κώμυρος 1228 Λαβραδεύς 559 f. 572 Λαβράνιος 598 f. Λαβραϋνδεύς 1228 Λαβραϋνδιος 962₀ Λαβράϋνδος (Λαμβράϋνδος, Λαβραύυνδος, Λαβραάϋνδος (?), Λαβραίυνδος, Λαβράϋνδος (?), Λαβράενδος, Λάβρενδος, Λάβρανδος (?), Λαβρανδεύς, Λαβραδεύς, Λαβρανδηνός) 576 f. 585 ff. 585₃ 597 ff. 598₁ 614 663 846 848 884₀₍₀₎ 963₇ 1220 1228 Λαβρένδιος 962₀ Labrios (?) 599₅ Labryandius 588₁ Λακεδαίμων 436 Laodicensis (?) 320₀ Laodicenus (?) 320₀ Λαοδικεύς (?) 320₀ Λαοδικηνός (?) 320₀ Λαπέρσιος 599 Laprius 588₁ 599 Λαράσιος 958₀ ff. 962₀ Λαράσιος Σεβαστὸς Εὐμενής (=Hadrian) 959₀ f. Λαρισαῖος 892₅ 958₀ 1144₂ Λαρίσιος 957₃ f. Λαρισσεύς 893₀ 1144₂ Λατιάριος 941₀ Λάφριος (?) 599 Λαφύστιος in Boiotia 899₁ Λαφύστιος in Thessaly 904₁ 1226 Λέψυνος 962₀ Λίθος (=Iupiter Lapis) 546₀ λιμενοσκόπος 343₀ Λιταῖος 1099 1100₀ Λοφείτης 873 f. 949₃ Λύκαιος 187 761 849 891₃ 927₁ 1013 1092 1105 1167 Λυκώρειος 901₂ 902₀ Μαζεύς (?) 294₀ 570₀ μάκαρ 954₀ 955₀ μακάρων μακάρτατε 337₄ Μαλειαῖος 488₀₍₀₎ 890₄ Μάνης 312 312₅ μαντικός 1097₂ μεγαβρόντης 727₃₍₁₎ Μέγας 344 f. 350₁ μέγας 295₂ 298₂ 321₁ 342₀ 569₇ 727₃₍₃₎ 925₁ 940₀ 1099₂ 1122₉ 1130₁ 1160 1160₄ μέγας ἀρχὸς ἀπάντων 1028 μέγας βοῦς 345₄ Μέγας Βροντῶν 835₆ 836 μεγασθενής 693₃ Μέγισστος 585₃ Μέγιστε Κοῦρε... Κρόνιε 931₀ Μέγιστος 807₂ 885₀₍₂₉₎ 956₀ 983₂ 985₁ (?) 1157₅ (?) (See also Μέγιστε Κοῦρε...Κρόνιε) μέγιστος 728₀ 950₀ Μέγιστος Κεραύνιος 807₅₍₁₎ Μέγιστος Σωτήρ 956₀ Μέγιστος "Υψιστος 886₀₍₀₎ 983₂ Μειλίχιος 291₂ 321 (?) 715 1037 1061 1091 ff. 1154 1155 1156 ff. 1159 f. 1161 1173 ff. 1177₂ Μείλιχος 1149 1160 μείλιχος 1092₈ Μελησός 280₁ Μελισσαῖος 928₀ 1112₆ Μελίχιος (=Μειλίχιος) 1147 1149 μέσσα 1027 f. 1033₁ Μηδεύς (Μηδινεύς) 312₅ Μήλιος 918₁ Μηλίχιος (=Μειλίχιος) 1156 1157₄ Μηλώσιος 918₁ μητίετα 1025 1147 μητιέτης 259₀ μητιόεις 716 721₃ 1017 1147 Μητίων (?) 1146 Μηχανεύς 1144₂

Zeus (cont.)

Μιλίχιος (=Μειλίχιος) 1105 1108 1115 1142 1144₃ (?) 1157₁ Μίλιχος (=Μείλιχος) 1151 Μοιραγέτας 231₈ Μοιραγέτης 187₁ 231 1137₀ Molio 588₁ Μοννίτιος 723₀ Μόριος 204 502₂ Μυλεύς 260₀ 824₄ 824₉ Νάιος 350₆ 763₁ 826 869₀ 1117 (?) Νάκρασος (?) 714₃ Νεαυλείτης 285₀ 1217 f. Νεικήτωρ 836₃ Νέμειος 259₀ 1143₅ 1186 1187₀ νεφεληγερέτα 723₀ 727₃₍₁₎ 950₀ 1177₂ Νικηφόρος (Νεικηφόρος) Κεραύνιος 1225 νόμου μέτα πάντα κυβερνῶν 855 Νόσιος 317₂ Νωδαῖος (?) 932₁ ξείνιος 1097₂ ξείνιος, ὃς ξείνοισιν ἅμ' αἰδοίοισιν ὀπηδεῖ 1097₀ 1101 Ξένιος 260₀ 617 723₀ 727₃₍₁₎ 887₀₍₃₁₎ 983₉ 1097₂ 1101 1102₀ 1102₇ 1142 1176₅ 1176₄ 1177₂ 1229 Ξένιος καὶ Φίλιος 1177₂ οἰκοφύλαξ ὁσίων ἀνδρῶν 1125₀ ὄλβιος 337₄ 955₀ ὀλοποιός 1030 Ὀλύβριος or Ὀλύβρις 980₁ Ὀλύμπιος 343₀ 695₀ 723₀ 727₃₍₂₎ 941₀ 1074 1157₀ Ὀλύμπιος at Akragas 911₀ Ὀλύμπιος at Athens 1078 1118 1121₀ 1123 Ὀλύμπιος in Bithynia 815₅ Ὀλύμπιος in Chios 1157₁ Ὀλύμπιος at Corinth 916₀ Ὀλύμπιος at Daphne, near Antiocheia on the Orontes 1191 Ὀλύμπιος at Elis 728₀ Ὀλύμπιος at Ephesos 962₂ Ὀλύμπιος in Lykia 972₁ Ὀλύμπιος in Mysia 953₂ Ὀλύμπιος at Olympia 18 758₀ 761 1188 Ὀλύμπιος at Pergamon 956₀ Ὀλύμπιος at Prousa ad Olympum 964₂ Ὀλύμπιος at Seleukeia Pieria 869₁ Ὀλύμπιος at Syracuse 915₂ 916₀ 917₀ Ὀλύμπιος (=Hadrian) 959₀ Ὀλύμπιος Πεισαῖος 962₀ Ὄμβριος 897₅ 897₆ 898₀ 1226 Ὁμοβούλιος 962₀ Ὁμόγνιος 1176₃ 1176₄ 1177₂ ὁμόγνιος 723₀ 1177₂ Ὁμολώιος 857₆ 900₁ 901₀ 904₄ 1227 Ὁμολῶος 857₆ Ὁμονῶος 857₆ Ὁμόριος (?) 1090 ὁ πᾶς κόσμος 1028 f. Ὁπλόσμιος 290₀ Ὀπωρεύς 1074 Ὁράτριος (=Ϝράτριος) 342₀ 723₀ Ὄρειος 868 Ὀρέστης (?) 1179 1183₃ Ὀρθώσιος (=Iupiter Stator) 422₁ 708₅ Ὄριος (=Iupiter Terminus or Terminalis) 1090 Ὄρκιος 569₄ 722 722₅ 726 f. 727₃₍₁₎ 1176₄ 1177₂ ὄρκιος 723₀ Ὀρομπάτας 869₀ Ὀσογῶα 578₄₍₃₎ 579₀₍₈₎ ₍₁₀₋₁₂₎₍₁₄₋₁₆₎₍₁₋₅₎ 582₀₍₀₎₍₇₎ 598₁ 616₁ 663 715 790₀ 846 963₇ 1220 Ὀσογῶα Ζηνοποσειδῶν (Ζανοποτειδᾶν) 578₄₍₂₎₍₄₎ Ὀσογῶα Σωτὴρ καὶ Εὐεργέτης τῆς πόλεως 579₀₍₁₃₎ (?) Ὀσογῶα Zeus Ζηνοποσειδῶν 578₄₍₃₎₍₅₋₇₎ 579₀₍₉₎ Ὀσογῶος (?) or Ὀσογῶου (?) 579₀₍₁₁₎₍₁₎ Ὄσσαιος 904₃ ὁ τὰ περὶ τῆς φιλίας ἐπισκοπῶν 1176₅ 1177₀ ὁ (τῆς) φιλίας ἔφορος 1176₅ 1177₀ ὁ τῆς φιλίας προστάτης 1177₀ ὁ τῶν θεῶν κορυφαῖος 1188₇ ὁ τῶν θεῶν ὕπατός τε καὶ ὑπέρτατος 891₀ Ὀτωρκονδέων

Zeus (*cont.*)

579₀(2) 580 580₁₀(1) 581₀(5)(1–5) Οὐ-δαῖος (= Plouton) 343₀ Οὐράνιος 436 869₁ 1065 1158 Οὐράνιος ῞Υψιστος Σααρναῖος Ἐπήκοος 886₀(30) 983₄ Οὔ-ριος 707 f. 917₀ 918₀ πᾶ (?) 294₀ 570₀ παγγενέτης 1122₉ παγκρατὲς αἰεί 855 παγκρατὲς γάνος 931₀ Παγχαῖος 342₀ (?) Παῖς 742 f. 749 826₆ Παλαμ-ναῖος 260₀ 1097₂ 1098 1098₅ 1099₁ 1101 παλαμναίων τιμήορον ἱκεσιάων 1097₂ Παλάμνιος 1099₀ πάμμεγας 349₂₀ Πανάμαρος 587 714₃ 963₈ 1195₃ (See also Πανημέριος, Πανήμερος) πάνδωρος 858 Πανελλήνιος 894₃ 895₀ 895₁ 1119₄ 1120₀ Πανημέριος 963₈ Πανήμερος 963₈ (See also Πανάμαρος) Πανκτήσιος 1067 Παννύχιος 941₀ Πανομφαῖος 1097₂ 1211 Πανόπτης 1130 παντοτινάκτης 1100₁ πάντων διατάκτωρ καὶ ὅλου τοῦ κόσμου 1023 1051 πανυπέρτατος 321₁ Παπαῖος 292₄ Πάπας or Παπᾶς 292 Παπίας 292₄ Παππῶος 292₄ Παρνήθιος 897₆ πασι-άναξ 1113₀(2) Πάσιος 1095₀ πάτερ (voc.) 271₁ 584₁ 693₃ 728₀ 855₂ 858 922₅ 950₀ 957₂ 1094₀ 1130₁ πάτερ εἰρήνης βαθυκά[ρπου] 875₁(2) Πατήρ 836₂ 836₃ πατήρ 1023 1030 πατρα-λοίας 942₀ Πάτριος 1141 Πατρῷος 233 244 280₁ 723₀ 902₂ 950₀ 1066 1095₀ Πατρῷος Ἐπιλόφιος (?) 948₄ παυσίλυπος 1123₇ 1124₀ Πεισαῖος 962₀ Πελασγικός 960₀ Πελινναῖος 923₀ Περικλύμενος (?) 1075 περίφαντος 1122 Περίφας (?) 1122 Περφερέτας 496₀ 1220 Πῖκος 697₀ (See further Pikos who is also Zeus) Πίστιος (= *Fidius*) 724₀ Πλουτοδότης 251₂ 385₀ πνοιὴ πάντων 1027 Πολιεύς 260₀ 869₁ Πο-λιεύς at Athens 897₂ 897₃ Πολιεύς at Delphoi 231 Πολιεύς in Kos 238₀ Πολιεύς at Lindos 923₀ Πολιοῦχος 941₀ πολύξενος (?) 1113₀(2) πολυξενώ-τατος 1113₀(2) πολύσταχυς 295₂ 569₇ Πολύτεχνος (?) 693 πολυώνυμος 855 πόντου ῥίζα 1027 Ποτεύς (or Πότης or Πότις) 285 287₁ Ποτηος (accent unknown) 285 πρευμενής 1098₄ Προ-γονικός 1225 Προπάτωρ 941₀ προσ-τρόπαιος (προστροπαῖος) 1097₂ 1098 f. 1099₀ 1101 πρῶτος 1027 f. πυθμὴν γαίης τε καὶ οὐρανοῦ ἀστερόεντος 1027 f. Ῥεμβήνοδος (?) 714₃ Σαάξιος (for Σαάξιος = Σαβάξιος) 284₀ Σααρ-ναῖος 886₀(30) 983₄ Σαβάξιος 282 285₀ 287₂ 664₁ (?) 745₁ 954₀ 957₂ 975₀ 1184 1217 Σαουάξιος (= Σαβάξιος) 285₀ 1217 f. Σάραπις 1171₃ cp. 773₀ (See also Σέραπις) Σαώτης 599₂ 1151 Σεβαστός (= Hadrian) 959₀ f. σει-σίχθων 1100₁ Σέραπις 714₃ (?) (See also Σάραπις) Σερεανός 883₀(0) Ση-μαλέος 4 897₆ Σημαντικός 280₁ σκαται-βότης (?) 15₁ 1211 Σκύλιος 723₀

Zeus (*cont.*)

Σκυλοφόρος (= Iupiter *Feretrius*) 111₀ Σολυμεύς 973₁ f. Σόλυμος 974₀ Σπάλαξος (less probably Σπάλωξος) 1220 Σπάλωξος 587 Στάτωρ (= Iupiter *Stator*) 708₅ στεροπηγερέτα 806₈ Στήσιος (= Iupiter *Stator*) 708₅ Στόρπαος 815 850 1095₀ Στρατεῖος 591₂ Στρατηγός 707 f. 848 918₀ Στράτιος 111₀ 585 591 591₂ 594 594₈ 595 (?) 595₀ 598₁ 705 713 715 722 846 848 884₀(0) 963₇ 974₁ ff. Συκάσιος 1103 σχέτλιος 727₃(1) Σώζων 987₀ Σωσίπολις (?) 1151 (cp. i. 58) Σωτήρ 233 294₂ 317₂ 321₁ 343₀ 434₃ 727₃(3) 728₀ 763₁ 884₀(0) 955₀ 962₀ 970₀ 1121 1123 1129₀ 1133₁ 1141 1142₁ 1144₂ 1147 1151 1156₁₃ 1159 1162 1169 1191 1228 f. [Σωτὴρ ἅπαν]τος ἀνθρώ-πων γένο[υς] 280₁ [Σωτὴρ] τοῦ σύμ-παντος ἀν[θρωπείου γένους] 280₁ Σω-τὴρ Τέλειος 1123₇ σωτήριος 1123₇ 1124₀ Ταλαιός 948₁ Ταλετίτας 890₂ 948₁ Ταλλαῖος 948₁ ταμίης πολέμοιο 734₃ Ταουιανός 754₁ Ταραντταῖος 32₃ Τέλειος 1076 f. 1089 1123₇ 1124₀ 1147 1150 1156₁₃ 1159 1162 1163₂ 1175 Τέλειος Σωτήρ 1124₀ Τελεσιουργός 1228 Τελεσφόρος 838 1089 τελεσ-φόρος 1089 τελέων τελειότατον κράτος 337₄ Τεράστιος 31 1211 Τερμινθεύς 962₀ τερπικέραυνος 502₂ 779 ff. 806₈ 822 1067 1070 1097₀ Τετράωτος 322 842 Τηρεύς (?) 693 697 Τιμωρός 874₂ 1099₀ 1101 τοῦ κατὰ χθονός | Διὸς νεκρῶν Σωτῆρος 1125₀ Τρεφώνιος or Τροφώνιος 233₀ 794 1061 1073 ff. 1112 Τριφύλιος 1095₀ Τροπαῖος 110₉ 111₀ 956₀ Τροπαιοῦχος 111₀ Τρο-παιοῦχος (= Iupiter *Feretrius*) 111₀ Τροπαιοφόρος (= Iupiter *Feretrius*) 111₀ Τροφώνιος (See Τρεφώνιος) Τρώιος 571₆ τῶν περὶ Λάκιον 1156₁₀ τῶν περὶ Ὀλυμπιόδωρον 1156₁₀ τῶν περὶ Πολύξενον 1156₁₀ τῶν φιλικῶν καθηκόντων ἔφορος 1177₀ Ὑδηνός (?) 1227 f. Ὑέτιος 164₅ 164₆ 318₀ 869₁ 1144₂ ὑέτιος 276₁ Ὑμήττιος 897₅ Ὑνναρεύς (Ὑνναρεύς ?) 987₁ Ὕπατος 163₄ 737 875 890₃ 897₂ 898₁ 898₂ 956₂ (?) ὕπατος 271₁ ὕπατος βασιλεὺς διὰ παντός 856 ὕπατος θεῶν 1125₁ *Ὑπερβερέτας 496₀ ὑπερμενής 1028 Ὑπερφερέτης (= Iupiter *Feretrius*) 111₀ 496₀ ὕστατος 1027 f. ὑψιβρεμέτης 830₁ 838 ὑψίδρομον (Pierson cj. ὑψί-βρομον) πυριαυγέα κόσμον ἐλαύνων 830₁ ὑψίζυγος 830₁ ὑψιμέδων 875₁(2) 907₂ Ὕψιστος 231₈ 293₀ 876 876₁ ff. 891₂ 892₃ 897₃ 898₃ 906₂ 907₁ 922₁ 922₂ 953₁ 956₀ (?) 963₂ 963₅₋₉ 983₂ 983₄ 983₆ 983₉ 1144₂ ὕψιστος 893₁ Ὕψιστος Βρονταῖος 834 f. Ὕψιστος καὶ Ἐπήκοος 885₀(29) 886₀(0) 983₀ Ὕψιστος Ἐπόπτης (?) 949₂ Ὕψιστος Μέγιστος

Zeus (*cont.*)

Ἐπήκοος 885₀(29) 983₂ Φαλακρός 874₂
893₁ 1099₀ 1144₂ 1226 Φερέτριος
(= Iupiter *Feretrius*) 111₀ Φερφερέτας 496₀ 1220 Φηγός (?) 413₂
φιλάνθρωπος 1177₂ Φίλιος 260₀ 723₀
727₃(1) 727₃(2) 728₀ 956₀ 1061 1092₈
1119₀ 1141 1160 ff. 1173 ff. 1186
1196 f. φίλος 1167 φίλτατος 1167₅
φοινικοστερόπας 806₈ Φράτριος 723₀
728₀ 730₀ 1177₂ Φύξιος 902₀ 1097₂
1144₂ 1177₂ φύσεως ἀρχηγέ 855
φυτάλιος 1100₁ φυτάλμιος 260₀ 1177₂
Χαριδότης 1065 Χθόνιος 829 878₀(3)
1100₁ 1119₀ 1155 Χρυσαορεύς or
Χρυσαόριος 722 848 Χρυσ-
αορεύς 884₀(0) ὠδαῖος (?) 932₁ Ὡρομάσδης 386 980₆

Festivals : Aitnaia 908₁ Basileia 900₀
Boukatia 235 Daidala Megala 977₀
Deia 320₀ Deia Sebasta Oikoumenika
320₀ Diasia 1138 ff. Διὸς βοῦς (See
Rites) Eleutheria (?) 974₀ Homoloïa 900₁ Ithomaia (Ithomaïs) 890₆
Megala Panhellenia 1121₀ Meilichia
1091 f. 1092₅ New Year's Day 931₀
Olympia 964₂ Panhellenia 1119₄
pentaeterís 1179 Traianeia Deiphileia 1180 *trieterís* 934₀ Xan-
thikos 23 981₁ f. yearly sacrifice
and *panégyris* 576₂

Rites : altars at Olympia and Pergamon made from ashes from thighs of
victims 955₀ ἀνιπτόποδες at Tralleis
959₀ f. banquet for all present at
sacrifice to Zeus Στράτιος 974₁
bovine omophagy 539 cp. 934₀
burial of bull 345 539 ceremonial
purity 934₀ communion-feast 1173
daily oblation to sceptre of Zeus at
Chaironeia 547₂ Διὸς βοῦς 318₀ Διὸς
κώδιον 1065 effigy worn by votaries
299 ff. first-fruits 872₀(5) funeral
offering in Idaean Cave 934₀ 942₀
god killed and eaten in form of
bull 345 hecatomb sacrificed to
Zeus Κάσιος on Mt Kasion in Syria
982₀ 1192 hecatomb sacrificed to
Zeus Νέμειος at Argos 1144₂ human
consort 128₄ 210₂ (See also *infra*
παλλακίδες) human sacrifice to
Zeus Ἀταβύριος in Rhodes (?) 924₀
human sacrifice to Zeus Ἰθωμάτας
890₆ human sacrifice to Zeus Λαφύστιος at Halos 904₁ (?) human
sacrifice to Zeus Λαφύστιος on Mt
Laphystion 899₁ human sacrifice
to Zeus-like deity Θυέστης at Mykenai (?) 1022 incubation 232 982₀ (?)
initiation 1186 jars of Zeus Κτήσιος 1054 ff. libation from first
krater to Zeus and Hera 1123₇
1124₀ libation from first *kratér* to
Zeus Ὀλύμπιος and the Olympians
1123 libation from third *kratér* to

Zeus (*cont.*)

Zeus Σωτήρ 1123₇ 1124₀ 1125₀ libation from third *kratér* to (Zeus)
Σωτήρ and Ὀλύμπιος 1124₀ libation
from third *kratér* to Zeus Σωτήρ or
Τέλειος 1123 libation from third
kratér to Zeus Σωτήρ Τέλειος 1123₇
libation to Zeus Διδυμαῖος with ivy-
leaves 317₁ libation and prayer to
Zeus Ἰδαῖος 950₀ libation to Zeus
Κτήσιος 1058 libation to Zeus
τερπικέραυνος 1097₀ love-feast 1197
lying prone 835 mysteries at Antiocheia on the Orontes 1186₆ mysteries in Crete 345 mysteries at
Pergamon 288₀ new fire (?) 1149₂(1)
νηφάλια 1142₃ no wine- or animal-
offerings on altar of Zeus Ὕπατος
at Athens 875₁(2) oak-brides burnt
on Mt Kithairon 977₀ oath taken
over boar 726 f. 728₀ offering of
meal (?) 18 omophagy 934₀ cp. 539
παγκάρπεια 1058 παλλακίδες at
Thebes in Egypt 960₀ παλλακίδες at
Tralleis 959₀ f. (See also *supra*
human consort) πέλανος 1058 procession up Mt Pelion 870₀ proces-
sions at Pergamon 288₀ purification by figs (?) 1103₄ 1103₇ purification in cult of Zeus Φίλιος 1186
sacrifice by Labyadai (Boukatia)
235 sacrifice of bull to Zeus Βρονταῖος 835 sacrifice of bull to Zeus
Στράτιος 975₀ sacrifice of nine bulls
to Zeus Κήναιος 902₂ sacrifice of
cakes moulded into forms of animals 1138₂ 1140 sacrifice of seven
cakes to Zeus Πολιεύς 238₀ sacrifice
of goat to Zeus Ἀσκραῖος 872₀(5)
sacrifice of humped bull to Zeus
Σολυμεύς 973₁ sacrifice of milk,
honey, wine, oil, incense to Zeus
Στράτιος 974₁ 977₀ sacrifice of ox to
Zeus Ἑρκεῖος 728₀ sacrifice of three-
year-old ox to Zeus 287₂ 954₀ sacrifice of three-year-old ox to Zeus
Βάκχος 287₂ 954₀ sacrifice of pig to
Zeus Βουλεύς 1105 sacrifice of pig
to Zeus Εὐβουλεύς 1105 sacrifice of
pig to Zeus Λύκαιος 1105 sacrifice
of pig to Zeus Μειλίχιος 1105 ff.
1140₂ (?) 1142 1157 sacrifice of pig
to Zeus Φίλιος 1161 sacrifice of ram
to Zeus Λαφύστιος 904₁ sacrifice of
ram to Zeus (? Μειλίχιος ? Φίλιος)
1175 sacrifice of sheep to Zeus
Μειλίχιος 1138₂ 1140 sacrifice of
white ox to Zeus Κτήσιος 1065 1067
(See also white victims) sacrifice of
singed victim to (Zeus) Μηλίχιος
1156 sacrifice to Zeus at Olympia
on logs of white-poplar 467 sacrifices to Zeus Στράτιος on mountain-
tops 974₁ ff. taboo on onions among
devotees of Zeus Κάσιος at Pelou-

Zeus (*cont.*)

909_0 Themis 37_1 willow-goddess (?) 947_0

consults Nyx 1029 consults Nyx and Kronos 1027 creates the world anew inside himself 1027 deposited by Typhon in Corycian Cave 449_0 Deukalion builds altar of Zeus Ἀφέσιος 892_4 Deukalion sacrifices to Zeus Φύξιος 902_0 Dionysos sewn up in thigh of Zeus 957_2 Διὸς ἀπάτη 1020 f. Dirke 1019 drives out Kronos 933_0 941_0 942_0 drives Kronos out of Assyria 693_4 694_0 Erechtheus 24 794 exiles Apollon to land of Hyperboreoi 484 493 Flumen 477_7 founds city on Mt Dikte 928_0 929_0 Ganymedes 188_0 189_0 281_4 933_0 Gigantomachia 752_4 830_7 gives Dionysos to Ma to nurse 565_2 gives golden vine to Tros 281_4 gives ring to Prometheus 990 golden hound 1227 golden ram 899_1 golden rope 1029 1211 golden vine 281_4 has Aigokeros or Capricornus for foster-brother 932_1 933_0 has sinews of his hands and feet cut out by Typhon and hidden in a bear-skin under the care of Delphyne 228 449_0 Hektor 950_0 helped by Aigokeros or Capricornus against Titans 933_0 hidden from Kronos by Korybantes 940_0 hidden from Kronos by Kres 928_0 infancy in Dictaean Cave 928_0 929_0 infancy on Mt Ide in Crete 932_1 infancy on a Phrygian mountain 968_{1-3} 969_2 Io 782_1 Ixion 1098_4 jars of good and evil 1067 f. Kapaneus 23 824 f. Kasios 981_1 Kekrops founds altar of Zeus Ὕπατος $875_{1(2)}$ Korybantes drown cries of infant Zeus 928_0 Kouretes drown cries of infant Zeus 928_0 961_0 968_{1-3} leaps upon Phanes and swallows him 1027 Leda 941_0 lets fall drops of blood, from which men arise 1032 lets fly eagles from west and east 179 makes cosmic mantle 351_1 makes Kronos drunk on honey 448_1 1027 Melissa 928_0 Merops 1132_1 mutilated by Typhon 448_2 mutilates Kronos 448_1 685 1027 nurses transformed into bears 227 f.

nursed by Adrasteia 933_0 Amaltheia 928_0 Ithome and Neda 890_6 Nymphs on Mt Ide in Crete 932_1 Rhea 961_0 968_{1-3} 969_2

nurtured by bears 928_0 939_0 bees 928_0 929_0 1112_6 doves 928_0 eagle 928_0 goat 928_0 961_0 968_0 goat Amaltheia 932_1 933_0 pig 928_0

Oidipous 829 Omphalian Plain 190 Ophiuchus 1087 Periphas 1121 ff. Perseus sacrifices to Zeus Ἀπεσάντιος 892_4 piles Mt Aitne on

Zeus (*cont.*)

Enkelados 909_0 piles Mt Aitne on Typhon 909_0 places heart of Dionysos or Zagreus in gypsum image 1031 Polytechnos 693 pounds heart of Zagreus into potion and gives it to Semele to drink 1031 prince slain by wild boar and buried in Crete 522 cp. 727 *psychostasía* 733 ff. quitting Assyria follows Kronos and becomes king of Italy 694_0 943_0 reared by Kouretes on Mt Dikte 928_0 929_0 refitted with his sinews by Hermes and Aigipan 449_0 Rhea gives Kronos stone instead of him 793_8 901_1 Rhea, pregnant with him, is protected against Kronos by Hopladamos (Hopladamos?) 291_0 Rhea rescues him from Kronos 928_0 Salmoneus 833 1122 *Seleucides aves* 981_1 Semele 24 ff. 731 ff. (?) succeeds Kronos as king of Italy 694_0 swallows Metis 12 348_2 Sykeas or Sykeus 1103_8 Thetis 45_1 thrusts Kronos down below earth and sea 1020 Titanes 218 1031 f. 1103_8 transforms Aigokeros or Capricornus and his mother Aix into stars 933_0 transforms Aigolios into owl 929_0 transforms himself into Eros when about to create the world 316 transforms Kallisto into bear 228_7 transforms Keleos the Cretan into green woodpecker 929_0 transforms Kerberos the Cretan into bird 929_0 transforms Laïos the Cretan into blue thrush 929_0 Typhon (Typhoeus) 228 448_2 722_2 731 826 839_6 981_1 Ursa Maior 928_0 Ursa Minor 928_0 visits Hera clandestinely 1020 wraps *aithér* round the world and ties up the bundle with golden cord 1029

Metamorphosed into Apollon 228_7 Artemis 228_7 1217 bear 229 bull 348 449_0 929_0 1131_1 1167_5 cuckoo 893_2 1144_2 eagle 187_8 228_7 752 909_0 (?) 941_1 1133 f. Eros 316 fly 782_1 gold 1131_1 hoopoe 697 1130 f. human lover 941_0 snake 941_0 1029 1061 1151 stranger 1096_4 swan 941_0 1015 1015_7 1131_1 vulture 909_0 woodpecker 524 693 (?) 693_4

Genealogy : b. of Ouranos 940_0 f. of Aiakos by Aigina d. of Asopos 894_3 f. of Aphrodite 1029 f. of Apollon and Artemis by Leto 453 f. of Apollonios of Tyana 569_4 f. of Arkas by Kallisto 228_5 f. of Arkeisios by Euryodeia (Euryodia) 1152_1 f. of Artemis 164_8 342_0 453 f. of Athena by Koryphe 869_1 cp. i. 155 f. of Attis 294 f. of Atys and Kotys (?) 312 f. of Chryses by Hesione d. of Danaos 1150_2 f. of Dardanos 8 f.

Zeus (*cont.*)

faring 987$_0$ sender up of souls 1058 sky 298 344 353 458 601 663 823 sleep 231 f. snow 1 343$_0$ solar 285$_0$ 840 948$_1$ 1130 1130$_7$ specialised into Poseidon 786 850 spinner of fate 1219 starry sky 436 stars 840 869$_1$ storm 267 591 705 848 streams 869$_0$ sun (See solar) suppliant 1096 1098 1101 suppliant-boughs 1149$_{2(2)}$ thunder 1 4 344 833 ff. 851 f. 941$_0$ 945$_2$ 1155 thunder and lightning 280$_1$ 817 thunderbolt 179 722 ff. 850 f. trees 946$_0$ trophy 110$_9$ 111$_0$ turnips (?) 260$_0$ underworld 1158 (See also chthonian) universe (See cosmic) upper world 1158 victor 758 victory 489$_{0(0)}$ 812$_1$ 813$_2$ violence 1098 war 705 ff. 848 water 1117$_3$ (?) weather 1 ff. 840 894$_3$ wind 444$_7$ (?) witness 728$_0$ f. world (See cosmic) a younger Zan 340 ff.

Etymology: 259$_0$ 855$_2$ 928$_0$ 1102$_8$ 1228

Attributes: *agrenón* 574 592 *aigis* 781 1187$_0$ apple (?) 831$_1$ bay-wreath 266 597$_3$ 714$_2$ 756$_1$ 924$_0$ 1187$_4$ 1192 f. 1223 bronze bulls 924$_0$ bronze oxen 924$_0$ buskins 1178 1184 car (*benna*) (?) 883$_{0(0)}$ chariot 436$_1$ 851 Charites (Moirai? Horai?) 232$_0$ *chitón* 597 f. 744 744$_4$ *chlamýs* 731$_1$ 744 ff. cock 946$_0$ 947$_0$ corn-ears 754$_1$ *cornu copiae* 1105 1162 crab 577 f. cup 1178 cypress 932$_1$ dagger 714$_1$ 722 diadem 597$_3$ double axe 283$_0$ 559 ff. 601 614 615 (?) 664$_1$ (?) 705 714$_1$ *drépanon* 448$_0$ eagle 283$_0$ 575 f. 577 f. 707 751 f. 808$_{0(0)}$ 833 836 838 956$_0$961$_0$968$_0$1133$_1$1143 1161 1185 f. 1188 1208 eagles 231 239 841 Egyptian head-dress (?) 987$_0$ female breasts 592 ff. flower 1224 (?) goat 987$_1$ (?) globe 980$_0$ golden ball 933$_0$ golden calf 354 golden *liknon* 933$_0$ golden vine (?) 281$_4$ grapes 281 287$_1$ 883$_{0(0)}$ hammer 945$_2$ *hárpe* 449$_0$ helmet 705 f. *himátion* 1082 *himátion* of gold 916$_0$ *himátion* of wool 916$_0$ Horai 1138$_5$ jar 1054 ff. jug 1117 *kálathos* 577 592 f. 593 (?) 597 597$_3$ 598 *kratér* 283$_0$ leaf-shaped lance 709 *liknon* 933$_0$ lily-wreath 740 lion (?) 575 f. lioness (?) 575 599$_2$ lion-skin (?) 947$_0$ lotos 771 1224 mattock 806$_1$ Moirai 1138$_5$ moon 980$_0$ necklace 593 Nike 873$_{0(8)}$ 1143 1145$_0$ 1190 1192 1193$_1$ oak-branch 1177 (?) oak-wreath 348 388 763$_1$ 1187$_4$ olive-branch 1177 (?) olive-wreath 323$_1$ palm (?) - tree 284$_0$ panther (?) 575 599$_2$ pectoral 574 *phiále* 881$_{0(21)}$ 906$_3$ 1105 1116 (?) 1143 1145$_0$ 1161 f. 1175 1184 pillar 818 pine-wreath 951$_0$ plane-trees 590 976$_0$ plough 281 836 pome-

Zeus (*cont.*)

granate 986$_0$ radiate crown 980$_0$ scales 734$_3$ sceptre 258 266 547$_2$ 709 731 ff. 763 788$_0$ 1105 1116 1143 1145$_0$ 1188 *sélinon* (?)-wreath 1187$_0$ shield 578 705 712 silver knife 354 *skýphos* 754$_1$ snake 283$_0$ 284$_0$ 285$_0$ 819 820 823 1111 spear 577 f. 704 ff. 722 848 957$_0$ stag 575 1220 star 980$_0$ 1187$_0$ stars 980$_0$ stick 1102$_0$ sun 980$_0$ sword 591 615 (?) 705 712 ff. 722 848 tall head-dress 980$_0$ (See also tiara) thunderbolt 283$_0$ 722 ff. 785 848 ff. 1145$_0$ *thýrsos* surmounted by eagle 1178 tiara 386 (See also tall head-dress) tortoise 895$_1$ trident 577 798 two doves (?) 872$_{0(5)}$ two eagles 179 f. two oaks 872$_{0(5)}$ two ravens (?) 872$_{0(5)}$ two spears 283$_0$ two thunderbolts 722 726 f. vervain 396$_0$ 397$_0$ vine 836 838 vine-staff 909$_0$ whip 851 willow 946$_0$ 947$_0$ winged chariot 43 321$_1$ woodpecker 518$_3$ (See further Pikos who is also Zeus)

Types: advancing with thunderbolt in lowered right hand and eagle on outstretched left 745 advancing with thunderbolt in raised right hand 26$_0$ 795$_3$ advancing with thunderbolt in raised right hand and eagle on outstretched left 739 ff. 818 f. 963$_0$ 1139$_0$ 1143 1222 f. advancing with thunderbolt in raised right hand, eagle on outstretched left, and snake at his feet 851 advancing with thunderbolt in raised right hand and sceptre as well as eagle in outstretched left 1223 advancing with thunderbolt in raised right hand and sceptre in outstretched left 25$_0$ 26$_0$ 27$_0$ 709 733 advancing with thunderbolt in raised right hand and spear (?) in left 708 f. amours with Leda, Semele, Kallisto, and Ganymedes 228$_7$ androgynous (?) 292$_4$ 594 androgynous with golden wings and heads of bulls and snake 1022 f. archaistic 744$_1$ Aristonous 1222 Assyrian 697$_0$ 938$_0$ bearded head as pendant 302 bearded head at either end of whip-handle 301 beardless 285$_0$ 742 748 946$_0$ f. 1224 (?) birth of Athena 709 f. 753$_3$ 785 boy with whip (?) 826$_6$ bronze statuette of 'Geometric' age representing Zeus fulminant (?) 1222 bronze statuettes inlaid with silver eyes 503$_0$ Bryaxis (?) 921$_0$ bull (?) 924$_0$ bust as medallion on wreath 301 bust as support for arm of Attis 297 bust between horns of crescent 712$_3$ bust facing, with thunderbolt and sceptre to his right and left 887$_{0(0)}$ bust supported on eagle

Zeus (*cont.*)

1061 1107 ff. 1174 soldier 705 f. standing with Artemis Ἐφεσία in right hand 962_2 standing with eagle in left hand 751_5 standing with eagle in right hand 751_5 standing with eagle in right hand and sceptre in left 319_4 951_0 957_0 968_0 standing with Nike in right hand and sceptre in left 1145_0 standing with *phiále* in right hand and sceptre in left 280_1 $881_{0(21)}$ standing with sceptre (?) in raised right hand and *phiále* (?) in left 752 f. standing with sceptre in raised right hand and thunderbolt in lowered left 749_1 820 f. standing with sceptre in right hand and eagle beside him 1143 1230 standing with spear or sceptre in raised right hand and left covered by *himátion* 918_0 standing with spear in right hand and eagle at his feet 707 standing with spear in right hand and thunderbolt in left 957_0 standing with thunderbolt in lowered right hand 280_1 standing with thunderbolt in lowered right hand and sceptre in left 734 f. 745 ff. 1145_0 standing with thunderbolt in outstretched right hand and sceptre in left 917_1 standing with thunderbolt in raised right hand and eagle on outstretched left 737 739 $819_{0(5)}$ standing with thunderbolt in raised right hand and sceptre in lowered left 833 standing with wreath in outstretched right hand 1192 statuette held by Laodikeia 319_7 320_0 with supported foot 266_1 surrounded by seven stars 238_0 syncretistic 850 τετράγωνος 1147_8 Theokosmos 1138_5 theriomorphic 1151 three-eyed 892_5 1144_2 traveller 1102_0 with trident, eagle, and crab 577_2 with trident, thunderbolt, and eagle 798 with trident, thunderbolt, and sea-monster 798 trophy 111_0 upborne on eagle 951_0 (See also seated on eagle) upborne on eagle between horns of crescent 712_3 winged 1028 *xóanon* 1196 youthful 861_5 1030 1185 youthful figure holding pomegranate 986_0 Ζᾶνες at Olympia 349

Identified with Adad 983_7 Adonaios 293_0 Agamemnon, the god (?) 1069 Ahura Mazdâh 976_0 Âmen-Râ 926_0 Amoun 293_0 Asklepios 1076 ff. Attis 292 Baal 869_0 Ba‘al Milik (Melek, Molok) (?) 1108 Ba‘al-šamin $886_{0(0)}$ 889 Bakchos 287 1184 Celtic Janiform god 1102 Chrysor, the Phoenician Hephaistos 715 1037 Daimon 1160_4 Dionysos 282 287 f. 288_0 Epopeus 445 Erechtheus 793 Eros

Zeus (*cont.*)

1028 Great Ox 354 Hades 582_4 1058 Hephaistos 715 Ianus 328_7 Jehovah 889 elder Kabeiros 664_1 Ḳaṣiu 983_0 (?) Keraunos 12 f. 119_1 Kragos 972_0 974_0 Mars 50 Melqart or Melqarth (?) 1109_0 Metis (masc.) 1028 Pan 349 1023 1024 1039 Papas 836 Pikos 220_6 342_0 693_4 694_0 695_0 696_0 697_0 Poseidon 582 ff. Poseidon and Ares 1225 Protogonos 1023 1039 1051 Roman emperors (See *Personated by*) Sabaoth 293_0 Sabazios 275 1184 Sarapis 714_3 (?) 745_1 773_0 1158 Solymos (?) 974_0 Theos Hypsistos $882_{0(22)}$ $883_{0(0)}$ $884_{0(0)}$ $886_{0(30)}$ 969_3 Trophonios (Trephonios) 1075 Velchanos 946_0 ff. the world 1028 f. (See also *Functions* cosmic) Zan 220_6 341_6 342_0 345 942_0

Assimilated to Apollon 986_0 Chaos 1051 Dionysos 1178 Poseidon 327_2 (?) (See also *Identified with*) Zagreus 980_5

Associated with Acheloios 1092_2 1138_5 Acheloios and Kallirrhoe (?) 1117 Agathos Daimon 925_0 Agdistis and Attis 1229 Aigokeros 938_0 Apollon 317 317_2 Apollon and Themis 730_0 Artemis and Athena 1144_2 Athena 259_0 920_0 923_0 955_0 1101_3 Athena Νικηφόρος 287_2 Athena Σώτειρα 1169_4 Athena and Apollon 458 1094_0 Athena and Herakles 1078 Athena, Herakles, Apollon $875_{1(2)}$ Boule (?) 260_0 *daimones* 931_0 Demeter and Kore 258_3 259_0 Dike 1029 1033_1 Dione 974_0 1029 Dionysos and Athena 925_0 Dioskouroi 1209_2 Enhodia and Polis 1155 Ge 266 f. 292_4 Ge and Athenaia 1115 Ge and Helios 729_0 $884_{0(0)}$ Ge, Helios, and Erinyes 728_0 f. goddess bearing wheat-ears (*cornu copiae*?) and torch (sceptre?) 820 hearth 728_0 Hekate 714_2 714_3 835_6 838 Helios 1114 Helios, rivers, earth, and chthonian powers 728_0 Helios, Selene, Asklepios, Hygieia, etc. 259_0 Hephaistos 972_1 Hera 259_0 592 707 776_3 893_2 894_1 900_0 1137 1144_2 1150 1157 Hera and Athena (= Capitoline triad) 319_7 Hera, Demeter Θεσμοφόρος, Kore, Baubo 259_0 Herakles $492_{0(0)}$ 1157_1 Herakles Ἀνίκητος 294_4 Herkyna 1073 1075 Hermes (?) 957_0 Hestia 259_0 317_2 960_0 1228 Horai 94_2 Kabeiroi 664_1 (?) Kouretes 587 938_0 Men 285_0 Meter 950_0 Meter ἐν Ἄγρας (?) 1142_3 Moira and Erinys 1102_7 Muses 898_5 Nike 853 1100_1 Nomos 1029 οἱ Σεβαστοί 951_0 Persephone 893_0 Philia and Tyche Ἀγαθή 1163 Polis $878_{0(6)}$

Zeus (*cont.*)

933_0 sacred stone of 982_0 f. in the Salian hymn (?) 328 ff. salt pool of 616_1 scales of 734_3 sceptre of 956_2 1026 1030 1058 1131 1132 shoulders of, *aér* 1028 sinews of 228 449_0 450_0 spear of 15_0 547_2 704 ff. spring of 569_4 590_3 890_6 1118 f. staff of (vervain) 396_0 397_0 swathing-bands of 929_0 sword of 591 705 712 ff. 848 threatens to cut men in halves 672_1 three gods of the name Zeus (Iupiter) distinguished 941_0 throne of 343_0 475_7 838 1082 1131 toast of Zeus Σωτήρ 1129_0 tomb of 219 341_6 348 354 556_0 694_0 695_0 696_0 934_0 940_0 ff. touch of 961_0 tower of 343_0 354 travestied 1033 treasury of 23 triad of Zeuses 1093_1 watch-tower of 343_0 354 whip of 260_0 824 ff. 851 will of 14_1 261_0 winds as horses of 830_7 wings of 1028 wisdom of 258_3 wrath of 1097_2 1098_1 1098_2

Zeus, as name of a ship 987_0

Zeus *Hýpatos*, as name of a ship 876_0

Zeus, king of Crete 940_0 941_0 942_0

Zeus, the planet

    Function: γένεσις 558_0

Zibeleïzis

    Cult: Getai 822 851

    Etymology: 823

Zio See Ziu

Ziobe See Zougo

Zioter (Zeter) 1212

Ziu 50 ff.

    Functions: sky 50 81 storm 81 sun 81 warrior 50

    Identified with Ares 50

    Attributes: spear 76 swan (?) 51_1 sword 77 thunderbolt 75_1 76 thunderdrum (?) 83 wheel 77_2 78_1 78_2

    Types: bearded 74 ff. beardless 74 f. driver of two-horse chariot 75 rider on horse supported by male giant 74 ff.

    Identified with Dings (?) 50 f. Er 50 f. 114 Iring (?) 51 f. Irmin 52 114 Sahsnot 50 f.

    Assimilated to Iupiter 74 ff. 78_2 80_2

    In relation to Wodan 62_1

    —— name of, attached to Runic letter 1212 f.

Zobe See Zougo

Zogui See Zougo

Zonos 353

Zophasemin

    Genealogy: children of Mot 1038

    Etymology: 1038

Zoroastres 33 ff.

    Genealogy: descendant of Ninos and Semiramis Rhea 694_0

    Etymology: 33 ff.

    Identified with Er, s. of Armenios 54_1

    —— perpetual fire on mountain of 33 977_0

Zougo (Zogui)

    Cult: bearded and breasted goddess (? Zobe ? Ziobe) 595 f. 846 1220

INDEX II

SUBJECTS   AUTHORITIES

The larger numerals refer to pages, the smaller numerals to foot-notes.

Ábata of Zeus on Mt Oite 903_2 of Zeus Δικταῖος 928_0 of Zeus Καταιβάτης 21 f. of Zeus Φίλιος 1178

Abbott, G. F. 3 36_3 480_7 1112_7 1164_1

Abeken, W. 708 918_0

Abel, E. 12_3 1019 1029

Abrahams, Miss E. B. 515_2

Acclamation of imperial house 980_0

Acieris 630

Acorn of Iupiter (walnut) 775_0 of Zeus (chestnut or other species of nut) 775_0

Acorns 405 407_0 410_0 523 802 965_0 1166_1

Actors, Etruscan 378

Acy, E. d' 690_1

Adam, J. 44_3 44_4 54_1

Adamant 447_8 449_0

Adelphoí in cult of Theos Hypsistos $883_{0(25)}$ $885_{0(0)}$

Adler, E. N. $888_{0(0)}$

Adler, Frau $807_{3(3)}$ 873_2 907_0 981_1 982_0 983_0 987_0

Adulterers in Tenedos slain with two sacred axes 668 f.

Ádyta of Asklepios at Trikke 1088 of Zeus Ὀλύμπιος at Agrigentum 915_0 1227

Adze held by statuette 387_4 (?) in Egypt 545_0 tombstones of Gallia Lugudunensis dedicated *sub ascia* 547_0

Adze-worship of Gaul 547_0

Aér 611_2 949_5

—— conceived as shoulders, breast, and back of Zeus 1028

Aeraki, G. 935_0

Aerolite 983_0 (?)

Agápe, the 'love-supper' of the early Christians 1173

Agnus castus 517_3 (?) 972_1 1118

Agonistic *amphorae* (?) 1064 tables $490_{0(5)}$ $491_{0(0)}$ urns $490_{0(5)}$ $491_{0(0)}$ 562

Agrenón 167 170_3 181_1 187_4 192 574 592

Agyieús-pillar 160 ff. 499 676 841 f. 844

—— compared with Diana-pillar 160 confused with herm 160_5

Ahlwardt, C. W. 855_1

Ahrens, H. L. 294_0 344 463_1 495_6 582

Aigís Salian shield as 377 worn by emperors 1194 worn by Zeus (See Index I Zeus *Attributes*)

Aithér 611_2 840 949_5 950_0 1026 1029

—— conceived as ear (?) of Zeus 1028_8 conceived as mind of Zeus 1028 f.

Akropóleis sacred to Zeus 873_0

Akrotéria 16_1 1102_8

Alábastron 305_0

Albers, C. 868_6

Alberti, J. 665_0 1218

Alders 472 949_5

Allegorical (?) figure of Kairos by Lysippos 859 f.

Allen, J. Romilly 604

Allen, T. W. 353_1

Allène, H. 118_2

Almonds 154_0 298 300

Almond-tree 295 969_4 970_0

Altar, 'baetylic' 193_2

—— bearing image of Mt Argaios 978_0 before sacred tree 285_0 blood poured over 517_1 decorated with double axe 1228 entwined with snake and flanked by snakes 1175 garlanded 1193 1194_4 holed 1056 1058 in two stages 975_0 of Apollon 163_4 of ashes at Olympia 21 955_0 of ashes at Pergamon 955_0 1181 of brushwood in Skythia 547_3 of Chians at Delphoi 170_2 of horns in Delos 1227 of roughly squared stones in Crete 926_0 of rude stones at Athens 1117 of rude stones on vase 903_0 of silver in Persia 34_1 of wooden blocks on Mt Kithairon 898_6 of Zeus 1141 of Zeus Ἀφέσιος 892_4 of Zeus Βουλαῖος 259_0 of Zeus Ἰδαῖος in Crete 937_0 of Zeus Ἰδαῖος in Phrygia 950_0 ff. of Zeus Καταιβάτης 15 ff. of Zeus Κεραύνιος 1228 of Zeus Λαβραϋνδεύς 1228 of Zeus Λαβράϋνδος 1228 of Zeus Λιταῖος 1099_2 1100_0 of Zeus Λύκαιος 187 1105 of Zeus Στράτιος 975_0 f. of Zeus Τέλειος 1147 of Zeus Ὑέτιος 1144_2 of Zeus Ὕπατος $875_{1(2)}$ of Zeus Φίλιος 1180 of Zeus Φύξιος 1144_2 portable 1128_0 rock-cut 937_0 952_0 f. stepped 263 surmounted by ritual horns 517 with boar in relief 1063 with festoon-bearing eagle 302 with four legs and central stem 193_2 pl. xi with hollow for libations 983_0 See also Pillar-altars, Table-altar

Altars, bilingual, from Palmyra $885_{0(29)}$ $886_{0(0)}$ dedicated to Zeus on mountain-tops 873_1 fire-altars (?) 426 of Zeus 231_8 twelve dedicated to Ianus as god of months 336_8

Hands (*cont.*)
outwards, the other in profile 536 suppliant $881_{0(0)}$ $889_{0(33)}$ 944_0 votive, in bronze $886_{0(30)}$
Hanging 1104
Hannig, F. 720 1018_3
Harding, P. J. 419
Hardouin, J. 1041
Hare 152_0
Harnack, A. 307_1
Hárpe a sickle-knife invented by Thracians 550_1 found among many peoples of Asia Minor 550 of Demeter 448_0 of Kronos 447_8 549 f. of Perseus 718 721_0 721_7 1084 of Saturn 70_1 550 on taurobolic altar 306_4
Harris, J. Rendel 133_3 248_0 291_2 318 428 429_3 430_1 434 442_4 447_6 451 452 487 ff. 487_3 $488_{0(0)}$ 692_9 693_4 697_0 824 844 851 1014 1064 1072 1219
Harrison, E. 412_7
Harrison, Miss J. E. 49_1 118_2 120_2 120_3 121_3 131_5 152_0 160_3 165_0 170_3 177_0 207_0 243_3 258_1 262_7 280_0 313 f. 315_3 375_1 432_4 450_1 458_1 458_5 495 511_1 516_6 517_3 520_5 692_6 693_4 791 931_0 932_0 1022 1030 1039 1056 1058 1062 1067 1083 1089 1095_0 1105_3 1105_9 1107_4 1110 f. 1111_0 $1114_{0(6)}$ 1125_1 1136_0 1137_0 1151_8 1151_9 1160_5 1161 1161_3 1163_3 1213
Harry, J. E. 805_6
Hartland, E. S. 291_0 294_1 451_1 960_0 1018
Hartung, J. A. 365_4
Hartwig, P. 460_2 473_1 473_{3-5} 473_7 475 479_1
Harvest-rites 498_2 1096_3
Hasluck, F. W. 835_2 $881_{0(21)}$ 943_0 1082
Hat of bifrontal sky-god 385 f. of Odhin 386 winged 388
Hatch, L. P. 1219
Hatchet See Axe
Hatzfeld, J. 1217
Hauck, A. 604_4
Haug, F. 57_3 57_5 70_0 70_1 71_{1-3} 71_6 71_7 74_4 75_1 76_0 77_2 87_2 87_3 88_1 88_2 1212
Hauser, F. 473_3 475_7 902_2
Haussoullier, B. 318_0
Hauvette-Besnault, A. 580_4 586_1
Havercamp, S. 1172_0
Haverfield, F. 91_1
Havet, L. $329_{0(2)}$
Hawes, C. H. 166_1 341_3 538_3
Hawes, H. 538_3
Hawk as embodiment of Horos 774_0 as shield-boss (?) 938_0 Egyptising 553 in relation to hoopoe 1131_2 on lotos 774_0 on pillar 1133_1
Hawk-headed god (Râ) 774_0 snake (Kneph) 1127_0
Hays, W. J. 1219
Hazel-tree 403_0
Hazzidakis, J. 925_1 935_0
Head as means of divination 290_0 as seat of the soul 290_0 291_0 buried separately 290_0 1218 of Archonides preserved in honey 290_0 of deceased treasured in

Head (*cont.*)
family (Africa), or buried separately from body and replaced by stone image (ancient Egypt) 1218 of priest of Zeus Ὁπλόσμιος denounces murderer 290_0 of Publius prophesies 290_0
Heads of gods (*struppi*) placed on sacred couches 1170 ff.
Head, B. V. 162_1 225_6 254 313_8 363_1 429_5 430_0 447 $491_{0(0)}$ 563_1 570_1 572_2 575_5 660 660_3 662 705_9 794_5 810_0 909_0 961_0 1042 1192_9 1224
Head-dress, Egyptian 987_0 of crab's claws 1185 Oriental 980_0
Headlam, W. 345_5 1098_2 1098_3
Healing gods: Asklepios, Hygieia, Telesphoros See Index I. Dionysos Ἰατρός 250_3 Zeus Ὕψιστος $877_{0(0)}$
Health bestowed by dead kings 1071
Heart of Dionysos or Zagreus 1031 of Liber 1031
Hearth, common, of the Arcadians 1148 invoked 728_0 of Zeus Ἀστραπαῖος 815
Heberdey, R. 728_0 757_1 972_1
Hecatomb sacrificed to Zeus Κάσιος on Mt Kasion in Syria 982_0 1192 sacrificed to Zeus Νέμειος at Argos 1144_2
Hecatombs sacrificed to Zeus Μειλίχιος at Athens 1141
Hedén, E. 1102_7
Hedgehog 964_3
Hedýosmos, taboo on 987_0 See also Mint
Heeren, A. H. L. 858_1
Hehn, V. 279_3 466_4
Heim, R. 410_0
Heiss, A. 1040
Helbig, W. 103_0 144_1 154_0 158_2 160_0 165_0 392_9 393 f. 398_1 400 473_7 641_1 652_3
Hellebore, white 903_2
Helm, K. 50_1
Helmet, horned 110_8 miniature 930_0 of Wodan 62_1 of Zeus Ἄρειος 705 f. plumed 376_1 376_2
Hempl, G. $330_{0(8)}$
Henderson, W. 1002
Henzen, W. 804_0
Hepding, H. 124_0 292_4 293_3 306_4 307_1 969_4 f.
Herald of Zeus 1141
Heraldic device 189_1
Herbig, G. 378_2
Herm, double, of Dionysos 381 f. ithyphallic 645_4 1091 of Augustus impersonating Iupiter 1091 of Diana 149 of Hermaphroditos 1091 of Hermes 152_0 384_0 834 955_0 of Homer with Hesiod 389 of Octavian 1091 phallic 384_0 1150_9
Hermann, G. 296_4
Hermann, K. F. 327
Hermet, F. 690_2
Hero appears as snake 1064 1151 ff. blinds one-eyed giant 988 ff. buried in precinct of god 953_2 buried in sanctuary of goddess 944_0 1152 1155 engulfed in chasm 923_0 escapes by clinging under

Miller, Eliza B. 137_0
Miller, J. 222_3
Millet 1172_4
Milliet, P. 731_2
Millingen, J. 131 162_9 273_4 717_1 717_2 1154_1 1154_5
Mime-performer $882_{0(0)}$
Minervini, G. 131_1 273_3 379_4
Minns, E. H. 293_0 $493_{0(7)}$ 495_5 510_{1-3} 540_4 632_6 $884_{0(0)}$ 925_0 1203 1204_1
Mint 1166_0 aphrodisiac 1165_1 taboo on 987_0 See also *Hedýosmos*, Water-mint
Mirabella, V. 917_0
Mirror, as toy of Dionysos 251_2 face of Klytaimestra seen in 206_2 made by Hephaistos 1030 of Kairos (?) 863_1 of Venus 70_1 609_1 showing whole world 1005 1016
Mirrors, Etruscan 100 f. 258_1 431 f. 432_2 560_3 708 ff. 713 848 Roman 1205_6
Mistletoe, Baldr stabbed with lance of 305_0 called *Donnerbesen* 642 on apple-trees 420_1 on oak-tree 643
Mitre of high priest symbolises sky 386_5
Models offered to gods and heroes 539_2
Modius dedicated by M. Modius Maximus 299 of Agathe Tyche 1128_0 of Agathos Daimon 1128_0 of Diana *Nemorensis* 149 of god from Idaean Cave 938_0 of Isis (Isityche) 1129_0 of Pluto 802 of Sarapis 1129_0 with oak-leaves and acorns 802 See also *Kálathos*
Mogk, E. 110_5 533_2 844_6
Mohl, J. 611_6
Mohnike, G. C. F. 854_9
Molinet, C. du 626_1
Mommsen, A. 233 240_2 486_3 1089 1092_3 1121_0 1139
Mommsen, Th. 328_3 364 440_4 440_5 619_4 803_2 1172_0 1195_0
Monier-Williams, Sir M. 660_1
Monogram, Christian, at Chedworth 604 f. Christian, at Frampton 604 Christian, in relation to trophy-cross and double axe 613 f. 846 Christian, on coins of Constantine the Great 604 Christian, on shields 602 Christian, on top of pillar 606 Christian, within wreath as standard of Constantine the Great 603
Monómmatoi (*Monómatoi*, *Monomátai*) 993_2
Monotheism, general trend towards 889
Monseur, E. 504_4
Monster, headless 305_0 three-bodied 805_6 1225 wolf-headed 305_0
Montelius, O. 529_1 618_1 636 637_1 647_4 687_2 788_1 1221
Montfaucon, B. de 319 626_1
Montgomery, J. A. $888_{0(0)}$
Month, sidereal or lunar, division of 236_5 synodical, division of 236_5
Months: Ἀγριάνιος 924_0 $948_{0(3)}$ (?) Ἀνθεστη-ριών 1139 Ἀνθεστηριών 1 equated with *kalendae Martiae* 1139_7 Ἀπελλαῖος 982_0 Βοηδρομιών 1121_0 Βακίνθιος $948_{0(3)}$ Γα-

Months (*cont.*)
μηλιών 1142 Διονύσιος 930_0 Ἑκατομβαιών 1091 f. 1139_5 Ἐλάφιος 554_2 Ἐλάφριος 599_7 Ἐλχάνιος $948_{0(3)}$ Ϝελχάνιος (?) $947_{0(2)}$ Κρόνιος 1091 Λώϊος 901_0 Μαλο-φόριος $489_{0(0)}$ Μεταγειτνιών 1121_0 Ξαν-θικός 982_0 Ὁμολόϊος 901_0 Ὁμολώϊος, Ὁμολῶος, Ὁμολούϊος 900_1 Τύβι (*leg.* Τυβι *vel* Τῦβι) 1127_0 Ὑπερβερεταῖος 495_8 496_0 Ὑπερβέρετος 496_0 Φεβρουάριος 1142_2
Moon as egg 1015_7 (?) 1035 as eye of Zeus 117 1028 golden, on breast of princess 1012_1
Mooney, G. W. 824_4
Moor, E. 150_2
Mordtmann, A. D. 195_1
Mordtmann, J. H. 270_3
Morell, A. 357_1 358_0
Morey, C. R. 135_1 1134_4
Morey, P. 79_1
Morgan, M. J. de 766_1
Morgan, T. 604
Morpurgo, Miss L. 392_8 392_9 393_1 393_2 398 ff. 398_0 420_1
Mortillet, A. de 686_3 687_1
Mosaic of sacred cistern on Mt Kynthos 919_0 920_0 922_0
Mosso, A. 520_1 544_3 643 646
Moth as soul 645_4 on bronze double axe from Phaistos 643 ff. 847 on golden disks and *plaques* from Mykenai 645
Moulds, stone, from Palaikastro 623 ff.
Moulton, J. H. 33_4 50_1 313_1 1036
Mountain climbed by children in 'Expulsion' tales 1008 f. 1011 1016 cosmic, two-peaked $888_{0(0)}$ cults of Zeus on 354 868 ff. glass 1012_1 opening at mid-day 1005
Mountain-god, recumbent 962_2
Mountain-top worshipped by Samaritans $888_{0(0)}$
Mourning-women 1065
Mouth, bad spirits may enter through 1162_3
Movers, F. C. 675_4 715_4 1038 1110_0
Mowat, R. 373_5
Much, R. 52_7
Müllenhoff, K. 52_7 53_3 844_6
Müller, C. 22_3 132_0 270_4 696_0 945_2 1023
Müller, C. O. See Müller, K. O.
Müller, F. Max 383_7 1035
Müller, G. A. 80_2 109_1
Müller, H. D. 549_6 1021 f.
Müller, K. O. 16_1 102_0 130 199_2 228_4 241_3 327 384_0 457 $491_{0(6)}$ 744_3 1042 1045 1048 1151_8 1151_{10} 1191_5 1197_3
Müntz, E. 106_2
Mulberry-trees 946_0
Mule, hind foot of 757_6 must not enter precinct of Elektryone 499_5
Mules, victims torn asunder by 1008 1019
Multiple blades of double axe 624 654 breasts 410_0 ears 322 eyes 446_1 892_5 893_0 types of deities 322_4 341_0 367 893_0
Muñoz, A. 863_1 865_2 866_0 867_0 867_2 867_3

Waser, O. 99_1 309_3 315_3 504_4 641_2 642_0 645_4 803 1025 1045 f. 1050 1087 1160_5
Water as gift to the dead 977_0 1056 1058 as primal element 1021 1022 as seminal fluid of deity 306_4 Dancing 1008 f. 1010 f. 1016 healing 115 in Indian cosmogony 1035 f. 1039 of immortality 1004 of life 1005 1012_1 salt, appears far inland at Athens, Mantineia, or Mylasa 581 salt, changes its nature 581 salt, in relation to Zeus 581 ff. 616_1 symbolised by reed and urn 1050 1083
Water-divinities 393 f. (?) 399 (?) See also River-god
Waterhouse, C. O. 124_2
Water-mint, aphrodisiac properties of 1165_1 1166_0 at Greek weddings 1164
Water-snake 833_0 See also Index I Hydra
Watkins, W. A. 1205
Waxen man in charm to secure wealth 1127_0
Weapon-worship 544 ff. 548_1 1132_6
Weather in relation to Zeus 1 ff. 840
Weather-forecasts 482
Weaving in Chinese myth 66_0 479_{10} in relation to Athena 66_0 1029 in relation to Minerva 66_0
Weber, Sir H. 657
Weber, O. 482_7
Weber, S. 1050
Weber, W. 986_0
Wedd, N. 1178_8
Week, days of the 69 ff.
Weicker, G. 721_1 782_1 1150_2
Weil, H. 12 243_3
Weil, R. 759_1
Weinreich, O. 1085 1228
Weizsäcker, P. 437_6 625_5 1123
Welcker, F. G. 160_3 164_6 315_1 315_2 350_4 383_7 498 693_1 697_2 706_5 786 800 802 802_7 868_6 $877_{0(0)}$ $878_{0(3)}$ 954_0 1069 1072 1087 1131_2
Well, holy, associated with holy tree 88 in garden of Zeus 1119 of St Michael 115 See also Fountain, Spring, Water
Wellmann, M. 230_1 447_7 782_1 1122_3
Wells, J. 311_9 436_8 455_1
Weltenmantel 1137_0
Welter, G. 1229 f.
Wendling, E. 76_1
Weniger, L. 238_1 242_6 262_8 466 928_0 1151_7
Wentzel, G. 160_3 $872_{0(5)}$ 1122_2
Were-wolves 414_2
Wernicke, K. 102_0 115_2 160_3 212_3 241_3 264_2 264_3 380_2 410_1 453 484_5 486_3 501 630_2 692_1 744_3 752 753_2 786_0 $878_{0(5)}$ 1070 1088 1098_6 1100_1 1125_1
Wessely, C. 410_0
West, E. W. 1036
Whatmough, J. 331_0 342_0 444_9 1220 1226
Wheat mixed with honey to make *pyramides* 1162 mixed with honey and sesame to make *élaphos* 1140_4 offered to Apollon Γενέτωρ 223_3

Wheaten flour 1140_4 See also Meal
Wheaten straw used in sacrifice by women of Thrace and Paionia 500 f. wrapped round Hyperborean offerings 497 498_2
Wheel as Corallian standard 108 as solar emblem in bronze and iron ages 109_1 magical 1030 of Fortuna 57_6 of Iupiter 57_6 of Kairos 863_1 of Mars 57_6 of Nemesis 1095_0 of personification of the Course 479 of Phaethon's car 473 of Ziu 77 f. solar 109_1 473 624 (?) 990
Wheels of bronze dedicated to Semo Sancus (Sangus) 724_0 winged 866
Wheeler, J. R. 597_2
Whip, Corcyraean, at Dodona 826 of *Archigallus* 300 f. of Eros 1048 of Kairos 863_1 of Zeus 260_0 824 ff. 851 strung with knuckle-bones 300
Whisper of worshipper heroïfied or deified as Psithyros 1044
White garments worn in precinct on Mt Kynthos 922_0 ladder in dream of Brother Leo 1215 ox sacrificed to Zeus Κτήσιος 1065 1067 stone in folk-tale of Kyklops 989 victims sacrificed to Zeus 'Ακραῖος $871_{3(1)}$
White, H. G. Evelyn 1154_4 1211 f.
Whitehouse, O. C. 426_5
White-poplar as substitute for storax $492_{0(0)}$ brought by Herakles from Acheron 469 brought by Herakles from Thesprotia 467 843 grows beside Acheron 467 ff. in land of Chalybes 472 in Elysian fields 469 in story of Astraios 230 names of, in Greek, Latin, and English 471_1 sacred to Hades 471 sacred to Helios 469 470_0 sacred to Herakles 469 symbolism of 469_1 471 the finest tree in modern Greece 470 turns its leaves at solstice 470_0 used at Olympia for sacrifice to Pelops 471 used at Olympia for sacrifice to Zeus 467 cp. 471 wreath of, in rites of chthonian Dionysos 471 wreath of, worn by victors at Athens and in Kos 470 wreath of, worn by victors in Rhodes 469
Whittaker, E. T. 1017_4
Wick, F. C. 124_4
Wickhoff, F. 1050 1181_0
Wide, S. 123_0 413_3 692 693_3 891_0 1069 1102_0 1218
Wiedemann, A. 544_3
Wiedemann, O. 570_0
Wiegand, T. 757_1
Wiener, L. 79_1
Wieseler, F. 23_7 102_0 124_1 161_2 195_1 197_1 221_5 372_3 372_4 476_{12} 478_3 478_4 $491_{0(6)}$ 717_2 744_3 802_8 802_{10}
Wieten, J. H. 118_2 118_3 119_0 119_1 120_3
Wilamowitz-Moellendorff, U. von 249_2 296_4 385_0 451_1 453 455 ff. 476_{12} 496_0 627_1 641_2 854_9 856_2 856_3 857_1 857_2 857_4 857_5 858_{1-3} $873_{0(11)}$ $878_{0(8)}$ 899_1
Wilcken, U. 987_0